M000290731

FROM HASTINGS TO THE *MARY ROSE*

THE GREAT
WARBOW

MATTHEW STRICKLAND
& ROBERT HARDY

SUTTON PUBLISHING

First published in the United Kingdom in 2005 by
Sutton Publishing Limited · Phoenix Mill
Thrupp · Stroud · Gloucestershire · GL5 2BU

Copyright © Matthew Strickland and Robert Hardy, 2005

All rights reserved. No part of this publication may be reproduced, stored in a retrieval system, or transmitted, in any form, or by any means, electronic, mechanical, photocopying, recording or otherwise, without the prior permission of the publisher and copyright holder.

Matthew Strickland and Robert Hardy have asserted the moral right to be identified as the authors of this work.

British Library Cataloguing in Publication Data
A catalogue record for this book is available from the British Library.

ISBN 0-7509-3167-1

Typeset in 11/14.5pt Berkeley Old Style.
Typesetting and origination by
Sutton Publishing Limited.
Printed and bound in England by
J.H. Haynes & Co. Ltd, Sparkford.

Contents

Part I: The Weapon

Part II: The Longbow Before Crécy

Part III: The Hundred Years War and Beyond

Acknowledgements

his book has had a long evolution, and in its course I have benefited enormously from the help of many friends and colleagues. My first tentative researches into the history of the longbow before the Hundred Years War were stimulated by Sir James Holt, whose own knowledge of archery stemmed from his own extensive work into the Robin Hood legend. My subsequent interest has been fuelled by Robert Hardy, who generously invited me to be his co-author, and whose good fellowship I have enjoyed over many years. Professor Archie Duncan very kindly read through the greater part of the text and has furnished a host of insights and references which have done much to improve this work. Dr Andrew Ayton, whose own major study of the battle of Crécy is soon to appear, readily shared his expertise on military affairs of the fourteenth century and made many helpful suggestions. Dr Graeme Small has been equally generous with his knowledge of later medieval France and Burgundy, and has given frequent assistance with translation of medieval French. Professor Anne Curry kindly supplied me with the texts of Tito Livio and the Pseudo-Elmham, as well as valuable comments. Dr Alan Williams has not only kept me steadily supplied with off-prints of his articles and papers on the metallurgy of armour, but offered expert advice on armour as well as on the crossbow. In addition to unwavering encouragement, Mr Bill Zajac has supplied many references and not least kept me abreast of the latest scholarship on Welsh castles and the fine publications of Cadw. I am particularly indebted to Debra Strickland, for her support and wise counsel as much as for her remarkable

scholarship and expert advice on medieval art and much else beyond, which is reflected, however faintly, in the following pages. Special thanks are likewise owed to Mr George Hope, who provided invaluable assistance in the final stages of the book, meticulously checking the notes and working tirelessly to compile the bibliography. All these friends have saved me from many errors, and those which undoubtedly remain are mine alone.

I would also like to record my gratitude to the following, who have contributed directly or indirectly to shaping this book: Dr Stuart Airlie, Dr Stephen Alford, Dr Ian Archer, Professor Rob Bartlett, Dr Steve Boardman, Dr Davie Broun, Dr Toby Capwell, Professor Sam Cohn, Professor Ted Cowan, Mr Bryan Dick, Dr Steve Driscoll, Mr David Edge, Professor John Gillingham, Professor Colum Hourihan, Dr Michael Jones, Professor Angus Kennedy, Dr Tig Lang, Dr Steve Marritt, Mr Patrick Parsons, Professor Carole Rawcliffe, Mr Graeme Rimer, Dr Andrew Roach, Mr David Sherlock, Dr Jim Simpson, Dr Tom Tolley, Mr Guy Wilson and Mr Bob Woosnam-Savage. The Department of History at the University of Glasgow kindly awarded me a precious period of sabbatical leave during which much of the second part of this book was written, while Mr Trevor Graham and his team at the University's Photographic Unit provided swift and excellent support. In Messrs Daryll Reach and Christopher Feeney we have been extremely fortunate in two commissioning editors who have shown exemplary patience and unfailing courtesy; the successful conclusion of this long project owes much to their unflagging commitment and gentle coaxing. Thanks are also due to all the team at Sutton Publishing, and in particular to Jane Entrican for her truly heroic efforts with the picture research. We are grateful to Bow Watkinson for his preparation of the maps and plans.

The pleasure in recording all these thanks is tinged with sadness owing to the untimely deaths in 2004 of two friends and colleagues, with whom I had the privilege of working and from whose friendship and learning I have greatly benefited over many years. Both helped directly with this book. Professor John Thomson, a distinguished historian of the later Middle Ages, with typical generosity provided me with a steady stream of references to archery, longbows and warfare discovered during his own indefatigable researches, even during his final courageous battle with cancer. Mr Michael Kennedy, a gifted scholar and superb latinist, not only gave me free access to his extensive library but was in the process of advising on the translation of some particularly challenging Latin passages at the time of his tragically premature death. My greatest debt, beyond expression, remains that to my late parents, John and Elizabeth Strickland.

Matthew Strickland

Abbreviations

Ailred	Ailred of Rievaulx, *Relatio venerabilis Aelredi abbatis Rievallensis, de Standardo*, ed. R. Howlett, *Chronicles of the Reigns of Stephen, Henry II and Richard I*, III (London, Rolls Series, 1886).
Alexiad	Anna Comnena, *Alexiad*, trans. E.R.A. Sewter, *The Alexiad of Anna Comnena* (London, 1969).
Ambroise	*L'Estoire de la guerre sainte*, ed. G. Paris (Paris, 1897).
Anderson	*Early Sources of Scottish History, AD 500–1286*, trans. A.O. Anderson, 2 vols (Edinburgh, 1922, repr. Stamford, 1990).
Ann. Dunstable	*Annales Prioratus de Dunstaplia, A.D. 1–1297*, ed. H.R. Luard, *Annales Monastici*, III (Rolls Series, 1866).
Ann. Worcester	*Annales Prioratus de Wigornia, A.D. 1–1377*, ed. H.R. Luard, *Annales Monastici*, IV (Rolls Series, 1867).
Anonimalle	*The Anonimalle Chronicle 1307–1334*, eds W.R. Childs and J. Taylor, Yorkshire Archaeological Record Series, cxlvii (Leeds, 1991).
Anonimalle Chronicle	*Anonimalle Chronicle 1333–1381*, ed. V.H. Galbraith (Manchester, 1927).
APS	*Acts of the Parliaments of Scotland*, ed. T. Thomson and C. Innes, 12 vols (Edinburgh, 1814–75).
ASC	*Anglo-Saxon Chronicle*, ed. D. Whitelock, *English Historical Documents, c.500–1042*, I (2nd edn, London, 1979), 145–261.
Avesbury	Robert of Avesbury, *De gestis mirabilibus regis Edwardi tertii*, ed. E.M. Thompson (Rolls Series, 1889).
Barber	*The Life and Campaigns of the Black Prince*, ed. R. Barber (Woodbridge, 1986).
BIHR	*Bulletin of the Institute of Historical Research*.
Bridlington	*Gesta Edwardi de Carnarvon auctore canonico Bridlingtoniensi cum continuatione ad AD 1377*, ed. W. Stubbs, *Chronicles of the Reign of Edward I and Edward II*, II (Rolls Series, 1883).
Bruce	John Barbour, *The Bruce*, ed. A.A.M. Duncan (Edinburgh, 1997).
Brut	*The Brut*, ed. F.W.D. Brie (Early English Text Society, original series, cxxxi, London, 1906).

Cal. Anc. Corr. Wales	*Calendar of Ancient Correspondence concerning Wales*, ed. J.G. Edwards (Cardiff, 1935).
Cal. Docs. Scot.	*Calendar of Documents relating to Scotland*, ed. J. Bain, 4 vols (London, 1881–8); vol. V ed. R.R. Sharpe (London, 1901).
Cal. Lib. Rolls	*Calendar of the Liberate Rolls Preserved in the The National Archive*, 6 vols (London, 1916–64).
CBP	*Calendar of Letters and Papers Relating to the Affairs of the Borders of England and Scotland*, ed. J. Bain, 2 vols (Edinburgh, 1894).
CCR	*Calendar of Close Rolls (1892–).*
Chandos Herald	*Life of the Black Prince by the Herald of Sir John Chandos*, ed. M.K. Pope and E.C. Lodge (Oxford, 1910).
Chronique Normande	*Chronique Normande du XIVe siècle*, ed. A. and E. Moliner (Paris, 1882).
Chronographia	*Chronographia regum Francorum*, ed. H. Moranville, 3 vols (Paris, 1891–7).
CPR	*Calendar of Patent Rolls (1891–).*
Coggeshall	*Raduphi de Coggeshall Chronicon Anglicanum*, ed. J. Stevenson (Rolls Series, London, 1875).
Devizes	*The Chronicle of Richard of Devizes*, trans. J.T. Appleby (London, 1963).
Diceto	*Radulfi de Diceto Decani Londiniensis Opera Historica*, ed. W. Stubbs, 2 vols (Rolls Series, London, 1876).
Documents	*The antient calendars and inventories of the treasury of His Majesty's exchequer, together with documents illustrating the history of that repository*, ed. F. Palgrave, 3 vols (London, 1836).
DNB	*Dictionary of National Biography*, ed. L. Stephen, 63 vols (London, 1885–1900).
EHD	*English Historical Documents.*
EHR	*English Historical Review.*
English Chronicle	*Chronicle of the Reigns of Richard II, Henry IV, Henry V, and Henry VI, written before the year 1471*, ed. J.S. Davies (Camden Society, London, 1856).
Eulogium historiarum	*Eulogium historiarum*, ed. F.S. Haydon, 3 vols (Rolls Series, London, 1858–63).
Expugnatio	Giraldus Cambrensis, *Expugnatio Hibernica. The Conquest of Ireland*, ed. and trans. A.B. Scott and F.X. Martin (Dublin, 1978).
Flores	*Flores Historiarum*, ed. H.R. Luard, 3 vols (Rolls Series, London, 1890).
Foedera	*Foedera, Conventiones, Litterae et Acta Publica*, ed. T. Rymer, 4 vols (Record Commission, 1816–69).
Fulcher	Fulcher of Chartres, *Historia Hierosolymitana*, ed. H. Hagenmeyer (Heidelberg, 1913).
Gesta	Roger of Howden, *Gesta Henrici II et Ricardi I*, ed. W. Stubbs, 2 vols (Rolls Series, London, 1867).
Gesta Henrici Quinti	*Gesta Heinrici Quinti*, ed. F. Taylor and J.S. Roskell, *The Deeds of Henry the Fifth* (Oxford, 1975).
'Gregory'	William Gregory, *Chronicle*, ed. J. Gairdner, *The Historical Collections of a Citizen of London in the Fifteenth Century* (London, 1876).
Guisborough	*The Chronicle of Walter of Guisborough*, ed. H. Rothwell (Camden Society, 3rd series, lxxxix, London, 1957).
Hemingburgh	*Chronicon domni Walteri de Hemingburgh de gestis regum Angliae*, ed. M.C. Hamilton, 2 vols (London, 1848).
HGM	*Histoire de Guillaume le Maréchal*, ed. P. Meyer, 3 vols (Paris, 1891–1907).

Historia Aurea	V.H. Galbraith, 'Extracts from the *Historia Aurea* and a French 'Brut' (1317–47)', *EHR*, xliii (1928), 203–17.
Howden	Roger of Howden, *Chronica*, ed. W. Stubbs, 4 vols (Rolls Series, 1868–71).
Huntingdon	Henry of Huntingdon, *Historia Anglorum*, ed. D. Greenway (Oxford, 1996).
Itinerarium	*Itinerarium Peregrinorum et Gesta Regis Ricardi*, ed. W. Stubbs (Rolls Series, London, 1864).
JMMH	*Journal of Medieval Military History.*
JSAA	*Journal of the Society of Archer-Antiquaries.*
Knighton	Henry Knighton, *Chronicon*, ed. J.R. Lumby (Rolls Series, London, 1895).
Lanercost	*Chronicon de Lanercost, MCCI–MCCCXLVI*, ed. J. Stevenson (Edinburgh, 1839).
Langtoft	*The Chronicle of Pierre de Langtoft*, ed. T. Wright, 2 vols (Rolls Series, London, 1886).
Le Baker	Geoffrey le Baker, *Chronicon*, ed. E.M. Thompson (Oxford, 1889).
Le Bel	Jean le Bel, *Chronique de Jean le Bel*, ed. J. Viard and E. Déprez, 2 vols (Paris, 1904–5).
Le Fèvre	*Chronique de Jean Le Fèvre, seigneur de Saint-Remy*, ed. F. Morand, 2 vols (Paris, 1876–81).
Le Muisit	Gilles le Muisit, *Chronique et Annales*, ed. H. Lemaître (Paris, 1906).
Lescot	Richard Lescot, *Chronique (1328–1344), suivie de la continuation de cette chronique (1344–1364)*, ed. J. Lemoine (Paris, 1896).
Liber recuperationis	*Liber recuperationis Terre Sancte*, ed. P.G. Golubovitch, in *Biblioteca Bio-Bibliografica della Terra Sancta*, II (Florence, 1913).
Matthew Paris	*Matthaei Parisiensis, Monachi Sancti Albani, Chronica Majora*, ed. H.R. Luard, 7 vols (Rolls Series, London, 1872–83).
MGH	*Monumenta Germaniae Historica:*
Capit	*Capitularia regum Francorum*
SRG	*Scriptores rerum Germanicarum in usum scholarum separatim editi*
SRM	*Scriptores rerum Merovingicarum*
SS	*Scriptores*
Monstrelet	*La Chronique d'Enguerrand de Monstrelet*, ed. L. Douet-D'Arcq, 6 vols (Société de l'Histoire de France, Paris, 1857–62).
Murimuth	Adam Murimuth, *Adae Murimuth. Continuatio Chronicarum*, ed. E.M. Thompson (Rolls Series, London, 1889).
Orderic	Orderic Vitalis, *Historia Ecclesiastica*, ed. M.M. Chibnall, *The Ecclesiastical History of Orderic Vitalis*, 6 vols (Oxford, 1969–80).
Parl. Writs.	*Parliamentary Writs and Writs of Military Summons*, ed. F. Palgrave, 2 vols (London, 1827–34).
Philippidos	William the Breton, *Philippidos*, ed. H.-F. Delaborde, *Oeuvres de Rigord et de Guillaume le Breton, historiens de Philippe-Auguste*, 2 vols (Paris, 1882), II, 1–385.
Récits	*Récits d'un bourgeois de Valenciennes*, ed. K. de Lettenhove (Louvain, 1877).
Reg. Scott. I	*Regesta Regum Scottorum, I. The Acts of Malcolm IV, King of Scots, 1153–1165*, ed. G.W.S. Barrow (Edinburgh, 1960).
Reg. Scott. II	*Regesta Regum Scottorum, II. The Acts of William I, King of Scots, 1165–1214*, ed. G.W.S. Barrow (Edinburgh, 1971).
Reg. Scott. V	*Regesta Regum Scottorum, V. The Acts of Robert I, King of Scots, 1306–1329*, ed. A.A.M. Duncan (Edinburgh, 1988).
Religieux	*Le Religieux of Saint-Denis*, ed. L. Bellaguet, *Histoire de Charles VI*, 6 vols (Paris, 1839–52), V.

RHC	*Recueil des historiens des croisades*, ed. Académie des Inscriptions et Belles-Lettres (Paris, 1841–1906).
RHF	*Recueil des historiens des Gaules et de la France*, ed. M.L. Delisle, 24 vols (new edn, Paris, 1869–1904).
Richer	Richer, *Histoire de la France*, ed. R. Latouche, 2 vols (Paris, 1930).
Rigord	Rigord, *Gesta Philippi Augusti*, ed. H.-F. Delaborde, *Oeuvres de Rigord et de Guillaume le Breton, historiens de Philippe-Auguste*, 2 vols (Paris, 1882).
Rishanger	*Willelmi Rishanger, Chronica et Annales*, ed. H.T. Riley (Rolls Series, London, 1865).
Rot. de Lib.	*Rotuli de Liberate ac de misis et praestitis, regnanate Johanne*, ed. T.D. Hardy (London, 1844).
Rot. Litt. Claus.	*Rotuli Litterarum Clausarum in Turri Londinensi Asservati*, ed. T.D. Hardy, 2 vols (London, 1833, 1844).
Rot. Parl.	*Rotuli Parliamentorum*, 7 vols (Record Commission, 1783–1832).
Rot. Scacc.	*Magni Rotuli Scaccarii Normanniae*, ed. T. Stapleton, 2 vols (London, 1840–84).
Rot. Scacc. Scot	*Rotuli Scaccarii Regum Scotorum*, ed. J. Stuart and G. Burnett, 23 vols (Edinburgh, 1878–1908).
Rot. Scot	Macpherson, D. *et al.*, *Rotuli Scotiae in Turri Londinensi et in Domo Capitulari Westmonasteriensi asservati*, 2 vols (Record Commission, London, 1814, 1819).
Scalacronica	Sir Thomas Gray, *Scalacronica*, ed. J. Stevenson (Edinburgh, 1836).
Scotichronicon	Walter Bower, *Scotichronicon*, ed. S. Taylor, D.E.R. Watt and B. Scott, 9 vols (Aberdeen, 1987–98).
Settimane	*Settimane di Studio del Centro italiano di studi sull'alto medioevo* (Spoleto, 1953–).
SHR	*Scottish Historical Review*.
Tito Livio	*Titi Livii Foro-Juliensis Vita Henrici Quinti*, ed. T. Hearne (Oxford, 1716).
Topographia	Giraldus Cambrensis, *Topographia Hibernica*, in *Opera*, ed. J.F. Dimock and G.F. Warner (Rolls Series, London, 1867), V.
Torigny	Robert of Torigny, *The Chronicle of Robert of Torigny*, ed. R. Howlett, *Chronicles of the Reigns of Stephen, Henry II and Richard I*, IV (Rolls Series, London, 1889).
TRHS	*Transactions of the Royal Historical Society*.
Trokelowe	John de Trokelowe, *Chronica monasterii S. Albani*, ed. H.T. Riley (London, 1866).
Usamah	Usamah ibn Munquidh, *Kitab al-I'tibar*, trans. P.K. Hitti, *Memoirs of an Arab-Syrian Gentleman or an Arab Knight in the Crusades* (Beruit, 1964).
Vita Edwardi	*Vita Edwardi Secundi*, ed. N. Denholm-Young (London, 1957).
Walsingham	*Thomae Walsingham, quodam monachi Sancti Albani Historia Anglicana*, ed. H.T. Riley, 2 vols (Rolls Series, London, 1863–4).
Waurin	Jean de Waurin, *Recueil des croniques et anchiennes istories de la Grant Bretaigne, a present nomme Engleterre, 1399–1422*, ed. W.L. Hardy and E.L.C.P. Hardy, 5 vols (Rolls Series, London, 1864–91).
Wykes	'Chronicon vulgo dictum Chronicon Thomae Wykes, 1066–1289', *Annales Monastici*, ed. H.R. Luard (Rolls Series, London, 1864–9), IV.
Wyntoun	*Androw of Wyntoun's Orygynale Cronykil of Scotland*, ed. D. Laing, 3 vols (Edinburgh, 1872–9).

Introduction

'hooting in the longbow', wrote the Tudor scholar Roger Ascham, was for the English the activity 'whereunto nature hath made them most apt, and use hath made them most fit'.[1] Such sentiments vividly reveal the impact of the longbow on the psyche of sixteenth-century Englishmen, for whom it was automatically associated with an earlier age of military greatness and the resounding victories of kings such as Edward III and Henry V in their wars against the French. Nor was the military importance of the longbow seen only as a thing of the past. When Ascham astutely presented his famous treatise on archery, *Toxophilus*, to Henry VIII in 1545 on his return from campaigning in France, a prefatory verse proclaimed that 'through Christ, King Henry, the Boke and the Bowe' England would overcome all her enemies, and especially 'the Scot, the Frenchmen, the Pope and hersie'. The longbow, together with the English translation of the Bible, was nothing less than a pillar of Henry VIII's Reformation.[2]

Ascham could never have imagined, however, that a naval disaster occurring earlier in the same year in which *Toxophilus* was published would come to play a crucial role in recovering the secrets of the longbow's effectiveness, lost to posterity as military archery waned then finally vanished. For in July 1545 Henry VIII's great warship the *Mary Rose* had sunk in the Solent during an engagement with the French fleet, taking to the bottom not only its crew but its armaments, including 250 yew longbows. The rediscovery of this ship, and the excavation from 1979 onwards of 138 of these longbows and over 2,000 arrows, represents an archaeological find of the first importance which, by remedying the almost complete dearth of surviving longbows from the central and later Middle Ages, has come to transform our knowledge of the longbow. It was Robert Hardy's close involvement with the conservation and testing of the *Mary Rose* bows, coupled with my own research interests in Anglo-Norman warfare and the history of the longbow before the Hundred Years War, that subsequently led to our partnership in the writing of this book.

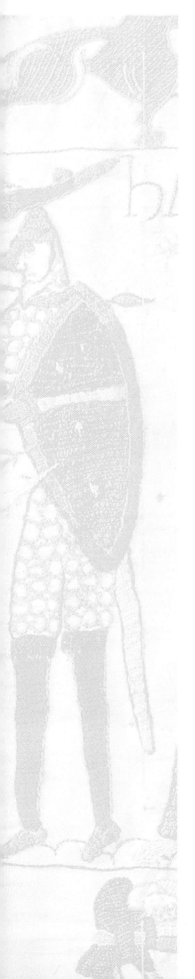

We had originally intended to produce a revised and enlarged version of Robert Hardy's *Longbow. A Social and Military History*, still in print (in its third edition) since its first publication in 1976 and translated into French and Italian. But as our researches developed, it soon became clear that *Longbow* should remain as the quintessential overview of the longbow from prehistory to modern sporting archery, and that what was needed was a new study that would focus exclusively on the medieval period. Nevertheless, the task of tracing the longbow's history over a thousand years is a daunting one, and a broad synthesis such as this must naturally be indebted to the researches of many scholars, who have been acknowledged as fully as possible in the notes. As the Tudor veteran Thomas Audley noted around 1550 in the preface to his *A. B. C. for the Wars*, no soldier can be expert in all branches of war, 'wherefore it is good to hear divers men's opinions and to consider them together and to take the best'.[3] Given the work's scope, it equally makes no claim to be either exhaustive or definitive; rather, it is intended as a contribution to an ongoing area of research and debate which happily shows little sign of abating.

This, then, is a book on the medieval longbow at war. Part 1 examines the nature of the weapon itself. Robert Hardy, who brings to this study a wealth of practical experience and the eye of an archer and bowyer, discusses in detail the conservation and testing of the longbows discovered on the *Mary Rose*, in which he has played so important a role. We also examine something of the circumstances of manufacture of medieval longbows and the craft of the bowyer. Drawing on the practical experiments undertaken on modern but carefully matched 'approximations' by the archer Simon Stanley, he outlines the awesome power of these great yew bows and sets out in the Appendix some of the data on their performance as revealed by recent tests at the Royal Military College of Science, Shrivenham. But these bows come from the twilight of English military archery. A fundamental question therefore must be to what extent such heavy bows were the product of development in the later Middle Ages. For the traditional and still remarkably prevalent orthodoxy holds that the longbow which contributed to the triumphs of English arms at battles such as Crécy, Poitiers and Agincourt was a new weapon, evolving from the weak and ineffectual 'shortbow' during the late thirteenth and early fourteenth centuries. Accordingly, Chapter 2 brings together a range of archaeological, iconographic and written evidence to demonstrate not only that powerful longbows had existed from at least the Iron Age, but also that heavy bows with similar general characteristics to those found on the *Mary Rose* were used in warfare in medieval Europe well before the fourteenth century.

But if powerful longbows existed throughout the medieval period, why then was it only in the fourteenth century that armies containing large numbers of English and Welsh bowmen began to inflict bloody defeats on French armies? And if the weapon was so ubiquitous, why was it that it emerges as the predominant infantry missile weapon in England and Wales but not in other European countries? These questions lie at the heart of this study, and to begin to answer them the second part of the book traces the military use of the longbow – and equally crucially of the crossbow – from the Anglo-Saxon period through to the eve of the Hundred Years War. The role of the longbow is examined in differing theatres of conflict, including Anglo-Welsh warfare, the Anglo-Norman campaigns of conquest in Ireland from 1169 onwards, and as the weapon of outlaws, foresters and poachers in the forests of thirteenth- and fourteenth-century England. It seeks to explain why crossbowmen none-the-less continued to remain an elite in twelfth- and thirteenth-century Britain as well as in Europe, discussing the intimate connection between the crossbow and the development of increasingly scientific provision for the missile defence of castles. Looking further afield, it examines the part played by the longbow and crossbow in crusading warfare in the Latin East where Frankish armies were pitted against Muslim forces, whose light horse-archers wielded the composite bow with great agility and astonishing accuracy. Moreover, the extensive use of the composite bow in southern and eastern Europe throughout the Middle Ages (and, indeed, well beyond in countries such as Hungary, Poland and Russia) is an important reminder that the impact of the longbow, even during its apogee in the fourteenth and fifteenth centuries, would always be limited by the question of its tactical suitability in military contexts markedly different from those of north-west Europe. Within Britain itself, a study of archery during Edward I's conquest of Wales and in the Anglo-Scottish wars from 1296 reveals the clash of divergent military traditions, and their subsequent interaction through prolonged conflict. Bitter years of defeat at the hands of Robert Bruce led the English to far-reaching military reforms and to the rediscovery of the crucial combination of dismounted men-at-arms and archers which decimated the once-invincible formations of Scottish spearmen at the battles of Dupplin Moor, 1332, Halidon Hill, 1333, and Neville's Cross, 1346.

The third and final part of the book combines a series of thematic chapters with an analytical survey of the longbow's role in warfare from the Hundred Years War, through the English civil wars of the fifteenth century, to the Tudor period when the weapon began its slow descent into obsolescence. It begins with a discussion of the changing organisation of English armies from the fourteenth century, including the development of indentured retinues and the increasing use of mounted archers, which provides an essential background to the tactical success of English arms from the reign of Edward III onwards. This also stresses the key, but too often overlooked, role of the men-at-arms, without whom the archers could not have operated effectively. Just how such bowmen *did* operate, and how they were arrayed by English commanders to achieve their maximum impact, is by no means fully understood. In Chapter 16, however, Robert Hardy carefully weighs the evidence and by applying the latest technical information derived from tests on 'approximations' from the *Mary Rose*, together with an intimate knowledge of many of the key battlefields, suggests new interpretations and challenges some existing orthodoxies. The question of the longbow's effectiveness against armour, raised in Chapter 1, receives more extensive treatment in Chapter 15 and is set within the context of the steady improvement in knights' defences and in metallurgy, while the treatment of arrow and bolt wounds is also examined.

These broad thematic chapters are complemented and contextualised by a chronological overview of the main engagements in the Hundred Years War and beyond. They not only assess the role of the longbow but as importantly also trace the nature of the French response to the seemingly invincible English battle formations. Such an approach reveals, for example, that the bloody débâcle at Crécy stands in marked contrast to the earlier attempts of Charles of Blois to counter English deployments, and to Philip VI's own earlier success in refusing to commit himself to a major battle with Edward III. In the wake of the catastrophic defeat of King Jean II at Poitiers in 1356, a strategy of non-engagement with English field armies became central to the successful war effort of Charles V, yet his military reforms not only included the beginnings of a standing army but also an attempt in 1367 to impose universal archery practice. Both Charles and his successors, moreover, encouraged the formation of urban confraternities of crossbowmen and

archers, which were to play an increasingly important role in the civic life of France and the Low Countries. There would be many reasons for the French defeat at Agincourt in 1415, but lack of an adequate supply of trained missilemen – including longbowmen – was not to be one of them.

If the methods by which the French sought to combat English tactics is a central theme running through Part 3, and one taken up to their successful culmination in the final expulsion of English forces from Normandy and Gascony, another is the spreading influence of English tactical thinking, carried beyond Britain and France by English troops serving abroad either as mercenaries or as allies. Thus in Italy English longbowmen served under Sir John Hawkwood, leader of the famous White Company and one of the most famous *condottieri* of the Quatrocento, while in Portugal the influence of English military advisers was nowhere more strikingly demonstrated than at the great battle of Aljubarotta, 1385, in which the dismounted Portuguese men-at-arms, with archer support, inflicted a devastating defeat on the Castilians. The resumption of the Anglo-French war in 1413 and Henry V's resounding victory at Agincourt witnessed an intensification of this process, and particular emphasis has been given to the developing role of archers in the armies of Burgundy and of Scotland during the fifteenth century.

No study devoted to the longbow could be deemed complete without a detailed analysis of Agincourt itself, an engagement which epitomises the quintessential elements of English military success in the triumph of a small but highly disciplined force of archers and men-at-arms against a far larger but poorly organised army. There will undoubtedly be some who regard the study of such engagements as at best peripheral, and at worst the outmoded preserve of retired soldiers. Yet the discipline of medieval military history has been transformed since the works of earlier historians such as Sir Charles Oman or Lieutenant-Colonel Alfred Burne drew criticism for their myopic, 'battle-centric' approach. Not only has far greater emphasis has been placed on organisation, logistics, siege and economic warfare, as well as on conduct in war and the experience of conflict, but a new generation of scholars has looked afresh at the strategic, tactical and psychological significance of battle, bringing to the subject a more critical and sophisticated methodology. Some of these approaches are reflected in the following pages. For Agincourt itself we offer two different perspectives on the battle; as part of Chapter 16, Robert Hardy first discusses the central but much debated issue of where and how the archers were deployed, while the following chapter places Agincourt in its wider military context and uses the exceptionally full source material for the engagement to offer a case study of the nature of battle.

Nevertheless, one needs only to read the superb introductory essay to John Keegan's groundbreaking study *The Face of Battle* to appreciate the complexity of the experience of combat, and the profound difficulties encountered in attempting plausibly to reconstruct even an engagement on the scale of Waterloo.[4] And if such problems exist for the eighteenth, nineteenth and even twentieth centuries, they are greatly multiplied for the Middle Ages. The difficulty in gaining reliable estimates of troop numbers in the frequent absence of muster lists or accounts, or in piecing together the often fragmentary or contradictory accounts of medieval chroniclers, are but some of the pitfalls discussed in the following chapters. The location of battles, moreover, and hence the effect of topography upon them, is rarely known with any precision. We have included a limited number of maps and diagrams in this book, in the belief that they will assist the reader, but do so with the caveat that they are nothing more than tentative suggestions and make no claim to a specious exactness. Yet the historian of the longbow has little choice but to confront all these challenges as best he may: one cannot study a weapon without at least attempting to discover how it performed in the role for which it was principally intended. And if justification for such a venture was needed, few better could be found than that expounded in 1531 by Sir Thomas Elyot in his *Book of the Governor*. The longbow, he wrote,

> is, and alway hath ben, the moste excellent artillerie for warres, whereby this realm of Englande hath bene nat only defended from outward hostilitie, but also in other regions a fewe englisshe archers have ben sceene to prevayle agayne people innumerable, also won impreignable cities and strongholdes, and kepte them in the myddes of the strength of their enemies. This is the feate, whereby englisshe men have ben most dradde [feared] and had in estimation with outwarde princes, as well enemies as alies.[5]

How this came to be so is the subject of this book.

Matthew Strickland

I would add very little to Matthew Strickland's Introduction, except to suggest that Chapter 17 be read before Chapter 16, and to list some of those who have been, and in many cases still are, crucial to the discovery, the research and the study of the *Mary Rose* military archery equipment, and in the use and investigation of the properties of modern versions of the great warbows from the *Mary Rose*. My heartfelt thanks are offered to:

Dr Margaret Rule CBE, the guiding spirit of the *Mary Rose* enterprise; Professor John Levy of the Imperial College of Science and Technology, Professor of Wood Science; Professor Anne Curry, whose brilliant analyses of the Hundred Years War and whose unique archival work, has always been both tutor and encourager; Professor Anna Crowley, of the Royal Military College of Science, who crucially organised the testing of bows and provided the technical appendix; Dr B.W. Koor of Amsterdam University, whose computer modelling of the bows startled the research team, and still astonishes many in the archery world; Dr Alexsandra Hildred, who leads the work on the *Mary Rose* and her artefacts today, and all those of the *Mary Rose* Trust and its officers who have helped and supported my efforts since 1979; Roy King, bowyer to the *Mary Rose* Trust, who made all the early test bows, and John Cave, bowyer, who made test bows; Simon Stanley, without whose skill, strength perception, knowledge, friendship and dedication our enterprise would have foundered short of practical research; W.M. Garcin and Janet Lord, who were unfailing assistants, labouring with the preservation of the bows and the preparation of the reports; and principally in memory of Professor Peter Pratt, sometime Dean and Emeritus Professor of Crystal Physics at the Imperial College, whose patience in guiding us non-scientists, and whose energy and profound scientific knowledge pushed the research forward.

To these people I dedicate the results of their work which are written in this study.

Robert Hardy

PART I

The Weapon

Shotte of yron. Shotte of Stone.
and Leade.

for Cannon. for portepecys CC
for Dimicas two

CHAPTER 1

The Mary Rose *Experience*

n 19 July 1545, the Tudor warship the *Mary Rose*, flying the flag of Henry VIII's vice-admiral, sank during the early stages of battle against a huge French fleet which outnumbered the Spanish Armada of forty-three years later. The disaster was due less to French action than to indiscipline and overcrowding on board, and probably to a sharp change in wind speed and direction. Her gunports wide open, the *Mary Rose* heeled over too far, taking in water when her lower gunports went under; she filled with shocking speed and sank, carrying the greater part of her complement with her, trapped beneath the anti-boarding nets stretched right across her weather deck. There may have been as many as 700 men on board, fewer than 40 of whom escaped. The whole tragic story is told in various editions of Dr Margaret Rule's book *The Mary Rose* and in Ernle Bradford's *Story of the Mary Rose*.[1] She lay in 6 fathoms, her masts jutting from the sea. The ailing Henry VIII had watched the disaster from Southsea Castle, surrounded by his army gathered to resist the French. The wife of the drowning vice-admiral, Sir George Carew, was at the king's side and all had heard the cries of the sailors as the great ship toppled and went down. The king ordered immediate attempts to raise her. Not only was she filled with expensive guns and weapons of all kinds, she was also named after the king's favourite sister, she was the pride of the fleet, and had done sterling service as a warship for thirty-five years.

The details of the failed attempts to raise her hardly concern us, and gradually even the memory of the event, certainly its exact location, faded. Then during the period 1834–6 and later in 1840 the Deane brothers, newly equipped for diving, were working at the behest of the Royal Navy in the Solent on the wreck of the *Royal George*, sunk towards the end of the eighteenth century. Told by local fishermen that their nets were often entangled not far from the *Royal George*, the Deanes dived on a second wreck, and found the *Mary Rose*. They brought up guns, timber, various personal items – and longbows, several of them, which together with many of their other trophies were auctioned to the public in 1840. Three bows, survivors of this first recovery, are still to be seen, two in the Royal Armouries collection, the other, with a metal bolt through its handle, at the National Army Museum in Royal Hospital Road, London. The rest probably ended up as walking sticks – the likely fate of thousands upon thousands of the war bows of the later Middle Ages, which we continually seek and never, for certain, find. If a bow was broken it was useless, except as a stick or firewood.

Once again the *Mary Rose*, filled with the treasures of long service and full commission, faded into oblivion, her broken hull covered in thick silt, her location again forgotten – until the 1960s when Alexander McKee, who had long held that it must be possible to rediscover the wreck, came upon her. This thrilling find opened the way for the slow excavation and final recovery of the *Mary Rose*.

In 1979, well before the raising of the ship, and while the exploration of her interior was slowly and carefully progressing under Dr Rule's direction, a diver surfaced alongside the *Sleipner*, the control vessel, holding in one hand a long stave of wood. The list of armaments, stores and equipment of the entire fleet is to be found in the Anthony Roll manuscript in the

Pepys Library of Magdalene College, Cambridge. In many of the ships' inventories appear 'bows of yew', bowstrings and arrows. The Admiral's ship *Henry Grâce à Dieu* carried 500 bows, a much smaller ship of 60 tons, the *George*, carried 30, and even a 20-ton 'row-barge' called the *Rose Slype* carried 10; the total of bows in the fleet was 2,949. In the *Mary Rose* list (transcribed into modern English) were 'Bows of yew 250 – Bowstrings 6 gross – Livery arrows in sheaves 400'. 'Livery' means army issue arrows, and a sheaf contained 24 arrows,[2] so at least 9,600 arrows were in that issue. In a similar inventory to the Anthony Roll, but of 1514, there are equally detailed references to longbows: for instance the *Trinity Sovereign* carried two chests of 'bows of yew' and two of 'witch hazel' bows, and the *John Baptist* 151 bows of yew and 84 of witch hazel, while

the *Rose* galley carried 55 yew bows and 40 'elm' (that is wych-elm) bows.[3] In the later roll, as in this of 1514, the *Henry Grâce à Dieu* and the *Mary Rose* are listed as carrying only yew bows, which has suggested to Dr Charles Knighton, who kindly passed the idea to me, that the respective ships of the admiral and the vice-admiral of Henry VIII's navy were not to be equipped with inferior bows. As to such inferiority, Thomas, Lord Howard wrote to the Council on 8 June 1513:

> . . . as touching the receiving of bows and arrows I shall see them as little wasted as shall be possible. And where your Lordships write that it is great marvelled where so great a number of bows and arrows be brought to so small a number, I have enquired the causes thereof; and

Below: The first longbow is carried through the murk of the Solent by a *Mary Rose* diver.

as far as I can see, the greatest number were witch bows, of whom few would abide the bending.[4]

Dr Rule was convinced the stave that had just surfaced after 434 years under water was a longbow, but might it be a pikestaff? Her desk was piled with books and manuscripts covering the many disciplines she and her team would have to master in understanding and cataloguing the mass of objects that were daily being brought up from the wreck. Among those works of reference was the first edition of my *Longbow*, published in 1976. Margaret Rule said, roughly speaking, 'Get this man!'

Already in charge of the timbers of the wreck was John Levy, Professor of Wood Science at the Imperial College of Science

and Technology in London. A colleague of his, Peter Pratt, one time Dean and Professor of Crystal Physics at Imperial College, was already a friend of mine. We had met at a symposium on history and archaeology at Reading University and had together profoundly disagreed with those speakers who, we thought, underestimated the technical abilities of our medieval ancestors. The three of us raced down to Portsmouth in a high state of excitement, and there on a table before us, dark, almost black from its long inundation, lay 6½ feet of timber, slightly bent, rather knobbly, blotched with oyster-spat, carefully tapered from the centre to both tips – the first Tudor longbow to see the light of day since the Deane brothers' dives. As I have said elsewhere,[5] the sight of Excalibur rising from the mere could not have thrilled the eyes of this beholder more than that of the longbow held by Adrian Barak on the deck of *Sleipner*: longbow no. 80A 812.

Professor Pratt and the author seeing the first two *Mary Rose* bows and the first arrows to surface, watched by Jon Adams and Andrew Elkerton. (© *The Mary Rose Trust*)

The excitement was tempered a little by the knobs on 812. They showed the skill of the bowmaker certainly, in leaving proud the knots in the timber, but my idea of a late medieval or Tudor war bow was conditioned by those fine fifteenth-century illustrations to Froissart in the Bibliothèque Nationale, the St Sebastian paintings of Hans Memling, and the marvellous drawings of bowmen in battle from the Beauchamp Pageant in the British Library. Rough as it might be, 812 was plainly a formidable weapon that must have had a draw-weight of well over 100lb (45.3kg). The draw-weight of a bow is the weight held momentarily by the archer when he has drawn back the arrow to its full length before he looses it. An archer's draw-length depends not only on the length of his arrows, but on his build and his anchor, the point to which he draws the nock of the arrow on the bowstring before release: this may be the angle of his jaw or his ear, or some other familiar spot about his head or neck. The average length of the *Mary Rose* arrow-shafts is

30in (76.2cm); although there are big men who can draw more than 33in (83.8cm), livery arrows could not accommodate individual tastes, and the anchor point might have to be adapted. Beyond the full-drawn shaft was the head of the war-arrow, which would be either barbed or sharp sided, so the head could not be drawn over the first knuckle of the bow-hand. Taking the average shaft length as 30in (76.2cm), this means that the overall length of war-arrows would be increased by anything from 2–6in (5–15cm), depending on the type of head and its date, though some ¾–1¾in (2–4.5cm) must be allowed for the insertion of the shaft into the socket of the head.

It was not long before more longbows were brought to the surface from various locations about the ship, though the find positions could not always be trusted in evaluating their use at the time of the sinking. There was tumbling at the impact of the ship on the sea-bottom and movement through the long years of the hull's disintegration to be taken into account, and indeed the result of a possible explosion set off by the Deane brothers to open up the ship's interior and get rid of the ribs above the silt that snagged the fishermen's nets. This explosion is discounted by Margaret Rule,[6] who believes the disappearance of the ship's port side is due to the actions of marine creatures and the 'tides of time', though some parts of the port side have been found during the later dives of 2004, which might suggest the report of the Deanes' explosion is true. Archaeological attitudes and concerns in the 1830s were not those of the late twentieth century. For instance, even the great and meticulous Charles Darwin, investigating the field of the battle of Shrewsbury, fought in 1403, recorded the finding of many iron arrowheads 'in a field . . . a little north of Shrewsbury', but forbore entirely to say where.

Some of the bows were finer than that first survivor, and some were broken. One was fixed in the braced position, sunk with the string taut, and by the time micro-organisims or larger creatures had consumed the string the saturated timber was fixed in a curve. All the bows were oyster-spatted and to varying degrees encrusted and dilapidated. Then came a wonder: the divers with their big hoses sucking away the thick soft silt came upon a chest, and they could see through a broken part of the lid that it was full of longbows. They were working in the weather deck, and it was not long before they found another chest in the orlop, the storage deck of the ship. The first chest contained 48 bows, the second 36. Of these boxed bows, one or two that had protruded through the broken lid had been attacked by gribble and teredo worm and other smaller burrowers, before all was covered in the silt which kept everything safe beneath its anaerobic shroud, free from feeding creatures and oxygen contamination. One of the upper deck bows which must have lain exposed longer than most others was so worm-eaten that it was a kind of filigree in wood, light to handle, and complete in form, but skeletal, ghostly. Of course it is quite possible that other bows, too long exposed above the silt, went beyond the filigree stage and were entirely consumed and so were never seen.

But the glory of the bows from the two bow-chests was that most of them were perfect, and in their first saturated state gleamed almost like new staves, showing clearly the distinction between sap and heartwood. It should be explained at this stage that yew timber cut from the bole of *Taxus baccata* or *Taxus brevifolia* was and still is the prime and perfect material for the making of single stave, unlaminated longbows. Throughout the military usage of longbows the timber was cut as 'self-staves' in lengths to allow the fully worked and tillered weapon to measure 6–7ft (1.82–2.13m) in length. Nowadays the much weaker longbows made for sport are usually constructed from a pair of sister-split billets, fish-tail jointed in the handle. There is not such strain on the timber of sport bows but they are usually made with a single rise, or swell, in the handle section for greater security in the joint; they are not subjected to the rigours of campaign and battle, and instead they lead a gentler, safer life.

By the time it was clear that the wreck site had yielded up all its bows, and the greater part of some 6,000 arrows, the Old Bond Store in Portsmouth Naval Dockyard was crowded with an enormous variety of objects large and small, the products of the famous *Mary Rose* 'time capsule' which attracted so much attention. By now, too, the consulting team of Professors Pratt and Levy and I had been charged with the conservation of the bows, which meant that we could suggest changes in their treatment and later in their storage. The *Mary Rose* conservators had so far tried various methods of treatment: the majority of the bows were laid in running fresh water, some were dried in air (sadly, owing to a major fault in the original humidifying machinery, some of these suffered considerable contortion), and some were treated with polyethylene-glycol (PEG) which has darkened their appearance permanently. The greatest number, removed from their fresh water and encased in damp wrapping, were delivered into the hands of the consulting team and transported to specially prepared racks in the cellars in my house in the country. There, in simply controlled humidity, they were allowed to dry at their own pace for nearly two years. But their life was not all peace: to begin with, every day they were wiped with soft cloths, to remove any surface salts, and every day they were weighed and replaced to lie free of each other and relax. And relax some of them did, losing to a slight extent the contortions which had resulted from the shocks of the sinking and the distortions caused by their positions in the wreck, as well as by the malign humidifier in Portsmouth dockyard.

Gradually their saturated weight reduced, at such a steady rate that the exhaustive daily doctoring, weighing and wiping gave way to weekly, much to the relief of my overworked assistant in these matters, Wendy Garcin. Steadily the excretion of salt lessened as the timber dried and the wiping could be reduced to once a month. During the first twelve months the bows lost up to half their initial saturated dead-weight. When their weights rose and fell with changing humidity, it was plain that in an average atmosphere they could be considered dried, but another six months were allowed before further treatment was started. For a full analysis of all the treatments and the full history of all the bows and arrows, and their differences, recourse must be had to the complete report on all the *Mary Rose* finds,[7] from the ship itself to the hairlice that lodged in the fine-toothed combs of the mariners; from now on this study deals with the best of the bows, including the few that the consulting team was commissioned to test 'if necessary in the case of one or two, to the point of breakage'.

Once all traces of salt had been removed and saline exudation had ceased, the treatment next used was an application of boiled linseed oil, as soon as this method had been approved as harmless and appropriate by the Professor of Wood Science. When that had thoroughly dried and the bows had been lightly rubbed to obtain the soft polish that linseed allows, pure beeswax was applied and polished several times until the bows glowed. Both these treatments correspond to what is regarded as good practice in the preservation of new yew-wood longbows today, and was advocated by the English scholar Roger Ascham at about the time of the sinking of the *Mary Rose* in 1545.[8] Ascham advised that 'you must have a herden or waxed wool cloth, wherewith every day you must rub and chase your bow, till it shine and glitter withal. Which thing shall cause it both to be clean, well favoured, goodly of colour, and shall also bring as it were a crust over it . . . so slippery and hard that neither any wet or weather can enter to hurt it.' Similarly, the Elizabethan Sir John Smythe, in his *Certain Discourses Military* of 1590, noted that in times past:

> the archers did use to temper with fire a convenient quantity of wax, rosin and fine tallow together, in such sort that, rubbing their bows with a very little thereof laid upon a woollen cloth, it did conserve them in all perfection against weather of heat, frost, and wet. And the strings, being made of very good hemp, with a kind of water glue to resist wet and moisture, and the same strings being by the archers themselves with fine thread well whipped, did also very seldom break. But if any such strings in time of service did happen to break, the soldiers archers had always in readiness a couple of

strings more ready whipped and fitted to their bows to clap on in an instant. And this I have heard of divers yeomen that have served as soldiers archers in the field.[9]

So excellent was the appearance of bows treated in this way that we felt they were in almost pristine condition. This turned out not to be true, once we embarked on the commissioned programme of testing, which revealed that in all tested cases the strength of the bows was reduced by a minimum of 50 per cent, owing to deterioration of the cell structure of the wood.

If the good-looking bows were rather a disappointment in elastic performance, the arrows, which looked shrunk and enfeebled, were worse. They broke easily, often when barely moved, and their apparent feebleness has given rise to a host of ill-judged opinions on the part of many who have had access to them. So considerable is their structural collapse that it is almost impossible to tell which of them are made from 'coppiced' wood and which from planked timber. Though we have sectioned some shafts to determine whether growth rings are circular or lateral, we have not yet found one that can offer conclusive proof either way. We have been keen to find coppiced shafts, believing that timber cut from complete, growing stems makes for stronger, more enduring arrows, because there is no cut in the grain – shaping possibly, but no real transverse cut. That both were used is illustrated by May 1484 Ordinances governing the trade by the Worshipful Company of Fletchers, which speak of a sum of 16*d* to be paid to arrowmakers for 100 best quality, bearing (i.e. heavy and

Above: Adrian Barak, of the salvage team, holds the first longbow to be recovered, on the deck of the recovery ship *Sleipner. (© The Mary Rose Trust)*

Right: Longbows from the *Mary Rose* on open shelves at the author's home.

strong) shafts 'well and cleanly cross notched after the best manner, peeled and varnished'. Dowelling cut from timber does not require 'peeling', so this must refer to coppiced shafts.[10]

In December 1359 William de Rothewell, Keeper of the Wardrobe, was ordered 'to buy and fell timber and wood for arrow making at a reasonable price',[11] which must refer to standing timber, to be planked and dowelled. It is also worth noting that at the same time he was ordered 'to buy 1,000 bows, 10,000 sheaves of good arrows [a minimum of 240,000], 1,000 sheaves of best arrows [24,000], with heads hard and well steeled for the King's bodyguard of archers, 100 gross of bowstrings [14,000], feathers of geese and other necessaries for the fletchers' craft'.[12]

A measure of the arrows' shrinkage is given in certain cases by a ring of copper glue applied in the sixteenth century to seal and preserve the fletchings, which makes a larger circle round the shaft of the arrow that has collapsed within it. One chest of arrows, found on the upper deck, held 1,248 shafts or 52 sheaves, tied with cord in bundles of 24, and laid head to head, but so destructive of metal was the Solent water and silt that all those heads were no more than a soft concretion in the middle of the crudely carpentered collapsing chest. Every effort was made to distinguish a single head from the decomposed metal of these and a thousand more arrows, but without success. Professor Pratt and I did identify a kind of 'negative' shadow in a few cases on some shafts where arrowheads had overlain the shafts of arrows packed beneath them, leaving a ghost of their shape below them as they decomposed. These shapes did suggest a short barbed head (called Type 16 in the London Museum Catalogue, and M4 in Oliver Jessop's new typology),[13] but a suggestion is all I would claim. Margaret Rule

Above: Dr Margaret Rule spraying the first of two boxes of longbows to be brought aboard *Sleipner*. Alex Hildred, head of conservation, takes notes. (© *The Mary Rose Trust*)

Below, left: The author, wearing surgical gloves and using a microscope, examines a longbow tip by his racks.

Below, right: The author in his workshop with a *Mary Rose* longbow and an 'approximation' arrow.

Some of the thousands of arrows recorded showing the metallic degradation at their pile ends. (© *The Mary Rose Trust*)

offers some arrow statistics, which to my mind do not represent original sizes before shrinkage and debilitation, whereas such is the nature of yew-wood that the bows' statistics today, in the case of good specimens, can be relied on as their original measurements, weight in hand alone being excepted. Margaret Rule's measurements are given as: 'arrows . . . 0.80m (2ft 6in) long with an average diameter of 0.01m (½in) . . . although no flights remained, traces of green-tinted glue or sealing compound and the spiral impression of binding thread indicate . . . the flights were about 0.15m (6in) long'.[14] She goes on to describe the nocks cut in the ends of the arrows, transversely reinforced by slender horn inserts. Very few of these inserts survive, because horn, being keratin, dissolves eventually in seawater and it was obviously attractive and nutritious to micro-organisms. Of the archers' leather 'bracers',

wrist-guards for the bow arm, 24 have survived, but only one horn bracer, and this only because 'a coil of tarred rope had fallen across the archer and the protein in the horn had been preserved by the biocidal action of the tar'. The same sort of chance preservation allowed just a very few arrows to keep their nock-end slips of horn, but no horn buttons or lanthorn horn panels were found. Most importantly, until recently no horn bow-nocks had been recovered. This brings us back to the examination and interpretation of the bows themselves.

As the polishing of the dried bows continued, their first deceptive wet brightness was regained in a surer form, and some of the best of them looked not much older, though certainly much larger, than Victorian bows. Yew-wood when new displays a sapwood that is almost ivory in colour; in ageing this turns to a soft honey colour. This sapwood is the finest known timber for resisting tension; in a completed bow it lies on the outside of the bend, away from the archer, on what is perhaps confusingly called the 'back'. The 'belly' is composed of the darker heartwood, which lies inwards from its own sapwood towards the centre of the tree. In new timber the heartwood varies in colour from a dark chocolate brown to a much lighter orangey beige, and this heartwood is the best known timber for resisting compression. Thus, with the sap on the outer bend and the heart in the inner, there is in a simple yew stave the perfect wooden spring. As bows grow old the sapwood is liable to fracture, and once cracks are noticed repairs should be made to a shooting bow. The sapwood of the *Mary Rose* bows is still in some cases astonishingly firm and elastic, while in others it is perished and untrustworthy.

There was much to study in all the bows, starting with the bow-tips. It was clear from the outset that at the tips of all the complete bows, or at the one tip of a part-broken or part-degraded bow, there showed an average 2 in (5cm) length of paler-coloured wood on that part which was cone-shaped and usually ½in (1.27cm) across and across the section at its base. The paler section was the result of lesser exposure of the timber, protected by the horn nocks as long as they remained. The silt allowed the horn a longer life, but even in the case of tips left exposed above the silt, and subsequently attacked by marine organisms, the position of this horn on the timber was clearly visible. Sometimes there was a slight ridging at the lower part of this coned tip. This was probably the result of whittling the bow wood for a short space below the position of the horn nock, possibly by individual archers who wanted their weapons 'whip-ended'; this can increase the cast of the bow by speeding up the return of the limbs from full draw to the braced position on release of the arrow. The plain conclusion was that the bows originally had horn nocks fitted to bear the wear of the string loop or knot. The bow-tips also bore slots for the tillering strings, one on the left side of the upper tip, another on the right of the lower.

Tillering is the process of tapering the bow from the centre to the ends, during which the bow has frequently to be held on the tiller by some firm grip at its centre, before being drawn to a gradually increasing depth with the aid of a pulley, to ensure that the weapon is properly balanced. In the earlier stages of this process the stave is much stronger than it is when fully tillered: a 150lb (68kg) bow might well be 200lb (90kg) or more at its early bendings. Some kind of pulley system is thus vital, and very strong bracing strings are needed to fit into the tillering nocks at the bow-ends, which are left thick enough to withstand such stress until the last stage of bowmaking. When the bow is finally tillered the tips are 'coned' to fit into the drilled-out horn nocks, made from the tips of cow or stag horn,[15] and in this process the tillering nocks are more or less worked out, depending on their depth and placement in the first instance. We see it on longbow tips made today, and we saw it on all the surviving *Mary Rose* bow-tips. Some had double tillering nocks that were only partly worked out, the higher being less defined than the lower; perhaps the bowyer felt the higher nock was dangerously near the very end of the stave and abandoned it. Others showed no tillering nock at all, the coning process having worked it out completely, and in a few cases the very tip of the wood was cleanly cut off at a forward angle – proof that the old practice was, as ours sometimes is, to have a neat little horn, more like a deep ring, to protect the wood under it from the working of the string but without weighing down the limb-ends with cumbersome hornery. A glance at the bows in Memling's 'Martyrdom of St Sebastian' in the Musée du Louvre, probably painted some seventy-five years before the *Mary Rose* sank, shows just such neat little horns. I labour this point because there was at the time of the first exhibiting of any of the bows much pother about there never having been horn tips at such an early date, and more stubbornly a determination among some that these great bows were not complete bows at all but unfinished staves awaiting the bowyers' hands – in a ship at sea, in battle! That argument has at last died away. During the bows' sojourn on the racks I invited chosen bowyers and one or two dissenters to view all of them in my care, and the inevitability of the bows' completeness and of their being horned gradually spread among the unbelievers. Every *Mary Rose* bow was complete and ready for use, and some, as we have indicated, were actually *in use* as the ship foundered.

There was no indication on any of the bows of a handle binding, such as we use today to protect the wood from sweat, and the handles themselves were in no way shaped to make the grip easier, nor the middle of the bow stiffer.[16] Those who have inwardly disgested the chapter on bow-making in *Longbow*

Six *Mary Rose* longbow tips which clearly show where horn nocks had been originally fitted.

should make particular note that what I then regarded as a generality in the shaping of bow handles and the stiffening of the bow's centre I now realise is a development that came gradually to the bowyer's craft *after* the military use of bows had ceased. It was for the comfort of the shooter's hands and the removal of stress away from the centre, partly as a result of the use of jointed staves and partly because draw-strengths decreased and the even spread of stress was no longer so vital. I should have known better, but it was not until we began tentatively and with the utmost care to test some of the *Mary Rose* bows that we finally understood what Roger Ascham meant when he described the longbow in his book *Toxophilus* ('Lover of the Bow') published in 1544 and presented to Henry VIII. He was the first writer to set down detailed advice for archers both military and civilian.

He wrote that when you had chosen a well-made bow, you should first 'shoot in him' until you were satisfied you had 'good shooting wood in him' and then 'have him again to a good, cunning and trusty workman, which shall . . . dress him fitter, and make him come round compass everywhere, and whipping at the ends, but with discretion, lest he whip in sunder'.[17] The concept of the 'round compass' was echoed by Maurice Thompson, the American archer, in 1877: 'So long as the new moon returns in heaven a bent, beautiful bow, so long will the fascination of archery keep hold of the hearts of men.' And that is what we saw when we finally achieved a 30in

Left: A detail from the *Martyrdom of St Sebastian* by Hans Memling (*d.* 1494), showing two archers stringing and shooting powerful longbows, very similar in appearance to those recovered from the *Mary Rose*. Their horn nocks are clearly visible. *(Musée du Louvre, Paris)*

Below: Archers drawing heavy bows, from *Sebastian's Altar* by the Meister der Heilige Sippe, *c.* 1493. The artist has carefully depicted the heartwood and sapwood of the bows. On the left a crossbowman spans his weapon using a cranequin. *(Richartz Museum, Cologne)*

(76.2cm) draw with MR1648 on a modern mechanical tiller. The 'new moon', the 'round compass', began to emerge as soon as we progressed from gentle, separate exercise of the bow-limbs. We put the bow first on a simple wooden tiller and with a pulley began inch by inch to draw and immediately relax the bow, until days later we had reached about a 7-inch tip deflection. Then we saw the bow's centre begin to move into action. By the time we had reached a full draw, again days later, on a more sophisticated machine, we had before us a perfect segment of a circle. Like a living creature, the bow first responded to the drawing of the string with a steady deflection of the limb ends, the movement gradually inching inwards towards the centre, and then at a given moment, just as an archer's shoulder muscles come into play as the strain increases across his back, the very middle of the bow began to move, adding its strength to the weight, and so to the power, of the bow. It was a lovely thing to see. That bow was drawn over a hundred times before any crack appeared. The other bows we tried with the same regime indicated imminent collapse before we got more than a 24in (60.96cm) draw and we immediately desisted, but not before we had gained enough information from separate tip deflections and whole bow drawing to deduce their draw-strengths at full draw.

All the tested bows were fitted with cow horn nocks, just as they would have been originally. There is no doubt that a few more bows, given the MR1648 treatment, would have stood up to full draw, but here we ourselves drew the line. Though drawn, 1648 was never shot; the fear was that the shock of speedy release from tension might destroy the bow. There are two other important points to note: in 1997 one of the Mary Rose Trust conservators, Maggie Richards, working on a piece of concreted metal, found within it a complete horn nock, surviving for the same reason that the horn bracer survived. It was slotted for the string, just as the tillering nocks had been, on one side only. This was proof of our belief in horns, but it also posed problems. The old Scots custom was also to have such diagonally grooved horns, and it has perplexed archers today, who find that with a modern string, knotted at the lower nock and looped for easy bracing and unbracing at the upper, there is a tendency for the loop to slip too far towards the single groove, which means an uneven brace and a more uneven draw, as it were diagonally across the length of the bow's belly. My colleague and master bowman Simon Stanley has found an answer: he uses a bowyer's knot, or timber hitch, at both ends. This keeps the string straight and central down the belly, but it is the devil to unbrace, because in shooting the knots become extremely tight. Nevertheless Tudor bows seem to have been single slotted. Simon's experience has again offered an explanation: finding that double-slotted nocks on a

170lb (77kg) bow repeatedly broke away, he realised it was because all the weight was exerted on the front of the horn; with a single-slot nock and a timber hitch the weight is transferred all around the bow, thus spreading the stress. He also says that the timber hitch is easy to remove with the use of a simple bastard string.

Now came a much greater puzzle: the draw-weight of 1648 was about 60lb (27kg) at 30 inches (72.2cm); the other bows, tested in part, suggested weights higher than 1648, but all quite obviously had much lower draw-weights than they would have had originally. Microscopic examination revealed a wide range of cellular deterioration. How could we get at the original weights? Professor Pratt contacted a colleague in Holland, Dr B.W. Kooi, then at Groningen University, now at the University of Amsterdam, and author of a profound study entitled *The Mechanics of the Bow and Arrow*.[18] An experimental programme was planned to compare and contrast the directly measured strengths with theoretical experiments based on Dr Kooi's computer modelling. Dr Kooi has kindly supplied for this study some explanation of his 'mathematical modelling philosophy'. When it was explained that there was a groundswell of disbelief in the results of his modelling among archers in England (who are unable to manage such weights of bow), he wrote: 'In my opinion, that people do not believe the results is not important; what matters is *why* they do not believe the results', and continued:

Mathematical models only mimic the physical reality. Models consist of mathematical expressions that are formulations of physical laws and constitutive relationships. Assumptions are made during this modelling process in order to keep the model tractable. Often the solution of the models has to be approximated by numerical simulations on the computer. The errors due to such approximations are generally much smaller than other sources of inaccuracies. Besides stated variables, the mathematical expressions consist of parameters. The values of these parameters (length of bow, draw length and so on) have to be measured. Some parameters can be measured more accurately than others, and furthermore the sensitivity of errors in some parameter values are larger than other errors. In our case the modulus of elasticity of the wood of the *Mary Rose* bows is unknown for sure and has to be estimated, while the draw-weight of the bow is proportional to this modulus of elasticity. That weight is also proportional to the cube of the height of the cross-section, while it is only proportional to the width of the limb. Last but not least, these bows are made of natural materials and there are always stochastic

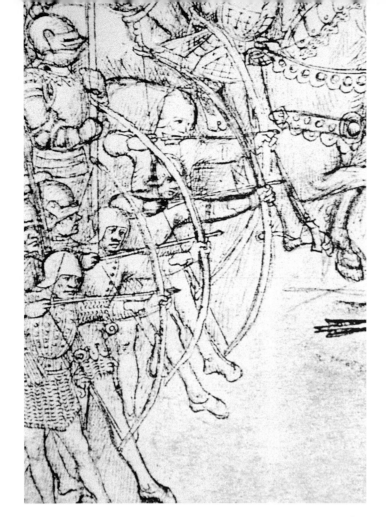

Longbowmen at the battle of Shrewsbury. Heavy and big bows, drawn back to the jaw, the full length of the arrow, which have three- on four-sided heads, for piercing plate armour. The drawing hand in each case is two-, not three-, fingered, which gives rise to the fabled two-fingered salute or victory sign. From the Beachamp Pageant, British Library, Cotton MS Julius E IV, f. 20v. (© British Library)

Archers, handgunners and canon – the contested landing of Alexander the Great in Scythia, c. 1480. From Paris, Bibliothèque Nationale, MS fr 6440, f.173. (Bibliothèque Nationale, Paris)

fluctuations in the properties of the wood. This is partly corrected by the bowyer. We assessed the influence of measurement errors on the draw-weight of most of these parameters by the experiments with the *Mary Rose* 'Approximations'. Of these bows Pratt was able to measure all parameters accurately including the modulus of elasticity and specific mass. For the *Mary Rose* bows themselves there are some extra uncertainties, which were taken into account in your final numbers for the bow weights.[19]

The faction dedicated to keeping the projected *Mary Rose* bow weights down to what they felt were manageable proportions received a boost from a report published in the *Journal of the Society of Archer-Antiquaries* in 1981 in which the late Commander W.F. Paterson RN quoted Dr David Clark's mathematical estimate of the draw-weight of bow number A812 as being between 70lb and 80lb (32–36kg). This claim forced Dr Kooi into reworking his model – and his figures still seemed right. When he told Professor Pratt of his conviction, the latter contacted Dr Clark, who in turn reworked *his* model – and found that he had made an error by the factor of two in his calculations. He now estimated the

draw-weight of A812 as 153lb (69kg), which was slightly over Dr Kooi's projection. Commander Paterson regretted being a party to the publication of so important an error, and sent off corrections to his report for inclusion in the following year's publication.[20] Commander Paterson still doubted that the arrows which he had examined from the 3,000 or so brought up from the wreck so far were stout enough to 'stand' in bows of such weights. I hope my own reaction to those arrows and their obvious shrinkage and profound deterioration may go some way to convince those who share the late Commander Paterson's doubts.

It had already been realised that if we were to come up with real answers we should make copies of the *Mary Rose* bows in new and comparable wood. This very difficult task was given to a bowyer of great reputation, Roy King, who was appointed Bowyer to the Mary Rose Trust. He studied the Tudor bows on the racks very closely and then, using some staves of English yew but mostly staves from Oregon, he began to make some *Mary Rose*-type bows.

Professor John Levy of the Imperial College of Science and the early bending of *Mary Rose* longbow 1648.

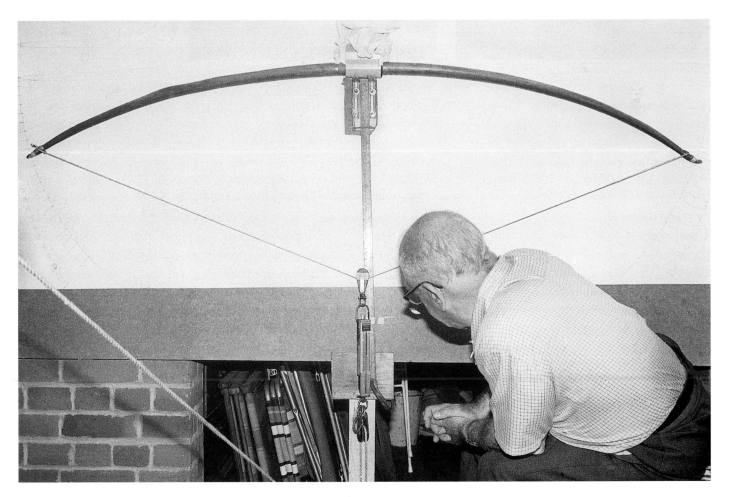

Simon Stanley shooting an early 'approximation' made by Roy King; left, at point-blank range, right, at extreme range. He draws, medieval fashion, behind and below the jaw, but using three, not two, drawing fingers. He draws 33½in (just over 85cm).

Oregon timber was felt to resemble most closely the type and quality of the timber imported from Europe in such enormous quantities throughout the Middle Ages, because it had grown in roughly similar climatic conditions to trees grown in Italy, Spain, Austria, Switzerland, Poland and Scandinavia: in other words enduring colder winters and hotter summers than are usual in the softer climate of the British Isles; this makes for closer year rings and denser timber. There is almost no suitable yew left in Europe which is allowed to be cut; much of it came to Britain in the past and much else was destroyed in the endless wars in Europe. Oregon was also chosen because there lives Don Adams, a brilliant longbow-maker who chooses his trees, tends them, cuts them, staves them and makes them into peerless weapons for hunting and for sporting archery. When approached for big staves, suitable for our *Mary Rose* 'approximations', he at once donated two to the Trust and sent us others as we ordered them. When bow timber was in military demand, and the Royal Wardrobe and the Armouries at the Tower of London regularly sent huge orders to Europe for thousands and thousands of bowstaves (Henry VIII asked permission from the Doge of Venice and was granted leave to import 40,000 staves in 1510 alone),[21] yew trees were specifically grown for the purpose in big

plantations, closely planted and tended by foresters throughout their growth, so that they grew straight and without pins and shoots to spoil the grain of the timber. Because available timber in modern yew stands is so ill-adapted for the cutting of straight staves, it is generally accepted that in England too yew plantations were formally organised. The remains of some of those plantations are still to be seen, but they are ancient now, uncared for, twisted, fasciated, gnarled, forgotten. One example of the use of English yew, from the year of Henry V's Harfleur–Agincourt campaign must suffice here: the King ordered Nicholas Frost, his principal bowyer, to go round England to gather yew for bows,[22] but expressly forbade him to take timber from any ecclesiastical land, which rather pokes a finger in the eye of the old belief that churchyard yews were grown for longbow timber. Nevertheless, foreign timber was clearly preferred where possible; references from the early fourteenth century suggest that the importing of yew from Spain, the Baltic and even from Ireland was common, while in the later fourteenth and fifteenth centuries the government's concern to ensure a ready supply of imported bow-wood was reflected in the injunction that every ship bringing goods into the kingdom must carry a stipulated number of bow-staves as well.[23]

Dr Kooi's computer modelling gave us bow-strengths we could hardly believe, ranging from a moderate 110lb (50kg) draw-weight to an incredible 185lb (84kg) at 30in (76.2cm). An attempt was also made to estimate the draw-weights of the two *Mary Rose* bows in the Royal Armouries, which came out at 98lb (44kg) and 101lb (46kg) respectively, but these estimates were made without the full data that was gathered from the Portsmouth bows. Whether those two bows had been sensibly dried in the nineteenth century, and properly cleaned of all salt exudation, one cannot tell, but they feel comparatively light in hand and are perhaps more dessicated than the Portsmouth weapons. Professor Pratt felt that the huge *Mary Rose* 1607 bow, Kooi-rated at 185lb (84kg), would be likely to break at full draw and suggested it might survive a lesser draw, say at 28in (71.12cm), which would reduce the draw-weight to 172lb (78kg) – which happens to be exactly the same as Howard Hill's hunting bow[24] and is a draw-weight that Simon Stanley can command completely. Simon does not feel happy with a draw-weight of 190lb (86kg); he can shoot it, but has said 'that's why the *Mary Rose* archers had twisted spines!'[25]

According to the Kooi method, then, the draw-weights ranged from around 100lb (45kg) to around 180lb (81.5kg). The largest weight group among the bows was in the 150–160lb range (68–72.5kg). Our later work has confirmed that these are the most likely weights of bows required to shoot the types of late medieval arrows able to inflict the sort of

Above: Roy King working on a first vice-held bend of an 'approximation' bow, in his Lancashire workshop.

Right: *Left*, the backs of an 'approximation' (L) and a *Mary Rose* bow (R), which shows Cambium layer still on the sap; this is safer than modern trimming, which can cut into the sap. *Right*, the bellies of the same pair, the *Mary Rose* bow showing discolouration from undersea contamination.

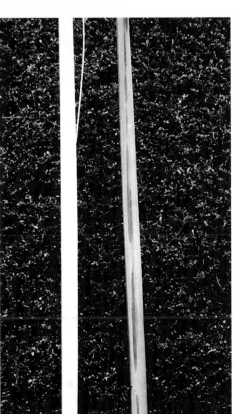

damage evidenced in contemporary descriptions, and account for the outcome and the death-toll in many recorded battles, as will be seen later. Further to fill out the picture of these Tudor/late medieval war bows, they ranged in length from just over 6ft (1.82m) to just under 7ft (2.12m), and their centre (or handle) measurements from a width of 1.61in (41.36mm) and a depth of 1.46in (37.68mm) down to a width of 1.33in (34.17mm) and a depth of 1.2in (31mm).

Faced with such high estimates we were sceptical. By this time Roy King had completed three bows of different weights, from 102.5lb (46kg) to 135lb (61kg), which Simon Stanley was busy breaking in. These were new bows, and we knew their vital, verifiable statistics to the last decimal point. So we sent the same statistics for these bows to Dr Kooi as we had for the *Mary Rose* bows. Back came the answer from his elegant computer model, giving the exact draw-weights of each bow at various draw-lengths. No doubts could remain in our minds about the accuracy of the Kooi estimates.

But great doubts *were* expressed throughout the archery world, and there were many attacks on our conclusions, some of them expressed in less than courteous terms. We have been called fantasists, fools and prattlers (a vile play on Professor Pratt's name) and frankly disbelieved. This disbelief is being gradually undermined, but is still obstinately held to in some surprising quarters. Many still cannot grasp, or will not accept, the fact that Tudor archers could shoot bows so much stronger than they themselves can use: they will, however, admit that Simon Stanley exists and they even allow that he shoots very heavy bows with accuracy, at great length and with alarming penetration. It is extremely difficult to simulate medieval attack and defence properties; for instance when Stanley agreed to shoot in recent tests mounted for television purposes, the target intended to show whether medieval plate-armour could be pierced by longbow arrows was far thicker than any medieval cuirass or helmet, and of a steel not manufactured in the Middle Ages; furthermore the metal sheet was not properly supported, as it would have been by a human body, but was allowed to give and so absorb a good deal of the striking force before penetration. There are archery displays at historic sites, given by good bowmen in medieval costume, wielding good bows no doubt, and some offer the spectacle of not being able to pierce quite thin reproduction plate-armour at quite short distances, proving what exactly? That we did not consistently destroy French and Scottish armies, as long as the archers were properly deployed in battle,[26] and that the archers on opposing sides in the Wars of the Roses did not consistently destroy each other and give rise to truly appalling death-tolls? The sad fact is that if an archer today can command a 90lb (40kg) bow but not a 150lb (68kg) one, he seems unable

to accept the fact that his forebears thoroughly outclassed him. And the disbelievers speak loud and long, and you will doubtless come across their opinions in the majority of written, spoken and televised versions of 'old, unhappy, far-off things, and battles long ago'. Of course you will not penetrate a plate helmet or any other piece of plate-armour, whether made in the year 2000 or the year 1400, if your bow has not the strength to do it, and if your arrow is not designed to penetrate it.

So what should be our next direction of research or experiment? By now the chief controller of our team, Peter Pratt, was dead, much mourned, much missed. We lacked our scientific adviser and we needed help. By a stroke of good fortune and the kindness of the then Chief of the General Staff, Sir Charles Guthrie ('Had he a ballistics expert up his sleeve?'), we were put in touch with Professor Anna Crowley of the Department of Ballistics at the Royal Military College of Science. Stanley and I met her and some of her colleagues; to our joy they were interested in the project and promised that when we were ready and they had the proper tracking machinery on hand they would work on arrow flight, and should be able to deduce impact force and thence penetration possibilities. For the first time in my life I was going to have to abandon foot-pounds as a measurement and learn to understand joules.

Archer Stanley, as he trained himself to these huge bows, began to discover extraordinary things: arrows of the weight and type that we know were used throughout the late medieval period could not be shot with good effect from bows weighing less than about 101lb (46kg), and that the heavier types of arrows, weighing 3½oz (100g) or more, demanded bows in the 143–165lb (65–75kg) range. With this kind of partnership, arrows between 3½ and 4oz (100–115g) shot from such bows would fly at least as far as 240 yards (220 metres). And with the help of Dr Crowley's team, Doppler radar and Stanley's test shooting we were able to assess that such arrows from such bows would over such ranges only lose between 15 and 30 per cent of their initial velocity, regaining at extreme range some of the speed lost during the middle (climbing) part of their flight, and thus regaining some of their power of impact, because gravity increased their downward trajectory. (See the Appendix)

For the moment we must return to the bows in storage and to the years 1980–5. Twenty-two bows, the first batch recovered, found not in boxes but about the ship, were retained at the Old Bond Store, Portsmouth, which, as explained above, contributed to their distortion, though this was not realised until some time had passed. Their retention was intended to offer comparison between the freeze-drying method, drying in air without washing and desalination (apart from the post-recovery freshwater immersion); treatment with polyethylene-glycol; and the method that I was using. By September 1982 all the bows were in my care; there were 138 complete bows, some half-bows, various bits of bows and small fragments. All the complete bows newly arrived from Portsmouth were put into the same system as the other residents: very dry salt dust was removed until there was no sign of it, and the oiling and waxing began in due time. They will never regain the lustre of the boxed bows, and they are lighter in weight being more dessicated, but their weight in hand does fluctuate a little in response to changing humidity. The bows that were boxed and then protected by fine anaerobic silt for 436–7 years or so are almost certainly better preserved than they would have been if they had spent the same period exposed to air.

There are two further observations to be made about the bows' appearance, concerning their shape and the marks on them. Bows that had been in use, apart from the one or two that plainly went down fully braced, show just the amount of 'string-follow' one would expect from good yew bows today, that is a slight bend towards the belly (known as a 'decurve'). Some bows lie straight or almost straight, suggesting newness in 1545, but the majority of the boxed bows show a 'recurve', that is they bend towards the back, or in bowyers' terms are 'set back in the handle'. This is easily achieved in more recent bows made from pairs of billets, and its advantage is that it helps to lessen string-follow in used bows, which in turn means a slightly longer distance to be travelled by the bow's outer limbs from the drawn to the release position, and possibly a faster return and a better 'cast'. The cause of recurve in the *Mary Rose* bows has been much argued. One theory suggests that in water the sapwood shrinks faster than the heartwood, and pulls the heartwood forward. This has been largely disproved. Another suggests it is the result of heat treatment during the bow-making process, but the dangers of heating the timber probably outweigh any possible advantage. A third idea, resulting from much earlier Scandinavian and North German longbow finds (which are closely comparable to the *Mary Rose* finds though almost always smaller and lighter, and almost always recovered from long immersion in lakes, marshes or peat-bogs), was that the Scandinavians made their bows 'the wrong way round', which is impossible, and would mean that the Tudor bowyers did so too. This leaves the two most likely answers: either that the timber was selected from slightly bent trees, where on one side the sapwood and heartwood would show a recurve, and/or the possibility that upon splitting from the bole, even in a straight tree, yew staves tend to enjoy the freedom of release and bend outwards towards the sap, which would allow a slight recurve in staves cut from the whole circumference of the log.

Four Scandinavian longbows (*c*. ninth or tenth century) at Schloss Gottorf, Schleswig-Holstein. The furthest from the camera shows an extreme string shape. The nearest, from Hedeby, is a big string bow in the 100+ range.

The marks are a different matter, sometimes puzzling, sometimes pretty clear. In many cases the geographical centre point and the holding position of the bows appears to be indicated by incised, pricked or even stamped marks. The precise implications of these have not been, and perhaps never can be, fully understood, and such a question may well seem outside the necessities of a study which seeks to throw light on the history of the war-bow of the English and Welsh, but it is my view that we should pursue any detail that might take us nearer to the time of Tudor bowyers and Tudor archers, and so to their predecessors of the fifteenth, fourteenth and earlier centuries. In our opinion there is no reason to suppose the *Mary Rose* bows are not the same as the bows of Agincourt, Poitiers, Crécy and before, the only limiting factor being that of the defence against which the bows and arrows were used, which will be investigated shortly.

The 'centre' of a longbow is midway in its whole length, but to accommodate the differing forces exerted upon and demanded from the weapon on draw and discharge, the 3.9in (10cm) long hand-grip is positioned slightly off-centre, about 1½in (4cm) above and 2.4in (6cm) below the median line. What is known as the 'arrow pass', where the arrow runs above the bow-hand and against the bow-wood, is just above the hand-grip and in modern longbows is protected by a little plate made of mother-of-pearl, metal or leather. The *Mary Rose* bows have no arrow-plate, but about a hundred of them bear in that position what we have called a 'bowyer's mark'. The message thus cut or punched into the left side of 'livery' or 'issue' bows from the *Mary Rose* seems to convey to the archer that 'this is the arrow-pass position, this the upper, this the lower limb'. A full analysis of the bow-marks can be found in chapter 11 of the 1990 and later editions of *Longbow*, but briefly the majority of them seem to have been made with the edge of a chisel or 'float' blade, the float being the multi-edged tool used by bowyers to reduce and shape their staves (the arms of the Worshipful Company of Bowyers, which as a Guild existed well before Crécy, bear three floats). These marks are firm and made in little groups, rarely covering an area of more than ⅝ × ⅝in (1.5 × 1.5cm), though there are examples of double and even

triple marks, which suggest either the personal identification of a bow or an alternative arrow-pass. It is possible, for instance, to drop the bow-hand a little, which would somewhat increase the draw-weight, without danger to the bow. There is a variety of circular marks, sometimes plain, sometimes with interior points or crosses, and there are various crosses, with or without points. The circles appear to have been made with some sort of stamp, the crosses with a blade. Some of the marks are to be found on more than one bow, with some appearing on several, and it is this which inclined us to believe they were made as claims by the bowyers. The known names of bowyers can be found in *Such Goodly Company* by Barbara Megson,[27] and it is perfectly possible that we now have, from the *Mary Rose*, bows made for example by Edward and George Balldocke, Robert Bowier, William Buckstead, John Fynche and Henry Pyckman (there are three Pyckmans) or by apprentices such as William Bennet and Richard Starkey. The victors of Agincourt should have been grateful to Robert Breton, John Bristoll and Tom Burton – certainly to Nicholas Frost, appointed Maker of the King's Bows in 1403.[28] William Barelle, Tom Coton, Robert Lincoln and John Derneford and their colleagues probably made many of the bows used at Crécy. Most of these makers probably liked to mark their bows in some manner; longbowmakers of the last 250 years certainly mark theirs. But several of our *Mary Rose* bows have no mark at all; they are well-preserved bows, so there is little chance of the marks being unseen, and none of them seems of lesser quality, in timber or in manufacture, than the marked bows. Are they apprentice bows? Were they perhaps made elsewhere in Britain, not under direct London Guild control?[29] Or were they made by someone too careless or too proud to add a mark?

There are, too, some marks that do not look at all official – little groupings or lines made apparently with the tip of a knife-blade. These scatterings of marks may have been made by archers, as messages of performance, perhaps distances, or just personal identifications. Whatever conclusion may be reached, the bowmarks add an extraordinarily personal touch to these weapons whose makers and users have long vanished.

Robert Hardy

BOW SUPPLY, BOWYERS AND MISTERIES

If, as we shall see, the Hundred Years War resulted in the rising status of the archer and the possibilities of upward social mobility, so the predominance of the longbow also offered opportunities for those craftsmen who could supply the vast quantities of bows and arrows demanded by the king. For the effectiveness of English armies depended on a ready supply of

arms and ammunition.[30] As the campaigns of Edward I and Edward II had already amply demonstrated, the well-developed central and local administration of England allowed kings readily to exploit the country's considerable resources of men and materials. The onus on supplying men raised by muster had originally fallen to the individual or the counties in which they were raised, but under Edward III the crown provided much of the equipment issued to troops, and the onset of the war with France resulted in a hitherto unprecedented and sustained demand for bows, arrows and bowstrings.[31] In 1341, for example, 7,800 bows were ordered from the counties, while in 1356 alone Edward III ordered 240,000 'good' arrows, and 24,000 'best' arrows, the latter being distinguished by having 'heads hard and well steeled'.[32] In early 1356, in preparation for his major campaigns in France that year, Edward III ordered 5,600 'white' bows (to distinguish them from 'painted' bows) and 9, 900 sheaves of arrows, at a period when 'white' bows were selling at 18*d* each and a sheaf of arrows at 16*d*, while steel arrowheads could fetch 2*s* 6*d* per hundred.[33]

On receiving a demand for a stipulated number of bows and arrows from the king, the sheriff sent his agents into the shires to gain all available supplies by purveyance (the king's right to mandatory purchase), which were then packed, the bows being wrapped in canvas, and sent either to the Tower of London or directly to a port of embarkation.[34] During the reign of Edward II the royal department known as the Wardrobe had established the Tower as its base, and from then on the Tower served as the realm's principal arms depot.[35] As well as a storage base, the Tower was also a centre of manufacture, with bowyers, fletchers, smiths and other artisans working under the supervision of the king's artiller (*attilator*), while supplies of staves, feathers for fletching and steel for making arrowheads were also assembled.[36] Similar munitions depots were established at Bordeaux to supply armies operating in Gascony, and, after its taking by Edward III in 1347, at Calais.[37] The kind of quantities involved may be gauged by the fact that between 1353 and 1360 the Keeper of the Wardrobe, William de Rothwell, obtained 4,062 painted bows, 11,303 white bows, 4,000 bow staves, 23,643 sheaves of arrows and 341 gross of bowstrings to augment existing stocks in the Tower, but even such quantities were deemed insufficient.[38]

Virtually every county was expected to supply quotas of bows and arrows, but writs ordering purchase between 1341 and 1359 reveal that after London, which was to supply 2,500 bows in 1341, highest demand was from Lincolnshire. While quotas sought from other counties ranged between 100 and 500 bows, Lincolnshire furnished 1,000 bows in 1341, another 1,500 in 1356 and a further 800 in 1359.[39] By contrast, in 1341 the greatest demand for arrows was from Surrey and Sussex, where the order for 2,000 sheaves reflected the rich resources of the Weald and the prevalence of iron-working there. Other counties where iron-working facilitated greater arrow production included Staffordshire, Yorkshire, Shropshire and Gloucestershire.[40] Within counties, the production of arrows could be spread among a number of towns. In 1346, for

example, the sheriff of Somerset and Devon purchased 120 bows from Wells, but his supplies of arrows came from Somerton, Bridgwater, Taunton, Sherborne, Bristol and Fleetbridge.[41]

For the crown to order such quantities was one thing, but for the counties to provide for the voracious demands of the royal commissariat was quite another. Often the quotas could not be met in full or by the appointed date; batches of bows and arrows must have continued to reach the Tower by dribs and drabs, while the crown was ready to accept a payment from the shires in lieu of outstanding orders. When need was most pressing, however, such as in 1359 which saw great military preparation, the king impressed bowyers, fletchers and arrowsmiths, who worked at a set wage to fulfil the required order, thereby ensuring a priority for crown supplies.[42] Even so, demand could still outstrip supply, and it was noted in the same year that 'no arrows can be obtained from England because the king has taken for his use all the arrows that can be found anywhere'.[43] Measures were taken to prohibit the export of these vital supplies of arrows and bows, and to retain the craftsmen who produced them within the kingdom. In 1355, for example, armourers in London were forbidden on pain of imprisonment to travel to Gascony or take service in the retinues of great lords going overseas on service.[44] In 1373, fearing the loyalty of religious establishments whose mother houses were in France, it was ordained that 'no alien prior was to dwell within twenty miles of the sea coast lest they send abroad bows and arrows and other weapons'.[45] Even shipments of bows, arrows and other munitions within the realm itself or to Calais required pledges and sureties that such arms would not be diverted to the enemy.[46]

Nevertheless, the demands of the war boosted those industries producing armaments, and led directly to the flourishing of the craft guilds of bowyers and fletchers. In London a community of bowyers and fletchers was already in existence in Ludgate by 1300, but by the 1340s these craftsmen were thriving, profiting from their proximity to the Wardrobe's operations at the Tower. The centre of their trade was at Bowyer Row, immediately to the west of St Paul's Cathedral, where several masters operated, largely from hired premises.[47] The Company of Bowyers first appears by name in 1363, and its formation may well have been the result, as Barbara Megson has suggested, of royal legislation that year ordering all craftsmen to choose between membership of only one Mistery or guild. This measure, designed to ensure the quality of artisans' work, now forced those craftsmen who had made both bows and arrows to specialise, and equally led to the emergence of a distinct Company of Fletchers.[48] By the mid-fifteenth century, when a considerable number of wills survive, it is clear that many London bowyers were men of some substance.[49]

York, a city which had already benefited from the voracious demands for supplies and arms of English armies operating against the Scots, emerges in the later fourteenth century as a major centre for bow production. The bowyers' ordinances registered there in 1395 and subsequent additions to them give an invaluable insight into the concerns of the guild to regulate its trade and safeguard its monopoly.[50] Bowyers themselves were not allowed to work outside the city itself, nor could they take any bows out of York for sale between Martinmas (beginning on 11 November) and Easter. Anyone taking more than one and a half horse loads of bows to the great Chester fair (around the Feast of St Helena, 18 August) faced a fine, for the bowyers of Chester were perceived as dangerous rivals for business, particularly for supplies of bows to garrisons in the principality of north Wales and to royal forces operating against the Welsh.[51] Bowyers or their servants were only to sell their bows in person, and not through any middleman, in order to ensure a stable price. Masters and their servants were forbidden to work at night on pain of a crippling fine of £10, while a penalty of 6s 8d was levied for any caught working on Sundays and on feast days.[52] Such restrictions, which effectively enforced a 'work to rule', were intended to prevent any members of the guild from gaining an unfair commercial advantage by over-production, and also aimed to maintain good quality of workmanship. It was absolutely forbidden for any servant to gain money by teaching those in the countryside the bowyers' craft (lart de bowers), with the gravity of the offence being reflected in a fine of 100s. A further set of ordinances, intended to supplement those of 1395 and probably issued not long after, established 'searchers' to ensure guild regulations and standards of manufacture were met 'for the profit of the king and his people'.[53] Similar provisions for the checking of the quality of arrows and arrowheads, and for the prohibition of working at night, were made in the Ordinances for the Fletchers Company in 1403.

Masters themselves could not practise their trade until they proved to the searchers that they were suitably skilled and able 'to serve the king and his people in his aforesaid craft'.[54] No apprentice was to be taken on for less than the statutory term of seven years.[55] Apprentices were to be honest, able-bodied, free-born – as opposed to unfree villeins – and English by birth, and were not to be taken on until approved by the guild's searchers.[56] Something of the strict conditions of apprenticeship can be gauged from a surviving contract that was drawn up in 1371 between a master bowyer of York, John de Bradlay, and Nicholas, son of John de Kyghlay. The master pledged to instruct his apprentice in 'bowercraft' to the best of his ability and to teach him all he could without concealing anything. He would provide him with board and lodging,

clothing of both linen and wool, shoes and other necessities. In return, John was to receive 6s 8d a year for the first three years of the apprenticeship from Thomas de Kyghlay, chaplain, one of Nicholas's kinsmen and possibly his uncle, while a fellow guild member stood surety for John's adherence to the contract, which was witnessed by a number of other bowyers. For his part Nicholas pledged to obey his master promptly and willingly, to keep his secrets and counsel to himself, and not to waste or damage his goods. He was not to absent himself by day or night without his master's permission, and was not to play at dice or frequent gaming houses, inns or brothels. In a scenario of anticipated domestic infidelity worthy of Chaucer himself, adultery or fornication with the master's wife or daughter was forbidden on pain of doubling the period of apprenticeship, thus giving the master an extended period of cheap labour even if it kept a sexual rival under his roof![57]

Such an apprenticeship would normally begin at about fourteen in the fourteenth century, but by the later fifteenth century the normal age of entry had risen to sixteen. Apprentices entering into this 'close quasi-familial relationship' were subject to the discipline of their masters as they had been to their fathers, including corporal punishment, but the master was expected not to abuse his position of authority, and some contracts for other guilds stipulate that the apprentice was not to be given menial tasks, for as a trainee craftsman he certainly was not a mere servant.[58] Conditions of service must have varied widely. If a master died, any years of apprenticeship still owed might be passed on to the master's heir as an asset or remitted by him in his will. It was not uncommon for masters to leave their apprentices tools and other bequests.[59] In some cases the apprentice actually did become a member of the master's family. The contract of John Derneford (d. 1392/3), the first known warden of the London Company of Bowyers, stipulated that during his apprenticeship of ten years his master, Thomas Huberd of London, was to hold John's paternal lands, but that if John married Thomas's daughter Juliana, these lands would then be settled on the couple.[60] John Derneford had clearly bought into his master's business, but entry into the guild following the completion of the apprenticeship was not always guaranteed, and there were some trained bowyers who worked as journeymen for established masters. But provided there was room in the guild, and adequate sponsorship was forthcoming, an apprentice might make the crucial transition to membership of the Mistery, which conferred considerable status and certain rights as a freeman within the city itself. The master himself might pay the entry fee, which in York was set at 6s 8d. Nicholas's career was probably successful, for in 1420 we find one Richard Kyghlay, perhaps a son or relative, among the fourteen masters of the York bowyers guild.[61]

High demands by the crown for bows sometimes led to the sacrifice of quality for quantity. In 1369 the London bowyers asked the city authorities to confirm an ordinance banning working by night, 'by reason that bows cannot in any manner be made as well or as profitably for the King and his people by night as by day'.[62] The supplementary ordinances of the York bowyers were clearly a response to perceived abuses taken by some of their number. They included the stipulations that no one was to paint any bow before it had been examined by the guild's searchers, even if it was due to be so painted, on pain of a fine of 3s 4d.[63] This strongly suggests that whatever 'painting' involved, it could be used as a means of disguising flaws in the bow or poor workmanship. It was the same story with arrows. In 1369 the king ordered the sheriffs of London and Middlesex to procure 1,000 sheaves of arrows 'of good and seasoned wood, and not of green wood' or they will answer to the king himself and be made an example of, 'that their punishment shall be a terror to others who neglect the execution of the king's commands'.[64] The renewal of the war with France in 1415 had once again led to demands for enormous quantities of arrows, and the following year the London fletchers complained to Parliament that although 'fletchers have always used Aspen to make arrows, and nothing else' the pattenmakers in the city had also taken to using Aspen for manufacturing pattens and clogs, so that 'fletchers cannot get enough Aspen to furnish the King and his realm with arrows'.[65] Though the king accordingly forbade the pattenmakers the use of aspen, pressure on supplies of seasoned wood remained acute and corners were cut. In 1432 the London fletchers again complained that 'the servants and workmen of the said Mistery, hired to make good and lawful arrows and other kind of artillery (dartelrie) for the good of the king and his people, do oftentimes work by night and in secret and change good stuff (estuffe) and dry wood for green wood and other false stuff, and therefrom make unserviceable arrows and other sort of artillery, to the prejudice and dishonour of the petitioners'. They accordingly asked, and were granted, that no member of the guild be permitted to work by night and that 'no freeman of the Mistery shall henceforth have a workman elsewhere than in his own house, so that his work can be overlooked, under a penalty of a fine of 6s 8d'.[66]

The problem of controlling the quality of work of journeymen (and unscrupulous masters who hired them) had equally been in the minds of the York bowyers when they compiled a new ordinance in 1420. They laid down that within York and its suburbs qualified artisans (known as taskemen) working for a master, and who earned money by piecework (taskewerk), were not to work on more than 100 bows at any one time, and that they should perform everything related to such taskewerk willingly and without murmur.[67] A distinction was made between these taskemen and others 'called journayman', who were not proficient enough to perform the more highly skilled piecework, but who instead worked for a weekly wage. These less skilled artisans were to receive 1s a week and food from the Feast of the Purification (2 February) to Michaelmas (29 September), but in the intervening period between October and January they were only to receive 8d and food per week, with the differential possibly reflecting a seasonal drop in demand over the winter months.[68]

What the skilled piecework involved is detailed in a passage of great interest for the light it sheds on the manufacture of longbows, with the Latin text giving the contemporary English terminology for the various operations:

> And, so that it should be better known what the work which is called taskewerk should be, and what should be received for the same, it is ordained that each taskeman should receive for chipping 16d for every hundred bows; for thwytyng, 20d per hundred, and for dressyng by his own work, 20d per hundred; and if he dresses (in English, 'dresse tham') those hundred bows at his own expense, 4s. And for bendyng, 5s for each hundred, and for hornyng for each hundred, 6d, and for drilling out one thousand horns (in English, boryng), 15d; and for cleansing (in English, clensyng uppe) 6d for each hundred, and for afterbendyng, 20d for each hundred, and for polyssyng and skynnyng, 20d for each hundred. And whoever violates this act is to pay for each offence 13s 4d, to be equally put to the use of the community and of the aforesaid guild, [and which is to be paid] through that master who has violated this act.[69]

This clearly set out the respective stages of bow manufacture.[70] The rough bowstave or billet from which the bow was to be worked was first cut down to its approximate size (chipping) with a small axe, before the bowyer began to shape the limbs more closely by paring (thwiting), which he did with a thwiting or draw knife or float. The bow was then bent (bending), usually over a tiller or fixed frame, to see its shape at the draw and assess whether further work was needed in its shaping. After being hollowed out to the required width (boring) and cut to receive the bowstring, horn nocks were fitted over the tips of the bowstave (horning). The bow was then bent once more (afterbending) for final adjustments, before being polished with wax or linseed oil to form a protective layer over the wood (polishing and skinning).

Perhaps the most acute problem facing both bowyers and those seeking to obtain supplies of bows for English armies from the fourteenth to the sixteenth centuries was obtaining

A rare illustration of a bowyer's workshop from the Behaim Codex, 1505, recording a variety of German guilds and craftsmen settled in Cracow. The bowyer is seen in discussion with his clients, two of whom hold crossbows. Note the bench with a screw mechanism for spanning crossbows. *(Jagiellonian Library, Cracow)*

following the king's death in 1422, notified his intention of launching an attack on the heretical Hussites in Bohemia. 'Archers of England', he noted, 'will be among the other nations on this expedition. It has proven necessary to make this decision and it will be soon announced publicly. And since we fear that a shortage of bows, the sort which our English archers are most skilled and experienced at using, might hinder the effort our forces shall make, as we have written to Prussia, we have decided to send and have sent our great friend, the Master of the Blessed Order of Mary of the Teutonic [Knights] of Prussia, to that same region for the purpose of transmitting without delay two ships laden with wood and materials suitable for the making of bows to the Port of London.'[73] Dependence on external supply for so vital a commodity was clearly a potential danger to national security as well as to the capabilities of overseas expeditions. Relations with the Hanse were often strained, not least because of the activities of English privateers. The problem had grown particularly acute from the 1370s and 1380s, and by 1405 had led to an embargo on the export of all Baltic goods to England.[74] Further trouble flared up, notably in the 1430s and 1440s at the very time when the land war in France was going very badly. In 1449, for example, the seizure by English vessels under licence from the government of over a hundred Hanse, Flemish and Dutch ships led to reprisals and the seizure of English goods and merchants at Danzig.[75]

Scarcity could lead directly to profiteering by unscrupulous merchants and to a serious inflation in bow prices. It was probably such fears of hoarding that caused the London bowyers to obtain an ordinance in 1394 requiring that bowyers were not to obtain more than 300 staves at any one time, and were to distribute any surplus among fellow members of the company.[76] By 1472 the Commons were complaining to Edward IV that there was an acute shortage of bowstaves being imported into England, and that those available were being sold at outrageous prices 'whereby the exercise of archery is greatly discontinued and almost lost'. The quality of the wood, moreover, was often poor. In the past, they noted, 100 of the best staves could be purchased for 40s or 4 marks, and the 'wrack' or poorest staves, fit only to make children's bows, sold at 10s or at the most 10s 4d. In better times yeomen could buy a bow for 8d, 10d or, for the best bows, 12d. But now 100 staves cost 100s or 10 marks, and the buyer had to 'take one with the other, ill and good, to the universal hurt of all your people'. Bows were accordingly selling 'at such an excessive price, that is to say some at 10s, some at 6s 8d and some at 5s, whereby the said occupation of shooting is thus discontinued and almost abandoned, and the said yeomen, in default of such bows, now use unlawful occupations', such as dice and cards, to the shame of the kingdom and the comfort of its enemies.

bow wood of suitable quality in sufficient quantities. Some wood, as we have already noted, could be obtained within England, and sheriffs might be granted permission to obtain yew trees from royal manors.[71] Yet indigenous supplies of good yew were limited, and production relied heavily on the import of yew bowstaves from abroad, most notably from Spain, the Baltic and the Adriatic. Little is known about the quantity of such imports before the later fourteenth century, brought by both English merchants trading in the Baltic and by other carriers, though by inference they must have been very substantial. Thereafter customs records reveal merchants of the Hanseatic League importing bowstaves along with other produce from the Baltic such as tar, pitch, wax and iron. In 1396, for example, one vessel entering King's Lynn carried 600 staves worth £6. The record evidence remains patchy throughout the fifteenth century but reveals that in 1467 one cargo at Lynn contained 200 bundles of bowstaves valued at £400, while the ship of Matthew Finkelburg of the Hansa carried 300 bundles of bowstaves at £60 10s. Native merchants continued to be involved in such trade; in 1503/4 Thomas Greenway imported 100 staves worth 20s into the same port.[72]

Nevertheless, difficulties in supply are evident from at least the early fifteenth century. In a letter of 1427 or 1428 to the city of Lübeck, Cardinal Beaufort, Henry V's uncle and one of the most influential figures in the Lancastrian government

Accordingly, it was decreed that every ship entering the kingdom from Venice or any land which had been accustomed to supply good bow wood was to bring four staves for every tonne, with a fine of 6s 8d for each missing stave. At each port these staves were to be examined by two sworn officials 'most expert', appointed by local mayors or sheriffs, and marked as being fit or otherwise, so that 'your liege people may have knowledge of them without defraude'.[77] That these measures had little immediate impact is suggested by the fact that a decade later Edward IV was moved to regulate the price of 'long bows of yew' and other bows, which were not to exceed 3s 4d each, since prohibitive prices demanded by bowyers were discouraging the practice of archery by those otherwise 'perfectly disposed to shoot'.[78] Richard III subsequently received a further petition from the bowyers of the realm, complaining that 'by the seditious confederacy' of Lombard merchants controlling the import of bowstaves into the kingdom, they could only be obtained at the 'outrageous' price of £8 per 100, and that good and bad staves were being sold bundled together. Accordingly, it was decreed that every merchant from Venice or elsewhere was to import ten staves ' of good and hable stuff' for every butt of Malmsey or Tyre wine they imported, that bowstaves could only be sold to the king's subjects, and that they were not to be sold in bundles of mixed quality ('garbelled').[79] In 1488 Henry VII restated that no bow was to be sold for more than 3s 4d on pain of a 40s fine to the king, 'for as much as the great and ancient defence of this realm hath stand of the archers and shooters in long bows', and in 1503 accepted the petition that no customs duties should be paid on any imported bowstaves of 6½ft or above.[80]

Despite such measures, reliance on such ad hoc methods of supply was clearly inadequate. Henry VIII sought to remedy the problem by importing massive quantities of bowstaves from Dalmatia, supplied through the Venetians; in 1510 alone he bought 40,000 staves.[81] This may perhaps be seen as a response to the activities of the Hanse, but the vagaries of Henry's own foreign policy meant that Venice would not always remain an ally. By the mid-sixteenth century problems of supply were once again becoming acute. In 1547, shortly after the death of Henry VIII, Bishop Tunstall informed Protector Somerset that:

> We doo fynde in our countre great lack of bowes and arrowes, and especially of bowes, whereof there is almost none in the countree of ewe. The cause is . . . that a merchant of Danske hath of late time engrossed up and gotten into his hands alone, the byinge of all bowstaves in Eastland [i.e. the Baltic], which were wont to be

brought hyther by diverse merchauntes, and then they were plenty and good cheap, and nowe one man havinge theim alone, enhaunceth the prices as he lyste.[82]

Similarly, he noted, the king's bowyers (presumably those based in the Tower) had established their own monopoly of supply to other bowyers' workshops, all of which had driven the prices of bows so high that many could not afford them, and had created a dangerous shortage for the army. Though the longbow would remain in use throughout much of the remainder of the century, it may well be that one of the underlying factors in the gradual transition from bows to firearms in English armies was less the respective (and hotly debated) merits of the weapons themselves, but the sheer difficulty in maintaining supplies of good bow timber and thus bows at affordable prices.

Matthew Strickland

Let us return to the *Mary Rose* bows themselves. As to the quality of the bowmaking, it is wonderful. A well-made longbow today excites admiration, and it will be varnished and polished till it flashes like glass. These Tudor bows are not so finely finished; the sweeping float lines can be seen quite clearly on the best preserved bows, in some cases as clear and regular as the fluting on the stem of a glass. Plainly these craft masters knew so well the tolerances of their materials that for

The winged and blindfolded God of Love draws a powerful bow to the ear, from a mid-fifteenth-century tapestry from the South Netherlands.

them a bow had no need to be made a museum specimen, though now of course they are just that. They are worth the most painstaking examination by visitors to Portsmouth, for our admiration for the skill of their making brings us closer to the men themselves, who were under constant pressure to produce fine weapons in enormous numbers. If we assume that 30,000 bows a year might be made in times of war or national danger, which a broad inspection of contemporary orders conservatively suggests, then between 1300 and 1550 we are speaking of some seven million bows in the 250 years of the military longbow's greatest usage.

Looking down the long lists of medieval bowyers' names for the period from 1293 to 1580,[83] one realises the continuity of their skills. Basically the making of longbows seems to have changed very little in that period; an efficient bow is an efficient bow and there may be need for change in only one direction: draw-weight. As armour became more efficient at resisting arrows and better designed to deflect them, and shields became more stout, arrow weights had to increase and arrowheads develop. As arrow weights increase, so bow strengths must increase, both to keep the range as long as possible,[84] and to increase the power of their impact and their penetration. Figures given in Longbow in 1992 suggest that an arrow weighing 2–2.6oz (58–75g) could be shot 320 yards (292.6m), and one weighing 1.1–1.5oz (31–42g) 350 yards (320 metres), from bows weighing 160–75lb (70–9kg). With bows of 100lb (45kg) the distances are reduced to 220 and 250 yards (201 and 229 metres) respectively. But could arrows of those weights really 'stand' in bows of 150–75lb (68–79kg)? Arrows that are too light for a bow may either break on release, the shaft not being able to withstand the force imparted by the bowstring, or if they survive will be deflected from true flight and proper speed; their vital initial velocity will be reduced. Our subsequent research makes us believe that by the time plate-armour was in partial use, as at Crécy and Poitiers in the mid-fourteenth century, arrow weights took a leap and bow-weights with them; and that by the time of Agincourt in 1415, when plate-armour was more complete, the necessary weight of arrows to achieve dangerous penetration must have been up to 4oz (113g). Some 250 years later King Charles II is reputed to have complained: 'No one is left to shoot a quarter-pound arrow!'

In the days of mail armour, long bodkin arrowheads were the most effective for penetration. They would slip their needle points in between the links of the mail and, as the heads penetrated, their broadening sides would distort and break the links, inflicting deep wounds on the wearer – often deep enough to cause death or incapacity. Police estimates today of the degree of penetration needed to incapacitate a fit young man in violent action, a depth that naturally depends on the part of the body struck, can seem quite slight: 2–3 inches (5–7.5cm). One eminent physician who is also an archer confirms this and emphasises that the place of penetration is of course vital: 1½ inches (3.8cm) through the left rib cage into the heart would suffice to kill; whereas with proper medical care, complete penetration of muscle to a depth of 4 inches (10cm) could be survived, even if temporarily incapacitating the victim. In medieval warfare septicaemia and poisons in wounds caused an incalculable proportion of deaths, in addition to those killed outright. The French sometimes accused the English of using poisoned arrows, which most have discounted as a false accusation, but recent evidence from the Mary Rose arrows shows that the French may have been right, though it was not a case of intentional chemical warfare.

A copper-based compound was used to protect the fletchings and to help firm the glue that held them on the arrow shafts, and traces of the same copper sulphate have also been found on the business ends of some arrows. It was probably used to firm the glue that held the head to the shaft; some plainly leaked on to the shafts, and could well have entered wounds and caused speedy mortification. If such usage went back to the Hundred Years War, French doctors may have detected it in some noble wound, and thus launched their accusation. My medical informant went on to say that a knife thrust would most likely come from below the ribs, and thus the necessary penetration was minimal, whereas an arrow tends to strike from above, and thus, in order to reach a vital organ, requires greater penetrative force. In subsequent chapters the tactical use of archery in battle will be fully discussed, but it is worth saying at this point that in our view the greatest effect was obtained at relatively short range, from 100 yards down to point-blank distance, where heavy arrows from such bows as we are discussing would be able to achieve a very considerable degree of penetration, as long as deflection did not cause the arrows to fly off their targets.

The development of armour and the extent to which it was proof against arrows is dealt with more fully in chapter 15. Here let us note that deflection became more and more likely as part-plate and whole-plate armours developed. Even a slight angling of the target surface would greatly lessen the chance of good penetration and increase the likelihood of bending or breaking a long-pointed arrowhead. So the arrowhead was shortened, thickened and made heavier, and shaped so that it had cutting edges, usually three or four, in a trihedral or tetrahedral head. As the head became heavier, a thicker and so heavier shaft was needed to carry it, along with a heavier bow to discharge the arrow. The heavier, thicker shaft required a bigger socket on the arrowhead. It is by examining the type of arrowhead and the size of the socket that we may well be able to date much more accurately than had previously been thought the many hundreds of arrowheads that survive in the museums and private collections of Europe and America. It is possible that many later arrowheads previously thought to be crossbow bolt-heads are indeed arrowheads from arrows heavy enough to match heavy longbows. One can make quite a nuisance of oneself, in antique shops that deal in arms and armour, looking at the bolt-heads offered for sale and telling the proprietors that they are selling arrowheads.

There are limits: a head with a socket interior measurement wider than ½in (14mm) is almost certainly a bolt-head, and a bodkin head with a socket interior measurement of less than ⅓in (10mm) is more likely to be an arrowhead from before the main development of plate-armour. Great broadheads or phaeons which are of the old hunting head type are either early or late, but latterly were used only for the chase because they could not cut through mail links except at very close range. They gave rise to the so-called Type 16, a much narrower, two-sided, bladed and barbed head, ballistically much more effective and able to penetrate mail, though not as easily as the bodkin of the kind clearly shown in the Beauchamp Pageant drawings. At short range it could be effective against plate, but it was deadly at almost any range against lightly armed men and appallingly destructive among horses. It is this type of head which I have always thought Froissart was alluding to when he spoke of 'the English bearded arrow'.[85] (Simon Stanky believes Type 16 heads were the result of much sharpening of arrows such as those seen overleaf.)

Yet, in thinking of the very many who died of their wounds, we must also remember the firm evidence from medieval battle casualties of horrendous wounds that healed. Skeletons from a small mass grave, casualties from the battle of Towton, have recently been excavated and examined with the most meticulous forensic care, the results of which have been published in *Blood Red Roses*.[86] The bloodiest battle ever fought in England, on Palm Sunday 1461, Towton was allegedly responsible for as many as 20,000 deaths. Some of the skeletons exhibit not only the horrible wounds that presumably caused their deaths, but also sure evidence of old wounds, in some cases causing severe deformation. But these had healed and were survived, and the men who bore them were able once again to take their place in the fighting line. The second example is the arrow wound to 15-year-old Prince Henry of Wales (later Henry V) at the battle of Shrewsbury in 1403; it was severe enough for those around him to try to make him leave the field, which he refused to do (and he fought on, materially shifting the balance of the battle). We know how serious the injury was because the surgeon who treated him, John Bradmore, wrote up the case in detail, and if the portraits showing the left side of his face, where the arrow struck, are anything to go by the extraction of the arrowhead was

very neatly done.[87] Although many survived, there is no doubt that the majority of the wounded, especially among the ordinary soldiers, succumbed from lack of care. It is worth repeating that huge casualties on *both* sides, such as occurred at Towton, Shrewsbury and Tewkesbury, only occur when the longbow is ranged against the longbow; where the longbow is effectively and massively deployed against armies without matching missile support, there are few casualties on the side of the longbow but enormous loss of life among the opposition, as at Dupplin, Halidon, Crécy and Agincourt.

If we are right about the weights of the *Mary Rose* bows there are three questions we must attempt to answer. What sort of men were able to master them? Why can so few men nowadays do so? Thirdly, did bows like those sunk in the Solent in 1545 see action at Bosworth only sixty years before, at Towton twenty-four years before that, or at Agincourt only forty-six years before Towton? Can we take them further back, perhaps to Poitiers, fifty-nine years earlier than Agincourt, or to Crécy, ten years before that? If the answer is that we reasonably can, then how much earlier in history can we assume there were bows of *Mary Rose* weight? Did Edward I have such bows in his Welsh and Scottish wars?

Let us attempt some answers. The first two questions are closely related. The greater part of the men who provided the archer corps for the three Edwards, for Richard II, for the Lancastrian Henrys and the Yorkist Edward IV and Richard III were drawn from those who worked on the land, in one way or another. They were men who in their daily lives were accustomed to hard physical labour, facing the kind of unremitting demands which we only see nowadays among a few farm workers who rely more on their bodies than their machines, or the most highly trained athletes. They endured hard living conditions, and they were used to surviving cold, flood, disease and times of dearth, but they also enjoyed times of plenty. Their lives encompassed Nature's ruthless mix of riches and privations. It is possible that their metabolism was more efficient than ours; if so it would mean that in good times and bad they converted their diet, rough and insufficient as it may have been for some, more immediately into strength and energy than our bodies are accustomed to do today. More certainly, studies of agricultural workers have shown that by the fifteenth century men ate more wheat bread and more meat than their thirteenth-century counterparts, accustomed to barley bread, cheese and only a little meat or salted fish.[88] Such an improved diet, together with hard and frequent practice with the bow, would make them strong and efficient archers. Being mostly countrymen, whether small farmers, labourers, the better off and even sometimes the very poor, they had access to good meat, good bread, fruit in season and milk products, except in

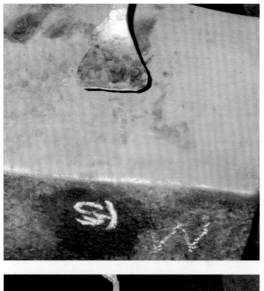

The making of a barbed arrowhead. Clockwise from left: the metal is flattened to make the ferrule, which is then coned to take the shaft. The barbed cutting edges are separately forged before being heat-welded onto the socket. *(© Simon Stanley)*

the worst of times, and they could hunt wild game, depending for the most part on the countryman's weapon, the bow. As we shall see in Chapter 8, hunting was only allowed officially in certain areas; in the royal forests those without special licence could not use sharp arrowheads or broadheads, only blunt piles – or to put it in Norman French: '*Arkes et setes hors de foreste, et en foreste arkes et piles.*' According to one historian:

> The moment the idea of controls upon peasant archery enters the picture, a figure can be seen fitfully among the forest trees, a figure in Lincoln Green, with his companions, their longbows in their hands; the greatest outlaw in history, but the hardest to pin down to a reality, just as he was the hardest to catch in those distant days.[89]

The elusive Robin Hood is so elusive because, whether he actually lived or not, he was a potent symbol of those who reject harsh authority, those who carry broadheads in the royal forests

– and there were always plenty of such men. The men of the countryside, of heath and hill and forest, were used to violence as well as hard living and hard labour. We need only look at the number of pardons granted to archers during the long years of the French wars: H.J. Hewitt in his illuminating study points out that these were times of violence, and that there were many murderers about who were declared outlaws, but 'it was held that murder (and other crimes leading to outlawry) could be expiated by notable service', and pardons could be granted by the King.[90] Taking up arms in time of war of course was not only militarily useful but was also the most effective way of offering 'notable service'. In 1339 and 1340 'at least 850 charters of pardon were granted to men who had served in the wars'.[91] At the time of Crécy and the subsequent siege of Calais, and for service against the Scots, 'several hundred' more pardons were granted; for service at the siege at least 1,800.[92] After the Poitiers campaign of 1356 there were 140 pardons, 'and in 1361, over 260'. Hewitt adds that 'the proportion of murderers in these numbers is considerably above three-quarters'. These

figures are taken from the Calendar of Patent Rolls. So we are thinking of tough, life-hardened, dangerous men in many cases, many of whom would have been accustomed to the bow, and of whom the majority, in obedience to the laws or for their own benefit, would have regularly practised at the butts, established in most towns and villages throughout the land, every week and on high days and holidays. Those who broke the laws and disappeared on practice days were likely to be using their bows none the less, for less worthy purposes. The use of indentured retinues in the fourteenth and fifteenth centuries meant that those archers chosen were the best, and by 1415 some at least were yeomen, even minor gentry, so they would have been comparatively well fed.

Those who went to France or Scotland in the thirteenth-, fourteenth- and fifteenth-century campaigns, and earlier, depended for their lives on their weapons, and therefore weakness, poor shooting speed and inaccuracy through lack of practice were widely seen to be suicidal. They worked hard in those campaigns: they marched long distances, although from the 1330s more and more of them were mounted. It is true that they repaired broken bridges and built causeways from whatever materials were at hand, as they succeeded in doing at

Tudor archers flank a scene depicting the temptation of Eve, from a sixteenth-century oak chest at Cothele Hall, Cornwall. The size of the arrow (but not the bow) held by the archer on the right has been greatly exaggerated. *(Courtesy of the National Trust)*

the two crossings of the Somme, upriver at Voyennes and Béthencourt in 1415;[93] they also sacked towns and villages when they were allowed to, stole when they could, drank when they had the chance, brawled and quarrelled among themselves and with those from other parts of England and Wales. Much of that we still seem able to do, though nowadays we cannot pull the big bows. Why? Because we do not start to shoot at seven or eight years of age, we do not practise as they did, and because there is no point in having great heavy bows any more, unless we are determined big game hunters with the bow and arrow. The furthest distance shot in longbow competition is now 'twelve score', or 240 yards (218.4m), but the more usual distances are 180 yards (163.8m) and 100 yards (91m) and so on down the scale, but at any of the distances we have no need to penetrate or destroy, merely to hit the target. I have the greatest respect for modern British professional soldiers and their fitness. We all know something of the toughness of their lives, if only from television documentaries, and I have no doubt that many of today's soldiers could be trained to shoot the great bows, but it would take ages of practice and they would have little time for anything else. It is worth repeating here the often-quoted words from a sermon preached by Bishop Latimer in 1549, four years after the *Mary Rose* foundered, in the presence of the boy king Edward VI, Henry VIII's son. The bishop was complaining about the decline of shooting among his contemporaries:

> The art of shooting hath been in times past much esteemed in this realm. It is a gift of God that He hath given us to excel all other nations withall . . . whereby He hath given us many victories against our enemies . . . Let there be sent forth proclamations to the justices of the peace . . . for they be negligent in executing these laws of shooting. In my time, my poor father was as diligent to teach me to shoot as to learn me any other thing, and so I think other men did their children. He taught me how to draw, how to lay my body in my bow, and not to draw with strength of arms as other nations do, but with strength of the body. I had my bows made me according to my age and strength; as I increased in them, so my bows were made bigger and bigger, for men never shoot well, unless they be brought up to it.[94]

Latimer was soon to be burned to death in Oxford in one of Queen Mary's *autos-da-fé*, but he was not the only man to voice such an opinion. Lord Herbert of Cherbury's complaint, written in the early seventeenth century is also worth quoting because it sheds light on the causes of the decline and also offers links to our own time and attitudes: 'Since the use of arms is changed, and for the bow (proper for men of our strength) the caliver (hand-gun) begins to be generally received, which . . . may be managed by the weaker sort.'[95] Not only was the population falling but the countryman was not so stout a yeoman as his ancestors. The tillers of the soil were increasingly driven from common lands which were being turned into sheep runs, and 'a few sheep masters could serve for a whole shire . . . and none left but a few shepherds, which were no number sufficient to serve the King at his need' and anyway 'shepherds be but ill archers'.[96] There had been bubonic plague in the 1540s and 1550s which, together with a 'sweating sickness', seems to have killed about a third of the able-bodied population. There was a lowering of living standards, a general loss of sheer physical strength among men 'pinched and weaned from meat', but that physical strength, maintained by good diet and the robust work of the old agriculture, was a necessity for the men who used the great bow. The wages of archers even, were whittled away by inflation: 'Sixpence a day now will not go as far as fourpence would . . . and therefore you have men unwilling to serve.'[97] The social changes that were taking place, the inflation, the extravagance that was much complained of, the reduction of the size of households and the loss of belief in the ideas of duty and service, all worked together against the continuation of great numbers of strong and willing archers.[98] All this is in the middle of the sixteenth century, not in the twenty-first, but how curiously familiar it all sounds, if you simply replace 'archers' with 'servicemen'.

The pathologist Dr A.J. Stirland, in her study of the *Mary Rose* skeletons, found evidence of childhood malnutrition. 'Given their average ages this is hardly surprising. Most of them will have been born in the 1520s, a time when famine was periodically widespread . . . in particular the severe winter famine of 1527–28.'[99] She points out that most of the bones affected by osteomalacia were well healed, and that in general the young men of the *Mary Rose* seem to have been a good deal healthier than many of their contemporaries. The exceptional state of so many of the bones (like the bows, well preserved in Solent silt) afforded evidence of high muscle and tendon activity, and encouraged Dr Stirland to try to identify archers' bones as opposed to mariners', and she came across examples of changes in shoulder blades which could only have resulted from heavy work. This might result from marine work on ropes and sheets and heavy tackle, but equally it might result from the frequent use of heavy bows. She decided to assess 'only complete pairs of shoulder blades' and found 'a slightly increased frequency of os acromiale (the condition in question) in the left side of the group of paired shoulders'. It is encountered more usually bilaterally, so what could this mean? Dr Stirland concludes that overall there was sufficient evidence to suggest that 'there was a group of specialist, or professional archers among these men', who were 'largely young', with 'average height within the range of today's recruits . . . a group of men who were in many ways rather like us in appearance'.[100] Moreover the skeleton of one of the two archers found on the ship's companionway showed distortion of two of the central vertebrae, almost certainly caused by twisting round and forward to the left – the result of the stress of drawing powerful bows. The other had developed nodes on some of his thoracic vertebrae, caused by persistently lifting heavy objects (or possibly by compression fracturing).

Dr Stirland brings out another very important point: *Mary Rose* bows 'between 135–160lb draw-weight (61–73kg) . . . needed arrows to be 3½–4¼oz (100–120g) to absorb all the energy of these very heavy bows and attain their targets with full effect'. And she adds a rider, resulting from our studies, to the effect that assuming the computer modelling of the *Mary Rose* bows is correct, that their draw-weights ranged from 100lb (45kg) to 175lb (79.2kg) at a 30in (76.2cm) draw, and the results of the experiments with our modern replicas, the so-called *Mary Rose* Approximations, run very close to those predictions. *But* she points out that the growth rings in some of the *Mary Rose* bows run much closer than those in the Oregon timber which we have largely used, and that 'means that the older yew was much denser and therefore stronger than the modern yew, since it had grown much more slowly. It is likely therefore to have produced even higher draw-weights . . . than predicted.'[101] This conclusion, which means the best European yew is a stronger timber than that from America, is backed up by Simon Stanley from his own experience, by Roy King, Bowmaker to the Mary Rose Trust, and by John Cave, another fine bowyer who is widely experienced in both types of timber. I have quoted Anne Stirland at some length, not only because she backs many elements of our case but also to persuade the reader to have recourse to her wholly fascinating account of her experiments with some of the crew of the King's ship *Mary Rose*, before they were given honourable reburial on shore.

I will add some thoughts that I delivered in Paris in April 2000, during a symposium at the Musée de l'Armée, entitled L'Homme Armée, before such alarmingly experienced and knowledgeable medievalists as Professor Philipe Contamine and Professor Bertrand Schnerb. After quoting some of Stirland's conclusions I told them that Stanley admits to lumbar changes, such as Dr Stirland observed in her studies, as a result of shooting heavy bows, and to both pain and deformation in his drawing elbow, hand and fingers; it is possible that scapula X-rays might show changes, or signs of similar stress to that seen in the *Mary Rose* archers, in his shoulder blades. Our researches, led in this respect by Stanley, also showed that arrows of the weight and type we now felt certain were used throughout the late medieval period could not be shot with good effect from bows weighing less than 100lb plus (46kg) and that heavier types of arrows weighing well over 3½ or 4½oz (100 or 115g) shot from bows of matching strength would fly at least as far as 240 yards (220m) without losing a critical amount of their initial velocity. As we have seen, tests carried out at the Royal Military College of Science, using Doppler radar to track the arrows, suggest that the loss of velocity over the full range was between 15 and 30 per cent, partly due to the addition of gravity from the zenith of the arrow's high parabola; also that the initial velocity of an arrow of 3.8oz (108g), shot from a 150lb bow (68kg), is about 57 yards (52m) per second, giving a kinetic energy of 146 joules – roughly the equivalent of suspending a sharp arrowhead with a load of 150lb+ (68kg) behind it a foot above the ground, and then letting it fall. At the shorter ranges referred to earlier, it would very probably pierce good plate-armour, provided that it was not deflected by inclined metal surfaces.[102] Lighter arrows, of the Westminster Abbey type, barrelled and thus strengthened in mid-shaft so they could still stand in heavy bows, could be shot 300 yards (270m) and more; perhaps, as some claim, about the limit of accuracy of the Martini-Henry rifle, before which such a distance was out of the effective range of any hand-held firearm. Winston Churchill, in his *History of the English Speaking Peoples*, puts it concisely, and more safely. At the time of Crécy he says: 'At two hundred and fifty yards the arrow hail produced effects never reached again by infantry missiles at such a range until the American Civil War.' And Churchill hardly had access to the results of the latest research.

It is worth a glance at the development of the musket and rifle to see how true such claims may be. Charles Chenevix-Trench in his *History of Marksmanship* is a reliable guide: 'In a carefully observed and recorded test held in 1776 a marksman with a heavy German rifle at . . . 150 yards (136m) shot a ball six times out of eight within the circumference of the crown of a hat.'[103] But the smooth-bore musket, 'as a weapon of war, was still on balance the better weapon, because the rifle ball was still inaccurate as to size and reaction to the rifling and the rim-bullet had not yet been perfected'. The 'Tower' musket or 'Brown Bess', used by British infantry from the reign of William III until the 1840s, fired a ball of about 1oz (28g), but the fact that the ball was smaller than the barrel bore led to inaccuracy because the ball 'bounced' from side to side during its passage through the barrel.[104] Changes were made and accuracy improved, but 'fired from a rest at a target 11½ feet by 6 feet (3.5 × 1.82m) ten shots at 250 yards (228.5m) all missed . . . [while] at 150 yards (137.1m) only half the shots hit'. Though the Germans developed an elite corps of Jägers, drawn from among foresters, hunters and gamekeepers, they could not compete with line infantry firing en masse though less accurately. This underlines perhaps the most important battle-winning attributes of military longbow archery: the mass volley.

The famous Kentucky rifle of the American War of Independence 'was not in all circumstances a better weapon than the German rifle or the musket'.[105] A further improved rifle, the Ferguson, was accurate at 200 yards (183m) but even in expert hands could only average four shots a minute, whereas the longbowman *could* shoot ten a minute and more, though Stanley says that with the heaviest bows he does not like to try for more than six a minute, and argues that three a minute would still produce an 'Agincourt result'. The Baker rifle, which followed the Ferguson, was inaccurate beyond 200 yards . . . and so on. What seems true is that only in very skilled hands could the muskets and rifles of the late eighteenth and early

The 'double-armed' man. A suggestion for a Jacobean archer to have both bow and pike. Sir John Smythe wrote ferociously against the disappearance of the longbow from military use. These illustrations are from a watercolour set in the author's possession, after the woodcuts in Smythe's *Double Armed Man* (1625).

nineteenth centuries achieve as much as the longbow used to accomplish, until, as Churchill says, the American Civil War, though I grant it is a general indication rather than a fact proven in detail. It remains a fact that the calivers and other hand-guns which banished the longbow from military use were far less effective than longbows, though admittedly, as long as they actually worked, the weather was not too wet or windy, and they did not blow up, they were easy to learn to use and required minimal skill and scarcely any strength.

To return to the Westminster Abbey arrow,[106] and to a sad story. It is the one arrow remaining in England which may well date from the early fifteenth century, 130 years before the *Mary Rose* arrows. It is the property of the Dean and Chapter of Westminster Abbey, and can be seen in the museum in the cloisters, together with Henry V's saddle, shield, sword and great helm, which formerly hung above his tomb in the Henry V Chantry Chapel. There, in 1878, the arrow was found, and was presumed to have been used against marauding pigeons in perhaps the seventeenth or eighteenth century. With its lethal, barbed head it seems an inappropriate

missile both for the target and for the sacred precinct – a bird blunt would have served much better and would have been safer for the environment. Peter Pratt and I contacted the Dean and were granted access to the arrow, and were able to examine, weigh and measure it. Its 'spine', or 'bendability', suggested that it would best be shot out of a bow in the 150lb (68kg) range.[107]

What we needed was a date for the arrow, which meant taking a small sample of the shaft timber. The Oxford University Carbon Dating facility stood ready, but the Chapter refused permission. Time passed and our research and testing crept forward. It became increasingly clear how important it was to date the Abbey arrow. Not long before Peter Pratt's death we tried again. There were new people in charge and our hopes were high. We made our case with care. We argued that to refuse permission to remove the head, drill out a minute bore of wood from the shaft no bigger than a pencil lead, fill the tiny hole and replace the head, made a nonsense of the reason for refusal: that the arrow was too precious to risk. While its date is unknown, the relic has nothing to tell us; there can be no label attached to advance public knowledge, so it is not precious, merely a question mark. We went to great lengths to explain the safety of the projected method, that there would be highly qualified archaeologists in attendance, but still the answer was, and remains, 'No'. One day perhaps it will be realised how precious a relic they might hold, if it could be dated to a period that covered the reign of Henry V *or* earlier. Even if it is of the Tudor period, it is in far better condition than the thousands of survivors from the *Mary Rose*. Whatever its date, it would help to place the concept of 150lb longbows in a definite time-scale.

A final word about arrows and arrow woods from Roger Ascham. In the light of our knowledge that the *Mary Rose* arrows are made from several types of wood, Ascham's contemporary list is doubly interesting: he writes of

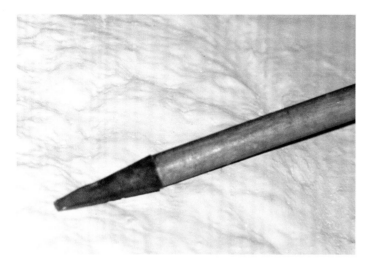

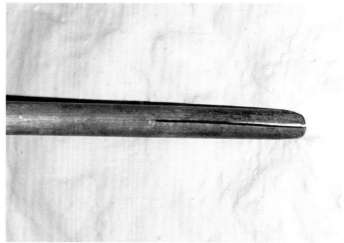

fifteen different woods, the more recognisable being brazil, birch, ash, oak, blackthorn, beech, elder, asp (aspen or poplar) and 'sugar cheste' (Spanish chestnut).

> Birch, hardbeame [hornbeam], some oak and some ash being both strong enough to stand in a bow, and also light enough to fly far, are best for a mean [average] . . . As concerning sheaf arrows for war (as I suppose) it were better to make them of good Ash, and not of Asp as they be nowadays. For of all other woods that ever I proved, Ash being big is swiftest, and again heavy to give a great stripe withal, which Asp will not do.[108]

The heavier the arrowshaft, consonant with good range, the greater the inertia when the arrow hits the target, and so the better the penetration, which is what Ascham means by a 'great stripe'. The Westminster Abbey arrowshaft is of ash.

This study examines in detail the military use of the longbow in Europe, and though our conclusions may not meet with universal agreement, at least from now on no one can attempt any conclusions without taking into consideration the 138 bows that have been brought to us from the past through the death of the *Mary Rose*. Such historians as have chosen to play down the effectiveness of the military longbow will have to fly now in the face of facts which only emphasise what so many contemporary chronicles of the Hundred Years War affirm: that until the French learned *not* to attack English and Welsh archers and men-at-arms under pitched battle conditions, and instead developed the use of gunpowder artillery, the longbow accounted for a long run of massive French defeats. But, as I have often said, when French eyes have flashed at talk of English victories, 'Remember Joan of Arc; remember Castillon.'

Robert Hardy

Three photographs of the Westminster Abbey arrow. *Clockwise from left:* the neat little Type 16 head, the barbs compressed against the ferrule; the arrow nock with the split where the horn insert would go, across the grain, to resist string impact; the whole arrow, showing the remains of paint and glue to hold the fletchings – the shaft is 'bob-tailed', i.e. slender towards the nock end. It is 'barrelled' for strength near the centre of gravity, and thus slightly reduced towards the arrowhead.

CHAPTER 2

Origins and Antecedents: the Myth of the Shortbow

he evidence from the *Mary Rose* provides a vivid impression of the awesome power of the Tudor longbow. Yet these bows stem from the twilight of effective military archery in England. The key question is whether these were the kinds of weapon in use at Dupplin Moor and Halidon Hill, Crécy, Poitiers and Agincourt. What, indeed, was the origin and ancestry of the longbow? Was the 6ft yew bow, as was long thought, the result of technical development stimulated by Edward I and his grandson Edward III, and thus part of the 'military revolution' of the late thirteenth and early fourteenth centuries? Or was it rather that the self-bow employed by the archers throughout the medieval period was essentially the same weapon, and that what brought the longbow into increasing prominence from the early fourteenth century was its mass deployment by English armies and tactical developments on the battlefield? These are fundamental questions which lie at the heart of this study.

THE MYTH OF THE SHORTBOW

As a potent symbol of English military greatness, it was not surprising that the longbow should attract much attention from late nineteenth- and early twentieth-century scholars such as Sir Charles Oman, J.E. Morris, H.B. George and T.F. Tout. In particular, these historians sought to trace the tactical origins of the battle-winning combination of dismounted men-at-arms and archers. One of the central themes of Oman's influential two-volume *History of the Art of War in the Middle Ages* was the evolution of the tactical combination of archery and cavalry, the only two military elements in medieval armies he regarded as being of any real value.[1] Oman believed that the genesis of the battle-winning English tactics of the Hundred Years War lay in the reign of Edward I (1272–1307) when 'the longbow first comes to the front as the national weapon'.[2] 'To trace the true origin of

the longbow is not easy,' admitted Oman, but he nevertheless believed that its use by English armies 'was originally learnt from the South Welsh'. Edward I, he argued, had found the Welsh using the rough bow of elm described a century earlier by Gerald of Wales,[3] and was quick to grasp its potential. He employed large numbers of Welsh archers first in his conquest of North Wales, then from 1296 in his attempted subjugation of Scotland. For Oman, the longbow's first serious military deployment was against the army of William Wallace at Falkirk in 1298.[4]

Oman's views received modification by J.E. Morris in an influential work, *The Welsh Wars of Edward I*, one of the first detailed studies of Edward I's armies based on the extensive surviving record material, particularly army pay rolls.[5] Morris laid to rest the theory that Edward's Welsh wars had acted as the catalyst

A rough sketch of a Welsh archer from the margins of the Treaty of Montgomery, 1267, contained in the *Littere Wallie* (London, The National Archive E36/274). *(The National Archive)*

for Edward's adoption of a significant archery arm; not only had the possession of bows and arrows been enjoined on the poorest ranks of freemen by Henry III's Assize of Arms of 1242, but English archers were visible well before Edward I's first Welsh campaign in 1277. Bowmen can be found among the infantry in the 'Barons' wars' of 1264–7, while archers from Nottingham-shire, Derbyshire and other English counties served from the outset of Edward's operations against Wales.[6] What Edward's Welsh campaigns did witness, Morris argued, was the genesis of the crucial tactical combination of archers and men-at-arms, which first occurred not, as Oman had believed, at Falkirk, but at the battles of Irfon Bridge (1282) and Maes Moydog (1295), where the English had used mixed formations of knights and bowmen to break up the tight formations of Welsh spearmen.[7]

But supposing Edward I was the founder of an effective archery arm in English armies, what then of military archery before the mid-thirteenth century? For as both Oman and Morris

realised, the bow had been in use for centuries previously, and was visible in Anglo-Norman warfare of the eleventh and twelfth centuries.[8] Indeed, had not William the Conqueror employed an effective combination of bowmen and cavalry at Hastings, in tactics that seemed closely to mirror those of Falkirk – only two hundred years previously? Yet the answer appeared simple. The Normans and their Saxon opponents at Hastings were not employing the longbow – for, it was argued, this did not yet exist – but rather the weak 'shortbow'. This latter weapon, in the words of Morris, 'was then held of no account: the string was pulled only to the chest, and the arrow, except at close quarters, was shot high . . . a high trajectory being in itself a confession of weakness'.[9] It was the alleged impotence of this shortbow, supposedly drawn to the chest not the ear, that explained the absence of effective archery on the medieval battlefield before the reforms of Edward I. Further evidence of the shortbow's insignificance was the absence of the bow from Henry II's Assize of Arms of 1181, an edict which enjoined all freemen to possess specified arms and armour according to a sliding scale of wealth.[10] Equally, the clear dominance of the crossbow in the armies of Henry II, Richard and John could only be accounted for by the inferiority of the shortbow: it was impossible to believe that a commander as gifted as Richard the Lionheart (1189–99) would have favoured the crossbow if he had known the military value of the true longbow of the fourteenth century.[11]

Yet contemptible though it was, the shortbow nevertheless was 'capable of great development'.[12] As Morris explained:

> The bow of Edward I was probably at first not much more powerful than the short bow of Hastings and Northallerton [i.e. the Battle of the Standard, 1138], but it was a longbow because it could be improved up to the standard of Crécy and Poitiers, whereas a shortbow, drawn to the chest, does not admit of improvement.[13]

Quite why the shortbow was incapable of improvement, or given this, how and whence the longbow was 'developed', were flaws in logic that did not seem to trouble Morris. *A priori*, the weaker a bow, the easier it is to draw further; this is why numerous illustrations of the composite bow – a weapon made of a combination of wood, horn and sinew – show the archer drawing his shaft to, or even past his ear.[14] Sceptical voices, indeed, were raised early against this theory of technical development. Already in 1900 the great German military historian Hans Delbrück had noted that 'the fact that the further one pulls the string, the stronger the shot, cannot have been any new discovery, and there were, of course, strong men also in the earlier periods . . . good marksmen have certainly always bent their bows as strongly and as far as their physical strength allowed'.[15] He further pointed out that although incorrect, the appealing idea of a technical leap forward achieved by greater draw-length was nothing new. In his *History of the Wars*, written *c*. 550, the Byzantine historian Procopius compared the efficacy of the bow-armed heavy cavalry of the Emperor Justinian (527–65) to the ineffectual archers of classical times:

> They were so indifferent in their practice of archery that they drew the bowstring only to the breast, so that the missile sent forth was naturally impotent and harmless to those it hit. Such, it is evident, was the archery of the past. But bowmen of the present time . . . draw the bowstring along by the forehead about opposite the right ear, thereby charging the arrow with such an impetus as to kill whoever stands in the way, shield and corselet alike having no power to check its force.[16]

Procopius, however, was mistaken. Persian, Greek, Roman and other archers in the earlier classical period had always drawn their composite bows to the ear, and there is nothing to suggest their weapons were any less powerful than those of the Byzantines. Nevertheless, for Morris the idea of a technical improvement of the longbow itself went hand in hand with an increase in its use by indigenous troops during the reign of Edward I and his successors:

> The rise of English infantry to be a real power in Europe depended upon this bow being a true long bow drawn to the ear, and, the attitude once learnt, it could be developed in both length and strength. That the weapon patronized by Edward before his Welsh wars was the real thing is proved by its rapid development. It only remained for him and his grandson to get the English to become expert at it by practice, to improve their range and to learn discipline.[17]

The final step was to hit upon a tactical system which allowed this new weapon to be deployed to its full effect. In Wales and in Scotland at Falkirk Edward I had used his archers in an essentially supportive role, to soften up the formations of enemy spearmen and allow the heavy cavalry to charge through the gaps they created. The battle-winning formula of archers combined with dismounted knights which was to dominate English formations in the Hundred Years War was the discovery of Edward III (1330–77), achieved, after the military humiliations of Edward II's reign at the hands of the Scots, through a chain of tactical developments from Dupplin Moor (1332),

Halidon Hill (1333) and Morlaix (1342) to Crécy (1346). The whole process was one of steady progression. Technical development went hand in hand with ever-increasing numbers of archers mobilised. As their numbers rose so the role of archery changed from one of essentially supporting cavalry to being the mainstay of English fighting power, now itself supported by dismounted men-at-arms. Such at least was the theory.

This view of the technological development of the longbow from the later thirteenth century as a prime factor for the massed deployment of archers and the English victories of the Hundred Years War was highly influential, and indeed still remains so. Many historians continue to write of the shortbow as a distinct category of weapon preceding the 'proper' longbow. The supposed impotence – and hence unimportance – of earlier bows led to a virtual neglect by historians of the role of medieval military archery before the later thirteenth century, and with it an important aspect of the deployment and value of infantry. The appearance of Jim Bradbury's important study *The Medieval Archer* did much to redress this imbalance.[18] Bradbury argued for the importance of military archery long before the reign of Edward I, not least in the first half of the twelfth century when Anglo-Norman tactics of combining archers with dismounted knights anticipated the English tactical formations of the Hundred Years War. Nevertheless, he too believed there was a development in the weapon itself from 'the ordinary wooden bow' to the longbow, though this transformation was gradual rather than the result of some technical revolution:

> . . . probably the ordinary bow in England did have a longer stave in the later middle ages, but this should not be emphasized to the point of treating the weapon of the fifteenth century as something quite divorced from that used at Hastings. Between the eleventh and the fifteenth centuries, bows were improved, but there were more drastic changes in the crossbow than in the ordinary bow.[19]

He notes that 'longbows in the eleventh century might have been about 5ft in length, gradually increasing to become about 6ft by the fifteenth century', though he points to bows of around 6ft existing in the earlier Middle Ages. Though Bradbury does not attempt to pinpoint how or why such an increase in bow length occurred, he crucially notes that 'there is no need to seek for the invention of a new weapon, and there is certainly no evidence that this new weapon was developed'.[20]

Others, in effect reverting to the thesis of Oman and Morris, have none the less attempted to place such a technological development more precisely, seeing a crucial improvement in the bow as part of the 'military revolutions' of the later thirteenth and early fourteenth centuries. Thus one scholar of the Hundred Years War has recently argued that the English contribution to the 'Infantry Revolution' of about 1302–46 rested on the development of 'the six foot yew longbow, substantially more powerful than the approximately four-foot Welsh elm bows of the early thirteenth century'. Like Oman and Morris, Clifford Rogers has argued that this bow was now drawn to the ear, not to the chest like the 'Welsh bow' and that this increased draw-length of several inches significantly increased the energy stored in the bow:

> Those extra few inches are . . . of critical importance. Thus, a six-foot longbow which at a twenty-eight inch draw had the same draw weight as a four-foot-eight-inch bow, would have a substantially higher draw weight at its full thirty-two-inch-draw, and would in total store about half again more energy than the shorter bow at the shorter draw. It seems reasonable to hypothesize that this increase could make the difference between ineffective-ness and lethality when attempting to penetrate an enemy's armour.[21]

If true, this concept of a technical leap forward, dated to the decades around 1300, is clearly of fundamental importance in explaining the rise to prominence of English archery. Yet its validity rests on being able to demonstrate the existence of an earlier, shorter and weaker weapon, used as the predominant

form of self-bow (that is, a bow made only of wood and not of composite construction) until the later thirteenth century. To posit an increase in bow length, one must prove that earlier bows, such as the Welsh elm bow, really were only some 4ft (1.22m) long. Such an assumption, however, is based on nothing more than a too literal reading of specific medieval illustrations, notably the two marginal sketches of archers preserved in the *Littere Wallie* or royal correspondence relating to Wales, one of which appears in the margins of a copy of the Treaty of Montgomery, drawn up between Henry III and Llewelyn ap Gruffyd of Gwynedd in 1267 (see p. 35).[22] Such illustrations, which are little more than rough cartoons and may even be caricatures of England's 'barbarian' opponents,[23] cannot be taken at face value as accurate representations of contemporary weapons. In fact, the shortbow as a specific category of weapon forming the impotent forerunner of the longbow simply did not exist.[24]

The word shortbow, or its Latin and French equivalents, does not occur in medieval Latin or French sources, while the term longbow, itself not common until the sixteenth century, was almost always used to contrast it with the crossbow.[25] As Sir James Holt pithily explains:

> Some historians have been misled by a semantic confu-sion. Almost inevitably the longbow has been contrasted with the shortbow, which is alleged to have preceded it as the conventional weapon of the twelfth and and thir-teenth centuries. But the longbow was so described to distinguish it not from a short, but from the crossbow. There were short bows. There were short men. Women

A lady hunts a stag, from the Queen Mary Psalter, English, *c.* 1310–20 (British Library, MS Royal 2.B.VII, f.153r). *(© British Library/Heritage Images)*

also used the bow, and then, as now, children played with bows and arrows. But the shortbow as a category of weapon was invented by the military historian Sir Charles Oman in the nineteenth century.[26]

The point is well made that not all bows produced during the Middle Ages were heavy war bows. Doubtless for many of the poorer sort, a single powerful weapon served for both war and the chase, as cases revealing poachers armed with longbows clearly reveal.[27] But if one could afford choice, a lighter weapon was far more suitable for hunting. In his famous *Livre de chasse*, written between 1387 and 1389, the expert hunter Gaston Phébus, count of Foix, recommended that the bow be not too strong, for it was essential to be able to draw stealthily and hold while a deer approached, in order to gain the best shot without scaring off the beast by the movement the draw would entail. He suggested a bow of yew or boxwood of around twenty hands (about 6ft 6in or 2m), strung with a silken string, and shooting an arrow of eight hands long (about 30in or 76cm) which carried a broadhead the width of four fingers from barbs to tip.[28] Ladies in particular might use lighter bows for hunting, and these would almost certainly be tailored to their individual needs.[29] In 1530, when Anne Boleyn's star was in the ascent at court, Lady Lisle sent her a gift of a bow, 'which she did greatly esteem, and commanded a string to be set on it and assayed it, but it was somewhat too big'.[30] As for women, so for children, who would require a range of bow sizes and weights as they grew. In the fifteenth century children's bows sold for 10s or 13s 4d per 100, and in 1542, in order to make bows readily available for obligatory practice at the butts, they were ordered to be sold at a range of prices between 6d and 1s each.[31] It is noteworthy that in his *Strategikon* the Byzantine Emperor Maurice (582–602) recognised the potential disparity in the strength among archers by permitting unskilled or weaker men to use less powerful bows than those used by regular or elite troops, though in Byzantine armies it was the composite bow that was predominant.[32]

Some less powerful longbows than those from the *Mary Rose* have survived. A bow of fifteenth- or sixteenth-century date in the Germanisches Nationalmuseum, Nüremberg, whose quality of finish suggests it was intended for the hunt rather than for war, is made of high-quality yew with the limbs being of rounded cross-sections at the grip and at the ends of limbs, but pentangular for the rest of its length. It measures 5ft 6in (1.68m) long and 1in (2.5cm) deep at the grip.[33] Similarly, a bow, probably of yew, formerly preserved in the collection of British and Roman antiquities at Alnwick Castle, measures some 5ft 4in (1.63m) long, 3⅜in (8.5cm) at its widest girth and 1⅛in (2.9cm) at its narrowest, and has been estimated as having a pull of only around 45–50lb (20.5–22.5kg).[34] The weapon is probably medieval, but has not been scientifically dated and is only linked to the minor battle of Hedgeley Moor in 1464 during the Wars of the Roses by local tradition. It is important also to remember that particularly once longbows had begun to be produced in their hundreds of thousands, the quality – and hence the performance – of such weapons could vary considerably. In 1542 a statute could set the price of 'bows of the best sort' at no more than 3s 4d, those 'of the second sort' at 2s 6d, and those 'of the third sort' at 2s.[35]

Holt also rightly doubted whether much reliance could be placed on artistic conventions concerning bow length or the archer's draw to chest or ear. Though he did not develop this point, it goes straight to the heart of the matter. The concept of the shortbow and arguments about bow length and length of draw stem principally from a too literal and too unwary interpretation of the iconography of the bow in medieval art, a form of evidence which must be carefully studied in the light of artistic conventions of the time. In reality, what changed from the thirteenth century was not the bow itself but rather the manner in which many artists depicted bows, with an increasing stress on proportion and naturalism. Significantly, scholars who preceded Oman had been unaware of either the term shortbow or the distinction from the longbow which it implied. Thus John Hewitt, one of the first serious academic students of arms and armour, employed the term longbow without hesitation for bows existing from early Frankish and Anglo-Saxon times onward.[36]

The argument for continuity in the basic form of the longbow is powerfully borne out by a combination of archaeological, written and iconographic evidence. Archaeology demonstrates beyond doubt the existence of longbows of well over 5ft from the early Middle Ages, and indeed, from prehistoric times. By contrast, archaeology has yielded scant traces of the medieval shortbow. The Berkhamstead bow, a 4ft (1.2m) yew stave discovered in 1931 in the moat of Berkhamstead Castle, was originally believed to be a shortbow of the thirteenth century, but has now been shown to be a limb from a crossbow of the same period, being far too powerful to be bent by hand.[37] Nor do we find any chroniclers or contemporary observers remarking on a major technical improvement in bow design or a military 'big bang' in the weaponry of English armies during the decades spanning the end of the thirteenth century, as one might expect if such a significant transformation had taken place. Rather, the testimony of Gerald of Wales, describing powerful Welsh longbows made of elm in the 1180s, suggests a continuity in use of the type of longbows found in early medieval graves, and this is strongly supported by the continuous importance of military archery in the centuries before the wars of Edward I.

BOW FINDS AND BOW FRAGMENTS: THE ARCHAEOLOGICAL EVIDENCE

Far from being developed in the later thirteenth century, the longbow has a venerable ancestry. A yew longbow, known from its finding place as the 'Rottenbottom Bow' and dated by radiocarbon analysis as early as 4040–3640 BC, was discovered in a peat bog in the Tweedsmuir Hills, while two fragments of longbows from the Mesolithic period were found at Stellmore, near Hamburg, both being deeply 'stacked' – that is having a deep 'D' section formed by a close width to depth ratio.[38] A number of Neolithic longbows have been excavated in England, northern Europe and Switzerland, mostly of yew, and in length the majority 'convincingly out-top the mean average stature of Neolithic males from the region'.[39] One found at Ashcott Heath in the Somerset Levels, dating to *c.* 2665 BC, had been cut from a yew billet, then shaped into a 'D' section which has a thickness-to-width ratio of 1:1.1, exactly the same as some examples from the *Mary Rose*.[40] Though only half of the weapon had survived, its overall length has been estimated at about 5ft 2½in (1.59m).[41] It is unsurprising to find bows of such length at so early a date, for when using bow woods such as yew, elm and pine a length of over 5ft is required to obtain the ideal combination of strength and safety from breakage.[42] While ethnic self-bows, such as those used in Africa or by native American Indians might demonstrate a variety of lengths, it is striking that sixteenth-century European explorers

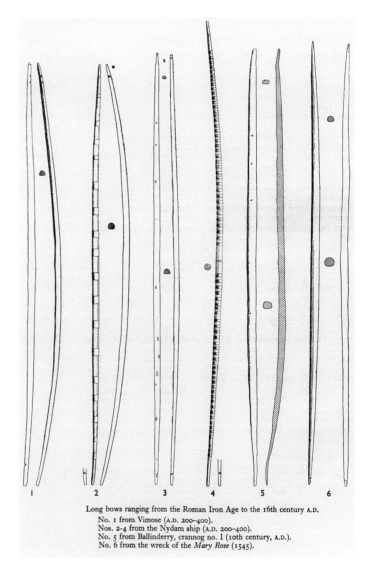

Long bows ranging from the Roman Iron Age to the 16th century A.D.
No. 1 from Vimose (A.D. 200–400).
Nos. 2-4 from the Nydam ship (A.D. 200–400).
No. 5 from Ballinderry, crannog no. I (10th century, A.D.).
No. 6 from the wreck of the *Mary Rose* (1545).

A comparative drawing of Iron Age and early medieval longbows with an example from the Mary Rose. From J.G. Clark, 'Neolithic Bows', *Proceedings of the Prehistoric Society*, 1963. *(Reproduced by kind permission of the Prehistoric Society)*

	Length	Thickness	Width	Thickness/Width	Museum
Nydam	197·5	2·60	2·75	I : I·I	Copenhagen
——	178	2·60	2·80	I : I·I	——
——	182·5	2·05	2·75	I : I·3	——
Vimose	178·5	2·50	3·25	I : I·3	——
	169·5	2·50	2·70	I : I·I	——
Heechterp	151+ (originally *c.* 168)	2·45	2·45	I : I·0	Leeuwarden
Mary Rose (1545)	187	3·20	3·50	I : I·I	Royal Armouries
——	190	3·25	3·50	I : I·I	——
——	188	3·00	3·25	I : I·I	Roy. United Services Inst.
Ballinderry, I	185	2·86	3·80	I : I·3	Dublin

Table showing the comparative dimensions of bows from the Younger Roman Iron Age (AD 200–400), a Viking bow from Ireland and specimens from the *Mary Rose*. From J.G. Clark, 'Neolithic Bows', *Proceedings of the Prehistoric Society*, 1963. *(Reproduced by kind permission of the Prehistoric Society)* on the eastern seaboard of America recorded indigenous peoples already carrying powerful longbows.[43] It is the combination of length and depth which distinguishes the longbow from other types of self-bow such as the 'flat bow'.[44] The Ashcott Heath longbow and its continental cousins are, as its excavators noted, the recognisable forerunners of the weapons drawn by English archers in the Middle Ages.[45]

Though the bow seems to have experienced a marked decline in use with the advent of bronze and later iron weapons, the considerable quantity of finely crafted bows recovered from the bog deposits at Thorsbjerg, Vimose and Nydam in Denmark and Schleswig-Holstein, ranging in date from the second to the fourth centuries AD, prove unequivocally that the longbow was known to the continental ancestors of the Anglo-Saxons.[46] No fewer than thirty-six longbows, together with several hundred arrows, tipped either with iron or bone, were found in the Nydam ship. Prehistoric bowyers, hampered by the limited capabilities of flint tools, may have used the shape of the original tree or sapling to reduce the amount of woodworking necessary, but with better tools, particularly of iron, had come greater sophistication.[47] Staves could now be cut from larger and more mature trees, allowing bows a wider back. In form, length and depth the bows from Nydam and Vimose bear a strikingly similarity to those of the *Mary Rose*. One example from Nydam was 5ft 8in (1.73m) long, 1.1in (2.8cm) wide and 1in (2.5cm) deep, compared to a typical *Mary Rose* example measuring 6ft 1in (1.85m) long, 1.4in (3.6cm) wide and 1.3in (3.3cm) deep.[48] Another example from Nydam was even longer (197.5cm) than the *Mary Rose* bows in the Tower (187cm, 188cm, 190cm), and though in all cases the earlier bows were less thick (2.5–2.6cm thick as opposed to 3–3.25cm for the *Mary Rose* weapons), they generally retained the same thickness-to-width ratio as the later bows.[49] The anonymous Germanic bowyers who shaped these bows, which were later ritually thrown into sacred bogs as an offering to the gods, did not have access to the fine imported yew that was available to their Tudor counterparts, nor to the level of sophistication of manufacture that was the product of a highly developed industry stimulated by the longbow's prominence in later medieval England. But the essential difference – and it is not great – is in the thickness, not in the length, width or general form; the bows of the second to fourth century AD and of the sixteenth century are undeniably the same basic weapon. As Robert Hardy noted in *Longbow*, the Nydam bows 'are not, on the whole, quite as sturdy as the *Mary Rose* bows . . . but they are very similar to look at: no Tudor archer would have found these bows anything but familiar'.[50] The Nydam bows in themselves should lay to rest the idea of the 'shortbow' as the pre-

dominant but ineffectual weapon of early medieval Europe until the emergence of longbows in the later thirteenth century.

The outlines of decomposed bows over 5ft in length contained in pagan Anglo-Saxon inhumations at Bifrons (Kent) and Chessel Down (Isle of Wight) demonstrate the continued use of longbows in post-migration areas of settlement.[51] With the conversion of the Anglo-Saxon peoples to Christianity throughout the late sixth and seventh centuries, the pagan practice of burying grave-goods with the dead ceased, and with it we lost an invaluable source of bows and archery equipment in a datable, social context. Nevertheless, continental evidence reveals the continued use of longbows. Bows of over 6ft in length were found in the graves of eighth-century Alemannic warriors at Oberflacht in Swabia, while Viking sites have yielded numerous parts or fragments of bows.[52] A yew longbow found in a crannog at Ballinderry in Ireland, and presumed to be Viking, was 6ft 1in (1.85m) long, 1⅛in (2.86cm) thick and 1½in (3.8cm) wide, compared to a *Mary Rose* example of 6ft 2in (1.88m) long, 1³⁄₁₆in (3cm) thick and 1¼in (3.25cm) wide, with the thickness-to-width ratio being 1:1.3 and 1:1.1 respectively.[53] This was clearly a powerful weapon, differing little in its essentials from the Tudor bows. Similarly, a tenth-century yew bow found at the great Danish trading emporium of Hedeby is a deeply stacked weapon some 6ft 3½in (1.92m) long, which has been estimated as having a pull of over 100lb.[54] From literary references as well as archaeological finds, we know the Vikings used bow woods such as yew and elm, while burials throughout the Viking world have yielded abundant evidence of the ubiquity of bows, doubtless serving a dual purpose for hunting and for war, and many graves of warriors contain arrowheads among other military equipment.[55]

As the Vikings themselves were converted to Christianity, however, they too stopped burying weapons and other grave-goods with their dead, so that from the eleventh century a primary context for the survival of bows disappears. Finds of bows from later periods consequently are haphazard and rare in the extreme. A fragment of a 'D'-sectioned longbow of yew was excavated from the castle of Wawel in Krakow, Poland, dating between the tenth and eleventh century.[56] Another such find was a fragment of a yew longbow found at Wood Quay in Dublin, excavated from a thirteenth-century level.[57] Unfortunately, the very few extant examples of longbows which may be from the central or later Middle Ages lack any reliable provenance and are hard to date with any precision. Such is the case with the yew longbow formerly in Wakefield City Museum, measuring a massive 6ft 7in (2m) in length with a circumference at the grip of 5¼in (12.8cm), and with a draw weight of well over 100lb (45.5kg).[58] Given the hundreds of

Above: The death of Cain, from the Holkham Bible, English, *c.* 1327–35 (British Library, Add. MS 47682). In the apocryphal story the blind Lamech, wishing to have some venison, instructs a boy to direct his aim at what he believes to be a deer in the undergrowth. Instead, he accidentally slays Cain, who is collecting wood, thereby fulfilling God's vengeance for the murder of Abel. Wounds inflicted by such large hunting broadheads as depicted here were often fatal. (© *British Library*)

Right: Modern replicas of a range of medieval arrowheads, including (from the top) four armour-piercing heads, a bodkin, a large hunting head, three Type 16 heads and another hunting broadhead (bottom right). (*Author Collection: forging by Simon Stanley*)

thousands of bows that were produced in England alone during the medieval period this scarcity is ironic, yet not altogether surprising. Their very ubiquity and cheapness to buy meant that an old or damaged bow was simply discarded, unlike swords or armour which could be pressed into continued service. And unlike crossbows which might be elaborately decorated with carving or inlay, such a plain and plebeian weapon as the bow must rarely have been used to decorate hearth, hall or manor house.

Yet if we are thus left with a serious hiatus in securely datable bow finds between the tenth-century Hedeby bow and the *Mary Rose* bows, we can supplement this deficiency with a

variety of literary and iconographic evidence. From the later thirteenth century record evidence and in particular court inquests describe weapons that are unquestionably longbows. Thus, for example, the de Banco Roll of 1298 describes in detail a bow used in the slaying of one Simon de Skeffington, of Skeffington, Leicestershire. The weapon, which was of yew, was 6in (15.2cm) in circumference (thus about 2in or 5cm thick), and an ell and a half in length. The ell was a medieval unit of measurement, gauged in England at 45in or a yard and a quarter (1.14m), making this bow some 5ft 7½in (1.68m).[59] The arrow, three-quarters of an ell long (about 34in or 86cm) and 1in (2.5cm) thick, had a shaft of ash, was feathered with peacock feathers and carried a broadhead 3in (7.6cm) long and 2in (5cm) broad.[60] This is an early reference to arrows fletched with peacock, made famous by Chaucer's portrait of the Yeoman in the Prologue to *The Canterbury Tales*,[61] and praised by his contemporary and fellow poet John Lydgate:

> Through al the land of Albion
> For fethered arwes, as I reherse can,
> Goos is the best, as in comparison,
> Except fetheres of pekok or of swan.[62]

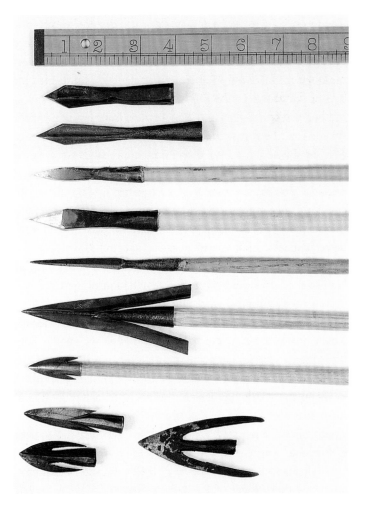

Though Roger Ascham criticised peacock as being 'rough and heavye' and rarely able to stabilise an arrow for shorter range shooting, the inventory of the archery equipment of Sir John Dynham drawn up in 1422 clearly shows that while flights of swan or white and grey goose were used, those of peacock were the most favoured.[63] This also indicates that some arrows, probably intended for the hunt or target shooting, were decorated with bindings for the fletchings in gold and coloured silks, while one sheaf of twelve arrows had the peacock feathers enriched with gold foil.[64] Geese, however, were far more common than peacocks, and hence it was the feathers of the goose that proved more suitable to the mass production of arrows. That many of the shafts loosed against the French at Agincourt had been feathered with goose is suggested by the fact that as part of Henry V's preparation for his second French expedition in 1417 the sheriffs were ordered to have three feathers plucked from both wings of every goose in the shires, save for breeding birds, which were then to be packed and sent to London.[65] In the following century Ascham opined that 'the Goose is the best fether for the best shooter', for no other feather 'hath all comodities in it'.[66]

Important details of bows are similarly furnished by a court case in Staffordshire in 1315, recording the murder of Robert of Essington.[67] Why Robert was slain we do not know, but according to his wife Margaret, who had raised the hue and cry after his assailants, seventeen in number, they had been thorough in their work. Robert, it was claimed, had been shot by several arrows in the chest and back, struck with staves, stabbed with a dagger and had his left foot severed with a sword. That the accused men in the case of Robert of Essington were finally acquitted by the county court suggests either a gross miscarriage of justice or that few believed Margaret's colourful version of events. Whatever the truth, the value of the case for us lies in the detailed information supplied concerning the bows of the assailants, which may well have been submitted and examined as evidence.

One of the attackers, John, son of Roger de Swynnerton, had 'a bow of Spanish yew, two ells in length, and of the thickness of four men's thumbs', shooting a barbed 'clotharewe'.[68] This would give John's bow a massive length of 7ft 6in (2.29m), which may well be an exaggeration, although we should note the comment of Sir John Smythe in 1590, who believed that the bows used by medieval archers had been longer than those in use in the 1580s. Because of the risk of breaking, he noted, 'there was special care that all livery or war bows, being of the wood of yew, were longer than now they use them and so very well backed and nocked that they seldom or never brake'.[69] Two other assailants drew bows of Irish yew, and one of elm, while another, Roger of Byshebury, had shot 'a bow called

Turkeys' of Spanish yew, one ell and a half in length, and with a barbed arrow called a 'Wolfarewe' made of ash and three-quarters of an ell in length. The natural assumption is that a 'Turkish bow' would be the name given to a form of composite bow made of wood, horn and sinew, yet the weapon here described was clearly a yew self-bow, and, as we have seen, in his *Livre de chasse* Gaston Phébus refers to a bow of yew or boxwood approximately 6ft 6in (1.98m) as being called an English or Turkish bow – though he does not explain the reason for such an appellation.[70]

It is not clear what distinguished the various types of arrow mentioned in the indictment, such as a 'Wolf arrow', a 'Dog arrow', or a barbed arrow called a Scottish arrow ('Scotis arewe') 'made of a wood called in French *boul* (birch), an ell in length, and feathered with the red [sic] feathers of a peacock'. All were barbed, and may have been forms of hunting broadheads. This was certainly the case of arrows described in charges of poaching as 'Welsh arrows' (*sagittis waliscis*), which were broadheads for hunting deer.[71] Perhaps the 'small arrow' (*sagitta minuta*) mentioned in an Oxford coroner's record of 1297, which had fatally wounded one John Metescharp 'in his left side half a thumb in width and five thumbs in depth',[72] was by contrast not so much one with a shorter shaft but one possessing a smaller head for war, such as the common Type 16 arrowheads so favoured by English archers in war.[73] The Dynham inventory of 1422 refers to 'spearheads' and 'broad hooked' arrows, probably referring to small barbed warheads and hunting broadheads respectively, to heads of 'bykker', probably bodkin heads, and to 'duckbill' heads whose form is uncertain. It is possible that such heads were for birding or target practice, but the fact that they occur in the inventory in large numbers makes more plausible the suggestion that these were possibly small barbed heads similar to Type 16.[74]

The case of Robert of Essington is an important indication of the diversity of weapons and bow woods in use among a group of local men of modest social standing – some of whom were even in minor clerical orders – and there is no reason to suppose that in this regard early fourteenth-century Staffordshire was in any way atypical. Here we glimpse, one year after Bannockburn, the kind of bows that the archers of Edward I and Edward II brought to the host, in a period when the majority of troops were expected to provide their own weapons or be equipped by their shires. While some were still choosing bows of elm, like Gerald of Wales's Gwentian archers in the 1180s, imported Irish and Spanish yew was clearly readily available and was, by implication, relatively inexpensive. A purchase of 180 dozen bows of Spanish yew costing £36 is recorded in Edward II's reign.[75] In 1283 Peter de la Mare purchased seven bows for use by the king's archers for 18s 6d,

The martyrdom of St Edmund of East Anglia, who according to legend was shot to death by the Vikings in 869/70 near Hoxne, Suffolk, as depicted in a psalter of *c.* 1250 (British Library, MS Royal 2 B VI, f.10r).
(© British Library)

and in 1289 bought eight bows for use by Queen Eleanor's foresters of Feckenham for 11*s* 6*d* (i.e. 1*s* 5*d* each), though in neither case is it stated whether these bows were made from imported wood.[76] Bows of yew are mentioned in the thirteenth-century pleas of the forest. Thus, for instance, in 1253–4 seven clerks and a chaplain were taken by the foresters in Stangate, Huntingdonshire, for having been seen carrying bows in the forest; the justices were presented with five bows

of yew with their strings and three Welsh arrows and a 'bosun' (a bolt?) as evidence.[77] The valuable evidence furnished by the Skeffington case of 1298 and the Essington case of 1315 provides a firm *terminus post quem* for the existence of heavy and powerful longbows, and allows us to be reasonably certain that the bows drawn at Halidon, Crécy and Agincourt were indeed weapons of a similar size and power to those found on the *Mary Rose*.

It must be remembered, however, that we lack this form of detailed deposition for earlier periods: few comparable court rolls are extant before the second half of the twelfth century, and even if subsequent rolls do mention bows, they rarely if ever give precise detail such as measurements before the thirteenth century. We must, therefore, be careful not to confuse a new type of source with the advent of a new weapon. Indeed, that the longbow had continued in use in the centuries before the campaigns of Edward I is strongly suggested by the remarkable account of Gerald of Wales.

GERALD OF WALES AND THE BOWMEN OF GWENT

Among our most valuable pieces of evidence for the military use of the longbow in the twelfth century is the testimony of Gerald of Wales, a churchman and scholar of mixed Norman and Welsh parentage, and one of the great literary figures of the twelfth-century renaissance.[78] In 1188 Gerald accompanied Baldwin, Archbishop of Canterbury, on a preaching tour of Wales to drum up support for the Third Crusade, and shortly thereafter he wrote up his travels in his *Journey Through Wales*. In this work, of singular importance for our knowledge of medieval Wales, Gerald tells of the skill of the men of Gwent in using the bow, and adds:

> The bows they use are not made of horn, nor of sapwood, nor yet of yew. The Welsh carve their bows out of the dwarf elm-trees in the forest. They are nothing much to look at, not even rubbed smooth, but left in a rough and unpolished state. Still, they are firm and strong. You could not only shoot far with them, but also they are powerful enough to inflict serious wounds in a close fight.[79]

It is worth examining this well-known passage closely, for it is in stating what the Welsh bows are *not* made of that Gerald is

most revealing. He clearly knew of the composite bow, made from layers of horn and animal sinew glued to a wooden core, which was the weapon par excellence of eastern horse-archers but was also in more limited use in the West.[80] What type of wood Gerald meant by sapwood (*alburnum*) is less obvious.[81] But his reference to yew shows that he regarded this and not elm as the more usual material for fashioning bows.[82] Not only this, but the weapons with which he was familiar were finished to a high standard of smoothness. Gerald does *not* say the longbow was used only by the Welsh, or that the weapon originated there. Rather, what struck him about Welsh bows was their power despite their rough, unfinished appearance. Here it is worth reiterating a point made in *Longbow: A Social and Military History*, namely that in the most widely available translation of Gerald's *Journey through Wales*, Lewis Thorpe renders the last sentence of this passage, 'You could not shoot far with them; but they are powerful enough to inflict serious wounds in a close fight'. If, however, we read 'not only . . . but also' for '*non tantum . . . sed etiam*', the passage makes far more sense. Not only could these bows shoot a great distance, but they could also inflict severe wounds at close range.[83] Significantly, this was the translation as rendered by Morris himself in his *Welsh Wars*, though he did not grasp its implications.[84] As Gerald goes on to say, these bows were almost (but by implication not quite) as powerful as a crossbow. He gives two anecdotes to illustrate the strength of these bows and the men who bent them. During a Welsh attack on Abergavenny Castle in 1182 two Anglo-Norman soldiers fled into the keep:

> The Welsh shot at them from behind, and with the arrows which sped from their bows they actually penetrated the oak doorway of the tower, which was almost as thick as a man's palm. As a permanent reminder of the strength of their impact, the arrows have been left sticking in the door just where their iron heads struck. William de Braose also testifies that, in the war against the Welsh, one of his men-at-arms was struck by an arrow shot at him by a Welshman. It went right through his thigh, high up, where it was protected outside and inside the leg by his mail chausses, and then through the skirt of his leather tunic; next it penetrated that part of the saddle which is called the *alva* or seat; and finally it lodged in his horse, driving in so deep that it killed the animal. An arrow pinned the thigh of another soldier to his saddle, although the tassets of his leather tunic were there to protect him outside and inside the leg. He tugged on the reins and pulled his horse round in a half circle, whereupon another arrow, shot by the same bowman, hit him in exactly the same place in the other thigh, so that he was skewered to his horse on both sides. What more could you expect from a crossbow?[85]

Gerald had doubtless seen the arrowheads in the keep door at Abergavenny, for he was Archdeacon of Brecon and very familiar with South Wales, and was also on close terms with the great marcher lord William de Braose, who was his informant for these events. We must, however, exercise some caution. Gerald was a great raconteur, and, like his fellow Welshman Walter Map, revelled in tall stories and tales of the marvellous. Doubtless the tale of William de Braose's man-at-arms being skewered to his horse had grown in the telling. Yet Gerald's testimony, even if taken with some scepticism, is none the less precious, as few chroniclers or observers of this period cared to record the nature or effect of missile weapons in such detail, if indeed at all. Gerald was an acute observer of military affairs, and, as we shall see, fully recognised the value of archers for operations in Wales and Ireland.[86] There can be little doubt that the weapons he describes in use by the men of South Wales were longbows, and it is hard to see how such weapons could 'develop' much further. It is worth noting, moreover, that even in the mid-sixteenth century Tudor bows were still being made from dwarf elm as well as from yew.

If the powerful archaeological evidence and the testimony of Gerald of Wales point to the existence of longbows well before their supposed development from the reign of Edward I, how was it that Oman, Morris and others came up with the notion of the shortbow as a distinct earlier category of weapon? To answer this, we must turn to the Bayeux Tapestry and the depiction of bows in medieval art.

THE ICONOGRAPHY OF THE BOW

The great Bayeux Tapestry, probably embroidered in the 1070s or 1080s for Odo of Bayeux, depicts in one of its central panels a group of Norman archers who draw awkwardly to the chest bows considerably shorter than the height of the bowmen themselves (see p. 63).[87] Nearly two centuries later marginal sketches from the Treaty of Montgomery, made in 1267 between Henry III and Llewelyn 'the Last', Prince of Gwynedd, show Welsh archers drawing short, knobbly bows to mid-chest. Such representations contrast sharply with later medieval illustrations of archers in manuscripts such as the early fourteenth-century Luttrell Psalter (see pp. 163, 197) or the late fifteenth-century Beauchamp Pageant, which show archers drawing powerful longbows fully to the ear (see p. 14). At first sight, then, a comparison between the types of bow depicted in the art of the earlier and later Middle Ages would seem to support the idea of the development of the longbow from the earlier shortbow, and points to such a transformation occurring by the early years of the fourteenth century. Indeed, the portrayal of the Norman archers from the central panel of the Bayeux Tapestry was almost certainly the *fons et origo* of Oman's idea of the shortbow. Equally, the marginal sketch from the Treaty of Montgomery has more recently been cited as the principal evidence for the existence of shortbows of some 4ft (1.2m) in length before the supposed Edwardian revolution of the weapon.[88] Yet can this rough drawing, penned by a royal clerk whose artistic abilities were to say the least limited, really stand such a conclusion?

Such a deduction is misleading for a number of reasons. First, in the earlier Middle Ages much iconography was heavily stylised and, not least in relation to the depiction of bows, profoundly influenced by classical models and earlier exemplars, rather than accurately reflecting the types of bow in use by the artist's contemporaries.[89] By contrast, the fourteenth and fifteenth centuries witnessed an increasing (but by no means universal) adoption of more naturalistic depictions, often reflected in the case of archers by greater emphasis on the proportion of weapon to user. We thus must be careful not to confuse a change in the nature of the evidence with the advent of a new weapon: to contrast the archers depicted in the Luttrell Psalter with those in the Bayeux Tapestry or the early twelfth-century Life of St Edmund is primarily to contrast artistic style and convention, not actual weapon types. This point becomes still more apparent in the fifteenth century, as the superb representations of longbows in the paintings of Hans Memling (see p. 12), and the highly detailed 'hyper-realism' of fellow early Flemish artists like Jan van Eyck and Rogier van der Weyden, have few if any parallels in the earlier Middle Ages.[90] Secondly, longbows and the archer's draw to the ear are depicted in manuscript illumination and other media long before the supposed development of the true longbow in the later thirteenth century. Conversely, more stylised or crudely executed images of archers either with shorter bows or depicted as drawing their weapons to mid-chest occur in Britain throughout the later Middle Ages and into the sixteenth century, despite the ubiquity of the longbow.

While the historian or archaeologist might yearn for naturalistic depiction in illumination or sculpture to furnish insights into arms and armour, combat techniques and battle formations, such realism was rarely if ever the intended goal of early medieval artists, who worked within a different conceptual framework in terms of perspective and naturalism, and who were often heavily influenced by existing iconographical conventions. Thus, for example, in the Bayeux Tapestry, a work brilliantly impressionistic and highly stylised in its design, a lone, unarmoured Anglo-Saxon archer crouching beneath the shield wall of Harold's housecarls is deliberately portrayed as a smaller and more insignificant figure in order to symbolise his social inferiority to the aristocratic warriors.[91] Clearly, such perspectival conventions make it unwise to place too much reliance on the proportions of bows depicted in such a context.

Moreover, in an age where emulation and faithful transmission were seen as virtues rather than artistic plagiarism, many illuminators were content to copy or develop pre-existing images, often themselves of considerable antiquity. They are thus rarely if ever a reliable guide to the types of weapon in use when the copy itself was made. This problem is particularly acute for bow iconography in the early Middle Ages. Carolingian manuscript painting, for example, was heavily influenced by classical models, while in turn these Carolingian manuscripts were widely disseminated and copied elsewhere, such as in Anglo-Saxon England. A good example of the difficulties this raises is shown by the Utrecht Psalter, produced despite its name at Hautevillers Abbey near Rheims in about 820–35; it depicts warriors using recurve composite bows, but these illustrations were heavily influenced by late Roman exemplars (see below).[92] In turn, the Harley Psalter, written at Canterbury in about 1000, closely copied the Utrecht Psalter, and again depicts archers with recurve bows (see p. 54).[93] Although it is not in itself impossible that the Carolingians made some use of composite bows, it would be dangerous to state from the evidence of the Utrecht Psalter alone that the Franks in the age of Charlemagne were using the 'double convex bow',[94] and still more so to conclude from the Harley Psalter that archers in the late Anglo-Saxon period were also using composite bows. The influence of classical models, moreover, continued to remain strong in particular images depicting archers, such as centaurs or the zodiac sign of Sagittarius, which throughout the Middle Ages frequently depict recurve bows, and such trends were naturally reinforced by the classical leanings of Renaissance art.

From the twelfth century onward a greater diversity in the representation of bows becomes apparent. The manner in which

An archer on horseback, from the Utrecht Psalter, MS 32, f.25r, c. 820–35, illustrating Psalm 43. (Utrecht, University Library)

medieval illuminators or sculptors chose to depict bows and archers at the draw varied widely from illuminator to illuminator, and was dependent on a variety of factors such as medium, stylistic convention, available exemplars and artistic expression. Some artists, such as the mid-thirteenth-century illuminator of the Maciejowski Bible or the late fifteenth-century master of the Beauchamp Pageant, painted or drew with an accuracy that suggests close personal observation and familiarity with military equipment. Indeed, so detailed are the depictions of arms and armour in the Maciejowski Bible that it has been suggested that the artist had himself seen active service (see pp. 80, 108).[95] Others, by contrast, simply drew stylised bows, often so tiny that there can be no suggestion of naturalism, as for example that given to an archer attacking an elephant and castle in a late twelfth-century English bestiary,[96] the puny weapon shot from horseback by Tristan on a lead-glazed tile of the mid-thirteenth century from Chertsey Abbey, or the little bow carried by the huntsman in the lower margin of the Hereford *Mappa Mundi*, executed in about 1283.[97] The latter illustration itself serves as a perfect example of the manner in which available space as well as social distinction directed perspective; the map's patron rides past the tiny figure of a huntsman fitted into the curving space beneath the orb of the world.

The extent to which artists might differ in their depiction of archers and their bows is strikingly illustrated by a comparison of two almost exactly contemporary English manuscripts from the early fourteenth century. In a famous image the Luttrell Psalter (produced in the 1330s) depicts archers practising at the butts and drawing smooth, finished longbows to the ear. Few would doubt that here is the classic longbow, which inflicted such great defeats on the Scots at Dupplin Moor in 1332 and Halidon Hill in 1333. The patron of this richly decorated psalter, Sir Geoffrey Luttrell, was in a position of authority on such matters: between 1297 and 1322 he had been summoned on several campaigns against the Scots, and had lived to see the triumph of English archery over the once victorious Scots in the opening years of Edward III's reign.[98] Yet by contrast, the artist of the contemporary Holkham Bible (*c.* 1320–30) portrays bowmen in an awkward stance bending shorter bows which are depicted as rough and knobbly (see pp. 41, 151). At first sight one might be tempted to see the portrayal of rough and knotty bows as an attempt at verisimilitude, echoing Gerald of Wales's remark about the Welsh bows of elm being left knotty and unpolished, but it seems more likely that this was merely an artistic convention, which can be traced in a related series of late thirteenth- and early fourteenth-century manuscripts.[99] Even artists from the same workshop, who drew on similar models, might depict bows very differently. Compare, for example, two early fourteenth-century manuscripts of the

Apocalypse produced in the same Fenland workshop. In the Canonici Apocalypse the crowned horseman in the opening of the First Seal carries a mighty longbow and a broadheaded arrow, while in the contemporary Crowland Apocalypse the same horseman bears a similar broadheaded arrow but a tiny bow, so small as to negate any suggestion of realism.[100] Similarly, in their respective depictions of 'the war of the dragon', the first artist depicts an archer shooting a thick, powerful bow, while his fellow illuminator depicts a smaller, more insignificant weapon, though drawn to the ear.[101]

Crucially, moreover, depictions of bows which are proportionally longbows occur before the period of supposed technical development under Edward I. The images of shortbows, such as from the Bayeux Tapestry and the *Littere Wallie*, are, in other words, not only stylised but also selective. The Bayeux Tapestry itself depicts numerous Norman bowmen in the bottom margin of the battle scenes, drawing bows which are as tall as the archers. While the Life of St Edmund of about 1120 portrays the king's Danish executioners using thin, slight bows (see p. 58), a carved font from Alphington, Devon, of about 1120–40, unequivocally portrays a huntsman with a powerful longbow. An archer from the Stuttgart Passional of about 1120 draws a very long weapon, while other archers depicted in the same manuscript have bows longer than those drawn by Matthew Paris in the mid-thirteenth century.[102] The illustration of Psalm 4 from the Eadwine Psalter, produced at Canterbury in about 1147 but ultimately deriving from the Utrecht Psalter, contains an archer loosing a longbow, while though far more stylised, a centaur shoots a stag with a powerful bow on a capital from the church of St Aignan (Loire-et-Cher), dated to the first half of the twelfth century.[103] An early thirteenth-century illustrated version of Gerald of Wales's *Topography of Ireland* shows archers holding bows that are as long as they are tall (see p. 92), while a carved capital of about 1170 in Adel Church near Leeds shows a Sagittarius figure bending a stout longbow. In a bestiary from the London region of about 1220–30 an archer draws a powerful bow, seemingly to the ear (see p. 81).[104] The Trinity Apocalypse of about 1250 similarly shows a number of archers bracing and shooting longbows, while any lingering doubts that these and other contemporary representations are intended to be longbows are rapidly dispelled by comparison with the contemporary psalter from St Albans, compiled after 1246, which shows one of St Edmund's assailants drawing a massive longbow (see p. 43).[105] Only the style and technical execution of the illumination or carving distinguish these longbowmen from those of the Luttrell Psalter. All these examples, moreover, were executed prior to the marginal doodles of the *Littere Wallie* depicting Welsh archers with their supposed shortbows.

THE DRAW TO THE EAR

'That fellow handles his bow like a crow-keeper,' Shakespeare's King Lear says, 'draw me a cloathier's yard.'[106] Oman and others were misled not simply by the proportion of bow to archer in the Bayeux Tapestry's central panel, but by the depiction of these weapons being drawn to the chest, which they regarded as an important indicator of the weakness of the shortbow. Yet this again is to interpret an artistic convention too literally. While drawing to the breast or 'to the pap' was not unknown, a draw to the chin (employed by most modern archers) or to the ear (still used in field shooting) was far more common. Its ubiquity is well illustrated by the comments of Guillaume de Lorris in his *Roman de la Rose*, written in France in about 1230–5, who describes how he was struck by the God of Love who 'took an arrow, and, when the string was in the nock, drew the bow – a wondrously strong one – up to his ear and shot at me in such a way that with great force he sent the point through the eye and into my heart'.[107] A bowman hunting magpies in the Ashmole Bestiary of about 1200 draws his weapon to the ear, as do the archers drawn by Matthew Paris in his *Chronica Majora*, executed in the 1240s (see p. 48).[108] Many artists, however, encountered difficulties in accurately portraying an archer at full draw. If the figure faces to the left, all details save his protruding right elbow are hidden by the back of the head and body, while if to the right, much of his face is obscured by his raised right hand, arrow and bowstring. Except in the hands of a skilled artist, such as the highly accomplished silverpoint illustrations in the fifteenth-century Life of Richard Beauchamp, Earl of Warwick (see p. 14), the result could be visually very unsatisfying. The famous illustration from the mid-fourteenth-century Luttrell Psalter of longbowmen practising at the butts is a case in point (see p. 197) – the fletchings of the archer at full draw at first sight give him the appearance of a wide, toothy grin! It was therefore natural for many artists to move the draw hand down to the centre of the chest for clarity, ease of representation and a more pleasing symmetry. Such a technique is still clearly apparent in later portraiture, such as Joshua Reynolds' painting of Viscount Sidney and Colonel Ackland. One of the two young men has not yet drawn his small composite bow, but the other, with a longbow fully bent, is represented with a draw to the chest in order to keep his profile clear.[109] The problem is yet more skilfully dealt with by Raeburn in his portrait of Sir Nathaniel Spens, where the artist adopts a bold almost frontal view of his subject, thereby allowing the face to remain unobscured by the draw of the arrow to the chin.

That the draw to the chest was merely an artistic convention is clearly shown by its continued use long after the supposed replacement of the weak shortbow by the longbow. Thus the

Far left: Archers and hand-gunners, assisted by clerics, assault a castle defended by ladies, in an allegorical illustration from Martin le Franc's *Champion des Dames*, Burgundy, late fifteenth century (Brussels, Bibliothèque Royale Albert I, MS 9466, f.4r). The artist has depicted the archers drawing their bows awkwardly above their heads. *(Bibliothèque Royale, Brussels)*

Left: A striking portrait by Sir Henry Raeburn of the surgeon Sir Nathaniel Spens in the livery of the Royal Company of Archers of Scotland, completed by 1793. *(From a Private Collection)*

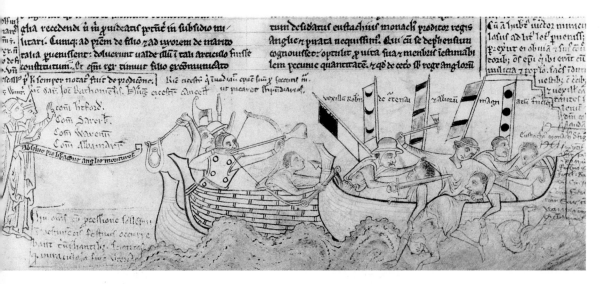

An English archer draws his bow to shoot a bag of quick-lime, intended to blind French sailors at the naval battle of Sandwich in 1217, from the *Chronica Majora* of Matthew Paris, completed in the 1240s (Corpus Christi College, Cambridge, MS 16, f.37r). To his left a companion prepares to throw a pot containing the same substance from a staff-sling. (*By permission of the Master and Fellows of Corpus Christi College, Cambridge*)

murals of about 1450 in the Church of St Peter and Paul, Pickering, depicted archers in a martyrdom scene of St Edmund whose weapons are proportionally longbows, but who are given the stiff, stylised draw to the chest (see p. 382). The same posture is given to the poet John Gower, who draws an impossibly thick longbow, in an early fifteenth-century manuscript of his *Vox clamantis*. As late as around 1610 a hunting mural at Madingley Hall, Cambridgeshire, contains a bowman drawing a shortbow awkwardly to his mid-chest in a stance almost identical to that of the archers on the central panel of the Bayeux Tapestry. At both Pickering and Madingley the no-doubt local artists were attempting to portray the bow most commonly known to them – the longbow – but in their attempted pictorial naturalism they fell far short of the master of the Beauchamp Pageant, who was capable of portraying longbowmen in faultless perspective and technical detail. We equally find distortions of scale in some later representations: a fine mid-Tudor Welsh chest at Cothele Hall in Cornwall depicts a number of archers holding longbows but with arrows that are massively out of proportion to the human figures (see p. 29). Numerous manuscript illuminations of the later Middle Ages, moreover, emphasise the continued difficulty encountered by artists in depicting an archer at full draw. Hence, for example, the illuminator of a fifteenth-century Burgundian manuscript depicting a series of archers drawing large, powerful bows has attempted to depict the two-tone appearance of the bow caused by the sapwood and heartwood, but the bowmen themselves are clumsily portrayed drawing their bows in an impossible position above their heads (see p. 47).

In short, it is very unsafe to use medieval illumination or sculpture to posit a 'development' from shortbow to longbow. As more artists became more skilful in the use of proportion and perspective and broke free more readily from existing exemplars, so the longbow and the draw to the chin or ear becomes recognisable in more illustrations. With the paintings of Hans Memling, we reach an almost photographic realism in the depiction of bows, which are virtually identical to those raised from the *Mary Rose* (see p. 12). Yet sufficient illustrations from the twelfth and thirteenth centuries exist to demonstrate that some artists were attempting to portray the powerful self-bows used by their contemporaries and their forebears. The testimony of Gerald of Wales describing the Welsh using what can only be powerful longbows in the late twelfth century serves to reinforce the archaeological evidence, which demonstrates the existence of longbows of well over 5ft (1.5m) from the Neolithic period onwards and unequivocally disproves the supposed technical leap forward of the late thirteenth century.

The myth of the shortbow left many unfortunate historiographical legacies. Not the least of these was an almost complete neglect of the role of archery in warfare before the later thirteenth century and the wars of Edward I. It was merely assumed that because of the weakness of the weapon supposedly used, the missile arm of pre-Edwardian armies was unimportant and therefore unworthy of detailed examination. With the 'shortbow' discarded, however, the realisation that the archers at Hastings (1066), the Standard (1138), Falkirk (1298) and Crécy (1346) were using weapons of a similar general specification prompts a fundamental reappraisal of the military role of archery. For if the longbow itself was a constant, why was it that the tactical deployment of the longbow en masse with such devastating effect as at Crécy and Agincourt had to wait until the fourteenth century? If we are to explain the prominence of archery in English armies and the battle-winning tactics employed in the fourteenth and fifteenth centuries, we must look to other factors than sudden improvement in the bow itself.

Matthew Strickland

PART II

The Longbow Before Crécy

CHAPTER 3

Before Domesday Book: the Bow and the Crossbow in Early Medieval Warfare

 t dusk on 14 October 1066, on Senlac Ridge, hard by the hoary apple tree, the last Anglo-Saxon King of England fell.[1] Wounded first by an arrow in his eye, Harold Godwineson was probably then cut down by Norman horse-men.[2] His death marked not only the collapse of his exhausted army but the beginning of the end of Anglo-Saxon England itself, soon to fall under the sway of Duke William of Normandy and his Franco-Norman followers.

Few historians would now hold with the notion that Hastings was the inevitable victory of a newly developed and invincible Frankish feudal cavalry over the outmoded infantry tactics of the old Germanic world. For though they customarily rode to battle and then dismounted to fight on foot, the Anglo-Scandinavian housecarls and thegns of Harold's army had put up a fierce and prolonged resistance to the Norman invaders since dawn on that autumn day, and at one crucial phase in the battle, when William's left wing had broken in flight and rumours spread that the duke had been slain, Harold had come within an ace of victory.[3] Throughout the medieval period well-disciplined infantry in close formation were usually able to repel the attacks of cavalry, and in some cases inflict a defeat upon them.[4] In this Hastings was no exception, for during the majority of the long battle the Normans could make no headway against the English ranks which 'were so tightly packed together that there was hardly room for the slain to fall',[5] while the housecarls took a terrible toll of both men and horses with their favoured weapon, the great two-handed Danish axe. But the manner of Harold's death also symbolised the tactical reasons for his defeat. After a day of bitter fighting, which had raged since first light, William had finally triumphed by a combination of a powerful cavalry arm with the massed shooting of archers and crossbowmen. By contrast the Anglo-Saxon army appears to have lacked any significant force of archers, a fatal weakness that did much to cost Harold the battle, his life and the freedom of his kingdom. But before turning to the role of the bow in this great engagement, it is necessary to provide a context by briefly examining what little is known of archery in warfare among the Anglo-Saxons, Vikings and Franks up to the eleventh century.

THE BOW IN ANGLO-SAXON AND VIKING WARFARE

Bows were commonplace among the Anglo-Saxon peoples who invaded and occupied much of lowland Britain from the late fifth century AD. As the bog deposits of Nydam, Vimose and Thorsbjerg so strikingly reveal, their ancestors, hailing from

The death of King Harold, from the Bayeux Tapestry (detail). *(Victoria and Albert Museum)*

Schleswig-Holstein and the Danish peninsula, had used longbows in war at least as early as the third century AD. The bow's continued use in the new lands carved out at the expense of the native Romano-British by a number of Anglo-Saxon warrior kings is shown by traces of such bows in pagan inhumations, together with large numbers of arrowheads, most commonly socketed and of leaf-shaped form.[6] A skeleton found at Eccles in Kent with an arrow embedded in one of the vertebrae confirms the natural assumption that such weapons were used for more than merely hunting.[7] Archers subsequently appear on sculpture, such as the archer shooting a bird on the Ruthwell Cross, Dumfriesshire, dating to about

750–850, while one of the scenes on the superb whalebone box known as the Franks Casket, probably produced in Northumbria in about 700, depicts Egil, brother of the legendary smith Wayland, defending his house with a bow against an assault by armed warriors.[8] Such a depiction of the bow in combat, however, is rare, while in sculpture and manuscript illuminations throughout the Anglo-Saxon period representations of archers are often highly stylised and heavily dependent on earlier models. Thus as we have noted, the short recurve bows in the Harley Psalter produced in about 1000 at Canterbury are borrowed directly from their Carolingian exemplar, the Utrecht Psalter of about 820 (see pp. 45, 54). Occasionally, however, one finds bows, such as that illustrated in a late tenth- or early eleventh-century manuscript of Aelfric's *Hexateuch* or the fine representation of Ishmael the archer

Egil the archer, identified by the runic inscription above him, defends his home against attack, from the lid of the Franks Casket, probably Northumbrian, c. 700. (By permission of the Trustees of the British Museum)

carved on an eleventh-century reliquary cross from Canterbury, which more closely resemble the kind of weapons suggested by archaeology.[9]

Yet if we may be fairly confident as to the presence of long, deep-sectioned bows in pre-Conquest England, it is a sad truth that 'the role of the archers in the Anglo-Saxon military force is a matter of great obscurity'.[10] Though noblemen might not shun its use in certain circumstances, the bow was not an aristocratic weapon like the sword and so does not feature in surviving Anglo-Saxon wills nor in the lists of death duties (heriots) paid by the aristocracy to the king in armour, weapons and horses. This also largely explains why in heroic poetry the bow, if mentioned at all, is referred to in perfunctory terms, though it appears in the more homely genre of the riddle.[11] Hence the great heroic poem *Beowulf* speaks only of 'the rain of iron when a storm of darts sped by the bowstrings came flying over the shield wall'.[12] We learn only a little more from the famous Anglo-Saxon poem on the battle of Maldon fought in 991 between the local forces of Earldorman Byrhtnoth of Essex and a Viking army, which tells how the combatants were initially separated by the tidal waters of the River Panta, so that 'none of them might harm another, unless a man should meet his death through an arrow's flight'. Once battle was joined, 'bows were busy' (*boga waeron busige*), but we know nothing of the proportion of archers to other elements of Byrhtnoth's forces or of their tactical disposition.[13] The poem gives the impression that bowmen were few in number and did little to

affect the outcome of the battle – the Vikings were clearly not mown down by a storm of arrows once they had crossed the causeway from Northey Island to the mainland, nor did they attempt to force a passage by advancing under a barrage from their own bowmen. It is important, however, to remember that the *Battle of Maldon* was not the factual dispatches of a war correspondent, but an epic poem celebrating fallen heroes who had died fighting steadfastly against a pagan foe.

But if we turn to chronicle and narrative sources we are confronted, as for so much else connected with Anglo-Saxon military organisation and warfare, with almost complete silence. Despite the high instance of warfare in the six centuries between the Anglo-Saxon invasions and the Norman Conquest, almost nothing is known concerning the raising, deployment and numbers of archers among the Anglo-Saxons. It is probable that archers were among the combatants in the battles between the kings of the heptarchy or in the many engagements between the Anglo-Saxons and their Viking enemies, such as Alfred the Great's triumph over Guthrum at Edington in 878, Edward the Elder's subjugation of the Vikings of the Five Boroughs at Tettenhall in 910, Aethelstan's great victory over a Norse and Celtic coalition at Brunanburh in 937, and the fateful battle of Ashington in 1016 which witnessed the defeat

Far left: Defeated
opponents succumb
to a shower of spears
and arrows, from the
illustration to Psalm 2
in the Harley Psalter,
Canterbury, *c.* 1000
(British Library, MS
Harley 603, f.2r).
(© British Library)

Left: Ishmael the
archer depicted on an
eleventh-century
English walrus ivory
pectoral cross.
*(Victoria and Albert
Museum)*

of Edmund Ironside by Cnut of Denmark, but the sources fail us. Speaking of the battle of Stamford Bridge in 1066, fought between King Harold Godwineson of England and the Norwegian army of King Harald Hardrada, the *Anglo-Saxon Chronicle* makes a passing reference to English archers, who tried without success to remove the lone Norse axeman who barred King Harold's passage over the Derwent, buying time for Hardrada and his men to make hasty preparations for battle: 'There was one of the Norwegians there who withstood the English host so that they could not cross the bridge nor win victory. Then an Englishman shot an arrow, but it was no use, and then another came and stabbed him under his mail shirt.'[14] But this indictment of English shooting (to say nothing of a sense of fair play) is, however, a late twelfth-century addition to the *Chronicle*, reflecting what were clearly legendary oral traditions concerning the great battle circulating over a century afterwards.[15] Nor, alas, can we place any reliance on the vivid and detailed account of the battle of Stamford Bridge furnished by the great Icelandic saga-writer Snorri Sturluson in his *King Harald's Saga*, in which Snorri describes Harold Godwineson's army employing combined assaults of cavalry and archers against Harald Hardrada's shield wall.[16] For not only was Snorri writing in the first half of the thirteenth century (he died in 1241), over a century and a half after the event, but it can be demonstrated that his lively tale is a work of dramatic fiction, consciously or mistakenly reworking incidents probably derived from earlier accounts of the battle of Hastings. Thus the Anglo-Saxon horsemen repeatedly execute a 'feigned retreat', the Norwegians break ranks and are cut down by the cavalry who wheel round against them, and for good measure Hardrada is struck down by an arrow, not in the eye like Harold but in the throat.[17]

LONGSHIPS AND LONGBOWS: VIKING ARCHERY

Comparatively more is known about the Vikings' employment of archers, though like their Anglo-Saxon opponents they prized the sword, axe and spear for hand-to-hand fighting. The Danish chronicler Saxo Grammaticus, writing before 1222, believed that the Norwegians placed great reliance on their archers.[18] The power of Viking bows, moreover, is suggested by his account of the legendary battle of Bravalla between the Danes and the Swedes, in which King Harold Wartooth of Denmark was slain, and during which 'the men of Gotland, skilful archers, would string their bows so hard that their shafts could pierce even shields. No instrument proved more deadly. The arrowheads penetrated breastplates and helmets as if they had been defenceless bodies.'[19] Norwegian law codes of the twelfth and thirteenth centuries list the bow as among the arms freemen were to bring to the muster, while from far earlier times the host was summoned by the circulation through the land of the 'war-arrow', whose very symbolism suggests that the bow was a widespread weapon.[20]

As Saxo notes, 'a wooden arrow that looked like iron was passed everywhere from man to man by way of an announcement, whenever sudden and unavoidable war fell on them'.[21]

Indeed, for such warrior farmers, traders and raiders, the bow must have been an essential multi-purpose weapon for war, hunting and self-defence, and its ubiquity is confirmed by the extensive finds of arrowheads in early Scandinavian society.[22] Somewhat surprisingly, many of these early Viking arrowheads, of which some 1,200 are known from Sweden alone, are tanged rather than socketed – a less effective design which was more likely to split the shaft on impact.[23] Examples from the later Viking period, by contrast, tend to be predominantly socketed.[24] The great thirteenth-century Icelandic epic *Njal's Saga*, written in about 1280 but purporting to describe events in the late tenth century, gives a glimpse of how

A modern replica of a Viking longship under sail. Scandinavian warriors employed archery not only in naval battles but also to cover landings ashore. (© *Ted Spiegel/Corbis*)

needful such a weapon might be in a society where feuds and localised violence were commonplace. In an incident which bears a striking similarity to the depiction on the Franks Casket of Egil defending his home with his bow while his wife sits behind him, the saga relates how Gunnar had been attacked in his farmstead at Hlidarend by a number of enemies, but had warded them off first with his spear then with his bow until its string snapped. Turning to his wife Hallgerd, he asked for two locks of her hair to plait into a new bow-string. 'Does anything depend on it?' asked Hallgerd. 'My life depends on it,' replied Gunnar, 'for they will never overcome me as long as I can use my bow.' 'In that case,' said Hallgerd, 'I shall now remind you of the slap you once gave me. I do not care in the least whether you hold out for a long time or not.' 'To each his own way of earning fame,' replied Gunnar; 'You shall not be asked again.' Gunnar had, it seems, earlier struck his wife for stealing, but he paid for his act of domestic violence with his life as his foes now overwhelmed and slew him.[25]

With the ninth century came the great age of Viking expansion through exploration, war and settlement, and graves of warriors throughout the Viking world contain arrowheads among other military equipment. Thus, for example, a Viking grave at Kaldarhofthi in Iceland contained a sword, two spears, two axes, a shield boss and three leaf-shaped arrowheads, while that of a Viking warrior at Donnybrook in Dublin had a spear and three iron arrowheads as well as a sword which marked the man out as being of some rank.[26] Arrows were found along with a sword, spear, axe and shield in a warrior's grave at Westness, Rousay in Orkney, whose high status is equally suggested by this being a boat burial, while another grave from the same site contained the skeleton of a warrior who apparently had been shot with four arrows.[27] Similarly, a boat burial of a male warrior at Kiloran Bay on Colonsay contained arrowheads as well as an axe, shield and spear, while an elaborate Norse ship burial at Scar, Orkney, contained a quiver of arrows along with a silver and brass-hilted sword and a set of gaming pieces.[28] Bows were clearly not restricted only to those of humble status. Surviving arrows show that some could be elaborately constructed. The tenth-century Hedeby boat grave which yielded a powerful longbow also contained nine arrows with bronze nocks, attached by means of a tang into the end of the shaft. These arrows were of birch wood and showed signs of binding, either to secure the nock or to attach the flight feathers.[29] A similar Danish ship burial at Ladeby also contained arrows, as did both the great Norwegian ship burials of Gokstad and Oseberg, though sadly the bows, as with the shafts of spears and the arrows, had not survived.[30]

These swift, sleek, dragon-prowed longships were rightly famed and feared as the Vikings' key offensive weapon, and many of the great battles between rival Scandinavian rulers were fought at sea. In these engagements the bow played an important role as a long-range weapon, being used to pick off enemy leaders and to rake the decks of opponents' ships before boarding and fighting hand to hand. Later sagas portray Viking leaders and marksmen shooting from ships,[31] such as the thirteenth-century *King Olaf Trygvasson's Saga* by the great Icelandic saga writer Snorri Sturluson, which dramatically portrays the last battle of this fierce sea-king during the naval engagement of Svold in 1000. According to Snorri, Olaf had been lured into battle against a numerically superior Swedish and Danish fleet, and soon Olaf's great longship *Long Serpent* was coming under heavy attack. Olaf plied his bow, as did one his best archers, Einar Tambarskelve, whose name literally translates as 'one who twangs the gut-string [of a bow]' and who shot arrows at one of the leading enemy commanders, Jarl Erik. Erik in turn ordered his own marksman, Finn, to shoot back, and as Einar again drew his bow, Finn's arrow struck the centre of Einar's bow, splitting it into two.

> 'What is that', cried Olaf, 'that broke with such a noise?'
> 'Norway, king, from thy hands', cried Einar.
> 'No, not quite as much as that', says the king; 'Take my bow and shoot', flinging the bow to him. Einar took the bow, and he drew it over the head of the arrow.
> 'Too weak, too weak', said he, 'for the bow of a mighty king', and throwing the bow back to him, he took a sword and shield, and fought.[32]

Finally, as his ship was overrun, Olaf, resplendent in a gilded helmet and red cloak, plunged into the sea, never to be seen again. The story of Einar is doubtless apocryphal, intended to symbolise the fall of a great king, but while the sagas are notoriously unreliable on specific events the picture they give of naval warfare is perhaps not too wide of the mark.[33] The use of the bow in this and other naval battles is confirmed by the much earlier poetry of the tenth and eleventh centuries, known as skaldic verse, contained like flies in amber within these later sagas. Intended to extol the martial prowess of a king or ruler, and often dazzling in their technical virtuosity, these courtly poems were highly stylised and formulaic, making much use of elaborate metaphors known as kennings.[34] Thus arrows could be called 'wound-bees' and a warrior 'the speeder of arrows'.[35] The *Ólafsdrápa* of Hallfreth the Troublesome Skald noted that at the battle of Svold, 'fast

through the air arrows sped forth', while the poet Egil Skalla-Grímsson, speaking of a naval victory gained by the Viking king and ruler of York Erik Bloodaxe (d. 954), noted:

> Darts splintered and points bit;
> Bow-strings sped arrows from the bow.
> The flying javelin bit, peace was broken;
> The elm-bow was spanned, the wolf rejoiced at it,
> The leaders of the host defied death,
> The yew-bow twanged when swords were drawn.
> The prince bent the yew, wound-bees flew.
> Eric offered corpses to the wolves from his fight at sea.[36]

Other verse similarly reveals the importance of the bow in Viking warfare. In his poem *Vellekla*, Einar Helgasson noted how Earl Hakon Sigurdson of Norway 'shook his shield free from showers of arrows falling fiercely, the ravens' feeder fended him in battle'. Later he notes how Hakon shot with his bow, 'the shower of ice-cold arrows falling on the throngs of warriors'.[37] The *Knútsdrápa* in praise of Cnut of Denmark spoke thus of one of his engagements during his invasion of England in 1016: 'The bow screamed loud. You won no less renown, driver of the leaping steed of the roller [i.e. the longship], on Thames's bank.'[38] Though highly formulaic, such contemporary verse demonstrates that the bow was a widely used weapon, worthy of inclusion in heroic verse, and that kings themselves did not disdain its use in combat at a distance.

If bows were used by the Vikings as ship-to-ship weapons, they might also be used for ship-to-shore attack. When in 1098 a Norwegian fleet led by King Magnus Bareleg approached the coast of North Wales, the great Norman lord Hugh of Montgomery, Earl of Shrewsbury, hastily gathered his forces on the shore in Anglesey to oppose any potential invasion. As he was riding along the beach, however, two Norwegian archers, one of whom was probably King Magnus himself, took aim and shot at him. The first arrow struck the nasal of Hugh's helmet and was deflected, but the one loosed by Magnus struck him through the eye and penetrated into his brain. He fell dead into the sea and his body was only recovered with difficulty when the tide ebbed.[39] How far offshore the Viking ships were, and thus the range involved, is unknown, but their marksmanship appears grimly impressive. In 1103, however, Magnus was himself slain when his landing in Ulster was repelled by force, despite the efforts, according to the thirteenth-century *Magnus Bareleg's Saga*, of the Norwegian archers to cover the king's withdrawal.[40] *Magnus Erlingsson's Saga* relates how in 1161 Erling's forces made a successful seaborne assault against their enemies guarding

Tonsberg, first by blinding them with smoke from a fireship, then by sustained shooting against the closely packed men defending the quays.[41] Given the crucial importance of warships to the military power of Scandinavian kingdoms, the bow continued to play a key role in naval warfare, a prominence reflected in the stipulation of the thirteenth-century Frostathing Law that in every warship 'there shall be a bow lying at each thwart. The two bench mates who row together shall provide the bow and two dozen arrows.'[42] Such a provision was echoed three centuries later in the Anthony Roll, listing a stipulated number of yew longbows among the ordnance aboard each of Henry VIII's warships.

ST EDMUND OF EAST ANGLIA

Perhaps the most famous victim of Viking archery was St Edmund, King of the East Angles, who was supposedly shot to death by pagan Vikings in the winter of 869/70.[43] Yet although at first sight Edmund's death might provide one of the most striking symbols of the Vikings' predilection for the bow, we must be wary. The most contemporary account, that of the *Anglo-Saxon Chronicle*, merely notes the conquest of East Anglia by the 'great heathen army' and the death of Edmund, but the manner of his demise is not recorded.[44] It was not until over a century later that the distinguished continental scholar Abbo of Fleury, visiting the fenland monastery of Ramsey in 985–7, was commissioned to write a detailed account of the king's life and death, *The Passion of Saint Edmund King and Martyr*. According to Abbo, the Viking leader Ingvar, having defeated and captured Edmund, had him bound to a tree, mocked and scourged and then for sport had him shot full of arrows, before finally cutting off his head. The head was left where it lay, but a wolf miraculously guarded it from harm until Edmund's loyal men finally came, rescued the head and rejoined it to the dead king's corpse in burial. Abbo claimed to have heard the story from Archbishop Dunstan (909–88), who in turn had heard it from none other than an eyewitness, Edmund's own armour-bearer.[45] While the chronology of this oral transmission is inherently possible, Abbo's own account is an amalgam of half-truths and pious invention:

> Falling into a fury, his opponents shot his whole body through with arrows as if in sport with him as a target, multiplying the harshness of the torment by the repeated discharge of missiles, since wounds dug into wounds as arrows gave way to arrows. And this was done until he bristled just like a hedgehog, or a thistle hairy with spines, in a similar manner to the passion of the illus-trious martyr Sebastian.[46]

The close similarity of Edmund's death to the fate of Sebastian, a late third-century Roman soldier executed for his faith under the Emperor Diocletian supposedly by being shot with arrows, is cause for no little suspicion, for the story may well have served as Abbo's model.[47] It is thus impossible to know if the historical King Edmund was actually riddled with arrows by his Viking captors. Nevertheless, the legend rapidly passed into accepted medieval tradition and exercised a profound influence over the iconography of the saint. Among the earliest known representations of Edmund's death is that contained in the

The martyrdom of St Edmund, from a fifteenth-century spandrel in St Lawrence's Church, Norwich. Note the wolf's head at the bottom of the scene, alluding to the wolf which guarded Edmund's severed head until it was rescued by his followers. *(M. Strickland)*

The martyrdom of St Edmund at the hands of the Danes, from the *Life of St Edmund*, Bury St Edmunds, *c.* 1120 (New York, Pierpont Morgan Library, MS M. 736, f.14). (© *2004, Foto Pierpont Morgan Library/Art Resource/Scala, Florence*)

magnificently illustrated life and miracles of the saint pro-duced in about 1124–5 at the great Suffolk abbey of Bury St Edmunds, which claimed the king's body as its most hallowed relic and was to become one of the foremost pilgrim-age sites in England.[48] The image of the king's martyrdom by shooting became very popular in English religious art, not least because, together with Edward the Confessor, Edmund became one of England's leading patron saints. The saint is also frequently represented as crowned king, holding one or more arrows as his attribute, such as on the famous Wilton Diptych, where St Edmund appears as one of the heavenly sponsors of Richard II.[49] Although the utter destruction of the abbey of Bury St Edmunds following Henry VIII's suppression of the monasteries has robbed us of what must have been among the richest of iconographical sources for scenes of the

king's legendary death, images of his martyrdom have survived the ravages of the Reformation in church wall-paintings as far afield as Kent and Yorkshire, on carved misericords and in more durable stone roof bosses such as at Tewkesbury and Norwich.[50] Such scenes furnish an important visual source for the study of the longbow, paralleled on the continent by the enormous popularity of images of the martyrdom of St Sebastian. This latter cult burgeoned in Europe in the later fourteenth and fifteenth centuries, and also attained popularity in England, in large part because Sebastian was held to have powers to ward off plague from those who invoked his aid, while his image also appeared on armour as a protective talisman against arrows.[51] With fine irony St Sebastian also became the patron saint of many of the confraternities of archers and crossbowmen that flourished in France, the Low Countries and Italy during the later Middle Ages.

If the actual shooting to death of King Edmund by members of 'the great heathen army' in 869/70 is open to question, it nevertheless seems certain that archers played a role among the great Viking armies which harried both Britain and Frankia in the ninth and tenth centuries. Thus, for example, Abbo of St Germain mentions the Vikings raining arrows upon the Frankish defenders of Paris during their hard-pressed but unsuccessful siege of the city in 888–9.[52] Similarly, the East Frankish chronicler Regino of Prüm recorded how in 891 a Viking army repelled a disorganised Frankish attack, 'then as is their custom, the Northmen rattled their quivers, raised their shouts to heaven and joined battle'.[53] Though almost nothing is known of how these archers were organised in land warfare, such a practice at least suggests that the possession of bows was widespread among Viking armies. Around the year 911 one such force, composed of warbands under the leadership of the Danish chief Rollo, was ceded a large tract of territory in northern Frankia by the Carolingian ruler Charles the Simple, in return for them guarding the land against other Viking predators. These early Scandinavian settlers rapidly assimilated the language and customs of their Frankish neighbours and subjects, together with many of their military institutions, and their land, soon enlarged by further expansion, was quickly to become the powerful duchy of Normandy. The transition to warfare dominated by castles and heavy cavalry cannot have been too difficult or abrupt for warriors who for over a century had made skilful use of fortifications and heavily defended camps during their raids on Frankia and Anglo-Saxon England, who were capable of mounting major sieges with engines as at Paris in 888, and who had long made use of horses for rapid mobility in war. Equally, Viking use of the bow was re-inforced by a long-standing tradition of Frankish military archery.

THE BOW IN FRANKISH WARFARE

According to Gregory, Bishop of Tours (538/9–594) and author of the *History of the Franks*, one of our most valuable sources for the Merovingian period, the Frankish tribes who came to occupy much of France during the fifth and sixth centuries had used the bow from at least the fourth century. He cites an earlier authority, Sulpicius Alexander, who recounts how the Franks ambushed a Roman force penetrating deep into the forests across the Rhine, shooting arrows smeared with poison as if from 'engines of war', from behind piled-up tree-trunks and barricades.[54] Early Frankish law codes confirm the use of poisoned arrows with ordinary bows and lay down fines for wounding by them.[55] Though sixth-century Byzantine observers like Procopius and Agathias could remark on the general absence of bows among Frankish armies operating in Italy, this was probably unrepresentative of Frankish forces, who seem always to have had elements of their armies using the bow.[56] Arrowheads are commonplace in Merovingian graves,[57] while one of the very few extant Frankish bows was discovered in the mid-sixth-century grave of a Frankish youth, probably of royal birth, which was excavated under Cologne Cathedral in 1957. This six-year-old was laid to rest with a fine helmet made of gilt-bronze ribs and horn plates, and a full complement of adult weapons including an axe, a long sword, two spears, a leather-covered shield and a bow with three arrows.[58] While it is possible that such a bow was used simply for hunting, a striking description by Gregory of Tours of his bitter enemy Count Leudast suggests that even noblemen of the highest rank could carry bows for war. The count, notes Gregory, entered the Church of St Martin at Tours 'in his cuirass and mailshirt, with his quiver hanging round him, his javelin in his hand and his helmet on his head. He could trust no one, for he himself was every man's enemy.'[59] Somewhat later Doda, a palace official of Pepin II (d. 714), had a military household containing warriors 'armed in mail shirts and helmets, with shields, lances and swords, and quivers of arrows', indicating that archers might not be simply the poorer sort but that bows could be carried by well-armed and well-equipped warriors.[60] Long 'D'-sectioned bows such as those found in Alemannic graves (one of which was some 6ft or 1.8m long)[61] appear to have been the most common Frankish bow type. Nevertheless, while Carolingian manuscript illuminations depicting recurve bows, such as those found in the Utrecht Psalter of about 820–35 (see p. 45), are heavily influenced by classical models, it is not impossible that the Franks may have made limited use of the composite bow.[62]

As with so much concerning warfare of the early Middle Ages, we know little or nothing about the number of archers in any given host or their role in battle during the Carolingian period. But from the reign of Charlemagne (778–814) a wealth of royal legislation, often expressed through edicts known as capitularies, allows us to glimpse the organisation of the great hosts that were raised on an almost annual basis.[63] On parchment at least, such organisation was impressive, with the king decreeing in 806 that the army should be well supplied with victuals and fodder, and that the accompanying wagons should carry 'axes, planes, augers, boards, spades, iron shovels, and other utensils which are necessary in an army'.[64] The Capitulary of Aachen, issued in 802–3, illustrates the type of equipment the infantry were expected to bring to the muster when summoned by the count, the main royal official responsible for local government, and suggests the importance placed by the Carolingians on the bow. When the army is summoned, the count should inspect the muster and 'see that they are properly equipped, that is, with a lance, a shield, a bow and two bowstrings, and twelve arrows'.[65] It was further stated that no soldier should be armed with a cudgel (*baculum*) but rather with a bow. Here the bow was regarded as the weapon suitable for the poorest classes, doubtless because of its low cost and ready availability, but the attempt to replace the club, the simplest weapon of all, with a more effective offensive arm has been seen as a major military development,[66] and may be compared to the insistence on the bow as the basic weapon in the English Assize of Arms of 1242 and the Statute of Winchester in 1285.[67]

We should be mindful that such legislation often reflects the wishful thinking of government more than actual practice, but it is none the less striking that Charlemagne intended each of his infantrymen to have both a spear and a bow, a provision which stands in marked contrast with later medieval armies, such as those of Edward I, in which footsoldiers came to the muster with either spear or bow but rarely if ever both. Charlemagne's infantry thus could have both an offensive and defensive capability, though frustratingly we know almost nothing about the actual combat methods and battle formations of Carolingian armies. Certainly siege warfare played a central role, and in such engagements the ability to field large numbers of bow-armed infantry would clearly be a major advantage. Though the writings of the Carolingian court scholar Rhabanus Maurus (d. 865) drew heavily on the *De Re Militari* of Vegetius and on the classical past, they none the less seem to reflect the importance with which the bow was regarded by contemporary Frankish commanders. He notes that only the best recruits should be trained as archers, and that target arrows should be shot at bundles of reeds or sticks. He also estimated the range of the bow at 600 Roman feet.[68]

Carolingian warriors confront lightly armed horse-archers, probably intended to portray Avars, from the Stuttgart Psalter, St Germain, *c.* 820–30 (Württembergische Landesbibliothek, Cod. Bibl., f.3). *(Württembergische Landesbibliothek)*

If it comes as little surprise to find the bow as a standard weapon among the poorer elements of the army, it is more striking to find that Charlemagne also intended his cavalry to carry bows. In a letter of summons to Abbot Fulrad of St Quentin in 806, the Emperor commands that the abbot should come to the muster in Saxony with his men 'well armed and equipped . . . that thence you may be able to go well prepared in any direction whither our summons shall direct; that is with arms and gear also, and with other equipment for war in food and clothing, so that each horseman shall have a shield, lance, sword and dagger, bow and quivers with arrows'.[69] How these cavalrymen were to use their bows is, however, far from clear. It has been suggested that Charlemagne had been influenced by his campaigns against the Avars, a powerful steppe people who made effective use of horse-archers armed with the composite bow; in response Charlemagne had attempted to create a body of cavalry which was not only skilled with lance and sword, but which could also shoot bows from the saddle.[70] Such a view,

however, has been strongly contested, and it may be significant that in the early ninth-century Stuttgart Psalter the Carolingian heavy horsemen who confront lightly armed eastern horse-archers, very probably Avars, are not armed with bows.[71] Nevertheless the idea is not wholly implausible; the Byzantines possessed such multi-purpose cavalry, and the *Psalterium Aureum* of about 880 from St Gall depicts a heavily armed Frankish warrior on horseback shooting a bow.[72] Yet the carrying of bows by mounted men does not necessarily mean these weapons were primarily intended to be used on horseback, as the case of the English mounted archers during the Hundred Years War amply shows. It may be that Charlemagne's *cabalarii* were tactically flexible, able to fight either as well-drilled cavalry or dismounted with bows and other weapons, not least in the vital context of the defence and attack of the fortifications which feature so prominently in Charlemagne's campaigns. Certainly the illustrator of the Stuttgart Psalter felt able to depict a Carolingian archer as well equipped with helmet and a form of scale-armour which also covers his thighs.[73] In the absence of other sources, the question remains moot, but however the emperor envisaged his horsemen employing their bows, the experiment seems not to have survived for long, and by the tenth century at the latest the bow seems to have been relegated to use by the common infantryman.

The use of archers in siege warfare, however, continues to be attested. At the siege of Laon in 938 the Frankish king Louis IV covered the approach of a siege-tower with archers, while an illustrated version of the *Liber Maccabeorum* of the early tenth century shows a group of archers assailing the defenders of the city while horsemen make an assault.[74] In 985, during an attack on Verdun, Lothar brought up a siege-tower by having oxen pull ropes around stakes acting like capstans so that they moved away from the walls themselves and out of effective arrow range.[75] By the tenth century, moreover, the crossbow appears in military use in Northern France.[76] The chronicler Richer, writing in 995–8, recorded its use by the citizens of Soissons against the forces of Hugh the Great in 948, and subsequently remarked that an attack on the city of Senlis the following year by Louis IV had been checked by the fortifications and the shots of *arcobalistae*.[77] In 985 the forces of Lothar deluged the defenders of Verdun with arrows and bolts from crossbows.[78] Such weapons were also used outside the context of siege, for Richer relates how in 984, at Brisach on the Rhine, local forces had barred the advance of Lothar by placing archers and crossbowmen (*sagittarii cum arcubus et balistis*) behind felled trees.[79] The crossbowmen in the service of Duke Charles of Lower Lorraine, during his capture of the key city of Laon in 986, are mentioned as being especially skilful.[80] From the tenth century too comes our first reliable depiction of early medieval crossbows in Europe, with the weapon being familiar enough for it to be carefully illustrated by Haimo, a prominent scholar in the abbey of St Germain in Auxerre, in his commentary on the Old Testament Book of Ezekiel written in about 1000.[81] Here two bowmen, lacking any protective armour but holding crossbows with long trigger mechanisms,[82] flank wheeled battering rams and shoot at a fortified city.

The rise of the crossbow was to have a profound impact on medieval warfare, and in particular on the subsequent history of the longbow, with whose story it is inextricably linked. More powerful yet slower to load, physically less demanding yet more costly to produce, the crossbow was to remain a potent rival to the longbow throughout the Middle Ages, until both were eclipsed by effective hand-held firearms. Given this importance, we need briefly to examine the nature of the early medieval crossbow and its antecedents.

THE EARLY CROSSBOW

The crossbow of tenth-century Europe had a venerable ancestry. Though the weapon was known to the Chinese perhaps as early as the sixth century BC,[83] it was the Greeks who developed the *gastraphetes* or 'belly-bow', so named from being spanned by placing the stock against the stomach to push a slide forward to lock with a trigger mechanism.[84] Less complex weapons without slides but probably with composite bow arms are found represented on Roman paintings and grave steles dating to the late first and second centuries AD from Solignac and Velay in Aquitaine, though these appear to be hunting weapons.[85] In his highly influential treatise *De Re Militari*, written in about 400 AD, the late Roman author Flavius Vegetius Renatus noted that 'the weapons which they now call *manuballistae* [hand crossbows] formerly were called *scorpiones*; they were so named because they inflict death by means of small and slender darts'.[86] It is probable that mounted infantry (*ballistarii*) with hand-held crossbows formed part of a strike force deployed by the Emperor Julian against the Alemanni in 365.[87] Nevertheless, the hand-held crossbow seems to have played a far less significant role in Roman warfare than the larger frame-mounted ballista, a highly adaptable light-artillery piece used extensively in both sieges and warfare in the field.[88]

Much practical expertise concerning siege warfare was inherited from the late Roman and Byzantine world by the barbarian successor kingdoms of the West, and knowledge of both the ballista and the hand-held crossbow appear to have been included in this technical legacy.[89] Known to the late Roman author Ammianus Marcellinus, the crossbow is mentioned in use by the Goths and also appears in Visigothic Spain in the seventh-century laws of King Reccaswinth in the context of the hunt.[90] Most intriguing of all are two Pictish symbol stones which may depict crossbows used for hunting.[91] The Drosten stone, dating from the ninth or tenth century, depicts a hooded hunter confronting a boar with a bow that unmistakably has some form of tiller, though he seems to be drawing back the string with one hand. Perhaps he is spanning his weapon, but even allowing for the highly stylised nature of these Pictish stones, the grip seems unusual for a crossbow and it may be that some form of hunting trap or spring-bow is intended.[92] Nevertheless, given contact in trade and war with Roman garrisons it is not impossible that the weapon was known to the tribes of north-east Britain, and may have continued to be employed until the seventh or eighth century in Scotland.[93] Two heavy iron bolt-heads were found at a crannog at Buston, Ayrshire, but unfortunately finds of crossbow trigger-nuts made of antler from this site and others are of an indeterminable date, though the seventh to eighth century has been suggested.[94] Similarly, finds at Burbage in Wiltshire included a crossbow nut of antler, a tiller pommel and fragments of decorated bone plaques, closely resembling those of Roman crossbows, but the dating is disputed and might be as late as the eleventh century.[95] Whether the crossbow was used in war or the hunt by the Merovingians or Carolingians is uncertain, though the description of the Viking siege of Paris in 888 by Abbo of St Germain suggests that the city's Frankish defenders had siege *ballistae*.[96] Similarly, the *Annals of St Bertin* seems to refer to crossbowmen when it notes that in 884 a Viking force that had raided Toulouse moved south into Galicia but was destroyed partly by a tempest but also 'partly by the attack of *ballistarii*'.[97]

The type of early crossbows depicted by Haimo of Auxerre lacks stirrups attached to the tiller, suggesting that they were simply spanned by hand, or by the bowman placing his feet on the bowstave either side of the tiller and drawing the string up with his hands. This latter method of spanning is clearly shown on a group of late eleventh- and early twelfth-century sculptures from the great abbeys of St Sernin at Toulouse, St Isidore at Leon and St James at Compostela.[98] It was also described in some detail by the Byzantine princess Anna Comnena in her *Alexiad*, a laudatory account of the deeds of her father the

Above: The prophet Ezekiel (bottom right) paints a picture of the siege of Jerusalem including crossbowmen supporting an assault with wheeled battering rams, from *The Commentaries of Hamo on Ezekiel, c.* 1000 (Paris, Bibliothèque Nationale, MS lat. 12302). Note the archers' lack of armour, and the long trigger mechanism of these early weapons. *(Bibliothèque Nationale, Paris)*

Above, right: A hooded Pictish huntsman prepares to shoot an oncoming boar, from the Drosten Stone, probably tenth century. The weapon may be a crossbow, or perhaps a form of trap-bow. *(© Crown Copyright reproduced by courtesy of Historic Scotland)*

Emperor Alexius I (1081–1118), written between 1118 and 1148:

> The crossbow (*tzagran*) is a weapon of the barbarians, absolutely unknown to the Greeks. In order to stretch it one does not pull the string with the right hand while pushing the bow with the left away from the body; this instrument of war, which shoots weapons to an enormous distance, has to be stretched by lying almost on one's back; each foot is pressed forcibly against the half-circles of the bow and the two hands tug at the bow, pulling with all one's strength towards the body.[99]

Anna was probably wrong in stating that the crossbow was unknown to the Byzantines.[100] Nevertheless, the Frankish weapon she describes was already formidable:

> In the shooting the string exerts tremendous force, so that the missiles, wherever they strike, do not rebound; in fact they transfix a shield, cut through a heavy iron breastplate and resume their flight on the far side, so irresistible and violent is the discharge. An arrow of this type has been known to make its way right through a bronze statue, and when shot at the wall of a very great town its point either protruded from the other side or buried itself in the wall and disappeared altogether. Such is the crossbow, a truly diabolical machine. The unfortunate man who is struck by it dies without feeling the blow; however strong the impact, he knows nothing of it.[101]

As a further illustration, Anna describes how Marianus, a Byzantine commander attempting to board a Frankish galley, was shot at by crossbows; the first bolt went clean through his helmet but missed his head; the second 'pierced his shield, bored through his breastplate of scale-armour and grazed his side'.[102] Though Anna was writing a considerable time after the First Crusade (1096–9) and other events she described, it seems probable that this was the type of crossbow in widespread use in eleventh-century France, and which was employed by the crossbowmen who accompanied Duke

William of Normandy on his expedition to England in 1066. The remarkable survival of a partially intact crossbow dated to the eleventh century was found in a waterlogged site at Lake Paladru near Charavines, north-west of Grenoble; it had a short stock 20in (51cm) long, with the span of the bow being approximately the same.[103]

THE BATTLE OF HASTINGS, 14 OCTOBER 1066

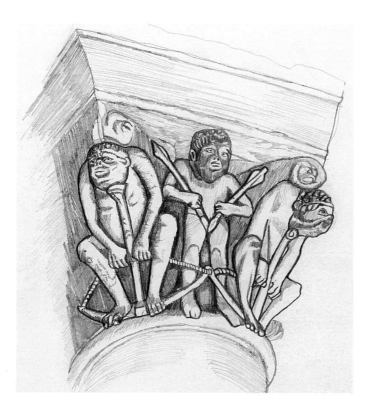

The significance of archery in the Frankish world by the eleventh century is nowhere more strikingly illustrated than by the large body of archers and crossbowmen which William, Duke of Normandy was able to raise for his army of invasion in 1066, and by the great military importance he placed upon them. Many of the duke's bowmen may have come from Normandy itself, but his powerful force was heterogeneous, raised not only from among his Norman vassals but from many of the principalities of France, with mercenaries flocking to his standard in the hope of pay, booty and rich pickings.[104] No reliable figures are available for the size of the expedition which finally sailed from the north French port of St Valéry on 27 September 1066, nor for what proportion of these troops were missilemen, but estimates for William's total strength vary between about 7,000 and 14,000 combatants.[105] A later Norman writer, Master Wace, writing his *Roman de Rou* (*The Romance of Rollo*) in about 1170 for the court of Henry II, gives a vivid description of how, on landfall at Pevensey on 28 September, William's archers leapt ashore to cover the disembarkation:

Above: Demons spanning crossbows, from the church of St Sernin, Toulouse, *c.* 1110, reflecting ecclesiastical censure of a weapon deemed fit only for the denizens of Hell. *(Martin Latham)*

Right: Norman archers from the Bayeux Tapestry. The figure wearing a hauberk and helmet may well depict a captain of archers. *(Victoria and Albert Museum)*

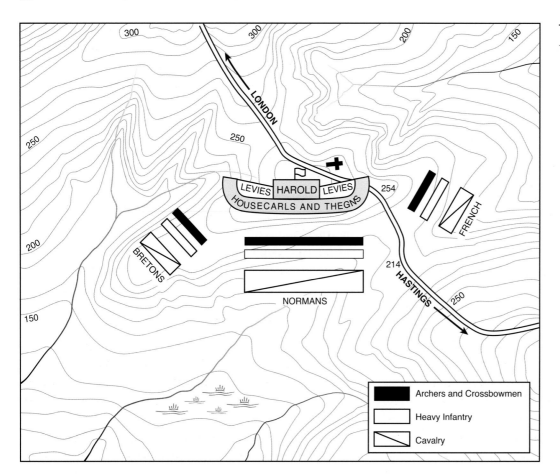

The battle of Hastings, 14 October 1066.

The archers disembarked, the first to set foot on land, each with his bow bent, his quiver and bowcase [*coivre et tarchais*] hanging at his side; all were shaven and shorn, and all clad in short tunics, ready to attack, ready to flee, ready to turn about and ready to skirmish. They scoured the whole shore, but not an armed man could they find there. When the archers had gone out, then the knights disembarked, all armed and armoured . . . they placed themselves next to the archers on the ground which had been seized.[106]

Though writing a century after Hastings, Wace was often very well informed, having access to a large body of oral tradition now lost to us, and may himself have received military training before he became a cleric.[107] His earlier mention of archers in engagements in pre-Conquest Normandy, such as at Varaville in 1057, cannot be confirmed, but his description of the Norman archers at Pevensey so closely echoes the depiction of the Norman bowmen on the central section of the Bayeux Tapestry that it is almost certain that Wace, who was a canon of Bayeux Cathedral, had studied this great embroidery.[108] Certainly the role he assigns the archers in securing William's beachhead is plausible enough, but for the impact of bowmen during the battle of Hastings itself we have the more con-

temporary account of Duke William's own chaplain, William of Poitiers.[109]

Once alerted to William's landing, King Harold had hoped to surprise the Norman forces by a lightning march south from Yorkshire, thereby repeating the tactics he had used so successfully to defeat the Norwegian king Harald Hardrada at Stamford Bridge on 25 September. His plan, however, was foiled by the vigilance of the Norman scouts. William had kept his troops in arms all night, expecting an attack, and now, forewarned, he seized the initiative, launching a pre-emptive strike against Harold before even a third of the Anglo-Saxon army was fully deployed.[110] As Harold had not intended to fight a defensive engagement, he had had no time to strengthen his position by digging the kind of concealed pits and ditches with which the Viking warleader Olaf Haraldson had broken the charges of Frankish horsemen in both Brittany and Aquitaine in 1014.[111] Nevertheless, he was able to adopt a strong if confined defensive position along a ridge whose height deprived the Norman assaults of much of their impetus.

William had drawn up his army in three main lines. The first line was of missilemen, including archers, crossbowmen and possibly also slingers. Behind them came the heavy infantry, clad in mailshirts, and lastly, behind this protective screen of foot-soldiers, came the mounted knights.[112] The initial assault is described by William of Poitiers, whose *Gesta Guillelmi* or *The Deeds of William* provides the fullest, if utterly partisan, account of the battle:

> Undeterred by the roughness of the ground, the duke with his men climbed slowly up the steep slope. The harsh bray of trumpets gave the signal for battle on both sides. The Normans swiftly and boldly took the initiative in the fray . . . the Norman foot-soldiers closed to attack the English, killing and maiming many with their missiles. The English for their part resisted bravely, each one by any means he could devise. They threw javelins and missiles of various kinds, murderous axes and stones tied to sticks. You might imagine that our men would have been crushed at once by them, as by a death-dealing mass. The knights came to their rescue, and those who had been in the rear advanced to the fore. Disdaining to fight from a distance, they attacked boldly with their swords . . . The English were greatly helped by the advantage of the higher ground, which they held in serried ranks without sallying forward, and also by their great numbers and densely packed mass, and moreover by their weapons of war, which easily penetrated shields and other protections. So they strongly held or drove back those who dared to attack them with drawn swords. They even wounded those who were hurling missiles at them from a distance.[113]

Poitiers's account of the opening phases of the battle demonstrates the importance William had placed on his missilemen, whose primary role was to try to break up the close Anglo-Saxon formations by their shooting, allowing the Norman cavalry whom they had been screening to ride in and exploit the disorder created by the showers of arrows and bolts. We glimpse here too an early instance of the unconcealed disdain of a man who had formerly been a knight before taking clerical orders for the comparative unworthiness of fighting with missiles at a distance in comparison to the close-combat techniques of the horsemen.

Yet with their assaults frustrated by the closeness and good order of the English ranks, the lightly equipped archers and the better protected heavy infantry were now highly vulnerable to the major counter-attack by an element of the Anglo-Saxon army which now seems to have followed. As Poitiers admits, 'terrified by this ferocity, both the foot-soldiers and the Breton knights and other auxiliaries on the left wing turned tail; almost the whole of the duke's battle line gave way . . .'.[114] This was the critical moment of the battle. Had Harold committed the whole of his army to an all-out attack, he might well have won

the day and driven the demoralised and panicked Norman soldiers back to their ships. But though sizeable, the English attack was seemingly more piecemeal than en masse, and William was able to rally his men. Riding in the path of those fleeing, the duke removed his helmet to scotch the rumour that he had been killed, crying, 'Look at me. I am alive and with God's help I will conquer.' With his forces regrouped and steadied, the duke succeeded in cutting off and slaying most of the English who had charged down from the safety of their former positions.[115]

With new heart the Norman army then renewed its assaults on Harold's main forces, but as before they could make little impression on the Anglo-Saxon ranks. According to William of Poitiers, it was now that the Normans, learning from the success of their earlier recovery from a real retreat, employed the tactics of the 'feigned flight'. Twice groups of Normans pretended to flee, drawing bodies of the English down from their main positions before suddenly wheeling around and cutting them down.[116] Despite some sceptics who have claimed that medieval cavalry lacked the discipline to execute so dangerous a manoeuvre in the face of the enemy, most scholars would now accept that the high level of training and professionalism of the Franco-Norman knights made such tactics inherently possible, a conclusion strengthened by earlier references to Norman cavalry employing the feigned flight at St Aubin le Cauf in 1051 and at Messina in 1060.[117] Poitiers certainly believed that this manoeuvre, repeated twice 'with the utmost success', marked a turning point in the battle. For although the remainder of Harold's army was 'still bristling with weapons and most difficult to encircle', nevertheless the nature of the struggle had changed: 'a combat of an unusual kind began, with one side attacking in different ways and the other standing firmly as if fixed to the ground. The English grew weaker . . .'[118]

Forced back on to the defensive by repeated Norman attacks, the dense nature of the Anglo-Saxons' formation made them vulnerable to the Norman bowmen, who renewed their showers of arrows, and even the housecarls' heavy defensive equipment could not withstand the impact of crossbow bolts. The *Carmen de Hastingae Proelio*, a Latin poem attributed to Guy, Bishop of Amiens, speaks in particular of the destructive power of the Normans' crossbows, according well with the later testimony of Anna Comnena: 'The foot-soldiers [*pedites*] ran ahead to engage the enemy with arrows (against crossbow bolts shields are of no avail!).' 'First', he adds, 'the bands of archers attacked and from a distance transfixed bodies with their shafts and the crossbowmen destroyed the shields as if by a hail-storm, shattered them by countless blows.'[119] The later chronicler Henry of Huntingdon, probably writing the earlier

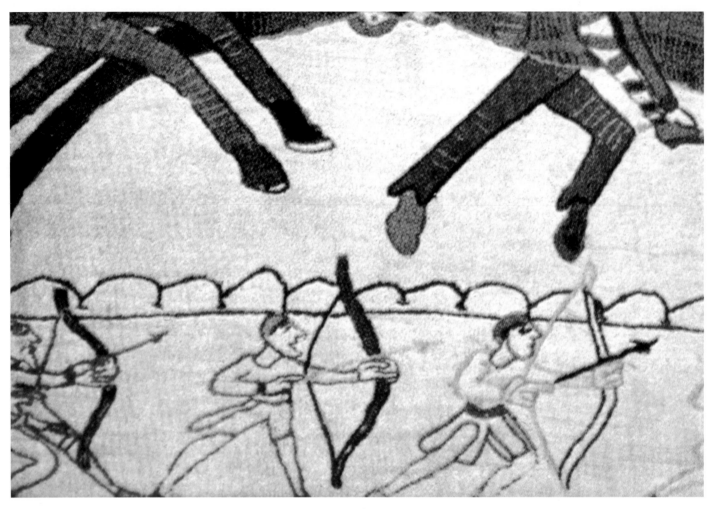

Norman archers, filling the bottom margin of the Bayeux Tapestry, support the cavalry above them, who attack the shield wall of the Anglo-Saxons. *(Victoria and Albert Museum)*

books of his *History of the English* before 1129, believed that Duke William 'instructed the archers not to shoot their arrows directly at the enemy, but rather into the air, so that the arrows might blind the enemy squadron', and that this ploy 'caused great losses among the English'.[120] It has been suggested that Henry, like Wace, had also seen the Bayeux Tapestry and that his description here was influenced by its depiction of a series of archers aiming upwards from the Tapestry's lower margins.[121] But such a tactic is not wholly implausible; the sixteenth-century chronicle of Olaus Magnus records how the crossbowmen of Götaland in southern Sweden shot their shafts high to pierce the helmets, upper bodies and even the backs of their opponents (see p. 283), while the excavators of the mass grave from the battle of Wisby in 1361 suggested that injuries to the upper part of several crania had been caused by arrows or bolts striking at such an angle.[122]

Yet whether or not they shot with a high trajectory, the steady attack by William's archers and arbalisters began to take its toll. This deadly rain of missiles may well have tipped the scales of victory by allowing the Norman cavalry finally to make full advantage of their great war-horses, driving in among the Anglo-Saxon ranks, now thinned and losing cohesion, to prise open their hitherto impenetrable wall of shields. Harold's brothers Gyrth and Leofwine had fallen earlier in the battle, and now Anglo-Saxon resistance centred on the position of King Harold, marked by the royal standards of the dragon of Wessex and Harold's own banner of the Fighting Man. Huntingdon relates a tradition of how twenty picked knights fulfilled their vow to cut their way to the English royal standard and seize it, and that 'meanwhile the whole shower sent by the archers fell around King Harold, and he himself sank to the ground, struck in the eye'.[123] The Tapestry famously depicts the king's arrow-wound, but the falling figure in the next 'frame' in all probability also shows Harold being cut down by a Norman knight (see p. 52).[124] The king's death was the signal for a general flight, although the fierce pursuit was briefly halted by a rearguard action by some English fighting around an old earthwork, which proved costly to the unsuspecting Norman cavalry and subsequently earned the soubriquet 'Malfosse' or 'evil ditch'.[125]

How is one to account for the fatal imbalance in missile forces between the Norman and Saxon forces at Hastings? In a speech of exhortation given to William before the battle of Hastings, Henry of Huntingdon has the duke tell his men that the English are 'a people devoid of military knowledge, a people that does not even possess arrows'.[126] Huntingdon was demonstrably wrong on both counts; on the eve of the Conquest Anglo-Saxon England possessed a highly sophisticated military organisation and a new king who had proved himself an able commander.[127] Moreover, though meagre, both archaeology and literary sources show beyond doubt that, as we have seen, the bow had long been known to the English for war and hunting. His strange claim, however, may reflect an awareness in post-Conquest England that the lack of adequate archery was a major factor in the Anglo-Saxons' defeat. This deficiency had equally been strongly hinted at much earlier by the Bayeux Tapestry's depiction of a solitary and ineffectual-looking Anglo-Saxon archer who alone confronts the serried ranks of Norman bowmen in the margins and main panel. The Tapestry perhaps here depicts another truth: that the highly trained and finely equipped military elite of housecarls and thegns who tower over the lowly bowman placed the hopes of their army on their own skill at close fighting with axe, sword and spear, and regarded such archers as essentially peripheral.

It has been suggested that many of Harold's archers, who would have been poor infantry unable to afford horses, had been unable to keep pace with the king's horsed warriors during the lightning march south from Stamford Bridge to Hastings, though it should be noted there is no contemporary evidence for Anglo-Saxon archery at Stamford Bridge.[128] Yet while Harold had notoriously failed to halt his advance in London long enough to await reinforcements, it seems likely that men had rallied to his standard as he marched south, particularly levies summoned from the southern shires, some of whom must have been bowmen. Yet the type of weapon such poor fyrd men brought to the levy was presumably a matter of personal choice and local custom, rather than conscious planning by military leaders to create balanced units of spearmen and bowmen. Be that as it may, the ultimate answer to the question of imbalance in archery lies in the fact that the army confronted by the Anglo-Saxons at Hastings was not a typical force as raised by the dukes of Normandy or their Frankish neighbours but an exceptionally powerful army of invasion containing a high number of stipendiaries, both horse and foot. Little wonder then that those farmers and herdsmen of Kent, Sussex and other shires who took up their bows, spears and cudgels to answer the summons of their lords to defend their land and homes stood little chance against William's large and hand-picked force of missilemen, drawn from the fighting elite of France.

The Normans may well have had the edge not only in professionalism but in technology, for the crossbow seems to have been largely unknown in England before 1066. Unfamiliarity with the weapon may account for its absence from the Bayeux Tapestry, which was almost certainly commissioned by William's half-brother Odo, Bishop of Bayeux, but was probably embroidered by Anglo-Saxons.[129] It is also reflected by the need of the *Anglo-Saxon Chronicle* to resort to the French loan-word *arblaste* to describe the weapon which slew Toki, son of the important Anglo-Saxon noble Wigod of Wallingford when he was fighting in the Conqueror's forces during the battle of Gerberoi in Normandy in 1079.[130] The later Norman writer Baudri of Bourgueil certainly believed the Anglo-Saxons had been ignorant of the weapon, and made play of the fact that the Normans had taught them a new way to die.[131] Certainly the ability of the crossbow to penetrate shields and armour, whether of mail or lamellar, may well have been an important factor in William's eventual triumph at Hastings, helping to thin the closely packed ranks of Harold's thegns and housecarls, whose strong defensive formation was highly effective at repelling the attacks of the Norman cavalry but made them far more vulnerable to intensive volleys of missiles. A striking epilogue to the importance of the Franco-Norman archers at Hastings is provided by a penitential edict issued in about 1070 by the papal legate Ermenfrid of Sion. Hastings had been a blood-bath, and both William and the papacy who had supported his adventure were keen to set the seal of moral probity on the Conquest. Thus a tariff of penances was laid down, according to the number of men each soldier had slain, and to the intention of the combatant – for to kill in hatred or out of greed for booty was a grave sin. A special clause dealt with the archers, who were enjoined a set penance, as it was recognised that in loosing their shafts they could have no real idea how many men they had killed or wounded.[132]

In the years following 1066 crossbowmen must have become a familiar sight in occupied England, as members of Norman garrisons and field forces. In 1075, when William's rule was threatened by a serious baronial rebellion, the key rebel stronghold of Norwich Castle was taken by men loyal to the king and garrisoned with a powerful royal contingent of 300 knights and many crossbowmen and engineers under the command of Geoffrey, Bishop of Coutances, William de Warenne and Robert Malet.[133] Crossbowmen may well have formed part of the large mercenary army raised by William in 1085 to meet the danger posed by the great invasion fleet being assembled by Cnut IV of Denmark, but the sources do not permit us to see the composition of his army. Nevertheless, the lethal nature of the weapon, together with its relatively high cost of manufacture, meant that crossbowmen were already regarded as a *corps d'élite*. Some were of enough social standing to witness ducal charters, such as one Fulcher 'arcibalister', who appears at Courdemanche in 1060 as a testator to a confirmation by Duke William of a grant of land to Saint-Père de Chartres.[134] More certainly, the great land survey of Domesday Book, undertaken as a direct consequence of the alarms of 1085, reveals a number of crossbowmen as landed tenants, such as one Odo *balistarius* holding land from King William in Yorkshire. This again suggests their comparatively high status, while from the late eleventh century there is further evidence of serjeantry tenure by service with a crossbow.[135] Material evidence of the crossbow's dissemination is furnished by the find of an eleventh-century antler crossbow nut at the seigneurial residence of Goltho in Lincolnshire, and of another crossbow nut from the first half of the twelfth century at Wareham Castle.[136]

The introduction of the crossbow into England by the Normans has equally been seen as part of a wider dissemination of superior military technology, which also included heavy cavalry and castles, from a central zone of Europe, formed predominantly by the Frankish and German heartlands, out to the peripheries of Europe by means of an aggressive diaspora of a militarily effective and land-hungry warrior elite. Thus the Franco-Norman invasion of 1066 brought such influences first to England, then rapidly to the Celtic lands, while swift and highly successful Norman expansion in southern Italy and Sicily had brought these military techniques to the Mediterranean.[137] In turn, the widespread use of the crossbow by the Italian maritime states helped further to disseminate this weapon. The Genoese, who were to become famed through Europe as mercenary crossbowmen, are recorded using crossbows as early as 1012 along with their great rivals the Pisans in the conquest of Sardinia, then again in operations in Corsica in 1072, developing what was to be a long-standing connection between the crossbow and naval warfare.[138] The Norman adventurers who had carved out principalities for themselves in southern Italy during the eleventh century seem to have supported their cavalry with archers,[139] and subsequently the great Norman leader Robert Guiscard was also to use crossbowmen to great effect, notably at the battle of Durazzo (Dyrrachium) in 1081 against the Byzantines and the Anglo-Saxons of their Varangian guard.[140] And we have already noted how Anna Comnena was struck by the awesome power of a weapon she believed to have been unknown to the Byzantines. Crossbowmen were also to play a key role in crusading warfare, where the Muslim opponents of the Latins soon gained a healthy respect for this weapon.

In tactical terms Hastings had witnessed the successful use of offensive archery combined with cavalry, while the mixture of archers and crossbowmen gave the Normans the advantage of the bow's rapidity of shooting combined with the penetrative power of the slower but more powerful crossbow. Though the manner of deployment of missilemen in field engagements in later tenth- and early eleventh-century France is obscure, it is most unlikely that William's tactics at Hastings were wholly an innovation, and the composition of William's army of invasion in 1066 is eloquent testimony to the importance of archers and crossbowmen in pre-Conquest Normandy and its northern French neighbours. Nevertheless, the continuing significance of missilemen in Frankish armies is well illustrated by the campaigns of the First Crusade (1096–9) in Asia Minor, Syria and Palestine, which represented a major military effort by the territorial principalities of France. Faced with new enemies and new tactics, the Franks, as we shall see in Chapter 6, quickly adapted their methods of war to meet these challenges, and in so doing highlighted still further the vital role of both archers and crossbowmen, not least in warding off the constant attacks of the Turkish horse-archers, whether on a 'fighting march' or in battle itself. In the Anglo-Norman realm there was not to be a pitched battle on the scale of Hastings until that of Tinchebrai in 1106, waged between two of the Conqueror's sons, Henry I of England and his brother Robert Curthose, Duke of Normandy. Yet archers remained an integral element in Anglo-Norman warfare, and we must now turn to the early decades of the twelfth century, which were to witness the emergence of a powerful tactical synthesis of dismounted knights supported by bowmen.

Matthew Strickland

CHAPTER 4

Tactics Found and Lost: Dismounted Knights and Archers in Anglo-Norman England

The best fighters were placed in the front rank as strikers. Those on right
and left flanks were crossbowmen and archers. The better and the larger
part of their army dismounted from their horses and, in the middle of the
field, on foot drew up their ranks in good order. They cut their lances
down and abandoned their heraldic devices. They advanced at a slow
march to fight through the mêlée in a body, so that no one should lose
his place nor any man turn in flight.[1]

ne could easily be forgiven for believing that these words were describing the battle tactics of the English in one of the great engagements of the Hundred Years War. Flanked by wings of missilemen, a disciplined body of dismounted men-at-arms forms the core of the army, their lances cut down to make them easier to wield on foot. Yet this remarkable passage was written in the 1160s for the court of King Henry II by the Norman poet Wace in his *Roman de Brut*, a legendary history of Britain beginning with its eponymous founder, Brutus. In Wace's poem this description forms part of an imaginary battle between the mythical British leaders Belin and Brenne against the Romans, but in fact it reflected the military practice of his own day. For in the 1160s Wace could look back over half a century in which dismounted knights, sometimes supported by archers, had formed a key element in Anglo-Norman battle dispositions. Though Edward III and his commanders may not have realised it, the tactics of the English in the Hundred Years War were no innovation. As Chaucer wisely observed in his *Knight's Tale*, 'Ther is no newe gyse that it nas old' – there's nothing new under the sun.[2]

DISMOUNTED KNIGHTS

Between 1106 and 1141 a series of battles took place in England and Normandy which were distinguished by the use of dismounted knights fighting on foot in close order.[3] At Tinchebrai (1106), Brémule (1119), Bourgthéroulde (1124), the Standard – also known as Northallerton (1138), and Lincoln (1141), significant elements of the Anglo-Norman forces fought on foot with the support of cavalry and, at least in the case of Bourgthéroulde and the Standard, of archers. This

Three knights on foot, from the Temple Pyx, (?) English, c. 1140–50. (Burrell Collection/Glasgow City Council (Museums))

phenomenon is of great importance, for such tactics show that commanders of the twelfth century had already discovered the potent tactical combination of dismounted men-at-arms and archers in a defensive position.

The widespread adoption of such dismounting tactics by Anglo-Norman armies has been variously attributed to the impact of Hastings on Norman military thinking, to the influence of the First Crusade, or to pre-existing Frankish custom.[4] There are difficulties with each of these theories. There is little doubt that Hastings, which had so forcefully demonstrated the effectiveness of closely formed and heavily armoured infantry to withstand cavalry, made an enormous impact on Norman consciousness. In this context it may well be significant that Robert de Beaumont, one of Henry I's closest advisers who fought for him at Tinchebrai, had as a youth served with distinction at Hastings.[5] Anglo-Saxons, moreover, continued to serve in the armies of William I and his sons, and in 1101 Henry I is reported to have shown his infantry levies the defensive tactic of holding their levelled spears so as to strike the chests of oncoming horses.[6] It is possible then that the long Anglo-Scandinavian tradition of fighting on foot did affect subsequent Norman practice, but it

must be remembered that the Conquest had all but annihilated the Anglo-Saxon military elite, and that Tinchebrai was fought half a century after Hastings.

Equally, writing before 1129, Henry of Huntingdon noted that Robert Curthose and his forces gained initial success at Tinchebrai in 1106 because of their military experience 'in the Jerusalem wars', but he does not say that the technique of dismounting, which was employed by elements on both sides, was adopted from crusading experience.[7] Knights rarely dismounted in pitched battle in this eastern theatre of war if they had the option, and the major victories won by the Franks such as Dorylaeum (1097), Antioch (1098) and Ascalon (1099), were won by a combination of cavalry and supporting infantry. As John France has shown, however, losses of Frankish horses on the First Crusade were so severe that in many engagements a high number of knights were forced to fight on foot through lack of replacement mounts.[8] Dismounting, moreover, had long been a recognised Frankish practice both for siege warfare and when faced with a crisis in battle.[9] Nevertheless, we do not find examples in earlier Frankish warfare of the use of archers in formation with dismounted knights, although this may be due simply to meagre sources. Certainly by the early twelfth century the practice was in evidence beyond the Anglo-Norman realm; at the battle of Alençon in 1118 Henry I's army was worsted by an Angevin force attacking in units each containing 100 dismounted knights and 200 archers.[10] Nevertheless, the deployment of knights on foot seems not to have been such a regular tactical feature in the warfare of the French territorial principalities as it was in Anglo-Norman engagements between 1106 and 1141.

It has also been suggested that the catalyst for the adoption of dismounting tactics in the early twelfth century was the increasing effectiveness of the mounted charge with the couched lance.[11] There is, however, little convincing evidence that the decades around 1100 witnessed a significant development in cavalry warfare, and the technique of the couched lance was already in use by Norman cavalry at Hastings. If dismounting tactics were designed to counter more effective cavalry, moreover, it is hard to see why these tactics become far less prominent during the second half of the twelfth century, at a time when the spread of mail barding for horses and increasing complexity of armour made cavalry heavier. Indeed, evidence of the deployment of dismounted knights supported by archers is notably rare in the later twelfth and thirteenth centuries, the very period which seemingly witnessed a renewed predominance of cavalry in battle. More convincing is the argument that the discipline and professionalism of the military households of the Anglo-Norman kings, which in effect furnished a small standing army, allowed commanders to dismount significant numbers of knights in tactics which were more favourable to group cohesion than the potentially indisciplined cavalry charge. Such an elite could also be used to good effect to stiffen the infantry levies which formed an important element of the military legacy of late Anglo-Saxon England.[12]

Yet if the origins of such tactics are disputed, their military effectiveness is clear. The dismounting by knights to fight on foot in a defensive formation had many advantages. One was psychological. Without horses, flight by heavily armed knights was difficult if not impossible. The sending of horses to the rear was thus an overt statement of resolve by the knights, and one which must have boosted the morale of the common infantry, who otherwise might be abandoned by their mounted masters if the battle turned against them.[13] As Orderic Vitalis has Amaury de Montfort say on seeing the leader of Henry I's household dismount his troops at Bourgthéroulde: 'A mounted soldier who has dismounted with his men will not fly the field; he will either die or conquer.'[14] Moreover, in a period when cavalry sometimes lacked the cohesion and discipline to regroup and charge afresh, the outcome of battle was often decided by the success or failure of the first assault. Well-equipped knights on foot in close formation could successfully withstand such an enemy charge, particularly if supported by archers who could break its impetus by their volleys. When operating offensively in open ground archers were always very vulnerable to the assaults of enemy cavalry and even opposing infantry. Protected by dismounted knights, however, they could hold their position more securely and keep up a steady rate of shooting.[15] It was this crucial combination of dismounted men-at-arms and archers, usually in a defensive formation, which was to bring the longbow into such prominence from the 1330s. Yet it was already visible two centuries earlier.

At the engagements of Tinchebrai, Brémule and Lincoln, where units of knights dismounted to fight on foot, there is no direct evidence for the role of archers, though at Brémule, fought in 1119 between the forces of Henry I of England and Louis VI of France, there is a strong hint of their presence. Here, Henry I dismounted many of his knights and successfully received the charge of the French and rebel Norman cavalry. The statement of Orderic Vitalis that the horses of William Crispin and the French knights were 'quickly killed' in the

A group of knights charging, from the *Life of St Edmund*, Bury St Edmunds, c. 1120 (New York, Pierpont Morgan Library MS M. 736, f.7v). Such a charge was broken by the volleys of Henry I's household archers at Bourgthéroulde in 1124. *(Pierpont Morgan Library/Art Resource/Scala, Florence)*

initial charge against Henry I's front ranks may well imply that they were shot down by archers.[16] This was certainly the case at the small but tactically significant battle of Bourgthéroulde in 1124. It is worth examining this engagement, and the battle of the Standard (1138), in some detail, for they provide the clearest and most sustained picture of the role of archery in open battle in the Anglo-Norman realm since Hastings.

BOURGTHÉROULDE, 26 MARCH 1124

In 1124 Henry I was facing widespread revolt in Normandy in favour of his nephew William Clito, who claimed the Norman duchy, held by his father Robert Curthose until his defeat and capture at Tinchebrai in 1106. During the hostilities a cavalry force led by two of the principal rebels, Count Waleran of Meulan and Count Amaury de Montfort, encountered a force of 300 troops from King Henry's military household led by Ralph of Bayeux, Odo Borleng and probably William de

Tancarville, Henry I's chamberlain.[17] Assuming a defensive position, the royal troops dismounted part of their forces, keeping a mounted reserve as was common Anglo-Norman military practice. According to Orderic, whose account of the battle is the fullest, forty archers were placed in front of the men-at-arms, but another well-informed chronicler, Robert of Torigny, believed the archers had been placed on the left wing sloping obliquely forward in order for them to shoot at the unshielded right sides of their opponents.[18] It is clear from what ensued, however, that the royal archers were ordered to shoot at the enemy's war-horses, not at the riders themselves, and it is more probable that, as at the Standard, the archers were mixed in with the front rank of knights for their protection. Seeing this defensive formation, the older and wiser Amaury urged caution and withdrawal. But the hot-headed young Count of Meulan would have none of this, believing he could sweep away in a single charge these household knights whom he despised both as stipendiaries and as his social inferiors. But Waleran had badly misjudged the situation. His impetuous charge was stopped in its tracks as the horses of his knights were mown down by the archers of the royal household 'before they could strike a blow', and he and his companions were quickly overpowered. Amaury escaped the rout, but Waleran, captured with over eighty other knights, was to pay for his folly by five long years in Henry's prisons.[19]

Though only a small engagement, Bourgthéroulde is highly revealing. Odo Borleng and his men were clearly well versed in the tactics of combining cavalry, dismounted knights and

archers, a factor which lends weight to the suggestion that archers had played a role at Brémule five years earlier. It is also significant that archers formed part of the elite military household of the king (known as the *familia regis*), just as a 'master of the archers' appears in the household of King Baldwin I of Jerusalem in 1103.[20] This was in effect a small but highly professional standing army, which not only served as the king's escort and retinue but also formed the core of larger armies and provided garrisons for royal castles. Such garrisons might be drawn together, as at Bourgthéroulde, to form a fast-moving field force.[21] The presence of archers in this detachment of the *familia* at Bourgthéroulde shows the importance attached to them,[22] as does the fact that they were provided with mounts for rapid mobility. Robert of Torigny calls them '*equites sagitarii*' – mounted archers, who like their counterparts in the Hundred Years War rode to battle but who, as at Bourgthéroulde, normally shot on foot.[23] While we need not regard Orderic's figures as exact, the proportion of archers within Odo Borleng's unit was considerable, and Torigny notes that there was a great number of such archers in the king's army.[24]

These mounted archers can scarcely have been an innovation in the 1120s. William the Conqueror must have had mounted elements of his missilemen for campaigns such as those of 1069–70 where large distances were covered at speed, and it may be significant in this context that the last surviving scene of the Bayeux Tapestry depicts an archer shooting from horseback among the Norman troops pursuing the fleeing Saxons.[25] They were probably present among the

A mounted archer, well armed in mail and with a shield, is attacked by a knight, from the *Chanson d'Aspremont*, French, *c.* 1225–50 (British Library, Lansdowne MS 782, f.10). Though illustrations of them are rare, such mounted bowmen were probably an integral part of royal and baronial house-holds from at least the twelfth century. *(© British Library)*

household troops of all the Anglo-Norman kings. Robert of Gloucester, the illegitimate son of Henry I, who, like his great opponent King Stephen, had gained experience of their value while serving in his father's household, employed them among his own forces; in 1139, when leaving Arundel, Robert slipped through King Stephen's territory with ten knights and ten mounted archers to reinforce the garrison of Wallingford.[26] Mounted archers become increasingly visible in the twelfth century, and as we shall see they formed an important element of the forces taken to Ireland by the Anglo-Norman marcher lords from 1169.[27]

Except in scale, baronial households mirrored that of the king, and many would doubtless have contained huntsmen and archers for the chase such as those mentioned in the *Constitutio Domus Regis*, or the 'Establishment of the Royal Household'. This tract, written shortly after the death of Henry I in 1135, sets out the wages and allowances in kind paid to the king's household officials, and among the numerous huntsmen and dog-handlers it is noted that each of the archers who carried the king's bow, together with the other archers, was to receive 5*d* a day.[28] That bowmen might also form part of a lord's retinue as a guard is suggested by a notorious incident that occurred in 1083 during a bitter dispute between the monks of Glastonbury and their new Norman abbot Thurstan. After an altercation in the chapter house the abbot summoned his household troops and the terrified monks fled to the abbey church where they were pursued. Then, noted the *Anglo-Saxon Chronicle*: 'the Frenchmen broke into the choir and threw

missiles towards the altar where the monks were, and some of the retainers went up to the upper storey and shot arrows down towards the shrine, so that many arrows stuck in the cross that stood above the altar; and the wretched monks were lying around about the altar, and some crept under it . . .'.[29] Three brothers were killed and nineteen wounded in the attack. Particularly in the early years of the Conquest, when Norman rule was not yet firmly established, the employment of such archers or crossbowmen must have been common among the retinues of Norman secular and ecclesiastical lords. This was certainly the case during the troubled reign of King Stephen (1135–54). Part of the rebel garrison at Exeter in 1136 contained bowmen, while in 1143 some of the bishops filled their castles 'with stocks of arms, knights and archers'.[30] In 1144 William of Dover established a large troop of mercenary knights 'and also bands of archers' at Cricklade to operate against Stephen.[31]

Indeed, although the Standard in 1138 is the only pitched battle during Stephen's reign in which massed archery is visible, the abundant and unusually detailed chronicle accounts for this period of civil war allow us to see the ubiquity of archers and their importance in a wide variety of other military operations, providing an important indication of the limitations of studying set-piece battles in isolation. In conjunction with knights they might form small, mobile field forces, as in 1136 when Stephen sent 200 knights 'with a large body of archers' to receive the surrender of Baldwin de Redvers's castle at Plympton.[32] At the critical engagement at

A suggested reconstruction by Peter Scholefield of the powerful earth and timber defences of the Norman castle at Stafford in the later eleventh century. Even after the spread of stone castles from the twelfth century onwards, many outer defences continued to be of wood, while wooden shutters and hoardings were extensively used on wall heads to give defending archers and crossbow-men additional protection. *(Courtesy of Stafford Borough Council/artist Peter Scholefield)*

A crossbowman and two archers with composite bows cover the operation of a traction trebuchet worked by Henry VI of Germany's Bohemian knights during the emperor's siege of Naples in 1191, from Peter of Eboli's *Carmen in Honorem Augusti*, composed and illustrated *c.* 1200 (Switzerland, Berne, Burgerbibliothek, Cod. Bern. 120, *c.*16). The knight wounded by an arrow in the face is the Sicilian commander Count Richard of Acerra. Note that the crossbow lacks a stirrup and was thus still spanned by bracing two feet against the lath. *(Burgerbibliothek, Berne)*

Winchester in 1141 some of Stephen's men arrived to aid his queen and his brother Henry, Bishop of Winchester, 'with a body of knights and archers very ready for action'.[33] We do not know if archers were used by Stephen to harass the approach of Robert of Gloucester's forces at Lincoln in 1141, or whether the Angevin army with their Welsh allies used bowmen offensively in their major victory over the king.[34] But the following year Matilda's forces used bowmen to dispute Stephen's approach to Oxford, 'doing very grievous harm to his men from the other side of the river by vigorous archery'.[35] Above all, archers appear as key troops in siege operations, often in conjunction with crossbowmen, and it was siege, not pitched battle, which dominated the warfare of the period. Archers and crossbowmen could be placed in siege towers, designed to overlook an enemy's ramparts and sweep the walls with missiles. At the siege of Pont Audemer in Normandy in late 1123 Henry I had built a belfry which towered 24 feet above the walls, from which archers and crossbowmen poured volleys down on the defenders.[36] Archers could also be used as patrols to guard against enemy sallies or attempts to revictual the besieged. During his siege of Bampton in 1136 King Stephen posted archers to act as pickets at night, while in 1145 when he besieged Faringdon he posted 'an encircling ring of archers in very dense formation'.[37] In conjunction with knights, archers could man siege works or 'counter-castles', erected to blockade an opponent's fortress. It was from Stephen's siege castle at Burwell, built to contain the rebel Earl of Essex's depredations from the Fens, that a royal archer fatally wounded Geoffrey de Mandeville in 1144, while Stephen's siege castle of Crowmarsh, on the opposite side of the Thames from the great Angevin stronghold of Wallingford, contained at least 60 archers in 1153.[38] Even such temporary fortifications might have powerful defences of earth and timber, and, as in more firmly established castles, defending archers and crossbowmen would have been protected on the towers and curtain walls by wooden hoarding, probably fitted with loops and shutters.[39]

Once in position, archers could keep up withering volleys or exploit their ability to shoot rapidly to cover frontal assaults. At the siege of Miles de Beauchamp's castle at Bedford in 1137–8 Stephen 'made a skilful reconnaissance round the castle, and posted bodies of archers in the vulnerable sectors, with orders to shoot at a high trajectory or keep close to the battlements, assail the enemy with frequent volleys of arrows, prevent them from having an unharassed look out and make every effort to throw them into confusion'.[40] At Winchcombe in 1144 Stephen's archers advanced 'shooting clouds of arrows' to cover the assault.[41] Stephen's continental opponents employed similar tactics. During an assault on Le Sap in Normandy in 1136 by Count Geoffrey of Anjou, 'about 3000 archers attacked with arrows and many slingers directed showers of stones against the garrison, so that they crushed them by the violent storm of their assault'.[42] Similarly, at Geoffrey's siege of Arques in 1145 one of his archers slew the garrison commander, William 'the Monk'.[43] Such references make it clear that archers formed an integral element not just of Anglo-Norman armies, but of the forces of the other territorial principalities of northern France, just as they had when Duke William had been recruiting missilemen for his invasion of England in 1066.

One is left with the powerful impression that there was an abundance of skilled bowmen in the England and Normandy of the mid-twelfth century, ready to take the wages of a lord, whether he be the king, a bishop or a local baron, or to bring his bow and shafts to the muster of the shire levy in times of crisis. How such men could be deployed is nowhere more strikingly illustrated than at the battle of the Standard in 1138.

THE STANDARD (NORTHALLERTON), 22 AUGUST 1138

The battle of the Standard in 1138 is still more important than Bourgthéroulde for the light it sheds on the tactical value of archers in the Anglo-Norman period.[44] In 1138 Archbishop Thurstan of York and many of the leading Anglo-Norman barons of northern England gathered an army near Northallerton to resist an invasion by David I of Scotland. The core of the army was formed by the retinues of the Anglo-Norman lords and a force of knights sent by King Stephen, but was bolstered by the county levies of Yorkshire, and probably by the civic militias of York, Ripon and Beverley.[45] Indeed, to meet the Scots' invasion Archbishop Thurstan had taken desperate measures and had, by edict throughout his archdiocese, summoned every able man to the host, to be led thither by parish priests 'with cross and banners and relics of the saints'.[46]

To counter David's powerful army, the Anglo-Normans decided to fight 'massed into one column', and predominantly on foot so as to prevent possible flight.[47] In the words of Abbot Ailred of Rievaulx, author of a valuable tract describing the battle, 'the most vigorous knights were placed in the first front, and the spearmen and archers so distributed through them that they were protected by the arms of the knights, and could with equally greater vigour and security either attack the enemy or receive his attack'.[48] The other knights formed up with the barons around a standard which gave its name to the battle, comprising a ship's mast upon which were hoisted the king's standard, the banners of St Wilfrid of Ripon, St John of Beverley and St Peter of York, and a pyx containing the consecrated host. This flagpole, reminiscent of the *carrochios* of the Italian city states, served as a command post and rallying point, as well as a spiritual power-house, invoking the aid of the great saints for the English cause against the sacrilegious Scots.[49]

David's army, by contrast, was large but hybrid, composed of an unstable mixture of native Scottish and Galwegian troops, his own Anglo-Norman knights, and mercenaries. Knowing that the majority of his Scottish soldiers possessed little or no defensive armour, King David had intended to deploy those knights and archers he had to the best effect, so that, in Ailred's words, 'armed men should attack armed men, and knights engage with knights and arrows resist arrows'.[50] This disposition, however, provoked the anger of the men of Galloway, who claimed the ancient privilege of being the first into the attack. They had recently defeated an English force at Clithero, and now hoped to repeat their success and inflame the Scots army by the example of their wild onrush. Ugly words were exchanged between David's Anglo-Normans and the Galwegians, between whom no love was lost, and to avoid open conflict within his own ranks, David reluctantly allowed the Galwegians to lead the first charge. The archers were accordingly placed in the second line together with a force of cavalry under the king's son, Earl Henry, while David and most of his own knights dismounted to fight on foot.[51]

The ferocity of the Galwegian charge initially 'compelled the first spearmen to forsake their post; but they were driven off again by the strength of the knights, and the spearmen recovered their courage and strength against the foe'.[52] Meanwhile, the English archers poured volleys of arrows into the dense ranks of the poorly armoured Galwegians. 'The archers,' noted Henry of Huntingdon, 'mingling with the knights and letting off clouds of arrows,' pierced the Scots, 'for of course they were without armour.'[53] Ailred described the rain of English arrows more poetically:

> the southern flies swarmed forth from the caves of their quivers, and flew like closest rain; and irksomely attacking the opponents' breasts, faces and eyes, very greatly impeded their attack. Like a hedgehog with its quills, so you would see a Galwegian bristling all around with arrows, and none the less brandishing his sword and in blind madness rushing forward now smite a foe, now lash the air with useless strokes.[54]

Unable any longer to withstand the rain of arrows, the Galwegians broke and fled, leaving at least two of their leaders, Ulgric and Donald, dead.[55] Similarly, after their earl had been slain by an arrow, the men of Lothian broke in flight.[56] Seeing this, David's own division and the bulk of the Scottish army began to disintegrate and turn in flight. Earl Henry made a valiant charge with his mounted knights, breaking through one wing of the Anglo-Norman army and attacking those guarding the horses.[57] But 'his mounted knights could by no means continue long against knights in armour who fought on foot, close together in an immovable formation'.[58] King David was compelled to leave the field to escape capture, as the victorious Anglo-Normans gave pursuit to the routed Scots.

We would like to know far more about the tactical positioning of the English archers among the dismounted knights, what their numbers were, and whence they hailed. Some may have been trained troops, serving in the retinues of the Anglo-Norman barons, but it seems probable that the majority would have been levies from the shires, following the sheriff, their lords or even their parish priests into battle with their bows and quivers. William Peverel, for example, had brought contingents from Nottinghamshire and Robert de Ferrers others from Derbyshire.[59] Whatever the archers' origins, however, their significance was fully appreciated by the chroniclers. 'By them', noted John of Worcester, 'the army of the Scots was greatly injured.'[60] 'And so,' noted John of Hexham, 'the Scots and the Picts [i.e. the Galwegians] held out with difficulty from the first hour when the struggle commenced to the third; for they saw themselves pierced and transfixed with the arrows, and overwhelmed and distressed.'[61] Such a remark could well have been made by fourteenth- and fifteenth-century chroniclers commenting on French or Scottish defeats at the hands of Edward III's longbowmen during the Hundred Years War.[62] The Standard, moreover, emerges as the first of a long series of engagements, reaching a crescendo with the battles of Dupplin Moor (1332) and Halidon Hill (1333) but stretching well into the sixteenth century, which

highlighted the extreme vulnerability of unarmoured Celtic infantry to massed archery. Indeed, because of the unusually detailed nature of the accounts of the Standard, we can see the role of the Anglo-Norman bowmen as clearly, if not more so, than that of their successors at the battle of Neville's Cross against the Scots in 1346.[63]

In studying these remarkable Anglo-Norman battles of the first half of the twelfth century Oman recognised that the tactics of combining dismounted knights and archers in some sense prefigured those employed so successfully by the English in the Hundred Years War. Nevertheless, there seemed to be no tactical link between the two periods and, despite the powerful evidence which should have given him pause for thought, the myth of the shortbow caused him to dismiss the worth of archery before the later thirteenth century. Yet there is nothing to suggest that the bows of the royal archers at Bourgthéroulde or of the Yorkshire levies at the Standard were any less powerful than those of the archers of Gwent described by Gerald of Wales in the 1180s or those bent by their fourteenth-century successors in the Hundred Years War. The series of engagements from Tinchebrai to Lincoln, moreover, may well provide an example of the kind of chain of battlefield experience and dissemination of military wisdom among a cohesive military community that can be traced in the tactics of Edward III and his commanders from Dupplin to Halidon Hill, Morlaix, Crécy and beyond, in the generalship of Henry V, Bedford and their commanders in the later stages of the Hundred Years War, and in the tactical thinking of Yorkist and Lancastrian leaders in the Wars of the Roses.[64] We have already noted the presence of Robert de Beaumont at both Hastings and Tinchebrai, forming a link with an earlier military tradition.[65] Henry I was personally involved at Tinchebrai and Brémule, while it was an element of his military household that fought at Bourgthéroulde. Stephen, whose forces dismounted at Lincoln, had served in Henry's household, as had several of the barons at the Standard.[66] It is quite possible that David I's own formations were influenced by his knowledge of his brother-in-law's campaigns, for David had not only married Henry's sister but been brought up as an Anglo-Norman magnate in Henry's own court. Presence at one battle, of course, does not necessarily imply influence in arraying a battle order in another, and such links must remain speculative, for as has been rightly noted, 'military theorising was part of an oral, vernacular and secular

Opposite: Archers aid knights to defend the walls of King David's palace, from Stephen Harding's Bible, Cîteaux, 1109 (Dijon, Bibliothèque Municipale, MS 14, f.13v). Such bowmen formed an integral part of the military households of the Anglo-Norman kings. (Bibliothèque Municipale, Dijon/Bridgeman Art Library)

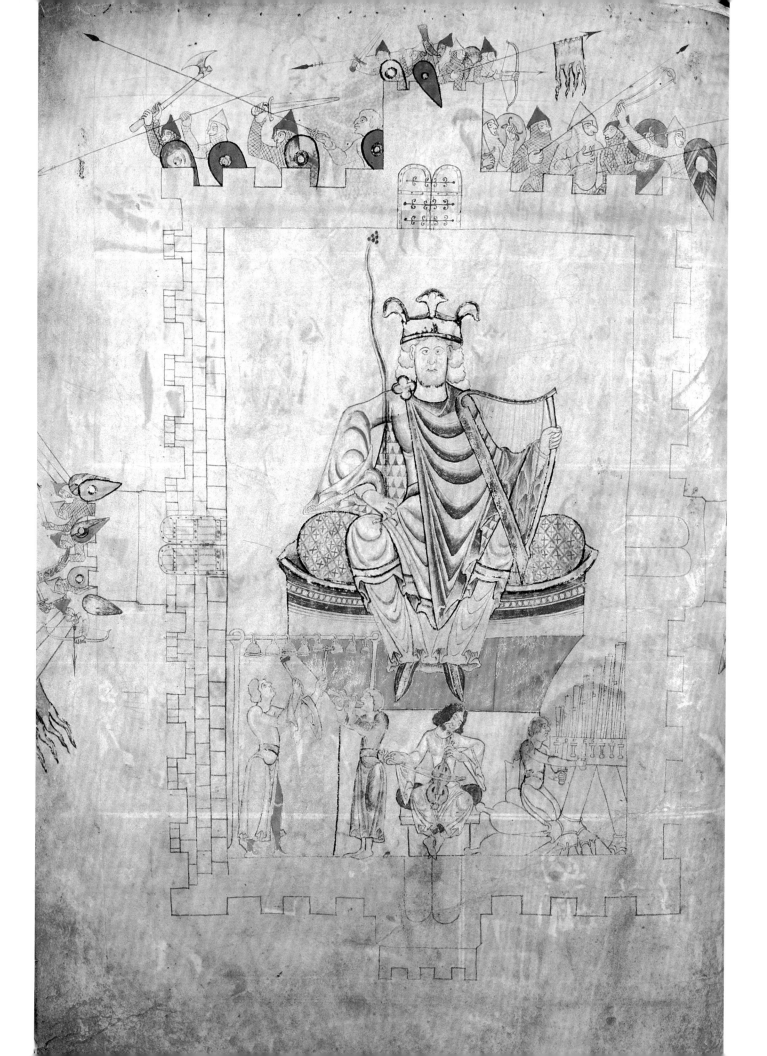

culture, which rarely survives in writing'.[67] Yet taken together, they strongly imply a tactical coherence, forged among seasoned veterans conscious of successful precedents in deploying for battle and well aware of the numerous advantages of fighting defensive engagements.

But if Anglo-Norman archers drew bows that were essentially the same as those of their fourteenth- and fifteenth-century counterparts, and if Anglo-Norman tactics anticipated the combination of bowmen with dismounted men-at-arms, why then do we not find in the twelfth century a bloody victory with high numbers of noble casualties of the kind suffered by opponents at Halidon Hill, Crécy or Poitiers? Overall numbers may have been a factor. Philippe de Commynes, counsellor to the dukes of Burgundy and later to King Louis XI of France, made a telling point in his *Mémoires* (completed in 1468) when he remarked, 'in my opinion, archers are the most necessary thing in the world for an army; but they should be counted in thousands, for in small numbers they are worthless'.[68] The numbers of bowmen deployed in the major Anglo-Norman engagements of the first half of the twelfth century are unknown, but armies in general tended to be smaller than those of the fourteenth and fifteenth centuries, and archer contingents are unlikely to have been anywhere near the scale of those in the armies of Edward III or Henry V. Nevertheless, from 1154, when the Exchequer accounts known as the Pipe Rolls survive in a continuous run, Henry II and his successors can be seen employing considerable numbers of Welsh archers not only within Britain but also in their continental campaigns.[69]

A far more significant factor is thus likely to be the context of battle and the attitude of warriors towards the slaying of fellow knights. Recent historians have placed much stress on the reluctance of eleventh- and twelfth-century commanders to commit their forces to pitched battle, a reassessment prompted in large part by the need to dispel the clearly untenable caricature of 'feudal' armies as a motley collection of brave but undisciplined knights, who lacked strategic or tactical skill and relied on impetuous charges to secure victory and personal glory. By contrast, it has been argued that pitched battles were a rarity, even in the careers of men like William the Conqueror, Henry II, Richard I and William Marshal who spent a lifetime in arms.[70] Conflicts like Hastings, where William's strategic vulnerability meant he needed a decisive encounter as soon as possible after landing while Harold sought to contain William on the coast, were outcomes of exceptional circumstances. In many cases the risks were enormous, the outcome too uncertain and often the opposing forces too evenly matched to stake all on one all-out conflict. There is much truth in these observations, although as with much important revisionism, the case has perhaps been overstated.[71] In many instances com-

manders wished for a major battle but were denied one by their opponents. That Henry II never fought a pitched battle, for example, was due to the wise reluctance of Louis VII ever to face him in the open field, while earlier in 1153 at Crowmarsh, when both he and King Stephen had sought a pitched battle to break the strategic stalemate, the magnates on both sides prevented them by making a peace.[72] Similarly, at Fréteval in 1194 Philip Augustus beat a hasty retreat when Richard I sought a decisive engagement, and such examples could easily be multiplied. Nevertheless, there does seem to be a marked difference between the role of battle in eleventh- and twelfth-century England and France and that in the campaigns of Edward III and his captains. Edward, it has recently been argued, pursued a deliberate battle-seeking strategy against his Scottish and French opponents, so as to deploy his tactical combination of dismounted knights and archers with often devastating results. He did not hesitate to unleash the full force of thousands of longbowmen against the knighthood of France in order to achieve a decisive victory against his Valois opponent, for only by inflicting the maximum possible casualties among his enemy's ruling elite could he break the strategic and political deadlock and achieve his ultimate goals.[73]

An important reason underlying this disparity was the nature of chivalric mores in the twelfth century, which emphasised the desirability of capturing noble opponents for ransom where possible rather than slaying them. While the high incidence of sieges and of small-scale skirmishes resulted in a steady number of fatalities, killing in major engagements could sometimes be remarkably limited.[74] Thus, for example, knightly casualties at Tinchebrai appear small, while at Brémule Orderic believed that only three knights were slain out of some 900 knights engaged, and over 100 French and Norman knights who had been in the thick of the fighting were captured.[75] Moreover, several of these Anglo-Norman engagements were fought within the context of civil war, which, in marked contrast to the later internecine strife of the Wars of the Roses, led to a sustained attempt to limit bloodshed and to spare friends or kinsmen on the opposing side. In such contexts an important element in restraint was the deliberate limitation of the killing power of archers and crossbowmen. Thus in 1098, when repelling the assault of William Rufus's knights, the elite French garrison of the key fortress of Chaumont

took care out of chivalry to spare the bodies of the attackers and turned the full force of their anger against the costly chargers of their enemies. So they killed seven hundred horses of great value with arrows and darts; the dogs and birds of France were gorged to repletion on their bodies. In consequence, many who had crossed the

Epte as proud knights on their foaming horses returned home with the king as foot-soldiers.[76]

Similarly at Bourgthéroulde Odo Borleng ordered his archers only to shoot at the horses of their opponents and not at the riders. For despite being in rebellion, Waleran de Beaumont was among the very greatest magnates in the Anglo-Norman realm, and the royalists sought only his defeat, not his death and that of his knights in a hail of arrows. The same considerations may have been true at Brémule, where Louis VI's forces contained a significant element of Norman dissidents among the cavalry launching the first charge against Henry I's dismounted knights.[77] Certainly at the second battle of Lincoln in 1217, where the supporters of Henry III faced many of their friends and kinsmen allied with the forces of Prince Louis of France, the royalist commander Fawkes de Bréauté ordered his crossbowmen to shoot at the war-horses of the opposing knights, not at the riders.[78] In such circumstances the direction of massed archery against one's knightly opponents was generally eschewed. And significantly, the one battle of this period where we *do* see archers taking a heavy toll of the enemy was the Standard, fought against the Scots; for the native Scots and Galwegian troops who were shot down were regarded as scarcely human savages, barbarians beyond the restrictions of civilised, chivalric conduct. Strikingly, none of Earl Henry's knights, considered by the Anglo-Normans as their own, is recorded as being slain or even wounded by archery, despite their valiant charge. By the same token Anglo-Norman commanders did not scruple to deploy considerable numbers of archers against their Welsh or Irish opponents.[79]

By contrast, when in 1187 the armies of Henry II and Philip Augustus faced each other at Châteauroux, a major battle was averted by wise counsel and parley – a phenomenon that would surely not have happened at Crécy and did not happen at Poitiers.[80] Similarly, when in late 1195 Richard I entrapped the army of Philip Augustus at Issoudun, the King of England chose to extract an advantageous peace even with his hated rival rather than launch an all-out attack.[81] Indeed, while in individual combat between the men-at-arms, concepts of chivalry and the desire to spare noble opponents was just as much in force as in the twelfth century, one of the most

important developments of fourteenth-century warfare was the infliction, whether by English and Welsh longbowmen or by Scottish, Flemish or Swiss spearmen, of massive and unprecedented casualties among noble and knightly opponents. Watching the flower of French chivalry being mown down by the archers at Crécy, some knights from the Empire serving as Edward's allies remonstrated with the king, and in so doing summed up the earlier view of warfare: '"Sire, we wonder greatly that you allow so much noble blood to be shed, for you could make great progress in your war and gain a very great deal in ransoms if you were to take these men prisoners." And the king replied only that they should not marvel, for the matter had been thus ordered, and thus it had to be.'[82]

Such an outlook goes far to explain why massed archery was not deployed on many twelfth-century battlefields in western Europe, despite the availability of powerful longbows and already deadly crossbows. The restriction on slaying knights with missile weapons was, however, by no means absolute, and a considerable number of individual lords fell victim to marksmen, very largely during siege warfare. The corollary was that captured missilemen might face execution or mutilation in reprisal for casualties inflicted. Orderic recounts how when a lowly archer mortally wounded the Norman lord Richer de Laigle, he would himself have been instantly put to death by the knight's companions had not Richer ordered his life to be spared.[83] At the siege of Crowmarsh Duke Henry, soon to become Henry II, ordered the beheading of 60 archers from Stephen's garrison, presumably because of their effectiveness against his own men, while after the fall of Rochester Castle in 1215 John spared the garrison except the crossbowmen, whom he had hanged.[84] At Bedford in 1224 the high rate of casualties inflicted on the besiegers by the defending crossbowmen was one of the reasons which led Henry III to hang the whole garrison, and in 1264 Henry ordered the beheading of over 300 archers who had harassed the royal army as it passed through the Weald.[85] The threat by French knights in the Hundred Years War to mutilate captured English archers by cutting off the first two fingers of their right hands was thus grounded in a long-standing tradition, reflecting the antipathy of the mounted aristocrat to the humble archer, born not only of class consciousness but of fear of the death-bringing power of his weapon.

TACTICS LOST: THE DECLINE IN DISMOUNTING

Two further factors limited the role played by longbowmen in battlefield tactics from the mid-twelfth to the late thirteenth century: the increasing dominance of the crossbow in field armies and garrisons, a phenomenon which we will examine in

Chapter 7, and secondly, and perhaps more immediately, the disappearance of the dismounting tactics which had so characterised Anglo-Norman warfare in the first half of the twelfth century. It remains a striking fact that despite its

Two archers, well equipped in hauberks and conical helmets, draw their composite bows to the ear, assisting an attack by mounted knights in this representation of the death of King Saul at the hands of the Philistines, from the Maciejowski Bible (New York, Pierpont Morgan Library, MS 638, f.34v, detail). (© 2004, Foto Pierpont Morgan Library/Art Resource/Scala, Florence)

effectiveness the Anglo-Norman practice of dismounting groups of knights largely disappears in the second half of the twelfth century, and with it the potential for deploying archers in open battle to their optimum effect. After the battle of Lincoln in 1141 there are few examples in England or France during the later twelfth century of knights dismounting to fight a major engagement on foot, still less one in which they combined in a defensive formation with archers. Most of the sizeable engagements which occurred in England or the continental domains of the Angevin kings after the accession of Henry II in 1154 were to be dominated by cavalry actions. The abruptness of such a transition should not be overstated. Despite the deployment of dismounted tactics by Stephen's forces at Lincoln in 1141, the Angevins had attacked success-fully with cavalry,[86] suggesting that unlike at the Standard and in contrast to the considerable numbers of archers often seen under his command, Stephen lacked a significant number of bowmen at this crucial time. It is clear, moreover, from other engagements during Stephen's reign that the dismounting of knights was far from universal; the sizeable engagements of Dunster (1139), Winchester (1141) and Wilton (1143) appear to have been predominantly cavalry engagements, though our

knowledge of all these battles is very slight. Equally, however, the Norman poet Wace, as we have seen, could still describe the dismounting of knights with archers in his *Roman de Brut* as late as the 1160s, while Richard the Lionheart's victory at Jaffa against the Turks in 1192 again witnessed the successful com-bination of spearmen, missilemen and knights in a defensive position.[87]

Nevertheless, the trend towards a renewed emphasis on cavalry is apparent. Thus at Fornham in 1173 the royalist forces under the justiciar Richard de Lucy surprised a mercenary force of Flemings commanded by Robert of Leicester and defeated them 'in the twinkling of an eye' by a cavalry charge which drove them into a marsh.[88] The following year a fast-moving group of English knights ambushed and captured William the Lion of Scotland as he besieged the castle of Alnwick. The same is true for Richard the Lionheart's campaigns in the west, where his defeats of Philip Augustus at Fréteval in 1194 and at Gisors in 1198 were less pitched battles than successful interceptions of the French forces on the march. At Fréteval Philip's rearguard was pursued and overwhelmed as the French attempted to avoid a face-to-face confrontation, while similarly at Gisors Richard's army fell upon Philip's column, forcing the king and his knights into such precipitous flight to the safety of the castle that the drawbridge broke under their weight and many French knights were drowned.[89] In the Holy Land Richard's victory at Arsuf in 1191 had showed the classic combination of a protective screen of infantry coupled with offensive cavalry charges, and cavalry continued to be employed in charges by Frankish knights against their Muslim opponents.[90] During the Albigensian crusade in Languedoc Simon de Montfort the Elder won the battle of Muret in 1213 by an impetuous cavalry charge.[91] At the great battle of Bouvines in 1214, where Philip Augustus defeated a powerful allied coalition of imperial and Angevin forces, infantry played an important role, but the majority of the knights were mounted and the battle was won by the superior close-combat skills of the French cavalry.[92] By the time of the second battle of Lincoln in 1217 cavalry warfare was so dominant that the French barons and their royalist attackers even fought on horseback in the narrow streets of the medieval city.[93] The importance of cavalry was to remain a marked feature of European warfare throughout the thirteenth century, while in England the battles of Lewes (1264) and Evesham (1265) were decided by cavalry forces.

Such an abandonment of dismounting tactics by men-at-arms in favour of offensively deployed cavalry is not without parallel. The second half of the fifteenth and the beginning of the sixteenth centuries were likewise to witness a renewed emphasis on heavy cavalry after over a century in which English, Burgundian and to a considerable extent French men-at-arms had come to fight predominantly on foot. Yet why were the tactics of dismounting that had proved so effective for the Anglo-Normans in the first half of the twelfth century abandoned? Why was it that the combination of men-at-arms on foot and archers that won the day at Bourgthéroulde and the Standard seemingly disappears from the battlefields of England and France until the early fourteenth century?

The causes of this change seem as opaque as those which led to the initial adoption of dismounting tactics. We cannot rule out the intangible factors of military tradition or fashion and the personal predilection of commanders. Too often we speak of the 'development' of tactics as some inexorable process of cumulative change, a kind of military 'Whig history'. But medieval commanders were not officers studying Clausewitz at a nineteenth-century staff college. Custom and inherited experience were important influences in tactical thinking, but particularly after prolonged periods of peace this could often be lacking. Thus by the time of the Barons' Wars of 1264–7 few English commanders had experience of a major battle; by contrast, it was the French who were seen to be the leaders in military technology and experience, and the baronial leaders looked for guidance to Simon de Montfort 'the precious flower, who knew so much of war (la flur de pris, qe taunt savoit de guere)'.[94] Simon himself would have been well aware of his father's successful charge at Muret in 1213, and French tactical influence may in part explain the predominance of cavalry in the battles of Lewes (1264) and Evesham (1265), and the apparent insignificance of archery – or at least its relegation merely to an auxiliary role – on the battlefield. Moreover, those military manuals that were studied were classical texts like Vegetius's De Rei Militari, not usually lessons from the more recent past. Indeed, military thinking of the later thirteenth and early fourteenth centuries shows no hint of familiarity with the tactical deployment and dismounted tactics of their Anglo-Norman forebears, and one must assume that the poems, songs and accounts of these great battles had either long vanished or were regarded as being of no practical military value. Rather, Edward III and his commanders had to reinvent the tactic of dismounting their men-at-arms in combination with archers, a lesson learned in the crucible of defeat and the hard school of the Anglo-Scottish wars.

There are, however, factors which go some way to explaining the predominance of cavalry. For the second half of the twelfth century witnessed the spread of horse armour in the form of

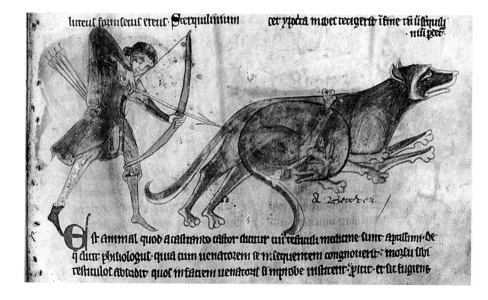

An archer hunting a beaver, from a bestiary, London region (?), c. 1220–30 (Cambridge, Fitzwilliam Museum MS 254 (Bestiary), f.19). (Fitzwilliam Museum, University of Cambridge)

mail barding and the increasing complexity and weight of knightly equipment, which may well have given cavalry warfare renewed impetus, just as it has been argued that the development of the lance-stop (*ârret de cuirass*) on solid plate breastplates gave a new power to cavalry attack from the late fourteenth century.[95] Moreover, though the tournament was in evidence from the early twelfth century at the latest, its popularity seems to have reached a new zenith in northern France during the 1170s and 1180s, which must surely be connected with the perceived importance of cavalry warfare. Texts such as the *Histoire de Guillaume le Maréchal* make it clear that the emphasis in tournaments was not on individual jousts, but firmly on group cavalry manoeuvres, where cohesion and discipline won the day. One of the principal reasons why Richard I licensed tournaments, hitherto banned in England, in 1194 was because the knights of his Capetian rival Philip Augustus had the edge over English knights in close combat skills due to their constant practice in tourneys.[96]

One might expect the corollary of such trends to have been a still greater emphasis on defensive tactics to counter the impact of cavalry. Certainly the use of tightly formed infantry continued to be a widespread response to the threat of horsemen. Though the Lombard League could itself command some 4,000 cavalry, it was its infantry who were pre-eminent in attaining a victory over the forces of the German emperor Frederick Barbarossa at Legnano in 1176, and later at Cortenouva in 1237 they again held off the repeated attacks of Frederick II's imperial cavalry.[97] The knights and foot-soldiers of Brabant formed a closely packed formation at Worringen in 1288, while the Flemish militia, armed with pikes and goedendags, were to triumph over the chivalry of France at Courtrai in 1302, as were the Scottish spearmen over the English knights at Bannockburn in 1314. But these were the tactics of the common infantry, and it was rare to find substantial bodies of knights dismounting in the thirteenth century. As had been noted, 'by the time of the Barons' Wars in the mid-thirteenth century, there was no question of knights fighting other than from the saddle'.[98] Whatever its causes, moreover, in Anglo-Norman warfare the disappearance of the practice of dismounting by men-at-arms crucially seems to have resulted in the eclipse of the tactical role of archers in battle. Archers rarely feature prominently, if at all, in thirteenth-century battles fought in the open field in England or France before the reign of Edward I, and where missilemen do feature, as at Lincoln in 1217 or at Taillebourg in 1242, they are crossbowmen. This was because, as we shall see in Chapter 7, the crossbow had become the pre-eminent missile weapon in a type of warfare dominated by siege. Yet to deduce from this that the role of military archery as a whole decreased from the 1140s or that the longbow was somehow in abeyance under the Angevin kings would be a mistake.

HENRY II AND THE ASSIZE OF ARMS, 1181

In 1181 Henry II, Stephen's successor on the throne and ruler of a vast empire stretching from the Cheviots to the Pyrenees, issued an 'assize' or royal edict in England, laying down what arms and equipment men should possess according to a sliding scale of wealth. All who possessed a knight's fief had to own a hauberk (*lorica*), helmet, shield and lance – the basic equipment of a knight.[99] Every free layman who had goods or income of 16 marks a year also had to possess a hauberk, helmet, shield and lance, while those with goods or income of 10 marks should have a short hauberk (*aubergel*), an iron headpiece and a lance. Thereafter, all burgesses and 'the whole body of freeman' were to have a gambeson (*wambais*), an iron headpiece and a lance.[100] The bow, however, is not mentioned. To Oman, and many subsequent writers, this absence seemed to confirm the insignificance of the bow – which, of course, was held to be the lamentably weak shortbow. The subsequent appearance of the bow in the Assize of Arms of 1242 issued by Henry III was thus seen as an important innovation, presaging the rise of the true longbow. Such a view, however, is untenable. The aim of the assize was not to lay down the blueprint for an army's weaponry, but rather only to ensure that men possessed the minimum defensive equipment for their rank when the shire levies were called out for local defence or peace-keeping duties. As we have noted, some if not the majority of the archers who played so vital a role at the Standard in 1138 were shire levies, and the presence in the same battle of spearmen suggests that when the sheriff issued a summons to muster, men chose the weapon of their preference, whether spear or bow. Long before Henry II's English Assize of Arms, moreover, the Norman poet Wace noted the prominence of bowmen, and their mixture with spearmen, in describing a Norman levy. Wace's description, supposedly of the forces of Duke Richard I at his victory over the French on the River Béthune in 986, but in all likelihood echoing the practice of his own day, well conveys the mixture of infantry weapons that the lower ranks would have brought to the host:

The French were in greater numbers than the Normans, but they were checked at the stream because the footmen defended it, with archers and squires, who gave them no mercy . . . There were archers and peasants on the level ground, in their hundreds and thousands lining the riverbank, here a man carried a bow, here an axe, here a long pike [*grant lance geldiere*]; they killed so many horses in the front and rear ranks . . . When the king saw his losses, he led off his troops.[101]

It is clear that the bow was in widespread use not only in war but for sport and hunting. The *Laws of Henry I*, compiled before 1135 but drawing heavily on earlier Anglo-Saxon legislation, enjoins monetary compensation for anyone accidentally slaying another 'in a game of archery (*in ludo sagittandi*)'.[102] Similarly, in his life of Thomas Becket, written between 1170 and 1183, William fitz Stephen speaks of archery among those sports practised by the young men of the city of London. In addition to ball games and mock combat, he notes that 'on feast-days throughout the summer, the young men indulge in the sport of archery [*excercentur arcu*], running, jumping, wrestling, slinging the stone, hurling the javelin beyond a mark and fighting with sword and buckler'.[103]

Moreover, at Le Mans at Christmas 1180, only a few months before the promulgation of the English Assize of Arms, Henry II had issued a similar assize relating to his continental lands, which *did* enjoin the use of the bow. All those owning less than 25 pounds Angevin were required to possess a gambeson, iron helmet, lance and sword 'or a bow and arrows'. This decree, adds Roger of Howden, was imitated by both the French king Philip Augustus and Count Philip of Flanders.[104] Why this injunction does not appear in the English Assize of Arms as we now have the text is uncertain. It may simply be due to its brevity: even Howden's précis of the continental assize is more inclusive than his record of the English edict in its list of weapons. Thus, for example, swords are wholly omitted from all social categories in the English assize, but clearly must have been a vital part of the equipment of most ranks save the very poorest. Only three years after the Assize of Arms Henry himself felt anxious enough about the prevalence of bows in the hands of poachers to forbid the unauthorised carrying of bows and arrows in the royal forests in his Assize of the Forest in 1184.[105]

Royal edicts, moreover, often reflected aspiration or wishful thinking on behalf of the king and his councillors rather than social reality. Thus remarkably, at the Council of Woodstock in 1175, held in the aftermath of the great revolt of 1173–4, Henry II forbade his previous enemies to come to court without permission or to arrive before or after sunrise, and prohibited all men in England east of the Severn from carrying arms, especially 'bow and arrows and sharp-pointed knife'.[106] What prompted such an edict is unclear; Henry may have feared the threat of assassination, for these might be the weapons of an assassin, as was the cover of night; or he may have simply been attempting to keep the peace in the troubled months following the 'great war' when crime and localised violence were rife. West of the Severn, of course, men needed their weapons to guard against the threat of the Welsh. Such a prohibition, however, was hardly realistic, and as Roger of Howden noted it was observed only for a short time.[107]

Above all, archers continued to form a key element in Angevin armies under Henry II and Richard I. If in the second half of the twelfth century it is hard to trace the tactical role of the longbow in major battles in England and Normandy, its importance is strikingly revealed in other theatres of war. Archers were to form an essential element in the forces of Richard I during the Third Crusade, with his deployment of missilemen reflecting almost a century of Frankish military experience against the Turks and their highly manoeuvrable horse-archers. Less further afield, the widespread deployment of archers in Anglo-Welsh warfare and the operations of Anglo-Norman marcher lords in Ireland from 1169 saw longbowmen playing a crucial part in warfare on the peripheries of the Plantagenet lands, coming into their own in operations in difficult terrain.

Matthew Strickland

CHAPTER 5

The Longbow in Wales and Ireland

THE BOW AND MARCHER WARFARE

'It is worth mentioning, or so I think,' wrote Gerald of Wales in his *Journey through Wales*, 'that the men of Gwent, for that is what they are called, have much more experience of warfare, are more famous for their martial exploits and, in particular, are more skilled with the bow and arrow than those who come from other parts of Wales.'[1] By contrast, the men from Merioneth and northern Wales 'are very skilful with their long spears'.[2] Gerald could speak with some authority. He was himself from a marcher family from South Wales, and because of his mixed Norman and Welsh ancestry he had seen extensive diplomatic service in Wales on behalf of Henry II and Richard I in their dealings with the Welsh princes. Gerald was proud of his countrymen's prowess with the bow, and as we have seen he described their feats of marksmanship and the power of their rough elm longbows with delight and fascination.[3] He was less proud, however, of the conduct of his nephew, Gerald de Barry, whom he took to task for neglecting his books in favour of archery, and for preferring to speak Welsh rather than the French and Latin expected of the educated man. 'It is written in Genesis', Gerald sermonised, 'that Ishmael, son of Abraham, grew up to be a young archer, and Esau, son of Isaac, grew up to be a huntsman; but rarely does Holy Writ mention archers or huntsmen in a good light.'[4] Rather than application to letters, 'you used to get up very early – about dawn – every day, take your bow, arrows and darts and almost always spend your time on the art of archery, and very frequently on hunting the hare until breakfast and later'.[5] Gerald's very reproaches, however, reveal the kind of habitual hunting and practice with the bow that made the young men of South Wales so proficient both in archery and in moving swiftly through woods and hills.

Gerald, who took a keen interest in military affairs, has left a striking picture of Welsh equipment and warfare:

The Welsh people are light and agile. They are fierce rather than strong, and totally dedicated to the practice of arms . . . They use light weapons which do not impede their quick movements, short mailshirts, handfuls of arrows and long spears; but rarely helmets, shields and iron leg armour. The leaders ride into battle on swift, mettlesome horses which are bred locally. Most of the common people prefer to fight on foot, in view of the marshy, uneven terrain. The horsemen will often dismount, as circumstance and occasion demand, ready to flee or to attack. They go barefoot or else wear boots from untanned leather roughly sewn together. By marching through the deep recesses of the woods and climbing mountain peaks in times of peace, the young men train themselves to keep on the move both day and night. In peace, they dream of war and prepare themselves for battle by practising with their spears and arrows.[6]

In commencing hostilities, he notes, the Welsh raise terrible cries and launch a formidable charge, hurling javelins; but if this first onrush is checked, then their tendency is to withdraw from the combat, though 'they will frequently turn back and, like the Parthians, shoot their arrows from behind'. Because of their light equipment, they cannot compete with the Anglo-Normans in open battle 'but they harass the enemy with ambushes and their night attacks'.[7]

Yet though vivid, Gerald's picture of Welsh warfare as essentially hit-and-run guerrilla tactics has been shown by recent scholarship to be an oversimplification. While the relative poverty of Wales's predominantly pastoral economy meant that the majority of troops could not afford defensive armour and fought as nimble light infantry, the Welsh princes kept military households or *teuloedd*, which comprised well armed and well mounted retainers, often possessing mailshirts and other defensive armour.[8] Though not numerous, such retainers formed an elite core of Welsh armies, and allowed

Above: Two huntsmen from a later thirteenth- or fourteenth-century copy of the *Novum Digestum* of Franciscus Accursius, formerly owned by the Abbey of Neath (Hereford Cathedral Library, MS P.viii. II). *(Copyright of the Dean and Chapter of Hereford and the Hereford Mappa Mundi Trust)*

Left: Wales and the Marches in the twelfth and thirteenth centuries.

them to fight – and not infrequently to win – pitched battles against their Anglo-Norman enemies or Welsh rivals.[9] Continuous contact with Anglo-Norman marcher lords and settlers in southern Wales and the borders, moreover, meant that the Welsh began to adopt aspects of their neighbours' military methods, including the building of castles and the development of siege tactics and equipment.[10]

Nevertheless, fast-moving guerrilla tactics still remained an important element in Welsh warfare and the mountainous terrain and dense woodland which covered much of medieval Wales provided ideal cover for ambush and harassing attacks for which the bow remained the pre-eminent weapon.[11] Earlier, in a moving lament for the loss of Welsh lands to the Normans, the poet Rhigyfarch (1056–99) reflected this reality as well as classical allusions when he bemoaned that 'You, Wales, do not dare to carry the quiver of arrows on your shoulder, nor stretch the bow with tight bow-string . . .'.[12] Many, however, did so dare. In 1121, when an army under Henry I invaded Powys, the Welsh prince Maredudd 'sent young men to waylay the king, to a certain counter-slope the way along which he was coming, in order to engage him with bows and arrows and to cause confusion amongst his host with missiles'. One arrow even struck King Henry himself, but he was saved by his hauberk.[13] William of Malmesbury, whether reworking this incident or recounting a separate event, records a similar story. When Henry I was en route with his army towards Wales, he was shot at by a distant archer, who then quickly escaped. The king, who had been saved from injury by the quality of his mail coat, immediately swore that the arrow which struck him was not let fly by a Welshman, but by one of his own subjects.[14] What led the king to make such a categoric assertion remains a mystery; was the archer's clothing or appearance distinctively English? Or was Henry, who lived in daily fear of assassination, more paranoid about internal treachery than Welsh aggression? For as Malmesbury observes, at the time of the attack the army was marching slowly in its own lands, not in an enemy's territory, 'and therefore an ambush was the last thing to be expected'. Whatever the reason, the natural assumption had been that the marksman was Welsh. It had been to prevent just this sort of ambush that in 1102, on his march to lay siege to Robert of Bellême's castle at Shrewsbury, Henry I had ordered his pioneers to clear away the dense undergrowth and trees along the *Huvel hegen* or 'evil hedge', which for a mile 'was so narrow that two horsemen could barely ride abreast, and was overshadowed on both sides by a thick wood, in which archers used to lie hidden and without warning send javelins or arrows whistling to take their toll of passers by'.[15] Nevertheless, Welsh marksmen may have claimed other important victims. In 1136 the powerful Anglo-Norman marcher lord Payne fitz John was

shot through the head by a missile 'while pursuing the Welsh, the only man of his company to be killed'.[16] The fact that earlier in that year a still greater lord, Richard fitzGilbert de Clare, had alone of his men been slain in a Welsh ambush strongly suggests that he too was the victim of a Welsh sniper.[17]

Against such fast, mobile troops as the Welsh, operating in broken terrain, the conventional forms of warfare practised by the Anglo-Normans and French involving siege, the *chevauchée* and cavalry combat in open ground were of little use. In particular, heavy cavalry, whose equipment was becoming more complex as the twelfth century wore on, were well-nigh useless among the hills, bogs and forests of Ireland and Wales. As Gerald explained in a telling comparison between the nature of Celtic and Franco-Norman warfare:

> there is a great difference between warfare in France on the one hand, and in Ireland and Wales on the other. In France men choose the open plains for their battles, but in Ireland and Wales rough, wooded country; there heavy armour is a mark of distinction, here it is only a burden; there victory is won by standing firm, here by mobility; there knights are taken prisoner, here they are beheaded; there they are ransomed, here they are butchered. When two armies meet in battle out on the plains, that heavy armour, consisting of several layers of linen or steel, gives soldiers excellent protection and is most becoming. But equally, when the fighting takes place only within a restricted space, or over wooded or boggy ground, where there is scope for foot-soldiers rather than horsemen, light armour is far superior. For light arms are quite sufficient for use against enemies who are not armoured. Any battle against these is either won or lost immediately, generally in the very first encounter. In that situation, it is inevitable that an enemy who is mobile and in retreat over confined or difficult terrain can only be routed by an equally mobile force pressing hard on them, and only lightly armed. For owing to the weight of that armour with its many layers, and saddles which are high and curved back, men have difficulty in dismounting, even more difficulty in mounting, and find advancing on foot, when the need arises, most difficult of all.[18]

Despite being part Welsh himself, Gerald devoted part of his *Description of Wales* to advice on the manner in which Wales could best be conquered, writing with the potential patronage of the Angevin kings Henry II and his sons in mind. Gerald's blueprint for the subjugation of Wales deserves to be quoted at length, for it is remarkable in its strategic acumen, and clearly outlines the vital role light troops were to play. The conquest of

Wales, he argued, could not be achieved by a decisive battle, or even by sieges, for the Welsh refused to allow themselves to be penned up in strongholds. What was required was a war of attrition, which demanded the undivided attention of a ruler for at least a year. Castles, both on the marches and further into Wales, were to be well garrisoned and stockpiled with supplies, while an economic blockade should prevent the Welsh from receiving vital imports of salt, corn and cloth. Then:

> Later on, when wintry conditions have really set in, or perhaps towards the end of winter in February and March, by which time the trees have lost their leaves, and there is no more pasturage to be had in the mountains, a strong force of infantry must have the courage to invade their secret strongholds, which lie deep in the woods and are buried in the forests. They must be cut off from all opportunity of foraging, and harassed, both by individual families and larger assemblies of troops, by frequent attacks from those camped around. The assault troops must be lightly armed and not weighed down with a lot of equipment. They must be strengthened with frequent reinforcements, who have been following close behind to give them support and provide a base. Fresh troops must keep on replacing those who are tired out . . .[19]

Ironically, it was to be nearly a century before an English monarch implemented this strategy in campaigns that were to be an important catalyst for the rising prominence of the longbow. Yet Edward I's grandfather King John had come close to attempting such a conquest in 1212, when he amassed a vast army by land and sea to crush the powerful Prince of Gwynedd, Llwelyn ap Iorwerth. Whether John had ever read Gerald's works is uncertain, but Gerald had been part of his entourage from 1185 to around 1194, and it is likely that the archdeacon gave the king the benefit of his accrued military wisdom on the value of archers and light infantry in Welsh and Irish campaigns. Exchequer records reveal the extent of John's military build-up in 1212, including the summoning of 8,430 axemen, carpenters and ditchers, but the discovery of a baronial plot either to assassinate him or abandon him to his Welsh enemies forced the king to cancel his planned invasion of Wales and to turn instead against his internal opponents.[20]

Long before Gerald was writing, however, the English had appreciated the vital importance of light infantry in warfare on the marches or in Wales itself. From the earliest days of the Conquest, Anglo-Norman kings and marcher lords had deployed their own light troops to counter the guerrilla warfare of the Welsh in broken country, and in so doing they were merely continuing Anglo-Saxon practice. Though contemp-

orary details of the expedition are lacking, the highly successful campaign of Harold Godwineson and his brother Tostig against North Wales in 1063 was cited approvingly by John of Salisbury in his *Policraticus* (completed in 1159) as a prime example of the value of light troops in campaigns in mountainous terrain, and also made a deep impression on Gerald himself.[21] John, drawing on an unknown source, relates that Harold's men wore leather armour, and fought with javelins and small round shields, though he does not mention archers. As early as the 1080s the marcher counties had developed a system of border patrols by lightly armed horsemen, known in Shropshire as *muntatores* and elsewhere as *homines equitantes*. These horsemen, whose speed and manoeuvrability proved highly effective in intercepting Welsh raiding parties which were normally on foot, formed the mainstay of the garrisons of key border castles such as Clun, Montgomery, Shrewsbury and Oswestry.[22] They were not, it seems, mounted archers, but early examples of the kind of troops subsequently known as hobelars, armed with lances and wearing iron caps and shorter mail shirts than the great hauberks and additional defences of the knights.

Archers were also important. *The History of Gruffyd ap Cynan* believed that Earl Hugh of Chester had deployed horsemen and archers to garrison the castles he had erected during his conquests in North Wales in the 1090s.[23] But such garrisons might operate offensively, launching patrols or laying ambuscades in attempts to beat the Welsh at their own game. The Welsh *Brut y Tywysogyon* (*The Chronicle of the Princes*) tells in some detail how, when in 1116 the forces of Gruffyd ap Rhys approached Aberystwyth Castle in order to besiege it, 'the garrison, as it is the way with the French to do everything with diligence and circumspection, sent archers to the bridge to shoot at them and annoy them'. Once they had succeeded in galling the Welsh into attacking, they fell back as if in flight, and the trap was sprung as a sudden counter-attack by mounted knights defeated the now disorganised and exposed Welsh.[24] The same year Owain ap Cadwgan of Powys was ambushed and killed by Flemish archers based in Dyfed, while in 1151 Cadell ap Gruffydd was surprised by knights and archers from the garrison of Tenby while hunting in the forest of Coed Rhath and was badly injured.[25] Until 1154 we are reliant for references to Anglo-Norman archers largely on the anecdotal evidence of chroniclers. Thereafter the continuous series of Exchequer accounts known as Pipe Rolls yield haphazard references to archers serving in garrisons in Wales or the marches.[26] Thus, for example, a group of ten archers were stationed at Wrockwardine in 1172–3, with a further ten at Chepstow in 1185, while the accounts for the honour of Chester recorded the payment of thirteen archers at the high

The south-west tower of the upper barbican at Chepstow Castle, built between 1219 and 1245 by the sons of William Marshal to provide a formidable defence for the castle's vulnerable western and landward approach. Of sophisticated design, the once timber-backed tower consists of three storeys, profusely equipped with loops, as well as a fighting platform at roof level. (M. Strickland)

rate of 6 pence per day, suggesting a skilled unit.[27] A large company of 40 mounted archers served with 20 knights and 450 foot serjeants at Gloucester Castle in 1193, doubtless intended to provide a powerful military threat in the earldom held by Count John, whose loyalty to his brother King Richard was highly suspect.[28]

Archers were equally an integral part of Anglo-Norman field armies operating against the Welsh. On hearing news of Welsh risings in 1135, Henry I had attempted to cross the Channel from Normandy 'with a strong force including picked archers'.[29] The following year his successor King Stephen, faced with a massive Welsh revolt, deployed 'knights and archers whom he had hired at very great expense', as did marcher lords such as Baldwin fitzGilbert, who in the same year hired 500 'valiant archers' as well as knights for operations against the Welsh.[30] Some of these stipendiary archers were drawn from Normandy, France or Flanders, but others were English, raised from the marches themselves or even further afield. In 1157, for example, Henry II's expedition into Wales was accompanied by archers from the Shropshire marches led by the sheriff William fitz Alan.[31] Perhaps they formed part of the light troops Henry used on this occasion to outflank the main force of Owain Gwynedd which barred the road from Chester to Rhuddlan at Basingwerk; the manoeuvre forced the Welsh to abandon their position, but not before the column was badly mauled and the king had nearly met his death in an ambush in the high forest ground to the south of the coastal road.[32] It may well have been as a response to the effectiveness of Welsh

archers that during his 1165 expedition Henry II equipped his Brabançon mercenaries not only with spears but with large defensive shields, ensured supplies of arrows, and, as he advanced from Oswestry into the forest of Dyffryn Ceiriog, had the woods cleared to prevent ambushes.[33] By the thirteenth century the Hundred Rolls and the Calendars of Inquisitions reveal numerous small-holdings held for archer service, such as at Faintree, Chettington and Havercote in Shropshire, while others were held by the provision of a serjeant (*serviens*) armed with a spear.[34] This suggests the aim was to provide a group of local infantry whose type of weapons provided mutual support. Such tenures existed considerably earlier and were not restricted to the marches. As early as 1185 serjeantry tenure is recorded on land in Suffolk worth 20s for service with 'a bow and arrows . . . for the service of the Lord King when he shall go with the army to Wales'.[35] This specification of service in Wales clearly reveals royal recognition of the need for such missilemen in campaigns against the Welsh.

It was the Welsh themselves, however, who furnished a highly significant proportion of light troops for Anglo-Norman and Angevin armies, operating both in Wales itself and further afield. Anglo-Saxon and subsequently Anglo-Norman lords had a long tradition of hiring Welsh friendlies as allies and mercenaries, whether in wars of conquest or of defence against Welsh princes, or in rebellion against their own sovereign; the Earls of Mercia, for example, had used Welsh allies in the 1050s in their political struggles, and in 1067 the English resistance leader Eadric 'the Wild' did so again in his warfare against the Norman invader. The great Norman marcher lord Robert of Bellême continued this trend in his rebellion against Henry I in 1102. Orderic Vitalis believed that the Welsh employed by Robert of Gloucester and Rannulf of Chester against King Stephen played a significant part in the victory of Lincoln in 1141, though whether archers played any role in their success is unknown.[36] When in 1191 the strained relations between Richard's chancellor William Longchamp and the king's brother Count John came near to breaking point, both men drew on Welsh troops; John brought 4,000 Welsh to Winchester as support during a peace conference, while Longchamp called out not only a third of the knight service of England but also 'the Welshmen of the king's levy'.[37] Later, when John moved into open revolt in 1193, Welshmen were among the troops placed in his castles at Wallingford and Windsor, who ravaged the land between Windsor and Kingston.[38] Equally, in the same year one of Richard's loyal co-justiciars, William Marshal, raised 500 infantry from the Welsh marches, who, together with 67 slingers and 66 well-armed serjeants, laid siege to Windsor.[39]

The Angevin kings made extensive use of Welsh troops not only for insular warfare but also for their campaigns in France. It has been rightly noted that 'fighting men from the Welsh mountains were . . . the Gurkhas of the twelfth century'.[40] Henry II, who had first-hand experience of the excellence of the Welsh at ambush, was quick to deploy them in the context of guerrilla operations against the French. In 1167 Henry II's Welsh executed a bold coup by swimming across the River Epte and burning Louis VII's key arsenal at Chaumont while Henry's main force led a diversionary attack against the garrison.[41] In 1174 1,000 Welsh were among the troops Henry II took to Normandy, and during his relief of Rouen they were sent across the Seine to cut French supply lines through the surrounding forests; their seizure of a major baggage train, whose carters were either slain or made captives, caused terror among the French, who believed the woods to be alive with Welsh.[42] When in June 1188 Philip Augustus made rapid gains in Berry, Henry II ordered his justiciar in England, Ranulf de Glanville, to raise an army of Welsh mercenaries, but the force also contained men, possibly archers, from Shropshire, Herefordshire and Gloucestershire.[43] Richard I took a large number of Welsh skilled with bow and spear with him on the Third Crusade,[44] and on his return he continued to employ such troops in his continental campaigns. Thus in 1195 five shiploads of Welsh crossed to Normandy to aid Richard in his war against Philip Augustus, and in that year they may well have been involved in ambushing a French force returning from a raid on Dieppe.[45] The Norman Exchequer records the payment of 3s for transporting wounded Welsh from Vaudreuil to Rouen, and we find them again operating in wooded territory along the Norman border.[46] The rolls also reveal something of the organisation of these units.[47] The government contracted for groups of Welsh mercenaries, who operated under a captain, either English or Welsh, who was responsible for their wages. In 1195, for example, William Marsh, a West Country lord with close connections to the Welsh march, received £296 10s for himself 'and his Welsh', while in 1210 the Welsh captain Lleision ap Morgan was at the head of 200 Welsh in John's service.[48]

How many of these Welshmen were archers? Unfortunately, the chroniclers and the rolls rarely if ever specify the arms used by the Welsh mercenaries, referring to them simply as 'Walenses'. Some may have been spear- or knife-men. A few may even have been crossbowmen; the Norman Exchequer rolls refer to one Richard the Welshman 'who made the king's crossbows' and was paid the considerable sum of 2s 6d a day.[49] One wonders if this Welsh artificer was using his bowyer's skill to craft wooden limbs for the royal crossbows or, as seems likely, was working with horn, sinew and other material that made the powerful composite crossbows. Nevertheless, many, perhaps indeed the majority, of the Welsh serving in the Angevin armies were certainly archers. *The History of William the Marshal*, written in about 1220, records a telling incident that occurred during mounting hostilities between Henry II and Philip Augustus in 1188. During a tense parley between the two kings at the great castle of Gisors on the Norman border, one of Philip's knights rashly – and, says the *History*, discourteously – began to taunt Henry's Welsh for their rude manners and appearance. Goaded by this, one Welshman drew his bow and let loose at the Frenchman, wounding him in the head. With the arrow still lodged in his head, the knight went to complain to King Philip who withdrew his forces in anger.[50] Philip's own biographer, William le Breton, described at some length the Welsh employed by Richard I in Normandy, noting

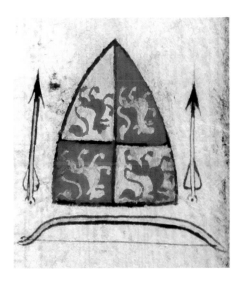

The inverted shield of David, Prince of Gwynedd, surrounded by a bow and arrows to mark his obit, 1246, from Matthew Paris's *Chronica Majora* (Corpus Christi College, Cambridge, MS 16, f.198). *(By Permission of the Master and Fellows of Corpus Christi College, Cambridge)*

their hardiness, agility and aptitude for war, their forest operations and their ruthlessness. They lacked armour and were armed with bows and arrows, as well as spears and axes.[51] Indeed, such was the close association of the bow with the Welsh in the minds of contemporaries that when the St Albans chronicler Matthew Paris recorded the death of David, Prince of Wales, in 1246, he depicted his coat of arms flanked by two barbed arrows and with a bow beneath (see p. 89).[52] The strongest indication that the majority of these Welsh troops were archers, however, comes from a comparison with the make-up of the contingents raised by Anglo-Norman marcher lords for their expeditions to Ireland from 1169.

THE COMING OF STRONGBOW: WELSH ARCHERS IN IRELAND

In 1166 the Irish King of Leinster, Dermot MacMurchada, had been driven into exile and took refuge in England. He received Henry II's permission to raise troops and began recruiting among the Anglo-Norman marcher lords of South Wales.[53] Here he found ready swords for hire, and attracted the support of Richard de Clare, lord of Striguil (or Chepstow), to whom he promised the hand of his daughter in marriage and with her succession to the kingdom of Leinster. We do not know if Richard himself was skilled with the bow, for although he is called 'Strongbow' by some near-contemporary Irish and Anglo-Norman chroniclers, it seems he inherited the epithet from his father, Gilbert de Clare (d. *c.* 1148), who is named 'Strongbowe' in a charter of 1206 for Tintern Abbey.[54] Intriguingly, the reverse of Gilbert's equestrian seal depicts him holding not a bow but a large feathered javelin, a form of weapon which occasionally appears in manuscript illumination, such as the Trinity Apocalypse of about 1255–60, and which also seems to have been favoured in Ireland. In 1399 the French esquire Jean Creton noted that the Irish King of Leinster, Art MacMurrough, 'carried in his right hand a great long dart, which he cast with much skill'.[55] Whatever was intended by this unusual image, the fateful impact of Gilbert's son and his companions in arms upon Ireland is beyond doubt. An advance party, led by Robert FitzStephen, landed from three ships at Bannow in May 1169. This force was reinforced by other contingents, and in 1170 Earl Richard himself arrived. Dublin fell, and by 1171 the Normans had carved out an enclave powerful enough to alarm Henry II. Anxious to reassert overlordship over his

The seal of Gilbert de Clare, Earl of Pembroke (d. *c.* 1148), bearing the shield of the Clare family but unusually depicting him without armour and holding a large feathered javelin (British Library, Lansdowne MS 203). *(Author Collection)*

erstwhile vassals, as well as to bring Ireland within his political hegemony, Henry mounted a major expedition in 1171, which overawed both the Norman adventurers and the majority of Irish princes into a formal act of submission. The fortunes of Ireland were henceforth irrevocably bound up with those of England.

We are fortunate indeed in having a highly detailed, if also highly partisan, account of the process of Norman invasion and settlement from the indefatigable pen of Gerald of Wales. Several of his relatives had been closely involved in these events, and it was in large part to highlight and extol their role that Gerald wrote his *Conquest of Ireland* in 1188. Gerald himself had accompanied Prince John on his first expedition to Ireland in 1185, and his observations on natural history and the miraculous tales he garnered there furnished material for his most popular work, *The Topography of Ireland*. Together with a contemporary Anglo-Norman poem, *The Song of Dermot and the Earl*,[56] which often provides an important corrective to Gerald, the *Conquest of Ireland* provides some of the most valuable evidence we possess for the continued military importance of the longbow at a time when the tactical combination of archers and dismounted knights fades from the battlefields of England and France.

Crucially, moreover, Gerald provides not only details of the campaigns but also of the numbers and composition of the various Norman contingents. According to Gerald, Fitz-Stephen's first contingent comprised 30 knights from among his kin and friends, 60 other *loricati* (probably less heavily equipped serjeants but still possessing mail hauberks), and 300 foot-archers 'from among the military elite of Wales'.[57] That of Maurice de Predendergast, which arrived the following day, comprised two ships containing 10 knights and a large, but unspecified, number of archers.[58] Possibly this contingent was the same strength as that of Maurice FitzGerold, FitzStephen's half-brother, who subsequently landed at Wexford with two ships carrying 10 knights, 30 mounted archers, and around 100 foot-archers.[59] The following year, 1170, FitzStephen's nephew, Raymond le Gros, reinforced his uncle with 10 knights and 70 archers.[60] Strongbow himself followed with

200 knights 'and about 1,000 others', raised on his journey to St David's and Milford Haven, from the pick of the fighting men from the coastal regions of South Wales.[61] Subsequently, in 1173, Raymond returned from Wales to Wexford with 30 knights from his kin, 100 mounted archers and 300 foot-archers 'chosen from the best fighting men in Wales'.[62] While Gerald's figures can only occasionally be corroborated, notably with *The Song of Dermot*, there seems little reason to doubt their essential validity. Even if we regard his estimates as rough approximations, the implications are important. They reveal the ready availability of a pool of skilled Welsh or Anglo-Welsh archers from southern Wales and the marches. By analogy, this strongly suggests that the majority of the *Walenses* employed by the Angevin kings at this time were also archers, and that the 'Welsh horse and foot' of the Pipe Rolls probably equate primarily with Gerald's '*arcarii equestres*' and '*sagitarii pedestres*', that is, to mounted and foot-archers.[63] The same emphasis on bowmen is apparent in the make-up of royal expeditionary forces to Ireland. Henry II's own army in 1171 contained 500 knights and 'many mounted and foot-archers'.[64] In 1185 John arrived at Waterford with around 300 knights and a 'large number of archers, mounted and on foot'.[65] If the usual proportions of 1:10 apply, John's force may have contained some 3,000 archers.[66] These were very significant numbers of bowmen, leaving no room to doubt the primary importance placed on archers by Anglo-Norman commanders.

These Anglo-Norman forces afford an important corrective to the novelty sometimes attributed to English armies of the Hundred Years War. Here, in the later twelfth century, we already find 'mixed retinues' of knights, *loricati* – who in later centuries would be referred to as men-at-arms – and archers, an important element of whom were mounted. Though it would take the catalyst of the Scottish wars to see their widespread adoption in Edward III's armies, the mounted archer was not, as has sometimes been claimed, an innovation of the fourteenth century.[67] While the ratio of archers to men-at-arms in Anglo-Norman forces often appears higher than in many fourteenth-century English armies, it compares with similar ratios found in English expeditionary forces in the latter stages of the French wars. The mounting of units of archers indicates once more the recognition of the enormous value of having highly mobile bowmen who could keep up with the knights or operate on forays. The implication, already suggested by the presence of mounted archers in the royal military household of the Anglo-Norman kings, is that some archers were of a higher rank or economic standing, able to afford mounts, and accordingly to command higher wages. The archers who accompanied Strongbow and his companions were very probably stipendiaries, who saw in service in Ireland a welcome

escape from the economic hardships of their own lands, and an opportunity for adventure and booty as well as pay. Though Anglo-Norman lords could call on their Welsh tenants for military service, this was only for a limited duration and geographical radius, and it is very unlikely that they could compel such men to serve abroad. There is, however, as yet no evidence of any written indentures of service, although Anglo-Norman kings were entering into written contracts for the service of mercenary Flemish knights from at least 1100. For the Irish campaigns terms and conditions, as with the sizes of contingents mustered by individual lords, were probably still a matter of oral agreement and negotiation.

We catch a glimpse of these Anglo-Welsh archers – albeit a distorted and disparaging one – though the miracles and tall stories which abound in Gerald's *History and Topography of Ireland*, written in 1185. In this the Welsh archers of the Anglo-Norman nobles habitually appear as ruffianly perpetrators of misdeeds, used by Gerald as foils to demonstrate the vengeful, even vindictive nature of the Irish saints. Thus, he tells us, one of Robert FitzStephen's archers shot one of the sacred teals of St Colman on a lake in Leinster, but the bird refused to cook, emerging raw even after hours in the pot. When an archer in Strongbow's army attempted to offer a penny to a cross in the Church of Holy Trinity, Dublin, venerated for its miraculous properties, it twice flung the penny back at him, accepting it only after he had confessed to having robbed the archbishop's residence that day. Another archer in the earl's retinue unwisely attempted to blow on the sacred fire of St Brigid at Kildare, which was said to be inextinguishable and which was surrounded by a precinct hedge which men were forbidden to cross; he immediately went mad, running around and blowing on any fire he saw, till becoming parched with thirst, he drank so much water that he burst his stomach and died miserably. Still worse befell one of Hugh de Lacy's archers who raped a woman in the sacred mill of St Fechin at Fore in Meath, for he 'was stricken in his member with hell-fire in sudden vengeance and immediately began to burn throughout his whole body. He died the same night.'[68] Gerald, aware that many in his audience would not believe these and other moralistic yarns, loudly protested their authenticity.[69]

In reality, however, the Welsh archers brought to Ireland from 1169 were no more or less lawless than other medieval infantrymen – the Cheshire archers were to gain an unenviable reputation in the late fourteenth century as Richard II's hired thugs – but more sober evidence suggests that discipline was a perennial problem. Thus at Portsmouth in 1194, while waiting to embark for Normandy, a bitter fight erupted between the Welsh and Richard's Brabançon mercenaries, and the king had to hurry back from Stanstead, where he had been hunting,

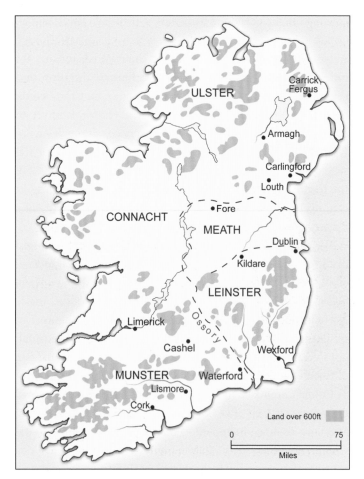

Above: Ireland in the twelfth century.

Right: A nobleman with infantry and archers, from an early thirteenth-century manuscript of Gerald of Wales's *Topographica Hiberniae* (Cambridge University Library F, f.1.27). *(Cambridge University Library)*

continue to form a major element in the armies of English kings and came again to prominence in the campaigns of Edward I.

The combination of Anglo-Norman lords fighting alongside such Welsh or Anglo-Cambrian marksmen reflected more than a century of marcher warfare and co-existence, which had produced a formidable military force. In examining these Anglo-Norman campaigns in Ireland, some military historians such as Oman and Hayes-McCoy placed much emphasis on the role of archers in pitched battle, where their support of the Anglo-Norman cavalry was taken as a key example of the successful tactical combination of horse and missile arms.[74] In fact, while archers and cavalry were used in close coordination to great effect in raids, marches and other operations, they were less prominent in engagements in the open field than was formerly believed.[75] In the first battle between the Normans and Irish, for example, the role of the newcomers' archers was hardly distinguished. In 1169, following a raid into Ossory, the joint forces of Robert FitzStephen and Dermot MacMurchada were being pursued by MacGillapatric of Ossory, but decided to utilise open terrain near Gowran to turn and attack their pursuers. The Normans placed forty archers in a thicket to ambush the Irish as they passed, but in the event the enemy

to quell the disturbance.[70] A century later Edward I was to find the Welsh archers he employed in large numbers to be similarly turbulent. On the eve of the battle of Falkirk in 1298 a vicious fight broke out among Welsh and English troops after the near-starving men had consumed several tuns of wine; many Welsh were killed, and in mutinous mood the rest held aloof from the opening stages of the battle and even threatened to go over to the Scots.[71] The Welsh, moreover, had earned a fearful reputation for not taking prisoners. Long before Crécy, where Froissart says their knifemen caused such slaughter among the wounded French knights, chroniclers noted the propensity of the Welsh to harry and slay without mercy, and to cut the throats of the enemy for good measure.[72] Their wild behaviour meant that their enemies might accord them little quarter in defeat. In 1189, during Henry II's precipitous retreat from Le Mans, many of his Welsh infantry perished at the hands of the forces of Philip and Richard.[73] Nevertheless, the Welsh would

numbers were so great that the archers dared not show themselves but remained in hiding. Instead, the battle was won by
the charge of the heavily armed knights, who rode down the
lightly armed Irish, many of whom were then beheaded by
Dermot's own Irish infantry.[76] The reality was that such engagements were rare, since the Irish quickly learned to exploit
the difficult terrain of bogs and woods to
neutralise the Norman cavalry.

Rather, the crucial function of the
archers was to defend the small numbers
of knights against ambush and missile
attack while on the march, out raiding
or advancing through difficult terrain.
Thus Raymond Le Gros is recorded as
leading a foraging party of 20 knights
and 60 archers into the area around
Lismore, returning to Waterford with
massive numbers of cattle.[77] When
Strongbow attacked the encampment of
Ruaidrí Ua Conchobair at Castleknock in
1171 he divided his force into three groups,
in each of which 20 to 40 knights were supported both by
archers and by the light horse and infantry of their Irish allies,
who acted as a protective screen.[78] As Gerald explained:

In any fighting in Ireland we must be particularly careful
to ensure that archers are always incorporated in the
mounted formations, so that the damage caused by the
stones with which they usually attack heavily armed
troops at close range, alternately rushing forward and retreating without loss to themselves because they are so
mobile, may be averted by volleys of arrows from our
side.[79]

In siege warfare, moreover, the archers supported the assault of
the knights, as during the attack by FitzStephen and Dermot
MacMurchada on Wexford in 1169.[80] They were equally
valuable in defending castles; in 1171, for example, Fitz-
Stephen, with only five knights and a few archers, was able to
defend Carrick against the host of Uí Chennselaig and the men
of Wexford.[81] Archers might even fight at sea, as in 1173 in the
harbour of Lismore when archers and crossbowmen in
Raymond's ships played an important role in putting to flight
an Irish fleet of thirty-two ships from Cork.[82]

The Welsh archers were particularly effective against the Irish
because, as with the Scots, very few wore defensive armour and
so were highly vulnerable to arrow wounds. Gerald believed
that at the time of the Anglo-Norman invasion the bow was
hardly used by the Irish, who relied instead on slings and stone

throwing. As a result, he saw archers and mailed horsemen as
the key to the Normans' initial successes in Ireland: 'For when
our people arrived there first, the Irish were paralysed and
panic-stricken by the sheer novelty of the event, and the
sudden wounds inflicted by our arrows, together with the
effectiveness of our well-armed troops greatly alarmed
them.'[83] He noted ruefully, however,
that the initial military advantage had
not been pressed home, and that the
first conquistadores and seasoned
veterans such as his Geraldine
kinsmen had been hampered and
replaced by inefficient and ignorant
royal officials, thus allowing the
enemy time to regroup and to adapt:

by usage and experience the natives
gradually became skilled and versed
in handling arrows and other arms.
Frequent encounters with our men,
and their many successes, taught them
how to set ambushes, whilst themselves guarding
against them. Consequently, this people, which to begin
with could have been easily routed, recovered its morale
and military strength, and was enabled to put up a
stronger resistance.[84]

As with his descriptions of Welsh warfare, Gerald's observations on the primitive state of Irish warfare must be treated
with some caution. Evidence from the Irish chronicles shows
that by the eleventh and twelfth centuries, Irish kings were
capable of mustering large armies for extended campaigns
which sometimes involved combined land and naval
operations. Use was made of fortified camps (or longphorts), as
well as more permanent fortifications (duns), which might be
made of stone as well as earth and timber, while the annalists'
use of the loan word *caistel* from the early twelfth century
suggests they saw little difference between some of the
fortifications erected by Irish rulers and the earth and timber
castles of the Normans.[85]

In terms of armament, the Irish had responded to the earlier
impact of Viking attacks by the adoption of new weapons, such

Above: The obverse of the Dublin City seal, mid-thirteenth century, showing
crossbowmen defending one of the gates of Dublin Castle, as strongly rebuilt by
King John from 1204 (Dublin City Archives). The crossbow gave the Anglo-
Norman invaders an important technological advantage over the Irish, whose
use even of the longbow in war appears to have been remarkably limited.
(By kind permission of Dublin City Council)

as the broad axe and the longsword.[86] Nevertheless, mail armour remained extremely limited because of the underdeveloped economy, and archery lagged behind as an offensive arm. The fact that the Irish *boga* (bow) is a loan word from Old Norse, coupled with the paucity of archaeological finds of iron arrowheads and of literary references to the use of the bow in Irish warfare, suggests that the Viking invaders of the ninth and tenth centuries had enjoyed a technical edge over the Irish by the deployment of archers as well as through their ability to equip more of their men with defensive armour and high-quality swords and axes.[87] The terror inflicted by such archery is well conveyed by the poetic language of the later Irish tract *The War of the Gaedhil with the Gael*, composed between 1086 and 1119, which noted of the Scandinavian forces confronting Brian Boru in 1012 that 'they had with them hideous, barbarous quivers; and polished, yellow-shining bows', which shot 'sharp, swift, bloody, crimsoned, bounding, barbed, keen, bitter wounding, terrible piercing, fatal, murderous, poisoned arrows, which had been anointed and browned in the blood of dragons and toads, and water-snakes of hell, and of scorpions and otters, and wonderful venomous snakes of all kinds'.[88]

The Irish did not shun the bow completely before the arrival of Strongbow; the will of the King of Connacht in 1156 mentions his 'bows, quivers and slings', while the tympanum of Cormac's chapel at Cashel (*c*. 1127–34), which itself epitomises Anglo-Norman architectural influence, depicts a

A centaur, wearing a conical helmet with nasal, draws a broadheaded arrow in his bow, from the tympanum of King Cormac's chapel, Cashel, Ireland, *c*. 1134. *(Conway Library)*

centaur wearing a conical helmet with a nasal, and drawing a large broad-headed arrow in his bow.[89] Yet it would seem that in his observations on archery Gerald was largely correct, and that the combination of mailed horsemen and archers did give the Anglo-Normans an important advantage. Such superior military technology should not be overstressed, for it was but one factor in the early successes of the Anglo-Normans; like Cortes in Mexico they made extensive use of local allies and skilfully exploited the internal divisions of their opponents. Nor were they invincible. Strongbow suffered a major defeat at Thurles in 1174, the Irish were often able to destroy castles despite their lack of siege engines, and – most crucially – only a partial conquest of the island was ultimately achieved.[90] Nevertheless, the deployment of large numbers of archers in the Anglo-Norman forces from 1169 was not accidental. Close economic, political and ecclesiastical ties afforded the invaders good military intelligence, and the vulnerability of the Irish to archers was already a matter of record in courtly circles by the 1150s. Thus in his *Roman de Brut*, a legendary account of the early history of Britain completed in 1155 and dedicated to Eleanor of Aquitaine, the Norman poet Wace included Ireland among King Arthur's conquests, and notes how Arthur's men, who shot fast and strongly with their bows, easily overcame the poorly armed Irish, who had no mail shirts or shields and did not know how to shoot with the bow.[91]

Strikingly, even after the Anglo-Norman invasion the bow never became the predominant infantry weapon of the native Irish. Well-armoured English and Welsh serjeants continued to serve as stipendiaries, possibly as archers, in Irish as well as English armies in Ireland from the later twelfth to the early fourteenth century, and the French squire Jean Creton, who visited Ireland in 1399, remarked that the Irish feared the arrows of the English.[92] Yet the favoured arm of the 'skipping kerns', the bare-legged, lightly clad Irish foot-soldiers, was the javelin, thrown with great speed and accuracy. From the thirteenth century the West Highland mercenary galloglasses, heavy infantry often with good defensive armour, preferred a two-handed axe (reflecting Norse elements of their ancestry) or sword, though they also might use javelins and in some sixteenth-century engravings are depicted as carrying bows as well.[93] Each galloglass was accompanied by two pages, who, according to a Tudor report of about 1540, themselves carried either javelins or bows.[94] As late as Elizabeth I's Irish wars, the Irish were deploying Scottish archers, who fought to good effect at the battle of Clontibret in 1595.[95]

Some Irish, however, may have used bows from horseback. Count Ramon de Perellós, a Catalan pilgrim to Ireland in 1397, described the forty-strong troop of cavalry under Niall Og O'Neill, King of Tir Eoghain, as 'riding without saddle on a

Irish galloglasses and kerns, from a facsimile of a drawing by Albrecht Dürer, 1521 (National Gallery, Dublin). Though the principal weapon of the galloglass wearing a long mail shirt is clearly his great two-handed sword, he carries a small bow and a number of arrows, whose different heads have been carefully depicted by Dürer. If such a weapon was not of composite materials, it can only have been of very limited power, and ineffectual against armour. *(National Gallery of Ireland/Kupferstichkabinett Museum, Berlin)*

cushion', wearing mail coats, bascinets with aventails, with long lances and swords 'like those of the Saracens which we call Genoese . . . and some make use of bows, which are as short as half a bow of England; but they shoot as far as the English ones . . . their manner of warring is like that of the Saracens, and they shout in the same way'.[96] What kind of bows can these have been? They can scarcely have been the supposed shortbow, for self-bows of around 3ft (0.91m), half the length of an English longbow, must have been remarkably weak and could not have delivered a cast such as Ramon describes. Bows that were short, and hence could be easily wielded by horsemen, yet could carry

An Irish archer drawn by Caspar Rutz, Amsterdam, 1588. The image is possibly based on observations of Irish troops serving with Sir Philip Sidney in the Netherlands in 1586, but there may equally be an element of artistic licence in the depiction of the recurve bow. *(Author Collection)*

Archers from a late fifteenth- or early sixteenth-century hunting scene, from a drawing of wall paintings in Holy Cross Abbey, County Tipperary. *(By permission of the Royal Society of the Antiquaries of Ireland)*

a great distance can surely only have been composite bows of wood reinforced with sinew and horn. Given its complexity of manufacture and the nature of the Irish climate, this seems remarkable. Yet an engraving by Dürer dated to 1521 shows an Irish galloglass armed with a short, seemingly recurved bow (see p. 95), while in an engraving of 1588 by Caspar Rutz, possibly based on the observation of Irish troops serving under Sir Philip Sidney in the Low Countries in 1586, the recurve of the Irish soldier's bow is far more pronounced.[97] One should not, however, set too much store by such depictions, which may have been subject to no little artistic licence to stress the exoticism of the subject. By contrast, surviving fifteenth-century wall-paintings in the abbeys of Holy Cross in Tipperary (see above) and Knockmoy in Galway depict more conventional longbows in a hunting scene and a martyrdom of St Sebastian respectively.[98] These were certainly the usual weapons carried by Scottish Highlanders, and, by implication, by those warriors from the Western Isles who formed a major source for galloglass troops fighting in Ireland. A French observer at the siege of Haddington in 1549 noted Highlanders 'were naked except for their stained [i.e. saffron] shirts and a certain light covering made of wool of various colours, carrying large bows (*portans grand arcs*) and . . . swords and bucklers'.[99] Nevertheless, despite a ready supply of native yew, which was being exported to England by at least the thirteenth century, and long exposure to English forces containing longbowmen, it seems some Irish or West Highland warriors were adopting a different weapon, better suited to their rapid, harassing forms of warfare, which struck the Catalan noble as very similar to the fast-moving,

skirmishing of the Muslims, whose manner of warfare he undoubtedly knew of from Christian–Moorish warfare in the Iberian peninsula.[100] It may have been to distinguish from this kind of weapon that an early Tudor proclamation in Ireland ordered that every man 'shall have an English bow and sheaf of arrows'.[101]

It is a great misfortune that Gerald, who had preached the Third Crusade so vigorously in Wales in 1188, never fulfilled his intentions to embark upon the crusade itself and to chronicle its achievements. One can only imagine what kind of perceptive observations he would have made about Turkish methods of warfare, of Frankish ways to combat them and of the personality and feats of arms of Richard I, to say nothing of the customs and marvels of the east. Yet he did dedicate a version of his *Conquest of Ireland* to Richard shortly before his coronation in September 1189. As Count of Poitou and Duke of Aquitaine, Richard must have already been familiar with the excellent Welsh archers employed by his father in many of his continental campaigns, and though he was never to set foot in Ireland he doubtless knew of the exploits of Strongbow and his companions. Indeed, Earl Richard and his men had returned from Ireland to aid Henry II against rebellion in 1173, in which the young Count of Poitou had himself been involved, and the marcher lords had played a part in the royalist victory at Fornham, Suffolk, over the rebel forces of the Earl of Leicester.[102] The outstanding general of his age, King Richard fully appreciated the importance of an effective missile arm, and the Angevin army which accompanied him on crusade clearly contained a powerful force of archers and crossbowmen. Here they would prove their worth in a very different theatre of war against a formidable opponent.

Matthew Strickland

Crusaders and Composite Bows

he army which landed with Richard I at the great coastal town of Acre in July 1191 contained a strong force of crossbowmen and archers drawn from the extensive continental lands of the Angevins as well as from England, Wales and the marches. Their ultimate goal was the recapture of Jerusalem and the holy places of Christendom, gained for the Franks by the First Crusade (1096–9) but recently retaken for Islam by Saladin following his great victory at Hattin in 1187. For almost a century the Franks and Muslims had engaged in sporadic warfare, with intense fighting punctuated by periods of truce or low-level hostilities, and it would not be until 1291 that the Franks were finally driven from Outremer – the 'land over the sea' – by the might of the Mamluk armies of Egypt. A study of the role of military archery in this theatre of war may seem a far cry from the 'mainstream' history of the longbow as it is often portrayed, with its preponderant emphasis on the Hundred Years War. Yet it would be a mistake to see crusading warfare as divorced from that of western Europe; the Franks took their military methods, including the use of archers and crossbowmen, with them to the east, and adapted their tactics to meet the challenges of opponents who were as, if not more, skilful, disciplined and technologically advanced as themselves. Missilemen played a vital role not only in sieges and pitched battles but on the march, forming a defensive screen with other infantry to protect the knights and their valuable destriers which were highly vulnerable to the constant harrying of the enemy's horse-archers.[1] For two centuries, while western Europe struggled to keep its

A lightly armed Turkish horse-archer shoots behind while at full gallop, from a fifteenth-century Turkish miniature. The short yet powerful limbs of the composite bow enabled such horse-archers to shoot from the saddle with great dexterity and astonishing accuracy. *(Topkapi Palace Museum, Istanbul, Turkey/Bridgeman Art Library)*

precarious foothold in the Latin East, the archers and crossbowmen who fought in the heat of the Syrian sun played a major role in the campaigns which sought to maintain the Frankish presence there.

TURKISH TACTICS AND THE COMPOSITE BOW

The armies of the various Islamic opponents encountered by the forces of the First Crusade varied considerably in composition and fighting techniques. Some, such as the armies of the Abbasid caliphate of Baghdad and the Fatimid caliphate of Cairo, contained units of heavily armed cavalry, some of them similar to the Byzantine *cataphracti*, as well as light horse, and almost all deployed archers, whether on horse or foot.[2] None, however, used the bow to greater effect than the Seljuk Turks, first encountered by the crusaders at Nicaea and Dorylaeum in 1097, who placed great tactical reliance on their highly mobile horse-archers.[3] Turkish tactics aimed at weakening and disorganising the enemy's ranks by constantly galling them with clouds of arrows. They often focused their attacks on an opponent's flanks, or in the case of a marching column on its rear, trying to pick off stragglers or exploit any gaps that appeared in the enemy formations. If attacked themselves, these light horsemen would scatter or hastily retreat on their swift steeds, so that the charge of the Frankish knights could not find a solid target on which to vent its impetus. A common tactic was to lure pursuing knights into an ambush, or suddenly to turn, regroup and attack their now disorganised pursuers.[4] As Ambroise, a Norman troubadour who probably fought in the Third Crusade, commented in his *History of the Holy War*:

> For the Turks have a serious
> Advantage, which cost dear to us:
> The Christians were with armour clad,
> And heavily. The Saracens had
> Mace, bow, and sword, and bore a spear
> Well sharpened and no other gear
> Except a knife that little weighs.
> When to pursue them one essays,
> Their steeds unrivalled like a swallow
> Seem to take flight, and none can follow;
> The Turks are so skilful to elude
> Their foemen when they are pursued
> That they are like a venomous
> And irksome gadfly to us.
> Pursue him, he will take to flight;
> Return and he renews his spite.[5]

Similiarly, Anna Comnena, when telling of the tactical formation devised by her father Alexius in 1116 to counter Turkish tactics, noted of the Turks that:

> As for the weapons they use in war, unlike the Kelts [Franks], they do not fight with lances, but completely surround the enemy and shoot at him with arrows; they also defend themselves with arrows at a distance. In hot pursuit, the Turk makes prisoners with his bow; in flight, he overwhelms his pursuer with the same weapon, and when he shoots, the arrow in its course strikes either rider or horse, loosed with such tremendous force that it passes clean through the body. So skilful are the Turkish archers.[6]

Turks had become the military elite in the armies of the great Muslim ruler of Aleppo and Damascus, Nur ad Din (d. 1174), and of his successor, Saladin (d. 1193), who created a powerful empire stretching from Egypt to northern Syria. Their forces also possessed more heavily armoured horsemen, and *ghulams*, a class of professional warriors purchased as slaves and trained from boyhood, who could fight close-in with spear, sword and mace as well as with the bow. They might shoot in disciplined formations, sometimes moving, sometimes at a standstill, whereas the auxiliary nomadic Turcoman tribesmen excelled in fast, harassing archery.[7] Turks from the Kipchak steppe were recruited in large numbers by the Mamluk sultanate, established in 1261, whose troops underwent rigorous training and attained astonishing skill with the bow.[8]

Western chroniclers were particularly struck by the range of the Saracen bows. The author of the *Deeds of the Franks* noted that at the battle of Dorylaeum in 1097, 'the Turks came upon us from all sides, skirmishing, throwing darts and javelins, and shooting arrows from an astonishing range'.[9] The Turks excelled at the sport of flight shooting, in which short, light arrows were shot from composite bows, usually with the aid of a *siper* or *majra*, a grooved arrow-guide which allowed the arrow to be drawn further back beyond the body of the bow itself. With this device great ranges could be achieved, exceeding 800 yards (730m). It is probable that in war archers used this method with light arrows to lay down a harassing barrage at about 400 yards. Even using longer arrows, however, an impressive range could be attained; in an exceptional case, in 1301–2, an amir using a 126lb (57kg) bow shot a remarkable range of 636 yards (582m).[10] Turkish archers could not only shoot at a great distance, but with great speed, so that contemporaries spoke of 'clouds of arrows' which darkened the sun. Ambroise, for example, recalls that at the battle of Arsuf in 1191:

> Well can I recount
> That neither rain nor snow nor sleet
> In winter's depth did ever beat
> More thickly or more densely fly
> (Many can tell ye if I lie)

Than did the foemen's shafts, which flew
Upon us and our horses slew.
In armfuls ye might there have found
And gathered them upon the ground
Like thatch upon a stubble field . . .[11]

A tangible glimpse of such an arrow storm has been revealed by recent excavations at the castle of Jacob's Ford on the River Jordan, begun by King Baldwin IV in 1178 and destroyed the following year by Saladin when still under construction; among the building works hundreds of arrowheads were found among the abandoned spades, hoes, chisels and axes of the workmen, who perished with the rest of the garrison.[12] A Frankish eye-witness to Saladin's assault on Jerusalem in 1187 bore a lasting reminder of the efficacy of such a rain of arrows:

Arrows fell like raindrops, so that one could not show a finger above the ramparts without being hit. There were so many wounded that all the hospitals and physicians in the city were hard put to it just to extract the missiles from their bodies. I myself was wounded in the face by an arrow which struck the bridge of my nose. The wooden shaft has been taken out, but the metal tip has remained there to this day.[13]

If hails of arrows had a psychological impact on the enemy, several Frankish chroniclers also allege that captured Franks were used as target practice. This fate supposedly befell some of Peter the Hermit's disordered followers in 1096, while Fulcher of Chartres claimed the Turkish garrison of Arsuf crucified some Frankish prisoners then riddled them with arrows.[14] William of Malmesbury had heard how Robert son of Godwine, a knight and faithful companion of Edgar Aetheling, was captured in battle at Ramlah, then taken to Cairo where, 'when he refused to deny Christ, he was set up as a target in the middle of the market-place and there, pierced through and through with arrows, achieved a martyr's death'.[15] Though such stories read like a topos, heavily influenced by the legend of St Sebastian, they none the less reflect the strong association in western minds of the Turks with archery; whether in battle or captivity, whistling death came with Turkish arrows. It was doubtless such associations that lay behind a story recorded by Roger of Howden, one of Richard I's own royal clerks, of how a Frank named René who had apostatised was captured among the Turkish garrison when the castle of Darum fell to the king just after Easter 1192. As an example, King Richard 'had him set up as a mark for arrows, and he was pierced to death'.[16] Whether or not the incident actually occurred, it must have seemed to Howden and his audience a fitting fate for one who had betrayed his faith to those infidels who martyred Christians in such a manner.

The weapon that gave such awesome range, speed of shooting and mobility to the Turkish horse-archers was the composite bow. The classic weapon of the eastern horsemen such as the Huns, Avars, Magyars, Mongols and Turks who broke in successive waves over the frontiers of Europe throughout the Middle Ages, the composite bow had a venerable ancestry.[17] Developed simultaneously in Mesopotamia, Anatolia and the northern Asian steppes during the third millennium BC, it was known to the Egyptians and Assyrians in a form known as the 'western Asian angular bow', and was in use from about 2400–600 BC.[18] Its development has been regarded as one of mankind's major technological breakthroughs, and its varying forms and uses, whether in the classical, near eastern or oriental worlds, have attracted a large scholarly literature.[19] In the Muslim world the curved composite bow was increasingly replacing earlier angular forms by the twelfth century.[20] The composite bow was a sophisticated weapon, formed by gluing layers of horn and sinew to a wooden core. Its size, shape and performance could vary widely. Turkish bows, for example, tended to be shorter and less powerful than Tartar bows.[21] Draw-weights might vary between 60 and 100lb (27–45kg) but could go higher, and a bow of 89.4lb (40.5kg) is recorded as shooting a 578.4g arrow over a distance of some 147–63 yards (135–49m).[22] A Persian composite bow examined by Payne-Gallwey measured 3ft 9in (1.14m) long, with the maximum width of each arm being 1⅛in (2.9cm). This bow, which weighed only 12½oz, had an impressive draw-weight of 110lb (49.8kg).[23]

Irrespective of size and shape, however, the method of manufacture was basically similar. The back (the outside of the bow, furthest from the archer) was formed by gluing varying lengths of animal sinew, if possible taken from the great neck tendon of an ox, to a thin wooden core. Sinew is extremely elastic, possessing a tensile strength estimated at about 20 kilograms per square millimetre, up to four times that of bow woods.[24] The belly (the inside of the bow) was formed from layered slivers of animal horn, which has natural compressive qualities, calculated at a maximum strength of about 13 kilograms per square millimetre – twice that of hardwoods.[25] The horn, best taken from water buffalo or young longhorn cattle, was boiled, shaped, then cut and glued to the inner side of the wooden core. The glue, a vital ingredient, was usually made from fish, especially the mouth of the sturgeon, and mixed with simmered sinew. The bow was then shaped over a former and dried very slowly. The whole was then covered with a protective layer of parchment, leather or bark, which might be painted or highly decorated.[26]

A finely decorated composite bow, with its red leather covering powdered with golden flowers, and a quiver of leather and velvet, enriched with carved and gilded mounts. Turkish, seventeenth century. *(The Hungarian National Museum)*

Such a method of construction – which may originally have been stimulated by the lack of suitable woods for self-bows[27] – and the resulting recurve shape once the bow was strung allowed the limbs of the composite bow to be made considerably shorter than those of self-bows, making them ideal for use in the saddle.[28] It was possible to shoot a longbow from horseback, but its length precluded the kind of agile movements constantly practised by eastern horse-archers, who were trained to shoot at the gallop with pin-point accuracy and even to turn and loose while facing backwards – the famous 'Parthian shot' (see p. 97).[29] Odo of Deuil, for example, noted that during an engagement on the Second Crusade with the forces of Louis VII the Turkish archers skirmished and retreated, shooting arrows from behind.[30] It has been estimated that a trained Muslim *ghulam* could loose up to five arrows in 2½ seconds.[31] The shortness and flexibility of the composite bow's limbs allow an arrow to be shot further and faster than from a self-bow of the equivalent draw-weight, and in modern tests a composite bow with a draw-weight of 59.5lb (27kg) shot the same arrow as fast as a replica medieval yew longbow with a draw of about 74lb (33.5kg), namely about 112mph (50m/s).[32] Many archers in the armies of the Seljuk Turks also made use of a *majra* or arrow-guide, a grooved wooden stave that could attach to the centre of the bow and allow the discharge of short darts rather than arrows, the arrow-guide thus serving very much like the grooved tiller of a crossbow for the discharge of bolts.[33]

Given the variety in size and methods of construction, composite bows must have varied considerably in range and power. It seems clear, however, from the accounts of western observers that the bows used by the Arabs and Turks in the eleventh and twelfth centuries were capable of shooting at great distances but that range, achieved by using comparatively light arrows, was bought at the expense of penetration. At shorter range arrows might pierce mail, as Gerard de Quiersy found to his cost on the First Crusade when a Turk he was charging shot an arrow through his shield and armour, fatally wounding him. Another crusader, Walter 'the Penniless', supposedly died when no fewer than seven arrows pierced his hauberk.[34] But in general the mail armour of the Franks proved highly effective in stopping the arrows of eastern composite bows. At Dorylaeum in 1097 Ralph of Caen noted that the Turks 'were helped by numbers, we by our armour'.[35] In 1107 the Byzantine emperor Alexius ordered his horse-archers to shoot at the horses of Bohemund's Frankish knights, 'for he knew that cuirasses and coats of mail made them almost if not entirely invulnerable; to shoot at the riders, therefore, would in his opinion be a waste of arrows and entirely ridiculous'.[36] In 1148, during the Second Crusade, Turkish arrows failed to penetrate Louis VII's hauberk, while at Jaffa in 1192 Ambroise records how Richard I rode deep into the Turkish ranks:

> But he was covered with such a sheaf
> Of arrows which the foe shot thick
> And fast at him and which did stick

In horse and horsecloth that, in fine,
He looked just like a porcupine.[37]

While the Turkish arrows might lodge between the links of the knights' hauberks, they seem often to have been unable to break through the links themselves or to pierce through to the padded garments such as a gambeson or aketon frequently worn beneath or over the hauberk.[38] As the twelfth century wore on, moreover, the defensive armour of the best equipped knights and their mounts steadily improved,[39] while commanders increasingly preferred to take smaller numbers of better armed and trained infantry than the unwieldy hordes which had accompanied the First Crusade. In the same decade in which Gerald of Wales was writing of the formidable penetrative power of the Welsh elm longbows in Gwent, Saladin's close aide and confidant Beha ad-Din remarked on the effectiveness of the Frankish infantry's armour against the Turkish bows during the Third Crusade: 'every foot-soldier wore a vest of thick felt and a coat of mail so dense and strong that our arrows made no impression on them . . . I saw some of the Frankish foot-soldiers with from one to ten arrows sticking in them, and still advancing at their ordinary pace without leaving the ranks.'[40] How good a protection such 'soft armour' afforded against these lighter Turkish arrows is revealed by Jean, sire de Joinville, who recounted in his memoirs how in 1250 at the disastrous battle of Mansourah in Egypt he and his men attempted to hold a small bridge against the Turks: 'We were all covered with the darts that failed to hit the sergeants. By some lucky chance I happened to find a Saracen's tunic, padded with tow. I turned the open side towards me and used the garment as a shield. It did me good service, for I was only wounded by the enemy's darts in five places, though my horse was wounded in fifteen.'[41] Against plate armour the composite bow was still-less effective; Bertrandon de la Broquière was to note in his *Voyage d'Outremer* of 1432 that the Turkish 'archers do not shoot as often as ours, nor from such a long range' – a comment at odds with that of earlier Frankish observers – and that the wearing of a brigandine or 'a light white armour'

A Muslim archer drawing a compact composite bow, from the bronze doors of Trani Cathedral, southern Italy, early twelfth century. The Norman kings of Sicily made extensive use of such archers in their armies. *(Cathedral of San Pantaleone, Ravello, Italy/ Bridgeman Art Library)*

would suffice for protection against their lighter arrows, which being tanged, could not withstand a strong blow.[42]

Yet although Turkish arrows might not be deadly against knights or well-armed infantry, they took a heavy toll of the knights' valuable war-horses, and this represented one of the principal dangers of Muslim archery for the crusaders.[43] For war-horses were not only very expensive and extremely difficult to replace in Outremer, but crucially the mounted charge was also one of the Franks' principal forms of attack.[44] The loss of horses through enemy arrows, disease and exhaustion was always an acute problem, and could critically hamper the offensive capabilities of the Frankish knights. At the battle of Antioch in 1098 the Franks may have had as few as 200 mounts, while at Jaffa in 1192 Richard I had fewer than fifteen horses for his knights; so apparent was his plight that in a truly chivalric gesture he was even sent two magnificent horses during the battle by Saladin's brother, al-Adil.[45] Given these factors, it was essential for crusading armies to protect themselves against the tactics of the Turkish horse-archers, and for this the careful deployment of their own longbowmen and crossbowmen was essential.

ARCHERS IN BATTLE AND ON THE 'FIGHTING MARCH'

The need for archers to guard against the attacks of horse-archers had long been recognised by the Byzantines.[46] In his *Taktica*, the Byzantine emperor Leo VI (865–912) noted the highly mobile tactics of the Magyars and Pechnegs, who were mostly light horsemen relying on the bow as their primary weapon, skirmishing in small groups and loosing volleys of arrows. On open ground the emperor advised a charge by the Byzantine *cataphracti*, or heavy cavalry, for whom they would be no match, but he cautioned against too reckless a pursuit, for such horsemen, and especially the Turks, were adept at feigning flight, only to turn and cut up their disorganised pursuers. Above all, however, he advocated the vital need for a missile arm, for 'foot-archers were their special dread, since the bow of the infantry soldier is larger and carries further than that of the horseman'. Though the archers in Byzantine armies were using composite bows, Leo's remarks are pertinent for the crusaders' later experiences:

> You will have many good archers. This arm is excellent and of great service, especially against the Saracens and the Turks, who put all their hope in them. We need archers, not only to oppose theirs, but also to shoot at their cavalry, which does them much harm and discourages them when they see their best horses killed. . . . they [the Turks] greatly fear infantry that maims their horses; and if they set foot on the ground, as they are not at all used to doing so, they suffer greatly. Nor do they like dealing with a tight line of cavalry in good order on an open plain.[47]

Similarly, another tenth-century treatise, the *Praecepta militaria*, attributed to the Emperor Nikephoros Phokas II, envisages a defensive formation against Arab horsemen formed by a hollow square in which three ranks of archers were placed between protective lines of the spearmen to the front and rear.[48]

The Frankish commanders of the First Crusade were no doubt advised by the Byzantine emperor Alexius Comnenus on the nature of the enemies they would encounter on their march from Nicaea into northern Syria. Nevertheless, the novelty of the Turks' tactics seem initially to have caught the crusaders off their guard. Remarking on the whitening bones of the slaughtered commoners of the People's Crusade near Nicomedia, the chronicler Fulcher of Chartres noted that the Turks, whom he calls 'a valiant race from the East skilled with the bow', had 'annihilated our people who were ignorant of the arrow and new to its use'.[49] He did not mean, of course, that archery was unknown in the west, but rather that the Franks had no previous experience of facing such highly mobile horse-archers who discharged clouds of arrows 'as was their custom'. Describing the first major engagement with the Turks at Dorylaeum in 1097, he commented: 'Meanwhile the Turks were howling like wolves and furiously shooting a cloud of arrows at us. We were stunned by this. Since we faced death and since many of us were wounded we soon took to flight. Nor is this remarkable because to all of us such warfare was unknown.'[50]

Nevertheless, the commanders of the First Crusade subsequently showed great skill in countering such tactics by the adoption of tight formations and the use of defensive bodies of infantry, and between 1097 and 1099 the crusader army became moulded by hard combat experience into an increasingly skilful and disciplined force.[51] At Dorylaeum the

Frankish foot helped to form a dense and immovable mass, which held the Turkish attacks and allowed the knights to launch counter-attacks.[52] At the battle of Antioch in 1098 the crusader army formed up in four divisions, each containing a unit of horse and foot, with the infantry in front to screen the knights, while at Ascalon in 1099, where the Franks faced a major Fatimid army from Egypt, they drew up their battle lines with 'infantry and archers' preceding the knights.[53] Fulcher of Chartres noted that the battle began with Frankish archery, before the knights launched their decisive charge, while following the rout of the Turks those who climbed trees to escape were shot down by Frankish archers.[54] At Jaffa in 1102 the Saracens were 'vigorously repulsed by the arrows of the infantry'.[55] How far such tactics drew on existing Byzantine practice is unclear; there must certainly have been considerable military dialogue between the Byzantines and the crusaders, and it is even possible that Alexius's own successful 'fighting march' in Anatolia in 1116 in turn reflected the successful formations adopted by the Franks against their Turkish opponents.[56] Equally, such engagements not only dispel the earlier belief that infantry played a poor role on the First Crusade and only gradually increased in professionalism during the twelfth century, but also qualify the view that 'the Franks had no technical response' to the composite bow.[57] Crossbowmen, whose importance had already been emphasised by their presence in William the Conqueror's invasion army of 1066, were certainly on the First Crusade, for they are recorded at the siege of Nicaea in 1097 giving covering volleys to the miners sapping the walls,[58] and though the sources give no details they must also have played a role in field engagements. Similarly, although hot, dry conditions may have adversely affected the performance of self-bows, the range of a longbow would have kept the Muslim horse-archers at a respectable distance.

Some of the bowmen on the First Crusade were poorly armed and ill-disciplined, for the expedition had many of the dimensions of a mass movement, attracting a large body of non-combatants and many whose weapons can only have been of the simplest. Thus during the winter of 1096/7, some of the poorer crusaders could not afford to winter in Sicily while waiting for the spring passage to the east, and so sold their bows, resumed their pilgrim's staves, and returned home.[59] But there were other archers who were well equipped and organised. In the engagement fought by King Baldwin I of Jerusalem outside Arsuf in 1102, the armour of the Frankish archers allowed them to withstand the archery of the Egyptians and return their volleys to good effect.[60] As early as 1103 Baldwin I is recorded as having had a 'commander of the archers' (*magister sagittariorum*), a post held by one Reinoldus, who was a *miles regis*, or king's knight, and himself a marksman of repute.[61] Though we have no further details of his role, the existence of a specific office suggests not only the importance of archers but the existence of a developed command structure; presumably his tasks included marshalling the bowmen and arranging their dispositions. Here we glimpse once more the close connection between the king's military household or *familia regis* and the provision of an elite force of archers, which was apparent in the forces of Henry I of England at the battle of Bourgthéroulde in 1124.[62] By the time of the Third Crusade, when the emphasis was on quality rather than quantity of crusading forces, the archers and crossbowmen possessed, as Beha ad-Din noted, good defensive equipment.

The Franks quickly came to appreciate the value of bowmen and disciplined infantry to screen and protect their formations when marching, for it was when on the move that their armies were particularly vulnerable to the constant harassing of the Turks. Archers played a significant role in Baldwin I's fighting march towards Hab in 1119, while on the Second Crusade in 1148 Louis VII, who had suffered badly from Turkish attacks on his column, stationed foot-soldiers and nobles who had lost their horses at the rear of the host to resist the attacks of the enemy with their bows.[63] Inexperienced crusaders who ignored these lessons did so at their peril, for a force lacking well-deployed bowmen was highly vulnerable. Odo of Deuil noted that as the Germans in 1147 had no bowmen, the Turks did not fail to attack them and shower them with a rain of arrows.[64] Similarly, Louis VII won Odo's praise for going to the aid of his followers, hard pressed by the Turks, although he was not accompanied 'by common foot-soldiers and serjeants armed with bows' and therefore was in great danger.[65] The catastrophic defeat at Hattin in 1187, where the army of Guy de Lusignan, King of Jerusalem, was annihilated by Saladin, furnishes the classic example of how the Muslims defeated the fighting march by cutting off the Franks from their water supply and wearing them down by constant harassment. The Frankish infantry finally broke, retreating up to the Horns of Hattin and refusing to rejoin the battle. Without their support the Frankish knights, with their horses increasingly exhausted, were hopelessly vulnerable.[66] Equally, lack of adequate archery protection might force the Frankish knights to charge prematurely or in disadvantageous situations. At Gaza in 1239 a Christian force was surrounded in a low valley and subjected to hails of arrows by Muslim archers. They were repelled by the Frankish archers and crossbowmen, but when these ran out of arrows and bolts the Frankish cavalry were compelled to charge, with ultimately disastrous results.[67] St Louis was similarly compelled to charge at Mansourah in 1250 because

Archers armed with composite bows and crossbows, together with heavily armed German knights, prepare to embark on the Emperor Henry VI's invasion of Sicily, from Peter of Eboli's *Carmen in Honorem Augusti, c.* 1200 (Berne, Burgerbibliothek, Cod. Bern. 120/II, f.131). The majority of the archers are only very lightly armed. *(Burgerbibliothek, Berne)*

his knights came under heavy Muslim arrow attack at a time when his own crossbowmen were absent.[68]

Such a disadvantage was not always one-sided. In his memoirs the Syrian emir Usamah ibn Munquidh recounts with not a little embarrassment how, after he and his companion Jum'ah, had routed a group of Frankish knights, they were approaching a bluff overlooking the castle of Afamiyah when

a small footman, who had climbed that steep ascent carrying a bow and arrows . . . shot his arrows at us while we had no way to hit back at him. So we ran away, hardly believing, by Allah, that we should escape with our horses safe . . . We then departed, with my heart laden with regret on account of that footman who put us to defeat while we had no access to him though we had defeated eight knights of the Franks.[69]

It seems that Frankish archers were capable not only of keeping Muslim horse-archers at a safe distance, but of discomfiting those Turkish horsemen who fought with heavier equipment and lances. It is interesting to note the shame felt by Usamah as a nobleman at having been worsted by a lowly Frankish bowman, and equal fear for the safety of their mounts as was displayed by Frankish knights. Usamah himself died in 1188 on the eve of the Third Crusade, and did not live to see the great battle at Arsuf in 1191 in which the Frankish forces under the command of Richard I routed Saladin's army. This engagement provides a classic and well-documented example of the fighting march, but the campaigns of the Third Crusade as a whole reveal the great importance of archers to the crusading forces.

ARSUF, 7 SEPTEMBER 1191, AND JAFFA, 5 AUGUST 1192

The archers and crossbowmen in the Angevin forces had already proved their worth in the fighting which occurred during Richard's outward journey via Sicily and Cyprus. When Richard took the Sicilian town of Messina by storm on 3 October 1190, he drew up a select force, which the Winchester monk Richard of Devizes estimated as 2,000 knights and 1,000 bowmen. Though his figures need not be taken literally, Devizes had access to a detailed account of the first part of Richard's crusade, and his description of the assault on Messina is instructive:

The king, who knew nothing better than storming cities and overthrowing castles, first let them [the defenders of Messina] empty their quivers. Then at length he made the first assault with his bowmen, who went in front of the army. The sky was hidden by a violent rain of arrows; a thousand darts pierced the shields extended along the ramparts, and nothing could save the rebels from the force of the javelins. The walls were left without guards, for no one could look out without getting an arrow in his eye immediately.[70]

Equally, archers and crossbowmen were to the fore during Richard's amphibious assault on Limassol in May 1191, which began his conquest of Cyprus from the Byzantine ruler Isaac Comnenus.[71] The missilemen were placed with knights in the small skiffs carried by Richard's transport ships, and as the crusaders rowed towards the shore, which Isaac had barricaded and manned with his own bowmen, they rained arrows upon the enemy: 'Our archers, likewise our crossbowmen, sent clouds of shafts upon their foemen. The Greeks recoiled before the shock . . .'[72] Leaping into the water, Richard led his knights on to the beach, with his archers preceding them and continuing their covering volleys. The crusaders now rushed upon the emperor and his forces, and, noted Roger of Howden, 'like a shower upon the grass did the arrows fall on those who fought',[73] so that soon the Cypriots had been put to flight.

Once Richard's army had arrived at the siege of the Turkish-held city of Acre, his archers and crossbowmen 'kept up an unceasing rain of arrows on the Turks' from a great prefabricated siege castle named Mategriffon, which Richard had earlier deployed outside Messina.[74] The Frankish archers were invaluable not only in attacking the city but in defending the

Richard the Lionheart's campaigns on the Third Crusade, 1191–2. The inset shows the defensive formation used by the Frankish army in their 'fighting march' from Acre to Jaffa in 1191.

Left: A horse-archer armed with a composite bow turns to shoot at a pursuing knight, from a late twelfth- or early thirteenth-century mural, designed to imitate a wall hanging, in the crypt of Massenzio, Aquileia Cathedral, Italy. *(Author Collection)*

crusaders' lines of circumvallation from the repeated attacks by Saladin's army, desperately attempting to relieve the garrison.[75] Beha ad-Din noted of Richard's infantry manning the ramparts and trenches of the Frankish camp that 'in truth, the enemy's foot presented a front like a solid wall; behind the shelter of their ramparts they defended themselves with their arbalists and arrows'.[76] A story was soon in circulation, recorded by the troubadour Ambroise, of a duel between a Welsh longbowman 'of some skill and craft' named Maradoc (perhaps a Norman's rendering of Madoc?) and a Turkish archer called Grair. The two marksmen repeatedly shot shafts at one another, till the Turk asked of his rival whence he came:

> 'I come from Wales,' our man replied,
> 'And you were mad to come outside.'

But the Turk then proposed a challenge. He would loose one shot at the Welshmen, who was not to move; and if he missed the Welshman could in turn take his aim at the Turk. The Welshman agreed, but the Turk missed his mark and demanded a second shot, saying that the Welshman could then take two shots at him.

> 'Gladly,' the man from Wales replied,
> And while his foe was occupied
> Taking a shaft from out his quiver,
> Standing close to the unbeliever
> The Welshman, who would have no part
> In such terms, shot him through the heart.
> 'You kept the pact not,' so he spoke,
> 'So, by Saint Denis, mine I broke.'[77]

Once Acre had been taken, the crusaders planned to strike down the coast of Palestine to occupy Jaffa, but knew they would come under constant attack from Saladin's forces as they marched south. Accordingly, in August 1191, before leaving Acre, Richard 'made all the archers of the host come before him and gave them good wages',[78] in order to retain those bowmen already in his service and to attract those who had formerly served in the forces of other crusade leaders. Though he had not seen combat against the Turks before, Richard had experienced the harassing tactics of light horsemen during his conquest of Cyprus in May 1191, when the Byzantine ruler

Muslim archers support horsemen in the defence of a town, from a fragment of a twelfth-century Egyptian painting. *(British Museum)*

Isaac Comnenus had made an unsuccessful attempt to ambush the rearguard of Richard's army as it moved inland towards Nicosia. As Ambroise relates:

> Then from the ambush where he lay,
> The emperor made a swift foray
> With force of seven hundred, which
> Their cowardice did sore bewitch.
> They sent their shafts at the foreguard,
> Who let them come straight on toward
> Them; skirmishing about the side,
> Like a swift Turcopole did ride
> The emperor, and swiftly sped
> Towards the rearguard, which Richard led,
> And at the king launched arrows two
> That had been dipped in poison brew.[79]

Unharmed, Richard had chased after Isaac, but could not catch him. Cyprus and the emperor subsequently fell into Richard's hands, but the incident must have been instructive. Once in the Holy Land Richard was well advised on Turkish tactics by the military experts of the Latin East, the military orders of the Templars and Hospitallers and the native Frankish barons of Syria, and, with the recent catastrophe of Hattin much in mind, he made his dispositions accordingly. To counter the Turkish assaults Richard's army marched along the coast, its right flank protected by the sea and the fleet which kept pace with it.[80] The infantry was divided into two main bodies; one formed a protective screen for the knights who formed units in the centre, while the other marched between the knights and the shore, carrying the baggage while their colleagues fought off the Turks. When the infantry facing the enemy grew tired, they were relieved by the other division, so they could rest in relative safety, while the sick or wounded were transferred to the ships. In the centre, guarded by the Normans and English, was the standard, from which flew the royal banner. This served as a rallying point and a place to which the wounded could be brought, and could be wheeled forward or withdrawn depending on whether the enemy withdrew or attacked.[81]

In describing the disciplined formation of the Frankish infantry on its march down the coast from Acre to Caesarea in 1191, Saladin's biographer Beha ad-Din does not hide his admiration for the dogged courage of these foot-soldiers:

> Their troops continued to advance . . . all the while maintaining a steady fight. The Moslems discharged arrows at them from all sides to annoy them, and force them to charge; but in this they were unsuccessful.

These men exercised wonderful self-control; they went on their way without any hurry, while their ships followed their line of march along the coast, and in this manner they reached their halting place. They never made long marches, because they were obliged to spare the foot-soldiers, for those of them who were not engaged in fighting used to carry the baggage and tents, as they had so few beasts of burden. One cannot help admiring the patience displayed by these people, who bore the most wearing fatigue without having any participation in the management of affairs, or deriving any personal advantage.[82]

But these troops could give as well as take punishment, for as Beha ad-Din recalls, 'they shot at us with their great arbalists, wounding some Muslim horses and their riders'.[83] Their greatest test, however, came on 7 September when Saladin, alarmed at his failure to prevent the slow but inexorable progress of the enemy, launched an all-out attack on the Frankish army as they approached the wood of Arsuf. Time and again the crusader archers and crossbowmen drove off the fierce assaults of the Turkish cavalry, who pressed ever harder, particularly against the rearguard.[84] Ambroise paid tribute to their steadfastness: 'That day our excellent crossbowmen fought nobly and did service yeoman, and good archers, who from aft the host sent many a well-aimed shaft.'[85] Such was the relentless Turkish attack that some 'craven folk and cowardly threw down their bows' and took refuge in the host. But the remaining infantry in the rearguard fought bravely on, marching backwards under the blazing Palestinian sun and shooting as they went. The ability to keep up such a steady rate of shooting must have required not only a cool nerve but a plentiful supply of arrows and bolts. Richard's great military ability extended to the careful provision of necessary supplies for his troops, and the Pipe Rolls for 1189 show that arrows and bolts had been ordered en masse in preparation for the crusade.[86] It seems very likely that, as with foodstuffs, it was the fleet which carried the requisite munitions, unloading them to the troops on the shore from skiffs before, or perhaps even during, the day's march.

Despite the efforts of the Frankish infantry, however, the rearguard of Richard's army came under such pressure that its commander, the Master of the Hospital, rode to the king and begged for permission to attack the Turks; his knights were losing many of their horses to Turkish arrows, and still worse their failure to strike back would brand them with cowardice and infamy. Richard, however, enjoined but a little more patience, for he was waiting until the crucial moment when the Turks became so closely engaged they could not escape the full force of the knights' charge; if this attack was premature or disorganised, the swift horse-archers would merely scatter before the Franks, only to turn and surround the knights once their charge had lost momentum and their mounts had become winded. He and his commanders had agreed that at the crucial moment six trumpet blasts should be sounded through the host to indicate the king's order to attack. But Richard's careful plan was nearly ruined when two knights, the Marshal of the Hospital and Baldwin de Carron, one of Richard's close friends, finally snapped under the pressure of having to endure the blows of the Turks without striking back effectively; breaking ranks against orders they put spurs to horse and charged out of the ranks, each slaying a Turkish adversary, and precipitating a general but premature attack. Such rashness could have ended in disaster, but Richard, quickly assessing the situation, immediately led the main contingents in a general charge which still succeeded in taking the Turks completely by surprise. Beha ad-Din was among the Saracen host and witnessed the terrifying Frankish charge:

> I myself saw their knights gather together in the midst of a protecting circle of infantry. They put their lances in rest, uttered a mighty war-cry, and the ranks of infantry parted to allow them to pass; then they rushed out, and charged in all directions. One division hurled itself on our right wing, another on our left, and a third on our centre, throwing our whole force into confusion.[87]

Arsuf was not a decisive battle, for it did not alter the course or outcome of the Third Crusade and Saladin's army, though badly mauled, remained very much in being. Nevertheless, it strikingly demonstrates the tactical effectiveness of the combination of disciplined infantry with heavy cavalry and epitomises the key role which missilemen could play in crusader armies.

Their importance is further revealed by Richard's subsequent engagements in the Holy Land. In June 1192 Richard led a daring attack on a rich Muslim caravan south of Hebron, having used a Bedouin and two turcopoles dressed as Saracens to spy out its position. As the enemy were forewarned, however, Richard 'sent his archers forward in the van with turcopole and crossbowman to skirmish with the Turks and strive to press them until he could arrive'.[88] 'His skirmishers', noted Ambroise, 'were letting fly their arrows, thick as dew at dawn' as the king launched his main attack in two divisions against the caravan, drawn up in defensive array, and successfully scattered its defenders.[89]

Yet perhaps the most remarkable use of missilemen by Richard was at Jaffa in 1192, when having successfully forced an amphibious landing in the face of Muslim opposition on the beach Richard had relieved the town from Saladin's forces at the eleventh hour.[90] But though the town was saved, Richard and his small force of knights, supported by spearmen and crossbowmen drawn largely from the Pisan and Genoese marines of his ships, found themselves confronted by a large Turkish army.[91] To counter this threat, on the morning of 5 August Richard drew up his infantry in a strong defensive position, with the spearmen crouching on one knee with their spear butts planted in the ground, and with wooden tent pegs hastily reused as stakes to give further protection from the enemy horsemen. Between every two spearmen, and so protected by their shields, the king placed a crossbowman, and behind him a companion to span a second bow and thus keep supplying the crossbowman with a loaded weapon.[92] According to Ralph of Coggeshall Richard also 'posted his fellow knights . . . by arranging them tightly together, and he stationed them steadily, each at the side of the other, so that no avenue for cutting through his unit in battle might lie open to the enemy from empty space'.[93] Such a tightly grouped formation of knights on foot echoes earlier Anglo-Norman tactics as well as the experience common to so many knights on crusade who had to fight on foot owing to the loss of mounts. The Muslims repeatedly charged at the crusaders' formation, but on nearing the immovable wall of spears they were forced to veer away each time, presenting excellent targets for the crossbowmen. Richard then took the offensive, ordering his infantry to advance carefully in front of the knights, the crossbowmen leading the way, shooting as they went. Though he had fewer than ten knights mounted on a sorry assortment of nags and even mules, Richard led a daring counter-attack, and after fierce fighting finally compelled the Turks to withdraw.[94] Ralph of Coggeshall, who had received an account of the battle from an eye-witness, noted that the crossbowmen were to be greatly praised for their 'incomparable courage' and role in this remarkable victory against the odds.[95]

Missilemen continued to play a significant role both in crusader field forces and garrisons until the Latin kingdom of Jerusalem was finally extinguished with the fall of Acre in 1291.[96] They were prominent on the fighting march of the crusaders south from Damietta during the Fifth Crusade, while during Louis IX's campaign in Egypt in 1250 crossbowmen were used to drive off Muslim horsemen, thereby permitting the Franks to engage successfully with the enemy's infantry.[97] It was recognition of this military value that led Henry III to order his sheriffs in 1255 to publish an edict in cities, towns and market-places throughout the realm that all those who had taken the cross were to practise shooting with crossbows.[98] Even after 1291 the tactical need for archers in subsequent operations in the east was recognised by those planning fresh crusades. That same year, in his tract *On the Reconquest of the*

Holy Land, the Franciscan friar Fidenzio of Padua advised at length on the necessity of archers: 'Horsemen should always have many crossbowmen and archers mixed in with them, so that they are able to repulse the malice of the Saracens by the crossbowmen and archers. For the Saracens shoot infinite arrows, and the Christian archers should [shoot] their arrows . . . so that they dare not make an assault against the Christians.'[99]

An archer, drawing a superbly rendered composite bow with its distinctive 'ears', wounds a knight in the face during a siege. From the Maciejowski Bible, a richly illustrated manuscript of Old Testament stories, Paris, *c.* 1250 (New York, Pierpont Morgan Library, MS 638, f.23v, detail). Though the simple conical helmet with nasal and the wide-brimmed *chapel-de-fer* (worn by the knight to the right) allowed better ventilation, the development from the late twelfth century of the great helm, worn here by several of the knights, afforded far greater protection from arrow wounds to the face. *(Pierpont Morgan Library, New York)*

Crossbowmen, he continues, should take every opportunity to slay the mounts of the Saracens, for they fear the loss of their horses and make poor infantry. As it was vital that the cavalry did not leave the archers behind, many thousands of picked archers should be given mounts, and in battle these should be kept safely in the middle of the formation – an emphasis on mounted archers which, we should again note, vividly anticipates English practice in the Hundred Years War. In drawing up infantry, Fidenzio added, spearmen should be ordered in tight formation, with shield-bearers next to them to protect them from the Saracens' arrows. From behind this defence 'like a castle wall', the archers and crossbowmen should shoot at the Saracens and their horses. It was essential for the infantry to possess bows or crossbows, he continues, for without them there is no way of withstanding the attacks of the enemy, who can destroy other infantry with their arrows. Accordingly, it is wise counsel that all the Christian infantry should learn to

shoot a bow or crossbow, and that they should also have good lances and swords, as well as good protective clothing that can stop Muslim arrows.[100] Here were the successful tactics of Richard's engagement at Jaffa writ large.

The same basic principle was reiterated later by Bertrandon de la Broquière in 1439, when he recommended that in battle against the Turk:

> a large part of the archers and crossbowmen should be sown amongst the men-at-arms, because the Turks are all archers . . . and they could not fire right into the said *bataille* [of Christians] if it was not for resistance by, and fear of, the archers and crossbowmen of the Christians . . . stationed among the men-at-arms or a little in front if necessary . . . because the Christian archers and crossbowmen shoot further; they can each have shot at least two or three arrows into the *bataille* of the Turks before the Turkish arrows can reach the Christians . . .[101]

Whether Bertrandon was correct in his assertions of comparative range and speed of shooting (which is unlikely), it seems certain that the deployment of crossbowmen in field armies gave the Franks a tangible advantage against their Turkish opponents. The weapon had long been known in the Muslim world,[102] and a treatise on armaments dedicated to Saladin by Mardi ibn 'Ali at-Tarsusi describes crossbows whose bows were made not only of composite materials but also of olive or yew. Muslim hand crossbows were generally spanned by the use of the belt hook, but windlass-spanned bows are mentioned, probably being large, frame-mounted siege weapons (*ziyar*).[103] Some were designed to cast vessels filled with Greek fire, and Frankish sources speak of the effectiveness of Turkish crossbows at sieges such as Acre in 1189–91.[104] The crossbow, however, was less well suited to use in the saddle than the composite bow, and its deployment by the Muslims appears to have been generally restricted to siege warfare. As the Muslim author Taybugha al-Ashrafi later noted in about 1368, 'My own view is that in the manoeuvres of [mounted] combat, in the desert and on expeditions the hand bow is a better and more serviceable weapon, whereas in fortresses, sieges and ships greater power and advantage will be derived from the crossbow.'[105] In the Iberian peninsula, however, where protracted political and military co-existence had resulted in widespread assimilation and cross-fertilisation of equipment and military thinking, the Muslims might also deploy crossbowmen in battle in favour of the composite bow. The thirteenth-century chronicler Ibn Said noted of Muslim princes in Al-Andalus that:

> Very often the Andalusian princes and warriors take the neighbouring Christians as models for their equipment. Their arms are identical, likewise their surcoats of scarlet or other stuff, their pennons, their saddles. Similar also is their mode of fighting with bucklers and long lances for the charge. They use neither the mace nor the bow of the Arabs, but employ Frankish crossbows for sieges and arm infantry with them for encounters with the enemy.[106]

Such military influences might work in both directions. The Franks of Outremer adopted the use of their own light horsemen, armed with the composite bow. Known as turcopoles, these were native troops who were often the product of mixed Christian and Muslim marriages, and they rapidly became an integral part of Latin forces in the East.[107] The Syrian emir Usamah calls them 'the archers of the Franks', and the military orders employed a Master of the Turcopoles (or Turcopolier) to organise their own contingents of these troops.[108]

THE COMPOSITE BOW IN THE WEST

Recognition of the military value of horse-archers had also led the Franks to employ Muslim troops themselves as mercenaries or allies almost from the inception of the crusader states, as the Normans had done following their establishment of power in Italy and Sicily during the eleventh century.[109] Following his own experiences in warfare against Saladin, Richard I even hired Muslims for his wars against Philip Augustus in Normandy from 1194. *The Old French Continuation of William of Tyre* says that following his victory at Jaffa he attracted over 300 Mamelukes into his service by his largesse, and of these he brought 120 back to France.[110] The testimony of this chronicle is confirmed by the Norman Exchequer Rolls, which show that *Saraceni* were placed at Domfront on the southern Norman border for defence of the Passeis in 1195. They were still in Normandy in 1198.[111] We would dearly like to know more about how Richard used these troops, and how they were regarded by his own men; for many who had fought in the east, religious hostility was tempered by an admiration for the superb fighting qualities of the Turks. Richard also employed other Saracens, as well as Greeks, as technical experts skilled in the construction of siege engines and in the manufacture of Greek fire.[112] The Emperor Frederick II similarly employed Saracen horse-archers, drawn from the Muslim colony he had established at Lucera in Apulia.[113] At the battle of Cortenuova in 1237 these Muslim horse-archers were used to harass the infantry formations of the Lombard League, though their role in subsequent battles by Frederick's descendants against Charles of Anjou does not seem to have been significant.[114] Whether in the armies of Richard I or Frederick II the numbers of such Muslim troops deployed in the west was probably too small to have made a really significant tactical impact. Unlike the adoption by Christian armies in the Iberian peninsula of the light javelin-armed skirmishers or *jinetes*, who were to confront the longbowmen of the Black Prince at Nájera in 1367,[115] the use of eastern horse-archers in Angevin armies was, it seems, a short-lived experiment.

Far more influential and lasting in its impact was the dissemination of the composite bow itself in parts of western Europe. Despite being the weapon par excellence of eastern horse-archers, the composite bow had been known in the west long before the crusades. In Anglo-Saxon England the *Beowulf* poet knew of the 'horn bogan',[116] while between the fifth and seventh centuries the composite bow appears to have been popular with the cavalry of the Alemanni, who were usually men of some wealth and status. The latest of such bow finds dates to about 700, and by contrast the eighth-century Alemannic longbows found at Oberflach were apparently used by poorer freemen, no doubt reflecting the relative cost of composite bows.[117] The composite bow may have been used by the Carolingians and certainly by their Avar and Magyar enemies.[118]

In addition to the military influence of steppe peoples, there was also the legacy of the classical world. The composite bow had been well known to the ancient Greeks, while subsequently the Roman Empire's absorption of Syria and the Levant and its strong eastern contacts with Persia and Mesopotamia helped to disseminate the composite bow widely throughout its provinces.[119] The Roman army itself had employed auxiliary archers armed with varieties of composite bows,[120] and it seems unlikely that this inheritance was ever wholly lost in the Mediterranean world. Knowledge of the composite bow may well have been reinforced by contact in war and trade with an expanding Islam from the seventh century, while it remained the main form of bow employed in Byzantine armies throughout the Middle Ages. Byzantine influence in southern Italy remained strong, and it was here, during their conquests of Apulia and Calabria from the early eleventh century, then of Muslim Sicily from 1060, that the Normans came into extended contact with the composite bow. Muslim archers wielding composite bows appear on the early twelfth-century bronze doors of Trani Cathedral and in other Siculo-Norman art (see p. 101),[121] while Peter of Eboli's *Carmen in honorem Augusti*, which records the conquest of Sicily by the German

emperor Henry IV in 1194, is an invaluable source for depictions of both composite bows and crossbows among the forces of Tancred, King of Sicily, and those of the emperor (see pp. 74, 103). Strikingly, the imperial archers, clearly labelled Bohemians in one illustration, also carry the same form of heavily recurved bow as their Sicilian opponents; if the artist is to be trusted, the presence of the composite bow in German forces may reflect the long influence of the Magyar horse-archers on the eastern marches of the empire.

The thirteenth century, however, witnesses a striking number of depictions of composite bows in illuminations or other media which, unlike Carolingian depictions of recurve bows, often appear less dependant on pre-existing artistic models.[122] The superb if now fragmentary statue of an archer, dating from the early thirteenth century, which once formed part of the façade of Ferrara Cathedral cannot but have been modelled on an actual composite weapon, while in the 1240s Matthew Paris, whom we have seen depicting longbows drawn to the ear, carefully portrayed what appear to be composite bows not only in the hands of the Saracens but also by one French archer at the battle of Bouvines in 1214 between the forces of Philip Augustus and the Emperor Otto IV.[123] Most remarkably, all of the bows (save for crossbows) depicted in the famous and near-contemporary Maciejowski Bible, produced in France in about 1250, are composite bows, drawn with fine detail and perspective and all shown drawn to the ear.[124] Used both on horseback and on foot, they are large weapons with a very thick belly, and with the limbs also terminating in the ears so characteristic of some composite bows. This strongly suggests that some composite bows were in use in French armies of the mid-thirteenth century, although how widespread and in what proportion to the self-bow we cannot say. Similarly, the fourteenth-century *Les Livres des Estoires dou Commencement dou Monde* depicts numerous archers, many wearing great hems, shooting composite bows, sometimes from the saddle. The weapon subsequently appears in numerous German and northern European woodcuts of the martyrdom of St Sebastian during the fifteenth century, and examples of the composite bow even appear in England; the magnificent stained-glass windows of the church at Fairford, dating from the early sixteenth century, contain the depiction of two archers with distinctive composite bows. The glass displays strong continental influence, and as the figures are among those representing persecutors of the Church their costume is a mixture of exotic and contemporary; one of the archers, for example, wears a gold decorated sallet, a mail shirt and a rich jack, as well as having at his waist a distinctive quiver, akin to those used by crossbowmen.[125]

It is thus possible that the experience of crusading stimulated the use of the composite bow in northern Europe

A finely rendered drawing of an archer, possibly a preparatory sketch for a painting of the martyrdom of St Sebastian, (?) French, late fourteenth century (Oxford, Christ Church Library, A.2). The type of bow intended here is unclear, though the pronounced swelling at the grip and the thickness of the limbs suggest a composite weapon. More certainly, the curved sword, the exotic head-dress and hairstyle, together with the quiver (more reminiscent of contemporary crossbowmen's quivers), indicate that the artist was seeking to suggest an eastern provenance for the archer. *(The Governing Body of Christ Church, Oxford)*

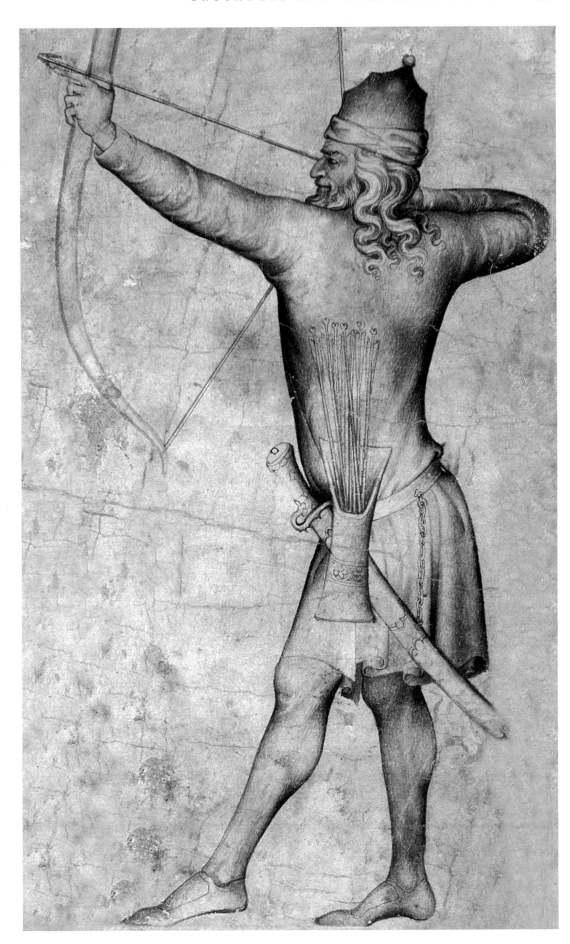

The Martyrdom of St Sebastian by Antonio di Jacapo Benci, known as Pollaiuolo, *c.* 1475. The two crossbowmen in the foreground span their weapons using a hook and pulley, which was more efficient than the more simple belt hook, while the archers draw composite bows with wide, flat limbs. *(National Gallery, London/Bridgeman Art Library)*

how, during a Turkish attack on the army of Baldwin and Bohemond in 1100, 'their bows and arrows failed them due to rain, for in those lands glue was used in making those weapons'.[128] The complexity of manufacture meant that costs would have been higher than for self-bows, for which good bow wood, whether indigenous or imported, was readily available. But in Italy and the Mediterranean world powerful cultural traditions ensured that, despite the capacity to export bowstaves of yew, the composite bow continued in use throughout the Middle Ages. In Italy it appears (with all due allowance given to the classical influences on Renaissance art) as the principal bow type in Italian painting and illumination until the sixteenth century. The martyrdom of St Sebastian by Antonio Pollaiulo (d. 1498) is an outstanding example, showing composite bows with wide, flat limbs being used in conjunction with crossbows. Still more significantly, central and eastern European kingdoms had for centuries been constantly exposed to a succession of enemies wielding various forms of the composite bow, of which the Mongols and the Ottomans were but the latest. The Hungarians still made use of horse-archers in their armies, as their Magyar ancestors had done, as did the Poles and Russians, while sustained Turkish influence on the borders of Christendom meant that the composite bow saw extensive use by a range of native and mercenary troops, both Christian and Muslim. At the great battle of Nicopolis in 1396, to give but one example, the allied army gathered against the Turks not only contained heavy cavalry from France, Burgundy and Hungary, but a large force of Hungarian horse-archers. And, with no little irony, it was to be a body of Serbian light cavalry – including horse-archers and fighting as auxiliaries for the Turks – who played a significant role in the ultimate defeat of their fellow Christians.[129]

Yet although the composite bow was never seriously threatened with replacement by the longbow, its military role was always overshadowed by the dominance of the crossbow, which was the weapon par excellence not only of the Genoese but also of the Pisans and other maritime city states. The crossbow, indeed, reigned supreme as the missile weapon of choice in Europe, and it is to the longbow's greatest rival that we now must turn.

Matthew Strickland

from the twelfth century onwards. The technology to make composite weapons was certainly known in the lands of the Angevin kings and in Capetian France,[126] for the specialists known variously as *balistarii*, *attilatores* and *ingeniatores*, who made and repaired the numerous crossbows stored in royal castles, were fashioning crossbow arms of composite materials as well as those simply of wood.[127] A number of factors, however, ensured that in Britain, France and much of northern Europe the use of the composite bow would remain comparatively limited. The climate was one such factor, for although composite bows were usually covered in leather or parchment to protect the materials beneath, rain could be a serious problem. Fulcher of Chartres records with satisfaction

The Reign of the Crossbow

he history of the crossbow and that of the longbow are inextricably linked. From at least the mid-tenth century, when the crossbow re-emerges in the narrative sources, both weapons had been frequently used in conjunction in siege operations and in engagements in the open field in western Europe as well as in the Latin East. Yet in the later twelfth and thirteenth centuries it is clear that it was the crossbow that reigned supreme as the missile weapon of choice not only in much of Europe but also in the lands of the Angevin kings of England. On the peripheries of the Anglo-Norman realm – in the marches, Wales and in Ireland – the longbow remained the ideal weapon for warfare in wooded, boggy or mountainous terrain against opponents lightly armed but swift of foot, and as we have seen Henry II and his sons readily deployed Welsh archers in their continental wars. Within England itself the longbow was the natural weapon of men from forest areas.[1] But for the Plantagenets and their Capetian rivals the *corps d'élite* of the infantry were crossbowmen, whether deployed as field forces or as garrisons in the numerous royal castles, defending against foreign attack from without or baronial rebellion from within. It was only from the late thirteenth and early fourteenth centuries, first with the massed deployment of the longbow, then with the evolution of the formidable tactical combination of dismounted knights and archers, that the emphasis of military archery in England and on the continent began radically to diverge. From then on, the longbow would become the mainstay of English infantry forces, while the crossbow remained the chief missile weapon for French and other European armies until the rise of the hand-gun. These two traditions were to clash head-on in the Hundred Years War,

A crossbowman, shooting from the shelter of a comrade's large shield, picks off defenders during an assault on a town, from the Maciejowski Bible, French, *c*. 1250 (New York, Pierpont Morgan Library, MS 638, f.10v, detail). He wears a heavy belt with a spanning hook, used in conjunction with the stirrup on the end of the bow's tiller. *(Pierpont Morgan Library, New York/Bridgeman Art Library)*

and at Crécy the rout of the Genoese crossbowmen by Edward III's archers painfully demonstrated the superiority of the rapid shooting longbow in the open field. How and why such a divergence occurred, why continental armies clung so resolutely to the crossbow, and the extent to which the armies of Burgundy and France *did* attempt to adopt the use of longbowmen *en masse* in the fifteenth century are questions fundamental to our study.

BALISTARII REGIS: ALL THE KING'S CROSSBOWMEN

Though major engagements in the field were comparatively rare in the Plantagenet lands during this period, the composition of field armies where known reveals the predominance of the crossbow. Crossbowmen formed a substantial element in the forces of King John on his expedition to Ireland in 1210, while the royalist army under William the Marshal which marched against the French and their rebel allies at Lincoln in 1217 comprised 406 knights and 317 crossbowmen.[2] Crossbowmen, many of whom were raised in Gascony, similarly formed a significant element of Henry III's infantry forces during the catastrophic Taillebourg campaign in 1242, when his Poitevin allies failed to hold a bridge over the Charente, exposing Henry's army to imminent defeat by a superior French army. Louis IX had quickly exploited this situation by rushing 500 of his own crossbowmen and a great number of infantry over the bridge to secure it, forcing Henry's army into a panicked flight to Saintes.[3] Units of Gascon crossbowmen served in Edward I's Welsh campaign of 1282–3 as part of a picked unit, and in Flanders in 1297 the king had a bodyguard of crossbowmen as well as archers.[4] In Scotland the force under Aymer de Valence which Edward I sent to put down Robert Bruce's rebellion in 1306 comprised 50 knights, 210 esquires, 140 crossbowmen and 1,960 infantry, many of whom were probably archers.[5] Edward also levied crossbowmen from the militias of English towns, as in 1277 when Winchester, Bristol and Gloucester sent 50–60 crossbowmen to a muster at Chester for service in Wales, and in 1295–6 when London furnished 500 foot-crossbowmen as part of the defence of the coasts.[6] It was envisaged that both archers and crossbowmen would be levied in large numbers from the southern counties for an expedition to France in 1295/6, but this never materialised.[7] And as late as 1314, following the catastrophe at Bannockburn, London, York, Lincoln and Northampton were ordered to furnish heavily armoured crossbowmen who would serve at the king's expense.[8]

Such a pattern was mirrored in Capetian armies. On the Norman border in 1202–3 Philip Augustus had a small but permanent army comprising 257 knights, 245 mounted serjeants, 71 mounted crossbowmen, 101 foot-crossbowmen and 1,608 foot-serjeants, together with some 300 *routiers* under the mercenary captain Cadoc.[9] Under Louis IX the significance of crossbowmen is highlighted by the king's creation of the office of the Grand Master of the Crossbowmen, who also commanded the engineers and artillerymen, while the prevalence of crossbowmen in Frankish armies in the east grew still more marked.[10] Some 4,000 crossbowmen had served on the Fifth Crusade (1217–21), where they played a key role.[11] A crusading confraternity, established at Châteaudun by Odo of Châteauroux for Louis IX's first crusade, was armed with crossbows, and the king probably took around 5,000 crossbowmen to Egypt with him in 1249.[12] While the troop numbers for Louis's great crusading expeditions can only be estimated, he spent the enormous sum of 39,000 livres on mounted crossbowmen and serjeants, and 60,000 livres on foot-crossbowmen and serjeants.[13] Crossbowmen were likewise among the 'French regiment' Louis left to aid in the defence of the Latin kingdom, while subsequent reinforcements from France in 1273 included 500 crossbowmen and 100 foot-archers.[14] Crossbowmen continued to form a key part of the forces of the military orders, with the Hospitallers similarly having the office of Master Crossbowman, while around the year 1260 the massive garrison of the great Hospitaller castle at Saphet included 50 knights, 30 brother serjeants, 50 turcopoles and 300 crossbowmen, as well as 820 workers and 400 slaves.[15] Similarly, the army which Louis's brother Charles of Anjou led through Italy in 1265 was reckoned to contain 6,000 horse, 600 mounted crossbowmen and several thousand foot, of which half were crossbowmen.[16]

The range and power of the crossbow meant that crossbowmen played an equally important role in war at sea, where ships' sides might offer both protection and a shooting platform.[17] During the later twelfth and thirteenth centuries it was crossbowmen who formed the main missile arm in the Angevin navy.[18] The crossbow was also the principal offensive weapon in the vessels of the Italian maritime states. In 1255 a Venetian code stipulated a set number of crossbows per size of ship for their defensive armament, and it has been argued that the deployment of such weapons, together with good defensive equipment for sailors and marines, played a significant role in Venice's development as a major naval power.[19] Similarly, there was an intimate connection between their maritime ventures and the prowess of the Genoese with the crossbow, with Genoa becoming known as one of the great centres for the manufacture of these weapons. It is thus unsurprising to find one Roger of Genoa in the service of King John, making and repairing royal crossbows.[20] During the Anglo-French war of 1294–8 Philip IV had galleys constructed by Genoese shipwrights at Marseilles and Normandy, and by 1295 a squadron of thirty was operating with other French vessels against the south coast of England.[21] The complement of crossbowmen aboard such Mediterranean galleys may be gauged by the fact that in 1258 there were 24 crossbowmen as well as crew in the Catalan galley *Bonanova*, while in 1323 galleys in the service of Aragon had around 30 crossbowmen in smaller galleys and some 40 in larger vessels.[22] Under Edward III longbowmen aboard ship were to out-shoot the Genoese at sea at Sluys in 1340, as they were to do on land at Crécy in 1346, but at sea the English forces contained crossbowmen as well as archers.[23] Indeed, the development of the cog with its high sides and prominent stern and forecastles provided an ideal fighting platform for crossbowmen, considerably offsetting their slow rate of shooting, and it is notable that though the English were eventually successful in naval engagements such as those in 1416 and 1417 they first sustained heavy casualties from the enemy crossbowmen.[24]

While some crossbowmen might be drawn from urban militias or local levies, many were professionals, often known personally to the kings who hired them, which suggests a high degree of individual skill. William le Breton, for example, says of Philip's crossbowmen that he had 'enriched them with manors, goods and money', and gives the names of some of the crossbowmen serving the king at the siege of Château Gaillard in 1203–4: Jordain, Paviot, Renaud Tatin, Pergias, Eldo and Clement Blondel.[25] Richard I granted land to one Turpin, his crossbowman, on 30 June 1190 at Vézelay, so it is likely he was one of those 'famous crossbowmen' Ambroise mentions as accompanying the king on crusade.[26] He was probably the same Turpin the *arbalistarius*, paid the goodly sum of 6*d* a day, who was sent with other members of Henry II's household to Ireland to assist his son John's expedition in 1184–5.[27] Some of those bearing the title *balistarius* were engineers who constructed and repaired the large *ballistae* and other siege engines kept in royal castles, men like Master Maurice, Master Ivo, Urric or Lupillin who played a crucial role in maintaining and operating the king's siege train.[28] Other *balistarii*, however, were certainly crossbowmen, and the rolls show royal gifts to them of horses, robes, oaks from the royal forests and sometimes even estates.[29] Henry III kept a small body of some 20 crossbowmen in his personal retinue, based at Westminster, while the constable of the king's crossbowmen in Gascony, Halingrat, was an important figure at court.[30] Matthew Paris recorded that one of those slain by the Welsh in 1245 was

'Raymond, a Gascon crossbowman, of whom the king used to make sport', revealing a close relationship between the king and his arbalisters.[31] Gascony, which throughout this period was ruled by the kings of England as its dukes, was a ready recruiting ground for crossbowmen.[32] Others were drawn from Anjou, Poitou, Flanders, Brittany and, owing to its proximity to the Gascon border, Spain.[33] Some came from still further afield. Genoese appear in Plantagenet service as early as the 1180s, while it was the skill with the crossbow of the Genoese and Pisan marines that significantly contributed to Richard's victory at Jaffa in 1192.[34] Following his return from crusade Richard even hired Frankish crossbowmen from Syria, whose prowess he had doubtless experienced there, with the Norman Exchequer recording payment to 'Peter de Tanentonne and Martin of Nazareth and their companions, crossbowmen'.[35] In John's reign we likewise find Peter the Saracen working at Northampton, making or repairing crossbows and drawing 6*d* a day.[36] The use of foreign troops was always an important element in the crown's defences against baronial rebellion, for provided their pay was readily forthcoming the loyalty of such mercenaries was rarely in doubt.

And wages were high. In 1198 crossbowmen in Normandy were receiving 4*s* a day.[37] Mounted crossbowmen in the forces of Philip Augustus received between 48 and 54 *deniers parisis*, while a mounted serjeant received only 36*d*, and similarly a foot-serjeant was paid only 8*d* in comparison to the 12 or 18*d* given to a foot-crossbowman.[38] This higher salary reflected not only their skill but the fact that they were often well equipped and had one or more mounts to provide for. Thus of a unit of 84 crossbowmen in John's service in 1200 no fewer than 26 had three horses each, 52 had two each, and seven had only one horse, indicating that there were distinct ranks within a given company.[39] Many illustrations depict crossbowmen as possessing a considerable degree of defensive armour, in contrast to the often lightly armed archers. The Maciejowski Bible of about 1250 depicts some crossbowmen in mail shirts and gambesons, with broad kettle hats or simple conical caps or *cervellières* (see p. 113), which accords closely with the description of the Frankish infantry on the Third Crusade given by Beha ad-Din.[40] In 1295 some 2,000 crossbows, 3,000 gorgets and 3,000 bascinets were collected at Toulouse and carted to Rouen and Paris, possibly intended for Philip III's invasion force against England.[41] By the turn of the thirteenth century not just stipendiaries but crossbowmen furnished by serjeantry tenure and urban militias were expected to be well equipped. A serjeant serving with a crossbow and a barded horse (*equus coopertis*), for example, appears among those proffering service at Carlisle in 1300, while in 1314 Edward II ordered London, York, Lincoln and Northampton to provide

Crossbowmen, well armed in mail, defend a ship during a naval engagement, from an Anglo-Norman French translation of Vegetius's *De Re Militari* made for the Lord Edward, *c.* 1265–72 (Cambridge, Fitzwilliam Museum, MS Marlay, Add. 1, f.86). *(Copyright of the Fitzwilliam Museum, University of Cambridge)*

crossbowmen well equipped with aketons, mail coats and bascinets of plate.[42] In 1351 King Jean of France issued an ordinance in which crossbowmen were required to have not only a crossbow and baldric (a spanning belt), but also 'plates', that is presumably body armour in the form of a 'pair of plates' or a brigandine, an iron cap (*cervellière*) and a gorget, and iron or leather arm defences, as well as a sword and knife.[43] In addition to their professionalism, the possession of this level of defensive armour was another reason why crossbowmen made good all-round heavy infantry.

How are we to explain this dominance of the crossbow, which, if the sources are not deceptive, appears to gather momentum in the second half of the twelfth century and to last in England well into the reign of Edward I? For undoubtedly the great military importance afforded to the crossbow, intimately linked to the predominance of siege warfare, goes far towards explaining the lack of prominence of the longbow in major field engagements in England and the continental lands of the Anglo-

Norman and Plantagenet kings before the fourteenth century. A considerable body of modern scholarship now exists on the weapon, whose significance in medieval Europe has become increasingly recognised.[44] But with the notable exception of Sir Ralph Payne-Gallwey, who produced one of the first serious studies of the crossbow in English, the crossbow was largely neglected by British historians of the later nineteenth and earlier twentieth centuries who were concentrating on the supposed genesis of the longbow and its apogee in the fourteenth and fifteenth centuries. This neglect was due to a combination of nationalistic prejudice, the concept of the 'development' from 'shortbow' to longbow, and a retrospective assessment of the poor military worth of the crossbow in the light of the Hundred Years War. Did not the triumph of the English longbowmen over the Genoese crossbowmen at Crécy demonstrate the clear superiority of the insular weapon? The crossbow, moreover, was seen as somehow distasteful, to be dismissed as mechanical, foreign and unsavoury, a weapon fit only for continental citizen militias or, still worse, for mercenary hirelings.

A DIABOLICAL WEAPON?

The crossbow's notoriety, it is true, had a venerable ancestry. Anna Comnena, perhaps with wishful thinking, viewed it as a barbarian weapon unknown to the civilised Byzantines, but she was not alone in regarding it as 'a truly diabolical weapon'.[45] For in 1139 the Second Lateran Council prohibited under pain of anathema the 'hateful and death-bringing art of crossbowmen' against fellow Christians.[46] Such sentiments were anticipated in a series of carvings from the early decades of the twelfth century,

found in the great pilgrimage churches on the way to Compostela (see p. 63), which depict demons spanning crossbows, while on the tympanum of St Foi at Conques (*c.* 1120s), the crossbow features as a fitting weapon for a demon among the legions of hell. The Church's ban of 1139 has often been regarded as an ecclesiastical reaction to a novel, lethal and underhand weapon.

Yet the crossbow was far from new in the 1130s, nor had it always been anathema to ecclesiastics; in the 1080s at least one

Christ with a hand-held crossbow as one of the Four Riders of the Apocalypse, from a Catalan copy of the Beatus of Liébana, *c.* 1086. *(Cathedral Library, Burgo de Osma, Soria/Institut Amatller d'Art Hispanic)*

Spanish illuminator had found nothing incongruous in having Christ himself wield a crossbow. Moreover, it is important to note that the Council's anathema extended equally to ordinary bows, and was thus an attempt to restrict the use of all missile weapons. As such, the Church's reaction in 1139 – which also included the prohibition of the tournament – may be seen as part of the wider movement of the Peace and Truce of God, by which the Church and secular rulers attempted to limit violence and bloodshed within Christendom and their own domains, caused in large part by feuding nobles. Thus between 1119 and 1124 Charles the Good, Count of Flanders, forbade the use of bows and arrows in his lands in order to enforce peace, while the German emperor Conrad III (1138–52) also prohibited crossbows.[47] Such secular legislation, however, was aimed primarily at curbing localised violence, brigandage and private war, rather than enforcing an absolute ban on missile weapons, and, as with other restrictions imposed by the Truce of God, it may be that the prohibition of missile weapons did not extend to the armed forces of the legitimate ruler entrusted to keep the peace. Equally, the ban has been seen as a means of limiting the potentially subversive impact of weapons available to the non-knightly class, and which seriously threatened the warrior elite in battle.[48]

Whatever the ideological or political reasons, however, behind the Church's prohibition in 1139, the essential military role of archers and crossbowmen ensured that the ban was almost universally ignored. Innocent III reissued the ban at the Fourth Lateran Council in 1215, which revealingly added that clerics were forbidden to command units of crossbowmen or mercenaries.[49] In theory, canon law forbade clerics to bear arms even on crusade, but in practice clergy are found plying crossbows against the infidel, such as at the siege of Acre in 1190 where 'there was also a certain priest who harassed the enemy constantly and tirelessly with shots from his crossbow'.[50] By the thirteenth century the papacy itself did not scruple to enlist the services of allies who employed crossbowmen, for the Lateran's prohibition of the crossbow was only for its use against catholics and good Christians, and its prevalence in the northern French armies operating in Languedoc against the Cathar heretics and their supporters was thus fully condoned. Moreover, as the papacy became increasingly embroiled in the politics and warfare of the Italian peninsula, notably against the Hohenstaufen, it was easy enough to proclaim campaigns against the enemies of St Peter as crusades, and the papacy accordingly saw nothing incongruous about maintaining crossbowmen in papal armies.[51] Meanwhile, academics and canon lawyers soon found ways to render the prohibition ineffectual for those not blessed with Rome's powers to bind and loose.[52]

Nevertheless, the prohibition could furnish a useful diplomatic stick with which to beat an opponent and to seize the moral high ground. Capetian apologists and at least one patriotic French historian (in 1916) might try to argue that the Church's ban had been observed by the pious Louis VII and would have been by Philip Augustus had not the widespread employment of mercenary crossbowmen by the unscrupulous Plantagenets Henry II and Richard I forced the Capetians reluctantly to follow suit.[53] Thus Philip Augustus's encomiast William le Breton exulted in Richard's death by a wound from a crossbow bolt, claiming it as a fitting irony since it was he who first introduced this dreadful weapon to the French.[54] Though demonstrably untrue – Louis VII is known to have employed crossbowmen as well as archers[55] – such an allegation made for a neat illustration of divine vengeance on the bloodstained and impious Plantagenet. This, however, was a game both sides could play; among a long list of grievances against the French king presented by Richard the Lionheart to Pope Innocent III in 1198 he complained that Philip had personally shot several of Richard's knights with a crossbow during the Lionheart's attack on Messina in 1191, despite the fact that Philip was supposed to be his ally and fellow crusader.[56] Intriguingly, moreover, Paris theologians in the circle of Peter the Chanter in the 1190s were

arguing that the crossbow could be employed against fellow Christians in the context of a just war.[57] It is tempting to regard this as an attempt to legitimise the extensive deployment of crossbowmen in Philip Augustus's struggle against his Angevin opponents.

To this ancient stigma of ecclesiastical censure, historians might add more contemporary prejudices. To those steeped in constitutional history the crossbow seemed irrevocably linked with the foreign hirelings who had supported King John in his tyranny. For had not Magna Carta, that great statement of the liberties of Englishmen, banned 'all those foreign knights, crossbowmen [balistarios], serjeants and mercenaries who have come with horses and arms to the harm of the kingdom'?[58] In reality, clause 51 of Magna Carta did not reflect a national distaste for the crossbow, but simply marked an attempt by the king's political opponents in 1215 to deprive him of some of his most reliable mercenary units and their captains who had risen to wealth and high office – too high for the liking of many – through service to the king. Only two years after the first issue of the Charter both the baronial forces and the royal forces which clashed at the second battle of Lincoln contained large numbers of crossbowmen, while as we have noted urban militias as well as stipendiary troops with this weapon were employed continuously throughout the reigns of Henry III and Edward I, the supposed 'father of the longbow'. Even when from the fourteenth century the longbow became the dominant missile arm in English armies, crossbows remained essential for siege warfare.[59]

More significantly, national pride in the achievements of the longbow might have as its corollary the denigration of the crossbow and those who used it. Even Sir Ralph Payne-Gallwey echoed nationalistic preconceptions when he noted, 'Our ancestors naturally despised the crossbow as a military weapon.'[60] For in disdaining to use this underhand mechanical device in favour of the longbow, a weapon of both skill and strength, the true English yeoman achieved a moral as well as physical superiority. Charles Ashdown, in his tellingly entitled *British and Foreign Arms and Armour* of 1919, took this view to its absurd extreme:

> There is little doubt that the crossbow was the ideal weapon for the ordinary soldier of an ordinary race, in as much as little intellect was required to direct the aim and little strength was necessary if the usual mechanical means were used to bend the bow. For efficient use of the longbow, on the contrary, a keen judgement was an absolute necessity, and it was only a race of considerable physical power that could put forth the strength and maintain the exertion which the longbow demanded. It is

undoubtedly a matter for national self-complacency to reflect upon the fact that while the British gradually discarded the crossbow and adopted the longbow almost entirely, the Continental nations proceeded in exactly the opposite direction.[61]

Such a caricature, however, hardly accords with the evidence. Though the crossbow certainly required less extended physical exertion than the longbow, particularly after the introduction of mechanical aids for spanning, its effective use in combat required skill and training. The Plantagenet, Capetian and Valois kings did not expend considerable sums on professional crossbowmen for nothing.

Yet though specious, such a theory fitted in well with the traditional interpretation of the shortbow and the 'development' of the longbow. Though Morris, Oman and others confidently assumed that the 'true' longbow was superior to the crossbow both in range and penetration – which was not necessarily the case, at least by the fifteenth century – they could not deny the evidence which pointed irrefutably to the predominance of the crossbow under the Angevins as the *arme blanche* of their stipendiary troops. The temporary dominance of the crossbow was, however, easily explained, for the weapon it outclassed until the later thirteenth century was merely the weak shortbow, whose insignificance was seemingly confirmed by its absence from Henry II's Assize of Arms of 1181.[62] Richard the Lionheart's predilection for the crossbow instead of six feet of good English yew could only be accounted for by the absence of this latter weapon. Richard was indeed a skilled marksman with the crossbow. At the siege of Acre in 1191 he delighted in picking off Turkish defenders with a crossbow, and among other victims claimed a Turkish emir who had presumed to disport himself on the walls wearing the captured armour of the recently slain Marshal of France, Alberic Clements. Even when lying sick of fever, he had himself carried on a litter within range to ply his crossbow against the Muslim defenders.[63] But he readily appreciated the value of archers, employing many, as we have seen, both on crusade and in his continental wars against Philip Augustus. In 1194 at the siege of Nottingham, held against him by the forces of his rebellious brother John, Richard personally slew a defending knight with a bow, after archers in the garrison had shot a knight standing next to the king, and he ordered 4,000 arrows to be sent to the besieging army in addition to shields and bolts.[64] And in Anglo-Norman operations in Wales and Ireland, as earlier at the battle of the Standard against the Scots, the value of longbowmen had been fully recognised.

There is no need for the myth of the shortbow and of the subsequent technical 'development' of the longbow to account for the crossbow's dominance in the Anglo-Norman and Angevin realms, for a number of key factors contributed to its ascendancy. First, the crossbow possessed not only great penetrative power but also the ability – unlike the longbow – to be steadily increased in power to counter developments in armour. Secondly, its use as a favoured weapon by professional troops meant that the skill and discipline of these stipendiary forces added to the innate value of the crossbow's ballistic properties. Thirdly, while the crossbow's slow rate of shooting was to prove a major disadvantage against English archers in the field during the Hundred Years War, it is important to realise that before the outbreak of the war in 1337 the tactical deployment of missilemen on the European battlefield meant that crossbowmen, used essentially as skirmishers or as a defensive screen for other forces, had rarely if ever been pitted against large formations of longbowmen in pitched battle, still less when the latter were deployed tactically in strong defensive positions as was to be the norm during the Hundred Years War. Fourthly, from the eleventh century onward the increasing ubiquity and growing sophistication of castles meant that sieges played a very significant role in warfare; and in defending or attacking strongholds, when speed of shooting was less important than it was in open battle, the crossbow's power and accuracy made it an ideal weapon. We have already discussed the professionalism of many crossbowmen. Now we must turn to the nature of the weapon, its use in siege warfare and its deployment in field engagements before 1337.

MANUFACTURE AND PERFORMANCE

It was the crossbow's great velocity and penetrative power that underpinned the enormous popularity of the weapon in medieval Europe. Muslims in the Holy Land particularly feared Frankish crossbowmen, and when in 1241 the Emperor Conrad IV drew up military measures to resist the Mongols it was surely the weapon's superior power that led him simply to state of the Christian infantry, 'Let them have crossbowmen.'[65]

Though in certain instances kings or their commanders might consciously seek to limit the fatalities inflicted by their crossbowmen, it was nevertheless the potential threat to knightly combatants by the crossbow that led to the high status of and military regard for these troops. We have already noted that by the time of Hastings and the First Crusade contemporaries had been struck by the awesome power of the

A crossbowman, whose tonsure suggests he is a cleric, spans a crossbow with the aid of a belt hook, from the Luttrell Psalter, English, *c.* 1320–30 (British Library, Add. MS 42130, f.56). Despite the increasing dominance of the longbow in English armies, the crossbow remained in use for siege warfare as well as for hunting and sport throughout the fourteenth and fifteenth centuries. *(British Library/Bridgeman Art Library)*

crossbow, and these were as yet weapons spanned only by hand or foot without mechanical aids. The record evidence which becomes increasingly available from the later twelfth and thirteenth centuries reveals that crossbows came in three basic types. In ascending order of size and power, there was the crossbow 'ad unum pedem' (literally, 'for one foot'), a larger size 'ad duos pedes' ('for two feet'), and crossbows 'ad turnum', spanned by a windlass, each of which required bolts of a differing size. Writing in about 1194, the Norman troubadour Ambroise mentions arbalists 'hand, wheel or twisted'.[66] With all types, the bow arm (known on crossbows as the lath) could be made either of wood (*de fusto*), whether of yew or elm,[67] or of horn (*de cornu*), that is of composite material with horn being usually, though not necessarily, the principal component.[68]

Though the distinction between crossbows 'ad unum pedem' or 'ad duos pedes' is often taken to refer to the fact that the latter weapon required not one but two feet to span it, the precise meaning of this designation remains unclear, and may have come to refer to the power and size of the bolt rather than the method of loading.[69] The crossbows described by Anna Comnena already required two feet for spanning, and one major development from the second half of the twelfth century

was the use of a special belt and hook which allowed the crossbowman to span his weapon while standing, and with only one foot. He placed one foot in a metal stirrup attached to the front of the stock, hooked the string over the claw attached to his belt and spanned the bow by straightening his back while pushing down on the stirrup with his leg.[70] Manuscript illuminations depict such crossbows, also referred to as crossbows 'ad estrif' or 'ad stritum', with increasing frequency during the thirteenth century.[71] These weapons have been estimated as having a maximum pull of about 330lb (150kg).[72] The larger crossbows 'ad duos pedes' may have been predominantly for siege use, and in some instances were spanned by using a combination of the old method of using both feet and the newer spanning hook and belt, a procedure which did not require a stirrup on the end of the tiller. The *Tabisirat*, a Muslim manual on arms written for Saladin by Mardi ibn al-Tarsusi in about 1180–90, describes this method. The bow 'is bent by the pressure of the two feet and the man with the strength of his back, because to draw it one needs a belt of ox-hide, well tanned and toughened, around the waist, at the end of which there are two iron hooks in which one puts the string. The man places his feet in the inside of the bow and pulls with his back the belt where the hooks are until the string reaches the latch of the guide [i.e. the crossbow nut]'.[73]

In 1304 Walter de Bedewynde, a royal clerk at Stirling, acknowledged receipt of 24 crossbows, four of which were of 'two feet', but also 24 baldrics – that is belts with spanning hooks – for the same, which confirms that such spanning belts were to be used with both sizes of weapon.[74] Weapons 'ad duos pedes' thus spanned may have had a pull of up to 460lb (209kg).[75] The earlier crossbows depicted in both the allegorical 'War of Cats and Mice' in the Johanneskapelle at Pürgg, of about 1160–3, and in the *Carmen in honorem Augusti* of Peter of Eboli of about 1197 (see pp. 74, 103), lack stirrups, and, as belt hooks are not in evidence, probably represent the earlier form of weapon. The records reveal that crossbows 'ad unum pedem' were the more numerous and less costly, though most castles contained a mixture of all types of weapon. In Europe crossbows came subsequently to be categorised in three basic sizes: full, half and quarter.[76]

Less ambiguous was the crossbow 'ad turnum', which was spanned by a windlass or winch. Some may conceivably have been large hand-held weapons, but before the fourteenth century, during which the windlass clearly appears on crossbows used in the field, such weapons were more probably large frame-mounted crossbows.[77] Some of these larger bows, such as those depicted in Walter de Milemete's *De Nobilitatibus, Sapientiis, et Prudentiis Regum*, written in about 1326–7, were spanned by means of a grapple and screw mounted inside the stock, with a large handle at the butt, while on others the spanning wheel was fitted laterally, as on the springald depicted in Edward II's charter for Carlisle in 1316 (see p. 176).[78] As this miniature reveals, such giant crossbows played an important role in the defence, as well as the attack, of castles.[79] Hence, for example, at Edward I's fortresses of Criccieth and Harlech in Wales, both situated on high coastal bluffs, such engines were probably used to cover the landing sites beneath the castle.[80] The great fortress of Krak des Chevaliers contains embrasures for such large frame-mounted bows, while in 1253 the defenders of Acre harassed Muslim attackers with these weapons. They could be used to defend field fortifications, as in 1219 when the Templars used one to repulse an Egyptian attack on the Christian camp on the Nile, and no doubt the Frankish lines of circumvallation at Acre between 1189 and 1191 were similarly equipped.[81] Their power, flat trajectory and range – greater than that of handbows – made them formidable anti-personnel weapons. During Edward I's siege of Stirling in 1304 Sir Thomas Gray was 'struck through the head below the eyes by the bolt of a springald'; he was initially taken for dead but recovered to survive his wound.[82] They could also be used to shoot fire arrows or other incendiary devices, as in 1194 when William de Mortemer, castellan of the great Norman border fortress of Verneuil, shot flaming bolts at the French army of Philip Augustus.[83]

The hand-held crossbow shot bolts or quarrels measuring on average 12in (30cm) and weighing between 1.5 and 5oz (42.5–142g), being shorter, thicker and heavier than ordinary arrows in order to withstand the enormous force exerted on release and the subsequent velocity.[84] The shaft often tapered from the butt-end to the bolt's heavy iron head, which lent the projectile the balance necessary because of its short length. Its thickness and shortness also meant that, unlike the longbow arrow, the shaft was less liable to break on impact. Because of the tremendous force exerted by the string, the shafts might be fletched with wood, horn, brass, leather or parchment instead of feathers. Bolt heads came in a variety of shapes including hunting broadheads, forkers for hamstringing game and blunt piles for birding or shooting smaller game.[85] But for warfare the most common form was the square-sectioned armour-piercing head, which gave the quarrel (Latin *quadrus*, 'a square', French *carré*) its name. With bolts, as with arrows, a lighter bolt achieves a greater range but, as it fails to absorb the maximum energy from the bow, distance is attained at the expense of penetrative power. A heavy bolt, by contrast, will have a shorter range, as a result of its lower exit velocity, but will be far more effective against armour.[86]

At least by the twelfth century, if not well before, crossbow bolts were capable of penetrating mail and its additional

defences, as witness the long list of rulers or nobles killed or fatally wounded by the weapon. Thus for instance, the crossbow claimed the lives of Matthew, Count of Boulogne, who died after being struck below the knee at the siege of Drincourt in 1173, Richard the Lionheart at Chaluz Chabrol in 1199, Eustace de Vesci, one of the leading baronial rebels against John, who was struck in the head by a bolt at the siege of Barnard Castle in 1216, and one of Edward I's knights during the storming of Berwick in 1296.[87] Others were severely injured. At Toulouse in 1218 Guy de Montfort's horse was hit by a bolt 'which drove half its length into its brain', before he himself was wounded in the groin, 'leaving the steel deep in his flesh'.[88] At the siege of Bedford in 1224 Richard de Argentan was severely wounded in the stomach when a bolt went through his armour, and six other knights were slain by bolts, while in a skirmish outside Monmouth Castle in 1233 Baldwin of Guisnes was shot in the chest by a crossbowman.[89]

Yet beyond the evidence of the chroniclers, assessing the actual power of medieval crossbows is problematic. By the twelfth century vernacular sources frequently mention distances measured as 'arbalestrée', that is by the shot of a crossbow, though what the exact distance was is unknown.[90] In Germany in 1232 the same distance could be described as 'the distance of a crossbow shot' ('*ad tractum ballistae*') by one witness and by another as the distance of two bowshots (*quantum bis iacere possit arcus*), though such estimates naturally were only a rough approximation of distance.[91] Only a comparatively small number of crossbows dating from before the fifteenth century are extant, and few of these can be tested.[92] Several modern experiments have either used weapons that do not approximate to military types of medieval crossbows with heavy poundages, or have used light bolts instead of the heavier armour-piercing types, with a concomitant effect on potential velocities.[93] Moreover, as the record evidence indicates, there were at any given time a variety of crossbow sizes and of methods of manufacture, which would have produced a significant range in performance. Crossbows of both 'one foot' and 'two feet' continued to be used into the sixteenth century, while lathes of wood were still manufactured alongside the more powerful but expensive composite bows. Similarly, composite and wooden lathes continued well after the appearance of the steel-bowed crossbow in the fourteenth century.[94] Early hand-spanned weapons may have had a poundage of around 150lb (68kg),[95] a draw-weight which was already equivalent to the middle to upper range poundages of the *Mary Rose* bows. This at least is the estimated strength of a large but probably hand-held crossbow whose yew lath was found in the moat of Berkhampstead Castle, probably dating to the siege of this castle by Prince Louis's forces in 1216.[96]

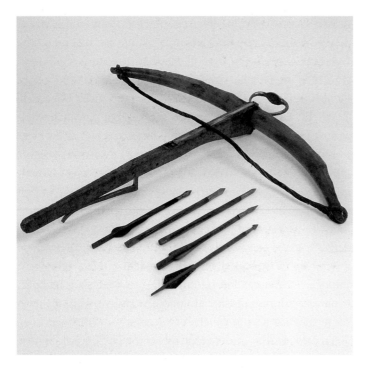

A rare surviving example of a crossbow with a bow (or lath) of yew and a walnut tiller (Glasgow Museums, E. 1939. 65.sn). Its date is unknown, but may possibly be as early as the fourteenth century. The roughly fashioned stirrup is hinged, allowing the bow to be removed. Note the knots in the bow, which have been left proud for strength as well as a form of decoration. Also shown are bolts with a variety of armour-piercing heads, and fletchings of wood or leather. *(Glasgow Museums)*

Crossbows constructed with composite bow-arms could be made far more powerful than those made simply of wood, but both types could be increased in strength well beyond the ability to be drawn by hand. The battle of Crécy is often taken as clear evidence that the longbow outranged the crossbow of the 1340s, yet we must exercise a degree of caution in dealing with the sources for this famous incident. While the valuable English chronicler Geoffrey le Baker believed the bolts of the Genoese fell short, few if any of the more contemporary and reliable French accounts mention this phenomenon, nor does the well-informed Italian chronicler Villani. Highly implausible tales that the crossbow strings of the Genoese became soaked by a rain shower and thus were rendered ineffectual must be seen as part of an attempt by subsequent French chroniclers to explain the catastrophic defeat of their army, largely by heaping blame on the hapless Genoese.[97] It is more likely that the Genoese were simply outshot by the rapid and deadly volleys of the longbowmen.

The spread of steel bows during the fourteenth century considerably enhanced the crossbow's performance. Little is known about the chronology of dissemination of this development, but one of the earliest references to steel crossbows comes in 1316 from the inventory of articles plundered from Countess Matilda of Artois by her nephew Robert, among which was 'a crossbow of gilded steel valued at 100 sous'.[98] This was clearly a deluxe weapon, probably for the hunt, but while steel-bowed crossbows may have been initially costly, their use became increasingly widespread as military weapons by the later fourteenth century. It has been demonstrated that shot at a 45-degree angle the average military crossbow of the fifteenth century could attain a maximum range of 370–80 yards (338–47m), though the effective aim was perhaps around 220 yards (201m).[99] If the composite crossbow was outranged in 1346, it seems unlikely that the same phenomenon would have occurred at Agincourt, had the French chosen to deploy their considerable numbers of crossbowmen in an effective manner.[100] As weapons became more powerful, however, so loading became slower, a factor which was comparatively unimportant in siege warfare but of much greater significance in field operations.[101] In 1417, prior to his second invasion of France, Henry V himself had specialist craftsmen brought to England from St Sever in Normandy to make steel bows for crossbows, still regarded as essential for siege work.[102] Such steel-bowed weapons, however, were not without their drawbacks. Poorly tempered bows might lose their strength or shed splinters of metal,[103] while cold weather could adversely affect their performance, so that for winter conditions the composite crossbow was often preferred. Steel bows, moreover, demonstrate a marked inefficiency in relation to their draw-weight, as their speed of recovery from the draw is slow: tests showed the efficiency of a heavy hunting crossbow to be only 43 per cent.[104] Nevertheless, bow-arms made of hardened and tempered steel meant that the power of crossbows could be greatly increased.

The later fourteenth century thus saw the emergence of the cranequin (see pp. 12, 226), a highly effective form of ratchet, appearing from the 1370s, and the simple but effective 'goat's-foot' lever, which like the cranequin had the great advantage of allowing the crossbow to be spanned much more easily while on horseback, and could be used on crossbows of up to 300lb (135kg) or more.[105] Similarly, the simple belt-hook gave way to the 'Samson belt', a more efficient but still comparatively cheap hook and pulley device which hung as before from the archer's belt. This might take various forms, but that consisting of a broad strap and roller doubled the effective spanning power of the crossbowman (see p. 112).[106] In addition, the windlass, long used to span siege crossbows, now became increasingly common for spanning hand-held crossbows used in the field, with one of the earliest references to such a device occurring in 1297.[107] Though cumbersome, the windlass could span bows of enormous poundages, for it was mechanically very efficient, though the cranequin was still more so.[108] By the fifteenth century a crossbow spanned by means of a cranequin might have very heavy draw-weights. A hunting crossbow in the Metropolitan Museum in New York has a pull of 1,090lb (490kg), while a much less powerful weapon with a draw-weight of over 400lb (181kg) achieved a range of around 500 yards (457m).[109] The increase in draw-weight, however, has diminishing returns. To double a crossbow's draw-weight does not increase its range or velocity by double but only by around a quarter, though an increased draw-weight does allow a heavier bolt to be shot without loss of range.[110] Nevertheless, some indication of the power of these weapons is indicated by the fact that using a large military crossbow of the later fifteenth or early sixteenth century, which was spanned by a windlass and had an enormous pull of 1,200lb (544kg, or over half a ton), Payne-Gallwey shot a bolt over 440 yards (402m) over the Menai Straits between Anglesey and the Welsh mainland.[111]

Thus despite the major drawback of its slow rate of shooting, the crossbow would always have one fundamental advantage over the longbow. Whereas a trained archer might draw a bow of 150lb (68kg) or even heavier weights, there was

nevertheless a physical limit imposed by the human body. It is clear that the poundages of the heaviest *Mary Rose* bows were reaching the absolute limits of performance, and as we have seen the skeletons of the archers on board reveal the deformities caused by continually drawing such massive bow weights.[112] Yet with a crossbow the draw-weight could be repeatedly increased with the development of effective mechanical devices to assist loading. This meant that in terms of power and penetration the crossbow was able to compete in the arms race against better defensive armour during the later fourteenth and fifteenth centuries in a way that the longbow could not. By the fifteenth century it was primarily the crossbow that was used to proof armour. In 1448 the statutes of the guild of armourers distinguished two types of proof, one by hand-drawn crossbows and longbows, and the other by more powerful windlass-spanned crossbows.[113] As has been well observed, 'To possess an armour stamped with a double armourer's mark, tested by crossbow at point-blank range, was clearly the best guarantee against sudden death in warfare' – or perhaps more correctly, this was *believed* to be the best guarantee, for metallurgical tests have clearly shown there was no correlation whatever between two armourer's marks and better quality armour.[114]

CASTLES AND CROSSBOWMEN

If the crossbow was at a disadvantage in open battle, it was supremely suited to the castle-based hostilities so central to medieval warfare. Fortifications had long played a major role in hostilities but before the later tenth century the majority of these had been large, communal defences covering a considerable ground area and needing substantial numbers of defenders. By contrast, the castles which increasingly spread through Europe from about 1000 were often far smaller, designed to protect a local lord and his retinue. Their design permitted effective defence by a comparatively small number of troops, and it has been suggested that it was the growing military importance of such structures that led to the increasing prominence of the crossbow in warfare.[115]

The rapid rate of shooting achieved by the longbow made it excellent for harassing the defenders during an assault, and for this reason archers were often used in conjunction with crossbowmen. In 1205, for example, Philip Augustus summoned horsed archers as well as knights and infantry for his attack on the great fortress of Loches in Anjou.[116] Archers are frequently to be found operating with crossbowmen in the mobile siege towers or belfreys which over-topped the walls of a castle, allowing the besieger's archers to sweep the enemy

ramparts with arrow-shot. At both the siege of Bedford in 1224 and that of Kenilworth in 1266 Henry III used two great belfries filled with archers and crossbowmen.[117] But for the often prolonged hostilities of a siege the crossbow came into its own. For when used behind the cover of ramparts and embrasures, or in attack from behind protective mantlets, the crossbow's chief defect – its slow speed of shooting – was far less of a disadvantage. The crossbow's design, moreover, meant that it was often better suited than the longbow to the confined spaces of castles' towers or fighting galleries. Even in some of the castles built by native Welsh princes during the thirteenth century the design of the embrasures seems to have been primarily for crossbowmen, as at Castell y Bere, begun by Llewelyn ab Iorwerth in 1221, and at Criccieth.[118] The Welsh can be found using crossbows in siege warfare as early as the siege of Dinefwr in 1213, and crossbowmen, probably stipendiaries, were employed by the rulers of Gwynedd.[119]

The one disadvantage the crossbow faced in defence was that when shooting downward at a steep angle the bolt might drop off the crossbow, for it simply sat, sometimes in a groove, on the top of the stock. By contrast, the longbow had no such

ꝛ q garda les citeins.
L es uenes. ꝛ les anciens.
P dafanse. ꝛ p la diutorre.
D e la fort tor. du capitorre.
⸿ poꝛ ce ausi uorrent.
Ql' meuz. ꝛ plꝰ gloꝛiousemt.
a pꝛeuenir de tor le mõde.

ꝛ mlt bone. ꝛ mlt ardauble.
⸿ e q̃ le translate ausimt.
L e referai mlt henu.
I e sai ce. q̃ plꝰ fort a fauc.
S oit ce q̃ des autours a trauc.
ꝛ e du recont p parole.
A insi q lon qte une fole.

A thirteenth-century depiction of a siege, in which a castle is assaulted by a variety of siege machines, including a ram, a 'cat' to cover sappers undermining the base of the wall, and a siege tower or belfrey (Paris, Bibliothèque Nationale, MS fr. 1604, f.57v). The crossbow was a siege weapon par excellence, and here crossbowmen assist in both attack and defence.
(*Bibliothèque Nationale, Paris*)

problem with plunging shots, provided that the embrasures allowed sufficient vertical room for the bow arms.[120] Nevertheless, unlike a longbowman who had to keep his weapon at the draw to aim and shoot, the crossbowman had the great advantage that his weapon could be pre-spanned and loaded, thus making the weapon very accurate in good hands. Roger Ascham noted the problem of the draw for a longbowman: 'Holdynge must not be longe, for it bothe putteth a bow in jeopardy, and also marreth a mans shoote.'[121] But the crossbowman could concentrate on taking aim without physical exertion, could use a wall or embrasure as a rest if need be to offset the heaviness of the weapon, and could shoot without undue movement should stealth be required.

It is probably no coincidence that some of our earliest references to the crossbow show it as a key weapon of defence in fortifications.[122]

From the second half of the twelfth century major developments in the art of fortification occurred which served further to enhance the defensive potential of archery. Provision for longbowmen was by no means neglected, but as the records for the supply of crossbows and their ammunition in royal castles so forcefully reveal it was crossbowmen who were intended as the mainstay of garrisons in Angevin and Capetian fortresses. From 1154 onwards the Pipe Rolls and other records of the Angevin kings refer frequently to units of crossbowmen serving in royal garrisons, sometimes in considerable numbers, but always more consistently than archers. Similarly, the intimate connection between crossbowmen and castles is well demonstrated by the numerous details furnished by the records of the manufacture, repair and storage of crossbows and bolts in royal castles.[123] Both the Angevins and the Capetians kept large numbers of crossbows and quarrels stored in key castles throughout their realms, and issued these to the crossbowmen in their pay. A list of munitions stored in 32 strongholds in the Capetian demesne between 1200 and 1202 records some 278 crossbows of varying sizes and 265,960 bolts, with Gisors, Pacy and Evreux forming the main arsenals on the Norman border.[124]

After the loss of Normandy to Philip in 1204 the Tower of London served as the principal place of manufacture and repair of crossbows for the Angevin kings. In 1258 the wages are recorded of Henry Teutonicus, 'maker of the king's crossbows' (*factor balistarum regis*), while in the 1240s Philip le Convers had received 4½*d* a day for repairing crossbows.[125] Crossbows could be sent to the Tower for repair, such as the 21 crossbows dispatched by the constable of Dover in 1229, or skilled 'engineers' (*ingeniatores*) might tour royal castles, as did Master Gerard who repaired the crossbows in the castles at Newcastle and Bamburgh.[126] Records show regular purchases of glue, horn and sinew to make or repair bows, together with material for bowstrings.[127] In 1242 Bertram de Cryoyl was ordered to test all the crossbows in Dover and the Tower so that the king could be confident that they worked effectively.[128] Such was the military significance of crossbows to the effective defence of royal castles that the king was quick to buy up supplies which became available on the death of a baron. In 1233, for example, Henry III ordered the crossbows of William Briwerre in Bridgnorth Castle to be assessed for purchase, and likewise those of the Earl of Chester in his Norman castle of St James de Beuvron.[129] Equally, however, gifts of crossbows or of supplies of bolts might be granted by the king from his stores as a mark of favour.

In England a number of castles served as principal strategic supply bases for the distribution of ammunition; Chester and Hereford served as major depots for the Welsh marches, Nottingham for the Midlands, Bristol, Corfe and Windsor for the south. The chief place of manufacture for quarrels was the castle of St Briavels in the Forest of Dean, where iron and wood for smelting, as well as for the supply of shafts, were plentiful.[130] From here, the castle's constable dispatched large quantities of bolts, transported packed into barrels, to royal castles or to the king's forces.[131] The output was prodigious. John Malemort, a master quarrel-maker resident at St Briavels, was paid the high daily wage of 7½*d* for making 100 quarrels a day and an extra 3*d* for feathering them, a number which suggests some form of production line and the aid of assistants.[132] In 1256 he was estimated to have made some 25,000 quarrels.[133]

Demand for bolts, however, was as enormous. Despite the comparatively slow shooting rate of a crossbow compared to a longbow, the number of bolts a crossbowman might expend in action, particularly during a siege, could be considerable. The injunction of Thibaud, Count of Champagne, in 1231 that

'everyone in my community of St-Florentin who is worth 20 pounds shall have a crossbow in his house and up to fifty quarrels',[134] indicates this to be the maximum that an archer could be expected to supply himself, and that thereafter more bolts would be supplied by the lord. For John's great continental campaign of 1214 30,000 bolts were shipped from Portsmouth.[135] In 1224 the young Henry III laid siege to Bedford Castle, held against him by the men of Fawkes de Bréauté, one of John's loyal captains who had fallen out with the new regime.[136] In addition to mangonels, stone-throwers, large siege ballistas[137] and a belfry drawn from various arsenals, the king ordered the castellan of Corfe to dispatch 12,000 bolts for 'one foot' crossbows and 3,000 for 'two feet' crossbows.[138] The constable of St Briavels sent a further 2,000, transported by four men and four horses, presumably pack animals.[139] The sheriffs of London were instructed to hire five or six smiths to work day and night, and their labours produced 2,300 bolts at the cost of £2 1*s* 8*d*, while another 4,000 were purchased for £3 6*s* 8*d*.[140] Remarkably, these supplies were still deemed insufficient, and more were ordered:

> The King to his bailiffs of Northampton, greeting. We command you that as you love Us and Our honour, as soon as these letters, that you cause to be made both by day and by night, by all the smiths of the town of Northampton who are skilled in the art of making quarrels, four thousand quarrels, and that you cause them to be well barbed (*inflecheari*) and winged (*inpennari*) and that you send them with all speed to Bedford.[141]

Similar quantities might be ordered to stock royal castles for their own defence and to issue to field forces when the need arose. In 1277, in preparation for his first Welsh campaign, Edward I ordered 200,000 bolts to be made at St Briavels.[142] The accounts of the constable of Bristol Castle similarly reveal the massive quantities of crossbow bolts which could be required, as in 1296 when expenses were recorded for the transportation of 50,000 bolts, received from the constable of St Briavels, from the castle to the harbour.[143] In 1297 100,000 bolts were collected in chests at Bristol and transported by sea to Edward's great new fortress at Caernarfon.[144] The same year a large shipment of munitions to Gascony to stock the strategically vital town of Bourg and other English-held strongholds included 3 springalds with 500 bolts; 12 'great crossbows' with windlasses and 36 other crossbows; 36 buckets with 1,000 bolts in each and 24 with 500 each; four coffers with 4,000 bolts with brass flights; and one coffer with 60 bows and bow strings.[145] By contrast, direct royal

An aerial view of Framlingham Castle, Suffolk, as rebuilt from the 1180s by Roger Bigod II. The castle was unusual in having no keep, and its defences consist of a series of towers flanking the curtain walls, with careful provision for archers and crossbowmen to sweep the ground approached by any attackers. *(Cambridge University Collection)*

production of arrows was limited indeed, for infantry summoned to the royal host were expected to bring their own bows and arrows. Some serjeantry tenures were held by the duty of supplying a number of arrows annually, such as the 200 arrows rendered to the king at St Briavels by Thomas de Laforge – whose name implies he was a smith – for lands he held.[146] But it was usually only on occasions of major sieges that the king ordered the wholesale purchase or manufacture of arrows. During Edward I's great siege of Stirling in 1304, for example, four arrow-smiths were employed during June and July, and bows and arrows were ordered from the counties: from Yorkshire 320, from Newcastle 59, from Lincolnshire 286 bows and 1,200 arrows, and from London 130 bows and 200 quivers of arrows – small quantities indeed.[147] All this would dramatically change in the fourteenth century, but before then it is crossbows and quarrels that fill the royal accounts.

TOWERS, LOOPS AND EMBRASURES: THE GROWING ART OF DEFENCE

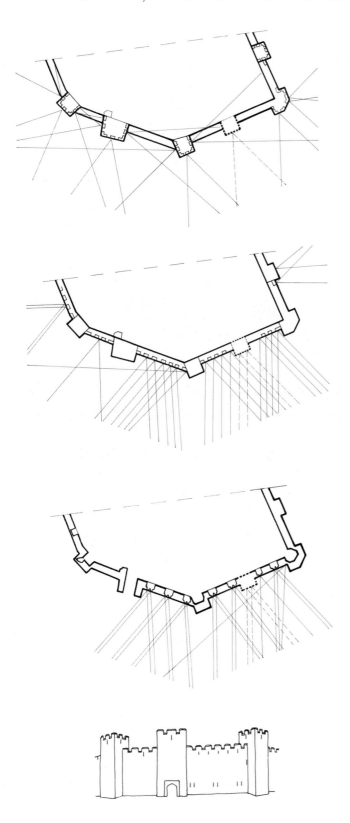

Comparative fields of shot from the three levels of loops on the south/south-east curtain wall of Framlingham Castle, covering the main approach to the castle. The later twelfth century witnessed an increasing sophistication in the planning for defensive archery in fortifications. *(Derek Renn/English Heritage)*

Castles themselves were evolving rapidly to exploit the defensive potential of crossbowmen and archers. The extent of provision for arrow-loops in most castles before the mid-twelfth century is uncertain, for the majority of fortifications were constructed of earth and timber and thus their wooden defences and superstructures have not survived. Nevertheless, one should not underestimate the sophistication of medieval carpentry, and artists' reconstructions of early Norman castles in Britain such as Hen Domen or Stafford (see p. 73) now envisage curtain walls with numerous loops, brattices or pierced shutters along the wall-walks, and even flanking towers of wood.[148] By contrast, in the great keeps of this period, whose primary role is increasingly being interpreted as domestic and residential rather than military, the majority of openings would appear to be only windows rather than defensive embrasures. In time of war wooden hoarding, doubtless equipped with loops, would have been constructed around the tops of such keeps, to furnish defenders with a fighting platform that overhung the base of the walls.[149] With the development of stone curtain walls, which increasingly came to replace earlier palisades of timber during the twelfth century, the process of more systematic defensive provision becomes easier to trace, though before the development of stone machicolations wooden hoarding was often still erected on stone curtains to provide a more effective fighting gallery.[150]

Though late Roman defences such as the Saxon Shore forts offered medieval builders extant examples of rounded mural towers for gates and at intervals along walls, thus allowing defenders to sweep the base of the curtain with missiles, their re-adoption was surprisingly slow. Some early stone curtains were strengthened with rectangular mural towers, as at Richmond and Ludlow, but provision for arrow-loops was slight or non-existent, with defence being essentially restricted to the wall-head.[151] By the reign of Henry II (1154–89), however, the use of square stone flanking towers pierced with arrow-loops on curtain walls was spreading. An early example, Orford, has now lost its curtain and towers, but it was probably the model for the outer defences of the great castle at Framlingham, built by Roger Bigod, Earl of Norfolk, in the 1180s, which survive in excellent condition. The curtain is defended by thirteen rectangular, open-backed towers, pierced on each of their three faces by arrow-loops immediately beneath the crenellations, designed to cover both the wall-walk and the base of the walls.[152] Further loops occur along the wall-walk itself, but the most remarkable feature of Framlingham is the powerful defensive provision for the south-east sector of the castle. Here, on the most vulnerable approach to the castle and to its main

entrance tower, there was not only a row of slits beneath the merlons of the wall-head but also a series of casemates some 6 feet above ground level along the curtain wall, housing pairs of arrow-loops (see p. 128). These casemates seem to have been designed for longbowmen, not crossbowmen, for they are very restricted laterally but not vertically, while the loops in the wall-head itself were far more suitable for crossbowmen. Taken together, these defences enabled the defenders to provide a withering barrage, and mapping the possible fields of shot demonstrates the relative sophistication attained in castle defence by this period.[153]

Embrasures with paired loops similar to those at Framlingham are found in the contemporary castles of Gisors, Carrickfergus and Dover, all dating from the 1180s, suggesting that systematic archery provision was becoming a standard feature of royal castles, as was the increasing provision of flanking towers with loops.[154] Having close analogies with classical and Byzantine types of arrow-loop, and possibly influenced by Frankish military architecture in Outremer, loops set within embrasures in the thickness of the wall are characteristic of fortifications within the Plantagenet realms.[155] By contrast, arrow-loops in the defences built between 1190 and 1225 by Philip Augustus of France were narrow and more restricted, being formed at the apex of a triangular embrasure, a design which sacrificed a wider field of shot for greater structural strength in the walls. Nevertheless, by the second half of the thirteenth century French royal military architecture had also adopted loops with broader embrasures, recognising their greater efficacy for use by crossbowmen.[156]

An equally remarkable example of the provision for concentrated shooting is provided by the Avranches Tower, a pillbox-like fortification constructed by Henry II's masons in the 1180s at Dover Castle, 'the key to England', in order to guard the outer curtain to the east of the great keep and its inner curtain, and to block the former entrance to the castle. This great polygonal tower, together with its 'traverse' or adjoining curtain with towers, bristles with loops, but was clearly designed only for crossbows owing to the loops' restricted vertical space. Their cramped grouping into pairs or threes indicates that one crossbowmen was assigned to each set of slits, giving him a varied field of view.[157] Dover itself provides an early instance of the concept of concentric defence, whereby the combination of a lower outer curtain wall with a higher inner curtain and still higher keep allowed defenders on all sets of walls to shoot simultaneously, thus increasing the shotpower encountered by attackers.[158] The thirteenth century witnessed a rapid development in the art of defence and

Opposite, top: The exterior of the southern curtain wall flanking the main gate at Framlingham, showing the extensive provision of loops at the tops of the towers, at the wall walk and at the lower-wall level. *(M. Strickland)*

Opposite, bottom: Embrasures with paired loops for archers, as seen from within the south curtain wall of Framlingham Castle, 1180s. *(M. Strickland)*

Above, right: White Castle, Gwent, as rebuilt by the English crown from the 1260s. The existing twelfth-century curtain walls were strengthened with large flanking towers and a powerful twin-towered gatehouse. *(M. Strickland)*

Right: The south-east curtain of White Castle, showing the distinctive arrow-loops with staggered horizontal slits, providing a combination of visibility with greater protection to the defending archers. The extent to which these carefully sited arrow-loops were felt to enhance the castle's defences is suggested by the fact that the earlier Norman keep was pulled down to make way for this new section of curtain wall with its flanking towers. *(M. Strickland)*

increasingly elaborate provision for defensive archery, reaching its apogee in the series of great castles built by Edward I from 1277 to secure his conquest of North Wales. The use of round or D-shaped mural towers containing embrasures for archers allowed the defenders to command the length of the walls. At the castle of Le Coudray Salbart in Poitou, whose construction in the first two decades of the thirteenth century was subsidised by the Angevin kings, the arc of view provided by such towers was augmented by the provision of shooting galleries for archers in the thickness of the curtain itself, an advanced defensive feature that would reach its most sophisticated expression at Edward I's Caernarfon.[159] Prior to the construction of Edward's great series of castles in North Wales, however, the great marcher lord Gilbert de Clare had, at Caerphilly in Glamorgan, built one of the most powerful castles yet seen. Designed as a response to the growing power of Llewelyn ap Gruffyd, Prince of Gwynedd, and raised with incredible speed between 1268 and 1271, Caerphilly was

defended not only by artificial lakes retained by a fortified dam but by highly developed concentric fortification. The central area of the castle consisted of a curtain wall strengthened by four large corner towers and two powerful twin-towered gate-houses, all generously provisioned with loops which allowed the defenders to shoot over the heads of those manning the lower curtain wall which formed the outer enclosure; any attackers could thus be exposed to a withering barrage from the garrison's crossbowmen and archers.[160]

Few castles were, however, built entirely *de novo*, and the desire for greater defensive power can also be seen in the upgrading of existing defences. Thus, for instance, the keep of Rochester Castle, damaged when King John had mined the south corner of the great tower keep in 1215, was subsequently repaired and further protected by a powerful two-storey drum tower, pierced with a series of arrow-loops with deep embrasures.[161] At White Castle, near Llantilio Crosseny in Gwent, Edward I replaced a small square keep and simple curtain wall with a twin-towered gatehouse, so characteristic a feature of castle design from the thirteenth century, and with flanking towers and curtains pierced with loops designed to give maximum field of view and to create an efficient 'beaten

Caernarfon Castle, begun by Edward I in 1283, seen from across the River Seiont. The triple rows of arrow-loops in the curtain walls are clearly visible, while the towers are equally well supplied with loops. *(© Dave Bartruff/Corbis)*

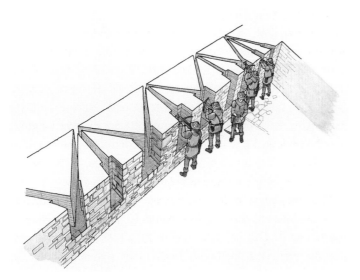

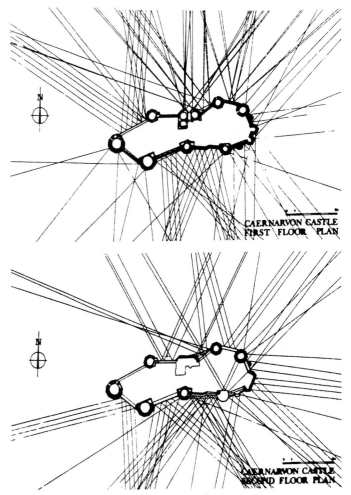

Above: A reconstruction by Chris Jones-Jenkins of the distinctive triple arrow-loops on the curtain walls flanking the Granary tower at Caernarfon Castle, part of the building phase dating from 1296 to 1323. *(Chris Jones-Jenkins/CADW)*

Right: Caernarfon Castle, mapping the possible arcs of shot from the loops of the curtain walls. The ability to deliver such a withering barrage, however, depended on the strength of the garrison, whose numbers were often remarkably small for such a great fortification. *(University of Liverpool)*

zone' with little dead ground.[162] The loops themselves are of an advanced design, with a larger opening or oillet at the base and staggered cross-slits to improve the archer's visibility. Experiments at White Castle have shown that bowmen did not stand in the embrasure itself close up to the loop – the length of a longbow makes this impossible, while for a crossbowman visibility would be restricted. Instead, the archers stood well back in order to gain a better field of vision and, for a longbow, to allow for the yaw or initial swerving of an arrow for the first 25 feet (8m) or so of its flight.[163] Such positioning was also safer, as it was quite possible for attackers to shoot into the castle's arrow slits; tests showed that at the comparatively close range of 25 yards (30m), 30 per cent of arrows shot by modern archers at a loop entered the slit. These considerations probably explain the staggering of the cross-slits, which considerably reduces the chances of enemy arrows entering the loop, in comparison to the more common cruciform slit, which offered an attacking archer a better target.[164]

Where he was in a position to build anew, Edward and his master masons constructed castles with a range of designs that blended military dictates with those of residential provision and imperial symbolism.[165] At Conwy, begun in 1283, the castle was deliberately built on the site of the dynastic monastery of the princes of Gwynedd, and such a political statement was felt to outweigh a number of disadvantages of the site, including large

areas of dead ground. To compensate for this the north curtain, which was the most vulnerable side, had six embrasures at ground level, supplemented by loops in the four great towers along its length (see p. 155). The merlons of the wall-head were pierced with alternate high and low loops, with those of the towers covering the courtyard within as well as the ground outside the castle.[166] The magnificent town walls of Conwy, constructed between 1283 and 1286, were also abundantly provided with arrow-loops, with no fewer than 480 slits piercing the merlons along the curtain itself, with the 3 twin-towered gates and the 21 flanking towers placed at roughly 50 yard intervals.[167] Caernarfon's defences, also begun in 1283, included a profusion of loops in flanking towers and two levels of mural galleries for archers in its high walls. In the curtain wall between the King's Gate and the Granary Tower, distinctive embrasures, reminiscent of those at the Avranches Tower at Dover, were constructed so that a single loop served three different shooting positions for crossbowmen.[168] By contrast, the castles of Harlech and Beaumaris took the concept of concentric defence to new heights.[169] The defences of Beaumaris, the last of Edward's great castles, which was begun in 1295 but never finished, marked the apogee of such design, and mapping of the potential arcs of shot here shows that scarcely any dead ground was left for attackers to exploit (see p. 131).[170]

Ultimately, however, a castle was only as strong as the garrison within it.[171] In heavily defended frontiers such as the Vexin, the militarised zone between Normandy and the Île de France, garrisons could be very substantial during wartime, and major border fortresses such as Berwick and Roxburgh were usually well manned. Such forces might be brought together to form small but professional field forces, while units of crossbowmen could be moved among the network of royal castles throughout the realm to reinforce garrisons in areas where internal or external danger threatened most. By contrast, peacetime garrisons were very small indeed, often comprising little more than a porter and a skeleton domestic staff. Even in times of hostilities the number of combatants was often relatively small. The baronial garrison which held Framlingham Castle against King John in 1216 contained 26 knights, 20 serjeants and 7 crossbowmen, implying that in this instance at least each of the thirteen towers and its intervening stretch of the wall-head was manned by four men.[172] In 1277 the marcher lord Bogo de Knovill, reporting to Edward I on the military strength of Oswestry and Montgomery at a time of substantial Welsh raids, reckoned that 10 to 12 crossbowmen for each castle would supply adequate defence, unless Llewelyn attacked in real strength, and provided they were supported by horsemen who could operate offensively from the castle.[173] Similar numbers appear during Edward I's campaigns. In 1283 the garrison he placed in Castel y Bere, the last Welsh stronghold to fall in the war of 1282–3, was 8 men-at-arms, 9 crossbowmen and 40 infantry,

reduced following the close of the campaign to 12 crossbowmen and 28 archers.[174] During the political crisis of 1297, when Edward strengthened certain royal castles, the great Midlands fortress of Tickhill was garrisoned with 13 crossbowmen and 20 archers.[175] Naturally, key fortresses in Scotland received sizeable garrisons of bowmen. In 1297 Robert Hastang agreed to garrison Roxburgh Castle with 18 men-at-arms, 20 crossbowmen and 92 archers, while in 1301 the constable of Edinburgh contracted to serve Edward I with 30 men-at-arms, 4 hobelars, 20 crossbowmen and 34 archers, as well as ancillary staff.[176]

The importance of Dover as the key defence on the Channel coast can be gauged by the fact that in 1242, during a period of conflict with France, there were 60 crossbowmen in the garrison, while the Avranches Tower alone was designed to be defended by up to 21 crossbowmen.[177] Following the Conquest, certain groups of estates or 'honors' were granted by the king to his lords with the duty of providing a specific number of men for castle-guard in royal fortresses, and (in theory at least) the 21 sets of slits on the Avranches Tower at Dover and its adjoining walls were manned by a contingent of 21 men supplied by the 'honor' of Avranches, which thus gave the tower its name.[178] Recent studies of castle-guard have revealed the great diversity of practice and local custom regarding periods of service, garrison strength, and whether such services continued to be performed in person or were commuted for a cash render. To give but one example, we catch a glimpse of bowmen as a part of the garrison of the royal castle of York in 1218–19, when a Yorkshire jury supplied the royal justices with information concerning some of the men who owed garrison duty:

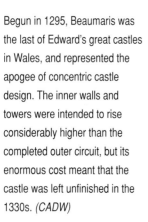

Begun in 1295, Beaumaris was the last of Edward's great castles in Wales, and represented the apogee of concentric castle design. The inner walls and towers were intended to rise considerably higher than the completed outer circuit, but its enormous cost meant that the castle was left unfinished in the 1330s. *(CADW)*

Touching the serjeants of the lord King they say that John le Poher holds in chief of the lord King 5.½ carucates of land in Yapham, Waplington, and Barmby Moor by the service of 1 bow a year at the castle of York. His land is worth 100s a year. Robert the crossbowman holds in chief of the lord King 4.½ carucates of land in Great Givendale by the service of 1 crossbowman a year at the castle of York. His land is worth 100s. Thomas of Walkeringham holds in chief of the lord King 4½ carucates of land in Great Givendale by the service of 1 crossbowman at the castle of York. His land is worth 6m a year.[179]

Here we see minor landowners, holding by feudal serjeantry tenure directly from the king in return for the service of castle-guard as crossbowmen in a major royal fortress.

Though the numbers of crossbowmen and archers often appear small, the increasing sophistication of the defences allowed even a handful of determined men to put up a sustained resistance. In 1404 a garrison of only 28 successfully defended Caernarfon against Owain Glyn Dŵr and his French allies.[180] At three of the greatest sieges in thirteenth-century England, that of Rochester in 1215, of Bedford in 1224 and of Kenilworth in 1266 – notably all in the context of baronial rebellions – the defending crossbowmen took a heavy toll of the lives of the attackers. At Bedford, where the only detailed figures are available, six of the king's knights were killed and another severely wounded by a bolt in the stomach, while over 200 serjeants and labourers working the siege machines were slain.[181] This was among the reasons why Henry III had the entire garrison, about 89 men in all, executed. In 1215 King John had spared the majority of the garrison of Rochester, but hanged at least one of the crossbowmen and possibly several others when the castle fell.[182] To counter such deadly attack, besiegers needed to protect their sappers and siege engines, and to supply defences for their own sharpshooters.

On Philip Augustus's arrival at the siege of Acre in April 1191, 'he ordered screens covered in iron that had been tinned so that they shone like silver to be erected around the city. He ordered his crossbowmen and archers to shoot continuously so that no one could show a finger above the walls of the city.' Ambroise recounts how he also brought up wicker 'hides' called circleia near the walls, from which he and his crossbowmen could shoot at the Turkish defenders.[183] Similarly, when in 1194 Richard laid siege to Nottingham Castle, held for his rebellious brother John, he 'had his men take strong, thick and broad shields; many a man carried these in front of him until he came up to the gateway . . . they protected themselves extremely well so that the crossbowmen

did not hurt them. In front of the king [his own] crossbowmen began to shoot and to do the best they could and held to their task until they took the barbican.'[184] Even such precautions, however, did not save Richard from the bolt of a sharp-eyed noble seeking revenge at the siege of Chaluz Chabrol in the Limousin in 1199, which struck the king despite his being accompanied by a shield bearer. Richard was not wearing armour and the bolt, which sank deep into his shoulder, gave him a mortal wound.[185]

It can be no coincidence that the great majority of nobles and leaders who fell victim to crossbow bolts did so during sieges, for those features which made the crossbow ideal for hunting game – the fact it could be pre-loaded so as to minimise movement or noise – also made it a highly effective weapon for marksmen. Leaders were especially targeted, for the death of a commander might well end a siege.[186] In 1214 the French defenders of the castle of La Roche au Moine in Poitou, perhaps inspired by the fate of Richard I, sought to kill his brother King John by an ingenious trick. John was in the habit of reconnoitring the walls, guarded as usual by a shield bearer. One of the defending crossbowman fitted a strong cord to one of his bolts, shot it through the pavise carried by John's attendant, then tugged on the cord, causing the unfortunate bearer to fall into the moat where he was promptly slain by rocks and missiles cast by other defenders. John, however, escaped unharmed, though he had presumably been shaken by the experience.[187] Other commanders had lucky escapes. Peter of Vaux de Cernay, a chronicler of the Albigensian crusade, noted how at the siege of Termes in 1210 Simon de Montfort had narrowly escaped death at the hands of a crossbowman, while Peter himself had a bolt lodge in his saddle bow during the siege of Moissac.[188] In 1304 at the siege of Stirling Edward I was nearly killed when riding without armour close to the walls in order to encourage his men. A bolt shot from the battlements pierced his garments without harming him and lodged in his saddle, whereupon Edward spat in contempt and swore to hang the crossbowman when the castle fell.[189] It was little wonder, then, that monarchs issuing licences for castle building might forbid or restrict the provision of loops in the fortifications held by their nobles. In 1223 Thibaut IV, Count of Champagne, granted Henry of Mirvaux 'to build a wall around his house fifteen-and-one-half-feet high and two-and-one-half-feet thick, but without towers and a moat, and only with loopholes for bows and crossbows appropriate for a plain wall'.[190] More restrictively, in 1239 Louis IX made the grant of a castle to the Count of Montfort 'in such a wise that we cannot allow in it any perpendicular loops for archers, nor any cruciform loophole for cross-bowmen'.[191]

THE TACTICAL DEPLOYMENT OF CROSSBOWMEN IN THE FIELD

The rout of the Genoese at Crécy was painfully to demonstrate the tactical superiority of the longbow over the crossbow in the open field. Nevertheless, it is important not to let hindsight of this battle distort an evaluation of the military effectiveness of crossbowmen in field engagements before the advent of the Hundred Years War. For Crécy was one of the first major engagements in which an army whose chief missile arm consisted of crossbowmen came up against longbowmen deployed against them in their thousands. The Angevin kings had used Welsh and English archers in their continental campaigns, but such bowmen had taken part in skirmishing and in guerrilla operations, and had never been unleashed en masse against Capetian armies. In the majority of continental warfare crossbowmen would face other crossbowmen, who loaded and shot at a similar speed, a situation in which numbers became the more decisive factor. Like the mounted archer who was to achieve such prominence in English armies from the fourteenth century, mounted crossbowmen provided highly adaptable troops whether for castle-based operations or in the field, and whose mobility allowed them to keep pace with the cavalry. The extent to which such crossbowmen fought from the saddle in this period is unclear; it is probable that in most engagements they dismounted to shoot, but a splendid mid-thirteenth-century tile from the abbey of Chertsey shows a knight with a pot-helm shooting a crossbow at the gallop.[192] Crossbowmen on foot frequently played a key role as advance guards or skirmishers, or formed protective screens for other forces, especially the cavalry. Hence crossbowmen covered the rear of Philip Augustus's army during his march from Mortagne to Bouvines in 1214.[193] At Lincoln in 1217 the crossbowmen advanced in formation about a mile ahead of the main body of knights, clearly a standard practice, for Matthew Paris could note 'crossbowmen always lead the way'.[194] As we have seen, the 'fighting marches' of the crusaders had relied heavily on crossbowmen and archers forming a protective wall around the cavalry, and similar tactics can be observed in the west. Thus according to the Catalan chronicler Desclot, when Philip III's army was on the march into Catalonia in 1285, units of heavily armed crossbowmen formed protective hedges all around the first two sections of the host, comprising the lightly armed infantry or 'ribauds', the first division of horse and other units.[195]

In battle itself, crossbowmen, supported by other troops, could form a defensive wall behind which cavalry could assemble to charge, then retire behind to reform. In 1233 the King of Aragon envisaged that in battle against the Moors formations should comprise a line of pavise bearers, then a line

of crossbowmen, then the cavalry.[196] Here the king was no doubt thinking of the particular threat posed by Moorish horse-archers and *jinetes*, the famous light cavalry whom the Black Prince was to encounter at Nájera in 1367. We have already seen how at Jaffa in 1192 Richard I had his crossbowmen operating in pairs behind makeshift defences and protected by spearmen, and how a variation of such a defensive plan was recommended in 1291 by Fidenzio of Padua for use against the Muslims in the Holy Land.[197] The use of such supporting spearmen or pavise bearers (who were themselves probably equipped with spears) was essential, as the crossbowmen's slow rate made them particularly vulnerable to cavalry attack. Even well-trained crossbowmen would only be able to discharge one or two bolts before charging horsemen were upon them, and in the sixteenth and seventeenth centuries a similar vulnerability required slow-firing arquebusiers and musketeers to be protected by pikemen. At the battle of Montaperti in 1260 the Florentine army contained 300 *pavesari* for their 1,000 crossbowmen, and the increasing use of such shield bearers in the Italian peninsula from the later thirteenth century had been seen as a reaction to a more widespread deployment of crossbows and bows in warfare in the region.[198] The use of pavises, however, occurs considerably earlier. Henry II issued *targie* to his Brabançon mercenaries operating against the Welsh in 1164, while at the great Norman fortress of Falaise in 1210 munitions included crossbows and other arms, with 20 shields (*scuta*) and 32 pavises (*targie*), presumably for use in the field as much as behind the castle's crenellations.[199] Pavises continue to feature in castle inventories, such as the munitions for Calais prepared in 1293 by Robert of Artois, which included armour, crossbows and pavises.[200] Given their defensive role, these paviseurs or 'talevassiers' needed to have good defensive armour; by 1351 those in the French army were required each to be armed with 'plates' or a habergeon, a bascinet with a camail, a gorget, harness for the arms and gloves, in addition to having side arms.[201] If such was the extent of defensive provision envisaged for crossbowmen, it is little wonder that the Genoese at Crécy, compelled to fight without their pavises and possibly even without their own armour, were at a serious disadvantage against Edward III's longbowmen.

One of the most striking uses of crossbowmen in thirteenth-century warfare was at the battle of Campaldino in 1289, fought between the Guelf Tuscan League headed by Florence and the Ghibelline forces led by Arezzo. The Ghibellines deployed their army with an advance and main division of cavalry followed by a third line of infantry, then a further line of cavalry in the rear. The Guelf formation, however, consisted of a central body of cavalry with two wings of infantry, comprising crossbowmen, pavise bearers and spearmen, who were thrown slightly forward in a crescent formation. Behind this deployment, which was masked from the enemy by a forward screen of cavalry, the Guelfs placed a row of wagons and then another strong force of spearmen and horse, to provide both a defended area for their cavalry to regroup and a powerful reserve. The Ghibelline attack which began the battle succeeded in driving back the Guelf cavalry in the centre, but as they advanced further, the Ghibellines became exposed to fierce enfilading shooting from the crossbowmen on the wings. Meanwhile, the Guelf reserve manoeuvred round the flanks of the enemy to attack them in the rear, completing a bloody defeat of the Ghibellines.[202]

Less spectacular but perhaps a more representative example of the function and effectiveness of crossbowmen in northern Europe is the role they played during the initial stages of the battle of Courtrai in 1302. The Flemish troops had drawn up in a very strong defensive position with their front protected by a series of streams and ditches. On seeing this, the French commander Robert of Artois ordered his crossbowmen forward. The Flemish archers thrown out in front of the main units of Flemish spearmen conducted an archery duel, but the power of the larger number of French crossbowmen began to tell. Their steady shooting so galled the Flemish foot that they withdrew out of bowshot, thereby yielding enough ground beyond the ditches and streams for Artois to get his cavalry across the obstacles yet still have room to reform and launch a charge. The crossbowmen and *bidauts* were then recalled, and managed to pass through or around the advancing units of French knights with only limited confusion.[203] Though the cavalry subsequently suffered a crushing defeat, the crossbowmen had accomplished their task with some success. At Mons en Pévèle in 1304 the Flemish protected their spearmen with large shields, presumably to guard against just such tactics.[204] Yet while a row of brightly painted pavises must have been an impressive sight,[205] their use must have hampered the tactical mobility of crossbowmen during battle. Extant pavises vary in weight, as some were clearly heavier versions intended for siege work, while representations occur of crossbowmen with smaller, more portable pavises. Even these lighter versions, however, must have been cumbersome to operate and to manoeuvre when troops were fighting in

formation.[206] By contrast, the faster-moving English archers became adept at using hedges, ditches and other natural features for cover, or if in close defensive positions, a laager of wagons, or even of horses tethered together. And for the English, 'the morale-breaking clouds of arrows shot by massed archers were in the end to be more important than the superior armour-piercing power of the quarrel'.[207]

Nevertheless, on the eve of the Hundred Years War the crossbow continued to reign as the primary missile weapon in the majority of European armies. Warfare within France, including fighting against the English in Poitou or Gascony, did not offer the same catalyst for the increasing prominence of archers as light troops as the Welsh and Scottish wars were to do for the armies of Edward I and his successors. The Albigensian crusade saw northern French armies operating in the high, rugged and often inaccessible terrain of Languedoc, but the focus on sieges, as well as the customary make-up of French forces, meant that crossbowmen remained the primary element of missilemen. The same was true of the forces of the defending southern lords such as the counts of Toulouse. In addition to the ubiquitous crossbow, some infantry in southern France or the Iberian peninsula carried composite bows, while others such as the Gascon and Navarese *dardiers* were lightly armed javelineers.[208] Other conflicts produced effective fighting forces of lightly armed mountaineers, but none was to adopt the longbow as their principal weapon. Thus the nimble Almogavars from the mountains of Catalonia and Aragon, 'a very strong, quick and agile people eager in pursuit and difficult to follow', were superb light troops, but, unlike their southern Welsh counterparts, they seem not to have favoured the bow above other weapons.[209] Equally, the men of the Swiss cantons who were soon to demonstrate their military potential by the ambush and defeat of an Austrian army at Morgarten in 1315 were to develop first the halberd then the great pike as their chief 'national' weapons, with supporting missilemen being almost wholly crossbowmen and later hand-gunners. But in South Wales and much of England it was the longbow which had long been the traditional weapon of many, providing the kings of England with a large reservoir of skilled bowmen on which to draw in times of war. And nowhere within England was this tradition stronger or more visible than in the forest areas which covered much of the country. Here archery had long flourished and it is to the forests that we now must turn.

Matthew Strickland

CHAPTER 8

The Woods So Wild: Archery and the Forest in the Thirteenth Century

Mery it was in grene forest
Amonge the leves grene
Where that men walke both east and west
Wyth bowes and arrowes kene.[1]

ARCHERY IN THE BARONS' WARS

he Barons' Wars which began in 1264 broke over an England which had seen few hostilities on its own soil since the invasion by Prince Louis of France in 1216–17, with the only serious warfare occurring during periodic flare-ups in Anglo-Welsh relations. There had been moments of political upheaval, such as the resistance of Fawkes de Bréauté and the resulting siege of Bedford Castle by Henry III in 1224, or the more sustained rebellion of Richard Marshal in 1233, but these were isolated campaigns. Abroad, the dismal record of military failures witnessed in John's reign with the loss of Normandy by 1204 and the catastrophic defeat at Bouvines in 1214 had continued unabated, with Henry III's last major expedition to France in 1242 ending in ignominious flight at Taillebourg.[2] As a result, when war between Henry III and a baronial coalition began in 1264 there was no immediate tactical experience of set-piece battles upon which to draw. The Anglo-Norman practice of dismounted knights supported by

archers had been long forgotten, and although large numbers of infantry feature in the campaigns between 1264 and 1266 archers and crossbowmen appear to have played a less important role in the two major pitched battles of the war at Lewes in 1264 and Evesham in 1265.

At Lewes, where on 14 May the baronial leader Simon de Montfort routed the royal army and took prisoner King Henry and his eldest son the Lord Edward, crossbowmen and slingers are mentioned as being present, though their contribution to this victory is unknown.[3] De Montfort's army had formed up in four divisions, and the royal army in three. Within these units only the formation of de Montfort's left wing is known; this comprised the Londoners, probably entirely on foot, preceded by a force of cavalry. It is possible that this deployment was mirrored in the other baronial divisions, but Walter of Guisborough believed that a large number of infantry clashed in the initial engagement, and at Evesham de Montfort is said to have favoured placing infantry in the front ranks.[4] It would

A tile depicting a hunting scene, *c.* 1250, from the chapter house of Westminster Abbey. The presence of such a subject even in an ecclesiastical context suggests the ubiquity of hunting as an aristocratic pastime, as well as appealing to the abbey's royal patrons. *(National Monuments Record/English Heritage)*

thus seem likely that at Lewes crossbowmen and other missile-men would have been placed forward, both as skirmishers and to act as a defensive screen for the cavalry units before their charges. The course of the engagement itself is less ambiguous. On the royalist right a furious charge by Edward's cavalry routed a force of Montfortian horse and then smashed into the Londoners, driving them from the field.[5] But while Edward gave relentless pursuit, Simon's other three 'battles' charged down the slope towards the town of Lewes, sweeping the royalist forces before them. By the following year the political and military tables had been reversed. In an early demon-stration of his skills as a general, Edward succeeded in out-manoeuvring de Montfort and used his superior forces to trap the earl within a bend of the River Severn at Evesham on 4 August.[6] Although de Montfort seems to have had several

thousand infantry, many of whom were Welsh, they did not confront Edward's cavalry with the same dogged resistance that he was to face at the hands of Welsh spearmen some years later during his invasion of Wales, nor was the royalist cavalry brought down by a hail of arrows. A newly discovered vernac-ular account of the battle tells how, as de Montfort prepared to leave Evesham for the battle, he found that Humphrey de Bohun, who was in command of the infantry, 'withdrew and remained in the rearguard', prompting Earl Simon to remark,

'Sir Humphrey, Sir Humphrey, that's no way to conduct a battle, putting the foot-soldiers at the rear. I know well how this will turn out.'[7] This remark only serves to confirm that commanders regarded the combination of infantry with cavalry as crucial, and that their tactical coordination was scarcely an innovation of Edward I, as J.E. Morris believed.[8] Fatally, however, such mutual support did not occur at Evesham. At the critical moment, when de Montfort charged the royalist lines, the foot remained behind at Evesham priory contrary to his orders, and then fled; a poem lamenting Simon's demise noted 'they fought the battle all on horse, which was the misfortune, without any foot'.[9] In an effort to break out of the royalist encirclement the earl seemingly chose to form up in a single tight formation, though its exact nature is uncertain. Wykes believed it to be 'in a thick mass in the form of a circle', though it has also been suggested that this was a wedge made up of cavalry.[10] The momentum of de Montfort's charge initially pushed Edward's men back, but the royalist line held. With their cavalry now able to push home the advantage, the royalists soon encircled de Montfort and his knights, who were fighting desperately on foot. They were shown little mercy by Edward's vengeful forces. Many fell at de Montfort's side, while the old earl's body was mutilated on the field of battle.[11]

If cavalry appear to have been the most significant arm in these major field engagements,[12] archers and crossbowmen were nevertheless prominent in other operations of the war, notably in sieges, guerrilla warfare and operations in difficult terrain. In siege warfare crossbowmen retained the prominence they had enjoyed in earlier Angevin forces. The king had crossbowmen with him at his assault on the rebel stronghold of Northampton in 1264 and likewise Simon de Montfort employed crossbowmen at the siege of Rochester the same year.[13] To attack the great castle of Kenilworth, which became the refuge for many of de Montfort's supporters following his death, King Henry deployed two great belfreys, one containing 200 crossbowmen, the other, known as 'The Bear', filled with archers, though to the king's anger and dismay both were destroyed by missiles from the castle's own stone-throwers.[14] County levies brought crossbows as well as bows to the muster. When, after Lewes, the baronial regency feared an invasion from France organised by Henry III's queen, Eleanor of Provence, they compelled the king to issue summons to all knights and freeholders to make ready to guard the coast, and extra infantry were to be called out from towns and vills. The sheriffs were to summon 'eight, six or four at the least, according to the size of such vills, of the best and most able foot-soldiers, well provided with befitting array, that is to say with lances, bows and arrows, swords, arbalests, and axes, and have them provided therewith at the common expense for forty days'.[15] More remarkably, during the royalists' storming of Northampton in 1264, some of the stoutest resistance came from a band of students from Oxford, who had been driven out when Henry III had set up his HQ there and had migrated with their masters to Northampton. Fighting under their own banner 'with utmost zeal', these students did 'more damage with their bows, slings, and crossbows than all the rest', so much so, indeed, that Henry resolved to have them executed when the town fell. He was only prevented by his nobles, who argued that the king should not risk offending the powerful families to which many of these young men belonged.[16] Students in the 1260s, it seems, shared something of the militancy of their fellows in the 1960s.

RESISTANCE IN THE FOREST

Most strikingly, however, archers played a key role in operations in wooded country and irregular warfare, much as they had done in Wales and Ireland during the previous century. Bowmen from the Weald had earned a formidable reputation in 1216–17 during the invasion by Louis of France, carrying out effective guerrilla operations under their leader 'Willikin of the Weald' against the French.[17] 'Willikin of the Weald', the name popularly given to William of Kensham (or Cassingham), was a young man in royal service operating with several hundred archers 'from deserted and densely wooded places', who had held out in the forest at a time when Louis had gained control of much of south-east England, harrying his forces, interrupting his communications with the coast, inflicting considerable casualties and in early 1217 almost succeeding in cutting Louis off at Winchelsea.[18] He and his men struck fear into the hearts of the French, picking off stragglers, breaking down bridges behind them, capturing unwary nobles and raiding the French siege camp at Dover.[19] Despite such exploits, and his not inconsiderable role in bringing about the defeat of Louis, William remains 'one of England's neglected heroes', though it is gratifying to note that the young Henry III was quick to reward him for his loyalty.[20] At about the same time the annals of St Augustine's Canterbury, completed by 1220, could tell the tale of how in 1066 the men of Kent had disguised themselves with the boughs of trees and trapped William the Conqueror in an ambush near Swanscombe; at a given signal 'they threw down their boughs, and drawing their bows and unsheathing their swords' they forced the king to cede the

Kentishmen their ancient rights and customs. Though wholly fictitious, the story reflects the reputation enjoyed by the men of Kent in guerrilla warfare within the forest.[21]

It was little wonder then that in 1264 King Henry was anxious again to have the archers of the Weald on his side. He ordered 300 'of the best archers of the Weald' to defend the port of Winchelsea, and while he was waiting for royalist troops being raised in the Weald news came that de Montfort was marching against him.[22] The Wealdians were summoned to join the king at once at Lewes, but this time the men of the forest chose instead to support de Montfort. They harassed Henry III's forces as they moved through the Weald, and on 2 May 1264 the king's cook, Thomas, was killed 'by the shaft of a low-born archer when out in front', as the army passed the priory of Combwell in Goudhurst. The king's response to such manifest treason was ruthless. Some 315 archers who, it was said, had been called deceitfully into the king's peace through the counsel of his brother, Richard of Cornwall, were beheaded in the royal presence at Flimwell. Some of these archers had been the men of the abbot of Battle, who accordingly had to fine 100m with the king to purchase his forgiveness.[23]

Nevertheless, this was a time of shifting allegiances and by 1265 the men of the Weald were supplying considerable numbers of archers for the king's forces, particularly in the royalist 'mopping up' operations of 1265–7 against remaining Montfortian supporters. Despite the crushing defeat at Evesham in August 1265 and the death of Simon de Montfort, Henry III's punitive policy of disinheriting many of the rebels ensured that there was continued resistance in the form of raids and sallies from remote marshland areas such as the Isle of Axholme on the Lower Trent, the Isle of Ely and the Fens and from forest areas in Sussex, on the borders of Essex and Hertfordshire, north and south of the Trent, parts of Oxfordshire and Sherwood.[24] The king's principal commander in conducting campaigns against these rebels in the south-east was Roger Leyburn, a Kentishman owning a number of manors in that county but also a 'king's knight' of considerable military experience in the Welsh marches. He had saved the king's life at the battle of Evesham, and Henry had made him Sheriff of Kent, Warden of the Seven Hundreds of the Weald and Deputy Warden of the Cinque Ports.[25]

Having secured London, which had supported de Montfort, Leyburn conducted a brief armed progress through the Weald to pacify it, leaving behind 200 archers, paid 3*d* a day for 46 days, to safeguard local markets and 'to clear the woods of those parts of robbers and those who lie in ambush in those areas, and to keep the peace of the lord king'.[26] In January 1266 he took the port of Sandwich by storm, using among other siege engines the same belfry known as 'The Bear' which

Archers, partly clad in green, shoot at oncoming deer, from the *Livre de chasse* of Gaston Phébus, count of Foix, written between 1387 and 1389 (Paris, Bibliothèque Nationale, MS fr. 616, f.111v). The type of hunting depicted here is 'bow and stable', where the archers each take a station close to a tree, and await the game driven towards them by beaters and dogs. *(Bibliothèque Nationale, Paris)*

would be deployed later that year against Kenilworth Castle, while he also deployed mounted crossbowmen drawn from the garrison of Dover Castle, paid at the much higher rate of 1s a day.[27] From there he joined forces with the Lord Edward to launch a joint land and naval attack on Winchelsea, and here no fewer than 577 archers from the Weald were in his pay.[28] In May, leaving 200 bowmen under the Earl of Surrey to ensure the continued submission of London, Leyburn took 500 archers, probably also from the Weald, together with a small group of knights, serjeants and seven crossbowmen on his campaign against rebels in Essex. When in June 1267 Winchelsea again rebelled, it was taken by 200 of Leyburn's

A hooded archer pursues a stag, from a fourteenth-century misericord in Gloucester Cathedral. *(Paulette Barton)*

archers.[29] The Exchequer rolls furnish some valuable details of these men 'in the service of the lord king', who in addition to the usual wage of 3*d* a day received expenses for travel, for they were serving outside their shire. They were grouped in companies of 100 – an early glimpse of the centenary that becomes familiar in the armies of Edward I and his successors – while 200 of them received tunics, costing 3*s* each, which may well have borne the royal livery.[30]

Archers also formed part of the garrison of the strategically important royal castle of Nottingham. Late 1266 and early 1277 had witnessed a resurgence of rebel activity in Sherwood, and though reinforced the royal garrison had suffered defeat at their hands.[31] It was again Roger Leyburn who held the custody of this stronghold, but occupied elsewhere he was represented by his deputy Alan de Kirkby commanding a force of 2 knights, 20 serjeants, 10 crossbowmen and 20 archers.[32] This permanent force, which once again reveals just how small a basic garrison might be even for a major royal castle, was reinforced as need demanded by larger units to undertake offensive operations within the forest, such as that led in 1266–7 by another royalist captain, Reginald de Grey. Grey's force comprised 2 knights and their sergeants, 20 mounted crossbowmen under a captain, 10 foot-crossbowmen and 20 archers, with the knights serving for 263 days and the others for 436 days 'to suppress the enemies of the lord king'.[33] Grey fought two engagements within Sherwood, in which his men lost a number of horses, but it was only following the rebels' defeat by a force under Leyburn's son William at Charnwood in September 1267 that the Montfortians in this area were finally pacified.[34]

Such operations, like the campaigns of the Anglo-Norman marcher lords in Ireland from 1169, reveal how valued archers were in operating in broken or heavily wooded country. Such experiences were not lost on the young Edward, who had undergone a hard but invaluable military apprenticeship in the 1260s. He would soon demonstrate his appreciation of bowmen by deploying them in large numbers in his Welsh campaigns, in which veterans like Reginald de Grey served with distinction.[35] By the same token, it may well have been his experience in these campaigns that led Henry III to make Leyburn his justice of the forest north of the Trent.

OUTLAWS, POACHERS AND FORESTERS

Such skirmishes between knights and archers deep in Sherwood readily call to mind the exploits of that greatest of bowmen and outlaws, Robin Hood.[36] The search for the 'real' Robin Hood and the origins of the legend has exerted as enduring a fascination among historians as the tales of the outlaw have done among a wider audience, though in Maurice Keen's words 'he has so far proved quite as infuriatingly elusive to nineteenth- and twentieth-century researchers as the Robin of legend proved to be for the Sheriff of Nottingham'.[37] Here is not the place to dwell at length on Robin Hood, for the extensive literature has been well reviewed elsewhere, but Sir James Holt's belief in a thirteenth-century origin for the legend has been strongly supported by recent scholarship.[38] It has been argued that the increasing popularity of the Robin Hood ballads was closely linked to the growing prominence of archers in English tactics and military organisation during the wars of Edward III, which led not only to the archer's rising status but to the swelling in numbers of those unemployed soldiers who, during periods of peace, took to the woods with their bows as brigands.[39] Doubtless all these factors added to the resonance of the Robin Hood legends, but the prominence of archers fighting in the forests in 1264–7 provides an earlier and more direct association of archery with outlawry and the greenwood. Indeed, in this context it is striking that the Scots chronicler Walter Bower, writing in the 1440s, chose to mention the exploits of Robin and Little John under the year 1266, believing them to have been among those disinherited by the king in the wake of Evesham for supporting de Montfort. He also placed the operations of 'that most famous armed robber (*sicarius*)' in the forest of Barnsdale, between Doncaster and Pontefract, several miles north of Sherwood.[40]

In fact, the name Robin Hood was already in common use as an epithet for an outlaw by the early 1260s, well before the activities of the disinherited in 1266–7. For in 1262 the plea rolls made mention of an outlaw named William, son of Robert Le Fevre, whose chattels had been seized without warrant by the abbot of Sandelford in Berkshire, and a royal clerk who compiled another roll recorded the same man as William 'Robehod', indicating that he was familiar with popular tales of Robin.[41] But if such tales were already current by the 1260s,

what was their ultimate origin? In many popular stories and films the adventures of Robin Hood are set during the absence of King Richard I on crusade and during his captivity in Germany (1190–4), with the outlaw hero loyally battling against the evil wiles of Prince John and his henchman the Sheriff of Nottingham until the king's eventual return. Such a tradition goes back to the *History of Greater Britain* of 1520 by the Scots historian John Major,[42] but there is, however, no contemporary evidence to suggest the activities of a Robin Hood at this date. Richard did indeed visit Sherwood Forest on his return to England in 1194, taking great delight from these woods which he had not previously seen, but of Robin Hood, alas, we hear nothing.[43]

Nevertheless, in 1226 Exchequer accounts record the sum of 32s 6d from the sale of the goods of one Robert Hod, *fugitivus*, whose case had been heard by assize judges at York the year previously, and the name of this outlaw was subsequently recorded on the rolls as Hobbehod in 1227 and 1228.[44] Though it cannot be proved that the two men were the same, David Crook has suggested that Robert Hod might be synonymous with one Robert of Wetherby, a notorious outlaw whose excesses were such that in 1225 the king empowered the Sheriff of Yorkshire to hire a force of serjeants to 'seek and take and behead' him as an 'outlaw and evildoer of our land'. The sheriff, Eustace of Lowdham, who had long been Under-Sheriff of Nottingham, seems to have succeeded, for he claimed expenses 'for a chain to hang Robert of Wetherby', which implies his body was left on public display for a considerable time.[45] It was natural for subsequent legend to transform such circumstances into more appealing tales of successful resistance by the outlaw and his band against the power of an oppressive sheriff, just as they no doubt transformed the character of the man himself.[46] Such a link must remain only speculative, but what seems clear is that the ballads of Robin Hood, whose earliest surviving forms are fifteenth-century texts bringing together earlier material, had their origins in the first quarter of the thirteenth century. Several instances of the name 'Robin-hood' occur during the last decades of the thirteenth century, such as, for example, the mention in the Sussex subsidy roll for 1296 of one Gilbert 'Robynhood',[47] suggesting it had become synonymous with notorious outlawry. Similarly, by 1309 Giles de Argentine, one of the most famous knights of his time, could be crowned 'King of the Greenwood' following his victory at a tournament in Stepney.[48] Familiarity with the tales

A woodcut used first to illustrate Chaucer's Yeoman in Richard Pynson's 1491 edition of the *Canterbury Tales*, then later reused to depict Robin Hood in the *Gest of Robin Hood*, as printed in the Chepman and Myllar tracts of 1508.

was such that by 1338 a clerk could enrol one of the archers of the garrison of the Isle of Wight as Robyn Hod, using the diminutive rather than the more formal name Robert normally occurring on such official lists, while the Robert of Sherwood who appears as an archer in the English garrison of Edinburgh Castle in 1335 may be an alias.[49]

Behind the evolving tales of Robin Hood lay the stark realities of life in thirteenth- and fourteenth-century England, which saw many a man who had been placed beyond the protection of the law flee to the greenwoods, and widespread brigandry by gangs of outlaws operating from the forests.[50] In 1221 the Gloucester assizes recorded that of 330 men accused of homicide 14 had been hanged, but 100 others had fled and were proclaimed outlaws in their absence.[51] Under Edward I a harsh royal response to a crime wave, caused in part by oppressive war taxation and a rising population, led many to despair of royal justice and flee to the forests. The author of *An Outlaw's Song of Trailbaston* spoke for many fellow outlaws: 'I have served my lord the king in peace and war in Flanders, Scotland, in Gascony, his own land; but now I do not know how to make a living . . . You who are indicted, I advise you, come to me, to the green forest of Belregard, where there is no annoyance but only wild animals and beautiful shade; for the common law is too uncertain.' Tellingly, he goes on to link such a lifestyle with skill with the bow: 'If I become a "companion" and know about archery (*et sache de archerye*), my neighbour will go around saying, "That man is of a company which goes to hunt in the woods and to do other follies; if he wishes to live, he will lead his life like a swine."'[52] Others took a similarly unromantic view of the hardships of the forest, such as the anxious lover in the fifteenth-century poem *The Nut Brown Maiden*:

> Yet take good hede, for ever I drede,
> That ye coulde not sustain
> The thoorney ways, the depe valeis,
> The snow, the frost, the reyne,
> The cold, the hete; for drye or wete
> We must lodge on the plan;
> And, us above non other roue,
> But a break, bussh or twayne.[53]

Nevertheless, by 1306 the problem of men fleeing from the royal justices was so endemic that Edward I ordered all the sheriffs throughout England to seize those who had left their own counties to 'lurk and dwell' in others, and who moved around suspiciously at night time.[54] The Statute of Winchester of 1285 had already ordered that highways to and from market towns were to be widened so that 'there may be no ditch, underwood or bushes where one could hide with evil intent

within two hundred feet of the road' on either side – in other words, within effective bow range.[55] The danger was illustrated in 1306 when a party of the king's men transporting the captive bishops of Glasgow and St Andrews to prisons in southern England increased the number of archers in their escort from 8 to 20 for the part of their journey from Pontefract to Tickhill, 'on account of Barnsdale'.[56] The area clearly already had a reputation as a refuge for outlaws, and it is in Barnsdale rather than Sherwood that some of the earliest ballads chose to locate Robin Hood.[57] So enduring was this connection that the phrase 'Robin Hode en Barnsdale stode' had even become a legal formula by the fifteenth century.[58]

Yet despite the grim social realities which underpinned the force and appeal of the Robin Hood legends, the potent image of woodsmen, skilled in ambuscade and use of the bow, was one readily exploited by the crown itself for political theatre and pageant. Nowhere is this more strikingly revealed than in 1356, when following the battle of Poitiers the Black Prince was escorting his captive, King Jean II of France, from the south coast to London. As the entourage was passing through a forest, they were 'ambushed' by 500 men wearing coats and mantles of green, and 'like robbers or wicked men' bearing bows and arrows, swords and shields. King Jean, as his host had intended, was suitably amazed, and upon enquiring who these fellows were received the reply from the prince that 'they were men of England, foresters who lived wild for their pleasure, and it was their custom each day to be thus arrayed'.[59] Though there was an element of chivalric sport in such display, the image being thus conveyed to King Jean – who after Poitiers must have needed little further convincing as to the power of English archery – was that England was a country full of hardy bowmen living rough by nature but ready to follow the prince back to France to ply their bows should he command.

It is striking to note that the garb of green, to become famous as 'Lincoln Green' after the colour of cloth woven at that city, was already the badge of the outlaw and woodsman. Forest assizes record one poacher dressed in green camouflage, complete with a mask of green.[60] The superbly illustrated *Hunting Book* of Gaston Phébus, Count of Foix, composed in 1387–9, provides several depictions of hunters clad in green, some even bearing foliage over their hoods and headgear for added camouflage, and the skilful poacher in the late fourteenth-century *Parlement of the Three Ages*, written in the north Midlands, likewise covers himself and his bow with foliage.[61] Similarly, *The Master of Game*, an English translation of sections of Phébus's work made between 1406 and 1413 by Henry V's brother Edward, Duke of York, who was to be slain at Agincourt, recommended that hunters should be clad in green.[62] From the earliest ballads it is the colour of Robin Hood

A huntsman and a nobleman from the Queen Mary Psalter, English, *c*. 1320 (British Library, Royal MS 2 B VII, f.151). Because of their skill with the bow, huntsmen and foresters were frequently recruited into the retinues of noblemen in times of war. *(© British Library)*

and his men, and in *A Gest of Robyn Hode* the outlaw even provides green cloth to the king and his retinue to make their livery from it.[63] In the later *Ballad of the Outlaw Murray* this practice has spread north of the border, for the men of this Scottish hero who fight against the English from their base in Ettrick Forest are 'in liverie clad of the Lincoln grene so fair to see'.[64] Such an image reflected social realities; in 1439 it was recorded how one Peter Venables of Derbyshire had gathered a band of outlaws, 'beyng of his clothinge, and in manere of insurrection wente into the wodes in that county like it hadde be Robyn Hode and his meynee [band]'.[65]

The actions of Willikin of the Weald's bowmen in 1216–17, the stubborn resistance of de Montfort's supporters in Sherwood, and the men who took to the woods with their bows as outlaws all serve to highlight the long-standing connection between archery and the forest. Medieval England was a densely wooded country, and a passion for hunting – whether lawfully or otherwise – was shared by all classes of society. Gaston Phébus, with a little false modesty, concluded his account of bow and stable hunting by remarking: 'I know little of hunting with the bow: if you want to know more, you had best go to England, where it is a way of life.'[66] If Waterloo was won on the playing fields of Eton, the great English victories of the fourteenth and fifteenth centuries against the Scots and the French had much to do with hunting in

England's forests. Hunting in all its forms had long been regarded as good training for war, and it is possible that some of the battle cries used by the English may have been taken from the chase, just as the 'hue and cry' raised by locals in chase after suspected criminals took its name from the French verb *huer*, meaning 'to shout when hunting', as a vocal imitation of the hunting horn.[67] It has been suggested that Sir Thomas Erpingham's famous command at Agincourt, recorded by Jean Waurin as 'Nestroque!', which has long mystified historians, may have been '*menée* stroke', that is the order to blow the stroke (or horn call) known as the *menée*. This call, according to *The Master of the Game*, written by Edward, Duke of York, who commanded the English right wing at Agincourt, was used when hunting the hart.[68] We shall probably never know the real form or meaning of Sir Thomas's command,[69] nor of the 'great cry which was a cause of great amazement to the French' made by the English after Erpingham threw his baton into the air, and which they repeated after their initial advance before loosing their shafts against the French vanguard.[70] But the conscious link between pursuing an animal and human quarry is apparent

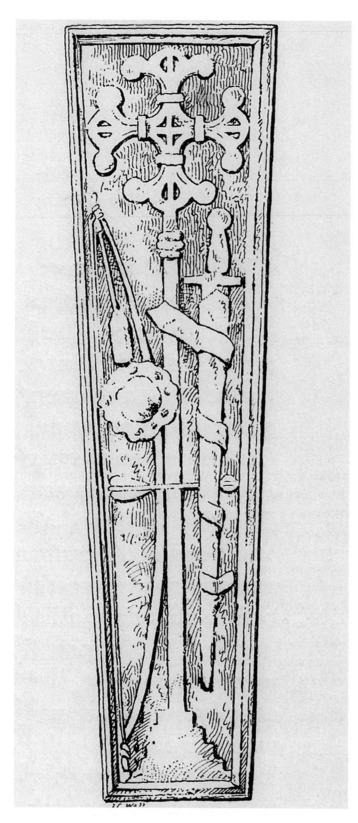

A chief forester's gravestone from the later thirteenth century, now in the Chapel of the Nine Altars, Durham Cathedral, depicting a bow and arrow as well as a sword and its belt, and what perhaps may be a forester's hat. The object lying in the upper part of the bow has also not been identified with certainty, though it has been suggested that it was a form of paddle indicating water or fishing rights. From J.C. Fox, *Royal Forests* (1905). *(Author Collection)*

in an incident which occurred at the start of the ill-fated Weardale campaign of 1327. The eye-witness Jean Le Bel records how after a major fracas broke out between English bowmen and troops from Hainault, the archers, snatching up their bows, pursued the Hainaulters with the hunting cry of 'Hahay, Hahay! – representing either the cry used to drive deer towards nets (*hayes*), or possibly that for calling the hunters together.[71] The concept of the enemy as game to be fiercely pursued is an aspect of the psychology of medieval warfare that would doubtless repay further study. Here let us simply note that the widespread participation in hunting – and indeed poaching, in what has been neatly termed 'fur-collar crime'[72] – by the English nobility would have left them with a knowledge of the bow and its potential, and, though they themselves wielded other weapons in war, with a professional respect for the men who drew the bow so effectively in battle.

BREAKING AND KEEPING THE FOREST LAW

Before the Conquest men might hunt as they pleased on their own lands provided they respected the king's own woodlands.[73] But with the coming of the Normans successive kings not only developed new hunting reserves such as the New Forest, but enforced a royal monopoly of hunting over extensive areas of the country through the harsh, arbitrary and detested forest law.[74] Designed in principle to protect the king's game by restricting hunting and disafforestation, the forest jurisdiction in addition quickly came to be a lucrative source of crown revenue, with itinerant justices of the forest exacting heavy fines not only for poaching but for taking wood or making clearings (assarts) for settlement and agriculture without permission. The Anglo-Norman and Angevin kings relentlessly expanded the technical bounds of the royal forests to include villages, towns and large areas that were not in fact wooded, so much so that at its high water mark under Henry II as much as one-third of England may have fallen within the forest law.[75] Little wonder that a curb on such a practice, together with reform of the frequently corrupt and oppressive behaviour of the royal forest officials, became a key target of political reform by the crown's opponents, and in 1217 the government was forced to cede not only a reissue of Magna Carta but a special Charter of the Forest.[76]

Within these forests the poaching of game was forbidden under threat of severe penalties, which might include mutilation or even death, while dogs within the forest areas were to be 'lawed' by having three claws from their forepaws cut off to prevent them from hunting. Weapons, and especially bows, were permitted only to those with appropriate authoris- ation. Henry II's Assize of the Forest of 1184 forbade 'that anyone should have bows or arrows or hounds or harriers in his [the king's] forests unless he shall have as his guarantor the king or some other person who can legally act as his guar- antor'.[77] To be caught bearing a bow without such permission risked being put at the king's mercy (*in misericordia*), that is being imprisoned to await trial before the itinerant justices of the forest.[78] One of the twelve questions asked by the royal justices in their 'Regard' or three-yearly inspection of the woods within the bounds of the royal forest was to elicit who had bows, crossbows or hunting dogs which might harm the king's venison, and the Pleas of the Forest record the prosecution of many such cases.[79] Thus, to give but a representative example, the forest eyre in Northamptonshire in 1209 recorded that 'Thomas, the son of Eustace and Thomas of Oswestry are in the king's mercy because they carried bows and arrows in the king's forest without licence; and the matter must be shown to the king'. Similarly 'Ralph Neirnut of Threwelton is in mercy because a crossbow and bow were found in his house without warrant'.[80] When in 1253 the jurors of Geddington and other neighbouring townships appeared before the justices in the same county, they noted 'that Simon the son of Roger of Geddington goes with bows and barbed arrows in the park at Brigstock. And he is not a sworn forester, wherefore they suspect that he is an evildoer to the venison of the lord king and privy to all the evil doers in the same park.'[81] The right to hunt with bows and dogs might be granted by the king as a special boon to favoured magnates or ecclesiastics. Thus the privileges of Lanercost Priory in Cumberland included not only

A woodcut of a mounted archer, with his sword and buckler, used to illustrate Chaucer's Knight in a 1532 edition of the *Canterbury Tales*. *(Author Collection)*

the right for the prior to have hunting dogs to hunt foxes and hares 'and all other animals which they call "clobest"', but also for the prior's men to carry bows and arrows throughout the barony of Gilsland provided they did not harm the animals in the forest.[82]

The majority of men authorised to carry bows, however, were the numerous foresters, woodwards and verderers who administered the forest areas either on the king's behalf or on that of lords who possessed their own woods and deer parks. The royal forests were overseen by wardens or keepers, who were in charge of a single forest or groups of forests, and who were answerable to the king's justices of the forest. Alongside the wardens, yet independent of them and answering to the king, were the verderers, often knights or men of some social standing, who were elected by the county court, and who were chiefly responsible for attending the forest courts and viewing and recording any trespass in the forest. Several verderers' grave slabs of the thirteenth and fourteenth centuries bear a depiction of an axe, symbolising his control over the felling of trees or the clearing of the 'vert', that is the undergrowth and trees which sheltered the game. Beneath these officials came the foresters, the equivalent in function to later gamekeepers, who were charged with the day-to-day upkeep of the forests, the oversee of the vert, the care of deer and the policing of the woods by the detecting and capture of poachers. Within a forest each forester had his ward or walks, sometimes known as bailiwicks, which he was to patrol. The number of foresters in any given woodland might vary, but in 1269 it was decreed by the justices that in Rutland Forest the warden should have no more than the customary five foresters on foot, one on horseback and a page.[83] Such 'riding foresters' were of higher rank and were sometimes known as 'bow-bearers' from their right always to carry a bow, whereas their subordinates needed the warrant of the warden so to do. In the early sixteenth- century rhyme of William of Cloudsley the hero is pardoned by the king with the words,

> I geve the eightene pence a day,
> And my bow shalt thou beare,
> And over all the north countre
> I make the chyfe rydere.[84]

This was a handsome sum, but the actual pay of medieval foresters was not insubstantial; in 1360 those of Clarendon received 2*d* a day, and they had certain perquisites including a limited supply of timber and venison.[85] Foresters played an important role not only in patrolling the forest, but in the hunting that occupied such an important role in the lives of kings and nobles. Here they would work in conjunction with those of the lord's household responsible for his hunting. As *The Master of the Game* explains:

> the master forester ought to show [the master of the game] the king's standing if the king would stand with his bow, and where all the remnant of the bows would stand. And the yeoman for the king's bows ought to be there to keep and make the king's standing, and remain there without noise till the king comes.[86]

The forester's equipment, which is proudly displayed on a number of grave slabs as symbols of their office, included not only a bow but also a hunting horn, normally worn on a broad baldric. This was used not only in the chase but to summon assistance when arresting malefactors in the forest. Such was the equipment of Chaucer's Yeoman in the Prologue to *The Canterbury Tales*, who with his bow, arrows, horn and green clothing, was the archetypal forester:

> And he was clad in cote and hood of greene;
> A sheef of pecock arwes, bright and keene,
> Under his belt he bar full thriftily.
> Wel koude he dresse his takel yemanly –
> His arwes drowped noght with fetheres lowe –
> And in his hand he bar a myghty bowe.
> A not heed hadde he with broun visage.
> Of wodecraft koude he wel al the usage.
> Upon his arm he bar a gay bracer,
> And by his syde a swerd and a bokeler,
> And on that oother syde a gay daggere
> Harneysed wel and sharpe as poynt of spere,
> A Christophre on his brest of silver sheene.
> An horn he bar; the bawdryk was of greene.
> A forster was he soothly, as I gesse.[87]

In his remarkable and challenging reinterpretation of Chaucer's Knight as an unscrupulous mercenary representing the very antithesis of chivalry, Terry Jones has argued that the Yeoman is not a forester, but a mercenary archer, part of the Knight's 'lance' or military retinue, who, like his master, may well have seen service in Hawkwood's White Company in Italy.[88] Not only is he heavily armed and wearing the green livery sometimes associated with Welsh archers, notes Jones, but 'the longbow which he carries was of course a military weapon not a hunting one, and the "peacock arrows" which he bears under his belt "full thriftily" would have been particularly long ones and illegal for foresters who by law were supposed to use only short arrows or bolts'.[89] Yet it is clear from the records of the Forest assizes that foresters and poachers alike used longbows,

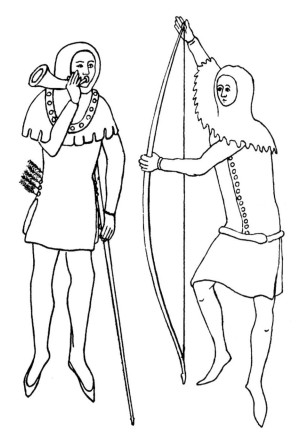

Two hunters, drawn after Stodhard (1811) from a now lost painting decorating the back wall of the tomb of Sir Oliver Ingham (d. 1344), Ingham church, Norfolk. Ingham had a distinguished military career under Edward II and Edward III, being seneschal of Aquitaine from 1333–43. The juxtaposition of a hunting scene with Ingham's military effigy underscores the intimate connection between war and the chase. From J.C. Fox, *Royal Forests* (1905). *(Author Collection)*

and that while legislation had proscribed barbed arrows to those dwelling within the forest bounds this restriction did not apply to foresters protecting the venison and vert. Nevertheless, the Yeoman is undoubtedly as much a soldier as a forester, and to Chaucer's contemporaries this vivid portrait of a skilled woodsman with his bow would have had powerful connotations not only with the tales of Robin Hood, but with the great victories of the recent past achieved by the prowess with the longbow of such men in the armies of Edward III and the Black Prince in France and Spain. Given their skill as bowmen, foresters were naturally among those selected for military service by commissioners of array or by those lords raising archers for their contract retinues.[90] In 1373, for example, John of Gaunt drew heavily on the personnel of the extensive forests and parks under his lordship to furnish men for the expedition of that year, for which he provided 200 archers from Lancashire and 100 from Yorkshire in addition to those raised by his captains under contract. His Yorkshire receiver was given the names of three parkers in particular, presumably because of their renown with bow, while the keeper of the forest of Leicester was ordered to offer recruits two oaks each as an incentive to join up.[91] Perhaps too there were darker overtones. Demobilisation in the late 1350s sent the crime wave soaring, and in 1358 a statute referred to 'those who have been pillors and robbers in the parts beyond the sea, and be now come again, and go wandering, and will not labour as they were wont in times past'.[92] Many such men took service with the king's armies to gain wages and pardons for their offences.[93]

Indeed, the sword, buckler and bow carried by the Yeoman is also a reminder that the forester's role in policing the forests and arresting poachers could be a highly dangerous one. Poachers used many ways to obtain venison, and snares and traps were the most characteristic methods of hunting by peasant poachers, possibly because bows were far more difficult to conceal.[94] As often as not, however, those who stole the king's deer were armed with bows or crossbows. The legal records known as the Pleas of the Forest reveal many instances of poachers violently resisting arrest. Thus in 1229 the chief foresters William of Northampton and Roger of Tingerwick were alerted to the presence in Rockingham Forest of poachers, there with greyhounds 'for the purpose of doing evil to the venison of the lord king'. Accordingly, they and their men

lay in ambush and saw five poachers in the lord king's demesne of Wydehawe, one with a crossbow and four with bows and arrows standing at their trees. And when the foresters perceived them they hailed and pursued them. And the aforesaid malefactors standing at their trees turned in defence and shot arrows at the foresters, so that they wounded Matthew, the forester of the park of Brigstock, with two Welsh arrows (*duabus sagittis waliscis*), to wit with one arrow under the left breast, to the depth of one hand slantwise, and with the second arrow in the left arm to the depth of two fingers, so that it was

despaired of the life of the said Matthew. And the foresters pursued the aforesaid malefactors so vigorously that they turned and fled into the thickness of the wood. And the foresters on account of the darkness could follow them no more.[95]

In 1248, while patrolling about midnight in the woods around Weybridge near Huntingdon, two foresters raised the hue against a gang of twelve poachers, of whom ten were armed with bows. They replied by shooting six arrows at the foresters, of which three were barbed. Unharmed, the foresters shot back with their bows, but the poachers made their escape into the night and the thick undergrowth.[96] As in many such cases, the arrows shot at the foresters were kept to be presented as evidence to the itinerant justices of the forest, which accounts for the details of such arrows being recorded.[97]

On other occasions the royal foresters might choose discretion rather than valour. In another incident in Rockingham Forest, recorded in 1272, a group of poachers hunted for a whole day, killing three deer and setting up a buck's head on a stake to mock the king's foresters. When they were finally spotted by the foresters, who raised the hue and cry, the poachers 'shot at them against the peace of the lord king', forcing them to flee.[98] That one of the poachers was a local woodward, Robert of Nowers, with custody of the wood of Bulax, suggests that connivance by minor forest officials was a frequent problem. Walking foresters could be bribed into acquiescence or even participation in poaching, while villages might be fined for failing to assist the foresters in pursuing poachers with the hue and cry.[99] Many such poachers hunted in groups, presumably for safety should they be discovered. In 1253 the jurors before the Northamptonshire eyre testified that

A king hunting on horseback, from a fourteenth-century manuscript of the *Decretals of Gregory IX* (British Library, MS Royal 10 E IV, f.255). *(akg-images/British Library)*

A very large hunting broadhead, probably dating to the fourteenth or fifteenth century. These large heads, intended to be used against deer or other large game, caused massive tissue disruption and meant that if not killed immediately, the quarry would quickly bleed to death. If used against humans, a wound to the torso invariably proved fatal. (© The Board of Trustees of the Armouries)

one James of Thurlbear 'hunted with his pack, and his greyhounds and his bercelets' and frequently assembled eighteen men with bows and arrows.[100] Strikingly, it has been observed that the majority of deer poachers were not peasants but 'barons, bishops, parish priests and the local gentry and their households', and that 'particularly for the nobility and higher clergy, poaching was both an entertainment and a way of solidifying connections with local clergy, knights and even royal officials'.[101] Nevertheless, while not uncommon, attacks on foresters by poachers 'seem typically to be the acts of a rough element among the lesser gentry, out for sport and excitement, and bearing arms'.[102] There has been considerable debate as to whether the intended audience of the Robin Hood ballads was of the gentry or yeomen classes.[103] Yet all elements of society must have savoured the irony developed in the Robin Hood ballads that when Robin feasts the disguised king within the greenwood as his guest, it is upon the king's own venison poached at will by the outlaw.[104]

Such accounts of poaching and outlawry clearly indicate that despite the forest law and its officers a considerable number of men possessed bows within the royal forests. Forest areas by no means had the monopoly of archers, but the Weald, Sherwood and Macclesfield are recorded as yielding notable numbers of bowmen from the thirteenth century. Thus, for instance, a picked force of archers from the king's own lands in Macclesfield served throughout Edward I's Welsh campaigns, drawing the high wage of 3d a day, while Nottinghamshire and Derbyshire were the only two counties save those bordering on Wales which sent infantry on all of Edward I's Welsh campaigns.[105] Later, in 1324, a commission was issued to select 300 foot-archers from the Forest of Dean, Berkleyhines and the county of Gloucestershire for service against the King of France in Aquitaine.[106]

There was clearly a major tension between the need to recruit skilled archers from such forest areas and the desire to protect the king's game and limit poaching. The Assize of Arms of 1230 enjoined that those with chattels of 20s or under were to have a bow and arrows, unless in the forest, in which case they were to have an axe or a lance.[107] More realistically, Edward I's Statute of Winchester of 1285, which reissued the Assize of Arms, now made legal the bearing of bows within the forest, but with 'bolts' – presumably blunt piles – rather than arrows.[108] Perhaps the most effective solution, however, was to press those caught poaching into military service. Some 300 outlaws were among those whom Edward I recruited in return for pardon for his wars in Aquitaine in 1294, the first known instance of his resort to this practice.[109] A generation later, in 1333, the archers who fought with such success at Halidon Hill in the army of his grandson included poachers from Sherwood pardoned on condition of entering the king's army[110] By then, however, English armies had undergone a profound transformation both in tactics and in composition, remoulded in the crucible of the bitter Anglo-Scottish wars in which Edward I would embroil England and its northern neighbour from 1296.

But such a struggle was not yet dreamt of in 1272, when Edward I succeeded his father on the throne of England. The young Edward, 'warlike as a pard',[111] had learned the harsh lessons of war and politics in the violent tutelage of the Barons' Wars, and had already shown his prowess at the battle of Lewes and his strategic skill at Evesham. Moreover, the lengthy process of subduing the Montfortian rebels in the aftermath of Evesham had given him and his commanders experience of operating in wooded or marshy terrain, such as Sherwood, the Weald and the Isles of Axholme and Ely, where the value of archers as light infantry came into its own.[112] Much of Edward's success in 1264–5, moreover, was due to his alliance with a group of powerful lords on the Welsh march, who had brought not only their forces but their military experience of border warfare to his aid. But it was Edward who was to transform the political situation on the marches by a series of campaigns intended first to subdue and finally to conquer the power of Gwynedd and of the princes of Wales.

Matthew Strickland

CHAPTER 9

The Hammer and the Anvil:
the Longbow in the Wars of Edward I

> Ynglis archais that hardy were and wicht
> Among the Scottis bykkerit with all thar mycht.
> That awfull schoyt was felloun for to byd.
>
> (English archers that were hardy and strong
> Attacked the Scots with all their might.
> That dreadful shooting was grievous to endure.)
>
> Blind Harry, *The Wallace* (*c.* 1476–8)

he reign of Edward I (1272–1307) was long regarded as a key phase in the technological improvement of the longbow and in its rise to military prominence as the 'national weapon'. The crucial catalyst for such developments was seen as the campaigns undertaken by the king in Wales, first in 1277 to contain and diminish the power of Llewelyn ap Gruffyd, Prince of Wales, then successfully to conquer Gwynedd itself in 1282–3, and finally to repress revolts against English rule in 1287 and 1294–5. To J.E. Morris, Edward's Welsh wars marked three significant developments, 'reform in organization, in the weapon of offence, and in combination of infantry with cavalry'.[1] Such advances, refined and reinforced by Edward's subsequent campaigns during his attempted conquest of Scotland from 1296, effectively laid the foundations on which Edward III built his successes in Scotland and in France.

More recent scholarship has seriously qualified such a view. Undeniably the conquest of Wales showed skilful strategy, tenacious and able leadership, highly sophisticated logistics 'on a massive scale which can certainly be regarded as revolutionary',[2] and the construction of the finest set of castles ever built in Europe, ringing Snowdonia with 'the towers of the bold conqueror'. Even here, however, it can be argued that Edward was but pursuing the strategy of earlier kings to their logical conclusion.[3] In terms of organisation, Edward's reign certainly saw the deployment of massive armies with unprecedented numbers of infantry, the majority of whom appear to have been archers drawn from both England and Wales. Yet high numbers belie the military effectiveness of such forces, which were often ill-equipped, poorly disciplined and could only be kept in the field for short periods.[4] As we have seen, moreover, the later thirteenth century did not herald any identifiable improvement in the bow, still less a radical change from shortbow to longbow. Nor did Edward's campaigns witness any great tactical innovations. In marked contrast to the campaigns of the Hundred Years War, where battles were very often begun on the defensive and frequently against superior odds, Edward I's armies in both Wales and Scotland significantly outnumbered their opponents in well-equipped troops, and, where the terrain and enemy tactics allowed, they attempted – and several times succeeded – to exploit their great superiority in heavy cavalry in offensive engagements. Rather than leading to innovation, such predominance ensured the continuation of, and strongly reinforced belief in, traditional tactics favouring the charge of heavy cavalry which had dominated military engagements in much of Europe during the thirteenth century. The deployment by Welsh and then by Scottish armies of large bodies of spearmen in defensive formations certainly reinforced the value of archers, who could be used to break up these units and allow the horsemen to penetrate the thinned and disordered ranks, but their role was still essentially supportive. And revealingly, in Flanders and Gascony, where the French were often more than a match for Edward I's forces, English and Welsh archers failed to make a significant impact; major engagements were eschewed and warfare was dominated by an equally traditional pattern of sieges, raids and minor skirmishes.

ORGANISATION

Edward I inherited a system of muster and recruitment for infantry that was little changed from the previous century. The obligation to serve at the king's command was enjoined on all free men between 15 and 60, who were required to possess weapons and equipment according to a sliding scale of wealth as laid down in the various assizes of arms issued from 1181 onward. These *jurati ad arma*, so called because they swore to use their arms in the king's service when required, were primarily intended to serve as a local peace-keeping force or the shire posse (*posse comitatus*), summoned 'from vill to vill with horn and hue' by the sheriff to pursue malefactors, or to act as an armed night-watch in towns and villages.[5] In times of more serious unrest such militias might assist at the siege of the castle of a disaffected baron, as at Rockingham in 1220 or Bedford in 1224, or in times of national peril be deployed in coastal defence, as in 1193, 1205 and 1265. Before the outbreak of the Barons' Wars Henry III's reign had seen only limited periods of external hostilities, but levies were also summoned on these occasions, such as for the expeditions against Wales in 1231, where many were to come with axes to help clear pathways, and in 1245.[6] Among a number of reissues of the Assize of Arms by Henry III that of 1242 stated that men holding between 40 and 100 shillings-worth of land or up to nine marks-worth of chattels were to serve 'with sword, bow, arrows and a knife', while those owning less were to be equipped with 'falces, gisarmes, small knives and other small arms (*arma minuta*)'. Men of greater wealth were, as previously, grouped as

Left: Edward I (1272–1307) and his queen, Eleanor of Castile, from the fourteenth-century gallery of kings on the west front of Lincoln Cathedral. *(© Mick Sharp)*

Opposite: Cavalry and infantry from the Holkham Bible, English, *c.* 1327–35 (British Library, Add. MS 47682, f.40). The horsemen wear a variety of helmets, either with full visors or with gorgets of plate, while the 'pair of plates' worn by the central figure is clearly shown. Several of the infantry, including the archers, wear heavily padded gambesons under their tunics and have padded coifs under their helmets. Note the use of small bucklers, which remained popular with English infantry until the sixteenth century. *(British Library/Bridgeman Art Library)*

Coment le grant peuple batallerent a cōtre le iour de iugemēt par orguil ꝑ enuie par couoitise.

Coment le cōmoune gent. checon leua a cōtre autre. luou dra autre octire ꝑ le auer. ꝑ ēue tise. E ceo est dunt nouс esperoūs bien ꝗ le iour de dreit iugemēt for mēt aproche.

well-equipped horsemen or as heavy infantry, protected by hauberks or gambesons, but it is noteworthy that those serving as archers were thus not envisioned as the poorest of society, but men of small landed holdings or a little portable wealth. The assize added, however, that 'all those who are able to shall have bows and arrows outside the forest; those in the forest shall have a bow and piles (*pilatos*)'.[7] Considerable weight was formerly placed by historians on the appearance of a separate category of archers by 1242 as indicative of the rising importance of the bowman in English armies. As we have seen, however, the absence of the bow from Henry II's Assize of Arms of 1181 is misleading as to the relative importance of military archery, while the use of archers throughout the intervening period suggests that the 1242 legislation was simply recognising the long-standing ubiquity of bows as a cheap but effective weapon among the poorer classes of freemen. In 1285 Edward reissued these provisions unchanged in the Statute of Winchester, stating that 'every man have in his house arms for keeping the peace in accordance with the ancient assize'.[8] It was not until the reign of James I (1603–25) that the obligation of all free men to keep arms was abolished by the repeal of this statute.[9] It is thus little wonder that bows feature as common weapons of offence in recorded acts of local violence. In 1292, for example, there was a flare-up of a long-running hostility between the men of Hales and of Clent in Shrewsbury, and in a skirmish one of the Clent villagers (among whose band had been the parish priest and a cleric) shot a man of Hales with three arrows from which he died.[10]

Once the royal summons to arms had gone out, recruitment was carried out by officers known as commissioners of array, who mustered all able-bodied men from the hundreds, the main subdivision of the shire, and from other local communities, then selected the best and most suitable men. The infantry, mobilised quite separately from cavalry forces, were formed into units of twenty commanded by a vintenar, who received double pay, while five of these units served under a centenar or constable.[11] Overall command and deployment of the foot in battle seems to have been the responsibility of the constable of the army, an important hereditary office held by the Bohun family.[12] The crown as yet did not supply arms and equipment to its troops save on exceptional occasions, when more specialised clothing might be issued. Thus, for example, armbands bearing the cross of St George were given to Edward's infantry in the Welsh war of 1282–3, and winter camouflage of white tunics and hose was supplied to the English garrison of Dolwyddelan in January 1283.[13] It is clear, however, that despite the injunctions of the assizes of arms some of the infantry served poorly equipped. In one notorious case one Hugo le Fitzheyr, who held land for service with a bow, shot the only arrow he had brought with him at the Scots then promptly left the army.[14] One wonders how such a man 'passed muster', and such extreme instances were probably not the norm. By contrast, men raised in Norfolk for service in Gascony in 1295 received from their local hundreds swords, knives and white tunics or *blaunchecotes*, whose high price of 3s each suggests these were some form of gambeson or soft armour.[15]

Yet although under Edward I the crown itself did not usually provide reserve supplies of bows or arrows – in stark contrast to the vast number of crossbow bolts issued – the sheer number of infantry serving as archers in Edward's armies suggests that large quantities of bows and arrows were being purchased by individuals or localities, with a concomitant stimulus in arms manufacturing. The prosperity of York in the fourteenth century may have owed not a little to its role in supplying English armies venturing north against Scotland, a boom that was shared by other northern towns; in 1315, for example, the artisans of Newcastle supplied Edward II with longbows, arrows, crossbows, siege engines and other munitions, and it is probable that they had furnished his father's armies with similar supplies.[16] Judicial records, moreover, such as the cases of Simon de Skeffington in 1298 and that of Robert of Esnyngton in 1315, indicate, as we have seen, that weapons of Spanish and Irish yew as well as of elm were readily available, as were a variety of arrow types.[17]

Already by Edward's first Welsh campaign of 1277 it appears that the majority of infantry were archers, though others served as spearmen; in 1277, for example, the border counties and Derbyshire supplied mixed units of archers and spearmen of the kind we can glimpse in the twelfth century.[18] By the time of the Scottish campaigns, beginning in 1296, almost all infantry are bowmen where their weapons are specified. The most striking feature of Edwardian armies was their sheer size. While few reliable figures are available for infantry contingents in the armies of earlier Anglo-Norman and Angevin kings, it is unlikely that they were ever consistently on such a scale.[19] Infantry had played an important role under Henry II, Richard and John, but such kings had preferred to use a smaller number of well-equipped serjeants, supplemented by mercenary Brabançon routiers – social outcasts but elite fighters – and by Welsh foot, whose numbers might be considerable, but were nothing like those seen under Edward I. Thus during Edward's first Welsh war of 1277 infantry numbers reached 15,000, of whom 9,000 were Welsh.[20] The campaign of 1282 saw the mobilisation of around 750 cavalry and 8,000 foot, while in 1287 11,000 infantry were raised, nearly two-thirds of whom were Welsh.[21] The greatest number of infantry assembled in the whole reign was in 1294, when Edward was forced to divert men and supplies intended for an expedition to Gascony to meet the serious threat of a widespread insurrection in Wales. Cavalry numbers are unknown, but infantry mustered in December 1294 numbered around 21,000 at Chester, serving under the king himself, with another 10,700 under the Earl of Warwick at Montgomery and a further 4,000 or more at Carmarthen under the Earl of Norfolk and William de Valence.[22] Massive numbers of infantry were also deployed in Edward's early Scottish campaigns, though numbers were markedly reduced in later forces. As many as 25,000 infantry may have served in his 1296 invasion of Scotland, while more certainly Edward commanded around 25,700 infantry at the battle of Falkirk in 1298.[23] 'Edward's intention', notes Professor Prestwich, 'appears to have been to crush the enemy by sheer weight of numbers.'[24] The use of mass infantry levies reveals the enormous resources of manpower on which Edward could draw, reflecting the growth both in population and in the royal bureaucracy which made the funding and mobilisation of such forces possible.

Nevertheless, quantity was undoubtedly obtained at the expense of quality, and scholars have generally thought little of the military worth of many of the infantry in Edward I's great hosts. In the first place, many who were summoned to muster never materialised, while the use of commissions of array allowed ample opportunities for peculation, profiteering and taking bribes for the avoidance of service –

Shakespeare's figure of Sir John Falstaff as a corrupt recruiting officer was far from new. In 1298, for example, 16,000 infantry were called up from Derbyshire, Nottinghamshire and the four northern counties, but of these only some 9,000 appeared.[25] Among those who did attend, discipline was poor and desertion an endemic problem, particularly in the harvest months of August and September, and during the winter. In 1295 the force commanded by the Earl of Warwick peaked at 14,500 in January, but had sharply fallen to only 2,489 by the time he fought the engagement against Llwelyn at Maes Moydog.[26] In 1300 an infantry force of some 9,000 had dwindled to only 500 by September.[27] Though the Welsh supplied a large proportion of the infantry, the hybrid nature of Edward's armies was potentially a source of serious trouble. In 1297 indiscipline among Edward's Welsh troops in Flanders had resulted in their pillaging of parts of Ghent, exacerbating the tensions between the king and this supposed ally.[28] The following year, during the Falkirk campaign, 80 Welsh were killed when a drunken affray was suppressed by the English cavalry, and the bad feeling that resulted led the Welsh to threaten to go over to the side of the Scots.[29] While Welsh elements had long served in Anglo-Norman armies, Edward I's demands for military service from the Welsh following his conquest of Wales undoubtedly did much to fuel such resentments and indiscipline.

DEFENCE AND CONQUEST: TACTICS IN WALES, 1282–95

While much of South Wales had been overrun by Anglo-Norman marchers by the end of the twelfth century, there were still large areas under native control in the west and most notably in the powerful northern principality of Gwynedd. A sustained period of military stalemate and coexistence, with frequent though not continuous hostilities, had resulted in considerable cross-fertilisation in techniques of war. Welsh archers and spearmen had become an increasingly important element in the armies of the Angevin kings, while in turn Welsh princes came to adopt aspects of Anglo-Norman military culture, including the construction of castles.[30] Nowhere was this more true than of the thirteenth-century rulers of Gwynedd, especially Llewelyn ap Iorwerth 'the Great' (d. 1240) and his grandson Llewelyn ap Gruffyd 'the Last' (d. 1282), who had engaged in a highly successful policy of expansion within Wales at the expense both of rival Welsh leaders and of the Anglo-Norman marchers. In order to retain and extend their hegemony they built and garrisoned castles, developed siege weapons, granted lands in return for what was effectively knight service, and even deployed cavalry with barded horses.[31] As

with parallel developments in Scotland from the early twelfth century, such measures were partly defensive imitation, to provide a greater ability to resist military threats from England, and partly to enforce a greater degree of control within the ruler's lands. Yet against a determined and skilful strategist like Edward, with the far greater resources of England at his disposal, neither castles nor heavy cavalry could avail.

The comparatively small and ill-defended castles of the princes of Gwynedd stood little chance against the weight of English numbers and the king's sophisticated siege trains, serving only to pin down Welsh forces to the defence of isolated strongpoints. Thus in April 1277, at the very opening of hostilities, Llewelyn's new castle at Dolforwyn surrendered rapidly to the English, while similarly in the very first stages of the 1282 campaign Prince Dafydd could hold neither Ewloe nor his new castle of Hope, which he slighted himself before withdrawing.[32] In early 1283 Dafydd attempted one last stand at Castel y Bere in Cader Idris, but his garrison was quickly contained and forced to surrender after only a ten-day siege by a predominantly infantry force of around

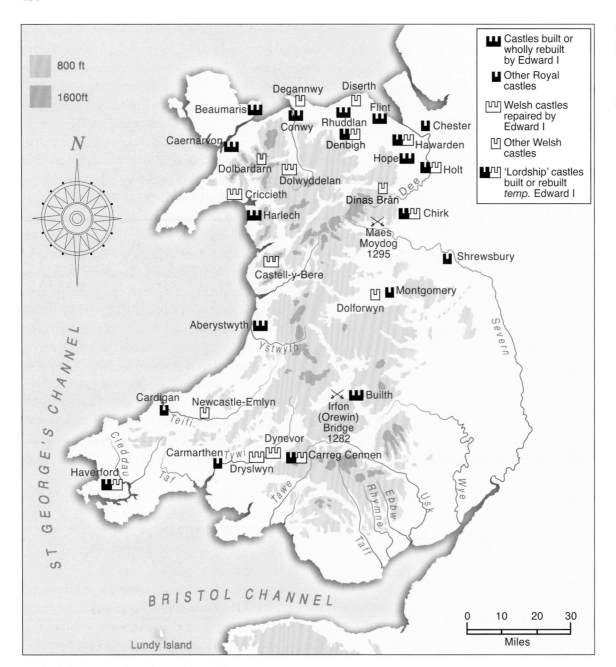

Edward I's castle-building in Wales (after *The History of the King's Works*, ed. H.M. Colvin *et al.* (1963)).

3,000, raised from Shropshire, Kidwelly and the southern Marches.[33] In 1287 the rebellion of Rhys ap Maredudd was soon reduced to the investment of his castle of Dryslwyn by a numerically far superior English force of 11,000 men under the king's brother Edmund of Cornwall, and within three weeks the castle fell.[34] Though there are few detailed accounts of fighting, the archers who formed much of the infantry contingents sent from England or their Welsh allies must have fulfilled their accustomed role of covering assaults, harrying the defenders and acting as pickets during these investments. Striking evidence of their presence is furnished by excavations, which revealed not only stone balls from trebuchets and other smaller artillery but over 100 arrow-heads, many of the bodkin type.[35]

Though the upkeep of heavy war-horses was ruinously expensive for the underdeveloped pastoral economy of Wales, Llewelyn obviously believed that the 200–300 barded horse which he could muster provided him with an important weapon against rival Welsh princelings or the marcher lords when unsupported by the English crown. Yet their absence from his campaigns of defence against Edward indicate that he recognised the futility of pitching so small a force against the numbers of heavy cavalry fielded by English royal armies.[36] Instead, the Welsh resorted of necessity to their time-honoured means of guerrilla attack and ambuscade, and by such means they achieved some successes, despite the formidable odds stacked against them. Edward's first campaign of 1277 against Llewelyn saw no major engagement, with the seizure of Anglesey and its

Conwy Castle, begun by Edward I in 1283 and substantially completed by 1287, showing the north curtain wall as seen from the town.
(© Sandro Vannini/Corbis)

grain harvest bringing the Welsh prince to submission without Edward having to penetrate into his fastness of Snowdonia itself.[37] But during the second war of 1282–3 the Welsh inflicted two substantial defeats on the English. In June 1282 a Welsh force ambushed the Earl of Gloucester, with casualties including William de Valence.[38] In the north Edward had made steady progress from his muster point at Rhuddlan along the northern coast, while a second force occupied Anglesey and constructed a bridge of boats across the Menai Straits. Despite such careful preparations, however, the English force on Anglesey led by Luke de Tany suffered a severe defeat in November, when, after making a rash and premature raid across the bridge without Edward's orders, they were attacked by the Welsh.[39] Whether, as Guisborough notes, they were unexpectedly cut off on the southern side of the bridge by the sudden tide, or whether the bridge broke down under the weight of men fleeing in the wake of defeat, the Welsh had been swift to exploit their enemy's difficulties and achieved a notable success.[40] According to the *Annals of Worcester*, 15 knights, 32 squires and 1,000 foot, 'terrified by the Welsh and fleeing from the face of the bow', were bogged down and drowned.[41] This victory is closely analogous to the defeat that the English – again in Edward's absence – would suffer at Stirling Bridge in 1297, when a rash advance over the Forth by Earl Warenne allowed the Scots to cut off and annihilate part of the English force on the north bank of the Forth.

Even when the king himself was in command, however, the army in Wales was still vulnerable to surprise attack. In December 1294, as Edward led his contingent through Denbighshire to Conwy, his baggage train was cut off and annihilated by the Welsh, leaving the king stranded at Conwy and with his men suffering a severe dearth of victuals for a time.[42] Nevertheless, certain factors helped to limit the effectiveness of Welsh guerrilla tactics in these campaigns. Edward employed large numbers of woodcutters to clear pathways through the dense forest to speed the passage of the army and to make ambush more difficult, as in 1277 when a swathe of wood was cleared between Chester and Flint.[43] As Edward continued with his policy of castle building, which eventually left Snowdonia encircled by castles, the English gained bases from which garrisons could attempt to interdict raids and launch offensive patrols. Many of the Welsh infantry serving in Edward's forces were men accustomed to fighting in rough terrain, and as skilled in the use of bow or lance as their Welsh opponents. Edward, moreover, made use of Gascon troops, some of whom may have been skilled in mountain warfare.[44] As Pierre Langtoft noted, in Edward's second Welsh war John de Vescy came 'from the king of the Aragonese with footmen without number of Basques and Gascons; they remain with the king, receive his gifts, in moors and mountains they clamber like lions. They go with the English, burn the houses, throw down the castles, slay the wretches.'[45] As a result, the Welsh did not have a monopoly on ambush and rapid strikes. In 1282 Robert Tibetot, aided by Rhys ap Maredudd and his men, had led the garrison of Carmarthen on a night raid which came close to seizing one of the Welsh leaders, Gruffyd ap Maredudd ap Owain, and took considerable booty.[46] The issue of winter camouflage clothing to the English garrison of Dolwyddelan in January 1283 suggests they were engaged in offensive operations,[47] while early in 1295 some of Edward's infantry based with the king at Conwy made a sortie in strength, inflicting substantial casualties on the Welsh and recovering at least part of the baggage lost the previous December.[48] The same year Reginald de Grey, who it will be remembered had commanded a force of archers and crossbowmen to pacify the insurgents in Sherwood Forest in 1267, carried out a similar foray from Rhuddlan Castle into the forests to flush out those of Madog ap Llewelyn's forces hidden there.[49] Concurrently, the Earl of Hereford lured a force of Welsh into a trap and defeated them.[50]

Significantly, the two principal engagements of Edward's Welsh wars were fought as a result of Welsh forces being brought to battle by the English through either ruse or ambuscade. In late 1282 Llewelyn ap Gruffyd had sought to break out of Snowdonia before Edward penned him up there, but marching south-east towards Builth he encountered an English force commanded by Roger Lestrange near the River Irfon at Orewin Bridge. Chroniclers differ as to the nature of the subsequent engagement, but both Guisborough and the Peterborough chronicle believed Llewelyn was surprised or ambushed by the English, and he may well have been lured there by treachery, expecting to receive the allegiance of Roger Mortimer.[51] What is certain is that the Welsh were heavily defeated with many casualties and the gallant Llewelyn was slain.[52] According to Guisborough, a unit of Welsh held Orewin Bridge while their main force remained on higher ground. Unseen by the Welsh a detachment of the English crossed a ford and attacked from the rear those holding the bridge. With these defeated, the main English division

crossed the bridge and advanced against the remaining Welsh forces, who were still in formation awaiting Llewelyn's return.[53] Meanwhile, hearing the noise, Llewelyn, who had been out on a recce with only one squire, tried to rejoin his army but was chased and run through by a knight named Stephen Frankton, who did not recognise who he was. The English forces, led by John Giffard and Roger Mortimer the younger, advanced up the hill, with the archers, who were interspersed with the knights, laying down a heavy covering barrage.[54] The Welsh were still expecting the return of their lord and held their ground bravely, but many were killed by the hail of arrows and the English forces exploited these losses to gain the victory.[55]

Events were to take a very similar turn in 1295, when the leader of the northern Welsh resistance, Madog ap Llewelyn, attempted to avoid encirclement by striking south, as Llewelyn had done in 1282. But he too was intercepted, this time at Maes Moydog in Powys by the English forces under the Earl of Warwick, operating from Montgomery. Whether they were forced or elected to engage in a pitched battle, Madog, 'with the elite of his Welshmen', fought stubbornly against a force of 2,500 infantry and some 119 cavalry. The chronicler Nicholas Trivet describes the ensuing engagement thus:

> The earl of Warwick, hearing that the Welsh were massed in great numbers in a certain plain between two forests, took with him a picked body of men-at arms, together with crossbowmen and archers, and, surprising them by night, surrounded them on all sides. They [the Welsh] planted the butts of their spears on the ground, and turned the points against the charging cavalry so as to defend themselves from their rush. But the earl placed a crossbowman between each two men-at-arms, and when the greater part of the spear-armed Welsh had been brought down by the bolts of the crossbows, he charged the rest with his squadron of horse, and inflicted upon them a greater loss, it is believed, than any which had been experienced by them in the past wars.[56]

To J.E. Morris, this battle marked an important step in the tactical evolution of the English armies towards perfecting the combination of missilemen and men-at-arms seen under

A Welsh spearman from the late thirteenth-century *Littere Wallie* (TNA E36/274). As with the archers depicted in the same text, it may be that one foot was left bare to gain added purchase on rough or slippery terrain. While not all Welsh troops were so simply equipped, the long spear proved a cheap and formidable weapon when deployed in disciplined formations against cavalry. *(The National Archive)*

Edward III, though in relationship to the development of the longbow itself he was forced to admit that 'the words of the chronicler and the evidence of high pay given to the crossbow-man show that he was the more important soldier in 1295'.[57] Morris's emphasis on the battle's tactical importance is problematic, for close cooperation between cavalry and infantry, particularly archers and crossbowmen, was scarcely new, as the Normans' tactics at Hastings, the crusaders' 'fighting marches', Anglo-Norman operations in Ireland, and the role assigned to crossbowmen and archers during the thirteenth century all indicate. It has been objected, moreover, that the key role of crossbowmen indicated by Trivet is hard to reconcile with the army's pay roll, which reveals the presence of only thirteen archers and crossbowmen in Warwick's division.[58] It is difficult to believe, however, that these were the only missilemen in so major an English force, and to square these accounts with Trivet both Morris and Prestwich are surely right in suggesting that other bowmen must have taken part in the engagement.[59] The tactics recorded by Trivet, furthermore, accord well with Guisborough's statement that at Orewin Bridge an attack was made 'by our archers who were mixed in with the knights', and with the advice of the *Liber recuperationis* of 1291 that on crusade 'horsemen should always have many crossbowmen or archers mixed in with them'.[60] Trivet's detail on just how the crossbowmen were 'mixed in' with the cavalry is of great value, as few other chronicles furnish such specific details. Perhaps a similar combination of one archer between two knights had been adopted earlier at the Standard in 1138, where we are told that archers were 'mixed in' with Stephen's dismounted knights, but are not told how.

A differing but equally important account of the battle of Maes Moydog, brought to light by Michael Prestwich, comes from a contemporary vernacular newsletter incorporated into the chronicle of the Premonstratensian house of Hagnaby in Lincolnshire:

> The prince's host awaited our men on open ground and they fought together, our men killing a good six hundred. Then our men from Llystynwynnan joined battle with

those who were transporting the prince's victuals, and killed a good hundred, and took from them over six score beasts laden with foodstuffs. And we lost only one esquire, the tailor of Robert FizWalter, and six infantry-men, but a good ten horses were killed. For the Welsh-men held their ground well, and attacked our men from the front, and they were the best and bravest Welsh that anyone has seen.[61]

This account is of greatest interest, for although archers are not recorded it strongly suggests that at some stage in the conflict the Welsh spearmen adopted the offensive – they 'attacked our men from the front'. This is not impossible to square with Trivet's account, for on being attacked the Welsh may have formed up into a defensive position to receive the initial charge of Warwick's cavalry, but then come on at the English. If so, this would be a very early example of the offensive use of such an infantry formation, anticipating by several years tactics that would become prominent with the Flemish defeat of the French at Courtrai in 1302 and with Bruce's victory at Bannockburn in 1314. We should be wary here, for as with Scottish tactics it may only be our dearth of evidence as to earlier Welsh formations in battle that creates the impression of innovation. As Gerald of Wales had pointed out in the previous century, the favoured weapon of the north Welsh was the long spear, and such infantry appear in the rough marginal sketches of the 'Liber A' (see p. 156).[62] The men of Gwynedd had faced the threat of heavy cavalry from the very onset of the Norman conquest, and it seems likely that they had found ways to maximise the spear's potential in battle long before 1295. Novel or not, however, the tactics of Madog's spearmen in 1295 failed to avert defeat, for the absence of adequate missile support left these formations of infantry highly vulnerable to enemy archers. By contrast, the implication of both Guisborough and Trivet is that bowmen in Edward's forces had played a significant role in achieving the victories at Orewin Bridge and Maes Moydog. Only three years later the same tactical imbalance would lead to the bloody defeat of William Wallace's army at Falkirk.

EDWARD I IN SCOTLAND

When Edward I invaded Scotland in 1296 he enjoyed, as he had done in his conquest of Wales, an enormous advantage in men, material resources and military organisation. Scotland was a poor land in contrast to its wealthy and economically developed southern neighbour, with little urbanisation and a largely pastoral economy. As the Anglo-Scottish wars were to

reveal, this very poverty and the problems posed by the land's geography were to be a great natural defence: in France the great *chevauchées* of Edward III and his commanders yielded riches and plunder, but in Scotland it was almost impossible to live off the land. Sophisticated though the logistics and commissariat of Edward I and II were by contemporary standards, armies frequently ran out of food, while lack of booty sapped morale. Scots commanders learned – though it took initial defeat to drive home the lesson – that the best way to defeat an English invasion force was to withdraw before it into the mountains or forest, if possible scorching the earth and removing livestock and any sustenance. Cheated of a static target against which to deploy their powerful armies, the English were soon forced through lack of supplies, exacerbated by cost and desertion, to head homewards and think again. They might leave garrisons in powerful castles, but even here the problems of victualling in hostile territory ultimately proved insurmountable in all but the castles of the southern lowlands.[63]

Though known to earlier Scottish kings and commanders, these lessons were only adopted gradually by the Scots in the face of Edward I's aggression. For the nobility of Scotland was largely Anglo-Norman in origin, and shared much of the chivalric culture and concepts of waging war of their English counterparts with whom they were interrelated by marriage and cross-border landholding. To fight a war using guerrilla tactics of night raids and commando attacks was considered by many to be unchivalric, cowardly and dishonourable; despite its effectiveness, Robert the Bruce himself was criticised by some of his nobles for just such a strategy.[64] Rather, men trained to fight in tournaments as heavy cavalry yearned for the glory of feats of arms in the open field. Thus it was that only a matter of weeks after Edward had crossed the border into Scotland in 1296, the Scots, most of whom had not seen serious military action,[65] attempted to give battle to John, Earl of Warenne, at Spottsmuir, close to the castle of Dunbar. As the Scots advanced, abandoning a strong hill-top position, the English cavalry attacked as they redeployed over difficult terrain and swiftly routed them. The Scottish horse 'broke up and scattered more swiftly than smoke', and many of the Scottish nobility were taken prisoner.[66] The Scottish leaders should have known better, for John Comyn, Robert Bruce (the future king's grandfather) and John Balliol had all been taken captive at Lewes in 1264, when they were overwhelmed by the charge of Simon de Montfort's forces.[67] Little is known of the role of the English infantry at Dunbar, but a surviving snatch of a popular song, very possibly sung by the common soldiers themselves, attributes to them a significant part in the battle and in the plundering that followed:

> The foot folk (*fote folk*)
> Put the Scots in the poke,
> And bared their buttocks (*nackened their nages*)
> By way
> Never heard I say
> Of readier boys

> To rob
> The robes of the rich
> That fell in the field
> They took of each man;
> May the rough ragged fiend
> Tear them [the slain Scots] to hell![68]

Dunbar painfully demonstrated the lesson learnt at such cost by David I at the Standard in 1138 and by William the Lion at Alnwick in 1174, that fighting the English in the open field was to invite disaster. The English armies of Edward I were superior in numbers, equipment and experience. Above all, no force of horse mustered by the Scottish nobles could hope to match the formidable numbers of heavy cavalry which the English could field.[69] This imbalance could be met by negotiation or flight; in 1297 Robert Bruce, Bishop Wishart and James Stewart mustered their forces at Irvine, but capitulated as soon as they were confronted by an English army under Robert Clifford and Henry Percy, while at the Cree in 1300 the Scots formed up into three 'battles' of cavalry but fled precipitously when charged by the English horse.[70] At Falkirk in 1298 William Wallace chose a third way: the stubborn resistance of tightly grouped infantry in defensive formations.

The disaster at Dunbar had profound military consequences. With a large element of the Scots nobility now languishing in English prisons, the leaders of the Scottish resistance had no choice but to place their reliance almost wholly on the common foot-soldier. The Scots infantry had already given an indication of their mettle against the English horse at Dunbar, where they 'would have stood firm had not the knights showed their heels so readily'.[71] As the flames of revolt spread through the land only a year after Edward's seemingly rapid and complete subjugation of Scotland, such men flocked to the standards of William Wallace and Andrew Murray, and in August 1297 their army inflicted a humiliating defeat on an English force under Earl Warenne at Stirling Bridge.[72] The Scots had occupied a strong hill-top position on the Abbey Craig at the base of the Ochils, overlooking the narrow bridge that crossed the Forth. Rashly believing the Scots would not dare to engage an English field army, Warenne and Hugh de Cressingham, the corpulent and hated English treasurer in Scotland, declined the wise advice of the Scottish knight Sir Richard Lundie to outflank the Scots by crossing the Forth upriver, and instead ordered part of their army across the bridge in the face of the Scots army. With astute timing the Scots swept down from their position, cut off this unit on the north bank and annihilated it, slaying Cressingham and forcing Warenne, who was powerless to assist on the other side of the river, into a headlong flight. Stirling Bridge has been hailed as

Above: Caerlaverock Castle, Dumfriesshire, built in the later thirteenth century by the Maxwell family. Though it has been rebuilt, the essential design is that of the castle besieged by Edward I in 1300. Excavations of the moat have yielded a number of tanged and bodkin-headed arrows, very probably dating from that brief but fierce assault on the castle. *(Historic Scotland)*

Right: Skipness Castle, Kintyre, seen from the south-west. The curtain wall, with its careful provision for arrow-loops, was erected in the late thirteenth or early fourteenth century to enclose an existing stone hall, possibly on the orders of Edward I. *(© Crown Copyright reproduced courtesy of Historic Scotland)*

one of the first triumphs of predominantly infantry forces over more heavily equipped 'feudal' armies in which cavalry were dominant, though it could be viewed more as an ambuscade, like the victory of the Swiss over the Austrians at Morgarten in 1315, than a pitched battle.[73] The triumph enormously boosted Scots morale, just as it spurred Edward to mount a major expedition in reprisal the following year. But its primary importance was that it encouraged Wallace, flushed with success and mindful of the resentment towards the English, to pit his spearmen in open battle against the full might of Edward I's army. Whether Andrew Murray, Wallace's fellow author of the victory, would have agreed with this plan is unknown, for he died of wounds received at Stirling Bridge. Before we turn to the battle itself, however, let us pause to place the Selkirk archers who fought and died with Wallace at Falkirk within a broader context and examine the evidence of Scottish military archery up to the close of the thirteenth century.

SCOTTISH ARCHERY BEFORE 1300

Like so much relating to Scottish military affairs before the later thirteenth century, our knowledge concerning the use of archers is scant. Bowmen appear on the tenth-century Sveno Stone from Forres, which though very badly weathered shows archers preceding a group of infantry armed with swords and small round shields.[74] Archers are mentioned among David I's forces at the battle of the Standard in 1138, where it seems the king had originally intended to deploy them in conjunction with his knights.[75] We do not know, however, whence these bowmen came. The Scots kings had two main sources of military recruitment. For the defence of the kingdom they could summon 'the common army' or a general levy of free-men, recruited on a local basis by earldoms. Known as 'Scottish service' north of the Forth, this supplemented a much smaller but more professional force of knights and serjeants raised by the tenure of land held in return for service as a fully equipped knight or a less heavily armed serjeant.[76] Both types of service yielded archers. From the reign of David's grandson Malcolm IV there is evidence for a number of tenures owing the service of an archer, who had to be mounted and might be required to possess a haubergel or short hauberk.[77] This suggests that from at least the mid-twelfth century the Scots kings could command a small but well-equipped and mobile force of bowmen, either for escort or to support their knights. Bowmen equally made up a part – though how large a part it is impossible to say – of 'the common army'. Matthew Paris noted that the Scots army drawn up to resist Henry III's proposed expedition in 1244 contained knights and infantry, the latter armed with axes, spears and bows.[78] We glimpse such troops among the force that drove off the fleet of King Haakon Haakonsson of Norway at Largs on the Ayrshire coast in 1263. *Haakon's Saga* relates that the Norwegians encountered 'a great army of foot-soldiers, well-equipped with weapons; they had mostly bows and Irish axes'. The Scots had shot at the Norwegian ships at a distance from the shore, and seem to have harassed them with archery during the ensuing struggle on the shoreline.[79] Some of these troops may have been crossbowmen, as the Exchequer records reveal payment in the same year for the purchase of 36 yew staves for the laths of crossbows at Ayr Castle.[80]

As in England and Wales, crossbows formed an essential element in the munitions of royal, and probably baronial, castles; in 1264–6, for example, 3,000 bolts were ordered for the strategically vital border castle of Roxburgh, together with 14 shields (*targis*).[81] In 1300 archers and crossbowmen were among those defending Caerlaverock Castle in Galloway against the assault of Edward I, with a contemporary French poem noting how the Scots 'bend their bows and cross-bows, and shoot with their espringalds'.[82] Military architecture such as at Caerlaverock similarly reveals increasingly sophisticated provision for defence by bows and crossbows. Existing curtain walls of stone, but of simple design, were strengthened with round mural towers, as at Rothesay and Kildrummy, to provide enfilade shooting. At Rothesay the long, thin loops in these mural towers terminate in spade-shaped openings set into the splay of the towers' base,[83] while at Kildrummy the most complete surviving tower, the north-west or Warden's tower, is of fine ashlar and contains carefully sited loops, served by wide internal embrasures, on two storeys, commanding the north-west and north-east curtain and the postern gate.[84] Such flanking towers were incorporated *ab initio* in the design of great thirteenth-century castles such as Bothwell, Direlton, Caerlaverock and Inverlochy, which, like Kildrummy, reflected the close ties of the Anglo-Scottish nobility with architectural trends both south of the border and in northern France.[85] Even in the more simple structures of the west coast embrasures for loops were provided at the wall head, or, as at Dunstaffnage (Argyll), in the north-west tower and at regular intervals along the south-west and south-east curtains.[86] Many of the defences constructed in Scotland by Edward I consisted of 'peels', heavily defended and no doubt generously provided with embrasures for missilemen, but they were made of wood and have accordingly not survived. But the formidable battery of cross-looped slits which guard the south and west curtain walls of the comparatively small castle of Skipness on the eastern coast of the Mull of Kintyre may be the result of payments made by the king to strengthen 'one of the major medieval fortresses of the western seaboard'.[87]

Though Scots archers are not mentioned at Wallace's victory at Stirling Bridge, it seems likely that some were among the infantry that formed the mainstay of his army. An English poem on the Anglo-Scottish wars imagines the Scots saying before the battle, 'O William Wallace! Send us to them [the English]. Arrows can penetrate the hard mail. Let us call together our archers . . .'.[88] At Falkirk many of the archers were drawn from Selkirk (now Ettrick) Forest, and Guisborough notes they were 'tall and handsome men'.[89] Wallace had used Selkirk Forest as a base in 1297 and continued to do so until his eventual capture in 1305. Doubtless the archers of Selkirk played the same role in harassing English troops as the bowmen of the Weald had done in 1216–17 and 1264–5 against the forces of Louis of France and Henry III respectively. The English realised the dangerous potential of the Forest for guerrilla operations in 1301: their strategy had been to contain it by taking Selkirk and Peebles,[90] while they themselves launched fast mounted raids into the Forest, even in winter. In February 1304 a unit under Seagrave, Clifford and Latimer raided into Selkirk Forest and defeated Wallace and Fraser.[91] Wallace himself was believed by at least one English chronicler, William Rishanger, to have been an archer – and thus by implication an outlaw and brigand – who had offered his bow in the service of the Guardians of Scotland against the invading English. There was, he notes:

> a certain young man by the name of William Wallace (le Waleis), an archer, who sought his living by his bow and quiver. Of lowly birth and reared as an outlaw, once he had tested his daring in many places (as is the habit of brave men) he sought permission from the Scots to intercept the English where possible and also to resist their army with his bow; the Scots were also to supply him with aid and he would protect their army.[92]

Striking confirmation of Wallace's link with archery has come from an important recent find. Only one original document issued by Wallace is known to be extant: a letter of 1297 to the merchants of Lübeck, noting that following the Scots' victory at Stirling Bridge the country's ports were again open for trade. Though the text of this latter document was well known, the reverse of the seal appended to it had not been reproduced and had gone unnoticed until 1998, when Mr Ashby McGowan rediscovered in Glasgow's Mitchell Library a cast of both sides of the seal made in 1912, when the letter had been on loan to

an exhibition in Kelvingrove Park. The obverse of the seal bears the royal arms of Scotland, a lion rampant within its tressure and fleur-de-lis, but remarkably the reverse depicts a bow and arrow, with a hand on the string. The inscription around the image has been read by Professor Duncan of Glasgow University as '[Willelm]vs Filivs Alani Walais', that is 'William son of Alan Wallace'.[93] This new evidence not only strongly suggests that Wallace came from Ayrshire, where his father Alan was a crown tenant (and not from Elderslie in Renfrewshire as was traditionally believed), but also that he regarded the bow as his distinctive weapon, and used it as his rebus.[94] Wallace's reputation as a skilful archer was developed in the legends which grew around him, and is reflected in the fifteenth-century poem *The Wallace* by Blind Harry, probably written in about 1476–8. In this colourful but historically unreliable epic, shaped as much by the political situation of Harry's own day as by Wallace's own career, the poet tells how Wallace defended himself against an English raid into Short Wood, north of Perth:

> A bow he bair was byg and well beseyn
> And arrows als bath lang and scharpe with-all.
> No man was thar that Wallace bow mycht drall.
> Rycht stark was he and in-to souir ger
> Bauldly he schott amang thai men of wer.
> Ane angell hede to the hukis he drew
> And at a schoyt the formost sone he slew.[95]

> He bore a bow which was big and well furnished
> And also arrows that were both long and sharp.
> There was no man who might draw Wallace's bow.
> He was very strong and wearing trusty armour,
> Boldly he shot among the warriors.
> He drew a broad arrowhead to the barbs
> And slew the foremost man with a single shot.

The seal of William Wallace. The choice of a bow and arrow as a device supports the belief of one contemporary chronicler that Wallace was a powerful archer. *(By courtesy of the Mitchell Library, Glasgow)*

Few of Wallace's men, noted Harry, were good archers, for they preferred to fight as equal opponents with sword or spear. But though wounded in the neck by a shaft from a Lancashire bowman, Wallace himself shot down fifteen of the enemy until he at last ran out of arrows.[96]

Influenced by the theory of the shortbow, some historians have regarded the Scots as possessing only an inferior kind of bow to their southern opponents, and being seriously disadvantaged as a result.[97] Yet there is nothing to suggest the weapons used by Scottish archers in this period differed markedly, if at all, from those used by their Welsh and English counterparts in Edwardian armies. There is little if any extant material comparable with the English court records that give such valuable details of bow size and wood types, but later Gaelic poetry mentions bows of both yew and elm, with arrows of birch and feathers of grey goose or eagle.[98] The so-called 'Flodden bow' is without reliable provenance or secure date, and as such cannot be taken as representative of Scottish weapons of the thirteenth to fifteenth centuries. Certainly no contemporary authority ever suggests that Scottish archers were defeated by their English counterparts because of a technical inferiority in their weapons. Indeed, as we shall see, the large numbers of Scottish archers who were recruited to serve in French armies in the latter stages of the Hundred Years War strongly imply that these bowmen were looked to as being an effective antidote to English archers.[99] But in 1298 the Scots would place their chief hope not in their archers but in their spearmen.

THE BATTLE OF FALKIRK, 22 JULY 1298

In 1298 a vengeful Edward led into Scotland a massive army comprising around 3,000 horse, 14,800 English infantry and a further 10,900 Welsh.[100] The English took a number of castles in Lothian but the problem of supply was acute, and they were on the verge of withdrawing south when contact was made with Wallace's army near Falkirk.[101] We have no comparative numbers for Wallace's force, though it appears to have been sizeable and its general composition is apparent. There was a small cavalry force but most were infantry, raised from the earldoms of Scotland by common levy or 'Scottish service'.[102] If we may believe the later testimony of the chronicler Walter Bower, Wallace had reformed and trained this levy, taking four men as a sub-unit and making the fifth man their officer; making the tenth man the officer of every nine, the twentieth the officer of nineteen, and so on up to units of 1,000, with obedience enforced by the death penalty. Similarly, he was said to have demanded lists from every shire, barony and town of all able-bodied men between sixteen and sixty, and hanged any who failed to attend the army.[103] The majority of such levies were armed with the long spear, a simple, cheap yet effective weapon when deployed in disciplined formations. Wallace formed his spearmen into four closely packed units or 'schiltroms', each bristling with spears, and according to one chronicler with ropes staked around the formations for added cohesion.[104] 'Their spearmen', noted Guisborough, 'had their spears sloping upwards, and they stood shoulder to shoulder with their faces outwards.'[105] Pierre Langtoft expressed it more poetically:

> In their vanguard back was placed against back,
> And point of lance on point, in ranks so serried,
> Like castle on plain surrounded with wall.[106]

Though the marked similarity between the battle of Stirling Bridge and the Welsh victory over Edward's forces crossing the Menai Straits in 1282 is probably no more than coincidence, it is nevertheless highly likely that Wallace would have known of this and other engagements such as Orewin Bridge and Maes Moydog fought by the Welsh against Edward's forces. Yet it is also important to remember that the long spear had been known to the Scots for many centuries; Anglo-Norman writers noted that it was the favoured weapon of the Galwegians at the Standard in 1138, while it is depicted much earlier on the famous Aberlemno stone, which probably represents the Pictish victory at Nechtansmere in 685 over the Northumbrian king Egfrith. On this stone a Pictish infantryman, flanked by two companions, holds a long spear with both hands, in a manner reminiscent of the pikemen in the Greek phalanx, with a shield hanging from his neck by a baldric. Opposing him is a heavily armed Northumbrian cavalryman. It is possible that here we have a very early schematic representation of the 'schiltrom', deployed by poorly equipped infantry against the might of heavy horsemen.[107] At Dunbar in 1296 the spearmen had held their ground, while the Lanercost chronicler notes that at Falkirk the Scots formed up 'as was their custom'.[108] What we can say is that Falkirk marks the first engagement where we have a certain and fairly detailed record of the Scots adopting the use of massed spears in a defensive formation. There is an important analogy here with the longbow. Neither weapon was invented or 'developed' around the turn of the thirteenth century, for they had been known since time out of mind. Rather, what occurred in the Anglo-Scottish wars was that a traditional weapon was deployed en masse and in a new manner, with profound tactical results, just as under Edward III

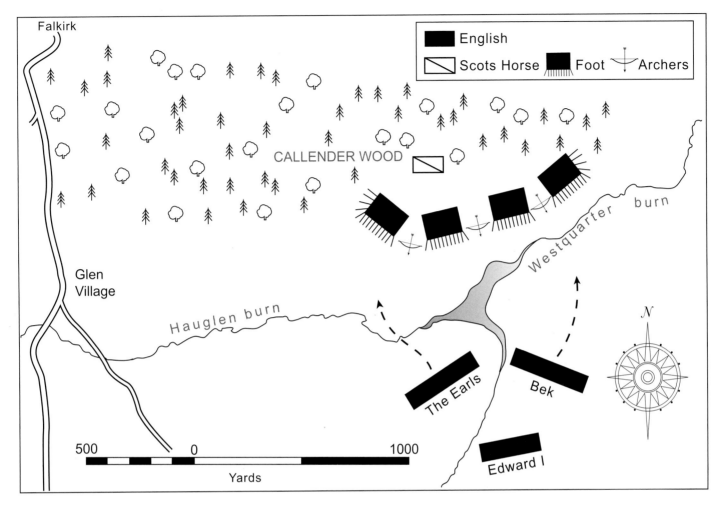

Above: The battle of Falkirk, 22 July 1298.

Left: An English archer bracing his bow, from the Luttrell Psalter, English, c. 1320–30 (British Library, Add. MS 42130, f.56). *(British Library/Bridgeman Art Library)*

tactics were implemented which allowed the pre-existing longbow to be used to its maximum effect.

At Falkirk Wallace drew up his ranks on high ground, with his front protected by a burn and boggy terrain. What cavalry he possessed were kept to the rear, while between the schiltroms he placed a significant force of archers, under the command of Sir John Stewart of Jedburgh. It is striking that unlike at the Standard in 1138, where the English archers had been mixed in between the dismounted knights and spearmen, the Scottish archers were placed outside the protective formations of pikemen. Why this was so is not certain; possibly the schiltroms needed to be densely packed to withstand the shock of the English cavalry, and that consequently there was insufficient space between the spearmen for the archers to shoot effectively. The archers, however, were not protected by pits or fosses, and as events were to show all too soon they were thus highly vulnerable.

Prevented by the burn from making a direct frontal assault, Edward's forces attacked the Scottish formations from the flanks. The chronicle formerly attributed to John of Fordun and its continuation by Walter Bower both assert that not only was Robert Bruce, the future King of Scots, fighting in King Edward's army, but that he even guided Anthony Bek's squadron around a hill to attack Wallace's positions from the rear.[109] Whatever the truth of this allegation, it is clear that the unsupported English cavalry brigades charged Wallace's schiltroms before any of their archers were brought up, in marked contrast to the earlier battles of Orewin Bridge and Maes Moydog, where the English bowmen had initiated the assault or worked closely with the cavalry in their attack on the Welsh formations. If Roger Lestrange or the Earl of Warwick had communicated their experiences of how to defeat such infantry formations, the lesson was now ignored. In part, this may have been due to indiscipline, for Guisborough noted that the second battle (or division) under Anthony Bek, the warlike Bishop of Durham, pushed on too fast 'so as to have the honour of attacking first'. His command to slow down and wait for the king's own battle was greeted by the angry retort of Ralph Basset of Drayton that he should go and say mass and not lecture soldiers on their job.[110] Yet more significantly, this unsupported assault reflected the supreme confidence of heavy cavalry in the thirteenth century. As we have seen, this was the period in which knights, increasingly heavily armed and usually mounted on 'barded' horses with mail and leather defences, played a highly prominent role in pitched battle. Cavalry had played a dominant role in the victory of the Sienese over the Florentines at Montaperti in 1260, and at the battles of Benevento (1266) and Tagliacozzo (1268) between Charles of Anjou and the Hohenstaufen.[111] Edward must have remembered his own successful cavalry charge at Lewes in 1264, and his defeat of de Montfort's army at Evesham the following year seems to have been primarily a mounted engagement until its final stages, with little evidence for a significant role played by missilemen in either engagement.

At Falkirk too, it seemed that initially the cavalry might indeed sweep the field in their first assault. Faced by the charging English knights, the Scots horsemen 'fled without striking a blow as at Dunbar', while the exposed archers were ridden down with heavy casualties and their commander slain.[112] In isolation, however, the English cavalry could make little impression on the bristling hedges of spears. As Guisborough noted, 'our men concentrated their attack on the spearmen in their rings who were like a thick wood, and could not force their way in because of the number of spears, though they struck and stabbed some on the outside'.[113] But now Edward's archers and slingers were brought to bear against the static schiltroms, themselves deprived of both cavalry and missile support. 'Our foot shot at them with arrows', continued Guisborough, 'and some with stones which lay there in plenty. So many were slain and the front ranks pushed back on the rear ranks in confusion, and then our horse broke in and routed them.'[114] Casualties among the Scots infantry are unknown, but must have been heavy. Though Wallace himself escaped, his military reputation and political position among a fractious and divided Scottish leadership were irreparably damaged; as an English song gleefully noted, 'Wallace, thy reputation as a soldier is lost; since thou didst not defend thy people with the sword, it is just that thou shouldst now be deprived of thy dominion'.[115] The impact of the defeat on Scottish morale was evident two years later when the Scots and English armies again confronted each other across the tidal estuary of the Cree in Galloway. Initially the Scots archers bickered with their English counterparts over the river, but once the tide receded sufficiently for the English to launch a cavalry attack the Scots forces broke up and quickly fled into the rough terrain. This time a lack of lightly armed Welsh troops in Edward's forces meant the English were not able to pursue them further.[116]

Crucially, it was the defensive formations adopted by the Scots at Falkirk that once more threw the role of archery in English armies into prominence. The tactical resemblance between Falkirk and Hastings has often been noted: only by a combination of missilemen with cavalry could disciplined infantry in a defensive formation be defeated. At Hastings, however, William had begun the assault with his archers and crossbowmen, who had been placed in the front ranks. Edward was a very capable commander, but it would seem he initially believed that the sheer weight of numbers of his heavy cavalry would win the day, and only after they were repulsed did he adopt the successful combination of cavalry with archers that his lieutenants had employed with good effect against the Welsh. Falkirk also demonstrated the extreme vulnerability of archers when not adequately protected either by their own infantry or by the kind of natural or man-made obstacles which the English were soon to employ with such proficiency during the Hundred Years War. In 1314 at Bannockburn, however, it was to be the English archers who would be taught a bloody lesson on the dangers of being caught by enemy cavalry on open ground.

Edward's policy of employing great numbers of infantry has generally been regarded as unsuccessful, in that their military worth ultimately did not justify the huge cost in wages, the massive logistical effort and problems of transport and supply. Equally, the reign had not given rise to any great tactical innovations. Nevertheless, if we avoid hindsight of the disastrous defeat of Edward II's huge army at Bannockburn and limit analysis to the period before Edward I's death in 1307, it should be noted that Edward's military policy of throwing great numbers and resources at the enemy, wasteful though it undoubtedly was, had achieved considerable success within Britain. Wales had been conquered and two rebellions suppressed. Scotland had been invaded, and despite a series of long and gruelling campaigns the Scots had finally been worn down and forced to accept a peace settlement recognising Edward's kingship in 1305. As an English song crowed,

Tprot! Scot, for thy strife
Hang up thyn hatchet and thy knife,
While life lasts to him
With the long shanks.[117]

Although Robert Bruce's *coup d'état* in 1306 shattered this political settlement, Edward I lived long enough to see his forces under Aymer de Valence rout Bruce at Methven, and at the time of the king's death Bruce was still on the run as a defeated and politically isolated fugitive.

FAILURE IN GASCONY AND FLANDERS

It is, however, important to set Edward's military successes in Wales and Scotland and the role of the longbow into the broader context of his continental wars, for the Anglo-French war of 1294–7 sharply reveals both the limitations of Edward's military capacity and the lack of any devastating new weaponry or tactics.[118] Of all Edward's wars this was arguably the most important to him, for it was fought to retain Gascony, the rump of the once extensive Angevin possessions within France, and Edward greatly prized his position as Duke of Aquitaine. Infantry were raised in large numbers from England and Wales to serve in Gascony, such as the 25,000 infantry summoned for the expedition of 1296, the majority of whom were archers.[119] Such troops were augmented by Gascon serjeants recruited within the duchy, many of whom came as part of the retinues of Gascon lords serving under Edward's banner, and by Catalan foot, who included crossbowmen.[120] Even given the disparity between the numbers of infantry summoned and those who actually attended muster and took ship to Gascony, Edward's army was greater than many of the English forces which were to win notable victories in France during the next century. Yet in contrast to the successes of Edward and his commanders within Britain, English campaigns in Gascony proved much more inglorious, and are well characterised as 'the last of the series of thirteenth-century military failures on the continent'.[121] This was for a number of reasons. Edward's opponent, Philip III, was more than a match in terms of men and resources, at a time when Edward had to face renewed insurrection in Wales and the onset of his war against Scotland from 1296. The fighting in Gascony was left to Edward's lieutenants, who were outnumbered and out-generalled by the capable French commander Robert of Artois, while Edward operated from Flanders at the head of an allied coalition that was ruinously expensive and achieved virtually nothing of strategic worth.

Above all, as Malcolm Vale has noted, 'the war in Aquitaine was to be primarily a war of sieges, skirmishes and counter-sieges, in which infantry and siege equipment had an important part to play'.[122] But whereas within Britain Edward could bring a formidable siege train to bear against his opponents, the expeditionary force of 1296 led by his brother Edmund of Lancaster did not possess heavy siege engines and accordingly achieved little; his Anglo-Gascon forces, for example, failed to take Bordeaux, and were forced to raise the sieges of St Macaire and Dax.[123] These engagements only give the briefest glimpses of the nature of the fighting. Hence at Bordeaux the French garrison sallied out against the English, who pretended to withdraw and then turned on the French, driving them back with casualties to the city gates, but some of the English, venturing in too far, were trapped and captured.[124] At Dax the besieging forces made daily, though fruitless, assaults against the town, while the French garrison made many sorties and fought with the besiegers.[125]

The role of Edward's infantry in open combat is still harder to assess, for the only major engagement in Gascony occurred at Bellegarde in February 1297, when an Anglo-Gascon army under Henry de Lacy, Earl of Lincoln, was routed by the forces of Robert of Artois. Lincoln, who was hastening to relieve the bastide of Bellegarde, had been informed by a spy that the French forces besieging the town were few in number. The English pushed on even though dusk was falling, marching in three divisions, with their supply wagons laden with grain placed between these formations.[126] Close to the town, however, they passed through a wood, and as the first division debouched from the trees on to open ground they found Artois's army, ranged in four divisions, lying in wait. Attacked by surprise, the English vanguard disintegrated, falling back in confusion and colliding with the oncoming middle and rear divisions, causing panic.[127] John of Brittany and Lincoln attempted to rally their men but found it impossible. Many fled, and the infantry subsequently refused to come out of the woods. Though some fighting took place, confusion reigned as night came on, with friend not recognising foe in the darkness. John de St John and several knights were caught up with the French forces as they withdrew towards Bellegarde and were captured.[128]

Similarly, Edward I's own operations in Flanders reveal something of the composition of his forces, but little about tactical dispositions in the field. He had assembled an army which from August to November 1297 included some 870 cavalry and 7,810 infantry. The latter comprised 5,297 Welsh archers, led by 45 mounted constables and the captain of the north Welsh, and 2,285 archers from England and the marches led by 21 mounted constables. In addition, there were 150 Irish foot, 48 archers and 22 crossbowmen of the king's wardrobe, and 10 lancers attending on the king's person.[129] The Flemish chronicler Lodewyk van Velthem has left us a vivid picture of the Welsh troops serving under Edward, and one which accords well with the observations of Gerald of Wales and William le Breton a century earlier:

> Edward, King of England, came to Flanders. He brought with him many soldiers from the land of Wales, and also some from England . . . There you saw the peculiar habits of the Welsh. In the very depth of winter they were running about bare-legged. They wore a red robe. They could not have been warm. The money they received from the King was spent in milk and butter. They would eat and drink anywhere. I never saw them wearing armour. I studied them very closely, and walked among them to find out what defensive armour they carried when going into battle. Their weapons were bows, arrows and swords. They also had javelins. They wore linen clothing. They were great drinkers . . . They inflicted much damage on the Flemings. Their pay was too small and so it came about that they took what did not belong to them.[130]

Such were the lightly armed but hardy Welsh, with their linen tunics and red cloaks, who had fought both for and against Edward I in his conquest of Wales, and who now had been summoned to ply their bows and javelins in the king's foreign wars. Nevertheless, Edward's expeditionary force was felt to be too small to challenge effectively Philip's main army, and it failed to undertake any offensive action before Edward abandoned his ally the Count of Flanders by negotiating a truce with the French.[131] Thus despite being able to field a sizeable force of missilemen to support their men-at-arms, such troops were restricted in Edward's continental campaigns primarily to siege warfare. Strikingly, Walter of Guisborough noted that despite its numbers the French army did not try to stop Edward's march from Bruges to Ghent, 'for they feared the infantry of the King of England, because there were many archers among them'.[132] Yet though this indicates the French knights already had a healthy respect for English and Welsh archers, there is little to suggest that, had a major engagement taken place between Anglo-Gascon and French forces, such bowmen would have played any more prominent a role than they had done in the civil war battles such as Lewes and Evesham in the 1260s. The point is significant. Record evidence, as we have seen, demonstrates unequivocally that longbows of over 6ft were commonplace in English society, yet in Edward's Gascon wars there were no battles such as those in the 1340s and 1350s in which small expeditionary forces triumphed over far larger French armies. The bow itself was thus not the catalyst for military change and the subsequent successes from the 1330s; the essential elements were to be organisational and tactical.

Edward I's reign had seen military activity remarkable not only for its geographical range but for its intensity and scale. Yet tactically his reign witnessed little change, for there had been scant reason for military innovation. Cavalry continued to retain the importance they had enjoyed throughout the century, though the need for archers and crossbowmen in an effective supporting role had been driven home by the defensive formations of Welsh and Scottish spearmen. The astute deployment of both arms had allowed Edward's lieutenants to defeat the spear-armed Welsh in open combat, and enabled the king himself to break the massed formations of Scottish spear-armed infantry at Falkirk. Robert of Artois, who had routed the English forces at Bellegarde, failed to achieve such a breakthrough against the Flemings at Courtrai in 1302, and was slain at their hands. Ironically, it was English successes in Scotland under Edward I which of necessity compelled the spear-armed infantry of the Scots into increasing prominence, and helped to forge an army which, after the bloody lesson of Falkirk in 1298, would itself develop the offensive use of massed infantry formations to crush the great army of Edward II at Bannockburn in 1314. It was not the triumphs of Edward I that spurred fundamental military reform of English arms, but the dark years of England's defeat and humiliation at the hands of Robert Bruce.

Matthew Strickland

CHAPTER 10

The Crucible of Defeat:
Bannockburn to Boroughbridge

 he three decades following the death of Edward I were of critical importance in the history of the longbow. They witnessed a remarkable transformation in the military successes of the Scots under the bold and capable leadership of Robert Bruce, who reversed the strategic and tactical initiative formerly enjoyed by the English, inflicting upon them at Bannockburn one of the greatest defeats to be suffered by English arms during the Middle Ages, and turning northern England as far south as York into a war zone. Yet under the hammer blows of defeat, English forces gradually underwent a profound change in both organisation and methods of fighting. Crucially, the dominance of heavy cavalry, smashed on the spears of the Scottish schiltroms, gave way to the readoption of the tactical combination of dismounted men-at-arms and archers in defensive positions, not seen in insular warfare since the first half of the twelfth century. Deprived of Bruce and other gifted military commanders, a new generation

of Scots were confronted by a young, able and ambitious English monarch, burning for revenge and able to use such tactics to terrible effect.

Sir Geoffrey Luttrell, magnificently mounted and accoutred, from the Luttrell Psalter, which he commissioned between *c.* 1320 and *c.* 1330 (British Library, Add. MS 42130, f.202v). Despite the growing tactical predominance of dismounted men-at-arms supported by archers from the 1330s, mounted knights continued to play a significant supporting role in English armies. *(British Library/Bridgeman Art Library)*

ENGLAND'S COURTRAI: BANNOCKBURN, 24 JUNE 1314

From the outset of Edward II's accession in 1307 the English crown had been paralysed by the bitter dispute between the nobility and Edward II over his hated favourite, Piers Gaveston. Robert Bruce had fully exploited this weakness to take castle after English-held castle within Scotland, and to launch effective military campaigns against the Comyn family and his other Scottish enemies. From 1311, after the dismal failure of an English expedition into Scotland in 1310, Bruce relentlessly harried the northern counties of England, making his army rich on booty and payments made by the localities to buy off devastation. In November 1313, moreover, Bruce had issued an ultimatum to his Scottish opponents: they had one year either to acknowledge him as king or else suffer perpetual disinheritance.[1] The position of those among the Scottish aristocracy who were hostile to Bruce and who favoured Edward would soon collapse unless the English king brought speedy and effective assistance. Added incentive was given to Edward II by the fact that in mid-summer 1313 the constable of Stirling Castle, which was the strategic key to eastern lowland Scotland, had agreed with Bruce's brother Edward to yield the fortress to the Scots unless he was relieved by Midsummer's Day (24 June). Accordingly in mid-June 1314 King Edward marched north with a formidable army. He had summoned over 22,000 infantry, including 3,000 Welsh, together with an additional 4,000 Irish, intending to advance on two fronts in the west as well as the east. How many of these troops actually served is unknown, for the pay rolls for the campaign are lost, and it is salutary to note that of similar numbers summoned in 1319 only a quarter actually mustered;[2] but his final strength at Bannockburn has been estimated at around 11,000 infantry and 2,000 horse.[3] Bruce's numbers are similarly unknown, but may have comprised some 5,000–6,000 infantry, with a small detachment of light cavalry.[4]

Hitherto, Bruce had been careful to eschew battle with a major English army, waging instead a highly successful guerrilla war of ambushes, raids and stealth attacks. Not only had he been mindful of the crushing defeat suffered at Falkirk by William Wallace, but at Methven in 1306 he himself had been surprised and routed by the cavalry of Aymer de Valence, Edward I's lieutenant in Scotland. When again forced to confront Valence's forces the following year at Loudoun Hill, Bruce only engaged after heavily fortifying his position with three lines of deep ditches dug at right angles to the road along which the English had to approach. Gaps were left in these defences in order to funnel the English horse into a constricted position where they were easily repulsed by the Scots spearmen.[5] If Barbour's narrative can be credited, it was a small but morale-boosting victory which showed his troops that the seemingly invincible English cavalry could indeed be defeated, though it should be noted that Valence's forces subsequently succeeded in pushing through to Bothwell Castle.[6] Now, in 1314, Bruce chose to bar the English approach to Stirling, though leaving himself the option of withdrawing northward if the need arose. The exact site of the battlefield is uncertain.[7] As with the great majority of medieval battles, contemporary descriptions of Bannockburn lack accurate topographical detail, while surprisingly, given the significance of Bruce's victory, a votive chapel was not founded on the battle site.[8] It seems probable, however, that Bruce took up a strong defensive position athwart the road where it passed through the New Park, a royal hunting reserve a little to the south of the castle. The site was far stronger than that adopted by Wallace at Falkirk, for the woods offered considerable protection against the English cavalry, as did the marshy ground around the Bannock and Pelstream burns to the east. As Barbour has Bruce tell his men, 'If we fight on foot, perfay, then we shall always have the advantage, for in the park among the trees horsemen are always disadvantaged, and the streams down below will throw them into confusion.'[9] To these natural defences the Scots added rows of 'pots' or holes 'a foot in diameter and all as deep as a man's knee, so thickly placed that they could be compared to a wax-comb that bees make'.[10] These were dug on either side of the main approach road – in a tactic echoing that of Loudun Hill – and hidden with grass and brushwood. Such preparations suggest that at this stage the most Bruce was contemplating was a defensive engagement. The Scots army was probably divided into three divisions under Bruce, his brother Edward, and his nephew Moray, though Barbour alone has Douglas lead a fourth division.

The battle developed over two days.[11] On the afternoon of the first day, 23 June, the English van under Humphrey de Bohun, Earl of Hereford, and the young Earl of Gloucester attempted to drive through the New Park. During their initial advance there occurred the famous single combat in which Bohun's nephew Sir Henry de Bohun was slain by Bruce, mounted on a little palfrey, who swerved aside from the English knight's charge and split Bohun's skull with his axe. The advancing English, unaware of the strength of the Scots' position, were repulsed by Bruce's division after bitter fighting in which the Earl of Gloucester was unhorsed. Meanwhile, a division of some 300 cavalry under the veterans Sir Henry Beaumont and Sir Robert Clifford attempted to outflank the Scots by sweeping round the New Park to the north-east towards Stirling Castle, over the hard ground between the woods and the boggy carse. They were intercepted, however, by

Bruce's nephew Moray, who rushed the Scottish van out into the open ground and attacked the English cavalry.[12] Taken completely unawares by this bold strike, Beaumont's knights found themselves with too little room to launch an effective charge; unable to operate in close formation, they could not penetrate the serried ranks of Moray's schiltrom. In vain they spurred their chargers towards the wall of spears, in their frustration even throwing maces and swords at the enemy beyond the reach of their lances or blades. Finally, the English broke off badly mauled, their disarray clear evidence of the vulnerability of heavy cavalry against disciplined foot-soldiers when lacking infantry support of its own. In the case of Clifford's fast-moving mounted strike force, such an absence is readily intelligible, but it is more surprising that archers were not effectively deployed in the action of the main vanguard under Gloucester. It is possible that Gloucester's division had not initially appreciated the strength of the Scottish position, and was merely probing; the *Vita Edwardi* noted that the English had spotted some Scots 'straggling under the trees as if in flight' and that accordingly Sir Henry de Bohun had led a force of Welsh towards the woods in pursuit, only to make his fateful encounter with King Robert.[13] Nevertheless, it seems clear that a major engagement subsequently took place, serious enough for Bruce's division to have need of reinforcement by that of his brother Edward Bruce. We can only conclude that, as at Maes Moydog, Falkirk and Loudun Hill, the cavalry initially sought to decide the day alone, and were accordingly worsted.

The reverses of that day should have alerted the English to the folly of attacking Bruce in so strong a defensive position, and doubtless at their counsel of war that evening some of Edward's experienced commanders advocated delay until Bruce moved off.[14] But others urged that their main force had not yet seen action, and that their chief objective remained to bring the Scots to a major battle in which English superiority in heavy cavalry, archers and overall numbers would, as at Falkirk, achieve a decisive victory. If the Scots were allowed to melt into the hills to wage a guerrilla war, the effectiveness of Edward's great host, levied at such enormous cost, would be set at nought. It seemed certain, moreover, that Bruce would indeed stand and fight, so much so that the English feared an imminent night attack. Edward of Caernarfon was no coward, and had seen action in his father's armies in Scotland. But he was as poor a commander as he was a leader of men, and as Langtoft noted sagely, 'Who is leader in war, and is un-acquainted with craft, often does harm to his company'.[15] The king agreed with the fateful decision to move much of the army across the Bannock burn, 'an evil, deep marsh with streams', in order to occupy the hard level ground south of Broomridge known as the Carse of Balquhiderock. From here, it was hoped, a major attack on the Scots could be launched the next day. Using makeshift bridges cobbled together from roofs, doors and other material taken from local houses in order to help men and horses cross, a large contingent of infantry and most of the cavalry struggled across the boggy ground, spending a

The evocative modern statue of Robert Bruce by Pilkington Jackson, erected in 1964 at Bannockburn near the Borestone where Bruce traditionally had his headquarters on 23 June 1314. *(© Michael J. Stead)*

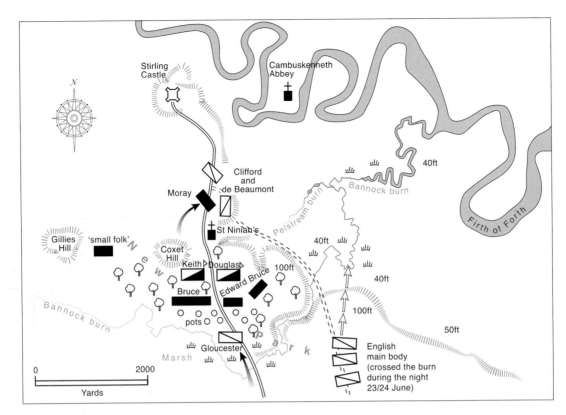

The battle of Bannockburn, day 1, 23 June 1314.*

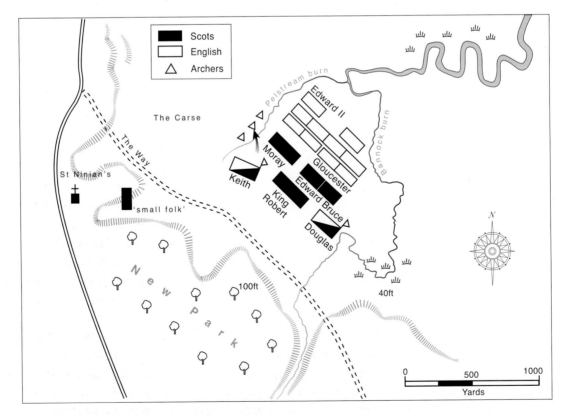

The battle of Bannockburn, day 2, 24 June 1314.*

*   Both plans follow Duncan, *The Bruce*, 445, in assigning Douglas a body of light horse attached to Edward
    Bruce's division, rather than a separate division of his own.

wretched night camped on the carse, exhausted, sodden and demoralised by the day's defeats.

Despite his success, Bruce had in fact intended to withdraw into the fastness of Lennox that night. Even though the English had been blooded, their army was still intact and Bruce was loathe to risk all his hard-won gains since 1306 on the uncertain chance of battle. At this crucial moment, however, a deserter from the English camp, Sir Alexander Seton, came to Bruce, reporting the enemy's low morale and urging him that the time was ripe to launch a major attack the following day.[16] Bruce must have realised that the English had placed themselves in a dangerously confined position, with the path of retreat hampered by the marshy ground and the Bannockburn. Thus encouraged, the Scots made the bold decision to take the offensive. In the morning of Monday 24 June, possibly as early as 4 a.m., the Scots heard mass, took a simple breakfast and then advanced out of the wooded New Park on to hard, open ground in three divisions. Those under Moray and Edward Bruce drew up abreast, with Bruce's own division held back in reserve. The Scots, noted the *Vita Edwardi*, wore 'light armour, not easily penetrable by a sword. They had axes by their sides and carried lances in their hands. They advanced like a thick-set hedge, and such a phalanx could not easily be broken.'[17] According to Barbour, the English were formed in one great body, except for a powerful vanguard in front.[18] The Scots knelt briefly in prayer. According to Barbour, Edward II, astounded to see common infantry coming on so boldly, supposedly mistook this for a gesture of surrender and remarked, 'Yon folk are kneeling to ask mercy'. He was quickly disabused by Sir Ingram de Umfraville, who said: 'They ask mercy, but not from you. They ask God for mercy for their sins. I'll tell you something for a fact, that yon men will win or all die – none will flee for fear of death.' 'So be it,' replied the king, and had his trumpets sound the attack.[19]

The sources disagree as to the opening stages of the battle, and thus to the role of the archers. The Lanercost chronicler, who claimed to have his report from an eye-witness, believed that hostilities commenced with a sharp archery duel: 'the English archers were thrown forward before the line, and the Scottish archers engaged them, a few being killed and wounded on either side; but the King of England's archers quickly put theirs to flight'.[20] Such an opening archery engagement echoes that fought at the Cree in 1300 between English and Scots archers, and its occurrence at Bannockburn gains further support from Trokelowe: 'the English leaders put infantry with bows and lances in the front line; they placed the knights behind, divided into wings'.[21] Such a deployment would suggest that, learning from their costly experience the day before at the hands of the Scottish spearmen, the English had placed bowmen, supported by spearmen, in the front of the van. John Barbour, however, gives a very different account. He does not mention an initial archery exchange between the bowmen, but has the Scots' forward schiltroms immediately attack the English. Despite the length and great drama of his account, it must be remembered that his narrative was written considerably later, in about 1375, and is often confused and unreliable. According to Barbour, the English rallied and launched cavalry charges against the Scots, but despite fighting fiercely were unable to make any impression against the schiltroms and were gradually driven back. It is only at this point that Barbour mentions the English archers, who presumably had been brought up to assist the cavalry, though he does not state their position:

> The arrows, too, flew so thickly there, that those who saw them could well have said that they made a horrible shower, for wherever they fell, I promise you, they left tokens behind them that needed medical treatment. The English archers loosed so fast that if their shooting had persisted, it would have gone hard for the Scotsmen.

But now King Robert, 'who knew well what a danger their archers were, with their hard and right hurtful shooting', ordered Sir Robert Keith, the Scots marshal, to take his small force of cavalry and ride down the English bowmen.[22] Keith took 500 horsemen, 'armed in steel, who were well horsed on light steeds, to gallop among the archers and so attack them with spears, that they would have no opportunity to shoot'. Accordingly, when Keith

> saw the archers shooting boldly, with the men of all his company rode quickly against them, and came upon them at a flank; he rode among them so forcefully, spearing them so relentlessly, knocking them down and slaying them in such numbers without mercy, that one and all they scattered: from that time on none gathered to try such shooting.[23]

The success of Keith's cavalry gave fresh heart to the Scots' own bowmen: 'When the Scottish archers saw that they had been driven back like that, they grew bold, shot eagerly with all their might among the horsemen who rode there, and made terrible wounds among them, slaying a very great many of them.'[24] The impact of the Scots archers on Edward's knights is suggested by a pious anecdote concerning a Gascon knight, whose horse was badly wounded by Scottish pikes, and who was caught up in the arrow storm. In his need he prayed to St Francis, who promptly appeared and personally warded off

Left: An English archer from the Luttrell Psalter (British Library, Add. MS 42130, f.45). As with all the archers depicted in this famous psalter, he is shown in 'civilian' dress, but in time of war he would have been more extensively equipped with a helmet, sword and shield, as well as body armour in the form of a gambeson worn with or without a short mail shirt. *(British Library/Bridgeman Art Library)*

Below: The battle of Bannockburn as imagined in William Hole's late nineteenth-century mural in the Scottish National Portrait Gallery, Edinburgh. *(The Scottish National Portrait Gallery)*

the Scottish arrows.[25] Barbour's account would thus place the English archers loosing galling volleys during – not before – the main engagement, which has led some authorities to place them on one flank of the main English force.

It is hard to reconcile these varying accounts, though greater trust must be placed in the more contemporary narratives. It may be that the archers of both sides played their principal role before the Scots spearmen engaged the main English forces, and that the English archers were driven off by Keith's cavalry at an early stage in the battle,[26] or that the Scots cavalry succeeded in routing archers brought up during the main engagement to help the English knights achieve a break-through. Whatever the reality, however, it seems that Edward and his commanders cannot be accused of neglecting the role of their archers, or of positioning them where they were of little value. If an opening archery duel did take place, this was more than had happened at Falkirk. And whether in the van or on a flank, all sources agree that a significant number were brought into action. It is only Geoffrey le Baker, also writing considerably later, who says that the English archers were placed in the second line behind the horsemen, together with the other foot 'who were appointed for the chase of the adversaries'.[27] When, however, they saw the English horse in difficulties, they shot at a high trajectory, but succeeded only in wounding and killing their own men.[28] If this was not retrospective justification for defeat, perhaps these were other bodies of archers who had not been posted in the van or to a flank, and who now found themselves unable to deploy effectively in the confined position into which the English had penned themselves. Four years later at the battle of Faughart, fought in Ireland between the invading army of Edward Bruce, Robert's brother, and the English commander John de Bermingham, the English archers seem to have made a far greater impact and Bruce's force was heavily defeated, though unfortunately the course of the battle is obscure.[29] At Bannockburn, however, either because they were driven from the field or because they were poorly positioned – or a combination of these factors – the English archers were not able to bring to bear enough sustained shooting against the Scottish formations to halt their advance or disorganise their ranks.

Their ultimate failure was crucial. The sources are in agreement that the Scots had taken the offensive, leading by their right under Edward Bruce, and that the English horse soon spurred to meet them. The young Earl of Gloucester, who had not donned his surcoat, rode ahead into the Scottish ranks but was soon struck down and slain. 'When both armies engaged each other', noted the *Scalacronica*, 'and the great horses of the English charged the pikes of the Scots, as it were into a dense forest, there arose a great and terrible crash of spears broken and of destriers wounded to the death.'[30] The Scottish divisions, now deployed in line abreast, inexorably drove back the increasingly compressed and disordered ranks of the English amidst bitter fighting. Sensing that the battle had reached its critical phase, Bruce now committed his own division, containing the Highlanders and men of the Isles, to the Scots' right flank. Under this onslaught from men fresh and in a terrible battle-fury, the English began to give more and more ground, so that among the Scots ranks the cry was raised, 'On them! On them! They fail!' As the English were forced back towards the marshy burns, the 'small folk' – those baggage handlers, servants and others whom Bruce had, as at Loudun, kept well to his rear – rushed down to join the mêlée.

Mistaking these for fresh Scottish reinforcements, the English army wavered and began to disintegrate. The Scots had penetrated the English ranks as far as the king himself, who beat back some dismounted Scottish knights with his mace as they tried to seize his horse's trapper. But finally, and with great reluctance, the king allowed himself to be led off the field by his bodyguard to make good his escape.[31] The Earl of Pembroke and a large unit of Welsh retreated in good order to Carlisle, but many of the English were not so fortunate; pursued by the Scots they floundered in the bogs and pools flanking the Bannock burn, while some who attempted to swim the Forth were drowned by the weight of their armour. A large party, including the Earl of Hereford and other lords, reached the apparent safety of Bothwell Castle, only to be betrayed to the Scots by its castellan.[32] One earl and at least seventy barons and knights lay dead, including veterans such as Robert Clifford, Payn Tiptoft and Giles d'Argentan, though the Scots' desire for prisoners to ransom averted the kind of carnage that had been witnessed among the French knights at Courtrai.[33] As the English writer of the Lanercost chronicle was forced to admit, 'After the aforesaid victory, Robert de Brus was commonly called King of Scotland, because he had acquired Scotland by force of arms.'[34]

The causes of the English defeat were many. Bruce's fine generalship triumphed over a king whose personal courage was not sufficient to offset his lack of military acumen or political wisdom. The English army was fatally hampered by indiscipline and divided counsel at the highest level,[35] which perhaps goes far to explain their greatest error – a choice of ground which was hopelessly restricted. The difficult manoeuvrings over the pows of the Bannock burn had been intended to gain the only ground suitable for deploying their cavalry, but this dry ground was limited, and did not allow for the contingency of withdrawal should the charges of the heavy horse fail. Crucially, it created a front narrow enough to allow the Scots to concentrate their forces while at the same time preventing the effective deployment of English reserves. According to the *Vita Edwardi*, more than 200 knights never had a chance to close with the Scots because of the ranks in front of them, and were forced to flee without striking a blow. Had the knights succeeded in breaking through or outflanking the Scots formations, as at Falkirk, all might have been well. But once their assault was checked and they were forced on to the defensive, the lack of space to manoeuvre became critical. Divided leadership, poor discipline, the neutralising of a numerical advantage by a poor choice of terrain, and the ensuing crush resulting from an initial advance being checked: all these were to be recurrent features of the dismal litany of French defeats in the Anglo-French wars to follow.

Tactically Bannockburn had been a vivid testimony to the offensive capabilities of the schiltroms, and to the skill and discipline of the Scottish infantry. This aggressive use of Bruce's formations of spearmen had taken the English completely by surprise, for even at Courtrai the Flemish militiamen had fought an essentially defensive action behind streams and ditches, which had broken the charge of the French knights. 'O famous race unconquered through the ages,' lamented the English monk who penned the *Vita Edwardi*, 'why do you, who used to conquer knights, flee from mere footmen? At Berwick, Dunbar and Falkirk you carried off the victory, and now you flee from the infantry of the Scots. . . . Indeed, I think it is unheard of in our time for such an army to be scattered so suddenly by infantry, unless when the flower of France fell before the Flemings at Courtrai, where the noble Count Robert of Artois was killed.'[36] Yet the Scottish army before which the English now fled had undergone a radical transformation from the knightly but amateur forces which Edward I's men had swept aside at Dunbar in 1296 into a highly effective fighting force under the leadership of Bruce and extremely able lieutenants like his brother Edward Bruce, James Douglas and Thomas Randolph.[37] The second two decades of the fourteenth century had witnessed the forging of a professional military community through years of bitter campaigning, evolving tactics and equipment to suit the changing needs of strategy. The social effects of prolonged warfare were also profound, for as Ranald Nicholson notes, 'a husbandman who was expected to wield a sixteen-foot spear in the schiltrom could no longer be expected to be content to be tied to the soil'.[38] Yet if it was the spearmen who won glory at this great engagement, one should not allow concentration on this one major battle to obscure the important supporting role which archers in Scottish forces continued to play.

SCOTTISH ARCHERS UNDER ROBERT BRUCE

In the years following his *coup d'état* in 1306 Robert Bruce had become a highly successful proponent of the warfare of stealth, ambuscade and rapid movement. On the run from Edward I's vengeance in 1306–7, his had been a harsh tutelage, and his narrow escapes from capture among the woods and bogs of south-west Scotland during this nadir in his fortunes had quickly become the stuff of legend. One tale told how he escaped from almost certain capture by wading down a stream to hide his scent from a tracker dog used to hunt him by the men of John of Lorn, the implacably hostile Lord of Argyll. But as Barbour reported, men told another version of how one of the king's companions, 'a good archer', realising the peril caused by the bloodhound, lay in ambush and slew the dog before vanishing back into the woods.[39] Here again is the bow in popular legend, first oral then written, as the weapon of forest ambuscade. Barbour similarly relates how, when in hiding in 1307, Bruce was out hunting and alone but for two hounds when he was attacked by three men armed with bows, seeking vengeance for the death of John Comyn, Bruce's great rival whom he had slain the year previously:

They went quickly towards the king, bending their bows when they were near, and he, who had a great fear of their arrows because he was without armour, quickly made an overture to them, saying, 'You ought to be ashamed to shoot at me from afar, perdé (by God), for I am one and you are three. But if you have the courage to come close to attack me with your swords, defeating me in this way if you can, you will be all the more esteemed.' 'Indeed,' said one of the three, 'no man is going to say we fear you so much that we will kill you with arrows.' With that they threw away their bows, and came on fast without delay.[40]

This sense of honour, however, cost the men their lives, for the king, aided by his dogs, cut them down in turn. One need not give credence to the story, which forms but one version of a group of tales illustrating the king's prowess in combat against the odds, but it certainly suggests that an attack by bows at a distance, particularly in such circumstances, might be regarded as unworthy and cowardly.[41]

Conversely, however, Barbour does not hesitate to recount how his other great hero, James Douglas, led archers in numerous engagements, and Bruce himself clearly recognised their value in the kind of war needed to defeat the English. During Bruce's struggle to assert dominance over his Comyn rivals and their allies within Scotland, both sides made use of archers. During his 1308 campaign against Buchan, Bruce's men took refuge in an area of wooded marshland as Bruce himself had fallen ill. The Earl of Buchan's forces advanced against their position with archers preceding more heavily armed men, but their attack was driven off by Bruce's own bowmen.[42] The same year Bruce's forces were ambushed beneath Ben Cruachan by the men of Lorn, who rolled rocks down upon them as they passed along the precipitous track-way. Foreseeing this trap, however, Bruce had sent James

Douglas with 'all the archers' to climb the hill higher above John of Lorn's men and shoot down upon them, 'wounding them with swift arrows' before closing with their swords and routing them.[43] Douglas again deployed his archers to good effect at Lintalee in 1315. Forewarned of an English raid into Jedburgh Forest, he organised an ambush by a large company of archers positioned in the trees at a point where the way through the woods narrowed, and where he had knitted together young birch trees in order to prevent the enemy from riding through. The English force was badly worsted by the archers, with one of its leaders, Sir Thomas Richmond, among the slain.[44] Douglas's connection with the archers of these forest areas must have been confirmed and strengthened by the subsequent grants to him of Jedburgh and its forest and wardenship of the royal forest of Selkirk, among other major estates awarded to him in recognition of his outstanding service.[45]

To regain effective control of Scotland, however, Bruce needed to take key castles and strongholds. He became a master of seizing English-held castles by night assault, stealth or guile, but where such methods failed recourse was had to siege, and here Scots archers can be seen playing an equally vital role. In 1314 archers were employed during Douglas's assault on Roxburgh Castle.[46] The following year the Scots laid siege to Carlisle with an array of siege engines. While their main force launched an assault on the east side of the city, Douglas led a picked force to launch a surprise attack at a place in the western wall where attack was to be least expected: 'There they set up long ladders, which they climbed, and the bowmen, whereof they had a great number, shot their arrows thickly to prevent anyone showing his head above the wall.'[47] The defenders, however, succeeded in repelling the attack and throwing down the ladders, though a Scots archer claimed the only English casualty of the siege. In 1318 the English constable of Berwick, Roger de Horsley, lost his eye to a Scottish arrow during the eleven-week siege of the castle which followed the seizure of the town by the Scots.[48] Rather than slighting this strategically vital town, the Scots chose to hold Berwick against the inevitable English counter-attack, and installed a powerful garrison under Walter Stewart; Barbour believed it to contain some 500 men as well as crossbowmen, archers and spearmen, together with many engines and springalds.[49] Berwick was subsequently besieged in early September 1319 by a major English army, which included the former Berwick garrison containing 44 crossbowmen and 98 archers, who may well have been regarded as an elite force.[50] That some were badly wounded in the ensuing action is revealed by the fact that in 1320 ten disabled archers of the garrison were sent to religious houses, presumably for

convalescence or longer-term support – a reminder that monastic houses might provide some of the most advanced medical treatment then available.[51] The English covered their assaults on Berwick by bowmen, who 'had been assigned to shoot at each embrasure that was there', but although 'the shooting there was so intense that it was remarkable to watch', the Scots succeeded in repulsing the attacks.[52] During one of the fiercest assaults, 'when the shot too was thickest, women with child and small children collected up arrows in armfuls, carrying them to those who were on the wall'.[53] Interestingly in the light of this Walter, Steward of Scotland, is found in 1318 granting an estate on Bute in return for 'the service of one archer in the king's army'.[54] We have seen how at Falkirk many of the Scottish archers came from Ettrick Forest, but archery was by no means restricted to the lowlands; many Highlanders fought as bowmen until as late as the seventeenth century.[55]

The majority of such archers were, as previously, drawn from the poorer elements of society, for the bulk of better-off fighting men were expected to serve as spearmen.[56] In a statute of 1318 King Robert decreed that every man who had possessions worth 10 pounds must possess an adequate aketon, bascinet and 'gloves of war', or a haubergel 'or a good iron piece for the body', iron cap and gloves, together with a spear and sword. In the wake of Bannockburn, which had so dramatically demonstrated the potential of the Scottish spearmen in battle, Bruce was trying to ensure that the infantry who formed the schiltroms – or at least their foremost ranks – were well protected by defensive armour, and each year after Easter the sheriff and local magnates were ordered to hold a view of arms or 'wappinschaw' to check that men were properly equipped.[57] By contrast, those worth only a cow – a basic unit of exchange in a society where coin was still limited – were to have either a good spear or a good bow with a quiver of twenty-four arrows.[58] He also attempted to increase the number of better-equipped archers at his disposal by granting land in return for archer service. Such tenures were not in themselves new, but Bruce can be seen substituting older obligations of knight service with that for bowmen, in a process apparently intensifying in the 1320s.[59] Hence in 1309 he regranted the barony of Manor in Tweedale, formerly held by the service of one knight, in return for the service of ten archers, and that of Cessford in Roxburghshire, formerly held by knight service, for the provision of four archers.[60] Annual fees or money fiefs were also used to obtain archers.[61] The number of bowmen yielded for the king's service by such provision appears from surviving documents to have been modest,[62] but in what was a clear trend the king's barons in turn granted out land in return for archer service. As Duncan

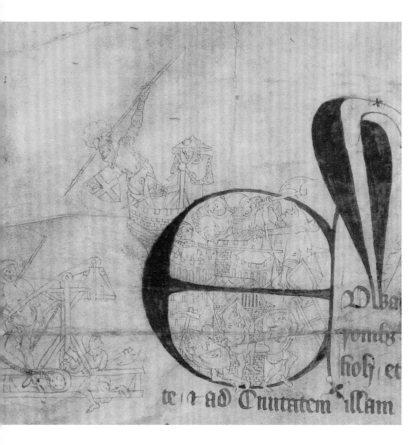

This illuminated initial prefacing the charter given by King Edward II to the city of Carlisle in 1316 shows the successful defence of the city against the Scots the year previously. An archer is among the Scottish infantry assaulting the walls, while to the left a javelin thrown by the garrison commander Sir Andrew Harclay transfixes another bowman standing beside a trebuchet prepared for firing. On the walls a soldier next to Harclay spans a springald by means of a windlass. Note the Scots' lack of defensive armour, though their unusual headgear may be an attempt to represent helmets of *cuir bouilli*. (Reproduced by kind permission of Carlisle City Council)

serjeantry tenure is seen in the grant by Bruce to James, Lord Douglas, of the land in Polmoody (Dumfriesshire) in return for an annual render of 12 broad arrows (*sagittas latas*), a traditional render which must in origin have been linked to providing equipment for the royal hunt.[64]

There are sadly no extant records allowing us to glimpse the activities of Scottish bowyers and fletchers in the fourteenth century, as we can increasingly do for their English counterparts. Yet with Flemish privateers acting in their service, the Scots during Bruce's reign and beyond were able to trade with Europe despite English naval activity, and it is possible that better bow wood was being imported along with other munitions that were traded in the Baltic and Low Countries for Scottish wool. It is also likely that the Scottish raiders who harried northern England almost at will in the decade following Bannockburn sought arms as well as cash and supplies in lieu of the protection money they extorted from the near-defenceless towns and villages of Northumbria and Cumbria, while it is certain that in the chaotic conditions of Edward II's later reign some English merchants are known to have provided the Scots with contraband weapons and supplies.[65]

notes, 'it is possible that as the king's major supporters were rewarded with baronies, the available resources for further knight service feus shrank, and that the recognition of this fact led to a deliberate policy of strengthening archer service, for archers were the best defence against opposing cavalry'.[63] If as seems likely such archers were mounted, Bruce may also have been seeking to provide his fast, mobile raiding forces of spearmen with an element of missile support. A more nominal

A range of arrowheads excavated from Urquhart Castle on Loch Ness, Inverness-shire, including bodkin heads of various lengths, three heads with broader cutting edges, and what may be a crossbow bolt head. To the left is a corroded mass of arrowheads, suggesting that a large bundle of arrows had been stored in a canvas or fabric bag. The stone cannon balls are from a later period. (© Trustees of the National Museums of Scotland)

Bannockburn had not in itself decisively ended the war with England, for the failure to slay or capture Edward meant that Bruce would have to wait until 1328 before the English officially recognised his kingship and Scotland's independence. Nevertheless, in its wake Bruce was able to lead plundering raids virtually at will deep into northern England, seizing booty, cattle and prisoners. With the collapse of effective resistance beyond a few key strongholds, towns and local communities were repeatedly forced to buy off destruction with the payment of large ransoms, which helped to replenish Bruce's coffers, pay his troops and further strengthen his war effort.[66] For such raids the Scots used lightly armed men on stout ponies, travelling fast and light. A famous description of these hardy troops is given by the Hainault chronicler Jean Le Bel, who accompanied Edward III's Weardale campaign of 1327 against the Scots:

When they want to pass into England, they are all mounted, except for the camp followers, who are on foot; the knights and esquires are mounted on good, large rouncies, and the other Scots on little hackneys. They bring no carts because of the mountainous terrain, nor do they carry any supplies of bread or wine. They are so little addicted to luxury that, in time of war, they can subsist well enough for a long time on half-cooked meat, without bread, and good river water, uncut with wine. They do without pots and kettles, since they cook their meat inside the hides of the animals which they have skinned, and they well know that they will find a great abundance of cattle in the country they are raiding. So they carry no other supplies, except that each one carries a large, flat stone in his saddle bags, and ties behind him a sack of oatmeal. When they have eaten so much of this badly-

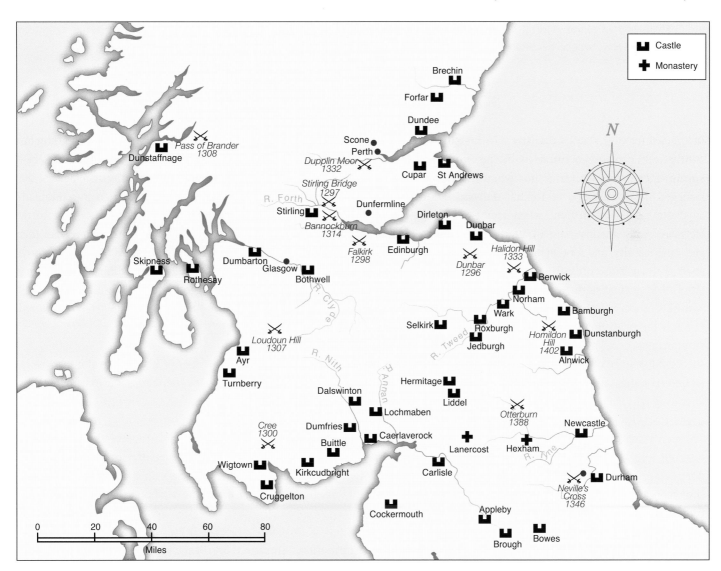

Southern Scotland and northern England in the late thirteenth and fourteenth centuries (after *The History of the King's Works*, ed. H.M. Colvin *et al.* (1963)).

cooked meat that their stomachs feel weak, they throw this stone into the fire, and mix a bit of their oatmeal with water. When the stone is hot, they make a sort of biscuit on it, which they eat to restore their stomachs. So it is no marvel that they make longer marches than other people . . . They enter into England, and burn and devastate the country, and find so many cattle that they don't know what to do with them all.[67]

Speed of movement and tactical flexibility lay at the heart of the Scottish successes, combining the swiftness of light horsemen with the defensive or offensive potential of the spearmen in disciplined formations. Yet despite the success of Bannockburn, Bruce and his commanders generally took care to avoid field engagements with major English forces. When, for example, Edward II led a large army to attempt to retake Berwick in 1319, Bruce resisted confronting this powerful force directly and instead sent a major raiding force into England under Douglas and Moray, whose devastations achieved his desired

goal of forcing the English to raise the siege. In turn, when these commanders were faced by a force of English levies at Swale in Yorkshire, the Scots initially drew up their spearmen in a defensive formation. Only when they perceived their opponents to be a motley though brave force of local levies, clergy and friars collected by Archbishop Melton, did they attack, routing them before remounting to engage in a bloody pursuit in which so many of the local clergy fell that the engagement earned the mocking nickname 'the Chapter of Mytoun'.[68]

Yet through their rough handling by the Scots between 1307 and 1329 the English were beginning to adapt and improve their own methods of warfare, melding existing strengths such as their powerful archer arm with elements of their enemy's winning tactics. This process of imitation and assimilation emerges clearly at the battle of Boroughbridge in 1322, ironically fought not against the Scots but between the forces of King Edward and those of his baronial opponents led by Thomas, Earl of Lancaster.

BOROUGHBRIDGE, 16 MARCH 1322

In the winter of 1321/2 Lancaster and his supporters had conducted secret negotiations with the Scots, and in the spring open rebellion broke out when Lancaster's forces besieged the royal castle of Tickhill. Edward II mustered a large army at Burton-on-Trent, where Lancaster and the Earl of Hereford made an unsuccessful attack 'with barons, knights and other cavalry, and foot archers', but 'the earl's forces were soon thrown into confusion and retired before the king's army'.[69] Retreating north with the intention of joining forces with their Scots allies, the rebels found their passage over the Ure was barred at Boroughbridge by Sir Andrew de Harclay, a veteran northern commander who had conducted the successful defence of Carlisle against Bruce in 1315. On being alerted to Lancaster's movements, Harclay, 'that valiant and famous knight',[70] had stolen a march on the earl, hastening by night from Ripon to seize the bridge at Boroughbridge. Through years of border warfare he had forged an effective fighting force from troops of the northern shires, placing particular emphasis on the use of hobelars, mounted spearmen who, like their Scots opponents, could ride fast over rough terrain and dismount to form effective infantry units.[71] In 1319 Harclay had led a powerful force of 980 archers and 354 hobelars to the English siege of Berwick, the larger part of which force was subsequently sent to intercept the Earl of Moray's raiding party returning from Yorkshire.[72] The force Harclay now commanded at Boroughbridge, summoned to

arms 'under very heavy penalties' from the shire levies, knights and gentry of Cumberland and Westmorland,[73] thus contained seasoned men who had learned much from warfare against the Scots, as was soon apparent from the formation they adopted. We are fortunate in possessing a detailed account of the battle from the continuation of the chronicle of the Franciscan friar Richard of Durham, preserved in the *Lanercost Chronicle*, which shows a keen observation of northern affairs and military matters, and it has been suggested that the author may even have been a knight before becoming a friar.[74] Richard noted how

> sending his horses and those of his men to the rear, he [Harclay] posted all his knights and some pikemen on foot at the northern end of the bridge, and other pikemen he stationed in schiltrom, after the Scottish fashion, opposite the ford or passage of the water, to oppose the cavalry wherein the enemy put his trust. Also he directed his archers to keep up a hot and constant discharge upon the enemy as he approached.[75]

Such a formation clearly drew directly on the Scottish formations employed by Bruce and his commanders. The location of the archers in relation to the spearmen is not clear, though as with Scottish deployments at Falkirk and Bannock-burn it would seem the bowmen were in separate units to the side, or in the case of those guarding the ford, in front of the spearmen, and not mixed in with them.

Lancaster's forces offered a sorry contrast with Harclay's disciplined and well-led northerners. Many had already deserted the earl's cause, and those that remained, probably numbering fewer than 700, were fearful and demoralised.[76] For even a powerful force to have attacked Harclay's strong defensive position would have been difficult and unwise, but, with the king hot on their heels and their attempts to win Harclay over to their cause rebuffed, Lancaster and Bohun had little choice but to force a crossing. They decided that Hereford, with his son-in-law Sir Roger Clifford, should attack the bridge, while Lancaster's cavalry should attempt to force a crossing at the ford. The attack, however, was catastrophic, 'for when the Earl of Hereford (with his standard bearer leading the advance, to wit Sir Ralf de Applinsdene) and Sir Roger de Clifford and some other knights had entered upon the bridge before the others as bold as lions, charging fiercely upon the enemy, pikes were thrust at the earl from all sides'. The earl was slain by a spearman thrusting upwards from under the bridge, 'for knights, not expecting to be struck from under the feet, do not protect their private parts'.[77] With him fell his standard bearer, Sir William de Sule and Sir Roger de Berefield, while Clifford, 'though grievously wounded with pikes and arrows' and driven back, escaped with difficulty along with the others.[78] Meanwhile, things were going equally badly for Lancaster:

> The earl's cavalry, when they endeavoured to cross the water, could not enter it by reason of the number and density of arrows which the archers discharged upon them and their horses. This affair being this quickly settled, the Earl of Lancaster and his people retired from the water, nor did they dare to approach it again, and so their whole array was thrown into disorder.[79]

With Bohun dead and his forces routed, Lancaster was forced to seek a truce with Harclay, by which the earl would either give him battle on the morrow or surrender to him. But the bloody reverse at Boroughbridge caused such desertion among Lancaster's forces during the night that the following day he had no option but to surrender to Harclay. Judged a traitor, he and many of his supporters were executed by a vengeful Edward II.

The tactical significance of Boroughbridge is considerable. Harclay's deployment of his men-at-arms and hobelars in schiltroms provides a striking instance of the 'defensive imitation' of an adversary's superior methods of war; Clifford, whose father Robert had died charging the Scottish spears at Bannockburn, was fatally wounded attacking the schiltrom of an English commander. Harclay, however, also combined these formations with a powerful force of archers placed in a strong defensive position. Archers had been combined with the schiltroms at Falkirk and at Bannockburn, but in 1298 they had been easily ridden down by the English cavalry, while in 1314 the course of the battle meant that the Scottish bowmen did not face a direct assault by English horse. Though Lancaster had employed archers of his own at Burton, it is uncertain what role, if any, they played at Boroughbridge; they are not mentioned by the *Lanercost Chronicle*, and the *Brut* notes only vaguely that 'then one could see archers drawing [their bows] on one side and on the other'.[80] But the deadly effect of volleys of arrows against the earl's unsupported charge at the ford demonstrated the extreme vulnerability of cavalry, twenty years before the French were to discover this for themselves at Morlaix. One can only speculate what Harclay's military acumen might have achieved had he been given a powerful voice in deploying a major royal army against Bruce, or had lived to see the accession of the young Edward III. But within a year of his being rewarded for his victory by the grant of the earldom of Carlisle, Harclay himself was charged with treason for attempting to make peace with the Scots without authorisation, and suffered a terrible death. It was a measure of Edward II's political incompetence as well as his vindictiveness that he had removed the one man who was capable of defending the north against the Scots, but who had never received the military support to do so effectively.

THE WEARDALE CAMPAIGN, 1327

In 1323 Edward II had obtained a truce from the Scots for thirteen years, but his deposition in 1327 at the hands of his queen Isabella and her lover Roger Mortimer soon led to renewed hostilities, with the Scots once again invading England in force. The English army which mustered at York against this threat was a powerful one, nominally under the command of the 14-year-old Edward III, and contained many archers and foot-serjeants.[81] The English had already made moves to respond to the swift Scottish raiders, for the number of hobelars was increased to form one-quarter of the army, and many of those summoned to the host were instructed to bring 'swift, strong and hardy rounceys to ride and pursue' the

Scots.[82] The majority of infantry, however, still remained on foot, and the cumbersome force had little hope of catching the rapidly moving Scots force over the rugged terrain of Northumberland. Try as the English might to bring the Scots to bay for a decisive engagement, the forces of Douglas, Mar and Moray repeatedly eluded them; even when the cavalry abandoned the infantry and its supply train they could not catch up with the Scots, 'crafty and tough, mounted on their little hackneys'.[83] Finally, the English were led to the Scottish position by a squire captured but then released by the Scots, who were apparently eager to give battle. The reason soon became apparent, for the Scots had drawn up in three divisions in a defensive position of great strength on the north bank of the Wear close to Stanhope Park, their front protected not only by the river but by a steep and craggy hillside.[84] Wise heads in Edward's camp immediately appreciated the futility of a direct assault; even if the English were to cross unmolested, the ground between the bank and the Scots' position was not adequate to allow them to deploy effectively, inviting the same catastrophe as the English knights experienced on the carse at Bannockburn, trapped between the Scottish spears and the

burn. Faced with this impasse, Edward's commanders attempted to provoke the Scots into abandoning their position by sending a body of archers across the river to harass them, but as at Bannockburn a counter-attack by the Scots horse soon drove the archers back.[85] Both sides now moved camp and in an attempt to break the deadlock the Scots succeeded in launching a bold night attack that came close to Edward's own tent. Nevertheless, after several days of stalemate the raiders finally slipped away under cover of night, leaving the young Edward to weep tears of bitter frustration.[86]

The campaign had been a humiliating failure. Indeed, the worst fighting had actually occurred not against the Scots but between the English archers and John of Hainault's men at York on 7 June, prior to marching against the enemy. A game of dice led to a brawl between some archers and the servants of the Hainaulter knights, which rapidly escalated into a serious

The Scots assume a strong defensive position against the English during the Weardale campaign of 1327, as imagined in a late fifteenth-century Flemish manuscript of Froissart's *Chronicles* (Paris, Bibliothèque Nationale, MS fr. 2643, f.18). *(Bibliothèque Nationale, Paris)*

skirmish. Jean le Bel, who found himself caught up in the trouble, related, 'all the other archers of the town and the others who were encamped among the Hainaulters gathered up all their bows, [crying] *hahay hahay* like pigs, and wounded many of the servants and forced them to retire to their hostels . . . [and] these archers, of whom there were a good two thousand, had the devil in their bodies and shot, with amazing skill, to kill everyone, both lords and varlets'. The Hainaulter men-at-arms, however, armed themselves, rallied and led a fierce counter-attack through the streets of York into the midst of the archers, leaving 316 archers of the Bishop of Lincoln slain.[87] Le Bel's remarks concerning the quality of English shooting are noteworthy, demonstrating that a well-informed continental observer already regarded English bowmen as remarkably proficient, and reinforcing the impression of their effectiveness given in accounts of Bannockburn and Boroughbridge. The Leicestershire canon and chronicler Henry Knighton recorded in an obituary of Sir James Douglas, Bruce's inseparable companion and lieutenant who was killed fighting the Moors in 1330, that he was in the habit of cutting the right hand off any English archer he caught, or putting out their right eye, taking terrible revenge without mercy 'on account of their bows and arrows'.[88] Douglas's reprisals, which considerably antedate known French threats to mutilate captured archers during the Hundred Years War, are a grim reflection of the efficacy of the English bowmen against the Scots. Skilled bowmen, available in large numbers and shooting powerful weapons, had long been present before Edward III's own imminent victories over his northern enemy.

Despite its failure, however, the Weardale campaign marks an important turning point,[89] for the recognition of the wisdom of fighting on foot was grasped before the campaign even began. In the proclamation summoning the army, it was stated that all should be prepared to fight on foot if it seemed necessary, should battle be given to the Scots – an order, it was noted, which was to apply to the magnates as well.[90] Accordingly, when the army, stationed at Durham, first located the Scots by the fires of burning villages, they drew up on foot in three great battles, each flanked by wings of cavalry.[91] Though they were not able to give battle, such a formation indicates that by 1327 the English were responding to the extreme vulnerability of cavalry against the disciplined Scottish schiltroms, and were prepared to deploy their men-at-arms on foot against enemy spearmen – just as the Austrians were subsequently to do against the Swiss halberdiers at Sempach in 1386.[92] As with the earlier combination of dismounted knights with cavalry in the Anglo-Norman period, units of cavalry were retained, both to protect the flanks and for rapid movement.

A revealing incident which occurred at Norham Castle on the Tweed at some time in the 1320s shows the growing use of dismounting tactics by English men-at-arms as a response to the effectiveness of Scottish spearmen. A knight called William Marmion had come to the castle, renowned as 'the most dangerous place in Great Britain' at the behest of his lady, who had given him a helmet with a gilded crest, urging him to gain glory with it. Accordingly, when a Scots force approached the castle, Marmion prepared to sally out, 'all glittering with gold and silver, marvellous finely attired, with the helmet on his head', and mounted on a great charger, for as the constable Sir Thomas de Gray had told him, 'it is more meet that deeds of chivalry be done on horseback than afoot'. Yet disciplined group combat required other tactics; when Marmion was wounded and unhorsed by the opposing Scots horsemen, de Gray and his men rushed to his aid not on horseback but on foot, 'with levelled lances which they drove into the bowels of the horses so that they threw their riders'. The dismounted English routed the Scottish cavalry, slaying many and taking fifty costly war-horses as booty, then they mounted their own horses which had been brought out from the castle by their womenfolk and gave fierce pursuit as far as Berwick. Like his fellow northern veteran Sir Andrew Harclay, Sir Thomas de Gray had adapted his methods of combat to the conditions of Anglo-Scottish warfare. The Weardale campaign itself, moreover, had demonstrated the caution of the English commanders, who had consistently refused to give battle to the Scots in strong defensive positions – an abandonment of the offensive which their French counterparts were much slower to concede. Thus on the eve of Edward III's assumption of direct rule in 1330, many key elements of subsequent English military success were already emerging, or perhaps more correctly given their Anglo-Norman antecedents were re-emerging: the mounting of elements of infantry, the dismounting of men-at-arms to fight and their remounting for the pursuit, the adoption of the defensive and the use of supporting archery. What Edward's reign was to witness was a radical improvement in army organisation, a highly able leadership and an aggressive, battle-seeking strategy which sought to deploy the formidable tactical combination of dismounted men-at-arms and archers. A new invention may also have made an early appearance in 1327, for Barbour notes that it was in this campaign that the English employed 'crakys of war' – early cannon.[93] Though at Crécy in 1346 the English guns were said to have caused consternation among the Genoese, the Scots seem to have been much less impressed by such pyrotechnics, though Edward employed them again at the siege of Berwick in 1333.[94] Before then, however, the English had unleashed something far more devastating on the unsuspecting Scots.

Matthew Strickland

CHAPTER 11

A Terrible Reckoning: from Dupplin Moor to Neville's Cross

'Every English archer beareth under his girdle twenty-four Scots.'
Roger Ascham, *Toxophilus* (1544)

his grimly arrogant proverb, evidently still current in the reign of Henry VIII, starkly epitomised the automatic connection in the minds of Englishmen of the longbow with victories over the Scots.[1] The telling advantage of English archers over the majority of Scottish troops, lacking any defensive armour, had been demonstrated as early as 1138, where longbowmen were instrumental in breaking the wild charge of the Galwegians at the battle of the Standard. Doubtless by 1330, when the young Edward III assumed full powers as King of England, few men would have had any recollection of this distant triumph. Yet within three years two remarkable victories, won using the same combination of dismounted men-at-arms supported by archers but now adopting a devastating tactical deployment, had not only reversed English fortunes in the Anglo-Scottish wars but had ushered in the age of supremacy for the longbow in war.

DUPPLIN MOOR, 9 AUGUST 1332

In 1332 Edward Balliol, son of King John Balliol who had resigned his throne to Edward I in 1296, gained tacit permission from Edward III to lead an expeditionary force to attempt to gain the throne of Scotland. The moment seemed propitious, for King Robert's son David had succeeded him in 1329 aged only five, and the deaths of James Douglas in 1330 and Thomas Randolph in 1332 had deprived the Scots of their most able and experienced military leaders.[2] Balliol was supported by a group of lords including Henry de Beaumont and Gilbert de Umfraville; known as 'the disinherited', they were heirs to those opponents of Robert Bruce who had forfeited their lands in Scotland. Despite the fact that Edward was bound by the peace treaty of 1328 with the Scots, and that his sister Joan had married Bruce's young son David, the expedition was allowed to sail and made landfall at Kinghorn, Fife, on 6 August.[3] The size of the force raised by Balliol and Beaumont was not large; the well-informed canon of Bridlington estimated its strength at 500 men-at-arms and 1,000 infantry and archers.[4]

The vital role of archers and infantry was apparent from the first, for it was they who succeeded in driving off the Scottish levies who opposed their landing at Kinghorn, before the knights' war-horses could be brought ashore.[5] Advancing inland towards Perth, however, the disinherited soon found themselves in danger of being caught, as the Scottish chronicler Wyntoun put it, 'as fish in a net' in a pincer movement between the northern forces of Donald, Earl of Mar and recently appointed Guardian of the Kingdom, which barred the approach to Perth, and a second large Scottish force under Patrick of Dunbar, Earl of March, which had crossed the Forth from Lothian into Fife and was hastily marching against them.[6] With the courage born of desperation, they resolved to do battle with Mar's force before he could be massively reinforced from the south. The bridge over the Earn was held by a strong Scottish force, but by night the disinherited secretly crossed the river by a ford and launched a successful raid on the Scottish camp at Gask, killing many of the grooms and infantry they found there and scattering the rest. They soon realised, however, that the main Scottish force remained intact, and as dawn broke on 12 August the English quickly prepared to meet Mar's army, now alerted and advancing rapidly against them. The disinherited drew up in a position which allowed the enemy to advance on them only through 'a streite passage', and where the dismounted men-at-arms could hold a narrow front only some 200 yards long.[7] The archers were posted on the wings of the men-at-arms, perhaps on the rising ground; as the Bridlington chronicle notes, the men-at-arms were formed up 'with the archers disposed so they could attack the columns of the enemy from the flanks'.[8] Some 40 German mercenaries were held back as a mounted reserve,[9] presumably to reinforce the line where needed, and in case of victory to launch a counter-attack and effective pursuit. Balliol had distributed to the strongest men in his force a supply of 500 new pikes, oak-shafted and with long iron heads, which they had captured among other supplies at Dunfermline shortly after their landing.[10] These had been ordered by the late regent Thomas, Earl of Moray, who with his schiltrom had fought so well at Bannockburn, and who appreciated the great value of such weapons in the hands of the Scottish spearmen. How Balliol in turn deployed these weapons is unknown, but he must either have armed his infantry with the pikes to strengthen the main body of men-at-arms, or given them to the men-at-arms them-selves to give them greater reach in dismounted combat. It has been plausibly suggested that the English centre was four deep, with three ranks of men-at-arms and spearmen in the fourth.[11]

Whence did the inspiration for such a tactical deployment come? We shall probably never know for certain who had the inspired idea of flanking the men-at-arms with archers, all forced on the defensive by the paucity of their numbers.

Nevertheless, one of the most likely candidates is Henry de Beaumont, the driving force behind the campaign and who, as a veteran of Falkirk and Bannockburn, had witnessed profound military changes during his career in arms.[12] Yet whoever it was, the English formation at Dupplin was radically different from either of these engagements, and its results were to have a profound impact on the nature of English tactical thinking for over a century.

The Scots attacked immediately, and since no source mentions the digging of defensive pits or ditches by the disinherited we may assume they had no time to do so before receiving the first onrush of the enemy. The Scots, formed into two great battalions led by the Earl of Mar and by Robert Bruce, illegitimate son of King Robert, advanced 'in the form of a wedge', with the infantry in front.[13] According to the *Brut*, it was at this very moment that Mar was accused by Bruce of collusion with the disinherited, with the regent resolving to disprove the charge of treachery by being first into the attack. Bruce thereupon attempted to outstrip him and both led their units in a disordered advance against the enemy.[14] Whether or not such a dramatic exchange actually took place, it seems clear that Bruce's battalion attacked first, but the bristling mass of spearmen was quickly met by a hail of arrows from the English archers volleying into their flanks. Though the number of archers present was relatively small, their effect was deadly. As the *Lanercost Chronicle* noted, 'the Scots were chiefly defeated by the English archers, who so blinded and wounded the faces of the first division of the Scots by an incessant discharge of arrows that they could not support each other'.[15]

Nevertheless, the Scots spearmen closed with the English men-at-arms and at push of pike drove them back some 20 to 30 yards. At this critical moment Lord Stafford is said to have rallied his colleagues, urging them to form a tighter and less vulnerable formation by crying out, 'Ye English! Turn your shoulders instead of your breasts to the pikes'. 'And when they did this', noted the Lanercost chronicler, 'they repulsed the Scots immediately.'[16] The English line held, and the Scots formation, unable to make a frontal breakthrough, now began to lose both momentum and coherence. The Scots chronicler Wyntoun had heard it said 'right firmly' that the Scots could still have been victorious at this point had they been allowed to fight unhampered, and if the Earl of Mar had brought up the second battalion on their flank.[17] But fatally, Mar advanced in haste and threw his men forward *behind* the now faltering first battalion, causing it to become hopelessly compressed. 'Their advanced guard was stopped for a little on feeling the lance points and the arrows,' noted the soldier and chronicler Sir Thomas Gray, 'when their rearguard charged in such disorderly fashion that, in their furious charge, they bore to the

Archers cover an amphibious landing from large cogs, from a late fifteenth-century manuscript of Giovanni Boccacio's *La Teseida* (Österreichische Nationalbibliothek, Vienna, MS 2617). *(Österreichische Nationalbibliothek, Vienna/Bridgeman Art Library)*

ground a great number of their advanced guard between themselves and the enemy, who fell upon them so fiercely that they fell back one upon the other, so that in a short time you might see a heap of men's bodies growing as the strangers [i.e. the disinherited] surrounded them.'[18]

The terrible bunching effect caused by the rear ranks pressing forward was exacerbated by the movement inward by the Scots on the flanks, trying to distance themselves from the deadly rain of shafts pouring into them. 'There was the disaster so cruel', noted Wyntoun, 'that whoever in that great throng fell never had the chance to rise again.'[19] The struggling mass was now hopelessly vulnerable to both archery and the sword and lance blows of the English men-at-arms. But, as several chroniclers reported, most of the casualties among the Scots were due to suffocation. As the Bridlington chronicle observed, 'the forward troops of the enemy were heavily wounded by the arrows and driven to close up to the main force; jammed together in a small space, one was crushed by another. Suffocated by each other, and beaten by that rather than by blows of

swords, they fell in a remarkable way in a great heap. Pressed together in this way, and squeezed against each other as if by ropes, they perished miserably.'[20] Similarly, the *Scalacronica* records that the Scots 'were nearly all smothered, for each one lay beneath another, and died in the manner described without any stroke of weapon'.[21] As the bodies piled up so the English men-at-arms stabbed into the heaving mass. The Scots' rear ranks under the Earl of Fife now began to retreat, joined in flight by any who managed to escape from this fearful press, but the English men-at-arms remounted and gave fierce pursuit, striking down the fugitives.[22] Meanwhile, their infantry and archers had been ordered to surround the great mass of the

fallen and to slay any still alive. Doubtless with some exaggeration, chroniclers estimated the heap of bodies to be a spear's length in height.[23] Scottish losses were grievous, and included the regent Mar, Robert Bruce and the Earls of Moray and Mentieth. The Bridlington chronicler noted that there also fell '18 bannerets, 58 knights, 800 horsemen (equites), 1,200 men-at-arms, and a great number of foot-soldiers, besides the men in the heap, whose number no one knows'.[24] By contrast, English casualties were slight, including 2 knights and 33 squires but, purportedly, not a single archer or foot-soldier.[25]

The battle of Dupplin Moor was of great significance, for it marked the turn of the tide of English defeats that had dogged the English since the death of Edward I in 1307, and began the long roll-call of victories which brought such prominence to English arms and English archers. In demonstrating that the schiltroms could be defeated in the open field and shattering their aura of invincibility, Dupplin was to the Scots what the battle of Bicocca in 1522 was to the Swiss, when their seemingly unstoppable pikemen were broken by the gunfire and strong defensive position of the Spanish arquebusiers. Crucially, Dupplin witnessed the re-emergence of the deadly application of longbowmen with dismounted men-at-arms in a strong defensive formation which had not been seen since the battle of the Standard in 1138. The wise policy followed by King Robert I and his commanders of avoiding pitched battle unless in exceptional situations had been discarded with fatal results, because the small number of the disinherited had made the Scots overconfident. 'The English were insignificant in their own eyes,' noted the canon of Bridlington, and the night before the battle the Scots army drank and caroused, sending to Perth for wine and ale.[26] The Scots chronicler Andrew Wyntoun was moved to censure such rashness: 'But none should do so if they were wise; wise men should dread their enemies. For underrating [the enemy] and over-confidence often leads to defeat.'[27] Drawing on the teachings of Vegetius, he added that cornering an opponent made him courageous, for 'despair gives courage'. Accordingly, as Scipio counselled, a good general always left his enemy a chance of escape, 'for thus men could easily be defeated, for whoever gives himself over to flight loses heart and might'.[28] The moral was clear: 'Hereby men may take example that in fighting, discipline is sometimes better than strength or might. As Cato says, in other matters men can often put things right when they err; but in a battle, when men are not properly ordered matters cannot be well amended again – for you get it in the neck!'[29] In short, good order and discipline counted for far more than superiority in numbers. It was a lesson the Scots, and later the French, would ignore at their peril.

HALIDON HILL, 19 JULY 1333

The battle of Dupplin Moor led directly to Edward Balliol's inauguration as King of Scots at Scone. But in reality his political position was precarious, and a pro-Bruce revanche soon forced him to seek refuge with Edward III. In return for a recognition of English sovereignty over Scotland and grants of lands in the Scottish lowlands, including Berwick, Edward allowed Balliol to gather fresh forces and lay siege to Berwick. The Scots attempted to raise the siege by raiding into Cumberland, but their attacks only served to give Edward III a *causus belli*, and he soon marched north to reinforce the siege of Berwick in May 1333. Eventually, the beleaguered garrison came to an agreement that they would yield up the city on 19 July if the Scots had not defeated Edward in the field, or had not succeeded in placing 200 men-at-arms in the town or in crossing the Tweed at a stipulated point.[30]

Edward III and his commanders had created a situation whereby the Scots would be forced to take part in an offensive engagement on ground chosen by the English, or lose the great town of Berwick with its valuable commercial resources.[31] Douglas, who had left the relief effort till the very last day stipulated in the convention of surrender, namely 19 July, planned to engage the English, and, whatever the outcome of the main battle, to drive a relief force through to Berwick. On learning of the advance of the Scots, Edward left a strong force to prevent a sally by the town's garrison,[32] while he took up a strong defensive position on Halidon Hill, an area of high ground 2 miles north-west of Berwick. The royal army was divided into three divisions, each with two wings.[33] The centre of the vanguard was led by the Earl of Norfolk, the king's younger brother John de Eltham, Earl of Cornwall, Edward de Bohun and Henry de Beaumont, with its right wing, closest to the sea, under David, Earl of Athol, and its left under Gilbert de Umfraville. The centre was commanded by Edward himself, and the rearguard by Edward Balliol. 'Archers', noted the Bridlington chronicler, 'were assigned to each wing.'[34] In addition, 'as the chief and supposed cause of the immediate battle was that 200 horsemen . . . ought to enter the town that day, the king carefully chose out horsemen who would fight together and stop the sally of the enemy'.[35] Save for these cavalry, the English men-at-arms dismounted to fight on foot, and after exhorting his men from horseback Edward III also dismounted.[36] Although Geoffrey le Baker commented that the English dismounted 'contrary to the ancient custom of their fathers', such tactics had been part of the English response to the Scottish formations as early as the Weardale campaign.[37] English numbers are uncertain but have been estimated as perhaps considerably fewer than 10,000 men.[38]

Strikingly the formation of each English division consciously recreated the deployment at Dupplin, with dismounted knights flanked by wings containing archers. Doubtless on the advice of those veterans of Dupplin such as Umfraville, Balliol and Walter Mauny now present in his army, Edward was seeking to replicate the tactical situation which had brought such astounding success the year previously. With the trap set and

Berwick as bait, he would now lure the Scots to still greater destruction. Edward's deployment at Halidon is of great significance, for it marks the emergence of what Oman, Morris and many subsequent historians have regarded as the classic English formation that would be repeated many times throughout the Hundred Years War, with wings of archers flanking each 'battle' or division. Where divisions were positioned in line abreast, each wing of archers, thrown forward to provide enfilade shooting along the front of the men-at-arms, might meet up with the neighbouring wing to form 'wedges' of bowmen. As we shall see, this interpretation has been challenged, notably by Jim Bradbury, who has argued that wings of archers were usually only posted on the extreme flanks of the English army, and not as wings to each division. Yet whatever may have been the case in subsequent battles, the sources are explicit that at Halidon Hill the archers formed the wings of each division, and were not merely on the flanks of the army as a whole.[39] The *Brut* supports the testimony of the Bridlington chronicler, stating unequivocally 'and tho hade every Englislisshe bataile ii wenges of pris Archiers'.[40] How the three main divisions were aligned in relation to one another, however, is less clear, though as Nicholson notes, 'the rounded slopes of the hill would have prevented the troops being drawn up in a straight line: the three divisions must have been disposed on a curve following the contour of the hill'.[41]

The Scots, marching from Duns, approached from the north via a ridge known as the Witches' Knowe which overlooks Halidon Hill, and might have offered a good defensive position were the Scots not compelled to attack to secure their objective. They too divided their army into three or four divisions,[42] and sent away their horses to the woods in their rear.[43] Their numbers are uncertain, for as usual the figures given by most chroniclers are hopelessly exaggerated, but the continuator of Walter of Guisborough, who had access to an unusually detailed source for the composition of the Scots army, stated that the Scots fielded 13,500 spearmen and 1,200 men-at-arms.[44] If the *Anonimalle Chronicle* is to be believed, the Scots waited until the Tweed was at full tide, 'because they then well imagined that they might drive the King of England and his men into the River Tweed or into the sea to drown them'.[45] To make their ranks distinct, the Scots wore white shirts over their armour.[46]

'The Scotsmen', noted Wyntoun, 'arrayed themselves soundly, and advanced against them in open battle. But they had not considered the terrain: for there was a large, marshy creekbed between them, with steep rising ground on either side. They came together at that valley, where they first had to go down the declivity, then climb up to their enemies up a slope where a single man might defeat three; but that they

could not see beforehand.'[47] The first Scottish division under Moray came on towards the rearguard under Edward Balliol, 'in order that they might first meet and attack the division of him who . . . laid claim to the kingdom'.[48] As the Scots approached, the flanking bodies of archers in Balliol's division 'shot arrows as thickly as the rays in sunlight, hitting the Scots in such a way that they struck them down in their thousands; and they began to flee from the English in order to save their lives'.[49] The Lanercost chronicler similarly stresses the withering volleys of the English archers: 'Now the Scots marching in the first division were so grievously wounded in the face and blinded by the host of English archery, just as they had been formerly at Gledenmore [Dupplin] that they were helpless, and quickly began to turn their faces from the arrow flights and to fall.'[50] Edward had taken care to lay in plenty of ammunition for his archers; the sheriffs of London are known to have sent 195 sheaves of 24 arrows packed in tuns to York, and these must only have been a small proportion of the arrows required.[51] Moray's division, it seems, was defeated before the Scottish divisions joined battle. These attacked the English van and main battles but were rapidly repulsed. There was fierce fighting on the English right as the picked force of Scots under Archibald Douglas detailed for the relief effort bravely tried to cut their way through to their comrades in Berwick: 'The troops of Scots in which the best soldiers were placed, who were to enter the town, rushed with the ferocity of a lion against the foremost English line. A bloody battle developed there; for the Scots struggled to reach the town, and wanted to fulfil their oath; on the other hand the English resisted manfully . . . In this prolonged struggle there perished 500 of the strongest and choicest of all the people of Scotland, in the spot called by the local inhabitants "Heavyside".'[52]

Seeing the rout, the servants and grooms 'pricked the horses of their masters with spurs in order to save themselves from peril, leaving their masters cold'.[53] The Scots in the rear took flight, but as at Dupplin Moor the English now remounted and charged the disordered Scots: 'but the English pursued them on horseback, felling the wretches as they fled in all directions with iron-shod maces'.[54] 'Many times', noted the *Cleopatra Brut*, 'they rallied in diverse companies, but always they were defeated. And thus it came about, as God willed, that the Scots on that day had no more numerical superiority against the English than twenty sheep would have against five wolves.'[55] The English pursued the Scots for seven leagues, until nightfall forced them to return to their encampments. The heavy toll of Scottish dead included Ross, Lennox, Sutherland, Carrick, Mentieth, Athol and Archibald Douglas, 'who was chiefly responsible for leading them on to

Right: A king and his knights, from
The Romance of Alexander, Flemish,
c. 1338–44 (Oxford, Bodleian MS Bodley
264), depicting the kind of armour worn by
Edward III and his nobles in the opening
decades of the Hundred Years War. Note
the various forms of helmet and body
armour, and the solid plate defences for
the arms and legs. *(Bodleian Library,
University of Oxford)*

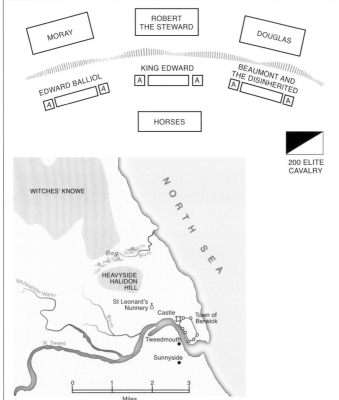

Left: (*above*) A schematic representation of the battle of Halidon Hill, 19 July
1333. The exact positioning of the flanking units of archers is unknown, as is
the precise relation of the three English divisions to one another. (*below*) The
general location of the battle (after R. Nicholson, *Edward III and the Scots*
(1965)).

such a fate', and some 27 bannerets.[56] English chroniclers
record implausibly small casualties among Edward's forces – a
knight, an esquire and 12 infantrymen[57] – but it nevertheless
seems that as at Dupplin the Scots did not succeed in closing
with the English archers.

Though much less well known than Crécy, Halidon Hill was
in many respects the most significant victory in the history of
the longbow for it marked the full-scale adoption by Edward III
of the devastating tactics pioneered by the expeditionary force
at Dupplin. Henceforth, English armies would utilise, in
varying depositions, the battle-winning combination of dismounted men-at-arms and archers against their opponents in
Scotland, France and, indeed, beyond. There had been no
technical development in the bow itself under Edward, only
the discovery, or perhaps more correctly the rediscovery, of the

Lightly armed longbowmen, wearing linen coifs and carrying bundles of arrows thrust into their belts, confront two heavily equipped crossbowmen, from *The Romance of Alexander, c.* 1338–44 (Oxford, Bodleian MS Bodley 264). *(Bodleian Library, University of Oxford)*

powerful defensive formations in which its power and speed of shooting could be used to maximum effect. And it is especially significant that such tactics were evolved against the Scots, where the full power of the bow had much greater impact against the poorly armoured spearmen.

It was to be another thirteen years before English and Scots forces clashed again in another major engagement. By the time they did English armies had successfully repeated the devastating tactics of Dupplin Moor and Halidon Hill against the French in a number of engagements, beginning with Morlaix in 1342 and culminating at Crécy in 1346. As Neville's Cross was to show, moreover, such a method of warfare had been fully absorbed by the wider military community, for it was an army largely composed of the levies of the northern shires which met and defeated the Scots outside Durham. For their part the Scots had taken some measures to avoid a repetition of the two crushing defeats of 1332 and 1333, and had no doubt studied the equally dismal experiences of their French allies at the hands of Edward III and his commanders. Nevertheless, at Neville's Cross they neither avoided a pitched battle nor abandoned the offensive – and once again the result was to be a disaster for them.

NEVILLE'S CROSS, 17 OCTOBER 1346

Edward III's great victory at Crécy on 26 August 1346 allowed him to lay siege to the major port of Calais, which, if taken, would give the English a vital bridgehead in France. As a result the Valois king Philippe VI appealed to his Scottish allies to launch an invasion of northern England, which he hoped would draw Edward away from his objective. David II had his own pressing reasons for launching a major campaign into England over and above expelling the remaining English garrisons in the Scottish borders: to force Edward III's recognition of the legitimacy of his kingship and to assert his authority over powerful Scottish lords who during David's exile in France (1333–41) had grown increasingly independent of royal power.[58] According to Knighton, the Scots 'had been told that there was no one left in England, everyone having gone to the siege of Calais except for helpless and feeble farmers and shepherds, and clergy'.[59] While the Scots were far less credulous than Knighton and other English chroniclers wished to think, King David nevertheless reckoned that with so great an army preoccupied at Calais the military resources of England must have been significantly depleted, and this was a major reason why he was confident in taking on the English forces in a major battle. In fact, with the threat of Scottish invasion a distinct possibility, Edward had made provision for the defence of the north while he was campaigning in France; no men had been levied from shires north of the Trent and, as was soon apparent, several able commanders were to hand in the north.[60] Taking the border fortress of Liddell, David's army of invasion entered England in early October, laying waste as it went in time-honoured fashion and sacking the religious houses of Lanercost and Hexham. Crossing the Tyne at the ford between Newburn and Ryton, the Scots encamped just west of Durham in the bishop's park known as Beaurepaire or the Bearpark, while the terrified monks pledged to pay an indemnity to save the community and its estates from destruction.[61] There is no reason to doubt one chronicler's belief that David intended to march via Beverley on York itself.[62]

To meet this threat an English army mustered at Richmond under the command of two of the leading northern magnates, Ralph de Neville and Henry de Percy, together with William Zouche, the Archbishop of York and Thomas Rokeby, Sheriff of Yorkshire.[63] Significantly Neville was joined by his son John, who had fought at Crécy only eight weeks previously and no doubt relayed details of Edward III's victory to the English commanders.[64] Veterans of earlier victories over the Scots were also present, notably Gilbert de Umfraville, Earl of Angus. The tale of Jean Le Bel, subsequently adopted by Froissart, that the army was presided over and encouraged by Edward's queen Philippa (who was in fact in Flanders), is merely a romantic fiction.[65] Marching via Barnard Castle, the English spent the night of 16 October some 8 miles south of the city at Auckland Park. Then on the next day, after making confession and hearing mass, they advanced north, meeting and putting to flight a force of 500 Scots foragers under Sir William Douglas, the famous 'knight of Liddesdale'.[66] Forewarned by Douglas, David's army hurriedly formed up and adopted a defensive position 'in a fairly steep place to await the English'[67] – doubtless hoping thereby to avoid the disaster that had resulted from taking the offensive at Dupplin and Halidon. The English commmanders, seeing this, in turn took up a defensive position just north of a stone cross a little to the west of Durham itself, where the terrain offered them a strong position.[68] The two armies, separated by about a quarter of a mile, thus awaited the assault of the other. Reliable figures for the Scottish army are lacking, though it was composed of some 2,000 well-armed men and a large but unrecorded number of more lightly armed infantry.[69] As the Scots formed up in three main divisions, 'they filled the land with the sound of trumpets and bugles'.[70] William Douglas and John, Earl of Moray, led the Scots vanguard on the right wing, King David himself commanded the centre, while the rearguard, which was the strongest division, was under Patrick, Earl of March, and Robert Stewart, the king's nephew.[71]

The exact location of the battle remains unknown,[72] but it is possible that the English had drawn up their formation along a pronounced ridge some 1,000 yards wide on Crossgate Moor, where to their left the land fell away to the River Browney and to the right there was a steep gulley known as Flass Vale.[73] The army was divided into the usual three battles. The vanguard, under Percy, Neville and Angus, was formed of the men from Northumberland, the centre under the archbishop comprised the men from the lands of St Cuthbert – Durham and its many dependent estates – while the rearguard, under Thomas Rokeby, John de Mowbray and John Leyburne, contained the men drawn from lands south of the Tees.[74] The numbers of the English force are uncertain, but as the summons to defend the country against invasion had gone out to all able-bodied men between 16 and 60 the resulting army may have been of a fair size, containing at least around 1,000 men-at-arms and 5,000 archers and other troops, and possibly considerably more.[75] The account roll of John de Wodehouse allows a portion of the army to be recovered in detail. It corroborates the statement of Geoffrey le Baker that archers from Lancashire were present, recording wages for 4 knights, 60 men-at-arms, 960 mounted archers and 240 foot-archers 'led from Lancashire to the battle near Durham'.[76] Yorkshire furnished at least 3,020 mounted archers, 29 hobelars and 15 men-at-arms.[77] Contingents from the other northern counties for which no pay rolls survive – Cumberland, Westmorland, Northumberland and Durham – may have provided an additional 4,000–5,000 men.[78] The army also contained a large number of local clergy who had mustered at Beverley at the summons of the archbishop to do battle against the Scots, and 'who, taking off their shoes and their hoods, showed themselves with swords and arrows at their waists and bows under their arms'.[79] According to canon law, clergy were not supposed to bear arms, but as in 1138 and 1319 the defence of the *patria* against an enemy who plundered and burned churches was regarded as a form of holy war. The description of these militant clergy strongly reinforces the impression given by court cases that many local clerics were just as adept at wielding a bow as their lay companions, and were often equally belligerent.

The men-at-arms, drawn from local gentry and the retinues of the magnates, formed the centre of each battle.[80] Where were the archers? Only one source, the Meaux chronicle, mentions the position of the bowmen, and then only in vague terms: 'Both the armies, the English and the Scots, divided their men into three lines, with the archers placed on the flanks.'[81] Does this mean the flanks of each division, as was certainly the case at Halidon Hill, or merely the outer wings of the army? It is possible that the narrowness of the ridge favoured the latter deployment, but the matter must remain uncertain. Burne suggested that the archers initially formed the first rank along the whole English position; after loosing their volleys they would have retired through gaps in the men-at-arms once the Scottish spearmen began to close.[82] Though speculative, evidence from battles in the Wars of the Roses certainly shows the possibility of such a deployment. The positioning of archers in the Hundred Years War, moreover, did not necessarily follow a rigid blueprint, as Jim Bradbury, Robert Hardy and Matthew Bennett have emphasised, and there must have been considerable fluidity of movement around the formations of men-at-arms to exploit changing tactical situations. Indeed, the Meaux chronicler noted how, prior to the main engagement, '500 English archers ran on

The battle of Neville's Cross, 17 October 1346.

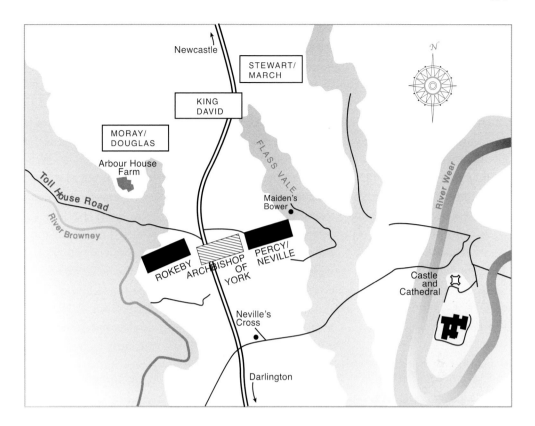

in advance, and by piercing them through many times with their missiles forced the Scots to abandon the place they had occupied, and provoked them to seek battle'.[83] Wyntoun similarly noted how, while the Scots were deploying, 'The English archers came so near that shoot among them well might they.'[84] Whatever their exact formations, what seems clear is that the English, desiring to remain on the defensive, succeeded in goading the Scots into the attack – just as Henry V was to force the French into advancing at Agincourt in 1415 – and thus into abandoning their defensive position.

The course of the ensuing battle is very hard to reconstruct with any certainty, for few of the sources give more than the briefest account of the fighting.[85] It is particularly unfortunate that the relevant portion of the *Scalacronica*, written by Sir Thomas Gray of Heton, is lost, for Sir Thomas himself fought in the battle.[86] It may, however, have been in the opening moments of the battle, as the advance unit of English archers launched their galling volleys at the motionless Scots, that Sir John Graham, Earl of Mentieth, requested command of a hundred cavalry to attack them, and thus to try to repeat the successful tactics of Sir Robert Keith at Bannockburn. In Wyntoun's words:

> Then good Sir John de Graham did say
> To the King, 'Get me no more
> Than a hundred horse with me to go,
> And all yon archers scatter shall I;
> So shall we fight more securely.'[87]

Yet remarkably – and fatally – either King David refused such a plan or, as the later chronicle of Walter Bower has it, Graham could find no one willing to venture upon so rash an escapade as to charge a substantial body of English bowmen. Graham showed his courage as well as his frustration by riding almost alone into the English bowmen and laying about him, before losing his horse to an arrow and retiring back to the main Scottish ranks.[88] The arrangement of the three Scottish schiltroms is by no means clear, but Alexander Grant has argued that rather than being in line abreast, the restricted ground meant that they were formed in echelon, with Moray and Douglas ahead and to the right of David's division, and the largest division under Stewart, probably containing the bulk of the more poorly armed troops, to the left and rear of the king.[89] The Scots' right wing now advanced but soon became hampered by the terrain, for as Wyntoun notes, 'at high dykes assembled they, and those broke wholly their array'.[90] If we accept the general location of the battlefield between the valley of the Browney and Flass Vale, the ridge to the south of the Scots would have narrowed, and close to where Arbour House Farm now stands they would have encountered a small but steep gulley. They would thus be forced to descend into a valley criss-crossed with ditches and fences before ascending again towards the English positions, a manoeuvre that unsurprisingly caused their ranks to lose cohesion just at the time they came within range of the archers in Rokeby's division.[91] The impact of Moray's division may

A coloured reproduction of the brass of Sir John III d'Aubernon (d. 1327), made *c.* 1340–5, from the parish church of Stoke d'Abernon, Surrey. This clearly shows, below the surcoat, the decorated rivets of the metal plates of his body armour, worn over a hauberk and a thickly padded aketon, while his arms and legs are protected by early forms of plate armour. Such armour was becoming increasingly common among English men-at-arms during the 1330s. *(By kind permission of the Heraldry Society/ICI)*

possibly have been greater than Wyntoun suggests. In a letter written shortly after the battle, Thomas Samson noted that 'twice our archers and common soldiers retreated, but our men-at-arms stood firm and fought stubbornly until the archers and the foot-soldiers rallied'.[92] Moray's initial assault may have been the cause of one of these re-treats, with the Scots men-at-arms forcing the archers and infantry either in front or on the flanks of the English men-at-arms to withdraw. The fact that this happened twice suggests that the archers and other infantry were reformed, and once again brought to bear against the Scots before a second advance compelled them to withdraw to a safer distance behind the men-at-arms.

According to Geoffrey le Baker, 'the Scottish nation, not accustomed to flee, resisted them [the English] stoutly. Their dense formation attacked the English and, with heads inclined and covered with iron, with polished helmets and tightly fastened shields, they frustrated the arrows of the English at the beginning of the battle. But the first rank of the men-at-arms were greeted by the enemy with deadly blows.'[93] This state-ment, which echoes Bower's remark that the Scots army con-tained around 2,000 very well-armed men (*excellenter armatorum*)[94] is very striking – the English archers were defeated by the defensive armament of the Scots, in particular their bascinets and their shields. As such, this anticipates by a

decade the first references to the armour of the French defeating longbow arrows, which occurred at Poitiers in 1356, and thereafter at subsequent engagements such as Cocherel and Auray, where the French were said to have been so well armed and pavised that the arrows had no effect.[95] It is possible, indeed probable, that such high-quality armour had been obtained from the Scots' French allies. Certainly by the later Scottish–French treaty of 1371 Charles V agreed to supply armour for 500 men-at-arms and esquires, as well as for 500 serjeants.[96] Grant has intriguingly suggested that it may have been this very failure of the English archers to make an initial impact on the Scots' ranks that caused David II to believe victory was indeed possible and to launch his main assault.[97] Be that as it may, it does seem that the Scots had attempted to solve the problem of the English archers faced at Dupplin and Halidon by increasing the defences of their leading spearmen. Given the poverty of the majority of Scots infantry, we must assume that, much like the practice of the Swiss and Landsknechts in the sixteenth century, the men with the best armour were placed in the front ranks. What kind of shields the Scots used is uncertain, for wielding the long spear required both hands, and it may be that, like the Macedonian phalanx, the infantry wore a targe strapped to their left arms.

Knighton makes the intriguing remark that the Scots were arrayed 'in the form and manner of the French'.[98] Could it be that here we have an analogy with Flodden over 150 years later, where the Scots had French military advisers fighting in their ranks, who had instructed them in the use of the newly adopted 16ft pike? Here too the English arrows had little effect on King James's heavily armoured men-at-arms, who also seem to have had pavises.[99] As a young man David had spent the years from 1334 to 1341 as an exile at the French court, where he may well have become acquainted with French military practices.[100] Certainly both the Italian chronicler Giovanni Villani and Geoffrey le Baker believed that Philip VI had sent mercenaries, including many Genoese, to aid David in 1346.[101] It would have been difficult if not impossible for David to re-equip his men in the aftermath of Crécy, for this was but two months previously, but it is not difficult to believe that the Scots and their French allies had been in close contact in the early 1340s and had consulted over the military threat posed by Edward's armies. This can only be speculation. But the implication of Baker's comments is important: the archers failed to stop the Scots' onrush, and it was the men-at-arms who held and broke their attack.

Unfortunately the course of the battle itself is obscure and much must remain conjecture.[102] After its initial impact the attack by the Scots' right under Moray was halted by the

English and then defeated with heavy losses, though the sources disagree as to whether this division was 'soon discomfited', as Wyntoun believed, or broke only after a sustained fight. With Moray himself slain, the survivors attempted to join King David's division, but finding that the king's position was so constricted that they could not fight there properly, the remnants of the earl's division moved further back from the front line to join the rearguard under Stewart, for 'thare had thai rowme to stand in fycht'.[103] Either during, or more probably after, the collapse of the Scots' right, David's division attacked the centre of the English line. This assault probably accounts for the second of the retreats by the English archers and infantry mentioned by Samson. The mention by the *Historia Roffensis* of three pauses in the battle would accord with an initial attack by Moray, a pause before David's first assault, followed by fierce fighting, then another pause before the combat was renewed.[104] Yet as to whether the Scots' centre again pressed home the attack or was in its turn assaulted, Wyntoun notes that:

> Then both the first forces right there
> At that assembly vanquished were.
> For of arrows such a shooting there was
> That lots were wounded in that place.[105]

As David's division engaged in fierce hand-to-hand fighting, it would seem that Stewart's division remained unengaged behind it. This may well have been due to the terrain rather than to any lack of courage or the treachery later ascribed to Robert in the aftermath of defeat. If David's division was so crowded that men could hardly fight properly, there would have scarcely been any room for the Stewart to bring his own schiltrom up in support, save from behind. This constriction is also suggested by Baker, who noted, perhaps with some hyperbole, that the Scots were so tightly bunched that one blow felled ten men.[106] If, moreover, the terrain had forced the Scots middle ward and rearguard to deploy one in front of the other, the dispersal of Moray's division would have left both flanks of David's division exposed to attack. The ability of the English archers to shoot at the Scots' flanks might well explain why they were able to inflict greater casualties than in the first encounters, for they would now be able to shoot at the less well-armed infantry behind the front ranks of the heavily armoured men, causing grievous wounds as in earlier Anglo-Scottish battles to men who probably lacked any form of iron armour.[107] The English now took the offensive, pressing in on David's division, though the Scots 'stood about him like a round tower', protecting the king in their midst and preferring death to flight.[108] 'The English archers', noted the *Historia*

The capture of King David II at Neville's Cross in 1346, from a fifteenth-century Flemish manuscript of Froissart's *Chronicles* (Paris, Bibliothèque Nationale, MS fr. 2643, f.165v). *(Bibliothèque Nationale, Paris/Bridgeman Art Library)*

Roffensis, 'surrounded the Scots so that they were not able to raise their heads.'[109] It was probably at this stage that Stewart and the Earl of Dunbar, rightly 'thinking that their men were losing and the English were prevailing, fled straightaway',[110] probably without a blow being struck.[111] According to Wyntoun, the king's division was still fiercely engaged,

> For when the fleears two miles and more
> Were fled, the banners were still standing,
> Face to face still fighting . . .[112]

Perhaps Stewart had little choice, but his withdrawal sealed David's fate. Being in the rear, the third division probably had guard of the horses of the men of the other two divisions; they could thus make good their escape but left their comrades, including the king, stranded.[113] Something very similar would happen at the battle of Poitiers in 1356, where after the repulse of the first French division the second division under the Duke of Orléans abandoned the field without fighting, leaving King Jean's division to be overwhelmed by the Black Prince's men.

Despite bitter fighting the king's division, attacked on three sides, began to disintegrate. David himself was taken prisoner by an English squire, John Coupland, either in the mêlée or, as another tradition relates, during the rout while hiding beneath a bridge at Aldingrange. Though badly wounded by two arrows, the king managed to knock out two of his assailant's teeth in the struggle.[114] Realising the enormous political significance of capturing David, as well as the size of the reward he could expect, Coupland rode off with him at full speed to the fastness of Bamburgh Castle, to prevent any Scottish attempt to rescue their king. Here David received medical treatment and, once fit to travel, was dispatched to London, though Coupland refused to yield him up to anyone save Edward III in person.[115] Meanwhile the English, now assisted by the lately arrived forces of Lord Lucy,[116] launched a fierce pursuit as far as Prudhoe and Corbridge, for which they almost certainly must have remounted. A letter written to the Bishop of Durham by Prior Fossor suggests that some of the Scots attempted to rally at Findon Hill, some 3 miles north of Durham, but were driven off.[117] Scottish losses included the Earls of Moray, Sutherland and Strathearn, several nobles and over 100 knights, but King David himself and an immensely valuable haul of prisoners had been taken.[118] Neville's Cross had been the third great military catastrophe suffered by the Scots in fourteen years. The monks of Durham, who had been watching the engagement from the great central tower of the cathedral, sang praises for victory, an event which was repeated annually until the 1640s.[119] The same cathedral was to see a form of belated revenge by the Scots, for in 1650 Scottish prisoners captured by Cromwell at the battle of Dunbar were imprisoned in the church, where they badly mutilated the fine alabaster effigies of Ralph Neville and his son John, together with those of their wives.[120]

Yet despite the magnitude of the English victory at Neville's Cross and the capture of King David II, the contrast between this engagement and those of 1332 and 1333 is marked. Whereas Dupplin and Halidon were won relatively quickly, with the shooting of the archers and the bunching of the attacking Scots being key features, several sources stress that Neville's Cross was a much longer and more bitterly contested struggle.[121] The *Anonimalle Chronicle* believed that the battle lasted from 8.30 a.m. to around 5 p.m. though the letter of Thomas Samson gives the more plausible duration as between Nones and Vespers, that is from 1.30–2 p.m. to around 5 p.m.[122] Indeed, so intense was the fighting that by agreement the two sides paused two or three times to rest before fighting recommenced.[123] This may, as we have seen, reflect the better armour of the picked Scots men-at-arms in the foremost ranks of the divisions of Moray and King David, and possibly also the terrain which affected the English deployment. One would like to know far more about the exchange of military intelligence between Scotland and France, the two partners of the Auld Alliance against England, during this period. But it seems likely that the Scots had been apprised of the experiences of the French against Edward III's forces on their own soil since the outbreak of the Hundred Years War in 1337. As the English had already discovered, the victories of the early 1330s over the Scots had not been so easily repeated in France; by the close of 1345 not only had the French forces of Philip of Valois displayed a wise reluctance to be drawn into a major engagement against defended positions, but combats such as Morlaix in 1342 had – like Neville's Cross – proved to be a close-run thing, largely decided not by archery but by the handstrokes of the men-at-arms. David II's use of heavily armoured men-at-arms on foot may simply have been a logical development of the Scottish tactics of massed spearmen offensively deployed, but they parallel the measures adopted against the English by the capable French commander Charles of Blois, who, as we shall see, attempted to counter the effect of English archery by the use of dismounted men-at-arms supported by cavalry from a comparatively early stage in the war. The French débâcle at Crécy, as Chapter 13 suggests, was an anomaly, scarcely representative of their best contemporary military practice, and thus must have been all the more shocking to contemporaries.

Matthew Strickland

PART III

The Hundred Years War and Beyond

Archers and crossbowmen as depicted in a collection of poems and romances presented to Henry VI's queen, Margaret of Anjou, French, *c.* 1445. (British Library, Royal MS 15 EVI, f.207). *(© British Library)*

'The Noblest and Finest Warriors that Are Known': the Transformation of English Armies, 1330–1415

'A hundred Frenchmen neither dared to meet twenty Englishmen in the field, nor to give them battle.'
Anonimalle Chronicle, s.a. 1356

espite containing large numbers of longbowmen, English armies during the reign of Edward II had been hampered by a sense of defeatism born of poor leadership and tactics, and a string of humiliating reverses at the hands of the seemingly invincible Scots. Yet the crushing defeats of the Scots first at Dupplin Moor in 1332 then at Halidon Hill the following year had not only arrested this process but instilled a high morale in the English armies Edward III was to lead against the French following the

outbreak of the Hundred Years War in 1337. This *élan* grew ever stronger as the tallies of victories in the 1340s and 1350s mounted, with the tactical synthesis of dismounted men-at-arms and archers developed against the Scots being employed to devastating effect against French armies seemingly overwhelming in their numbers. The three decades between 1330 and 1360 were to witness the apogee of the longbow, and the great battles of Crécy in 1346 and Poitiers in 1356 are indelibly linked with the prowess of the English archer. This same period witnessed what has been described as the

English archers practising at the butts, from the Luttrell Psalter, *c.* 1320–30 (British Library, Add. MS 42130, f.147v). Such shooting, which blended recreation with military training, was widespread long before Edward III made it compulsory for all able-bodied adults in 1363. Note the bulbous pile arrowheads, designed only for target shooting.
(British Library/Bridgeman Art Library)

'remilitarisation' of the English aristocracy, and by the 1360s Jean Le Bel could call the English 'the noblest and finest warriors that are known'.[1]

How are we to account for these remarkable successes? Tactics were a crucial element, and English deployment in battles, together with developing French responses to the defensive combination of men-at-arms and archers, will be explored in detail in subsequent chapters. The power of the longbow as a weapon undoubtedly played a key role, and its performance against armour and the wounds it might inflict will be examined in chapter 15. Yet underpinning both these elements were other vital factors, particularly the development of a highly efficient form of army organisation which, coupled with excellent leadership, helped forge a disciplined and superbly effective fighting force. The period between Edward III's first Scottish campaigns from 1327 and the Treaty of Brétigny in 1360, which marked the end of the first stage of the Hundred Years War, witnessed a radical transformation in the raising and structure of English armies, characterised by some scholars as no less than a 'military revolution'. Among the most crucial elements of change were the development of raising troops by indenture; the increasing proportion of archers who served mounted; the more balanced proportions of mounted archers to men-at-arms in comparison with cavalry–infantry numbers in many earlier armies; and the creation of mixed retinues of mounted archers and men-at-arms.[2]

CONTRACT ARMIES AND INDENTURED RETINUES

One of the most far-reaching developments affecting the efficiency of English armies under Edward III and his successors was the increasing use of armies serving wholly for pay and raised by written contracts of military service known as indentures. This important aspect of military organisation has been extensively discussed,[3] and here we need only a brief overview of its principal features. Neither paid service nor indentures were in themselves new; payment for service had become widespread under Edward I, and a limited number of written indentures begin to appear from the 1270s.[4] Their development was probably stimulated by the need to provide a specified number of men-at-arms and other troops for garrisoning key castles and to facilitate the organisation of forces in areas of conflict such as Gascony and Scotland on occasions when the king himself (and hence much of his administration) was absent.[5] Nevertheless, the bulk of the armies of Edward I and Edward II continued to be raised by the slow, cumbersome and inefficient systems of feudal summons for the cavalry and by separate commissions of array for the infantry right up until the dismal Weardale campaign of 1327. By contrast, an army summoned in 1337 for service in Scotland in the king's absence was raised by the voluntary service of nobles and knights, who negotiated contracts to provide a specified number of men-at-arms.[6] During Edward III's reign the use of these far more efficient contract armies was to become increasingly widespread. By this process the king contracted with his lords and captains, who each agreed to provide a retinue containing a specified number of men-at-arms, archers and, as required, other troops. Thus, for instance, in 1347 the king contracted with Thomas Ughtred to provide the service of 20 men-at-arms and 20 mounted archers for a year.[7] The nobles and knights who had undertaken these contracts then raised their promised retinues, often by sub-contracting with knights and archers in similar indentures. In 1372, for instance, William, Earl of Salisbury, contracted for the service of Reginald Mautravers, with two 'valet archers' to serve with him for two years.[8] In 1381 Sir Thomas Felton had contracted with the crown to serve in Brittany for six months with 499 men-at-arms and 500 archers. Fifteen of the sub-contracts survive by which he assembled his retinue, and they reveal a wide range in the size of constituent sub-retinues from the largest, containing 59 men-at-arms and 60 archers, to the smallest containing just one man-at-arms and one archer.[9] The contract or indenture, of which a copy was kept by both parties, often stipulated details such as the length of service, the place of service, pay and expenses, conditions such as the division of booty and the payment of a bonus or 'regard', and the equipment required.[10] It was not uncommon for the sub-contracts between a retinue captain and his men to differ in their terms and conditions from that agreed between the captain and the crown, particularly in relation to pay and the division of the spoils of war, enabling the captain to make a substantial profit.[11]

The 1330s and 1340s have been seen as a period of fundamental transformation, which witnessed the decline of massed infantry levies and the rising importance of the retinue, whose mounted archers were better trained and equipped, and who were drawn from a more affluent section of society, than the often poor and lowly foot-soldiers of the armies of Edward I and Edward II.[12] Nevertheless, the adoption of indentured retinues did not take place as a sudden, single reform but developed gradually as Edward III's reign progressed, and there remained a considerable overlap between the old and new systems of recruitment. In the 1330s and 1340s, for example,

Edward continued to raise men-at-arms by issuing mandatory summonses to serve in return for the king's wages, and a scheme for a proposed expedition to France in 1341 by which nobles contracted to serve with the king himself was as yet still experimental.[13] Formal indentures, moreover, were not used for those armies led by Edward III in person, such as those for the Crécy and Calais campaigns in 1346–7, or for the great expeditionary force of 1359, as these continued to be administered directly through the royal financial department known as the Wardrobe.[14] During this transitional period the traditional methods of raising archers and other infantry through commissions of array continued alongside the use of contracts. Thus the majority of Edward's mounted archers in his army of 1335 serving in Scotland had been raised by commissions of array, and only about one-third by contract.[15] It is probable that a large number of the infantry for the siege of Calais in 1346–7 were still raised by commissions of array, and levies continued to be drawn in this way from cities and the shires until the 1360s.[16] In his principality of Cheshire the Black Prince contracted with knights and squires to raise archers, but continued to hold commissions of array, with his captains often appointed as commissioners to select the best men.[17] Similarly, for his French expedition of 1355 the Black Prince raised most of his force by contract, but the Welsh archers continued to be raised by commissions of array.[18]

Moreover, even though his armies were becoming increasingly professional, Edward III was concerned to ensure a large reservoir of skilled archers on which either his retinue captains or the commissioners of array could draw. Hence in 1363 he issued the first of what would be a regular series of royal decrees stretching well into the sixteenth century, commanding that on feast days every able-bodied man should in his sports use bows and arrows, pellets or bolts (suggesting that the use of slings and crossbows was not discouraged) 'and shall learn and practice the art of shooting'. To this end, men were forbidden to either play or watch 'vain games of no value' such as the hurling of stones, loggats or quoits, handball, football, club ball, cambuc and cockfighting, through which, the statute claimed, the art of shooting, 'whence by God's help came forth honour to the kingdom and advantage to the king in his actions of war', was now almost wholly disused, and the realm was likely to find itself without archers.[19] Such rhetoric can hardly be taken at face value only seven years after the victory at Poitiers, but it does reveal the extent to which the longbow had become regarded as the universal weapon. In 1388 the Statute of Cambridge again commanded that all artisans and labourers shoot at the butts every Sunday and on feast days, and the act was reissued in 1410.[20]

The use of contract armies was, as Andrew Ayton has shown, a highly effective mechanism of raising and administering forces in a military situation which saw several of Edward's forces fighting concurrently under subordinate commanders in several different theatres of war such as Aquitaine, Brittany and France. Equally, by devolving recruitment on to lords and captains the use of indentured retinues served to relieve the crown of much burdensome fiscal and military administration.[21] Nobles themselves had long been entering into contracts with their own retainers for service in peace and war, and often – though not invariably – such men-at-arms would form the core of wartime retinues, while archers and others might be drawn from a noble's estates.[22] After 1359, when Edward III no longer commanded in person, the indenture system was increasingly adopted as the principal method of raising armies.[23] The retinues of members of the royal family or of the great earls who acted as the king's commanders were often small armies in themselves. For the expedition of 1359, for example, the Black Prince's own retinue consisted of 587 men-at-arms and 900 archers, and that of John of Gaunt 582 men-at-arms and 423 archers.[24] In 1415 the Duke of Clarence commanded a retinue of 960 men, and Henry V's other brother, the Duke of Gloucester, one of 800.[25]

Indentured retinues continued to form the basis of Henry V's armies of 1415 and 1417, though the subsequent conquest of Normandy and the need to maintain permanent garrisons in Lancastrian France were to have a profound impact on the nature and organisation of English armies.[26] In 1415, for instance, Thomas Tunstall contracted with Henry V to bring 6 men-at-arms and 18 archers, while an example of a sub-contract is furnished by the indenture between Thomas, Earl of Dorset, and John Le Boteler, squire, who agreed to serve for a year with 2 men-at-arms and 6 archers, who were to receive 12*d* and 6*d* per day respectively.[27] The force that sailed to France with Henry that year comprised, in addition to miners, armourers, artillerymen and other ancillary units, at least 290 retinues containing 10,533 men. As Anne Curry has shown, this represented an usually high number of retinues because many men, often bringing only small detachments, had indented directly with the crown.[28] Thus, for example, the contingent led by Henry's brother Humphrey, Duke of Gloucester, comprising 190 men-at-arms and 610 archers, was made up of 56 separate retinues, 24 of which contained only a single man-at-arms accompanied by between 2 and 4 archers.[29] In some cases even archers themselves contracted directly with the crown, or as individuals with the leader of a major retinue.[30] By contrast, the contingents from South Wales, Cheshire and Lancashire were raised not by indenture but from the localities by the crown's local officers.[31]

These methods of recruitment allowed English kings to field very large armies. The army Edward took to Scotland in 1335 contained around 15,000 men, while that proposed in 1341 was to have a strength of 13,500.[32] His army on the Crécy campaign in 1346 has been estimated at over 15,000 men, comprising some 2,700 men-at-arms, 3,250 mounted archers and hobelars, 7,000 foot-archers and 2,300 Welsh spearmen.[33] For the siege of Calais in 1346–7 Edward's host numbered at its peak some 5,000 men-at-arms, 5,000 horse-archers, 15,000 foot-archers and 600 hobelars, plus Welsh spearmen and foreign troops; it was probably the largest English army to be raised before the sixteenth century.[34] Pay rolls indicate the English army of 1359 numbered almost 10,000 men, one of the largest armies (together with those of 1385 and 1400 against Scotland) to be raised until 1415, when Henry invaded France with a force numbering over 12,000 men.[35] Nevertheless, such were the losses incurred during the siege of Harfleur through attrition and the ravages of disease, which forced many to be invalided back to England, that by 25 October the king had with him at Agincourt around only 900 men-at-arms and 5,000 archers.[36] Yet these great armies were exceptions, and the majority of English forces operating in France were usually far smaller.[37] The

Archers aid men-at-arms to take a bridge near Ivry in 1358 (British Library, MS Royal 20 CVII, f.137). Note the thickly padded gambesons or jupons worn by both archers and men-at-arms, in the latter case almost certainly over a hauberk and other body armour. (© *British Library*)

army in Brittany in 1342, for example, has been calculated at 2,000 men-at-arms, 1,780 mounted archers and 1,750 infantry.[38] Similarly, English forces sent to Lancastrian Normandy from the 1420s were rarely more than a few thousand strong. That of 1430–1, raised as a deliberate show of strength following Charles VII's coronation at Rheims and numbering 1,352 men-at-arms and 5,593 archers, was unusually large.[39]

If contract armies generally tended to be smaller than the great hosts of the first two Edwards, they were far superior in quality, and the increasing deployment of contract armies had profound consequences on the military effectiveness of English armies. Whereas the earlier system of raising cavalry and infantry separately had hampered their effective coordination on campaign and deployment in battle, the indentured retinue ensured that cavalry and infantry (who were to become horsed in increasing numbers) were raised together in a single unit, thereby greatly improving cohesion and command structure. Both the men and their equipment, moreover, were subject to regular checks, and the crown's purchase of massive stocks of bows and arrows may well have helped to provide a greater standardisation – though perhaps not quality – of weaponry.[40] Crucially, captains could now ensure the selection of consistently dependable troops, whether men-at-arms or archers, and as the war progressed many of those thus selected were veterans. Men raised from the same estate, village or hundred might fight together on several campaigns, thereby increasing the cohesiveness and effectiveness of their units. Equally, the core of many

magnates' retinues was formed by members of their own households or 'affinities', who were already contracted to serve their lord in peace and war, so on campaign and in battle itself a lord was surrounded by trusted servants and proven men. It is likely, moreover, that as with the Yeoman in the retinue of Chaucer's Knight, some of those who served in the mixed retinues of archers and men-at-arms were men who in times of peace had brought their bows to the aid of their lords in licit or illicit hunting, which, it has been argued, helped form powerful bonds between nobles and their retainers.[41] To such retainers were often added friends and kindred, so that in Jonathan Sumption's evocative phrase, these retinues were 'a miniature of English provincial society projected onto the battlefields of France'.[42] The cohesion of some units might be further enhanced by the provision of uniforms. Troops raised by the counties might be 'clothed in one suit', though the colours of such uniforms are unknown save for those of Cheshire and Flintshire, who wore caps and tunics of white and green, while it is probable that from the later fourteenth century the archers in the retinues of at least some lords would have borne their badges of livery.[43] In order to provide a greater degree of uniformity throughout the army, however, Richard II's Ordinances of War, issued in 1385, stipulated that 'everyone, of what estate, condition or nation he may be, so that he be of our party, shall bear a large sign of the arms of St George before, and another behind, upon peril that if he be hurt or slain in default thereof, he who shall hurt or slay him shall suffer no penalty for it'.[44]

Though Richard's ordinances are the first surviving set of English military regulations, it is very probable that such a provision was in force much earlier, at least from the start of the French wars, and marked a development of Edward I's practice of requiring his men to wear armbands with the red cross of St George.[45] Henry V, whose own ordinances of war issued at Mantes in 1419 were based on those of Richard II, similarly required all his men to wear the red cross of St George.[46]

The use of contracts ensured the king a known supply of trained troops, which greatly aided logistical and strategic planning, whereas with earlier feudal musters there had almost always been a marked disparity between the number of troops summoned and the actual number appearing on campaign.[47] Even when raised by commissions of array, the inducements of wages and booty, together with pardons for those with criminal convictions, ensured that there were many volunteers, particularly after the 1340s and the string of successful operations in France. In 1355, for example, over half the able-bodied men of seventeen Derbyshire manors were in military service, while in 1359 there were more volunteers for Edward's expedition than the king could use.[48] Similarly, in 1415 recruiting seems to have been easy. Several retinue leaders are recorded as bringing more troops than they had contracted to provide – Sir Thomas Erpingham, for instance, brought an additional 4 men-at-arms and 12 archers – while many were willing to serve without the customary full payment in advance.[49] The problem of desertion, which had plagued earlier

Thomas Holland, Earl of Kent, Duke of Surrey and one of Richard II's closest confidants, with his uncle, the Duke of Exeter, with a retinue of mounted archers, from Jean Creton's *Histoire du roy d'Angleterre Richard II*, c. 1401–5 (British Library, MS Harley 1319, f.25). *(© British Library)*

armies, particularly under Edward I and Edward II, was considerably diminished, though far from eradicated.[50]

Though the command structure of such armies is still imperfectly understood, the retinues, which were themselves often composed of several smaller units, gave the assembled army a vital degree of cohesion, flexibility and discipline. The ordinances of Richard II and Henry V reveal the primacy of the retinue in the order of march, with men forbidden to move ahead of or in any way beyond the pennon of his lord or captain, and to remain within the 'battle' or division to which the retinue had been assigned. Strict regulations prevented men from leaving their own retinue to join another, thereby disrupting the coherence of the retinue, while similarly the potentially explosive issue of billeting was controlled by each retinue having its own *herbergeour*, an officer assigned to provide lodging, who worked under the direction of the constable or marshal.[51] The primacy of the commander of the 'battle' was asserted in controlling foraging and the personnel involved, and though the regulations say little about command in battle itself the importance within the 'battle' of the retinue captain, clearly identifiable by his pennon or banner if he was of the rank of knight banneret, is clear.[52] Even those units not raised by indenture might have considerable coherence. The composition of a Welsh contingent in the 1334 Scottish campaign, for instance, suggests a high degree of organisation and command. It was led by its captain, Rhys ap Griffith, with a '*subconductor*', both paid 2*s* a day, 8 men-at-arms and 4 centenars at 12*d*, 444 Welsh, including 23 hobelars at 6*d*, a chaplain, 10 standard bearers, 20 vintenars, one beadle or cryer, and a surgeon (these men receiving 4*d*, all others 2*d*).[53] Similarly in 1359–60 a unit of 1,100 Welsh, comprising 920 infantry, was grouped into centenaries under 10 constables and 50 vintenars, with each centenary having its own standard bearer, crier, chaplain and doctor.[54] Why these crucial elements only appear in records of Welsh contingents and not in those of English companies is unclear, but must surely be a matter of bureaucracy, and it may not be too rash to envisage a similar provision within centenaries of English troops. In 1415 the fact that Cheshire archers were raised from the shire's individual hundreds suggests there may have already been a degree of familiarity between troops, while those levied from Lancashire served in units of 50, each led by a knight or esquire, who was no doubt a prominent local figure.[55] While it is probable that men-at-arms were often, though certainly not invariably, separated from the archers when battle formations were drawn up, it is a reasonable inference that the Cheshire and Lancashire archers retained their formations as sub-units within any larger formation of bowmen in which they were placed. Melded by bonds forged through service in royal or noble households, local ties and repeated campaigning in the same units, and highly motivated through pay and the desire for booty, such retinues provided English armies with a skill and professionalism denied to the French until the formation of the *Compagnies d'Ordonnance* in the 1440s.[56]

THE MOUNTED ARCHER: MILITARY AND SOCIAL MOBILITY

Initially, archer forces drawn from both retinues and the shires had been formed from foot as well as mounted bowmen. As the French wars progressed, however, the number of archers serving on foot declined markedly and the great majority of bowmen became mounted.[57] Edward III's Scottish campaign of 1334–5 was long hailed as the earliest appearance of the mounted archer or *eques sagittarius*, and it was natural for historians such as J.E. Morris to link the appearance of the mounted archer with the development of the longbow.[58] Horsed archers, however, were hardly an innovation of the fourteenth century, for as we have seen they appear in royal and baronial retinues in the twelfth century and were prominent in the forces serving under Anglo-Norman lords in Ireland from 1169. As he re-emerges in the 1330s the mounted archer was a logical extension of the versatile hobelar or mounted spearman who had come to prominence in the Anglo-Scottish wars of Edward I and Edward II as well as in Ireland.[59] A text of the 1320s speaks of a unit of 103 '*hobelarios sagittarios ad equites*' from West Yorkshire, and it is likely that the term hobelar disguises the earlier use of mounted bowmen.[60] The English experience of campaigning in Scotland reinforced the enormous value of mounted infantry, and by 1322 it is probable that a significant element of the forces of Sir Andrew Harclay at the battle of Boroughbridge consisted of mounted archers.[61] Given their numbers in 1334 it seems likely that mounted archers had been in service for some time before, including perhaps on the Halidon Hill campaign, while by the campaign of late summer 1335 their overall numbers had risen to 3,500.[62] Their operational value was demonstrated as early as 1336, when Edward III led a fast-moving mounted force of 400 men-at-arms and 400 horsed archers and hobelars to the relief of Lochindorb Castle, completing the successful expedition by widespread plundering in Aberdeenshire.[63] Such tactics of speed and surprise by a force of horsemen unimpeded by slow-moving infantry clearly echo those which Bruce had employed to such good effect against northern

England, but had the added advantage of providing archer support for the men-at-arms. Mounted archers now began to serve in large numbers in continental expeditions; in 1339 there were around 1,500 present in the English army in the Low Countries, and 1,780 mounted archers in Brittany in 1342.[64] From this period onward almost all the archers serving in the retinues of the king or his captains were horsed; in 1334–5 the retinues brought by nobles comprised almost entirely mounted men-at-arms and archers in virtually equal numbers.[65] In 1355 the Black Prince's retinue was unusual in having not only 433 men-at-arms and 400 mounted archers, but also 300 additional foot-archers.[66] Equally, many cities and shires increasingly sent mounted archers raised through commissions of array, as well as foot-archers. Edward III's army which marched on Rheims in 1359 comprised around 4,000 men-at-arms and more than 5,000 mounted archers.[67]

The increasing use of mounted archers has been seen as an important reason for the reduction in the size of most English armies, as horsed troops were naturally more expensive to raise.[68] But increased mobility more than compensated for loss of numbers. The use of mounts allowed supporting archers to move at the same speed as the men-at-arms, and thereby allowed the development of the *chevauchée* as one of the principal methods of English strategy.[69] It also meant that archers could operate effectively with men-at-arms in an offensive role in combat itself. When in 1346 the Earl of Derby came to the relief of the English garrison of Auberoche in Gascony, his force of only 300 men-at-arms and 600 archers surprised and routed the large French besieging army by launching a fierce cavalry charge into their encampment as they sat at dinner. The archers and Gascon crossbowmen supporting Derby dispersed any groups of French who managed to come together on open ground, while the English force quickly defeated the troops of the second French camp, aided by a mounted sally from the English knights within the castle.[70] At the battle of Poitiers in 1356 the Captal de Buch led a force of mounted archers and men-at-arms in his decisive flanking attack on the French rear, and 'the archers he had taken with him wrought great havoc'.[71]

Recognition of the effectiveness of the mounted archer led to their forming an increasing proportion of English armies. As early as the winter campaign in Scotland in 1334–5 Edward III's army contained some 6,200 men, comprising around 1,240 men-at-arms, 40 foot archers and 1,200 mounted archers serving in the retinues of the king and his nobles, while a number of shires provided a further 70 men-at-arms, 460 hobelars and horsed archers, and 1,750 foot-archers, together with 100 men from York and a contingent of Welsh, whose arms are not stated.[72] The overall proportion of mounted archers to men-at-arms raised from retinues was thus nearly

equal, while this proportion was reflected in the composition of many of the retinues themselves.[73] The same balance, both in the army as a whole and in individual retinues, is also visible in the English force in Brittany in 1342–3, which comprised some 1,800 men-at-arms and 1,800 horsed archers,[74] and in several other armies, such as that of Sir Robert Knollys in northern France in 1369, containing 2,000 men-at-arms and 2,000 mounted archers.[75] In naval forces by the end of the fourteenth century the ratio of men-at-arms to archers was also roughly equal.[76] Such proportions, however, were far from rigid. While the overall total for the continental expedition of 1338–9 was 1,600 men-at-arms, 1,500 horsed archers and 1,650 foot-archers, several retinues brought more men-at-arms than mounted archers.[77] The great army of 1359 comprised 5,000 mounted archers and 4,000 men-at-arms, although the individual retinues were more balanced in their numbers. Thus, for example, the retinue of the Earl of Northampton contained 160 men-at-arms and 200 mounted archers, and that of the Earl of Warwick 120 men-at-arms and 120 horsed archers.[78] In some retinues archers could considerably outnumber the men-at-arms. Thus in 1345 the Earl of Derby's own retinue comprised 7 bannerets, 92 knights, 150 esquires, 250 mounted archers and 300 Welsh archers.[79] The retinue of John of Gaunt for the Calais expedition of 1369 comprised 499 men-at-arms, 1,000 mounted archers, 300 Welsh spearmen and bowmen, and 40 miners.[80] In expeditions between 1369, when the French war was renewed, and 1380, when the last force to be sent to France that century was dispatched, the ratio between men-at-arms and archers was normally equal, but as the century wore on the proportion of archers in retinues tended to increase.[81] During the reign of Richard II the ratio of archers to men-at-arms was normally 2:1 or 3:1, proportions which subsequently became the norm by the early fifteenth century.[82] Retinues at Agincourt generally show a ratio of 3 archers to 1 man-at-arms, and for the 1415 expedition archers comprised at least three-quarters of the whole army.[83] Such a composition meant that whatever the size of individual forces English armies had far more 'hitting power' per capita than any opposing French or Scottish armies. Henry VI's reign witnessed the appearance of retinues with still higher ratios, possibly due to the difficulty in obtaining men-at-arms or to the lower cost of the mounted archer's wages. Thus, for instance, while many retinues in the expeditionary army of 1430–1 continued to have a ratio of 1:3, the Bastard of Clarence brought 50 men-at-arms and 700 archers, Sir John Kyghley 30 men-at-arms and 500 archers, and William Heyward esquire 6 men-at-arms and 120 archers, while the joint retinue of squires Thomas Burgh and Henry Fenwick contained 80 men-at-arms and 600 archers. In the forces of 1450 and 1453 the normal ratio had become 1:10.[84]

THE ARCHER'S RISING STATUS

These changes had important implications not only for the tactical and strategic potential of English armies, but also for the social status of archers themselves. Many of the infantry archers in Edward I's armies had been drawn from the poorer sort, yet the mounted archers of Edward III's armies were increasingly raised from the more prosperous yeoman classes.[85] The social category covered by the term yeoman was a broad one, but usually denoted a reasonably well-to-do freeholder or tenant, who might still cultivate his own land, and was distinct from poorer husbandmen and labourers, and still more so from unfree villeins and bondmen.[86] After the terrible ravages of the Black Death from 1348 onwards, many smallholders had prospered, taking advantage of the depressed land market to augment their estates. It was such men, some of whom might possess considerable standing in local society, who now served as mounted archers, drawing the considerable pay of 6*d* a day, double that of a foot-archer. This was at a time when a ploughman's annual wage might be some 12*s* and the price of an acre of good arable land stood at around 4*d*.[87] Accordingly, such men often possessed superior equipment, and, in an age profoundly conscious of status, were separated from other infantry by the very fact of being mounted. An archer's hackney might cost around 20*s*, a substantial sum.[88] A writ of arms issued by the king in October 1344 or January 1345 stated that all men with £5 of land were to be ranked as mounted archers, those owning £10 as hobelars with more extensive equipment, and those owning land valued at over £25 as men-at-arms.[89] Those ranking as '£2 tenants' were to serve as foot-archers, possessing a bow, arrows, a sword and knife. But even such archers were the social superiors of several lesser ranks with smaller holdings, who were to have gisarmes, swords and knives.[90] This is a very different picture from the lowly status of the archer in the Assize of Arms of 1242.

The status of the mounted archer may be gauged by the fact that in the fourteenth century, when an annual income of £5 may have denoted eligibility for entry into the ranks of the lesser gentry, it has been estimated that not including barons, earls and dukes, who formed the highest echelons of the aristocracy, there were around 1,100 knights possessing incomes over £40, and some 10,000 other families were in receipt of annual incomes of between £5 and £40.[91] By the early fifteenth century the number of knights earning between £40 and £400 had fallen to under 1,000, while some 6,200 landowners with an income of between £5 and £39 were assessed in the taxation of 1436. Later in the century Sir John Fortescue regarded an income of £5 as 'a fair living for a yeoman', while in the ranks of the lesser gentry a 'gentleman'

needed at least £10 income a year, and an esquire over £20.[92] In Cheshire the status of the mounted archer was particularly high, and as early as 1334 a body of 200 mounted archers from Cheshire under John Ward were chosen for the bodyguard of Edward III.[93] As Philip Morgan has noted, 'in Cheshire there were many whose standing, within the context of county society, was analogous to that of men-at-arms raised elsewhere in England, but who took service in the [Black] Prince's retinue as mounted archers'.[94] In 1355 the Cheshire archers drew pay of 6*d* a day compared to those of North Wales and Flintshire who received only 3*d*.[95] The practice of recruiting royal bodyguards from the area continued and reached its apogee under Richard II, whose Cheshire archers gained an unenviable reputation as an instrument of an oppressive regime.[96]

But if the Cheshire archers were a corps d'elite, other factors led to the rising status of mounted archers in general. As Jim Bradbury has pointed out, the series of victories achieved by the English between 1332 and 1367 must have done much to augment the military profile and standing of the archer,[97] and the same may have been true of later victories such as Agincourt and Verneuil. The social gap between man-at-arms and archer was becoming less sharply defined than in earlier centuries, just as the category of man-at-arms included both knights and esquires, united in their capacity as warriors fighting in full harness, but of very mixed origin.[98] Indeed, 'a typical royal army would probably include many archers and men-at-arms of a roughly similar social status', while the category of mounted archer could itself embrace a broad social spectrum.[99] It was not uncommon for a family to send one member to fight as a man-at-arms, while another, perhaps a younger brother or son, would serve less fully equipped as an archer. This trend could only be furthered by the levying of archers together with men-at-arms in contract retinues. The later evidence of the composition of the retinues of John, Lord Talbot, between 1439 and 1442 reveals a number of men who had served as archers subsequently being recruited as men-at-arms.[100] Richard II's Ordinances of War of 1385 provide a particularly graphic indication of the greater social status of the mounted archer and the perceived gulf between him and the archer on foot. If a man-at-arms or a mounted archer in the host raised the unauthorised cry to mount or any other 'escry' by which the cohesion of the army could be put at risk, he was to forfeit his best horse – but if he was a foot-archer or a valet he was to lose his right ear. No doubt precisely because of their mixed backgrounds, mounted archers thus now enjoyed the exemption from mutilation shared by gentlemen.[101]

War could be a means for rapid social advancement, and just as some of the minor gentry enriched and ennobled themselves by distinguished service in the French wars, so archers of yeoman status might themselves gain preferment through military service and its perquisites.[102] As Sir Thomas Gray noted in his *Scalacronica*, by the 1350s there were many 'young fellows who hitherto had been but of small account, who became exceedingly rich and skilful in this war . . . many of them beginning as archers and then becoming knights, some captains'.[103] It was reputed that Sir John Hawkwood and Sir Robert Knollys began their military careers as archers.[104] Speaking of the men-at-arms and archers taken by Knollys to the assistance of Charles of Navarre in 1358, the chronicler Henry Knighton remarked that 'together they despoiled all the countryside all around, and many of them were made immensely rich and opulent, so that they seemed rather lords of the land than soldiers. And many who went out as mere boys and servants (*garciones vel valetti*) became experienced knights and came home rich men.'[105] By 1421 Henry V could grant a commission to local knights to raise from the counties of Yorkshire and Lancashire 400 'fitter and sufficient archers who are of gentle progeny (*de progenie generosa*) or men called "yomen" or sons of men called "yomen"' for service in France.[106] Over a century later a vivid glimpse of a yeoman archer still some way below the gentry class is provided by Archbishop Hugh Latimer in a sermon to the young Edward VI in 1549. Looking back nostalgically he told how his father, who had taught him to shoot the longbow from boyhood, 'was a yoman, and had no lands of his own; only he had a farm of 3 or 4 pound by year at the uttermost, and hereupon he tilled so much as kept half a dozen men. He had walke [pasture] for an hundred sheep, and my mother milked 30 kyne. He was able, and did find the king a harness, with himself and his horse.'[107] Such a condition was probably shared by many yeoman archers in armies of the previous two centuries.

In attempting to reconstruct the 'military community' of later medieval England, Andrew Ayton has remarked on the difficulties of tracing the background or careers of any but the nobility and gentry; mounted archers and other infantrymen can rarely be identified beyond the lists of names, or even just numbers on the rolls.[108] One exception is the army of 1415, and the forces occupying Lancastrian Normandy, and the further researches of Anne Curry will doubtless shed important light on the backgrounds of the archers as well as the men-at-arms in the first half of the fifteenth century. What can be said is

that archers in later medieval armies were probably drawn from a comparatively wide social spectrum; some might be the scions of gentry families, many would be farmers or minor landholders of varying prosperity, while others might be comparatively poorer artisans. Thus while the social status of the archer in later medieval England had undoubtedly waxed, there nevertheless might still remain a significant social divide between many archers and the men-at-arms in whose retinues they served. Chaucer's Yeoman, who epitomises a well-equipped archer of the late fourteenth century, is still very much the armed servant of his master, the Knight. Indeed, one definition of the term yeoman was exactly that of an armed retainer, a rank more emphatically rendered in the French equivalent *valet de guerre*. Such social disparity was reflected in pay, with an archer receiving only half the wages of a man-at-arms; in 1415, for example, an archer received 6*d* a day and a man-at-arms 1*s*.[109] French observers, moreover, not only made a clear distinction between the English nobles and their archers, but also noted that many of the latter were poorly equipped. Pierre Cochon, a priest of Rouen probably writing in the 1430s, regarded many of the soldiers landing with Henry V at St Vaast-la-Hogue in 1417 with disdain, noting with some hyperbole that they were 'young men from various lands, some Irish, all with bare feet and no shoes, dressed in scruffy doublets made out of old bedding, a poor scull cap of iron on their heads, a bow and a quiver of arrows in their hand and a sword hanging at their side. That was all the armour that they had. There was also a large quantity of scum (*menues merdailles*) from several lands.'[110] As the French chronicler Monstrelet noted, at Agincourt most of the English archers 'were without armour, dressed in their doublets, their

Archers, protected by heavy shutters, shoot from a wheeled wooden siege tower, giving cover to sappers and a scaling party (British Library, Royal MS 14 E IV, f.281v). (© British Library)

hose loose around their knees, having axes or swords from their belts. Many had bare heads and were without headgear.'[111] Others had 'hunettes or cappelines' of boiled leather, and 'some of osier on which they had a binding of iron'.[112] In the later stages of the war in France, moreover, there were a significant number of archers among those 'gens vivants sur le pays', those former soldiers from disbanded garrisons or field forces who roamed English-held Normandy as militarised vagabonds and who in the 1430s and 1440s might comprise up to 40 per cent of English field forces.[113] As Monstrelet noted cynically of the English slain at Patay in 1429, 'among the dead were a certain number of the leaders, the rest were men of middling or low degree – the sort who are always brought from their own country to die in France'.[114]

Nevertheless, the increased social status of many English archers in the fourteenth and fifteenth centuries had significant military implications. As Matthew Bennett has noted of the archers at Agincourt, 'they were soldiers with a high degree of individual skill, proud of their craft (like guildsmen) and capable of independent action'.[115] Not for nothing did Henry V's Ordinances of War issued in 1419 forbid 'that no assault be made on a castle or fortification by an archer or any other of the commons without the presence of a man of estate'.[116] In physical terms such men were not impoverished peasants on a subsistence diet, but comparatively well-fed and healthy, as they needed to be to train effectively and wield their powerful bows. In social terms the enhanced status of many archers and the nature of the indentured retinue helps to explain a key factor in English military success: the close cooperation and mutual interdependence between the archers and men-at-arms. Their close association is suggested by references in muster and retinue rolls to 'each man-at-arms with his archer' (chescun home darmes avec son archier),[117] affording an analogy with the role of the 'gros valet' or coustillier accompanying French and Burgun-dian men-at-arms of the later fifteenth century, and again reminding us of Chaucer's Knight, accompanied by his squire (his son) and the yeoman archer.[118] The skill and professionalism of the archers made them an indispensable element in English armies, which could rarely match the numbers of men-at-arms fielded by the French. The contrast here with French armies is very striking, for despite the reforms attempted by Charles V to create an effective archer arm the French continued to rely heavily on crossbowmen, who were often foreign stipendiaries, and to deny their own archers real military significance.[119] Indeed, as Agincourt was so painfully to demonstrate, many of the French nobles treated their infantry with unconcealed disdain, and were to pay a heavy price for so doing.[120]

Conversely, defeat at the hands of archers who, whatever the complexities of their actual social background, were perceived by French chroniclers and French men-at-arms alike as mere commoners was accordingly seen as a terrible disgrace. Thus the Religeux of St Denis bemoaned that at Agincourt 'the nobility of France were taken prisoner and put to ransom as a vile troop of slaves or else perished under the blows of a faceless soldiery. O eternal dishonour! O disaster for ever to be deplored! If it is usually a consolation for men of heart and a softening of their sadness to think that they have been beaten by adversaries of noble origin and of a recognised valour, it is on the other hand a double shame, a double ignominy, to allow oneself to be beaten by unworthy and vile men.'[121] Such contempt for the common soldier made defeat at their hands a bitter experience, and helps to explain the readiness to slay or mutilate English archers should they be vanquished. Though this was to prove a rare occurrence, an English defeat might give rise to a situation in which a member of the lesser gentry who fought as a man-at-arms would be accorded the right to parole and ransom by his French opponents, but one who fought as an archer might suffer mutilation or death.

THE UNIVERSAL SOLDIER

The corollary of the increasing reliance on archers in English armies was a gradual decline in the numbers of other types of infantry. Spearmen, predominantly from Wales, continued to be deployed in significant numbers in the first part of Edward III's reign. In the continental campaign of 1338–9 Welsh spearmen served in an army whose English contingents consisted wholly of men-at-arms and archers (both horsed and on foot), while in 1341 the king's council envisaged an expeditionary force of 10 earls, 49 bannerets, 589 knights, 1,946 men-at-arms, 1,012 'armati', 7,952 archers (including 2,000 Welsh archers) and 2,000 Welsh spearmen.[122] Heavy infantry were deployed in the early stages of the war in Gascony, and a force planned for a campaign in Brittany in 1342 was to include 2,000 men armed 'with large lances and burnished bascinets'.[123] The Welsh, and probably these other spear-armed 'gentz armez', may well have been intended to afford protection to the archers, or, as in Edward's deployment at La Flamengerie in 1339, to defend the front of the army against direct cavalry attack.[124] Welsh spearmen likewise served on the Crécy campaign, but their role decreased as the Hundred Years War progressed and as English archers moved from the use of potholes, ditches and hedges for cover to the adoption of defensive stakes from the 1415 campaign onwards.[125] Equally, many of the functions of the mounted spearman or hobelar could be performed by the versatile mounted archer, 'a superior breed of fighting man because of his potent weapon'.[126] Mounted archers thus largely replaced the hobelar in expeditionary armies, though these 'border spears' remained invaluable as 'prickers' in northern campaigns and saw extensive action against the Scots and Irish well into the sixteenth century.

The numbers of crossbowmen, who had played an important role in the forces of Edward I, dwindled in English field armies, though some continued to be employed in siege operations and as marines at sea. In 1333 Edward III had some crossbowmen at Halidon Hill, where they had presumably been deployed in the siege of Berwick, while in 1336 and 1340 crossbowmen are found aboard English ships.[127] Henry V had a small number of Gascon crossbowmen in his army of 1415, though once again they had probably been hired for siege work at Harfleur.[128] There was still a need for specialist engineers to supervise the construction and repair of siege engines, springalds and crossbows, and large quantities of crossbows and bolts continued to be produced for the munitions of royal castles.[129] It is thus unsurprising to find a number of 'arbalisters' still working in London, such as the two who appear as beneficiaries of the will of a bowyer.[130] The use of foreign stipendiary archers, which can never have been high, largely disappeared.[131] The proportion of Welsh archers, who had served in such large numbers in the armies of Edward I, also declined. There was a substantial contingent at Crécy, and though in 1355–6 a small force of only 170 Welsh accompanied the Black Prince, archers were summoned in 1356 from all of Wales and the south and Midlands of England for the army intended to reinforce Lancaster in Normandy.[132] In 1359–60 the army contained a force of 1,100 Welsh, while 400 Welsh foot-archers are known to have served in John of Gaunt's retinue on the 1369 expedition, but thereafter they appear to have played little if any role in subsequent forces sent to France in the last decades of the fourteenth century.[133] In the wake of Owain Glyn Dŵr's rebellion Henry V had cause to doubt the loyalty of troops from northern Wales, but in 1415 the counties of Brecon, Carmarthen and Cardigan provided substantial contingents amounting to 20 men-at-arms, 23 mounted archers and 473 foot-archers.[134]

Thus it was that the archer became the universal soldier in English armies, a mounted infantryman deployed in virtually every kind of action. We shall examine the tactical role of archers in battle in subsequent chapters, but it is important to remember that despite the battle-seeking strategies of many English commanders such major engagements would have formed only a small (if momentous) part of an archer's military

experience. Much more time was spent in the numerous raids, skirmishes and sieges that constituted the great majority of the fighting during the Hundred Years War, and in the more mundane but equally essential task of garrisoning castles and fortified towns. This role in siege and garrisoning, long of importance in Gascony, became increasingly essential as the English made territorial gains in France. It was still more pronounced during Henry V's campaigns in Normandy from 1417 to 1420, as English policy became one of conquest and settlement, a pattern that was maintained by Bedford's subsequent expansion of English control into Maine and Anjou. By 1421 English garrisons in Normandy and other territories totalled some 4,000 men: the highly sophisticated military organisation involved in retaining these lands through a combination of magnates' retinues, feudal military service from English and French lords, permanent garrison forces and expeditionary armies has been the subject of major studies by R.H. Newhall, Christopher Allmand and Anne Curry.[135]

As in earlier conflicts archers continued to prove invaluable in siege warfare, playing an essential role not simply in the great set-piece investments of cities such as Calais in 1346–7, Harfleur in 1415 or Rouen in 1419, but in the attack and defence of innumerable castles and fortified towns. They could defend lines of circumvallation, such as during Edward III's siege of Tournai in 1340 when the archers were instrumental in repulsing a major French sally by 100 French men-at-arms, or man siege towers, such as the three built by the Black Prince to take the castle of Romorantin in 1356.[136] Above all, their rapid volleys gave vital cover to the men-at-arms launching an assault. During his initial attack on Bergerac in 1345, for example, the Earl of Derby used archers to great effect to cover the attacks first of his cavalry then of his dismounted men-at-arms.[137] Two days later, when Derby mounted a ship-based attack on the side of the town facing the Dordogne river, the archers in the ships 'kept up so quick an attack with their arrows, that none dared show themselves, unless they chose to run the risk of being killed or wounded'.[138] Later in the same campaign, when he laid siege to Roche Millon, Derby sent forward sappers with picks to undermine the walls, while he 'had his archers advance to the barriers, where they shot so well that none dared appear to defend them'. Under the cover of their bowmen the English were able to break down the defences to such an extent that the garrison agreed to surrender on terms.[139] Froissart describes how, on laying siege to Castelnuadry during the Black Prince's *chevauchée* of 1355, the English

spread out around the town and their assault parties began to throw themselves against the walls. Their archers were formed up in divisions (*estoient arouté*) and

Archers and crossbowmen shooting from ships support an assault on a town, from a collection of poems and romances presented to Henry VI's queen, Margaret of Anjou, French, *c*. 1445 (British Library, Royal MS 15 E VI, f.207). *(© British Library)*

shot volleys of arrows so dense that the defenders could no longer hold their positions on the walls. Then the assault parties pressed their advantage and poured across the defences to capture the place.[140]

Some idea of the hail of shafts launched in such assaults may be gauged by a dispatch written in 1359 by the two consuls of the town of Issoire in the Auvergne; they proudly noted that an attack by an English force of 800 men had been successfully repulsed, despite the enemy having shot 1,500 arrows into the town, a figure that may not have been too much of an exaggeration.[141] Rapid shooting made archers equally effective in defence, whether manning ramparts or engaging in sallies. In 1342, for example, a force of men-at-arms and 300 archers under Sir Walter de Mauny, who had reinforced the besieged town of Hennebont in Brittany, led a major sally out by night, destroying a large trebuchet that had been bombarding the town, for the archers 'shot so well that those who guarded the

machine fled'. When the besieging French rallied and counter-attacked, the knights made a stand to cover the retreat of the others, but the rest of the garrison issued out in their aid, and 'ranging themselves upon the banks of the ditch, made such good use of their bows that they forced the enemy to withdraw, killing many men and horses'.[142] During the Lancastrian occupation of Normandy English archers doubtless helped man the great entrenchments built by Henry V around the city of Rouen in 1418, and were instrumental in driving off a major French attempt to relieve the second English siege of Harfleur in 1440, when they shot rapidly from behind their lines of contravallation.[143] Their importance in assault is equally seen in the ordinances issued by the Earl of Salisbury, probably for the Maine campaign in 1425, which stipulated that every man was to make 'a good substantial faggot of 13 foot in length without any leaves', for use at 'bolewerkes and ditches', that every seven men-at-arms were to have one ladder of fifteen rungs, and that every two yeomen were to make a pavise, the one to hold it while the other shot from behind it.[144]

Nor should we overlook the key role archers played in naval warfare. At sea archers were deployed from the 'castles' which formed the fortified sterns or prows of vessels in maritime warfare, as well as from fighting tops on the mastheads.[145] In

1340 they played a vital role in securing Edward III's great naval victory at Sluys. Here, archers were deployed in two squadrons of ships placed on the flanks of a central squadron of vessels containing men-at-arms, though surely others must have been placed with the men-at-arms themselves.[146] One English chronicler, Thomas of Burton, remarked that 'the French and the Normans were defeated by the English through fierce shooting',[147] though as in so many land engagements it was the combination of bowmen with men-at-arms that won the day, with the latter succeeding in boarding the line of French ships under the cover of the volleys of their archers. The naval victory of 'Les Espagnols sur Mer' in 1350 against a Castilian fleet was similarly won by the hand-to-hand combat of the English men-at-arms supported by their archers.[148] English naval forces attempting to guard the seas might contain substantial numbers of archers as well as men-at-arms. In 1341 it was envisaged that all the major vessels carrying the army for Edward III's proposed expedition should have 50 soldiers, double the normal complement, to create an effective fighting force at sea.[149] In 1378 a fleet under the Earl of Arundel and John of Gaunt contained 5,000 sailors and as many troops, the latter raised, as with land armies, by retinue. Thus Arundel's retinue comprised 400 men-at-arms and 400 archers, and that of Gaunt 500 men-at-arms and 500 archers.[150] In 1416 the English fleet carried 600 men-at-arms and 1,200 archers.[151] The presence of such bowmen, however, did not always ensure victory; in 1372 an English fleet carrying a force under the Earl of Pembroke to Gascony suffered a crushing defeat at La Rochelle at the hands of a larger squadron of Castilian galleys.[152] The skill of the men-at-arms

and the accuracy of the English archers initially kept the enemy at bay, but when battle was rejoined the next day, 23 June, the Castilians sprayed oil on to the rigging and decks of the English vessels and set them alight with fire arrows.[153] The large carracks used by France's naval allies also gave opposing crossbowmen an advantage. In 1416 an English fleet under Bedford won a hard-fought victory in the mouth of the Seine, thereby helping to secure Harfleur, against a powerful French, Spanish and Genoese fleet, including nine large Genoese vessels each bearing 100 crossbowmen. The English ships had repeatedly closed with the enemy vessels, only to be driven back each time by a hail of bolts and javelins cast from the higher stem and stern castles of the Italian ships. In a fight which lasted some seven hours before the Genoese were finally taken or scattered, English casualties amounted to some 700 men-at-arms killed or wounded and a higher number of sailors and other troops.[154] In such engagements, where the Genoese enjoyed considerable protection from their ships' superstructures, the volleys of the English archers were far less effective. A very similar pattern of engagement occurred the following year, in June 1417, when an English squadron under the Earl of Huntingdon joined battle in the Channel with an enemy fleet, which in addition to French, Spanish and Biscayan vessels contained nine large Genoese carracks carrying 700–800 Genoese troops. The English initially suffered heavy losses from their bolts, but won the day when they succeeded in grappling and boarding the enemy carracks.[155] It was precisely to counter such a threat from these great Genoese vessels that Henry V constructed his own large warships, which would restore the advantage to English archers and men-at-arms.[156]

Archers aboard ship might similarly cover the landings of troops. At Kinghorn, Fife, in 1332 it was the archers who had cleared the shore for the disembarkation of the disinherited, while at Cadzand in November 1337 the English bowmen under Sir Walter Mauny drove off the French crossbowmen and other troops who sought to bar their landing.[157] The ability to lay down a heavy barrage of arrows was equally valuable in effecting opposed river crossings. On 24 August 1346 archers supported the mounted men-at-arms of Edward III's army as they forced the crossing of the ford over the Somme at Blanchetaque in the face of fierce resistance from a large French force, including many crossbowmen.[158] Similarly, when Henry V finally succeeded in finding a crossing over the Somme at the fords near Voyennes and Béthencourt on 19 October 1415, he

The naval battle of Sluys, 1340, as portrayed in a fifteenth-century Flemish manuscript of Froissart's *Chronicles* (Paris, Bibliothèque Nationale, MS fr. 2643, f.72). (*Bibliothèque Nationale, Paris/Bridgeman Art Library*)

first sent a force of 200 archers on foot followed by 500–600 men-at-arms under Sir John Cornwall and Sir Gilbert Umfraville to establish a bridgehead and protect the rest of the army from attack by the enemy as they made their crossing.[159] Three years later, in June 1418, Henry's archers once again played a vital role in forcing a crossing of the Seine at the heavily defended town of Pont de L'Arche, which barred the approach to Rouen. After their initial attempts to take the town had failed, the English built a pontoon bridge to an island in the middle of the river some 400 yards downstream of the bridge, then launched a surprise raid in small boats to secure the northern bank of the Seine, covered all the while by volleys from the English archers drawn up on the island.[160] It is probable that archers were once again prominent during John, Lord Talbot's successful crossing of the Somme at Blanchetaque in 1437, in the face of opposition from Burgundian forces.[161]

MEN-AT-ARMS: THE ARMY'S BACKBONE

Crucial as the archers were, however, it would be a mistake to regard bowmen as the sole factor in English victories during the Hundred Years War. Any analysis of the engagements of the Hundred Years War must acknowledge the equally vital role of the English men-at-arms, who formed the armoured core of English armies. It was around their formations that units of archers were deployed, and it was on the resilience and steadfastness of the men-at-arms that the security of the archers and the chances of victory ultimately depended. Archers could wreak havoc upon opposing cavalry and their volleys might throw lines of advancing men-at-arms on foot into disorder. Yet no matter how effective, it would have been impossible for the archers to bring down or disable all oncoming French men-at-arms; whether we posit the archers placed in units on the wings of each division, on the extreme flanks of the formations of the English men-at-arms, or even as units mixed in with them, there must have been a proportion of enemy knights in the centre of advancing units who were protected from the bowmen's enfilading volleys. From the 1350s, moreover, developments in plate armour afforded increasing protection from arrows. At Cocherel in 1364, where Du Guesclin triumphed against an Anglo-Navarese army under the Captal de Buch, Froissart noted: 'And when the archers were forward, then they shot fiercely together, but the Frenchmen were so well armed and so strongly pavised that they took but little hurt, nor letted not for all that to fight, and so entered in among the Englishmen and Navarrois, and they in likewise among them, so that there was between them a cruel battle.'[162] He records in near identical language the same phenomenon occurring at Auray in the same year, though here the English archers, finding their shafts had little impact, threw down their bows and attacked the French with their side-arms.[163] Equally, in several smaller engagements archers were present only in comparatively small numbers and their presence seems not to have been decisive.

As a result, in the great majority of battles groups of French men-at-arms succeeded in closing with their English counterparts and engaging in what was often a fierce, prolonged and bloody mêlée. Though at Crécy repeated French cavalry charges failed, sufficient numbers of the French, probably now on foot, succeeded in converging on the Black Prince's division and pressing it hard enough for reinforcements to be sought from Edward III. 'In this battle', noted Geoffrey le Baker with

Archers aboard ship confront crossbowmen, from the Beauchamp Pageant, English, c. 1483–4, representing an incident in 1416 when Richard, Earl of Warwick, captured two French carracks in the Seine estuary (British Library, Cotton Julius E IV). (© British Library)

considerable exaggeration, 'a handful of men in the front line held their ground together with the prince, whom the French repeatedly attacked.'[164] At Nájera in 1367 Sir John Chandos found himself pinned down by a huge Spanish man-at-arms who tried to stab him through his visor, though Chandos eventually succeeded in killing his assailant.[165] Similarly at Agincourt there was fierce fighting between the leading ranks of the French vanguard and the English men-at-arms; the Duke of York was killed, and at one stage of the battle Henry V fought with his feet astride the prostrate body of his brother Humphrey, Duke of Gloucester, who had been badly wounded by a sword thrust, until he could be carried to safety. Henry himself is said to have received a blow which lopped off one of the fleurs-de-lis from the crown on his helmet.[166] Such examples could be multiplied, and they represent the kind of desperate engagements that must have been repeated all along the battle-line. Given this ability of the French to close to sword and lance strokes, battles in France stand in striking contrast to the terrible effects the volleys of English arrows had upon the much less well-equipped Scots at Dupplin and Halidon, though as we have seen Neville's Cross appears to have been far more of a slogging match; the English archers fell back at least twice, and victory hinged on the ability of the men-at-arms to hold the line and rally their more lightly armed troops.[167] In most engagements the English archers had protected themselves against direct attack by French men-at-arms by the use of man-made pits and ditches, as at Crécy, by natural obstacles such as marsh, hedges, bushes or undergrowth, as at Poitiers, or from 1415 onwards by the use of sharpened stakes, as at Agincourt. But in each case, if the formations of the English men-at arms had given way the archers' position would have become perilous.

If the English men-at-arms proved decisive in defensive and offensive combat on foot, they could be just as effective on horseback. The adoption of dismounting tactics from the Weardale campaign of 1327 onwards by no means signalled the demise of cavalry as an effective arm in English armies. When Sir Geoffrey Luttrell chose to have himself depicted as a splendidly caparisoned knight on his great destrier in the magnificent psalter he commissioned between 1325 and 1335, he was not invoking a vanishing relic of a bygone age, and the *Scalacronica* of Sir Thomas Gray reveals that fighting on horseback was still regarded as being preferable where possible.[168] During almost all the major battles of Edward III's reign the men-at-arms initially fought on foot; their horses were placed in the rear, but were near enough to hand for the knights to remount quickly either to launch a counter-attack or give pursuit to a defeated enemy. The crucial role of

mounted knights is nowhere more striking than at Poitiers in 1356. The *Anonimalle Chronicle* noted how after recrossing the ford of the River Miosson at the beginning of the engagement, the Earl of Warwick's men, all still mounted, 'struck and defeated' the French shield bearers, only then dismounting to take up defensive positions. Subsequently the Captal de Buch led a flanking attack with mounted men-at-arms and archers which caused much dismay among the French, while the turning point in the battle came when the Black Prince and his men remounted and led a fierce counter-attack downhill against King Jean's dismounted knights.[169] Cavalry, moreover, were essential to press home an effective pursuit. Thus at Halidon Hill, after the Scottish assaults had been successfully defeated, Edward's knights mounted and gave chase to the routed Scots for several miles. Though at Crécy the danger that the French might regroup and attack again caused Edward to keep his army in formation that evening, le Baker noted that Edward III had 'kept back the war-horses with his supply train for use in pursuit of the retreating enemy', and he makes the same observation about the Black Prince at Poitiers.[170] At Nájera in 1367 the prince kept back a cavalry reserve under King Jaume of Mallorca, which he launched against the disintegrating Castilian division of Enrique of Trastamara, and which fiercely pursued the scattered enemy.[171] Nor was it simply in the great set-piece engagements that mounted English knights played an important role, but in a host of small engagements and skirmishes, while patrols and reconnaissance in strength played a vital part in the *chevauchées* and expeditions of English and Anglo-Gascon armies.

Above all, whether on land or at sea, a constant factor in English success was the close cooperation between men-at arms and archers. An excellent example of their mutual support is provided by the Earl of Derby's attack on Bergerac in 1345. During his initial engagement with the French defenders in front of the gates of the town, Derby combined a barrage from his archers with a highly successful mounted assault by his knights. The English advanced in good order and, noted Froissart, 'the archers began to shoot thickly', forcing the French infantry and poorly armed country folk back on their own men-at-arms. 'The archers continued to shoot with great quickness, doing much mischief to them,' while the English knights advanced 'mounted on their excellent coursers, with lances in their rests, and, dashing into the midst of this infantry, drove them down at pleasure, and killed and wounded the French men-at-arms in abundance; for they could not in any way exert themselves, as these runaways had blocked up the road'. The English archers were then posted on the side of the road to clear the enemy from it, before covering a new assault by the men-at-arms, this time on foot, which succeeded in taking the town's suburbs.[172] By contrast, when at Caen in 1346 some of Warwick's archers attempted to attack a strongly fortified bridge 'without accord and without array', they 'had hard fighting' against the French men-at-arms; fearing they would be badly mauled without the support of English men-at-arms, Edward III ordered their withdrawal. Only by a combined attack of archers with men-at-arms was the bridge finally taken, while lightly armed Welshmen swam across the River Orne and attacked the French from behind.[173]

LEADERSHIP, DISCIPLINE AND MORALE

Further crucial factors in English military success were the quality of leadership and the skill and discipline of forces in the field. In marked contrast to the lamentable failings of Edward II, Edward III showed himself to be a highly able tactician, strategist and warleader. He has been called 'a genuinely outstanding military commander, one indeed who must be ranked among the most successful of European history',[174] while his son the Black Prince has been called 'an even greater soldier than his father'.[175] A born warrior, King Edward endeared himself to his aristocracy by his aggressive and successful prosecution of the French war. Even in times of peace he delighted in tournaments, and would often honour his knights by fighting in their retinues either incognito or by wearing their coats of arms. His creation of the Order of the Garter imbued his wars with the mystique of Arthurian romance and gave tangible form to an elite military brotherhood forged by Edward's Scottish and French campaigns.[176] But Edward's charisma touched not only his nobles but also the archers and other infantry in his forces. Contemporaries were struck by the king's ability to encourage his men while at the same time maintaining strict discipline. Geoffrey le Baker, for instance, records a revealing incident (which had clearly grown in the telling) which occurred at Calais in 1350, when a small pursuit force of men-at-arms and archers led by Edward was confronted by a far larger body of French men-at-arms. Edward, who up till then had remained incognito, threw away his scabbard and 'encouraged his men and spoke to them courteously, saying, "Do your best, archers; I am Edward of Windsor." Only then did the archers realise that the king was with them, and how necessary it would be to fight well; they bared their heads, arms and chests, and each one concentrated on not wasting a single arrow.'[177] Equally, le Baker was impressed by the military sagacity of the Black Prince during the 1356 campaign: 'Nor did he fail in the skills of a wise commander; but he appointed the distinguished knights John Chandos, James Audley and their companions, all skilled in warfare, to act as scouts in the enemy countryside lest they laid ambushes in woods for our men. He himself took charge of the camp, seeing that it was moved each day when the road had been inspected and provided with defences against night attacks. He also saw that the usual watch was kept, and went round them himself with his more valiant comrades, each part of the army being visited in case something out of order exposed it to danger.'[178]

As le Baker recognised, success depended not only on the military capacity of the king and his sons, but on the skill and experience of their captains. For though dictates of status and constraints of finance meant that major armies were invariably led by members of the royal family, the strategy of fighting on several fronts, combined with the system of contract armies, encouraged the emergence of talented and resourceful

Edward III granting Aquitaine to the Black Prince in 1362, from an illuminated initial on deed of title (British Library, MS Cotton Nero D VI, f.31). *(Private Collection/Bridgeman Art Library)*

commanders both from the higher aristocracy and from the lesser nobility.[179] In certain subsidiary theatres of war, such as Brittany, men like Sir Thomas Dagworth or Sir Walter Bentley enjoyed considerable autonomy.[180] Captains like Sir Hugh Calveley or Sir Robert Knollys, who possibly served at Crécy, Poitiers and Nájera, had gained experience not only in English armies but also as leaders of the Free Companies, enriching themselves through pay and plunder. Edward's reign witnessed the creation of an increasingly experienced cadre of able commanders, a community of professionals capable of planning and executing complex strategy and able to pool their respective tactical experiences. A number of veterans of Dupplin Moor, such as Thomas Ughtred (whose long career in arms stretched back to Bannockburn) and Richard Talbot, subsequently fought with Edward III at Halidon Hill, while many of Edward's captains at Crécy had also seen action at Halidon Hill, including the Earls of Arundel, Oxford, Warwick, Suffolk and possibly Northampton, together with Ralph Basset and Bartholomew Burghersh.[181] Significantly, the Earl of Warwick and Sir Reginald Cobham, a veteran of Sluys, Morlaix and perhaps also Halidon, were among those chosen by Edward to select the most suitable site for a battlefield at Crécy, while Northampton, who had led the English forces at Morlaix, was placed in command of the left wing.[182] In turn, many veterans of Crécy were with the Black Prince at Poitiers, including Oxford, Warwick and Stafford, together with Sir James Audley and Sir Reginald Cobham.[183] Edward III possessed an 'essential gift for picking his subordinates and for recognising, at an early age, the military abilities of his aristocratic contemporaries'.[184] Though it was an act rich in political symbolism, one of the primary aims behind Edward III's establishment of the Order of the Garter in 1348 had been to honour the leading men of the 1346–7 campaigns, and the creation of an elite military confraternity that included not just the royal family and the greatest nobles but knights and lesser captains of proved military worth must surely have provided an important forum for the exchange and discussion of strategic and tactical experiences.[185]

English command, however, was not wholly without rash leadership or internal quarrels. At Falkirk in 1298 Antony Bek had been unable to restrain the knights of his own division, while divided counsel and accusations of cowardice rashly thrown cost the English dear at Bannockburn.[186] In 1338 an English force was defeated by the Scots at Presfen, near Wark on Tweed, 'having, on account of imprudent, angry talk, broken their ranks and hotly engaged upon unsuitable ground'.[187] The presence of an able and undisputed leader such as Edward III, the Black Prince, Henry V, Bedford or one of their leading commanders made such problems rare. But

where overall command was more ambiguous, cohesion could quickly suffer and defeat follow. Thus at Cocherel in 1364 the English were defeated when John Jouel rashly led his men down from a strong defensive position in pursuit of the withdrawing forces of Bertrand du Guesclin, heedless of the Captal de Buch's orders and his warning that this could be a ruse.[188] A primary reason for the failure of Sir Robert Knollys's chevauchée in 1370 was a shared command, resulting from resentment of his lack of nobility – he was referred to as 'the old brigand' – and doubts concerning his ability and social standing to command the unqualified obedience of his colleagues and men.[189] Though English armies usually enjoyed much better discipline than their French opponents it might nevertheless sometimes be hard to get men nourished on ideas of chivalric prowess and personal pride to take secondary positions. At Auray in 1364 Chandos requested that Sir Hugh Calveley command the rearguard, which had the essential task of reinforcing the line wherever it was hardest pressed, but Calveley indignantly refused, wishing instead to win honour in the front rank; he finally only reluctantly consented after much pleading by Chandos.[190] Elmham recorded the story that at Agincourt Henry V intended that his brother Edward, Duke of York, should guard the baggage, and hence the army's rear, but he likewise refused and instead was given command of the vanguard.[191] Even with a prince of the blood valour might outweigh sense. At Baugé in 1421 Thomas, Duke of Clarence, committed his force to battle, despite unfavourable terrain, superior enemy numbers and the absence of his own infantry, with disastrous consequences, because he had not yet won honour in battle and thus felt compelled to fight.[192]

Clarence had failed to do what the author of Knyghthode and Bataile, a mid-fifteenth-century translation of Vegetius, advised all commanders – to heed the advice of veterans, 'olde and exercised sapience'.[193] Occasionally the chroniclers directly note the influence of such men. At Poitiers Robert Ufford, Earl of Suffolk, a veteran who was one of the commanders of the rearguard with Salisbury, 'passed through each rank, encouraging his men, restraining the young knights from advancing against orders and bidding the archers not to waste their arrows'.[194] At the same battle Sir John Chandos remained constantly at the prince's side not only to guard but to advise him, while Froissart notes that it had been Sir James Audley who had advised on the drawing up of the English positions, 'for he was a most wise and valiant knight'.[195] It was Chandos who was in de facto command of John de Montfort's army at Auray in 1364, while similarly at Nájera Chandos 'that day did like a noble knight and governed and counselled that day the duke of Lancaster in like manner as he did before the prince at the battle of Poitiers, wherein he was greatly renowed and praised'.[196] At Agincourt the archers were famously arrayed and exhorted by the hoary-haired Sir Thomas Erpingham, and a similar role may have been performed by Sir Thomas Ughtred at Crécy.[197] Henry V is said to have chosen the battlefield 'with the advice of experienced soldiers', and during the preceding night had sent knights to examine the battlefield by moonlight, to gain a good sense of the ground on which to fight.[198] In King Henry the English had another outstanding military commander, but also both Edward, Duke of York, and Thomas, Lord Camoys (see p. 326), who commanded respectively the right and left of Henry's divisions of men-at-arms at Agincourt, had considerable military experience in Wales and France, and in the case of Camoys, also against the Scots.[199] The same phenomenon of the transmission of battlefield experience can be seen in the later stages of the Hundred Years War, in the careers of able commanders such as John, Duke of Bedford (see p. 348), Henry V's brother and the victor of Verneuil in 1424 and of the great earls such as Exeter and Salisbury. The latter was described by Monstrelet as 'a veteran soldier with a great reputation in war . . . the most experienced and skilful as well as the most fortunate of all the princes and captains of England',[200] while Sir John Fastolf, who had made a fortune from ransoms won at Verneuil, went on to command the English force which won the battle of Rouvray in 1428. The most famous commander of the later stages of the war, John Talbot, Earl of Shrewsbury (see p. 357), had gained widespread military experience in Wales, Ireland and France in a career in arms that may have begun in 1403 fighting for Henry IV at the battle of Shrewsbury, and only ended in the earl's death at Castillon aged around 66.[201]

Such experienced and skilful leadership was doubtless reflected at a lower level of command by the leaders of constituent retinues,[202] and many men-at-arms had long battle honours. The example of Henry Tilleman, a man-at-arms who had been on the Black Prince's Spanish campaign and had seen continuous service up to the battle of Verneuil, where he carried Bedford's standard, can hardly have been unique.[203] The epitaph to Sir Sampson Meverell in the church of Tideswell, Derbyshire, records how he served first Nicholas, Lord Audley, then John Montagu, Earl of Salisbury, who made him 'captain of divers worshipful places in France; and after the death of the said earl, he came to the service of John, Duke of Bedford and so being in his service, he was at XI great battles in France within the space of two years'.[204] Were the sources available, such battle honours could no doubt be mirrored in the careers of many archers. In battle itself, as we have noted earlier, the personal retinues of leading nobles, whether princes of the blood, earls, lords or knights banneret, formed up under their standards and banners, would have formed tightly knit

and cohesive units with the main formations of the men-at-arms. Chandos Herald gives a vivid glimpse of the importance of such standards in his account of how, immediately before the battle of Nájera in 1367, the Black Prince promoted Sir John Chandos to the rank of knight banneret by giving him the banner with the words, 'God grant that you may do nobly with it'. The herald continues: 'So Chandos took his banner, and set it up among his comrades, saying, "Sirs, here is my banner, guard it as if it were your own, for it is yours as much as mine". His companions were delighted by this. Then they continued on their way, not wanting to wait any longer for the battle.'[205]

Example and exhortation were ruthlessly backed up by the enforcement of strict discipline. At Crécy Edward combined cheerful encouragement with the command that 'on pain of the noose, none should break ranks, nor seek gain, nor despoil either living or dead, without his leave; for if the affair went in their favour, each would have enough time to pillage, and if fortune turned against them, then nothing they could do would gain them anything'.[206] Keeping tight and well-ordered ranks was absolutely vital, particularly when, as was often the case, the English were outnumbered; if soldiers broke ranks and ceased fighting to pillage the dead or take prisoners for ransom, there was a grave danger that the enemy might quickly exploit any gaps to prise the English formations apart with catastrophic results. Only the army's commander could permit the cry 'Havoc', allowing soldiers to break ranks to plunder and take prisoners at will, and the ordinances of war of Richard II and Henry V, clearly here echoing earlier practice, punished the unauthorised use of this cry by beheading.[207] Even after nightfall following the battle of Crécy Edward kept his men to arms and in their ranks, for there were still substantial French units at large.[208] Similarly, in mid-September 1356, when he was readying his army for an imminent engagement with the French, the Black Prince 'gave orders that none, upon pain of death, should proceed without permission in front of the troop of the marshals'.[209] At the battle of Poitiers itself, after the defeat of first the initial French attack and then the Dauphin's battle, the English refrained from any pursuit, using the respites to draw breath and reform, with the vanguard and the centre battles merging.[210] It was only in the context of this orderly regrouping following the assault of the Dauphin's division that 'our men placed their wounded beneath the thickets and hedges, while others took lances and daggers from the fallen to replace their own broken weapons and the archers hastened to pull their arrows out of wretches who were still half-alive'.[211] The fact that many men-at-arms and archers were experienced troops must have made such cohesion easier, for seasoned men no doubt appreciated that the chances of victory, and indeed of very survival where they were heavily outnumbered, depended on maintaining close order and a cool nerve. Flight in the face of the enemy, which endangered the lives of all, could be summarily punished by death. Following the battle of Mauron in 1352, in which one unit of archers had broken and fled when ridden down by French cavalry, the English commander Sir Walter de Bentley had 30 archers beheaded for cowardice.[212] The night before Agincourt Henry V enjoined silence on the English camp on pain of the loss of horse and equipment for a gentleman, and the loss of an ear for a yeoman or any of lesser rank.[213]

Though the formation of armies by indentured retinues brought many military advantages, their temporary nature and the fact that the primary legal bond was between troops and their retinue commander required the issue of specific and more universal ordinances for each army raised.[214] Problems of control were exacerbated by the practice of recruiting murderers and felons into the army in return for pardons, and also by the fact that the desire for plunder and booty to supplement wages was a major motivation to serve for men of all ranks. In recognition of this, many of the regulations in the ordinances of 1385 and 1419 seek to strike a balance between maintaining effective military cohesion and allowing troops the profits of war, while seeking to avoid further quarrels over their division. In Maurice Keen's words, 'even when the dogs of war had been formally unleashed, licensed greed needed to be equitably restrained'.[215] Whatever its ultimate strategic goals, the burning and harrying process of the *chevauchée* served the invaluable function of allowing troops to plunder with such licence, and such operations might be controlled and directed to a considerable degree. The 1385 ordinances prohibit any foraging without permission of the commander of the 'battle', while Henry V's ordinances of 1419 not only reiterate the immunity afforded by the earlier ordinances to the Church and its members, but also afforded extensive protection to non-combatants; no child under fourteen was to be taken captive, women were to be safe from any robbery or disturbance, the agricultural tools and beasts of ploughmen and labourers were not to be taken, and there was to be no burning without the king's express command. Any areas entering into the king's

The brass of Sir Hugh Hastings (d. 1347), Elsing, Norfolk, one of the finest of its period, as depicted in an engraving after Craven Ord in 1782, made before several more parts were lost. Sir Hugh is portrayed in the latest armour, complete with a visored bascinet and solid gorget of plate, and is surrounded by eight of his comrades in arms as 'weepers'. These include Edward III and the Earls of Lancaster, Warwick and Pembroke, as well as Ralph Lord Stafford and Sir Hugh Despencer. In the canopy above angels carry Hugh's soul heavenward, towards St George who acts as guardian, while at the very top the Virgin is blessed by Christ. (Author Collection)

obedience were to be spared robbery or pillage on pain of death.[216] Yet there were limits to the effective enforcement of discipline, particularly over scattered foraging parties. It seems that when Edward III disembarked in the Cotentin in 1346, his initial plan was to win over the Normans to his allegiance, for there were already a substantial number of nobles disaffected with Philip of Valois, and to this end he forbade unauthorised looting or burning on pain of death or mutilation. He found it impossible, however, to control his men, some of whom plundered around the landing area and sacked Barfleur and Cherbourg. As the army advanced into Normandy, towns which had capitulated on terms, such as Valognes and Carentan, were fired despite the king's protection.[217] In his own progress through eastern Normandy in 1415 Henry V had greater, though not complete, success in forbidding looting and pillaging in a duchy he claimed as his own, and a soldier caught stealing a pyx near Nesle was hanged.[218] Even French chroniclers admitted his troops were well disciplined, with the Religieux of St Denis contrasting the behaviour of the English with the brigandry and exactions of French troops.[219] In the 1346 campaign the Welsh seem to have been particular offenders in flouting the king's decrees, and at least one chronicler accuses them of beheading their prisoners, an allegation which was quite in keeping with what we know of their customary conduct in war.[220] In the immediate aftermath of Crécy it was the Welsh and Cornish knifemen who, much to Edward's anger, began to kill and despoil the French wounded.[221] Such pillaging of the dead

was, however, a normal aspect of war. When, on the morning after Agincourt, Henry V rode past the battlefield, the bodies of the thousands of slain had already been stripped almost naked by pillagers from the English army, who had been engaged in a busy night's work.[222]

Given such conduct, it is hardly surprising that when a town which had resisted by force fell to the army, there were often appalling excesses by the archers and other infantry. According to the laws of war, an attacker was obliged to offer peace and terms to a town or fortified place, but, if the inhabitants refused to yield and the town was subsequently taken by assault, the lives and property of all inside were forfeit, as Shakespeare famously has Henry V remind the citizens of Harfleur in 1415. Once a city fell, it was well nigh impossible for commanders to keep control of their men. In 1346 at St Lô and Caen, for example, there were violent scenes of pillage and rape.[223] Jean le Bel gives a grim account of how at Caen Edward's archers ran riot, raping women and slaying indiscriminately, although some of the men-at-arms attempted to stop such conduct. Caen was to suffer again in 1417, when many of the townsmen were slain during its storming and in the subsequent sack, though Henry V had ordered that no women or ecclesiastics were to be harmed.[224] Such instances could be greatly multiplied and were, of course, by no means particular to English armies. But they serve as a salutary corrective to a too rosy and over-romanticised view of the 'yeoman bowmen' of English armies, and help to ground their activities in the brutality which characterised so much of medieval warfare.

Soldier looting (British Library, MS Royal 20 C VII, f.41v. Commanders often found it impossible to prevent such indiscipline, particularly when a town was captured after hard fighting. (© British Library/Bridgeman Art Library)

One final factor in the success of English armies must be noted, that of morale and psychology. The combination of efficient army organisation, excellent leadership and highly effective tactics led not only to victories in the field but to a concomitant development of a self-confidence and élan that struck many contemporaries. 'The English,' noted Froissart, 'and all the various men-at-arms on their side, never let it worry them if they were few in numbers.'[225] Success breeds success, and knowledge of victories in the recent past must have helped steady the nerve of men in combat. English sources written with hindsight of victory might play up this sang-froid in the face of great odds; the mid-fifteenth-century *Brut* noted that at Agincourt, 'our archers shot no arrows off target . . . for they were shooting that day for a wager'.[226] More certainly, well-timed war cries were used to boost morale and discomfit the enemy. Thus at Agincourt, after Sir Thomas Erpingham had thrown up his baton as a signal, 'all the English suddenly made a great cry which was a cause of great amazement to the French',[227] while at Verneuil, after the English lines were broken by a powerful French cavalry attack, Bedford's men quickly rallied and after reforming gave a great shout to demonstrate their continuing resolve.[228] In many situations, as at St Pol de Léon, Poitiers and Agincourt where the English were heavily outnumbered, there was a realisation that only discipline and audacity would save them, while a sense of desperation may well have fuelled a particular ruthlessness in combat. Thus at Agincourt, noted Tito Livio, 'the English were increasingly eager to kill, for it seemed that there was no hope of safety except in victory', and they only began to take prisoners when it became clear that the French vanguard was disintegrating.[229] This was not merely the retrospective rhetoric of the victors, for the Religieux of St Denis notes the same phenomenon: 'They kept themselves with advantage in the middle of this bloody mêlée, not without losing many of their own men but fighting with so much passion, for they knew that for them it was a matter of life or death.'[230]

In the case of the archers their resolve was further strengthened by the fear of mutilation should they be captured. According to the French herald Jean Le Fèvre, who was with the English army at Agincourt, Henry V told his men on the day of battle 'that the French had boasted that if any English archers were captured they would cut off the three fingers of their right hand so neither man nor horse would ever again be killed by their arrow fire'.[231] Thomas Walsingham likewise noted that before the battle 'the French published abroad that they wished no-one to be spared except certain named lords and the king himself. They announced that the rest would be killed or have their limbs horribly mutilated. Because of this our men were much excited to rage and took heart, encouraging one another against the event.'[232] Accordingly, the English soldiers 'seeing those who on the previous day had sworn to bring about their deaths or mutilations . . . were made hot with indignation, and forgot all their exhaustion, misfortune and weakness'.[233] The English author John Strecche similarly believed that when before the battle of Valmont (or Ouainville) in March 1416 the French commander the Count of Armagnac gave the Earl of Dorset the chance to surrender, he insisted that the men-at-arms must surrender for ransom but the archers would lose their right hands. Dorset indignantly refused, and battle was joined despite heavy odds against the English.[234]

The ensuing engagement furnishes one of the most remarkable instances of the discipline, cohesion and nerve of English forces, and serves as a fitting conclusion to this chapter. Dorset had been leading a raiding force of 1,000 men from Harfleur when he was surprised by a French force under Armagnac at least three times its size.[235] The earl dismounted his men into single line, with the horses and baggage to the rear, and succeeded in holding off the French attacks for a considerable time. His archers inflicted heavy losses on the horses of the French cavalry, but eventually some of the enemy horsemen succeeded in breaking through the English line and attacked his baggage train. Dorset, however, skilfully managed to reform his men in a large garden where they were better protected by a ditch and hedge. Armagnac now attempted to induce the English to surrender, but his demands were rejected and with night falling he withdrew to the town of Valmont with the intention of returning to finish off the enemy in the morning. But Dorset used the cover of darkness to slip his little force away, and succeeded in evading the French. Marching his men along the coast back towards Harfleur, using the shore to cover their left flank, Dorset had almost regained safety when at the cliffs of St Andress they were again intercepted by a French detachment under Marshal de Loigny. Yet as the French charged in disorganised fashion down the cliffs, the English formed up and attacked the enemy so vigorously that the French were utterly routed. When Armagnac's main force arrived on the scene the English proceeded in turn to storm up the cliffs and routed the French, whose discomfiture was completed by a sally from the garrison in Harfleur.[236] In Burne's words, the engagement at Valmont stands almost without rival in the Anglo-French wars for 'pluck, endurance, and sheer doggedness, for coolness, discipline and hitting power when cornered – in short, for all those military virtues that made the reputation of the English army in the Hundred Years War'.[237]

Matthew Strickland

Apogee: English Victories and French Tactical Responses, 1337–64

'I will heap mischiefs upon them; I will spend mine arrows upon them . . . I will make
my arrows drunk with blood, and my sword shall devour flesh . . .'
Deuteronomy, 32: 23, 42

he onset of Edward III's long struggle with the Valois kings of France which began in 1337 would see the English king and his commanders deploy the devastating tactics developed at Dupplin Moor and Halidon Hill against his French opponents. It has been forcefully argued that Edward's great confidence in the efficacy of English battle tactics was such that his strategy throughout his French wars was vigorously to pursue a battle-seeking strategy in an attempt to draw his opponent into a decisive engagement in which his dismounted men-at-arms and archers would inflict a knock-out blow.[1] At Crécy in 1346 Edward was to achieve a resounding victory over Philip VI, while ten years later his son Edward the Black Prince was to inflict another terrible defeat on the French at Poitiers and even capture their king, Jean II. Yet despite these and other losses in the field, compounded by chronic internal dissension and a crippled economy, Valois France remained remarkably resilient. Although he fielded one of the largest armies ever taken by an English king to France, Edward's attempt to take Rheims in 1359 was frustrated, and with it he lost any serious prospect of gaining the throne of France. At the treaty of Brétigny in 1360 he renounced his claims in return for

the cession of extensive territories south of the Loire, which restored much of the former Angevin possessions lost to France in the early thirteenth century.

The longbow is often hailed as a 'decisive weapon', above all in relation to the great engagements of the French wars such as Crécy, Poitiers and Agincourt. In this and in subsequent chapters, we shall examine the extent to which the longbow *was* the decisive factor in many of the English victories of the Hundred Years War. But it is also important to keep its impact and that of English battle tactics in a broader perspective; the very duration of Edward III's wars is itself testimony to the fact that neither brought about instant or complete victory. Though they undoubtedly played an important part in wearing down the French through high casualties and a massive financial outlay in ransoms, few if any of Edward's battlefield victories could be said to be truly decisive in the way that, for example, Hastings or Bouvines had been. He and his commanders may have sought to give battle wherever possible, but in reality the war continued to be fought predominantly through sieges and devastating raids. Victories in the field covered Edward III, the Black Prince and their nobles with glory, greatly boosting their martial prestige as well as their revenues in an age in which martial prowess and 'worship' or respect gained through feats of arms were essential elements in political success. Yet they were none the less only part of an extended war effort that finally succeeded in forcing the French into major territorial concessions not by irresistible tactical or technological superiority but by attrition.

In discussing the tactical and technological developments of the Hundred Years War, Clifford Rogers has argued for the concept of a 'punctuated equilibrium', whereby each military advance, whether in tactics, gunpowder weaponry or fortifications, created an initial advantage for the innovator. This in turn, however, stimulated the enemy by emulation or fresh invention to match these developments, thus restoring the status quo or military equilibrium.[2] This concept is of particular value in suggesting an approach to the impact of English tactics and the use of the longbow during the Hundred Years War. Our purpose in the following chapters is not only to examine the nature of these tactics and to assess what the sources reveal about the role of archery, but also to explore the ways in which French commanders sought to respond to the threat which they posed.[3] How did the French attempt to defeat defensive formations of dismounted men-at-arms and archers, and with what success? Did they ever come close to achieving a restoration of the military equilibrium at any stage or stages during the wars? It is only by setting the longbow within such a context that the extent, and the limits, of its impact can be adequately gauged.

THE SNARE AND THE FOX: LA FLAMENGERIE, 23 OCTOBER 1339

It would be a mistake to regard the French as suddenly surprised by the formidable new tactics of the English once Edward's campaigns in France had begun, and being rudely awakened to the capabilities of English arms first at Morlaix in 1342 then at Crécy in 1346. It is hard if not impossible to believe that the French did not receive reports about the manner in which their Scottish allies had been discomfited at Dupplin Moor and Halidon Hill at the hands of the English, and Philip VI was anxious not to make similar costly mistakes. Indeed, Philip VI showed exemplary caution when in October 1339 he first confronted Edward in the field at La Flamengerie. From the outset of the 1339 campaign, his first on French soil, Edward III had intended to draw his Valois opponent into a major engagement. To this end he had besieged the important city of Cambrai, hoping thereby to force the French to give battle in order to raise the siege – just as he had successfully done to the Scots at Berwick in 1333. When they declined so to do, Edward proceeded systematically to lay waste the Cambrèsis, causing terrible devastation in order to sting the French into action.[4] As Edward calculated, the pressure on the French king to avenge these injuries became enormous: Philip VI eventually felt compelled to send a challenge to Edward, bidding him select a suitable site for battle 'unobstructed by wood, marsh or water'.[5] On the contrary, however, Edward adopted a very strong defensive position, drawing up his formations on high ground between the villages of La Capelle and La Flamengerie, with his front protected by a deep ditch. In addition to a large number of men-at-arms and troops from his continental allies, Edward's English forces included some 1,600 men-at-arms, 1,500 horse-archers, 1,580 foot-archers and a number of Welsh spearmen.[6] He placed the English in the van, the German Hainaulters and the margrave of Juliers in the centre battle, and the Brabanters in the rearward, with archers posted on each flank and with Welsh spearmen protecting the deep ditch that ran across his front line. Tellingly, Edward's German allies had never seen such a formation, 'but seeing that it was a strong position, cunningly laid out, and that the king was content, they were satisfied'.[7]

The careful selection of a strong defensive position as seen at La Flamengerie was to be one of the keys to English tactical success in the ensuing French wars, but on this occasion the French, unlike the Scots at Halidon Hill, did not take the bait. Forewarned by good reconnaissance and the capture of some German knights who revealed Edward's dispositions, Philip's counsel of war decided to withdraw and in turn the French dug in their army, fortifying their positions with tree-trunks.[8] This move proved unpopular with many of the French, for such caution smacked of cowardice, and the king and his advisers were taunted for their 'reynardie' or fox-like cunning. Yet Philip's decision was a sound one, for, as Jonathan Sumption notes, 'had it not been made La Capelle might have been as famous a name as Crécy'.[9] Such caution had been visible, indeed, in Philip's first major campaign following his coronation in 1328, when at Cassel he had refused to take the offensive against the rebel Flemish army drawn up in a strong hill-top position.[10] Much to Edward's frustration, Philip displayed a similar unwillingness to commit his forces to a major engagement throughout Edward's siege of Tournai, and, save for his naval victory at Sluys, the Treaty of Espechin in 1340 saw him still cheated of his sought-after battle.[11]

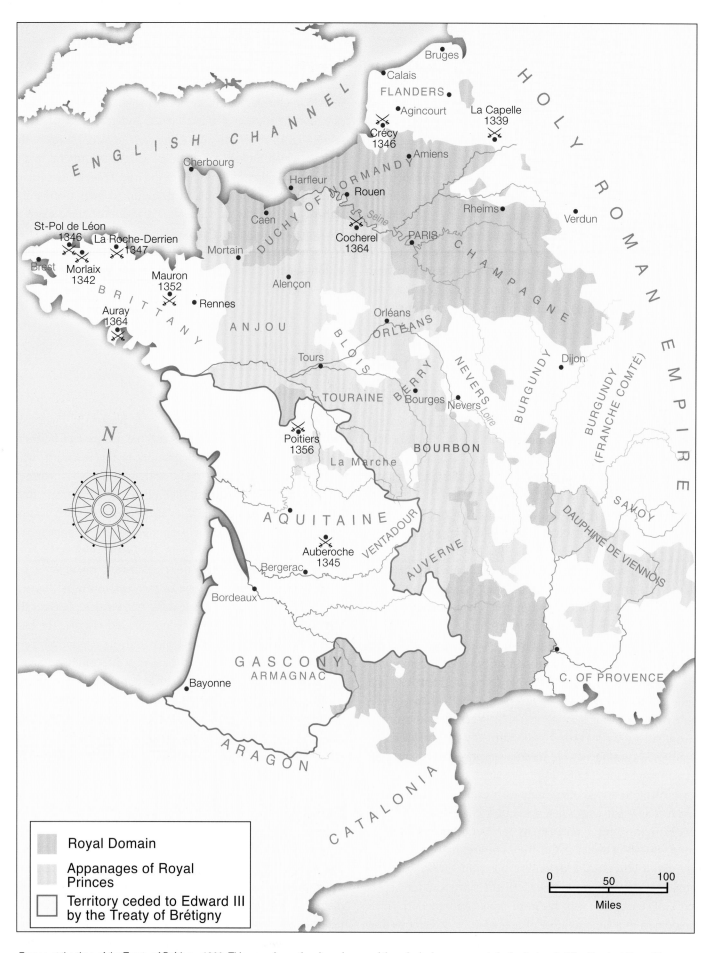

Bruges

Calais

FLANDERS

Agincourt

La Capelle
1339

Crécy
1346

Amiens

ENGLISH CHANNEL

Cherbourg

Harfleur

Rouen

Rheims

Verdun

Caen

DUCHY OF NORMANDY

Seine

Cocherel
1364

PARIS

St-Pol de Léon
1346

La Roche-Derrien
1347

Mortain

CHAMPAGNE

HOLY ROMAN EMPIRE

Brest

Morlaix
1342

Mauron
1352

Alençon

ANJOU

Orléans

ORLÉANS

BRITTANY

Rennes

Auray
1364

Tours

BLOIS

BERRY

Dijon

TOURAINE

Bourges

Nevers

BURGUNDY

Nevers

Loire

BURGUNDY
(FRANCHE COMTÉ)

N

BOURBON

Poitiers
1356

La Marche

SAVOY

AQUITAINE

VENTADOUR

AUVERNE

DAUPHINE DE VIENNOIS

Auberoche
1345

Bergerac

Bordeaux

GASCONY

ARMAGNAC

C. OF PROVENCE

Bayonne

ARAGON

CATALONIA

Royal Domain

Appanages of Royal
Princes

Territory ceded to Edward III
by the Treaty of Brétigny

0   50   100

Miles

France at the time of the Treaty of Brétigny, 1360. This map shows the sites of some of the principal engagements in the first part of the Hundred Years War.

MORLAIX, 30 SEPTEMBER 1342

It may thus have been no coincidence that the first major land engagement of the war was fought not between the Kings of England and France but by their respective lieutenants in Brittany, following Edward III's intervention in the succession to the duchy in the wake of the death of Duke Jean III in 1341. On 30 September 1342 an expeditionary force under William Bohun, Earl of Northampton, which had been dispatched by Edward III to support the pro-English candidate Jean de Montfort, was confronted at Morlaix by the army of his French rival, Charles of Blois, who was Philip VI's nephew.[12] A contemporary newsletter preserved by the chronicler Henry Knighton records that the English, faced with the approach of a considerably larger French force, used the cover of darkness to prepare a strong position 'about a league from the enemy, near a wood, and dug pits and ditches round about, and covered them with hay and brushwood'.[13] Though there are similarities here with Bruce's defences at Bannockburn, Northampton and his fellow commander Robert of Artois had seen action in Edward's 1340 campaigns and were clearly drawing on the dismounted, defensive formations that were by now becoming standard English military practice even in the smallest engagements. For example, in April 1340 a force of a few hundred men-at-arms and about 2,000 infantry, including some archers, led by the Earls of Salisbury and Suffolk 'by want of prudence in a foolish reconnaissance', had approached too close to Lille, and had been cut off by a powerful French sortie. The English dismounted and fought bravely, but were finally overwhelmed and captured.[14]

Details of the course of the battle of Morlaix are unfortunately very scanty and Northampton's dispositions are unknown. His force numbered some 2,400, of whom at least half were bowmen, though some of these men had been killed or wounded in the unsuccessful assault on the town of Morlaix prior to the battle. Charles's army was larger, though not overwhelmingly so, containing at least 3,000 cavalry, 1,500 Genoese, and a quantity of Breton light infantry.[15] In the light of Edward's known dispositions at La Flamengerie and at the earlier victories in Scotland, it is quite probable that the earl placed archers on his wings. Yet it is important to note that no chronicler actually mentions their role in the fighting, despite the extrapolations made by Burne and subsequent commentators as to their part in the battle.[16] Their presence is perhaps suggested by the fact that the initial French attacks by a force of cavalry under the leading French knight Geoffrey de Charny, which formed the first of three French divisions, were quickly routed.[17] Charny's cavalry, however, are not recorded as having met the fate of the second wave who fell into concealed pits and

ditches, and it is thus possible that the initial charge represented an attempt to sweep round one or both of the English flanks. This can only remain conjecture, but it was with just such a flanking attack that the French had won the battle of Cassel in 1328 against the Flemish,[18] while at St Omer in 1340 the French had gained initial success against the forces of Robert of Artois by a flank attack, although they lost the battle itself.[19] Certainly such a tactic would become a key feature of their subsequent attempts to neutralise the English formations of dismounted men-at-arms and archers. Significantly, Knighton records that Charles was able to regroup his forces and take counsel after the defeat of the first French wave.[20] Accordingly, the horsemen of the second French division 'spurred their horses on recklessly to ride them [the English] down', hoping to take advantage of the paucity of English numbers. But they quickly fell foul of the hidden pits and ditches, and 'they fell into them one upon the other in heaps'. Yet despite the effectiveness of the concealed obstacles, the French – many of whom must now perforce have been fighting on foot – succeeded in closing with the English and the battle became hard-fought on both sides. The English men-at-arms held firm, however, and the French were finally repulsed with heavy losses. Many, including Charny, were captured and some 50 knights

A life-size model of a Welsh archer, *c.* 1400, from the National Museum of Wales. He wears the distinctive green and white livery of troops raised from the principality of Wales, and is equipped with a sword and small buckler, a thickly padded gambeson and a simple, open-faced helmet. His dagger is modelled on an original found near Dolwyddelan, and the arrowheads on specimens found at Criccieth Castle. (© *National Museums & Galleries of Wales*)

and a large number of others were killed.[21] None the less, Northampton was still heavily outnumbered by the remaining French forces and felt it prudent to withdraw into the wood at his rear, using it as a natural defence against further attack.[22]

It was clear that Morlaix had been a close-run thing. Charles's men-at-arms had fought hard and well against the English, and though they were repulsed Northampton had been forced to abandon the field. Writing in the 1350s with hindsight of many subsequent engagements, the English chronicler Geoffrey le Baker remarked that neither at Halidon Hill nor Crécy, nor indeed in the whole French wars before the capture of King Jean at Poitiers, did the French fight so bitterly or at such length in hand-to-hand combat in the open field.[23] His remarks in part stem from a desire to praise the Earl of Northampton, with whose family le Baker had close connec-

tions.[24] But they are nevertheless significant in suggesting that unlike at Dupplin or Halidon, the shooting of the English archers did not primarily decide the day. Whether as in later engagements the archers joined in this mêlée with their side-arms is unknown, but once the French had succeeded in closing and engaging in bitter hand-to-hand combat it seems it was ultimately the stamina, discipline and cohesion of the English men-at-arms which saved Northampton's army. In this, Morlaix highlighted what was to become a consistent feature of almost all the major engagements of the war. Equally significantly, Charles of Blois, who emerges from the engagements of the 1340s as one of the most intelligent and resourceful of the major French commanders,[25] responded to his experiences at Morlaix by devising what he hoped would prove a tactical solution to the problem of English defensive tactics.

THE TRIUMPHS OF SIR THOMAS DAGWORTH: ST-POL DE LEON, 9 JUNE 1346, AND LA ROCHE-DERRIEN, 12 JUNE 1347

It is often assumed that the French began to adopt dismounted tactics to counter the English only after the catastrophe at Crécy in August 1346.[26] But in a much less familiar but tactically significant engagement fought several months earlier on 9 June 1346 at St-Pol de Léon (Finistère) in Brittany against the forces of Sir Thomas Dagworth, the French under Charles of Blois dismounted a sizeable element of their men-at-arms to attack the English defensive positions. An unusually detailed account of the battle is contained in the *Historia Aurea* of John, vicar of Tynemouth, based directly on a dispatch by Dagworth himself describing his victory.[27] In response to a major offensive by Charles, Dagworth, who was acting as deputy for the Earl of Northampton, had ridden out from La Roche-Derrien to reconnoitre, taking with him a small force of some 80 men-at-arms and 120 mounted archers.[28] Suddenly coming across the entire French army, which massively outnumbered him, Dagworth was unable to withdraw and accordingly formed his force up on foot, sending the horses and wagons to the rear.[29] Seeing their small numbers, one of the French captains, Guillaume de la Heuse, nicknamed 'Le Gallois', vowed to bring Dagworth to Charles as a prisoner, and accordingly selected a picked force of 500 French and German men-at-arms and a large body of crossbowmen and infantry. This force now divided into two in an attempt to catch the English in a pincer movement. The main body, under the Lords of Beaumanoir and Montauban with Pagan de Fontenay, the Captain of Rennes, dismounted to fight on foot, sending their horses to the rear.[30] A smaller force of 40 barded horse, supported by a large force of crossbowmen and foot, attacked

the English position from the rear.[31]

The French dispositions clearly reflect the impact of Charles of Blois's earlier discomfiture at Morlaix; having realised the vulnerability of cavalry in a direct frontal assault, Charles had his men dismount, in what appears to be one of the very earliest instances of the French adopting this practice. It is important to remember, however, that French men-at-arms, as much as English, would have trained with weapons on foot as well as on horseback, and that the ubiquitous siege warfare would have given them ample opportunity to hone these skills; in siege after siege from the start of the Hundred Years War we read of English and French men-at-arms engaged in combat on foot 'at the barriers', those outworks of timber, earth or stone that were erected before the gates of town or castle,[32] and specialised weapons for foot combat were developing, above all the poleaxe. Nevertheless, to advance on foot in good order, particularly when facing the volleys of longbowmen, was another matter altogether.[33] Charles of Blois now combined this dismounted element with a smaller cavalry force, which could, it was hoped, gain some protection from the enemy archers by sweeping round to attack in the rear, and by ensuring the mounts were armoured. At this date such horse armour was probably of mail, though the wealthiest may also have had defences of 'jaseran', made of metal lames either attached to mail or possibly stitched within a fabric lining.[34] This use of a selected force of horse to attack the archers was to be a recurrent theme of French tactical thinking, seen again, for example, at Poitiers in 1356, Agincourt in 1415 and at Verneuil in 1424. But it is noteworthy that the plan of using such an elite force of cavalry in conjunction with an attack by dismounted men-at-arms was conceived a decade earlier than Poitiers by Charles of Blois.

The two French forces attacked Dagworth's men simultaneously, and a fierce battle raged from the first to the ninth hour of the day. But eventually the French were beaten off with heavy losses. Guy de Rochefort and many other knights and nobles were slain, and Guillaume de la Heuse, Rolland de Dinan and Pagan de Fontenay were captured.[35] Though details are lacking, Dagworth had probably used his wagons as a laager to defend part of his positions, which would explain the ability of the English to repulse the attack in their rear. In several subsequent engagements the English also formed their horses, tethered together by muzzle and tail, into a living defence, and that they did so at St-Pol de Léon is suggested by the very high casualties Dagworth's force suffered among their mounts on this campaign, with 66 horses of the men-at-arms being lost along with 120 hackneys of the archers.[36] As the bloodied French forces returned to Charles's position, the weary English took the opportunity to snatch some rest. But around vespers Charles himself advanced against them with his forces drawn up in three divisions, all on foot. Charles seems to have deployed these battles against the English front, flanks and rear, for Dagworth's men found themselves attacked from all sides. Despite the onslaught, the English held fast, and Charles was finally compelled to withdraw, whereupon Dagworth's force fell back towards Quimperlé. It had been a remarkable feat of arms, and one which strikingly demonstrated the enormous advantage of the defensive over the offensive. As Dagworth commented in his letter to the king, not one man-at-arms had been killed, but almost every man in his tiny force had been wounded.[37] Dagworth was subsequently rewarded by being created the king's lieutenant in Brittany on 10 January 1347, and was soon to vindicate Edward's trust by his surprise attack and capture of Charles of Blois at La Roche-Derrien on 12 June 1347.

In 1347, when Charles laid siege to the English-held town and castle of La Roche-Derrien, he again showed initiative in attempting to combat the threat of the English bowmen by having the countryside around his siege lines stripped of anything which might act as cover for the enemy archers. As Dagworth reported in his dispatch to Edward III, 'the lord Charles had made great entrenchments round about him, and outside his stronghold had caused to be levelled and razed, for a half league breadth of the country round about him, all manner of ditches and hedges, whereby my archers might not find their advantage over him and his people, but they needs must in the end fight in the open fields'.[38] Nor had Charles neglected his own missile arm, for Dagworth estimated his force as containing '1,200 men-at-arms, knights and squires, and 600 other men-at-arms, and 600 archers of the countryside, and 2,000 crossbowmen, and of commons I know not how many'.[39] Forewarned by his scouts of the approach of Dagworth's relief army of 300 men-at-arms and 400 archers,[40] Charles kept his men standing at arms all night. But when the attack came, shortly before dawn on 12 June, the French, who were encamped in four main positions, seem to have been taken largely unawares by the English strategy. In a remarkable display of the effectiveness of men-at-arms and archers in an offensive role, Dagworth succeeded in launching an attack with all his troops against each French force in turn, defeating them in detail before one could reinforce another, while the English garrison made a powerful sally to catch the French in the rear. Though as at Morlaix the nature of Dagworth's deployment and the positioning of his archers is unknown, the result was a crushing French defeat, in which Charles himself and a great number of nobles were taken prisoner, while Dagworth estimated that between 600 and 700 French men-at-arms had been killed.[41] Together with the Earl of Derby's success at Auberoche, this remarkable victory clearly reveals that from a comparatively early stage in the war the English were not wedded to defensive tactics and were equally formidable in the assault.

Between Dagworth's victories at St-Pol de Léon and La Roche-Derrien, however, an English success had occurred which was to overshadow all the triumphs of Edward III's commanders in Brittany. For on 26 August at Crécy-en-Ponthieu King Edward himself at last achieved the all-out battle he had so long sought.

'THE FEARFUL FACE OF WAR': CRECY, 26 AUGUST 1346

To understand fully the catastrophic French defeat at Crécy it is necessary to set the engagement within a broader strategic context. In July 1346 Edward landed in Normandy at St Vaast-la-Hogue with a powerful army, estimated as roughly 2,700 men-at-arms, 3,250 mounted archers and hobelars, 7,000 archers on foot, 2,300 Welsh spearmen and other troops.[42] Marching through the duchy, he took and sacked the great city of Caen, then, laying waste the countryside as he went, Edward moved east to the Seine. Despite being shadowed on the right bank by Philip's army, he eventually managed to cross by rebuilding the bridge at Poissy. As Edward hoped, the destruction of lands and royal demesne so close to Paris led

Philip to issue the English a challenge to battle. For although historians have been divided on the purpose of Edward's *chevauchée*, Burne's view that Edward was deliberately seeking to provoke Philip VI into a major battle has recently been strongly re-emphasised by Rogers.[43] Nevertheless, Edward declined to face a French army nearly twice the size of his own on open ground that was of his adversary's choosing. Instead, with Philip's army in hot pursuit, he marched north into Picardy en route for Calais. In Ponthieu, which was Edward's own county by marriage, he hoped to join forces with the forces of his Flemish allies. He had already advised Philip by formal challenge that 'at whatever hour you approach you will find us ready to meet you in the field, with God's help, which thing we desire above all else', but Edward intended that any such encounter should only happen once his army had crossed the Somme. For as early as 29 July, when Edward was in Caen, he had ordered reinforcements of men-at-arms and archers, together with fresh supplies of bows, arrows and bow strings to be sent to Le

Crotoy, at the mouth of the Somme.[44] As on the Seine, Philip's forces attempted to bar Edward's crossing of the Somme while the French king's main army drew ever closer. Once again, however, Edward managed to force a crossing at the ford of Blanchetacque just below Abbeville on 24 August, and – not by coincidence – only a few miles upstream from Le Crotoy, where he expected to find fresh supplies – though it seems in fact that they did not arrive. By now the French were so close that Philip's advance guard reached the ford just as the last of Edward's rearguard had crossed. The French declined Edward's offer of an unopposed crossing in order to give battle, preferring to move up to Abbeville and cross the Somme in safety. Meanwhile, Edward's army moved slowly the 9 or 10 miles north to Crécy, where on 26 August the king deployed his army. Edward was not, as often believed, run to ground by Philip and finally forced to turn at bay to fight a major engagement he had sought to avoid. Rather, his whole strategy had sought to provoke Philip into a decisive engagement at a time and place of Edward's choosing. As Kenneth Fowler has remarked, 'in view of the speed with which he took up position after crossing the Somme, the battlefield must have been reconnoitred in advance'.[45] Philip now fell directly into the King of England's trap.

The battle of Crécy has been much discussed.[46] In particular, the disposition of the English army, the positioning of the

The battlefield of Crécy on a modern map. Probable positions: A – Edward III with the reserve battle; B – Black Prince with vanguard battle; C – Rearguard battle; D – English baggage park and horses; E – The steep drop; F and G – The two possible directions of French attack; H – Line of French approach; I – Central terracing.

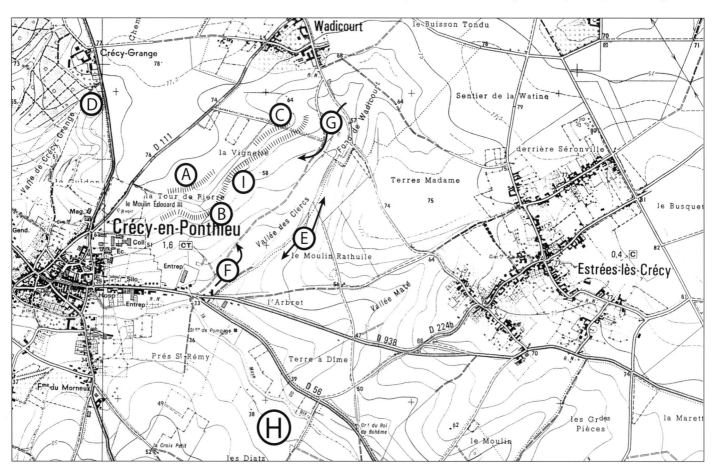

archers and what Froissart meant by the term 'herce' in relation to their formations had been hotly debated ever since Jim Bradbury challenged the traditional consensus.[47] The issue of whether the archers were placed only on the outer wings of the army, as Bradbury suggests, or formed wings on *each* English division will be discussed more fully by Robert Hardy in Chapter 16, but here the course of the battle itself needs to be examined in some detail. Edward was careful not to repeat the events of La Flamengerie, where the English position had been so strongly entrenched that Philip had refused to give battle. But his site was well chosen. He drew up his forces between the villages of Crécy and Wadicourt on the high ground that rises up from what is now known as the Vallée des Clercs, while to his rear lay the woods of the Bois de Crécy Grange. His right was thus protected by the village of Crécy itself and the valley of the River Maye, while it is possible that a number of agricultural terraces gave added protection to the centre of his position. His young son the Black Prince was given command of the vanguard on the right wing, while the Earls of Northampton and Arundel led the rearguard on the left flank. Edward III himself, who oversaw the battle from a windmill near the top of the ridge, commanded the centre division, which kept back at some distance. A general sense of the division of the English forces is given by Jean Le Bel's estimate that the right wing under Edward, Prince of Wales, contained 1,200 men-at-arms, 4,000 archers and 3,000 Welsh, the left under Arundel, Suffolk and the Bishop of Durham, some 1,200 men-at-arms and 3,000 archers, and King Edward's reserve division 1,600 men-at-arms and 4,000 archers.[48] Though his figures are probably far from exact, Le Bel's statement assumes that each division had its own force of archers, suggesting that whatever their exact formation units of bowmen may well have been deployed with each 'battle' and not simply on the outer wings of the army.[49] By contrast, the well-informed chronicler Geoffrey le Baker states explicitly that 'the archers were also assigned a place apart from the men-at-arms, so that they were positioned at the sides of the king's army almost like wings; in this way, they did not hinder the men-at-arms, nor did they meet the enemy head on, but could catch them in their cross volleys'. Though Northampton is traditionally said to have commanded the English left wing, Andrew Ayton has suggested that both he and Warwick (as Constable and Marshal respectively) were with the Black Prince on the right wing, following the dispositions detailed by the *Acts of War of Edward III* for 15–17 August.[50]

To further strengthen his position against an attack from the rear, Edward ordered a laager to be made, forming 'all the carts and wagons of the army into a large enclosure with only one entrance, and he had all the horses put inside'.[51] Similarly, as at Morlaix the English 'quickly dug a large number of pits in the ground near their front line, each a foot deep and a foot wide, so that if the French cavalry approached, their horses would stumble in the pits', and it is likely that these were hidden with grass and foliage.[52] Some authorities have followed the statement by a number of French chroniclers that in addition to the wagon laager in the rear, the formations of archers on the English flanks were also surrounded by circles of baggage carts, and that Edward's artillery pieces were placed under these carts, but this has not met with general acceptance.[53] Such striking dispositions are not mentioned by Le Bel, Froissart or Geoffrey le Baker, and have thus been regarded more sceptically by other writers on the battle.[54] It seems very likely, however, that Edward did employ cannon at Crécy, perhaps numbering as many as 100 ribalds and some other heavier pieces, and these may well have been placed on the flanks.[55] It is also possible that some of the English archers made use of hedges to provide additional defences; the *Chroniques des quatre premiers Valois* speaks of bowmen 'embuschiés', while the *Chronique normande* says their position was defended not only by carts but by 'de fortes haies et d'autre targement'.[56]

Chroniclers also differ as to Philip's intentions on 26 August as the long columns of his army snaked along the road from Abbeville towards Crécy. Jean Le Bel, clearly anxious to exonerate Philip from the ensuing defeat, paints a detailed picture of a cautious and able commander swept unwillingly into battle by the indiscipline and insubordination of his men.[57] Philip, he notes, was careful to obtain good information, first sending outriders to establish the English position, then once this was known deputing 'a knight who was very valiant and experienced in arms' with four others to reconnoitre Edward's strength and deployment. Returning to the king, these scouts reported that the English were in formation only a league away. They advised Philip to camp for the night to allow his army, mostly still on the march, to regroup, for 'your host is very spread out over the fields'. If the French moved north to Labroye, they could encamp in a position blocking Edward's progress. They should attack the next day, rested and in full strength. The king was in full agreement, and accordingly had his heralds proclaim 'that each person should draw back his banners, for the English were arrayed nearby'.[58] This order, however, was not so easy to implement among the contingents of knights whose blood was up from a fierce pursuit of the English. As Le Bel notes:

> None of the lords wanted to turn back unless those ahead of them would turn back first, and those who were forward did not want to pull back, for it seemed shameful to them. So they held still without moving, and the others who were behind rode ever forward, and all this

was through pride and envy, which destroyed them . . . riding thus, through pride and envy without order, one after another, they continued until they saw the English ranged in three battles, well arrayed, awaiting them. Then, when they had seen their enemies so close, the shame of retreating would have been even greater.[59]

Realising that there was now nothing for it but to give battle, Philip at least managed to bring light infantry and the Genoese to the fore, to provide the attacking knights with some missile support.

This version of events, however, flies in the face of almost all the accounts by French chroniclers, who assign the decision for a rash and ill-prepared attack squarely on Philip. These writers aver that the king would not listen to wiser counsel which urged him to wait for the rest of his army, much of which was still on the road from Abbeville.[60] Seeing the enemy within striking distance, Philip was so inflamed with anger against the English that he refused to delay, and accordingly drew up those lords he had with him and placed his Genoese crossbowmen and light infantry in the van.[61] There can be no doubt that this

A crossbow with a steel bow, south German, mid-sixteenth century, with a cranequin and bolts. Though steel bows were being developed during the fourteenth century, it is probable that the majority of crossbows used by the Genoese at Crécy still had composite laths. (© The Board of Trustees of the Royal Armouries)

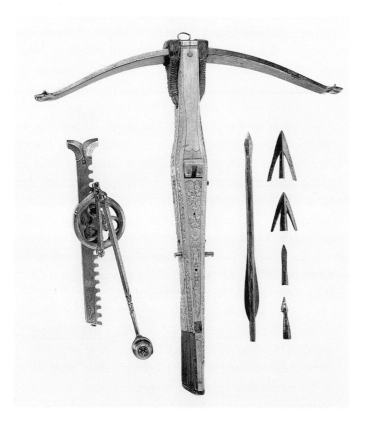

latter version of events is closer to the truth than that of Le Bel, for it would surely have been impossible to have organised the Genoese crossbowmen in the vanguard had the French lords been so impetuous.[62] Philip had consistently showed himself a cautious and able commander who had thwarted Edward's previous attempts to draw him into battle. Yet 'by 1346 his reputation could not bear a stalemate any more than a defeat' and the political pressure to achieve a notable blow against the English was becoming acute.[63] His hasty decision to attack, however, was to prove catastrophic. Had Philip waited for his full host, Edward would have had to confront a massive French army, and the French could have had time to work out an effective tactical plan. Louis, Count of Blois and brother of Charles of Blois, the veteran of Morlaix and St-Pol de Léon, was present among Philip's commanders on 26 August 1346.[64] But if Louis had urged the king to employ his brother's tactics, Philip utterly ignored his advice concerning the wisdom of dismounting his men-at-arms and of deploying cavalry only in flanking manoeuvres against the English defences. As the *Chronicle of St Omer* put it, the king attacked 'against the wishes of those who knew the ways of war' (*contre le volente de ceulx qui de guerre savoit*) and strikingly the only French contingent known to have dismounted at Crécy was led by a captain who had served with Charles in Brittany.[65] For although the forces already with Philip probably significantly outnumbered the English, the extemporised attack soon showed a complete lack of tactical forethought or coordination. Hence it must be stressed that Crécy – so often seen as representative of all that was wrong with French organisation and tactical thinking – was in fact an anomaly when compared to French deployment in battles both before and after.

Chroniclers, particularly among the French, were well aware of this and stress Philip's rash conduct and the ensuing lack of French discipline. Froissart, writing considerably later but with the ability to set Crécy in a wider context of Anglo-French conflicts, remarked, 'There is no one, even among those present on that day, who has been able to understand and relate the whole truth of the matter. This was especially so on the French side, where such confusion reigned.'[66] He went on to draw a telling comparison with the battle of Poitiers, where the French were far better organised:

You read earlier in this chronicle about the battle of Crécy, and heard how unfavourable fortune was there to the French. At Poitiers similarly it was unfavourable, fickle and treacherous, for the men-at-arms were at least seven to one in trained fighting men. But it must be said that the battle of Poitiers was fought much better than Crécy. Both armies had better opportunities to observe and weigh up the enemy, for the battle [at Crécy] began without proper preparation in the late afternoon, while Poitiers began in the early morning, and in good enough order, if only luck had been with the French. There were incomparably more fine feats of arms than at Crécy, though not so many great lords were killed.[67]

Philip's army encountered difficulties almost immediately. His Genoese crossbowmen, under the command of Ottone Doria and Carlo Grimaldi, were well-trained, professional troops, but crucially their great pavises, so essential to their effective operation in battle, together with much of their ammunition and possibly even some of their defensive armour were still in the baggage carts following behind the army.[68] Although the Genoese 'would have sooner gone to the devil than fight at that moment' because of their long march that day, they nevertheless formed up and began to advance in good order. As they approached they uttered three great cries, aiming and loosing their bolts after their third roar.[69] According to Geoffrey le Baker, 'The French crossbowmen began the attack; their crossbow bolts did not reach the English, however, but fell a long way off. Much to the terror of the crossbowmen, the English archers began to pick off their closely-packed enemies with arrows, and they ended the hail of crossbow bolts with a rain of arrows.'[70] The reasons for the poor performance of the Genoese has long been a matter of debate. As Burne comments, it is highly unlikely that a unit of such professionals would have all misjudged the range so badly when they began shooting, particularly as the English had not yet begun shooting when the Genoese loosed their first volley.[71] Some French chroniclers repeat a story that rain had soaked the bowstrings of the Genoese, rendering them ineffectual, but this was more likely a retrospective fiction, designed to help explain such a catastrophic French defeat and to cast blame on foreign mercenaries. Not only is such a tale absent from better-informed and earlier French accounts and from that of Villani, but the incident itself is implausible. Crossbow strings would doubtless have been waxed, as were longbow strings, to protect them from the possibility of getting damp, as to remove and refit a crossbow's string was a complex operation which required a special bench with a windlass, and thus was impossible to perform in combat situations. The very fact that the story of drenched bowstrings arose, moreover, presupposes that range would not have been a problem had the weapons not been defective and their strings been dry.

There are more plausible explanations for the defeat of the Genoese than lack of range. Though chroniclers' estimates of the number of Genoese in Philip's force vary greatly, the figure of 2,000 given by the *Chronique Normande* may well be closer to

reality than the much higher numbers claimed by other chroniclers.[72] How many of the English bowmen actually engaged the Genoese is unclear, but even if their numbers had been equal the crossbowmen were heavily disadvantaged by the rapid shooting of Edward's archers. Unfortunately, we do not know what kinds of crossbow the Genoese were using in 1346, whether steel or composite, or the means of spanning, though it has been estimated that if they were using the belt and hook system, which seems probable, they might at best have been able to loose four or five bolts a minute.[73] Without their pavises, and possibly also with only a limited supply of ammunition, the Genoese were very vulnerable in the open ground, and were simply shot to pieces by the rapid and deadly volleys of the longbowmen.[74] Such was the force of the English archery that the two French marshals had already withdrawn their light infantry back to the king's battle-line, but in a fury Philip would hear nothing of retreat, saying he himself would be the constable and marshal that day.[75] Even as the king urged his men forward, however, the Genoese ranks were beginning to disintegrate under the English volleys. The English archers 'poured out their arrows on the Genoese so thickly and evenly that they fell like snow. When they felt those arrows piercing their arms, their heads, their faces, the Genoese, who had never met such archers before, were thrown into confusion. Many cut their bowstrings and some threw down their crossbows. They began to fall back.'[76] Though the effect of the English bombards must have been more psychological than anything else, Villani asserts that the Genoese were also badly shaken by the firing of the English cannon, which further hastened their panicked retreat.[77]

It should have been possible for the Genoese to fall back and regroup behind the ranks of the French men-at-arms who followed. This had been successfully achieved at Courtrai in 1302, while later at Poitiers in 1356 there is no hint that the crossbowmen accompanying the divisions of the Dauphin or King Jean were unable to allow the men-at-arms to pass. At Crécy, however, the French men-at-arms not only barred the way of the retreating Genoese, but even began to ride them down. According to Le Bel, this was as a result of French indiscipline, for 'the battles of the great lords were so inflamed by envy, one against the other, that they did not wait for one another, but attacked completely disordered and mixed together without any order whatsoever, so that they trapped the light infantry and the Genoese between them and the English, so that they could not flee, thus the war-horses fell over them, and the others trampled them, and they tumbled over each other like pigs in a heap'.[78] Other sources, however, state that the men-at-arms were actually ordered to attack the Genoese, either by the Count of Alençon, King Philip's younger brother, or by Philip himself, believing them to be guilty of cowardice,

A falling knight, struck in the back by an arrow, from a misericord, *c.* 1370, in the choir of Lincoln Cathedral. As he wears no surcoat, the arrangement of the lames of his body armour are clearly visible. *(Paulette Barton)*

or worse still of treachery.[79] 'Quick now, kill all that rabble,' Froissart has Philip say, 'They are only getting in our way!'[80] The rear ranks of the French, believing the terrible cries of the Genoese to be those of the dying English, pressed forward for 'every Frenchman strove to follow those who had already charged; foremost in such rashness and boldness were newly made knights, of whom there were a good number in the army, all eager to gain the glory which they thought they would earn by fighting the English king'.[81]

As a result the French attack was quickly plunged into terrible chaos. The assault of their first division against the English positions lost much of its momentum as the French horsemen pushed and hacked their way through their own crossbowmen, and 'the French line of battle was badly disorganized by stumbling horses'.[82] Meanwhile 'the English continued to shoot into the thickest part of the crowd, wasting none of their arrows. They impaled or wounded horses and riders, who fell to the ground in great distress, unable to get up again without the help of several men.'[83] The terrible effects of the arrows against the horses threw the advancing cavalry into further confusion. 'The archers', noted Le Bel, 'shot so marvellously that when the horses felt these barbed arrows (which did wonders), some would not go forwards, others leapt into the air as if maddened, others balked and bucked horribly, others turned their rumps towards the enemy, regardless of their masters, because of the arrows they felt. Some, unable to avoid it, let themselves fall. The English lords, who were on foot, advanced and pierced through these men, who could not help themselves, by their own efforts or by their

horses.'[84] Nevertheless, enough French men-at-arms managed to close with the Black Prince's division to involve the English in fierce fighting. One chronicler claimed that the Prince's standard was seized by the Court of Alençon before he was slain,[85] while according to a tradition developed by Froissart the prince became so hard-pressed that Sir Thomas Norwich was dispatched to King Edward to seek reinforcements. The king asked if his son was badly hurt or slain, and was told that he was not, but was under such fierce attack that he needed assistance. Edward famously replied, 'Sir Thomas, go back to him and those who sent you and tell them from me that they are not to send to me for help, whatever happens, so long as my son is alive. Tell them that my orders are that they are to let the boy win his spurs; for I wish the day to be his, if God so wills it, and that he and his companions shall have the honour of it.'[86] Geoffrey le Baker, writing in about 1358–60 and probably drawing his information from members of the prince's household, noted that the sixteen-year-old 'displayed marvellous courage against the French in the front line, running through horses, felling knights, crushing helmets, cutting lances apart, avoiding the enemy's missiles; as he did so, he encouraged his men, defended himself, helped fallen friends to their feet and set everyone an example; nor did he rest from his labours until the enemy retreated, leaving behind a heap of dead bodies'.[87]

Although the ground in front of the English right wing was littered with the bodies of fallen men and horses, the second French division pressed home its attack. Among its leaders was John, the blind King of Bohemia, who ordered his knights to lead him into the attack with their bridles tied to his; after the battle he was found dead with his household knights beside him.[88] But the sheer weight of French numbers meant that the prince's division again came under severe pressure. The prince himself was beaten to the ground, but was saved by his standard bearer, Sir Richard FitzSimon, and Sir Thomas Daniel.[89] This time, King Edward dispatched a group of knights under the Bishop of Durham to reinforce his son's ranks.[90] The ferocity of such fighting is an important indication of the extent to which English success relied on combined arms; the volleys of arrows served to break much of the force of the French attacks and to disorganise their advance, but the engagement ultimately hinged on the ability of the English men-at-arms to stand their ground. Though it is the battle of Agincourt that is best remembered for the terrible deaths by suffocation of many French knights, le Baker noted a similar result at Crécy: 'When they attacked the well-armed English, they were cut down with swords and spears, and many were crushed to death, without a mark upon them, in the middle of the French army, because the press was so great.'[91] The nature of the well-chosen terrain seems to have funnelled the charging French men-at-arms into a restricted killing zone in front of the Black Prince's division. Indeed, so effective was their deployment that King Edward never had to commit the bulk of his own division to the engagement, and was said never even to have donned his helmet. Similarly, the left wing under Suffolk and Arundel may well have helped to reinforce the prince's division, but it seems not to have been engaged in the same fierce struggle.

By now the French forces were in a state of chaos. Nevertheless, they continued to launch wave after spontaneous and disorganised wave, and though the sun set the fighting continued by moonlight. 'So the fearful face of war was displayed', noted Geoffrey le Baker, 'from the setting of the sun until the third quarter of the night, during which time the French raised a general war-cry three times and charged fifteen times.'[92] But each assault which faltered before the English lines merely added to the mass of dead and wounded men and horses obstructing a concerted and effective strike. One chronicler estimated that the French lost over a thousand war-horses in the battle, which, given the great price of such destriers, must have represented a staggering financial loss.[93] King Philip had fought bravely, having two horses slain under him and being wounded in the face by an English arrow.[94] But as his army began to disintegrate in confused flight, he reluctantly allowed himself, like Edward II at Bannockburn, to be led off the field by his bodyguard, and the king's departure marked the end of effective resistance.[95] The English kept the field, but stood to arms during the night. According to a later source, but one

drawing on local knowledge, Edward had the windmill he had used as his command post filled with wood and set alight, to act as a beacon.[96] In the moonlight, as the pillagers began to strip the slain and the dying, the magnitude of the French defeat could only be surmised, and it was only once the heralds had completed their grim task of identifying the noble dead by collecting up their heraldic coat armour that the appalling carnage inflicted on the French was truly revealed: the blind King of Bohemia, the king's brother the Count of Alençon, the Count of Flanders, a number of great lords and, according to Edward III's own estimate, 80 bannerets, at least 1,542 knights and esquires, and a large but unascertainable number of the common soldiery.[97] The extent of such slaughter, including

A stylised depiction of Crécy as a cavalry engagement, from a fifteenth-century copy of Froissart's *Chronicles*, with the arms of some of the nobles who fought in the battle (New York, Pierpont Morgan MS 804, f.101v). *(Pierpont Morgan Library, New York)*

some of the greatest nobles in Europe, was unprecedented and shocking. 'It was said', remarked Le Bel, referring to the bloody rout of the French by the Flemings in 1302 and the crushing defeat of Manfred of Hohenstaufen by Charles of Anjou in 1266, 'that for a long time no one had heard of so many princes killed in a single day, not at Courtrai, nor at Benevento, nor anywhere else.'[98] In stark contrast to the battle of Poitiers ten years later, where the English netted a huge haul of valuable prisoners, few if any prisoners were recorded as being taken in the fighting at Crécy.[99]

The English had achieved their crushing victory through a number of factors. Edward's strategy of provocation had finally succeeded in goading the enemy into a hasty and poorly organised attack against a strong and carefully selected defensive position. Crécy had been the triumph of a disciplined and well-organised army, led by experienced captains, over a larger but heterogeneous and poorly organised force of mercenaries, feudal cavalry and infantry levies.[100] Once again, the tactical combination of archers and men-at-arms had proved devastating. Froissart, writing a considerable time after the battle, reflected, 'I tell you that that day the English archers gave great support to their side, for many said that by their shooting the affair was won, even though there were also several valiant knights there in their ranks who fought valiantly hand-to-hand, and made many fine openings [among the French ranks] and great recoveries. But it should be well known and recognised that the archers did a great feat there, for by their shooting at the outset the Genoese, who numbered 15,000, were discomfited, which was a great advantage from them.'[101] Had they been allowed adequate rest, plentiful ammunition and above all the essential protection afforded to them by their pavises, the Genoese, as Froissart implies, might have proved much more formidable, and could have inflicted significant casualties among the English.

In truth, the French had done much else to rob themselves of any chance of victory. Failure to allow the Genoese to withdraw caused confusion from the outset and broke the force of the charge of the first French attacks. Though they may have been formed up into as many as sixteen different units, the French did not attempt to attack the entirety of Edward's positions or to deploy formations to turn the English flank, but instead allowed themselves to be corralled – as Edward had intended – towards a killing zone in front of the prince's battle. The crucial failures to regroup effectively, to take counsel – as Charles of Blois had managed to do at Morlaix after the defeat of the first French attack[102] – and to deploy their great numbers to better effect were the major reasons for the French defeat at Crécy. The sources give the impression of an abundance of courage but a total lack of communication and overall command, with the battle providing a classic instance of the reinforcement of defeat. If, moreover, the battle had begun with indiscipline, defeat was followed by complete confusion among the French. Many were disoriented and 'went in bands, three here, four there, like lost men; and none of them knew if their lords or relatives or brothers were dead or had escaped'.[103] Whereas the English kept in formation that night, the French were hopelessly scattered, and the following day surviving contingents found themselves attacked and bloodily defeated by English scouting parties operating in strength.[104]

The French disaster at Crécy allowed Edward to take the strategically vital port of Calais, though it was to cost a huge effort in men, money and logistics in a siege lasting eleven months before the town finally fell on 3 August 1347.[105] In a last desperate bid to relieve the town, Philip VI had challenged Edward to leave his powerful siege fortifications around Calais and fight a battle on open ground chosen by four knights from each side. Such was Edward's confidence in his army, as well as 'in God and our right', that he enthusiastically accepted, but once their bluff was called the French quickly backed down from a major engagement, leaving the gallant garrison no option but to surrender.[106] A revealing incident which occurred some three years later at Calais, on 2 January 1350, shows how Edward's skilful eye for choosing good terrain, witnessed at Halidon Hill, La Flamengerie and Crécy, could be applied in microcosm. Following a carefully planned ambush of French forces attempting to take the castle at Calais by stealth, Edward had sallied out in pursuit of a far larger body with a smaller force. The exploit doubtless grew in the telling, with the king's band being reckoned at only some 30 men-at-arms and the same number of archers, though in reality he may have commanded some 250 bowmen.[107] Realising their superiority in numbers, the French turned about to attack Edward, who encouraged his men and drew them up in a strong defensive position. As Geoffrey le Baker notes, he

posted the archers to one side of the men-at-arms on dry islands in the marsh, surrounded by muddy swamps so that the heavily armed horsemen and foot-soldiers would be unable to reach them without sinking in the mire . . . they greeted the oncoming French bitterly enough with a shower of sharp arrows. All the men-at-arms stood on a hard causeway, which was only broad enough for twenty men to march abreast; on either side lay the marsh, where armed men could not go and where the archers were safe, out of the way of their own men and showering the enemy with arrows from the flank. So the king and his men in the centre and the archers on each side killed and took prisoners, and put up a brave fight until the arrival of the Prince of Wales put the French to flight.[108]

Even in an extemporised position, we see the adoption of the key tactical elements of dismounted men-at-arms on a limited front with their flanks protected by both natural obstacles and enfilade shooting from archers, themselves carefully positioned to protect them from direct attack by French cavalry. In the ensuing fight the French suffered heavy casualties, including some 200 men-at-arms.

HOW TO DEFEAT THE ENGLISH? FRENCH TACTICAL RESPONSE BETWEEN CRÉCY AND POITIERS

Subsequent French attempts to tackle the problem of English formations reinforce the impression of Crécy as a disastrous shambles unrepresentative of the real capabilities of French arms or tactical thinking. At Lunalonge in Poitou in 1349 an Anglo-Gascon force, led by the Captal de Buch (who was soon to play such a prominent role in the battle of Poitiers), drew up on foot in a strong position to confront a French army under the seneschal of Poitou, Jean de Lille, and Lord Boucicaut.[109] The contemporary account in the French *Chronique Normande*, written by a soldier from the lesser Norman nobility, describes how the French launched two simultaneous cavalry attacks, one directly at the English position but the other sweeping round behind the Anglo-Gascon position. This outflanking manoeuvre succeeded in capturing all the enemy's horses, probably formed up as usual with the wagons behind their main position, and was intended to cut off their chances of flight or preclude them from launching a mounted counter-offensive or pursuit. The French frontal attack, however, was repulsed and thrown back on their main formation, with some 300 French being slain or taken prisoner. The great strength of the Anglo-Gascon position deterred the French from further attacks,[110] and a stand-off occurred between the two forces until vespers, when the French finally withdrew. The Anglo-Gascons used the cover of darkness to march away on foot, since their horses had all been seized.[111]

The defeat at Lunalonge may have hammered home to the French the extreme vulnerability of their war-horses in a direct assault on English defensive positions, for at the battle of Taillebourg on 8 April 1351 the young French marshal Guy de Nesle dismounted the majority of his men-at-arms to fight but kept two wings of cavalry in support, thereby resorting – whether consciously or not is unknown – to the tactics of Charles of Blois at St-Pol de Léon. A league to the north-west of Saintes, by the little chapel of St George, Guy had intercepted an Anglo-Gascon raiding force, though unfortunately for the French he delayed long enough in making his dispositions for the English to receive reinforcements of 300 to 400 men from

nearby Tonnay-sur-Charente and Taillebourg. Regrettably little is known of the course of the battle, or of the role of either the archers or the flanking bodies of French horse. But although the engagement was hard-fought, there seems little doubt that the French suffered a marked reverse, being driven off with considerable losses, including 600 men-at-arms slain or taken, and with the prisoners including Marshal Guy himself and Arnoul d'Audrehem.[112] Nevertheless, only two months later on 6 June the tables were turned when a French force led by the Lord of Beaujeu engaged an English force under John de Beauchamp, the captain of Calais, at Ardres. The French force greatly outnumbered Beauchamp's force of some 600 men, who sought to defend themselves in a bend of a river by digging a trench around their positions. As was by now usual, the French sought to combat the English by a combination of dismounted men-at-arms and flank assaults by cavalry. Early in the attack the French commander was slain, but the French were able to bring up fresh troops and after a long fight the English archers ran out of arrows before the attack of the third French division. As a result the French cavalry were able to outflank them and badly cut them up. The French men-at-arms fought so well that the English were defeated, losing several hundred dead or wounded, and with Beauchamp being captured.[113] That a French force operating in a different theatre of the war was employing dismounting tactics so soon after the engagement at Taillebourg is striking, and may well reflect a process analogous to the sharing of strategic and tactical ideas visible among the English military command.[114]

It is also striking that the readoption of dismounted combat by Guy de Nesle came only three months after the famous 'Combat of Thirty' in Brittany between thirty French and English knights, which took place between Josselin and Ploermel on 26 March 1351.[115] This bloody duel, fought *à outrance* with weapons of war and not those of the tournament, had been the result of a personal challenge from Jean de Beaumanoir, castellan of Josselin and the English captain of Ploermel, with each selecting a team of picked knights. The

English, whose number included Sir Robert Knollys, Sir Hugh Calveley and John Dagworth, nephew of Sir Thomas Dagworth, fought dismounted, as did the majority of their opponents, but the French kept four or five of their companions mounted – a disposition which in microcosm echoed many of their subsequent battle formations.[116] The engagement was long and bitter, but was punctuated by a pause for a drink of wine. According to a verse account of the duel, however, when after more intense fighting Beaumanoir sought to suspend the battle again for another drink, one of his companions, Geoffroi de Boves, retorted, 'Drink your own blood, Beaumanoir, your thirst will pass!' The engagement readily demonstrated the abilities of both the French and English knights at foot combat, but significantly it was the intervention of one of the French mounted knights that finally swung the balance in favour of the French.[117] Though six of the French lay dead, the fatalities were more numerous among the English, and, as they refused to flee, all the survivors were captured.

Brittany, where the deeds of the Thirty were to be long remembered, was soon to be the scene of another sizeable engagement in which the French came very close to repeating their victory at Ardres. On 14 August 1352 at Mauron, a small village a little to the north of Ploermel, Guy de Nesle again gave battle, this time to a small Anglo-Breton force under the command of Sir Walter de Bentley.[118] Not only was Bentley heavily outnumbered, with the *Chronique Normande* giving his force as 1,500 men including 800 archers,[119] but also, as he noted in his dispatches, the ground 'was upon the open fields, without woods, ditches or other defences'.[120] Nevertheless, he positioned his men on foot on rising ground in front of a hedge, which served to protect their rear, and placed his archers on the flanks.[121] As at Taillebourg, Guy de Nesle dismounted all his men, save for a cavalry force under the Lord of Hangest placed on his left wing, whose task was to ride down the archers. Although the dismounted French men-at-arms found it hard going advancing up the slope, which was covered in thick scrub, they closed with the English and drove them back to the hedge. Meanwhile, the French cavalry attacked and routed the archers on the English right flank, slaying a great number of them. In the centre, however, the premature withdrawal of a large group of French under the Lords of Hambuie and Beaumanoir allowed the English to regroup, and the archers on the left flank, who had repulsed a force of French infantry and chased them back down the slope, may have now turned to attack the exposed right flank of the French centre. In the fierce fighting that followed, the French centre was defeated with heavy losses. Guy de Nesle and Alan, Viscount Rohan were slain, along with several important lords, 7 bannerets and 44 knights, while some 800 other men-at-arms were killed or captured.[122] Among the prisoners were 45 knights of the elite Order of the Star, founded only the year previously as the French equivalent to the Order of the Garter. Its members 'in their profession had sworn never in fear to turn their backs on their foes', and now they left another 89 members dead on the field.[123] Bentley, who was himself badly wounded, 'ordered thirty of the archers to be beheaded, because at the height of the battle, frightened by the numbers of the French, they had fled'.[124] Here we glimpse the grim reality of military discipline which underpinned the cohesion vital to the effective operation of such small numbers of professionals in combat against the odds.

Mauron was a significant battle, for the French had come close to victory. Why some of their men-at-arms retreated at a crucial moment is unclear, though the heavy French casualties may well have occurred in the press as the French were driven back down the slope. Nevertheless, their cavalry had succeeded in riding down the archers, who seemingly had not been protected by ditches or pits, and were thus highly vulnerable. As Sir Robert Keith's crucial charge against the English archers at Bannockburn had also revealed, cavalry *could* close with bowmen with success. Though the battle itself was lost, the effectiveness of flanking cavalry at Mauron goes far to explain the tactical plan of the French at the great battle of Poitiers in 1356.

'THIS GREAT AND TERRIBLE BATTLE': POITIERS, 19 SEPTEMBER 1356

In 1356 the Black Prince had led a major *chevauchée* from Gascony north into Poitou, repeating the successful campaign of pillage and devastation he had carried out in south-west France the year before. By 17 September a powerful French army under King Jean II had given chase and confronted the Black Prince, whose forces were heavily laden with a mass of booty, close to the town and abbey of Nouaillé, a few miles south of the city of Poitiers. The circumstances of the battle have been much debated. Was the prince brought to bay and forced to give battle as the only way to escape from disaster, or was he actively seeking battle? Rogers has argued convincingly that from an early stage the prince was deliberately seeking battle with Jean's forces during his northward march towards Tours. The whole strategy of the *chevauchée* had, as in 1346, been to provoke the French into a decisive battle, and to the same end the prince had laid siege to the castle of Romorantin to entice Jean towards him.[125] The French in turn had sought to cut off the prince's retreat south, and briefly succeeded in so doing. In a later letter the prince stated that he had intended to give battle to the enemy on 16 September close to Chauvigny, probably as the French had already barred his line of retreat. Froissart believed that the French simply had to wait things out, for the English 'were beginning to feel great want of stores, which was a great concern to them, for they did not know where to go to forage, so closely were their exits blocked; they could not leave their camp without danger from the French. Indeed they did not fear a battle as much as that they would be blockaded where they stood.'[126] The prince may well have been running short of supplies, but it is hard to see how the army could have been without water when their left flank rested on the River Miosson. More importantly, by 17 September the English had in fact outmanoeuvred Jean's army to place themselves once again south of the French, and though the French were hard on their heels escape was possible.[127]

The exact location of the battle is a matter of considerable uncertainty, but what is clear is that the prince had succeeded in placing his army in a very strong natural position ideally suited to defensive tactics (see map on p. 229).[128] Geoffrey le Baker describes how the Black Prince had reconnoitred the ground and found a suitable hill on which to deploy, with the vanguard under Warwick and Oxford to his left, his own division in the centre, and the rearguard under Salisbury on the right:

> Between our men and the hill was a broad deep valley and marsh watered by a stream. The prince's battalion crossed the stream at a fairly narrow ford and occupied the hill beyond the marshes and ditches where they easily concealed their positions among the thickets, lying higher than the enemy. The field in which our vanguard and centre were stationed was separated from the level ground by a long hedge and ditch, whose other end reached down to the marsh. The Earl of Warwick, in command of the vanguard, held the slope down to the marsh. In the upper part of the hedge, well away from the slope, there was a certain open space or gap, made by the carters in autumn, a stone's throw away from which our rearguard was positioned, under the command of the Earl of Salisbury.[129]

The great wood of Nouaillé was to their rear, while the marshy ground around the River Miosson gave their left flank added protection.[130] On their most exposed flank, probably their right, 'they had placed their carts and other tackle as fortifications, so that they could not be attacked from that quarter'.[131] Along the front of the English line archers were 'positioned in safe trenches

The gilt bronze effigy of the Black Prince (d. 1376), in Canterbury Cathedral. *(Canterbury Cathedral, Kent/Bridgeman Art Library)*

along the ditch and beyond the hedge'.[132] The men-at-arms kept their horses close by 'so that they could mount without delay if need arose', while a body of 300 knights and as many mounted archers were placed on their right flank to move round the enemy's position behind the cover of a low hill.[133] No pay-rolls are available for the Poitiers campaign, but according to a letter of Burghersh the prince's army comprised around 3,000 men-at-arms, 2,000 English and Welsh archers, and some 1,000 Gascon infantry,[134] while King Jean's army has been estimated at 8,000 men-at-arms and 3,000 infantry.[135] The English were thus significantly outnumbered, but as events were to fall out one-third of the French army was never to strike a blow.

All through 18 September the two armies glared at each other while the French cardinal Talleyrand attempted to avoid the imminent bloodshed through negotiation, but in vain. Froissart believed that during this day of truce the English worked hard to strengthen their defences further, with the archers 'digging ditches and setting up defences around them'.[136] French scouts had carefully observed the English positions and reported their great strength to King Jean. As Froissart has Sir Eustace de Ribemont tell the king:

> They have chosen a road strongly fortified with hedges and undergrowth, and have posted their archers along this hedge on both sides of the road, so that one cannot approach to attack the army save between these rows of archers. This road has no other entry or issue, and is only wide enough for perhaps four men-at-arms to ride abreast. At the end of the hedge, among the vines and thorn bushes, where one cannot go on foot or ride, are their men-at-arms, all on foot; and they have placed their

men-at-arms all behind their archers in the manner of a herce (*et on mis leurs gens d'armes tout devant yaus leurs arciers à manière d'une herce*). All this, it seems to us, is most skilfully planned, for if we could fight our way to that point we could not penetrate further without coming up against the archers, whom it would be no light task to dislodge.[137]

Nevertheless, the French decided to attack. Jean was no doubt painfully aware of the catastrophe that had befallen the French a decade earlier at Crécy when they had assaulted an English army in a strong defensive position. But the situation now appeared very different. Unlike Philip VI, Jean had not attacked over-hastily after a long march, but had gained good intelligence as to the enemy's position, while his army, which considerably outnumbered the English, was rested and had ample opportunity to organise itself into three main units, each with two wings.[138] The first division was led by the eighteen-year-old Dauphin Charles and the Scottish lord Sir William Douglas, the second by the Duke of Orléans, with King Jean bringing up the rear. At least in theory the army also had greater cohesion and better internal discipline than that of 1346. It was not, as at Crécy, encumbered by a mass of poorly equipped and ill-disciplined foot-soldiers raised by the *arrière-ban*, for the king had dismissed most of these, keeping only the better-trained infantry including a strong force of crossbowmen. By an ordinance of 1351, moreover, King Jean had attempted to introduce major reforms to the structure of the host.[139] French kings were able to field impressive numbers of men-at-arms, but although troops raised from an area or from the feudal dependants of certain lords might sometimes be formed into 'battles' from the outset of a campaign, the great majority of men-at-arms came to the host with only a very small following, and their arrangement thereafter into larger units by the marshal or constable was often haphazard. This meant that French knights and esquires often had few if any personal ties with the lords commanding their divisions and very little experience of fighting in established units.[140] They thus lacked the discipline and esprit de corps that many of the retinues under Edward III had achieved through years of campaigning together, and such factors only served to exacerbate the individualism and ill-discipline among some of the men-at-arms. Accordingly, in 1351 King Jean had issued a royal *ordonnance* stating that all men-at-arms were to be grouped in units of between 25 and 80, known variously as *compagnies*, *routes* or *bannières*, which were to be led by knights banneret or other men of rank, while the infantry were to be formed in units of 25 to 30, known as *connestables* or constabularies. Further regulations also aimed to secure the adequate provision of equipment.

Unlike at Crécy, the king and his commanders had ample time to draw up a coherent battle plan. They chose to dismount the majority of their own men-at-arms, a decision Geoffrey le Baker ascribes to Douglas, 'a ferocious adversary of the English', now fighting with King Jean with 200 men-at-arms. For the Scots, noted le Baker, 'were well aware that throughout the wars of the present King of England the English were mostly accustomed to fighting on foot, imitating the Scots, ever since Stirling [i.e. Bannockburn]. So William preferred to follow his nation's style of fighting and attack on foot rather than on horseback, and he persuaded the usurper [King Jean] and the rest of the French to fight in a similar fashion.'[141] Froissart, however, attributed the advice to dismount the main force to the veteran French knight Sir Eustace de Ribemont, and it is very improbable that Douglas's counsel did any more than reinforce a decision made by the French themselves based on their own past experiences.[142] As we have seen, the French had already begun to adopt such tactics as early as 1346 at St-Pol de Léon, while one of the French marshals, Arnoul d'Audrehem, had fought and was captured at Taillebourg where the French had again dismounted, and Geoffrey de Charny, who at Poitiers was to bear the great Oriflamme banner, had taken part in the French victory at Ardres.[143] Similarly, the French had enjoyed other successes on foot, as for example at Combourg in the spring of 1354, where the French under Audrehem had defeated the English garrison of Becherel under Hugh Calveley and taken him prisoner.[144] Accordingly, it was ordered 'that those who had lances should shorten them to a length of five feet so that they could be more easily wielded, and that they should also remove their spurs'.[145]

The advance of these dismounted men-at-arms, however, was to be preceded by a mounted attack by a picked force of cavalry, who were to force a path through the archers positioned by the gaps in the hedge. As Froissart has Eustace de Ribemont advise Jean: 'three hundred horsemen of the boldest, strongest, toughest and most enterprising, well armed and mounted on the finest chargers . . . will break through the lines of archers for your own battalions to follow in quickly and fight hand-to-hand with their men-at-arms and overcome them by the fierceness of their attack'.[146] These horses – who may have actually numbered more like 500 – were to be well barded to protect them from arrows as they attempted to ride down the English archers,[147] and were supported by an additional mounted reinforcement of German cavalry under the Counts of Saarbruck, Nido and Nassau.[148] The French vanguard also contained pavise-bearers and crossbowmen, together with infantry armed with swords and javelins, suggesting that the French had attempted to provide some missile cover for their mounted attack.[149]

On the morning of 19 September the prince made preparations for battle, but then ordered the left wing under Warwick to begin to withdraw across the Miosson. Was this a genuine attempt to withdraw from battle against a powerful force,[150] or a feint to lure the French into attacking an otherwise impregnable position? Accounts of the circumstances of the battle and its opening phases are contradictory and often confused. While Froissart and others thought the Black Prince awaited the French army in a strong defensive position, le Baker, Chandos Herald and the *Anonimalle Chronicle* all believed that the Black Prince was attempting to withdraw from his initial positions when the French launched their attack. This latter version has the prince sending the vanguard under Warwick to transport his baggage over the stream, but with the earl then being forced to about face and advance back to the English position on learning of the French onslaught.[151] The French, it seems, were equally uncertain as to the prince's intentions, and the two marshals, Clermont and Audrehem, disagreed violently as to the appropriate response. Clermont did not believe the English were really withdrawing, but was taunted by Audrehem for his view that the French should not attack so strong a position but rather should wait for hunger to force the prince's withdrawal.[152] Audrehem, believing the English were trying to slip away, urged an immediate attack lest the French lose contact with them, and in order to avoid the slur of cowardice Clermont was forced to join in the assault. Chandos Herald vividly imagines their heated exchange:

> D'Audenham said, 'Your delay will make us lose them very soon.' Then Clermont replied: 'By St Denis, marshal, you are very bold,' and added angrily: 'But you will never be bold enough to get your lance in front of my horse's backside.' So, full of bad temper, they set out towards the English.[153]

Nevertheless, the fact that Audrehem's force of half the heavy horse attacked the English left under Warwick and half under Clermont attacked the right under Salisbury suggests that despite their disagreement and rivalry, they were operating on a preconceived plan to hit the flanks of the English positions as had been the pattern in earlier engagements.

Clermont's cavalry now attempted to drive through the gap in the hedge but they were confronted by Salisbury's archers, who 'shot volleys thicker than rain on the two sides facing the armed horses'.[154] The *Chronographia Regum Francorum* similarly noted how 'by the archers' arrows the horses of the French were slain, so that their falling riders were suffocated in the press'.[155] Meanwhile, Audrehem's cavalry, supported by a powerful force of crossbowmen, had attacked the other flank of

the English army, which in Warwick's absence would have been formed by the left flank of the prince's division. It was now that Warwick recrossed the ford, and launched a mounted counter-charge which caught the French crossbowmen and their pavise-bearers out in the open, quickly routing them. As the *Anonimalle Chronicle* notes, Warwick's men-at-arms 'all on horseback, struck and defeated the pavise-bearers. Dismounting, he arrayed his division, the vanguard striking the front of his enemies.'[156] For protection against the French horsemen, Warwick seems to have placed some of his archers in the marshy ground below the hill on which the main English positions were situated. As le Baker noted:

> the archers of our vanguard were safely positioned in the marsh, where the cavalry could not reach them; but they were of little use there. For the cavalry, designed to ride down the archers and protect their companions from them, stood beside the other French troops and offered the archers as a target only their forequarters, which were well protected by steel plates and leather shields, so that the arrows aimed at them either shattered or glanced off heavenwards, falling on friend and foe alike. The Earl of Oxford saw this and left the prince to lead the archers to one side, ordering them to shoot at the horses' rear quarters; when this was done, the wounded chargers reared, throwing their riders, or turned back on their own men, throwing not a few of their masters to the ground, who had intended a quite different conclusion. Once the war-horses were out of the way, the archers took up their previous position and shot directly at the French flank.[157]

With the initial cavalry attack repulsed, the first French division, led by the Dauphin, advanced towards the English on foot. As they did so, they suffered heavy casualties from the archers as they attempted to penetrate the gaps in the hedges along the English front.[158] Fierce hand-to-hand fighting ensued between the men-at-arms, but the English held their ground. According to Chandos Herald, Warwick's men had advanced up the hill from their earlier positions and assisted in driving back part of the Dauphin's battle from a gap in the hedge.[159] The bitter struggle lasted for some two hours before the French were finally forced to withdraw. King Jean at this stage may have instructed the Dauphin to be led away to safety, lest the English exploit this disengagement and counter-attack, though perhaps an all-out effort by the king at this stage might finally have overwhelmed the exhausted English.[160]

So far, the French had been worsted, but two-thirds of their army was still fresh, while the English were all but spent, with many wounded. Yet remarkably, the second division under the

The battle of Poitiers, from a fifteenth-century Flemish manuscript of Froissart's *Chronicles*, depicting the attack by Oxford's archers on the cavalry of the French vanguard (Paris, Bibliothèque Nationale, MS fr. 2643, f.207). Note the large arrow bag at the feet of the leading archer. *(Bibliothèque Nationale, Paris/Bridgeman Art Library)*

This late fourteenth-century depiction of the battle of Poitiers vividly emphasises the thick cover used by the English archers as a defence against the French cavalry (Österreiche Nationalbibliothek, Vienna, MS Cod. 2564, f.413). *(akg-images)*

king's brother the Duke of Orléans took the withdrawal of the Dauphin's division as a signal not to attack in his turn once the way was clear, but to abandon the field without a blow struck. It was little wonder that contemporaries subsequently attributed cowardice and even treachery to the shameful retreat of Orléans's men. Their departure must have given new heart to the English, and also brought them a much-needed breathing space to rest and regroup, while the archers collected up arrows, even recovering them from the bodies of the slain. Conversely, Orléans's departure must have badly shaken the morale of King Jean's division, no doubt already sapped following the repulse of the marshals' cavalry attack and the withdrawal of the Dauphin's division.

Nevertheless, Jean's remaining battle was still very powerful and posed a grave threat to the prince's army. English chroniclers readily admit the fear of the prince's men at this stage. 'Our men', noted le Baker, 'were frightened not only by the numbers of the enemy but also by their own weakened state. Many of our men had had to withdraw from the fighting because they were wounded, the rest were very tired, and the archers had used up their arrows.'[161] As it finally began its steady advance up the slope, the French king's battle was preceded by crossbowmen protected by pavise-bearers, and it is noteworthy that, in contrast to Crécy, no chronicle records them being suddenly swept from the field by the shooting of the English archers. The archers continued to harass the oncoming French with enfilade shooting, but the sources are at odds as to the effectiveness of the English bowmen at this stage. The *Chronique Normande* noted that 'there were many English there who turned to flee, but the French began to pile up because of the great shooting of the archers, which fell upon their heads, so that a great many were not able to fight and they fell back one against another. From that point on, the French were discomfited.'[162] Geoffrey le Baker, by contrast, believed that the French knights advanced in close formation, 'protecting their bodies with joined shields, [and] turned their faces away from the missiles. So the archers emptied their quivers in vain, but, armed with swords and shields, they attacked the heavily armed enemy, anxious to buy death dearly since they expected to meet their end that day.'[163] Knighton corroborates this, noting that 'so strong and hard was the fight that the archers ran out of arrows, and picked up stones, and fought with swords and lances and anything they could find, and they defended themselves with marvellous courage'.[164]

In such combat the lightly armed archers enjoyed greater manoeuvrability than the heavily armed French knights, but nevertheless the situation was beginning to look desperate for the English. Yet the Black Prince had one ace left to play. The Captal de Buch, Jean de Grailly, had manoeuvred in a wide arc round the French flank with a force of 60 men-at-arms and mounted archers, using the terrain to obscure his movements.[165] He now launched a devastating attack on the rear of King Jean's battle, during which 'the archers he had taken with him wrought great havoc'.[166] The Captal's surprise attack was the turning point in the battle, for the prince, who had

meanwhile ordered many of his men-at-arms to remount, took this as the signal to launch an all-out charge. The English knights, led to the fore by Sir James Audley, thundered down the slope into the dismounted French men-at-arms, who were now at a grave disadvantage. Assaulted from the rear and the flank as well as from the front, 'the French battle line was completely broken up'.[167] The archers, including those from Warwick's left flank, continued to hack and stab at the mass of French knights, now terribly vulnerable to the attack of these nimble and deadly troops. A vivid and prophetic glimpse into the fear and resolve of knights facing the enemy in just such a situation is provided by the leading French knight Geoffrey de Charny, who bore the Oriflamme banner signifying war to the death. He describes the harsh realities of conflict:

> You will have to put up with great labour before you achieve honour from this employ: heat, cold, fasting, hard work, little sleep and long watches and exhaustion . . . You will needs be afraid when you see your enemies bearing down on you with lances lowered to strike you and swords ready to attack you. Shafts and quarrels come at you and you do not know how best to protect your body. Now you see men slaughtering one another, fleeing, dying and being taken prisoner, and your friends dead, whose corpses lie before you. But your horses are not killed, you could well get away. Through them you could save your skin; you could ride off without honour. If you stay, you will have honour ever after; if you flee you dishonour yourself. Is this not a great martyrdom?[168]

Charny, true to himself and his chivalric code, chose to stay and was slain fighting beside his lord and king. King Jean fought just as bravely, with 'the zeal of a young knight, doing great deeds, maiming some, killing others, cutting or bruising faces, gutting or beheading others'.[169] But acts of individual prowess could not save the French division, whose cohesion had been hopelessly shattered. Many fled, but Jean, with his young son Philip at his side, was finally overwhelmed and captured along with some 3,000 others, including 14 counts, 21 great lords and bannerets, and 1,400 knights.[170] The French dead numbered around 2,500 men-at-arms and an unknown number of other ranks, compared to about 40 English men-at-arms and an unknown tally of archers.[171]

So ended what Chandos Herald called 'this great and terrible battle'.[172] Ultimately, the combination of an exceptionally

The battle of Poitiers, from *Les Guardes Chroniques de France*, late fourteenth century, from British Library, MS Cotton Nero E ii (Part II). *(British Library © 2003, Foto Scala, Florence/HIP)*

strong defensive position, enfilade volleys by the archers and a resolute defence then counter-attack by the English men-at-arms achieved victory. As one French chronicler noted, recording contemporary opinions on the causes of the catastrophe, 'others said that the cause of the defeat was because it was impossible to close with the English, for they were stationed in too strong a position, and their archers shot so strongly that the men of the aforesaid King of France were not able to endure their shooting'.[173] Yet despite the magnitude of the French defeat, Poitiers had been a far more hard-won victory for the English than Crécy, where Edward III's division had not even been engaged. Whether the Duke of Orléans's division would have swung the day for the French had it attacked, or whether it too would have been bloodily repulsed, will never be known. But in a telling observation, the *Eulogium*

historiarum noted that whereas in the past the way a battle would go could be judged by the first three to four, or even six volleys of arrows, at Poitiers the outcome was uncertain even after 100 volleys.[174] Indeed, it is clear that by the time the Treaty of Brétigny in 1360 brought the first phase of the Hundred Years War to a close, English archery had gradually lessened its effect against the French. The adoption of heavier armour and large pavises by dismounted French men-at-arms meant that they could better withstand English volleys, and in such circumstances English forces could be defeated in the field. In 1356 near Coutances the archers in a combined English and Navarese force under Geoffrey de Harcourt had shot in vain against the French, who were well guarded by large shields. In the ensuing mêlée, moreover, the French kept better discipline than the English, who were put to flight.[175]

COCHEREL AND AURAY, 16 MAY AND 29 SEPTEMBER 1364

A similar pattern can be seen in Bertrand Du Guesclin's victory at Cocherel in 1364. Though the Kings of France and England were at peace, Charles the Bad, King of Navarre, had taken up arms against the Dauphin Charles over the succession to the duchy of Burgundy, and in an attempt to threaten Paris he enlisted some of the roving bands of the Free Companies. On 15 May one of these companies, made up of English, Gascons and Navarese and led by the veteran of Poitiers, Jean de Grailly, the Captal de Buch, was confronted by the French commander at Cocherel near Mantes.[176] The Anglo-Navarese force, perhaps numbering some 700 men-at-arms, 300 archers and 500 infantry, had drawn up in a defensive position on foot on a small hill close to the town on the right bank of the River Eure, and had sent their pages and baggage into a small wood that protected their rear.[177] They were formed up into three battles, with the English men-at-arms and archers in the van under Sir John Jouel, and the Captal in command of the second battle. The Captal had his standard hoisted on a tall bush, guarded by sixty men, to act as a rallying point.[178] Du Guesclin, whose mixed force of Bretons, French and Gascons seems to have been similar or even slightly smaller in size than that of his opponents, realised it would be folly to launch a frontal attack uphill. Accordingly, he appealed to the Captal's chivalry by requesting that de Grailly would either choose another place for battle, or break three lances with him, with the winner choosing his preferred site for the ensuing engagement. Doubtless mindful of the crucial role a strong defensive position had played at Poitiers, the Captal declined to yield his ground, and early the following morning, 16 May, the French were seen to withdraw in good order towards the bridge over

the Eure. One contemporary believed that this manoeuvre was because Du Guesclin was running seriously short of supplies, but it may well have been a feint, designed to draw the Anglo-Navarese from their hill-top position.

Whatever the French commander's intention, the result was the same. Anxious not to let the French escape, the English captain John Jouel rashly led his men down the slope, heedless of the Captal's orders and his warning that this could be a ruse. Once Jouel had committed his forces to the attack, however, de Grailly could do little else but follow in support – only to see, as he had feared, Du Guesclin's army turn and reform for battle.[179] Realising their error, the Anglo-Navarese fell back and attempted to regroup, making way for their archers, who moved to the front and began to shoot strongly. But the archers were unable to make a significant impact on the French, partly due to their paucity of numbers but also to the fact that the French men-at-arms, who were also fighting on foot, were too heavily armoured and well shielded. As Froissart notes: 'And when the archers were forward, then they shot fiercely together, but the Frenchmen were so well armed and so strongly pavised that they took but little hurt, nor letted not for all that to fight, and so entered in among the Englishmen and Navarrois, and they in likewise among them, so that there was between them a cruel battle.'[180] In the fierce mêlée which ensued, the French were initially driven back with considerable loss, and the battle hung in the balance. But Du Guesclin had kept back a mounted reserve of some 200 Bretons, stationed with the baggage train, which he now committed to a flank attack.[181] The intervention of these fresh troops was decisive, and as the French men-at-arms redoubled their efforts, with cries of 'Notre

Dame! Du Guesclin!', the Anglo-Navarese line began to disintegrate, with some of the Captal's men turning in flight. John Jouel was mortally wounded, and the Captal, fighting on to the last with a war-hammer, was finally overwhelmed and taken.[182] Du Guesclin's victory at Cocherel had been the result of his caution in not attacking a strong defensive position, the ability of his force to switch effectively from withdrawal to attack in the face of an enemy onslaught – whether the move was intended or not – and his timely use of a mounted reserve.

This effective use of a supporting body of horsemen was very much in line with the French tactical thinking visible in the engagements of the 1350s, although Du Guesclin had wisely not attempted to deploy his cavalry against archers in defended positions. In all of these engagements the French cavalry had continued to play a significant role, closely analogous to that given to units of horsemen in support of dismounted men-at-arms in the Anglo-Norman period. The parallels are not coincidental: they reflect the tactical need of an army that has committed a substantial element of its force to a more solid but slow-moving dismounted formation to retain a more flexible and rapid element to create or exploit disruptions among the enemy ranks. So too the English, as we have seen, either kept a mounted reserve or remounted elements of their men-at-arms to deliver a counter-attack once the enemy had been broken by their defensive formations. While the increasing deployment of the longbow undoubtedly rendered frontal cavalry assaults dangerous if not suicidal, the continuing and sometimes successful use of cavalry by the French should dispel the long-held idea that the impact of the longbow witnessed the obsolescence of the mounted man-at-arms. Historians have long noted that by the close of the fifteenth century the use of heavy cavalry had witnessed a resurgence, which must in part be attributed to the use of the lance stop, a short bar affixed to the solid breastplate which not only allowed knights to steady their lances but also prevented a heavy cavalry lance from slipping backward when impact was made, thus allowing the delivery of a far more effective blow at the charge.[183] The use of such *arrêts*, however, was developing during the later fourteenth century, made possible by the concomitant emergence of breast defences made of one or more solid plates to which the *arrêt* could be firmly secured. Chaucer, writing his *Knight's Tale* between about 1380 and 1400, was familiar enough with the technique to note that as knights charged against each other in the tournament between Palamoun and Arcite, 'in goon the speres ful sadly in arest'.[184]

Nevertheless, even with reduced efficiency against the best armour – always in limited supply – archers showed their great value as infantry at Auray in Brittany, only a few months after Cocherel, where it was the turn of Du Guesclin to be heavily defeated. Learning that his rival Jean IV de Montfort had laid siege to the important castle and port of Auray, Charles of Blois had collected a relief army at Josselin and marched against him.[185] Du Guesclin, who because of Charles V's peace with England was fighting not in his capacity as captain general of Normandy but as one of Charles of Blois's Breton vassals, came with his retinue of around 100 lances formed from his relatives and Norman and Breton followers, with his ranks further swelled by a small number of French knights and other men-at-arms he had collected from the garrisons under his command. De Montfort had substantial English aid, including the service of the two experienced captains Sir John Chandos and Sir Robert Knollys, with around 1,000 archers and 1,800 men-at-arms, the majority of whom were veterans of the Free Companies. The English, forewarned of the French advance, took up position on a raised plateau on the right bank of the River Loche, below which the ground was marshy, and prepared for a defensive engagement. Chandos seems to have formed his ranks into three main battles, each of some 500 men-at-arms and 300–400 archers, with a reserve force under Sir Hugh Calveley, which he instructed to reinforce any part of the line that became too hard-pressed.[186] Knollys, with Walter Huet and Sir Richard Burley, commanded the first battle; the second was led by Oliver de Clisson, Eustace Aubrichecourt and Matthew Gournay; and the third by de Montfort, with 400 archers and 500 men-at-arms.[187]

By the morning of 29 September the Franco-Breton force had crossed the River Loche and formed into three main battles, with Bertrand du Guesclin in the first, the French under the Lords of Auxerre and Joni in the second, and the Bretons under Charles of Blois in the third, while a fourth unit was held in reserve.[188] The French advanced in good order, so closely formed, noted Froissart, that one could not have thrown an apple without it hitting a lance or a bascinet.[189] The men-at-arms had cut down their lances to 5 feet (1.5m) in length, and carried short axes at their sides.[190] The French van under Du Guesclin closed with that of the English under Knollys. The archers immediately began to shoot, but once again, as at Cocherel, the French men-at-arms were too well armoured and shielded for their arrows to have much effect.[191] Consequently, the archers 'who were big men and light' threw down their bows, and – in a move that was to be repeated on a much larger scale at Agincourt – attacked the French on their flanks, wrestling the axes from some of the knights and using them lustily on their former owners.[192] Charles of Blois's battle engaged that of Jean de Montfort and succeeded in driving it back, but they rallied after receiving timely aid from Calveley's reserve force. Chandos then attacked the battle of the Count of Auxerre, locked in combat with the third English battle, and under this joint onslaught it was routed. Du Guesclin's battle fought fiercely but, according to Froissart, the French were not able to keep their lines in as good order as the English and Bretons. Calveley's ability to support the English line seems also to have helped tip the balance, and the French forces eventually broke. Many of the leading French lords, including Du Guesclin himself, were captured, but the valiant Charles of Blois was slain.

The death of this intelligent and resourceful French commander marks an appropriate conclusion to a tactical analysis of the first phase of Anglo-French warfare. His military experiences against the English, spanning over twenty years from Morlaix to Auray, symbolise the French attempts to adapt their tactics effectively to counter English battle formations, but his defeats and final demise illustrate their failure to do so successfully. Whether under Charles or other French generals, the French, as we have seen, had quickly learned to dismount large elements of their men-at-arms, who by the 1350s and 1360s were becoming better armoured and better defended by shields against the penetrative power of the longbow. Cavalry nevertheless retained a key role, with elite units of the best-armoured men-at-arms, often on barded horses, aiming to outflank English positions and break up their formations of archers. Yet despite several near-run battles and some minor successes the French were consistently defeated in most of the major engagements, and had not, in tactical terms, succeeded in either restoring the military equilibrium or tilting it in their favour. This was because of a number of factors. Though they regularly deployed crossbowmen, sometimes in considerable numbers, to precede the main attacks by men-at-arms, the slow rate of shooting of the crossbow compared to the rapid shooting of the longbow meant that although they might loose a few damaging volleys such missilemen could not give their advancing troops either sufficient or sustained cover. Crucially, the French almost always assumed the offensive, which allowed the English to exploit their tactical synthesis of archers and dismounted men-at-arms to its best advantage, very often when deployed in strong defensive positions.[193] Where fear or indiscipline took hold among the English archers, as at Mauron, a flanking cavalry attack might achieve success. Yet so long as an adequate number of archers remained steady and secure behind natural or artificial defences, or had the immediate support of a body of men-at-arms, the vulnerability even of barded horses usually ensured the defeat of such cavalry assaults.

Moreover, because the efficacy of the longbow meant that the majority of their men-at-arms now fought dismounted, the French were immediately placed at a major disadvantage. Looking back at over a century of warfare the veteran French soldier Jean de Bueil remarked around the year 1450, 'Everywhere and on all occasions that foot-soldiers march against their enemy face to face, those who march lose and those who remain standing still and holding firm win.'[194] Exceptions can be found to this *dictum*, the Black Prince's victory at Nájera in 1367 being among the most prominent, but it was an acute observation. Retaining tight formation even over level terrain was extremely difficult, and well nigh impossible on broken or sloping ground in the face of volleys of enemy arrows. It is a tribute to the discipline and tenacity of the French men-at-arms that in almost every engagement they succeeded in closing with their English counterparts despite the arrow storm. Chroniclers' statements that the English were driven back 'a lance's length' may be regarded as a topos, but it is clear that in battles such as Morlaix, Poitiers and Auray the English men-at-arms were very hard-pressed, and occasionally, as at Coutances, French cohesion might prevail. But though the adoption of more effective armour during the 1340s and 1350s and the use of large shields gave the French knights increasing protection from arrows, the added weight of such equipment meant that they would often reach their opponent's lines already tired, and thus hampered in the ensuing hand-to-hand combat. As English commanders had long realised, if the French could be provoked into attacking, the natural advantages of the defensive over the offensive would help offset the numerical odds against them and give them a greater chance of victory. Their philosophy of battle was perfectly summarised by Du Guesclin's biographer Cuvelier, who has Sir John Chandos tell Jean de Montfort at Auray:

> Let them come on, and the French attack first'
> Let's hold our horses without plunging in too soon,
> For it is often the case, let me tell you,
> That he who attacks first suffers misfortune.[195]

At Cocherel, by contrast, the English had launched an uncoordinated attack and had been defeated. Yet rarely could major victories be won merely by a static defence. Northampton had badly mauled Charles of Blois's forces at Morlaix, but he lacked the manpower to counter-attack and so failed to inflict a crushing defeat on them. Dagworth's tiny force was still less able to exploit the bloody repulse of Charles de Blois at St-Pol de Léon. Crécy may thus be seen as an anomaly, for here the French suffered terrible casualties as their cavalry repeatedly dashed themselves against Edward's powerful defensive positions. It is possible that the Black Prince's division took opportunities to advance some way into the disorganised French lines, but Edward III did not order a major counter-attack. At Poitiers, by contrast, the Black Prince's mounted counter-attack delivered a decisive blow at a stage in the battle where the exhausted Anglo-Gascon army might well have suffered a reverse had they continued simply to fight on the defensive.[196] Indeed, the great strength of English tactics was their flexibility as much as their great defensive potential. Dagworth's assault at La Roche-Derrien and that of Derby at Auberoche showed an equal mastery of aggressive assault. Nowhere would this be more powerfully demonstrated than at the Black Prince's victory at Nájera, where Du Guesclin's defensive position was overwhelmed by the sustained force of the English assault.

THE BLACK PRINCE IN SPAIN: NÁJERA, 3 APRIL 1367

In 1365 Bertrand du Guesclin had led a powerful force of *routiers* across the Pyrenees, including Englishmen such as his former adversaries Sir Hugh Calveley and Matthew de Gournay, and deposed King Pedro the Cruel of Castile in favour of his illegitimate half-brother Enrique of Trastamara. This *coup d'état*, however, posed a very real threat to Edward III. Now firmly allied to Charles V, Castile not only posed a grave danger to English rule in Aquitaine, but its powerful galley fleet could wreak havoc with English convoys to and from Gascony and even to shipping in the Channel. Thus it was that in February 1367 the Black Prince led a hybrid Anglo-Gascon, Navarese and Castilian army from his duchy of Aquitaine into Spain in an attempt to restore Pedro I and in turn expel Enrique de Trastamara.[197] The strength of his army is uncertain, but was possibly between 6,000 and 8,000 men.[198] At its core were the retinues of the prince and his leading supporters, including his brother John of Gaunt, who brought a force of 400 men-at-arms and 800 archers, and some 1,600 archers summoned from England, supplemented by Gascon lords and several bodies of men raised by Sir John Chandos from the Free Companies.[199] The prince's attempt to outflank Enrique's position at Zaldiaran by a hard march north-west through the rugged terrain of Alava was frustrated by the Castilian ruler, who, on the advice of Du Guesclin and other French commanders, as yet refused open battle and instead harried the English forces with his light cavalry known as *jinetes*.[200] A night assault on the English camp by these horsemen under Enrique's brother Don Tello and the French marshal Arnoul d'Audrehem was successful and resulted in considerable Anglo-Gascon casualties. Withdrawing from this position, the Black Prince crossed the Ebro at Logrono with the intention of marching directly on the capital Burgos, but he was met by Enrique who barred his crossing of the River Najerilla at the town of Nájera (also known as Navarette).[201] Instead of merely blocking the prince's path, however, and exacerbating his mounting logistical difficulties, Enrique chose to cross the Najerilla and fight him in the open field, stung by a mutual exchange of challenges and the fear that his wavering political support would melt away if decisive action was not quickly taken. As at Crécy, the dictates of honour and political support gained sway over military pragmatism. Nevertheless, Enrique attempted to gain some defensive benefit, choosing a site close to the village of Aleson where the enemy's direct approach would lead them to the River Yalde, swollen by the spring rains and deep enough to offer a significant obstacle to dismounted

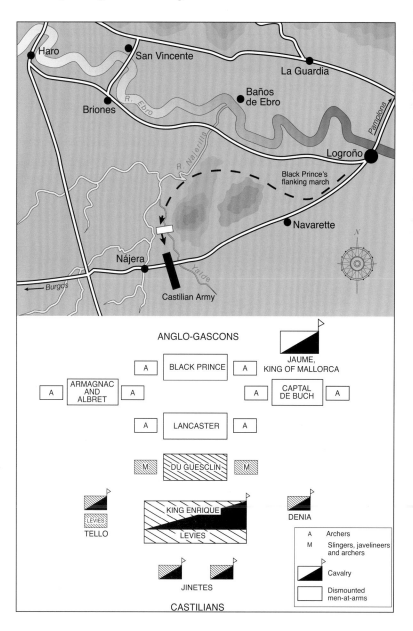

(*Above*) the location of the battle of Nájera, showing the Black Prince's flanking manoeuvre. (*Below*) a schematic plan of the opposing forces at Nájera. (Note: the positioning of the archers is conjectural, save for those in Lancaster's division.)

men-at-arms.[202] According to the account of Pero Lopez de Ayala, who fought in the battle as Enrique's standard bearer, the Castilians had 4,500 lances and a large but unspecified number of light cavalry and infantry.[203]

The plan of battle, employing a powerful vanguard, seems to have reflected French practice, particularly Du Guesclin's earlier experiences at Auray. In this vanguard Enrique placed Du Guesclin, Audrehem and his French and Aragonese mercenaries, together with the Castilian knights belonging to the Order of the Band, an elite force upon which Edward III's own Order of the Garter had in part been modelled. They were to fight on foot and were supported by crossbowmen, slingers and javelineers, though it seems the quality of these missilemen, drawn from Castilian levies, was not high.[204] By contrast, the force of Andalusian *jinetes* under Don Tello who formed the left wing had already shown their potential. The Castilian right wing comprised the brother knights of the Orders of Calatrava and Santiago, and Aragonese knights under Alfonso de Villena, Count of Denia.[205] Enrique himself commanded the main battle, formed of Castilians and some Aragonese, together with a large body of levies.

The prince and his advisers, realising the strength of the Castilian position, decided on a bold flanking manoeuvre. Under cover of darkness they mounted and struck off to their right, swinging round behind a long ridge known as the Hill of Cuento, which hid their advance from Enrique's scouts, and at dawn they emerged on the Castilian left flank, dismounting to form up and attack. The prince's deployment mirrored that

which the army had adopted from the outset of its march.[206] The van, led by Lancaster and Chandos together with the two marshals of Aquitaine, Stephen de Cosington and Guichard d'Angle, was formed predominantly of English men-at-arms and archers. The prince took the centre with his personal retinue, troops from Gascony, Pedro with those Castilian men-at-arms who still supported him, a detachment of Navarese men-at-arms, and squadrons drawn from the Free Companies. Two wings were formed primarily by Gascons; on the right were Gascon lords under the sire d'Albret and the Count of Armagnac, while on the left, under the Captal de Buch, were men of the Count of Foix and others of the Free Companies. The strength of the prince's army by the time of the battle is unknown, but Russell plausibly estimates that the direct approach from their camp at Navarette would be restricted and drawing up his army behind a stream, contained some 3,000 men, the prince's division around 4,000, and the two wings some 2,000 men each.[207]

Even before the engagement began, the rapid defection of some Castilian levies and units of *jinetes* to the forces of Pedro and the Black Prince showed how uncertain was the support for Enrique. But notwithstanding the fact that his position had been turned, Du Guesclin wheeled his own van round and launched a fierce attack on Lancaster's oncoming division, driving the English back a little before they rallied.[208] There was hard fighting between the experienced men-at-arms on both sides, and 'many held their spears in both their hands, foining and pressing at each other, and some fought with short swords and daggers'.[209] At one stage Chandos was pinned to the

A stylised depiction of the battle of Nájera, 1367, from a late fifteenth-century Flemish manuscript of Froissart's *Chronicles* (Paris, Bibliothèque Nationale, MS fr. 2643, f.312v). The Black Prince, in a helmet adorned with ostrich feathers, and his men-at-arms are shown as mounted, rather than on foot, but an attempt has been made to represent the Castilian slingers and javelineers, who proved no match for the English archers. *(Bibliothèque Nationale, Paris/Bridgeman Art Library)*

ground by an enormous Castilian knight, Martin Fernandez, who attempted to stab him through his visor, but Chandos managed to draw the dagger at his side and slew his assailant.[210] 'The archers volleyed thicker than ever rain fell,' noted Chandos Herald, while the Castilian crossbowmen returned their volleys.[211] That the archers were able to keep up their shooting as the men-at-arms clashed together suggests that they were positioned on the flanks of the English van in positions where they could readily avoid close contact with the French men-at-arms. For unlike in the majority of earlier battles, the English forces were deployed on the offensive, and hence the archers could not protect themselves by the usual means of pits, ditches or hedges. Realising this, Enrique attempted to exploit their vulnerability by sending against them his left wing, comprising the powerful body of light horse under his brother Don Tello, supported by infantry levies. But the archers shot so effectively against the lightly armoured *jinetes* that they abandoned the field and Don Tello fled. The Gascons of the prince's right wing, advancing to close up with Lancaster's men, soon dispatched the unsupported Castilian levies and now attacked Du Guesclin's force from the flank and rear.

The prince's battle engaged the Spanish right wing which, also attacked from the flank by the Gascons under the Captal de Buch, was soon in grave difficulties. Now only the main Castilian battle under Enrique himself remained. The large body of crossbowmen and slingers in this unit seems to have had some initial effect against the prince's main battle as the two divisions closed; according to Froissart, 'the Spaniards and Castilians had slings, with which they hurled stones in such a way that they clove in and broke many a bascinet and helmet and injured many men, and cast them to the ground'. But it was not long before they were driven off by the intense shooting of the English archers, who 'shot fiercely and hurt the Spaniards grievously and brought them to great mischief'.[212] For 'when their cast was past and they felt the sharp arrows light among them, they could no longer keep their array'.[213] Enrique himself attempted to lead a charge of the Castilian armoured cavalry, but the horsemen, seeing how the archers were taking a heavy toll of their horses, refused to ride further into the lethal zone created by their arrow shot.[214] By now the French and the knights of the Order of the Band had been overwhelmed, with many captured, including Du Guesclin and Audrehem. Lancaster's division could thus join the prince's forces in an all-out attack on the Castilian centre which disintegrated under their combined assault, despite Enrique's

repeated efforts to rally his men. The Castilians turned in headlong flight towards the bridge at Nájera, their discomfiture completed by a fierce pursuit headed by the prince's small mounted reserve under King Jaume of Mallorca. Many were slain fighting around the bridge, and others drowned in their attempt to cross the swollen River Najerilla, but Enrique managed to make good his escape and fled to Aragon.

The battle of Nájera set the seal on the Black Prince's reputation as an outstanding commander. Whereas at Poitiers he had launched a successful counter-attack only in the last stages of the battle, at Nájera the prince took the offensive from the outset and fully demonstrated the effectiveness of his men-at-arms and archers in such a deployment. It also illustrates the continuity of French tactical thinking, for, as at Auray in 1364, Du Guesclin had placed his hopes on a powerful vanguard of dismounted knights, supported by missilemen and flanking cavalry. But the Castilian crossbowmen, slingers and *jinetes* were simply unable to match the powerful shooting of the prince's longbowmen, while they, by contrast, wreaked havoc among Enrique's heavy cavalry. Nevertheless, despite the brilliance of the prince's victory, Nájera is an outstanding example of a tactical triumph yielding few if any long-term gains. Whereas the capture of King Jean at Poitiers had had enormous ramifications, Enrique of Trastamara was neither killed nor captured but survived to overthrow Pedro after his brief restoration to power – then to murder him with his own hand at Montiel in 1369. Worse still for the English, Pedro had defaulted on the massive sums he owed to the Black Prince, leaving the latter with a heavy debt which had severe repercussions on the political stability of Aquitaine. Attempts to raise funds to pay off his men led to an appeal by disgruntled Gascon lords to Charles V against the prince's taxation and heavy-handed rule, which in turn sparked off a renewal of the Anglo-French war in 1369. Yet at this time of crisis the English were robbed of the outstanding military leadership they had enjoyed in the 1340s and 1350s. Edward III was by now in his dotage, while the debilitating illness which the Black Prince had contracted on his Spanish expedition left him unable to wield effective military or political command, and led to his premature death in 1376, one year before that of his father. As the great Tudor historian Samuel Daniel gloomily noted, Edward III went to his grave 'hauing seene all his great gettings, purchased with so much expence, trauaille and blood-shed, rent cleane from him'.[215]

Matthew Strickland

CHAPTER 14

Reverberations: the Impact of the Longbow, 1360–1403

The years between the outbreak of the Hundred Years War in 1337 and the Treaty of Brétigny in 1360 had witnessed the first high water mark of English arms, as the tactical techniques develped against the Scots in the early 1330s were applied with devastating success against French armies. The resulting defeats had forced French commanders to respond with their own tactical innovation or adaptation, and by limited reform of military structures, though with little immediate success. In stark contrast, the three decades from the renewal of the war in 1369 to Richard II's conclusion of a 28-year truce with France in 1396 were marked for the English by failed strategy, defeat and the loss of much of their territorial gains. It is small wonder that there is a tendency in some older military histories to pass quickly over this 'dreary tale of ineptitude and failure'[1] and hasten to the study of Henry V's great triumph at Agincourt in 1415. Burne disparagingly dismissed the campaigns between 1369 and 1396 as 'the Duguesclin sub-war', in which, he noted with evident disappointment, 'nothing worthy of the name of battle was fought', and that therefore 'the war is thus rather lacking in military interest, for there was remarkably little actual fighting'.[2] Yet for a study of the longbow the period between Brétigny and Henry V's renewal of the French war is of considerable significance, for it witnessed the ripple effect of English tactical influence on contemporary warfare not only in France but well beyond. In France, the able Charles V not only developed a highly effective strategy which avoided major engagements in the field against the English but also created a standing army and even, in emulation of the English, attempted to enforce on his own subjects universal archery practice. At the very time, moreover, when English fortunes were at a low ebb in France, the impact of the victories of Edward III and his commanders was becoming manifest, whether directly through the active involvement of English forces or by emulation, in both the Iberian peninsula and in Italy. In these lands the effects of this 'military diaspora' were to be limited in extent and duration, but they anticipate the more extended influence of English organisation and tactics on Burgundian, Scottish and French military thinking in the decades following Agincourt.

Any discussion of such influence must begin by the acknowledgement that while it is useful shorthand (and is retained as such) to speak simply of 'English' tactics during the Hundred Years War, it is misleading in that it fails to recognise the important role played by Edward's continental subjects and allies in the campaigns and battles of the war. Edward III's employment of Hainaulter men-at-arms, of which Sir Walter Mauny was but the most famous, must have helped further disseminate English military influence, while in Brittany English troops had fought alongside both their Montfortian allies as well as the Navarese troops of Charles the Bad in the near-constant warfare which wracked that unhappy duchy. The victory of Jean de Montfort at Auray in 1364 over his long-standing rival Charles of Blois was in reality won by the veteran English knights Sir John Chandos and Sir Hugh Calveley. Yet within France itself, those most rapidly and profoundly affected by the impact of Edward's tactical deployments were his own Gascon subjects, for Gascony, which had been the ultimate *causus belli*, not only played a crucial role in Edward III's strategic thinking, but also supplied him with large numbers of men-at-arms and troops. Campaigns such those of the Black Prince in 1355 and 1356 in France, and his 1367 expedition to Spain, were conducted by Anglo-Gascon armies, with Gascon commanders such as Jean de Grailly, the Captal de Buch, playing key roles. The nobility of a large area of south-west France thus played an integral part in the King of England's military ventures, and, while having a distinctive organisation, shared in the tactical thinking that characterised the deployment of his armies in the field.[3]

That the impact of English tactical thinking might spread beyond the king's Gascon vassals is strikingly illustrated by the battle of Launac, fought on 5 December 1362 a little to the north-west of Toulouse, in which the forces of Gaston Phébus, Count of Foix, inflicted a crushing defeat on the numerically more powerful army of his local rival Jean I, Count of Armagnac. Armagnac possessed few infantry but a superior force of heavy cavalry drawn from many of the nobility of Gascony, while Foix crucially had a significant number of archers among his troops, which included a number of the Free Companies. Armagnac, who clearly had profited little from the military lessons of the preceding twenty years, immediately threw his cavalry into a frontal attack on Foix's defensive positions. The centre of Phébus's line held the onslaught, however, and meanwhile he sent his archers under cover of a copse to encircle and attack Armagnac's cavalry from the rear. Their volleys of arrows rapidly threw the mounted knights into confusion, and in the ensuing rout Armagnac and many of his nobles were captured. Their subsequent ransoms furnished the Count of Foix with a vast sum of at least 600,000 florins or 2,124kg of gold. It was little wonder that Phébus had murals of his victory painted in the great hall of his castle at Orthez and continued to celebrate the anniversary of the battle throughout his lands as a great feast day.[4] The Count of Foix's flanking attack clearly echoed that which his fellow Gascon, the Captal de Buch, had launched at Poitiers, and at least one of the companies in his service in 1362 was led by an Englishman, John Amory.[5] Nevertheless, the Count of Foix was not simply reliant on English bowmen, for he had raised a select force of well-trained archers from within his own lands – a telling instance of what might have been achieved by the French monarchy on a wider scale.[6]

Amory's presence at Launac suggests that at least some of the Free Companies played a significant role as a conduit for the wider dissemination of the tactical combination of dismounted men-at-arms and archers. The Treaty of Brétigny in 1360 had brought a period of peace between the crowns of England and France, but there were many for whom peace meant a loss of their livelihood, and for whom a return home might mean only poverty and unemployment. In Froissart's words, such professional soldiers who had profited from regular wages and booty 'could not live without war and did not know how to'.[7] So it was that after the demobilisation of the kings' armies, many old soldiers remained in France, banding together in companies and living by pillage and extortion, holding the countryside to ransom.[8] The Free Companies added to the miseries of a land already weakened by the ravages of war, but also formed a reservoir of skilled veterans, whether fighting as men-at-arms, archers or other kinds of troops, who were readily employed by lords pursuing their own local quarrels and by foreign rulers. After plundering at will in France, one of the largest bands, known as the Great Company, marched down the Rhone Valley, seized the Pont-Saint-Esprit and held the Pope at Avignon to ransom. The Great Company, which already contained several English captains, split up in 1362.[9] Some of 'these villains commonly called English' ravaged the Rhineland, while the largest unit, known as the White Company, commanded by the German Albert Sterz but with a number of English among his lieutenants, entered Italy in the service of the Marquis of Monferrat.[10] Other bands of the Free Companies continued to terrorise central France, and at Brignais in 1362 they defeated a French royal army sent to destroy the menace of these *routiers*. Though it seems likely that they were concentrated under English or Anglo-Gascon captains, it is difficult to know how many longbowmen were serving in the Great Company and its constituent bands; in many of the Companies men-at-arms were predominant, as in contemporary French armies, and many of their supporting infantry were crossbowmen. In 1368, for example, the force Bertrand Du Guesclin proposed to lead to Sardinia comprised 1,200 lances but only 400 missilemen, while the 1,000 infantry to be supplied by Charles V were to be crossbowmen and pavise-bearers.[11] Certainly at Brignais no mention is made of archers despite the presence of Englishmen such as John Hawkwood, Robert Birkhead and John Cresswell.[12] The Companies lured the French army into a frontal assault up a wooded slope against their centre, which had been made to look deceptively weak, then hit them with a major flank attack and an encirclement from the higher ground. In terms of missiles, however, the men of the Companies seemingly could only resort to throwing stones down upon the attacking

French, albeit with considerable effect, for they had collected many cart loads of flints for this purpose.[13] As we have seen, men of the Companies fought on both sides at Cocherel and Auray in 1364, when the renewed conflict between Charles of Navarre and the new French monarch Charles V and the resumption of the war over the succession to Brittany gave the Free Companies fresh employment. Longbowmen may well have served with Sir Hugh Calveley in Spain, first alongside Du Guesclin, then against him as part of the Black Prince's expedition that culminated in the battle of Nájera, but details as to their numbers or their manner of deployment in the hybrid forces of the Companies are few.[14] With the operations of Sir John Hawkwood, however, and the White Company in Italy, the role of archers comes into clearer focus.

SIR JOHN HAWKWOOD AND THE LONGBOW IN LATER FOURTEENTH-CENTURY ITALY

Hawkwood, the second son of an Essex tanner, served in the Anglo-French wars, possibly in the retinue of the Earl of Oxford, but by May 1360 he appears as a member of the Free Companies besieging Avignon, and in 1361 is found as the marshal to one of the Companies commanded by the English captain Walter Hoo.[15] These loose confederations of mercenaries repeatedly formed and reformed under different names and captains, and when, after a period of fighting in the service of Pisa, the White Company split up in 1364 Hawkwood led off one of its constituent groups under the same name.[16] Though the White Company was all but destroyed by the German Company under Bongarten between Arezzo and Cortona, Hawkwood was soon able to raise a new Company, that of St George, which in turn disbanded after suffering defeat in 1367.[17] Yet Hawkwood was never short of fresh volunteers. As the chronicler Matteo Villani noted in 1363, 'these English were all lusty young men, most of them born and brought up in the long wars between England and France; warm, eager and practised in rapine and slaughter . . . with very little care for their personal safety but in matters of discipline very obedient to their commanders'.[18] Such men,

like Hawkwood himself, were attracted by good wages, rich pickings in booty and, perhaps equally important, a far greater independence than was possible in the more rigid social hierarchy of England. Though there was a well-established command structure among the Companies, leaders were elected, conditions of service were favourable, and there was a higher degree of consultation and debate among the soldiery, who could otherwise express their dissatisfaction simply by leaving for another Company.[19] Contract service in an English captain's retinue in the Anglo-French wars had been appealing, but that in Hawkwood's Company must have been still more so. If Terry Jones is right in his intriguing suggestion that Chaucer's Knight represents a travel-worn mercenary, not the epitome but rather the antithesis of the chivalric ideal, then Chaucer's exquisitely ambiguous pen has drawn an unforgettable portrait of the kind of man-at-arms, with his squire and his archer, who would have fought for Sir John under the Tuscan and Romagnol sun.[20]

The longbow cannot have been completely unknown in the Italian peninsula before the advent of the White Company south of the Alps in 1361. An intriguing mural of about 1340

Archers and infantry in combat, from a fresco of the Tuscan school: *c.* 1340, in the Camera della Guardie, Castello di Avio, near Verona. *(Castello Avio/Scala)*

in the castle of Sabbionara at Avio in Lombardy, which represents a battle between Guelphs and Ghibellines, contains a force of archers among the Guelph infantry who draw long weapons. The pro-papal Guelphs, however, were the enemies of the Ghibelline or pro-imperial patrons of the work, the Castelbarco family, and both the costumes and the weapons of these archers have been deliberately 'orientalised' by giving the men highly exotic headdresses and the bows greatly exaggerated recurving tips, in order to suggest a sinister eastern provenance for these troops.[21] Whatever type of bow the artist intended to portray, however, the predominant missile weapon in Italian warfare continued to be the crossbow, employed not only by elite mercenaries such as the ubiquitous Genoese but also by the communal militias which formed the bulk of troops raised by the endlessly warring city states. In 1231, for example, Siena had in its pay 400 Genoese crossbowmen and probably another 300 from the area around Spoleto.[22] Crossbowmen (balestrieri) predominate among infantry forces included in late thirteenth-century condotte, or contracts for mercenary service, from Bologna, with the city undertaking to supply bolts.[23] Of the 6,000 infantry deployed by Florence at the siege of Pistoia in 1302, 1,000 were foreign stipendiaries, but most of the remaining 5,000 were crossbowmen and shield-bearers from the city's urban and rural militias. The crossbowmen of Florence had played a major role in the victory over the Ghibelline forces of Arezzo at Campaldino in 1289, and later in the ambush and defeat of the German and Hungarian cavalry of the Great Company at Le Scalelle in 1358.[24] In 1356 Florence had been able to field an impressive 4,000 crossbowmen from its militia, the bulk of whom came from its contado or rural hinterland, while in 1378 the Italian peasant uprising in Florence known as the Ciompi had levied a force of 1,000 crossbowmen to secure its position in power.[25] Crossbowmen also formed part of Siena's militia, with 100 being drawn from each of the city's three districts or terzi; they were normally paid 20 soldi each per month. Not only did they guard the city, but these units, each under a centurione, fought in the field against Hawkwood in 1375 and in subsequent engagements against the Companies.[26]

Archers also served in Italian armies, though to a more limited extent. In 1270 archers were among the small group of berrovieri, or men under the command of the podestà, entrusted with policing Sienese territory. The Libro di Montaperti, which provides a partial record of Florentine troops raised for the great battle at Montaperti in 1260, suggests that the city could field 1,000 crossbowmen and perhaps as many archers. Such troops, like the city's other infantry and cavalry forces, were raised from Florence's six regions or Sesti, each with a designated area of manpower from the contado. The number of Sesti sending troops to the army varied, depending on the importance and duration of the campaign, but within the forces of each Sesto units of crossbowmen and archers were kept distinct, serving under their own banners, whereas the other foot-soldiers were organised in regional companies (popoli) grouped in units of 25.[27] After the intervention of King Lewis of Hungary against Naples in 1347 many of his Hungarian light cavalry, armed in the eastern manner with composite bows and lances, stayed on in the peninsula after the king's return home and served for several years as mercenaries there.[28] The evidence of iconography strongly suggests that the great majority of native Italian archers were also using composite bows which, as we have noted, had been long deployed in the Italian peninsula.[29] While the influence of classical models in the art of the trecento and quatrocento was naturally strong, the fact that artists such as Signorelli, Pisanello, Polliauolo and Carpaccio depict contemporary crossbows in great detail, capable of corroboration with extant weapons, suggests that they applied the same accuracy of observation to the composite weapons they depicted. Certainly, Italian contemporaries, familiar with the crossbow and composite bow, were struck by the great bows bent by the English. As the chronicler Pietro Azario noted, 'the foot-soldiers have big and powerful bows that reach from their heads to the ground, and being drawn, shoot great long arrows'.[30] Similarly, Matteo Villani noted of the English that 'others of them were archers, and their bows were of yew, and long, and with them they were prepared and well trained, and made a good showing with them'.[31]

A combination of the power of their weapons and their skill in shooting made the services of English archers highly prized by Italian states. The military contractors for Lucca in 1379 insisted that all the archers should be English, 'good and valiant men' (inghelise, boni et valenti homini) well skilled in the use of the longbow.[32] They were also well equipped. In 1368 the Florentines expected English archers in Hawkwood's service to have a helmet (cappellino) or bascinet and a mail coat (panciera) or breastplate (cuirasse), gloves of mail, and a sword, dagger, bow and arrows.[33] We would like to know more about how these archers replenished their supplies of bows and arrows. In 1365 Cardinal Albornoz and the Neapolitans attempted to buy off the White Company for six months with a promise of 160,000 florins and 100 English bows, suggesting that weapons finished in England (though possibly of imported yew) were being widely exported.[34] Certainly the fourteenth century witnessed a flourishing arms trade from Milan and north Italy to Europe and Britain, and it is probable that the same merchants who exported fine Italian armour north of the Alps might bring back supplies of longbows and arrows to sell to the compagnie degli inglesi.[35] But it is possible that some finished weapons could be obtained in Italy. In 1390 the Signoria of Florence made a gift to Hawkwood of 100 good bows, noting that 'we will send to Lucca for the best kind of bows, for they are not good here'.[36] Not only was the longbow a more powerful weapon than the composite bow, but the English Companies had a greater ratio of archers to their men-at-arms than those of other mercenary Companies. Thus, for example, the 'Grand Company' led by the Provençal captain Walter of Montreal, known as Fra Moriale, was composed among others of Germans, Italians, Catalans and French mercenaries but contained only 2,000 crossbowmen to 7,000 men-at-arms.[37] By contrast, at the battle of Castagnaro in 1387 Hawkwood's own force consisted of 500 men-at-arms and 600 mounted English archers. When in 1379 Lucca sought to recruit eighteen 'lances' of English troops, each consisting of one knight, a man-at-arms and a page, the English suggested that a brigade of twenty lances was preferable, and requested that an additional archer should be included in each lance.[38]

The monument to Sir John Hawkwood by Ucello in the Cathedral, Florence, 1436. (Florence Cathedral © 2002, Foto Scala Florence).

The presence of English longbowmen was not the only distinguishing feature of the White Company and subsequent English units. The Catalan, German, Provençal and Italian men-at-arms who fought as stipendiaries, whether directly for cities like Florence or as part of the great mercenary bands such as the Company of St George or the Great Company, had invariably been hired as heavily armed cavalry and fought as such. By contrast, the men-at-arms of the White Company fought, like those in Edward III's armies, predominantly on foot. Nevertheless, their manner of fighting was distinctive, for they gave greater emphasis to the offensive qualities of the heavy cavalry lance. French men-at-arms had used their lances on foot at battles such as Poitiers, as had the Austrians at Laupen and later at Sempach, but on these occasions they had cut their weapons down to make them easier to wield on foot.[39] The men of the White Company seem to have favoured the greater reach of the longer lance employed like a pike, relying on the greater impetus of a weapon handled by two men in close formation. While their pages held their horses in readiness for a possible pursuit, the men-at-arms advanced in tight formation, with two or even three men holding one lance, while archers formed the rear ranks.[40] As far as is known, this technique was not employed by the English in the Anglo-French wars, but it must surely have been developed from experience born of the frequent close combat between men-at-arms in which cohesion, discipline and impetus were crucial factors in tilting the fortunes of the mêlée. The name White Company, moreover, came from their habit of keeping their armour gleaming, as Villani noted:

> For armour, almost all of them wore mailshirts (*pancerones*), and in front of the breast heart-pieces of steel (*un'anima d'aciaio*), arm, thigh and leg-pieces (*braccaiali di ferro, cosciali e gamberuoli*), daggers and sharpened swords, all with lances in position, which they willingly used dismounted, and each of them had one or two pages, some more, depending on how powerful they were. When they removed their armour, these pages kept it so polished that when they appeared at a skirmish, their arms resembled mirrors, making them all the more frightening.[41]

Pietro Azario, however, believed that many chose to be much more lightly armed: 'For their custom is, when it is necessary to fight in the open, to dismount from their horses. Many of them are armed only in a thick doublet (*sola diploide armati*) and either have a single iron plate upon their chests (*placa una ferrea supra pectus*) and, as many do, leave their heads uncovered, or else they wear only a small barbuta (*cupo barbute*) and [carry] great lances.'[42]

English troops gained a reputation not only for combat, but for their versatility and endurance in campaigning in winter and for effectively executed marches at night, 'a thing', noted Villani, 'unusual even among the Romans'.[43] Hawkwood himself executed a number of brilliant withdrawals in difficult conditions, not only before Castagnaro in 1387, but still more famously in 1391 in the same area, when he rescued his army from Milanese attack through the flooded countryside bordering the Adige.[44] The English, and the other foreign troops who were sometimes lumped together under the title '*inglesi*', were also feared for their rapacity and ruthlessness. As the contemporary saying ran, '*Inglese italianato e un diavolo incarnato*' – an Englishman become an Italian is a devil incarnate. Nevertheless, their impact on the tactics used in the unremitting warfare between the rival Italian city states was limited by their comparatively small numbers and the resulting need often to fight as part of larger forces accustomed to their own methods of fighting. In 1387, for example, Hawkwood commanded only 600 English bowmen. Yet the eagerness with which the Italian states sought to employ them suggests their military value far outweighed their relatively scant numbers. Nowhere was this better demonstrated than by Hawkwood's most famous victory at Castagnaro on 11 March 1387, a battle which reveals not only the influence of the English tactics developed under Edward III, but also the way in which these might be adapted to suit the armies available in Italy.[45]

In 1387 Hawkwood was a veteran, well advanced in years and so closely established in the affairs of the Italian states that he had married the daughter of Bernabo Visconti, Lord of Milan. Though still in the service of Florence, which he had entered in early 1380, he had been permitted by the Florentines to assist the ruler of Padua, Francesco Carrara the Elder, who was conducting a war against the Della Scalla of Verona. An unsuccessful blockade of Verona by the Paduan army from February to early March had to be abandoned because of effective enemy disruption of their over-extended supply lines, but Hawkwood conducted a masterly withdrawal of his forces while hotly pursued by the Veronese under the command of Giovanni dei Ordelaffi. Hawkwood's initial aim had been to fall back to his supply base at Castelbaldo on the Adige, but instead, on 10 March, he stopped at Castagnaro, a few miles from his destination. Just as Edward III had lured his pursuers into attacking a heavily defended position at Crécy, and the Black Prince had similarly stood at bay to fight the French at Poitiers, so Hawkwood decided to fight a rearguard action against his own pursuers, thereby giving himself an element of surprise. It is possible that he had been present at both these earlier battles,[46] but even if he had not he and his men must have been familiar with the tactics of Edward III and

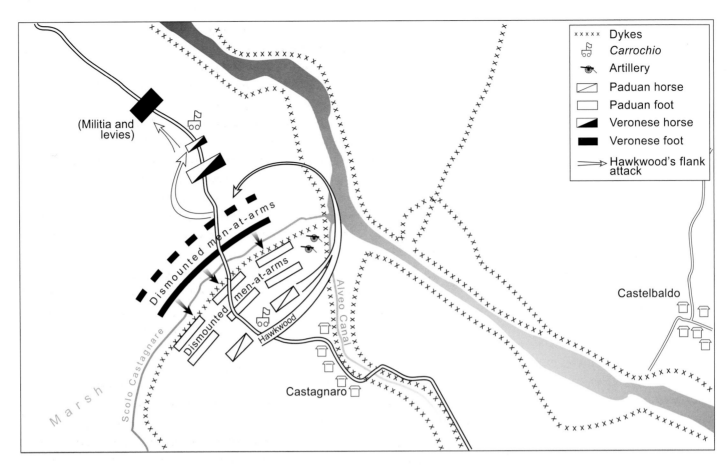

The battle of Castagnaro, 11 March 1387 (after D. Nicolle, *Medieval Italian Armies* (1983)).

his eldest son, and as events would soon reveal Hawkwood had studied the Black Prince's victory at Poitiers with care.

As day dawned on 11 March it became clear how well Hawkwood had chosen his ground; though there was no rising ground as at Crécy, nor dense hedges as at Poitiers, the area was criss-crossed with drainage ditches, offering ready-made and effective defences, while the low-lying ground was heavy and sodden with the winter rains. He drew up his front along a large drainage ditch, protected to the left by a swamp and to the right by a canal linking the Adige with the Tartaro. In addition to his own force of 500 English men-at-arms and 600 mounted archers, he commanded 6,400 men-at-arms raised by other captains and an additional 1,000 infantry.[47] The dispositions of the army reflected a mixture of English and Italian practice. Instead of the usual three 'battles', there were two lines of dismounted men-at-arms, each divided into three 'battles'. In the third line was the *carrochio* of Padua, a mobile wagon carrying the city's banners and religious images which acted as a rallying point for the army, and on either side were two units of mounted men-at-arms and Hawkwood's personal retinue. He retained his 600 mounted English archers with him as a strike force, while along the bank of the canal to his right

he placed his crossbowmen, protected by their great pavises which in effect formed a palisade, and his few pieces of ordnance.

Faced with Hawkwood's strong position, Ordelaffi drew up his forces, consisting of about 9,000 men-at-arms, 1,000 infantry and 1,600 crossbowmen and archers, together with a large force of local militia and peasants. Keeping a strong mounted reserve, he deployed the majority of his men-at-arms on foot in two lines, with the militias to the rear behind the Veronese *carrochio*. As Hawkwood had expected, the Veronese launched a frontal assault by their dismounted men-at-arms, for the ditches made a direct cavalry attack impossible. By heaping fascines into the irrigation canal, the Veronese managed to establish a foothold on the opposite bank, but all the while they had suffered from an enfilading barrage from the Paduan crossbowmen and gunners. The Paduan men-at-arms succeeded in holding their front, though the commitment by Ordelaffi of his second line put great pressure on them and they slowly gave ground. Meanwhile, however, Hawkwood was executing a bold flanking manoeuvre with his mounted English detachments. Racing along his right flank, positioned on the canal and probably unseen behind its banks, he crossed the canal with ease at some point discovered in his previous reconnoitring, and swung round to launch his horsemen in an attack on the Veronese rear. This tactic has such a close parallel with the Captal de Buch's famous flanking move at Poitiers that it is tempting to see a direct emulation here. Hawkwood's archers, and other missilemen that he had ordered to follow him from the right flank, supported their horsemen with a withering barrage of arrows, while in a pre-arranged manoeuvre his second-in-command Giovanni d'Azzo degli Ubaldini led the main battles of the Paduan army into the attack. The Veronese lines, attacked from two sides, began to crumble, and the press to the rear effectively hampered an attempt by Ordelaffi to launch his reserve cavalry into a counter-attack. In a *coup de grâce* Hawkwood turned from the smashed left wing of the Veronese positions to seize the enemy *carrochio* – a final blow to Veronese morale – and to scatter their levies in headlong flight, while Ubaldini pressed home the advantage by committing his own mounted reserves to the pursuit.[48]

It has been rightly noted that while Castagnaro revealed striking tactical similarities to English victories in France, it avoided their terrible death tolls among the defeated. This may be explained in part by the relatively small numbers of longbow-men available to Hawkwood, in part by the pragmatic recognition of defeat by the Veronese, and in part by the differing political circumstances from the English war aims of the 1340s and 1350s. While some 716 were slain (many of these being among a brave band of levies who had refused to abandon their revered *carrochio*) and 846 wounded, many more were taken prisoner. These included Ordelaffi and many of his captains, around 4,600 men-at-arms and 800 infantry.[49] Casualties among Hawkwood's army were estimated at around 700.

Hawkwood's victory at Castagnaro has been described as 'a triumph of his old age'.[50] In 1390 he became Captain-General of all of Florence's forces, and soon after at Bologna he defeated his long-standing rival Jacopo Dal Verme, who led the forces of Milan. On his death in 1394 Hawkwood was accorded the honour of burial in the Duomo of Florence – ironically something denied to Dante – but at the request of Richard II his remains were returned the following year for interment in the church of his native Sibil Hedingham in Essex. As a result the proposed tomb in the Duomo was never built, but in 1436 the memorial fresco painted at his death by Taddeo Gaddi and Giuliano d'Arrigo was replaced by the famous fresco by Paulo Uccello.[51] One wonders what became of Hawkwood's fellow Englishmen, men-at-arms and archers alike, who had served in the Companies under his command. Some, perhaps, returned home rich in memories and perhaps also in booty, but others may have settled and married locally, as was later to happen with a number of Scots serving in France from 1419 onwards.

By the time of Hawkwood's death the flood into Italy of English lances and bows for hire was drying up, and with the accession of Henry V in 1413 there would soon be fresh opportunities for employment in northern France. And whereas the majority of Companies in the period from the 1340s to the 1380s had been formed from foreigners, the last decades of the century witnessed the increase of native Italian *condottiere* such as Alberigo da Barbiano and his Company of St George.[52] Warfare in fifteenth-century Italy would be dominated by heavy cavalry, supported by infantry whose principal missile weapon remained the crossbow, a combination vividly depicted in Uccello's famous series of paintings of the Rout of San Romano. It has also been suggested that the composite bow gained a new lease of life as a result of 'the influence of newer, post-Mongol forms of oriental-style composite bows on such trading states as Venice and Genoa'.[53] In such Italian armies, moreover, cavalry usually greatly outnumbered infantry, the latter containing not only crossbowmen but spearmen, pavise-bearers and, increasingly, hand-gunners.[54] From the 1440s and 1450s companies of hand-gunners or *schoppettieri* become increasingly prominent in the armies of city states such as Venice and Milan, and the militia of the latter city adopted hand-guns in 1449.[55] With the disappearance of the English Companies, their influence on military thinking in the peninsula, which had always been limited by their small numbers and the hybrid nature of the forces available to city states, soon faded. Their fleeting impact may perhaps be reflected in a fine late fourteenth-century mural in the Valeri chapel in the cathedral at Parma, which depicts scenes from the life and martyrdom of St Christopher. In this, archers drawing powerful longbows shoot at the bound saint, only for their arrows to ricochet harmlessly off.

'THE WAY OF PORTUGAL': ALJUBAROTTA, 14 AUGUST 1385

In marked contrast to Italy, English tactics seem to have exerted a direct influence on the Portuguese conduct of war against their Castilian opponents during the 1380s, culminating in the great battle of Aljubarotta. In 1381, in an attempt to counter the damaging alliance of Castile and France, an English expeditionary force had been sent to assist King Ferdinand I of Portugal, led by Edmund of Langley, Earl of Cambridge, Sir William Beauchamp, who had served on the Nájera campaign, and the veteran captain Matthew Gournay, who had campaigned in Brittany, Gascony and with the Free Companies under Calveley in Spain.[56] The expedition itself was a fiasco; frustrated by Ferdinand's temporising, a lack of decisive action and poor leadership by Langley, mutiny broke out and the English returned ignominiously in 1382.[57] But the presence of the English had at least allowed the talented young Portuguese nobleman Nun'Alvares Pereira the opportunity to discuss tactical and organisational matters with the English captains. In 1384, although aged only 24, Nun'Alvares was made *condestabre* or commander-in-chief of the Portuguese army, to lead the kingdom's defence against a Castilian invasion, and on 6 April 1384 at Os Atoleiros in Alemtejo he put these lessons to good use to win a resounding victory over the mounted knights of a larger Castilian force.[58] He drew up his force of some 300 Portuguese 'lances' on foot – a new method of fighting for these men-at-arms – and formed them into a square formation in a strong defensive position on rising ground with a small stream in front. Though Nun'Alvares only had 100 crossbowmen, these were placed in two wings, supported by some 1,000 other infantry. The Castilian cavalry attempted a direct assault on the Portuguese square, but with their lance butts planted in the ground the dismounted men-at-arms repulsed them, while the crossbowmen and javalineers assailed their flanks with missiles. The Castilian soldiers, who may have outnumbered their opponents three to one, were quickly seized with panic and fled, leaving at least 77 mounted men-at-arms dead, but with no Portuguese casualties.[59]

The following year a small Portuguese force once again encountered a larger Castilian raiding party near Trancoso; they dismounted and took up a defensive position in a ploughed field. Unable because of their small numbers – about 300 men-at-arms – to form a square as at Atoleiros, and lacking missilemen to place on their flanks, they drew up in a single line, with a force of poorly equipped levies at their rear. The Castilians, perhaps in turn drawing on French tactics, themselves dismounted and attacked on foot, but hastily and in a poorly organised manner, while they sent their *jinetes* to attack the Portuguese infantry. These raw levies might well have been scattered, but being attacked in the rear they were hemmed in between the enemy and their own men-at-arms, and were thus forced to fight off the Castilian light cavalry. The Portuguese men-at-arms now counter-attacked, and after a long struggle defeated the exhausted Castilians. Many Castilian men-at-arms were killed, for they could not regain their mounts to flee.[60] The battle once again indicated the inherent strength of a defensive stance, even when men-at-arms were unsupported by archers. By now, however, the Portuguese had appealed to King Richard II for aid, and King João of Portugal was soon able to swell his forces with a detachment of some 700 English and Gascon men-at-arms and archers, intended as an advance party for further reinforcements.[61]

As a general Nun'Alvares was a passionate exponent of a battle-seeking strategy as opposed to that of siege or attrition;

the influence of Edward III and the Black Prince again suggests itself here, aided perhaps by a horoscope allegedly recorded at the *condesabre*'s birth, which announced that he would never be defeated. At a council of war he successfully argued for such a course to counter a new invasion threat by King Juan I, whose far larger army was marching on Lisbon.[62] Thus it was that on 14 August 1385, in an attempt to halt the Castilian advance, Nun'Alvares deployed the Portuguese on a high bluff overlooking the ford through which the main road to Lisbon passed, with streams protecting his position on two sides. Seeing that a frontal assault on such an extremely well-defended position would be folly, the advancing Castilians executed a lengthy flanking movement, wheeling round in order both to come between the Portuguese and their way of retreat, and to gain a more accessible approach to their positions. Meanwhile, however, Nun'Alvares had countered this move by turning his army about – always a difficult and dangerous manoeuvre with the enemy in proximity – and with great skill redeploying it only 1¼ miles (2km) further south around the little hermitage of St Jorge, in a position which kept the advantage of high ground and the flanking protection of the two streams, and allowed the enemy to approach only on a narrow front some 300 yards wide. He himself commanded the vanguard, composed of around 600 Portuguese men-at-arms, supported on the right by a body of elite knights and on the left by the Anglo-Gascon men-at-arms under Guilhem de Montferrand. Behind the vanguard came the main Portuguese battle under King João himself. According to Ayala, the Portuguese adopted the novel deployment of concentrating some of their archers behind the wings of the vanguard.[63] The Castilian army appears to have been significantly larger, with some 5,000–6,000 men-at-arms, 2,000 *jinetes*, a large number of bowmen and light infantry, and 16 light cannon.

The site of the battle can be determined with a precision usually lacking for the majority of battlefields, for two reasons. The first is the existence of the chapel of St Jorge, near where Nun'Alvares planted his standard. The second is that part of the battlefield, principally to the south of this chapel and thus the site of the Portuguese left wing, was subject to extensive excavation between 1958 and 1960. This revealed not only a ditch 200 yards (182m) long which ran across the front of the Portuguese position, where Nun'Alvares's vanguard was stationed, but also hundreds of pits, dug in rows converging on other ditches which afforded in-depth protection.[64] These pits varied in size, but were roughly 1m long, .5m wide and .3m deep, while the distance between the pits in each row varied from .35m to 1.6m, and the distance between the rows themselves varied from 2.3m to 2.6m. To the west and south the defensive system was seemingly bounded by further ditches, while the rows of pits were aligned in a herringbone pattern on another ditch running roughly at right angles to the Portuguese front. The excavators found no evidence of stakes or other obstacles in these pits, but according to the *Cronica del Despensero* they were hidden by brushwood. Froissart's attribution of the choice of site and these defensive measures to the English captains in João's service may well underestimate the experience of Portuguese commanders, who, as we have seen, had in previous years demonstrated their aptitude in fighting successful defensive engagements.[65] The right flank of the Portuguese position has not yet been excavated, but it is nevertheless striking that the extensive system of pits and ditches guarded the position held by the Anglo-Gascon contingent. Hence this remarkable discovery provides tangible evidence of the kind of defences which had played such an integral part in many of the English tactical deployments of the Hundred Years War. As Froissart notes, 'then on the side next the fields they cut down the trees and laid them one over another, to the intent that horsemen should not come with full course on them. They left one way open, not very large, and such archers and crossbows as they had, they set them on every side of the way, and their men of arms all afoot in a plain within the way and the church on their one side.'[66]

The Castilians sent one of their most experienced knights, Pero Lopez de Ayala, the chronicler and veteran of Nájera, to parley and to reconnoitre the enemy's position. What he saw made him urge King Juan to avoid battle that day. The strength of the Portuguese position, flanked by two watercourses, meant that the Castilians could only attack on a narrow front, where their van could not receive effective support from the wings and would itself be subjected to both frontal and enfilade shooting from the bowmen stationed in the rear of the Portuguese van, shooting over the heads of their men-at-arms.[67] Their army had, moreover, made a long and exhausting march in the fierce heat, while their own archers and infantry were still approaching with the baggage train. The wisest course, Ayala informed the king, was to wait, for while the Castilians had ample supplies the Portuguese were low on food. Avoidance of battle was also strongly counselled by the French ambassador Jean de Rye, who had served at both Crécy and Poitiers, and who also emphasised the need for the van to be supported by wings in any attack. The king agreed, but such a counsel of caution was angrily opposed by his young and hot-headed captains; earlier battles and a terrible epidemic which had ravaged his army at the siege of Lisbon in 1384 had removed the majority of his veteran commanders, men who could recall the catastrophe of Nájera, and accordingly there was a lack of cautious counsel to counter the firebrands. The matter, however, was decided when some of the Castilian

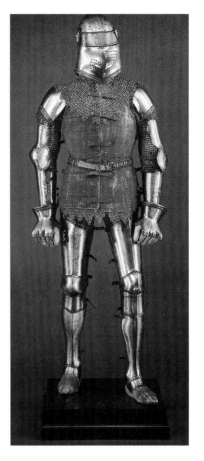

A composite Italian armour *c.* 1390–1400, from pieces found at Chalcis, Greece. The breastplate, worn over a hauberk, is formed from two pieces bucked together and covered with red velvet. Quality armour from Milan such as this was being exported throughout Europe from the second half of the fourteenth century. *(Metropolitan Museum, New York)*

nobles began the attack in defiance of the king's orders.[68] Accordingly, the Castilian cannon opened fire on the Portuguese vanguard, while detachments of *jinetes* attacked the infantry formed in a square around the horses and baggage in the Portuguese rear. As at Trancoso, however, this blocked any means of flight for the Portuguese levies and compelled them to stand their ground. King Juan now had little option but to engage his other forces, and the Castilian vanguard, which included a detachment of French men-at-arms, advanced on foot. Hampered by the ditches and pits, however, which lessened the impetus of their attack, they now came under heavy enfilade shooting from the English archers and Portuguese crossbowmen. In Froissart's words, 'because the entry was so narrow, there was great press and great mischief to the assailants, for such English archers as there were shot so wholly together that their arrows pierced men and horse, and when the horses were full of arrows, they fell one upon another'.[69] Froissart's account seems incorrect in suggesting elements of the vanguard were mounted, but Ayala also notes that the narrow front put the Castilians at a great disadvantage; while the Portuguese wings could harass the flanks of their vanguard, this could not receive any support from the wings of Castilian infantry and missilemen. Nevertheless, the Castilian attack succeeded in driving back the Portuguese vanguard some way, until the main battle under João moved forward to reinforce it. Further assaults by mounted knights and *jinetes* on the Portuguese rear were driven off. Now, however, without effective missile support and with its flanks under a constant barrage, the Castilian vanguard began to falter. After fierce fighting the fall of the royal standard began a general collapse, and Juan himself was led away by his bodyguard to ride fast for refuge in Santarem. News of the king's departure hastened the rout of his army. Many who fled were cut down by local peasants, but the heaviest losses had occurred in the short but bitter fighting in the centre of the battlefield.

The analogies between Aljubarotta and Crécy are striking. At Aljubarotta, the field defences had played a vital role in funnelling the Castilians into a narrow front, which minimised their numerical strength, hampered effective manoeuvre and left their flanks dangerously exposed first to volleys of arrows, bolts and stones, then to direct attack. A similar effect had been achieved against Philip VI's cavalry, though only excavation of the battlefield will reveal whether the English employed such extensive field defences at Crécy, or whether it was more the lie of the land itself that helped to corral the French towards a killing zone. Like Crécy, Aljubarotta witnessed a horrific number of casualties, with perhaps as many as 2,500 men-at-arms being slain, including many high-ranking nobles as well as Geoffroi de Parthenay, the leader of the French contingent, and

Jean de Rye.[70] Froissart, who noted that more Castilian nobility perished here than at Nájera, in part accounts for the high noble fatalities by recording that many of the prisoners taken during the defeat of the Castilian vanguard were subsequently ordered to be put to death when it was feared that the main battle under King Juan would renew the assault – an anticipation of Henry V's actions thirty years later at Agincourt. Though many were reluctant to slay their valuable captives, the risk that they would take up arms again if battle was renewed seemed too great, and others among the Portuguese were found ready to do the killing. From that point of the battle on, the Portuguese took no prisoners.[71] While some of the leading lords received honourable burial, it seems that the bodies of many were left where they lay, prey to wild animals; the excavators found a quantity of bones close to the chapel of St Jorge which showed signs of combat.

Both the battles of Aljubarotta and of Castagnaro, in which longbowmen played differing but significant roles, illustrate the diaspora of English military thinking and the manner in which it had been both applied and adapted to the differing forms of warfare in Iberia and Italy. Yet to English observers at home, these victories would have stood in stark contrast to the military reverses suffered by English arms once the Anglo-French war recommenced in 1369.

CHARLES V, ARCHERS AND THE 'ARMY OF THE RECONQUEST'

As a result of the incapacity of both Edward III and the Black Prince, and of the political disaffection rife within Gascony as a direct result of the latter's 1367 Spanish expedition, the French were able to achieve remarkable military successes within the space of a few years. By 1374 the English had lost almost all the territories ceded to them in 1360, and inroads had even been made into English-held Gascony. The French, led in the south-west by Louis of Anjou, Charles V's capable brother, and in the north by Du Guesclin, promoted to Constable of France in 1370, had been able to exploit the military and political weaknesses of the English to great effect. At sea the French had an able admiral in Jean de Vienne and a powerful ally in the Castilian fleet, which inflicted a catastrophic defeat on an English naval force at La Rochelle in 1372. Although the English responded by launching major *chevauchées* in 1369 under John of Gaunt, in 1370 under Sir Robert Knollys and in 1373–4 once again under Gaunt, these expeditions achieved little. The English had failed to adapt their strategy to a defensive war, for once their raiding armies had returned home the French simply continued their gradual but inexorable advance, retaking English-held towns and castles.[72] Unlike in

1346 or 1356, moreover, the French did not allow themselves to be drawn into a major battle in the field. As regent after his father's capture at Poitiers, Charles had applied the tactics of containment and avoidance with considerable success in 1359–60 to thwart Edward III's attempts to strike at Paris and Rheims. Now Du Guesclin, as Constable, did likewise; in 1370, for example, he shadowed Knollys's *chevauchée* on its return journey, harassing it then finally falling on and defeating its rearguard at Pontvallian, near Le Mans.[73] Here the English contingents were taken completely by surprise, and routed in detail; in one of these engagements at Rillé, Du Guesclin's men-at-arms and those of the English fought fiercely, but the English lines were finally broken by the charge of 60 newly arrived French lances – a successful implementation of the tactics attempted by French commanders in the 1350s.[74] Only when he was sure of favourable circumstances, as at Chizé in 1373, did Du Guesclin commit his forces to battle. Historians have been divided over their assessment of Du Guesclin's military talents, but whether this new-found caution was a result of his own chastening experience of being defeated and captured twice at Auray and Nájera, or whether wiser counsel was imposed upon him by King Charles, the result was a sustained period of French military recovery. Ultimately, it was such Fabian tactics that had proved the most effective counterstroke to the power of the longbow. It was a lesson that was ignored with terrible consequences in 1415.

Charles V's successes, however, were also due to major military reforms and the creation of France's first standing army.[75] This project had been set afoot by Jean II in an ordinance of 1363, which envisaged a permanent force of 6,000 men, based on quotas raised from each diocese and paid for by the *fouage*, a dedicated hearth tax, and by duty on wine.[76] The figure was unrealistic, and an army of only 1,500 was raised.[77] But with the outbreak of the war in 1369 Charles revived these measures, and secured increased taxation to support a regular force of some 3,000 men. This was to be supplemented by a small but elite and permanent force of crossbowmen; in 1373 it was stipulated that their number was to be only 800, selected and regularly reviewed by a captain-general.[78] Further missilemen could also be called upon from confraternities of archers or crossbowmen established in major towns. From at least the time of Philip Augustus (1180–1224), towns had been important in supplying infantry to French royal armies, and crossbowmen had numbered among these well-equipped serjeants. During the fourteenth century, however, shooting guilds were becoming increasingly common in both the Low Countries and in France. Mention is made, for example, of confraternities of crossbowmen at Ypres in 1302, St Trond in 1310, Noyons in 1316, St Quentin in 1330 and Carcassonne in 1335, while a guild of archers is found at Namur in 1266, Ghent in 1322, Chimay in 1338 and at Rheims at about the same period.[79] The Anglo-French war naturally acted as a stimulus to the French crown to encourage further such groups; confraternities of crossbowmen appear at Rouen in 1347, Caen in 1358 and Paris in 1359, and those of archers at Châlons sur Marne in 1357 and Loan in 1367.[80] These confraternities were afforded special privileges by the crown (particularly exemption from certain taxes), often in recognition of their loyal service in wartime. In 1367, for instance, Charles granted exemption from all subsidies, just as he had to the crossbowmen of Rouen, to a 'constabulary' of sixteen crossbowmen at Lagny sur Marne for their assistance at the sieges of Étampes, Nogent and Marrolez.[81] The following year he confirmed the privileges and regulations of the crossbowmen of Compiègne, twenty-strong under the constableship of their 'king', the aptly named Simon le Flechier, while in 1373 the crossbowmen of La Rochelle were granted exemption from military expeditions, because, noted the king, under the English occupation they had been called out so many times by Edward III and the Black Prince for

'sieges, hosts, *chevauchées* and armies at sea' that the men had declined to practise shooting.[82]

Most strikingly, however, Charles had also attempted to build up a powerful archer arm. In 1367 he had ordered that a register was to be made of all archers and crossbowmen in each of his '*bonnes villes*', so that the king knew how many bowmen he might call upon. Furthermore, all young men were encouraged to learn and practise the art of shooting.[83] The immediate stimulus for these measures was the threat posed by the return to France of the Free Companies which had been campaigning in Spain with the Black Prince, and they were part of a comprehensive plan of defence.[84] As with his subsequent strategy against the English, open battle with the Companies was to be eschewed wherever possible, and any fighting was to be conducted from the safety of walled towns or castles. Accordingly, key fortifications were to be strengthened, while those not thought worthy or capable of repair were to be razed lest they offer the Companies bases for future depredations.[85] Seen in this context, Charles's archer force was intended not so much as part of a field army but as a major contribution to communal defences. Nevertheless, these measures might be used to good effect in the war against England; two years later, in an ordinance that may well have taken its inspiration from Edward III's own statute forbidding games and encouraging shooting, Charles decreed that his subjects were to abstain from a range of games and were to exercise by shooting bows and crossbows in suitable places, and that there should be prizes for those who shot the best.[86] It should be noted that the king was not attempting to impose the exclusive use of the longbow on his subjects, nor was he seeking to introduce a new weapon; his ordinances assume the bow was widespread, and simply sought to encourage as many men as possible to shoot, whether with longbows or crossbows. Shooting ranges were created or repaired. In 1371 the accounts of the pay-master of the city of Paris, Simon Gaucher, record payments for the erection of two new butts (*muttes*) for crossbowmen on the Ile de Notre Dame, and the repair of two other butts for archers which already existed on the same island. In 1379 crossbow-men are also found shooting in the 'champs des arbaletriers', a field running the length of the city walls between the old Rue du Temple and the Coulture de Ste Catherine.[87]

The French chronicler Jean Juvenal des Ursins believed that this attempt to create large numbers of bow-armed infantry had to be abandoned through fears of peasant insurrection,[88] and his remarks have been widely accepted as the reason for the French failure to adopt the longbow *en masse*. Yet this explanation is problematic. It is true that the great peasant rebellion in northern France in 1358 known as the Jacquerie caused grave alarm among the French aristocracy, who

Left: Bertrand du Guesclin's forces, covered by archers, storm Melun, from the *Chanson de Bertrand du Guesclin de Cuvelier, c.* 1400 (British Library, Yates Thompson MS 35, f.62). (*© British Library*)

Below: Sir Hugh Calveley (d. 1393), from a drawing based on his effigy in the choir of Bunbury church, Cheshire. A leading commander of the Free Companies, Calveley commanded the reserve division at Auray in 1364, and fought for the Black Prince at Nájera against du Guesclin, his former business partner in war. (*By kind permission of the Heraldry Society/ICI*).

repressed it with great brutality. Yet if Charles or his counsellors had had qualms about encouraging archery among the lower orders, it did not prevent them issuing the ordinances of 1367 within a decade of the insurrection, and as we have seen nobles such as Gaston Phébus in 1362 were recruiting local archers for their forces, just as Charles of Blois had drawn on 'archers of the countryside' in the 1340s. Nor were any such fears expressed when from 1448 Charles VII moved to establish a large reservoir of bowmen by his creation of the Francs-archers. In large part this lack of concern must be explained by the comparative ease with which peasant bands could be defeated by regular troops, and nowhere was this more graphically demonstrated than at Meaux. Here on 9 June 1358 a peasant force under Jean Valliant and Pierre Gilles was utterly routed by a small force of only some twenty-four knights who launched a surprise mounted sally from the town's fortress, the Marché. It was symbolic of aristocratic class solidarity in the face of peasant insurrection that both French and Anglo-Gascon knights fought together in this group of men-at-arms, whose number included both the Captal de Buch and Gaston Phébus.[89] A potentially greater military danger was posed by the Jacques (the name given to the peasant rebels) led by Guillaume Cale, who, expecting an attack from the forces of Charles of Navarre, had drawn up his men at Silly, north-east of Paris, in a defensive position which may well have drawn its inspiration from Flemish and English tactics. With his flanks protected by carts and trenches, he placed his archers in the front of his two ranks of men, and had even created a small mounted

reserve. How his force would have fared in battle under his leadership, however, was not to be known, for on 10 June Cale was treacherously seized during a parley. This was a severe blow to the peasants' morale and cohesion, and when Charles's mounted men-at-arms launched their charge the Jacques broke in utter panic, only to be savagely cut down.[90]

After such events it must have been clear to all that even if they were equipped with bows or other weapons, poorly trained and organised labourers and artisans were no match for even the small forces of seasoned troops in open combat. If many French nobles dismissed with contempt the contribution of the levies of the *arrière-ban* to the feudal host, they must have had still greater disdain for any such force so rash as to presume to meet them in battle. As with a similar plan by James I of Scotland in the 1430s, Charles V's scheme to raise a large indigenous force of archers did not wither on the vine because of the aristocracy's fear of arming a discontented and rebellious peasantry. Rather, successes in the war, followed by a long period of comparative peace with England, meant that the scheme fell into disuse largely through lack of pressing need and practical difficulties of enforcement, just as fiscal pressures gradually led to the disbanding of Charles's standing 'army of the reconquest' under his successor, and the need for its recreation by Charles VII in the 1440s. Tellingly, when Charles VII looked to supplement his *Compagnies d'Ordonnance* with an archer levy in 1448, he abandoned any plans to enforce universal practice with bow or crossbow in favour of a more select force raised through the proffer of privileges and tax-exemptions.[91] For field operations during the reign of Charles V's successor, however, crossbowmen were still regarded by the French as the elite troops. The expeditionary force dispatched under Jean de Vienne in 1385 to aid the Scots in an attack on England had originally been intended to contain 1,000 men-at-arms and 600 crossbowmen, but in the event the force that sailed to Leith comprised 1,350 men-at-arms and only 300 crossbowmen. The reduction in the latter's numbers seems to have been due to difficulties in raising sufficient crossbowmen, but even the proportions of men-at-arms to crossbowmen in the intended strength of the force reflected the continuing French tendency, despite Charles's reforms, to underrate the value of missile elements in their armies.[92]

PEASANT ARCHERS AND ROYAL THUGS

Many of the same considerations concerning the use of the longbow by potentially dissident elements also held true for England. Certainly the longbow could prove a threat to society in the hands of brigands and outlaws, few of whom drew their bows with such discrimination and noble intent as the Robin Hood of the fifteenth-century ballads.[93] Where there were affrays and local riots, such as at Norwich in 1272 when the townsmen attacked and burned the cathedral and its monastic precinct,[94] it was natural that men should take up bows as well as other weapons which the assizes of arms enjoined them to possess and which were often carried as a matter of course. Yet major insurrections were remarkably infrequent in England, and none is known of before the Peasants' Revolt of 1381.[95] This 'Great Rising', like the Jacquerie of 1358, demonstrated not only the potential threat of armed and discontented elements of society, but also their military limitations. There can be little doubt that the men of Kent and Essex who rose in early June 1381 were comparatively well organised; not only did the Kentishmen order all those living within 12 miles of the sea to remain behind to guard against potential French raids, but the rebels were able to cover 70 miles in two days during their march from Canterbury to Blackheath in London. Froissart believed one of the principal leaders, Wat Tyler, to have been a former soldier, and though former soldiers do not appear as prominently in 1381 as they were to do in the revolt of Jack Cade in 1450, it seems likely that at least some of the rebels had gained some military experience in the Anglo-French wars.[96] The young Richard II, not yet fifteen, had achieved the dispersal of many of the Essex men after agreeing to the rebels' demands at an assembly at Mile End on 14 June, but the following day a meeting with Wat Tyler and the Kentishmen at Smithfield nearly proved catastrophic. During an altercation between Tyler and the Mayor of London William Walworth, Tyler was slain and the angry commons began to draw their bows.[97] The chronicler Thomas Walsingham records the dramatic sequel:

Immediately the commons saw Tyler's downfall, they cried with sorrow for his death: 'Our captain is dead; our leader has been treacherously killed. Let us stay together and die with him. Let us shoot our arrows and staunchly avenge his death.' And so they drew their bows and prepared to shoot. But the king, with marvellous presence of mind and courage for so young a man, spurred his horse towards the commons and rode around them saying, 'What is this, my men? What are you doing? Surely you do not wish to shoot at your own king? Do not attack me and do not regret the death of that traitor and ruffian. For I will be your king, your captain and your leader. Follow me into that field [St John at Clerkenwell] where you can have all the things you would like to ask for.'[98]

It would have been no small irony had the son of the Black Prince been struck down by an English clothyard arrow. Yet the events which immediately ensued revealed the true weakness of the rebels. Rashly believing the king's promises and deprived of effective radical leadership, the quiescent commons

Following the death of Wat Tyler (left), the young Richard II addresses the rebels (right) during the climax of the Peasants' Revolt, 1381, from Froissart's *Chroniques de France et d'Angleterre* (British Library, MS Royal 18 E 1, f.175r). It is unlikely that many of the rebels were as well equipped as depicted here. *(British Library/Bridgeman Art Library)*

soon found themselves surrounded by a force of men-at-arms hurriedly raised by Walworth, which included professionals led by the veteran commander Sir Robert Knollys. There may have been a sprinkling of former soldiers in their ranks, but most of the insurgents were merely farmers or artisans unused to war, with one chronicler noting that their number included 'decrepit old men and young men armed with rusty axes and arrows, bows and sticks'.[99] Against the trained royalist forces, they realised they had little chance, and sought the king's mercy, flinging down their bows and other arms. To his credit Richard II prevented Knollys from massacring the now demoralised and disorganised commons, whom one chronicler describes as sheeplike ('*come berbiz en caules*'), for the king realised that many had taken up arms unwillingly.[100]

It thus seems evident from the thirteenth-century assizes of arms, the subsequent legislation by Edward III enjoining universal archery practice and prohibiting other sports, and the continued reissue of such statutes after 1381 that the English crown did not regard a peasantry armed with bows as an inherent threat to the social order. The rising social status of the mounted archer during the fourteenth century meant that many of the men who had gained military experience in France were of a rank who would feel more threatened by than in sympathy with the kind of rising seen in 1381. Indeed, for medieval English kings the danger of sporadic insurrection was more than outweighed by the advantages in having all freemen equipped with arms compatible with their wealth and status to assist in local policing and in the defence of the shires, and to swell the ranks of royal armies through commissions of array. The price was not the threat of repeated insurgence which might overthrow the social order but rather localised violence, ubiquitous but of low intensity, whether in the form of poachers and brigands bending their bows in the forests and byways, or of the numerous homicides involving antagonists ready to settle quarrels with bows as much as with swords, daggers and other side-arms. It was a price that rulers were willing to pay, for outlaws, homicides and other men with a proclivity for violence, whether men-at-arms or archers, could always be drafted into the king's army for service abroad.

If the early years of Richard II's reign saw the bow used in a popular uprising against the abuses of government and lordship, its closing years were to see a body of archers in the king's service used for repression and political intimidation.[101] English kings from at least the reign of Edward I had retained a small personal bodyguard of archers, usually numbering only 24.[102] These bowmen received a wage of 6*d* a day, sometimes granted for life, while Edward III gave each of his archer guards one mark at Christmas to buy robes.[103] But as the troubled reign of Richard II unfolded, and the king grew increasingly at odds with an opposing faction within the nobility, he increased his personal retinue and engaged much larger numbers of archers. From at least 1387 the majority of these additional bowmen were raised from the county of Cheshire, of which he was earl and to which he showed particular favour in order to build up a power base in what was effectively his private lordship, while spearmen were also drawn from North Wales.[104] Unlike the small core of yeoman archers of the crown who were paid by the Exchequer, the Cheshire archers were financed through the resources of Richard's own palatinate earldom and were very much a 'private' force. The knights and squires retained by Richard in his affinity wore the famous badge of the white hart, but the majority of his Cheshire archers and other archers of the crown in the king's immediate service instead bore a livery badge in the form of gold and silver crowns.[105] During the years of Richard's mounting insecurity from 1397 to 1399 the core of these troops was a personal bodyguard of 312 archers divided into seven 'watches', each led by a squire of proven loyalty, with each watch guarding the king's bedchamber all night for one day each week. But in times of particular crisis the number of Cheshire archers might be greatly increased. In 1397, as a prelude to his own *coup* against the Lords Appellant, Richard attempted to raise a large force of Cheshire archers, possibly numbering over 2,000, which he used to overawe the Parliament summoned in September.[106] This assisted him in forcing through the exile of Thomas Arundel, Archbishop of Canterbury, and the condemnation of his brother Richard, Earl of Arundel, whom the archers then escorted to the scaffold on Tower Hill. The chronicler Walsingham believed that Arundel's ghost haunted Richard in his sleep, and that the king was afraid to go to bed without his bodyguard of 300 Cheshire archers.[107] Not only was this small private army expensive – at Michaelmas 1398 the wage bill for his retained knights, esquires and archers totalled £5,000, of which the archers accounted for four-fifths – but it became increasingly un-popular as a symbol of the king's despotism. A combination of the high-handed behaviour of these yeomen and their perceived over-familiarity with the king had rendered the Cheshire archers an object of loathing.[108] Some measure of this hatred can be gauged by the fact that after the deposition of Richard II Henry Bolingbroke, now Henry IV, had Peter de Legh, a close retainer to Richard and probably responsible for recruiting the Cheshire archers, beheaded, while other captains and members of the Cheshire archers had to obtain special pardons from the new king.[109] The use of hired archers or other retained men to overawe opponents was not, however, restricted to the crown, and would become a growing problem in the fifteenth century. An early example occurs in 1402, when Margaret, Countess of Warwick petitioned Henry, Bishop of Norwich to take action against the parson of Beeston, who, in her hundred of Wayland, had held a hundred court in the name of the Earl of Arundel and there exercised 'maintenance' – armed intimidation – with 100 archers.[110]

Unlike their forebears or comrades at Crécy and Poitiers, the Cheshire archers were not destined to draw their bows against the French during Richard II's reign. In 1377 it had been intended that Richard, now Prince of Wales, was to command a retinue of 600 men-at-arms and 600 archers in the large army planned to invade France that year, but the death of Edward III caused the expedition to be cancelled. Had it entered the field, the course of the Anglo-French war and Richard's subsequent prosecution of it might have been very different. But as it was, Richard's greatest military efforts were directed not against France, but against Scotland and Ireland. Major expeditions were launched against the Scots by John of Gaunt in 1384 – the first since 1357 – and by a royal army led by Richard in person in 1385, but while these inflicted considerable economic damage they failed to bring the elusive Scottish forces to a decisive engagement. As always, supply problems and the difficulties of living off the land led to rapid withdrawal, though the 1385 expedition had succeeded in putting paid to an effective attack on northern England planned by the Scots and French forces under Jean de Vienne.[111] Unusually, the army of 1385 was raised by feudal summons and was exceptionally large, numbering over 12,000 men, with Richard's own household officers commanding 450 men-at-arms and 550 archers, nearly a tenth of the entire army.[112]

Though the army saw little actual fighting the campaign saw not only the promulgation of the first surviving ordinances of war for a medieval English army, but also a royal summons for all clergy to be arrayed in arms, including as archers. In spite of the prohibition by canon law on clerics bearing arms, this practice had been instigated by Edward III in 1369 to meet the threat of French invasion.[113] Bishops were ordered 'to cause all abbots, priors and men of religion and other ecclesiastical persons of your diocese whatsoever to be armed and arrayed'. The clergy were to be arrayed just like the laity, although separately and by ecclesiastics, and all able-bodied clerics between 16 and 60 were to be furnished with arms, 'each according to his estate', and 'put in thousands, hundreds and twenties, so that they shall be ready with the king's other lieges to march against the said enemies of the realm'.[114] Such measures had been repeated by Edward in 1372 and 1373, and by Richard himself in 1377, 1381 and now in 1385, when he ordered bishops and abbots to bring their men to Newcastle for the defence of the realm against the Scots. Clergy were grouped into the categories of mounted men-at-arms, hobelars, archers

and a lesser catch-all category of men armed with glaives, pole-axes and other staff weapons, and the instructions issued by Thomas de Brantyngham, Bishop of Exeter, in 1372 reveal that these were based on a sliding scale of wealth. Stipendiary priests without lands should serve with a bow and arrows, while rectors or vicars holding benefices worth 10 marks were to serve as archers, presumably with better equipment; those with benefices worth £10 would serve as men-at-arms, while those with more substantial holdings were to provide retinues appropriate to their income. Thus those with benefices worth £20 should serve as men-at-arms each accompanied by two archers, those worth £40 should provide two men-at-arms and two archers, and so upward to the wealthiest, holding benefices of £100, who were to furnish five men-at-arms and six archers.[115] Some of these troops may have been furnished by proxy, but the evidence suggests that service was more usually by the clergy in person and as such was simply a continuation, albeit in a more highly organised manner, of the military service performed by clergy in earlier centuries in times of threatened invasion.[116] The practice continued under Henry IV in 1400 and 1402, and under his son in 1415 and 1418. In the latter year, for example, the bishop's return for the diocese of Norwich lists 'armed men, all appearing with lances', hobelars and 'archers arrayed with hauberks, bows and arrows, swords, shields and daggers'.[117]

The most striking use of archers in Richard's campaigns came in his first Irish expedition in 1394. Faced with the growing power of the Leinster Irish, and especially that of Art MacMurrough Kavanagh, the position of the English lordship had become critical, and from 1389 the Justice of Ireland, Sir John Stanley, had been struggling to maintain the lordship with a retinue of only 5 knights, 94 men-at-arms, 300 mounted archers and 100 foot-archers. As he had done for the Scottish campaign of 1385, Richard raised a large host, numbering at least some 6,000 men, but the logistics and strategy of the Irish campaign were far better planned and far more successful. A great armada was prepared, a vast quantity of arms and munitions were sent from the Tower to Dublin Castle, and careful thought was given to the provision of food, including protecting the royal officers sent to raise supplies of meat and corn from the native Irish with a powerful bodyguard of 190 mounted archers and 9 foot-archers.[118] Among the archers of the main army were 'each and every one of our yeomen and archers of the crown holding our wages and fees', now summoned by Richard, and units of the Cheshire archers.[119] Not since the days of King John had there been such an expedition, prompting Froissart to observe that 'it is not in memory that ever any King of England made such apparel and provision for any journey to make war against the Irishmen, nor such a number of men-at-arms or archers'. To counter the guerrilla warfare which the Irish had long employed to such effect, the campaign began from Waterford on 19 October, once autumn had stripped the woods and undergrowth of their leaves, denying the enemy the cover needed for their ambuscades. While a fleet prevented supplies from reaching Leinster by sea, a ring of fortified bases or 'wards' was established as a cordon around MacMurrough's lands. From these, mounted archers harried his forces both by fast raids and by slowly but surely diminishing his areas of movement. By January 1395 MacMurrough had made his submission.[120]

Such a campaign, using the onset of winter, an economic blockade and fast, highly mobile troops, bears a striking similarity to the kind of warfare Gerald of Wales had advocated in the 1190s for the conquest of Wales, and which Edward I had put into operation against Gwynedd. The combination of speed and missile power supplied by mounted archers made them ideal for the difficult terrain of Ireland, and as we have seen they were used there from the earliest intervention of the Anglo-Normans in 1169. Richard was, however, unable to repeat this success on his second Irish expedition in 1399. Though the army was smaller, being less than 5,000 men, archers were once more prominent in the retinues of the magnates, which had mostly been indentured for a whole year's service, while 900 Cheshire archers supplemented the king's immediate bodyguard of 300 Cheshire bowmen. As before, great quantities of munitions, including 32 cannon, 1,500 bows and thousands of arrows, were dispatched from England. Yet the campaign, dogged by financial problems and overshadowed by domestic dissension, was fought in summer rather than in late autumn, and the policy of systematic containment and raids was replaced by an unsuccessful attempt to bring the Irish to a decisive engagement involving heavy cavalry. MacMurrough, probably with larger forces and alerted by the English strategy of 1394, was able effectively to harry Richard's army as it marched through Wicklow to Dublin, forcing it to return to Waterford with little to show for a campaign that would ultimately contribute to Richard's own downfall.[121]

'À PERCY! À PERCY!': OTTERBURN, 19 AUGUST 1388, AND HOMILDON HILL, 14 SEPTEMBER 1402

For all his efforts Richard II had failed to gain a martial reputation and indelibly to link his name to a great victory in the field, as his father and grandfather had done. In marked contrast, the young Henry Percy, son of the Earl of Northumberland, nicknamed 'Hotspur' for his daring and impetuosity,[122] gained lasting renown in chronicles and ballads, and his name is inextricably linked to three of the greatest battles fought in the decades spanning the turn of the fourteenth century. In each, the longbow was to play very different roles. In the first engagement, fought at Otterburn as night fell, the use of the longbow was minimal. At the second, Homildon Hill, the English archers achieved such a complete victory against the Scots that the English men-at-arms were scarcely engaged but for the pursuit. And in the third, at Shrewsbury, English longbowmen were for the first time pitted *en masse* against other English longbowmen in a bloody internecine conflict.

In 1385 the Scots had wisely chosen to avoid battle with Richard II's great army. Three years later, however, a large Scottish raiding force under James Douglas was forced into a major engagement when probably on 19 August 1388 the

Richard II embarks on his expedition to Ireland, surrounded by his guard of Cheshire archers, from a late fifteenth-century manuscript of Froissart's *Chroniques de France et d'Angleterre* (British Library, Harley MS 4380, f.166b). *(© British Library)*

Scots camp at Otterburn in Redesdale suffered a surprise attack by Henry Percy. The Scots had undertaken a major invasion of England, with their main thrust directed towards Carlisle and the western march. In the east, however, the Earl of Douglas had led a smaller but still powerful force into Northumbria, ravaging up to the gates of Newcastle itself, where angry challenges were exchanged between Douglas and Percy.[123] Hurrying to catch the Scots as they made their way back across the border, laden with spoils, Hotspur threw his men into a precipitate attack on the Scots camp even though night was falling. Though Douglas had halted at Otterburn with the express intention of accepting Percy's earlier challenge to battle, the Scots were caught completely unawares by the sudden English onslaught as they sat at dinner, and scarcely had time to arm before the fight was upon them.[124] The ensuing battle, made famous by the border ballads, was far more than a mere skirmish between the feuding families of Percy and Douglas. In Anthony Goodman's words, it was 'one of the most important battles of the fourteenth century', with profound effects on border society as well as on the course of the Hundred Years War,[125] and though the number of combatants is hard to ascertain it was the largest Anglo-Scottish engagement since Neville's Cross in 1346. Nevertheless, the circumstances of the battle meant that, ironically, archery would play a more limited role than in any other major engagement fought that century by English forces.

The English plan had been for Percy to launch a frontal attack while a second force (led according to various sources either by Sir Matthew Redmayne, Sir Thomas Umfraville or Robert Ogle) was to outflank the Scots' position and attack their camp from the rear. But, noted the *Westminster Chronicle*, 'Sir Henry Percy was so rash as to make his assault about the time of Vespers without on this occasion drawing up his troops in battle formation'.[126] Fortunately for Douglas, moreover, the brunt of Percy's main attack had unwittingly been made against that part of the camp occupied not by the Scottish men-at-arms but only by their servants. These were quickly put to flight, but in the confusion Douglas was able to send infantry and armed valets to prevent the English advancing further into the camp and to win enough time for him to launch a surprise counter-attack. That he was able to respond so quickly was because he and his commanders had carefully surveyed the surrounding area the day before and had made contingency plans based on possible English attacks, which included a flanking manoeuvre. Froissart, who had spoken to men of both sides soon after the battle, noted, 'it was this that saved them [the Scots], for it is a great thing for men-at-arms who are exposed to a night attack to know the ground round them thoroughly and to have already concerted their plans'.[127] Hastening unseen under the

A statue of Henry Percy, known as 'Hotspur', from Beverley Minster, Yorkshire. *(Wells Cathedral, Somerset/ Bridgeman Art Library)*

cover of dense thickets, Douglas's horsemen rode around the flank of Percy's main force, then dismounting they suddenly charged from cover yelling their war cries.[128] Meanwhile, the English attack on the Scots' rear had succeeded, but it seems that by this time the majority of the Scots had left the camp to engage Hotspur.

Douglas's attack had taken Percy's division by surprise, but the English quickly rallied and through their superior numbers they began to prevail. The archers, however, had to fight with other weapons than their bows. The fading light made shooting difficult, although there was a moon, but perhaps more significantly, as Froissart noted, there was little place for the archers to shoot in this battle because both sides were locked so closely together.[129] Chronicle accounts stress the intensity of the hand-to-hand fighting between the men-at-arms. Douglas fell mortally wounded after a recklessly brave attack, though the claim by English sources that he was killed by Percy himself is not corroborated in Scottish accounts.[130] Fortunately for the Scots, his death seems to have been little noticed in the confusion of battle, for in other circumstances the fall of a leader often shattered an army's morale and caused it to break in flight. A fierce onslaught by another Scottish knight, Sir John Swinton, seems to have opened up just enough space among the English ranks to allow the Scots to break through, pushing home with their spears and prising apart the enemy formation just as the

English had done so often in battles against the French.[131] The battle raged through the long summer evening and well into the night, but the English began to tire more quickly because of their earlier forced march, and the Scots eventually succeeded in overwhelming Henry and his brother Ralph de Percy, who were both captured. The English suffered heavy casualties, put at 550 by a well-informed source, while the Scots 'carried off some doughty soldiers as their prisoners', including many men-at-arms and archers.[132] Though Douglas had been slain the Scots had won the field, and Percy was taken together with a rich haul of prisoners. 'The calamity that befell our countrymen on this occasion at Otterburn', noted the *Westminster Chronicle*, 'was due in the first place to the heady spirit and excessive boldness of Sir Henry Percy, which caused our troops to go into battle in the disorder induced by haste; in the second place because the darkness played such tricks on the English that when they aimed a careless blow at a Scotsman, owing to the chorus of voices speaking the same language it was an Englishman that they cut down; and in the third place they were disappointed in the help and support arranged between them and the Bishop of Durham.'[133] In tactical terms it must be added that crucially the English had lacked an effective opportunity to weaken the Scots by archery before joining in close combat.

In marked contrast, the battle of Homildon Hill, fought on 14 September 1402 and in which Hotspur avenged his earlier defeat, shows the importance assigned by the Scots to their archers, but demonstrated once more the overwhelming superiority of the English bowmen. Hoping to exploit the preoccupation of the English with the rising of Owain Glyn Dŵr, a Scottish army had raided into Northumberland, only to find its retreat north barred at Milfield, north-west of Wooler, by a strong force of men-at-arms and archers, estimated at some 12,000 lances and 7,000 archers under the Earl of Northumberland and his son Henry Percy.[134] The Scots quickly took up a defensive position on Homildon (now Humbleton) Hill, arraying their own archers and men-at-arms, and awaited the attack, just as Douglas had intended to do at Otterburn. The impetuous young Percy wished to oblige them by making an immediate assault, which given the Scots' strong hill-top position might have invited a second defeat for Hotspur. But according to Bower's *Scotichronicon*, the Scottish lord George of Dunbar, Earl of March, who was fighting with the English, 'reined Percy back, saying that he should not move, but should send archers who could easily penetrate the Scots as targets for their arrows and defeat and capture them'.[135] Accordingly, the sizeable body of English archers may have occupied Harehope Hill, within easy bow range of the Scots but separated from Homildon Hill by a ravine, a natural defence from direct attack that allowed the archers to operate in the open without the

direct support of men-at-arms. Alternatively, as argued in Chapter 16 by Robert Hardy, they were sent up the main slope of Homildon to harass the Scots. As Walsingham, who gives one of the fullest accounts of the engagement, relates:

> When our men saw this, they left the road in which they had opposed the Scots and climbed a hill facing the Scots. Without delay our archers, drawn up in the dale, shot arrows at the Scottish formation (*cuneum*) to provoke them to come down. In reply, the Scottish archers directed all their shooting at our archers; but they felt the weight of our arrows, which fell like a storm of rain, and so they fled.[136]

The rapid discomfort of the Scottish archers has led to the deduction that they were using weaker bows, but as we have already noted there is no evidence that this was the case.[137] Not only did the Scots archers acquit themselves well at Bannock-burn, according to Barbour, but it is inconceivable that they neither had access to suitable bow wood nor could have allowed to pass by a century of defeats in which the longbow played a major role without the simple expedient of copying the weapon of their southern neighbours. It seems equally inconceivable that French monarchs and the Dukes of Burgundy would hire Scottish archers if they considered their weapons to be second-rate, and such bowmen can be found in French pay as early as 1391, when a unit of 100 archers received 1,100 francs.[138] Certainly by the 1440s a manuscript of Virgil's *Aeneid* depicts an archer, very probably intended to be a Highland Scot, holding a longbow that looks no whit less powerful than those drawn by archers south of the border.[139]

It is possible that at Homildon the Scottish archers were heavily outnumbered: the *Scotichronicon* places the total strength of the Scots army at 10,000, but chronicle figures for either army are hardly reliable and the proportion of archers to men-at-arms and other troops in Douglas's force is unknown, though Bower's reference to lances suggests that spearmen still made up part of the infantry force. We know nothing too about weather conditions or the prevailing wind at Homildon, but this may have played a significant role in the defeat of the Scots, as it certainly did for the Lancastrians at Towton in 1461, where a headwind made their volleys fall harmlessly short – and here there can be no question of deducing that the Lancastrians drew weaker bows! So at Homildon both sides used a similar weapon, but what probably accounted for the English archers' victory was their superior training and experience: for exactly the same reason English archers were hired in Burgundy, Flanders and other parts of Europe because of their high degree of skill, even though records and iconography clearly reveal that fine and powerful longbows were available to native archers in these areas.

The *Scotichronicon* vividly describes the effect of the English archers, who 'advancing towards the Scots, smothered them with arrows and made them bristle like a hedgehog, transfixing the hands and arms of the Scots to their own lances. By means of this very harsh rain of arrows they made some duck, they wounded others and killed many.'[140] According to the same source, a valiant group of Scots, rallied by Sir John Swinton, advanced downhill and managed to close with some of the English, 'and it was sworn on oath by some Englishmen, as I have heard, that if the other Scots who had stood on Humbleton Hill had fallen on them with like vigour, either the English would have fled, or the Scots would have achieved victory over them'.[141] Yet Bower protests too much, and such sentiments read like an attempt to salvage some credit from a total defeat. Walsingham, by contrast, believed that the Scots commander, Archibald, Earl of Douglas, attempted to counter-attack with a cavalry charge against the English archers, 'trusting too much in his equipment (*armatura propria*) and that of his men, who had been improving their armour for three years'. One would like to know more about Walsingham's sources for these interesting remarks, and about the kind of armour possessed by the better-off Scottish nobles, who, like the picked force of the French marshals at Poitiers, hoped that better defences of plate would render a swift cavalry attack invulnerable. Faced with the oncoming Scots cavalry, however, the archers fell back in good order,

> but still shooting, so vigorously, so resolutely, so effectively that they pierced the armour, perforated the helmets, pitted the swords, split the lances and pierced all the equipment with ease. The Earl of Douglas was pierced with five wounds, notwithstanding his elaborate armour (*sumptuosissima armatura*). The rest of the Scots who had not descended the hill turned tail, and fled from the flight of arrows. But flight did not avail them, so that the Scots were forced to give themselves up, for fear of the death-dealing arrows.[142]

Many of the fugitives were captured, but a considerable number were drowned trying to cross the Tweed. In this remarkable victory, concluded Walsingham, 'no lord or knight received a blow from the enemy; but God Almighty gave the victory miraculously to the English archers alone, and the magnates and men-at-arms remained idle spectators of the battle'.[143]

Homildon was to be the last great pitched battle between the English and Scots in Britain until Flodden in 1513, though they were soon to fight bloodily in France. Not only did it bring 'to a decisive end the border warfare which the Scots had conducted with some success for over a generation',[144] but it may well have been the catalyst needed by the Scots to undertake more far-reaching military reforms and to imitate the composition of the English forces in their ratios of men-at-arms to archers. Certainly by 1419, when the English and Scottish forces were to clash again – this time in France – the Dauphin Charles was relying on the Scots to provide a major archer arm as well as men-at-arms for his forces. Yet if Homildon brought peace to the Anglo-Scottish border, it ironically contributed directly to the major rebellion led by the Percys against Henry IV the following year, which culminated in the battle of Shrewsbury.

In the opinion of the early fifteenth-century *Chronicle of London*, the first major bloodshed in the context of civil war 'between Englysshmen and Englysshmen was the sory bastaill of Schrovesbury'.[145] The battle of Boroughbridge in 1322, where the forces of the Earls of Lancaster and Hereford were mown down by the arrows of Sir Andrew Harclay's archers, might claim the dubious distinction of having been the first engagement during the later Middle Ages in which English longbowmen loosed volleys against English opponents. Lancaster's own forces, however, seem not to have used archery to any effect, and in tactical terms the battle reflected the triumph of defensive formations of spearmen and archers over a largely unsupported cavalry assault. At Shrewsbury, by contrast, both sides employed longbowmen to devastating effect.

SHREWSBURY, 21 JULY 1403

In the summer of 1403 numerous personal grievances with Henry IV provoked the powerful northern family of the Percys into revolt.[146] A small force led by Hotspur and his uncle the Earl of Worcester marched into Cheshire where they quickly succeeded in raising a powerful army, for this area had been fiercely loyal to Richard II and, as we have seen, had furnished his notorious archer bodyguard. The rebels initially proclaimed that Richard was still alive and, as they were fighting in his name, some bore his livery badge of the white hart.[147] Many

local priests had come armed to the rebel army, perhaps leading the men of their localities; some may even have fought as archers themselves, as many clerics had done at Neville's Cross in 1346.[148] With their forces swollen with Cheshiremen as well as many Welshmen from Flintshire and Denbighshire, the rebel forces moved towards Shrewsbury.[149] Extensive border warfare on the northern march had given the Percys much military experience, and Hotspur himself had already taken part in two pitched battles. Indeed, his prisoner from

Sir Robert Swynburne (d. 1391) and Sir Thomas Swynburne, from a brass of 1412 from Little Horksey Church, Essex, showing how defences of plate and particularly protection for the face and neck had developed by the early fifteenth century (From C. Boutell, *Monumental Brasses and Slabs* (1847)). *(Author Collection)*

Homildon, the second Earl of Douglas, now served in Percy's forces at Shrewsbury. King Henry IV himself had a glittering chivalric reputation, had seen service with the Teutonic knights in Prussia, and had conducted a major, though uneventful campaign against the Scots in 1400.[150] Yet despite distinguishing himself at the engagement at Radcot Bridge in 1387 between the Lords Appellant and Robert de Vere, Henry possibly had less comparable knowledge of major engagements than the Percys, and may have relied on more experienced commanders such as the Earl of Dunbar, who only the year before had fought with the Percys against his fellow Scots at Homildon.[151] He was also supported by his eldest son Henry, who, as Prince of Wales from 1399, had gained considerable military experience against the Welsh following the great rising under Owain Glyn Dŵr in 1401.[152] The royalists may have had the advantage in numbers, with Henry IV's army being estimated by one chronicler at some 14,000, though as so often little confidence can be placed on such figures.[153] Nevertheless, the king's force certainly contained at least 2,500 archers, in addition to any who had been raised from shire musters on his march westward to Shrewsbury.[154] In strategic terms, moreover, Henry IV had succeeded in bringing the rebels to battle before they could either join forces with the Welsh leader Owain Glyn Dŵr or receive further support from Hotspur's father, the Earl of Northumberland.

The battle took place in open fields some 3 miles to the north of Shrewsbury, possibly within sight of nearby Haughmond Abbey. While the exact location of the respective forces cannot be gauged with any certainty, the general site is marked by Battlefield Church, founded on the site of his victory by Henry IV as a collegiate chantry for his soul and those of the slain, and built over a mass burial pit.[155] Several chroniclers comment that the site favoured the Percys, who may have occupied a ridge of rising ground with a gentle dip before it.[156] The tangled crop of peas in the fields before their front presented some obstacle to the royalist advance;[157] if they attempted to create more significant defences with pits or trenches this is nowhere mentioned, and the use of stakes by archers was not seen until Henry V's campaign of 1415. The formation adopted by the Percys is still more obscure. Oman's statement that they employed the traditional formation with archers on the wings and men-at-arms in the centre finds little corroboration in the chronicle accounts, though nearly all the sources agree that the Percys' bowmen played a key role in the initial stages of the battle.[158] It is possible that a powerful body of archers was drawn up in front of their main formation, a suggestion supported by the statement of the valuable *Annales Henrici Quarti* that on seeing the rebels' battle formation, 'and especially the archers grouped together', Henry IV drew up his own army in three divisions, with the van commanded by the Earl of Stafford, the centre by the king, and the rearguard by the young Prince Henry.[159]

The conflict, preceded by lengthy but ultimately futile negotiations, began only a few hours before nightfall, but its course remains largely conjectural. The king, who according to several sources broke off the parley with the command 'Advance banner!', may have begun the combat by moving forward against Percy. If so, he was attempting what so many French armies had done in launching a frontal attack against a force on the defensive which contained a powerful body of archers, though alternatively the battle may have opened with an archery duel between units of bowmen in the front ranks of each army. The Burgundian chronicler Waurin, though writing many years after the battle, was an experienced soldier who had fought with the English in France and was present at Agincourt. He noted how the van of the rebel army, led by Douglas, advanced:

> and then when they came in sight of each other, the archers dismounted, uttering a loud and horrible cry which was dreadful to hear, and then began to march at a good pace in good order against each other, and the archers to draw so fast and thick that it seemed to the beholders like a thick cloud, for the sun which at that time was bright and clear then lost its brightness so thick were the arrows . . .[160]

Percy's archers, 'of whom none better could be found in the county of Cheshire', unleashed furious volleys, and their shafts took a heavy toll.[161] Walsingham believed the royal archers returned harmful volleys in their turn, and that many fell on each side, 'like apples fallen in the autumn, when stirred by the south-west wind'.[162] But the large number of casualties so quickly inflicted by the strong shooting of the Cheshire and Welsh archers, combined with a rumour that the king himself had been slain by an arrow, caused a part of the royal forces – possibly the van – to break in flight.[163] It was this confusion which may have led Hotspur and Douglas now to launch an assault on Henry IV's main battle. Ignoring the hail of arrows and the formation of the men-at-arms, Percy, Douglas and a picked force of 30 men-at-arms 'made a lane in the middle of the ost til he cam to the kyngis baner', in an attempt to kill the king and thus gain victory at a stroke – just as at Bosworth Richard III was to make a direct assault on Henry Tudor.[164] Several of those defending the king, including the royal standard bearer Sir Walter Blount, were slain, as was the Earl of Stafford and two knights wearing the royal arms – a common policy to save the person of the real king from just such targeted attacks.[165] According to one source, Henry IV was unhorsed several times by Douglas but fought resolutely, though it is more likely that at this stage he was moved to a place of greater safety by the Earl of Dunbar. If Waurin is to be trusted, it was not just the king but considerable numbers of men-at-arms who fought on horseback; he noted that the cavalry of the advance guards clashed with couched lances, and implies that Henry IV came to the aid of his collapsing vanguard with a force of horsemen.[166]

Meanwhile, the fall of arrows continued to inflict many casualties on both sides, and at some stage – either now or in the initial arrow storm – Prince Henry was badly wounded by an arrow in the face, which lodged in the bone below his eye.[167] A matter of inches and the future victor of Agincourt would himself have fallen victim to the longbow. Henry refused to leave the field, however, and at this crucial point in the battle he launched his rearguard in a counter-attack to support his father's heavily engaged battle. Breaking through the opposing division he then turned to attack Percy's formation from the rear.[168] The conflict became a confused mêlée, in which it became hard to tell friend from foe. Though Percy's men tried to rally to the cry of 'Henry Percy, King!', Hotspur had in fact been slain, perhaps soon after his attempt to kill the king, when he would have found himself in the thick of the royalist press with only a handful of men.[169]

According to the *Annales Henrici Quarti*, Henry IV returned their rallying cry with the shout that Percy was dead.[170] For the rebels, hard-pressed on all sides and with night falling, the death of Henry Percy, 'the flower and glory of Christian knighthood',[171] marked the end and their army broke in flight. That the pursuit was fierce, despite the oncoming darkness and an eclipse of the moon, was indicated by the fact that the bodies of the slain were said to have been spread for 3 miles around.[172] Estimates of the fallen, stated to be some 1,600 on both sides, with a further 3,000 wounded, are impossible to corroborate, but Waurin was moved with pardonable exaggeration to note that, 'as I have heard tell by word of mouth and by writing, it is not found in any book of this chronicle that there was ever in the kingdom of England since the conquest of Duke William so horrible a battle or so much Christian blood spilled as in this'.[173]

The fierce fighting endured by Henry IV's archers at Shrewsbury, 'a strong and an hard bataille',[174] is indirectly revealed by some of the rewards and compensations awarded by the king in the aftermath of victory. Richard de Croke, a squire, who with his sons served with the king's archers in the battle, was given more than £26 because one of his two sons had been wounded and he himself had lost his horse and harness.[175] Another squire, Adam de Lever, was granted £40 out of taxes levied for the war, because he and his sons 'together with all the bowmen with them were in our company and train' in the campaign and battle, in which two of his sons were wounded and a third slain.[176] The fact that both Richard de Croke and Adam de Lever lost 'horse and harness' suggests that as squires they may have served mounted as men-at-arms and lost their horses in action. Here we have a valuable glimpse of the kind of troops that would have formed the core of the king's army, with local gentry bringing their sons and tenants to serve as bowmen. The supply of sufficient arrows must have been a crucial part of Henry IV's ultimate victory, and William Stersacre, 'keeper of our artillery' – that is bows and arrows as well as guns – was rewarded 'for his good service' by a grant of land in York taken from one of the rebels.[177] These were lessons that were not lost on the young Prince Henry, who had seen at first hand the terrifying effects of an arrow storm and had endured an agonising arrow wound to his face. As he drew up his forces to confront the French at Agincourt in 1415, it is hard to believe his mind did not briefly cast itself back to his experiences at Shrewsbury, but with the knowledge that twelve years later the archers of England were now united under his banner against a common enemy.

Matthew Strickland

CHAPTER 15

Attack and Defence: Armour, Arrow Penetration and Wounds

he longbow's effectiveness in battle did not depend solely – perhaps not even principally – on its performance against armour. The impact of dense clouds of arrows on the cohesion of an advancing enemy as well as upon their morale must have been devastating, while massed archery crucially rendered frontal assaults by cavalry well-nigh impossible.[1] Forced to dismount most of their forces to attack, an enemy thereby placed himself at a severe disadvantage against the defensive formations of men-at-arms and archers, while the effects of enfilade shooting might cause the enemy formations to bunch and become fatally compressed, as the outer ranks moved inward away from the rain of arrows and pressed in on their comrades who became increasing unable to fight effectively. Such a terrible occurrence, whereby as many perished through trampling or suffocation in the crush as by English arrows, had befallen the Scots at Dupplin Moor in 1332 and Halidon Hill in 1333, and, if the *Gesta Henrici Quinti* may be believed, had also happened to elements of the French at Agincourt in 1415.

Nevertheless, the question of the longbow's powers of penetration continues to exert a perennial fascination, provoking disagreement and debate among scholars and scientists alike. For those who posit the development of more powerful bows in the later thirteenth or early fourteenth century the issue of increased penetrative power is clearly central. Others, by contrast, reacting to what they regard as technological determinism, have argued that the claims made for the longbow's powers, and hence its abilities as a decisive weapon, have been considerably exaggerated. While massed volleys of arrows might indeed break up enemy formations or slay horses, it has been argued that the penetrative ability of the longbow

The terrible effect of arrows against horses is graphically conveyed by this battle scene from a late fifteenth-century Flemish manuscript of Jean Waurin's *Chronicle of England* (British Library, Royal MS 14 E IV, f.201v). *(© British Library)*

against armour was significantly limited by the steep trajectory needed to achieve the necessary range, and by the ability of plate armour, as suggested by some modern tests, to defeat arrows except at certain specific angles of strike.[2] In turn, such views have recently been countered by a strong reaffirmation of the longbow's powers not only to wound armoured men but also to kill considerable numbers of combatants, based on the explicit statements to this effect by a wide range of fourteenth- and fifteenth-century chronicles.[3] This chapter aims to discuss some of the available evidence for the penetrative powers of the longbow, and the problems inherent in such material. The nature of arrow wounds and how they might be treated by medieval surgeons will also be explored.

There can be little doubt that to many medieval observers – English, French, Scots and Flemish alike – the longbow appeared to be a devastatingly effective weapon. To give but one example, Thomas Walsingham noted that at Agincourt, 'volleys of arrows struck helmets, plates and cuirasses. Many of the French fell, pierced by arrows, here fifty, there sixty.'[4] Yet though of considerable value, the anecdotal evidence of chronicles and other literary material none the less has significant limitations. Narrative sources suffer from a chronological imbalance, with a general paucity of evidence in the earlier period compared to the rich vein of chronicle material available for the Hundred Years War, much of which, significantly, was written in the vernacular and took a keener interest in military affairs. The observations of Gerald of Wales concerning the penetrative powers of the Welsh elm bows thus stand in virtual isolation, while fellow ecclesiastics were often less well informed and might offer contradictory evidence; hence one chronicler believed that in 1264 arrows had no impact on mailed knights, while a close contemporary made the opposite comment.[5] More significantly, medieval chroniclers of whatever period rarely if ever provide any technical details concerning range, materials used in bow manufacture, the types of arrow, or the quality of armour worn by those being shot at. By contrast, inquests and legal records often supply the size of the bow, types of arrow and sometimes the nature of the wounds received in considerable detail, but these show the effects of arrows, whether accidental or intentional, not in war but in a civilian context against men who were in the majority of cases not wearing defensive armour. Similarly, manuscript illuminations frequently show arrows penetrating mail or plate armour, and killing or wounding men and horses, with the Bayeux Tapestry, the Maciejowski Bible, or the numerous fifteenth-century manuscripts of Froissart's *Chronicles* being notable examples. But, as we have already noted, iconographic conventions mean we should be cautious in reading such images literally without supporting evidence.

Such evidence must come from modern ballistic tests, which can be used to discover the velocity, impact and penetrative ability of arrows, though it is crucial that both the arrows and the armour used in such tests approximate as closely as possible to medieval exemplars. Medieval armour might vary considerably in quality and strength, depending on whether it was made of wrought iron or steel, and whether it had been quenched or heat-treated.[6] The performance of armour depended on its composition (in particular the absence of slag), as well as on its hardness, thickness and shape: good-quality armour made of steel would be at least twice as effective as armour made of iron with a low carbon content. In this regard, our knowledge of the manufacture and strength of medieval armour has been greatly enhanced by research on the metallurgy of armour. The microstructures of an increasingly wide range of armours have been analysed and their hardness measured. Hardness is determined by measuring the size of an indentation made by a diamond under a standard load and recorded on the Vickers Pyramid Hardness (VPH) scale.[7] Such experiments can to a limited extent be augmented by the burgeoning discipline of battlefield archaeology.[8] Before exploring these approaches further, we need to set them within a chronological framework of the development of armour and the level of protection it might afford.

DEFENCE AND PENETRATION: THE AGE OF MAIL

From the early Middle Ages till at least the mid-fourteenth century the basic form of defence for the well-armed warrior was the hauberk or mail shirt, formed of thousands of interlocking rings of iron or steel,[9] a garment so costly that it long remained the *sine qua non* of knighthood. By the twelfth century this flexible defence had come to reach to just above the knee, often supplemented by mail leggings, and had extended to cover the forearm, sometimes with bag-mittens for the hands. A mail coif or hood might be integral to the hauberk or worn separately. Literary sources repeatedly state the efficacy of hauberks at warding off sword cuts or dagger thrusts,[10] but vary in their accounts of the degree of protection they afforded against arrows. Thus according to William of Malmesbury, Henry I was saved from an assassin's arrow by the quality of his hauberk, and as we have seen the mail armour worn by crusaders proved effective against the arrows shot from Turkish composite bows, at least at longer ranges.[11] A fiscal record from Savoy in 1390 mentions 'a hauberk of steel proofed against all

A hauberk or shirt of mail, with a bascinet and aventail of mail, c. 1340. Worn over a thickly padded aketon, the hauberk remained the principal defence of knights and men-at-arms, and even after the spread of plate armour often continued to be worn under such defences. (© The Board of Trustees of the Royal Armouries)

blows', while the *Chronicon Colmariense* noted that in 1398 knights wore 'mailshirts, made from iron rings, through which no arrow was able to wound a man'.[12] By contrast, we have already noted the testimony of Gerald of Wales concerning the ability of the twelfth-century Welsh longbows of elm to pierce both mail and other protective layers of leather and cloth.[13]

It is evident that the interlocking rings of mail afforded better protection against a broader-headed arrow than a bodkin, which could penetrate more easily between the links, and it is therefore unsurprising that the latter type of arrowhead was employed from an early date. Examples survive from Danish bog deposits of sacrificed arms dating to the second and third centuries AD, while later Scandinavian graves contained slim but quadrilateral and trilateral arrowheads, whose principal purpose can only have been to cut through or prise apart mail.[14] Similarly, bodkin heads appear regularly from excavated sites within Britain from at least the eleventh century, with slender bodkins dating from about 1000–80 being found at the Lincolnshire fortified manor house of Goltho, and others of twelfth-century date from the Norman castle at Castle Acre in Norfolk.[15] These were perhaps the kind of arrowheads referred to by Gerald of Wales which he had seen embedded in the door of Abergavenny Castle, though other arrowheads of this date, such as those excavated at Laugharne Castle, have flat, triangular heads with no barbs. Bodkin heads dating from the 1270s have been found at the castles of Rayleigh and Dyserth, and also at Caerlaverock, probably dating from the early fourteenth century.[16] Tests undertaken by Stephen Grancsay, a former curator of arms and armour at the Metropolitan

Museum in New York, showed that at a range of 15ft an arrow from a comparatively weak 68lb (31kg) longbow could penetrate mail with ease.[17] This was point-blank range, however, and it is regrettable that Grancsay did not extend his testing to more representative battlefield ranges.

As with later plate armour, however, a number of variables would have affected the penetrative qualities of arrows against mail: the nature of the arrow and the quality of its head, the strength and quality of the mail, and the extent of additional defences worn over or above it. Mail might vary widely in quality, depending on the nature of the iron or steel wire used to make the rings, on the size of the rings (for the smaller the rings, the more per unit area), on whether the rings were flat or rounded (*mailles rondes*), and on whether the individual rings were welded or riveted. The use of two rivets may have been thought to provide a more sturdy armour, and such garments were doubtless more expensive than ones in which the links received only one rivet (*demy cloues, demi cloies*).[18] Thus in 1316 the inventory of King Louis X of France (1314–16) speaks of a hauberk and mail sleeves '*de roondes mailles de haute clouer*', that is mail of high quality with rounded rings, but then refers to a similar garment but 'of stronger steel'.[19] In 1369 Italian arms dealers in Avignon were selling mail shirts whose varying quality was reflected in a price range of 3 to 14 livres.[20] Literary and record evidence, moreover, refers to 'double mail' and garments such as a '*haubert à maille double*' or a '*haubert doublier*', in which two or more rings might be used in place of the normal one ring. This would give the armour a greater thickness, and thus better protection, but the increase in weight must have limited the practicality of such garments and extant examples are unknown. Where such an increase in thickness could work well, however, and give added stiffness, was in smaller pieces of armour, notably coifs and neck defences, such as the 33 '*gorgieres doubles de Chambli*', that is neck pieces of double mail made at the famous armour-producing town of Chambli, that were also recorded in the inventory of Louis X.[21] Equally, it has been suggested that the distinctive square flaps on the chests of some of William's knights on the Bayeux Tapestry may represent a mail reinforce.[22]

Assessing the penetrative abilities of arrows against such armour is made still more problematic by the fact that the hauberk would have been worn in conjunction with heavily padded garments known as aketons, which might absorb the impact of an arrow which had succeeded in piercing the hauberk itself.[23] Sometimes, however, an arrow is recorded as piercing both mail and the aketon worn beneath, as a chronicler described at the siege of Dunbar in 1337: 'And now I shall tell you of a great shot made as they skirmished there one day, that caused them much wonder. The arrow pierced the blazon of

William Despencer, and through three folds of mail armour, and through three plies of the acqueton, and into the body, so that he lay there dead of the blow.'[24] The wonder of the onlookers, however, and the care taken by the chronicler to record the incident suggest that such a feat was rare. It is also unclear whether the unfortunate Despencer's blazon was simply a thin heraldic surcoat, or a more substantial quilted tunic, of the kind that would soon be referred to as 'coat armour'. For while the aketon or the similar thickly padded gambeson often formed the sole body armour of infantry or less well-equipped serjeants, late twelfth- and thirteenth-century sources frequently refer to an aketon, hauberk and gambeson together, as if they were an entity intended to be worn in conjunction.[25] These thickly padded surcoats were often richly coloured or embroidered, while in addition they might also have a stiff gamboised collar forming an early type of gorget, such as that worn by a knight on the west front of Wells Cathedral, dating to about 1230–40.[26] The monument of Sir Robert de Shurland at Minster in the Isle of Sheppey, of about 1330, is of exceptional interest in depicting not only such a gambeson worn over the hauberk, but one which was decorated with the arms of his lord, Sir William de Leyburn, under whom he fought in Scotland. Such padded 'coat-armour' or jupons continued to be worn over armour until the later fourteenth century, and must have continued to provide an additional degree of protection against arrows.[27] A few elaborate specimens of fourteenth-century jupons survive, notably that of the Black Prince, that which Charles of Blois is said to have worn to his death at Auray in 1364, and that belonging to the Dauphin Charles.[28]

This form of 'soft armour' offered a surprisingly effective defence, owing to the considerable quantities of folded tow, cotton or sendal with which they were tightly packed. Ordinances in England and France attempted to regulate the quality of these garments carefully, to ensure that they were adequately filled with good material and that sub-standard stuffing was avoided.[29] A Parisian ordinance of 1311 stated that a gambeson was to contain 3lb of new cotton, while in 1450 a regulation of Louis XI stipulated that jacks of fabric should comprise 29 or 30 layers of linen with a covering of deerskin.[30] Between 1462 and 1471 John Howard, the future Duke of Norfolk, ordered a 'doublet of defence . . . eighteen-fold thick of white fustian, and four-fold of linen cloth', while jacks in Sir

A statue of St George, from a Flemish retable, commissioned by Duke Philip the Bold of Burgundy (1363–1404), showing the thickly padded coat armour or *pourpoint* worn over the plate defences for the arms and torso. Such 'soft' armour afforded added protection against arrows, and was sometimes also worn over the mail aventail attached to the bascinet. *(Musée des Beaux-Arts de Dijon)*

John Fastolf's inventory of 1459 show that they could be stuffed not only with cloth but with mail and horn.[31] The *Chronicle of Bertrand du Guesclin* believed that in 1383 a lance thrust that had penetrated a shield and coat of plates had been finally defeated by an aketon of buckram.[32] Tests conducted on the resistance of wrought iron, similar in quality to medieval munition armour, demonstrated that the presence of padding underneath (in this case 16 folds of linen) required an extra 50 joules of energy for a point to penetrate the armour plate, and 80 joules for a blade.[33] What is needed to assist our understanding of the efficacy of such defences is controlled modern tests of the relative resistance of such a combination of an aketon, a good-quality mail shirt and a gambeson against longbow arrows and crossbow bolts.

'LAPP'D IN PROOF': THE SPREAD OF PLATE ARMOUR

Despite the significant degree of protection offered by a hauberk in conjunction with soft armour, attempts to reinforce the mail hauberk yet further had occurred as early as the 1180s. William le Breton describes both Richard the Lionheart and the French champion William des Barres wearing a protective iron plate under their hauberks and gambesons when engaging in single combat in 1188.[34] The same author speaks of solid breast protection during his account of the battle of Bouvines in 1214, and noted the increasing efficacy of the knights' armour:

> But even then, iron cannot reach them unless their bodies are first dispossessed of the armour protecting them, so much has each knight covered his members with several layers of iron and enclosed his chest with armour, pieces of leather and other types of breastplate . . . . While misfortunes multiply, precautions against these multiply as well, and new defences are invented against new kinds of attack . . .[35]

Such reinforcements, also mentioned by Gerald of Wales, are visible in several illustrations by Matthew Paris, which depict gambesons with rigid shoulder protection, probably attached to some form of solid body defence worn beneath the surcoat.[36] The *Rule of the Temple*, dating in its existing form to 1257–65, mentions additional shoulder pieces or *espalières* over the hauberk, and metal *soliers d'armer* for the feet over the mail stockings or chausses.[37] During the thirteenth century poleyns (knee defences), either of iron or *cuir bouilli* (boiled and hardened leather), become increasingly common in illustrations and on effigies, while forms of solid body armour begin to appear, worn over the aketon and hauberk but under the surcoat. An effigy of a knight in Pershore Abbey, dating to the second half of the thirteenth century, clearly shows some form of solid body armour, probably of *cuir bouilli*, forming a breast and back defence buckled at the side over the hauberk but beneath the surcoat. By the second half of the thirteenth century sculpture and illustration begin to show the use of surcoats reinforced with numbers of small plates, presumably of metal, a body defence known as a 'pair of plates'.[38] In 1260 knights in the service of Florence were expected to wear such body armour or *lamières* over their hauberks, and such was the kind of armour which chroniclers report was worn by German knights at the battle of Benevento in 1266 and Tagliacozzo in 1268.[39] Similarly, the inventory of the Count of Nevers in 1266 refers to '*paires de cuiraces*', though hardened leather may have continued to play an important part in such defences.[40] Development of body armour to supplement the hauberk seems thus to have been a gradual but continuous process from at least about 1200 rather than any sudden response to the growing effectiveness of archery or any marked increase in the longbow's power. Concurrently attempts were made to protect the knights' costly war-horses, always vulnerable to arrows, and by the mid-twelfth century references increase concerning the provision of bardings of cloth, leather or, for the wealthiest,

mail. When in 1198, for example, Richard the Lionheart routed Philip Augustus's forces near Gisors, he captured many prisoners and 140 horses covered with mail bardings.[41]

Until the mid-fourteenth century, however, medieval armourers were confronted by major limitations in the raw materials and processes available to them. The basic form of manufacturing iron was by smelting in a furnace known as a bloomery hearth, in which charcoal was burned with iron ore. The iron ore was reduced at 800°C to iron, which never melted, but non-metallic impurities from the ore and the furnace lining would react with some of the iron ore to form slag, a glass-like material which liquefied at around 1,200°C. If this was allowed to flow away, most of it (but not all) could be separated from the iron, which would then aggregate to form a 'bloom' or porous mass. Further slag might be removed by reworking the iron bloom, though this was time-consuming and thus expensive. The existence of steel was known, but its controlled manufacture was extremely difficult. If a bloom or pieces of a bloom were left in the furnace for a longer time, at a suitable temperature and without oxygen, the iron might absorb enough carbon (up to 0.5 per cent) to become steel. Alternatively, it might easily absorb enough carbon (2 per cent) to form a liquid of lower melting point (1,150°C), known as cast iron. While this material was subsequently used to cast guns, it was far too brittle to make armour.[42] Given these constraints, it was extremely difficult to produce large sheets of properly homogenised iron or steel as the majority of iron contained slag or iron particles, which might lead to flaws and splits when the metal was worked. It was for this reason that early medieval helmets were rarely worked out of single pieces of iron or steel but used the 'spangenhelm' construction of a number of plates riveted to a frame,[43] and why some leg harness even by the later fourteenth century was made from splints of iron riveted to fabric rather than being hammered as single pieces. Similarly, body armour could rarely be forged into large plates, and so the most common form of construction remained the 'pair of plates' formed by riveting a series of broad lames to a fabric base.[44]

Twenty-five sets of such armour were excavated from the grave pits at Wisby. Though used in the battle in 1361 between Danes and Gotlanders, they were probably considerably older and regarded as outmoded by the conquering Danes.[45] Subsequently, a less cumbersome defence known as a brigandine, made of a larger number of smaller plates, became popular and with its variant the jack remained in use until well into the sixteenth century. The significant difference in quality between armours used contemporaneously is demonstrated by tests on lames from three of the 'pairs of plates' from Wisby. One was made of wrought iron, another of a low-carbon steel (0.1 per cent), but the third was of better-quality steel (0.6 per cent carbon) with a microhardness of 266 VPH.[46] By contrast, a lame from a similar 'pair of plates' excavated from Knüssnach Castle, Canton Schwyz in Switzerland, and antedating the castle's destruction in 1352, was of a heterogeneous steel made from carburised iron which had been 'slack-quenched' then heat-treated, producing an impressive average hardness of 390 VPH.[47] To set this in context, the hardness of modern mild steel is around 100 VPH, of unhardened tool steel around 250 VPH, and of hardened tool steel 500–600 VPH.

The first half of the fourteenth century witnessed great strides in the development of plate armour. The Hainaulter chronicler and soldier John Le Bel was guilty of exaggeration when he remarked that before the time of Edward III the English did not know of plate armour, 'nor of bascinets with gorgets (ne de bachines a barbière).[48] Royalty and the wealthiest nobles certainly had access to quite considerable amounts of plate; prior to 1306, for example, accounts reveal that the young Edward of Caernarfon (the future Edward II) possessed cuisses, greaves, sabatons and gloves of plate, while the kind of helmet probably referred to by Le Bel, with a hinged gorget of plate, appears in the Holkam Bible (see p. 151), dating from the 1320s, and 'gorgeret de plates' are recorded in the inventory of Raoul de Nesle in 1302.[49] Nevertheless, it is from the 1330s that effigies, brasses and manuscript illuminations begin regularly to show knights with plate arm and leg defences, often worn over mail.[50] The bascinet, rounded to deflect the blows of edged weapons and missiles, became increasingly popular, worn in conjunction with an aventail of mail attached to them (see p. 268), while the great helm might be worn over the bascinet. The 'pair of plates' continued to be the principal form of defence for the torso, and by 1335 even hobelars were required to possess them.[51] In his English translation of Pierre Langtoft's rhyming French chronicle, completed in 1338, Robert Manning of Bourne gives a vivid and suitably updated account of the arming of King Arthur, and of the kind of equipment an affluent knight might possess:

> He himself was finely armed
> With sabatons, and spurs, and greaves of steel,
> A doublet, cuisses [thigh-pieces], with very richly
>   decorated poleyns,
> Gussets, a groin-proction of mail, armoured breeches
>   without equal,
> A hauberk, with very well burnished plates,
> Vambraces and rerebraces with couters of steel,
> And over this a padded aketon of silk.[52]

The brasses of knights such as Sir John III d'Aubernon (c. 1340–5) and Sir Hugh Hastings (c. 1347) clearly show this armour and give an excellent idea of the kind of equipment in use by leading knights in the armies of Edward III by the late 1340s (see pp. 192, 215). It was just such equipment which, at the siege of Tournai in 1340, saved the French lord Godemar du Fay from English arrows, for he 'was shot in the plates of armour, and the arrow remained stuck in it'.[53] At this period such harness was relatively expensive. An earlier attempt by Edward II to compel infantry to serve in Gascony with plate armour as well as mail had to be dropped on the grounds of cost.[54] It has been suggested that Edward III's introduction in the 1340s of a bonus payment known as a regard to those men-at-arms serving in his continental campaigns was to help cover the cost of plate armour, and certainly on the Neville's Cross campaign in 1346 a group of Lancashire men-at-arms and the men serving with them received a bonus payment of £20 from the king 'for good equipment'.[55]

Such developments in armour have been seen in part as a reaction by the military elite to the 'infantry revolution' of the later thirteenth and early fourteenth centuries, which saw the increasing deployment of larger numbers of infantry armed with staff weapons or bows. Yet the weapons deployed by fourteenth-century infantry such as the Scots and Flemings were not in themselves new, and earlier staff weapons anticipated even the fearsome halberd of the Swiss. Equally, the longbow was no novelty, and the crossbow had clearly posed a major threat to knights from at least the eleventh century. Instead, the increasing availability of plate armour may well have been primarily the result of major advances in armour production occurring during the fourteenth century.[56] Larger and more powerful bloomery furnaces with bigger shafts were developed. These made the production of larger blooms easier and, because of the higher temperatures they attained, speeded up the absorption of carbon. This eased the effective separation of liquid slag from the iron and facilitated the production of steel, which, unlike iron, can be hardened by quenching.[57] Though the carbon content might vary in steel thus produced, hammer-ing and refolding could help to spread the carbon content throughout the plate.[58] Because it now contained less slag, the iron or steel could be fashioned into larger plates, and it is from the mid-fourteenth century that the 'pair of plates' begins to be replaced by breastplates forged as a single piece of armour.[59]

Not only could larger plates now be made, but the armourers of northern Italy developed a process of hardening their armours. If heated steel is rapidly quenched by plunging it into water (full-quenching), the crystalline structure is altered, and in the right conditions martensite is produced, which is extremely hard. Brittleness could then be reduced by a process of reheating or tempering the steel. This process of rapid quenching and tempering required great skill, carefully controlled temperature and time, and homogeneous steel of a consistent quality.[60] Until the mid-fourteenth century most armour (except that made for the greatest) seems to have been of iron or low-carbon steel, for it was probably difficult to keep the true curvature of forged pieces while quenching without the armour warping.[61] As a result many armourers left the worked steel simply to air cool, which would still yield a much better armour than one made of iron. But in addition the armourers of Milan and northern Italy began from the mid-fourteenth century to produce high-quality armours made of medium-carbon steel, often also 'slack-quenched' to make it harder still.[62] This involved plunging the red-hot pieces of armour into oil or other less rapid coolants, or allowing a space of time to elapse before quenching. Full-quenching and tempering (the modern method) entails plunging the red-hot steel into water to obtain the maximum hardness, and then gently reheating it to reduce hardness but to achieve maximum toughness. This was (and is) extremely difficult to control, and the method was seldom practised before the sixteenth century, and then by only a tiny minority of armourers. Nevertheless, the Milanese armourers of the fourteenth and fifteenth centuries were able to produce armour of impressive hardness,

Parts of a late fourteenth-century armour, made in Milan for a Vogt of Matsch, from the great castle armoury of Churburg in the Tyrol. This is one of the earliest extant armours of plate, and the breastplate, intended to be worn over a mailshirt and without a backplate, is still made of a number of separate plates, which curve around the torso. *(akg-images/Erich Lessing)*

often full-quenched and tempered, which could achieve great resilience. Thus, for example, a steel bascinet made in Milan in about 1330–40 attained a hardness of 300 VPH, while a late fourteenth-century steel breastplate, probably also Milanese, had been hardened by heating to around 340 VPH.[63]

Such a chronology accords well with chronicle evidence concerning the effectiveness of armour. As we have seen, at least some of the Scottish men-at-arms at the battle of Neville's Cross in 1346 were so well armoured that, according to Geoffrey le Baker, the English arrows did them little harm, while at the siege of Bergerac in 1345 the armour of the well-equipped Genoese protected them from Derby's archers.[64] The same phenomenon is reported in 1356 at the battle of Poitiers, where the arrows of Oxford's men had little effect on the breastplates of the French knights forming the initial cavalry strike, who had probably been selected because they possessed the latest high-quality armour.[65] The English bowmen were compelled to shoot them from behind, where they were less well protected, for in this transitional period it was common to wear only a breastplate, strapped over the hauberk, without an accompanying backplate.[66] A fine example of such a breastplate survives as part of a brass-edged Milanese armour from Churburg Castle in the Tyrol (see left).[67] The breast defence is still composite, being made of a larger central plate with smaller lateral lames, all carefully rounded to offer a glancing surface, yet though these lames curve around the torso of the wearer there is no backplate. Perhaps offering as much protection as the breastplate itself (if not more in the mind of the warrior) are the religious invocations etched over all the brass edgings, both on the breastplate lames and on the visor of the bascinet – a common medieval practice designed to seek the assistance of God and his saints in warding off danger.[68] The dating of the Churburg breastplate has been a matter of considerable dispute, with suggestions ranging from the 1360s to between about 1380 and 1400.[69] What is clear, however, is that solid breastplates, whether worn as part of a pair of plates, such as is indicated on the tomb of Mahiu de Montmorency (1360) at Tavergny, or as separate pieces, were becoming widespread in the second half of the century.[70] Early composite forms gradually gave way to breastplates forged in one piece and increasingly fitted with lames on their lower edge to extend the defence to the lower torso.[71] By 1369 the city of Florence expected its men-at-arms to serve with cuirass or *panciera* (breastplate) as well as a coat of mail, and with armour for the arms and legs, together with gauntlets, and fines were levied if any of these items were lacking.[72] The funeral effigy of the Black Prince (d. 1376) in Canterbury Cathedral gives a fine example of the kind of harness worn by the greatest lords by the 1370s (see p. 233),[73] and by about 1400 the brasses and effigies of numerous English lords and knights reveal that such complete suits of 'white harness' had become commonplace (see pp. 264, 324, 326).

Armour of such quality was naturally in high demand, and was soon being exported in large quantities throughout Europe by merchants such as Francesco di Marco Datini, the Pratese entrepreneur who plied a lively trade in arms from his base in Avignon. After the Anglo-French truce of Bordeaux in 1357 he sold considerable amounts of armour not only to the soldiers of the Free Companies and other adventurers, including Bertrand Du Guesclin, but to towns in southern France seeking defence against these very brigands.[74] Though some armour was probably produced in England, the Low Countries and in France – Lyons, for example was producing bascinets 'of the latest fashion' and leg harness in the 1370s and 1380s – the lion's share of the fourteenth-century market was dominated by Milanese workshops, with armour being wrapped in straw and canvas and sent by mule across the Alps.[75] Northern Italy and Milan in particular witnessed a marked industrial expansion to meet demand, while some armourers, notably the famous Missaglia family of Milan, even produced their own steel and became major dealers in arms on the European market.[76]

Such mass production and export made plate armour far more widely available. An inventory of Datini's shop in 1367 included 25 bascinets, 3 war hats, 10 cervellières, 60 breast-plates, 20 cuirasses, 12 coats of mail, 23 pairs of gauntlets, mail sleeves, cuisses of plate and other armour,[77] while a Bohemian merchant in London in 1387 possessed 33 breastplates as well as 600 'white plates' and 50 'long plates', presumably the necessary raw material for armourers.[78] Though armour of the highest quality was still expensive, the overall price of plate armour had fallen.[79] An inventory drawn up in 1374 of the Leicestershire knight Sir Edmund Appleby of Appleby Magna, who had served on the Poitiers campaign and was later in the affinity of John of Gaunt, shows the equipment available to a knight of fairly modest means.[80] It records one bascinet with its aventail valued at 2 marks, one hauberk and two haubergeons together worth 13 marks, two pairs of plate gauntlets at 6s 8d, and two kettlehats and two 'plates' (paletta) – perhaps 'pairs of plates' or separate breastplates – worth 6s 8d.[81] The quality of Sir Edmund's armour is unknown, but clearly it was comparatively inexpensive to possess the basic equipment needed by a man-at-arms in the later fourteenth century.

There is thus an important chronological element to the question of the protection afforded by armour against the longbow. In the first stages of the Hundred Years War quality plate armour was comparatively rare, and knights fully equipped with good steel armour would have represented only a minority of the combatants at engagements such as Morlaix in 1342 and Crécy in 1346. The brass of Sir John Clifford (d. 1348) at Bowers Gifford in Essex, for example, shows arm and leg defences still only of mail, while as late as the 1350s and 1360s it is likely that many less affluent men-at-arms might still be protected only by mail, worn with 'soft armour' such as a gambeson and perhaps reinforced with cuir bouilli.[82] The continuing vulnerability of limbs is demonstrated by the remarkably detailed account of the Tournai Chronicle, which lists many of the French defenders of this city in 1340 as being wounded by English arrows in the arms, thighs and knees.[83] It is important to remember, moreover, that some of the French nobility became impoverished by the wars, and could not afford full 'white harness' even when it became less expensive. In 1369, for example, the Sire de Courcy was reduced to borrowing a bascinet and an old pair of gloves from the merchant Datini.[84] Much armour must have been handed down and reused, giving the men-at-arms of any given host a very heterogeneous appearance. While good-quality breastplates forged from single sheets were increasingly widespread by the 1380s and 1390s, the brigandine remained favoured by some. A composite armour of about 1390–1400 in the Metropolitan Museum in New York, containing elements from the hoard of Italian armour from Chalcis, has a body defence comprised of two plates covering the upper chest, with other smaller plates for the torso, all riveted to a fabric lining and covered with velvet (see p. 253).[85] The quality of protection afforded by a high-quality brigandine or jack is indicated by an incident which took place during the Peasants' Revolt in 1381. Having plundered John of Gaunt's palace of the Savoy, some of Wat Tyler's men 'seized one of his most precious vestments, which we call a "jakke", and placed it on a lance to be used as a target for their arrows. And since they were unable to damage it sufficiently with their arrows, they took it down and tore it apart with their axes and swords.'[86]

Not only cost, but military fashion and utility led many men-at-arms to abandon the full panoply demanded of knights in the first decades of the century, rejecting crested helms, heraldic ailettes and other finery in favour of lighter, more practical and work-a-day equipment. Writing between 1352 and 1356 Jean Le Bel looked back with nostalgic regret to the 1330s when,

> at that time the great lords did not count men-at-arms if they did not have crested helmets, whereas now men with glaives, panchières, haubergeons and chapeaux-de-fer are counted. So it seems to me that the times have certainly changed from what I remember, for barded horses, crested helms, with which one used to bedeck oneself, plates, and armbands with coats of arms have all disappeared, and the haubergeons, which are now called panchières, the gambesons and the chapeaux-de-fer have all come to the

fore. Nowadays, a poor servant is as well and as nobly armed as is a noble knight.[87]

His contemporary Jacques de Hemricourt, a clerk of Liège, similarly bemoaned that whereas in the past knights had fought on chargers with rich trappings and high saddles, 'nowadays, each one is armed in a coat of mail called a *panchire*, rides a small horse and is dressed in a jupon of fustian, regardless of the fact that one cannot distinguish one man from his companion . . . thus is all honour and nobleness perished'.[88] Such a fusion evidently reflected the process whereby the distinctions clearly visible on the battlefield around 1300 between knight, squire and serjeant had blurred, being replaced by the more amorphous grouping of 'men-at-arms' to cover any warrior possessing the minimum equipment and mounts necessary.

A full suit of 'white harness' was not particularly heavy; a Milanese harness of about 1450, complete but for its missing tassets, weighs 57lb (25.9kg), while a German Gothic armour of about 1480 weighs 59lb 12½oz (27.1kg).[89] Yet its weight might none the less quickly cause fatigue if a man-at-arms had to move any distance on foot and fight dismounted; this proved fatal to the French knights at Agincourt. As a result many chose to sacrifice added protection for greater manoeuvrability, wearing only select pieces of plate armour. The men of the White Company, for example, seem to have favoured being more lightly armed, wearing a haubergeon with a steel breastplate as well as arm and leg defences, but discarding the *corazza* (either a coat of plates or a full cuirass of breast- and backplates) and gorget.[90] At Auray in 1364 Sir Hugh Calveley and the knights of his mobile reserve took off their leg armour to allow them to move swiftly along the Anglo-Gascon line to reinforce it where necessary.[91] Neither Hawkwood nor Calveley's men, however, ever had to confront the rapid shooting of massed longbowmen, and it is far less likely that French men-at-arms would have chosen to remove elements of armour, if they possessed it, when advancing on foot against English defensive formations.

Of equal if not greater significance, much plate armour worn in the fourteenth century would have been made not of steel, for this was extremely expensive, but of wrought iron, the ability of which to withstand arrows was considerably poorer. Thus, for instance, the great helm from the tomb of Sir Reginald Braybrook (d. 1405), formerly in Cobham Church, Kent, has been shown to be of very low carbon (below 0.1 per cent), being virtually wrought iron, with an average hardness of only 108 VPH, while that from the tomb of Sir Nicholas Hawberk (d. 1407) from the same church is of a superior medium-carbon steel which ranged in hardness from 110 to 195 VPH.[92] Similarly, a bascinet of 1390–1410, possibly Italian but lacking any armourer's marks, and a contemporary German bascinet were made only of a poor-quality steel, scarcely better than wrought iron.[93] Hence even as the availability of plate armour widened, there remained marked differences in its quality and thus effectiveness, and such a disparity would remain on the European battlefield throughout the period when armour was worn. Common infantrymen with munition-quality armour, still more the lightly armed troops such as the French *bidauts* or Castilian *jinetes*, would have remained extremely vulnerable to the arrows of the English archers.[94]

Nevertheless, for those who could afford full 'white harness', the design and manufacture of plate continued to improve. By the time of Agincourt solid breastplates with a fauld of overlapping plates protected the torso, besagews helped to defend the vulnerable areas of the armpits, and increasingly the use of steel gorgets affixed to the lower half of the bascinet, replacing the older aventail of mail, gave the throat added protection.[95] Such armours were now often worn over a padded arming doublet with mail reinforcing at the exposed armpits and inner elbows, as described in detail by a fifteenth-century treatise on arming for foot combat,[96] though some still wore a complete hauberk under their harness for added protection.[97] By the early fifteenth century, if not before, it would seem that armours of the very best quality, made of hardened steel, would have been able to defeat the arrows and bolts of longbows and crossbows. The chronicler Monstrelet noted that at the battle of Othée in 1408 the Burgundian duke John the Fearless 'was so well protected that although he was frequently hit by arrows and other missiles' he 'did not, on that day, lose a drop of blood'.[98] At Agincourt the French chronicler Jean Juvenal des Ursins noted that 'the French were scarcely harmed by the arrow fire of the English because they were well armed', though the *Gesta Henrici* noted that the English arrows 'by their very force pierced the sides and visors of their helmets'.[99]

From around 1440, moreover, the quality of Italian and southern German armour improved still further. A total of 45 out of 72 specimens of marked north Italian armour dating to 1340–1510 tested by Alan Williams were of hardened steel, especially those dating after 1440, and ranged in hardness between 300 and 400 VPH. Only four were made of iron.[100] Not only did the Italians produce better-quality steel, they also began to make significant design improvements, with increasingly large pauldrons, smooth rounded surfaces which offered few surfaces where a point might easily bite, and several areas where plates overlapped, offering extra thickness against attack. This is well illustrated by the superb Milanese armour, known from one of the religious mottos it bears as the Avant armour, now in the Kelvingrove Museum in Glasgow.[101] This, in common with many Italian armours of the period, has a two-part breastplate, with the lower plate extending high up the chest and buckled to the underlying upper plate, thereby giving a double thickness to much of the chest and abdomen.[102] Similarly, each plate of the fauld overlaps, while the very large pauldrons give excellent protection to the shoulders. Extra pieces could be added, such as reinforces for the right and left pauldron, while the gradual abandonment of the shield meant the left arm could be further protected by enlarging the couter or by fitting it with a reinforce known as the pasguard. Such armour, similar to that depicted on the effigy of Richard Beauchamp, Earl of Warwick (1453–6), and worn by many of the better-off protagonists in the Wars of the Roses, offered the best protection yet available against arrows. The thinner armour of vambraces and cuisses, however, might still prove vulnerable. Prior to the battle of Towton in 1460 the Earl of Warwick was wounded in the leg by a Lancastrian arrow, while at Barnet in 1471 Sir John Paston was wounded by an arrow in the left arm just below the elbow.[103]

Warriors of the period did not, of course, have access to sophisticated metallurgical tests to ascertain the quality of the armour they were purchasing. Instead, they had to rely on the marks of proof stamped by the armourers on their finished pieces, which were required by armourers' guilds to ensure the standard of their products. In 1448 the statutes of the armourers of Angers enjoined craftsmen to make white harness and brigandines with two proof marks to indicate an armour 'fully proofed' (*de toute éprouve*), which could withstand a shot from a windlass-drawn crossbow, with one mark for an armour 'of half proof' (*demie espreuve*), which had withstood the impact of a bolt from a crossbow spanned by a cranequein (*arbaleste à crocq*) and an arrow shot from a bow.[104] Nevertheless, metallurgical testing of armour has revealed that while armour bearing marks was usually of better quality than armour without them, there was no correlation whatsoever between the quality of the metal and the number of marks.[105] The surest way for a patron to discover the quality of the armour was to test it for himself. Thus, for example, in 1455 two crossbowmen hired by the Bishop of Toul, Guillaume Fillastre, were paid for breaking sixteen bolts against armour purchased for the bishop's men.[106]

From the mid-fifteenth century high-quality export armours were available not only from northern Italy but also from centres of armour production in southern Germany such as Innsbruck, Augsburg, Nüremburg and Lanshut.[107] The best German armourers in particular developed the tempering of armour to a fine art, replacing slack-quenching by full-quenching and producing harness that offered a very significant degree of protection. Of 23 specimens tested from Augsburg and Innsbruck, dating between 1460 and 1510, 15 achieved a hardness between 400 and 500 VPH.[108] The two centres produced armours of distinctive design and form, with Italian armours emphasising smooth, rounded surfaces while German armours of Gothic form were more angular and often had

The AVANT armour, Milanese, c. 1450, so called from one of the religious invocations it bears, and typical of Italian export armours worn by the wealthier protagonists in the Wars of the Roses. By the mid-fifteenth century north Italian armourers had succeeded in combining high-quality steel with designs whose gracefully curving surfaces helped to deflect strikes by arrows. Though shown here with an open-faced barbuta, the armour would originally have been worn with an armet, offering greater protection to the face. *(Glasgow City Council (Museums))*

fluted surfaces (see p. 388). It has been suggested that such differing styles reflected not only aesthetic tastes and considerations of climate, but also forms of warfare; the glancing surfaces of Italian armour with large pauldrons and couters reflected an emphasis on cavalry warfare with lance and sword in a theatre of war where the longbow was rarely deployed, whereas the fluted surfaces of German armour afforded better protection against arrows and bolts, and the sallet, with its often elongated neck guard, might guard against vertical archery.[109] It is certainly true that cavalry warfare was more predominant in Italy than in England, France and Burgundy until the later fifteenth century, when the practice of dismounting men-at-arms which had dominated tactical thinking since the 1350s began to wane. Yet it should be noted that Italian export armour, which was no less proof against crossbow bolts, was worn by English, French and Burgundian men-at-arms alike just as much as suits of German manufacture. Indeed, Italian armourers even produced armour in Gothic and other north European styles for export. English lords who saw action in the Wars of the Roses must surely have bought such armour with the threat of longbow arrows in mind as much as that of swords, lances or poleaxes.

In terms of head protection the more open-faced barbuta favoured in Italy would have been unsuitable for warfare in northern Europe where, as in the Wars of the Roses, there was a high instance of missile shot. But the armet, with its sloping surfaces and complete face protection, offered as good if not better defence against arrows than the sallet. While the tail of the sallet afforded good protection against sword cuts to the neck and the rear of the shoulders, there is little evidence of vertical arrow shot being a perceived threat; most shafts would have struck at a more direct angle, and unless shot at retreating men-at-arms it would have been very difficult for an arrow to strike the back of the neck. Not all versions of the sallet, moreover, were long-tailed, and those of possible English or Burgundian manufacture have considerably shorter neck guards than many German examples. Equally, while the armet could be fitted with a 'wrapper', or reinforce, which gave additional protection to the throat and lower face, the sallet required a separate beavor, which, while offering better ventilation, gave less complete protection.[110] When advancing on foot against a hail of arrows, men-at-arms had a tendency to incline their heads forward, a phenomenon noted of the Scots at Neville's Cross and the French at Agincourt.[111] It is thus natural to find bascinets of the early to mid-fifteenth century, such as the fine example from Bourg en Bresse, fitted with reinforcing plates on the brow, which could serve equally well to strengthen the helmet against sword blows. Similar reinforcing plates appear on some armets and sallets later in the fifteenth century. For the same reason the 'great bascinet' continued to enjoy popularity in northern Europe. A fine example of an export Milanese bascinet 'alla francesca', of about 1445–50, has a heavy 'frog-mouthed' visor which would have afforded excellent protection against the risk of an arrow penetrating the sights, a deep gorget of plate, and beneath this and the lowered visor a solid plate instead of a mail aventail protecting much of the lower face (see p. 348).[112] An arrow would thus have to defeat two layers of plate armour to wound its wearer in the face or throat. How much protection this afforded its wearer against nimble archers wielding mauls, axes or daggers is another matter.

The effectiveness of high-quality armour against arrows continued to increase in the late fifteenth and early sixteenth centuries. By the time of the battle of Flodden in 1513 the armour of the front ranks of King James's column was largely effective against Surrey's archers.[113] As has been rightly observed, 'a variety of reasons have been offered for the decline of the longbow but undoubtedly inadequate performance against hardened armours must have been one of them'.[114] As we have seen, the longbow was already beginning to lose its battle against good-quality plate armour as early as Neville's Cross and Poitiers. If there was any time when bows became increasingly powerful, it would logically be from the second half of the fourteenth century, as higher poundages were attempted in order to gain extra penetration. It must be stressed, however, that there is no direct evidence of such an increase, and, unless archaeology produces new bow finds that prove the contrary, it is likely that a longbow bent by an archer at Towton in 1461 differed little in draw-weight and power from that used by his forebears at Poitiers in 1356 and at Crécy in 1346. Be this as it may, the archer was ultimately bound to lose the arms race against the armourer, for the limits of the human body meant that an impassable ceiling was quickly reached, while the armourer's craft consistently improved through the fifteenth and early sixteenth centuries. Only the crossbow, with its steel bow and windlass, could attempt to keep pace. Yet even the finest of armour was to prove of little defence against the enormously greater penetrative power of the hand-gun, rapidly disseminating through European armies in the fifteenth century and becoming lethally effective by the early sixteenth century.[115] Tests carried out on a replica of an arquebus from the *Mary Rose* penetrated two 2mm sheets of mild steel using 65 grains of power, while a charge of 90 grains nearly penetrated 6mm of sheet steel.[116]

TESTING ARROWS AGAINST ARMOUR

Anecdotal evidence concerning the effectiveness of armour gleaned from chronicles and other written evidence can to a certain extent be tested against modern scientific experiments. The extent of arrow penetration, however, depends on a complex variety of factors: the amount of energy (measured in joules) delivered by the arrow or bolt; the thickness of the armour; whether the armour is of iron or steel, and if it has been heat-treated for hardness; the slag content of the metal, a very significant factor as this strongly affects the fracture toughness of the armour; the range of attack; the angle of strike; and the type and quality of manufacture of the arrow itself.[117]

Given that the amount of medieval armour surviving from before about 1500 is extremely small, and that museum curators are naturally reluctant to allow such prize pieces to be subjected to potentially destructive tests, experiments must be conducted on reproduction armour or metal plates which resemble as closely as possible the kind of wrought iron or steel used in the Middle Ages. Yet as we have seen, armour could vary enormously in quality and thus strength, while some arrows were of far higher quality than others, as witnessed by the distinction in accounts between 'good' and 'best' arrows, the latter having heads of hardened steel.[118] In 1419 'arrows of proof', used to test armour, cost 8s per dozen but ordinary arrows only 4s.[119] The vast quantities of arrows demanded by the English government during the Hundred Years War clearly led to problems not only of supply but of ensuring the requisite quality, for in 1405 Henry IV legislated against arrowsmiths producing inferior arrowheads that had not been properly tempered and were thus too soft. Such potential disparity in the quality and thus penetrative power of arrowheads is corroborated by tests which revealed a wide range of hardness for medieval arrows, from 120 to 400 VHN (Vickers Hardness Number), though the majority were very hard, on average 350 VHN.[120] Analysis of a small Type 16 barbed head (Jessop M4) showed that a higher-quality blade (of iron containing 0.35 per cent carbon) had been hammer-welded to a lower-carbon iron ferrule.[121] A bodkin head, by contrast, had been forged in one piece, with the blade section case-hardened (pack carburised).[122] Modern tests thus need to allow for the fact that some medieval arrowheads may have been of poor quality and their penetrative qualities thus diminished, while conversely the best steel-bladed examples may have outperformed modern replicas.

Some of the earliest scientific tests were conducted in 1954 by Stephen Grancsay, on sixteenth- and seventeenth-century armour from his private collection.[123] Understandably, the armour thus sacrificed was munition-quality for troops rather than the high-quality steel armour of the nobility, which Grancsay was at pains to stress would have offered considerably greater protection.[124] A greater limitation of the tests was that, in line with pre-*Mary Rose* research as to the power of the medieval longbow, the bow used was only of 68lb (30.9kg), made of Osage orange and backed with rawhide (as with many native American bows), and was thus less than half the poundage of some of the larger *Mary Rose* bows. The test arrows, weighing around 2½oz (70g), were made of beech, with case-hardened steel bodkin heads. At 15ft (4.5m) the arrow, achieving a velocity of 91.2mph (40.8m/s) at 20ft, penetrated a sixteenth-century mail shirt, made of alternate solid and riveted rings, which had been stuffed with a bag of feed. The arrow penetrated the bag and broke links in the back of the mail shirt. Clearly, this was at extremely close range, and did not take into account the probability of a padded gambeson or arming doublet worn underneath the mail shirt. Unfortunately, no further tests were conducted for greater ranges, with Grancsay merely surmising that at a distance of 200 yards 'an arrow might kill an unprotected man but it would not penetrate a shirt of mail'.[125] Shooting at a seventeenth-century cabasset, the arrow pierced the helmet when it struck full square, but merely glanced off when the archer aimed for the side of the helmet.[126] Similarly, a 1.15oz (33g) bolt, with a pyramid-shaped head of steel, shot at the same 15ft (4.5m) range from a crossbow with a 740lb

(336kg) pull, penetrated the helmet when it struck the weak point of a lining rivet, but other bolts glanced off its rounded surfaces. The weight of the bolt, which achieved only a velocity of 94.6mph (42.3m/s), was probably significantly too low.[127] These tests, then, only give us some indication of the performance of wrought-iron armour as worn by infantry at very close range, but they do suggest that unless the angle of strike was nearly full square a helmet or other curved plate would have offered a significant chance of deflecting the arrow or bolt.

Further tests were carried out by Peter Jones at the Royal Armament Research and Development Establishment at Fort Halstead.[128] Jones used arrows with carburised wrought-iron bodkin heads against sheets of Victorian soft wrought iron of varying thicknesses: 3mm to represent the average thickness of the front of medieval helmets; 2mm representing a breastplate; and 1mm for leg armour.[129] The arrows were shot by John Waller with a yew longbow of 70lb (32kg) pull against the plates that were set at an oblique angle to simulate the angle of strike of an incoming arrow. At a range of 33ft (10m) they penetrated the 1mm plate to between 1½–2in (4.5–5cm), which would have inflicted a seriously debilitating wound to the arm or leg. The 2mm plate was penetrated, but only to 1.1cm, 'insufficient to cause fatal wounding of the thorax'. No account, however, was made for the dampening effects of a heavily padded undergarment (or padded coat armour worn over a knight's body armour), so it is unlikely that this degree of penetration would have wounded the wearer significantly, if at all. The arrows were defeated by the 3mm plate,[130] indicating that even helmets of wrought iron might offer significant protection, at least in the front of the skull where the metal tended to be made thickest.

Such tests, however, had significant limitations. First, a flat plate is far less effective in resisting arrows than the rounded forms of forged helmets (as Grancsay's earlier tests clearly revealed), still less than shaped plate armour, so that on the battlefield itself many arrows would, as the armourers intended, have been deflected by the sloping surfaces of armour.[131] Secondly, the wrought iron used would only reflect the poorer-quality armour of those unable to afford steel.[132] While a poor-quality armour of wrought iron could be penetrated by a pointed weapon such as an arrowhead or spear exerting around 150 joules, it is probable that an armour of good-quality steel might offer as much as twice the resistance to penetration than a poorer armour of wrought iron, and would thus offer significant protection against arrows and bolts.[133] Even in tests using a flat plate of iron, penetration was only achieved through the 2mm plate at 0° angle of obliquity, and at 20° the arrow was defeated. Penetration of the 1mm plate occurred at 20° but not at 40°, where the arrow was not only defeated but itself fragmented.[134] Subsequent tests by Jones using a bodkin head against a 1.5mm plate of mild sheet steel again revealed the great significance of the angle of strike in determining the effectiveness of penetration. At 0° angle of obliquity, the optimum angle of attack, the steel was fractured and penetration occurred. At 45° the armour was pierced to a less significant extent, at 60° the arrow penetrated slightly before the head fractured, while at 70° the arrow ricocheted off the plate.[135] Given that 1.5mm was the thickness only of thinner pieces of armour such as the visor or vambraces, the extent of penetration of thicker steel plate such as for breastplates or the brows of helmets must have been considerably less.[136]

Most important, however, all these experiments were based on tests with bows with comparatively limited draw-weights not exceeding 70lb (31.8kg). More recently, heavier poundages were used in a series of ballistic tests conducted by the staff of Vickers Defence Systems at Royal Ordnance, Ridsdale, including the measuring of arrows shot by John Waller from three longbows of 72, 78 and 90lb (32.7, 35.4 and 40.8kg) at a 28in (0.71m) draw. Poplar arrows of 28in, with a Type 16 head and weighing 1⅝oz (45g), shot from the more powerful 90lb bow achieved an initial velocity of 99.54mph (44.5m/s), with an average velocity of 99.32mph (44.4m/s), while with a bodkin head they reached an initial velocity of 97.45mph (43.6m/s) and an average velocity of 97.24mph (43.5m/s). When shot at 2mm of mild steel (at an unstated range) the arrows were successfully resisted by the plate, as were bolts shot by a steel-bowed crossbow with a pull of 440lb (200kg).[137] Given the evidence presented above, however, even a poundage of 90lb (40.8kg) does not represent the full potential of the *Mary Rose* bows. Similarly, the calculation of the kinetic energy of 80 joules available to a longbow, used in a recent examination of the penetrative power of medieval weapons, was based on experiments by E. McEwen using a longbow and arrows that may well be considerably less powerful than their fifteenth- and sixteenth-century equivalents.[138] By contrast, the most recent

experiments, undertaken by Simon Stanley and Robert Hardy, have used both heavier bows and arrows. As Robert Hardy has indicated in Chapter 1, a 3.8oz (108g) arrow shot from a 150lb (68kg) longbow possesses a kinetic energy of 146 joules.

What this represents in terms of the penetration of armour is suggested by the collaborative researches of David Blackburn, David Edge, Alan Williams and Christopher Adams. Their tests indicated that a bodkin-headed arrow just penetrated a 1.9mm wrought-iron plate at 20 joules, but at 75 joules it created a hole 6mm in diameter. As we have seen, however, armour would have been invariably worn over a thickly padded garment, and to defeat the same wrought-iron armour suitably padded required a considerably greater force of 125 joules.[139] Putting together these researches, we may conclude with reasonable safety that even at a range of 240 yards heavy war arrows shot from bows of poundages in the mid- to upper ranges possessed by the *Mary Rose* weapons would have been capable of killing or severely wounding men equipped with armour of wrought iron. Higher-quality armour of steel would have given considerably greater protection, which accords well with the experience of Oxford's men against the elite French vanguard at Poitiers in 1356 and des Ursins's statement that the French knights of the first ranks at Agincourt, which included some of the most important (and thus best equipped) nobles, remained comparatively unhurt by the English arrows. The closer the range, however, the more effective the shooting of the English would become, while as our anecdotal evidence from the fifteenth century suggests the thinner plates on the arms and legs even of the better armours might not stop penetration. What are now needed are tests of the effects of heavy arrows shot from *Mary Rose* weight bows over a spectrum of ranges against accurate approximations of armour made from better-quality steels, with examples reflecting the range of hardening and tempering processes used, as well as the deflective shapes of items of plate armour. Only then will the longbow's true potential and its ballistic limitations be fully understood.

AIMING FOR THE FACE

However good a suit of armour may have been, it could not guarantee complete protection. It seems that where possible, archers did not take a chance that their shafts would be defeated by defensive equipment but instead chose to aim at the faces of their assailants. Chronicle sources furnish a remarkable number of instances where nobles and knights were killed or injured by arrow wounds to the face. Until the late twelfth century the principal form of head protection was the simple conical helmet with a nasal, worn over a mail coif which

had a flap or ventail which covered the lower part of the face. This still left areas of the face vulnerable to either a chance arrow, as probably in the case of King Harold at Hastings, or a well-aimed shaft (see p. 108). Thus during the siege of Sainte-Suzanne in 1084 the Norman lord Richer de Laigle received a mortal wound below the eye from a low-born archer, while in 1098 Hugh, Earl of Chester was struck in the face by arrows shot from Norwegian ships as he attempted to drive off from the Welsh shoreline a marauding force under King Magnus

Bareleg.[140] The temptation to loosen one's ventail or remove one's helmet for ventilation during a lull in the fighting could prove fatal. At the siege of King Stephen's earthwork castle at Burwell in Cambridgeshire Geoffrey de Mandeville inadvisedly removed his helmet within bow-range and a royal archer seized his chance to give him his death wound.[141] This practice of aiming for the face of the enemy is apparent from an early period in Anglo-Scottish warfare, where the bowmen could take ready advantage of the general lack of helmets as well as effective body armour among the Scots rank and file. At the Standard in 1138 Ailred of Rievaulx noted how the English archers wounded the 'breasts, faces and eyes' of the onrushing Galwegians, just as two centuries later at Dupplin 'the English archers, by a continuous volley of arrows, so blinded and wounded in the face the first division of the Scots that they were helpless'.[142] At Halidon Hill in 1333 the archers again went for the faces of the Scots in the first division, who were 'wounded in the face and blinded by the multitude of English arrows'.[143]

For those able to afford the best equipment, protection for the face improved markedly with the development of the great helm from the last decades of the twelfth century, and it is perhaps significant that there are fewer references to facial arrow wounds in this period.[144] Yet the great helm was heavy, cumbersome and restricted visibility, and many warriors continued to wear either the old conical helm, the broad-brimmed *chapel de fer* or simply a mail coif with or without an accompanying steel cap or *cervellière* over or under it, despite the increased danger of facial wounds. From the close of the thirteenth century the bascinet, with its sloping surfaces to deflect blows, movable visor and aventail of mail, became the predominant form of head protection for men-at-arms, though the great helm could be worn over the bascinet for added protection. In all likelihood it is precisely because of the spread of and improvements in plate body armour that references to wounds in the face become still more marked in the fourteenth and fifteenth centuries, as archers sought to counter the increasing effectiveness of knights' defences. At Poitiers the *Chronique Normande* noted that the French men-at-arms of King Jean's division were thrown into disarray by the volleys of arrows shot at their heads.[145] Earlier, at Crécy, Philip VI not only had two chargers slain beneath him, but had also been wounded by an arrow in the jaw, and possibly also in the thigh,[146] while in the same year King David II of Scotland was struck in the face by two arrows at the battle of Neville's Cross.[147] As kings, David and Philip VI must have been accoutred in the very best armour of the time, and yet they received serious facial wounds. Similarly the veteran commander Sir Thomas Dagworth met his death in Brittany, cut down after being blinded in one eye by a lance and wounded five times by crossbow bolts in the face.[148] While there are some early instances of gorgets of plate, such as that on the brass of Sir Hugh Hastings (d. 1347) (see p. 215), the primary neck defence until the close of the fourteenth century continued to be the aventail of mail, which must have been vulnerable to the attack of bodkin-headed arrows. The future Henry V was wounded in the face by an arrow at the battle of Shrewsbury in 1403, while during the Wars of the Roses the Duke of Buckingham was wounded in the face and King Henry VI himself wounded in the neck by an arrow at the first battle of St Albans in 1455.[149] In many of these cases it is probable that arrows struck when a visor was raised to facilitate the giving of commands or to gain air, or when a bevor was ill-attached or left off,[150] though in other instances longbow arrows succeeded in penetrating helmets. In 1356 the French lord the Bastard of l'Isle was slain at the siege of Castelsagrat 'by an arrow which went through his head'.[151]

ARROW WOUNDS AND BATTLEFIELD ARCHAEOLOGY

There can be no doubt that against unarmoured men arrow wounds to the torso were frequently deadly. The place of penetration is of course vital: 1½ inches through the left rib cage into the heart would suffice to kill, while with proper medical care, 4 inches, or complete penetration of muscle, could be survived, even if the wound resulted in temporary incapacitation. A 2-inch wound in the thorax is enough to lead to death within 15 minutes.[152] Broad-headed arrows used for hunting caused extensive tissue disruption,[153] making them effective against game and lethal should they strike humans. This is unambiguously attested by the numerous instances from records such as the Coroners' Rolls where death from a stray arrow during hunting or shooting accidents was almost instantaneous. Thus, for instance, Richard, son of Walter de Aspele, accidentally killed his brother William when 'he was shooting at a kite and the arrow in falling fell on William and killed him'.[154] In 1277 two friends, William and John, were hunting with their lord William Comyn in his park near Fakenham. 'A deer came between William and John, and William thought he had shot it, but the arrow glanced on the branch of a tree and killed John by misadventure.'[155] In 1367 a chaplain, Walter Auncel, had gone out with some friends on the king's highway to Egbaston 'to sport at archery'. A traveller coming the other way, seeing their sport, placed his cap on the road and said 'Shoot at my cap.' Walter loosed, but the arrow fell on a stone, and glancing off, struck 'Roger, son of Adam, who had been sitting by the highway under a bramble bush, piercing him above the navel and killing him'.[156] Equally, judicial records furnish numerous cases of wounding or slaying in brawls or other altercations. In 1265, for example, Robert Cariman and a band of robbers had tried to steal some cattle from the abbey of Kirkstall. But as the abbot's men tried to protect the cattle, one of them, Gilbert Palfreyman, shot an arrow at Robert, but it accidentally struck his own comrade Thomas le Mouner in the back and he died instantly.[157] Nicholas and his brother William Koc, 'armed with bows and arrows', tried to break into the tavern of Alard de Bokland at Sutton following an earlier altercation, but when Nicholas broke down the door Alard shot and killed him with an arrow.[158] In some cases, as we have seen, details of the arrow's penetration and effects are given, and indicate just how lethal the impact of an arrow could be, particularly when few if any of the protagonists were wearing defensive equipment.[159]

What can we learn of arrow or bolt wounds sustained in combat, beyond the indications furnished by chroniclers? The developing science of battlefield archaeology goes some way to increasing our knowledge of the effect of arrows and bolts on the human body, though there are significant limitations. First, there have been remarkably few scientifically excavated grave-pits from medieval battles. The excavation of 1,185 bodies from the battlefield of Wisby in Gotland, fought in 1361 between the royal Danish army and a hopelessly outmatched group of peasants and townsmen from Gotland, has until recently stood in virtual isolation as a large-scale excavation, and there has as yet been no systematic excavation of a major battlefield of the Hundred Years War.[160] This in turn is partly because the location of the vast majority of burials following medieval battles is often as uncertain as the location of the fighting itself; recent digs at Shrewsbury, for example, failed to discover any grave-pits from the battle in 1403.[161] In some instances, as probably at Shrewsbury, churches or chapels were erected directly over the site of mass burials, making future excavation unlikely. It is probable, moreover, that mass graves contain a higher percentage of the common soldiery, rather than providing a social cross-section of combatants; as the unusually detailed evidence for the fate of the fallen at Agincourt reveals, several of the high-ranking men who fell in the battle were removed for more fitting burial elsewhere. By contrast, some of the English dead were placed in a house or barn which was then burned on Henry V's orders, while the bodies of the Duke of York and the Earl of Oxford were boiled, so their bones could be brought back to England.[162] Nor was this an isolated occurrence. When in May 1405 a small force of English men-at-arms and archers had suffered heavy losses in an unsuccessful attempt to take Ardres, the survivors heaped together their dead, numbering between 40 and 50, in a house by the walls and set it on fire.[163] Such cremation may have reflected not only the impossibility of transporting corpses back to England, but also perhaps the fear of desecration of burials in hostile territory.

Lack of excavation is also due to the fact that in other cases, such as Crécy, where some graves are probably marked by a later calvary, local sensitivities and the respect for war graves, albeit ancient ones, preclude any intrusive investigation. It is noteworthy in this regard that the graves of 38 soldiers slain either in or after the battle of Towton were discovered in 1996 only by accident, during building work on the extension of a house. No doubt there will be other such discoveries in the future, but it is likely they will occur by equal happenstance. The Towton excavations have furnished important new insights into late medieval warfare, and have resulted in a publication that is a model of interdisciplinary collaboration.[164] Nevertheless, it remains uncertain as to whether these men – ranging in age from 16 to 50, with 30 being the average age at death[165] – died fighting during the battle or were cut down during the bloody rout which ensued. The majority of head wounds caused by blunt instruments, probably including poleaxes, were to the left side, consistent with hand-to-hand combat, while a high proportion of wounds were to the right hand or arm, sustained by parrying blows. One man (Towton 25) appears to have fought off an attack, but after receiving repeated blows was slain by a head wound that came from behind, receiving two further blows while on the ground. Other injuries, such as repeated cuts to the backs of the upper arms, suggest the desperate attempts of unarmed men to ward off the repeated blows of assailants. Several wounds were to the back of the head, while many skulls revealed multiple cuts by edged weapons; a total of 113 wounds were found on the sample of 27 crania examined, with 2 having as many as 10 wounds each. While men fleeing the battle may have thrown away their helmets, the high incidence of head wounds points rather to the massacre of men deliberately stripped of their defensive armour before being repeatedly hacked at, probably while on the ground. The location of the shallow grave, moreover, was not on the site of the main engagement but near the village of Towton, towards which the Lancastrian fugitives fled in the rout. It may be these circumstances which explain the comparative rarity of arrow wounds on the Towton victims; only two were found, both on skulls. That of one man (Towton 40) had been struck on the left frontal by an armour-piercing arrow of diamond section, whose head had penetrated up to the socket, while an arrow, perhaps similar to the Type 16, had punctured the occipital of another (Towton 2) to a depth of ⅜in (1cm). It is possible that two square puncture wounds on another skull (Towton 41) were caused by crossbow bolts, but they more likely represent the beak of a war-hammer or poleaxe.[166]

The ambiguity of such wounds highlights perhaps the most significant limitation of battlefield archaeology in respect of assessing wounds inflicted by the longbow, for even when they are found skeletal remains have long since lost soft tissue and internal organs. Thus while cutting or crushing weapons often left significant traces of trauma on bones, a skeleton cannot reveal whether a man suffered an injury or fatal wound from an arrow or bolt unless the arrowheads struck bone or remain in situ.[167] Not only this, but almost invariably the dead were stripped of their armour, a costly commodity, and even their clothing after battle. Several chroniclers note, for example, that on the morning after Agincourt the French dead had been stripped all but naked by English pillagers and local peasants. In the absence of such armour, it is impossible to assess the amount and quality of defensive equipment the slain would have worn in combat, and to gauge the extent of its efficacy by relating it to visible wounds.

In all these respects the Wisby graves remain unique and invaluable. For reasons that are not clear – possibly because of the speed with which decay set in in the summer heat, or the Danes' urgency in conquest – those slain, the majority of whom were probably the defeated Gotlanders, were placed in burial pits still wearing their armour. Accordingly, many skeletons were still clad in mail coifs or armour and provided unambiguous evidence of battle wounds and of the deadly effect of crossbows. Examinations revealed that around 125 men, over 10 per cent of the bodies discovered, had received one or more bolt wounds to the head. It is likely that many more received other bolt wounds, which are no longer traceable.[168] Several of the skulls showed wounds, sometimes multiple, from crossbow bolts, some of which were still lodged in the bone or had penetrated right through and were found inside the cranium; thus, for example, one had penetrated the frontal bone, another had penetrated the roof of the cranium, while a third had a bolt lodged in the cranium having entered through the nose.[169] There was a predominance of bolt wounds to the left side of the crania, possibly explained by the fact that in battle warriors would instinctively turn a little to the right to shelter behind a shield or when raising a sword or weapon in

The collection of the dead and their burial in mass grave pits, in this case following the Swiss victory over the Burgundians at Morat in 1476. From the *Berner Chronik* of Diebold Schilling, *c.* 1483. *(Burgerbibliothek, Berne)*

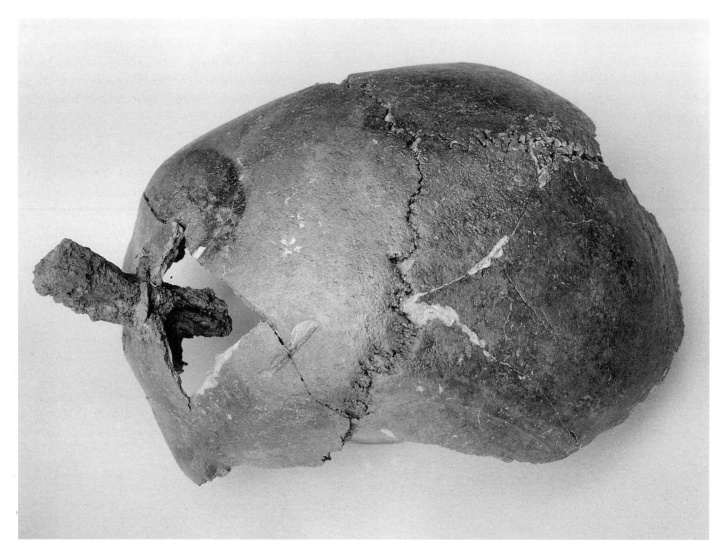

A skull from the battle of Wisby, 1361, with a frontal bolt wound to the cranium.
(© Riksantikvarieämbetet/Antikvarisk-topograpfiska arkivet, the National Heritage Board, Stockholm)

their right hands.[170] Many (47.2 per cent) of those who received bolt wounds to the head also received other severe blows, suggesting that the men were cut down after being wounded with bolts, while the high percentage of such wounds sustained by those found in common grave 1 (73.5 per cent) may indicate that this group of warriors was in the forefront of the Gotlanders' battle line.[171] The distribution of skeletons wounded by bolts suggested that crossbows had been used across the whole battlefield by the Danish army. It would also seem that the defenders' armour had given them scant protection against the shower of bolts.[172]

The wounds also suggested the crossbowmen's manner of attack; some bolts 'had been shot at a rather large angle of elevation and had then fallen more or less vertically', while it was clear that others had been shot more directly as they struck horizontally. Possibly the battle began with a rain of arrows from above, with crossbowmen then shooting at a more horizontal trajectory as they closed with the Gotlanders – though by analogy with Hastings this sequence may have been reversed, with a high angle used to break a tight formation of men sheltering behind shields. That some were struck on both sides of the head suggests that they may have been caught in enfilade shooting.[173] The vanquished Gotlanders were harried by bolts even when fleeing; eight crania had bolt wounds which struck the occiput, or back of the skull, which could only mean that the warriors had their backs turned to the enemy.[174] One wonders whether such a vivid picture will ever be revealed in relation to the impact of the longbow?

Such evidence can be supplemented by a small, and essentially haphazard, number of analyses of knightly burials in churches, which have thrown intriguing light on the bodily stresses inflicted by a life of arms. The right arm of Sir Bartholemew Burghersh was extended through use in a lifetime of sword play, while the skull of Sir Hugh Hastings, who died in 1347 (see p. 125), showed that during his campaigning days he had suffered a major blow to the face which had removed

5 or 6 teeth and made eating difficult. His skeleton also displayed signs of osteoarthritis, probably resulting from repeated wielding of weapons, and his teeth had been ground down by the grit often found in coarse brown bread, suggesting perhaps the rigours of campaigning.[175] Nine of the skeletons excavated at Towton revealed previously healed wounds to the skull, doubtless from earlier combats, with one remarkable cut to the jaw which may have disfigured the individual but had not put him out of continued military service (Towton 16).[176] Written evidence paints a similar picture. Of those recruited into the Provençal army in 1374, about one in four displayed serious scarring on hands and faces, presumably reflecting the absence of adequate gauntlets and the widespread use by infantry of helmets lacking visors.[177] At Edward 1's siege of Stirling in 1304 Sir Thomas Gray was struck by a springald bolt but lived to recount his wound to his chronicler son, while in the next century an English soldier, Thomas Hostell, petitioning the king for financial aid, told how at the siege of Harfleur in 1415 he had been 'smyten with a spingolt through the hede, lesing his oon ye, and his cheke boon broken'.[178]

TREATING ARROW WOUNDS

How were those who were wounded by archery treated? Those fortunate or wealthy enough might have their wounds given professional attention by a surgeon, such as the one who treated Sir John Paston after Barnet in 1471.[179] Such a doctor might be conversant with some of the medieval medical manuals which dealt explicitly with the problems caused by arrow or bolt wounds. A good example is the *Chirurgia* of Roger of Salerno, written in 1180, a highly popular text reflecting the wisdom of the famous medical schools of Salerno, which was translated into several languages including English and French. A version translated into Occitan, the language of southern France, in verse sometime before 1209 counsels the physician thus:

Take out the piece of iron expertly and carefully: pay attention to how it may have entered, whether it penetrates deeply or whether the injured man may live, and consider carefully anything else that may happen. Our elders in Salerno make a dressing out of lard, when the wound is superficial, and there is no other cause for alarm; when it is deep, they make the dressing very thick, out of cloth, and make it absorb molten lard from which it draws out the humour. Don't do anything especial in the case of an arrow or crossbow bolt. The fate of the wounded man is in God's hands, and if you cannot remove it without injury or the patient crying out, leave it

Crossbowmen shooting their bolts at a high trajectory against cavalry, from a sixteenth-century woodcut. After Olaus Magnus. (© The Board of Trustees of the Royal Armouries)

where it is – and I'm giving sound advice here. For I have certainly seen it happen, and this has often been the case, that wounded men live well with the whole piece of iron left in, with only a slight reduction in their strength, and if it had been removed, they would have all very easily died.[180]

Centuries later, similar medical opinion was to leave many a veteran of the world wars with lead or shrapnel as a permanent fixture. That the practice of allowing arrowheads to remain in place if it was deemed too dangerous to extract them was commonplace is suggested by the *Miracles of Our Lady of Rocamadour*, which relates several stories of how it was only after a visit to this great pilgrimage site in Quercy that several men were finally cured of arrow wounds. One man had had an arrowhead lodged in his chest for three-and-a-half years, another had part of an arrowhead remaining in a stomach wound below his navel, while the wound of a knight struck close to his eye had become infected, making it impossible to remove the arrowhead.[181] It was commonly recognised that attempting to extract an arrow was a highly dangerous business. As Chaucer notes in the *Franklin's Tale*,

And wel ye knowe that of a sursanure [a superficially healed wound]
In surgerye is perilous the cure
But men mighte touch the arwe or come thereby.[182]

If it was felt that the arrow could be removed but the head was barbed, the surgeon is advised by the *Chirurgia* to place tubes of metal or goose quills over the barbs before attempting to draw the arrow out.[183] Such a process was far more difficult if an arrow or bolt had lodged itself into bone. If a man is struck in the skull by a bolt,

and the wounded man is not mortally injured, make a cruciform cut in the skin at the point of exit of the iron. Next day, with a trepan, begin to prepare and enlarge the passage where the bolt is; bend your hand and work as well as you possibly can and draw out the iron, if God is willing to help you. Trust your hand on the shaft where it is entered and draw it out forthwith, gently and smoothly. I'll not tell you about the rest of the treatment for this is not difficult, it is so much in daily use.[184]

It is possible that this form of trepanning was used on the unfortunate David II of Scotland, struck in the face by two arrows at Neville's Cross in 1346. Badly wounded, he was taken by his English captors to Bamburgh Castle, where he was

treated by two barber surgeons summoned from York, Masters William of Bolton and Hugh de Kilvington, who were paid the considerable sum of £6 for their efforts.[185] Subsequently, his own doctor, Hector Macbeth, was one of the first Scots allowed to visit David in captivity.[186] Nevertheless, it seems David was still suffering from one of his wounds many years later, as the tip of one of the arrows 'could not be extracted by any doctor's skill'. It was only following his visit to the shrine of St Monans sometime between 1365 and 1370 that the king believed he had been miraculously cured, thereafter rebuilding the church at considerable expense as a thank offering.[187] Prince Henry, son of Henry IV and future victor of Agincourt, was wounded in the face by an arrow at the battle of Shrewsbury in 1403, but was fortunate in being attended to by a skilled doctor, John Bradmore. Bradmore may have been in royal service under Richard II, but the first unequivocal reference to him is in this year when he appears as royal surgeon (*chirurgico domini regis*) to Henry IV.[188] We are fortunate that Bradmore left a detailed description of the operation in his *Philomena* (*The Nightingale*), a book of surgery, which even includes a drawing of the instrument he used to extract the arrow (see p. 285).[189]

And it should be known that in the year of Our Lord 1403, the fourth year of the reign of the most illustrious King Henry, the fourth after the Conquest, on the vigil of St Mary Magdalene, it happened that the son and heir of the aforesaid illustrious king, the Prince of Wales and Duke of Aquitaine and Lancaster, was struck by an arrow next to his nose on the left side during the battle of Shrewsbury. The which arrow entered at an angle (*ex transverso*), and after the arrow shaft was extracted, the head of the aforesaid arrow remained in the furthermost part of the bone of the skull for the depth of six inches. The aforesaid noble prince was cured by me, the compiler of this present *Philomena gratie* [*The Nightingale of Grace*], at the castle of Kenilworth – I give enormous thanks to God – in the following manner. Various experienced doctors came to this castle, saying that they wished to remove the arrowhead with potions and other cures, but they were unable to. Finally, I came to him. First, I made small probes from the pith of old elder, well dried and well stitched in purified linen cloth [made to] the length of the wound. These probes were infused with rose honey. And after that, I made larger and longer probes, and so I continued to always enlarge these probes until I had the width and depth of the wound as I wished it. And after the wound was as enlarged and deep enough so that, by my reckoning, the probes reached the bottom of the wound, I prepared anew some little tongs, small and hollow, and with the width of an arrow. A screw ran through the middle of the tongs, whose ends were well rounded both on the inside and outside, and even the end of the screw, which was entered into the middle, was well rounded overall in the way of a screw, so that it should grip better and more strongly. This is its form [illustration]. I put these tongs in at an angle in the same way as the arrow had first entered, then placed the screw in the centre and finally the tongs entered the socket of the arrowhead. Then, by moving it to and fro, little by little (with the help of God) I extracted the arrowhead. Many gentlemen and servants of the aforesaid prince were standing by and all gave thanks to God.

And then I cleansed the wound with a syringe [*squirtillo*] full of white wine and then placed in new probes, made of wads of flax soaked in a cleansing ointment. This is made thus. [Item] Take a small loaf of white bread, dissolve it well in water, and sift through a cloth. Then take a sufficient quantity of flour of barley and honey and simmer over a gentle heat until it thickens, and add sufficient turpentine oil, and the healing ointment is made. And from the second day, I shortened the said wads, soaked in the aforesaid ointment, every two days, and thus within twenty days the wound was perfectly well cleansed. And afterwards, I regenerated the flesh with a dark ointment (*unguentum fuscum*). And note that from the beginning right up to the end of my cure, I always anointed him on the neck, every

Above: A simple sketch of the surgical instrument used by the surgeon John Bradmore to extract an arrowhead from the face of Prince Henry, wounded at the battle of Shrewsbury in 1403, from Bradmore's medical treatise *Philomena* (British Library, MS Sloane 2272, f.137r). *(© British Library)*

Left: Count Richard of Acerra, wounded in the face by an arrow during the siege of Naples in 1191, is treated by a surgeon, from the *Carmen in Honorem Augusti* of Peter of Eboli. *(Burgerbibliothek, Berne)*

day in the morning and evening, with an ointment to soothe the muscles (*unguentum nervale*), and placed a hot plaster on top, on account of fear of a spasm, which was my greatest fear. And thus, thanks be to God, he was perfectly cured.

Bradmore himself was doubtless well rewarded for saving the prince's life,[190] and he was thus careful to record his successful operation for posterity.

A far more violent and dangerous method of removing a bolt was to use a crossbow itself. A clamp was fixed to the shaft or head of a bolt lodged in a wound, which was then affixed to the string of a drawn crossbow. When the bow was shot, the force pulled the bolt out with great speed. An illustration of this process occurs in the thirteenth-century Spanish *Cantigas de Santa Maria*, depicting the unsuccessful attempts to remove a Moorish bolt from the neck of a Christian knight, first with

forceps, then with a crossbow. Only when the knight invokes the aid of the Virgin does the bolt miraculously come out.[191] Similar treatments appear in the fourteenth-century medical manuals of Guy de Chauliac, the papal physician, and of Ian Yperman in Ghent.[192] Joan of Arc, wounded by an English crossbow bolt at the fort of Les Tourelles as she attempted to raise the siege of Orléans in May 1429, was fortunate enough not to require such extreme measures. As her colleague in arms Dunois noted, 'Joan was wounded by an arrow which penetrated her flesh between her neck and shoulder for a depth of six inches', but despite this she carried on fighting, to the encouragement of her troops and the dismay of the English.[193] Rejecting the advice of her men to use magic charms on the wound, she instead had it dressed with a poultice of lard and olive oil, which successfully healed the injury within two weeks.[194]

Perhaps the greatest risk to the victim was gangrene or other infection, caused either by the wound itself or by surgery to remove the head. Sir John Smyth had heard Frenchmen of his day allege that in former times the English used to smear poison on their arrows, because many of those wounded could not be cured and subsequently died. Smyth angrily rejected the charge, noting sensibly that these 'impostumations [infections] proceeded of nothing else but of the very rust of the arrowheads that remained rankling in their wounds'. It was this factor, he added, that made arrow wounds far more lethal that those inflicted by muskets, 'and by the common experience of our ancient enemies (that we have so often vanquished), not only the great but the small wounds of our arrows have always been found more dangerous and hard to be cured than the fire of any shot unpoisoned'.[195] Nevertheless, recent evidence from the *Mary Rose* arrows shows that there was some substance in the French complaint. As noted in chapter one, a copper-based compound was used to protect the fletchings and to help firm the glue used to fix them on the arrow shafts. It is possible that the copper sulphate may (albeit unintentionally) have served to exacerbate a wound inflicted by the arrow head itself.

Be this as it may, a long list of fatalities from arrow or bolt wounds that were not in themselves lethal supports Smyth's belief about the dangers of infection. Thus, for instance, at the siege of Pevensey Castle in 1088 the great Norman lord William de Warenne was wounded in the leg by a bolt and died soon after.[196] Geoffrey Martel, Count of Anjou, was wounded in the arm by a crossbow bolt at the siege of Candé in 1106 but died the next day, while similarly Matthew, Count of Boulogne, struck in the leg by a bolt at the siege of Drincourt in 1173, perished shortly after.[197] It took Geoffrey de Mandeville, Earl of Essex, almost a month to die after he had been wounded in the head by an arrow in 1144.[198] Undoubtedly the most famous victim to fall prey to a bolt wound, however, was Richard the Lionheart. In 1196 he had been struck in the knee by a bolt shot by the French *routier* captain Cadoc while attacking the fortress of Gaillon.[199] But it was a bolt wound received during his siege of the little castle at Chaluz Chabrol in the Limousin in 1199 that gave him his death wound. While reconnoitring the walls, only lightly armed with an iron cap but no hauberk, Richard was shot at by the nobleman Peter Basil, with the bolt striking the king in the shoulder and penetrating deep into his side. With his characteristic bravado Richard made light of the wound, and in attempting to remove the bolt snapped off the shaft, leaving the head embedded. He was treated by the surgeon of Mercadier, his faithful captain, who succeeded in removing the barbed head but in so doing may well have exacerbated the wound. Whether or not the king flouted instructions to remain inactive as some chroniclers allege, the wound became fatally infected and Richard died of gangrene a few days later, on 6 April.[200] As one contemporary sourly observed, 'Valour, avarice, crime, unbounded lust, foul famine, unscrupulous pride and blind desire have reigned for twice five years; all these did an archer with hand, art, weapon, strength lay prostrate.'[201]

Matthew Strickland

CHAPTER 16

The Tactical Deployment of Archers

he tactical disposition of archers is inherent in much of the preceding examination of English armies in the early and late Middle Ages. What may be described as 'inherent' in the contemporary accounts often means that comprehension is taken for granted and very little detail, or none, is offered. So our understanding of medieval archer tactics is not only scant, but the subject of long, confusing and sometimes obtuse debate. And as I tried to show in Chapter 1 there is an on-going debate about the relative capabilities of medieval and Tudor military archers and about the strengths, qualities and performances of their weapons. We must enter this debate, armed with what we know for sure, what we can reasonably surmise and with a determination to remain practical in our analysis.

We need also to look at the archer himself, who represents a much broader swathe of medieval society, certainly by the fourteenth and fifteenth centuries, than has frequently been thought the case, and so is harder to typify than is often imagined. But think of the ranks of skilled, semi-skilled and unskilled soldiers, sailors and airmen of the two world wars and you will find an equally baffling mix: at one end of the scale are men of low intellect or poor education and unhelpful background; at the other are men of intelligence and good upbringing, with the ability to absorb swiftly technical skills, some of whom inevitably go on to be officers. On the one hand there are men who have been released from prison for the express purpose of going to war, and who at any moment might deserve to be imprisoned again, on the other are men of

great potential and broad outlook, who if they survive the war and return to a civilian life may gain access to the highest and most rewarding activities in any stratum of society. Of course the difference between such men serving in the forces in 1914–18 or 1939–45 and the medieval archer is that every archer had to have or acquire the strength, skill and knack of using heavy bows and war arrows to an acceptable and demanding standard, a skill requiring a great deal more effort than the ability to use a crossbow, a hand-gun, a musket or a rifle to an effective level.

This is not the place to repeat details of recruitment, travel, conditions and pay, much of which can be found in the preceding pages, with further signposts towards study in the Bibliography, but I would recommend the reader especially to refer to H.J. Hewitt's *Organisation of War under Edward III*[1] and the equally well researched and illuminating *Muster and Review* and *The English Conquest of Normandy* by R.A. Newhall.[2] For the less academic reader there is my own attempt to portray the life of a late medieval archer in *Longbow*,[3] while Professor Anne Curry is now opening her massive research hoard to public view, from time to time and as it were page by page, drawn from her long research into the Lancastrian occupation of Normandy. I have her permission to quote some of her references to English archers in the army of occupation.[4] I first heard her speak at an Oxford symposium on the Hundred Years War some 15 years ago, when she said that the records of the military and bureaucratic administration of the forces of occupation from the Treaty of Troyes to the English eviction from France would supply enough information to keep her

This picture of a battle with longbowmen on either side shows archers across the front of both armies as well as in wedges, hearses, blocks, *à choix*, on the armies' wings. *(Bibliothèque Nationale, Paris/akg-images/Jerome da Cunha)*

occupied until 2020. She has since said that this was a large under-estimation. What is so particularly riveting is that her work, and that of others toiling to illuminate this period of Anglo-French history, will reveal among other things the names of almost every archer sent to France beteen the battle at Agincourt and the final débâcle at Castillon.

From her recent studies we know that there were regular inspections, for instance of billeting arrangements in occupied France, and regular musters to keep an eye on the soldiery. Just such a muster took place in Honfleur at 9 a.m. on 26 September 1430. It is also recorded that an archer had been excused appearance at the March muster because he was ill in bed, but he was only off duty for five days and so lost no pay.[5] The musters recorded were carried out quarterly, but it is possible that they were more frequent. They may have included checks on equipment; there is some indication that a mounted man-at-arms would be demoted to the foot force if he lost his horse, and 'the counter roll for Gournay of the quarter March to June 1446 records three archers entering on 1 April, four on the 5th, five on the 6th, four on the 8th and four on the 9th . . . which suggests the maintenance of a daily record'.[6] Six archers from Caudebec were allowed absence to attend a joust at Pont-de-l'Arche, 'during the truce, so we must ask whether jousts were being held because war-time military service was now lacking and men had to be given the opportunity to let off steam. . . . The lot of the peace-time soldier', adds Curry, 'has never been easy.'[7] Cooperation with the French was encouraged, but carefully, and only where they themselves were cooperative. Sometimes archers were 'loaned' to native garrisons, and sometimes French soldiers were loaned for English service. One over-officious Frenchman in English pay, whose job it was to note absentees and to see to the fining of offenders, so enraged the guard-archers at Alençon that they lay in wait for his emergence to his duties at 9 o'clock one morning and lynched him. There was need one day for an archer who could speak French, and to act as '*trompette*' or bugle-caller for parades and so forth, to carry messages and to act in some sort as a spy. One can imagine the vintainer lining up 20 men and asking 'Which of you lads can parler the lingo?

Right, you three forward. Now which of you lot can blow a trumpet?'

But in 1436 18 archers were sent off the garrison at Fresnay for 'fraternising' with the 'enemy', while 21 archers who took part in a sortie that captured a ship from Brittany were apparently allowed to keep the proceeds from the sale of their loot, which 'netted over £2 each'.[8] Another 53 archers from Harfleur took part in what sounds like piracy, but was probably justified as security action, seizing French inshore craft and selling the proceeds in Calais, further up the coast. Curry notes, 'It is surely significant that they made efforts to be back in base for Christmas.'[9] Some archers were seconded to units enforcing military law, acting in fact as military police. They also took on other duties. Four men from Domfront were absent with leave for seven days on escort duty for the Lady Scales, while another 20 archers from Harfleur escorted Lord Talbot, Sir John Popham and others across the Channel. Archers could be detailed off to collect wages, and were even sent to accompany a man-at-arms on a visit to his sick brother.

Inevitably there were endless language difficulties between the occupiers and the occupied, which sometimes turned ugly. One French report tells of an Englishman shouting 'Parle anglois, tu scez bien parler anglois!' How often has one heard such refrains with rising tempo and increasing volume? These were the boys who referred to the Quai de Caux as 'Kidcaws' or 'Kidcocks', and to *cuir bouilli*, the stiffened, boiled and pitched leather headpieces so many wore, as 'querbole'. There was also a keen awareness of rank, class and status, and Professor Curry quotes the case of one 'Pacquinton', the controller of Bayeux, who killed a member of the garrison because he spread rumours 'that Pacquinton had been in trade before joining the army' – *plus ça change* . . .

Then there is the admirable account by the chronicler Geoffrey le Baker of Oxford, who tells us that during an earlier truce in 1352 a captured English archer, John Dancaster, held to ransom in the castle of Guines, had no money to pay the ransom but was freed on condition that he stayed and worked with the French. This is just six years after Crécy, four before Poitiers. 'Now this fellow used to lie with a laundrymaid who was his strumpet', from whom he learned that there was a causeway across the moat, just under the water. He escaped from the castle but not before he had 'measured the height of the castle wall with a thread'. He made straight for Calais, where he collected thirty tough lads from the garrison with ladders of the right length; returning to Guines, they scaled the walls, killed the guards and threw them into the moat, then 'fell on the ladies and knights that lay there asleep . . . or playing at chess or hazard' and shut them all up. Releasing all the English prisoners held there, they 'treated them to a feast'.

Next morning they let the ladies go, with their horses and belongings, and sent for more help from their friends in Calais. Thus installed, they refused entry to both French and English, and in the end sold the castle to the highest bidder, who happened to be the King of England. The story is well worth reading in all its details in le Baker, as it illustrates so many of the attributes of British soldiery – their individualism, daring, aggression, lawlessness and a certain charming kindness – which have caused frustration and not a little admiration through the ages.[10]

It is clear that by the time of Richard II's wars, his great enlargement of the royal bodyguard of archers and the creation of the 'Archers of the Crown', that military archery was not mainly in the hands of the lowest levels of society. Richard's recruitment, both for political force and for personal safety, of skilled and loyal bowmen, his awarding of badges of silver or gold crowns for them to wear, and his allowing the smaller band of his own bodyguard to wear the royal livery of the stag, tended to encourage an elite group of bowmen, mostly raised from his earldom of Chester, which caused envy among the other far larger but less privileged groups of military archers. Sayings such as 'There's many a good archer outside of Chester' and 'The best longbowmen are not all Cheshire bowmen' became common.[11]

The force of archers King Richard brought to London to impose his will on Parliament in 1387 probably numbered about 2,000 men, almost all of them archers from the principality of Chester,[12] though his own bodyguard, the royal bodyguard, which had existed in his great-great-grandfather's time, was probably never more than some 300-strong. These men were profoundly loyal, and were even on easy terms with the king. Such familiarity, according to the *Kenilworth Chronicle*,[13] gave rise to many complaints about them addressing the monarch 'in the mother tongue': 'Dycun, slep sicury quile we wake, and dreed nouzt quile we lyve seftow', and though these complaints were brought to Richard's notice he 'made no effort . . . to administer justice or remedy, but . . . favoured these same men in their evil doings'. But as Hutchinson wrote in his biography of Richard II, 'they [the Cheshire archers] were probably neither better nor worse than the average fighting man of the day'.[14]

What J. Gillespie's research shows is that many of the Cheshire archers were yeomen of some standing, some of whom were related to important Cheshire families. 'Within the watches' of the king's permanent bodyguard 'were about fifty men who were associated with manorial families, and another hundred who were drawn from the yeomanry'. Even outside the immediate guard there were some 'ten members of gentry families, and thirty-five yeomen'.[15]

Perhaps the best known example of archers of the yeomanry is given by the Jodrell family. The 'Jodrell pass', written on paper rather than the less expensive parchment, and signed by Edward the Black Prince himself, is still preserved in the Mostyn-Owen-Jodrell family. It reads: 'Know all that we, the Prince of Wales, have given leave . . . to William Jauderel, one of our archers, to go to England. . . . Given at Bordeaux 16th December, in the year of grace, 1355.' Did he get home in time for Christmas? This William was a descendant of one Peter Jauderel who served under Edward I. He bore his own coat of arms, as do his descendants to this day. Originally from Yeardsley in Derbyshire, the Jauderels soon settled at Jodrell, as in today's Jodrell Bank, on land which was acquired by the family at a later date. William or his brother, perhaps both of them, fought for the Black Prince the following year at Poitiers, where one of them 'liberated' a silver salt 'ship' from the French king's baggage, which the Black Prince coveted and *bought* from Jodrell. On William's return to England he was granted two oak trees from the royal forest at Macclesfield towards the repair of his Derbyshire house at Whaley Bridge, where the Jodrell Arms Inn, until recently at least, sported the Jodrell blazon.

It is worth bearing in mind that archers' wages were substantial. A mounted archer in the mid-fourteenth century would be paid more 'than skilled workmen in the building trades', and their income even rivalled that 'produced by many small manors'.[16] There is now vast and ever-increasing scope for the evolution of a very full portrait of the late medieval archer. But how was he organised and how did he function tactically in the armies of the Hundred Years War? I mean to examine several battles, fought in differing conditions, but especially the battle of Agincourt, although we should bear in mind that great, and even lesser, battles were rare events. For long stretches of the Hundred Years War the archers were on duty at sieges, serving in garrisons, marching from garrison to garrison, fighting in sorties and skirmishes, providing escorts – in fact doing a myriad of jobs, not necessarily always of a military nature. We need to find out, if it is possible, why and how the archers from Wales and England were so much more effective than archers from anywhere else, and why and how they greatly influenced battle after battle, often against astonishing odds, until the French learned how to avoid them, to surprise them and eventually to beat them with gunnery.

In the opening chapter we saw that the archers were trained to become a powerful and effective weapon. Exactly *how* they were trained it is now hard to find out; as Professor Prestwich has said, 'how far men were trained in archery is difficult to determine from the surviving evidence', but he added, wisely, that 'to have been as effective as they were . . . the English archers of the 14th century must have had ample practice'.[17] It

was during the fifteenth and sixteenth centuries that kings and prelates kept trying to reinforce the rules concerning archery practice, often complaining that 'our strong shooting is laid in bed'.[18] As I know well enough from my own experience, and more specifically from that of my strong-shooting colleague Simon Stanley, without rigorous practice not only is one's own shooting poor, but there is grave chance of physical injury. Big bows of the medieval weight demand both knack and great physical exertion; the effective archer with powerful bows, drawing between 140 and 160lb (63.5–72.6kg), must be fit, in practice and relatively young. With the far lighter longbows shot today I am glad to say one can go on shooting into old age – but not without practice.

Prestwich argues that 'shooting wholly together', an often-used phrase of contemporary chroniclers, was an absolute necessity for effective volleys in battle, and that such discipline 'demanded a degree of drill; but there is nothing in the written records . . . yet pictorial representations of armies in battle . . . show archers carefully lined up, bows all drawn, and it would not be wise to dismiss this as mere artistic licence'.[19] He speaks elsewhere of the mistake made by historians who 'assume that battles were disorganised affairs, waged by men who could not control their troops and who could do little more than encourage the outbreak of chaos'.[20]

There is no written record detailing anything to do with the practice of military archery until Roger Ascham wrote about it all in 1544, and that is largely because the use of archery was so common, and so much a part of English and Welsh life that there was little need to codify it. While the man-at-arms was brought up to a tough discipline of war and war-games, the practice of arms and methods of combat – methods that would allow a sword-wielder to decapitate a man at a stroke, or even cut a man in half, and an axe-wielder to split a head in half, or open a man up from belly to chin – the archer, drawn mainly from levels of society that did not train for that kind of expertise, was nevertheless not unused to physical combat and the use of hand weapons, and was obliged to practise regularly at the butts.[21] The folk who would be archers in wartime were encouraged by their very way of life to use the longbow, for their meat, for their defence and for unlawful attack as well; such men must have been hard to control in battle, and perhaps they sometimes got out of hand, but there are many occasions when it can be seen that a successful result came from discipline on the field of battle, from tactical positioning and from skilful manoeuvring.

The development of armour to protect against attack, particularly arrow attack, meant increases in both weight and coverage especially for the head of the wearer. These innovations must have seriously increased the difficulties that faced fully armed men in battle; their sight and hearing were hampered, and the sheer physical work was harder; in contrast the lightly armed archer enjoyed unimpaired vision, hearing and movement, so that functioning in battle must have been easier. This can be seen clearly at Agincourt, where, once their arrows were exhausted, the archers were free to dance round the heavily armed French, to use whatever space was available, to climb the heaps of dead and dying, and to wreak the most terrible havoc on the crowded and suffocating masses of their enemy. The archer was still able to see how he stood among his fellows, to understand the larger picture, at least in his vicinity, to hear trumpet calls and orders from the 'criers', the vintainers who were only in charge of twenty men, or the centenars, who no doubt passed their orders to criers or trumpeters; it was easier too for archers to see how and where to respond to orders, and to identify banners, flags and pennons. At Agincourt all these advantages and disadvantages came together in monstrous form.

Dr Strickland, who is responsible for the bulk of this study, shows us most of what is known from contemporary sources about the battles, sieges and skirmishes that were fought, and how their reporters, even in a few cases their participants, spoke of them, through a large part of the Middle Ages. It is my purpose now to take a few examples from the long list available and attempt to make tactical sense of them in terms of military archery. Colonel Alfred Burne tried it a while ago,[22] and cast much light about him. It is now the fashion to decry much of his work, and pour scorn on his watchwords 'inherent military probability'. I prefer to use the phrase 'practical possibility', in the light of what we now know of the weapon under discussion, of new studies of terrain, and new examination of contemporary records to which Burne did not have access. Much must necessarily be speculative, but after all modern historians who reject Burne's surmise that at Agincourt the archers were placed in projecting wedges between three 'battles' of men-at-arms, are themselves offering no more and no less than surmises. I have long thought that whatever conclusion we may reach upon the way the fight at Agincourt developed, if, as in Michael Crichton's *Time Line*, we were suddenly time-slipped back to that October day in 1415, we would be not only profoundly shocked at the horror of it all, but totally astonished at how different it all was from our surmises.

In 1314 when the Scots won their great victory over Edward II's forces at Bannockburn, the English defeat was largely due to lack of command and cohesion, and to extremely canny defensive tactics on the part of the Scots, notably their skilful use of the terrain and their digging of pits to slow and disrupt the eager and uncoordinated attacks of the English cavalry.[23] But Edward had a good force of archers; what happened to them? Unsupported by the men-at-arms they never really got into the battle, before being separated and routed. Unsupported archers were very vulnerable, open to flank and rear attack unless their own flanks were secured by woods, water or some other natural feature which prevented them from being turned. At Bannockburn they were not intelligently used, though it is possible that the king had in mind his father's tactics at Falkirk, where the archers were used late in the battle to break up the static, defensive and impenetrable Scots schiltroms. Their arrows broke up the Scots formations and opened gaps through which the English cavalry poured. By the time of the battle at Dupplin in 1332 it had been well learned that mutual support between archers and men-at-arms was a potentially battle-winning tactic. Ten years earlier at Boroughbridge, archers protected by a river, shooting across it at the enemy on the other side, had shown what they could do if the terrain was intelligently used. The battle-front at Dupplin was narrow, so that the archers massed on either wing, forward of the central battle of men-at-arms and evidently well protected by woodland, were able to pour volley after volley into the flanks of the advancing Scots. They were also able to cover the whole front so the space in front of the English army, into which the Scots drove with great ardour, became a killing ground; the heaving mass of Scottish soldiers was squeezed from the sides by the arrow storm, pressed from behind by their own advancing men and battered in front by the English men-at-arms. A similar horror would take place at Agincourt 83 years later. It is probable that the English army at Dupplin was no more than 2,000-strong, of whom perhaps three-quarters were archers. The *Lanercost Chronicle* describes how the piles of dead and dying grew 'as high from the ground as the full length of a spear' – the sort of claim later made for the French disaster at Agincourt, and dismissed by Sir John Keegan in his spendidly evocative *Face of Battle*. But I think such awful piling-up of bodies may well be possible, given the enormous pressure on the centre, from all angles, of hundreds and hundreds of men. The bodies would not slide off if there was nowhere for them to go; and we have seen such appalling heaps of bodies in photographs from Auschwitz and Buchenwald.

But at Dupplin there were certainly no archers among the piles of dead. The total English losses were 33 men, of whom none was an archer; the Scots' losses were disproportionately enormous. This was the stark result of massive archery correctly deployed, and such tactics were to be seen time and time again in the coming years.

In 1333 the young Edward III had with him the Dupplin commanders when he faced the Scots at Halidon Hill near

Archers at a siege, shooting high to keep the defenders' heads down. They are using heavy bows, arrows planted ready to hand. While the longbowmen shoot, the crossbowman still winds up his weapon. *(Bibliothèque Nationale, Paris)*

Berwick. He took up position on a wooded hillside, his back to its forested crest. He drew up his men-at-arms on foot in three battles, with flanking archers placed between and slightly forward of each division. Thus, if three Dupplin formations are put together side by side, the forward horns of archers on both flanks of the central, and each inward flank of the two outer divisions join together in a sort of triangular wedge. So arranged, they could unleash an increasingly close and murderous arrow storm, first at the enemy's front, then to their flanks as they closed with the men-at-arms. This is the formation which Colonel Burne believed was to become the classic arrangement in Anglo-Welsh armies during the Hundred Years War. But it needs examination. Such a defensive formation has received the closest attention of scholars and military historians for a long time, and there has been very much discussion on the subject of Froissart's 'herce'; this has been translated as 'harrow', 'hedge', 'hedgehog', 'wedge' – almost anything that sprang to mind – but it has remained rather a mystery, chiefly because it is not clear quite what Froissart meant when he described the English archers at Crécy being drawn up 'in the form of a herce'. Did he mean it to apply overall? To separate bodies of archers? Or to the actual formation on the ground into which archers were ordered, in any group or body? If it is translated as 'hedge', then it could apply overall, and would hardly imply anything specific. If it is 'hedgehog', it is equally inexact, though conveying an idea of overall and spiky defence. If it means 'harrow', and this is the most compelling in my view, then it suggests that the archers in any group, wedge or body were drawn up on the ground in a chequerboard fashion, with each rank slightly offset so that the second rank could shoot through the men in front of them, and the third and further ranks find space to see and shoot. On totally flat ground I cannot see the formation being able to shoot 'wholly together' in more than four ranks without constantly reforming, but on sloping ground, as at Crécy, with the advancing enemy below, that number of ranks could perhaps double yet still allow synchronised volleys to be shot. It is remarkable that whenever English commanders were able to deploy their forces on a slope, thus forcing the enemy to attack uphill, they used it to great advantage. Of course the slope could not be too severe or the enemy might refuse the challenge, but it is equally noticeable how often the French, by one means or another, were enticed or goaded into just such an attack, often overwhelmed by rage at the sight of a foreign army quietly waiting beneath their banners.

Let us go back to the putative Halidon formations of interior wings of archers meeting each other to form a 'triangle'. Some have suggested that the triangle had its point towards the enemy, while others envisage a kind of inverted triangle with its *base* towards the front. I can see no point at all in the latter. The archers on the 'base' would certainly be able to shoot at the foe, but those on the sides further back towards the apex would surely be useless. This leaves us with 'points towards the enemy'. The weakness of this formation is the narrowness of the apex, or what one might term the shooting front, shooting directly forwards; admittedly the archers on the triangles' sides would be well placed to shoot into the flanks of an attack, as long as the attack divided, as apparently it did at Agincourt, into columns that could be side-shot into; but what if the attack came on straight and solid? Could a narrow pointed formation withstand it: 'No,' say those who discredit Burne; they believe that the archers were placed only on the outer wings, as at Dupplin, not *between* the divisions of men-at-arms. But does this apply however broad the front? My belief is that where the front was too wide, as at Crécy and possibly Agincourt[24] and certainly Poitiers, for archers on the outer flanks only to cover the whole of the ground in front of the army's centre, then some other positioning must have been brought into play. I cannot be persuaded that armies with sufficient archers would not place them in such a way as to cover the whole front. It simply does not make sense to remove your whole archer force to positions where they can *only* shoot into the flanks of the enemy. Shooting into an enemy's rear ranks is a great idea if you can get at them, but in most battles that would be impossible. If your wing archers *can* reach the centre, or in other words if they are no more than about 500 yards apart, then at full range they can engage the centre ranks of an enemy attack, at closer range they can target enemy troops to right and left of a central attack, and at short range they can hit the troops closest to them.

At this point in the argument it is well to remember that it was the terrible power of archery to *stop* cavalry, and to *stop* and destroy the cohesion of infantry, that was the root cause of so many successes. They could very seldom win a battle alone, but if they could halt or slow the enemy's advance it gave the men-at-arms a better chance of standing their ground, even against superior numbers. In the grinding together of two opposing forces of men-at-arms, archers could be of crucial help, either by continuing to volley, or by picking off targets at close range, while those too embroiled in the crowded mêlée to use their bows, or who had shot all their arrows, could engage the enemy with their side-arms, swords, axes, mauls (battle hammers) and daggers. We shall see this at Agincourt in particular.

Let us look briefly at a battle fought in August 1352 at Mauron, which by rights the French should have won. The English drew up on a rise, but quite clearly with archers on the outer wings only. They faced a formidable army with an equally formidable commander, the Maréchal de Nesle. He saw that the archers on the English right wing, opposite his left flank, were vulnerable, having evidently been placed there without the protection of a hedge or bank. So he ordered a large force of cavalry to charge those archers, driving them back and

Crécy battlefield from the French position. The bosky terrace in the centre shows the middle of the Anglo-Welsh position. The Bois de Crécy-Grange is in the distance.

scattering them, and then he concentrated his main dismounted force against the English centre, which was soon in grave danger of being overcome. The day was saved for the English by the archers of the left flank, who volleyed into the right flank of the French attack, and then got behind them and volleyed into their backs, thus turning the tide of battle completely.

Several questions arise. How did those flank archers on the left escape de Nesle's attention? Were they in such a position that cavalry could not get at them? Did de Nesle not have enough cavalry to accommodate a double attack, one on each flank? We seem to have no answers to these questions. All we know is that those archers won the day. Their comrades on the right had fared far worse, and were to fare worse again, and offer another reason for the English successes while those successes lasted: discipline, of the toughest sort. After the battle the English commander Sir William Bentley, badly wounded and no doubt in a vile temper, had 30 of his retreating archers beheaded as an example to the others. This stiff lesson, of a kind recommended by Jean Sans Peur, Duke of Burgundy, illustrates the disciplinary strength that made English armies so responsive to command.

Going back six years, we can examine one of the truly great battles of the Hundred Years War, fought at Crécy on 26 August 1346. This is not the place to outline the whole campaign that led to some 12,000 English and Welsh soldiers, under the direct command of King Edward III, being drawn up just below the crest of a long downland ridge that runs between the little town of Crécy-en-Ponthieu and the village of Wadicourt. Behind the crest lay the Bois de Crécy Grange, where the baggage wagons and horses of the English were formed up into a defensive laager. Of the whole army some 6,000 or 7,000 were archers, with perhaps 1,000 Welsh spear and dagger men; we can use these figures as a rough estimate, but at the same time remember that trying to establish the actual numbers involved in medieval warfare is not only a number-crunching but a mind-crunching game. We should concentrate instead on what we know for sure about the battle: that the English had a large force of archers; that they were sited on a commanding but not too intimidating slope; that the openness of the downland allowed them a fine view of any attack; that the battle started late enough in the day for the westering sun to be to some extent in the attackers' eyes; and that on the right of the English army the ground dropped steeply towards the little town of Crécy, the small River Maye and the undrained area around this river, making any attack from that flank extremely difficult for the French.

More vulnerable was the English left, towards Wadicourt, where the slope is less marked. Nevertheless it is very likely that there was thicker woodland around the village than there is today, and the English would also have gained some protection from field terraces, some indications of which still survive, albeit much softened over the centuries. This terracing, called *raidillons* in local parlance, can still be clearly seen in what would have been the very centre of the English deployment. Even today getting a horse up the steep little escarpment there would be extremely difficult; in the context of war it would have been an impassable obstacle, which would mean there was an area in the middle of the English line that could be very lightly defended. Better still, it provided a high point from which archers could shoot down into the flanks of any attack on the Black Prince's, Warwick and Oxford's battle to the right or Northampton's battle to the left (on the Wadicourt side). It has been argued that the whole English deployment lay between the Crécy declivity and the central terracing, with the Prince of Wales's battle and the English left battle being jammed together, and archers positioned on the wings. But such a deployment would leave the easier part of the slope open to a French outflanking movement. I believe it must have been vital to deny them that opportunity. Moreover, it is known that the English third battle, under the direct command of the king, was kept to the rear of the other battles, while the king himself watched events unfold from his vantage point in a windmill (where today stands a tower) on the crest of the hill. Even when the prince's battle was dangerously engaged and sent for help, the king could see that it was unnecessary to engage his reserve fully, although he did send a small reinforcement to his son's aid, with the famous words 'Let the boy win his spurs!' I labour these positional questions in an effort to get at the basic question: how were the archers deployed at Crécy?

There is yet another, possibly vital, issue concerning the terrain at Crécy. Having visited the battlefield many times, I have always assumed that the steep and formidable drop in the ground to the south-east of the Vallée des Clercs, the shallow valley at the foot of the Crécy–Wadicourt ridge, was from its clean-cut elevation and its regular line, the result of large-scale earth-moving for agricultural or perhaps military purposes long after the battle. However, Sir Philip Preston, who lives in Crécy and has spent much time and labour in careful research into the battle, opened the question of this fall of ground to archaeologists and geologists, some of them local, others national, and the general opinion is that such a feature existed in 1346. If that is the case, it would very likely have been even more clearly defined and thus less negotiable than it is today. Sir Philip has pointed out that no historian or antiquarian writing about Crécy has brought this feature into the equation, which could be explained as far as earlier writers are concerned if it were *not* there in 1346. But it is clearly

THE TACTICAL DEPLOYMENT OF ARCHERS 295

shown on a mid-nineteenth-century map, and many good writers since then have ignored it, including such historians as Oman, Belloc, Burne, Sumption and many others. I too have written about Crécy and ignored the drop for the reason given above.

Now *if* that barrier were there in the fourteenth century, certain intriguing possibilities follow. It would mean, for example, that the French could not, as always supposed, have ridden straight down the slope south of the Vallée and then attacked up the other side towards the English lines, and instead that the initial deployment of Genoese crossbowmen and subsequent cavalry charges would have had to be made from either the east or the west end of the Vallée des Clercs. This would mean that the Genoese could have been caught by the longbowmen as soon as they launched their own attack, and thus would have been in no position to shoot disciplined volleys. Indeed, it is recorded that the English archers on the slope loosed their shafts 'so thick that it seemed snow', outranging the crossbowmen and causing the beginnings of the French disaster. Likewise the French cavalry, whether they approached the Vallée from the Crécy end (which I think most likely, if only because it was above the prince's and the king's battles that the great banners flew) or from the Estrées lès Crécy direction, would equally have had to swing hard left or right before being able to line up and charge, making them vulnerable to the archers. Another reason why I favour the Crécy direction for the French entry into the Vallée is the presence of a track known as 'le chemin de l'Armée', which tradition says is the French approach route to the battlefield; this track runs north-westwards, a little south of Fontayne-sur-Maye and south-east of Crécy, straight to the western end of the Vallée des Clercs. Tradition can deceive, but unless there is compelling evidence that tradition is wrong, it is well worth keeping it firmly in mind. (There is, for instance, a move at present to relocate the battlefield of Bosworth (1485), the scene of the death of the last Plantagenet King, Richard III, some 8 miles from its traditional site. Fine, if it can be proved. But why on earth should so firm a tradition arise in the first place? Did local farmers in 1486 say to one another, 'I know where it was really, but let's tell everyone it was here instead', or did their great-grandsons a hundred years or so later deliberately misplace the site? Again, why?)

The distance from the bottom of the Vallée des Clercs to what I take to have been the position of the prince's archers is some 350 yards, probably out of range of the crossbows of 1346 and very uncomfortably long range for longbows. If the Genoese, whose protective pavises were still in the wagons on their way from Abbeville, realised they were out of range,

they would have spread themselves out into shooting order, no doubt exchanging shouts of command and agreement, and then advanced to what they thought was their range and let off a first volley. This apparently fell short, at which point the longbowmen loosed off volley after volley to the very great shock and discomfort of the Genoese. Where were these longbowmen, and how many volleys were needed from how many men to bewilder and grievously hurt the Genoese order of battle?

Many writers offer neat battle maps using blocks differently marked as 'cavalry', 'men-at-arms', 'archers' and so on, but these very rarely correspond either to the proportional numbers engaged or to the practical likelihood of the situation. Jonathan Sumption's magisterial, mammoth and still emerging study of the Hundred Years War places the Crécy archers in little circles of protective wagons, apparently some 1,200 yards apart or more, and solely on the wings. But there is no way in which such dispositions could have hit either the Genoese or the subsequent French charges other than on their flanks, and since the French knew well enough the dangers of English archery they would simply have attacked out of the effective range of the archers. Plainly neither the Genoese nor the French were able to keep out of the archers' range on the day, so where *were* the archers?

The answer depends upon whether or not one believes that it was possible for medieval soldiers to learn and apply drill movements to facilitate manoeuvrability on the field of battle. Since victory depended on the minimising of casualties on one's own side, and since learning how to make the battlefield a safer place for oneself was important, soldiers could surely be persuaded to undertake such movements as might achieve both ends. It seems highly unlikely that commanders had not evolved and imposed methods of manoeuvring in battle, and that soldiers were unable to follow orders and deploy accordingly, as far as was possible amid the noise and confusion of joined battle.

In order to disrupt, or halt, an attacking force, the archers must have been positioned so that they could shoot solid volleys at whichever part of the attack seemed most dangerous. In order to do that at Crécy, the archers must have been so positioned as to cover the whole front of the prince's battle, and the whole front of the battle commanded by Northampton at the Wadicourt end of the English line. Further, if Sumption is correct in surmising that the three English battles were positioned one in front of the other, then that is all the more reason for the archers to be in the forefront when the Genoese opened the attack. If the archers were truly 1,200 or more yards apart then all the Genoese had to do was avoid the 250 yards at either end of their attack where the dispersed longbowmen

could have got at them, staying instead on a central front some 600 or 700 yards across, and let the unprotected men-at-arms have it good and hard, once they were in range. But could not the longbowmen have closed in from their wings? Not if they were neatly enclosed in their wagon circles.

But if the prince's front was about 500 yards wide *including wing archers*, then the story is very different. The Genoese could have been shot to pieces. The same is true on the other side of the line. If Sumption is wrong and Northampton's battle was also some 500 yards wide, then any Genoese attacking there

Opposite, top: Crécy battlefield with Wadicourt to the right and Crécy far left. Bois de Crécy-Grange is far centre, where the English baggage train and the horses were concealed.

Opposite, bottom: Crécy field from the approximate position of the Black Prince's battle looking towards the French arrival position. The 'long-drop' terrace spans the picture as a definite line.

Above: Crécy field from the top of the terrace at the English centre. The far 'long-drop' terrace is clearly visible, which would have prevented the French attacking straight ahead.

would have suffered the same fate. We know that the Genoese *were* shot to pieces. So what can we deduce? We know that the central part of the English line was well protected by the steep terracing; if the left flank archers of the prince's battle were themselves flanked by its protection, and the right flank archers of Northampton's division likewise, the terrace top could have been defended by just a handful of bowmen who could attend to anyone making a nuisance of themselves at the edges. Moreover, being high up, they might get in some extremely useful sharp-shooting at the dividing flanks first of the Genoese (if they ever got that far up) and then of the fifteen or sixteen cavalry attacks that followed through the August twilight and into the darkness.

How many archers were there? This is difficult of course to establish, but from the various claims 6,000 seems a minimum number, 10,000 a maximum. Plenty. How many volleys were needed to do the job? From Sumption, who quotes contemporary sources, we can understand quite clearly that Edward's archers were running short of arrows. After the failed attempts earlier in the campaign to take the castle at Caen (although the town was plundered), Edward, already planning to move north to the Somme and probably actively seeking battle with Philip of France, sent orders to England for 1,200 men, mostly archers, together with '2,450 bows and

6,300 sheaves of arrows' (totalling some 151,200 arrows, which suggests over 60 arrows per bow and 2 bows per man), and for ships to be made ready to bring these supplies of men and munitions. The king 'wanted all these arrangements completed by 20th August'. (The battle at Crécy was fought just six days later.) The small fleet necessary was to sail for Le Crotoy, on the estuary of the Somme, which Edward hoped to capture.[25] But when the English finally arrived there, they found no ships and no reinforcements. In fact the soldiers were not yet on board the ships, which were still gathering off the Kent coast.[26]

So Edward was moving towards a major confrontation with fewer men, especially archers, than he wanted, and to some degree short of his archers' weapons. Edward knew the country round Abbeville and Amiens and the Forêt de Crécy well from his youth. How detailed that knowledge was we can only guess, but as things turned out in 1346 he had enough time to find suitable terrain for a defensive battle – and he chose the Crécy–Wadicourt ridge. Even without a major impediment to a direct attack it was a strong position, but if that steep drop at the south-eastern side of the Vallée des Clercs were there at his front, just where a gathering attack would like to organise itself before committing to the gallop of horse or the steady advance of footmen, by its very existence it would make such a mass direct attack impossible. Whether Edward already knew it was there, or found it by great good fortune, he chose his ground quite brilliantly. The French, as we have seen, would have had to enter the Vallée des Clercs from one end or the other, and then wheel to attack the English up the slope. In the case of the Genoese we have already looked at a possible scenario; in the case of cavalry attacks, to trot or canter in column parallel to the enemy's front, then spread out and wheel before committing to the charge would have demanded great discipline, especially since they were already just within range of the longbows. Once within 250 yards of the archers the potential devastation could be appalling. And so it was. But *only* because the archers were able to cover the whole width of the charge; in other words they were placed opposite the charge, and not 1,200 yards apart on separate wings.

We know, furthermore, that after the defeat of the Genoese there was a great deal of panic, retreat and confusion. The French, enraged at the Italians' withdrawal, charged among them from behind, causing the Genoese to turn their crossbows on the French, in an effort to prevent themselves being ridden down. Certainly there was chaos in front of the English lines, of which the archers took terrifying advantage. They could only do that if they were within range, and opposite the French lines. I labour the point because it is so vital to any comprehension of the successes achieved by longbowmen used *en masse*.

Sir Philip Preston has long concentrated his research on the various possibilities of the battle, and his conclusions are about to be published in a collection of essays, the result of a symposium on the battle held at Crécy some three or four years ago, which illness prevented my attending. Professor Michael Prestwich, Dr Andrew Ayton and other scholars of high repute are among the contributors. Sir Philip and I have walked the field and discussed the battle at length, and what follows owes much to our conversations and his ideas.

We assumed that the archers were placed to best advantage, but that they could not afford to be reckless with their shafts; they had to be standing somewhere near the Black Prince, and able to see any enemy movement either directly in front or to left or right of him.[27] Preston suggested that if 1,000 archers could at a given moment bear on the Genoese, and shot three arrows apiece at them, the result would be dramatic. If 2,000 or 3,000 could bear, the figures double and redouble – and so does the effect. We know what the effect was – the Genoese were destroyed – so all we have to do is work back from the fact to the method, and the requisites for the method are outlined above.

After the Genoese débâcle there were fifteen or sixteen cavalry charges, thundering uphill into a storm of archery. Now think of three or four volleys at long range: killed and wounded horses – berserk, unmanageable, falling, kicking, screaming; killed and wounded men. Over and through this tangle of destruction must come the second wave, facing more volleys and more destruction, leaving a worse barrier of horror for the next wave, who would leave a still worse struggling mass of men and horses for the next. After each successive charge it became ever harder to find a way through the slaughter: the French cavalry had to twist and turn, run sideways searching for a gap, and all the time exposed to the volleys of arrows. We know some got through, that the men-at-arms were engaged and that the prince's guardian captains feared for his safety and sent for help. None of this could have happened if the archer corps were away on either side of the field, with each wing positioned at least 600 yards from the centre. They cannot have been. As the pressure from the French brought their charges nearer and nearer, the shooting of the archers became more and more deadly – but not over a distance of 600 yards.

Before embarking briefly on a discussion of the archer dispositions at Poitiers, fought ten years after Crécy, I would like to say that I have enormous admiration and respect for Sumption's great work in progress, and that if he can make alternative surmises to put my own out of court I would welcome them. The aim, after all, is to get at the truth, as far as we can at this distance. In his second volume of the Hundred Years War series, *Trial by Fire*, Sumption examines the Black Prince's campaign that led to the fight at Poitiers, and studies his motives and his

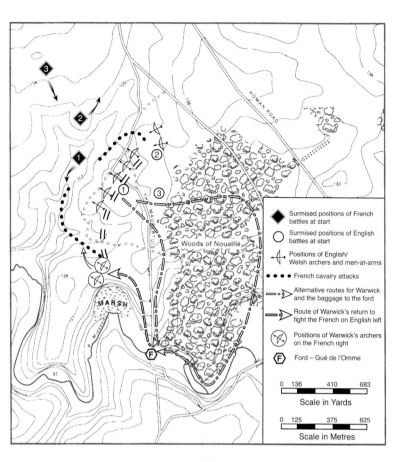

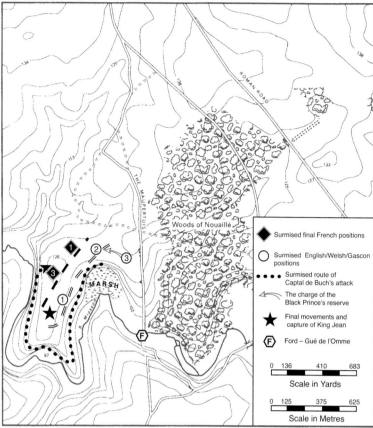

Key movements in the battle of Poitiers.

manoeuvres, and for this work there can be nothing but admiration. But in his map of the battle[28] in its early stages the inward wings of the far-separated archers on the flanks are at least 1,200 yards apart, while in the later stages of the battle, mapped two pages later, they are some 1,600 yards apart, according to his own scale. The arguments used against such positions at Crécy apply equally at Poitiers, though there are major differences in the way the battles developed. It might be argued that such mapping is only offered as a suggestion of possible positions, but if a scale accompanies the surmised placement of various troops then one must apply it, and if the application of scale leads to impossibilities then the whole map should be rejected.

The moves of the English army up to and during the battle of Poitiers are complicated, whatever motives are attributed to the commanders, whether they were seeking or trying to avoid a fight with a notably preponderant French army,[29] and the various interpreters of the battle through the last hundred years or so have even differed considerably in their defining of the battlefield. So what can be deduced from the contemporary sources that might affect our estimate of the value of archers there? Clifford Rogers, Assistant Professor of History at the United States Military Academy at West Point, whom I increas-

ingly admire, in his *War, Cruel and Sharp*[30] adopts the site (and its tactical use) suggested by Tourneur-Aumont,[31] who positions the main fight rather to the south and west of the usually accepted site. This replacement seems to fit the contemporary accounts rather better than, for instance, Colonel Burne's set of positions and movements. (The fact that it concurs with my own surmise, after many hours on many occasions walking the possible sites, is of course nothing to do with the matter.) Rogers also, almost alone, suggests that the final flanking move through dead ground with 60 men-at-arms and 100 archers under the command of Jean de Grailly, the Captal de Buch,[32] was not a sweep to the north-east but to the south-west, where there is much more dead ground, moving to the north-west of King Jean's last battle before displaying the banner of St George and both volleying and charging into the rear of the French forces, just as the Black Prince with his mounted escort and remounted men-at-arms cried 'Avaunt Baner!' and charged at the French front. The combination of shock tactics and the sudden final surge of energy from the English sealed the day, and soon the French king was taken prisoner.

Archers had been engaged throughout the Black Prince's *chevauchée* of 1356. They numbered 2,000 out of a total host of about 6,000, only 3,000 being men-at-arms, a high proportion which warns us not to hand the victory at Poitiers to the archers alone. In addition, there were 1,000 or so other infantry. These figures are given by Bartholomew Burghersh, who was there throughout and so probably knew; Geoffrey le Baker adds another 1,000 men-at-arms, while other chroniclers lessen the overall numbers, leaving roughly the same proportions, though John of Reading gives 1,900 each of men-at-arms and archers.[33] What is clear is that the Black Prince had a smaller army than his father's of ten years earlier, and far fewer archers. The wholly different proportions of a similar army at Agincourt, 59 years later, will be examined shortly. The fluidity of the positions during the early part of the fight at Poitiers is such that it is difficult to see exactly where the archers started, and where they went until finding a good

Left: Some of Oxford's longbowmen in the swamp at Poitiers putting French wing cavalry to rout on the south-west of the battlefield. This painting, by Andrew Boardman, is in the author's possession.

Below: Poitiers battlefield: the probable advantageous English position as the battle began. The French were at the lower end of the slope on the right, with the wood of Nouaillé in the distance.

position. They were certainly 'on the wings' but they were also mostly on the move, and after the first exchanges they were most likely still on the wings but no more than some 350 to 380 yards apart, according to Rogers' scale on his very detailed and persuasive maps.[34] According to le Baker, the Black Prince deployed his rearguard as a right wing and the Earl of Warwick's force as a left wing, while the men-at-arms of the centre stood behind a hedge running northeast to southwest, determinedly guarding two gaps in it, one large, one smaller, through which the French cavalry were trying, four abreast, to push. In guarding these danger points they were much assisted, as a double French cavalry attack opened the action, by the shooting of the rearguard archers (now on the right flank), who also formed up behind the hedge and on the right wing (or perhaps *among* the right wing's men-at-arms) close to the big woods of Nouaillé Abbey which bordered and defined the eastern limit of the action. I believe parts of the line of this hedge are still to be found, especially towards the south of the battlefield, bordering the Champ Alexandre, where King Jean's last stand was made. There was a body of archers to the right of the prince's initial position, in marshy ground where they could shoot in comparative safety from the cavalry. The Earl of Oxford, seeing that the archers would be more effective in a position where they could shoot into the sides of the cavalry, and then, as they rode on through, at their rear, led them almost due north on to the flank of the French right-hand cavalry attack. So at this point the English seem to have been fighting with a central mass of men-at-arms, and two large wings of archers, to right and left, who, if they were only 350–380 yards apart, would be able to cover all but the very centre of any general French attack. Oxford is said to have

realised that with strong French armour and shields defeating the arrows at long range he must get the archers to a better position, which is why he moved them to the flank. An alternative possibility is that the archers Oxford realigned had been positioned directly opposite a wing of the French and too far off to be effective, so that he moved them both closer and on to the enemy flank. It is almost impossible to tell exactly where this move took place, because it seems the prince moved north and east from his first position, but that it succeeded there is no doubt. The opening cavalry attacks were driven off by the archers to left and right, and by those with the men-at-arms by the hedge. If one follows Rogers' third map, the flank archers are something like 550 yards or more apart, which suggests to me that there certainly were archers, as we saw, with the men-at-arms by the hedge.

When the English men-at-arms held the first heavy attack of French dismounted knights, the French became 'sitting ducks' for what Rogers describes as the 'short-range' shooting of the longbowmen. 'Short range' demands that there were archers closer than the wing archers, if the latter were really 550 yards apart. They could certainly deal with the French on the wings, but it must have been more centrally positioned men who, according to le Baker, drove their shafts through the French armour.[35] No fewer than six contemporary chroniclers affirm without qualification that the first French battle was defeated by the arrows of the English.

Two other significant facts are known about the archers of Poitiers. One is that during a lull in the fighting, being short of arrows, they ran forward pulling arrows from the ground, and pulling them too from the dead and wounded men and horses, and then used them against the next French attack.

The second is that when those reclaimed arrows were exhausted, the archers became light men-at-arms, using their side-arms and whatever weapons they could find from among the helpless or wrest from the enemy in the fight, as they were to do with terrible effect at Agincourt.

Since the publication in 2000 of Professor Anne Curry's splendid *Battle of Agincourt*,[36] the simplest way to get an overview of contemporary chroniclers' and later accounts and the later interpretations of those accounts is by having recourse to her volume. If you do not want to be encumbered or confused by the very differing accounts that are presented, simply turn to the chapter entitled 'Conclusions' and see how she draws the strands together. In her introduction she points out that the contemporary chronicles offer differing versions of the great fight at Agincourt, disagreeing about its position, the deployment of troops on either side, the numbers (of course) and the duration; she also explains which chroniclers followed whom, copied whom, altered whom and so forth. She has printed everything in full, including other relevant sources of information such as letters, licences and petitions, making a study of the battle far easier than it has ever been. She concludes that no one present at a battle can have 'a full knowledge or understanding' of the whole affair. I would dispute this. The commander-in-chief, in this case Henry V, would have had access afterwards to anyone who took part in the battle, and from them he might learn about their experiences in any part of the field. Moreover, some battles were witnessed by privileged spectators, non-combatants who were there throughout and were in a position to see a great deal. Such a source we have for Agincourt, and I shall return to it and put great emphasis upon it.

Curry goes on to say that although no one can be sure of the precise numbers involved, the enormous numbers of dead on the French side, compared to the very small number among the English, and the low proportion of prisoners compared with those taken at Poitiers present a particularly horrifying picture, even by the standards of many medieval slaughters, but without doubt it was an overwhelming victory for the little English army. More than that, it represented a shift in the focus of contemporary accounts and reactions from the 'great and the good', which permeate medieval writings, 'towards the rank and file, the archers . . . As warfare itself developed . . . the military effectiveness of the archer became the central issue.' That the battle has generated 'a degree of mythology' is not to be denied, and there still persists today 'a sense of amazement' at the extraordinary victory of a David against a Goliath: 'even if we can now set the battle in a firmer context . . . the desire to "know Agincourt" is destined to continue'.

How firm is the context? Let us look at what we really seem to know: the English and Welsh army comprised about 6,000 fighting men, of whom a little less than 1,000 were men-at-arms, the rest, some 5,000, were archers. This is why anyone attempting to study the tactical use of archery in the wars with France *must* solve some of the puzzles of Agincourt. We know the English were tired, after enduring a much longer march from Harfleur than any of them, including the king, had expected. They were underfed, since in the last few days they had had little in the way of nourishment, while the 'flux' – dysentery – was rife, the very affliction which was to kill Henry V seven years later. The sources tell us the weather had been unseasonably wet and cold: 'Il fascoit très lait temps de pleuve et de vent',[37] 'Car il avoit bien longuement plue',[38] 'toute la nuit ne fit que pleuvoir',[39] 'prodiga inondacione pluviarium'.[40] We are told that the French army numbered somewhere between 20,000 and 50,000 (though here we must beware of the chroniclers' exaggeration), and that after a long chase they finally caught up with the English. The French chose the ground, but with fatal consequences because in the event it was too restricted for them to use their vast numbers effectively, except to their own destruction. We know the English first saw the French host late on Thursday 24 October, but that where they saw them was not in their final position for battle. But there's not much else we know for sure, except that the fight took place between the villages of Agincourt (now Azincourt), Tramecourt and Maisoncelles, and roughly equidistant from each. Nothing could really be more precise, though there are still those who say the place of battle is uncertain, one of whom offers a map which sets it to the east of Tramecourt, when it was without a shadow of a doubt to the west.[41] Also the map of marked blocks which we have come already to distrust suggests far more men-at-arms than archers on the English side. It is a very strange map, especially when, on the previous page, the author has written: 'The chroniclers make it clear that the battle was fought over muddy farmland that had recently been sown with corn, between the villages of Agincourt and Tramecourt.' Agincourt is west of Tramecourt, so if Bradbury puts the French to the east of it nothing makes any sense at all. One wonders if he or his map-maker were misled by the old picture map published in Sir Harris Nicolas's very detailed *Battle of Agincourt*,[42] which was the first major collection of all the sources available at that time. On page 405 there is a delightful hand-coloured map, with blocks of soldiers in the oddest imaginable groupings, facing the right way at least, but to the *west* of Agincourt. I have often felt this resulted from the printer reversing the block by mistake, but I think not; I believe Sir Harris thought the French were astride the Hesdin–Calais road, when in fact they were astride the Blangy-sur-

Ternoise–Calais road. But perhaps the former was the older road? No, say my local informants, the family who own the battlefield, and had owned it a long time before the date of the battle. They say there is not the slightest question that the battle was fought where the chroniclers say it was, and not where Nicolas or Bradbury think it was; and they are quite definite that the road concerned is the one that mounts the hill to the Agincourt plain and leads past Maisoncelles to its left, passing between Tramecourt on its right and Agincourt to its left, and then on through Ruisseauville and Fruges to St Omer and Calais.[43]

Bradbury quotes Monstrelet's claim that archers were placed forward overnight in the Tramecourt woods, 'that is to the left of the English position'. Were Bradbury right, the engagement must have taken place between Tramecourt and Ambricourt, which is the same distance from Tramecourt as Tramecourt is from Agincourt. So the battle would surely have been known as either the battle of Tramecourt or the battle of Ambricourt. Bradbury also says that 'from the site generally thought to be the battlefield it is further to Agincourt than to Tramecourt'. This is not true: from that site the two villages are equidistant. In any case there was a fortress at Agincourt, the foundations of which can still be traced, and a smaller fortress at Tramecourt, so the naming of the battle from the nearest large fortress or château fort was easy and obvious, and once again confirms the accepted place of battle. To my mind the clinching evidence is the great grave site dug by order of the Bishop of Thérouanne at La Gacogne where some 6,000 men are buried. That *must* have been close to where the greatest number of dead were found, naked and despoiled, on the morning of 26 October.

Let us seek a guide through the tangle of reports, both French and English, which describe the battle. Two men, Jean Waurin and Jean le Fèvre were there, fifteen-year-old Waurin on the French side, and nineteen-year-old le Fèvre with the English. They may have been among the heralds who remained together during the battle but separated to their grim duties afterwards. Waurin was also present with the English at the battles of Cravant and Verneuil ('a second Agincourt'), and later at the great French victory at Patay, fighting against the English. For a long time the chronicles of Enguerrand de Monstrelet were thought to be the most authoritative source for the battle of Agincourt (as for much else), but as Professor Curry points out, a comparison of the accounts given by Monstrelet, Waurin and le Fèvre shows many signs of copying one from another; she then helpfully prints all three battle pieces together in different typefaces so that one can compare similarities and differences. Both the younger men, for example, describe the English crossing of the

Somme, and Henry's reply to the French heralds who came to challenge him on the following day, Sunday 20 October. They then agree in ascribing to that day the king's order that each archer should have and carry with him a stake pointed at both ends.

We come now to their descriptions of the movements of both armies on the day before the battle, Thursday the 24th, which I take to be of vital importance. Neither of the two who were present is at all clear, except to say that after crossing the River Ternoise at Blangy Henry heard from his scouts that the French were 'before him' in great numbers, so he drew up his army, expecting battle. There follows a clue which may lead us to the truth, when both agree that after a stand-off 'the Constable arrived near Agincourt' (le Fèvre) 'at which place assembled all the French together in a single host. The English King . . . had all his battles *move off* to lodge at Maisoncelles' (le Fèvre and Waurin). The inference is that *both* armies *changed position* as the light failed, and that it was not until the following morning that positions were taken up which would lead directly to the final confrontation. There are many other versions of what happened and of how many were engaged, which are not really germane to the issue.

But our best guide? We have not yet consulted him, and it is time we did so on this crucial matter of the movements of the 24th. He is known as 'the chaplain' but it is not absolutely clear who he was. He might be Thomas Elmham, a monk of St Augustine's Abbey in Canterbury, or, as Curry thinks more likely, John Stevens, a canon of Exeter Cathedral, but his identity does not matter as much as the fact that he was a witness to the battle. Moreover, he had been through the entire campaign with the English and is firm, clear and specific on every point of fact he sees fit to mention.[44] He was there, he was a well-educated, intelligent priest and an acute observer, who had access to everyone's recounting of their participation, and he wrote it all down mainly in 1416, finishing it the following year. This cannot be said of anyone else, so I believe we should be very sure that he is wrong about this or that before we doubt his story. Here he is, on the 24th, just before the crossing of the Ternoise: 'Word was brought to the king by our scouts and mounted patrols that an enemy force of many thousands was on the other side (the north side) of the river about a league away to our right.' The English are about to cross by the bridge at Blangy; Maisoncelles and Agincourt are a little to the left (west), Tramecourt to the right (east), and the enemy are on the English *right* (east). The Chaplain describes crossing the river 'as quickly as possible' and continues, vitally, 'just as we reached the top of the hill on the other side we saw *emerging* from higher up the valley about half a mile away from us . . .

the compact masses, battles and columns' of the French, who took up position opposite the English in numbers, 'so great as not to be even comparable with ours . . . rather more than half a mile away . . . and there was only a valley, and not so wide at that (*vallem modicam*) between us and them.' The king then calmly drew up his small army 'in battles and wings' (note the plural) ready for action.

Then comes the story of Sir Walter Hungerford wishing for 10,000 more good English archers, and the king's reply, 'Oh, do not wish one more!' (So wrote Shakespeare, who followed the Chaplain's report of the speech very closely.) Then

there was a pause, and then 'while the enemy from their positions had watched us . . . they withdrew to a field, at the far side of a certain wood which was close at hand to our left, between us and them', while King Henry 'immediately moved his lines again, always positioning them so that they faced the enemy'.[45]

Not much about the archers there, you may say. Not yet, no, except that those plural 'wings' after plural 'battles' must apply to archers, if the 'battles', as is usual, applies to men-at-arms. More, this whole business of drawing up quickly for battle, and then the movement of the English lines 'always . . .

so they faced the enemy' speaks of decisive command, of clear orders being obeyed – in fact, discipline in manoeuvre. Do not forget we are speaking of a force of fewer than 1,000 men-at-arms and 5,000 archers, so we must believe that five-sixths of the army was as disciplined as the other one-sixth. Shortly after these manoeuvres, and the issuing of the orders for silence in the English host through the night, the king 'at once moved off in silence to a hamlet nearby [Maisoncelles] . . . and heavy rain [fell] almost the whole night through'.

Let us look at the terrain seen by the Chaplain through our own eyes. After crossing the Ternoise at Blangy the Calais road winds steeply uphill and as it reaches the top there is a little valley on the right, 'not so wide at that', across which I think the Duke of York first saw the French, and told the king who was waiting with the main-guard below. He then rode up to see for himself. It is easy to see where he would have drawn up his men to face a French attack across that little valley, easy to follow the eyes of the English searching for shelter as the night advanced and seeing the little white road leading off ahead and

Above: The lower slope of the English position at Poitiers, with a course of the Nouaillé wood in the distance, and the hedge (?) to the right.

Opposite, above: Poitiers. This shows the slope bending east from the previous pictures of the English position. The French would have started to appear on the skyline to the left. I think it just possible that the hedge across the centre represents, or is derived from, the original hedge with two gaps. The left of the picture is where the marsh begins.

Opposite, below: The marsh of the little river Miosson. It is photographed from the Gué de l'Omme and shows the modern footbridge. It was here that Warwick reached the ford and got the baggage train across before the French moved to prevent him.

to the left to Maisoncelles. What is clear also is that the French, after pausing to evaluate the strength of the English force, moved on behind the Tramecourt woods, which were, as the Chaplain says, 'on our left'. This caused the king to wheel his army, in battle order, to their left, anticipating that the French would attempt some sort of encirclement. This they did not do, but instead, in the open plain just beyond Agincourt and Tramecourt, they spread slowly over the whole area, occupying the villages round about, including Canlers and Agincourt but probably not Tramecourt, their whole vast array spreading back towards Ruisseauville to their rear. No doubt there was more woodland around the village then than there is today. Even fifty years ago Agincourt was well hidden, but now there is only a sparse fringe of new trees, which still mark the site of the old fortress. But I am assured that the ancient woods on the Tramecourt side have altered very little for centuries,[46] and the recent clearances to which Bradbury alludes have certainly not opened up much space on the eastern limit of the battlefield. In short, one can discern the limits to the open spaces where the fight took place, though orchards and hedges may well have been altered and indeed largely cleared. A little controlled marching and measuring can give us the dimensions of the ground on which the main clash happened, just north of the east–west lane from Tramecourt to Azincourt, and marked by the grave-pits on the French left at La Gacogne, passed by the Calais road a yard or two to the west.

Perhaps thirty years ago I saw a map of the battle contained in the *Grand Livre d'Or Historique de la Gendarmerie Nationale*, lodged in the church at Auchy-les-Hesdin. This showed clearly the first position of the English army as described above, and indeed until some five years ago there was an engraved map near the Agincourt memorial stone at the corner where the lane running north-eastwards from Maisoncelles joins the Calais road, together with a separate map first before Maisoncelles showing the other two positions of the English on the day of the battle itself, and after the advance, short of the grave-pits. When I was last there, just a year ago, the first position map had disappeared, although the other one was still there, possibly a newer version but still offering the same positions for the 25th.

I shall add a very brief note on why the monument is set where it is, short of what I take to be the true first deployment on the day of battle. When the late Abbé de l'Etoile, chaplain to the de Chabot-Tramecourt family, asked the then Vicomte, Antoine de Chabot-Tramecourt, for a suitable spot to erect a memorial, it was suggested that he put it where it stands, well away from the busy crossroads, where heavy lorries come and go, where it would be in the way, and where it would be quite dangerous for sightseers because of fast traffic travelling on both roads. So it is where it is, and at least it points the way to the truth.

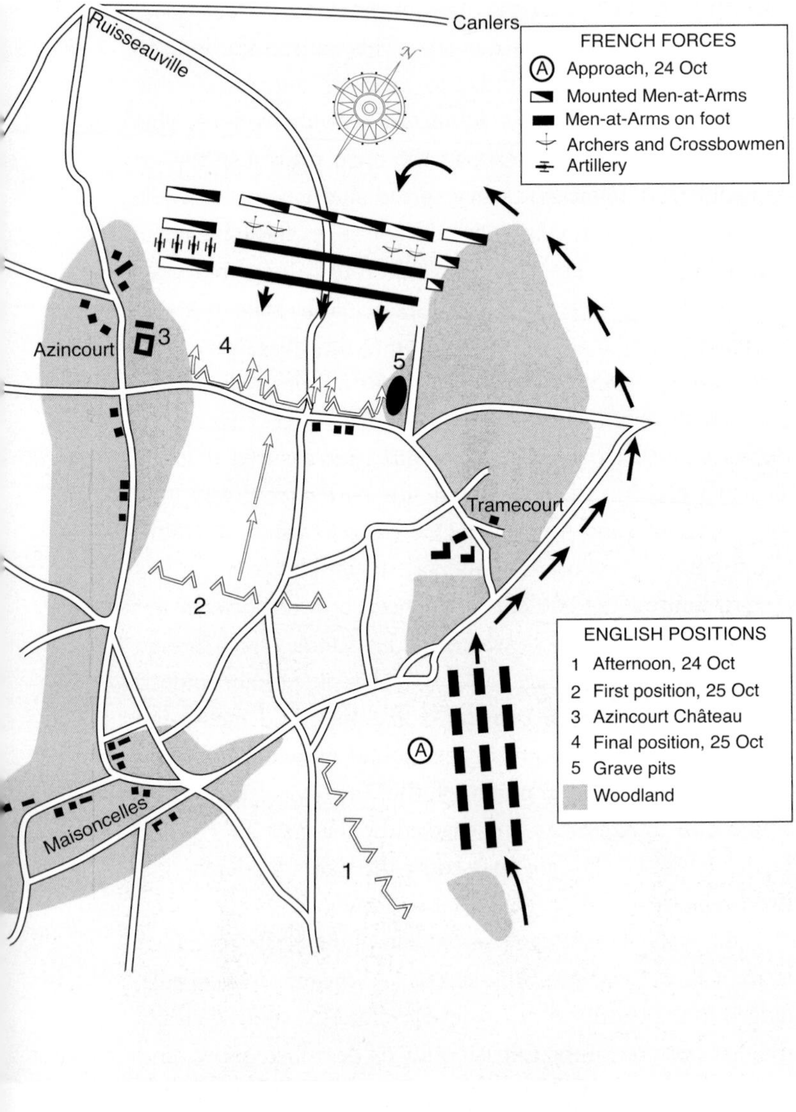

On the dispositions of both armies the Chaplain is quite clear. The massive first division, or battle, of the French had cavalry on each wing 'to break the formation and resistance of our archers', while their vanguard comprised dismounted men-at-arms 'drawn from all their nobles and the pick of their forces, with its forest of spears . . . and helmets gleaming . . . at a rough guess thirty times more than all our men put together' – which was either an estimate of the whole French army stretching back as far as the eye could see, or 'a scribal error' (as the editors of the Chaplain's account suggest), or perhaps flat panic. Now to the English:

> Meanwhile our king . . . made ready for the field, which was at no great distance from his quarters [at Maisoncelles], and in view of his want of numbers, he drew up only a single line of battle, placing his vanguard commanded by the Duke of York as a wing on the right, and the rearguard, commanded by Lord Camoys, as a wing on the left; and he positioned wedges [or bodies] of his archers in between each battle, and had them drive in their stakes in front of them.

So far, there is no doubt that we have three English battles side by side, four men deep,[47] and according to the Monk of St Denis (also known as the Religieux), whose account makes sense, there were archers *in between each battle* of some 300 men-at-arms; '*intermisisset cuneos saggitariorum*', says the Chaplain. The left battle was commanded by Lord Camoys, the centre by the king, and the right by the Duke of York. The Chaplain goes on to describe the start of the battle: 'When the enemy was nearly ready to attack, the French cavalry posted on the flanks made charges against those of our archers who were on both sides of our army, but . . . they were forced to fall back under showers of our arrows . . .' Note the phrase 'those of our archers who were on both sides of our army'. In other words there were other archers who were *not* 'on both sides of our army' – where were they? Wylie[48] explains it thus: 'Spanning his [King Henry's] whole front [quoting St Denis, '*in fronte aciei regiae*'; Pierre Fenin, '*tous ses archiers devant*'; and Monstrelet: '*au front devant*'] and circling it from flank to flank like a crown [quoting St Denis, '*ad instar corone*'] were placed the archers, clumped in triangular wedges, each block . . . of about 200 men each, in the usual open order, like a hearse or harrow'. All that is worth bearing in mind. He goes on to describe the archers planting their stakes in the ground 'beside' them, and then offers this rather wonderful passage:

Plan of the probable position of the French and English at Agincourt.

FRENCH FORCES
- (A) Approach, 24 Oct
- Mounted Men-at-Arms
- Men-at-Arms on foot
- Archers and Crossbowmen
- Artillery

ENGLISH POSITIONS
1 Afternoon, 24 Oct
2 First position, 25 Oct
3 Azincourt Château
4 Final position, 25 Oct
5 Grave pits
Woodland

Canlers
Ruisseauville
Azincourt
Tramecourt
Maisoncelles

We know enough of their bearing and equipment to enable us to estimate the value of their services on that memorable day. Trained from their boyhood by constant practice . . . these quick-eyed clever longbowmen could hit the prick of the oyster shell in the centre of the butt, with the nicety of a Thames fisherman garfangling an eel, while for nimble readiness in the field they stood unrivalled in the western world.

Let us now try to work out in practical terms how the archers might have been deployed. If there were 5,000 archers and 1,000 men-at-arms defending a 1,000-yard front, and if they were all in one line, as the Chaplain avows, and the ranks were four deep, then there would be 1,500 men in each of the four ranks, as long as the array was in a straight line. But set a proportion of the archers forward on each exterior wing, and one can imagine a straight front between the wings of some 800 men in each of four ranks, totalling 3,200 men in the line and 2,800 archers in those two forward-reaching wings, 1,400 on each side. Of course you may alter the proportions as you please, but not the total number. Next, 1,000 men-at-arms divided into three battles of four ranks each presents three short battle-fronts some 83 men wide. Perhaps the men-at-arms were in two ranks only, in which case the three short

battle-fronts would be some 166 men wide. In the first case the men-at-arms could cover some 166 yards, allowing two yards per man, in the second case some 333 yards. It is to be doubted if the men-at-arms would be ranged in a single line, so if we allow them two lines on a front of 1,000 yards there is still nearly 670 yards to be filled, *and* the two lines of their 333 yards to be made up to four. By whom but the archers, obviously? It was vital that no gaps were left in the English line, and to strengthen it there *must* have been archers in the main battle-front. Subtract from the 1,000-yard front the space laterally taken up by the butt-end of the outside wings of archers, and you still have far too long a central line to cover; if the back end of the outer wings were 50 yards wide at each side, the front is only reduced by 100 yards, and I believe it would be near the limit of plausibility for mass volleying to have archers in a crowd at the back ends, perhaps 25 or 30 men shooting from a quincunx formation. What are we left with? The near certainty that in between the three battles of men-at-arms were bodies of archers. I no longer believe that they were formed into triangles created by two forward-

An impression of the English right wing at Agincourt looking west towards the village. The French are moving in on foot, their wing cavalry charges already fouled. Painting by Andrew Boardman.

Above: View of Agincourt field from above the village, showing the narrowing of the woods that caused the French crush. Behind the fringe of trees is the site of Agincourt Castle. The clump of trees across the field marks the enormous grave-pits.

Left: The road to Calais through the field of battle: Maisoncelles to the near left, Azincourt beyond and Tramecourt woods to the right. Even today the defile between the woods can be seen to narrow dramatically.

inclined wings joining together at the apex. Having pushed long-suffering bodies of today's enthusiastic archers about, I have so far concluded that four ranks, in chequerboard or quincunx formation, is about right for volleying 'wholly together', so one must think of solid, four-deep bodies of longbowmen interspersed with the three small 'battles' of men-at-arms.

Dr Matthew Bennett, with whom I have had both public and private debate on this subject, surmises that *all* the archers were on the outside wings only, and that such was the usual battle formation of English armies, and there are many who agree with him. If this were true, then at Agincourt there were 2,500 archers on either wing, curving back into the flat line, with 1,000 men-at-arms in the middle, defending a quarter of that whole front, as shown below (and here come three plans with designated groups of soldiery, which we already know we should not trust, so be on your guard).

If, however, you have three separate battles of men-at-arms, with archers in between, the picture would look more like the plan shown at the top of p. 310.

In either case the forward ends of the outer wings of archers are fairly safe, though as the Chaplain takes pains to explain 'a very few' of the French cavalry, 'although not without losses in dead and wounded, rode through between the archers and the woodlands'. But he goes on to say that 'when the men-at-arms

had from each side advanced towards one another over roughly the same distance, the flanks of both battle lines . . . extended into the woodlands which were on both sides of the armies', and from then on, the archer wings seem to have proved impenetrable. There is another picture to consider, having in mind the phrases 'in the form of a coronet' or 'like a crown', 'all in front' and the like, and this is shown at the bottom of p. 310.

In this surmise, the 'coronet' archers could keep up their volleys from maximum range until they became vulnerable to the advancing French, and then retire through the ranks of men-at-arms and archers behind them, the main bodies of archers being protected by their stakes. Having pulled back, they could both reinforce the archer lines and shoot over the heads of the men-at-arms with high trajectories which would make the enemy keep their faces down and their shields up, and thus would help to disorganise their advance. The permutations are many, but no one can alter the fact that the proportion of five to one, archers to men-at-arms, must always be taken into account.

That the three battles of men-at-arms were separated from one another emerges from the Chaplain's account:

The French nobility, who had previously advanced in line abreast, and had all but come to grips with us, either from fear of the missiles, which by their very force pierced the

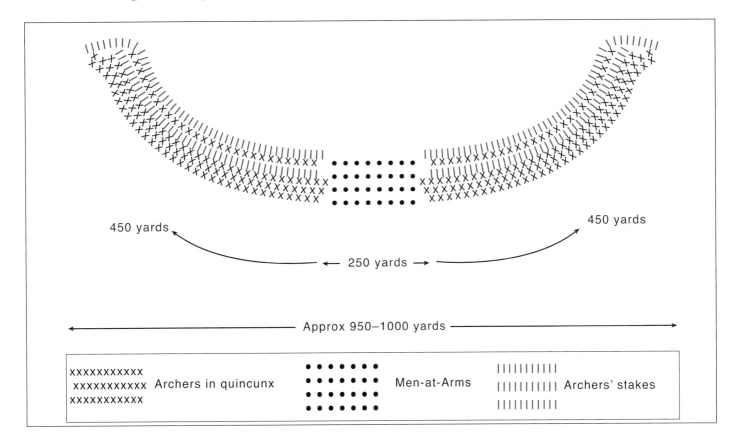

450 yards

450 yards

← 250 yards →

Approx 950–1000 yards

xxxxxxxxxx
xxxxxxxxxxx Archers in quincunx
xxxxxxxxxxx

Men-at-Arms

||||||||||
|||||||||| Archers' stakes
||||||||||

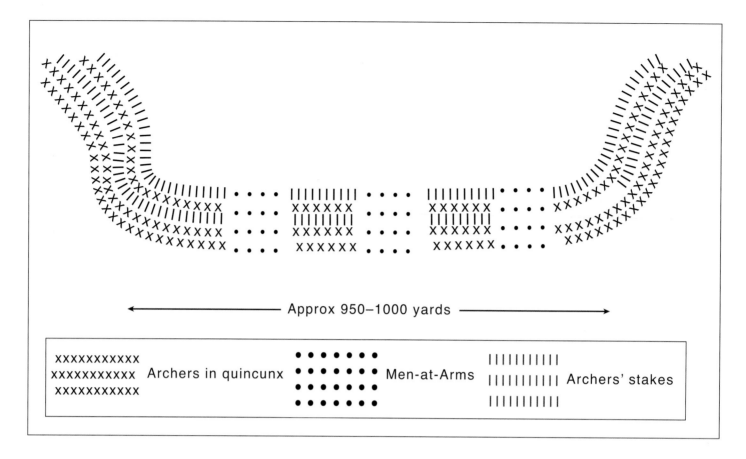

Approx 950–1000 yards

xxxxxxxxxx				
xxxxxxxxxx	Archers in quincunx	• • • • • •	Men-at-Arms	‖‖‖‖‖‖‖
xxxxxxxxxx		• • • • • •		‖‖‖‖‖‖‖ Archers' stakes
		• • • • • •		‖‖‖‖‖‖‖

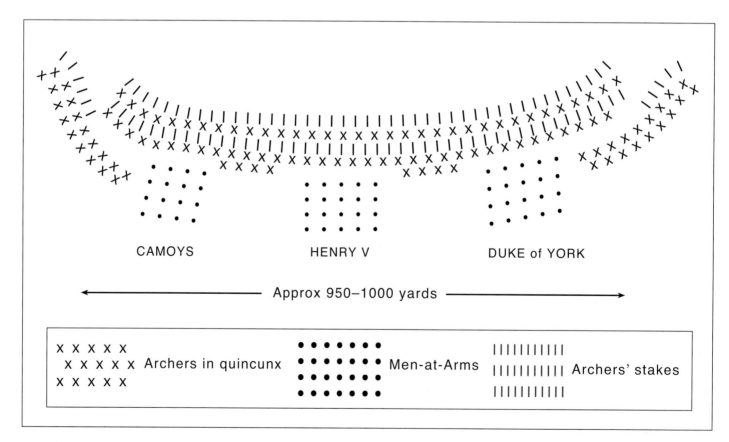

CAMOYS   HENRY V   DUKE of YORK

Approx 950–1000 yards

x x x x x				
x x x x x	Archers in quincunx	• • • • • •	Men-at-Arms	‖‖‖‖‖‖‖
x x x x x		• • • • • •		‖‖‖‖‖‖‖ Archers' stakes
		• • • • • •		‖‖‖‖‖‖‖

sides and visors of their helmets, or in order the sooner to break through our strongest points and reach the standards, divided into three columns, attacking our line of battle where the three standards were.

He goes on to say the attack came on so fiercely that 'our men . . . fell back almost a spear's length'.

Should we trust the Chaplain, and the accuracy of his observation? I think so, because he was right there, on his horse, waiting with the other priests behind the battle line, which we know was shallow. Before the battle was joined, he has this to say of the moments before the king decided to move from his early morning position before Maisoncelles: 'So he decided to move against them, sending for the army baggage in order to have it at the rear of the engagement lest it should fall as booty into the hands of the enemy. He had previously arranged that this baggage, together with the priests . . . should await him in the aforesaid hamlet.' (Just to the west of Maisoncelles older maps show a 'Bois des Anglais', where it is possible the baggage was parked at first.) The Chaplain describes how some of the baggage was laggard in coming forward, and that the enemy fell upon it 'owing to the negligence of the royal servants'. A precious crown and a sword, 'as well as all the bedding', were seized by the French – whereby hangs a long tale, but this is not the place to tell it. The king, thinking all the baggage was up close behind him, advanced to within bowshot of the French who themselves began to advance, stung into action by the first volleys from the archers. The Chaplain then recorded:

But then indeed, and for as long as the conflict lasted, I who am now writing this, and was then sitting on a horse among the baggage *at the rear of the battle*, and the other priests did humble ourselves . . . and also, in fear and trembling with our eyes raised to heaven we cried out that God would have compassion upon us.

He was there, and saw everything within his range; since he was a royal chaplain, I imagine he was behind the king's battle, and so would have been central. When his eyes were raised to heaven he may have missed a detail here and there, but why should we doubt that what he saw that day was burned into his memory?

The French began to fall to the arrows, and then to the men-at-arms; their own ranks already broken by their retreating cavalry, they began to pile up in front of the English line, while their oncoming flanks were volleyed into and driven, as at Dupplin, into an ever-growing and chaotic press. The French second rank pushed up behind the first and penned in the vanguard, while those on the wings pushed inwards to escape the arrows; as the supply of arrows dwindled and then ceased, the archers threw down their bows – 'nor, it seemed to our older men, had Englishmen ever fallen upon their enemies more boldly and fearlessly, or with a better will'. They had no choice, those 6,000 men; it was a case of massacre or be massacred. The Chaplain recorded:

When their arrows were all used up, seizing axes, stakes and swords and spearheads that were lying about, they struck down, hacked and stabbed the enemy . . . so great was the undisciplined violence and pressure of the mass of [French] men behind, that the living fell on top of the dead, and others falling on top of the living were killed as well, with the result that, in each of the three places where the strong contingents were, such a great heap grew of the slain and of those lying crushed among them that our men climbed up those heaps which had risen above a man's height, and butchered their enemies down below.

The rest of the story is well known. As victory was within the English grasp the French rearguard threatened to renew the attack, and the danger from the thousands of captured Frenchmen caused the king to order a massacre of the prisoners. This led many a more recent writer to declare that Henry was no more than a war criminal, though we should remember that no contemporary blamed him; they lamented the deaths, which added to the slaughter of the battle, but they did not think it an awful deed. This shows how very important it is for those writing about the past to study the ethos of the period enough to understand the actions and judgements of the time of which they write.

Henry V had trusted his archer force enough to risk a major battle with them as five-sixths of his whole force, and they had responded by giving him a victory which has so echoed down the ages that now at Azincourt itself they celebrate their 'page d'histoire en Artois' and welcome visitors to a fine new museum, where among other things you can test your strength on the 'Agincourt bow' machine. It draws all of 60lb (27kg). Multiply that by two-and-a-half times and you have the bows that won so many battles. Such bows also caused huge casualties in civil wars in England, when archers such as fought at Agincourt were ranged against each other in equal numbers and equal fury, particularly at Towton during the Wars of the Roses, where the appalling numbers of dead numbered between twenty and thirty thousand.

Of course the French eventually learned how to deal with the longbow threat, at Baugé, at Patay and at Castillon – but that is shown elsewhere in this study.

It would be wrong to leave the subject of Agincourt without remarking how many television programmes have put bad information and inference into the public mind. There is often much to object to which will of course enter the realms of received myth. I have seen it claimed that the arrows of the late medieval period could never have pierced plate armour; the range of the longbow and it strengths have been pitifully reduced; it was said in one television programme on Agincourt that dark secrets about the battle were revealed for the first time and that the 'accepted story was never challenged until now', when a mere glance at the long catalogue of literature on the subject represents a never-ending series of challenges. Every imaginable possibility, conjecture, explanation and claim has been put forward from both sides of the Channel for centuries. The bibliography is immense. But we are so often left with a few headline-grabbing phrases, which are thrown at us without justification. It has been claimed that archers were employed simply because they were cheap, not because of their skills as fighting men, or because of the remarkable power of their principal weapon, the longbow. As to cheapness, their pay was on a level with a skilled craftsman, a master carpenter or a joiner at home, and any reader who has got this far will know by now a good deal about the fighting archers of the Hundred

Above: An English foot soldier leads away noble prisoners, still fully armoured but with their hands bound, from the *Vigiles de Charles VII* by Martial d'Auvergne, late fifteenth century. At Agincourt the large numbers of French men-at-arms taken captive as the cohesion of French divisions collapsed posed a serious threat to the heavily outnumbered English in case of a renewed French assault. *(Bibliothèque Nationale, Paris/Bridgeman Art Library)*

Opposite: The brass of Sir Thomas Brounflet, cup-bearer to Henry V, from Wymington church, Bedfordshire, 1430 (from C. Boutell, *Monumental Brasses* (1847)). *(Author Collection)*

Years War and the weapon that in their hands pierced mail and plate, killed and wounded thousands upon thousands of their enemies, and won for Henry V the title 'Héritier de France' and for his infant son the very title of kingship.

There are shafts of light. Dr Alan Williams of the Wallace Collection has been sensible, as one would expect, about armour, though to speak of a 'sudden change' in quality, or as 'a new metal for a new age', is to belittle much earlier work on the process of steeling; swords, arrowheads and plate armour were gradually improved over many years and through much experience. For instance, when in the 1980s our little team of

consultants to the Mary Rose Trust had commissioned a substantial quantity of arrowheads to be made for our ballistic and penetration tests, using a modern spring steel as the likeliest approximation to the many fourteenth- and fifteenth-century arrowheads we had examined, a telephone call from Professor Pratt stopped the process in its tracks. He had obtained permission to carry examination to thorough analysis, and was permitted by the Royal Armouries to cut up and subject to total metallurgical breakdown a fourteenth-century head. He stopped us manufacturing 'approximations' because the arrowhead revealed an unguessed-at sophistication in its manufacture. The tip was steeled, as were the cutting edges, and these hardened extremities were bedded in a softer iron centre, with a considerably softer socket which would be less likely to split on the shaft upon impact.

But in many television stories the arrowheads are 'made of iron', an iron arrow tip curled over on striking a steel plate used to represent French armour, which was cited as proof that 'the weaker English bodkin would simply buckle where it hits steel . . . it fails . . . there is no way it would have gone through French armour'. In this case the impact of the arrowhead on this steel, descending on an Instron machine, was determined by the weight of the bows offered for our consideration. The figures suggested were for a 2¼oz (63g) arrow, with a velocity of 37.9 metres per second, which equalled an impact force of 38 joules – and the head could not even stand up to those demands. We should have seen tests made with steeled arrowheads under conditions dictated by the use of bows in the 140–150lb (63.5–68kg) range, when, as can be seen in Appendix 1, we would be looking at impact velocities of over 48 metres per second at 50 metres and over 41 metres per second at 200 metres, with impact energies of 103 joules at 50 metres, 86 at 100, 72 at 150 and so on, with matching impact energy/area (J/mm²) of 0.81, 0.68 and 0.57 respectively. (The Appendix explains the manner of tests made at the Royal Military College of Science, and the deductions recorded from them, during 2002/3.)

It is usually impossible in television programmes to guess at the strength of the bows used, though to a reasonably accustomed eye they often appear to be of modern target longbow power and appearance; never, either in what is supposedly test shooting, or in re-enactment shooting, have I seen any longbow fully drawn up to the length of the arrows. It is perhaps no wonder that after a good deal of this kind of evaluation commentaries pontificate that 'the longbow simply could not have been the decisive weapon history has claimed'. The kindest thing that can be said of those who put about such assertions is that they, as Churchill said of Hitler's apparent ignorance of the dangers of the Russian winter, 'must have been very loosely educated'.

There have been good investigations on TV: for instance, Tim Sutherland and Simon Richardson of Bradford University, who have published much interesting evidence from their geophysical work on the battlefield of Towton (1461), dug down to the depth of a metre into the Agincourt soil and sent samples to Professor Andrew Palmer at Cambridge. He explained that the Agincourt mud was of a particularly thick and sticky consistency, and so would have been very difficult to fight in. That is valuable evidence, and chimes with the majority of contemporary accounts, and with my own experience.

I have also seen a brilliant analysis of crowd collapse and mass chaos given by Dr Keith Still, a crowd analyst, on the subject of the French collapse at Agincourt. Nothing could diminish the force and horror of the disaster to the overcrowded French, which Dr Still vividly illustrated. But I think it must be realised that although the slope on the eastern (Tramecourt) side of the field might, as Professor Curry said to me personally, have meant that some of the French left flank could have advanced almost into the English archers before they saw them, what really squeezed the vast French numbers into a giant and lethal crowd-disaster was the narrowing of the woods, making a funnel into which they were driven by their determined advance and the enormous pressure from their own men in great numbers behind them. Without a shadow of a doubt the press was exacerbated by the lethal volleys from the archers on the wings, forcing the French on the flanks to move towards the centre. There was nowhere for them to go as long as the English line held – and miraculously it did.

In general it has to be said that science is often used as camouflage for ignorant ideas that ignore established facts. Naturally these are often attacks on the massacre of prisoners, which make no allowance for the fact that at Agincourt blame was never contemporaneously attached to Henry V for his order. There is little appreciation of the fact that perhaps the first duty of any historian is to think himself back into the ethos of the period which he treats. Television too frequently offers us falsity where truth, as far as it can be known, would have been a hundred times more interesting and compelling.

It is worth examining in further detail three battles which strongly suggest the use of archers across the battle-front of English armies. My own belief is that this was a more common tactical usage than is usually allowed nowadays, and the three fights in question seem to me to pose differing and strong reasons to believe that they are exemplars of the 'archers in front' deployment. That it is not often believed in by historians writing today is possibly because we have so little evidence of any drilled manoeuvre among the soldiers of the Middle Ages, and absolutely no written evidence of how such putative movements might have been put into practice, though a little thought may suggest perfectly simple ways in which retiring archers could slip into alleys left open between men-at-arms or disperse to the wings, while still shooting, Homildon-fashion. But there is a lot of what might be called evidence by inference: there are numerous battles in which the archer corps survived the initial stages of conflict, the 'archery duel', and reappeared alongside the men-at-arms fighting almost *as* men-at-arms, their bows discarded. We have seen it at Agincourt, at Poitiers and others, but to shed further light on the argument let us look again at the battles of Homildon Hill (1402), Shrewsbury (1403) and Towton (1461), with the position of the archers foremost in our minds.

When the Percys and their allied magnates of the north were still warding the northern counties against Scottish invasions, and still remained loyal to Henry IV, an invading Scottish force under Archibald, Earl of Douglas, which had reached as far as Newcastle and was returning north with great booty, was forced to face about and do battle with the intercepting English army under Northumberland and his son Henry Percy, the 'Hotspur' of both fact and fiction. Douglas had some 10,000 men (according to Walter Bower's *Scotichronicon*, or 12,000–13,000 according to the *Historia Vitae et Regni Ricardi Secundo*, which gives the English 7,000 archers over and above an army equalling the Scots), and most historians seem to settle for two fairly equal armies. Douglas took up a position of advantage on Homildon Hill, not far from Wooler in Northumberland. Percy, with George Dunbar, Earl of March, was below and facing him on level ground. Ahead of his right flank was a substantial second slope called Harehope Hill. It is on this hill that many have supposed the English archer force was flung forward against the Scottish left, separated from them by a steep defile, the Scots position on Homildon being such as to refuse their flank by forming an arc round the contour of the hill. This is the version, at first reporting, preferred by the Battlefields Panel of English Heritage, on which I sit. However, our new chairman (2003) Professor John Childs has made us re-examine the evidence, based on what he thinks may be a mistranslation of Thomas Walsingham's account of the battle in his *Historia Anglicana*. Rather than rendering the Latin as meaning 'our men climbed *a* hill opposite the Scots', and 'our archers who were drawn up in *a* valley', Childs suggests the passage in full can read, 'Our men left the road on which they were assembled in order to oppose the Scots, and climbed *the hill opposite* the Scots' (*montem Scotis oppositum conscenderent*). The Latin continues:

'*nec mora, nostri sagitarii, in valle constituti, sagittas miserunt ad Scotorum cuneum, et eos ad descensum quomodolibet provocarent*', which Childs suggests should be translated: 'Without delay, our archers, who were drawn up in the valley, volleyed at the Scottish schiltron to provoke them into coming down.'

The inference is that the Scots on Homildon were faced by the English in the valley at the hill's southern foot; the English archers thus advanced to their front and shot straight up the hill into the Scots formation in order to tempt them down, rather than that a major wing of archers on the English right climbed Harehope Hill and started shooting across *that* valley into the Scottish left. Childs goes on to suggest that Douglas, galled by arrows, would hardly have charged down into the defile that separates Homildon from Harehope; Walsingham, he says, indicates that Douglas charged down *the* hill, on which he stood, straight towards the English archers 'deployed before the main English force as it ascended the hill'.

Let us return to the outset of the battle, as seen by the *Scotichronicon*: 'As they stood on the plain facing the Scots, the English were impatient to attack them on Percy's order; but the Earl of March reined Percy back, saying that he should not move, but send archers who could easily penetrate the Scots as targets for their arrows and defeat and capture them.' This advice came from a Scot himself, who knew that the Scottish archery was not as strong as that of the English and Welsh. According to many, and indeed to our own original report for the English Heritage Panel, this sending of the archers was fulfilled by their marching right-handed up Harehope Hill, to enfilade the Scots' refused left flank; this was a dangerous manoeuvre, unless in some way these Harehope archers managed to be an extension of the English right wing position. Otherwise the Scots could have caught them before they were in position, and if they were detached from the English right the Scots could have cut them off – and as we know, unsupported archers are extremely vulnerable. The alternative, taking John Childs' 'up the hill' to mean the hill in front of them, would surely have been preferable in every way, and would certainly produce the results that occurred.

Again, Walsingham says the English archers shot 'without delay', and that they shot from where they were drawn up 'in the dale' – not after a manoeuvre and not on a hill to the side. But does he go on to say the archers climbed *a* hill, or *the* hill opposite the Scots? It must be *the* hill on which the Scots were drawn up, and down which the opening volleys were tempting them to charge. The Scots put in their own volleys, but, says Walsingham, 'they felt the weight of our arrows, which fell like a storm of rain, and so they fled'. 'They' must mean the Scots archers, who doubtless failed in their riposte because of poorer shooting or a lack of adequate numbers.

Let us follow Walsingham a little further: 'The Earl of Douglas . . . saw their flight . . . so he seized a lance and rode down the hill with a troop of his horse, trusting too much in his equipment and that of his men, who had been improving their armour for three years, and strove to rush on the archers.' Had he charged left-handed towards Harehope Hill he would have exposed his flank to the barely restrained Hotspur's cavalry. No, he charged straight down Homildon Hill at the archers who were ahead of the English main battle and had just scattered the Scots archers. Walsingham goes on: 'When the archers saw this they retreated, but still shooting, so vigorously, so resolutely, so effectively that they pierced the armour, perforated the helmets, pitted the swords, split the lances, and pierced all the equipment with ease. The Earl of Douglas was pierced with five wounds, notwithstanding his elaborate armour.' There in a few lines we have pretty clear evidence of the tactic of the archers' fighting withdrawal and the effectiveness of arrows shot from English longbows. The rest of the Scots army fled and were pursued by Hotspur's cavalry, released at last; many Scots were killed and many made prisoner, including Douglas. Walsingham concludes: 'in this fight no lord or knight received a blow; but God Almighty gave the victory miraculously to the English archers alone, and the magnates and men-at-arms remained idle spectators of the battle.' Had the victorious archers been on Harehope Hill, those idle spectators, with Hotspur in the lead, would have charged the Scots' exposed flank and so won their part of the triumph.

Henry Bolingbroke, uncertain still of his newly won authority, demanded Hotspur's prisoners; this was a grave political mistake, which led the following year to the Percy revolt and the two English armies that faced each other a little north of Shrewsbury. This is a fascinating battle to unravel, with little evidence to go on, but it also provides a grim foretaste of what was to come in the battles of the Wars of the Roses, and I believe it was another example of a contest in which archers right across both battle lines were ranged against each other with deadly effect.

Shrewsbury in 1403 was young Henry Plantagenet's first big pitched battle. Though he had already gained much experience in Welsh guerrilla campaigns, sadly enough under Hotspur's tutelage, this was his first set-piece. He was fifteen, rising sixteen, and he would have only one other such experience, as king, twelve years later at Agincourt. He took part in numerous sieges, fighting hand-to-hand in the mines, and many skirmishes, but only these two great battles. Here at Shrewsbury the rebel army had the advantage in archers, though it seems the royal army was the larger of the two overall. The rebels in their march south had recruited many of the finest archers from Cheshire and Flint, where many believed Richard II was

Opposite, above: Shrewsbury battlefield, looking from the royal army position up towards Hotspur's.

Opposite, below: Shrewsbury field, from Hotspur's position looking down to the royal position. Both are comparable to the Crécy situation.

still alive and the majority were loyal to his memory, but the sources for this battle offer such disparate estimates of numbers that it is not useful to try to enumerate the armies further.

It seems that Hotspur drew up his men on a rise, north-west of the present Battlefield Church. His choice of ground was typical of the general English positions selected as advantageous for the archer forces. Here the archers would be tilted (like the seating in a theatre), allowing clear sight-lines for their chequerboard ranks or 'herces', and it is hard to credit that given such choice ground English commanders would waste the advantage by relegating their archers to the wings. Of course on the flat plain at Agincourt Henry V could offer no such advantage to his 'yew hedge'. Here at Shrewsbury young Henry was on the left of the royal army waiting for the first flights of arrows. The rebels had the best of the initial archery exchanges, shooting, says Walsingham, 'so the place for the missiles was not on the ground . . . for men fell on the King's side as fast as leaves fall in autumn after the first hoar-frost', or in another account 'like apples fallen in the autumn . . . stirred by the south-west wind'. The king's division of the royal army suffered so badly it was said some 4,000 men fled the field, or at least out of bowshot. So far not a single blow with lance, bill or sword had been struck; it had been an archers' battle, won by the side with better, or more, bowmen. 'Nor did the King's archers fail to do their work, but sent a shower of sharp points against their enemies.' It is hard to see how this deadly archery duel could have happened unless the archers on both sides were deployed across the battle-front. Eventually Hotspur's charge and the Prince of Wales's counter-manoeuvre on the left must have pushed through the bowmen, who would be left to 'shoot as they bore' or turn to their side-arms. One version has Hotspur slain by an arrow in the face, either as he charged with visor raised to see better, or as he raised it to gulp air in the July heat.

The bitter Shrewsbury archery duel forecast the slaughter of the Wars of the Roses battles, of which Towton was the most terrible example. That battle was fought, at least to start with, in a snowstorm in March 1461. It began with an archery duel which may have been responsible for huge casualties. The Yorkist archers, facing roughly north with the wind and snow behind them, shot their first volley of heavy sheaf arrows into the Lancastrians opposite, evidently gauging the range well through the flurrying whiteness, then stepped back several paces so that when the Lancastrians blinded by snow shot back, their arrows fell short. The Yorkists advanced, pulled out the arrows sticking in the ground and shot them back. How long this grim line-dance lasted no one knows, as the two armies joined and fought, paused and fought again, but the resulting casualty figures are fearsome to read. Some say 28,000, others 36,000, were left dead on the field and along the paths of the rout when the Lancastrians broke and fled. Many were drowned in the swollen waters of the Cock Beck, which winds past Towton village along the northern side of the battlefield. Towton is well worth visiting today, since of all England's fields of conflict it has changed the least since the men loyal to their causes fought and died there in their thousands.

Only twenty years before Towton the final battle of the French wars had been fought at Castillon – the culmination of France's achievement in learning how to side-step, surprise, harass and finally outgun the English archers.

Robert Hardy

'That Mound of Blood and Pity': Agincourt, 25 October 1415

Then for sothe thate Knyghte comely,
In Agincourt feld he faught manly;
Throw grace of God most myghty,
He had both the felde, and victory.
Deo gratias
Deo gratias Anglia redde pro Victoria.

The Agincourt Carol, 1415

Agincourt, Agincourt!
Know ye not Agincourt?
Never to be forgot
Or known to no men?
Where English cloth-yard arrows
Kill'd the French like tame sparrows,
Slaine by our bowmen.[1]

Agincourt, or the Bowman's Glory, c. 1600

Few battles have achieved such lasting fame as that of Agincourt. For a medieval battle it is exceptionally well documented, a testament to its enormous impact on contemporary writers. It has entered national mythology, with each successive age recasting it to suit the needs of its own time, and by at least the time of the publication of the *Bowman's Glory*, it had come to represent the triumph of the yeoman archer over the proud chivalry of France.[2] Yet behind such enduring fascination lies the nature of the battle itself. For although

strategically Agincourt was not to prove decisive, in tactical terms it was a truly remarkable triumph of a heavily outnumbered force against a mighty army which should have crushed Henry V's tired and sickness-riddled force. Henry's campaign of 1415 and the battle of Agincourt have been much studied, so much so, indeed, that changing methods, agendas and assumptions of historians in their treatment of the battle can themselves provide an intriguing case study of trends in the writing of military history.[3] Accordingly, the following chapter is less a campaign history than an attempt both to evaluate the role of the longbow and of the English archers in achieving victory, and to analyse the broader military context of the engagement from the French as well as the English perspective.

The richness of the sources, moreover, allows an exploration of the *mentalité* of the combatants to an extent often impossible for other medieval battles.

FRENCH TACTICAL THINKING ON THE EVE OF AGINCOURT

Some five years prior to Henry V's momentous invasion of Normandy in 1415, the great French courtly writer Christine de Pizan produced her *Livre des fais d'armes et de chevalerie*.[4] This vernacular military manual may well have been commissioned by the Duke of Burgundy to aid the instruction of his son-in-law, the Dauphin Louis of Guyenne, whose guardian he had become in 1409.[5] The work was subsequently to become very popular. Ironically, John Talbot, Earl of Shrewsbury, the scourge of the French in the latter stages of the Anglo-French war, presented a collection containing the *Livre des fais* to Margaret of Anjou, wife of Henry VI, in 1445, while in 1489 Henry VII of England gave William Caxton a copy, commanding him to print an English translation of it.[6] Christine's work is in itself a remarkable insight into the perceptive understanding of war by a leading noblewoman at the French court. What is still more striking is the close correlation between her description of the ideal battle formation as recommended by contemporary commanders and an actual battle plan drawn up only a few days before Agincourt itself by the commanders of the French vanguard. Her observations thus shed an important light on French military thinking in the years immediately prior to the most famous, and in many ways the most remarkable, triumph of English arms during the Hundred Years War.

Christine drew extensively on Vegetius and other classical military authors, but in many places she sought to update the work, including an important and well-informed discussion of the use of gunpowder artillery.[7] Similarly, while she rehearses the various battle formations outlined in the *De Re Militari*, she also notes how contemporary battle formations differed from those of Vegetius's day, 'for then troops fought more commonly on horseback than on foot'.[8] In her own times, by contrast, the dismounting of men-at-arms had become commonplace, not only as a reaction to the mass deployment of the longbow by English armies, but to counter the effective infantry tactics of the Flemish and Swiss. Elements of the Franco-Burgundian army had fought on foot against the formidable Flemish infantry at Roosebeke in 1382, while at Sempach in 1386 the Austrian knights had dismounted and cut down their lances to engage the Swiss, though they met with bloody defeat. So familiar had the practice become that in the famous *Très Riches Heures*, Jean, Duke of Berry (d. 1416), son of King Jean II and

uncle to King Charles VI, is depicted as feasting in a hall decorated with tapestries which show knights riding to battle but then dismounting to fight opposing men-at-arms on foot.[9]

According to skilful military men, Christine continues, the best modern battle formation involves:

> making the advanced guard of considerable length, with men-at-arms arranged close together, so that one should not pass another, the best and most select being in the forefront, the marshals with them, following their standards and banners, and in wing formation at their sides the firepower, cannoneers along with crossbowmen and archers similarly arranged (*et fait on eles aux coustez devant esquelles est le trait*).

The van is to be followed by the main battle, 'where the main mass of men-at-arms is ordered by their captains', with the commander and banners in its centre, surrounded by picked men-at-arms. If the main battle is to include 'a considerable number of common people (*gent de commune*), these should be used to reinforce the wings in well-ordered ranks behind the firepower (*le traitt* [sic]), and they should be commanded by good captains, and also that they should be put in front of the major part of the formation, so that if they should be tempted to flee, the men-at-arms behind them would prevent it'.[10] Behind the rearguard come 'yeomen on horseback (*varlez a cheval*)', 'good men, holding the horses of their masters and forming an obstacle so that no one can attack the army from the rear'.[11] This use of horses as a living screen to protect an army's rear had long been in use by English armies when fighting on the defensive, but in a reflection of French practice from at least the 1350s Christine also notes that it is customary to have a select force of well-mounted men-at-arms stationed on the flanks, ready 'to come racing to break up and throw into disarray the battle formations of the enemy (*rompre et desrengier la bataille de les ennemis*)'. But, she continues, if there is a paucity of common infantry, some experts (*expers d'armes*) advise it best to form the men-at-arms into one single battle without advanced and rear guard, save for forward wings. Such a deployment, she notes, had been used successfully by Charles VI at Roosebeke in 1382 and by John the Fearless, the most militarily able of all the

Jean the Fearless, Duke of Burgundy (1404–19), militarily the most able of the Burgundian dukes and a commander who fully recognised the importance of archers as well as other missilemen. *(Louvre, Paris/ Bridgeman Art Library)*

Burgundian dukes, at Othée in his crushing defeat of the Liègeois in 1408.[12]

These two victories provide an important context for the subsequent engagement at Agincourt, for they demonstrate that, despite the series of defeats at the hands of the English in the first part of the Hundred Years War and the catastrophic battle against the Turks at Nicopolis in 1396, well-led French armies could still achieve major victories against powerful infantry forces. At Roosebeke in 1382 the French had repeated the tactics that had given them victory over the Flemish infantry at Cassel in 1328, when they had received and held the onslaught of the Flemish pikemen, then successfully counter-attacked with cavalry against their flanks. The Flemish commander at Roosebeke, Philip van Artevelde, had with him some 60 English archers, who had deserted from the garrison of Calais to make more money with Philip, but their slight numbers cannot have made them a very effective force; Van Artevelde placed them near him on one flank where he took up position on foot, and it is probable he regarded these archers primarily as a personal bodyguard.[13] According to Froissart, the Flemings chose to take the offensive, unwisely abandoning a strong defensive position, where their front had been protected by a deep ditch and their rear by thick brambles and scrub. The massed ranks of Flemish pikemen bore down on the dismounted men-at-arms of the French centre commanded by King Charles VI, but though this division was driven back a little way the French van and rearguard now launched mounted assaults on both flanks of the Flemings. Surrounding them, the French horsemen caused such a press that the Flemings were soon squeezed together so tightly that they were unable to fight, with many, including Philip van Artevelde himself, killed by trampling or suffocation in the overcrowded ranks.[14] The devastating effect of bunching up the enemy, caused at battles such as Dupplin Moor and Halidon Hill by the enfilade shooting of English archers, had here been achieved by the combined assaults of French mounted men-at-arms.

In 1408 at Othée, a little to the north of Liège, Duke John the Fearless had prepared for an attack by the men of Liège by dismounting his forces in a single battle, 'in order', as he subsequently wrote to his brother Antony, Duke of Brabant, 'to resist more effectively the shock and charge which the Liègeois were likely to give us'.[15] Not only had he anticipated fighting on the defensive, but still more strikingly he had placed two wings of bowmen and men-at-arms flanking this main body. This may represent a conscious imitation of English tactics, although, as Christine de Pizan observed, the battle of Roosebeke also seems to have served as a model for Duke John's deployments.[16] But though the Liègeois drew up their own formations, which included 100 English archers, they did not attack, and were content to let their guns play against the Burgundian ranks. Accordingly, John and his commanders decided to advance (as Henry V was to do in an analogous situation seven years later). This they did 'in handsome and excellent order', while they dispatched a force of 400 cavalry and 1,000 picked infantry to attack the enemy's rear. The ensuing battle was hard-fought, and, noted the duke, 'experienced people say that they have never seen men fight so well as they [the Liègeois] did; for the battle lasted nearly one and a half hours and, for at least half an hour, no one knew which way it would go'. The Burgundian plan, however, succeeded admirably; the combination of 2,000 archers shooting rapidly from the flanks into the Liègeois ranks with an attack from the rear by 400 mounted men-at-arms with infantry support led to a major victory, inflicting heavy losses among the defeated. John's conduct in the battle won him the sobriquet 'the Fearless', and demonstrated, in the words of his biographer, 'an element of military genius'.[17]

The importance placed on archers by Duke John was reflected in the marked increase in their numbers in Burgundian forces during his reign. At Roosebeke in 1382 the army of Philip the Bold had contained only around 12 per cent of archers and crossbowmen, but under John the Fearless this had risen to 27 per cent in 1405 and by 1417 to 40 per cent – a sharp increase which, together with the tactics adopted at Othée, undoubtedly reflected the increasing military influence of the English.[18] Juvenal des Ursins believed that in addition to 3,000 knights and squires John's army in 1411 contained

4,000 crossbowmen, each with two assistants (one at least of these presumably being a pavise-bearer), and over 5,000 archers, while his army of 1417 was thought to comprise 3,600 men-at-arms and 2,000 bowmen.[19] Some of these missilemen came from the Flemish towns, like the 1,000 crossbowmen and 9,000 infantry promised for his campaign against the Armagnacs in Vermandois in 1411, while others were English, such as the archers employed under the Earl of Arundel in 1411.[20] John had made good use of this substantial English force during his successful attempt to break the Armagnac blockade of Paris, attacking the outlying town of St Cloud so effectively that the Armagnacs withdrew, breaking up their siege. In contrast to English armies, however, John not only continued to use large numbers of crossbowmen, but was also equally anxious to harness the comparatively new technology of the hand-gun, and by 1411 he had over 4,000 hand-gunners in his service.[21]

THE 'SOMME PLAN'

Seen in the light of engagements such as Roosebeke and Othée, the débâcle at Agincourt, like Crécy before it, appears unrepresentative of French military capabilities in the field by the early fifteenth century. Such a conclusion receives added weight from the study of a battle-plan drawn up by the commanders of the French army's vanguard at some time between 13 and 21 October 1415, only a few days before Agincourt itself. This invaluable document, which has come to be known as the 'Somme Plan', was rediscovered by Christopher Philpotts in a badly burned manuscript in the British Library.[22] On 13 August 1415 Henry V had landed in Normandy with a powerful army, and after a hard-fought siege had succeeded in taking the great port of Harfleur. From there on 6 October he had set out to march his depleted and

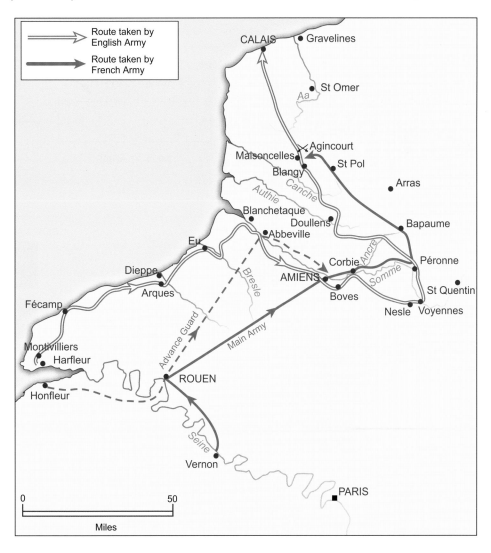

Movements of the French and English armies during the Agincourt campaign, October 1415.

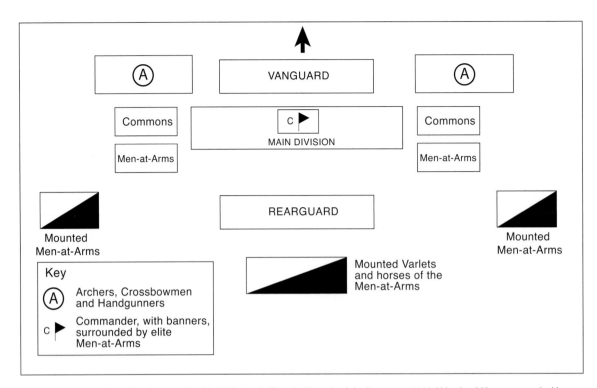

The recommended plan of battle as outlined in Christine de Pizan's *Livre des fais d'armes*, *c.* 1410 (this should be compared with John the Fearless' battle plan, p. 340).

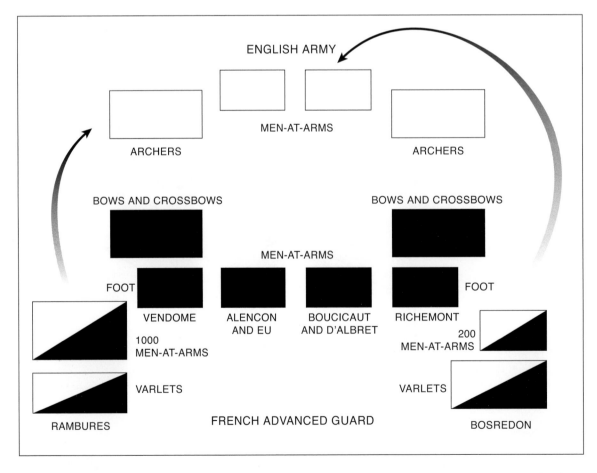

The 'Somme Plan', drawn up by Marshal Boucicaut and the Constable, Charles d'Albret, in October 1415 only a few days before the battle of Agincourt (after M. Bennett, *Agincourt* (1991)).

disease-ridden army north towards Calais, hoping, like Edward III in 1346, to cross the Somme at Blanchetaque. As the main French army mustered at Rouen, however, an element of the vanguard under the veteran commander Marshal Boucicaut shadowed Henry's army while the Constable, Charles d'Albret, had hurried to Abbeville with the remainder of his force and ensured that all bridges over the Somme were destroyed and other possible crossings were heavily guarded. Henry was accordingly forced to march away from the coast and, with his supplies running dangerously low, to seek a crossing further upstream in mounting desperation. The French vanguard, which had united on the 13th, shadowed his movements along the right bank of the Somme from their base at Peronne, but they were unable to prevent Henry V from stealing a march on them by masterfully exploiting a loop in the river and effecting a passage at the fords of Béthancourt and Voyennes on 18 October.[23] Boucicaut, Albret and other seasoned captains had already advised against joining battle with the English on any account, despite their apparently weakened state and smaller numbers. Their preferred strategy was to allow King Henry unhindered passage to Calais, but to contain his depredations en route by attacking his foragers and thus denying the enemy adequate supplies. For, as the French chronicler Juvenal des Ursins put it with hindsight of the ensuing catastrophe, 'even supposing that God gave victory to the French this might not be without great damage. For the matter was very doubtful, and often the events of a battle were risky and perilous. For once the English archers had engaged the French men-at-arms who were heavily armed, and once the latter had got out of breath, disaster might fall upon them. All they had to do was besiege Harfleur and they would get it back easily . . .'[24] Such caution, however, was to be rejected in favour of an all-out blow against Henry using the might of the combined French forces. Yet as the main French army moved from Amiens and on to Baupaume, where it arrived by 20 October,[25] the vanguard commanders shadowing Henry realised that they might be forced to engage the English on their own without their main army. Accordingly, they drew up a contingency battle-plan, which reveals much careful thought given to countering the essential elements of English tactics. Their astute provisions reflected the fact that some of these men had seen wide military service.[26] Boucicaut, for example, had been knighted at the battle of Roosebeke, had fought in Prussia with the Teutonic Knights, and been made Marshal of France in 1391. He had played a leading role in John the Fearless's contingent on the crusade which had ended in the disastrous defeat of the Christian forces at Nicopolis in 1396, and, having narrowly escaped execution at the hands of the Turks, he had been ransomed.[27] As with

Christine de Pizan's *Fais d'armes*, however, the French plan also directly reflects the tactical influence of John the Fearless himself.

Albret and Boucicaut were to form a large battle (*une grosse bataille*), with the Constable forming its right and the Marshal its left, while another battle under the Duke of Alençon and the Count of Eu was to be placed close by (*aupres de celle-la*). If, however, the English decided to fight in a single division (*bataille*), then these two French units were similarly to form up into one. These main French battles were to be flanked by two large bodies of infantry (*grosses helles de pie*), that on the right commanded by the Lord of Richemont, with the Lords of Comburg and Montauban, that on the left by the Lords of Vendome and Jaligny. In front of these two wings of infantry were to be placed 'all the archers of the entire company' (*toutes les gens de trait de toute la compagnie*), under captains assigned to them by the commanders of the wings. The French thus sought to place the full strength of their missilemen on their own wings, where it was hoped their volleys would engage those English archers stationed on the flanks, and thereby give support to their own dismounted men-at-arms.

Significantly, the plan assumes from the outset that the French would have to take the offensive. To weaken further the impact of the English bowmen, it was decided that a force of at least 1,000 cavalry, placed under command of the Master of the Crossbowmen David de Rambures, was to be drawn up 'a little apart, to the left and slightly to the rear of the other battles', its aim being 'to attack the archers and to do all in their power to break their ranks (*ferir sur les archers et ferra leur pouvoir de les rompre*)'. These horsemen were to be reinforced by half of all the available *varlets de guerre* who were to be mounted on their masters' best horses – a way of ensuring that while the men-at-arms fought dismounted, their squires or servants could utilise their costly and highly trained mounts, many of which would have been armoured. The assault of this cavalry force on the English archers, who presumably were to be attacked in the flank or the rear of the English right, was to be the signal for the men-at-arms in the centre divisions and the wings of archers to advance in unison. A second unit of 200 mounted men-at-arms under the command of Louis de Bosredon was to attack the English formation in the rear, 'in particular upon the varlets and their carts at the rear of their battle (*sur leurs varles et seur leur carriage*)', and was to coordinate its attack with that of the other mounted units under Rambures.[28] The use of mounted units for flank attacks against the English archers was, as we have seen, a common feature of French tactical thinking from the 1340s and 1350s, and the 'Somme Plan' shows its continued importance. It also shows the French attempting to exploit the enormous shock value of a mounted attack against the enemy's rear, which had proved so effective at Poitiers and at Othée. By seizing their horses, moreover, the French aimed to prevent the flight of the English, or, should Fortune prove fickle, their ability to launch a mounted counter-attack, as the Black Prince had done so effectively at Poitiers in 1356.

The 'Somme Plan' represents an effective tactical response to Henry's anticipated formations, and evinces a unity of purpose and military competence that was to prove singularly lacking among the leading French nobles at Agincourt itself. Had such a deployment been put into practice by the French vanguard, whose strength was approximately the same as Henry's army at Agincourt, the outcome of the battle fought on St Crispin's day might, perchance, have been different. For if forced to give battle, it is unlikely that men of such experience would have

chosen a constricted field which gave an enormous advantage to the enemy and would have frustrated their planned flank and rear attacks. It may be doubted that the cavalry units of Bosredon and Rambures at full strength and on better-chosen terrain would have achieved any greater success against the wings of archers and their protective stakes (of which the French were unaware when this plan was drawn up) than the undermanned units that rapidly came to grief in the opening stages of Agincourt. But what is clear is that key elements of the actual French defeat would have been avoided: the hopelessly divided command, the poor choice of battle site, and the poor tactical dispositions which crammed the men-at-arms into huge and unwieldy divisions and relegated the missilemen to an impotent role in the rear. Given their more manageable numbers and the plan's stress on the effective combination of archers, dismounted knights and mounted units, a battle involving the French vanguard alone on ground of their choice would in all probability have avoided the terrible overcrowding seen at Agincourt, which led to the deaths of many French by crushing and suffocation, while the dismounted French men-at-arms would have had the support of a substantial body of their own archers and crossbowmen.

What would have happened if Henry V had lost the battle – not of Agincourt, but, say, of Péronne where the French vanguard was when Henry crossed the Somme – is an intriguing counter-factual question that could be long debated. The plan itself, however, is firm testimony to the response of seasoned military men to English tactics at the renewal of the war in 1415, and Christine de Pizan's *Livre des fais d'armes* shows that such ideas were current some years before Henry's invasion. We need not, of course, envisage Boucicaut, Albret and their colleagues poring over a copy of Christine's book. For even if these men were not among Christine's informants (and it is very probable that they were), all alike drew on the comparatively recent experiences of French arms, and in particular on the spectacular victory of Duke John of Burgundy at Othée. Indeed, given his military competence, it was fortunate for the English that John the Fearless was not present at Agincourt. Though promising the French king that he would come, he never set out, and probably ordered his son Philip, Count of Charolais, to halt at Aire in Artois while en route to the French muster at Rouen.[29] His brother Anthony, however, who had not

Sir Simon Felbrigg, standard-bearer to Richard II, whose banner he holds, drawn from a brass of 1416 in Felbrigg church, Norfolk. A Knight of the Garter, Sir Simon wears full white harness over a hauberk whose lower border is just visible. The crosses of St George on his besagews (designed to defend the armpits) were intended not only for recognition but also to invoke the protection of the saint in battle. *(By kind permission of the Heraldry Society/ICI)* been present at Othée, arrived on the field of Agincourt late in the day and was slain there. He had attacked almost alone, without a helmet and in armour borrowed from his chamberlain, donning a banner taken from one of his trumpeters with a hole cut in it to make an extemporised surcoat.[30] Yet despite John's absence the 'Somme Plan' has strong echoes of his own tactical deployments, which he was subsequently to refine in the wake of the French defeat, and which he set out in his own battle-plan in 1417.[31]

Having successfully crossed the Somme, Henry continued his march towards Calais, while the French vanguard fell back from Péronne to link up with their main army at Baupaume.[32] On 24 October the English crossed the River Ternoise at Blangy, but the next day they found their way ahead barred near Agincourt by a formidable French host. Henry immediately drew up his vanguard, centre and rearguard into formation. The French, however, withdrew, causing Henry to fear that they would attempt to outflank him using the woods on the English left as cover. He accordingly 'moved his lines again, always positioning them so that they faced the enemy', but as the sun was setting no engagement occurred.[33] Camping at the village of Maisoncelles, the English army passed a troubled night in anticipation of the engagement they knew must come.

Religious preparation before battle played an important part in all medieval armies. It was widely believed – and particularly by the devout Henry V – that battle was a form of judicial ordeal, a trial by combat in which God would look favourably on the cause that was most just, and hear the supplications for aid of the humble and contrite. For the safety of one's individual soul, moreover, it was vital not to die unshriven, but as there was a shortage of priests in the English army 'many confessed to each other'. Many also took what they feared would be their last mass, 'for, as was later revealed by some prisoners, they expected to die on the next day'.[34] The next morning, prior to the advance, 'the whole English army knelt, [and] each soldier took a little piece of earth in his mouth' to symbolise that soon dust might return to dust.[35] Later in the century Duke Charles the Bold of Burgundy observed that before the advance at the siege of Neuss in 1475 the English archers in his service, 'according to their custom', made the sign of the cross on the ground, then kissed it.[36] To at least one English chronicler such an act could reflect not just piety but a resolve to fight to the end. The *Brut* records how on the morning of Agincourt Henry V told his men, 'in remembrance that God died on the cross for us, let every man make a cross on the earth and kiss it, and in token that we would rather die on this ground than flee'.[37] Doubtless many a man-at-arms and archer had also prayed to his tutelary saints, above all St George, both for safety in battle and for victory. The red crosses they bore, whether on their tunics, their banners or painted on the besagews of their armour, served as much as talismans to invoke divine favour and protection as badges of recognition. In the flush of victory the chronicler Thomas Elmham would even record the belief that at Agincourt 'St George was seen fighting in the battle on the side of the English', while other heavenly patrons had granted victory: 'St Maurice took Harfleur, St Crispin carried the battle of Agincourt.'[38] It was in just such a hope of aid from the saints that Henry V advanced to battle not only under the royal arms of England but under the red cross of St George, and with the banners of the Trinity, the Virgin and St Edmund.[39]

'GOD AND OUR ARCHERS MADE THEM STUMBLE:'[40] AGINCOURT, 25 OCTOBER 1415

The French had a massive advantage in numbers. No precise figures are extant, and chroniclers' estimates vary wildly, but their army may have been as large as 25,000 and contained perhaps as many as 14,000 men-at-arms.[41] Against this, Henry commanded some 900 men-at-arms and 5,000 archers.[42] Yet crucially, the English were led by a highly able and charismatic king,[43] whereas the French lacked a unified command. Their king, Charles VI, had been suffering from intermittent bouts of insanity, and his son the Dauphin Louis was young and inexperienced. Doubtless with the catastrophic political and financial consequences of King Jean's capture at Poitiers in 1356 firmly in their minds, the king's counsellors had decided that neither the king nor the Dauphin should personally take part in the battle. Consequently, overall leadership of the army fell to the great princes of the blood, especially the king's nephew the Duke of Orléans and John, Duke of Bourbon.[44] But there was 'great division' and suspicion between the Armagnacs supporting the Duke of Orléans and the Burgundians favouring John the Fearless, Duke of Burgundy. Bitter memories were harboured of how Orléans's father Louis had been assassinated in 1407 by Duke John's men, and in such a climate the duke himself held aloof from the campaign.[45]

Nevertheless, given their great superiority in numbers of men-at-arms, many of the French lords were supremely confident of victory, a fact not lost on the moralising chroniclers who were to narrate their defeat. 'It was said', noted the *Gesta Henrici*, 'they thought themselves so sure of us that

Lord Camoys, who commanded the left wing of the English army at Agincourt, and his wife, from a brass of 1419 in Trotton church, Sussex. Armed in a developed 'white harness', with a solid plate gorget and face guard, he wears the Lancastrian livery collar of linked 'S's and the garter of a Knight of the Garter (from C. Boutell, *Monumental Brasses and Slabs* (1847)). *(Author Collection)*

that night, they cast dice for our king and his nobles.'[46] The Duke of Bourbon, it was later said, refused to wait for large reinforcements under the Duke of Brittany, while the service of the Paris militia was haughtily rejected.[47] At a council of war at Baupaume, the Dukes of Bourbon and Alençon had overruled the cautious counsel of Albret, Boucicaut and other 'anciens chevaliers et escuyers' to avoid battle with the English. There was great pressure to avenge the insult of the English invasion, the fall of Harfleur and the subsequent depredations of Henry's army; one decisive battle against the weakened and numerically inferior English, it was argued, could wipe out any future threat from Henry. Accordingly, on 20 October Orléans and Bourbon sent heralds to inform the King of England 'that they would do battle with him before he reached Calais, although they did not assign a day or place'.[48]

At this same council it seems that a version of the plan already formulated by the vanguard was put forward, for 'it was ordered that there would be cavalry to charge the English archers in order to disrupt their shooting (*qui frapperoient sur les archers Anglois pour rompre leur traict*)'.[49] Crucially, however, this element of the French plan had already become known to the English by around 17 October. The *Gesta Henrici Quinti*, written by a chaplain in Henry's army, noted that as the English army prepared to cross the River Somme news was gained from some French prisoners that:

> the enemy command had assigned certain squadrons of cavalry, many hundreds strong and mounted on barded horses (*equis armatis*), to break the formation and resistance of our archers when they engaged us in battle. The king, therefore, had it proclaimed throughout the army that every archer was to prepare and fashion for himself a stake or staff (*unum palum vel baculum*), either square or round, but six feet long, of sufficient thickness, and sharpened at both ends; and he commanded that whenever the French army drew near to do battle and to break their ranks by such columns of horse, all the archers were to drive in their stakes in front of them in line abreast and that some of them should do this further back and in between, one end being driven into the ground pointing down towards themselves, the other end pointing up towards the enemy above waist-height, so that the cavalry, when their charge had brought them close and in sight of the stakes, would either withdraw in great fear or, reckless of their own safety, run the risk of having both horses and riders impaled.[50]

Good intelligence had thus given Henry V an important advantage; he was forewarned about one of the key elements in the French plan of attack, and had taken a simple but highly effective measure to combat the threat. Although the use of such stakes was an innovation among the English forces in 1415, it is clear from the *Gesta*'s account that Henry had already given careful thought to how such defences were to be laid out for optimum effect, creating a kind of chequerboard field of stakes among which the archers could manoeuvre and shoot, while protected from the direct onrush of enemy horse.[51]

As Matthew Bennett has noted, European commanders appear to have first encountered this form of defence at the fateful battle of Nicopolis on 25 September 1396, fought on the Danube in Bulgaria by a hybrid Christian army of French, Hungarians and Germans against the invading forces of Bayazid I.[52] On rising ground south of the town of Nicopolis, which was being besieged by the allies, the Ottoman sultan had drawn up his army, placing his first division of irregular cavalry to hide a field of thickly planted stakes a bowshot deep, 'set into the ground at an angle, the points turned towards our men, so high that they could enter a horse's belly'.[53] Behind this defence was Bayazid's main division, largely composed of infantry and archers, while out of sight over the skyline he held the elite Sipahi cavalry in reserve under his personal command. The charge of the French knights, led by the Count of Nevers (the future Duke of Burgundy) in the allied vanguard, successfully broke through the division of Turkish light cavalry, only to find its progress halted by the stakes and volleys of arrows from the Turkish foot-archers, whose shafts slew many horses and men.[54] With great difficulty and further losses, the knights, many of whom must by now have dismounted, forced a path through the stakes, uprooting them to make way for their comrades, assisted by supporting infantry.[55] They closed with the Ottoman foot, and after a fierce conflict scattered both them and the light horse of the first division which had regrouped behind its infantry. The Franks pressed on, chasing the retreating Turks up the steep slope, but as the now exhausted knights reached its summit they were attacked and rapidly overwhelmed by the charge of the fresh Sipahi cavalry.[56] Bennett also offers the intriguing suggestion that Henry may even have learned of such tactics from reading the *Livre des fais* of Boucicaut himself.[57] It is important to note, however, that a contingent of some 1,000 English, including men-at-arms and archers from Cheshire, had been present at Nicopolis, led by Henry IV's illegitimate brother John of Beaufort, Earl of Somerset.[58] Earl John died in 1410, but it is not hard to believe that he had regaled his young nephew Henry with tales of the battle and of the major role the defence of stakes combined with archers had played in the defeat of the Christian host. Perhaps some survivors of the catastrophe may even have been present in Henry's ranks at Agincourt itself.

If the idea of combining archers with protective stakes was already forming in Henry V's mind before the 1415 campaign, did his army practise some form of drill after 17 October to familiarise the archers with the setting-up of the stakes in the optimum manner? We have no direct evidence, but it would have been remarkable had they attempted such a novel tactic untried in the face of the enemy. There had been an opportunity for such a rehearsal on 20 October, when Henry allowed his army a day's rest around Athies after fording the Somme, and given that he was expecting the French to give battle on the 21st, such preparations would have been still more pressing.[59] Knowledge of the proposed French cavalry attacks would suggest that at the very least the archers set up their stakes when it seemed the armies would clash in the late afternoon of 24 October.

As the morning of the feast day of St Crispin and St Crispinian dawned, Henry drew up his 900 men-at-arms in three battles in a single line 'in view of his want of numbers'.[60] The king commanded the centre, the vanguard to the right was under the Duke of York, and the rearguard to the left under Thomas, Lord Camoys.[61] It is possible that Henry's main battle had two flanking units on its wings, a sub-division visible in Richard II's army in Scotland in 1385.[62] Sources disagree, however, as to the nature of Henry's deployment of the archers.[63] Here let us note the *Gesta*'s famous statement that Henry 'positioned "wedges" of his archers in between each "battle" (*intermisisset cuneos sagittariorum suorum cuilibet aciei*)'. Clearly, the most recent editors of the *Gesta*, Frank Taylor and John Roskell, were influenced in their translation of the Latin *cuneos* as 'wedges' by the traditional view of English formations as propounded by earlier authors such as Oman and Burne, and more recent commentators have preferred the more neutral term 'unit' or 'formation'.[64] Those who have argued that the archers were placed only on the wings of English formations have objected that the author of the *Gesta*, a chaplain in the army, was poorly informed as to the battle deployment and, by his own admission, was situated in the army's rear with the baggage during the battle. Yet wholly to dismiss the *Gesta*'s testimony on this matter is unwise; the author clearly had access to detailed military information on other issues, notably Henry's command for the archers to equip themselves with stakes, and in the aftermath of the battle must have had ample opportunity to gain eyewitness accounts of the fighting itself.[65] In this context we should note the French chronicler Robert Blondel's description of the English formations at the battle of Formigny in 1450: there were not only two wings of archers, but one in the centre, 'like three firm towers', each formed up at some distance in front of, not abreast with, the formation of men-at-arms.[66]

By contrast, however, Monstrelet believed that in drawing up the ranks at Agincourt Sir Thomas Erpingham placed 'the archers in the front and then the men-at-arms (*mettant les archer au front puis les hommes d'armes*). He made two wings of men-at-arms and archers, and the horses and baggage were placed behind the army.'[67] The subsequent accounts of le Fèvre and Waurin, however, diverge from that of Monstrelet by stating that Henry V ordered Erpingham 'to draw up his archers and to put them in the front in two wings (*pour ordonner ses archiers et les mectre au froncq devant en deux elles*)'.[68] Matthew Bennett proposes a convincing compromise to these conflicting accounts: 'It is possible to make sense of the final formation as having archers mainly on the flanks, but also surrounding the main "battles". It is not impossible that archers stood between the men-at-arms in the battle line, at least initially, before falling

A crossbowman from a fifteenth-century playing card. He wears a strap and roll spanning device suspended from a belt around his waist. Note the typical form of quiver and the spare bolt tucked in his hat. (© *Kunsthistorisches Museum, Vienna*)

back just before the enemy arrived at hand strokes.'[69]

As the English drew up their battle lines the archers planted their stakes in front of them.[70] Perhaps the overseeing of such defences was an important element in the remit of Sir Thomas Erpingham when he arrayed the archers before dismounting to join the king's division.[71] Though they were heavily outnumbered, the terrain favoured the English. Their rear was defended by the village of Maisoncelles and by their baggage train, while they faced the French across a field flanked by the woods of Agincourt and Tramecourt.[72] These woods were of critical importance and largely shaped the course of the battle. They made any flanking manoeuvre – particularly by cavalry – difficult if not impossible, thereby negating at a stroke the key offensive element in the French plan. Instead, the two wings of French horsemen designated to ride around the English flank and rear would have to try to force themselves between the archers on the English flanks and the woods. Still worse for the French, the comparatively narrow front meant that they could

not take the best advantage of their great superiority in numbers. If the massive French army had been able to deploy in line abreast, as Henry was forced to do by the paucity of his troops, the English would have been seriously outflanked and probably overwhelmed. According to Monstrelet, the first French battle contained 8,000 men-at-arms – more than the entire English army – supported by 5,500 missilemen. Behind this came the second battle of 3,000–6,000 men-at-arms and their well-armed valets on foot, while the rearguard consisted of some 8,000–10,000 mounted men-at-arms. The restricted nature of the battlefield, however, forced the French to deploy their vanguard, centre and rear each in front of the other, and to deploy each division in deep columns. Tito Livio believed that the French vanguard was 31 deep, compared to the English lines which were just 4 deep.[73] Such a formation meant that only a comparatively small number of the available men-at-arms could actively engage with the English at any one time. Agincourt was, in effect, a battle of line against column, and one in which the former held the key advantages.

There were, moreover, serious dangers inherent in the French deployment in a series of deeply formed columns. Should the front ranks or the vanguard as a whole need to withdraw, it would be extremely difficult for these troops to fall back past the centre division which blocked its path on the restricted battlefield. In addition, the French ranks themselves were ominously overcrowded. As the *Religieux* noted, the French vanguard, 'composed of about 5,000 men, found itself at first so tightly packed that those who were in the third rank could scarcely use their swords. That taught them that if a large number of combatants was sometimes an advantage there were occasions when it became a hindrance.'[74] Such deployment flew in the face of the advice given by Christine de Pizan in her *Livre des fais d'armes*, who had specifically warned against using too large an army on a confined battlefield.[75] In the words of Caxton's translation, 'nothyng profyteth more in a bataylle saith he [Vegetius] than to keep the ordre that ought for to be betwix every rowe, for men ought to see by grete cure that they overpresse not eche other and that they also large not nother the one from the other but shal kepe themself in covenable ordre togider. For they that were to nyghe eche other shuld lese theyre strokys and theyre fyghtyng for lacke of more rowme and space.'[76]

Such sentiments were later echoed by the anonymous author of *Knyghthode and Bataile*, who around the year 1460 translated Vegetius into English verse. Too great an army, he noted, was both cumbersome and potentially dangerous; it was far better to deploy a smaller, but better skilled force 'of proved and achieved sapience . . . a learned host'.[77] Henry's victory was to be the triumph of just such a small, well-disciplined force over a massive but disorganised and poorly controlled army.

'INJURY TO VERY FEW': THE TACTICAL RELEGATION OF THE FRENCH ARCHERS

One of the most striking features of the battle of Agincourt is the number of archers the French had at their disposal. Monstrelet noted that the French vanguard initially contained 8,000 men-at-arms, 4,000 archers and 1,500 crossbowmen, while the main battle also contained archers.[78] The day before the battle the Count of Richemont had been sent on a recce in strength of the English camp, taking 2,000 men-at-arms and archers, while among the supplies seized the following day by the victors from the French were many baggage carts 'loaded with provisions and missiles, spears and bows'.[79] Despite their experiences against the English in the previous century, the French had continued to favour the crossbow as their missile weapon of choice. Among the military reforms initiated by Jean II in 1351 it had been stipulated that all infantry were to be grouped in units of 25 to 30, each enrolled under a captain with his own pennon. At least twice a month this captain was to carry out a muster to ensure that all crossbowmen and pavise-bearers were suitably equipped, and the crossbowmen were to span their bows and shoot at least two or three times. Any default in equipment was punished by a fine, recorded by the Clerk of the Crossbowmen.[80] The introduction of the steel bow, coming into wider circulation by the end of the fourteenth century, had greatly increased the weapon's powers of penetration. Mercenary crossbowmen from Italy and Spain were hired in considerable numbers in the armies of Charles V and Charles VI, and crossbowmen, both mounted and on foot, had formed the permanent companies established by the Valois after 1369.[81] The Genoese were still regularly employed as elite crossbowmen, both in land forces and as marines. Genoese crossbowmen, for example, assisted in the defence of Caen in 1417 against Henry V, and the power of their bolts excited fear and sometimes anger among their English opponents.[82] In 1405, following their unsuccessful attack on Ardres, the English swore the Genoese had been using poisoned bolts, and it was only with difficulty that the Genoese prisoners were saved from the vengeful clamour of the men of Calais.[83] To supplement such stipendiaries, the French kings continued to encourage major towns to raise and maintain guilds or confraternities of crossbowmen, who swore to serve the king and defend their town as a well-trained and well-equipped unit, and in return received special privileges, including exemption from a range of taxes.[84] Such confraternities were already established in

many towns in the Low Countries and we have noted elsewhere Charles V's interest in promoting units of crossbowmen in select towns, but the French crown seems to have made a particular effort to foster existing fraternities and to create new ones early in the second decade of the fifteenth century. In 1410, for example, the confraternity of the crossbowmen of Paris, numbering some 60-strong and with a 'king', constable and master, was granted the same privileges enjoyed by their fellows in Rouen, Tournai and other *bonnes villes*.[85] The following year similar privileges were granted to the city's 120-strong confraternity of archers, 'to the honour and praise of God, the blessed virgin Mary, and Monseigneur Saint Sebastian', and to the crossbowmen of Rouen and Mantes.[86] In 1412 Charles VI granted the Lord of Waurin the right to establish a brotherhood of 60 crossbowmen, to aid in the defence of the town and castle of Waurin and the lands bordering on Burgundian and English-held territory, and in recognition of their notable military

Marshal Boucicaut and his wife at prayer before the Virgin, while to his left a saint holds his lance and bascinet. From the Hours of Marshal Boucicaut, Paris, *c.* 1408 (Paris, Musée Jaquemart-André, MS 2, f.26v). The heraldry has been altered to substitute the arms of a later owner of the manuscript. *(Institut de France – Musée Jacquemart-André, Paris)*

service. This sworn fraternity of crossbowmen were all to wear a livery of their choosing, each to bear a good crossbow and a baldric with three dozen good bolts, and were to have a constable and a 'dizennier' to command each unit of 10.[87]

The initial objective of creating such confraternities was to provide a reservoir of skilled missilemen in time of war, whose recreational shooting would provide a degree of cohesion and élan when serving in the host. The numbers raised by each town, however, were notably small, and it is clear that from their inception membership of such confraternities brought with it considerable social standing within the local community. Indeed, of ultimately greater significance than their military contribution was the important role these guilds quickly came to play in civic life, while elaborate shooting competitions were organised between the confraternities of neighbouring towns. The fierce pride which such brotherhoods might arouse is well illustrated by the demand from one of the crossbow guilds in Tournai that the town authorities recognise its privileges, which it claimed were established by King Dagobert in the seventh century![88] It was, however, indicative of the rivalries and organisational weaknesses in the French army that in 1411 Charles VI and his council had to intervene in a dispute between the Master of the Crossbows, John, Lord of Hengest, and Marshal Boucicaut, who claimed the right of the Marshal of France to muster and review archers and cannoneers, and to have jurisdiction over them.[89] The decision went in favour of Boucicaut, who clearly took a keen interest in the organisation and control of these troops, but the incident points to a division of command over archers and crossbowmen that must have hampered their operational effectiveness. Even in the 'Somme Plan' the Master of the Crossbows David de Rambures had been assigned not to command the missilemen but to lead the unit of cavalry which was to attack the English archers in the flank.

Nevertheless, as we have seen, the 'Somme Plan' shows that Albret, Boucicaut and their colleagues had sought to make full use of the available missilemen by placing them in front of the two wings flanking their dismounted men-at-arms. Yet now, on the day of battle, the huge numbers of men-at-arms available, combined with the restricted nature of the battlefield, led to the French missilemen being pushed into a secondary position where they could offer no effective support. As Jean le Fèvre noted, the French 'had plenty of archers and crossbowmen but nobody wanted to let them shoot. The reason for this was that the site was so narrow that there was only enough room for the men-at-arms.'[90] Similarly the Religieux of St Denis noted that 'four thousand of their best crossbowmen who ought to have marched in the front and begun the attack were not found to be at their post and it seems that they had been given permission to depart by the lords of the army on the pretext that they had no

need of their help'.[91] A small element may have seen action in the opening stages before being withdrawn; the *Gesta Henrici* recorded that 'the enemy crossbows which were at the back of the men-at-arms and on the flanks, after a first but over-hasty volley by which they did injury to very few, withdrew for fear of our bows'.[92] Thereafter the French archers played no further role in the battle. As a result the advancing French men-at-arms were deprived of any missile support, leaving them to face a storm of arrows without any ability to return such murderous shooting. Conversely, unlike at Poitiers, the English archers and men-at-arms were almost completely spared from the physical and psychological impact of enemy bolts and arrows, a factor which goes far to explain the remarkably low casualties they sustained in the course of the battle.

The fateful neglect of the French missile arm at Agincourt was symptomatic of a wider problem of *mentalité* among some of their nobility. Whereas in many campaigns English armies were heavily dependent on their archers not only for their withering volleys but for numerical strength, the superfluity of French men-at-arms heightened the tendency of French commanders to allow them to dominate tactical dispositions, thus relegating infantry, including missilemen, into a very secondary role. As the French chronicler Pierre Cochon noted, at Agincourt 'the French thought that they would carry the day given their great numbers, and in their arrogance had proclaimed that only those who were noble should go into battle. So all the men of lower ranks, who were enough to have beaten the English, were pushed to the rear.'[93] Effective tactical cooperation between French men-at-arms and their archers and crossbowmen was hampered by the unconcealed disdain of many of the aristocracy for non-noble combatants. In part, this was due to the poor showing of some levies. Thus many of those who had joined Philip VI's army in early August 1346 at Rouen were infantry raised from the towns who mustered 'amazingly ill-armed and unwillingly'.[94] Such was the low esteem in which troops mustered by the general levy were held that in his *Le Songe du Vieil Pélerin*, written in 1389, Philippe de Mézieres counselled Charles VI 'that you make little use of that royal right which is called the *arrière-ban*, which is the cause of many disadvantages which it would take too long to list'. For such forces 'will lack discipline, like men coming to a fair'.[95] Moreover, fewer infantry were mounted than in English armies, which slowed down movements of the French army, particularly when in pursuit of an English expeditionary force. The desire for more speed to catch up with the Black Prince's fast-moving army in 1356 caused Jean to make a fateful decision in August at Breteuil to pay off and disband the infantry raised from the northern towns, a decision which earned the censure of some contemporary observers, though significantly he retained a sizeable force of crossbowmen with him.[96]

But such disdain was also displayed towards better-armed and trained infantry. The French knights at Crécy had reacted with fury to the discomfiture of their own Genoese crossbowmen in the van of the French army, not only riding through them but even cutting them down.[97] And when, before Agincourt, the city of Paris offered the French king 6,000 well-armed infantry, one of the Duke of Berry's knights, Jean de Beaumont, is reported to have said dismissively that 'the king should not accept the help of these rude mechanics for we are already three times more numerous than the English'. 'He did not see', added the Religieux of St Denis, 'that plebeians were worthy of bearing arms, even though many such men had great honour by their deeds.' As this chronicler astutely pointed out, 'it can be seen in the histories of France that knights had used this kind of presumptuous talk at the battle of Courtrai and

soon they had been thrown headlong into deep ditches, cleverly covered by light planks, where they were killed by the Flemish. At Poitiers, the illustrious King John was taken prisoner, and in Hungary [i.e. Nicopolis], the Christians were overcome and massacred by the Turks. I do not think that one should agree with such a way of speaking.'[98] Similarly, the *Chronique de Ruisseauville*, probably reflecting opinions in the 1420s or 1430s, noted, 'it is said that the *gros varlets* might have fought well against the English' had they been allowed so to do.[99] It was in vain that the veteran commanders 'and several other knights and squires who had much experience in arms', and thus readily appreciated the potentially enormous value of infantry and missilemen, urged that if battle was given to the English 'they should employ the communes and that they should prove useful'.[100]

A HOUSE DIVIDED: THE FAILURE OF FRENCH COMMAND

Why then had the French committed themselves to such a poor choice of ground and, as a result, to a battle formation which threw away many of the advantages they should have enjoyed? They had, after all, blocked Henry's line of march, and could have elected to fight on more open ground. The answer lies in the problems of divided leadership and the absence of a single authoritative commander, which led to the overruling of the advice of seasoned campaigners like Albert and Boucicaut by men of higher rank but less military sagacity. For like the great Bertrand Du Guesclin before him, Boucicaut was, despite his Marshal's rank, only from a family of bourgeois origins. He had gained wealth and social elevation through military prowess and his marriage to Antoinette de Turenne, from a well-established family, but even his father-in-law had noted disparagingly that Boucicaut was 'not of a great lineage, and had only 200 livres a year'.[101] Christine de Pizan had earlier warned that in choosing the Constable and the Marshals of the army, 'greater attention should be given to perfection of skill in arms, along with the virtues and the character and good bearing that should accompany this, than to exalted lineage or blood'.[102] Tellingly, however, she is forced then to admit that if both experience and nobility 'were to be found in the same person it would be very useful, for the simple reason that the nobler the blood, the greater the esteem in which he would be held in exercising his office, a quality necessary to every leader'. The rage and frustration felt by Boucicaut as his social and political superiors first drew up their forces in the cramped fields between the villages of Tramecourt and Agincourt, then proceeded fatally to botch the careful tactical provisions of the 'Somme Plan' can only be imagined; regrettably, the *Livre des*

fais which chronicles his military feats ends in 1409, and one cannot blame him for not spending any of his years of captivity in England following Agincourt dictating memoires of so catastrophic a defeat.[103] To the deeply pious Marshal, who according to his biographer was accustomed to eat frugally on Fridays and to wear only black in honour of Christ's passion, it must have seemed portentous that this great battle with the English, in which God would give victory to the cause He considered most just, had fallen on a Friday.[104]

The problems of leadership were again graphically revealed when it came to assigning command to the various divisions of the army. According to Guillaume Cousinot, writing in the 1420s, 'all the lords wanted to be in the vanguard, against the opinion of the Constable and the experienced knights'.[105] Spurred on by desire for glory, noted the Religieux, many leading nobles 'flocked to the front in their rash and imprudent haste', for 'when it came to putting the army into battle formation . . . each of the leaders claimed for himself the honour of leading the vanguard. This led to considerable debate and so that there could be some agreement, they came to the rather unfortunate conclusion that they should all place themselves in the front line.'[106] Thus arrayed, at least old quarrels were put aside while they faced a common enemy. 'Some of them kissed', noted le Fèvre, 'and put their arms around each other's necks in making peace, and it was moving to see this. All troubles and discords which had been between them and which they had in the past were changed into great feelings of love.'[107] Such reconciliations, however, could scarcely offset the severe problems that this concentration of leaders caused. The great difficulties of battlefield communica-

Above: An anonymous portrait of Henry V (1403–22). *(National Portrait Gallery, London/Bridgeman Art Library)*

Right: English longbowmen from Beauchamp Pageant, *c.* 1483–4, depicting the battle of Shrewsbury in 1403. Although Henry, as Prince of Wales, had been wounded in the face by an arrow during the battle, Shrewsbury had given him invaluable military experience. Note the careful rendering of the heavy, armour-piercing arrowheads. (British Library, Cotton MS Junius E IV, f.4). *(© British Library)*

tions confronted all medieval armies, but were often more acute for French armies than for English in the Hundred Years War because of their greater size, their poorer internal cohesion and their frequent adoption of the offensive. At Crécy Philip VI had imposed his will to launch a frontal assault against a formidable English defensive position on his reluctant commanders, but once the attack was under way he was powerless to prevent the chaos which ensued from the French cavalry's attempt to press through the ranks of the retreating Genoese. Thereafter, failure to allow attacking divisions to withdraw before launching a fresh cavalry wave resulted in the attack's impetus being broken before it reached the English lines by the disorganised remnants of earlier attacks. Medieval kings, moreover, rarely directed their forces from a distant point of vantage, as they were expected to lead from the front and be in the thick of combat. But once the king himself or the army's main leaders became directly involved in the fighting, it was difficult if not impossible for them effectively to control other sections of the army.[108] Thus at Poitiers King Jean led the second French division in person, and as a result was unable to prevent the entire third battle, led by the Duke of Orléans, from withdrawing from the engagement at a critical moment, when it could have brought aid to the king's hard-pressed division and might have carried the day against the exhausted English. A notable exception is Edward III at Crécy, who commanded the engagement from the vantage point of a windmill on high ground, but he was represented in the front line by the young Black Prince, whose division bore the brunt of the fighting. With the defeats of Charles the Bold in mind, Philippe de Commynes later remarked on the vagaries of battle that God alone was the true arbiter, for 'I think no man's wisdom can guide or give order to such a great number of men and that things in the field seldom turn out as they have been planned.'[109]

If at Agincourt the concentration of so many leading nobles in the van would prove to be a serious problem once battle was joined, a further indication of the failure of command on a smaller scale can also be gauged by the poor organisation of the two flanking units of cavalry. The 'Somme Plan' had envisaged two units of horsemen playing a key role in outflanking the English and attacking their archers, and in theory this element of the plan was retained on the day of battle. Yet remarkably, despite the profusion of available men-at-arms, the cavalry wings that assembled on the field were hopelessly under-strength even from the numbers which had been posited when the vanguard alone faced the English. Instead of the 800 cavalry planned for the right wing, William de Saveuse found himself leading only between some 150 and 300 horsemen, while of the 1,600 horsemen envisaged for the left wing on the Tramecourt side a mere 120 mustered under the command of Sir Clignet de Brabant.[110]

'ADVANCE BANNERS IN THE NAME OF ST GEORGE': BATTLE IS JOINED

From around 8 a.m. the two armies faced each other, but the French did not attack. Perhaps some among the French still believed that the sheer size of the French army confronting the English would obviate the need for battle; faced with such odds, Henry would surely have no option but to sue for terms, despite the failure of negotiations the day before. Yet it may also be that the French were hoping in the initial stages of the battle to exploit the advantages of the defensive. All could see that the ground ahead, a newly ploughed field which had been soaked with rain, would be treacherous. Let the English come to them or surrender, for withdrawal was now impossible. In his turn Henry V 'realised the astuteness of the French in standing firm in one place so that they might not be exhausted by advancing on foot through the muddy field',[111] for the battlefield 'was newly sown with wheat. Here it was extremely difficult to stand or to advance because of the roughness as well as the softness of the ground.' Moreover, the field was 'newly worked over, and . . . torrents of rain had flooded and converted [it] into a quagmire'.[112] Well supplied and in high spirits, the French could afford to play a waiting game. But Henry could not. Recognising that any further delay would sap the morale of his men in the face of such fearful odds, Henry consulted with his commanders and decided to advance.[113] At his orders the English moved carefully forward, taking care to dress their ranks and keep tight formation despite the slippery ground. This was a dangerous manoeuvre, for it meant that they had to abandon the defensive positions on which they were so reliant, and that for the moment the stakes carried by the archers would be of no protection; if the French cavalry units were to launch a sudden charge at this critical moment, all might be lost. Those few hundred yards must have seemed interminable, but the French still made no move. As soon as they were within effective bowshot of the enemy, the king commanded the army to halt, and the archers hastened to replant their stakes, thankfully driving them as hard as possible into the muddy ground.

Though it was only the opening stage of the battle, this advance demonstrates the skill and discipline of the English. It also reveals the enormous importance of the stakes, which now gave the English a much greater tactical flexibility. No longer reliant on natural features such as slopes, hedges and ditches, the archers could carry their own defences to a site of their choosing. And it was this mobility that must have wrong-footed the French, who had anticipated an English attack but had not expected Henry to be able to re-establish his defensive formations. Henry's dispositions had not changed – indeed, the protection offered to his flanks by the woods was now greater – but the French had failed to exploit a key opportunity. Worse, the leading French ranks were now within range of the English archers, who 'began with all their might to shoot volleys of arrows against the French for as long as they could pull the bow',[114] thereby galling them into the attack they had so far resisted. Henry may also have secretly sent a small force of 200 archers towards Tramecourt to a meadow close to the French vanguard.[115] According to Monstrelet, as the main English formation advanced with a great cry, these hidden archers now similarly raised a great shout and began shooting hard and fast at the French.[116] Some historians have doubted whether this manoeuvre occurred, and the accounts of le Fèvre and Waurin record hearing it said 'and certified as true by a man of honour who was there on that day in the company of the King of England that nothing like this happened'.[117] There is a hint here that some regarded this as something of an underhand ruse, but there seems little reason to doubt the essential plausibility of Henry's attempt to offset the great odds ranged against him by the use of surprise.

The French now had little option but to attack, and the flanking cavalry units – who were least able to endure the stinging rain of arrows – were the first to charge. As the chronicler Thomas Walsingham noted, the French sent 'mounted men ahead who were to overwhelm our archers by

English archers confront crossbowmen, one of whom spans his powerful weapon with a windlass, from a late fifteenth-century Flemish manuscript of Froissart's *Chronicles* (Paris, Bibliothèque Nationale, MS fr. 2643, f.165v). Though the archers here are well equipped with brigandines, sallets and even poleyns of plate, many of the bowmen at Agincourt may have been much more lightly armed. *(Bibliothèque Nationale, Paris/Bridgeman Art Library)*

the barded breasts of their horses, and to trample them under their hooves'. But the attacks of these two bodies of horse, already badly under-strength, came to grief almost immediately despite the bravery of the French commanders and their men. For 'the archers simultaneously shot arrows against the advancing knights so that the leading horses were scattered in that great storm of hail . . . the horses were pierced by iron; the riders, turning round by means of their bridles, rushing away, fell to the ground amongst their army'.[118] Some of William de Saveuse's men actually managed to use the weight of their horses to knock down some stakes, loosened in the muddy ground, but William himself was unhorsed and killed.[119] The *Gesta* noted that the French cavalry 'were forced to fall back under showers of arrows and to flee to their rearguard, save for a very few who, although not without losses in dead and wounded, rode through between the archers and the woodlands, and save too, of course, for the many who were stopped by the stakes driven into the ground and prevented from fleeing very far by the stinging hail of missiles shot at both horses and riders in their flight'.[120]

Confronted with the rain of arrows, many of the horsemen were forced back on to the French vanguard, now slowly advancing on foot over the slippery ground. If we can accept the chronology of the battle given by Monstrelet, le Fèvre and Waurin, the vanguard had already endured sustained volleys of arrows which further slowed their approach. The French 'began to bow their heads, especially those who had no shields, because of the English arrows. The English shot so vigorously that there were none who dared approach them, and the French did not dare uncover themselves [i.e. raise their visors] or look up . . . before they could engage together, many of the French were wounded and hurt by the shooting of the English.' It was at this point, however, that the horses of the defeated cavalry wings, maddened by the wounds inflicted by arrows and impossible for their riders to control, careered into the oncoming French knights, 'causing great disarray and breaking the line in many places, making them fall back on to the ground which had been newly sown'.[121] Ironically, it had been this very vulnerability of their horses to sustained shooting, experienced in numerous earlier engagements, that had led the French to dismount the majority of their men-at-arms. But even without the chaos caused by the runaway destriers, the French knights were at a serious disadvantage when attacking on foot because of the weight of their armour.[122] The herald le Fèvre, who was with the English during the battle, noted that the French knights 'were armed with long coats of mail, reaching below their knees and being very heavy. Below these they had leg armour

and above white harness. In addition they had bascinets with aventails (*baschinés de cavail*).'[123] Advances in such plate armour meant that although protection was improved, moving any distance on foot would have required great exertion. As one English chronicler noted, 'the enemy was worn out under the weight of their armour',[124] and this factor gave the waiting English men-at-arms an immediate edge in the hand-to-hand mêlées which ensued when their French counterparts finally closed with them. As the author of *L'Apparicion Maistre Jehan de Meun* later commented:

> I'll tell you another thing –
> You equip yourselves with armour that is too heavy,
> So that when you are fully armed,
> You'll be defeated in a short while . . .[125]

At Agincourt, moreover, the difficulties caused by the weight of the French knights' armour were exacerbated by the heavy clay soil. The Religieux noted how they advanced, 'marching through the middle of the mud where they sank up to their knees. So they were already overcome with fatigue even before they advanced against the enemy.'[126] 'As the night had seen much rain,' Pierre Cochon remarked, 'the ground was so soft that the men-at-arms sank into it by at least a foot.'[127] Le Fèvre and Waurin noted that 'so heavy were their arms that as the ground was so soft they could scarcely lift their weapons'.[128] The Burgundian nobleman Olivier de la Marche was later to recount how at the battle of Dendermonde in 1452 the men-at-arms were so exhausted that they lent on the pages for support, lest they fall and be unable to rise.[129] But at Agincourt 'most had no one to help them up, because they had not wanted to take with them any of their lower ranks (*varlets*), for the gentlemen had wanted to have the honour deriving from the battle'.[130] As a result, knights who fell were in grave danger of being trampled or suffocated as the rear ranks pushed inexorably forward.

Accounts of the ensuing stages of the battle now differ. According to the *Gesta*, the English men-at-arms may have moved forward to meet the disorganised but still powerful French vanguard, but:

> the French nobility, who had previously advanced in line abreast and had all but come to grips with us, either from fear of the missiles which by their very force pierced the sides and visors of their helmets, or in order sooner to break through our strongest points and reach the standards, divided into three columns, attacking our line of battle at the three places where the standards were. And in the mêlée of the spears which then followed, they

hurled themselves against our men in such a fierce charge as to force them to fall back almost a spear's length.[131]

The validity of the Chaplain's account at this point has been doubted by some. But for others the fact that the French attacked at only three places and not along the whole line has added weight to the belief that between the English men-at-arms there were units of archers, whose vigorous shooting forced the French away from the archers' positions and funnelled them towards the three main divisions of men-at-arms. It has been objected that the French dismounted men-at-arms would have been able to overrun any formations of archers projecting beyond the line of men-at-arms, but it may well have been that the intensity of their shooting was such that the French could make no headway. This is supported by le Fèvre's comment that 'the English shot so vigorously that there were none who dared approach them', and it is important to remember that as the range decreased so the effectiveness of the English arrows against armour increased. Alternatively, we might envisage any groups of archers initially placed in front of or between the main English divisions shooting their volleys and then withdrawing behind their own men-at-arms once the French were getting too close. Certainly there is nothing to suggest that the bodies of archers on the extreme flanks were overrun, and they continued to pour arrows into the French flanks while their arrows lasted.[132] As the chronicler Tito Livio noted, 'the order of the English would have been thrown into disorder by the French knights if the greater part of the latter had not been killed or wounded with arrows and had been forced to retreat in terror'.[133] Given sheer weight of numbers, however, some of the French knights must have made it into the rows of stakes, but the more nimble archers could weave and dodge between these, and in such an encounter could use their side-arms to deadly effect against the lumbering men-at-arms.

Whatever the exact position of the units of archers, the *Gesta*'s account envisages bitter hand-to-hand fighting now raging between the heavily armoured English and French knights, thrusting and cutting at each other with lance, sword and poleaxe, that deadly staff weapon developed specifically for such foot combat.[134] But though the English had been forced to give a little ground, their lines held fast. In other circumstances the battle would probably have turned into a prolonged slogging match between the opposing men-at-arms, as was to happen in battles of the Wars of the Roses such as Towton in 1461, won ultimately by the side either with the greater stamina and cohesion, or which could bring any reserves effectively to bear. But at Agincourt not only did the intense shooting from the English archers on the flanks cause the men-at-arms of the French vanguard to bunch inward, but they were also quickly hampered in their ability to fight by their comrades in the rear ranks pressing on, who in turn were being driven forward by those behind them. In what has often been accepted as the classic interpretation of the battle, the *Gesta* believed that as a result, the French suffered

a great blow from which there could be no recovery. For when some of them, killed when battle was joined, fell at the front, so great was the undisciplined violence and pressure of the mass of men behind that the living fell on top of the dead, and others falling on top of the living were killed as well, with the result that, in each of the three places where the strong contingents guarding our standards were, such a great heap grew of the slain and of those lying crushed in between that our men climbed up those heaps, which had risen above a man's height, and butchered their enemies down below with swords, axes and other weapons.[135]

The archers then joined in the mêlée, attacking the flanks of the struggling mass of French men-at-arms, held to the front by their English counterparts. 'When their arrows were all used up', the *Gesta* relates, the archers continued the battle, and 'seizing axes, stakes and swords and spear-heads that were lying about, they struck down, hacked and stabbed the enemy.'[136]

The veracity, indeed the plausibility, of the great piles of French dead has been questioned. Certainly the *Gesta*'s vivid image contains an element of exaggeration, but it is worth noting that the accounts of le Fèvre and Waurin state that after the battle some French nobles, including the Duke of Orléans, were pulled out alive by the English from the heaps of the dead.[137] More importantly, we must contrast the *Gesta*'s version of the battle with the substantially different narrative furnished by the more detailed (and closely related) accounts of Monstrelet, le Fèvre and Waurin. These envisage an initial English attack, galling the French into an advance during which the knights of the vanguard were badly mauled by the storm of arrows. Then comes the under-strength charge by units of French cavalry, which is defeated by the shooting of the English archers, and the ensuing chaos among the French vanguard caused by the retreating horsemen. But for these chroniclers this is the critical juncture in the battle, for 'because of the cavalry, the French battle line was broken'.[138] They immediately record not a slogging match between men-at-arms but a vigorous counter-attack by the English archers against the hopelessly disrupted French vanguard; this attack

Left: The battle of Agincourt from the *St Alban's Chronicle* (Lambeth Palace Library, MS 6, f.243). Dating to the 1420s, this is one of the earliest representations of the battle, but its rendering of the combat and of the landscape are alike stylised, with the English men-at-arms shown fighting on horseback rather than on foot. The tunics of the infantry nevertheless reflect the stipulation in Henry V's ordinances of war that all should wear prominent crosses of St George as a form of recognition. *(Lambeth Palace Library, London/Bridgeman Art Library)*

Below: Sword and buckler fighting, from a South German fencing manual, *c.* 1300. The English were noted as being particularly skilled in this form of combat, and at Agincourt the archers put these side-arms, together with axes and mauls, to terrible effect in the mêlée against the French men-at-arms. *(© The Board of Trustees of the Royal Armouries)*

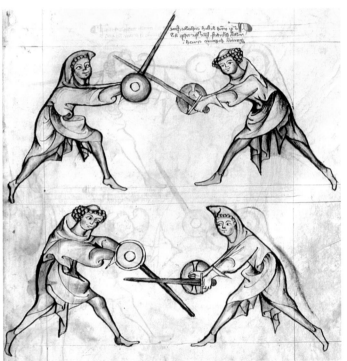

was so successful it penetrated through to the French main battle. 'And soon afterwards,' noted le Fèvre and Waurin,

> the English archers, seeing the breaking up of the French vanguard, came out from behind their stakes all together and threw down their bows and arrows, taking up their swords, axes and other arms and weapons. They struck wherever they saw breaks in the line. They knocked down and killed the French, and finally moved forward to the rear of the vanguard which had seen little or no fighting. The English advanced so far, striking from right and left, that they came to the second French battle which was behind the vanguard. They then attacked it and the King of England threw himself into the fight with his men-at-arms.[139]

This is a very different picture of Agincourt from that of the *Gesta*, and one which places the archers in the forefront of a daring but wholly successful counter-attack. It is important to remind ourselves here of the numerical predominance of the archers in the English army, who formed some five-sixths of the entire force. Their role could not simply be one of supporting the men-at-arms with their withering volleys, for of necessity they *had* to bear the brunt of the hand-to-hand fighting. Whence the order for a general attack came or how it was transmitted to the different units of archers – perhaps by a predetermined trumpet signal – we do not know, but they emerged from behind their defences '*tout ensembles*', not

piecemeal on individual initiative, and their success in prising apart the French ranks suggests they fought with discipline. We glimpse a clue to such cohesion in the ordinances for the army issued by Henry V, probably at Mantes in 1419, which stipulated that all men were to remain in their places under their captains' pennons, nor were to leave their formation (*bataille*) without orders.[140] The sources for Agincourt itself illustrate more vividly than for any other engagement of the period how the archers could rapidly transform from bowmen into superb light infantry. Though many had no armour, or only jacks, and some even were bare-headed as well as bare-footed,[141] their speed and agility on the muddy ground against exhausted and disorientated men-at-arms proved devastating. Darting in among the French men-at-arms, many of whom may already have been wounded by arrows, the archers cut swathes through the French lines.

The Religieux of St Denis, indeed, regarded the nimbleness of the archers as a key factor in the English victory: 'As they were lightly armed and their ranks were not too crowded, they had freedom of movement and could deal mortal blows with ease.'[142] The Burgundian chronicler Waurin noted that the archers used 'swords, hatchets, mallets, axes, falcon beaks (becs de faucquon) and other weapons' to good effect, while Monstrelet also mentions their use of the heavy bladed falchion.[143] But it was the lead maul that was most effective against opponents in good-quality plate armour. 'In addition,' noted the Religieux, 'many of them had adopted a type of weapon until then unknown – great lead-covered mallets from which one single blow on the head could kill a man or knock him senseless to the ground.'[144] It is often assumed that these lead mauls were short-hafted implements, like a modern mallet. But a Tudor tract of 1562 by Henry Barrett, a member of the Yeomen of the Guard, suggests they were something yet more formidable. Barrett recommended that archers should wear a simple burgonet to protect the head, and only the lightest of armours or none at all, and carry 'a maule of leade with a pyke [spike] of five inches longe, well stieled, sett in a staffe of fyve foote of lengthe with a hook at his gydell to take of and mayntayne the fighte as oure elders have donn, by handye stroaks'.[145] This was effectively a long-hafted staff weapon, akin to the Flemish goedendag which had wreaked such havoc on the French nobility at Courtrai in 1302, or to the poleaxe used by men-at-arms. With a stout pick for piercing plate armour and a heavy hammer head, and capable of being wielded in both hands, this must indeed have been a formidable weapon in the hands of lightly armoured infantry. If the maul described by Barrett is of the type used by the archers in 1415, we have a fresh insight into why the archers were so deadly in their close-combat encounters with French knights. Even if such weapons were a later development, the lead mauls they did use were clearly deadly, while the archers' agility on the muddy, slippery field of Agincourt gave them an enormous advantage over the heavily armoured French knights. They are even recorded as having untied their hose, normally attached to the doublet by laces, in order to give them more freedom of movement in combat.[146]

Using such formidable side-arms, the archers led the way in prising open the increasingly disorganised French ranks, creating gaps which their men-at-arms could then exploit. 'After the English archers,' noted Monstrelet, 'the King of England followed up by marching in with all his men-at-arms in great strength.'[147] Among the effects that overcrowding might have, Christine de Pizan had warned that 'they that were over large ordered shuld gyve to theyre ennemyses an entree thrughe them self, and so were thet in parell [peril] to be broken and sparpeylled [scattered] abrode, wherof the fere that they shuld have to see theyre ennemyes so comen wythyn them shuld yelde hem as dysperate and loste'.[148] So it was to prove at Agincourt. As the English drove deeper into their ranks, we must envisage isolated clusters of French men-at-arms, some fighting on, others attempting to surrender as the English surged past. 'Then the French were in great disarray', noted Pierre Fenin, 'and began to break up into little groups. Also the centre battle and rearguard did not assemble with all men and thus all took to flight, because the princes had placed themselves in the vanguard and had left their men leaderless. As a result, there was no control or discipline amongst their men.'[149] Now the failure of overall command was to prove catastrophic, for there was no unified leadership to rally, regroup or redeploy the French ranks. The Duke of Alençon, 'who until then had enjoyed a great reputation for wisdom' and who had been placed in charge of the second division, had already abandoned his command and, 'carried away by a foolish passion and by an overwhelming desire to fight', had plunged into the mêlée where he was slain.[150] Others, more fortunate, were helped off the field by their valets.[151] Faced with the utter disintegration of the vanguard and the assaults of the English, the disorganised second division now started to break up as French morale began to collapse. Monstrelet was struck by the cohesion and discipline of the English attack. They 'pushed further and further into the French, acting together and with great energy (conjoinctement et moult vigoreusement), breaching the first two battles in several places, knocking men to the ground and killing them cruelly and without mercy. . . . The English were so intent upon fighting, killing and taking prisoners that they did not bother to pursue anyone. The rearguard was still mounted, but seeing the first battles doing so badly, they took to flight, save for some of their leaders.'[152]

Not all the fight, however, had gone out of the French. The Gesta believed that after a lull in the fighting, which had allowed the English to begin to separate the living from the dead, 'a shout went up that the enemy's mounted rearguard (in incomparable number and still fresh) were re-establishing their position and line of battle in order to launch an attack on us, few and weary as we were'.[153] At this stage, or possibly earlier in the battle, the English had also suffered an attack on their baggage train, when a force led by a local lord, Isembard d'Azincourt, succeeded in moving undetected round the woods and fell upon the English wagons, inflicting casualties and pillaging some of Henry's regalia. It has been plausibly argued that this attack was not a spontaneous act of opportunism but an attempt to execute the flanking manoeuvre envisaged by the 'Somme Plan', and to repeat the kind of tactic used to good effect by John the Fearless at

Othée.[154] Almost two centuries later Shakespeare was to make much of the attack on the 'boys' of the baggage train; Captain Llewelyn claims that such an act was expressly against the laws of war, while Henry V is stirred to righteous anger. Yet in reality this was less a massacre of the innocents than an attack on those 'other ranks' who crucially guarded the wagons and the dismounted men-at-arms' horses, both of which served to defend the English rear; they were no more 'non-combatants' than the valets and pages in the French army who in the 'Somme Plan' had been instructed to ride their masters' war-horses as supporting cavalry. This assault on the baggage, combined with the threat of a powerful new attack by fresh units from the third French division, created a potentially disastrous situation for the English. All would be lost if the numerous French prisoners took the chance to seize the weapons strewn about the field and recommence fighting. Henry's cold but effective response was to order each man to kill his prisoners, save only those of highest rank, 'lest', noted the Gesta, 'they should involve us in utter disaster in the fighting that would ensue'.[155] Though ruthless, Henry's decision drew considerably less criticism from contemporary observers, including the French, than from some modern historians.[156] Many English knights did indeed balk at the order, which was eventually carried out by a unit of 200 archers led by a gentleman,[157] doubtless as much from a sense of professional and class solidarity as for the loss of rich ransoms such slaughter would entail. But they would have admitted that clemency and its profits depended on the circumstances of battle, and no commander would have been censured for placing discipline in combat above the urge of individuals to plunder or secure valuable prisoners. Hence at Crécy, Poitiers and Agincourt the raising of the French oriflamme banner symbolised the commencement of 'mortal war' in which prisoners were not to be taken, while similarly before Crécy Edward III had ordered that none should be taken for ransom until victory was assured.[158] At Aljubarotta the Anglo-Portuguese army executed the noble Castilian prisoners already taken in the engagement when faced with heavy odds and the prospect of renewed fighting, while the Anglo-Burgundian ordinance drawn up on the eve of the battle of Cravant in 1424 decreed that no one of whatever rank might take prisoners during the battle until the enemy was completely vanquished. Any prisoners who were taken in contravention of this order were to be put to death and their captors executed.[159]

The renewed assault, however, never came. The remaining French forces abandoned the field and Henry was informed by the French herald Mountjoy that the day was his. The carnage among the French had been appalling, and even the English themselves seem to have been awed by the slaughter they had managed to inflict.[160] 'As I truly believe,' noted the Gesta, 'there is not a man with heart of flesh or even of stone who, had he seen and pondered on the horrible deaths and bitter wounds of so many Christian men, would not have dissolved into tears, time and again, for grief.'[161] He referred to the great heap of French dead as 'that mound of pity and blood where had fallen the might of the French', and went on to record that 'of that great host there fell the Dukes of Bar, Brabant and Alençon, five counts, more than ninety barons and bannerets, whose names are set down in a volume of records, and upwards of one thousand five hundred knights according to their own estimate, and between four and five thousand other gentlemen, almost the whole nobility among the soldiery of France'.[162] By contrast, English losses had been remarkably few, Monstrelet estimating their dead to be around 600 of all ranks.[163]

Agincourt, more than any other engagement of the Hundred Years War, reveals the English tactical synthesis and army structure working at their most effective. The initial advance to provoke the French into an attack, as well as the aggressive yet cohesive counter-attack which destroyed the French vanguard and pressed through to the second division, revealed the cool nerve and discipline of the English archers and men-at-arms, whose paucity of numbers was offset by far superior leadership, cohesion and manoeuvrability. As an anonymous later fifteenth-century translator of Vegetius's De Re Militari put it, 'noght multitude and unkunnyng, ne strengthe untaught is cause of overcomynge, but craft, usage and exercise of armes getith victorie and overcometh enemys'.[164] The battle also highlights the remarkable tactical flexibility of the English archers. Sir Michael Howard has spoken of 'the dilemma – speed or firepower' which confronted many early modern armies, and the problem 'of how to combine missile weapons with close-action; how to unite hitting power, mobility and defensive strength'.[165] Yet the English archer had achieved an effective answer to all of this, long before the scientific military deployments applied to pike and shot by the likes of Maurice of Nassau and Gustavus Adolphus. Mounted for speed of mobility, capable of unleashing devastating volleys against the enemy on foot or on horse, and now protected by a movable field of stakes, the longbowman could as easily engage in close combat with his side-arms or other weapons once formations of opposing men-at-arms had become sufficiently disorganised. Until the advent in the eighteenth century of the socket bayonet, which transformed the defensive and offensive capabilities of musket-armed infantry and made the pike redundant, the archer was undoubtedly one of the most highly adaptable troops on the European battlefield.

Matthew Strickland

The English Way in War? The Impact of the Longbow in Fifteenth-Century Europe

he renewed successes of English arms under Henry V were to have a profound effect on both allies and enemies alike, and the first half of the fifteenth century was to witness a far more sustained period of emulation of or reaction to English tactics and military prowess than had occurred in the later fourteenth century. This process is best seen by a comparative study of the role of bowmen in the armies of Burgundy, Scotland and France, set within the context of the latter half of the Hundred Years War.

BURGUNDY AND THE INFLUENCE OF ENGLAND, 1415–35

Duke John the Fearless had, as we have seen in the previous chapter, been a leading proponent of the effective deployment of archers well before Agincourt.[1] At Othée, he had used powerful flanking units of archers to good effect against the Liègeois, and his influence on military thinking had been reflected in both Christine de Pizan's description of model battle formations and in the French 'Somme Plan' of 1415. In the wake of the disaster at Agincourt he was able to exploit the political vacuum left by the death or capture of so many nobles and princes of the blood to challenge Armagnac influence over Charles VI and eventually to occupy Paris. Two years after Agincourt the duke himself drew up a battle plan at Versailles on 17 September 1417, before he moved his large army against the Armagnac forces holding Paris.[2] This document, which was considered a unique survival of its kind until the discovery of the Agincourt plan, is an important reflection of Burgundian military thinking shortly after the catastrophe of 1415. Not

surprisingly, there are close similarities between this and the earlier plan, but important additional features and amendments, which indicate Duke John had revised his tactics in the light of Agincourt, make the ordinance worth citing in some detail. It is important to note that though here John was envisaging the Armagnacs as his chief opponents, there was a distinct possibility in 1417 that he might have to confront the invasion army of Henry V, which had already taken the great Norman town of Caen and was making major territorial conquests in Lower Normandy.

If the enemy took up a position near Paris, where they could benefit from plentiful cannon and other defensive measures, an engagement should be avoided at all costs and the army should withdraw, protected if need be by a strong rearguard. If the enemy assumed the offensive, however, the Burgundian van was to draw up on foot 'in the most advantageous position possible', with all the archers and crossbowmen of the army, save for a reserve of 300, being placed in front of the van in two wings. Each wing of bowmen 'shall be led by two notable and valiant gentlemen' who were to command the unit's standard. The importance of these archers is shown by the insistence that 'the captains of the companies of bowmen shall inform the two commanders of the bowmen of the numbers of reviewed men under them, so that they know how many bowmen are there in all'.[3] If space on the battlefield allowed, the main battle, led by the duke, was to draw up on foot on one side of the van, or some forty paces behind it, 'so that if the enemy forms one division only, our van and main division can join together in a single command'. If the site was too constrained, however, the main formation was to draw up

behind the van and its wings of bowmen. A reserve, stationed a bowshot behind, was to be formed by 400 mounted men-at-arms with their valets, and 100 bowmen, 'in case any of the enemy cavalry is ordered to attack our army in the rear', while the baggage wagons were to be drawn up behind them to strengthen their position.[4] Such a provision reflected John's attempts to prevent the kind of attack on the rear envisaged in the 'Somme Plan' and which had actually been carried out to some effect on Henry V's baggage train at Agincourt. Although this was intended as an initially defensive formation, John made provision for a powerful cavalry detachment, ready to launch an attack whenever circumstances best suited. A number of lords, comprising a force of 1,000 men-at-arms, in addition to all their *valets de guerre*, were to reinforce the van. On the enemy's approach this cavalry force was to 'withdraw

Duke John the Fearless' proposed plan of battle, 17 September 1417.

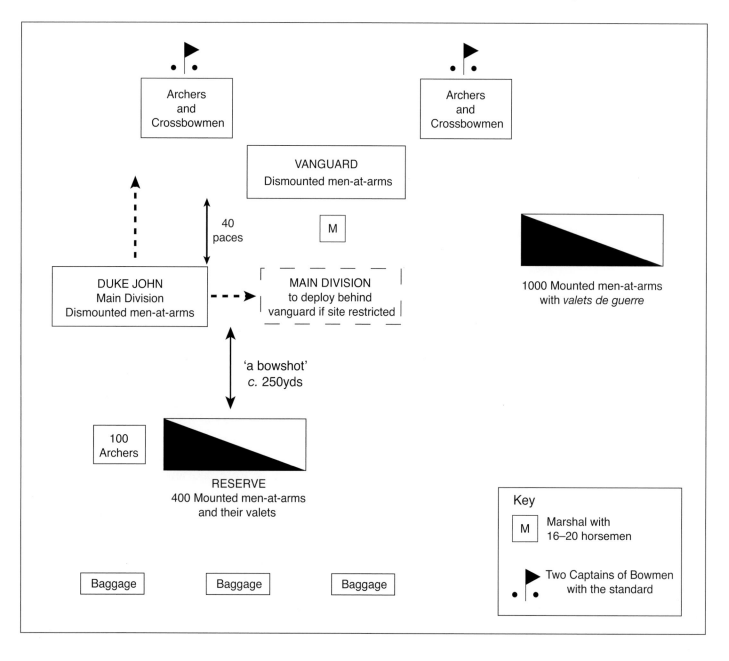

Heavily armed archers precede the army of King Arthur as he confronts the Saxons, from the *Chroniques de Hainault* (Flemish, 1468; Brussels, Bibliothèque Royale Albert, 9243, f.36v). *(Bibliothèque Royale Albert, Brussels)*

from the main division of the army and the van to one side, and, if they see any disorder in the approaching enemy's ranks, or any mix-up between their cavalry and infantry, they are to attack them vigorously'.[5] If the enemy approached in good order, however, this force should keep itself in readiness at some distance from one flank of the van, 'to do whatever they see to be expedient, whether this be to charge the enemy's cavalry, if he has any, or his bowmen, or to make their way round him to attack his rear, a manoeuvre which might prove of great value'.[6]

As Matthew Bennett has noted, the battle plan of 1417 shows Duke John ready to learn from the lessons of French defeat.[7] Thus emphasis was given to the adequate spacing of the army and its deployment commensurate with the nature of the terrain, to avoid the fatal overcrowding that had so hampered the French at Agincourt. Strikingly, the whole archer force was placed in the van, revealing a concern to deploy all of them as effectively as possible, and not, as had occurred at Agincourt, to leave the missilemen uselessly in the rear. Such considerations clearly outweighed any fear that if the main battle was deployed in line abreast with the van, one of its flanks would be unprotected by archers. Doubtless with the débâcle of the hopelessly inadequate and under-strength cavalry wings at Agincourt in mind, Duke John stipulated that the flanking body of horsemen were 'to exclude from their ranks those either poorly mounted or inexpert on horseback', and should their numbers fall below 1,000 they were to draw on other contingents to make up their full strength. Moreover, provision was made to steady any who waivered; the marshal and between 16 and 20 picked horsemen were to be posted immediately behind the van 'so that they can rally any who fall back and encourage them to do their duty' – at lance point – as well as stepping into any breaches occurring in the van.[8] Similarly, harsh disciplinary clauses, forbidding men to abandon the banners of their units and enjoining the death penalty for any fleeing the battle itself, sought to prevent the units in the rear from abandoning the field as had happened at Poitiers and Agincourt.[9]

How such an astute battle plan would have worked had it been put into operation cannot be known, for despite intensive military activity the duke was never to fight another major battle. His murder during a conference with the Dauphin on 10 September 1419 on the bridge at Montereau, some 20 miles upstream from Paris, removed this

unscrupulous politician and skilled general, but led his son and successor Philip the Good into an alliance with the English which lasted from 1420 to 1435.[10] Despite its vicissitudes, the Anglo-Burgundian alliance was vital to the successful retention of English conquests in Normandy and beyond, and served to intensify English military influence on the Burgundians. In July 1422, following an offensive by the Dauphin, Philip had requested Henry V to send him English archers to bolster his own forces, and the king had dispatched Bedford to his aid. A set of ordinances drawn up the following year at Auxerre on 29 July 1423 by a joint Anglo-Burgundian army on the eve of the battle of Cravant provide an intriguing glimpse of the process of English influence at work. Two marshals, one English and one Burgundian, were appointed to direct the troops, who were enjoined to live together in peace and amity. The army would be preceded in its march by 120 men-at-arms, half of them English and half Burgundian, who would be accompanied by 120 archers. Thus far the provisions were unexceptional. It was ordered, however, that on arrival at the battlefield all would dismount promptly when so commanded, and that any who refused would be put to death.[11] This draconian provision strongly indicates that there were still Burgundian men-at-arms who might resist orders to fight on foot, preferring to fight from the saddle as the majority of them (and their dauphinist opponents) seem to have done at Philip the Good's victory at Mons-en-Vimeu in 1421.[12] To ensure that none had the opportunity to remount against orders, it was decreed that all the horses were to be led half a league to the rear, and that any found nearer would be confiscated. All archers, moreover, Burgundian as well as English, were to supply themselves with a stake sharpened at both ends.[13] Despite the misgivings reflected in the ordinance, the adoption of English tactics was successful and the battle of Cravant was a resounding victory for the allies.[14] Burgundian archers also made a good showing on their own account, as in May 1430, when a Burgundian raiding party under Franquet d'Arras was attacked near Langy-sur-Marne by a larger French force led by Joan of Arc. The Burgundian archers carefully formed up together on foot in excellent order so that by virtue of their shooting the first and second French assaults achieved nothing. Only when the French were reinforced by a large number of crossbowmen, culvineers and other troops drawn from neighbouring garrisons were the Burgundians finally overwhelmed.[15]

If Cravant had been won by a combined English–Burgundian army, a largely Burgundian force, assisted by English military advisers, achieved a notable victory at Bulgnéville in 1431.[16] On 2 July a small force led by the Marshal of Burgundy Antoine de Toulongeon, but also containing English and Picards, was withdrawing from a *chevauchée* into Lorraine when it learned that the army of René of Anjou was in pursuit. As the enemy's advance guard under the Duke of Bar was close at hand, the Burgundians held a council of war and decided to fight. According to Monstrelet, they were advised in drawing up their formations by an English knight, Thomas Gargrave, and their subsequent dispositions certainly bore the hallmark of English tactical deployment.[17] They drew up on gently rising ground about one kilometre south of Vaudoncourt with their rear protected by a stream and by large bushes and hedges, and with the advantage of the sun to their backs.[18] The men-at-arms were ordered to dismount to fight on foot, but while the English and Picards readily complied there was dissent from the Burgundians who wanted to fight on horseback.[19] This was exactly the scenario which the pre-battle ordinance before Cravant had sought to counter, and it is noteworthy that eight years later the Burgundian men-at-arms and squires were still resistant to dismounting. The English and Picards, however, were absolutely insistent, and it was accordingly ordered that everyone, irrespective of rank, was to fight on foot on pain of death.[20] The horses, together with the baggage, were carefully arranged behind the army to further protect its rear. The archers, who now planted their stakes in front of them, were placed not only on the wings but in front of the line,[21] which stretched some 1,000m – yet another indication that the positioning of archers was flexible and not simply confined to the flanks of men-at-arms as some scholars have

suggested. A number of light artillery pieces were also placed both on the flanks and in the middle of the men-at-arms' units.[22]

On reaching the battlefield Duke René reconnoitred the Burgundian dispositions. Despite the advice of his most experienced captain, the French veteran Arnuad-Guilhelm, Lord of Barbazan, to avoid pitched battle, he decided to attack, being confident in his superior numbers. The duke's army formed into three battles, with the vanguard on the right, the main battle in the centre and the rearguard to the left.[23] The majority of the men-at-arms dismounted to fight on foot, but, as at Agincourt and in John the Fearless's battle plan of 1417, the Barrois kept a mounted unit of 200 lances on their left wing.[24] As the Barrois moved forward to the assault, the Burgundians sent up a great cry and their artillery opened fire to considerable effect, sending many of the attackers plunging to the ground to take cover and badly shaking their morale. No sooner had this bombardment ceased than the archers let fly their volleys, which took a heavy toll of the Barrois.[25] No doubt dissuaded by the ferocity of these missile attacks and the strength of the Burgundian position, the cavalry units on the left of Duke René's army seem not to have attempted a serious assault, and subsequently abandoned the field. Their right wing nevertheless succeeded in closing with the Burgundian left, only to be received by a fierce counter-attack in which its commander, the Lord of Barbazan, was slain, and its formation broken. All along the line, indeed, the Burgundians counter-attacked, taking advantage of the disarray caused by the volleys of arrows – a move closely analogous to the assault of the English at Agincourt. The Barrois formations began to disintegrate in panic, and Duke René, wounded but still fighting fiercely, was captured. The discomfiture of the Barrois was as complete as it was swift – the battle itself was over in only a quarter of an hour, and the victorious Burgundians launched a long and fierce pursuit in which they took a great haul of prisoners. While the victors only sustained around forty casualties, Duke René's men had suffered far higher losses, as was so typical in such attacks on a position defended by archers. These numbered at least some 1,000 dead, including many knights and squires from Bar, Lorraine and Germany, and the much-mourned Lord of Barbazan, whose sage counsel, grounded in his experience of war against the English, had been ignored to such cost.[26]

The success of engagements such as Cravant and Bulgné-ville goes far to explain why English influence on Burgundian military thinking extended beyond battlefield dispositions to the composition of armies themselves. Duke Philip, like his father, had readily appreciated the importance of a powerful missile arm; already in 1421 the small force he conducted in operations in Picardy comprised 541 men-at-arms, 245 crossbowmen and 200 archers.[27] But between 1430 and 1436, as Bertrand Schnerb has shown, missilemen came to comprise around 70 per cent of Burgundian armies, achieving a ratio of archers to men-at-arms of 3:1, the same as in many English forces of this period. Similarly indentures for military service drawn up between the duke and leading nobles reflected the English model.[28] Thus between 1404 and 1435 it was the Dukes of Burgundy, rather than the Kings of France, who had shown themselves most willing to absorb the tactical and organisational lessons suggested by the successes of English

arms. Only in the 1440s did Charles VII embark on radical reform of his armies, though when he did so his creation of a standing army followed not the English model but instead the precedent set by Charles V after 1369, when permanent companies of men-at-arms and crossbowmen had been established for the renewed war against England.[29] By the close of the fourteenth century, however, these companies had dwindled, and in the dark days following Agincourt Charles VII was first forced to turn for aid to a country that itself was undergoing a period of major military change which sought to bring the longbow to the fore – Scotland.

SCOTTISH ARCHERS AND THE AULD ALLIANCE

In 1417 Henry V had begun a slow but methodical reduction of Normandy by a series of protracted sieges, initiating what was to be a new English policy of direct territorial conquest and settlement in France. The Dauphin Charles, who had become Charles VI's heir apparent in 1417, had been driven from Paris the following year by the Burgundians, and was left to rule only the rump of 'the kingdom of Bourges' with the support of the Armagnacs. There was neither the time nor the capability for a major reorganisation of French forces, so in this state of acute crisis Charles resorted to expedients. He not only hired large numbers of mercenary crossbowmen from Italy and Savoy in the time-honoured manner, but also turned to Scotland, the old ally of France, for direct military aid.

There was already a tradition of Scots fighting in French forces stretching back to the mid-fourteenth century. In 1356 William Douglas, nephew of Sir James Douglas, and his cousin Archibald 'the Grim' had fought at Poitiers with a contingent of some 200 men-at-arms, while units of Scots had served in the Free Companies with Du Guesclin in Spain in the 1360s.[30] Alexander, Earl of Mar, had served John the Fearless in his campaigns of 1408 and had fought with him at Othée, while in 1413 the Burgundian duke had contracted with Archibald, 4th Earl of Douglas, for a force of 4,000 men, including archers.[31] But between 1419 and 1424 Charles took the unprecedented step of hiring major Scottish armies to fight in France. Already by 1418 Charles had Scottish archers in his bodyguard, and other detachments were soon stationed at key fortresses; there were, for example, 100 Scottish archers at Loches, while by May 1419 William Douglas of Drumlanrig was garrisoning Méhun-sur-Yèvre with a force of 150 men-at-arms and 300 archers.[32] Such troops, however, were but the advance guard of the expeditionary army of 6,000–7,000 men under the command of John Stewart, Earl of Buchan, Constable of Scotland and son of the regent, Albany, and

Archibald, Earl of Wigtown, which sailed from Dumbarton to La Rochelle aboard a hired Castilian fleet.[33] This force, 'probably the largest army to be sent abroad in Scottish medieval history',[34] was remarkable not only for its size but also for its composition. For what is striking about the Scots retinues operating in France in the early 1420s is that they contained a high proportion of archers, closely reflecting the English model and generally displaying the same ratios of men-at-arms to archers. This was in marked contrast to contemporary French forces, where the ratio of men-at-arms to archers was 2:1.[35] A major change seems thus to have occurred in the make-up of Scottish armies – or at least in those selected to form expeditionary forces – moving away from an emphasis on formations of heavy infantry armed with long spears to armies composed primarily of archers and men-at-arms.

How or when this transition occurred is not easy to trace, but the crushing defeat of the Scots by the archers of the Earl of Northumberland and Henry 'Hotspur' Percy at Homildon in 1402 suggests itself as a likely catalyst for, or at least an accelerator of, military reform.[36] Archers can be glimpsed in nobles' service in the few 'bonds of retinue' extant from the later fourteenth century, such as that in 1372 by which the Earl of Douglas retained Sir James Douglas of Dalkeith with 8 men-at-arms and 16 archers, in return for 600 marks.[37] But we would wish to know far more about how the Scottish commanders went about recruiting the great armies of 1419 and 1424 that served in France, as well as the other smaller retinues which saw service, and about rates of pay, terms and conditions of service and about the type of equipment the Scots archers possessed. For the raising of such forces was a remarkable phenomenon in a country whose population in about 1400 has been estimated at around only half a million.[38] In addition to existing indentured retainers, many

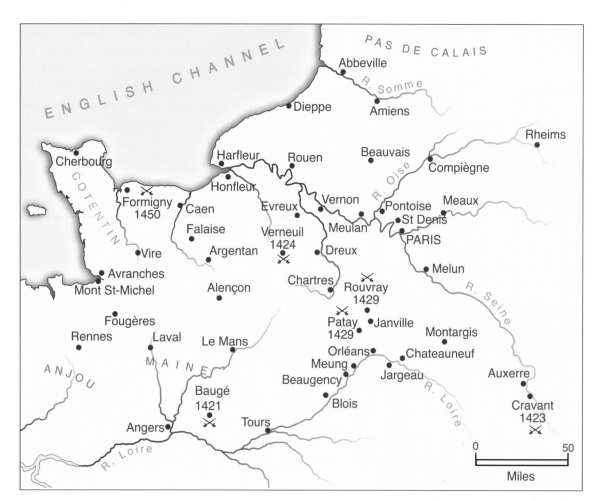

Northern France, showing some of the major engagements in the later stages of the Hundred Years War.

The effigy of Thomas, Duke of Clarence, from his tomb (dating to *c.* 1439) in Canterbury Cathedral. Clarence's decision to launch a surprise attack on the Franco-Scottish army without archer support proved catastrophic, and led to his defeat and death at Baugé in 1421. *(© Angelo Hornak/Corbis)*

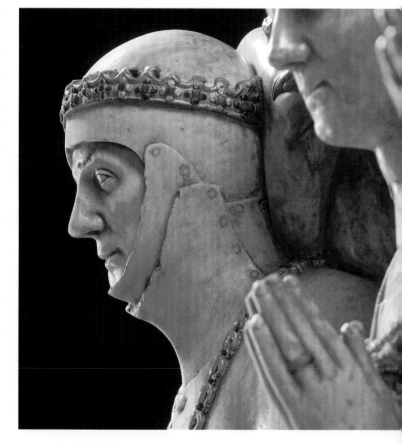

men must have been raised from the vast estates controlled by the ruling dynasty of the Stewarts, and by the Douglases, by far the most powerful noble family in Scotland at this time, but others may well have come from the Highlands, where a long tradition of archery was to last until the early eighteenth century.[39] Whether the heavy hand of the laird lay behind the service of some cannot be known, but no doubt all were attracted by the pay and the hope of booty, and some by the opportunity for a new life in a new land; after 1424 many Scottish troops stayed in France, and small groups continued to serve in French armies throughout the fifteenth century.

For the French, the initial results of Charles's scheme were unpromising. In March 1420 a joint Franco-Scottish force marching to the relief of Fresnay-le-Vicomte was ambushed and defeated with heavy losses by the Earl of Huntingdon. No details of the fighting are known, but the Scottish pay chest fell into the hands of the English.[40] During the rest of that year the great 'army of Scotland' was deployed by the French primarily to garrison a chain of fortresses both around Paris and in Maine and Anjou in an attempt to halt Henry V's relentless drive south and east from Normandy, with Buchan using the castle of Châtillon in the Touraine as his principal base.[41] The presence of so many foreign troops inevitably caused tension:

some of the French lords resented the influence of the Scots commanders and the local population, faced with billeting and supplying the Scots, complained loudly of the depredations of their would-be defenders. Moreover, because there had not yet been the hoped-for knock-out blow to the English, the Scots were derided as 'wine-bibbers and mutton-eating fools'.[42] Yet on 22 March 1421 a joint Scottish and French force achieved a notable victory at Baugé in Anjou, in which Thomas, Duke of Clarence, the brother and heir apparent of Henry V, was slain.[43]

During Henry V's absence in England, Clarence, acting as regent in Normandy, led a force of some 4,000 men, mostly drawn from the garrisons of Normandy, through Maine on a raid deep into Anjou as far as the Loire, attempting but failing to take Angers. The dauphinist army, comprising predominantly the Scots under the Earl of Buchan, but also with some French lords such as Etienne de Vignolles, otherwise known as La Hire, and a force of troops raised from Anjou, blocked his line of retreat and selected a site for battle at La Lande Chasles, some 6 miles south-east of Baugé where they had camped. Clarence had been unaware of this danger until some Scots captured by his foragers revealed the location and strength of the enemy. Despite the fact that most of his archers were scattered around the local countryside gathering supplies, the duke at once decided on a surprise attack, taking with him only a force of some 1,500 mounted men-at-arms. The Earls of Salisbury and Huntingdon and Gilbert de Umfraville were among the many wiser heads that cautioned him against such a rash advance without proper intelligence and against a far superior force. But Clarence, as the *Brut* put it, 'wold not be gouerned and have take hys ost with hym', even though he had ordered Salisbury to collect the archers and follow him as soon as possible.[44] Invalided home during the siege of Harfleur, Clarence had not been at Agincourt, and as several sources remark he was eager to win his own glory by a victory over the French.[45] But very strikingly, at least one chronicle, the *Vita et Gesta Henrici*, believed that Clarence left behind his main force of archers to give the lie to the French taunt that the English victories in France were achieved wholly by their bowmen.[46] Whether or not this was one of Clarence's real motives, the comment strongly suggests that the French had been mocking the English men-at-arms for their over-reliance on their archers, seen as men of inferior rank, and implying therefore that they were flinching from a 'fair fight' with their French peers. Be this as it may, the failure of Clarence to bring with him archer support was to prove a fatal blunder.

Clarence's mounted strike depended wholly on surprise for its success, but his advance was spotted by a Franco-Scottish reconnaissance party.[47] With the alarm raised, a small force of 30 Scots archers under Robert Stewart of Ralston rushed to hold the narrow stone bridge over the River Couasnon and prevented the English cavalry, whose horses were wounded by the arrows, from crossing long enough to be reinforced by a large group of Scots under Hugh Kennedy. Gradually, 'with the greatest difficulty and furious fighting and leaving their horses behind, the duke and his men gained a passage across the bridge on foot and sought the open country near Baugé'.[48] Brushing aside a small force of French under Jean de La Croix, Clarence's men-at-arms now remounted and rode for Baugé. By this time, however, the main Scots army had deployed and as Clarence's forces advanced they were met by Buchan's forces near the church at Vieil Baugé and a fierce conflict ensued. Regrettably, as for all the major engagements fought by the 'army of Scotland' in France, we have no details of the formation adopted by the Scots and thus where and how they deployed their archers.[49] The English in all likelihood dismounted once more, but, save for the archers in Clarence's own bodyguard, they had no force of bowmen to guard their flanks.[50] The accounts of the fighting itself are sparse and contradictory. All that is certain is that as Scottish and French reinforcements came up, Clarence's disordered forces were quickly overwhelmed, and the duke was killed together with possibly as many as 1,617 men-at-arms, including Sir Gilbert Umfraville and John Grey, Lord of Tancarville. Among the captured were the Earl of Huntingdon and John Beaufort, Earl of Somerset.[51] That disaster was not compounded by complete catastrophe was only due to Salisbury's highly skilful retreat with his force of some 4,000 archers through heavily wooded country towards La Flèche and then Le Mans, thereby eluding the Scots army which sought to finish off the remaining English. As Wylie notes, 'if they had caught Salisbury, Henry's chances of enforcing the Treaty of Troyes would have been ruined, and the verdict of Castillon would have been anticipated by thirty years'.[52] As it was, Salisbury gathered fresh forces and within two months had made a morale-boosting raid back into Anjou once more, challenging the French to a battle which they declined to accept.

Nevertheless, Baugé had been a major reverse as well as a bitter humiliation for English arms. For the Dauphin, who was sent Clarence's banner by Buchan and Douglas, it was a vindication of his policy of hiring Scottish forces, and it prompted Pope Martin V to make the famous remark, 'Truly the Scots are an antidote to the English!'.[53] The grateful prince created Buchan Constable of France and showered towns, castles and lordships on the Scottish commanders.[54] On returning to France in June 1421, burning with revenge,

Henry V at once marched a powerful English army towards Beaugency on the Loire to seek the Franco-Scottish army, but this time Buchan wisely refused battle, instead stripping the land of victuals to force an English withdrawal. Nor did Henry live to exact his vengeance, for he died of dysentery following the siege of Meaux on 31 August 1422. The 'army of Scotland' continued to play an important role in 1423 in consolidating Charles's position and in stemming the English advance towards Bourges. According to Bower, Sir John Stewart of Darnley achieved another notable success over the English at 'Brosignere', possibly Bazougers near Laval in Maine, where he defeated and captured John de la Pole, brother of the Earl of Suffolk, and inflicted heavy casualties.[55] But in July of that year, while Buchan and Wigtown were back in Scotland recruiting more troops, part of the Scots force under Darnley was destroyed by an Anglo-Burgundian army at Cravant-sur-Yonne.

'THE BOW OF THE BRAVE HAS BEEN OVERCOME': CRAVANT, 31 JULY 1423, VERNEUIL, 17 AUGUST 1424, AND ROUVRAY, 12 FEBRUARY 1428

A powerful Franco-Scottish force, bolstered by Lombard and Spanish troops, had been besieging the town of Cravant, whose fall would open the way to an attack on the heartlands of Burgundy. An army under the Earl of Salisbury was sent to the town's relief by John, Duke of Bedford, Henry V's brother and now regent in France on behalf of the child king Henry VI. At Auxerre Salisbury joined up with a Burgundian force and on 31 July 1423 they came within sight of the enemy drawn up outside Cravant, but in such a strong position on high ground that Salisbury wisely declined a direct attack.[56] Withdrawing some miles he crossed the River Yonne to its left bank, thus placing himself on the opposite side from the French, then executed a flanking march along the river to arrive opposite Cravant. If his intention had been to draw the Franco-Scottish force down from its commanding position then his plan had worked, for they now descended to oppose his crossing of the river. The armies faced each other across the Yonne for about three hours, before the allies 'advanced suddenly with the ardour of rash courage, and archers began to shoot all together'. As the bowmen laid down their covering volleys, the men-at-arms waded into the river, for at this point the water was only waist deep. With the cry of 'St George!', Salisbury led his men across while to his right Lord Willoughby forced a passage across the bridge a little further upstream.[57] The chroniclers give few or no details about the ensuing fight, save that the garrison of Cravant made a sally in strength against the rear of the Franco-Scottish army. Caught between these two forces, the French were overcome and many were slain in the flight.[58] Darnley, who had lost an eye in the battle, was captured.[59] Charles, now king since his father's death in October 1422, wrote cynically to his supporters in the Lyonnais not to lose heart since 'almost none of the nobles of our kingdom [were] there, but only Scots, Spaniards, and other foreign soldiers, accustomed to live off the country, so that the harm is not so great'.[60]

Horse armour by Pier Innocenzo da Faerno of Milan, *c.* 1450–60. Though this is the earliest surviving barding of plate, it was probably similar defences that allowed the Italian heavy cavalry to smash through the English line at Verneuil, although Bedford's men were able to regroup and eventually achieve victory. *(Vienna Museum)*

Such sentiments, however, were largely a reflection of the need to steady the nerve of his French supporters rather than an indication of the real value Charles placed on the Scots. For in 1424 he hired a second major Scottish army consisting of 2,500 men-at-arms and 4,000 archers, who arrived at La Rochelle in April. It was led by Archibald, Earl of Douglas, who was given the unfortunate nickname of 'the Tyneman', meaning 'the Loser', an epithet which, as Norman Macdougall puts it, 'may refer either to his defeats or to losing a portion of his anatomy at each of them'.[61] United with the remnants of the Scots force defeated at Cravant, this army may have totalled some 10,000–12,000 men, and thus represented a very significant field army.[62] Charles and his generals intended to deploy this powerful force in a battle-seeking strategy in order to inflict a decisive defeat on Bedford and the English army of occupation.[63] In so doing they hoped to repeat the successes achieved in the field by French armies the year previously, for in September 1423 at La Gravelle in Maine the Count of Aumâle, Jean d'Harcourt, had succeeded in defeating an English force by a flanking cavalry attack, thereby demonstrating that the plan so badly botched at Agincourt could work if correctly implemented.[64] In the same month the French had also defeated a Burgundian force at La Buissière in the Mâconnais, where a major role in the French victory had been played by Italian mercenary heavy cavalry.[65] Their success may well have been due to the development by Italian armourers of more effective protection for the horses. Though the earliest surviving example of full plate horse-barding is that made in Milan around 1450 by Pier Innocenza da Faerno (see p. 346),[66] it seems probable that such plate defences were emerging in the 1420s and it is significant that it was from Milan that in 1424 Charles recruited some 2,000 heavy cavalry. If so, such plate barding would have afforded a significantly higher degree of protection to the horses than the traditional horse trapper of mail and leather, with the only plate defence being the chamfron or head-piece.[67] Charles hoped that a combination of such cavalry with his Scottish army would shatter the English.

In August 1424 the Scots joined forces with French units under the Dukes of Aumâle and Alençon at Châteaudun before attempting the relief of the key Norman border fortress of Ivry, which was being besieged by Bedford. Initially pledging to join battle with Bedford on 15 August, the Franco-Scots reneged on their agreement, partly because of the strength of Bedford's position but largely because the Milanese cavalry on which they pinned their hopes had not yet arrived.[68] Once it had appeared, however, the Franco-Scottish army manoeuvred south-west on to an open field a little to the north of the town of Verneuil, where the terrain would best suit their heavy cavalry. The gravity of the French threat had led Bedford to raise a substantial army of some 8,000–10,000 men. In addition to the regent's military household and other retinues, a large number of men had been drawn from the English garrisons in Normandy and other territories, while those Normans under English rule who owed military service had been summoned to fight as men-at-arms.[69] He now had to face the French on open ground, with no hedges, ditches or natural obstacles to exploit, nor, as at Agincourt, with woods to protect his flanks. Accordingly, he defended his rear with the customary wagon-laager and with the army's horses tethered in a defensive screen, allocating a small reserve to guard this baggage formation. He drew up his men-at-arms in one central battle, with archers, protected by their stakes, positioned on the wings.[70] According to Monstrelet, he also placed a body of archers in front of the main formation.[71] This may well have been to counter the unexpected threat of a frontal cavalry assault, but it may also have reflected a common English practice in the opening stages of an engagement.[72]

Traditional interpretations of the battle, following chronicles such as that of Guillaume Cousinot, chancellor to the Duke of Orléans, have the French deploying their Lombard cavalry in an attempt to outflank the English position, and such does indeed accord with earlier French tactical practice. Such a move, however, is said to have failed, with the Italians expending their efforts in a vain assault against the English wagon-laager before dispersing to plunder. But in a masterly reinterpretation of the battle of Verneuil, Michael Jones has argued that the Milanese horse in fact carried out a full frontal assault on Bedford's position with devastating success. For just as at Poitiers the archers had made little impact on the plate armour of the French knights, so now at Verneuil their shafts failed to halt the onrush of the superbly armoured Milanese horsemen. The archers in the frontal positions were swept aside – their defensive stakes seemingly having little effect – and the cavalry proceeded to strike the main English battle with such impetus that they drove right through the ranks.[73] The English attempted to part their ranks to let the cavalry through as best they could. As the Norman chronicler Thomas Basin noted: 'the whole battle line of the English was deeply penetrated. The English themselves half opened to let the Italian cavalry pass through with the least possible harm.'[74] Nevertheless, their charge had effectively cut Bedford's army in half. The Lombard horse carried on their attack through to the English baggage train, whose substantial guard of at least 500 men broke in panic and fled, carrying the news of Bedford's defeat with them.[75]

Remarkably, however, the English now managed to regroup. Many of the front-line archers who had been scattered by the Lombards' charge rallied to Bedford's position; some had

survived the onslaught by throwing themselves to the ground to let the horsemen ride over them.[76] Now they reformed, uttering a great shout to boost the shaken morale of their forces.[77] They decided on an immediate counter-attack before the Lombard horsemen could be redeployed against them, and, as in the initial stages of Agincourt, the English now advanced, stopping occasionally to dress their ranks and once more to utter their customary shout.[78] The French moved to meet them, but their discipline and cohesion were poorer, and it seems that initially some units of the French advancing too fast may have been defeated in detail by Bedford's force. Once the main French battle closed, however, a fierce mêlée ensued, which long hung in the balance. At such close quarters many if not all of the archers must have been engaged in hand-to-hand combat, as they had been at Agincourt and at earlier battles such as Auray in 1364. Finally, however, the English prevailed, and a bloody rout ensued.[79] The Scots were a particular target for English vengeance; not only was Baugé to be avenged, but the 'army of Scotland' had sailed to France in de facto violation of a truce between England and Scotland, which had been a condition for the release of King James I.[80] Bedford ordered his men to give no quarter; the Scots force was virtually annihilated, and Douglas, who had recently been created Duke of Touraine, was slain. His body, together with that of Buchan, was ransomed from the English and buried with honour in the choir of the cathedral in Tours. Douglas's chaplain, John Carmichael, survived the battle and, on becoming Bishop of Orléans, instigated a mass for the souls of those Scots slain at Vernueil – a tradition that continued until the eighteenth century.[81]

Above: John, Duke of Bedford, kneels before St George, who wears the mantle of the Order of the Garter over his armour, and whose squire carries his helmet and shield. From the *Bedford Hours*, commissioned to celebrate John's marriage to Anne, sister of Duke Philip of Burgundy, in 1423 (British Library, Add. MS 18850, f.256v). As Regent of France following his brother Henry V's premature death in 1422, Bedford proved to be a capable military commander, and won a resounding victory over the French at Verneuil, called 'a second Agincourt', in 1424. *(© British Library)*

Left: A bascinet made in French style, Milan, *c.* 1450, from Churburg Castle in the Tyrol. The narrow eye slit was intended to give protection both against lance bows and missiles, while the solid plate gorget gave better defence to the throat than earlier aventails of mail. *(Paris, Musée de l'Armée)*

Opposite: The battle of Rouvray, 1428, also known as the 'Battle of the Herrings', in which an English force under Sir John Fastolf inflicted a heavy defeat on the Franco-Scottish army. From Jean Chartier's *Chroniques du temps de Charles VII* (Paris, Bibliothèque Nationale, MS fr. 2691). *(akg-images/Jerome da Cunha)*

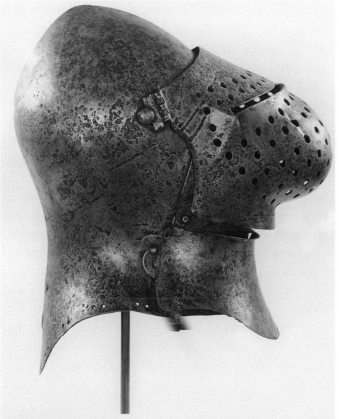

There remained a final, bloody epilogue to Charles's attempts to harness Scottish men-at-arms and archers to his war effort, for on 12 February 1428 at Rouvray the remains of the 'army of Scotland' suffered another major blow at the 'battle of the Herrings'. To victual the English army besieging the strategically vital city of Orléans, Bedford had sent Sir John Fastolf, grand master of his household, with a large supply column comprising some 400–500 carts and wagons, containing among other supplies a large quantity of salted herring, for it was Lent. According to Monstrelet, who provides the fullest narrative of the battle, he had a force of some 1,700 troops but also around 1,000 non-combatants. On 12 February, learning that a stronger French force of 3,000–4,000 French under the Duke of Bourbon, the Marshals of France and Sir John Stewart of Darnley was planning to attack them, Fastolf halted at the village of Rouvray between Janville and Orléans, where 'the English quickly set about forming their convoy of carts into a large enclosure, big enough to take them all and leaving only two openings which were covered by the archers. On the

better-protected side they placed the merchants, carters and pages and other non-combatant persons, with all the horses.'[82] There is an intriguing parallel between Fastolf's laager and the *wagenburgen* which the Hussites of Bohemia had deployed to such great effect against the attacks of the invading Germans from their victories at Luditz and Küttenburg in 1421 and beyond.[83] These involved a formation of wagons chained together, usually in a square; spear and flail-men guarded the gaps between them, while hand-gunners and crossbowmen shot from within the wagons, further protected by stout pavises or the wooden superstructures of the vehicles. Decimated by the fire and shot of the missilemen, an attacking enemy would then be counter-attacked by the spearmen emerging from within. To facilitate such a tactic two openings were left in the *wagenburg*, at the front and rear, protected by chains and wooden obstacles which could be quickly cleared to allow a sally – in a manner similar to that adopted at Rouvray. How far Fastolf knew of the successes of the Hussite tactics is unknown, and it may well be he was simply adapting existing methods; the

English, and indeed other western armies, had long used wagon defences to protect the rear or flanks of their armies, and such a laager was the only effective method of defending a convoy of these vehicles.[84] Whatever the case, Fastolf's tactics helped neutralise the numerical advantage of the enemy while giving excellent cover to his archers.

After a wait of some two hours the French arrived and formed up out of bowshot of the laager. Yet despite their superior numbers, there was disagreement among the allied commanders as to how best to attack. 'Some,' noted Monstrelet, 'particularly the Scots, wanted to fight on foot, while others preferred to fight on horseback' – the latter presumably hoping to be able to force an entry into the openings of the wagon defence. In the event a joint attack was launched, with the Scots all on foot but with some French still mounted, but 'the English archers began to shoot their arrows thick and fast from the cover of their wagons, and the accuracy was such that both riders and foot-soldiers were driven back'. A fierce attack by Darnley and the Scots on one of the openings was similarly repulsed, and the Franco-Scots withdrew badly mauled, leaving a number of French lords, around 120 knights and between 500 and 600 other attackers dead. The Scots had borne the brunt of the casualties, and both Darnley and his brother William Stewart were killed. Among the English, whose archers had been so well protected by the wagons, there was only one casualty of note ('des gens de nom'), one Bresanteau, nephew of Sir Simon Morbier.[85] After a brief rest to take refreshment, the English column moved off to the village of Rouvray where they spent the night, before setting off for Orléans which they reached in safety.[86]

As Monstrelet remarked, 'King Charles was sick at heart to learn of this further disaster to his fortunes'.[87] Later that year James I promised Charles a fresh Scottish army of 6,000 men as part of the negotiations that resulted in the marriage of his daughter Margaret to the Dauphin, but the Scots king never ratified this element of the treaty. By then, however, Charles had received far more potent aid from the most unexpected of sources, 'Joan the Maid', the young girl from Domremy whose religious fervour and seemingly heaven-sent visions reinvigorated the French. Her relief of Orléans in May 1429 marked an important turn in the fortunes of war, and was quickly followed by the capture of the Loire fortresses of Jargeau, Meung and Beaugency from the now demoralised English. On the same day that Beaugency fell, 18 June, the French army intercepted an English relief force marching from Paris close to the village of Patay. Even before the French attack the English commanders were in disagreement over their strategy; Fastolf, alarmed by the damaging effects of the French run of victories on the morale of his troops, urged a defensive policy of avoiding battle and withdrawing to key strongholds until reinforcements could come from England, while John Talbot, Earl of Shrewsbury, and other captains urged that battle should be given, no doubt arguing that a victory would restore confidence and might eliminate the threat posed by Joan.[88] As it was, however, the English were caught by surprise and, as Monstrelet noted, 'had no time to make their customary defences of sharp stakes stuck in the ground'. At the moment of crisis, moreover, when unified action was vital, they were divided about where they should deploy:

> Some wanted to take up their positions on foot near a hedge in order to prevent a surprise attack from the rear. Others, however, were not satisfied with this kind of strategy, and said they would find more advantageous ground; they turned round and retreated six or seven hundred yards from their former position, which was full of hedges and undergrowth. The French, who preferred to fight on open ground, nearly all dismounted from their horses and continued on foot, their vanguard impatient to attack the English, because they had lately found them to be ill prepared in defence. With a sudden bold onslaught they caught them before they could form up in any order, while Sir John Fastolf and the bastard of Thian, both knights, and their men, who had not dismounted, took flight across the open country to save their lives.[89]

Unable to form up properly, the English were quickly overwhelmed. They suffered heavy casualties, put by Monstrelet at 1,800 dead, while the Lords Scales, Talbot and Hungerford, Sir Thomas Rempstone and other knights were captured, together with much booty. Fastolf, the hero of Rouvray, was bitterly condemned for his cowardice, and was temporarily stripped of his membership of the Order of the Garter.[90] In the wake of the French victory at Patay, a number of key towns including Troyes, Chalons and Rheims surrendered to Charles, who was triumphantly crowned at Rheims on 16 July 1429. Yet Patay had been more of an ambush than a set-piece battle of the likes of Agincourt and Verneuil. It neither marked the collapse of English tactical success, nor led inexorably to the final military failures between 1444 and 1453.[91] When defeat came, it was to be at the hands of a radically reformed French army, and in far more adverse political and military circumstances.

In the meantime, despite the capture of Joan of Arc at Compiègne in May 1430, the French ruler was now far less reliant on Scots forces than he had been in the dark days since 1418. Scots archers and men-at-arms continued to serve with the King of France, such as the substantial force led by Sir Gilbert Kennedy in 1429–30,[92] but the era of major military intervention by the Scots in France during the fifteenth century was over. They left, however, one enduring legacy to the French crown in the form of the famous Garde Écossaise. Scottish archers had already served as bodyguards in the households of the greatest French lords, as in 1401–2 when Louis, Duke of Orléans, had engaged the services of David Lindsay, Earl of Crawford, with 3 men-at-arms, 6 esquires and 12 archers as part of his guard. Under Louis's son Charles, a Scottish esquire named John Stewart appears in 1412 as 'the captain of the archers of the prince'.[93] By 1418 the Dauphin Charles had a bodyguard of Scots archers commanded by John Stewart of Darnley, but as king he established the small but prestigious Garde Écossaise as a permanent feature of the royal household. From 1446 to the end of his reign this Scottish contingent numbered some 26 men-at-arms and 78 archers, supplemented by smaller units of French and German archers.[94] Berry Herald gives a vivid description of the splendour of the archer bodyguards accompanying Charles VII and some of his lords during his triumphal entry into Rouen in 1449:

And before them, in the first rank, were the archers of the King of France, all clad in jackets covered with gold embroidery, of the colour of red, white and green. Those of the King of Sicily, the Count of Maine, and many other lords who were there, to the number of six hundred archers, well mounted, all armed in brigandines and jackets (*jacquettes*) of many and different patterns, over their armour to their legs, and all their swords and daggers and side-arms were covered and ornamented with silver.[95]

Such an image accords well with Jean Fouquet's beautiful illumination of Charles VII as one of the three magi, surrounded by the Garde Écossaise in their splendid uniforms, contained in the Hours of Etienne Chevalier, *c.* 1448–52 (see p. 352).[96] Charles's successors continued to employ these elite Scottish archers, keeping their numbers at around 100 while generally expanding the size of the bodyguard itself. Thus after 1466 the guard comprised 100 archers of the Garde Écossaise and a 100-strong company of French archers, while under Louis XI the royal guard contained 160 gentlemen, 400 archers and 40 crossbowmen – in effect a small army in itself.[97]

JAMES I AND ARCHERY IN SCOTLAND

If by the end of the 1420s the age of the great expeditionary forces to France was over, in Scotland itself the process of military reform in favour of the longbow was still under way. A Scottish parliament at Perth in 1424 acknowledged the shift from an army reliant on formations of spearmen to a host of archers and men-at-arms by enjoining the practice of archery by all able-bodied Scots.[98] The king 'forbiddis that na man play at the fut ball', but instead, on pain of a fine, 'all men busk thame to be archaris' from the age of twelve. Butts (bowmerkis) were to be established in every £10 worth of land, and especially near parish churches, 'quhar upone haly dais men may cum and at the lest schute thrice about and have usage of archery'.[99] In the words of Walter Bower:

There was certainly one statute among the others which the king issued which was most useful for the kingdom and the public interest, namely that the archer's art (*ars architenencium*) should be practised by nearly everybody, at least on feast days, under the threat of fixed money fines, with targets for shooting prepared and erected in every village, especially at the parish churches.[100]

This statute was clearly modelled directly on existing English legislation, hardly surprising given that from his capture at sea by English pirates in 1406 to his eventual release in 1424, James I had been in honourable captivity in England and had seen the English war machine at work when accompanying Henry V on campaign in France in 1420. Presumably the attempts to reform the composition of Scottish expeditionary armies had been set in train under the governorship of Robert, Duke of Albany, but despite the mixed fortunes of the forces of Buchan, Douglas and Darnley in France, James himself, once back in power, rightly saw that an effective archer arm, coupled with a powerful siege train, was badly needed if the Scots were to engage the English on anything like equal military terms. The wappinschaws or regular musters four times a year were revived,[101] while at the same time as he enjoined upon his subjects practice with the bow, James was ordering large quantities of ordnance, including a massive bombard named 'The Lion', from Flemish gun foundries.[102] As early as 1425 merchants coming into the kingdom were, as in England, required to bring with them bowstaves as well as spear-shafts and other munitions.[103] Subsequently, in 1429, parliament laid down that men worth £20 per annum, or holding £100 worth

Depicted as one of the three Magi, Charles VII of France is accompanied by his Garde Écossaise in their resplendent uniforms, in this miniature from the Hours of Etienne Chevalier by Jean Fouquet, *c.* 1448–52. *(Musée Conde, Chantilly, France/Bridgeman Art Library)*

great border castle of Roxburgh, one of the two remaining strongholds in English hands, having issued 'a blanket summons to all laymen who were of the age of discretion (that is between the ages of sixteen and sixty)'.[106] Yet despite a massive bombardment from his new artillery and countless volleys from his archers, the 'Marchmount', as the fortress was known, well supplied and garrisoned by 80 men-at-arms under Sir Ralph Grey, remained impregnable. 'For fifteen days', wrote Bower, 'these men devoted themselves to the siege and earned no praise there; after rashly and incautiously losing enough shooting equipment (*artilia*) and arrows seemingly for the whole kingdom, our men returned home ignominiously without achieving their object.'[107] On the arrival of a powerful English relieving force, the Scots hastily abandoned the siege, leaving James's military reputation seriously damaged.[108] The king's assassination not long afterwards, moreover, saw a backlash against his repressive policies and a neglect of archery training. As Bower lamented in a telling passage:

> After and as a consequence of his sad death, nearly everyone gave up bows and archery equipment without a thought, and devoted themselves to riding with lances, with the result that now at a meeting of magnates you usually find out of one hundred men some eighty lances and scarcely six archers. For this reason the English can now truly say with the Psalmist about the Scots, 'The bow of the brave has been overcome'; and we in turn say of them: 'and the weak have been equipped with strength' [1 Samuel 2:4]. You should therefore read the old chronicles if you will, and you will find that the English have often beaten the Scots by means of their bows.[109]

One would dearly like to know what engagements Bower had in mind when penning these lines, and to which chronicles he would have referred his contemporaries in the 1440s, for the ravages of time have left us with precious little Scottish chronicle material before Bower's own enormous *Scotichronicon*. One glimpse of a Scottish archer may be furnished by a richly illuminated copy of Virgil's *Aeneid*, probably made by a Flemish artist for James I's youngest daughter Leonora before 1449, in which a fully equipped man-at-arms confers with an archer, clutching a longbow and arrows, who wears the traditional long saffron shirt and simple mantle of a Highland Gael in the later Middle Ages.[110] Archers would continue to form a significant element of Scottish forces. In 1455, for example, when there was fear of English attack, it was decreed that the border was to be defended by three forces; on the East and Middle March these were each to comprise 200 lances and 200 archers, while on the West March 100 lances and 100 archers.[111] James II,

of goods, were to serve in the army as mounted men-at-arms, while those worth £10 were to have a helmet, gorget, breast-plate, rerebraces, vambraces and gloves of plate, together with leg armour – presumably to swell the ranks of the men-at-arms with well-equipped spearmen. Yeomen worth £20 were to have 'a good doublet of defence, or a haubergeon, a war hat, with bow, sheaf, sword and buckler', while those worth £10 were to be armed with bows, arrows, sword, buckler and knife, or, if not archers, were to have an axe or a 'broggit [sharp-pointed] staff'.[104] The social status of archers was thus far higher than it had been in King Robert's 1318 assize of arms, when qualification for this weapon was merely the possession of a cow; as in England archers were now men of some substance. In 1431 James was to receive another reminder of the value of archers, this time from his own rebellious Highland subjects. Near Inverlochy a royal force under the Earl of Mar, sent to subdue Lochaber, was routed when confronted by the men of Donald Balloch and assaulted from the flank by 200 archers under Alastair Carrach, uncle of the Lord of the Isles.[105]

In 1436 the intended target of James's new weaponry and his archer levies became clear when the king laid siege to the moreover, continued to forbid football and golf in his statute of 1457, enjoining the practice of the bow on his subjects; each Sunday every man was to shoot at least six times, and 'at ilk paroch kirk a paire of buttis' were to be set up. In a nice touch the fine of 2*d* levied from absentees was to be used to buy drink for those shooting at these butts.[112] Towns and parishes were responsible for the maintenance of the butts, and at Peebles the fees known as 'burgess silver', paid by those newly admitted as burgesses, was allocated for this purpose.[113] Some Scottish archers even took up their bows to fight against the Turk. In 1458, for example, Pope Pius II granted a privilege and safe conduct to Alexander Preston, a canon of Glasgow Cathedral, who had been 'engaged for about a year with twelve archers and more in fighting against the infidel', and his case does not appear to be an isolated one.[114]

Nevertheless, to a well-informed observer like Bower, James I's death had marked the end of a military experiment, and had thus yielded back to the English their crucial superiority in archery. As Donald Watt has observed, 'the change from bows to lances between 1437 and the mid-1440s appears to have been remarkably rapid', and surely marks the reversion to the time-honoured use of the long spear by the bulk of Scottish infantry.[115] In 1471 an act of the Scottish Parliament decreed that no merchant should import billets for spears into the country shorter than 6 ells 'and of a clyft [all of one piece]', while no bowyer was to make spears of any shorter length – a valuable indication that the bowyer's craft might extend to the shaping of pikestaffs as well as bowstaves. Any yeoman 'who cannot deal with a bow' should have a good axe and a targe of leather, cheap because it required only the cost of a hide, 'to resist the shot of England'.[116] A subsequent act in 1481, which envisaged that men would come to the muster in time of war with 'bows, spears and axes', noted that such shields of wood and leather, intended to offer unarmoured infantry of the poorest sort at least some protection against the deadly shafts of the English, were to be modelled on the examples sent to each sheriff.[117] Yet to the great Scottish poet William Dunbar (*c.* 1460–*c.* 1513), it was the spear not the bow that was the

Crossbowmen shooting at the popinjay, watched by two fully armoured comrades holding pavises, from the Behaim Codex, 1505. From at least the reign of Charles V, French kings had encouraged the formation of urban confraternities of crossbowmen and archers, who in return for certain privileges provided a small but highly trained group of elite missilemen in times of war. *(Jagiellonian Library, Cracow)*

national weapon, when in a striking analogy he spoke of Scotland as 'the awfull Thrissill [thistle] . . . kepit with a busche of speiris [a bush of spears]'.[118] And when a major English and Scottish army would next clash, on the field of Flodden in 1513, the Scots, assisted by French military advisers, would attempt a new experiment, that of replacing their usual spears with the great 16ft pike that was beginning to dominate the battlefields of Europe.

ARCHERS OF THE *COMPAGNIES D'ORDONNANCE* AND THE FRANCS-ARCHERS: THE REFORMS OF CHARLES VII

By contrast, just as the Scots were abandoning their experiments in the mass training of archers, their old ally Charles VII was making bowmen an important element in his restructuring of the French military. And unlike his hapless ally James I, Charles was to achieve far greater success in implementing a series of military reforms which were to help turn the tide of war decisively against the English, and to see them driven first from Normandy by 1450 and from Gascony by 1453. Charles had made initial moves to create a standing force in 1439, but in 1445 he took advantage of the truce made the previous year with the English (intended to last twenty years) to create what was in effect a small but professional standing army, his

Compagnies d'Ordonnance.[119] This force consisted of some 12,000 men, formed into twenty companies, with each company comprising 100 *lances fournies*. The lance was a tactical unit, itself made up of one man-at-arms, a coustillier (a trooper armed with a long knife known as a coustille) and a page, two archers and a *valet de guerre* or another archer, all of whom were mounted.[120] Looking back on how Charles had successfully reconquered Normandy from the English, Gilles le Bouvier, Berry King-at-Arms, noted how well equipped and paid these lances were:

the King of France had brought his army and troops into such good order in regard to his men-at-arms that it was an excellent thing. That is to say, all his men-at-arms and archers were well and safely clad; the men-at-arms were provided each with three horses, one for himself, one for his page, and one for his servant (*varlet*); all were armed in cuirasses (*armez de cuirasses*), and armour for the legs, sallets and swords, all garnished with silver, and lances, which the pages of each carried. The said servants were armed with a sallet, brigandine, jack or haubergeon, and with an axe or guisarme. And each of the said men-at-arms had for his lance two mounted archers, armed for the most part with brigandines, armour for the legs, and sallets, many of which were ornamented with silver; and at the least all of them had good jacks or haubergeons. And the said men-at-arms and the archers on foot were paid and had their wages once a month, besides which they were allowed, during the said war of Normandy, to take prisoners, and to ransom horses or any other cattle whatsoever, provided that at the time the said persons were on the side of the English. But they might not take victuals of any kind without paying for them, in any place whatsoever, excepting from the English aforesaid and those persons who were on their side who were found making war and in arms. These they might lawfully take prisoners . . .[121]

These companies, well paid and provisioned, were stationed in royal castles and cities throughout Charles VII's domains, with fifteen kept in northern France, the Langue d'Oïl, and five in the south, the Langue d'Oc. Though they could be combined for major operations, each company was intended to be a flexible force, combining heavy and light cavalry with archers, mounted for rapid manoeuvrability, and now provided with the kind of mobile power of shot that English armies had enjoyed from their mounted archers from the outset of the war in 1337.[122] Like John the Fearless, Charles fully recognised the importance of longbowmen. Whereas in the early fifteenth century the ratio of men-at-arms to missilemen had been 2:1,

and the crossbow had been the weapon of preference, the archers of Charles's companies were in greater numbers and wielded the longbow.[123] 'When the king loses us, he'll lose his kingdom,' one of the archers of the *ordonnance* is recorded as having boasted.[124]

Though the archers of the *Compagnies* would generally have fought on foot, Charles, like his predecessors, still lacked an efficient infantry force. He had continued the earlier royal policy of encouraging urban fraternities of archers as well as crossbowmen.[125] In 1437 he confirmed the privileges of the 60-strong fraternity of crossbowmen of the city of Paris, and those of the archers of the same city.[126] In 1445 he granted permission for the establishment of a confraternity of 50 archers at Euregenies, near Tournai, with its own 'king' and constable like existing archery confraternities. His privilege explained how, although these men were renowned as the best archers in this region (on the marches of the Empire, Hainault and Flanders), they had up till then no sworn brotherhood, and as a result could not engage in competitions with confraternities in neighbouring towns and villages, so that their practice of archery was in danger of neglect.[127] The following year he also confirmed the statutes and privileges of the crossbowmen of Tournai. They were allowed to carry their crossbows and other weapons anywhere in the realm for their own protection, and to wear the king's livery badge on their coats or hats. If anyone was wounded or killed by accident when the crossbowmen were practising at the butts in a public place, the king granted his pardon, provided adequate safety measures had been taken to secure the shooting range.[128]

Yet though such measures provided a number of skilled marksmen, far more radical steps were needed to obtain an adequate supply of archers for war against the English. Charles thus sought to supplement the elite archers of the companies through the creation of a territorial militia known as the Francs-archers.[129] He no doubt called to mind not only the Scots' promotion of archery through legislation, but also the earlier reforms attempted by his grandfather Charles V, which had envisaged a universal obligation on his subjects to practise with bows and crossbows.[130] Charles VII, however, adopted a more realistic model for the creation of a skilled reservoir of bowmen, achieved through selection and financial incentives and better suited to a country in which, unlike England, the longbow was not the ubiquitous 'national weapon'. Yet such a scheme had already been put into operation by the Duke of Brittany in the 1430s, and it is likely that this formed the immediate inspiration of Charles's own measures.[131] By an ordinance of 1448 it was stipulated that in time of war all parishes in the kingdom were to provide archers or crossbowmen in the ratio of one archer from every 120, 80 or 50 hearths. The archer was

THE IMPACT OF THE LONGBOW IN FIFTEENTH-CENTURY EUROPE

to be well equipped with 'a sallet, dagger, sword, bow, sheaf, jack, and a short coat of mail'. These men were to be of some standing, to be selected by the regional royal officials (*prévôts*) 'from among the better endowed and more prosperous as may be found in each parish'. They were 'to prepare themselves with their above-mentioned equipment on all feasts and holidays, so that they may become more skilled and accustomed to the said way of life', and took an oath to serve the king faithfully against all men. In return, the bowmen gained freedom from the majority of taxation, and were not obligated to provide billeting for troops or to perform guard duty – hence the name Franc-archer ('free-archer').[132]

In addition, each Franc-archer received 4 francs a month, the same pay as archers of the *Compagnies d'Ordonnance*. It seems, however, there was little love lost between the two groups of archers. A plea for pardon of homicide records how one François Queret from the company of Anthoine de Chabannes, at a fair at Thors in the Saintonge, had asked one of the Francs-archers, Jean Guilloteau, to exchange daggers with him. Jean refused, saying the king himself had given him the dagger, but was met by the scornful response that the king had never heard of the likes of him. When François went on to boast how, by contrast, the archers of the companies were invaluable to the king, a fight broke out and Jean was slain.[133] A further edict of 1451 stated that each Franc-archer was to be equipped, at the expense of his local community, with a jack or brigandine, a sallet, sword and dagger. Royal inspectors were to make periodic reviews of local musters, and, as in England, legislation enjoined constant practice to maintain skilful shooting. Such organised reserves formed a reservoir of competent missilemen whose numbers under Charles VII probably reached around 8,000.[134] As Philippe Contamine has noted, the Francs-archers can be seen either as the extension into the countryside of the urban confraternities of archers and crossbowmen, or as 'a direct extension of the former general *arrière-ban*, no longer considered usable'.[135] As with many obligations to the crown, towns and local communities attempted to barter with the king. In 1448, for example, Poitiers managed to reduce its quota of 30 Francs-archers down to only 12, and again in 1467 from 24 to 18.[136]

The French chronicler Robert Blondel regarded the Francs-archers as being intended as a deliberate counter to the English longbowmen,[137] yet despite their numbers the impact of the Francs-archers on the final stages of the Hundred Years War is hard to gauge. They may well have played a useful auxiliary role in the siege warfare that dominated the campaigns following the expiry of the truce in 1449; that year, for example, 4,000 Francs-archers took part in the successful siege of Harfleur, and in 1450 there were 2,000 of them at the siege of Caen.[138]

Perhaps fortunately, however, they were never pitted against the English in open combat. That Charles's successor Louis XI initially believed them to be of value is indicated by the fact that in 1466, following the War of the Public Weal, he doubled their number to some 16,000. They were now organised into four regional groupings of 4,000, each commanded by a captain-general and subdivided into seven units. In an attempt to create mixed units of what in the sixteenth century would be termed 'pike and shot', the divisions of Francs-archers were also to contain pikemen and men armed with gisarmes.[139] Yet despite the increase in their strength, they performed poorly at Guinegatte in 1479, when their indiscipline played a large part in the defeat of a French force, numbering some 1,200 men from the *ordonnance* and 8,000 Francs-archers, by Duke Maximilian of Austria.[140] Like the 'select bands' of the Tudor shires to which they were likened by Oman, the real Achilles' heel of the Francs-archers was not the individual marksmanship of the bowmen but the lack of cohesion and effective training.[141] Thereafter Louis turned increasingly to pikemen, raised primarily from the Swiss, to provide the mainstay of infantry for French armies.[142]

A far more significant factor in Charles VII's ultimate triumph over the English was his formidable artillery train, developed by the famous Jean Bureau, the king's *maître d'artillerie*, and his brother Gaspard.[143] The French weapons were not necessarily more advanced in technological terms than those available to the English, but Charles had more guns and the logistics of his artillery were superbly managed, sieges being laid with methodical, even scientific precision.[144] 'He had such a great number of large bombards, large cannon, fowlers, serpentines, crapaudine, ribaudequines and culverins', noted Berry Herald, 'that no one can remember any Christian king ever having such great artillery.'[145] In some cases, as at Rouen in 1449, the outnumbered English garrisons found it impossible to effect a sustained resistance in the face of mounting hostility from townsmen and local inhabitants and were forced to yield towns and strongholds on terms. Where they stood their ground, however, the French guns and bombards methodically pounded the remaining English fortresses into submission. In 1449–50, in one year and six days, the Bureau's artillery was responsible for reducing no fewer than sixty fortified places in Normandy.[146] 'It was a wonderful thing', added Berry Herald, 'to see the bulwarks, approaches, trenches and mines which these said persons made before all the castles and towns which were besieged during the war. For in truth there was no place which surrendered which could not have been taken by the valour and skill of the troops who were there.'[147] Ironically, however, it was a pitched battle that was finally to seal the fate of

Lancastrian Normandy, for under the skilled leadership of the Count of Clermont and the Constable, Arthur de Richemont, the *Compagnies d'Ordonnance* were to forcefully demonstrate their determination and discipline by inflicting a crushing defeat on the English at Formigny, worse even than that of Baugé.[148]

'WELL-NIGH THE FIRST FOUGHTEN FIELD THEY GAT ON THE ENGLISH': FORMIGNY, 15 APRIL 1450, CASTILLON, 17 JULY 1453, AND THE ENGLISH EXPULSION FROM FRANCE

There had been few major engagements in the field since Patay, and as with Joan of Arc's campaigns in 1429–30 the final stages of the war were dominated by sieges, raids and ambuscades. The failure of the English siege of Orléans had witnessed the end of English attempts to expand the Pays de Conquête, and their position had been seriously weakened by the failure of the alliance with Burgundy in 1435, together with the loss of control over Paris and the Île de France, and the death of Bedford in the same year.[149] Nevertheless, they had made a significant recovery in the 1430s, and they achieved a number of notable successes, principally under the skilled command of John, Lord Talbot.[150] In 1437, for example, Talbot ambushed and routed a French force twice his number at Ry near Rouen, took the strategically vital town of Pontoise by surprise – his troops wore white clothes as camouflage in the snow[151] – and even attempted an assault on Paris itself. In 1438 he drove off a Burgundian force besieging Le Crotoy, and in 1440 launched a surprise attack at Avranches on the French army under the Constable, Richemont, putting it igno-miniously to flight.[152] Despite being neglected by domestic chroniclers, this latter engagement was a remarkable feat of

arms, whereby the English undertook a bold outflanking march by picking their way at low tide through the treacherous sands of the Cousenon estuary, feeling for the hard ground with their lance points. By so doing, they completely turned the flank of Richemont's forces, which were established in a strong position to bar any attempt to cross the river.[153] This was an offensive engagement worthy of comparison to Dagworth's victories at La Roche Derrien and Auberoche.

Many political, fiscal and logistical factors contributed to the final defeat of the English in the closing decades of the Hundred Years War, but these campaigns go a long way towards refuting the belief that among the most significant military factors was the stagnation of tactical thinking and a failure to adapt to changing circumstances. For Oman, the failure in France starkly revealed 'the inadequacy of the old English system of tactics, the game of the defensive battle accepted on an advantageous ground, to fit all the vicissitudes of war. Commanders who had received the tradition of Poitiers and Agincourt disliked assuming the offensive.'[154] While such criticism might be partially justified in Kyriel's failure to switch from the defensive to the offensive at a critical stage during the

Heavily armed archers lead an assault on a town, supported by crossbowmen who shoot from behind the cover of a large pavise. From a tapestry depicting the *Histoire du Fort Roy Clovis, c.* 1468, possibly owned by Philip the Good of Burgundy, in the Palais de Tau, Rheims. *(akg-images/Gilles Mermet)*

John Talbot being invested either as Earl of Shrewsbury or as Marshal of France by King Henry VI, from a miniature at the beginning of a copy of Christine de Pizan's *Livre des fais d'armes*, contained in the Shrewsbury Book, a collection of chivalric works and romances presented by Talbot to Margaret of Anjou, Henry's queen in 1445. (British Library, Royal MS 15 E VI, f.405). *(© British Library/Heritage Images)*

battle of Formigny, it hardly fits with the aggressive and often highly successful use of the offensive by Talbot. Nor does it square with the opinion of the French veteran Jean de Bueil, who in his *Le Jouvencel*, written about 1466, summed up French tactical thinking a decade after the close of the war. If battle was to be given, the commander should seek to deploy using the most favourable terrain available, placing his men-at-arms in the centre and archers on the wings:

> And first of all, for combat on foot, if you find yourself in formation drawn up without fortification, it is necessary that the main division should be elongated. And for this reason, the bulk of the men-at-arms should be placed in the centre, and the archers and other missilemen on the wings, if there are any of these. And to guard the missilemen, a certain number of men-at-arms need to be placed at the end of the wings, according to their available strength.[155]

There was little different here from the battle formations of Christine de Pizan, of the 'Somme Plan' or of John of Burgundy in 1417, but Le Bueil went on strongly to counsel against taking the offensive: 'A formation on foot should never march forward, but should always hold steady and await its enemies on foot . . . A force which marches before another force is defeated unless God grants it grace. And, therefore, take up a position as advantageous as possible and do it early.'[156] The French had lost at Agincourt and Verneuil for this reason, but so too, he noted, had the English at Baugé, Patay and Castillon,

and the Swiss at St Jacob-en-Birs. At Formigny, however, the French did succeed in taking the offensive successfully, as they were able to attack the English on two fronts.

Nevertheless, one major factor in explaining the absence of a decisive English victory on the scale of Agincourt or Verneuil in the last decades of the war was the caution of French commanders in avoiding such major engagements in the first place. At Meaux in 1439, for example, Richemont did not attempt to stop Talbot revictualling the garrison and refused his open challenge to battle. Talbot was eventually forced to withdraw, and Richemont took the town.[157] It had been Richemont's resolute adherence to a strong defensive position at Avranches that had compelled the English to adopt their bold but extremely risky flanking march in order to give battle on their own terms. French reluctance to risk a pitched battle was most graphically demonstrated in 1441, when the English under Warwick and Talbot played a remarkable cat-and-mouse game with Charles's army, with both armies crossing and recrossing the Oise and the Seine; the French finally escaped but came within an ace of being trapped by the two English forces in a superb display of generalship by Talbot.[158] So famous was this campaign that in 1476 at the reburial of Richard of York, Talbot's fellow commander, it was recalled with pride 'how he passed the river at Pontoise and drove away the French king'.[159] Had Charles been captured, the course of the war and the fate of Lancastrian Normandy might have been very different.

Effective prosecution of the war, however, was being increasingly undermined by bitter political divisions, ultimately stemming from the crucial failure of the incompetent and sporadically insane Henry VI, and by crippling fiscal problems. Changes in military organisation, moreover, which moved away from the traditional system of armies raised by tightly knit retinues under the sole command of figures such as Bedford, were hampering the effectiveness of the English forces. The English government had attempted to create an increasingly professional standing army in Normandy, through the appointment of military commanders, the implementation of a formal process of muster and review, and attempts to closely control the nature of recruitment – even to the extent of forbidding men involved in crafts, merchants and those who held land from joining up. In 1430 it was stipulated that in order to obtain men disinterested in local conditions of the occupation in Normandy, retinue captains were not to recruit from their neighbourhoods. No more than half of their men-at-arms could be drawn from native French troops, while significantly *all* archers were to be English, Irish, Welsh or Gascon.[160] This provision had less to do with an assumption of the superiority of bowmen from these areas, than with their greater reliability at a time of mounting hostility to English rule by the native population. Nevertheless, in the process the close personal bond between captains and the men of their retinues, which had formed so vital an element in the cohesiveness of English armies, had become increasingly eroded by a regular influx of new troops from English expeditionary forces and by the employment not only of 'creus' or additional troops not directly bound to a captain, but also of the 'gens vivans sur le pays', those leaderless and undisciplined soldiers who had been made redundant following the loss of English garrisons in the Île de France in 1435. Increasingly short periods of service, moreover, meant that there was too rapid a turnover of personnel in retinues. Only three months' service was common, giving captains no time to establish effective control over their men, leading to problems of desertion and of poor discipline, particularly in relation to the civilian population.[161] Above all, the prosecution of the war was fatally compromised by the increasing interference of the king's council in England in the operation of war, the concomitant reduction in independence and executive powers of commanders, and above all by the bitter court factionalism which directly affected both military policy and the appointment of key personnel in Normandy. This ultimately led to a disastrous failure in centralised military control and a complete breakdown in the ability to organise and pay troops at a time when military reverses made the supply of regular wages crucial as the only fiscal incentive available to soldiers.[162]

It had long become apparent that the system initiated by Henry V and Bedford, whereby land had been granted to men in return for specified military service, had failed to provide adequate forces even for defensive needs, making commanders heavily reliant on expeditionary forces from England for any effective operations. In 1435 Sir John Fastolf had recommended that the maintenance of the English position in France depended on a strategy which avoided protracted and expensive siege warfare, and in which the borders should be maintained by two permanent field forces of around 750 'lances' each, led by two commanders and capable of supporting both each other and any threatened garrisons. These forces were to undertake offensive operations by a relentless process of ravaging enemy territory each campaigning season from June to November, for a period of at least three years, to defeat Charles VII by a bitter war of attrition.[163] Fastolf's plan, however, was never implemented, and though the later 1430s had seen a number of armies dispatched from England, it was increasingly necessary to deplete garrisons to form field forces in order to counter French attacks. The Duke of York, for example, took no fewer than 300 lances and 900 archers from the Norman garrisons to enable him to besiege Tancarville.[164] In 1443 a sizeable army was scraped together, but under the incompetent leadership of John Beaufort, Duke of Somerset, it achieved nothing, save to spend the wages desperately needed by York's garrisons. Despite the bitter opposition of the Duke of Gloucester and others who favoured a vigorous prosecution of the war, Henry VI's marriage in 1444 to Charles VII's niece, Margaret of Anjou, led to the cession of the strategically vital county of Maine, for which the English gained not peace but only a truce which was ended by a French offensive in 1449. Starved of adequate supplies of money and of men, disastrously led by Somerset, and facing ever more vigorous resistance from many of the native French, the English position in Normandy had become critical.

The government responded by dispatching an expeditionary force of 425 men-at-arms and 2,080 archers under Sir Thomas Kyriel, which landed at Cherbourg on 15 March 1450 and soon recaptured Valognes. It was, however, indicative of the comparative weakness of Kyriel's army that the English had felt obliged to strip several of their remaining garrisons to swell its numbers: 600 men from Caen under Robert Ver, 800 from Bayeux under Sir Matthew Gough, and 400 from Vire under Henry Norbury.[165] Marching to the relief of Bayeux, the English force was intercepted at Formigny, between Carentan and Bayeux, by the Count of Clermont at the head of 600 *lances garnies*. This gave the French a force of some 3,000 men, comprising 600 men-at-arms, 1,200 mounted archers, 600 coustilliers and the same number of valets, supported by a body of local levies. As the French outriders began to engage with the English, their two leading captains, Kyriel and Gough, chose their ground and prepared a defensive position to the west of the village athwart the Carentan–Bayeux road, with their rear guarded by the little stream of the Ruisseau du Val. The description of their dispositions given by the French chronicler Robert Blondel, whose account of the battle is the fullest, is of particular importance:

> The battle lines of the English were handsomely drawn up. Three-fold ranks, like the solid wall of a city, drove away the attack of the enemy. Three units of archers, each composed of 700 men, were placed like three firm towers, two at the extremities of the battles and the other in the centre. Drawn up as a defence, these kept the attack of the enemy at a distance, lest it break the lines of the men-at-arms.[166]

Blondel further explains that the 'three-fold' ranks behind these archer formations had men-at-arms in the front row, but since these were so few in number the second row comprised billmen and the third archers.

The French did not attack immediately, for they were awaiting reinforcement by Arthur de Richemont, the Constable, who was marching to their aid from St Lô. This gave the English time to strengthen their position by digging a wide and deep trench across their front, while the archers placed their stakes before them.[167] 'They made large holes and trenches with their daggers and swords before them', noted Berry Herald, 'in order that the French and their horses should stumble if they attacked them. And at the distance of a long bowshot behind the English there was a little river, with a great abundance of gardens full of various trees, as apples, pears, elms and other trees; and they encamped in this place because they could not be attacked in the rear.'[168] At length, however, Clermont, apparently against the advice of his more experienced commanders such as Admiral Pegent de Coëtivy, ordered attacks against the English flanks, but the French assaults, supported by some 1,500 French archers, were thrown back.[169] To assist a breakthrough, the French master of the royal ordnance, Giraud, brought up two culverins (*columbrinas*) or field pieces, whose fire was sufficiently galling to cause a formation of archers to sally out in strength and attack the French, forcing their line back about the space of a bowshot. They succeeded in capturing the guns, which they dragged back to their lines.[170] Nevertheless, a French knight, Pierre de Brezé, rallied the fleeing French archers and in turn led a flanking unit of French men-at-arms to engage with those English archers who had moved beyond

their defences. After a sharp fight they succeeded in recovering the guns.[171] This seems to have been the critical stage of the battle, for had Kyriel launched an all-out counter-attack he might very well have succeeded in routing Clermont's forces before Richemont could come to his aid.[172] But instead of attempting to defeat the French in detail, the English commanders chose to remain on the defensive. The reasons for this decision, which earned Kyriel and Gough the opprobrium of several later historians,[173] is lost to us, but it was to cost the English dear.

As the English regrouped behind their defences, Clermont's forces launched a full-scale attack, dismounting their men-at-arms and fiercely engaging with Kyriel's line. For some time the engagement hung in the balance, but then Richemont's force, consisting of 300 lances (comprising some 1,200 men) and probably an additional 800 archers,[174] reached the field from the direction of Trevières to the south of Formigny. Richemont rode in person to find Clermont and they agreed how best to coordinate their attack. Richemont advanced his forces across the Ruisseau du Val, so that his left flank swung round to join forces with the right wing of Clermont's army, still hotly engaged with the English. Kyriel, alerted to Richemont's advance and finding both his rear and left flank now threatened, attempted to extricate himself from this dangerous position by turning the left flank of his army to meet Richemont's oncoming troops, while his right still held Clermont's divisions. But changing formations during a battle, even immediately prior to an engagement, was an extremely dangerous manoeuvre; planned withdrawal could all too easily be mistaken for flight, shaking the morale of even well-disciplined troops. Vegetius had strongly counselled against it, and in *Le Jouvencel* Jean de Bueil explicitly cites Formigny as an example of the practice leading to disaster.[175] Though Kyriel may have had no choice, it seems that his need to withdraw men from his existing front so weakened it that under a renewed assault by Clermont's division the English right collapsed in confusion. According to Chartier, Gough and Ver had fled at the approach of Richemont's force, and seeing this Kyriel fell back on the stream and village, but at the bridge a strong detachment of the Constable's archers dismounted and 'fought against the flank of the English formation', inflicting heavy casualties.[176] Caught between the attacks of the two French forces, the English formation disintegrated. Kyriel, Norbury and many men-at-arms were taken prisoner, but a bloody slaughter followed of the rank and file in which the French gave little quarter. At least some of the archers were cut down as they attempted to yield. The English army was virtually obliterated, and with it went any last hope that Normandy could be held. The dead, possibly not as many as

French cavalry attack the English force of dismounted men-at-arms and archers at the battle of Formigny, 1450, from Jean Chartier's *Chroniques de Charles VII*. From Paris, Bibliothèque Nationale, MS fr. 2691. *(Bibliothèque Nationale, Paris)*

the official French estimate of 3,774 but still very great, were buried in fourteen separate grave-pits around the site.[177]

When in his continuation of John Hardyng's *Chronicle* the Tudor historian Richard Grafton observed that Formigny was 'well-nigh the first foughten field they gat on the English', he was not ignoring the earlier defeats at Baugé and Patay.[178] Rather, he was drawing a distinction between these reverses and a defeat in a set-piece battle which had not begun suddenly and in which at the outset the English had had ample time to prepare defensive positions. The battle, however, hardly demonstrates the stagnation of English tactics; Formigny, as the French chroniclers freely admit, was a long and hard-fought battle. What might have occurred had Kyriel not attempted to redeploy but had stood his ground will never be known, but Richemont's skilled attack had caught the English in a pincer movement from which they could not recover. By contrast, as the French narratives also make clear, the archers of Richemont's companies must take a good deal of the credit for the eventual victory.[179] While several sources recount the fight over the French culverins in the first stages of the battle, their role should not be overstressed; they had been used to some effect to gall the English, but had only provoked a sally in strength from behind the enemy's defences, not a full-scale attack such as Henry V's archers had brought about by their mass volleys. It was without doubt, however, the guns of Jean Bureau that were to decide the final engagement of the war.

By the 1440s artillery defences in strongholds and in fortified field camps were becoming increasingly sophisticated,[180] and it was against the latter type of fortification that John Talbot led his men for the last time at Castillon on the Dordogne on 17 July 1453.[181] Rather than forming lines of circumvallation, the French besiegers of Castillon had constructed, under the direction of Jean Bureau, a strongly defended encampment, with a rampart of earth strengthened with tree trunks, bristling with serpentines, culverins and other pieces of artillery. If the English were to relieve the town, they would have to assault a formidable obstacle. Marching from Bordeaux, Talbot had struck with his usual speed and surprise, attacking with only his advance guard but routing a force of some 1,000 French archers posted in the outlying priory of St Laurent. Fatally, however, he mistook the fact that some French troops and horses were leaving the camp (to obtain fodder, it seems) for a general French panic and flight. He rapidly advanced on the camp with his men-at-arms, 'but without his foot-soldiers whom he had left behind'. Too late Talbot realised his mistake, yet despite the fact that the majority of his troops and his artillery had not yet arrived on the field, he none the less ordered the assault, despite the wiser counsel of Sir Thomas Evringham. But just as the English had cut down the French attackers at Mauleon and Guissen from their artillery *boulevards* or outworks in 1449,[182] so now the French guns took a terrible toll of Talbot's men. French crossbowmen, protected by their ramparts, also inflicted serious casualties.[183] Some of the Anglo-Gascon force reached the ramparts but their numbers were too few. Their fate was sealed when an elite force of Breton troops posted as a reserve well beyond the camp assailed the heavily engaged English from their right flank. Talbot himself, unhorsed by a cannon ball that hit his charger, lay trapped beneath it, and had his skull cleft by a French soldier's axe.[184] With the death of this great leader, the Anglo-Gascons broke and fled, suffering many further casualties in the rout which followed. Just as the defeat at Formigny had spelt the end for English rule in Normandy, so that of Castillon rapidly led to the final and complete French conquest of Gascony, marking the end of a struggle for control which had lasted since the twelfth century. Calais now remained the only English possession on French soil.

To regard the final English defeats in France as somehow representing the failure of the longbow and of English tactics is misleading. Had the English been united under a strong king who had been an able warleader, or who at least had possessed the capacity to appoint talented generals and furnish them with the money and men needed, the fate of Lancastrian France might have been very different. As it was, the catastrophic incapacity of Henry VI had resulted in domestic dissension which strangled the effective prosecution of the war at a time when the French were rallying under a determined and skilful monarch. While English resources were increasingly limited, the French had enjoyed an enormous advantage in manpower, which had allowed them to field several armies concurrently for joint operations – four in Normandy in 1449–50, for example, and three in Gascony in 1453. Even after the expulsion of the English, Charles 'always kept on foot an army of fifteen hundred lances and five or six thousand archers, who received regular wages as follows – for men-at-arms with three horses, fifteen florins a month from the royal mint, and for archers, seven florins a month. These sums were raised by taxes on the good towns and villages, and so regularly collected that the payments were never in arrears'.[185] For all its efficacy in battle, the longbow had never been a war-winning weapon, and could not by itself make up for the critical political, fiscal and strategic shortcomings which resulted in the ultimate failure of English arms in the late 1440s and 1450s.

Charles the Bold, Duke of Burgundy (1446–77), after Rogier van der Weyden (Dahlem Museum, Berlin). *(akg-images)*

Paradoxically, France, which for over a century had had the most exposure to the potentially devastating power of massed archery, proved the least successful in adapting the longbow to its own military advantage. By the later fifteenth century the pike was becoming the dominant infantry weapon in Europe, and French monarchs hired increasingly large numbers of Swiss pikemen and German Landsknechts. Such reliance on foreign infantry was to result in a comparative neglect of their own infantry forces, and the missile arm in particular; while crossbowmen continued to serve in considerable numbers until the 1520s, and the weapon itself finally disappeared only in the 1560s, the French were slow to develop the potential of the arquebus, with hand-gunners only becoming a significant force in the second half of the sixteenth century. With the expulsion of the English from Guienne and all of northern France save Calais, the main threat to the kingdom of France now came from the powerful and expansionist Burgundian state.[186] The true heir of Charles VII's reforms, and of the impact of the longbow on the continent, was Burgundy, a state growing increasingly powerful from the mid-fifteenth century, and which, under the energetic leadership of Duke Charles the Bold, would develop the most sophisticated standing army yet seen in medieval Europe.

'THICKER THAN ARROWS IN AN ENGLISH BATTLE': ARCHERY IN THE ARMIES OF CHARLES THE BOLD

In 1467 the youthful, energetic and boundlessly ambitious Charles the Bold succeeded his father as Duke of Burgundy. He inherited, as we have seen earlier in this chapter, a military legacy which placed considerable importance on the provision of archers and which was heavily influenced by English practice.[187] His reign was to see archers retain a key role in his extensive military reforms, and the duke doubtless agreed with the opinion of his former counsellor, Philippe de Commynes, that 'Archers are the most necessary thing in the world for an army; but they should be counted in their thousands, for in small numbers they are worthless.'[188] English influence had been remembered long after the collapse of the Anglo-Burgundian alliance in 1435. At the engagements of Oudenaarde, Ghent and Gavre in 1452–3 the army of Philip the Good broke up the enemy's formations of pike and archers with archers and gunfire, before charging with cavalry.[189] Similarly, in one of Charles's first major engagements, the battle of Montlhéry in 1465 against Louis XI of France, all the Burgundian men-at-arms had been initially instructed to fight on foot after the English manner. As Philippe de Commynes remarked,

> it was then the most honourable practice among the Burgundians that they should dismount with the archers, and always a great number of gentlemen did so that the common soldiers might be reassured and fight better. They had learnt this method from the English, with whom Duke Philip had fought in his youth in France for thirty-two years without truce.[190]

Similarly, prior to the main engagement, a Burgundian advance guard under the Count of St Pol had responded to the arrival of the French vanguard by dismounting its men-at-arms and archers to await reinforcements within a protective enclosure of wagons, as had been done by the English at Rouvray in 1428.[191] As the main Burgundian army drew up, the archers seem to have been redeployed behind defensive stakes, for as Commynes recorded, 'we found the archers with their boots off and with a stake driven into the ground before them, and there were many barrels of wine broached for them to drink. . . . I have never seen men more willing to fight, which seemed a good sign and was very comforting.'[192] Nevertheless, Charles the Bold was by no means wedded to the use of dismounted men-at-arms; in the preliminaries to Montlhéry he changed his mind from a general order to dismount to one for the majority of his men-at-arms to remount, although a number of knights and squires, including the Lord of Cordes and Sir Philippe de Lalaing, were to remain on foot. Such a change of heart, admitted Commynes, caused the Burgundians much inconvenience and lost a great deal of time, during which Charles could have seized the initiative.

Commynes's detailed description of the developing battle of Montlhéry allows us to see the role of archers in a way impossible for any contemporary engagements in England during the Wars of the Roses. The battle itself began when a fierce skirmish developed around the village of Montlhéry between the Burgundian archers, who 'were disorderly and without a commander as frequently happens when skirmishes

start', and the well-disciplined archers from the French *Compagnies d'Ordonnance*, sporting gold-embroidered uniforms. Strength in numbers, however, gave the Burgundians the advantage, and using doors from the houses to shield themselves they moved forward, firing the village and driving off the French. Nevertheless, as the main Burgundian force began to advance towards the French positions, crucial mistakes were made that hampered the bowmen's effective deployment in an offensive role. The Burgundian commanders had agreed before the battle that as the two armies were so far apart, and separated by fields full of ripe crops, their forces should rest twice during the advance 'to give the foot-soldiers time to catch their breath' and dress their ranks. In the event, Charles advanced at full speed and the archers, who were already in poor order as they began their march on foot at the head of the army, were exhausted by the time they reached the French positions. Then, as the French men-at-arms emerged from either side of a large hedge that had protected their front, the undisciplined Burgundian horse charged forward through their own archers, 'who were the pride and joy of the army, without giving them time to shoot'. By such a failure of discipline, reminiscent of the French at Crécy in 1346, 'they forfeited their chief hope of victory'.[193] On the right flank Charles achieved notable success with a cavalry charge and gave lengthy pursuit to the French, but the Burgundian left wing collapsed as its infantry were overwhelmed by the French horse. The battle ended in a confused stalemate, with both sides attempting to rally their scattered forces.

Despite their evident lack of cohesion in combat, as evinced at Montlhéry, Burgundian archers were clearly an essential element in Burgundian forces by the 1460s, and continued to play an important role in the battles of Montenaeken (1465) and Brusthem (1467). In the latter engagement the Burgundian vanguard, comprising dismounted men-at-arms and archers supported by field artillery, led a successful attack against the fortified village of Brusthem, held by a powerful force of Liègeois, storming the defences which included water-filled ditches and taking the enemy's artillery. Nevertheless, the subsequent failure of the Burgundians to direct adequate artillery fire against their opponents allowed the Liègeois to counter-attack. As Commynes notes:

> When our men shot and missed the Liègeois rallied and with their long pikes (very useful weapons) they charged our archers and their leaders in one mass and killed four or five hundred men in one moment. At that point, all our standards began to give way as if routed. Immediately, the duke ordered up the archers of his company, under the leadership of Sir Philip de Crèvecoeur, Lord of Cordes, and several other noblemen, who with a loud cry

attacked the Liègeois, who were likewise defeated almost instantaneously.[194]

Though the Burgundians had ultimately gained the victory, Brusthem had revealed the vulnerability of both archers and men-at-arms when caught in open ground by a charge of massed pikemen, and was to prove only a foretaste of their crushing defeats at the hands of the Swiss in 1476 and 1477.

Duke Charles not only recruited archers from his widespread lands, but also hired English archers in considerable numbers. As early as 1467 500 English archers are found among the ducal forces at the battle of Brusthem.[195] The renewed Anglo-Burgundian alliance led Edward IV to promise several thousand English troops in 1472, but only a small retinue of 11 men-at-arms, 27 mounted archers and 16 foot-archers is actually recorded as receiving pay that year.[196] By 1473, however, there were sufficient of them to play a notable role at the Burgundian siege of Nijmegen,[197] and the following year Edward dispatched 13 men-at-arms and 1,000 archers to Charles. Following the treaty of Picquigny in 1475 between Edward and Louis XI, some 2,000 Englishmen of Edward's former expeditionary force took service with the Duke of Burgundy. That year the ducal guard alone contained eight companies of mounted English archers, and by 1476 four 100-strong contingents of English bowmen were in Charles's pay. During his fateful campaigns against the Swiss, Charles retained more than ten companies of 100 English mounted archers, some of whom saw action at Morat in 1476, while many perished in the disastrous defeat at Nancy in 1477.[198]

These English archers had gained considerable renown for their fighting abilities. At the siege of Neuss, where Englishmen under the captaincy of Sir John Middleton had formed one of Charles's companies of ordinance, the Count of Chimay noted that 'the English have been more watched and admired in our army and better esteemed than were our robes of cloth of gold and costly adornments at the last feast of the Golden Fleece', the great Burgundian chivalric order of knighthood. Describing the hardships of the besiegers, he also remarked that 'shot from hackbutts and culverins flies at us thicker than arrows in an English battle'.[199] The English also lived up to their reputation for quarrelsome behaviour. During the same siege some English had come to blows with each other over a woman and Duke Charles himself went to break up the fracas, but he only narrowly avoided being killed when the English, not immediately recognising him, shot several arrows at him. This caused them in turn to be attacked by outraged Burgundian troops, but after some had been slain Charles eventually quelled the disturbance and pardoned the English 'for he regarded them as his friends and subjects'.[200] In March 1476, shortly after the defeat at Grandson, the duke was once again forced to intervene in a quarrel between some of his Italian troops and the English, who, noted the Milanese ambassador sourly, 'are proud people without respect and they claim superiority over every other nation'. Charles then had to quell an open mutiny by English archers demanding their pay.[201] Nevertheless, the great value placed on the English bowmen by the duke was reflected in their higher pay; when payment was made to the army at Morat in June 1476 other mounted archers received 16s each, but the English received 20s.[202]

Nevertheless, Charles always regarded the archers as but one element of the combined arms system which he attempted to develop. From his earliest military experiences, such as at

Archers and mounted men-at-arms, from the *Chronicles of the Counts of Flanders*, 1477. From Holkham Hall, MS 659, f.121v. *(By kind permission of Viscount Coke and the Trustees of the Holkham Estate)*

Montlhéry in 1465, it had become increasingly apparent to him that nothing short of a major reorganisation of the Burgundian military was needed to turn his ambitions into reality. The first moves towards reform of his forces came in an ordinance of 1468, which was largely concerned with discipline and logistics. The following year ideas were broached about the creation of companies of ordinance, which were to be directly modelled on those of Charles VII.[203] It was not, however, until his Abbeville Ordinance of 1471 that Charles laid down the blueprint for his 'new model army'. This was to consist of 1,250 'lances', with each lance or tactical unit containing a mounted man-at-arms, a mounted page, a coustillier or mounted swordsman (who was also equipped with a javelin),[204] 3 mounted archers and a crossbowman, a pikeman and a hand-gunner all on foot. The equipment and wages for each type of soldier were carefully specified, with the men-at-arms receiving 15 francs, the mounted archers 5 francs and the infantry crossbowmen and hand-gunners 4 francs. Archers were each to have a bow and thirty arrows (a larger sheaf than the customary 24 arrows used by English archers), a two-handed sword and a dagger, together with a jacket of livery in blue and white with the red cross of St Andrew. Here was a striking attempt to create a highly flexible force of combined arms, with a core of men-at-arms and their armed retainers, who might fight either on horse or on foot, and were strongly supported by a variety of missilemen, comprising some 3,750 mounted archers, 1,250 crossbowmen and 1,250 hand-gunners. Unlike the lances of Charles VII's *Compagnies d'Ordonnance*, where all the elements had been mounted, the Burgundian lance mounted only the archers, which, together with their numerical preponderance, illustrates the higher value placed on them. Nevertheless, the mixed composition of the infantry in the lance is a striking reflection of Charles's recognition of the continuing importance and power of the crossbow, his confidence in the hand-gun, and the appreciation of the need to defend his missilemen by a body of pikemen.

Charles took a deep interest in every detail of his army's organisation and continually strove to improve its composition and structure. Thus, following a year's campaigning against France, he issued a new ordinance in 1472 at Bohain-en-Vermandois which reduced the total force and altered its component elements to 1,200 men-at-arms, each with a page and coustillier, 3,000 mounted archers, 600 crossbowmen who were now also mounted, 2,000 pikemen, 1,000 foot-archers and 600 hand-gunners. Details of defensive equipment were also set out. Archers were to have a brigandine over a padded jacket, some armour for the forearms, and a sallet and gorgerin, while they were also to possess a lead hammer – another legacy from the English – and a sharp dagger in addition to their bows

and arrows. It is instructive to compare this equipment with the heavier armour required for pikemen and hand-gunners. Pikemen were to possess not only a sleeved jacket reinforced with plates but also a breastplate, a vambrace for the right arm and a targe for the left, while similarly hand-gunners were to have a breastplate, a sleeved mail shirt, a sallet and a gorgerin of either mail or plate.[205] The following year the ordinance issued at St Maximin en Trier made considerable changes to the internal structure of each company and laid down detailed regulations concerning billeting, leave and discipline, but it did not stipulate any changes to the basic composition of the lance. It did, however, lay down compulsory drill for both the cavalry and the infantry, which allows us a rare and important glimpse into the training and manoeuvres of both cavalry and infantry.

That cavalry drill was badly needed had been observed by Commynes in his account of the performance of the Burgundian horse at the battle of Montlhéry, where he noted, 'I do not believe that amongst the twelve hundred men-at-arms or thereabouts who were there fifty knew how to lay a lance in the *arrêt*. There were no more than four hundred armed with breastplates and there were no armed valets, because of the long peace . . .'[206] In his earlier ordinances Charles had remedied such a lack of equipment; in the Abbeville Ordinance of 1471 he stated that each man-at-arms should have a complete suit of armour, three horses, a chamfron and a war-saddle. Now the 1473 ordinance commanded that:

> in order that the said troops may be better practised and instructed when something happens, when they are in garrison, or have time and leisure to do this, the captains of the squadrons and the *chambres* are from time to time to take some of their men-at-arms out into the fields, sometimes partly, sometimes fully armed, to practise charging with the lance, keeping in close formation while charging, [how] to charge briskly, to defend their ensigns, to withdraw on command, and to rally, each helping the other, when so ordered, and how to withstand a charge.

Still more revealing are the instructions regarding archers. The ordinance stated that captains were also to train

> the archers with their horses, to get them used to dismounting and drawing their bows. They must learn how to attach their horses together by their bridles and make them walk forwards directly behind them, attaching the horses of three archers by their bridles to the saddle-bow of the page to whose man-at-arms they belong; also to march briskly forwards and to shoot without breaking rank. The pikemen must be made to advance in close formation in

A unit of Burgundian archers, protected by stakes, with their supporting infantry, reflecting the tactical flexibility planned by Charles the Bold. From an engraving, *c.* 1475, by Master WA, a Flemish artist working at the court of Duke Charles. *(akg-images)*

front of the said archers, kneel at a sign from them holding their pikes lowered to the level of a horse's back so that the archers can shoot over the said pikemen as if over a wall. Thus, if the pikemen see that the enemy are breaking rank, they will be near enough to charge them in good order according to their instructions. [The archers must also learn to] place themselves back to back in double defence, or in a square or circle, always with the pikemen outside them to withstand the charge of the enemy horse, and their horses with the pages enclosed in their midst.[207]

Here in 1473 is a remarkable attempt to order the effective coordination of what would in the next century be termed 'pike and shot'. But instead of the slow-firing hand-gun, the Burgundian drill envisaged the combination of quick-shooting longbowmen with pike formations, melding two of the most formidable weapons of the contemporary battlefield. The protection offered to the archers by the pikemen allowed them to move over open ground in much greater safety, obviating the need for defensive stakes such as Burgundian bowmen had used at Montlhéry in 1465, and which are shown in a series of contemporary etchings of Burgundian troops.[208] Jean de Waurin, describing the Flemish pikemen raised by Charles the Bold in 1471, highlights the great value of these troops, each armed with 'a sallet, jacket, sword and pike or a long lance with a slender shaft and a long sharp spearhead, cutting on three

sides . . . These pikes make very convenient poles for placing a spike between two archers against the terrifying efforts of cavalry trying to break their ranks, for there is no horse, which, if struck with a pike in the chest, will not unfailingly die. These pikemen can also approach and attack horsemen from the side and pierce them right through, nor is there any armour however good that they cannot break or pierce'.[209] Nothing akin to the formations outlined in the Burgundian ordinance of 1473 seems to have been attempted in contemporary English military thinking. Here, the combination of bow and 'brown bill' was predominant until the early sixteenth century, and was to prove its efficacy against the Scottish pike formations at Flodden in 1513. Yet even after Henry VIII's increasing commitment to wars on the continent led to a greater adoption of the pike by English armies, archers were still envisaged as providing only 'sleeves of shot' in support of bodies of pikemen, rather than operating as combined units as in the Burgundian model. A subsequent suggestion of 1625 to create 'The Double Armed Man' by equipping infantry with both pike and longbow was by then nothing but an antiquarian fantasy.[210] Yet though the Burgundian military ordinances of the 1470s were impressive in their attempts at innovation in theory, it proved a far more difficult task to put such drill into effective practice in battle itself. And as events were to show, there was good reason for the stolid conservatism of English arms.

THE TACTICAL DISPOSITION OF ARCHERS IN BURGUNDIAN ARMIES

Just how such troops might be deployed in the field is well illustrated by a detailed dispatch written by Duke Charles himself, describing the battle of Neuss, fought against the German emperor Ferdinand on 23 May 1475. The imperial

army had attempted to raise Charles's massive and prolonged siege of Neuss,[211] and had entrenched themselves in a fortified camp heavily defended by artillery. The Burgundian duke had responded by leaving a strong force to contain the garrison while he drew up his formations to attack the German positions. 'In the first battle,' wrote Charles,

> [we posted] all the infantry, pikemen of our [companies of] ordinance, and the English archers both of Messire Jehan Middleton's company and of our household and guard, together with the infantry belonging to [the companies of] the Lords of Fiennes, Roeux, Crequy, Haines, and Peene and other enfeoffed lords. [Among] all these pikemen were intermingled the archers in groups of four, so that there was a pikeman between every group of archers.[212]

Here in action was a version of the combination of pikemen and archers envisaged in the 1473 ordinance, in formations designed to allow both defensive and offensive operations. On either flank of these mixed units of archers and pikemen were two squadrons of mounted men-at-arms, with the hindmost units acting as a reserve. Thus the cavalry could support the infantry, while if the need arose the pikemen and archers could offer protection to the horsemen. Behind this formation came the second Burgundian battle, whose composition reflected more closely the formations seen in the earlier part of the century, such as the French battle-plan before Agincourt. The centre comprised 'gentlemen of the chamber' from the ducal household, with a strong mounted reserve, while to their right and left, set a little back from the central formation, were archers from the ducal bodyguard and other units of archers. These in turn were flanked by units of men-at-arms, with two of these in reserve.

As with so many of Charles's engagements, however, the careful tactical planning of the council of war was badly let down by the inability of elements of his troops to implement these manoeuvres effectively. After a heavy artillery bombardment the Burgundians advanced, to be countered by a major sally of imperial horse and hand-gunners. This force was eventually driven back by the right wing of the Burgundian van, comprising men-at-arms under Jacobo Galeoto and Sir John Middleton, and supported by the Count of Campobasso, but crucially the units of archers of the van's centre, under the Count of Chimay, had moved too far away for effective support. Lacking these archers, as the duke noted in his dispatch, 'it was not possible to attempt anything else against the enemy'.[213] The emperor pressed home his advantage by sending out a stronger force, estimated perhaps optimistically at some 3,000 cavalry and 6,000 hand-gunners,[214] who pressed these elements of the Burgundian van, now withdrawing under heavy artillery fire from the imperial camp. Charles urgently dispatched reserves of men-at-arms from his second battle and

the whole right wing of archers to remedy their lack of effective shot against the hand-gunners. But as at Montlhéry in 1465, the Burgundian horse quickly outstripped their archers, who were on foot, and joining their beleaguered van well ahead of the infantry they succeeded in driving the Germans back into their camp. Nevertheless, this force was now in exactly the same position as the one it had been sent to relieve, and 'because they did not have with them the archers of the right wing of the second battle' they were forced by heavy artillery fire to withdraw. Once again the imperialists counter-attacked, this time with a major force, which threw back both the van and the reserves of the Burgundian right wing, until Charles led fresh forces to the rescue. He rallied his disorganised men and in turn forced the imperial troops to retire.[215]

The engagements at Neuss are revealing, for they foreshadow a major factor in Charles's subsequent military failings against the Swiss, namely that while his tactical dispositions were carefully planned his ability effectively to execute manoeuvres was hampered by a lack of de facto coordination between units of his army once the enemy had become engaged. Charles's dispatch clearly shows his realisation that failure to achieve archery support for his men-at-arms was a decisive factor in the Burgundians' inability to press home their attacks; remedying the problem was far more difficult. Neuss also shows that while Charles still set great store by his archers, the imperial army had made much greater use of hand-gunners.[216] The same emphasis on hand-gunners and crossbowmen, rather than archers, in a supporting role to pikemen and halberdiers is to be found in the Swiss armies of the period. Equally, in the Italian contingents of Charles's army the mounted missilemen were all crossbowmen and not archers, and hence their rate of shooting was considerably slower.[217] This is significant, for from 1473 Italians formed an increasing proportion of the companies of ordinance, and by 1476 'the Burgundian army can appropriately be described as predominantly Italian, certainly as far as its numbers were concerned'.[218] This may help to explain why longbowmen seem not ever to have been deployed to their greatest effect in Charles's final campaigns against the Swiss. It may thus be in part that the predominance of Italian troops and their experience of war, as much as Charles's own tactical thinking, ensured that the Burgundian army's missile arm remained a mixture of archers, crossbowmen and hand-gunners, but with no single constituent being able to effect a major impact on the outcome of combat. Rather, each was intended to support other elements of the army, while Charles placed considerable reliance on his impressive collection of field artillery. On paper Charles's army was impressive in its sophistication and its emphasis on combined arms. Yet in reality, as Charles's disastrous wars of 1476–7 were to reveal, his forces lacked real unity, discipline and coordination, and proved woefully inadequate when confronted by the most formidable military organisation in Europe, the army of the Swiss confederation.

In the opening stages of the battle of Grandson in March 1476, fought on the north bank of Lake Neufchâtel, Charles deployed units of archers to skirmish with the advanced forces of the Swiss, but they were repulsed by hand-gunners from Schwyz with heavy losses.[219] His artillery, however, was initially used to good effect against the main pike square of the Swiss vanguard or *Vorhut*, though subsequently this successfully repelled repeated charges of the Burgundian horse. Disaster only struck when Charles attempted a planned withdrawal in order to lure the Swiss away from the rising ground which protected their rear, in order to allow his cavalry to attack their square from all sides. In a medieval battle such manoeuvres were always difficult and fraught with risk. It was Charles's misfortune that his attempts to reorganise his forces coincided with the arrival of the main Swiss division, and that the rear ranks of the Burgundian army mistook withdrawal for retreat. Soon, panic swept through his army and a full-scale flight began which Charles was powerless to prevent.[220] The Swiss did not press home their victory, being preoccupied by a mass of booty that they found in the Burgundian camp. As a result battlefield casualties were restricted, with the Burgundian losses numbering only a few hundred men despite their being utterly routed. The Swiss also sustained casualties, largely from arrows or hackbutt shot.

Nothing daunted by this defeat, Charles regrouped his army, rebuilt his artillery train and, mindful of the drastic failure of his forces' cohesion, issued a new ordinance at Lausanne in May. This led to significant changes in organisation, including the division of the army into eight units, each comprising of equal numbers of cavalry and infantry. The core of the army that Charles was soon to lead to a far worse defeat at Morat (or Murten) comprised some 1,241 men-at-arms, 4,062 mounted archers (of whom 1,377 were English) and 4,445 infantry, supplemented by 500 men from the ducal household and further units from Burgundy and Savoy.[221] Just as Edward III had used the siege of major towns such as Berwick and Tournai to try to provoke his enemy into a decisive engagement, so Charles laid siege to the Bernese-held town of Morat and goaded the other elements of the Swiss confederation, hitherto reluctant to aid Bern, to assist her by making major forays deeper into Bernese territory.[222] As the site for his encounter with the Swiss Charles selected his fortified siege camp around Morat, creating a long line of palisaded entrenchments strengthened at intervals with artillery bastions. Having experienced the power of the Swiss pike squares in open

ground at Grandson, Charles intended to draw the Confederates into an attack on a well-defended position from which his artillery could slaughter the oncoming pikemen. A similar tactic was to be planned by James IV in 1513, who sought to lure the English army under the Earl of Surrey to mount a suicidal uphill attack against the powerful Scottish gun positions on Flodden Edge.[223]

As events were to show, however, Charles's choice of ground was poor; his position was restricted, with his rear to Lake Morat, and with only the right wing of his army having a ready route for withdrawal. Had Charles been able to fight the engagement as he had envisaged, these factors might not have proved so crucial, but they were to become so through a catastrophic failure of generalship. Expecting an imminent attack, Charles drew up his army into battle formation on Friday 21 June, but though the troops stood to arms for six hours the onslaught did not come. By that evening, despite the advice of his captains, Charles had become convinced that the Swiss were not going to confront him and stood down his men, leaving much of his defences only thinly manned.[224] The following morning he continued to ignore reports of enemy troop movements, even though by now the Confederate army, which may have been as large as 25,000-strong, was advancing rapidly, making good use of the cover afforded by the wood of Murtenwald which lay to the front of the Burgundian positions. Sources disagree as to whether Charles had again drawn up his men into formation that day, only to be stood down once more, but what is certain is that the Swiss struck with complete surprise, when Charles was occupied with arrangements for paying his troops. Emerging from the woods the Swiss van rapidly bore down on the Grünhagen or 'green hedge' which formed part of the Burgundian lines of defence to the south of the hamlet of Burg. The skeleton garrisons comprising some Burgundian artillery and English archers made a brave effort to halt their advance but their resistance was soon overcome, and the Swiss smashed into the disorganised units of the main Burgundian army. Defeated in detail as they struggled to regroup, the Burgundians were swiftly routed and ruthlessly cut down, while one unit of Swiss attempted to cut off the main line of retreat westward along the lake shore. 'It all happened in less time than it takes to say a *Miserere*,' noted the Milanese ambassador Panigarola wistfully.[225] Though many, including Charles, managed to escape, it is estimated he had lost about a third of his total strength of around 12,000 men. Despite having four-fifths of the number of archers Henry V had commanded at Agincourt, a slightly larger number of men-at-arms and over 4,000 additional infantry, Charles had suffered a crushing defeat. His folly had prevented his archers and his powerful artillery train from deploying to any real effect.

The final act of Charles's tragic trilogy was to be played out the following year at the battle of Nancy.[226] As a result of Charles's defeats at Grandson and Morat, Duke René of Lorraine, who had been allied to the Confederates in 1476, had been able slowly to win back his duchy from earlier Burgundian occupation, and had laid siege to its capital, Nancy. As a result of the mutiny of the English troops in its garrison, the city was surrendered to René on 6 October 1476, prompting Charles's immediate military intervention. Despite the onset of winter, tenuous supply lines, a motley and under-strength army and the hostile activity of a string of René's garrisons, the Duke of Burgundy in his turn laid siege to Nancy. Meanwhile, René had succeeded in raising a powerful army of mercenaries from among the Swiss, who, with other units he had mustered, marched north from St Nicolas-du-Port toward Nancy. Accordingly, on 5 January 1477 Charles, no doubt with the catastrophe at Morat at the front of his mind, collected his army from their siege works and, as the snow fell heavily, drew up a battle formation in a strong position, with a forest to his right, his left flank guarded by the River Meurthe and his front, commanded by his guns, protected by a stream flowing through a ravine. The Swiss and their allies, who numbered some 20,000 against no more than 5,000 Burgundians, executed a bold flanking movement, with their van sweeping round Charles's right wing using the forest as cover. As their main division advanced to engage the front of the Burgundian army, the van launched a devastating surprise attack, scattering the cavalry on Charles's right flank and rolling up his line. Faced with attack on two fronts the Burgundian army, which had been cold and dispirited even before the fight, completely disintegrated, only to find themselves betrayed by the Count of Campobasso, commanding a force of Italian cavalry, who treacherously barred their flight towards Nancy. There followed a terrible rout and pursuit, in which Charles himself was slain. Two days later the duke's body was discovered, lying stripped and mutilated in the ice by a pool, one of his cheeks eaten away by wolves or dogs. When his corpse was retrieved, washed and examined, his head was found to have been split by a halberd from one ear to the jaw, while a pike or spear had pierced both his thighs and, presumably after he had been felled, another thrust up into his bowels.[227]

Charles's defeats, which marked the collapse of Burgundy as a great power, were due in part to a failure of generalship and in part to the structural failings of the Burgundian army. At Grandson, Morat and above all at Nancy, Charles was significantly outnumbered. As English victories such as Agincourt revealed, numerical inferiority was not in itself decisive, provided an army had cohesion, high morale and good leadership. In Charles's armies, however, all these factors were lacking. Vain, headstrong and impervious to the wiser counsels of his commanders, the duke had consistently underestimated the numerical strength, cohesion and fighting abilities of his enemies, while showing a culpable neglect of reconnaissance at critical times, thereby allowing himself to be surprised in all three battles.[228] Save for the opening stages of the battle of Grandson, Charles was accordingly never able to deploy his army as he intended, and hence failed to use his artillery, archers and other missilemen to their maximum effect. But perhaps the most critical factor was the lack of real cohesion within his forces. Charles's army reflected the fragmented polity of Burgundy itself, and was a hybrid creation of troops from different regions – Flanders, Holland, Picardy, Burgundy and Italy – and with different fighting skills, bound together only by the will and purpose of the duke. On paper the Burgundian army looked superb, with a sophisticated organisation emphasising the close interaction of combined arms, and enjoying the support of an abundant artillery train. Yet in reality the lack of discipline, cohesion and morale meant that the effective execution of manoeuvres was often thwarted and, worse, that Charles's armies disintegrated in the face of determined assault. All this stood in marked contrast to the earlier successes of Charles VII's *Compagnies d'Ordonnance* against the English in France up to 1453, and to the striking series of victories achieved by Duke Charles's contemporary Edward IV against his Lancastrian opponents. Though far less can be ascertained concerning the detailed structure of Edward's armies than those of the Burgundian duke, it is clear that he was able to win repeatedly not simply by his greater talents as a commander but also by the discipline and cohesion of his forces.

Surveying Charles's resounding defeats in 1476–7, Edward must have seen little reason to emulate his military reforms, nor, in the wake of his own destruction of the Lancastrians, those of the kingdom of France. None the less, Charles's death marked the end of a military tradition which had been heavily influenced by English tactics and archery. Just as from the 1360s in the wake of the Treaty of Brétigny, English men-at-arms and archers had campaigned in France, Spain and Italy as stipendiaries, so a century later Charles's military ambitions had given other English knights and bowmen the opportunity to gain wages and renown in the wars of Burgundy. Had these men been more fortunate in their commander, the role of archers might still have been an important one on the battlefields of Europe as the fifteenth century drew to a close. As it was, many of Charles's bowmen, both English and Burgundian, were to meet a swift and bloody end at the hands of the Swiss by the lakeside of Morat or on the frozen slopes below Nancy.

Matthew Strickland

CHAPTER 19

'Here Ourselves to Spill': the Longbow in the English Civil Wars of the Fifteenth Century

Thus, thou peculiar engine of our land
(Weapon of conquest, master of the field)
Renownèd Bow (that mad'st this Crown command
The towers of France, and all their powers to yield)
Art made at home to have th'especial hand
In our dissensions, by thy work upheld:
Thou first didst conquer us; then raised our skill
To vanquish others; here ourselves to spill.[1]

hus reflected the Tudor historian Samuel Daniel (1562–1619) in his *The Civil Wars between the Two Houses of Lancaster and York*, when describing the archery duel that began the fateful battle of Towton in 1461. Looking back from an age of English military decline, Daniel was acutely aware of the irony that the longbow, which had been instrumental in achieving victories abroad, had been turned against fellow Englishmen in the series of civil wars that have become known as the Wars of the Roses. If for Daniel the use of longbow against longbow was symbolic of internal dissension and a political malaise that had wracked England from the 1450s, subsequent historians have focused on the tactical interest of engagements in which both sides drew on a common military tradition. A significant element in the success of English tactics during much of the Hundred Years War had stemmed from the adoption of the defensive and the combination of dismounted

men-at-arms and archers. Clearly, however, such dispositions could not be adopted by both sides in a battle without an indecisive stand-off.[2] How, then, were tactics modified in the context of civil war, and what now was the role of archers?

For half a century after the bloodshed at Shrewsbury England enjoyed domestic peace while the fortunes of war in France flowed then ebbed away.[3] The first bows to be bent in anger against fellow Englishmen within the kingdom were those of the supporters of Jack Cade's rebellion in 1450, some of whom were veterans bitter at the incompetent management of the war and frustrated by the failures of government at home.[4] They had returned home 'in great mysery and poverte', and accordingly 'many of them drewe to thefte and misrule and noyed sore the commonalty of this land'.[5] By contrast, other veterans from Normandy had been hired by Sir John Fastolf to guard his house at Southwark during these same disturbances.[6] Cade, noted a royal writ, had marched on Blackheath 'with gret power of men of armes and archiers arraised', while he had fortified his camp 'as if it [had] been in the land of war'.[7] The dissident men of Kent had used the mechanisms of the county militia to raise their forces, mustering in the shire's hundreds and electing constables and captains to lead them.[8] Though the rising failed, the pool of available soldiers from the French wars, swollen after the loss of Normandy and the 'Pays de Conquête', provided nobles with a ready source of recruitment as the factionalism that was strangling the effective prosecution of the war in France grew ever more bitter. The chronicler known as 'Gregory' noted how Richard, Duke of York and other lords had ridden through London in 1451 with 'hyr retenowys of fensabylle men', which, he added sadly, 'was a gay and gloryus syght if hit hadde ben in Fraunce, but not in Ingelonde, for hit boldyd sum mennys hertys that hyt causyd after many mannys dethe'.[9] In March 1453 the Duke of Somerset persuaded Parliament to vote not only taxes for the war in Gascony but money to raise 20,000 archers for 'the defence of the realm', effectively a force intended to defend the king and the court party against the potential military threat posed by Richard, Duke of York.[10] But it was not until 1455 that the political divisions between the Duke of York and Margaret of Anjou, queen of the feeble and intermittently insane Henry VI, at last degenerated into open warfare. As John Hardyng lamented, 'In every shire with jacks and salets clean, misrule does rise, and makes the neighbours war.'[11] Unfortunately, for a period which may well have witnessed considerable diversity in military practice the sources are particularly poor, and it is impossible to reconstruct the deployment of armies or the course of the fighting for all but a handful of battles during the Wars of the Roses. Gone are the rich narratives of Le Bel, Froissart, Monstrelet and other such key sources; while contemporary or near-contemporary sources for the battle of Agincourt can fill a large book, those for Towton (1461) can scarcely fill a few pages.

SITTING TIGHT: ENTRENCHMENTS AND CANNON, 1455–61

It has been argued that in strategic terms pitched battles played a far greater role in warfare during the Wars of the Roses than did sieges, in marked contrast to contemporary European campaigns. This was due to the relative scarcity of significant urban defences and purpose-built artillery fortifications in England, whether in towns or castles (in contrast to English bastions in France such as Calais), and the concomitant superiority of developing artillery over outmoded defences.[12] Political considerations, moreover, meant that commanders, anxious not to lose popular support by extended campaigns of devastation, pursued a battle-seeking strategy to find and eliminate their opponents as quickly as possible after the outbreak of hostilities. Nevertheless, several of the early engagements in the wars reveal a strong emphasis on the defensive, employing either existing town defences or fortified field encampments of the kind that were being increasingly used in the later stages of the Hundred Years War. Such entrenchments and earthwork defences reflected the search for an effective means of deploying artillery, much of which was too cumbersome or too slow-firing to deploy safely in the open field.[13] Indeed, the year before John Talbot met his death at Castillon attempting to storm just such a camp, Duke Richard of York had, in the very first stages of Yorkist military action in 1452, drawn up his forces at Crayford in Kent in a strong defensive position with his flanks protected by the Thames and the River Cray, with a sizeable force of artillery drawn up in front.[14] Negotiation averted fighting on this occasion, but at the first battle of St Albans on 22 May 1455 the Lancastrians success-

Map of England showing the principal engagements in the civil wars of the fifteenth century.

fully held the town gates, strengthened with hastily improvised defences, against York's attack, until the Earl of Warwick led 600 archers through the back gardens of Holywell Street, thereby bypassing the main Lancastrian defences. Emerging into the market square, Warwick's bowmen rained volleys at close range upon the Lancastrians, including King Henry and some of his leading commanders, who were taken completely by surprise and 'out of array', with some even having removed their helmets.[15] According to an account of the engagement sent to the Duke of Burgundy, four of Henry's bodyguard were killed by Yorkist arrows.[16] Henry's army commander, the Duke of Buckingham, was struck in the face by an arrow, and wounded by two more, Lord Stafford was wounded by an arrow in the hand, while Henry Filongley, nephew of Sir John Fastolf, 'faught manly, and was shet throwe the armys in iii or iiij places'. Another arrow grazed the neck of the king himself – a wound that was grimly symbolic of the burgeoning civil war.[17]

The first battle to reflect the customary English defensive tactics of the Hundred Years War was possibly that of Blore Heath on 23 September 1459, when following the renewal of hostilities a Lancastrian force under James, Lord Audley clashed with the Earl of Salisbury as he attempted to join forces with York and Warwick. Given that Queen Margaret had raised this army largely from Cheshire, those knights and local gentry who took the Lancastrian livery badge of the white swan would

surely have numbered bowmen among their retainers or tenants. Nevertheless, Salisbury and his forces, drawn from the northern marches, were victorious.[18] Regrettably little is known about the battle itself, for no contemporary account of the fighting itself survives, and reconstructions have been based largely on the late and mainly uncorroborated account of Waurin.[19] Waurin states that the Yorkists, outnumbered and facing a superiority in Lancastrian cavalry, took up position on rising ground with the Wemberton Brook at their front. They dug a trench to protect their rear, defended their right flank with a wagon laager, and set stakes before them. After a feigned withdrawal by their centre to encourage a Lancastrian assault, the Yorkist archers defeated two charges by the Lancastrian horse, in the second of which Audley was slain. They then drove off a third attack, this time by dismounted men-at-arms.[20] If Waurin is to be believed, here was a tactical situation similar to so many engagements of the Hundred Years War. In 1459 there must still have been a considerable number of veterans from the French wars in service, and Salisbury's adoption of a classic defensive formation would help explain

Archers defend the wooden outworks of a castle, under attack from bowmen, crossbowmen and cannon, from a late fifteenth-century Flemish manuscript of Jean Waurin's *Chronicles of England* (British Library, Royal MS 14 E IV). *(© British Library)*

why a smaller force won so singular a victory. It is harder to know why the Lancastrian cavalry felt they could achieve what so many mounted French assaults had failed to do against such a position, but perhaps Audley's attacks reflected over-confidence in his numbers. A key factor in the Yorkist victory seems to have been the experience of Salisbury's men compared to the raw Cheshire recruits, but the battle was hard-fought and was said to have lasted four hours. The Lancastrians suffered heavy casualties, notably among the Cheshiremen, with the overall dead put at around 2,000.[21]

Nevertheless, in the wake of the battle the main Lancastrian army advanced against York's base at Ludlow, and York reverted to the tactics he had adopted at Crayford in 1452 and prepared to receive their attack at a heavily fortified camp at Ludford Bridge, a move informed by the Lancastrians' numerical superiority and the Yorkists' reluctance to attack a force led by King Henry VI in person. Yet although the camp was surrounded by 'a deep ditch, and fortified with guns, carts and stakes', York's position became untenable when the Calais garrison, an elite force which had been brought to the aid of the Yorkists by Warwick, defected to the king's forces, leaving York, Warwick, Salisbury and March little option but to flee abroad.[22] York's defensive stance at Ludford was to be mirrored by Henry VI's own dispositions at Northampton in July 1460, when confronted by the powerful army of the Yorkist lords who had returned from exile. The Lancastrian commanders had made a heavily entrenched camp, with the River Nene at their backs, allowing their powerful artillery to command the low-lying ground around.[23] Initial Yorkist attacks on this encampment by the forces of Edward, Earl of March, Warwick and Lord Fauconberg, Warwick's uncle, suffered from strong Lancastrian archery, and the engagement might have been another Castillon but for the fact that heavy rain rendered the Lancastrian guns ineffectual. While Yorkist superiority in numbers allowed them to attack in several places at once, the collusion of Lord Grey enabled the Yorkists to scale the western side of the royal encampment and the defenders were quickly overwhelmed. King Henry was captured in his tent by a Yorkist archer, Henry Mountfort.[24]

By contrast to Northampton, it was the premature abandonment of a heavily fortified camp that led to Warwick's defeat by Margaret of Anjou's forces at the second battle of St Albans on 17 February 1461, following her march south after the crushing victory over York at Wakefield. Warwick had advanced north from London to St Albans and 'pitched a field and fortified it full strongly'. In a crucial failing of intelligence gathering, however, the Yorkist lords, unaware that the Lancastrians were very close and almost upon them, 'like unwise men brake their array and took another' on Nomansland Common, a little to the north-east of the town.[25] Though Warwick seems to have been seeking a suitable site to deploy for a decisive field engagement, the Lancastrians took his forces by surprise, attacking St Albans from the north-west and thus attempting to get behind Warwick's army. Clothyard shafts once again flew in the streets of St Albans, as a small detachment of Yorkist archers stationed by the cross in the market square initially succeeded in driving back the assault of the Lancastrians into the town from the west up George Street.[26] But now it was Warwick's turn to be outflanked as Lancastrian forces used a back lane to skirt around the defenders, and having overcome a body of infantry barring the road to the north they marched against Warwick's main force. Nevertheless, the Yorkists succeeded in turning their positions about and for a while their van fought fiercely but then, whether through lack of support, a sudden loss of morale or, as Abbot John of St Albans believed, because the northern forces were more hardened to war by the cold climate, it then broke in flight. Lancastrian cavalry engaged in a fierce pursuit of the crumbling Yorkist army.[27] Among the prisoners taken was Sir Thomas Kyriel, 'that manly knight' and veteran of the French wars, who had survived defeat by the French at Formigny only now to be beheaded as a traitor by the victorious Lancastrians.[28]

Warwick had gathered a considerable amount of ordnance and had a number of Burgundian hand-gunners with him. But as the chronicler known as 'Gregory' noted, the Lancastrians fell upon them by surprise, so that 'before the gunners and Burgundians could level their guns, they were busily fighting, and many a gun of war was provided that was little avail or none at all'.[29] Though little can be gleaned from the meagre contemporary accounts of the nature of the fighting at the second battle of St Albans, 'Gregory', who may well have been among those forces levied from London present at the battle, gives an unusually detailed description of the defensive devices deployed by Warwick's Burgundian hand-gunners:

> The Burgundians had such instruments that would shoot both pellets of lead and arrows an ell in length with six feathers, three in the middle, and three at one end, with a very big head of iron at the other end, and wild fire, all together . . . Also, they had nets made of great cords four fathoms long and four feet wide, like a hedge (an haye), and at every second knot there was a nail standing upright, so that no man could pass over it without a strong chance of getting hurt. Also they had a pavise borne as a door, made with a staff folding up and down to set the pavise where they like, and loopholes with shooting windows to shoot out at. . . . And when their shot was spent and finished, they cast the pavise before them; then no man might come over the pavise because

A crossbowman and a handgunner from a misericord in St George's Chapel, Windsor, 1477–83. *(Paulette Barton)*

of the nails that stood upright, unless he wished to do himself a mischief. Also, they had a thing made like a lattice full of nails as the net was, but it could be moved as a man would; a man might squeeze it together so that the length would be more than two yards long, and if he wished, he might pull it wide, so that it would be four square. And that served to be at gaps where horsemen would enter, and many a caltrop.[30]

Presumably these defensive implements had been deployed as part of Warwick's fortified camp, but were now rendered of little value against the Lancastrians' sudden attack from the rear. Accordingly, 'Gregory' dismissed these devices as worse than useless, as the result of the battle showed: 'Therefore they are much neglected, and men betake themselves to mallets of lead, bows, swords, glaives and axes. As for spearmen [i.e. horsemen or 'lances'], they are only good to ride before the footmen and eat and drink up their victuals, and many more such fine things they do. You must hold me excused for these expressions, but I say the best; for in foot-soldiers is all the trust.'[31] Nevertheless, such devices are striking testimony to the need to provide a mobile defence for the slow-firing hand-gunners, particularly against cavalry, and mark ingenious developments from the crossbowman's pavise. They were clearly the equivalent of the stakes of the English archers, which were also being deployed by Burgundian bowmen in the 1460s and 1470s. It is noteworthy too that some of the guns were still firing projectiles designed like arrows as well as lead balls, reflecting an element of conservatism in the weapon's capabilities. Hand-guns were also prey to the vagaries of the weather; 'Gregory' noted that at St Albans the rain dampened their power, while the wind extinguished their slow matches.[32] Some commanders, however, did not share the chronicler's scepticism towards such new-fangled devices: when Edward IV

marched on London in 1471, after his arrival from Flanders, his army contained 'black and smoky sort of Flemish gunners to the number of 500'.[33] Both he and Warwick, with their close political connections with Burgundy, were doubtless well aware of the significant role hand-gunners had played in Burgundian armies from as early as the reign of John the Fearless and now in 1471 Edward readily accepted the loan of such hand-gunners from Duke Charles. The duke in turn must have been influenced by the precocious development of these weapons in the cities of the empire, while the introduction of corned powder, longer barrels and the first types of matchlock arquebus in the closing decades of the century significantly increased the effectiveness of hand-held weapons.[34] Nevertheless, hand-guns were expensive, and seem to have been generally restricted to more select forces, such as the men in the fleet of John, Lord Howard, who were armed with brass hand-guns as well as cannon for the combined naval and land operations with Richard of Gloucester against Scotland in 1481.[35] It is clear, however, that in England hand-gunners were never deployed in sufficient numbers to threaten the dominance of the bow as the primary missile weapon, nor did field artillery play anything like as significant a role as it was to do in continental warfare of the later fifteenth and early sixteenth centuries. In one of the few surviving muster rolls from the period, that from the Dorset town of Bridport in 1457, only one of the 100 or so men arrayed with equipment had a gun, and this was in addition to a bow and arrows. The commissioners were evidently unimpressed, for they ordered him to provide himself with another sheaf of arrows.[36] Hand-guns were still only in limited use, and were generally restricted to more elite troops.

REGAINING THE OFFENSIVE: TOWTON, 29 MARCH 1461, BARNET, 14 APRIL 1471, AND TEWKESBURY, 4 MAY 1471

After the second battle of St Albans the use of defensive encampments features less prominently in subsequent campaigns. It has been suggested that the youth of commanders such as Edward, Warwick and Henry, Duke of Somerset made them less hidebound and readier to adapt military methods than some who harked back to the more traditional forms of war used against the French.[37] As we have noted, however, English tactics in the final stages of the Hundred Years War can hardly be characterised as stagnant or wedded to the defensive; speed of movement and willingness to attack, using surprise to offset limited troop numbers, were the hallmarks of Talbot's campaigns. How far Edward IV was consciously drawing on such precedents is uncertain, but his own generalship was marked by an aggressive battle-seeking strategy and, perhaps more than any other commander in the Wars of the Roses, by a vigorous preference for the tactical offensive. Warwick, by contrast, relied more on the use of strong defensive positions.[38] The tactics of Edward's first major victory at Mortimer's Cross on 2 or 3 February 1461 are unknown, though his success here against the Welsh levies and mixed Breton, Irish and French auxiliaries of the Lancastrian Earls of Pembroke and Wiltshire may have owed much to the superior training of the Yorkist forces and perhaps to greater numbers.[39] It is probable that as is recorded at the later battle of Stoke in 1487 the Irish troops' lack of armour made them particularly vulnerable to Yorkist archery.[40] The interest of the chroniclers' scant notices, however, focuses primarily on the strange appearance of three suns in the sky, which Edward told his men was symbolic of the Trinity and hence revealed God's favour for his cause.[41] Doubtless heartened by his triumph as much as by this heavenly portent, Edward was soon to lead his forces to a much greater victory at Towton.

After being proclaimed king in London on 4 March, Edward raised fresh forces and marched north towards York to confront the Lancastrian army, which attempted to hold the crossing of the Aire at Ferrybridge. On 28 March the Yorkist vanguard successfully forced a passage, gaining the northern bank after a hard-fought engagement in which Warwick was wounded in the leg by a Lancastrian arrow and Lord Clifford slain by a Yorkist one, when he had unwisely removed his gorget 'either for heat or payne'.[42] The engagement was of considerable tactical and strategic significance, and the paucity of the sources may disguise a feat of arms by knights supported by bowmen as dramatic as the opposed river crossings of Edward III at Blanchetacque in 1346 and Henry V's crossing of the Somme in 1415.[43] The following day the Yorkist army deployed

for battle some 6 miles north of Ferrybridge at Towton, faced by the Lancastrian forces drawn up on the rising ground above a shallow valley known as Dintingdale. Though the armies appear to have been exceptionally large – three-quarters of the adult peerage fought at Towton – the precise numbers on both sides are impossible to ascertain.[44] Nevertheless, despite the enormous significance of this battle and the terrible casualties which are remarked on by almost all the sources, contemporary narratives of the ensuing engagement are remarkably slight. Historians have attempted fuller reconstructions, but in truth the known details are few.[45]

Around 9 in the morning, on Palm Sunday, 29 March 1461, the strong wind which had initially been against the Yorkists shifted, blowing snow into the faces of the Lancastrians. According to the Tudor chronicler Edward Hall, the Yorkist vanguard was led forward by William Neville, Lord Fauconberg, who:

being a man of great polecie and of much experience in marciall feates, caused every archer under his standard to shot one flyght (which before he caused them to provide) and then made them to stand still. The northern men, feling the shoot, but by reason of the snow not wel viewing the distance betwene them and their enemies, like hardy men shot their schiefe arrowes as fast as they might, but al their shot was lost and their labor vayn, for they came not near the Southernmen by 40 taylor's yerdes. When their shot was almost spent, the Lord Fawconbridge marched forwarde with his archers, which not onely shot their awne whole sheves, but also gathered the arrowes of their enemies, and let a great parte of them flye agaynst their awne masters, and another part they let stand on the ground which sore noyed the legges of the owners, when the battle joyned.[46]

Galled by the Yorkist barrage, the Duke of Northumberland and Andrew Trollope, leaders of the Lancastrian vanguard, had little choice but to assume the offensive and order the advance.[47] As the enemy came on, Fauconberg must have had his archers fall back to the main Yorkist positions. Command structures can only be glimpsed in these engagements, but Fauconberg had earlier been placed in charge of the Yorkist infantry and led the advance north from London on 11 March, while 'Gregory' noted that at Towton Sir Thomas Hammys was 'captayne of alle the foot men' of the Lancastrians.[48] Both men perhaps played a role similar to that of Sir Thomas Erpingham at Agincourt, assigning archers and other infantry to their stations and, in Fauconberg's case, leading them forward to begin shooting.

Though his is a late account, Hall's description of the positioning of archers in the opening stages of the battle is reflected in subsequent engagements such as Tewkesbury and Bosworth, and indicates what surely must also have been a common tactic in some battles during the Hundred Years War: a powerful body of archers thrown out in front of and screening the main positions to disrupt the enemy by their shooting and to provoke an attack, when they would then fall back into the protection of the main formation. What we unfortunately do not know is how and where the archers were positioned once they returned to the main divisions. It would seem likely that they were withdrawn to the flanks, for the main stage of the battle seems to have consisted of a long and bitter slogging match between the two opposing bodies of men-at-arms, which according to Warwick's brother George Neville, Bishop of Exeter, lasted from dawn until 'the tenth hour of the night'.[49] Only the later account of Waurin speaks of an initial cavalry attack by the Lancastrian vanguard under Exeter, Rivers and Somerset which routed Edward's horse and pursued them for several miles. He tells too of the failure by Northumberland to implement a similar attack on the other flank as planned, thereby allowing Edward to regroup and successfully counter-attack.[50] Given the dearth of more contemporary sources, it is impossible to gauge the validity of this account. If a successful Lancastrian charge did take place, the Yorkist archers were clearly unable to prevent it. Equally, the duration of the battle and the long stalemate after the initial volleys strongly suggest that the archers' role in the principal engagement – as bowmen at least – was far from decisive. It may be that, as in so many of the Hundred Years War battles, they had put aside their bows and joined in the general mêlée as light infantry. The deadlock was only broken in favour of the Yorkists 'when about noon . . . John, Duke of Norfolk with a fresh band of good men of war came in' and successfully attacked the Lancastrian left.[51]

Writing with the knowledge of victory, pro-Yorkist sources were quick to stress that in the critical phase of the battle both the generalship and personal prowess of Edward had been crucial, and there may well be substantial truth in this.[52] 'I prefer you should learn from others than myself,' Neville disingenuously informed the papal legate Coppini, 'how manfully our King, the Duke of Norfolk and my brother and uncle [Warwick and Fauconberg] bore themselves in this

The opening stages of the battle of Towton, 1461, as reconstructed by Graham Turner. To the right, Fauconberg's archers take advantage of the favourable wind to loose their shafts against the Lancastrians, while to the left the Yorkist men-at-arms advance, led by the standards of Lord Hastings and King Edward IV. (© Graham Turner)

battle; first fighting like common soldiers, then commanding, encouraging, and rallying their squadrons like the greatest captains.'[53] Another dispatch to the same correspondent, this time by Richard Beauchamp, Bishop of Salisbury, told how Towton was 'a very hard-fought battle . . . the result remaining doubtful during the whole of the day, till at length victory declared itself on his side, at a moment when those present affirm that almost all of our followers despaired of it, so great was the power and impetus of the enemy, had not the Prince single-handed put himself forward as nobly as he did, with the utmost of human courage'.[54]

Once the Lancastrian divisions had broken, the slaughter was fearful. Before the battle Edward had proclaimed 'that no prisoner should be taken, nor one enemie saved', and similar orders were given to King Henry's army.[55] Many Lancastrians drowned in the Cock Beck, 'not very broades, but of a great deapnes', while others, fleeing along the road north to Tadcaster, perished in the River Wharfe, as their forces had earlier broken down the bridge there.[56] Some of the Yorkist men-at-arms remounted for the chase, again reminiscent of earlier English practice in the French wars, and engaged in a bloody pursuit which left the countryside between Towton and York strewn with the fallen. 'Quite lately,' noted Bishop Neville, writing on 7 April, 'one might still see the bodies of these

unfortunate men lying unburied, over a space nearly six miles in length and three or four furlongs broad' – a grim picture of the swathe cut by a force of cavalry fanning out to cut down stragglers.[57] The 'official' number of slain claimed by Yorkist dispatches was 28,000.[58] Though this was almost certainly a great exaggeration, contemporaries regarded the slaughter as unparalleled, and certainly the Lancastrians suffered a heavy loss among their nobles. The Earl of Northumberland, Lords Dacre, Welles, Nevill, Willoughby, Scales and Mauley, Sir Henry Stafford and the able captain Anthony Trollope were among the dead, while 42 knights taken captive were summarily executed, as were the Earls of Devon and Wiltshire on being taken soon after. By contrast, the only Yorkists of note to fall were John, Lord FitzWalter, killed during the crossing of the Aire, John Stafford, kinsman of Sir Humphrey Stafford, and the Kentish captain Robert Home, while the losses of their 'commons' was put at between 800 – an implausibly low figure for an engagement of such size and duration – and 8,000 by a seemingly less partisan Italian report.[59] Most of the dead were initially buried in five great pits in a field near the church of North Saxton, but were later removed to Saxton churchyard. Richard III subsequently began building a church on the battle site for the Yorkist dead, but this was abandoned and the site as yet remains undiscovered. The battlefield itself has yielded a

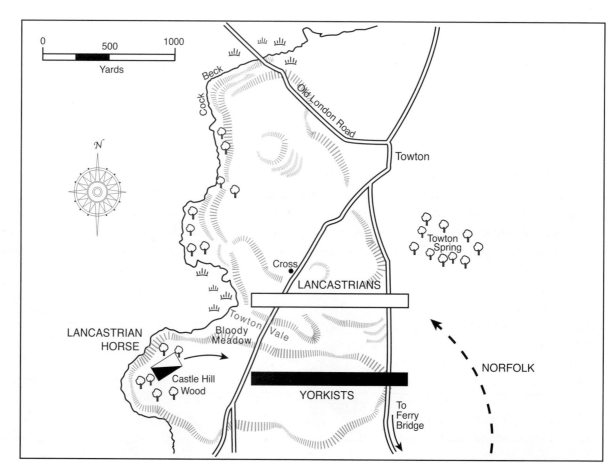

The battle of Towton,
29 March 1461.

number of arrowheads of bodkin type, while at least one of the skeletons from the recently discovered grave pits had suffered a severe arrow wound to the skull.[60]

A decade later, at the two great battles of Barnet and Tewkesbury, Edward IV's opponents adopted a stronger defensive position, utilising hedges and natural obstacles to a far greater extent than seems to have occurred at Towton, where the ground was more open. At Barnet on 14 April 1471 Warwick, who had become irreparably estranged from Edward, drew up his forces on a ridge of high ground, protected by hedges that covered part of his front, in a manoeuvre reminiscent of the Black Prince's position at Poitiers in 1356.[61] His bowmen were probably well supplied, for the city of London had earlier lent Warwick money for the purchase of bows, arrows and bowstaves.[62] Strikingly, the Tudor chronicler Polydore Vergil noted that he placed his archers in the centre of his line, rather than on the wings, suggesting that as at Towton the role of the archers was to provide opening volleys to disrupt the enemy and, in this case, to provoke them into an attack against a well-defended position. Warwick also had a considerable amount of ordnance, which he hoped would slaughter the attacking Yorkists. He had his guns fired throughout the night, but because of the lie of the land they had little effect other than to advertise his position.[63] As it was, Edward needed little provocation and once again adopted the offensive. Despite a dense mist he advanced at dawn in a sudden attack, 'and set upon them, first with shotte, and than and sone, they joined and came to hand-strokes, wherein his enemies manly and coragiously receyved them, as well in shotte as in hand-strokes'.[64] Presumably, as at Towton, the archers in the front ranks must have withdrawn once the Yorkists closed, but the conflict between the men-at-arms nearly proved catastrophic for Edward. Because the king had arrayed his force during the previous night, his formation was not drawn up exactly opposite that of Warwick but was further to the east, meaning that just as Edward's right could threaten to envelop Warwick's left, his own left flank was dangerously exposed to envelopment by Oxford's battle. Indeed, as the conflict developed, Edward's left under Hastings became so hard-pressed that it broke and fled.[65] The mist, however, saved Edward's weak position from being fatally exploited, as neither side realised what was occurring. In the confusion Warwick's men mistook the Earl of Oxford's men, returning from their rout of the Yorkist left back to the main engagement, for Edward's forces, for in the mist the livery badges of the Earl of Oxford, 'a star with streams', looked all too similar to Edward IV's 'sun in splendour' ('the sun with stremys'). As a result, 'the Erle of Warwick's menne schott and faughte ayens the Erle of Oxenforde's men', thereby putting his own right wing to

flight.[66] Meanwhile, Edward's own right division succeeded in overwhelming Exeter's battle and began rolling up Warwick's line, while Edward pressed into the centre of the enemy line with 'the welle asswred felowshipe that attended trewly upon him'.[67] Warwick himself was slain in the confusion, and his army routed.

At Tewkesbury on 4 May 1471 Edward achieved a second major triumph in under a month against a Lancastrian force commanded by the Earl of Somerset. Queen Margaret had been fleeing from Edward's pursuit, hoping to join forces with the substantial reinforcements raised in Wales by Jasper Tudor, Earl of Pembroke. Prevented by tides from crossing the Severn, however, her army turned to face the Yorkists in a strong defensive position at Tewkesbury. We are better informed concerning this battle by virtue of the account known as *The Arrival of King Edward*, possibly written by an eyewitness who calls himself 'a servaunt of the Kyng who presauntly saw in effecte a great parte of his exploytes'.[68] He noted that the Lancastrians had adopted 'a marvaylous strong grownd . . . full difficult to be assayled', in broken terrain to the south of Tewkesbury Abbey. They thus had 'the towne and the abbey at theyr backs; afore them, and upon every hand of them, fowle lanes and depe dykes, and many hedges with hylls and valleys, a ryght evill place to approche as could well have been devised'.[69] The Lancastrian right probably occupied the ruins of Holme Castle, whose walls added to the defensive strength of their position.[70]

Edward deployed his army into the usual three battles, which had formed his line of march, with his brother Richard, Earl of Gloucester, in the van, Edward in the centre and William, Lord Hastings with the rearguard to the right. Edward could not afford to bide his time, for he needed to defeat the queen's army before Pembroke could come to her aid. Unwilling to attack so heavily defended a site, however, he placed his bowmen and artillery to the fore with his vanguard so as to gall the enemy into an attack. 'The Kyng's ordinance', noted the *Arrival*, 'was so conveniently layde afotre them, and his vaward so sore oppressed them with shott of arrows that they gave them right-a-sharpe showre.' While the Lancastrians returned the hail of arrows and gunshot, they nevertheless 'had not so great plenty as had the Kynge'.[71] As Edward hoped, Somerset was provoked into an attack: 'wether it were that for he and his ffellowshipe were sore annoyed in the place where they were, as well with gonnes-shott, as with shott of arrows, which they would nor durst abyde, or els, of great harte and courage'. Somerset, 'knyghtly and manly avaunsyd' himself, and may have attempted a bold flanking manoeuvre, aimed at enveloping the Yorkist left, making use of a careful earlier reconnaissance of the ground. As the *Arrival* relates, he moved

The battle of Tewkesbury, 4 May 1471.

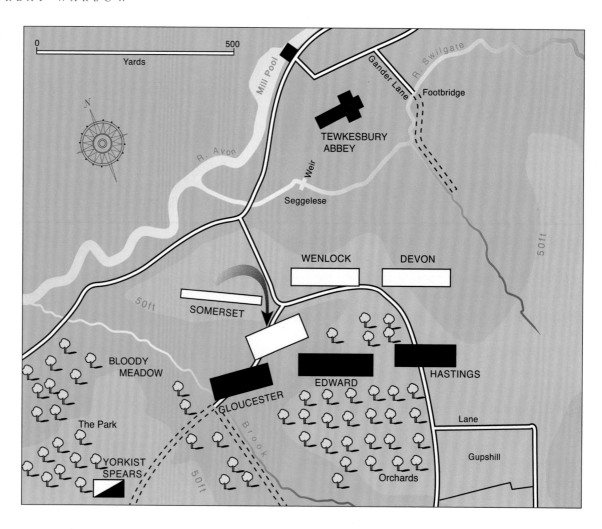

forward 'somehwt asyde-hand the Kyngs vawarde, and, by certayne pathes and wayes therefore afore purveyed, and to the Kyngs party unknown, he departed out of the field, passyd a lane and came into a fayre place, or cloos, even afore the Kyng where he was embattled, and from the hill that was in one of the closes, he set himself right fiercely upon th'end of the Kyngs battayle'.[72] Such a stroke might have proved decisive, but Richard of Gloucester, aged only eighteen, in turn led a vigorous counter-attack against Somerset's flank, allowing Edward's own battle to hold and rally.[73] Throwing his forces

against the Lancastrians, Edward 'full manly set forthe even upon them, enteryd and wann the dyke and hedge upon them, into the cloose, and with gret vyolence put them upe towards the hyll'. At this stage units of spearmen that Edward had concealed in woods on his left flank attacked Somerset 'asyde-hand, unadvysed [unawares]'. Under this combined pressure Somerset's division, which had failed to receive support from Lord Wenlock's division, began to collapse.[74] Edward now attacked this and the other remaining Lancastrian units who were swiftly overwhelmed.

BOWMEN, BILLMEN AND MIXED RETINUES: A DECLINE IN ARCHERY?

Edward's victories at Barnet and Tewkesbury serve to qualify Jean de Bueil's dictum that an army which attacks on foot against a dismounted force on the defensive would be sure to lose. Was this because his opponents could not bring to bear the kind of massed archery that had defeated so many French assaults in the Hundred Years War? Certainly these engagements, as with Towton, suggest that the primary use of archers was in the opening stages of the engagement, to gall the enemy

into abandoning a strong defensive position, and that thereafter they did not play a decisive role. As far as can be ascertained, neither the Yorkist nor Lancastrian forces consistently enjoyed any marked numerical superiority in missilemen which would have swung the tactical balance. Indeed, it is possible that archers were not always as predominant among the infantry forces raised during these internecine wars as they were in expeditionary armies to France, and that billmen or spearmen formed a significant minority of troops. As had been the case earlier in the century the core of most armies was formed by the retainers of the great lords, usually contracted to serve in times of need with a stipulated number of men, bolstered by troops raised in the shires by commissions of array and by civic militias.[75] Evidence concerning the composition of armies during the Wars of the Roses is more limited than for the French wars, but the Bridport Muster Roll of 1457 reveals that almost two-thirds of the 100 or so men present with arms and equipment were archers, while the others were arrayed with a variety of staff weapons such as bills, glaives, spears and poleaxes.[76] A list of 'fencible men' in seventeen vills in the half-hundred of Ewelme, Oxfordshire, perhaps dating to about 1480, lists the men available from each village together with the names of their constable, whether or not they have 'harness', i.e. defensive equipment, and in some cases gives their principal weapon, be this bow, bill or 'staff' (presumably some form of long-hafted weapon). Thus the entry for the village of Ewelme itself reads: 'Ewelme. Thomas Stauton, constable. Richard Slythurst, a harness and able to do the king's service with his bow. Thomas Staunton, John Holme whole harness and both able to do the king's service with bill. John Tanner, a harness, and able to do the king's service with a bill. John Pallyng, a harness and not able to wear it. Roger Smith, no harness but nevertheless an able man and a good

archer.' Entries for other vills are less full, and some simply state the number of men and how many have harness. Accordingly, an exact assessment of the proportion of archers to other troops is not possible, but of the 31 men whose arms are stated, 18 were bowmen, 7 were billmen, 5 had staffs and 1 an axe.[77]

What is more striking is that magnate retinues might now contain a mixture of archers and billmen, in marked contrast to the indentured retinues of the fourteenth and early fifteenth centuries, which comprised almost entirely men-at-arms and archers. In 1452, for example, the Westmorland squire Walter Strickland contracted with Richard, Earl of Salisbury, to provide a retinue of 290 men from his tenants comprising 'bowmen horsed and harnessed, 69; billmen, horsed and harnessed, 74; bowmen without horses, 71; billmen without horses, 76'.[78] Clearly here was a careful attempt to provide a balanced force containing near equal proportions of archers and billmen, and of foot and horsed infantry. What is unknown, however, is how such troops were deployed in the

The battle of Tewkesbury, 1471, as imagined by Graham Turner, at the moment Edward IV's forces stemmed the counter-attack of the Duke of Somerset in bitter fighting in the hedges and ditches below the Lancastrians' main position. In the distance to the right the division of the King's brother Richard, Duke of Gloucester, is shown advancing. (© Graham Turner)

field. Did the billmen and archers form separate units, or did the billmen serve to protect the archers in mixed units, in a similar manner to the combination of pikemen and archers set out in Charles the Bold's ordinance of 1473? Precise details of retinue composition, moreover, such as those furnished by the Strickland indenture, are regrettably rare, making it hard to gauge how exceptional such arrangements were.[79] In 1493, however, Henry VII could assume a retinue would be mixed when in July 1493 he commanded Sir Gilbert Talbot to bring to his aid a force of 80 men on horseback, 'whereof we desire you to make as many spears, with their custrells [armed attendants], and demi-lances, well horsed as ye can furnish, and the remainder to be archers and bills'.[80]

Nevertheless, it is clear that archers were still regarded as the infantry of choice. Commissions issued in 1457, with which the Bridport Muster Roll may well be linked, were specifically instructed to discover how many archers 'each hundred, wapentake, rape, city and borough . . . town, township, village, hamlet and all other places' in named shires might supply, and what goods and revenues were available to support the specified number of archers allocated to each shire. The total

An archer's leather bracer, with the inscription *Armilla*, found in the bilges of the Newport Ship, laid up on the banks of the Usk at Newport, south Wales, *c.* 1467. The meaning of the inscription is uncertain, for while in Latin *armilla* means a wrist or arm guard, there is also a town immediately south-west of Granada called Armilla. Was this town famous for its leather working in the later fifteenth century, and hence is the inscription a pun? The ship had certainly been trading with Spain and Portugal. Whatever the case, the find is a rare example of a bracer dating to the period of the Wars of the Roses. (*© Newport Museum & Art Gallery*)

number of archers required amounted to 10,993 from the shires and 1,602 from ten towns.[81] There is no indication of the criteria on which the assessments were made, and the quotas vary greatly. Northumberland, for example, was to furnish 60, Shropshire 192, Northamptonshire 346, Suffolk 429, Kent 575, Yorkshire 713, Lincoln 910, Norfolk (then a very populous and wealthy shire) 1,012, and so forth. London was to furnish 1,137 archers, while York and Norwich, the two greatest cities of the realm after the capital, supplied 152 and 121 respectively, with other major cities contributing in proportion to their size and wealth: Bristol 91, Coventry 76, Newcastle 53, Hull 50, Lincoln and Southampton 46, Nottingham 30.[82] Local evidence suggests the same priorities. In 1468 commissioners in Cornwall were instructed to array hobelars and archers, and form them into companies 1,000-strong, each containing the customary subdivisions of hundreds and twenties.[83] Similarly, in October 1485 the Duke of Suffolk commanded John Paston, as Sheriff of Norfolk and Suffolk, to bring to the king's aid all those 'defensible able to labour, as well archers and hobyllers'.[84] Archers likewise predominate in civic forces summoned during the wars. In 1455, for example, Coventry intended to send Henry VI 100 archers, while the city of York itself had sent 1,000 men, many of whom were probably bowmen, to join the Lancastrians at Towton in 1461.[85] In the wake of the battle the formerly pro-Lancastrian town of Beverley was required to send Edward IV 24 men-at-arms and a force of archers, all in new livery reflecting their new political allegiance.[86]

By contrast, when Edward IV assembled a great royal army in 1475 in order to mount an invasion of France, it was dominated by archers. Described by one observer as the 'finest, largest and best appointed force that has ever left England', it comprised the customary retinues of the great lords, household retainers and other captains, and numbered some 1,278 men-at-arms and 10,173 archers. The ratio of archers to men-at-arms was thus 7:1, much higher than the ratio of 1:3 common in the time of Henry V and closer to those of English expeditionary forces in the final stages of the Hundred Years War.[87] In some of the constituent magnate retinues it was higher. Sir Richard Tunstall, for example, agreed to serve 'with 10 spears himself accounted, and 100 archers well and sufficiently able, armed and arrayed'.[88] Sir William Trussell had contracted with the king to provide 6 'spears' and 60 archers for a year. Like Sir Nicholas Longford, who also commanded a force of 6 spears and 60 archers, Trussell was an indentured retainer of Lord Hastings, whose total force on the 1475 expedition amounted to 40 men-at-arms and 300 archers.[89] In addition, 2,000 archers were sent as a separate contingent to support Edward's ally the Duke of Brittany – this latter arrangement was similar to Edward's earlier offers of 3,000 English archers to Francis II of Brittany in 1468, and of 2,000 in 1472.[90] The composition of these forces clearly reveals not only that archers were still considered the pick of available infantrymen, but also the belief that for war against the French the old and tried ways were the best. Parliament had agreed, granting King Edward a tenth towards the expenses of 13,000 bowmen, each to receive 6*d* a day for a year.[91]

In the event this formidable army did not see action, for, deserted by Charles the Bold of Burgundy, Edward IV allowed himself to be bought off by the French in return for a massive subsidy at the treaty of Picquigny in August 1475. Such cold pragmatism drew criticism from some; the English ambassador to Spain, Louis de Bretelles, believed it such a disgrace that it overshadowed all of Edward's nine earlier victories in the field.[92] Nevertheless, the preparations undertaken for this expedition demonstrate once again how the resources of the kingdom could be directed to provide vast quantities of bows, arrows and other equipment. In December 1474, 'considering that among other ordinaunce, bowes and arrowes be most special and necessarie', large quantities of each had been ordered throughout the kingdom and purchased by specially appointed commissioners in preparation for the expedition the following summer. The king had prohibited any fletcher from making 'any maner of taccle for shooting but only shefe arowes', while bowyers were commanded to make all their bowstaves into bows, and fletchers, arrowhead makers and string makers were to produce as much as they could on pain of the royal displeasure.[93] Crossbows were also gathered as part of a formidable array of ordnance.[94] At least 10,000 sheaves of arrows were produced and taken on the expedition, while bowyers and fletchers accompanied the king's forces, as doubtless they had in earlier expeditions, as members of a small army of specialists.[95] Similarly, when a small force of 220 archers under Thomas Danyell, squire, was sent in April 1475 to Ireland in ships from Chester, Conwy and Beaumaris, bowyers, fletchers 'and other workmen for the artillery' were dispatched with them.[96]

Edward IV had continued his predecessors' legislation to encourage archery practice, and even extended it to the English settlers in Ireland. By a statute of 1465 every English town in Ireland was to have 'one pair of butts for shooting, within the town or near it, and every man of the same town between the ages of 60 and 16 shall muster at the said butts and shoot up and down three times every feast day' between March and July.[97] Such legislation forbidding other sports and enjoining archery practice has been taken as an indication of the decline in shooting by the later fifteenth century,[98] but we should beware of taking at face value the doleful protestations to this effect contained in the statutes' preambles. Such legislation was more concerned with preventing lax morals and social disorder, to which the honest and healthful pastime of archery offered a counter, than with any de facto decline in the number of skilled archers. Just as Edward III's statute of 1363 complained of a decline in shooting only a few years after the triumph at Poitiers, so Edward IV clearly had little difficulty in obtaining over 12,000 archers only five years after re-enacting once again a statute requiring mandatory archery practice. That there was little need for royal concern is suggested by the rare survival of a written challenge to an archery competition, sent in August 1478 from the married freemen of the Staple of Calais to 'our well beloved good brother Thomas Wryght and all other bachelors who are Freemen of the Staple'.[99] It runs as follows:

> If it should please you for your sport and pleasure to meet with us next Thursday on the east side of this town in the place called The Pane, you shall find a pair of butts (*a pere of prykys*), the length between the one and the other being 260 tailor's yards, measured out with a line. There we, the underwritten, shall meet with as many of your order and shoot with you at the same butts for a dinner or supper, price 12*d* a man. And we pray you for your goodly answer within twenty-four hours. Written at Calais on 8 August, in the year of Jesus, '78.

Ready to disport with you:

Wedded Men	Rob Adlyn	William Bondeman
	John Ekyngton	John Dyars
	Phelip Williamson	Richard Wylowly
	Seman Grantham	Rob Besten
	Thomas Sharpe	Thomas Layne
		John Wryght
		Rob Knyght

This splendid glimpse of a sporting competition, which incidentally gives us an exact range for their target shooting, only survives because it was incorporated with the papers of the Cely family, who were merchants closely involved in the wool trade, whose main continental outlet was the Staple at Calais. Though Calais was by now the only bastion of English occupation in France, the men involved in the shooting match were not, it seems, members of the elite military garrison, but merchants and artisans working or settled in the town. Nor was it merely yeomen who might shoot at a wager; in 1443–4, for example, the accounts of John Howard, Duke of Norfolk, record 8*d* 'for my master's losses at the pricks', and 20*d* 'lost at shooting'.[100] It was said of Sir Thomas Wortley, a Yorkshire noble and knight of the body to successive kings from Edward IV to Henry VIII, that 'he was much given to shootinge in the

Archers draw powerful longbows in a mural (heavily restored from 1876) on the north wall of the nave of the church of St Peter and St Paul, Pickering, Yorkshire, *c.* 1450, depicting the martyrdom of St Edmund. *(© Mick Sharp)*

long bow, and many of his men were cunninge archers, and in them he did much delite'.[101] Little wonder that when in 1489 William Caxton came to the discussion by Vegetius and other classical authorities of archery in his translation of Christine de Pizan's *Livre des Fais d'armes*, he added, 'in this art Englishmen are learned from their young age'.[102] Indeed, archery was so integral a part of social as well as military life in the later fifteenth century that contemporaries could readily think in terms of men as 'bows'. In 1517 a member of the Anglo-Irish gentry, Sir William Darcy of Platten, recalled the impressive physique of one Nicholas Travers of Corkelagh (d. 1486) when a guest at his wedding: 'as tall a man as ever he was and the best and strongest archer that was at that marriage. And at the least, to the said Sir William's remembrance, there were forty good bows [i.e. archers] there.'[103] It was just such reminiscences that Shakespeare had in mind when in Henry IV he has Justice Shallow recall the shooting prowess of 'Old Double', John of Gaunt's marksman.[104] Such real-life competitions call to mind the famous shooting match at Nottingham in the *Gest of Robyn Hode*, where the prize was to be a silver arrow for

He that shoteth allther best
Furthest fayre and lowe,
At a pair of fynly [goodly] buttes
Under the grene wode shawe.[105]

Not all men who drew bows, of course, were necessarily good archers. The value of the muster roll for the half-hundred of Ewelme is that it gives us a precious glimpse, albeit in only one rural microcosm, of the diversity of martial skills. The vill of Netylbede, for instance, could furnish 7 men, 6 of them with 'harness', of whom 2 were listed as 'a good archer'. In Huntyrcombend 2 men out of 9 (of whom 2 were 'not able') were recorded as good archers, while of Warboroghe's 12 men there were 4 with harness, 3 archers and 2 men 'able with a staff'.[106] In this context we may note the remarkable (and

An English king, intended to represent William the Conqueror, and archers, from Ricart's *Mayor's Calendar of Bristol, c.* 1480. The artist has clearly found representing the archers at full draw a challenge, and the illumination should be compared to the bowmen drawn in the almost exactly contemporary Beauchamp Pageant. *(Bristol Record Office)*

surely dubious) statement by Philippe de Commynes, speaking of the archers in the armies of Burgundy in the 1460s, that 'those who have never had a day's experience of their job are more valuable than those who are well trained; this is the opinion of the English, who are the world's best archers'.[107]

A valuable contemporary description of English infantry and their equipment survives from the pen of the Italian observer Dominic Mancini, who had visited England in 1482–3. Describing the large force summoned by Richard III from his estates and those of the Duke of Buckingham to London for his coronation, he noted:

There is hardly any without a helmet, and none without bows and arrows: their bows and arrows are thicker and longer than those used by other nations, just as their bodies are stronger than other peoples', for they seem to have hands and arms of iron. The range of their bows is no less than that of our arbalests; there hangs by the side of each a sword no less long, but heavy and thick as well. The sword is always accompanied by an iron shield; it is the particular delight of this race that on holidays their youths should fight up and down the streets clashing on their shields with blunted swords or stout staves in place of swords. When they are older they go out into the fields with bows and arrows, and even the women are not inexperienced at hunting with these weapons. They do not wear any metal armour on their breast or any other part of the body, except for the better sort who have breastplates and suits of armour. Indeed the common soldiery have more comfortable tunics that reach down below the loins and are stuffed with tow or some other soft material. They say that the softer the tunics the better do they withstand the blows of arrows and swords, and besides that in summer they are lighter and in winter more serviceable than iron.[108]

Commynes had earlier noted that such bowmen should be poorly mounted and 'men who would not mind losing their horses or not even provided with them'.[109] His comments are echoed by Mancini, who continues: 'Not that they are accustomed to fight on horseback, but because they use horses to carry them to the scene of the engagement, so as to arrive fresher and not tired by the fatigue of the journey; therefore, they will ride any sort of horse, even pack-horses. On reaching the field of battle the horses are abandoned, they all fight under the same conditions so that no one should retain any hope of fleeing.'[110] His description of sword and buckler play is particularly striking, and the development of

such skills may help to explain the success of English archers in close combat during the mêlée, in which they often proved so valuable.

Mancini's remarks on the archers' equipment and the value of the 'soft armour' receive some corroboration from the Bridport Muster Roll. Of the 180 men listed 60 were recorded as not having equipment, but 10 possessed the full requirement of sallet, jack, buckler and offensive arms, and at least 70 possessed some elements of defensive armour. Those without full equipment, moreover, were ordered by the commissioners to supply the missing items on pain of a fine.[111] Some levies raised in times of emergency were more poorly armed: 'Gregory' speaks of 'nakyd men' [i.e. without any defensive armour] that were compelled for to come with the kyng' when his army confronted York at Ludford Bridge in 1459.[112] By contrast, the archers in the Beauchamp Pageant are portrayed with short-sleeved mail haubergeons as well as jacks or brigandines, and with sallets. Edward IV's archers intended to serve in France on his expedition of 1475 may have been particularly well equipped, and the king had commissioned the making of brigandines.[113] Among the items some of the Bridport levies were ordered to provide were pavises, a valuable indication that defensive shields, doubtless of a variety of sizes, could be used by archers as well as by crossbowmen.[114] Though some may have been used in the field, others were probably intended for siege operations or for use in defended encampments. Sieges were remarkably few during the Wars of the Roses, and were largely restricted to the reduction of the great northern castles held by the Lancastrians. The only assault made on a walled town or city was that by Fauconberg's men on London in 1471, and here archers played a prominent role on both sides. There was, noted the *Arrival*, 'much shote of gonnes and arrows a grete while, upon both parties', but as the Kentish-men assaulted Aldgate the Earl Rivers sallied out with a picked force of 400–500 men 'and mighteley laied upon them with arrows and upon them in bands, and so killd and toke many of them, dryvynge them from the same gate to the water syde'.[115]

Doubtless those 'household men and feed men' who were retained directly by lords were better armed and equipped than many of the county levies. The evidence of Lord Hastings' retinues suggests that brothers or kinsmen of retainers serving as men-at-arms could also be retained as archers.[116] As with other retained troops, archers would have borne the livery badges of their lords. Parliamentary statutes had attempted to ban this practice without success, though it was lawful for men to wear their lords' badges of livery when serving with the king in time of war.[117] At the second battle of St Albans in 1461

'Gregory' had noted that all the Lancastrian forces wore their lords' liveries, 'that every man might know his own fellowship by his livery', while they also wore the livery of the Prince of Wales, a black bend with silver ostrich feathers.[118] In the 1475 expedition, for example, Lord Hastings' men, 40 men-at-arms and 300 archers, bore his badge of a black bull's head with a gold crown around the neck.[119] Similarly, when in the political turmoil of 1485 the Duke of Norfolk summoned John Paston to send him a retinue, he added 'I pray you ordain them jackets of my livery'.[120]

'LYKE A MOST STRONG TRENCHE OR BULWARK': ARCHERS AT BOSWORTH, 22 AUGUST 1485, AND STOKE, 16 JUNE 1487

Two further engagements, Bosworth (1485) and Stoke (1487), were to be fought in the context of civil war before an uneasy peace returned to the kingdom, but the role of archery differed significantly between them. Despite its enormous political importance, the course of the battle of Bosworth, which marked the accession of Henry Tudor and the end of the Yorkist dynasty, is difficult if not impossible to reconstruct in any satisfactory manner owing to the poverty of surviving sources.[121] Even the site is uncertain and a matter for considerable controversy. Arguments have been made for moving the battlefield a little to the south from its traditional location of Ambion Hill either to near the church of St James at Dadlington, where the bodies of many of the slain were buried, or to Atherstone, some 8 miles to the west.[122] Our focus here, however, is on what we can glean concerning the deployment of archers, and for this our principal source is the Italian Polydore Vergil, a Tudor apologist whose work was commissioned by Henry VII. Though he was writing in about 1503–13, and thus considerably after the battle, it is possible that he had access to details of the battle from the king himself, but the absence of other detailed accounts precludes corroboration of his account. Reliable estimates of the strength of the respective armies are lacking, but Vergil gives Tudor's force as scarcely 5,000, and Richard's as double this.[123] According to Vergil, King Richard arrayed his vanguard, 'stretching yt furth a woonderfull length, so full replenysyhd both with footmen and with horsemen that to the beholders afar of yt gave a terror for the multitude, and in the front were placed his archers, lyke a most strong trenche and bulwark; of these archers he made leder John Duke of Norfolk'.[124] Behind this came Richard himself with a picked force of men, though probably a considerably smaller division than the vanguard.[125] Vergil's phrase to describe the function of Richard's archers is striking; he clearly believed they were intended to act as a major defensive shield for the troops of the vanguard, in a position closely analogous to the role of the Yorkist archers at Towton. Richard had been too young to fight at Mortimer's Cross and Towton, but he had been in the thick of the fighting at Barnet, where he had been wounded and many of his men had fallen, while at Tewkesbury his intervention against Somerset's division may well have been the most critical act in the battle.[126] His knowledge concerning the best tactical use of bowmen, and indeed of artillery which was used on both

A typical infantryman's armour from the mid- to late fifteenth century, comprising a mail shirt, a brigandine and deep war-hat worn with a bevor. Made of many small plates riveted to a fabric lining, the brigandine afforded a light, effective and comparatively inexpensive form of body armour, which was also widely used by archers. *(© The Board of Trustees of the Royal Armouries)*

A series of eight distinctive loops on the south curtain of the outer ward of Coity Castle, Wales, of fifteenth-century date and probably designed for early hand-guns. *(M. Strickland)*

sides,[127] must have been heavily influenced by his brother Edward's generalship, but his deployment at Bosworth also echoes the advice of Vegetius, a copy of which he had commissioned:

> But one rule look thou take most heed of that whether thou fight with thy right wing, or thy left or thy centre, set thy strongest and mightiest and wisest fighters that thou hast, both horsemen, footmen and archers, there where the burden and brunt of the battle will be. For victory and overcoming in battle is not in great numbers but in a few strong, wise and determined warriors, who must be arranged to best advantage.[128]

As events would show, however, these words would apply more fittingly to Henry Tudor's army. Tudor drew up his smaller army, keeping the marsh which lay between the two forces on his right, 'that yt might serve his men instede of a fortress'.[129] By contrast to his opponent, he was obliged to make 'a sclender vanward for the small number of his people', with Gilbert Talbot commanding the vanguard's right wing and John Savage the left; and 'before the same he placyd his archers'

under the Earl of Oxford, who was in overall command of the vanguard.[130] It is possible that Richard's vanguard was similarly divided, for the Crowland chronicler noted that Norfolk commanded the wing of the vanguard which bore the brunt of the fighting against Oxford, while according to Molinet, the other was commanded by Sir Robert Brackenbury.[131] If Vergil is correct about its great length this would make sense in terms of effective command. As Michael Jones has recently argued, however, the greatest strength of Henry Tudor's army lay not in its bowmen but in an elite force of over 1,000 French pikemen under their captain Philibert de Chandée, who were placed in the van organised by companies of 100 each under their own ensign.[132] By the 1480s the pike was fast becoming the arbiter of the European battlefield, thanks to the phenomenal military success of the Swiss and the rapid dissemination of their military techniques. In Swiss tactics pike formations were supported not only by groups of halberdiers but by crossbowmen and hand-gunners, and it may be that the

Left: Archers in battle, drawn up in front of mounted men-at-arms, from a French translation of Caesar's *Commentaries*, Flanders, 1473 (British Library, Royal MS 16 G VIII, f.189). (© *British Library*)

Opposite: Pikemen in triangular formation, flanked by archers and hand-gunners, from Xenephon's *Cyropaedia*, Flanders, c. 1470–80 (British Library, Royal MS 16 G IX, f.76v). It was perhaps such pikemen in the service of Henry Tudor who broke Richard III's daring cavalry charge at Bosworth. (© *British Library*)

archers mentioned by Vergil were intended to act as a defensive screen for Tudor's mercenaries, bickering with the Yorkist bowmen until the pikemen could deliver their all-important charge. This, it seems, was intended to be launched obliquely, in tactics echoing the Swiss outflanking movements of Charles the Bold's army at Grandson (1476) and at Nancy (1477). The tactical parallel is unlikely to have been fortuitous; Swiss pikemen had been serving in French armies from 1474, even before the crushing defeats inflicted on Charles the Bold, while English troops, as we have seen, had served in the Burgundian armies.[133] The Burgundian chronicler Jean Molinet says that because of the firepower of Richard's guns, the French captains in Henry's army 'resolved, in order to avoid the fire, to mass their troops against the flank rather than the front of the king's battle. Thus they obtained mastery of the vanguard . . .'[134]

On seeing Oxford's advance past the marsh, noted Vergil, Richard's men 'making suddaneley great showtes assaultyd th'ennemy first with arrowes, who [Oxford's men] wer nothing faynt unto the fyght but began also to shoote fearcely; but when they cam to hand strokes the matter was delt with

blades'.[135] Here again, as at Agincourt, Verneuil and other engagements, we glimpse the use of a great shout by the archers to boost their morale and shake the enemy's resolve. An initial archery exchange is also mentioned in a surviving ballad, which notes how 'Archers they let sharp arrows flee . . .'[136] Oxford seems at one point to have regrouped his men, ordering that none should go ten feet beyond the standards, though whether this was to bring the pikemen to the fore or dress their ranks after an initial advance is unknown. After a brief respite he attacked again in close order, 'with the bandes of men closse to one an other . . . and in array tryangle vehemently renewed the conflict'.[137] Vergil's reference to a triangular formation, hitherto denied satisfactory explanation, makes immediate sense if Tudor's vanguard contained pikemen, who often attacked in a wedge-shaped formation (and in so doing lends more weight to the veracity of Vergil's account). Such a formation, protected by hand-gunners forming a 'sleeve of shot', is clearly illustrated in a contemporary Flemish illumination.[138] The movements of the respective forces once battle was joined must remain largely

speculative, though Henry's forces are reported to have had the advantage of the sun and wind at their backs, and the professionalism of his highly drilled mercenaries must have compensated to a considerable degree for their inferiority in numbers.[139]

Whatever the actual course of the battle up to this point, there is general agreement that its climax was marked by a furious cavalry charge led by King Richard directly at Henry Tudor, who seems to have been situated some way behind his vanguard and commanding only a comparatively small force. Whether or not this attack was a precipitate response to deliberate inactivity on the part of some of his supposed adherents (principally Northumberland and the rearguard), a strike to pre-empt possible treachery, or a bold and coolly deliberate counter-attack with a major division of cavalry, Richard clearly sought a rapid and decisive outcome by slaying his rival.[140] He nearly succeeded, killing Henry's standard bearer, William Brandon, and beating down the redoubtable Sir John Cheney.[141] Yet, just as all seemed lost, Henry made a remarkable recovery. Accounts have often suggested that at this critical juncture it was the final intervention of William Stanley, who had been waiting on the sidelines with a powerful force, that saved Tudor, but Michael Jones has argued instead that Richard's charge was broken by Henry's French mercenary pikemen.[142] Henry seems to have dismounted behind their protective spears, for as one of these French soldiers subsequently noted, 'he wanted to be on foot in the midst of us, and in part we were the reason why the battle was won'.[143] In this reading of events, it was only when Richard's counterattack had been seen to fail that Stanley committed his forces, and the arrival of his fresh troops proved decisive. The power of their charge spent and their cohesion lost, Richard's horsemen were overwhelmed, and the king, spurning advice to flee, fought on fiercely until he was slain. Richard himself was cut down by a Welsh halberdier, the first English king since Harold Godwineson to be killed in battle.[144] In the meantime, Oxford, 'after a lyttle bickering', put to flight Richard's rearguard, many of whom had come 'to the fielde with King Richard for aw and no goodwill', and had no stomach for the fight.[145] King Richard's charge, like that of Hotspur against Henry IV at Shrewsbury in 1403, was a highly dangerous gamble which failed, and recent historians have been critical of Richard's abilities as a general.[146] But there could be no doubt as to his great personal courage. As Polydore Vergil noted of the battle's close, 'King Richard alone was killyd fyghting manfully in the thickkest presse of his enemys'.[147]

Bosworth was thus a battle in which archery played only a subsidiary, supporting role, with bowmen being placed in the vanguards of both forces as had been customary through much of the Wars of the Roses. The hybrid nature of Henry Tudor's forces, made up of Welsh, Breton, Scottish, English and French troops, and in particular his reliance on foreign mercenaries, meant that archers must have formed a comparatively small part of his available infantry. How far the weakness in his rival's missile arm encouraged Richard to launch his cavalry assault cannot be known, but there is a certain irony that in a civil war the cavalry charge of an English king was thwarted not by volleys of longbow arrows but possibly by the massed spears of French pikemen. By contrast, when another hybrid force attempted to topple the reigning king by the fortunes of battle at Stoke in 1487, they met with a very different fate.

Only two years after his victory at Bosworth, Henry Tudor faced a serious rebellion led by Francis, Viscount Lovell and Sir John de la Pole, the Earl of Lincoln, who had crowned a pretender, Lambert Simnel, as Edward VI in Dublin, and had landed with a small invasion force at Furness in Lancashire.[148] They had been supplied with a force of 2,000 German mercenaries under their captain, Martin Schwartz, by Margaret of Burgundy, the sister of

Edward IV and Richard III. To this force, which probably comprised mainly pikemen, the rebel leaders had added a disaffected element of the Calais garrison, Irish troops under Thomas Geraldine, and forces raised locally by dissident Yorkists like Sir Thomas Broughton.[149] Henry VII decided to march directly against the rebels before their numbers could swell, and encountered them at East Stoke, south of Newark, on 16 June 1487. Polydore Vergil, on whom we are once again largely reliant for any details of the battle, notes that the king was accompanied by 'a great number of armed men', including experienced captains like George Talbot, the Earl of Shrewsbury, George, Lord Strange, John Cheyney and 'many others

Armour for horse and man, South German, Lanshut, c. 1475–85. *(Reproduced by permission of the Trustees of the Wallace Collection, London)*

well versed in military affairs'.[150] Coming across the enemy by surprise, the royal vanguard under the veteran Earl of Oxford, John de Vere, was forced to engage while the main and rearguard divisions were still some way off.

As at Towton, Tewkesbury and Bosworth, the engagement began with an exchange of archery, but this time the royalist army had a distinct superiority, not least against Geraldine's poorly equipped troops. 'The Irish,' noted Vergil, 'though they fought most spiritedly, were nevertheless (in the tradition of their country) unprotected by body armour and, more than the other troops engaged, suffered heavy casualties, their slaughter striking no little terror into the other combatants.'[151] This is corroborated by Molinet, who records that the Irish 'could not withstand the shooting of the archers of England'.[152] Suffering serious casualties from the arrows, Geraldine's men were forced into a precipitate charge down from the high ground the rebels had been occupying, despite the orders of Lincoln and Lovell to hold their position. The rebel commanders now had little choice but to commit the rest of their forces to a general attack, and at first Schwartz's onslaught pushed the royal vanguard back. 'Those rugged men of the mountains, the Germans, so practised in warfare, were in the forefront of the battle,' noted Vergil, but Oxford's division was a powerful one, containing seasoned troops, and they succeeded not only in containing the rebels' advance but in finally overwhelming their opponents, virtually unaided by Henry's other units.[153] Further details of the fighting are lacking, but by the end of the battle Lincoln, Lovell, Broughton, Schwartz and Geraldine all lay dead on the field.[154]

The deployment of French mercenaries at Bosworth and of German and Irish forces at Stoke led to a clash of differing troop types, which can only be glimpsed in the sources. Yet English military organisation appears to have been little affected by continental influence in the later fifteenth century. If England did not follow much of Europe in terms of the increasing prominence of pikemen, the widespread adoption of firearms and the development of purpose-built artillery fortifications, there was equally no attempt by English kings to imitate the military reforms of Charles VII of France or the creation of a 'new model army' by Charles the Bold of Burgundy. Lancastrian rule in Normandy and the subsequent 'Pays de Conquête' had necessitated the creation of a standing army of occupation which had achieved a considerable degree of sophistication in its organisation. But the *raison d'être* of this army was lost with these French territories, and there was neither the money nor the political will to recreate such a force within England itself. The only permanent forces to remain, other than the household retainers of the king and nobles, were the garrisons of Berwick and of Calais. Though in time the very notion of a standing army would be decried by the political nation as a hated symbol of foreign absolutism, English monarchs also feared that such a force might be turned against them by dissident nobles, and the potential danger had been well illustrated by the shifting allegiance of the commanders of the Calais garrison, which had played a significant military and political role in the civil wars.[155] As a result the tried and tested system of contract armies and magnate retinues was to continue well into the sixteenth century.[156]

Matthew Strickland

CHAPTER 20

Tudor Twilight

O what cause of reproche shall the decaye of archers be to us nowe liuyng? Ye, what irrecuperable damage either to us or to them in whose time nede of semblable defence shall happen? Which decaye, though we all ready perceive, feare and lament, and for the restauryng therof cesse nat to make ordinances, good lawes and statutes, yet who effectuelly puttethe his hande to continual execution of the same lawes and provisions? Or beholdyng them dayly broken, wynketh nat at the offendours? O mercifull God, howe longe shall we be mockers of our selfes? How longe shall we skorne at our one calamitie?[1]

Sir Thomas Elyot, *The Governor* (1531)

he sixteenth century was to witness the final demise of the longbow as a military weapon. Yet although men like Elyot (whose manual of instruction for the Tudor gentry became a bestseller and went into eight editions by 1580) perceived English archery to be already sunk in decline by the 1530s, the path of the bow to obsolescence was long and halting. The concept of a sweeping military revolution in the sixteenth century has been increasingly challenged, and replaced by an emphasis on more gradual change and adaption. Throughout Henry VIII's reign, the Tudor commissariat was to order many thousands of new bows, and when, just two years before his death, the *Mary Rose* went down with almost all hands, archers were still a key element of her complement. And in 1547, at Calais and Boulogne, the great English bastions on French soil, as well as in the numerous fortifications along the south coast of England, great stores of longbows and arrows remained as an integral element of the defence of the latest artillery fortresses.

Important factors would eventually tell against the longbow; its poorer powers of penetration of armour compared to the steadily improving hand-gun; the growing difficulty of obtaining imported bow wood, with a concomitant rise in cost and fall in quality of available bows; and – as Elyot saw – the disinclination of men to exert themselves in the regular practice needed for its proficiency. Against this, however, the longbow was still much cheaper than the arquebus; the government believed its encouragement was closely linked to the maintenance of social order; and, most significantly, its fast rate of shooting still allowed it to play a significant military role. It was not mere antiquarianism or misplaced nostalgia that led English veterans who had seen action on the continent to put up a prolonged and spirited rearguard action to retain its deployment. As late as the 1590s the debate over the respective merits of bow and hand-gun raged with passionate intensity, and it was only in 1595 that Elizabeth I's Privy Council ordered the general replacement of the bow with the arquebus by decreeing that the bow was no longer an acceptable weapon for any member of a shire's train-bands. Indeed, it has been remarked that 'so strong was the case for the bow that in discarding it and substituting "weapons of fire", the Privy Council showed courage as well as foresight'.[2] Yet when in 1509 the young, hugely ambitious and bellicose Henry VIII succeeded to the throne of England, the redundancy of the longbow must have seemed unimaginable.

A NATION OF ARCHERS?

Proficiency with the bow, whether in hunting or at the butts, was regarded as an integral part of the education of any renaissance prince. Henry VII had brought up all his children to shoot; his eldest son Arthur had begun as young as five-and-a-half, while when only fourteen his daughter Margaret is recorded as having killed a buck in Alnwick Park while journeying north to marry James IV of Scotland in 1503.[3] James himself was a keen shot, and the significance of archery at his court is reflected by the numerous references to shooting in William Dunbar's poem *The Golden Targe*.[4] He had a set of butts made for his private use in the gardens of Stirling Castle, and is found shooting at a wager, such as the 35 shillings he 'tint' at the Dumbarton butts in 1498.[5] Henry VIII excelled with the longbow and revelled in displaying his prowess with it. In 1510, as a young man of nineteen, he 'shot as strong and as great a length as any of his guard' of yeomen, while at Calais in 1513 Henry demonstrated his skill before the ambassadors of Maximilian. He 'cleft the mark in the middle and surpassed them all, as he surpasses them all in stature and personal graces'.[6] According to his fictionalised biography *Der Weisskunig*, Maximilian himself had been a fine shot as a young man, and was even better (or so the author claimed in a revealing statement of national one-upmanship) than the English mercenary archers in his service.[7] As late as 1531 the Venetian Ludovico Falieri reported that Henry 'jousts and wields his spear, throws the quoit and draws the bow, admirably'.[8] Henry's love of 'disguisings' and courtly pageants as well as archery led him to play the role of Robin Hood in the May celebrations of 1510, when he and his retinue suddenly rushed into the bedchamber of Queen Katherine of Aragon,

> all appareled in shorte cotes of Kentish Kendal, with hodes on their heddes, and hosen of the same, every one of them, his bowe and arroes, and a sword and buckler, like out lawes . . . whereof the Queen, the ladies and al other were abashed, as well for the straunge sight, as also for their sodain commyng, and after certain daunces and pastimes made, they departed . . .[9]

In 1515 200 archers from the king's bodyguard dressed in green and under the command of a 'Robin Hood' feasted with the king in a greenwood arbour 'made of boughs, with a hall, a

Maximilian I of Austria kneeling before St Sebastian, from the *Prayer Book of Maximilian I* by the 'Maximilian Master', commissioned probably just after he became Emperor in 1486 (Vienna, Österreichische Nationalbibliothek, Cod. 1907, f.61v). Sebastian, here unusually depicted in full armour and holding a longbow, was thought to offer protection from the plague, and was also a favourite patron saint of guilds of archers and crossbowmen. *(Österreichische Nationalbibliothek, Vienna)*

The meeting of Philip I of Castile (left) and Henry VII of England, from *Der Weisskunig, c.* 1517, the fictionalised autobiography of Maximilian I. In portraying Henry's guard with powerful longbows, the artist was reflecting the automatic association of this weapon with the English. Their full armour and elaborate dress suggest that they are gentlemen of the chamber. (© *The Board of Trustees of the Royal Armouries*)

great chamber and an inner chamber, very well made and covered with flowers and sweet herbs'.[10] Henry's maying festivities that year also included an archery competition,[11] and such May celebrations, when it was customary to go out and gather sprigs of greenery, invoked strong echoes of the forest and of hunting, as well as of amorous desires. A poem by King Henry himself plays on the chase as a metaphor for sexual conquest:

> Sore this dere stryken ys,
> And yet she bledes no whytt:
> She lay so fayre, I cowde nott mys:
> Lord I was glad of it![12]

Yet Henry's attachment to the longbow had a much deeper significance, for he yearned to repeat the military exploits of his royal predecessors against the old enemy France.[13] When as a young man he went to war in 1513, it was 'to create such a fine opinion about his valour among all men that they could clearly understand that his ambition was not merely to equal

but indeed to excel the glorious deeds of his ancestors'.[14] It was such a desire that caused Henry to encourage Lord Berners to translate Froissart's *Chronicles* into English, in order to inspire his subjects by reminding them of the great feats of arms of their forebears, and to commission a life of his namesake, Henry V, with whom he so strongly wished to identify.[15] It has been noted that 'there were men at his side whose grandfathers fought at Agincourt',[16] and on his army's first night on French soil in 1513 Henry consciously sought to imitate his hero's actions on the eve of Agincourt by remaining in armour till dawn and touring the camp to encourage his men. The realities of the situation, however, were very different; not only was Henry VIII supplied with sumptuous accommodation and every luxury, but there was to be no great hard-won victory.[17] In focusing on the long and costly siege of Thérouanne, the 1513 campaign was but a foretaste of the kind of warfare Henry's armies would fight on the continent in 1522–3 and 1544, which, despite their enormous expense, never yielded a triumph in the field to match those of his ancestors. Nevertheless, Roger Ascham doubtless struck a powerful chord when, by presenting the king with his treatise *Toxophilus* at Greenwich on his return from France in 1545, he implicitly linked Henry VIII with the longbow's glory days against the old enemy. The king's pleasure was reflected in Ascham's grant of a pension of £10 per annum.[18] It was this powerful symbolism of the longbow that caused Henry to flaunt English archers at great diplomatic meetings with his fellow European monarchs. Thus at his meeting with Francis I at the Field of Cloth of Gold at Guisnes in 1520 Henry himself took part in an archery competition and had 24 archers of his guard shoot before the French king.[19] Similarly, at the summit with Charles V and Francis, he took for his device an English archer in a green coat drawing an arrow to the head.[20]

Henry's perception of the longbow not only as the instrument of past but also of future victories also informed his renewed promulgation on the enforcement of archery practice among his subjects. In 1528, for example, the preamble to a statute forbidding the use of crossbows and hand-guns noted that under the king's predecessors,

there did insurge, increase and grow within the same realm great numbers and multitude of Francs-archers which not only thereby defended this his [the king's] said realm and subjects thereof against the danger and malice of their enemies, but also with a mean and small number and puissance, in regard and comparison to their enemies, have done many notable exploits and acts of war to the discomfiture of their said enemies; by reason whereof as well our said sovereign lord the King as also his noble progenitors have had and obtained great and triumphant victories against their enemies to the great honour, fame, renown and surety of his and their noble persons, and of this his said realm of England and subjects of the same, as also to the terrible fear and dread of all outward and strange nations attempting anything by the way of hostility to the hurt or danger of this his said realm.[21]

As early as 1512 Henry had expanded existing legislation, mindful that 'by the feate and exercise of the Subgiettes of this Realm in shotying in long bowes there hath continually growen and ben within the same gret nombre and multitude of good Archers'.[22] All men not 'lame, decrepute or maymed' under 60 'do use and exercise shotying in long bowes', except justices of the Bench and Assize judges. Any over the age of 24 were not to shoot at a mark at less than 220 yards – a recognition that shooting from the most powerful bows could only be attained with full physical maturity. Furthermore,

Every man having a man child or men children in his house shall provide, ordain and have in his house for every man child being of the age of seven years and above, till he shall have come to the age of seventeen years, a bow and two shafts to induce and learn them and bring them up in shooting, and shall deliver all the same bow and arrows to the same young men to use and occupy.[23]

Roger Ascham fondly remembered his boyhood training in the 1520s in the household of Sir Humphrey Wingfield, who 'at term times would bring down from London both bow and shafts. And when they should play he would go with them himself into the field, and he that shot fairest would have the best bow and shafts, and he that shot ill-favouredly should be mocked of his fellows till he shot better'.[24] Likewise, John Lyon, a Tudor yeoman of means who founded Harrow School, stipulated among his regulations that each child was to bring not only the necessary books, paper, ink, pens and candles, but also his own arrows, bowstrings and bracer.[25] Children as young as five-and-a-half or six could be provided with bows, and even those destined for a clerical career were taught to shoot as boys.[26] It was noted of Archbishop Thomas Cranmer himself that 'albeit his father was very desirous to have him learned, yet he would not that he should be ignorant in civil and gentleman-like exercises, in so much as he used him to shoot and many times permitted him to hunt and hawk and to exercise and to ride rough horses'. Even when archbishop, he

would spend some of his leisure time in hunting and hawking, 'and would sometimes shoot in the longbow'.[27] Equally, Bishop Latimer could, as we have already seen, tell the young Edward VI during a sermon how his father had taught him to draw the longbow from childhood, and had supplied him with increasingly powerful bows as he grew in age and strength, just as other fathers did with their sons.[28]

Foreign observers were equally minded of the continuing importance of archers to the English and their armies. An Italian diplomat writing in about 1500 remarked that the bow was 'decidedly the weapon of the English as the pike is that of the Germans'. 'They have', he also noted, 'a very high reputation in arms; and from the great fear the French entertain of them, one must believe it to be justly acquired.'[29] In 1519 the Venetian ambassador Giustiani reported to the Signory that the real military force of England lay not in men-at-arms, for she could raise but a small quantity of these, but in infantry, whose number he hazarded at some 150,000, and whose special weapon was the longbow. The English archers were equipped with a breastplate, sword, bow and arrows and two stakes, with which they made palisades. They insisted on monthly pay and were averse to hardship, but if given their comforts they would give battle daily, with a courage, vigour and valour that defied exaggeration. Above all, their prowess was in the bow.[30]

Nevertheless, although the reputation of the English archer remained high, the composition of Henry VIII's armies indicates that in actuality archers rarely comprised more than half the infantry forces. The remainder were made up primarily of billmen, whose role increasingly replaced that of dismounted men-at-arms. For whereas in the formations of the Hundred Years War and the Wars of the Roses it had been the men-at-arms, equipped with white harness, who had formed the armed core of the army, by the early Tudor period the number of fully equipped men-at-arms had fallen significantly, and recourse often had to be had to hiring stipendiaries on the continent for expeditionary armies. Nevertheless, as in the reign of Henry VII, the bulk of the army was raised through retinues brought by the nobility, supplemented by men raised from the shires through commissions of array. After 1512 the king dispensed with formal indentures, simply requiring service as a duty of holding offices, fees, annuities or land of the king's gift; in 1513, for example, nobles were summoned by signet letters to bring stipulated numbers of men, with the greatest lords being required to supply the most troops. The captain general of the rearguard, Charles Somerset, Lord Herbert, commanded 20 captains, 153 demi-lances and 883 footmen, while Charles Brandon, Duke of Suffolk, mustered 1,831 men, raised mostly from north Wales.[31] These larger retinues contained a mixture of infantry, horsed archers and light horse; that of Henry Bourchier, Earl of Essex, for example, comprised 255 infantry, 20 mounted archers and 30 demi-lances.[32] Smaller retinues contained around 100 men, comprising approximately equal numbers of bows and bills. Thus Robert Radcliffe, Lord FitzWalter, was to bring 50 archers and 50 bills, all on foot, 'sufficiently harneysed and appointed for the warres', while George, Lord Hastings brought 60 archers and 40 bills.[33] Such infantry were mostly raised by nobles from their household retainers and tenantry, although records of conduct money show some units came from towns. For every 100 men, there was a captain, petty captain and chaplain.[34] There was thus an important difference between the army of 1513 and that of 1415, in which archers had made up four-fifths of the whole force. Although Henry VIII had a substantial artillery train, this meant that the infantry itself had considerably less 'firepower' proportionally than had Henry V's army. For the 1513 campaign the king had purchased a number of hand-guns and larger arquebuses,[35] but the number of English hand-gunners remained small, and there was only a smattering of native pikemen, some of whom served as marines. Walter Devereux, Lord Ferrers, for instance, manned the *Trinity Sovereign* with a retinue of 420 men, including 300 pikemen, 100 archers and 7 billmen, suggesting that the pike was favoured in naval combat because of its great reach.[36] In the main, however, Henry relied for his pikemen primarily on the 8,000 German Landsknechte and Burgundians supplied by Maximilian.[37]

The significance of archers to the army of 1513 is revealed by the impressive logistical provision for them, on paper at least. Each of the three divisions or 'wards' of the army was allocated 5,200 bows, in parcels of 400, which required 13 wagons, 86,000 bowstrings contained in 20 barrels needing 2 wagons, 10,000 sheaves of arrows requiring 26 wagons, plus 5,000 archers' stakes (2 per man) and caltrops in large numbers, in addition to cavalry lances, 4,000 pikes and 5,000 bills.[38] The Statutes and Ordinances of War issued at Calais had commanded that at the first muster 'every archer have his bow and arrows whole; that is to wit, in arrows 30, or 23 headed and whole in a sheaf at the least'. All were to swear that their bows, arrows and armour belonged to them, or their master or captain, while significantly no one enlisted as an archer was to change to any other form of fighting without the king's special licence.[39] As the army advanced against the French outside Thérouanne the king was surrounded by his bodyguard of mounted archers, drawn from his Yeomen of the Guard.[40] The number of these yeomen varied from a minimum of 150 to over 600 in Henry VIII's early reign,

though subsequently he was to supplement them with a gentleman bodyguard known as the King's Spears, a force of 200 men, formed of 50 gentlemen each with his own archer, light cavalryman and mounted valet.[41] Some of these men were clearly close to the king's affections and must have shot with him regularly; when in 1512 one of Henry's yeomen, Richard Newbolt, had killed a man at Westminster Palace, the king ordered him to be hanged only with great reluctance, as he was a 'specyall archour'.[42]

As the campaign was dominated by siege we gain no clear idea of how the archers would have been deployed had a major battle been joined, though their traditional role as skirmishers was well demonstrated. During a minor French raid on the outskirts of the king's camp at Calais at low tide, for example, a force of archers waded into the harbour and repelled them, while at the siege of Thérouanne, it was the archers who protected Henry's army from enemy sallies and drove off a sortie by German mercenaries.[43] The only field engagement which occurred was a minor skirmish at Bomy, near Thérouanne, known as the 'Battle of the Spurs' owing to the precipitate flight of the French and the rapid English pursuit. Here, Henry's middle ward, numbering some 16,000 men, advanced against a French relief force, being covered by some light artillery drawn up on rising ground on one flank and by an advanced unit of archers, who in time-honoured manner used a hedge for cover. The archers so galled the horses of the French gendarmes that they quickly turned in flight, despite the barding of their mounts which the knights now discarded to speed their retreat.[44] Royal propaganda and self-delusion magnified this scuffle – the only engagement in the field that Henry's armies would fight in all of his French expeditions – into a triumph on a par with the victories of Poitiers and Agincourt.[45] Such a vaunt might with much more justification have been made for the defeat of the Scots at Flodden which had occurred while Henry was playing at soldiering in France, though the victorious commander, Thomas Howard, Earl of Surrey, was discreet enough not to make any such claims. For Henry's part, his relief at the removal of the threat of invasion on his northern border was tempered by jealousy of Howard's far better deserved military glory.[46] Flodden was undoubtedly one of the most significant military engagements of the period, witnessing as it did the deaths of the Scottish king and the flower of his aristocracy.[47] It revealed, moreover, that an English army composed of the traditional combination of bills and bows was capable of defeating massed formations of pikemen supported by heavy artillery. Yet it equally showed how limited a role the longbow had come to play in such a decisive engagement.

FLODDEN FIELD, 9 SEPTEMBER 1513

In 1513 James IV invaded northern England with one of the most powerful and best-equipped armies that Scotland had ever raised. The Scots had long been accustomed to fighting with large formations of infantry equipped with the long spear, but James had been determined to introduce the much longer pike in line with continental military practice, and to reorganise the army in new formations better suited to its deployment. In 1513 his French allies, who wished to use the threat of a Scottish invasion of England to weaken any expeditionary force Henry might use to attack France, sent military advisers to assist in training the Scots in the use of the new weapon, large numbers of which were now imported through the port of Leith or manufactured in Edinburgh itself. They also brought, no doubt at James's request, a large number of arquebuses, for the Scots king had readily appreciated the value of gunpowder weapons and had already done much to expand his artillery park.[48] At Flodden the Scots were deployed in five main columns, with a bowshot distance between each, while in turn each column was subdivided into two brigades.[49] Eight French military experts were stationed with each column. But more traditional arms were still in evidence alongside the new, for many Scottish troops, particularly those from the Highlands, were archers, swordsmen or axemen wielding their traditional long-hafted weapons. James's sheriffs had been ordered that year to provide adequate supplies of two-handed swords, halberds, Leith axes and Jedart staves, as well as bows, crossbows and hand-guns.[50] John Major, a lowland Scots author writing in 1527, described the distinctive appearance of such Highlanders or 'Wild Scots':

> From the mid-leg to the foot they go uncovered: their dress is, for an overgarment, a loose plaid and a shirt saffron dyed. They are armed with a bow and arrows, a broadsword and a small halbert. They always carry in their belt a stout dagger, single-edged but of the sharpest. In time of war they cover the whole body with a coat of mail, made of iron rings, and in it they fight. The common folk among the Wild Scots go out to battle with the whole body clad in a linen garment sewn together in patchwork, well daubed with wax or pitch, and with an overcoat of deerskin.[51]

Such men, drawn in part from the lands of the Gordon earl of Huntly, formed part of the left-most division of the Scots army which would soon lead the attack against the English.

To meet the Scottish threat the Earl of Surrey marched north with an army comprising the retinues of northern lords, including ecclesiastics such as the Bishop of Durham and the Abbot of Whitby, with the levies of Yorkshire, Cheshire, Lancashire and shires even further south, with a thousand marines under his son, the Admiral Thomas Howard.[52] Surrey's personal retinue consisted of 462 bows and bills, 22 light horsemen or demi-lances, and a single man-at-arms.[53] That such local contingents contained a mixture of bows and bills is well illustrated by a list in the church of St Oswald's in Arncliffe, Yorkshire, commemorating the men of Arncliffe and neighbouring Littondale and Hawswick who served in the battle. Once painted on to wooden boards and seemingly drawn from a muster list, each name is followed by the kind of weapon carried.[54] Thus from Arncliffe we find John Knolle, 'able horse and harnish'd', that is serving mounted and well armoured, probably as a man-at-arms and leader of the unit, together with Oliver Knolle 'a bowe' (perhaps John's son or brother, though the surname was a common one in the area), Robert Tylson 'a bille', William Firth 'a bowe', Richard Clemenger 'a bille', and so forth. These lists clearly show the mixture of bows and bills in these local contingents, most of whom appear to have served only as foot-soldiers.[55]

On 5 September the English made contact with the Scots, and found James's army drawn up in an impregnable fortified camp on Flodden Ridge, his flanks protected by a marsh and the River Till, and with the only approach up a very steep incline guarded by his ordnance, 'as goodly guns as have been seen in any realm'.[56] Realising a direct assault would be impossible, and failing to lure James down by an appeal to chivalric fair play, Surrey attempted a bold flanking manoeuvre. Marching north on the eastern bank of the River Till, as if perhaps to move on Berwick, he then swung his army south-west over the river, with the vanguard and the artillery under his son Thomas Howard crossing downstream at Twizel Bridge, while Surrey himself with the main battle crossed south of Etal Castle. The English army now stood between James and his route back into Scotland. But James's intelligence was good, and on seeing Surrey's deployment he hastened to turn his army about and occupy Branxton Hill, which also offered a strong defensive position. Some accounts suggest that James, on seeing that the English forces had separated to cross the Twill, decided to launch an attack against the admiral's division, in the hope of defeating it before Surrey could come to its support.[57] Writing with hindsight in 1514, the Scots privy council believed defeat had come from James's impatience to attack the English and the inexperience of his troops.[58] Yet the Scots king more probably intended to force Surrey into an uphill attack during which James's large guns

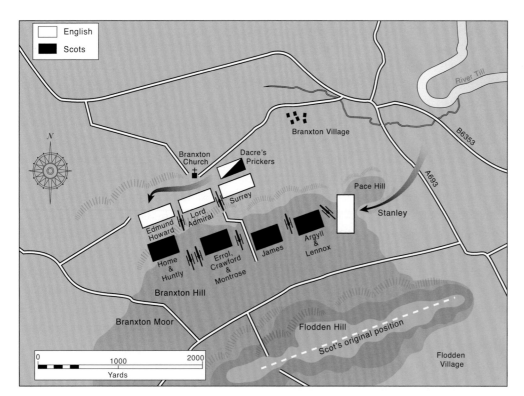

Left: The battle of Flodden, 9 September 1513.

Below: English billmen rout the pike formations of James IV's army at the battle of Flodden, 1513, from a woodcut by Hans Burgkmair from *Der Weisskunig*. To the left King James (wearing a crown) lies slain, though in reality he was cut down without being recognised in the fierce mêlée. (*© The Board of Trustees of the Royal Armouries*)

would sweep the English with fire before a devastating Scots counter-attack by massed pikemen.[59]

Instead, the English artillery was quickly brought to bear, and fired with great effect against the Scottish guns and formations, leaving James with little option but to order an all-out attack between 4 and 5 p.m.[60] Just as at Agincourt the shooting of Henry V's archers had galled the stationary French into launching an attack, now at Flodden Surrey's guns forced James IV to abandon his strong defensive position which he had hoped the English would have to assault, compelling him instead to fight the offensive engagement he had sought to avoid. But though the king had to change his plan of battle, the Scots advanced 'in good order, after the Almayns manner, without speaking a word'.[61] They attacked with their columns in echelon, some 'in grete plumpes, part of them quadrant [square or rectangular formation]' and some 'pikewise', that is being more wedge-shaped to the front, with the division of Lords Home and Huntly leading by the left, followed by that of Errol, Crawford and Montrose, and followed up by the largest division under James himself.[62] Each division contained eight French captains to help control and direct the formations of pikemen.[63] Initially it seemed this incisive strike would pay off as the Scots borderers under Lord Hume utterly routed the right wing of the admiral's division under his brother Edmund Howard.

The Scottish chronicler Pittscottie noted that in this first attack 'the Earl of Huntly's Highland men with their bows and two-handed swords fought so manfully that they defeated the Englishmen'.[64] It would seem likely that these men preceded

the closely arrayed border pikemen of Lord Hume, using their bows to skirmish as they came on before closing in with their great swords. Many of Edmund Howard's force, composed of men from Cheshire, Lancashire and Yorkshire, took to flight, but instead of regrouping to attack the admiral's exposed flank the borderers left the field in search of plunder, allowing Surrey speedily to dispatch a relief force under Lord Dacre with some

1,500 horse. Dacre's counter-attack just succeeded in holding the Scots, whose charge must now have lost some of its momentum and formation, though Howard himself was only narrowly saved from death or capture by the efforts of John, the Bastard of Heron.

Meanwhile, however, the second Scots division under Errol, Crawford and Montrose had advanced in good order down Branxton Hill against the admiral's division, while behind and to their right the king's own division advanced in turn against Surrey. As the Scots came within range the English archers loosed their shafts, but against the more heavily armoured troops who formed the front ranks of the pike columns their shafts had little impact. As the chronicler Hall wrote, the Scots 'were most assuredly harnassed and abode the most dangerous shot of arrows, which sore them annoyed, but yet [unless] it hit them in some bare place, did them no hurt'.[65] Although the *Trewe Encounter* noted that 'there was great wind and sodden rain, all contrary to our bows and our archers', it seems unlikely that the rain adversely affected the archers' bowstrings, for these were usually water-proofed by waxing.[66] Contrary winds might have made the archers' shafts fall short, as they had for the Lancastrians at Towton, but contemporaries were agreed that it was the quality of the Scots armour rather than the weather that effectively neutralised the longbowmen. 'The Scots', noted the *Trewe Encounter*, 'were so surely harnessed with complete harness, German jacks, rivets, splents and other habilments, that the shot of arrows in regard did them no harm.'[67] Writing to Cardinal Wolsey shortly after

the battle, Bishop Ruthal noted that the Scots 'were so well cased in armour that the arrows did them no harm, and were such large and stout men that one would not fall when four or five bills struck them'.[68] The only English archers who may have shot to any effect were on the English left, where Sir Edward Stanley's men faced far more lightly armoured Highlanders under the Earls of Lennox and Argyll.[69] Rather, it was the fire of the light English field artillery which, able to achieve a range of some 600 yards (twice that of the extreme range of the longbow) first put the heavy Scottish guns out of action and then fired murderous volleys into the densely packed Scottish units, scything paths through their ranks and throwing their formations into disorder.

The exact course of the critical stages of the battle which followed is far from clear. It may be that this second Scots unit experienced difficulties when its pike formation encountered a small but boggy stream lying at the foot of the hill in front of the Lord Admiral's position on the comparatively high ground of Piper's Knoll. The combination of this obstacle and the rising ground, also encountered further along the line by James's own battle, may have been sufficient to rob the Scots attack of its force, and to have allowed the English billmen to close with the first ranks of the Scots pikemen before being overwhelmed by the oncoming mass of their formations. Equally, the English artillery seems to have inflicted damage on the advance squares and disrupted their formation. Whatever the cause, it is clear that the English billmen were able to break in among

Above: An English bill, sixteenth century. The English version of the halberd, the 'brown bill' was the principal infantry weapon other than the longbow in English armies of the fifteenth and sixteenth centuries. (© *The Board of Trustees of the Royal Armouries*)

Right: A detail of the 'Flodden Window' in St Leonard's Church, Middleton, Lancashire, from a coloured engraving of 1845, showing a row of kneeling archers, headed to the right by their chaplain, Henry Taylor. Dressed in the livery of their lord, Sir Ralph Assheton, each archer has his name inscribed along his bow. (*Reproduced by courtesy of Geoffrey Wheeler*)

the pikemen, wreaking havoc with their weapons and exploiting emerging gaps in the Scottish ranks. The pike's great strength lay in its deployment in closely formed ranks but for close combat it was useless, and when forced to drop their great spears and fight with swords the Scots were at a clear disadvantage against men wielding the murderous bill.[70] As Bishop Ruthal put it, 'our bills shortly disappointed the Scots of their long spears', for 'they could not resist the bills that lighted so thick and so sore upon them'. Similarly Brian Tuke, Clerk to the Signet, noted that 'the men in the English army who are now called halberdiers decided the whole affair, for in this battle the affair so developed that the bows and ordnance were of little service'.[71] King James, whose own pike had been cut to pieces, and his men stood their ground, fighting fiercely till nightfall, but they were gradually overwhelmed. Nor could they receive support from the division of Argyll and Lennox, which was caught in the flank and rear by units from Sir Edward Stanley's forces on the English left wing.

The slaughter was terrible, for the English gave no quarter and the chase continued for 3 miles. As an observer noted, many more would have been slain had the English been mounted, and had night not intervened.[72] Among the Scottish losses were thirteen earls, the Archbishop of St Andrews, the Bishops of the Isles and of Caithness and several abbots. James himself had fallen, but such was the fierceness of the mêlée that his death – which if bruited abroad would probably itself have decided the day – went unnoticed, until his body was recognised the following morning by Lord Dacre. His corpse, noted Hall, had been pierced by 'diverse deadly wounds and in especial one with an arrow, and another with a bill as appeared when he was naked'.[73] Where this arrow wound was is not stated, though given the quality of James's armour it was probably in the face or neck, just as David II had been wounded by arrows in the face at Neville's Cross in 1346. The possibility of a facial wound is suggested by the fact that following the battle the king granted Surrey the right to bear an augmentation to the Howard arms. This took the form of the Scottish royal arms displayed in the bend of their own arms, but with an arrow piercing the mouth of a truncated lion – symbolising the death of the Scottish king and the dimidiation of the power of his realm.[74]

If Flodden revealed the limitations of archers against the plate armour of the early sixteenth century, it none the less produced one of the earliest surviving memorials to English archers. In about 1524 Sir Richard Assheton erected a fine stained-glass window in St Leonard's Church, Middleton, Lancashire, to commemorate the victory at Flodden, which among other scenes now badly damaged depicts Sir Richard, his wife and son at prayer, while beneath them are shown his retinue of archers from Middleton whom he led to the great battle. Sir Richard himself bears a sheaf of arrows at his waist, testimony to the ubiquity of archery among all levels of English society, while his son carries a bow, reminding us of the common practice in later medieval English armies whereby a local lord or squire might serve as a man-at-arms while his sons or kindred might also serve but as less heavily equipped archers. Most remarkable, however, is the depiction of the sixteen archers, shown, like Sir Richard, in civilian dress but all wearing blue jackets of livery, while each kneeling archer carries a bow, above which is inscribed his name.[75] As Sir John Hale remarks in his study of warfare in renaissance art, 'So totally unusual is this anticipation of the village war memorial that at first glance they [the archers] may be taken as a tribute to Sir Richard's loins rather than his tenantry.'[76] Nevertheless, this window is indeed one of the earliest known memorials to the common soldier, and as such is vivid testimony to the respect in which these yeomen archers were held by their lord. Present too at the head of the archers is their chaplain, Henry Taylor, a reminder of the continuing role such clerics played in accompanying troops into battle against the Scots, as they had done since the days of the Standard in 1138. Doubtless it would have gladdened Sir Richard to learn that in his *Toxophilus* Roger Ascham paid special tribute to the bowmen of his shire at Flodden, 'in which battel the stoute archers of Cheshire and Lancashire for one day bestowed to the death for their prince and country sake, hath gotten immortall name and prayse for ever'.[77]

HACKBUTT, CALIVER AND ARQUEBUS: THE RISE OF THE HAND-GUN

Both armies at Flodden had been equipped with the latest artillery, yet the one weapon that had been largely absent was the hand-gun. The later fifteenth century had seen significant improvements in the technology of hand-held firearms, which continued apace during the sixteenth century. The provision of more effective stocks improved aim, while the introduction of corned gunpower greatly increased range and penetrative power. If armour of the early sixteenth century could defeat a longbow arrow and a crossbow bolt save perhaps at extreme close range, the ball fired from an arquebus was capable of penetrating even the best plate at a respectable distance. Even using uncorned powder modern tests have shown that an

By contrast, the famous Gascon captain Blaise de Montluc noted how at Boulogne in 1544 English archers had to get within very close range to loose their shafts, which found it increasingly difficult to penetrate breastplates made to stop the ball of an arquebus.[82] When, following the siege of Leith in 1560, the English captain Humphrey Barwick asked a French captain what effect the archers had had, he was told that arrows had killed none of the garrison and wounded only one.[83]

Given its potential, it is not surprising that in Europe the arquebus rapidly displaced the crossbow. In skilled hands the crossbow was undoubtedly by far the more accurate weapon, but its rate of shooting was, if faster than that of the hand-gun, only marginally so. Moreover, not only was the arquebus a more powerful weapon, but it was cheaper than the crossbow, with its steel or composite bow and its more complex trigger mechanism. It has been argued that it was its comparative cheapness, rather than its military effectiveness, that led to the widespread adoption of the hand-gun by the Italian city states during the second half of the fifteenth century. Venice had replaced crossbows with hand-guns as early as 1490 and in 1508 decided to arm its newly created state militia with firearms. Castilian infantry had made increasing use of shoulder-fired arquebuses alongside crossbowmen in the wars of the Reconquista, while Spain's intervention in the Italian wars from 1495 gave a further stimulus to the widespread adoption of such weapons.[84] In 1503 at Cerignola the arquebusiers of the great Spanish commander Gonzago de Cordoba, firing from defensive trenches, inflicted a bloody defeat on the Swiss – thereby demonstrating what Charles the Bold might have achieved, had he been a more competent general, at Grandson in 1476 against the formations of Swiss pikemen. In the empire, where wealthy and powerful cities such as Nuremburg had played a major role in the precocious development of firearms, the hand-gun had long been in widespread use, and in 1517 the emperor was simply recognising a *fait accompli* when he declared the crossbow obsolete. France was more halting in its relegation of the crossbow, though it was increasingly relegated to the defence of fortifications. In 1523 the company of Blaise de Montluc was still comprised entirely of crossbowmen, but by 1527 there were 400 arquebusiers in his company of 800 men.[85] Francis I's catastrophic defeat at Pavia in 1525 at the hands of Charles V's infantry armed with arquebuses had provided an important catalyst for change; when in 1534 Francis attempted to reform the French infantry – choosing, as a true renaissance prince, a classical model for his new 'legions' – each new unit of 6,000 men was now to contain only pikemen and arquebusiers, with a small detachment of halberdiers. The new

Arquebus racks in the Tyrol Armoury, a miniature from the workshop of Jorg Kolderer, c. 1502–8. (© *Kunsthistorisches Museum, Vienna*)

arquebus could obtain a muzzle velocity of 340 metres per second, with an initial energy of 1,150 joules – a huge increase on that exerted by longbows or crossbows.[78] With corned powder, moreover, a sixteenth-century matchlock arquebus from the arsenal at Graz could shoot a 15mm lead bullet through 1mm of mild steel at 100m (and in doing so exerted 1,750 joules of energy, with a muzzle velocity of 428 metres per second).[79] The heavier musket which emerged from the 1550s and usually required the aid of a rest for shooting was still more powerful. A wheel-lock musket was capable of penetrating 2mm of steel at 100m (4,400j, 482m/s, using uniform-sized corned powder).[80] Tests using a German matchlock arquebus of about 1600 with a .75 bore and firing a ball weighing 30g (with a velocity of 190m/s) found that the ball penetrated through the front of a seventeenth-century lobster-tailed burgonet (*zischagge*) and exited through the back; a sixteenth-century breastplate was penetrated by two out of three balls, though this was not a heavy specimen, and a thicker backplate withstood shots from the same arquebus.[81]

importance of the gun was shown by the fact that out of a proposed force of seven 'legions' numbering 42,000 men, 12,000 were to be arquebusiers.[86]

In both England and Scotland, where the longbow had for centuries been the predominant missile weapon, the transition to firearms was far more gradual. In England it was scarcely complete by the end of Elizabeth's reign in 1603, while in Scotland, despite the growing preponderance of firearms, the longbow remained in military use well into the seventeenth century. The general use of the crossbow had been prohibited by Henry VII, not in favour of the hand-gun but lest it undermine the practice of the longbow, but the Scottish monarchs did not harbour such qualms. Crossbowmen as well as hand-gunners formed part of Albany's forces in 1523, while the crossbow was accepted at musters at least until 1540.[87] A comparable difference in attitude towards hand-guns seems to have existed between the two realms, at least in the first decades of the sixteenth century. The Scots king actively sought to promote the spread of firearms. In 1535 it was decreed that landholders were to have 'hagbuts of found' or 'hagbuts of Crochert', and now instead of bowstaves every merchant coming into the realm was to bring at least two hagbutts with them, as well as quantities of gunpowder.[88] In stark contrast, Henry VIII had reissued his father's prohibition on the use of crossbows and hand-guns without special licence to all but men worth £100 or more per annum.[89] This allowed nobility and gentry to use such weapons, primarily for the chase, but in 1528 the king extended the ban to all, irrespective of rank, and forbade the manufacture or importation of crossbows and hand-guns into the realm, except with royal permission.[90] In part, such legislation was an attempt to ensure a ready supply of skilled archers, and Sir Thomas Elyot reflected the government's paranoia in his belief that 'crosse bowes and hand gunnes were brought into this realme, by the sleighte of our enemies, to th'entent to destroye the noble defence of archery'.[91] Yet it also reflected deep-seated fears among the king's council that the widespread ownership and use of hand-guns among subjects would lead to social unrest and give robbers and outlaws too formidable a weapon.

Such legislation, however, did not mean that the English crown was blind to the increasing importance of firearms. Henry VIII might take great pride in the longbow but he was no Luddite when it came to military technology. A connoisseur of fine armour, Henry brought in German and Flemish armourers to work at the Tower and, hoping to match the centres of armour production in Germany and Italy, subsequently established workshops at Greenwich. He continued his father's efforts to develop a modern and impressive artillery arm.[92] Surrey had good ordnance with him at Flodden, and his

victory resulted in the extensive Scottish artillery park falling into English hands. Similarly, the French expeditions of 1513, 1523 and 1543–4 were well equipped with a range of heavy and light guns. At sea Henry fully realised the navy's significance and spent heavily on building new vessels or re-equipping others with the latest ordnance – as the range of guns recovered from the *Mary Rose* bears witness.[93] He was fascinated by firearms and owned some early examples of breech-loading matchlocks as well as the sophisticated but expensive wheel-lock pistols and rifles, while some of his guard carried ingenious combination weapons of buckler and pistol. During the later stages of his reign, moreover, he built a series of artillery fortifications along the south coast and continued to strengthen the great fortresses of Calais and Boulogne.[94]

If Henry did not rush to re-equip all his English forces with pikes and arquebuses in the manner of continental armies, there was good reason. Armies of bows and bills had defeated the German pike-armed mercenaries of Martin Schwartz at Stoke in 1487, and in 1489 Lord D'Aubeny, the Lord-Lieutenant of Calais, had won a notable victory over a combined force of French and Flemings at Dixmude, where he inflicted heavy casualties, took many of the enemy's artillery and 'gat hym there great worship'.[95] Above all, at Flodden bows and bills, well supported by good artillery and light cavalry, had annihilated one of the most impressive Scottish hosts yet fielded, fighting in the latest manner as pikemen. For warfare in Scotland and Ireland, moreover, such forces continued to be highly effective. Billmen could operate better in broken country than the large formations of pike whose effectiveness depended on cohesion, and while the arquebus was highly vulnerable to the vagaries of wind and rain, which might dampen powder, blow out a slow match or scatter the priming powder, the longbow could still operate effectively if bow and string alike were properly oiled or waxed. The fighting in the major pitched battle at Flodden had been an exception, and in the fast-moving raids and skirmishes between the forces of the borderers, mounted archers must have retained much of their efficacy. In late 1513 the force led by Sir Christopher Dacre on a raid in strength into the Scottish Middle March comprised 2,000 horse and 4,000 archers, while on the expedition of 1523 the retinue of the commander, the Earl of Surrey, contained 1,116 mounted archers as well as 1,028 infantry and 200 demi-lances, out of a total force of around 10,000 men.[96] When during his invasion Surrey invested the powerful border stronghold of Cessford, archers supported the English assaults, together with fire from a number of field guns.[97]

For the remainder of Henry VIII's reign, and indeed well beyond, bowmen continued to form an important part of

English forces operating against the Scots, whether as smaller raiding parties led by the Wardens of the Marches, or as larger invasion forces. In 1542, for example, archers formed an integral part of the small army raised by Sir Thomas Wharton, Warden of the West March, which succeeded in routing a far larger Scottish force at the battle of Solway Moss. As the Scottish invasion army manoeuvred past the boggy ground of the Solway Moss, they found their route south blocked by Wharton, who had drawn up his bills and bows on Hopesike Hill, including 200 archers drawn from Kendal under Walter Strickland. As the Scots came within range of the English archers, a force of 700 light border horse or 'prickers' under Sir William Musgrave launched a prearranged attack against the Scots' left flank. The Scots army, seemingly already demoralised and suffering from disputes over command, was quickly thrown into utter disorder as the attacks of the English light cavalry drove them into the Moss, where many drowned. Those slain in combat were few but the rout was total and the English captured a rich haul of prisoners and a fine artillery train.[98] As late as January 1560 the Earl of Huntly had advised the English to include one or two thousand archers in their army entering Scotland, and archers took part in the siege of Leith.[99] Archers likewise remained an integral part of Scottish armies. When Anglo-Scottish tensions had escalated in 1532, James V sent 500 Scots archers to assist insurgents against English rule in Ireland.[100] Highland archers, wearing only their saffron-dyed shirts and plaid, had fought at the siege of Haddington in 1549, while at the great battle of Pinkie the chronicler Pattan believed that among the Scottish forces were 4,000 'Irish' (Highland) archers under the Earl of Argyll.[101] A visitor to the Highlands in 1618 noted that 'their weapons are long bowes and forked arrowes, swords and targets, harquebusses, muskets, durks and Loquhabor [Lochaber] axes', which they might also take with them for hunting.[102] As late as 1669 an English clergyman, James Brome, visiting Scotland, commented of the Highlanders that:

> when they go to War, the Armour wherewith they cover their bodies, is Morion or Bonnet of Iron, and a Habergeon, which comes down almost to their very heels; their Weapons against their Enemies are Bows and Arrows, and they are generally reputed good Marks-Men upon all occasions; their Arrows for the most part are barbed or crooked, which once entered within the Body cannot be well drawn out again, unless the Wound be made wider; some of them fight with broad Swords and Axes, and in the room of a Drum make use of a Bag-pipe.[103]

Nevertheless, the absence of large numbers of arquebusiers and pikemen among the forces raised in Tudor England has sometimes been seen as symptomatic of the conservatism and insularity of Henrician armies, failing to keep abreast of continental developments in war. It has, for example, been remarked of Henry's 1513 expedition to France that 'fundamentally, the "army royal" was an old-fashioned force, raised by quasi-feudal methods, fighting with out of date weapons for an anachronistic cause'.[104] As Gervase Phillips has argued, however, the kind of specialist troops deemed necessary for warfare on the continent, such as pikemen, arquebusiers or heavy cavalry, could readily be obtained from allies or by the hire of mercenaries. This was not only cost-effective and secured well-trained and equipped forces, but was standard practice across Europe, as the dependence by French and Imperial armies on Swiss pikemen, German Landsknechts and, increasingly, Italian and Spanish arquebusiers, amply demonstrated. Military change was less a matter of sudden revolution than of adaption and the effective combination of old and new weapons and combat systems, and the continued survival and adaptation of the longbow was but a prominent example of this phenomenon.[105]

There could be no better symbol of the synthesis of tradition and innovation than the inventories of royal fortifications or 'bulworkes' made in 1547, the year of Henry VIII's death. Fearing French invasion, Henry had built a series of impressive new artillery fortresses along the south coast, and strengthened existing coastal defences with blockhouses and provision for guns. Yet at every place of strength there was a ready supply of bows and arrows; thus, for instance, at Dover there were 320 bows, at Carisbrooke 21 chests of bows, and even at the small fort at East Tilbury 49 yew bows, five dozen bowstrings and 64 sheaves of livery arrows. At Calais, which had been systematically refortified to the latest standards of artillery defences, the inventory reveals not only a formidable range of cannon, but a special 'Arrowe Lofte' in which were stored 4,600 sheaves of feathered arrows, 60 sheaves of feathered and cased arrows, 200 arrow cases of red leather 'with girdells', 2,000 heads for livery arrows and 66 sheaves of unfeathered arrows.[107] There was also 'the long bowe Chambre', containing 1,500 'long bowes of all sortes', 'the crossbowe Chambre', with a wide range of tools and material for their repair, and the 'Malle [Maul] Chambre', full of bills, spiked pole-arms known ironically as 'holy-water sprinklers', halberds and 824 leaden mauls, the traditional side-arm for English archers since the days of Agincourt.[108] Nor were these mere mouldering antiques, overtaken by the pace of modern warfare; in 1549 Protector Somerset, a highly competent commander well versed in continental developments, was still ordering large quantities of yew bows and livery arrows to be sent to Boulogne, along with 500 hackbutts, powder and other munitions. Similarly, 500 yew bows 1,500 sheaves of arrows and 30 gross of bowstrings were sent to Calais, in addition to a large quantity of pikes, lances and artillery equipment.[109]

It was in such a context, then, that the core of English armies during Henry VIII's reign retained bows and bills. For the expedition to France in 1523 the Duke of Suffolk relied on the emperor to furnish him with contingents of pike, as he had done for Henry's army in 1513. The same year Suffolk noted that for a new campaign against the Scots he would need at least 4,000 'Almayns' or German mercenaries, 'for the Duke [of Albany] will bring pikes with him, to which the English are not accustomed but will easily learn when they see the order of the Almayns'.[110] The duke's optimism, however, was not matched by any sustained attempt to replace the bill with the pike among English levies, while arquebusiers were still less in evidence. None is recorded serving in France in 1522–3, and it was only after the failure of the campaign that Henry's government made large purchases of 10,000 hand culverins and 5,000 hackbutts, as well as enough pikes and pikemen's armour to equip over 10,000 men.[111] These and subsequent purchases of firearms do, however, indicate that questions of cost were not a significant reason for the widespread retention of the longbow, even though it was considerably cheaper than the arquebus. Throughout Henry's reign the best kind of yew longbow could be purchased 'at the king's price' set by statute at 3s 4d. By contrast, in 1513 hand-guns were bought by the crown at 6s each, and larger arquebuses at around 12s each, in 1523 hand culverins cost 25 sous (complete with powder horns) and hackbutts 40 sous each, while in 1535 8 hagbutts cost 40s, and a culverin 28s.[112] Nevertheless, while arquebuses and other firearms might be purchased in large numbers – by 1547 there were 6,500 hand-guns and 20,000 pikes in the Tower alone[113] – the policy of forbidding subjects to own or shoot firearms in a domestic context meant that troops issued with them had little opportunity to practise effectively until on campaign.

Licences to retain arquebuses, however, must have been granted, as by 1544, when Henry undertook his last and largest continental venture, 'the enterprise of Boulogne', arquebusiers were being included in some though not all of the retinues brought by the nobles and gentry. Thus Lord Wriothesley's retinue contained 20 hackbuteers, 50 archers, 50 bills, 40 pikes, 20 light horse and 20 'demi-lances', but that of the Duke of Suffolk contained none. Presumably some of the nobility had obtained the king's permission, even perhaps his encouragement, to allow some of their more trusted retainers or tenants to possess and shoot firearms. Yet of the 28,000 English infantry raised in 1544 only around 2,000 were hand-gunners, with the bulk remaining bows and bills, with a leavening of pikemen. In one detachment of the main 'ward' or battle, for example, there were 181 arquebusiers, 380 pikes, 807 archers and 1,073 bills. Overall, bills now outnumbered bows, and in some retinues the proportion of archers was strikingly reduced. The Earl of Huntingdon, for instance, was summoned to serve with a retinue of 70 horsemen and '150 able footmen, whereof 29 to be archers, every one furnished with a good bow in a case to carry it in, with 24 good arrows in a case with a good sword and dagger'.[114] As on previous occasions, Henry sought to supplement his forces with Landsknecht pikemen, detachments of heavy cavalry from the Low Countries and four companies of elite Italian and Spanish arquebusiers.[115] The Duke of Somerset was also to hire elite units of arquebusiers for his campaign of 1547 against Scotland, in which they were to play a prominent role. Such a trend is striking; just as in the later twelfth and thirteenth centuries Angevin kings had hired elite crossbowmen from Gascony and beyond, so now specialists using the crossbow's successor were again employed by English rulers as the cream of available missilemen. The days of the English archer fulfilling this role in mercenary service throughout Europe were over.

The kind of consciously balanced force evinced by Lord Wriothesley's retinue in 1544 suggests that by the 1540s archers were being increasingly regarded not as the army's mainstay but as supporting troops to guard formations of bills and pikes. And it was in this role that the longbow would continue to play a part in tactical thinking for some decades. By about 1550 pikemen were becoming increasingly important in English armies. But as the engagements between Cerignola (1503) and Pavia (1525) had demonstrated, unsupported pikemen were vulnerable to the fire of arquebusiers and field artillery.[116] They were also threatened by cavalry, particularly when used in conjunction with firearms. At Marignano in 1515, for example, the French repeated Charles the Bold's tactics at Grandson by attacking the Swiss columns from the flanks with heavy cavalry, forcing them to halt in defensive formation, while artillery was brought to bear against their front. The French gendarmes attacked in relays of 500 horse, and, as Francis I wrote to his mother, doubtless with the humiliating 'Battle of the Spurs' in mind, 'this way more than thirty fine charges were delivered, and no one will in future be able to say that cavalry are no more use than hares in armour'.[117] The French Huguenot commander François La Noue noted in his *Discours* that even a small force of cavalry could rout a force of 5,000 arquebusiers on the move, and that a guard of pikemen was essential to cover them against attack by horsemen.[118] Accordingly, the unwieldy formation of pikemen needed the protection of their own 'shot', while in turn the formations of pikemen helped protect the arquebusiers, whose slowness of reloading made them vulnerable. While in European armies the supporting 'shot' comprised largely arquebusiers, English forces readily incorporated their archers into these defensive units of 'shot' in combination with men using the caliver or the heavier arquebus. Instead of defending formations of men-at-arms, archers now formed up on the wings, or as a covering screen, for bodies of pike. In his *A.B.C. for the Wars* written in about 1550 to instruct the young Edward VI, Thomas Audley drew on his experiences in Henry VIII's wars to lay out an ideal battle formation. Significantly, he noted that while in earlier wars the English had won battles by 'shot' alone, such forces were now very vulnerable to being overrun by the powerful pike formations which dominated the battlefields of Europe. He thus advised that the bulk of the army should be formed of a square of pikemen, bills and halberds, surrounded by a screen of 'shot', either four deep, with the ranks comprising two archers and two arquebusiers, or five deep with three archers and two arquebusiers.[119] Ascham had noted earlier that 'artillery, now-a-days, is taken for two things, guns and bows', and it is striking that even by 1550 Audley took it for granted that archers would form a significant element of the 'shot'.

This concept was shared by Henry Barrett, a veteran and member of the Yeomen of the Guard. In 1550 he produced a diagram demonstrating the ideal marching formations for an English army. The artillery is placed in the vanguard, with engineers and men of the ordnance, with the main body of infantry surrounded by a hollow square, with echelons of shot at each corner. Behind this come the supply wagons, livestock and another square of mixed infantry including shot. The rearguard contains archers, hand-gunners and the cavalry, both heavy and light.[120] In 1562, at a time when Elizabeth was preparing to supply military aid to the French Huguenots, Barrett produced a tract in which he similarly envisages an army whose infantry is comprised of hand-gunners (hagbutters), archers, pikemen, billmen and halberdiers, the last to act as the guards for the ensigns and to be an elite, well-armoured group. Barrett goes on to describe the equipment which the archers should possess in some detail:

> Those leadinge longbowes muste regarde that every man have a good and mete bowe according to the drawghte [drawing power] and strengthe of the man, their stringes whipped or trenched in the nock and myddes, waxed on the glew [glue]; a braser and shooting glove, a sheafe of arrowes in number xxiv whearof I wish viii of them more

flighter then the reste to gall and annoy the enimyes farder of then the usuall custom of the sheafe arrowes, whose sharpe hallshot [hail-shot] may not be indured, neither may th'enimyes putt up hande or face to incounter the same – so that the archers draw their arrowes to the hedd and delyver the same according to that arte which ys onely by God his provydence geven to Englishe men, who geve us grace to mayntayne the same as our elders have donn before us. Such [archers] weareth lighte armures or else none, a burganet or huslyn, a maule of leade with a pyke [spike] of five inches longe, well stieled, sett in a staffe of fyve foote of lengthe with a hook at his gydell to take of and mayntayne the fighte as oure elders have donn, by handye stroaks.[121]

Archers continued to form elements of Elizabethan companies into the 1580s. In Lancashire in 1584, for example, a company of 250 men contained 40 archers, 40 halberdiers, 80 arquebusiers and 80 pikes. When such a mixed company deployed, the role of the 'shot' was to form two wings or 'sleeves' on either side of the main body of pikemen, in whose centre were the ensigns, guarded by the halberdiers. The archers were placed nearest the pikemen, while the arquebusiers were on their flanks.[122] Even Barnaby Rich, one of the stoutest proponents of the merits of the arquebus over the longbow, admitted in *A Right Exelent and Pleasant Dialogue* of 1575 that the bow still had its uses.[123] These were spelt out by Sir John Smythe in 1590, who stressed the continued value of archers in guarding pike formations, noting that bowmen should be 'in great numbers and reduced into the form of herses or double herses as wings to a battle or squadron of pikes, that they may the more conveniently give their volleys of arrows'. They should not, however, be obstructed by other formations of caliver men, whose smoke could impair their aim. When the enemy came within range, 'then the archers are to give their volleys of arrows at the enemy approaching within eight, nine, ten or eleven scores. And to perform the same they might not have any other weapon placed before them that may anyways take away their sights to direct their arrows towards the enemies' faces.'[124]

The importance of the archers' ability to gall enemy horsemen with their lighter, long-range flight arrows noted by Audley was echoed nearly thirty years later by Sir Thomas Wilford, who had been High Marshal on Lord Willoughby's expedition to Normandy in 1590. First among the archer's continued uses, he explained, was the effectiveness of their arrows 'in the field against horsemen, though it be shot at the highest random, only with the weight and fall it galleth both horse and man, and though the wound be not mortal, yet both

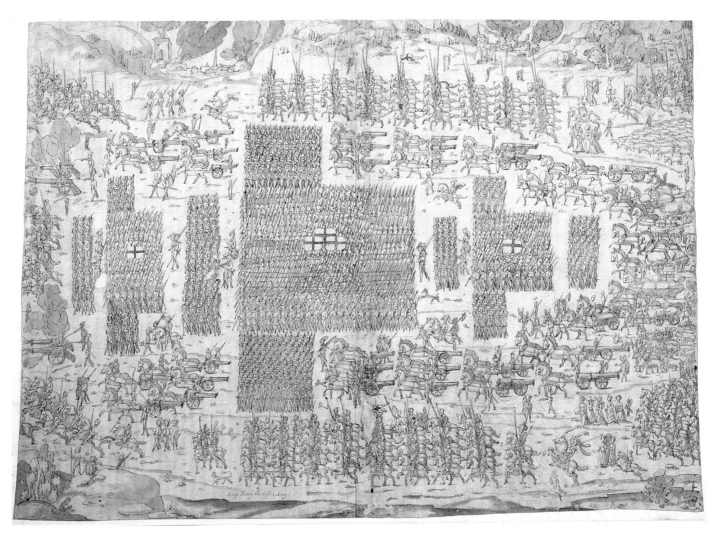

A Tudor drawing of an English army on the march, probably representing Henry VIII's French campaign of 1513 (British Museum, Cotton Augustus III). Each of the three divisions or wards consists of pikemen preceded and flanked by bodies of archers, while the whole army is screened by cavalry. (© *British Library*)

horse and man are made unserviceable then and long after, if so be they escape death'. Unlike the arquebus, he continued, the longbow was not affected by bad weather, and 'in the night it is both a ready and a secret shot, and doth not discover itself as doth the arquebusier both with his fire and blow'. Moreover, 'when men come near together, it is a very good weapon', and 'the use of it is good when it be in forcing the enemy's trenches, in sally out of town, or otherwise'. Above all, its rapid rate of shooting and its ability to shoot at a high trajectory over defences made it an ideal weapon in siege warfare in attack or defence:

> Fourthly, at an assault, when all the defences of a town are taken away, you deliver your arrows over the wall and rampires [ramparts] with its fall only. The like use we

have of them out of the town, when an assault is given, in delivering them into the enemy's trenches, and among men at their approach to an assault, though they be shot over the wall by chance. Fifthly, to shoot arrows with wildfire, to burn a gate or a drawbridge, to fire thatched or shingled houses. In France, when we were before Paris and divers other towns that we besieged, bows would have stood us in good stead and I did then wish that we had brought some bowmen with us. Surely we have no reason to give over the bow as we have done, for I hold that the worst bowman that can draw but his bow to be far better than a bad fire-shot.[125]

The longbow's speed of shooting also meant it remained an important part of naval armament in the Tudor navy as late as 1545, for its advantage over the arquebus in this respect would have given a marked advantage in attack or in repelling boarders. The same considerations caused the Venetians to arm their galleys with a combination of firearms and bows – in this case probably composite bows – and to carry archers among their complements well into the mid-sixteenth century.[126]

BAD BOW WOOD AND POOR SHOOTING

Recognition of the continuing military potential of the longbow was one thing, but obtaining an adequate supply of skilled archers, able to draw heavy war bows to their best effect, was quite another. At the very time when his modernising opponents were stressing the comparative ease with which men could be taught to use firelocks, Smythe was scoring an own goal when he stated in his polemic defending the longbow that he would not have anyone in the army who had not been trained in archery from boyhood.[127] This had always been the weapon's Achilles' heel. If, as we have seen, the repeated reissues of royal injunctions to practise shooting cannot always be taken at face value as a reflection of subjects' unwillingness to 'draw in the longbow', and that the theme of a falling off from a past golden age was a topos of long standing, the increasing proportion of bills to bows during the fifteenth century is more suggestive of a declining number of men who regarded their primary weapon as the longbow. By the 1530s the neglect of archery practice was openly acknowledged – and condemned – by men such as Sir Thomas Elyot. Towards the end of his reign Henry VIII reissued his earlier statute commanding regular practice at the butts, but as Roger Ascham himself had admitted, good shooting could not be fostered simply by royal fiat.[128]

Perceiving that part of the problem lay in the high cost of bows, the Tudor government had tried to regulate prices so that subjects could readily afford the necessary equipment required of them, and to provide bowyers with adequate supplies of imported bow wood.[129] In 1512 Henry VIII had ordered that for every yew bow produced bowyers were to make two cheaper bows of elm, a measure which also sought to ease the difficulties of obtaining sufficient imported bowstaves of good yew.[130] The latter concern, as we have seen, had long been a pressing issue. In 1528 the king voiced his concern that despite earlier goodly statutes the number of bowstaves being imported into the country had declined, and it was therefore ordained that until the time of the next parliament all bowstaves over 6ft 5in (1.96m) could be imported without custom duty.[131] Yet by 1536 Lord Lisle's agent John Husse was having trouble obtaining good bows for his lord, for as he complained 'under v mark the score I cannot be served of seasoned wood and good stuff', and on dispatching those he had obtained he commented wryly, 'touching their goodness, they are to be praised as they do hereafter prove'.[132] When in 1571 Elizabeth's council extended the obligation to import 10 bowstaves for every tun of wine to the foreign merchants trading from the extensive network of towns in the Hanseatic League, they were clearly fighting a losing battle.[133] In 1542

Henry VIII had renewed legislation capping the price of archery equipment; bows 'of the best sort' were to cost 3s 4d, 'of the second sort' 2s 6d, and 'of the third sort' 2s, with each sheaf of livery arrows 2s, better quality arrows 'of eight inch or nine inch the feather' 2s 4d per sheaf, a leather quiver 6d, a belt 2d, and twelve dozen bowstrings 3s 4d.[134] Yet in barely changing the prices of bows from those set by Henry VII back in 1488, the government was giving scant regard to the impact of inflation, in particular on the soaring cost of bowstaves, which had risen to £12 per hundred.[135] Accordingly, these measures seriously undermined the bowyers' ability to turn a profit, while the use of poorer wood further undermined sales, leaving them with large stockpiles of inferior bows.[136] In 1566 a new act allowed bowyers to charge more realistic prices, reflecting the fact that over a century the prices of imported bowstaves had risen from £2 to £12 per hundred. Now prices were set at 6s 8d for a bow made of best foreign yew, 3s 4d for second-best quality and 2s for bows of English yew – a striking indication of how poor native bow wood was considered to be compared to that from abroad.[137]

Contemporaries, however, sought a number of explanations for the country's military decline beyond a disinclination to practise at the butts and the high cost of bows. Enclosures, which replaced arable farming with sheep, had greatly diminished the number of good archers, for while ploughmen could, by virtue of their strength, draw powerful bows, 'shepherds be but ill archers'. It had been a matter of pride (and no little self-delusion) that 'Englishmen, by reason of their strong feeding, be much hardier and stronger in the wars than be the French peasants'. But now, soaring inflation and economic depression had greatly eroded the buying power of the yeoman's income or the soldier's wage. Unable to afford an adequate diet, their fighting ability diminished 'if they be pinched and weaned from meat'.[138] A good diet was acknowledged as essential for archers. In 1575 Humphrey Barwick argued that one of the reasons why arquebusiers were preferable to bowmen as troops was that they were less dependent on their physical strength. But as for the longbowman, 'If he have not his three meals a day, as is his custom at home, nor lies warm at nights, he presently waxes benumbed and feeble, and cannot draw so as to shoot long shots'.[139] The English captain Sir Roger Williams equally believed that particularly in harsh winter conditions few bowmen could adequately keep up the required strength, so that the effectiveness of their shooting declined and 'Few or none of these will then do any great hurt at twelve or fourteen score [240 or 280] yards'.[140]

As Jeremy Goring has shown, there were some elements of truth behind this gloomy picture of perceived physical and moral decadence. In the 1540s and 1550s the population seems to have been struck hard by epidemics of plague, and in particular by a virulent form of influenza known as 'the sweating sickness'. And whereas in the past noblemen's retinues had formed the core of royal armies, changing patterns of land ownership now meant the crown was far more reliant on a far larger number of lesser gentry, whose resources were less and who were unable to maintain the kind of households which earlier had supplied armed retainers. Tenants, moreover, were increasingly denying their obligations to serve in their military following.[141]

TRAIN-BANDS AND SHIRE ARCHERS

Nevertheless, many of the men raised by commissions of array in the shires continued to be armed with the longbow, particularly in the north of England. When the Earl of Sussex sought to muster shire levies to counter the rebellion of 1569 known as the 'Rising of the North', he found 300 pikemen and 300 arquebusiers among the men raised from the Midlands, but in Yorkshire only 60 out of over 2,000 men were found to be armed with the arquebus. Sussex remarked that those hand-gunners sent from the south were of such poor quality that he would rather have had good archers.[142] He was forced to rely on 300 arquebusiers drawn from the permanent garrison of Berwick-upon-Tweed, and to issue the levies with powder, which they largely lacked, supplied from Newcastle.[143] His report indicates the poor state of the militia, for he had discovered 'great default of armour and weapons, no spears for the horse, no arquebuses or powder for shot; all that the people had for armour was plate coats, jacks and sallets, with black bills, bows and arrows'.[144] It was in large part a response to such glaring shortcomings that in 1569 the Privy Council issued extensive proposals to local authorities in the shires for measures to increase the number of arquebusiers available in the kingdom and to provide for more regular shooting practice.[145] But their continuing fear that such weapons could be used for poaching, robbery or, still worse, popular insurrection was reflected in their stipulation that firearms should be kept in regional stores or 'artillery houses', and that from these the levies should be issued with arms, powder and shot for practice every fortnight under the supervision of the local justices of the peace.[146] As several counties told the Council, however, such a scheme was not only hopelessly impractical – only by being allowed to keep their weapons at home could men become proficient with them – but concentrating arms into such depots actually increased the chances of rioters or rebels gaining all the local supplies of firearms should they seize the arsenals. Essex, for instance, feared that 'shoemakers, tailors and weavers and other light persons' might do just such a thing.[147] The Council's continuing efforts, however, gradually bore fruit, and the number of men serving as arquebusiers rose substantially. By 1573 half the trained bands of London, totalling some 6,000 men, were being raised and trained as arquebusiers, and proportions of archers among the levies of southern and midland counties continued to decline.[148]

In the north of England and the borders, however, the survival of the longbow was more pronounced. In 1572 the Earl of Huntingdon issued articles of enquiry for the northern counties, including instructions 'to take order for the maintenance of artillery, that the laudable and allowable exercise of shooting in the long bow may be used, and butts made and used according to the good laws of this realm, that thereby other unlawful games be not so commonly used as they be, and this lawful exercise the more used for the better defence of this realm'.[149] The fortifications of Berwick might boast the very latest artillery defences with their 'trace italienne', but levies raised in the northern counties were still predominantly armed with bill and bow, with the better equipped possessing a jack and steel cap.[150] The continuing importance of the bow is also indicated by an inventory of 1580 for arms at Newcastle, which in addition to armour, pikes, lances and halberds contained 1,109 bows, mostly packed in boxes of 50, 4,940 sheaves of arrows and 279 lead mauls for archers, though there were also a respectable number of cannon and some 400 arquebuses.[151] Details of a muster by Lord Scrope in 1581 reveal that out of over 3,000 men fewer than a dozen possessed firearms, suggesting that the Wardens of the March regarded it as better to rely on the traditional weapon skills than to train elements of the county levies in new firearms drill. It also indicates that while the bow and bill predominated in the southern areas of the march, the men nearest the border were mostly equipped with a jack, steel cap and a spear, reflecting the long tradition of the spear's predominance as an infantry weapon in Scotland. Thus in the Leith Ward, Cumberland, there were only some 171 spearmen compared to over 1,000 bowmen and billmen, whereas in the Eskdale and Allerdale Wards there only 83 bowmen to over 2,000 spearmen.[152] The same phenomenon is visible in the muster of 1584, when the Eastern March, which was all in close proximity to Scotland, raised only spearmen, 2,173 in number, and no bowmen. The Western March, however, still supplied 2,500 archers and 2,500 billmen, all 'furnished', that is owning defensive equipment including a jacket or steel cap or both, and a further 2,682 abled-bodied but 'unfurnished' men whose weapons were not recorded. Similarly, the weapons and equipment of the men of the Middle March, which brought the total levy to over 15,000 men, were not specified.[153]

As late as 1583 bows were also still to be found among the equipment of some of the light horse of the Western March, who were armed with breast- and backplate or a jack, a steel helmet, sword, lance and buckler.[154] The same was true among infantry forces. In 1587 the Council stipulated that 40 per cent of a special force of 200 infantry for border defence should be gunners, with 20 per cent pikes and spears and 20 per cent bows.[155] In 1592 the elite garrison of Berwick still received 1,000 bows as well as 300 muskets and 300 calivers or lighter hand-guns,[156] and while the supply of such firearms reflected the government's recognition of the need to increase the numbers of shot, an inventory at the same arsenal in 1593 suggests that over 500 arquebuses had been allowed to decay through neglect.[157]

Further south, however, matters were different. By 1588, when England was threatened by the great Armada, none of London's trained militia was equipped with the bow. Levies from the counties of Wiltshire, Cambridgeshire and Hunting-donshire comprised solely pikemen, arquebusiers and caliver-men, while in other counties, even in the North and the Midlands, bowmen formed only between one-third and one-fifth of the troops.[158] There were still archers among the forces raised at Tilbury, but Sir John Smythe was scathing as to the manner in which they had been deployed, indicating an ever-diminishing awareness of how bowmen could be put to most effective use.[159] But for all his eloquent polemic, Smythe was fighting a losing battle. The efforts of the Privy Council to increase the number of arquebusiers was slowly but surely killing off the longbow as a military weapon. In 1570 the Council noted that men no longer practised shooting with the longbow 'imagining it to be of no use for service as they see the caliver so much embraced at present'.[160] This had not been the government's intention, for the year previously they had forbidden trained archers to practise with hand-guns, in order to retain at least an element of skilled bowmen. In 1577 they were moved to instruct local authorities that 'You shall signify to the people that it is not meant by the latter orders for training of shot (also a meet and necessary weapon for service), that the reputation of the bow should be in any way obscured or taken away'.[161]

But it was too late. There was now a widespread perception that men shot less strongly and less effectively than in the past. It was, of course, only natural that 'modernisers' like Barwick should play on the decay of shooting, and point up the growing inaccuracy of archers, particularly at long ranges.[162] But even Sir John Smythe admitted that some archers were now given to using the weaker draw, using only two instead of three fingers, and Sir Roger Williams, who had seen service in the Low Countries, explained that his preference for arquebusiers over archers was in part due to the decline in bowmen's ability. He believed that only about 1,500 out of every 5,000 archers could still 'shoot strong shots'.[163] The range of shooting at the butts was diminishing with men's skill and strength. Shakespeare himself reflected the transition from military archery to shooting as a pastime when he mocked those who drew their bows like 'crowkeepers' and had Justice Shallow dwell nostalgically on the skill of John of Gaunt's marksman 'Old Double'. It must have seemed a bitter irony to men who read Froissart, who saw Shakespeare's *Henry V* or who heard the ballads celebrating past victories over the French that such feats could no longer be achieved. As William Harrison noted bitterly in his *Description of England*, esteem for English shooting had now become so low that the French and Germans would 'turn up their tailes and crie "Shoote, English"'. But had they been facing Edward III's archers, 'the breech of such a varlet should have been nailed to his bum with one arrow, and another feathered in his bowels before he should have turned round about to see who had shot the first'.[164] England's poor military showing abroad in the later sixteenth and early seventeenth centuries only served to fuel a nostalgia that increasingly magnified the role of the longbow, which had come to symbolise the nation's greatness. Reviewing past triumphs, Samuel Daniel fondly hoped that such days were not, perhaps, lost for ever:

> And now how com'st thou to be out of date,
> And all neglected leav'st us, and art gone?
> And with thee, th'ancient strength, the manly state
> Of valour, and of worth, that glory won?
> Or else stay'st thou, till new prized shot abate?
> (That never shall effect what thou hast done)
> And only but attend'st some blessèd Reign,
> When thou and virtue shalt be graced again.[165]

Matthew Strickland

Appendix

INTRODUCTION

The trial was sought to establish the trajectories of arrows shot from the longbow in a number of different scenarios, in order to assess the effectiveness of the longbow as a weapon of medieval warfare. This required data on the launch velocity, the effect of air resistance on the flight, and the impact velocity at the target, so an experimental shoot was conducted, employing instrumentation more commonly used for recording the flight of gun-fired projectiles. With such data, standard trajectory simulation techniques will permit the calculation of trajectories for a range of different scenarios.

BACKGROUND

The trajectory of any projectile in the atmosphere is determined by the launch velocity, the angle of elevation at launch, the forces of gravity and drag due to air resistance, and the wind velocity. This trajectory may be accurately simulated provided that these factors are known, using the so-called point mass model. This approach neglects motion of the arrow relative to its centre of mass, as occurs when the arrow vibrates, but gives good results for the trajectory provided the arrow is stable in flight. Thus once the drag force is determined, the trajectory may be calculated for any choice of launch conditions, and the range and velocity at impact result. The science of aero- dynamics has established that the drag force depends on air density ρ the presented cross-sectional area of the body A, and the velocity v of the projectile in the following manner:

$$\text{Drag} = \tfrac{1}{2}\, c_D\, \rho\, A\, v^2,$$

and acts to oppose the motion of the projectile and slow it down. The factor c_D, which is known as the drag coefficient, depends on the shape of the body, being small for a streamlined projectile such as a rifle bullet, and higher for a blunt-nosed projectile. At subsonic projectile velocities the value of c_D for an individual projectile is approximately constant.

TRIAL SHOOT

Using the above information, if the release velocity and launch angle are known, the drag coefficient may be estimated by matching a simulated trajectory to the actual range measured in the trial. Shooting the same arrow several times and measuring the launch velocity and range each time gives improved confid- ence in the resulting estimate of the drag coefficient. A trial shoot was undertaken in October 2002, in which a variety of arrows was shot from a longbow made of Oregon yew, being an approximate replica of those found on the *Mary Rose*. As a result of that trial, we have results for the initial velocity from the Doppler radar measurements, and a measured range. The effect- ive drag coefficient may then be obtained by using the point mass model to fit the experimental results. The cross-sectional area of the arrow was measured where the shaft was thickest. For this part of the exercise it was assumed that the launch angle was 45 degrees, which is close to the angle for maximum range.

EXPERIMENTAL DATA

The same longbow, which draws 150lb at a 32in draw-length, was used for all shots except 16 and 17, for which a part fibre-glass flat-bow of 170lb draw weight was employed.

The wind speed was measured by anemometer as 9m/s, a tail-wind.

The details of the arrows are shown in Table 1.

Each arrow was shot 3 times, making a total of 15 shots.

Arrow	Mass (gm)	(ozs)	Shaft material	Diameter	(in)	Shape (mm)	Head	Feathers (in)	(cm)
1	53.6	1.9	Birch	10.0	.39	barrelled	Small bodkin	6 × ½	15.24 x 1.27
2	95.9	3.3	Birch	12.7	.49	bob-tailed	Large bodkin	8½ × ¾	21.59 x 1.90
3	74.4	2.6	Poplar	12.7	.49	bob-tailed	Fluted bodkin	8½ × ¾	21.59 x 1.90
4	57.8	2.0	Birch	10.0	.39	parallel	Small bodkin	8½ × ¾	21.59 x 1.90
5	86.6	3.0	Ash	12.7	.49	bob-tailed	Target blunt	7 × ¾	17.78 x 1.90

Table 1. Data for the arrows.

The recorded data, grouped by arrow shot, is shown in Table 2.

Arrow	Mass (gm)	(ozs)	Shot no	Velocity (m/s)	(yd/s)	Range (m)	(yd)
1	53.6	1.9	1	70.07	76.3	328.0	360
			6	64.29	70	313.8	345
			11	64.65	70.4	312.8	344
			16 (Flat bow)	73.85	80.4	387.7	425
2	95.9	3.3	2	NR		249.9	272
			7	53.36	58	234.7	256
			12	52.28	57	228.6	250
3	74.4	2.6	3	57.48	62.6	258.2	281
			8	57.77	63	258.8	282
			13	58.24	63.4	260.3	284
			17 (Flat bow)	63.95	69.7	294.8	321
4	57.8	2.0	4	62.25	67.8	299.7	327
			9	NR		291.1	317
			14	63.09	68.7	301.9	329
5	86.6	3.0	5	NR		239.0	260
			10	53.59	58.4	230.6	251
			15	53.52	58.3	231.2	252

Table 2. Recorded data on initial velocity and range.

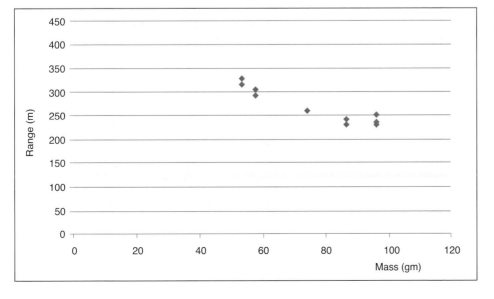

Fig. 1. Plot of range v. arrow mass shot from the same bow.

Fig. 1 shows the range achieved for the different arrows in the experimental shoot. The trend towards longer range with lighter arrows, resulting from their higher initial velocity, is clear.

Some mild anomalies appear in the data: compare, for example rounds 6 and 11, where for the same arrow a marginally lower initial velocity gives rise to a slightly greater range. It is believed that this is due to a minor variation in the launch angle corresponding to the shooter's stance, and possibly to wind variations.

ESTIMATED DRAG COEFFICIENT

Assuming that the launch angle was 45 degrees and the initial velocity was as recorded, the drag coefficient was estimated by adjusting its value and computing the corresponding range using the point mass model until good agreement was obtained between the recorded and computed ranges for all the shootings of each arrow with the longbow. The tail-wind of 9m/s was included in the simulation. The cross-sectional area of the arrow was taken as the given shaft diameter in each case. Table 3 below lists the drag coefficients and corresponding ranges for each of the rounds.

Arrow	Drag coefficient	Shot no	Exptl. Range (m)	(yd)	Computed range (m)	(yd)
1	1.8	1	328.0	357.5	352.9	384.6
		6	313.8	342	312.5	340.6
		11	312.8	340.9	315.0	343.3
		16 (Flat bow)	387.7	422.5	(379.0)	413
2	2.0	2	249.9	272.3	–	
		7	234.7	255.8	235.7	257
		12	228.6	249	228.4	249
3	1.8	3	258.2	281.4	256.7	279.8
		8	258.8	282	258.6	281.8
		13	260.3	283.7	261.3	284.8
		17 (Flat bow)	294.8	321.3	(299.0)	326
4	1.9	4	299.7	326.6	299.6	326.5
		9	291.1	317.2	–	
		14	301.9	329	305.5	332.7
5	2.1	5	239.0	260.5	–	
		10	230.6	251.3	230.7	251.4
		15	231.2	252	230.3	251

Table 3. Comparison of recorded and computed range with the estimated value of drag coefficient.

The estimated drag coefficients lie in a narrow range (1.8–2.1), and the variation is likely to be related to differences in the size of the head and the fletchings relative to the shaft diameter.

In the previous work by P. Pratt (*Longbow, Some technical considerations*, pp. 230–1) the drag was written in the form

$$Drag = K v^2,$$

so that

$$K = \tfrac{1}{2} c_D \rho A.$$

A quick calculation indicates that the drag coefficient values obtained here lead to similar drag force values to the K values listed in the above reference.

With the estimated values of drag coefficient the agreement in range is good for all arrows shot from the longbow, except for round 1. On examination of the recorded radar data there is an apparent discrepancy between the initial velocity and the remainder of the trajectory, the source of which is being investigated. From the simulation, using the estimated drag coefficient, the range measured corresponds to an initial velocity of 66.5m/s rather than 70m/s. The results are slightly less good for the arrows from the flatbow, which had somewhat higher initial velocity.

Where the initial velocity was not recorded, as for example in round 2, the initial velocity may be estimated once the drag coefficient has been determined; for round 2 this gives an initial velocity of 55.3m/s, similar to the other shootings of this arrow.

The model also gives the velocity of the arrow at impact, with which the energy delivered at impact can be calculated. It is usually considered that a penetrative projectile delivering 80J at impact is lethal. By this criterion the two heaviest arrows (2 and 5) are lethal, and there is little doubt that the others would be extremely unpleasant.

Arrow	Mass (gm)	(ozs)	Initial velocity (m/s)	Initial KE (J)	Impact velocity (m/s)	Impact KE (J)
1	53.6	1.9	64.3	111	48.9	64.1
2	95.9	3.3	53.0	134	43.3	89.9
3	74.4	2.6	57.8	124	44.9	75.0
4	57.8	2.0	62.25	112	48.3	67.4
5	86.6	3.0	53.55	124	43.0	80.1

Table 4. Impact velocity and energy with the estimated drag coefficients and 9.0m/s tail-wind as at the experimental shoot.

DISCUSSION

Having determined the drag coefficient of the arrows, the point mass model may be used to predict results with other initial velocities or elevations. As an example graphs are shown below for arrow 2 fired in still conditions. The first of these shows the variation in range with initial velocity, as might be achieved with different bows, and the second shows the variation in range with change of launch elevation at an initial velocity of 52.8m/s, the average of the values obtained with the longbow in this trial.

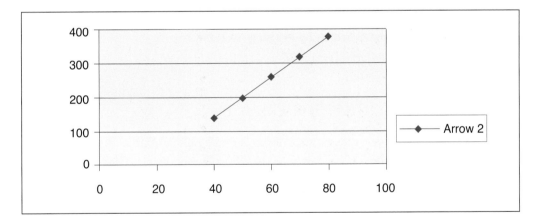

Fig. 2. Range (m) v. initial velocity (m/s) for arrow 2 at 45 degrees elevation.

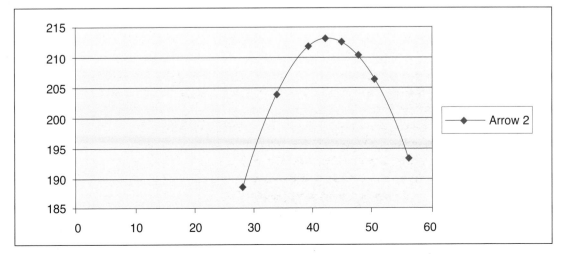

Fig. 3. Range (m) v. angle of elevation (degrees) for arrow 2 at initial velocity 52.8m/s.

IMPACT CONDITIONS

Once the drag coefficient for an arrow has been determined, the model may be used to simulate the trajectory from any initial conditions, that is, any combination of initial velocity and angle of elevation. It is of interest to examine the impact conditions at various ranges, to determine the likely effect at a target whether protected or unprotected. In the following plot the impact energy at a number of ranges is given for each arrow, assuming that there is no wind, and that the ground is level. For each arrow the launch velocity is taken as the average of the values recorded in the trial shoot.

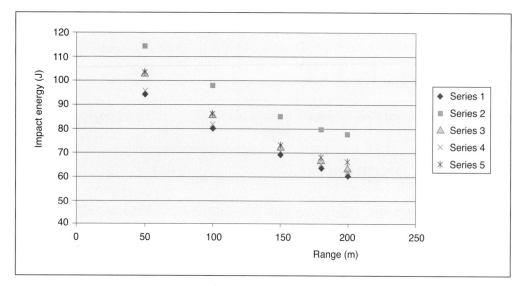

Fig. 4. Impact energy (J) v. range (m) for each of the arrows in the trial.

It is usually considered that a penetrative impact delivering 80J of energy to an unprotected person is likely to be lethal (clearly the part of the body hit will affect the outcome to some extent). Thus it is seen that all these arrows would be lethal for an unarmoured person at a range of 100m or less. Arrow 2, the likely common arrow of medieval warfare, is lethal against such targets up to a range of 180m.

EFFECT OF HEIGHT DIFFERENCE

The calculations above assume that both shooter and target are at the same height. If the shooter is above the target, by virtue of a position on a castle wall, or better still a hillside, then the horizontal range to target is considerably enhanced. Consider, for example, an archer on a hillside, with a target on the valley floor 300m below. The following graphs (Figs 5 and 6) show the variation in horizontal range to target with change in the angle of elevation for arrows 1 and 2 shot in still conditions

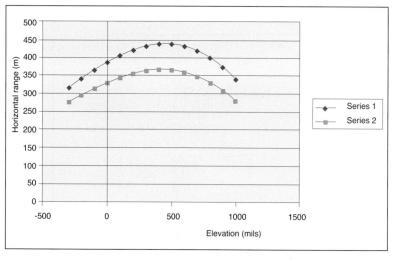

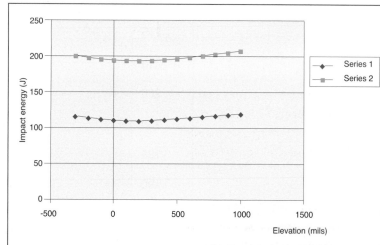

from the same yew longbow. It is immediately obvious that the horizontal range is considerably enhanced by the height advantage of shooter over target, in this case by some 100m, and hence the distance from archer to target is approximately doubled. Moreover, there is a choice of elevations to reach a specific target, a low angle and a higher angle.

As the arrow drops it is accelerated by gravity and the impact velocity is considerably raised, to the point where both arrows impart impact energy significantly above the 80J criterion for lethality, as shown in Fig. 6. Thus if a target is struck in these conditions penetration will be significantly enhanced. If the higher angle trajectory is employed, it can be seen from Fig. 6 that the impact energy is slightly greater than for the low angle trajectory.

Similar calculations were also performed for smaller height advantages, with the target 100m and 50m below the bowman, the latter perhaps being representative of the height difference between a defending archer on a castle wall and an attacker on the ground below. Fig. 7 shows the drop in horizontal range for arrow 2 as the height advantage reduces (compare with Fig. 4 showing range on horizontal ground). The corresponding impact energy is shown in Fig. 8, and is in excess of 100J for all these cases, and hence likely to be lethal to the unarmoured individual.

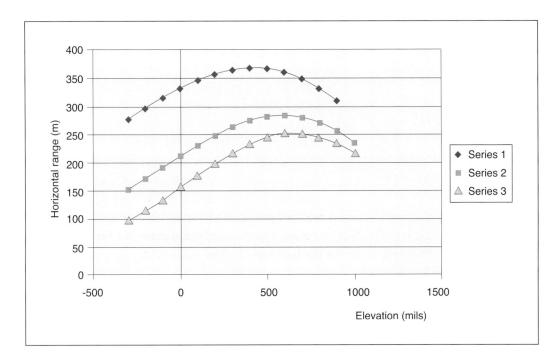

Left: Fig. 7. Graph of horizontal range (m) v. elevation (mils) for arrow 2 with three different height advantages: series 1, 300m; series 2, 100m; series 3, 50m.

Below: Fig. 8. Graph of impact energy (J) v. elevation (mils) for arrow 2 with three different height advantages: series 1, 300m; series 2, 100m; series 3, 50m.

Opposite, left: Fig. 5. Variation in horizontal range (m) with angle of launch (mils), when the target is 300m below the shooter. (45 degrees = 800 mils)

Opposite, right: Fig. 6. Graph of impact energy (J) v. elevation (mils) for a target 300m below the shooter.

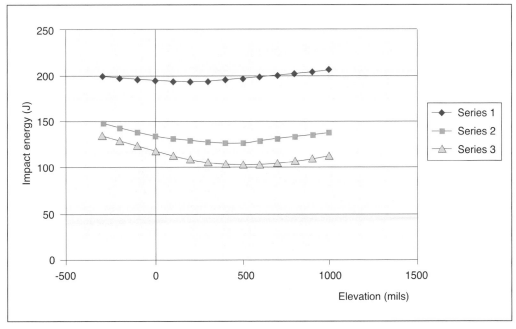

CONCLUSION

The measurements of initial velocity and horizontal range recorded during the trial shoot were reasonably consistent for each arrow, enabling reliable estimates of the drag coefficient for each arrow to be made. These drag coefficients lie in the range 1.8–2.1 for the arrows trialled here. With this information the arrow trajectory may be calculated for different scenarios, and leads to the unavoidable conclusion that the lighter arrows from this trial, shot from a replica of the *Mary Rose* longbow, would have achieved ranges in excess of 300m. However, at any given range that they could reach, the heavier arrows would carry greater energy, and hence would be more injurious. The range is considerably extended if the archer has a height advantage, as can be seen from Figs 5 and 7.

Anna B. Crowley
Professor of Ballistics and Computational Fluid Dynamics,
The Royal Military College of Science

COMMENTARY BY R. HARDY

I would add a few thoughts to Professor Crowley's detailed analysis:

(i) It is plain that the right arrow shot from a *Mary Rose*-weight bow is capable of inflicting serious or lethal damage, the lethal potential increasing as the range to the target lessens; it also depends on the quality of the protective armour worn by the target, which is self-evident.

   (a) It should also be remembered that an arrow wound can be more lethal than a bullet wound; that 80J is equivalent to 60ft/lb and that much less than that, e.g. 20ft/lb, has been known to kill a bear.

   (b) The arrow enters its target with a cutting edge, and the inertia of the long shaft behind it drives it in.

   (c) It is worth adding this rough table of retained Kinetic Energy and of retained velocity:

	Retained KE	Retained velocity
1	58%	76%
2	67%	82%
3	60%	78%
4	60%	78%
5	65%	80%

(ii) More tests, against targets that truly reflect the strength to resist penetration by arrows from such bows as were used in the tests, are necessary, but hard to achieve both because of the difficulty of reproducing accurately medieval protective clothing, and the fact that no museum or private collection will allow precious armours, whether 'soft', 'mail' or 'plate' to be shot at; further as regards attack on plate it is vital to achieve as credible an approximation of the defence as we have achieved in the weapons of attack.

(iii) Extraordinary claims have been made about the inefficiency of longbow attack; it has been said that a 'standard arrow' of some 52g (which is an invention of members of the British Longbow Society), shot from a 200lb (90.6kg) bow, only achieved 237yds (217m). Reference to the test figures above will show either that the bow was too stiff to work effectively, or that it was too strong for its arrow, which would cause it to fly off one-sided and so reduce its range, or that the archer was not the bow's master. It will be remembered that by the time of the Tudors shooting at targets under 240yds (219m) was discouraged.

(iv) It can be realised from the recorded measurements above that the energy of a shot arrow in attack is exerted upon the needle point of an arrowhead. The bow and arrow together are a delivery system, the details and potential of which have been clarified above.

Penetrative potential depends on the design efficiency of the arrowhead against various targets of defence. Efficacy of defence depends on the ability to repel or absorb arrow attack, and on the design of steel armours to deflect striking arrowheads. The age-old escalation from better defence to better attack can be seen throughout the pages of this whole study. The makers of longbows and the designers of arrowheads (and shafts) were leaders of ballistics in their day, and the forerunners of modern designers of projectors and projectiles. Those who deny or decry the effectiveness of the great warbow of the late Middle Ages deceive themselves and others.

Notes

INTRODUCTION

1. Roger Ascham, *Toxophilus*, ed. E. Arber (London, 1902), 16.
2. *Toxophilus*, ed. Arber, 11.
3. Cited in C.G. Cruickshank, *Army Royal. Henry VIII's Invasion of France 1513* (Oxford, 1969), 106.
4. J. Keegan, *The Face of Battle* (London, 1976).
5. Sir Thomas Elyot, *The Boke Named the Governour*, ed. H.H.S. Croft, 2 vols (London, 1883), I, 297–9.

CHAPTER 1

1. M. Rule, *The Mary Rose*, foreword by HRH the Prince of Wales (Conway Maritime Press, 1982); Ernle Bradford, *The Story of the Mary Rose* (Book Club Associates, 1982).
2. Sometimes a double sheaf of 48 arrows is also called a sheaf. The *Mary Rose* inventory is reproduced in Rule, *The Mary Rose*, 26–7.
3. PRO, E36/13, quoted in C.S. Knighton and D.M. Loades, *The Anthony Roll of Henry VIII's Navy* (Aldershot, 2000), 123, 138, 156.
4. *Letters from the Mary Rose*, ed. C.S. Knighton and D.M. Loades (Stroud, 2002), citing PRO, SP1/229 ff.193–4.
5. 'First report of the care of the bows to the Mary Rose Trust', Robert Hardy, Peter Pratt, John Levy, 1987.
6. Rule, *The Mary Rose*, 47.
7. To be published by the Mary Rose Trust, probably in 2005.
8. Roger Ascham, *Toxophilus*, ed. E. Arber (Westminster, 1902), 118.
9. Sir John Smythe, *Certain Discourses Military*, ed. J.R. Hale (Ithaca, New York, 1964), 69–70.
10. J.E. Oxley, *The Fletchers and Longbowstring-makers of London* (Court of the Worshipful Company, London, 1968).
11. *CPR, 1358–61*, 323.
12. *CPR, 1358–61*, 221, 323.
13. For arrowhead typology, see J.B. Ward Perkins, *London Museum Medieval Catalogue, 7* (London, 1940), 65–73, and the important revisions proposed by O. Jessop, 'A New Artefact Typology for the Study of Medieval Arrowheads', *Medieval Archaeology*, xl (1996), 192–205.
14. Rule, *The Mary Rose*, 174–5.
15. Bow nocks of *Mary Rose* date were made of cow or stag horn. In the USA today buffalo horn is often used as well.
16. Robert Hardy, *Longbow* (Patrick Stephens, 1976–92), 136.
17. Ascham, *Toxophilus*, 116.
18. B.W. Kooi, 'The Mechanics of the Bow and Arrow' (PhD thesis, Rÿksunversitat Groningen, 1983). See also B.W. Kooi and C.A. Bergmann, 'An approach to the study of Ancient Archery using Mathematical Modelling', *Antiquity*, lxxi (1997).
19. Dr B.W. Kooi, University of Amsterdam, September 2001, pers. comm.
20. *JSAA*, XXV, 1982. It is my belief that the correction was published in the next *Journal*, but there in print was a passport for those who disbelieved Dr Kooi's conclusions.
21. *Letters and Papers, Foreign and Domestic of the Reign of Henry VIII* (hereafter *Letters and Papers H.VIII*), ed. J. Gairdner and R.H. Brodie (London, 1920–32), 1, 67.

22. Hardy, *Longbow*, 186.

23. For Spanish and Irish yew, see p. 42; for bowstaves imported from the Baltic, and for mandatory imports of staves, see N.S.B. Gras, *The Early English Custom System* (Harvard, 1918), 288, 296, 435–6, 437.

24. Howard Hill is a famous American archer, author of *Hunting the Hard Way*, and other titles.

25. Dr A.J. Stirland, *Raising the Dead: the Skeleton Crew of Henry VIII's Great Ship the Mary Rose* (Chichester, 2002). See also Ch. 16.

26. See Ch. 16 on archers' tactics.

27. B. Megson, *Such Goodly Company. A Glimpse into the Life of the Bowyers of London* (Worshipful Company of Bowyers, London, 1993), 88–90, 79–81, 73–9.

28. Nicholas Frost served both Henry IV and Henry V. He died in 1433.

29. York was especially noted for the strength and good workmanship of its bows; *York Memorandum Book*, ed. M. Sellars (Surtees Society, CXX, 1911), 52–4.

30. A.E. Prince, 'The Army and Navy', in *The English Government at Work*, I, ed. J.F. Willard (Cambridge, Mass., 1940), 332–93, especially 365–76; H.J. Hewitt, *The Organization of War under Edward III, 1338–1362* (Manchester, 1958), 50–74, provides a detailed analysis of such logistics for the period up to 1362.

31. Demand on a comparable scale had been envisaged for Edward II's war in Gascony in 1324, when among other preparations it was proposed to purvey 100,000 goose feathers for the making of arrows, but the force and supplies actually sent were much smaller (*The War of St Sardos*, ed. P. Chaplais (Camden 3rd ser., lxxxvii, 1954), 66–8; M.C. Prestwich, 'English Armies in the Early Stages of the Hundred Years War: a Scheme in 1341', *BIHR*, CXXXIII (1983), 102–13, at 106).

32. Hewitt, *Organization for War*, 65, tables the demands for bows and arrows between 1341 and 1359; *CPR, 1358–61*, 323. In 1359 over 4,000 arrowheads, costing 52s 5d, had been assembled at Chester Castle (*Cheshire Chamberlains' Accounts*, ed. R. Stewart-Brown (Record Society, 1910), 273).

33. *CCR, 1354–8*, 244; H.J. Hewitt, *The Black Prince's Expedition of 1355–1357* (Manchester, 1958), 30; *idem, Organization for War*, 66; *CPR, 1358–61*, 222, 304.

34. Hewitt, *Organization for War*, 65–8.

35. For the Privy Wardrobe see T.F. Tout, *Chapters in Administrative History: The Wardrobe, the Chamber and the Small Seals*, 6 vols (Manchester, 1920–33), IV, 439–84, especially 455ff; J.H. Johnson, 'The King's Wardrobe and Household', in *The English Government at Work*, ed. J.F. Williard, I, 206–29, especially 223–6.

36. Hewitt, *Organization for War*, 68–70. The office subsequently developed of Master of the King's Bows in the Tower of London, which by the end of the fourteenth century entitled its holder to robes, a chamber in the Tower and a daily wage of 6d (*CPR, 1391–1401*, 98, 214; Megson, *Such Goodly Company*, 30).

37. Hewitt, *Black Prince's Expedition*, 59–63; *ibid.*, 30, 49.

38. Hewitt, *Organization for War*, 69; *idem, Black Prince's Expedition*, 92.

39. Hewitt, *Organization for War*, 64.

40. Hewitt, *Organization for War*, 64, 70. In 1355 ten fletchers from the Forest of Dean received a daily wage of 6d (Prince, 'The Army and Navy', 343, n. 13).

41. Hewitt, *Organization for War*, 65.

42. Hewitt, *Organization for War*, 66, 69; *idem, Black Prince's Expedition*, 30; *CPR, 1354–58*, 516; *CPR, 1358–61*, 222, 304.

43. *Register of Edward, the Black Prince*, ed. M.C.B. Dawes, 4 vols (London, 1930–3), III, 223.

44. *Calendar of Letter-Books Preserved Among the Archives of the Corporation of the City of London, 1275–1498*, ed. R.R. Sharpe, 11 vols (London, 1899–1912), G, 92, 44.

45. *Rotuli Parliamentorum*, 6 vols (Record Commission, 1767–77), II 320b (47 Edward III, 1373); *York Memorandum Book*, ed. M. Sellars (Surtees Society, cxx, 1911), xlviii.

46. Megson, *Such Goodly Company*, 42–3.

47. Megson, *Such Goodly Company*, 12–19, and for a vivid glimpse of life in Bowyer Row, 34–40.

48. Megson, *Such Goodly Company*, 23–4. This legislation also formed part of a series of acts designed to arrest the social and economic freedoms of labourers opened up by the impact of the huge depopulation caused by the Black Death in 1348–9. For the fletchers, see Oxley, *Fletchers and Longbowstring Makers*, 1ff.

49. Megson, *Such Goodly Company*, 46ff, provides a valuable discussion of the social, financial and religious conditions of bowyers revealed in these wills.

50. *York Memorandum Book*, 52–4, 61–3, and discussed at xlvi–xlviii. For York as a centre for arms making, see E. Miller, *War in the North* (Hull, 1960), 7, 9–10.

51. R.H. Morris, *Chester in the Plantagenet and Tudor Reigns* (Chester, 1893), 339, who notes the exodus of a number of Yorkshire bowyers to work in Chester in the early fifteenth century.

52. *York Memorandum Book*, 52–3, xlvi–xlvii.

53. *York Memorandum Book*, 61; *Calendar of Letter Books for the City of London*, I, 25.

54. *York Memorandum Book*, 62.

55. *York Memorandum Book*, 52.

56. *York Memorandum Book*, 61.

57. *York Memorandum Book*, 54–5, xlvii.

58. For the nature of apprenticeship and for master–apprentice relations see B. Hanawalt, *Growing up in Medieval London. The Experience of Childhood in History* (Oxford, 1993), 129–72; N. Orme, *Medieval Children* (New Haven and London, 2001), 311–13; and P.J.P. Goldberg, 'Masters and Men in Later Medieval England', in *Masculinity in Medieval Europe*, ed. D.M. Hadley (London and New York, 1999), 56–70.

59. Megson, *Such Goodly Company*, 15, 47–51.

60. S.L. Thrupp, *The Merchant Class of Medieval London* (Michigan, 1962), 219; Megson, *Such Goodly Company*, 27.

61. *York Memorandum Book*, 200.

62. *Calendar of Letter Books of the City of London*, G, 279; Megson, *Such Goodly Company*, 25.

63. *York Memorandum Book*, 62. It is suggestive of declining standards that this clause is a later insertion in English to the existing French text.

64. *CCR, 1369–74*, 57–8.

65. *Rot. Parl.*, IV, 103a. Pattens (from the French *patin*) were a form of shoe with a raised wooden base, like a clog.

66. *Calendar of Letter-Books of the City of London*, K, 140.

67. *York Memorandum Book*, 199.

68. *York Memorandum Book*, 200. No guild member was to hire such workers for longer than fifteen days if another member wished to employ them.

69. *York Memorandum Book*, 199–200. For similar regulations promulgated by the London Fletchers Guild in 1484, setting out the price for arrows of various types and quality, *Letter Book*, L, 212–13.

70. For the making of a longbow, see Hardy, *Longbow*, 186–93; and D. Adams, *Making the Boughstave Longbow* (Lincoln, 1988).

71. Hewitt, *Organization for War*, 70.

72. Gras, *The Early English Customs System*, 296, 435–6, 437, 611, 616, 666, 675. The references to bowstaves in such accounts are sometimes to bundles, made clear by the record of the 60 'bunches of bowstaves', each containing 800 staves, worth £300, brought to Lynn in 1503/4 by Le George of Dansk (Danzig) (*ibid.*, 646–7).

73. *The Crusade against Heretics in Bohemia, 1418–1437: Sources and Documents for the Hussite Crusades*, ed. T.A. Fudge (Aldershot, 2002), 242. I am indebted to Professor John Thomson for this reference.

74. M. Postan, 'The Economic and Political Relations of England and the Hanse from 1400 to 1475', in *Studies in English Trade in the Fifteenth Century*, ed. E. Power and M. Postan (London, 1933), 91–153, at 108–9.

75. C. Richmond, 'Royal Administration and the Keeping of the Seas, 1422–1485' (Oxford University D.Phil. Thesis, 1963), 295–6.

76. *Calendar of Letter-Books of the City of London*, H, 414; Megson, *Such Goodly Company*, 28.

77. *Statutes of the Realm*, 11 vols (London, 1810–28), II, 432 (12 Edward IV); *Rot. Parl.*, VI, 156a. By way of comparison, a stock of 1,200 bowstaves in London in 1381 had been valued at £12 (*Calendar of Pleas and Memoranda Rolls Preserved Among the Archives of the City of London*, ed. A.H. Thomas, 6 vols (Cambridge, 1926–61), II, 294–5).

78. *Statutes of the Realm*, II, 472–3 (22 Edward IV, c. 3).

79. *Statutes of the Realm*, II, 494 (1 Richard III, c. 11).

80. *Statutes of the Realm*, II, 521 (3 Henry VII, c. 13); II, 649 (*19 Henry VII, c. 2*). Customs records at Dunwich show that thitherto every 100 staves paid a levy of 2*d* (Gras, *The Early English Customs System*, 193).

81. *Letters and Papers*, I, 537.

82. *The Hamilton Papers*, ed. J. Bain, 2 vols (Edinburgh, 1890, 1892), II, 440, and cited by G. Phillips, *The Anglo-Scottish Wars, 1513–1550* (Woodbridge, 1999), 81.

83. Guild records quoted in Megson, *Such Goodly Company*.

84. See the section on Crécy in Ch. 16, pp. 294–9.

85. It is Simon Stanley's firm belief that what we call the Type 16 is only a much larger type of barbed head reduced by much sharpening. The large barb is easy to make, the Type 16 the very devil.

86. V. Fiorato, A. Boylston and C. Knüsel, *Blood Red Roses. The Archaeology of a Mass Grave from the Battle of Towton, AD 1461* (Oxbow Books, 2000).

87. See Ch. 15.

88. C. Dyer, *Everyday Life in Medieval England* (London, 1994), 77–100, at 87; idem, *Standards of Living in the Later Middle Ages* (Cambridge, 1989), 109–50. This whole subject needs a great deal of further research.

89. Hewitt, *Organization of War*.

90. *Ibid.*

91. *Ibid.* Also G. Wrottesly, *Crécy and Calais* (1897).

92. Hewitt, *Organization of War*.

93. On the march from Harfleur to Agincourt.

94. *The Sermons of Hugh Latimer*, ed. G.E. Corrie (Parker Society, 1844), I, 196–7.

95. Edward Herbert, Baron Cherbury (1588–1648). A soldier, statesman and philosopher, he was the brother of the poet George Herbert.

96. J. Goring, 'Social Change and Military Decline in Mid-Tudor England', *History*, lx (1975), 185–97, at 187.

97. *Ibid.*, 187–8.

98. *Ibid.*, 187–97.

99. A.J. Stirland, *Raising the Dead*.

100. *Ibid.*

101. Rule, *The Mary Rose*, 184–6; Stirland, *Raising the Dead*, 123–30.

102. As was the experience at Poitiers.

103. Charles Chenevix-Trench, *History of Marksmanship* (Longman, 1972).

104. *Ibid.*

105. *Ibid.*

106. Hardy, *Longbow*, 53–4.

107. See spine and bow-weight table in Hardy, *Longbow*, technical appendix.

108. Ascham, *Toxophilus*, 123–6.

CHAPTER 2

1. C.W.C. Oman, *A History of the Art of War in the Middle Ages*, 2 vols (London, 1924, repr. 1991).

2. Oman, *Art of War*, II, 57.

3. See pp. 43–4.

4. Oman, *Art of War*, II, 59–60.

5. J.E. Morris, *The Welsh Wars of Edward I* (Oxford, 1901, repr. Stroud, 1996, with a foreword by M. Prestwich).

6. Morris, *Welsh Wars*, 32–3; *ibid.*, 99, '. . . the longbow was not a

new weapon, the use of which was learned in the Welsh wars. It was already in the hands of some proportion of the English and their allies, the Welsh of the March.'

7. Morris, *Welsh Wars*, 182–4, 255–8, where these battles are referred to as Orewin Bridge and Conwy respectively. For these engagements, see pp. 156–7.

8. Oman, *Art of War*, II, 57, 'the bow had of course always been known in England'.

9. Morris, *Welsh Wars*, 26. Cf. Oman, *Art of War*, II, 58, 'the shortbow, drawn to the breast not the ear'.

10. See pp. 82–3.

11. Morris, *Welsh Wars*, 27–8.

12. Morris, *Welsh Wars*, 28.

13. Morris, *Welsh Wars*, 100.

14. For the composite bow, see below, Ch. 6, pp. 98–101.

15. H. Delbrück, *A History of the Art of War Within the Framework of Political History*, 3 vols, trans. W.J. Renfroe Jr (Westport, 1975), II, 386–7. Delbrück did, nevertheless, accept some elements of Morris's thesis, concluding that 'the techniques in the use of the weapon were raised to a level that no doubt had been reached earlier but now seemed to be new to contemporaries (*ibid.*, 387).

16. Delbrück, *A History of the Art of War*, II, 346.

17. Morris, *Welsh Wars*, 34.

18. J. Bradbury, *The Medieval Archer* (Woodbridge, 1985).

19. Bradbury, *The Medieval Archer*, 16. He notes further that 'the longbow is simply the result of the evolution of the ordinary wooden bow over a long period of time', and refers, perhaps more equivocally, to 'the ordinary wooden bow, which in a later age would be called the longbow' (*ibid.*, 15, 14).

20. Bradbury, *The Medieval Archer*, 74–5.

21. C.J. Rogers, 'The Military Revolutions of the Hundred Years War', *The Journal of Military History*, lvii (1993), 241–78, at 249.

22. PRO, E36/274. Bradbury, *The Medieval Archer*, 15, also takes these sketches at face value, noting that 'they seem to be using ordinary bows rather than longbows'.

23. H.F. McClintock, *Old Irish and Highland Dress* (Dundalk, 2nd edn, 1950), 25.

24. Bradbury, *The Medieval Archer*, 8, also rejects the shortbow as a distinct category of earlier self-bow (cf. *ibid.*, 73–5), but instead uses the term shortbow to describe the composite bow made of wood, horn and sinew. We prefer to retain the unambiguous term of composite bow and to discard the term shortbow altogether as misleading.

25. Bradbury, *The Medieval Archer*, 71–3, 152.

26. J.C. Holt, *Robin Hood* (London, 2nd edn, 1989), 79–80.

27. See Ch. 8, pp. 144–8.

28. Gaston Phébus, count of Foix, *Livre de chasse*, ed. G. Tilander (Karlshamn, 1971), 269–70; J. Cummins, *The Hound and the Hawk. The Art of Medieval Hunting* (London, 1988), 52.

29. For examples of ladies hunting with the bow see N. Orme, *From Childhood to Chivalry. The Education of English Kings and Aristocracy, 1066–1530* (London and New York, 1984), 200–1.

30. *The Lisle Letters*, ed. M. St Clare Byrne, 6 vols (Chicago and London, 1981), I, no. 32, 332–3. Anne, it seems, was a keen archer, and records of the King's Privy Purse for the same year record payment 'for bows, arrows, shafts, broadheads, bracer and shooting glove for Lady Anne, 23s 4d'. Two weeks later another 13s 4d was paid for four bows for Anne, the number of bows ordered for her perhaps reflecting the need to test out several until one most suitable to her strength and liking was found (*Letters and Papers*, V, no. 1799, 750). Bows appear to have been a popular gift, cf. *The Lisle Letters*, III, no. 588, 165, for the promise by Mary Basset of a bow to a gentleman.

31. Orme, *From Childhood to Chivalry*, 198–205.

32. *Maurice's Strategikon. Handbook of Military Strategy*, trans. G.T. Dennis (Philadelphia, 2001), Bk I, Ch. 2.

33. H. Riesch, 'Archery in Renaissance Germany', *JSAA*, xxxviii (1995), 66–7 and figs 9, 10.

34. H. Gordon and A. Webb, 'The Hedgeley Moor Bow at Alnwick Castle', *JSAA*, xv (1972), 8–9.

35. *Tudor Royal Proclamations*, ed. P.L. Hughes and J.F. Larkin, 3 vols (New Haven and London, 1964–9), I, no. 213, 313–14.

36. J. Hewitt, *Ancient Armour and Weapons* (Oxford, 1855, repr. London, 1996), 54, 156.

37. *The Antiquaries Journal*, xi (1931), 423; R.C. Brown, 'Observations on the Berkhamstead Bow', *JSAA* (1967), 12–17; D. Renn, 'A Bowstave from Berkhamstead Castle', *Hertfordshire Archaeology* (St Albans, 1971), 72–4. I am grateful to Mr Guy Wilson, Master of the Royal Armouries, for allowing me to examine this weapon, and for his expert advice on it (MJS). A comparatively short self-bow from Desmond Castle, Co. Limerick (now in the City Museum in Limerick), is possibly of fourteenth-century date, but D. Nicolle, *Arms and Armour of the Crusading Era, 1050–1350*, 2 vols (New York, 1988), I, 384, and II, 840, no. 1017, suggests this is probably a hunting weapon.

38. *Current Archaeology*, cxxxvi (1993), 147; Hardy, *Longbow*, 17.

39. J.D.G. Clark, 'Neolithic Bows from Somerset, England, and the Prehistory of Archery in North-western Europe', *Proceedings of the Prehistoric Society*, xxix (1963), 50–98, at 67–8.

40. Clark, 'Neolithic Bows', 54–6, 86. For his comparative measurements, Clark used the *Mary Rose* bows in the Tower, originally raised by the Deane brothers.

41. Clark, 'Neolithic Bows', 54–6, 57 (fig. 3), 90. Another near-contemporary bow, found at nearby Meare Heath and dating to 2690 BC, was by contrast made with wide, flat limbs, though this design was less common among prehistoric weapons than the D-sectioned longbows (*ibid.*, 55–9).

42. C.A. Bergman, R. Miller and E. McEwen, 'Experimental Archery: Projectile Velocities and Comparison of Bow Performances', *Antiquity*, lxii (1988), 660, 661. For self-bows, the ratio of bow length to the arrow draw-length must not be less than 2:1 without severe risk of breaking, and accordingly longbows tended to have a considerably higher ratio of overall length to draw-length (*ibid.*, 661).

43. Thus for example, the bow used by the Kamba tribe of Kenya was only 3ft in length with a 50lb pull, while by contrast the great bows employed by the Langulu to hunt elephant were as long and as powerful as the *Mary Rose* bows (Hardy, *Longbow*, 25). For native American longbows see, for example, the watercolour by John White, *c*. 1584–90, reproduced in Hardy, *Longbow*, colour plate opposite 113; and the superb drawings of Carriban Indians from the 1590s known as the 'Drake Manuscript' (*Histoire Naturelle des Indes. The Drake Manuscript in the Pierpont Morgan Library*, with introduction by V. Klinkenborg and translations by R.S. Kraemer (New York and London, 1996), especially folios 81, 85, 87–90, 92, 96v).

44. Hardy, *Longbow*, 9–10.

45. G. Clark and H. Godwin, 'Prehistoric Ancestors of the Weapons which brought England victory at Crécy, Poitiers and Agincourt: Neolithic Longbows of 4,500 years ago, found in the Somerset-shire Peat', *Illustrated London News*, 10 February 1962, 219–21.

46. Clark, 'Neolithic Bows', 82–6; H.C.C. Engelhardt, *Nydam Mosefund, 1859–63* (Copenhagen, 1865); C. Englehardt, *Denmark in the Early Iron Age* (London, 1866), and *idem*, *Vimose Fundet* (Copenhagen, 1929).

47. E. McEwen, R.L. Miller and C.A. Bergman, 'Early Bow Design and Construction', *Scientific American* (June 1991), 76–82 at 52–3. While the Ashcott, Meare and other Neolithic longbows of yew appear to have no sapwood, it has been suggested that the propensity of yew heartwood to split makes this very unlikely, and that the original bows may have been made from unseasoned wood (*ibid.*, 53).

48. Hardy, *Longbow*, 21–2.

49. Clark, 'Neolithic Bows', 86.

50. Hardy, *Longbow*, 21.

51. For Chessel Down bow, measuring 5ft (1.52m), see G. Hillier, *The History and Antiquities of the Isle of Wight* (London, 1850), 30, where it is also stated that arrows of hazel wood were discovered; and Clarke, 'Neolithic Bows', 89; for Bifrons, G.B. Brown, *The Arts in Early England*, 6 vols (London, 1903–37), III, 242, IV, 217, and cf. 748–9 (Chessel Down); C.J. Arnold, *The Anglo-Saxon Cemeteries of the Isle of Wight* (London, 1982), 24 and fig. 7. An archer's bracer may have been found at Lowbury Hill, Berkshire (V.I. Evison, 'Sugar Loaf Shield Bosses', *The Antiquaries Journal*, xliii, 38–96, at 46, n.).

52. W. Veeck, *Die Alamannen im Würtemberg* (Berlin and Leipzig, 1931), 20–1, and pl. 6b; G. Rausing, *The Bow. Some Notes on its Origins and Development* (Lund, 1967), 60. The length of these eight bows varied from 6ft (1.83m) to 6ft 7in (2.1m). For Viking bow finds, P.G. Foote and D.M. Wilson, *The Viking Achievement* (London, 1970).

53. H.O'N. Hencken, 'Ballinderry Crannog No. 1', *Proceedings of the Royal Irish Academy*, xliii (1935–7), 103–239, at 138; Clark, 'Neolithic Bows', 86.

54. E. Roesdahl, *The Vikings* (London, 1991), 143.

55. See Ch. 3, pp. 54–7.

56. A. Abratowski, 'The Bow in Poland', *JSAA*, xliv (2001), 16 (with illustration at 18).

57. Dublin, National Museum (E132 62239).

58. Hardy, *Longbow*, 54.

59. The ell, however, varied in length in different countries, with the Scottish ell measuring 37in, the Flemish 27in, and the Saxon ell 22in (Heath, 'The Medieval English War Arrow', *JSAA*, iii (1960), 19). In 1338 Nicholas Coraunt, the king's artiller, was ordered to buy 4,000 sheaves of arrows an ell long (*CPR, 1338–40*, 124). In this case the Scottish ell seems to have been intended: 45 inches is over-long, whereas 37 inches accords much more closely to the 'cloth-yard' of 36 inches.

60. G.F. Farnham and S.H. Skillington, 'The Skeffingtons of Skeffington', *Leicestershire Archaeological Society Transactions*, xvi (1929–31), 74–128; F. Cottrill, 'A Medieval Description of a Bow and Arrow', *The Antiquaries Journal*, xxiii (1943), 54–5; Bradbury, *The Medieval Archer*, 80–2.

61. See Ch. 8.

62. John Lydgate, *The Horse, the Sheep and the Goose*, ed. J.H.F. Jenkinson (Cambridge, 1906), ll. 211–14. Goose feathers were ordered by Edward III for his fletchers in 1359 (*CPR, 1358–61*, 323).

63. Ascham, *Toxophilus*, 129; J. Gendall, 'The Arundell Archive of Arrows and Arrowheads', *JSAA*, xliv (2001), 61–2.

64. Gendall, 'The Arundell Archive of Arrows and Arrowheads', 61–2, who notes the correlation between the red and black silk bindings with the colours of the Dynham arms, Gules, four fusills in fesse, Ermine.

65. T. Rymer, ed. *Foedera, Conventiones, Literae*, 20 vols (London, 1704–35), IX, 436; C.L. Kingsford, 'A Historical Collection of the Fifteenth Century', *EHR*, xxix (1914), 505–15 at 512; J.H. Wylie and W.T. Waugh, *The Reign of Henry V*, 3 vols (Cambridge, 1914–29), III, 44–5.

66. Ascham, *Toxophilus*, 129–30. He goes on to discuss the respective merits of feathers from young geese 'best for a swift shaft', and from older geese 'stiff and strong, good for a wind, and fittest for a ded shaft'.

67. 'Extracts from the Coram Rege Rolls and Pleas of the Crown, Staffordshire, of the Reign of Edward II, A.D. 1307 to A.D. 1327', ed. G. Wrottesley, in *Collections for a History of Staffordshire*, x (Staffordshire Record Society, 1889), 16–17 (Easter 8 Edward II); and noted in Prestwich, *Armies and Warfare*, 131.

68. Cf. 'Meryrick' (sic), 'On Cloth Yard Arrows', *Gentleman's Magazine*, April 1932; Heath, 'The English War Arrow', 17–19. It is possible, though less likely, that the Scottish ell was used here, giving a bow length of 6ft 1½in.

69. Smythe, *Certain Discourses Military*, 69.

70. *Livre de chasse*, ed. Tillander, 269–70. His contemporary, Geoffrey Chaucer, also uses the term in the *Romance of the Rose*, l. 923, and *The Knight's Tale*, l. 2895. (All references to Chaucer are to *The Riverside Chaucer*, ed. L.D. Benson (3rd edn, Boston, 1987), unless otherwise stated.) By the reign of Henry VIII, however, the

term 'Turkeybow' could also be applied to a crossbow, sometimes with steel arms, as well as to the more usual composite bow (*The Inventory of King Henry VIII*, ed. D. Starkey (London, 1998), no. 8157, 9598, 11648, 13199, 17482).

71. *Select Pleas of the Forest*, ed. G.J. Turner (Selden Society, 1901), 79, 90, 96, 101. In 1249 a boy was caught in the woods at Lockhawe, Northants., with a bow with barbed arrows and a Welsh arrow (*sagittis barbelatis et una sagitta valisca*), while in 1251 at Corby, near the forest of Rockingham, thirteen Welsh arrows were found in the house of Robert of Corby (*ibid.*, 90, 96 and cf. 101).

72. *Oxford City Documents, 1268–1665*, ed. T. Rogers (Oxford, 1891), 150; translated in *Documents illustrating the History of Civilization in Medieval England (1066–1500)*, ed. R. Trevor Davies (London and New York, 1926, repr. 1969). He had been shot after 'one Michael, maniciple of the clerks dwelling in Bolenhall in the parish of St Aldgate's and one John de Skurf, a clerk, and one Madoc, a Welsh clerk, went through the streets with swords and arrows and bows after the hour of curfew and molested all passers by'. When the hue and cry was raised, John and others came out of his house and John was shot by Michael before the rioters fled.

73. Ward Perkins, *London Museum Medieval Catalogue*, 65–73; Jessop, 'A New Artefact Typology for the Study of Medieval Arrowheads', 192–205. A similar arrow is mentioned in the forest eyre of 1251 in Northamptonshire: 'In the house of Geoffrey Gos was found a piece of venison from a buck upon a cart . . . a bow with a string, and seven barbed arrows, and a small arrow (*una parva sagitta*) and five fletches' (*Select Pleas of the Forest*, 96). For a selection of arrowheads found at York and ranging across the medieval period, see P. Ottaway and N. Rogers, *Craft, Industry and Everyday Life: Finds from Medieval York* (York, 2002); *The Archaeology of York*, ed. P.V. Addyman, vol. 17:15, 2967–9.

74. Gendall, 'The Arundell Archive of Arrows and Arrowheads', 61–2.

75. Prestwich, *Armies and Warfare*, 131, 359 n. 56.

76. *Accounts of the Constables of Bristol Castle in the Thirteenth and Early Fourteenth Centuries*, ed. M. Sharp (Bristol Record Society, xxxiv, Gloucester, 1982), 20, 26.

77. *Select Pleas of the Forest*, 78–9. In Northamptonshire in 1251 we similarly find reference to a yew bow, '*arcus de if et due sagitte barbate et tres sagittas genderese*' (*ibid.*, 96).

78. For Gerald see the excellent study by R. Bartlett, *Gerald of Wales, 1146–1223* (Oxford, 1982).

79. *Itinerarium Kambriae* (Bk I, c. iv) in *Giraldi Cambrensis opera*, ed. J.S. Brewer, J.F. Dimock and G.F. Warner, 8 vols (Rolls Series, 1861–91), VI, 54; '*Non autem arcu utuntur corneo, non alburneo, non taxeo: solum ex ulmellis silvestribus arcus formant, non formosus, non politos, immo rudes prorsus et informes: rigidos tamen et fortes; non tantum ad eminus missilia mittenda, sed etiam ad graves cominus ictus percutiendo tolerandos.*' The translation is based on *The Journey Through Wales and The Description of Wales*, trans. L. Thorpe (Harmondsworth, 1978), 113, but with the last sentence emended as suggested in Hardy, *Longbow*, 37.

80. See Ch. 6, pp. 109–12.

81. C.T. Lewis and C. Short, *A Latin Dictionary* (Oxford, 1879), give *alburnum* as 'the soft, thin, white layer between the bark and the wood of trees, sapwood, alburnum'.

82. Clark, 'Neolithic Bows', 51, notes that 'it seems that other woods [than yew] were used for bows only in territories in which the climate was too cold for the yew to make substantial growth; for instance in Schleswig Holstein and Denmark elm (Ulmus) was generally used'. It may have been such climatic conditions that prevented the growth of suitable yew in Wales.

83. Hardy, *Longbow*, 37–8.

84. Morris, *Welsh Wars*, 16, 'we get from Gerald a valuable picture of the archers of Gwent with their "bows made of wild elm, unpolished, rude and uncouth, not only calculated to shoot an arrow to a great distance, but also to inflict very severe wounds in close fight"'.

85. *Itinerarium Kambriae* (Bk I, c. iv), 54; trans. emended from Thorpe, *Journey Through Wales*, 113.

86. See Ch. 5, pp. 84–93.

87. D.M. Wilson, *The Bayeux Tapestry* (London and New York, 1985), 60. All subsequent references to the Bayeux Tapestry are to plates in this edition, unless otherwise stated. In an earlier edition of the Tapestry, *The Bayeux Tapestry*, ed. F.M. Stenton (London, 1957), 174, C.H. Gibbs-Smith commented on 'the comparatively weak and so-called Danish shortbow', reflecting another antiquarian myth that the bow was a Viking import. He noted inconsistently, and without evidence, that while the weapon could not penetrate the wood of the Saxon shields, it could pierce a hauberk at 50 yards.

88. Rogers, 'Military Revolutions of the Hundred Years War', 249.

89. Bradbury, *The Medieval Archer*, 24, 36–8, rightly points to some of the difficulties posed by medieval illustrations of bows and the influence of exemplars. Yet he none the less draws the conclusion from the marginal archers on the Bayeux Tapestry that they draw a 'bow of no great length' and that accordingly 'ordinary bows in the eleventh century were shorter than those in the later Middle Ages' (*ibid.*, 36–7). Similarly, he regards the marginal sketches of Welsh archers in the Treaty of Montgomery as representing an earlier form of weapon, namely 'ordinary wooden bows rather than longbows' (*ibid.*, 15).

90. Here too, however, artists' treatment of models could sometimes be complex. Thus, for example, in his depiction of the martyrdom of St Ursula, Hans Memling drew for the basic composition and attitude of the principal figures on a mid-fifteenth-century German illustration, which depicted the saint's slayer drawing a heavily recurved bow. Memling, however, not only transformed the crudely executed weapon of his exemplar into a beautifully depicted bow, but heightened its recurve (in contrast to the other longbows depicted on the same panel) to match the exotic orientalism of the Emperor's equipment. D. De Vos, *Hans Memling. Catalogue* (Bruges and Antwerp, 1994), no. 57, 180–1.

91. *Bayeux Tapestry*, 61–2.

92. *The Utrecht Psalter in Medieval Art: Picturing the Psalms of David*, ed. K. van der Horst, W. Noel and W. Wustefeld (London, 1996), 2, 60, 62, 169, 205.

93. *The Harley Psalter*, ed. W. Noel (Cambridge, 1996).

94. As does the great authority on prehistoric bows, Rausing, *The Bow*, fig. 23a.

95. *A Picture Book of Old Testament Stories of the Thirteenth Century*, ed. S.C. Cockerell (Roxburghe Club, London, 1924), 135.

96. BM Harley MS. 4751, f.8.

97. P.D.A. Harvey, *Mappa Mundi. The Hereford World Map* (Hereford and London, 1996), 2.

98. M. Camille, *A Mirror in Parchment. The Luttrell Psalter and the Making of Medieval England* (London, 1998), 66–73.

99. Peterborough Psalter, f. 14 (L.F. Sandler, *The Peterborough Psalter in Brussels and Other Fenland Manuscripts* (London, 1974), pl. 296); Tickhill Psalter (Notts, 1303–14).

100. Canonici Apocalypse (Oxford, Bodleian Library, MS Canon. Bibl. 62); Crowland Apocalypse (Cambridge, Magdalene College, MS 5); Sandler, *Peterborough Psalter*, 9–10, 62.

101. Sandler, *Peterborough Psalter*, pls 202–3.

102. *Das Stuttgarter Passionale*, ed. A. Boeckler (Augsburg, 1923), pls 99, 47, 90.

103. Cambridge, Trinity College MS R. 17.1, f.9, illustrated in *Romanesque Manuscripts, 1066–1190*, ed. C.M. Kaufman (London, 1975), no. 68, pl. 184; J. Bayet, 'Le symbolisme du cerf et du centaure à la Porte Rouge de Notre-Dame de Paris', *Revue archéologique*, xliv (1954), 52, fig. 4.

104. N.J. Morgan, *Early Gothic Manuscripts, I. 1190–1250* (Oxford, 1982), pl. 189 (Fitzwilliam MS 254).

105. British Library, Royal MS 2. B VI, f.10 (Morgan, *Early Gothic Manuscripts*, no. 86).

106. *King Lear*, Act IV, Scene VI, 88. Cf. Ascham, *Toxophilus*, 145 on poor shooting stances: 'An other coureth downe, and layeth out his buttockes, as though he shoulde shoote at crowes.'

107. *The Romance of the Rose by Guillaume de Lorris and Jean de Meun*, trans. C. Dahlberg (Princeton, 3rd edn, 1995), 54. (Cf. A. Blamires and G.C. Holian, *The Romance of the Rose Illuminated* (Cardiff, 2001)).

108. *Ashmole Bestiary*, Oxford, Bodleian Library, MS Ashmole 1511, f.48v, and for a reproduction, see *Vollständige Faksimile Ausgabe im Originalformat der Handschrift MS Ashmole 1511, Bestiarium* (Graz, 1992). Prestwich, *Armies and Warfare*, 130–1.

109. This portrait is reproduced in Hardy, *Longbow*, 151. *The Beauchamp Pageant*, ed. A. Sinclair (Donnington, 2004), now provides a fine new facsimile of these famous drawings.

CHAPTER 3

1. *Anglo-Saxon Chronicle (ASC)*, 'D', 1066. This and all subsequent references to the *Anglo-Saxon Chronicle* are to the translations in *English Historical Documents, I, c. 500–1042*, ed. D. Whitelock (2nd edn, London, 1979), for annals up to 1042, and *English Historical Documents II, 1042–1189*, ed. D.C. Douglas and G.W. Greenway (2nd edn, London, 1981, for 1042–1154).

2. Such is the implication of the Bayeux Tapestry (*Bayeux Tapestry*, 71); and for further discussion of Harold's death see M.J. Strickland, *War and Chivalry. The Conduct and Perception of War in England and Normandy, 1066–1217* (Cambridge, 1996), 4–7. The earliest explicit narrative account to relate that Harold was killed by an arrow in the eye comes from the chronicle of Amatus de Montecassino, written *c.* 1080 (now surviving only in a French translation); Aimé du Mont Cassin, *Storia di Normanni*, ed. V. de Bartholomeis (Rome, 1935), I:3, 11. The account of Harold being finally slain by Norman warriors received poetic elaboration in *The Carmen de Hastingae Proelio of Guy Bishop of Amiens*, ed. and trans. C. Morton and H. Muntz (Oxford, 1972), ll. 535–50, an incident discussed in Appendix D, 116–20.

3. Much has been written on the battle of Hastings, but see R.A. Brown, 'The Battle of Hastings', *Proceedings of the Battle Conference on Anglo-Norman Studies*, iii (1980), 1–21, reprinted in *Anglo-Norman Warfare: Studies in late Anglo-Saxon and Anglo-Norman Military Organization and Warfare*, ed. M.J. Strickland (Woodbridge, 1992), 161–81; S. Morillo, 'Hastings, An Unusual Battle', *Haskins Society Journal*, ii (1990), 95–103, reprinted with a selection of sources and reprinted papers (including Brown's article) in *The Battle of Hastings: Sources and Interpretations*, ed. S. Morillo (Woodbridge, 1996); and most recently, J. Bradbury, *The Battle of Hastings* (Stroud, 1998).

4. For the limitations of cavalry and the continued significance of infantry see, *inter alia*, S. Morillo, *Warfare under the Anglo-Norman Kings, 1066–1135* (Woodbridge, 1994), 150–62; M. Bennett, 'The Medieval Warhorse Reconsidered', in *Medieval Knighthood, V. Papers from the Sixth Strawberry Hill Conference, 1994*, ed. S. Church and R. Harvey (Woodbridge, 1995), 19–40; and *idem*, 'The Knight Unmasked', *Military History Quarterly*, vii (1995), 8–19.

5. *The Gesta Guillelmi of William of Poitiers*, ed. and trans. R.H.C. Davis and M. Chibnall (Oxford, 1998), 130–1; Henry of Huntingdon, *Historia Anglorum*, ed. and trans. D. Greenway (Oxford, 1996), 392–3, even describes the dense English lines as 'like a castle' (*quasi castellum*).

6. For a valuable survey of archaeological and other evidence for Anglo-Saxon, Frankish and other early medieval archery see J. Manley, 'The Archer and the Army in the Late Saxon Period', *Anglo-Saxon Studies in Archaeology and History*, iv (1985), 223–35.

7. K. Manchester and O.E.C. Elmhurst, 'Forensic Aspects of Anglo-Saxon Injury', *Ossa* (1982 for 1980), 179–88 at 181. It seems that despite this wound the warrior had probably been killed by a sword.

8. The varying interpretations of the symbolism of the archer on the Ruthwell Cross are discussed in R.T.A. Farrell, 'The Archer and

Associated Figures on the Ruthwell Cross – A Reconsideration',
in *Bede and Anglo-Saxon England*, ed. R.T. Farrell, *British
Archaeological Reports* (British Series), xlvi (1978), 96–117. For
the Franks Casket, see *inter alia*, L.E. Webster, 'Stylistic Aspects of
the Franks Casket', in *The Vikings*, ed. R.T. Farrell (London,
1982), 20–32; and *The Making of England. Anglo-Saxon Art and
Culture, AD 600–900*, ed. L.E. Webster and J. Backhouse
(London, 1991), 101–3, with illustrations and bibliography.

9. Aelfric's *Hexateuch*, BL, MS. Cotton Claudius B. IV f. 41v;
reproduced in Nicolle, *Arms and Armour of the Crusading Period*, I,
346 (no. 872), II, 816, and cf. C. Hart, 'The Bayeux Tapestry and
Schools of Illumination at Canterbury', in *Anglo-Norman Studies*,
xxii (1999), 117–68, at 136–7. The bow drawn by a huntsman
in the same MS, f. 36b, illustrated in Stenton, *The Bayeux
Tapestry*, 30, is smaller and more stylised. For discussion of the
reliquary cross, decorated in the style of the Canterbury school,
see R. Randall, 'An Eleventh-Century Ivory Pectoral Cross',
Journal of the Warburg and Courtauld Institutes, xxv (1962),
159–71 at 167, pl. 32d; J. Backhouse, ed. *The Golden Age of
Anglo-Saxon Art, 966–1066* (London, 1984), 122–3.

10. C.W. Hollister, *The Military Organization of Norman England*
(Oxford, 1965), 218.

11. A bow is the subject of Riddle 23 from the Exeter Book, while
Riddle 17 possibly refers to a ballista or siege engine (Bradbury,
The Medieval Archer, 18–19).

12. *Beowulf*, ed. and trans. M. Swanton (Manchester, 1978), l. 3117.

13. *The Battle of Maldon*, ed. D. Scragg (Manchester, 1981), ll. 70–1,
110. For the political, military and literary context of the battle,
see *The Battle of Maldon AD 991*, ed. D. Scragg (Manchester,
1991); and *The Battle of Maldon. Fiction and Fact*, ed. J. Cooper
(London, 1993). It is noteworthy that the Northumbrian hostage
fighting with Byrhtnoth uses a bow, at least initially, though he
would certainly be a noble (*Maldon*, ed. Scragg, ll. 265–72).

14. *ASC*, C, 1066.

15. For this interpolation see B. Dickens, 'The Late Addition to *ASC*
1066 C', *Proceedings of the Leeds Philosophical and Literary Society*,
v (1940), 148–9.

16. The most recent treatment of the battle, K. DeVries, *The
Norwegian Invasion of England in 1066* (Woodbridge, 1999),
regrettably does not display sufficient caution in its use of saga
material. For a more judicious treatment, see F.W. Brookes, *The
Battle of Stamford Bridge* (East Yorkshire Local History series, vi,
1956); and Bradbury, *The Medieval Archer*, 20–1.

17. *King Harald's Saga*, trans. M. Magnusson (Harmondsworth,
1966), 151–2.

18. Saxo Grammaticus, *Danorum regum heroumque historia*, ed. E.
Christiansen, 3 vols (Oxford, 1980–1), II, 484, III, 826, and cf. I,
24.

19. Saxo Grammaticus, *The History of the Danes, Books I–IX*, ed. H.
Ellis Davidson and trans. P. Fisher (Cambridge, 1979, 1980 in 2
vols, reprinted as one volume 1996), 242.

20. L.M. Larson, *The Earliest Norwegian Laws* (New York, 1935), 197,
c.309, requiring freemen to bring a bow and two dozen arrows,

319, c.13; and 197, c.312 for details of how the war-arrow is to
circulate.

21. Saxo Grammaticus, *The History of the Danes*, 142, and see note at
II, 81, where it is suggested that like the 'fiery cross' used to
summon men to arms in medieval Scotland, the war-arrow was of
charred wood (and hence its resemblance to iron).

22. J. Graham-Campbell, *Viking Artefacts. A Select Catalogue* (London,
1980), 12. Arrow types and Old Norse terminology are briefly
discussed in H. Shetelig and H. Falk, *Scandinavian Archaeology*
(Oxford, 1937), 390–3.

23. Graham-Campbell, *Viking Artefacts*, 12; Manley, 'The Archer and
the Army', 227–8. For an example of a tanged, leaf-shaped
arrowhead from the Viking site at Jorvik see R. Hall, *The Viking
Dig: The Excavations at York* (London, 1984), 110.

24. For later socketed heads, see for example, B. O'Riordan,
'Excavations at High Street and Winetavern Street, Dublin',
Medieval Archaeology, xv (1971), 73–85, at 76.

25. *Njal's Saga*, trans. M. Magnusson and H. Pálsson (Harmondsworth, 1960), 170–1 (for the slap, 122–3). Is the correlation with
the Franks Casket merely a coincidence, or was the saga here
reworking, consciously or otherwise, a motif from what was
clearly a well-known story from earlier Germanic legend?

26. J. Jóhannesson, *Islendiga Saga: A History of the Old Icelandic
Commonwealth*, trans. H. Bessason (University of Manitoba,
1974), 395, pl. 1; R.A. Hall, 'A Viking Age Grave at Donnybrook,
Co. Dublin', *Medieval Archaeology*, xxii (1978), 64–83, at 70.

27. J. Graham-Campbell and C.E. Batey, *Vikings in Scotland. An
Archaeological Survey* (Edinburgh, 1998), 118–19.

28. *Ibid.*, 135–7, 139–40.

29. M. Müller-Wille, 'Das Bootkammergrab von Haithabu', in *Berichte
über die Ausgrabungen in Haithabu*, ed. K. Schietzel (Neumünster,
1976), 80ff.

30. E. Thorsilen, *Ladbyskibet* (Copenhagen, 1957), 82ff.

31. For example *Orkneyinga Saga*, trans. H. Pálsson and P. Edwards
(Harmondsworth, 1981), 84; Snorri Sturluson, *Heimskringla*,
trans. S. Laing, 2 vols (revised edn, London, 1964), II, 394 and
206.

32. *Heimskringla*, I, 94–5.

33. On this naval warfare, see P. Griffith, *The Viking Art of War*
(London, 1995), 196–202, and cf. 163–4 for brief comments on
the Viking use of the bow.

34. For skaldic verse see *The Skalds: A Selection of their Poems*, ed. and
trans. L.M. Hollander (New York, 1947); E.O.G. Turville-Petre,
Scaldic Poetry (Oxford, 1976); and R. Frank, 'Skaldic Poetry',
Dictionary of the Middle Ages, ed. J.R. Strayer, 13 vols (New York,
1982–9), xi, 316–23 for a good introduction and bibliography.

35. Egil Skalla-Grímsson, *Head-ransom*, in *EHD*, I, 324–31 at 330;
Einar Helgasson, *Vellekla*, in *The Skalds*, ed. Hollander, 112.

36. Egil Skalla-Grímsson, *Head-ransom*, *EHD*, I, 330.

37. *The Skalds*, ed. Hollander, 105–6.

38. *The Knútsdrápa of Ottar the Black*, *EHD*, I, 335–6 at 336.

39. *The Ecclesiastical History of Orderic Vitalis*, ed. M. Chibnall, 6 vols
(Oxford, 1969–80), V, 222–5; E.A. Freeman, *The Reign of William*

Rufus and the Accession of Henry the First, 2 vols (London, 1882), II, 133 and Appendix II, 618–24, which collects and discusses the sources for this incident.

40. *Early Sources of Scottish History, AD 500–1286*, trans. A.O. Anderson, 2 vols (Edinburgh, 1922, repr. Stamford, 1990), II, 130.

41. Saxo Grammaticus, *Danorum regum heroumque historia*, III, 826.

42. *The Earliest Norwegian Laws*, 319, c.13.

43. For a detailed discussion of the legend and cult of St Edmund, see D. Whitelock, 'Fact and Fiction in the Legend of St Edmund', *Proceedings of the Suffolk Institute for Archaeology*, xxxi (1967–9), 217–33; G. Loomis, 'The Growth of the Saint Edmund Legend', *Harvard Studies and Notes in Philology and Literature*, xiv (1932), 83–113; S.J. Ridyard, *The Royal Saints of Anglo-Saxon England. A Study of West Saxon and East Anglian Cults* (Cambridge, 1988), 61ff.

44. *ASC*, 870.

45. Ridyard, *Royal Saints*, 63–9; C.E. Wright, *The Cultivation of Saga in Anglo-Saxon England* (Edinburgh and London, 1939), 58–9, and cf. 55.

46. *Abbonis Floriacensis passio Sancti Edmundi* in *Memorials of St Edmund's Abbey*, ed. T. Arnold, 3 vols (Rolls Series, 1890–6), I, 15.

47. The traditional version of Sebastian's death first occurs in a fifth-century life mistakenly attributed to Ambrose, bishop of Milan, by which the saint, having miraculously survived use as target practice, confronted Diocletian who thereupon had him (successfully) beaten to death with clubs. For Sebastian see *Acta sanctorum* (64 vols, Antwerp, 1643–), II, 257–96, and D.H. Farmer, *The Oxford Dictionary of Saints* (2nd edn, 1987), 380–1.

48. R.M. Thomson, 'Early Romanesque Book Illustration in England: the Dates of the Pierpont Morgan "Vitae Sancti Edmundi" and the Bury Bible', *Viator*, ii (1971), 211–15.

49. For a selection of representations of St Edmund see E.G. Tasker, *Encyclopedia of Medieval Church Art* (London, 1993), 124–5; and for the Wilton Diptych, D. Gordon, *Making and Meaning. The Wilton Diptych* (London, 1993), pl. 15.

50. For wall-paintings, see E.W. Tristram, *English Medieval Wall-Painting: The Thirteenth Century*, 2 vols (Oxford, 1950), I, 530–1, 290–3 and pl. 137. Images survive, for example, at St Helen's, Cliffe-at-Hoo, Kent, *c.* 1250, and in a very indistinct scene in one of the chapels of the north transept at Ely Cathedral. The church of Thornham Parva, Suffolk, contains a fine twelfth-century cycle of paintings illustrating the life and miracles of the saint, though regrettably the martyrdom scene was destroyed by the insertion of later medieval windows.

51. Farmer, *The Oxford Dictionary of Saints*, 381; M.G.A. Vale, *War and Chivalry* (Athens, Georgia, 1981), 110.

52. Abbo, *Bella Parisiacae urbis*, ed. H. Waquet, *Abbon. Siège de Paris par les Normands* (Paris, 1942), 18–19.

53. *Reginonis abbatis Prumiensis chronicon cum continuatione Treverensi*, ed. F. Kurze, *MGH SRG* (Hanover, 1890), 137; trans. in *Medieval Europe*, ed. J. Kirshner and K.F. Morrison (Chicago and London, 1986), 64.

54. Gregory of Tours, *Decem libri historiarum*, ed. B. Krusch and W. Levison, *MGH SRM* (Hanover, 1951); Gregory of Tours, *History of the Franks*, trans. L. Thorpe (Harmondsworth, 1974), 121 (Bk II, 9). Earlier, Caesar had noted that there were a very large number of archers among the native Gauls (*Bello Gallico*, VII, 31).

55. *Laws of the Salian and Ripuarian Franks*, trans. T.J. Rivers (New York, 1986), 61, c.2 and 149, c.1. The same text also prescribes compensation of 36 *solidi* for the loss of the index finger 'with which one shoots an arrow'; *ibid.*, 73, c.6, 173, c.7.

56. B. Bachrach, 'Procopius, Agathias and the Frankish Military', *Speculum*, xlv (1970), reprinted in *idem*, *Armies and Politics in the Early Medieval West* (Aldershot, 1993), 435–41; *idem*, *Early Carolingian Warfare. Prelude to Empire* (Philadelphia, 2001), 172 and n. 73.

57. E. Salin, *La Civilisation mérovingienne: d'après les sépultures, les textes et le laboratoire*, 2 vols (Paris, 1959), I, 356, II, 87, 239, 241; J. Werner, 'Bewaffnung und Waffenbeigrabe in der Merowingerzeit', in *Ordinamenti militari in occidente nell'alto medioevo*, Settimane, xv, 2 vols (Spoleto, 1968), I, 95–108, at 105.

58. P. Lasko, *The Kingdom of the Franks. North-West Europe before Charlemagne* (London, 1971), 54–5.

59. Gregory of Tours, *Libri historiarum*, I, I (Bk V, 48), 258; trans. Thorpe, *History of the Franks*, 315.

60. *Vita Landiberti vetustissima*, MGH SRM, IV, 353–84 at 365; R. Le Jan-Hennebicque, 'Satellites et bandes armées dans le mond franc (VIIe–Xe siècles)', in *Le Combattant au Moyen Age* (Paris, 2nd edn, 1995), 99.

61. P. Paulsen, *Alamanische Adelsgräber von Niederstotzingen (Kreis Heidenheim)* (Stuttgart, 1967), 122, pls 18, 10; and see p. 40.

62. S. Coupland, 'Carolingian Arms and Armour in the Ninth Century', *Viator*, xxi (1990), 29–50 at 49. For the composite bow, see Ch. 6, pp. 98–101.

63. F.L. Ganshof, 'L'armée sous les carolingiennes', *Ordinamenti militari*, I, 109–30; J.F. Verbruggen, 'L'armée et la stratégie de Charlemagne', *Karl der Grosse. Lebenswerk und Nachleben* (Dusseldorf, 1965), 420–36; J. France, 'The Military History of the Carolingian Period', *Revue Belge d'Histoire Militaire*, xxvi (1985), 81–99; and for a recent overview see T. Reuter, 'Carolingian and Ottonian Warfare', *Medieval Warfare. A History*, ed. M. Keen (Oxford, 1999), 13–35, and J. France, 'The Composition and Raising of the Armies of Charlemagne', *JMMH*, i (2002), 61–82.

64. *Karoli ad Fulradum abbatum epistola*, in *MGH Capit*, I, ed. A. Boretius (Hanover, 1883), 168 (no. 75); trans. P.E. Dutton, *Carolingian Civilization: A Reader* (Ontario, 1993), 73.

65. *Capitularia Aquisgranense*, ed. A. Boretius, *MGH Capit*, I (Hanover, 1883), 171 (no. 77), c.9; trans. H.R. Loyn and J. Percival, *The Reign of Charlemagne. Documents on Carolingian Government and Administration* (London, 1975), 83.

66. *Ibid.*, 172, c.17. Cf. H. Riesch, '"Quod nullus in hostem habeat baculum sed arcum": Pfeil und Bogen als Beispiel für technologische Innovationen der Karolingerzeit', *Technikgeschichte*, lxi (1994), 209–26.

67. See pp. 150–2.

68. *De Procinctu romanae miliciae*, ed. E. Dümmler, *Zeitschrift für Deutsches Alterum*, xv (1872), 413–81, at chs ix, xiii; Bachrach, *Early Carolingian Warfare*, 100–2, 107.

69. *Karoli ad Fulradum . . . epistola*, 172; Dutton, *Carolingian Civilization*, 73.

70. B. Bachrach, 'A Picture of Avar-Frankish Warfare from a Carolingian Psalter of the Early Ninth Century in Light of the *Strategicon*', *Archivum Eurasiae Medii Aevi*, iv (1986), and reprinted in *idem, Armies and Politics in the Early Medieval West*, 5–27, for an important discussion of Avar equipment; F.L. Ganshof, 'À propos de la cavalerie dans les armées de Charlemagne', *Comptes-rendus de l'Académie des inscriptions et belles-lettres* (1952), 531–6 at 532; *idem*, 'Charlemagne's Army', in *Frankish Institutions under Charlemagne* (New York, 1970), 65.

71. France, 'The Military History of the Carolingian Period', 81–99; and for the Stuttgart Psalter, Bachrach, 'A Picture of Avar-Frankish Warfare', 27.

72. For Byzantine mounted archers (*c*. 600) see A.D.H. Bivar, 'Cavalry Equipment and Tactics on the Euphrates Frontier', *Dumbarton Oaks Papers*, xxvi (1972), 283.

73. *Der Stuttgarter Bilderpsalter*, 2 vols (Stuttgart, 1965–8), I, *Faksmilie*, fol.3, also illustrated in Reuter, 'Carolingian and Ottonian Warfare', 23. As with other Carolingian illustrations, however, there is a strong possibility that this illustration and the kind of scale armour it depicts was borrowed from classical or Byzantine models; see Coupland, 'Carolingian Arms and Armour', 40–1.

74. Richer, *Histoire de la France*, ed. R. Latouche, 2 vols (Paris, 1930), I, 142.

75. Richer, II, 178.

76. C. Gaier, 'Quand l'arbalète était une nouveauté. Réflexions sur son role militaire du Xe au XIIIe siècle', in *idem, Armes et combats dans l'univers médiéval* (Brussels, 1995), 159–82, provides an excellent survey of the early medieval crossbow.

77. Richer, I, 272, 282.

78. Richer, II, 132–4.

79. Richer, II, 4–6.

80. Richer, II, 172–4.

81. E. Harmuth, 'Die Armbrustbilder von Haimo von Auxerre', *Waffen- und Kostümkunde* (3rd ser., xii, 1970), 127–30.

82. Fragments of such weapons have been discovered. A. Kluge-Pinsken, 'Bogen und Armbrust', in *Das Reich der Salier 1024–1125. Katalog zur Ausstellung des Landes Rhein-Pfalz* (Sigmaringen, 1992), 96–9, illustrates a find of one such long trigger from Braunschweig, made from antler or bone, dating from the tenth century, and catalogues others together with a drawing of a reconstructed weapon. A crossbow bolt with its shaft, found at Winetavern Street (Dublin National Museum, 398) has been dated to the tenth century.

83. L. White, *Medieval Technology and Social Change* (Oxford, 1962), 151–2, provides a bibliography on the Chinese crossbow and its dissemination; and cf. C.M. Wilbur, 'A History of the Crossbow', *The Smithsonian Report for 1936* (Washington, 1937), 427–38, at 428–30. Archaeological remains exist from the Han dynasty (206 BC–AD 220), but literary records refer to its earlier use, for example at the battle of Ma-Ling in 341 BC.

84. E.W. Marsden, *Greek and Roman Artillery* (Oxford, 1969), 5–12.

85. Gaier, 'Quand l'arbalète était une nouveauté', 163, and n. 6; D. Baatz, 'Die Römische Jagdarmbrust', *Archäologisches Korrespondenzblatt*, xxi (1991), 283–99.

86. Flavius Vegetius Renatus, *Epitoma Rei Militaris*, ed. L.F. Stelten (New York, 1990), Book IV, Ch. xxii, 258–61, and III, Ch. xxiv, 176–7. Vegetius was writing sometime between *c*. AD 383 and 450 for the Emperor Theodosius I or Valentinian III (423–55). Somewhat unhelpfully he adds that he thought it superfluous to describe 'the *arcuballistae . . .* which present use makes known', without explaining if or how such weapons differed from the hand crossbow or *manuballista*. He does, however, comment that in drawing up an army's battle lines, crossbowmen (*manuballistarii*) could be placed behind the infantry in the fifth rank, together with slingers, staff-slingers, and carriage-mounted ballistae.

87. D.B. Campbell, 'Auxiliary Artillery Revisited', *Bonner Jahrbücher*, clxxxvi (1986), 117–32 at 131–2; P.E. Chevedden, 'Artillery in Late Antiquity: Prelude to the Middle Ages', in *The Medieval City under Siege*, ed. I.A. Corfis and M. Wolfe (Woodbridge, 1995), 131–73 at 144–5.

88. This machine, fast to load, extremely accurate and firing a heavy armour-piercing arrow often stabilised with brass flights, had been developed to a high degree of sophistication by the Greeks and initially employed a large wooden or composite bow, which soon gave way to the more efficient torsion-driven engines in which two separate bow arms were inserted between tensed skeins of hair. By the late first century AD the Romans had developed a light, robust all-metal framed version, which could be mounted on mule-drawn carts for great manoeuvrability. For a detailed discussion of such machines and early Roman crossbows see Chevedden, 'Artillery in Late Antiquity', 131–73, including a very full bibliography.

89. For this inheritance see J. Bradbury, *The Medieval Siege* (Woodbridge, 1992), 12–19.

90. Ammianus, XII: 8; *Leges Visigothorum*, ed. K. Zeumer, *MGH LNG* (Hanover, 1902), I, 340 (viii, c. 23).

91. J.M. Gilbert, 'Crossbows on Pictish Stones', *Proceedings of the Society of Antiquaries of Scotland*, cvii (1975–6), 316–17.

92. Such bow traps have been suggested as a possible origin for the crossbow (Wilbur, 'A History of the Crossbow', 428), and it is striking that the Visigothic Laws mention such traps and *ballistae* in the same breath (*Leges Visigothorum*, I, 340). Such bow traps long remained in use, and one appears in the late twelfth-century version of the Tristan legend (Béroul, *The Romance of Tristan*, ed. N.J. Lacy (New York and London, 1989), ll. 1752–73). When a refugee from King Mark in the forest of Morrois,

> Tristan invented the Unfailing Bow.
> He set it up in the woods in such a way
> That it killed everything that came in contact with it.
> If a stag or deer came through the woods
> And touched the branches

It shot him high if the animal touched it high

And if he touched it near the ground

It shot him low . . .

The bow was well named, for it never failed.

93.   L. Alcock, 'Gwyr y Gogledd: An Archaeological Approach', *Archaeologica Cambrensis*, cxxxii (1984 for 1983), 1–18, at 12.

94.   The nut found at Buston crannog could date anywhere from Roman times to the eighteenth century, while that found at Urquhart is either Norman or late medieval; A. MacGregor, 'Two Antler Crossbow Nuts and Some Notes on the Early Development of the Crossbow', *Proceedings of the Society of Antiquaries of Scotland*, cvii (1975–6), 317–21; A.G. Credland, 'Crossbow Remains, Part 1', *JSAA*, xxiii (1980), who accepts the dating to the seventh or eighth century.

95.   Credland, 'Crossbow Remains, Part 1', 12–13. The Burbage nut is illustrated in W.F. Paterson, *A Guide to the Crossbow* (Society of Archer Antiquaries, 1990), 15, ill. c.

96.   Abbo, *Bella*, 22–4.

97.   *Annales Bertiniani*, ed. F. Grat, J. Vielliard, S. Clémencet and L. Levillain, *Annales de Saint-Bertin* (Paris, 1964), 884.

98.   R. Rey, *La Sculpture Romane Languedocienne* (Paris, 1936), fig. 65 (Toulouse); G. Gaillard, *Les débuts de la sculpture Romane Espagnole* (Paris, 1938), pls 27, 108 (St Isidore, naval capital; Compostela, Portal des Orfèvres). Another example occurs on one of the double capitals in the west cloister arcade of St Peter's at Moissac.

It is possible that a badly mutilated capital from the Roman-esque cloister of Norwich Cathedral depicts a crossbowman spanning his bow thus, rather than being an example of an archer lying on his back and shooting the bow with his feet in the manner of some south American tribes, as suggested by J.A. Franklin, 'The Romanesque Cloister Sculpture at Norwich Cathedral Priory', in *Studies in Medieval Sculpture*, ed. F.H. Thompson (Society of Antiquaries of London Occasional Paper, new series, III, 1983). An example of such 'pedestrial archery' does, however, occur in the Luttrell Psalter, where it clearly depicts a game (not, as stated by Bradbury, *The Medieval Archer*, 148, a crossbowman spanning his weapon, for the bow has no tiller).

99.   Anna Comnena, *Alexiad*, trans. E.R.A. Sewter, *The Alexiad of Anna Comnena* (London, 1969), 316, n. 36. See J. France, 'Anna Comnena, the Alexiad and the First Crusade', *Reading Medieval Studies*, x (1983), 20–32; and W. Rose, 'Anna Comnena über die Bewaffnung der Kreuzfahrer', *Zeitschrift für Historische Waffen- und Kostümkunde*, ix (1921), 1–10.

100. A weapon known as the *solenarion* is mentioned in the *Strategikon* of Maurice (XII.5), which has been regarded by some as a cross-bow, and by others as a bow with an arrow guide for shooting shorter darts. Similarly, the *cheirotoxobolistai* mentioned in use alongside bows on a Byzantine warship in 950 could be cross-bows, but might be frame-mounted weapons; Gaier, 'Quand l'arbalète était une nouveauté', 167–8; J. Haldon, '"Solenarion" – The Byzantine Crossbow', *Historical Journal of the University of Birmingham*, xii (1970), 155–7; and Chevedden, 'Artillery in Late Antiquity', especially at 142–51, which provides an extensive

discussion on the subject of the Roman and Byzantine crossbow and existing scholarly literature; cf. Bachrach, *Early Carolingian Warfare*, 111–12.

101. *Alexiad*, 317 (n.36).

102. *Alexiad*, 316–17.

103. R. Colardelle and M. Colardelle, 'L'habitat médiéval immergé de Colletière à Charavines (Isère)', *Archaeologie Medievale*, x (1980), 167–219, at 195; Paterson, *Guide to the Crossbow*, 16, and 17 ill. e.

104. It has been suggested that crossbowmen were particularly prevalent in Flanders, though this is based primarily on the earlier testimony of Richer (*The Carmen de Hastingae proelio of Guy, Bishop of Amiens*, 114, n. 2).

105. For a discussion of possible troop numbers, B. Bachrach, 'On the Origins of William the Conqueror's Horse Transports', *Technology and Culture*, xxvi (1985), 505–31, at 518–19.

106. Wace, *Roman de Rou*, ed. A.J. Holden, 3 vols (Paris, 1970–3) III, ll. 6, 481–508; trans. M. Bennett, 'Wace and Warfare', *Anglo-Norman Studies*, xi (1988), 37–58, repr. in *Anglo-Norman Warfare*, ed. M. Strickland (Woodbridge, 1992), 230–50 at 238–9.

107. M. Bennett, 'Poetry as History? The Roman de Rou as a Source for the Norman Conquest', *Anglo-Norman Studies*, v (1982), 21–39; and cf. E. Van Houts, 'The Ship List of William the Conqueror', *Anglo-Norman Studies*, x (1987), 159–83, at 163 and n. 22.

108. For Varaville, Wace, *Roman de Rou*, III, ll. 5, 204–5, 210; Bennett, 'Wace and Warfare', 245–7; Bradbury, *The Medieval Archer*, 26; and for Wace's connection with Bayeux and the Tapestry, Bennett, 'Poetry as History?', 22–3, who notes 'it is inconceivable that Wace should have been unaware of it'.

109. For this important text, see R.H.C. Davies, 'William of Poitiers and his history of William the Conqueror', in *The Writing of History in the Middle Ages*, ed. R.H.C. Davies and J.M. Wallace-Hadrill (Oxford, 1981), 71–100.

110. William of Poitiers, 122–5; *The Chronicle of John of Worcester*, 3 vols (Oxford, 1995–), II, ed. and trans. R.R. Darlington, P. McGurk and J. Bray, 604–5.

111. Olaf had defended his front line with trenches concealed with branches and sods, into which the enemy cavalry fell, allowing the Norse and their allies to kill or capture many of their opponents; M.J. Strickland, 'Military Technology and Conquest: The Anomaly of Anglo-Saxon England', *Anglo-Norman Studies*, xix (1996), 353–82.

112. William of Poitiers, 126–7; John of Worcester, II, 604–5, men-tions the slingers (*fundibalalari*), in describing William's landing 'with an innumerable multitude of knights, slingers, archers and foot-soldiers, for he had brought strong auxiliaries from the whole of Gaul with him'.

113. William of Poitiers, 128–9. The translation of the last sentence has been emended to reflect the ambiguity in the text of whether these troops were archers or javelineers (cf. the translation of D.C. Douglas in *EHD*, II, 240).

114. William of Poitiers, 128–9.

115. William of Poitiers, 130–1.

116. William of Poitiers, 133–4. This ruse is also mentioned by the *Carmen de Hastingae proelio*, ll. 423–4, and Baudri of Bourgeuil, *Les oeuvres poétiques de Baudri de Bourgeuil (1046–1130)*, ed. P. Abrahams (Paris, 1926), no. 96, ll. 419–20.

117. Brown, 'The Battle of Hastings', in *Anglo-Norman Warfare*, 176.

118. William of Poitiers, 132–3.

119. *Carmen de Hastingae proelio*, 24–5, 26–7 (ll. 381–2, 409–12). After much debate as to its veracity as a contemporary account, the Carmen has been rehabilitated as an important source for the battle. For the most recent study and bibliography see the new edition and translation by F. Barlow (ed.), *The Carmen de Hastingae Proelio of Guy, Bishop of Amiens* (Oxford, 1999).

120. Huntingdon, 394–5.

121. G.H. White, *Complete Peerage*, 12 vols (London, 1910–59), xii (1), Appendix, L, at 43–4.

122. J. Alm, *European Crossbows: A Survey*, trans. H. Bartlett Wells and G.M. Wilson (London, 1993), 52–3; B. Thordemann, *Armour from the Battle of Wisby, 1361*, 2 vols (Stockholm, 1939), II, 187–91, and see pp. 281–2.

123. Henry of Huntingdon, 394–5. See D.J. Bernstein, *The Mystery of the Bayeux Tapestry* (London, 1986), 144–61, for the intriguing suggestion that the blinding of Harold by an arrow was an example of a medieval iconographic motif symbolising divine punishment for perjury.

124. Evidence of the stitching reveals that the fallen figure also originally had an arrow sticking from his eye; Bernstein, *The Mystery of the Bayeux Tapestry*, 144–52.

125. For a discussion of the Malfosse incident and its place in the chronology of the battle see Brown, 'The Battle of Hastings', 178–81.

126. Huntingdon, 392–3, '*gentem arte belli cassam, gentem nec etiam sagittas habentem*'.

127. Cf. C.W. Hollister, *Anglo-Saxon Military Institutions on the Eve of the Norman Conquest* (Oxford, 1962); R. Abels, *Lordship and Military Obligation in Anglo-Saxon England* (Berkeley, 1988); and for Harold's military skills, K. De Vries, 'Harold Godwineson in Wales: Military Legitimacy in Late Anglo-Saxon England', in *The Normans and their Adversaries at War*, ed. R.P. Abels and B.S. Bachrach (Woodbridge, 2001), 65–86.

128. R. Glover, 'English Warfare in 1066', *EHR*, lxvii (1952), 1–18.

129. It has been suggested that the distinctive figure of an archer in the central panel of the Tapestry depicting the Norman archers may be an attempt to portray a crossbowman, as he alone of the archers wears a helmet and hauberk and bears a quiver at his belt (*Carmen*, ed. Morton and Muntz, 115). Given that his weapon appears the same as the others, however, it seems more likely that he is a captain of archers, a *magister sagittariorum*, an office occasionally mentioned in the twelfth century.

130. *ASC*, 1079.

131. Baudri, ll. 409–12.

132. H.E.J. Cowdrey, 'Bishop Ermenfrid of Sion and the Penitential Ordinance following the Battle of Hastings', *Journal of Ecclesiastical History*, xx (1969), 225–42.

133. *The Letters of Lanfranc, Archbishop of Canterbury*, ed. and trans. H. Clover and M. Gibson (Oxford, 1979), 126–7 (no. 35), where *balistariis* is strangely rendered as 'slingers' not crossbowmen.

134. *Recueil des Actes des Ducs de Normandie, 911–1066*, ed. M. Faroux (Caen, 1961), no. 147.

135. H. Ellis, *A General Introduction to Domesday Book* (London, 1833), lists those tenants in Wiltshire, Yorkshire and Norfolk given the title '*arbalastarius*'. J.H. Round, *The King's Serjeants and Officers of State with their Coronation Services* (London, 1911), 13–14.

136. MacGregor, 'Two Antler Crossbow Nuts', 317–21; D. Renn, 'The Keep at Wareham Castle', *Medieval Archaeology*, iv (1960), 56–68, at 61, fig. 19c.

137. R. Bartlett, *The Making of Europe: Conquest, Colonization and Cultural Change, 950–1350* (London, 1993), 60–84, and 64 for the rise of a professional elite of crossbowmen.

138. E. Harmuth, *Die Armbrust* (Graz, 1975), 23; and S.A. Epstein, *Genoa and the Genoese, 958–1528* (North Carolina, 1996), 99, 190–1.

139. William of Apulia, *Gesta Roberti Wiscardi*, ed. D.R. Wilmans, *MGH, SS*, IX, 266, l. 4; trans. M. Mathieu, *Guillaume de Pouille, La Geste de Robert Guiscard* (Palermo, 1961).

140. For Durazzo, *Alexiad*, 146–8; N. Hooper and M. Bennett, ed. *Cambridge Illustrated Atlas of Warfare. The Middle Ages, 768–1487* (Cambridge, 1996), 83.

CHAPTER 4

1. Wace, *Roman de Brut*, ed. I. Arnold, 2 vols (Paris, 1938–40), ll. 3, 123–36; trans. Bennet, 'Wace and Warfare', 56–7.

2. Chaucer, *The Knight's Tale*, l. 2,125.

3. Hollister, *The Military Organization of Norman England*, 127–9; and J. Bradbury, 'Battles in England and Normandy, 1066–1154', *Anglo-Norman Studies*, vi (1984), 1–12, reprinted in Strickland, ed., *Anglo-Norman Warfare*, 182–93, for a valuable survey.

4. Hollister, *The Military Organization of Norman England*, 127–9; Oman, *Art of War*, I, 383; Bradbury, 'Battles in England and Normandy', 192.

5. William of Poitiers, 130–1.

6. Hollister, *The Military Organization of Norman England*, 216ff; William of Malmesbury, *Gesta regum Anglorum*, ed. and trans. R.A.B. Mynors, R.M. Thompson and M. Winterbottom, 2 vols (Oxford, 1998–9), I, 716–17.

7. Huntingdon, 454–5, and for the chronology of Henry's composition, *ibid.*, lxvi–lxxvii; cf. Oman, *Art of War*, I, 383 who writes of Tinchebrai: 'Undoubtedly the juxtaposition of cavalry and infantry in each division of the royal army was learnt from crusading experience.' For Tinchebrai see M. Leroux, *La bataille de Tinchebray* (Tinchebray, 1972).

8. R.C. Smail, *Crusading Warfare, 1097–1193* (Cambridge, 2nd edn,

1995), 165–75; and for detailed analysis of these and other engagements, J. France, *Victory in the East. A Military History of the First Crusade* (Cambridge, 1994).

9. Bradbury, 'Battles in England and Normandy', 11–12, who quotes the *Taktica* of Leo the Wise (*c.* 900) on the Franks: 'when their soldiers are hard pressed in a cavalry fight they will turn their horses loose, dismount and stand back to back against superior numbers rather than flee'. Leo further noted that: 'If their cavalry is caught up in some defile, it dismounts, and forms up very well, just like infantry' (G. Chaliand, *The Art of War in World History: from Antiquity to the Nuclear Age* (Berkeley, 1994), 365).

10. *Chroniques des Comtes d'Anjou*, ed. P. Marchegay and A. Salmon (Paris, 2nd edn, 1871), 144–51; and for a full analysis of the battle and its sources, Bradbury, 'Battles in England and Normandy', 188–9.

11. Bradbury, *The Medieval Archer*, 57.

12. Morillo, *Warfare under the Anglo-Norman Kings*, 156–7.

13. Morillo, *Warfare under the Anglo-Norman Kings*, 156–7.

14. Orderic, VI, 350–1.

15. Bradbury, 'Battles in England and Normandy', 193.

16. Orderic, VI, 238–9. For other descriptions of the battle see Huntingdon, 462–5; *Chronica monasterii de Hida juxta Wintoniam*, in *Liber monasterii de Hyda*, ed. E. Edwards (London, Rolls Series, 1866), 317–18; Suger, *Vie de Louis VI le Gros*, ed. H. Waquet (Paris, 1929), 196–8.

17. Orderic, VI, 348–50. Though not mentioned by Orderic, Huntingdon, 472–3 and n. 213, names William de Tancarville as the main royal commander. If Huntingdon is right, it is significant that Tancarville also took part in the battle of Brémule (Orderic, VI, 234–6). Orderic suggests Odo, though a more lowly figure, had *de facto* command. For Odo, Bourgthéroulde and the royal military household see M. Chibnall, 'Mercenaries and the *Familia Regis* under Henry I', *History*, lxii (1977), 15–23, reprinted in Strickland, ed., *Anglo-Norman Warfare*, 84–92.

18. Orderic, VI, 348–51, who twice states the archers were in the front (*in prima . . . fronte*); Torigny's description occurs in his interpolations in William of Jumièges, *The Gesta Normannorum Ducum of William of Jumièges, Orderic Vitalis, and Robert of Torigni*, ed. E.M.C. van Houts (Oxford, 1992, 1995), II, 234–5.

19. Orderic, VI, 350–1. For Waleran and the political context of the battle see D. Crouch, *The Beaumont Twins. The Roots and Branches of Power in the Twelfth Century* (Cambridge, 1986), 13–23.

20. See pp. 102–3.

21. Chibnall, 'Mercenaries and the *Familia Regis*', 84–92; J.O. Prestwich, 'The Military Household of the Norman Kings', *EHR*, xcvi (1981), 1–37, reprinted in Strickland, ed., *Anglo-Norman Warfare*, 93–127.

22. A document relating to the officers of the royal household in the last years of Henry I's reign, the *Constitutio Domus Regis*, mentions royal archers but these were huntsmen, listed along with hornblowers and keepers of dogs, and regrettably the *Constitutio* does not detail the composition of the king's

household at war (*Dialogus de Scaccario and Consititutio Domus Regis*, ed. C. Johnson (London, 1950), 135).

23. *Gesta Normannorum ducum*, II, 234–5.

24. *Gesta Normannorum ducum*, II, 234–5.

25. *Bayeux Tapestry*, 72–3.

26. *The Chronicle of Robert of Torigny*, ed. R. Howlett, *Chronicles of the Reigns of Stephen, Henry II, and Richard I*, 4 vols (London, Rolls Series, 1884–9), IV, 137.

27. See pp. 90–3.

28. *Constitutio*, ed. Johnson, 135.

29. *ASC*, 'E', 1083.

30. *Gesta Stephani*, ed. and trans. K.R. Potter, with new notes and introduction by R.H.C. Davis (Oxford, 1976), 34–5, 156–7.

31. *Gesta Stephani*, 170–1.

32. *Gesta Stephani*, 36–7.

33. *Gesta Stephani*, 130–1.

34. For the battle see Orderic, VI, 542–4; *Gesta Stephani*, 110–14; Huntingdon, 724–38; William of Malmesbury, *Historia Novella*, ed. E. King and K.R. Potter (Oxford, 1998), 47–9; and for a detailed modern account, J. Bradbury, *Stephen and Matilda* (Stroud, 1996), 90–8.

35. *Gesta Stephani*, 140–1.

36. Simeon of Durham, *Historia regum*, ed. T. Arnold, *Symeonis Monachi Opera Omnia*, 2 vols (London, 1882–5) II, 274. For the siege see Crouch, *The Beaumont Twins*, 17–20.

37. *Gesta Stephani*, 30–1, 182–3.

38. The sources for Geoffrey's wounding are collected in J.H. Round, *Geoffrey de Mandeville* (London, 1892), 221, and for Burwell see Bradbury, *Stephen and Matilda*, 115–16. For the garrison of Crowmarsh, Torigny, 173–4.

39. See pp. 127–32.

40. *Gesta Stephani*, 48–9.

41. *Gesta Stephani*, 174–5.

42. Orderic, VI, 470–1.

43. Torigny, 150.

44. For reconstructions of the battle, A.D.H. Leadman, 'The Battle of the Standard', *Yorkshire Archaeological and Topographical Journal*, x (1889), 377–86; J. Beeler, *Warfare in England, 1066–1189* (New York, 1966), 86–92; Bradbury, *Stephen and Matilda*, 33–6; and for the political context, P. Dalton, *Conquest, Anarchy and Lordship. Yorkshire, 1066–1154* (Cambridge, 1994), 148–52, 205–6.

45. Beeler, *Warfare in England*, 86.

46. Richard of Hexham, *De gestis regis Stephani et de bello Standardii*, ed. R. Howlett in *Chronicles*, III (Rolls Series, London, 1886), 159–61; Ailred of Rievaulx, *Relatio venerabilis Aelredi, abbatis Rievallensis, de Standardo*, ed. R. Howlett in *Chronicles*, III, 181–3.

47. Ailred, 189, 191; Simeon of Durham, II, 293.

48. Ailred, 191; trans. A.O. Anderson, *Scottish Annals from English Chroniclers, AD 500 to 1286* (London, 1902), 201. This is corroborated by Richard of Hexham's statement that 'the greater part of the knights left their horses and became foot soldiers. The picked men of these, mixed with the archers, were arrayed in the front rank; while the rest . . . were massed with the barons in the

heart of the battle, near to and around the Standard' (Richard of Hexham, 162–3; trans. Anderson, *Scottish Annals*, 201). John of Worcester (III, 254–5) believed that the archers were place in front of the knights, but this would have left them far too vulnerable).

49. Ailred, 191–2; Richard of Hexham, 163; Huntingdon, 712–13.

50. Ailred, 189; trans. Anderson, *Scottish Annals*, 198.

51. Ailred, 189–91; Richard of Hexham, 163.

52. Ailred, 196; trans. Anderson, *Scottish Annals*, 198.

53. Huntingdon, 716–17.

54. Ailred, 196; trans. Anderson, *Scottish Annals*, 203.

55. Ailred, 197.

56. Ailred, 197; Huntingdon, 716–17. The earl was possibly Gospatric II, Earl of Dunbar (Anderson, *Scottish Annals*, 203, n. 4).

57. Ailred, 197–8.

58. Huntingdon, 718–19.

59. John of Hexham, *Chronica*, in *Symeonis Monachi Opera Omnia*, ed. T. Arnold, II, 284–332 at 294.

60. John of Worcester, III, 254.

61. John of Hexham, 294; trans. Anderson, *Scottish Annals*, 204.

62. Compare the numerous references to the longbow's effectiveness marshalled by C.J. Rogers, 'The Efficacy of the English Longbow: A Reply to Kelly De Vries', *War in History*, v (1998), 233–42.

63. See pp. 189–94.

64. See pp. 212–14.

65. See p. 70.

66. Simeon of Durham, II, 292, calls Bernard de Balliol 'very expert' in military affairs.

67. M. Bennett, 'The Development of Battle Tactics in the Hundred Years War', in *Arms, Armies and Fortifications in the Hundred Years War*, ed. A. Curry and M. Hughes (Woodbridge, 1994), 1–20 at 2.

68. Philippe de Commynes, *Memoires*, trans. M. Jones, *Memoirs. The Reign of Louis XI, 1461–93* (Harmondsworth, 1972), 72.

69. See pp. 88–90.

70. These views are most cogently expressed in a series of articles by J. Gillingham, 'Richard I and the Science of War in the Middle Ages', in *War and Government in the Middle Ages*, ed. J. Gillingham and J.C. Holt (Woodbridge, 1984), 78–91; 'William the Bastard at War', in *Studies in Medieval History presented to R.A. Brown*, ed. C. Harper-Bill, C. Holdsworth and J. Nelson (Woodbridge, 1989), 141–58; 'War and Chivalry in the *History of William the Marshal*', *Thirteenth Century England. Proceedings of the Newcastle upon Tyne Conference*, II (Suffolk, 1987), 1–14; all reprinted in Strickland, ed., *Anglo-Norman Warfare*, 194–207, 143–60, 251–63.

71. See now C.J. Rogers, 'The Vegetian "Science of Warfare" in the Middle Ages', *JMMH*, i (2002), 1–19; S. Morillo, 'Battle Seeking: The Contexts and Limits of Vegetian Strategy', *ibid.*, 21–41; and the rejoinder by J. Gillingham, '"Up with Orthodoxy!" In Defence of Vegetian Warfare', *JMMH*, ii (2004), 149–58.

72. Huntingdon, 766–7. At Lincoln in 1141, by contrast, Stephen successfully overruled counsel to avoid battle, while his opponent Robert of Gloucester was equally concerned to fight a decisive engagement (E. King, ed., *The Anarchy of Stephen's Reign* (Oxford, 1994), 21; William of Malmesbury, *Historia Novella*, 47–8).

73. C.J. Rogers, *War, Cruel and Sharp: English Strategy under Edward III, 1327–1360* (Woodbridge, 2000); see pp. 186, 218, 223–4.

74. On the nature of such warfare and the risks involved see Strickland, *War and Chivalry*, 132ff.

75. Orderic, VI, 238–41, who puts the number of captive knights at 140, while the *Chronica de Hida*, 318, says 114.

76. Orderic, V, 218–19.

77. Orderic, VI, 238–9.

78. Matthew Paris, *Chronica majora*, ed. H.R. Luard, *Matthaei Parisiensis, monachi sancti Albani, Chronica majora*, 7 vols (Rolls Series, London, 1872–3), III, 21; *L'Histoire de Guillaume le Maréchal*, ed. P. Meyer, 3 vols (Paris, 1891–1901), ll. 16, 314–24, where the order is ascribed to Peter des Roches, Bishop of Winchester.

79. See pp. 87–93.

80. For the stand-off at Châteauroux see J. Gillingham, *Richard I* (New Haven and London, 1999), 83–5.

81. Gillingham, *Richard I*, 296–7.

82. *Chronicle of St Omer*, cited in Rogers, *War, Cruel and Sharp*, 269.

83. Orderic, IV, 48–51.

84. Torigny, 173–4; Matthew Paris, II, 626.

85. K. Norgate, *The Minority of Henry III* (London, 1912), 296–8; D.A. Carpenter, *The Battles of Lewes and Evesham, 1264/5* (Keele, 1987), 16, and see p. 139.

86. William of Malmesbury, *Historia Novella*, 84–5.

87. For Jaffa, see p. 107.

88. Roger of Howden, *Gesta Henrici II et Ricardi I*, ed. W. Stubbs, 2 vols (Rolls Series, 1867), I, 62; Diceto, I, 377–8.

89. For these engagements see Gillingham, *Richard I*, 288, 315–17.

90. See pp. 104–7.

91. Oman, *Art of War*, I, 453–67; J. France, *Western Warfare in the Age of the Crusades* (London, 1999), 167–8.

92. G. Duby, *The Legend of Bouvines*, trans. C. Tihanyi (Cambridge, 1990); J.F. Verbruggen, *The Art of Warfare in Western Europe during the Middle Ages*, trans. S. Willard and S.C.M. Southern (Woodbridge, 2nd edn, 1997); and for important observations on the French cavalry tactics at Bouvines see J. France, *Western Warfare in the Age of the Crusades* (London, 1999), 169–71, and Appendix I, 'The Battle of Bouvines', 235–41.

93. For detailed reconstructions of this battle see T.F. Tout, 'The Fair of Lincoln and the "Histoire de Guillaume le Maréchal"', *EHR*, xviii (1903), 240–65; F.W. Brooks and F. Oakley, 'The Campaign and Battle of Lincoln, 1217', *Associated Architectural Societies' Reports and Papers*, xxxvi, pt 2 (1922), 295–312; D.A. Carpenter, *The Minority of Henry III* (London, 1990), 36–40.

94. Carpenter, *The Battles of Lewes and Evesham*, 17; *The Political Songs of England: from the reign of John to that of Edward II*, ed. T. Wright (Edinburgh, 1884), 125.

95. F. Buttin, 'La Lance et l'arrêt de cuirasse', *Archaeologia*, xcix (1965), 77–114; Vale, *War and Chivalry*, 118–19.

96. William of Newburgh, *Historia Rerum Anglicarum*, ed. R. Howlett, *Chronicles of the Reigns of Stephen, Henry II and Richard I* (London, 1884), II, 422–3; J. Barker, *The Tournament in England, 1100–1400* (Woodbridge, 1986).

97. Oman, *Art of War*, I, 494–6; M.E. Mallet, *Mercenaries and Their Masters: Warfare in Renaissance Italy* (London, 1974), 12.

98. Prestwich, *Armies and Warfare*, 317.

99. 'And let every knight have as many hauberks, helmets, shields and lances as he has fees in his demesne'. (W. Stubbs, *Select Charters and other illustrations of English Constitutional History from the earliest times to the reign of Edward the First* (9th edn, revised H.W.C. Davis, Oxford, 1913), 181–2; *EHD*, II, no. 27, 416–17.)

100. Stubbs, *Select Charter*, 181–2.

101. Wace, *Roman de Rou*, II, 3,928–30; 3937–41; 3,945. Bennet, 'Wace and Warfare', 49.

102. *Leges Henrici Primi*, ed. L.J. Downer (Oxford, 1972), c. 88.6, 270–1.

103. *Materials for the History of Thomas Becket*, ed. J.C. Robertson, 7 vols (London, 1875–85), III (London, 1877), 11; trans. *EHD*, II, 1029.

104. *Gesta*, I, 270. For the equipment of local levies, *Annales Monastici*, III, 32, 35.

105. Stubbs, *Select Charters*, 186–7; *EHD*, II, 451.

106. *Gesta*, II, 93.

107. *Gesta*, II, 93.

CHAPTER 5

1. *Itinerarium Kambriae* (Bk I, c. iv), 54; trans. Thorpe, *The Journey Through Wales*, 112–13.

2. *Descriptio Kambriae* (Bk I, c. vi), 177; trans. Thorpe, *The Journey Through Wales*, 230–1.

3. See pp. 43–4.

4. 'While Cicero says, "Most of my conversation is with my books", our nephew says, "Most of my conversation is with bows, arrows, lutes and the rest of my foolish pastimes"', Giraldus Cambrensis, *Speculum Duorum*, ed. Y. Lefèvre and R.B.C. Huygens, trans. B. Dawson (Cardiff, 1974), 138–41.

5. Giraldus Cambrensis, *Speculum Duorum*, 138–41.

6. *Descriptio Kambriae* (Bk I, c. viii), 181; translation emended from Thorpe, *The Journey Through Wales*, 233–4.

7. *Descriptio Kambriae* (Bk II, c. iv), 209–10; trans. Thorpe, *The Journey Through Wales*, 259–60.

8. For the *teulu* (plural: *teuloedd*), see D. Crouch, *The Image of Aristocracy in Britain, 1000–1300* (London, 1992), 156–61, 276–7; *idem*, 'The March and the Welsh Kings', in *The Anarchy of Stephen's Reign*, ed. King, 255–89 at 267–8.

9. S. Davies, 'Native Welsh Military Institutions, *c.* 633–1283' (Doctoral thesis, University of Wales College, Cardiff, 2000), 112–20.

10. Bartlett, *The Making of Europe*, 76–7; Crouch, *The Image of Aristocracy*, 155–63.

11. *Brut y Tywysogyon, or The Chronicle of the Princes, Peniarth MS. 20*, trans. T. Jones (Cardiff, 1952), 48 (1121).

12. M. Lapidge, 'The Welsh-Latin Poetry of Sulien's Family', *Studia Celtica*, viii–ix (1973–4), 68–106, at 90–1, and for classical models, 105 n. 52.

13. *Brut y Tywysogyon*, 48 (1121). The chronicler believed that this was a stray arrow, and that though unharmed Henry was badly shaken.

14. William of Malmesbury, *Gesta regum Anglorum*, I, 726–9.

15. Orderic, VI, 28–9.

16. *Gesta Stephani*, 24–5, where '*missilia*' here is translated as javelin, though the term is ambiguous and for a head wound an arrow seems as likely.

17. *Gesta Stephani*, 16–17. Certainly in a subsequent engagement in 1136 the Welsh compelled the defeated knights of Richard fitzGilbert to flee, pursuing them 'with shouts and arrows' (*ibid.*).

18. Giraldus Cambrensis, *Expugnatio Hibernica. The Conquest of Ireland*, ed. and trans. A.B. Scott and F.X. Martin (Dublin, 1978), 246–7.

19. *Descriptio Kambriae* (Bk II, c. viii), 218–19; trans. Thorpe, *The Journey Through Wales*, 267–8.

20. *Pipe Roll 14 John*, xv–xvi; W.L. Warren, *King John* (2nd edn, London, 1978), 199–200; and for broader context, I.W. Rolands, 'King John and Wales', in *King John: New Interpretations*, ed. S.D. Church (Woodbridge, 1998), 273–87.

21. *The Statesman's Book of John of Salisbury*, trans. J. Dickinson (New York, 1927), 194–5; *Itinerarium Kambriae* (*Descriptio*, Bk II, c. vii), 217; trans. Thorpe, *The Journey Through Wales*, 266: Harold 'advanced into Wales on foot, at the head of his lightly clad infantry, lived on the country, and marched up and down and round and about the whole of Wales with such energy that "he left not one that pisseth against a wall" [I Samuel 25:22, I Kings 16:11]'.

22. F.C. Suppe, *Military Institutions on the Welsh Marches: Shropshire, AD 1066–1300* (Woodbridge, 1994), 18–19, 63–87.

23. *The History of Gruffyd ap Cynan*, trans. A. Jones (Manchester, 1910), 133, 136–9, where the Normans defend their castles, 'shooting shafts in showers and arrows and quarrels'.

24. *Brut y Tywysogyon*, 42–3 (1116).

25. *Brut y Tywysogyon*, 44–5 (1116), 57 (1151).

26. For an important new study of garrison strengths see J.S. Moore, 'Anglo-Norman Garrisons', *Anglo-Norman Studies*, xxii (1999), 205–59. A principal difficulty is that often troops other than knights are classed simply as 'serjeants', with their weapons unspecified, making it impossible to ascertain the presence of archers or crossbowmen.

27. *Pipe Roll 19 Henry II*, 107; *Pipe Roll 31 Henry II*, 10; *Pipe Roll 33 Henry II*, 33.

28. *Pipe Roll 5 Richard I*, 148.

29. Orderic, VI, 444–5.

30. *Gesta Stephani*, 16–17, 20–1.

31. *Pipe Roll 3 Henry II*, 89.

32. J.E. Lloyd, *A History of Wales*, 2 vols (London, 1911), II, 496–9; Beeler, *Warfare in England*, 242–4; D.J. Cathcart King, 'Henry II and the Eight at Coleshill', *Welsh History Review*, ii (1964–5), 367–75; J.G. Edwards, 'Henry II and the Eight at Coleshill: Some Further Reflections', *ibid.*, iii (1966–7), 251–63; and J.D. Hosler, 'Henry II's Military Campaigns in Wales, 1157 and 1165', *JMMH*, ii (2004), 53–72.

33. *Pipe Roll 11 Henry II*, 31, 68, 73; Gaier, 'Quand l'arbalète était une nouveauté', 173 n. 27; *Brut y Tywysogyon*, 63 (1165); and for a detailed study of the campaign and its logistics, P. Latimer, 'Henry II's Campaign against the Welsh in 1165', *Welsh History Review*, xiv (1989), 523–52.

34. *Rotuli Hundredorum*, ed. W. Illingworth and J. Caley, 2 vols (London, 1812–18), II, 82, 105; *Calendar of Inquisitions Miscellaneous (Chancery)*, 7 vols (London, 1916–37), I, 85, II, 39; Suppe, *Military Organization*, 18–19.

35. *Rotuli de Dominabus et Pueris et Puellis de Donatione Regis in XII Comitatibus, 31 Henry II, 1185*, ed. J.H. Round (London, 1913), 59.

36. Orderic, VI, 542–4, though Huntingdon, 736–7, says the Welsh, drawn up on one flank, were routed by the Count of Aumale and William of Ypres. For the Welsh forces at Lincoln, see Crouch, 'The March and the Welsh Kings', 277–8.

37. Richard of Devizes, *Chronicon*, ed. and trans. J.T. Appelby (London, 1963), 33.

38. Gervase of Canterbury, *Opera Historica*, ed. W. Stubbs, 2 vols (Rolls Series, London, 1879–80), I, 515.

39. *Pipe Roll 5 Richard I*, 99, 148. In 1194 20 slingers came from Northampton to aid Richard in the siege of John's castle at Nottingham (*Pipe Roll 6 Richard I*, 43, 68, 175–6, 212, 251).

40. W.L. Warren, *Henry II* (London, 1973, repr. 1983), 158.

41. Stephen of Rouen, *Draco Normannicus*, ed. R. Howlett in *Chronicles of the Reigns of Stephen, Henry II and Richard I*, II, ll. 684–6; Howden, I, 282.

42. Newburgh, I, 195–6; *Gesta*, I, 74–5; Torigny, 265.

43. *Gesta*, II, 39; Ralph of Diceto, *Opera Historica*, ed. W. Stubbs, 2 vols (Rolls Series, London, 1876), II, 55; *Pipe Roll 34 Henry II*, 95, 106–7, 210. A force of 1,695 foot-soldiers and 107 mounted men crossed over to Normandy, many of whom were surely archers.

44. Gerald suggests as many as 3,000 Welsh took the cross in 1188, though this is probably a considerable exaggeration (II, 13: *Itinerarium Kambriae*, 147).

45. Rigord, *Gesta Philippi Augusti*, ed. H.-F. Delaborde, *Oeuvres de Rigord et de Guillaume le Breton, historiens de Philippe-Auguste*, 2 vols (Paris, 1882), I, 131–2; William the Breton, *Philippidos*, ed. Delaborde, *Oeuvres de Rigord et de Guillaume le Breton*, II, 1–385 at 198.

46. *Magni Rotuli Scaccarii Normanniae*, ed. T. Stapleton, 2 vols (London, 1840–84), I, 155.

47. F.M. Powicke, *The Loss of Normandy, 1189–1204* (2nd edn, Manchester, 1961), 226–8, provides a valuable collection of references, and cf. *ibid.* 243–4.

48. *Rot. Scacc.*, I, 236; Powicke, *Loss of Normandy*, 227 n. 109; *Rotuli de Liberate ac de misis et praestitis, regnante Johanne*, ed. T.D. Hardy (London, 1844), 88.

49. *Rot. Scacc.*, II, 314; Powicke, *Loss of Normandy*, 226–7.

50. *HGM*, I, 267–8, ll. 7,409–28; III, 87, and n. 3 cites the unflattering comments of a knight in Chretien's *Perceval*, 'Galois sont tuit par nature/Plus fol que bestes en pasture'.

51. William the Breton, *Philippidos*, ed. Delaborde, *Oeuvres de Rigord et de Guillaume le Breton*, II, 136.

52. S. Lewis, *The Art of Matthew Paris in the Chronica Majora* (Berkeley, 1986), 220.

53. For the context of the Anglo-Norman intervention into Ireland see M.T. Flanagan, *Irish Society, Anglo-Norman Settlers, Angevin Kingship: Interactions in Ireland in the Late Twelfth Century* (Oxford, 1989), and for a modern analytical narrative, A. Cosgrove, ed., *A New History of Ireland, II. Medieval Ireland, 1169–1534* (Oxford, 1987), 43ff.

54. A Tintern charter granted by William the Marshal the Younger dated at Chepstow 22 March 1206 mentions '*Walter, filius Ricardi, filii Gilberti Strongbowe, avi mei*' (*Monasticon Anglicanum*, ed. W. Dugdale, 6 vols (London, 1817–30), V, 267). For the epithet applied to Richard, see the references collected in the *Complete Peerage*, X, 352, including *Chronica de Mailros*, ed. J. Stevenson (Edinburgh, 1835), 88, '*Ricardus comes, cognomine Strangboge*', and the *Annals of Loch Cé*, ed. and trans. W.M. Hennessy, 2 vols (London, 1871), I, 143: 'Earl Strongbow came into Erinn.'

55. Jean Creton, *Histoire du Roy d'Angleterre Richard*, in J.A.C. Buchon, *Collection des Chroniques nationales française*, xxiv (Paris, 1826), 334–5; A. Gransden, *Historical Writing in England*, II (London, 1982), 172. The suggestion of L.H. Nelson, *The Normans in South Wales, 1070–1171* (Austin and London, 1966), 139, that Gilbert holds an arrow, 'a tribute to his proficiency with the national arm of South Wales', seems unlikely given its great size as well as the absence of a bow.

56. *The Song of Dermot and the Earl*, ed. and trans. G.H. Orpen (Oxford, 1892).

57. *Expugnatio*, 30–1, '*sagittariis quoque pedestribus . . . de electa Guallie iuventute*'.

58. *Expugnatio*, 293 n. 28.

59. *Expugnatio*, 50–1.

60. *Expugnatio*, 56–7.

61. *Expugnatio*, 64–5.

62. *Expugnatio*, 140–1. When John sailed with 60 ships for Ireland in 1185, he took 300 knights and a large body of archers (*Expugnatio*, 226–7; *Annals of the Four Masters, Annals of the*

Kingdom of Ireland by the Four Masters, from the earliest period to 1066, ed. J. O'Donovan, 7 vols (Dublin, 1851), 1185).

63. Thus, for example, in 1195 the Exchequer rolls record, '*in passagio Philippi de Estapedona et Walteri de Escudemore et Helye de Chigehan et sociorum eorum Walensium equitum et peditum in ii navibus* [to Barfleur] *viii li.*' (*Rot. Scacc.*, I, 275).

64. *Expugnatio*, 92–3.

65. *Expugnatio*, 227–8.

66. *Expugnatio*, 350 n. 459.

67. See, for example, J.F. Lydon, 'The Hobelar: An Irish Contribution to Medieval Warfare', *Irish Sword*, ii (1954–6), 12–16.

68. Giraldus Cambrensis, *Topographia Hibernica*, in *Opera*, ed. J.F. Dimock and G.F. Warner, v (Rolls Series, 1867), 117, 129–30, 131, 134; *The History and Topography of Ireland*, trans. J.J. O'Meara (revised edn, Harmondsworth, 1982), 86–7, 81–2. Several of these incidents are illustrated in a thirteenth-century manuscript of Gerald's *Topography* (Cambridge University Library, MS F f.1.27, f.34v, 35v), and are discussed by R. Knight, 'Werewolves, Monsters and Miracles: Representing Colonial Fantasies in Gerald of Wales's *Topographia Hibernica*', *Studies in Iconography*, xx (2001), 55–86, at 77–80. Regrettably, however, the artist chose to depict the archers in 'civilian' dress, wearing only simple tunics, rather than carrying their military equipment.

69. *Topographia*, 74–6; O'Meara, *History and Topography*, 57.

70. Howden, III, 251.

71. *The Chronicle of Walter of Guisborough*, ed. H. Rothwell (Camden Society, London, 1957), 324–5.

72. Strickland, *War and Chivalry*, 309–10.

73. *Gesta*, II, 68.

74. Oman, *Art of War*, I, 403–15; G.A. Hayes-McCoy, *Irish Battles* (London, 1969), 28–9.

75. For a valuable reassessment see R. Rogers, 'Aspects of the Military History of the Anglo-Norman Invasion of Ireland, 1169–1225', *Irish Sword*, xvi (1986), 135–46, to which the next two paragraphs owe much.

76. *Song of Dermot*, 50–9.

77. *Expugnatio*, 136–7.

78. *Expugnatio*, 82–3.

79. *Expugnatio*, 248–9.

80. *Expugnatio*, 32–3.

81. *Expugnatio*, 84–5.

82. *Expugnatio*, 136–7, and n. 220, which suggests this harbour was at Youghal; G.H. Orpen, *Ireland under the Normans, 1169–1333*, 4 vols (Oxford, 1911–20), I, 329–31.

83. *Expugnatio*, 230–1.

84. *Expugnatio*, 230–1.

85. M.T. Flanagan, 'Irish and Anglo-Norman Warfare in Twelfth-Century Ireland', in *A Military History of Ireland*, ed. T. Bartlett and K. Jeffery (Cambridge, 1996), 52–75. For Irish armies see K. Simms, *From Kings to Warlords: The Changing Political Structure of Gaelic Ireland in the later Middle Ages* (Woodbridge, 1987), Ch. 8, 'The King's Army', and T.M. Charles-Edwards, 'Irish Warfare

before 1100', in T. Bartlett and K. Jeffery, ed., *A Military History of Ireland* (Cambridge, 1996), 26–51.

86. E. Rynne, 'The Impact of the Vikings on Irish Weapons', in *Atti del VI Congresso Internazionale delle Scienze Preistoriche et Protostoriche, Roma, 1962* (Rome, 1966), 181–5; Simms, *From Kings to Warlords*, 117.

87. Hayes-McCoy, *Irish Battles*, 19; Simms, *From Kings to Warlords*, 117. Earlier flint arrowheads have been found, but those of iron are extremely scarce; E. O'Curry, *On the Manners and Customs of the Ancient Irish*, 3 vols (London, 1873), I, ccccii–cccliv, II, 272–3.

88. *Cogadh Gaedhel re Gallaibh. The War of the Gaedhil with the Gaill*, ed. and trans. J.H. Todd (Rolls Series, London, 1867), 158–9.

89. Flanagan, 'Irish and Anglo-Norman Warfare', 72, and ill. 3.5.

90. Flanagan, 'Irish and Anglo-Norman Warfare', 69–75. For subsequent Irish warfare, K. Simms, 'Warfare in the Medieval Gaelic Lordships', *Irish Sword*, xii (1975–6), 98–108; *idem, From Kings to Warlords*, 127; *idem*, 'Gaelic Warfare in the Middle Ages', in *A Military History of Ireland*, 99–116.

91. *Roman de Brut*, II, 510, ll. 9,679–86; Bennett, 'Wace and Warfare', 51. Equally, in Arthur's battle against the Roman general Lucius, 'arrows fell like hail' (*Roman de Brut*, ll. 12,547–8).

92. Simms, *From Kings to Warlords*, 119–20; Creton, *Histoire du Roy d'Angleterre Richard*, 326–31; his account is translated by J. Webb, *Archaeologia*, xx (1824), 13–239; and see also J.F. Lydon, 'Richard II's expeditions to Ireland', *Journal of the Royal Society of Antiquaries of Ireland*, xciii (1963), 135–49.

93. Hayes-McCoy, *Irish Battles*, 49–52; A. McKerral, 'West Highland Mercenaries in Ireland', *SHR*, xxx (1951), 1–14, at 10–12. For the galloglass see also J.F. Lydon, 'The Scottish Soldier in Medieval Ireland: the Bruce Invasion and the Galloglass', in *The Scottish Soldier Abroad, 1247–1967*, ed. G.R. Simpson (Edinburgh, 1992), 1–15.

94. L. Price, 'Armed Forces of the Irish Chiefs in the Early Sixteenth Century', *Journal of the Royal Society of Antiquaries of Ireland*, lxii (1932), 201–7, at 206, where kerns are also reported as carrying either a bow or three javelins.

95. J. McGurk, *The Elizabethan Conquest of Ireland* (Manchester, 1997), 229; and for the battle, Hayes-McCoy, *Irish Battles*, 87–105. Warriors from the Western Isles fighting in Ireland in 1594 were recorded as carrying 'bows carved out of wood strong for use' as well as two-handed swords (J.T. Dunbar, *History of Highland Dress* (Edinburgh and London, 1962), 32).

96. J.P. Mahaffy, 'Two Early Tours in Ireland', *Hermathena*, xl (1914), 7; D.M. Carpenter, 'The Pilgrim from Catalonia/Aragon: Ramon de Perellós, 1397', in *The Medieval Pilgrimage to St Patrick's Purgatory*, ed. M. Haren and Y. de Pontfarcy (Enniskillen, 1988), 99–119; Simms, 'Warfare in the Medieval Gaelic Lordships', 105, 107.

97. H.F. McClintock, *Old Irish and Highland Dress* (2nd edn, Dundalk, 1950), 30–1, 39–40, pls 17, 23. A similar short, heavily recurved bow appears in a French print of 1562 of an Irish warrior, while

as late as 1631 an engraving of 'Irish' troops, probably members of Mackay's Highlanders fighting under Gustavus Adolphus, shows two archers, though the artist's rendering makes the nature of their weapons unclear (Dunbar, *History of Highland Dress*, 165 and pls 6, 10).

98.   McClintock, *Old Irish and Highland Dress*, 58–61.

99.   *L'Histoire de la Guerre d'Ecosse*, 1556, cited in Dunbar, *History of Highland Dress*, 27.

100. For further discussion of this comparison, Simms, 'Warfare in the Medieval Gaelic Lordships', 107.

101. S.G. Ellis, 'The Tudors and the Origins of the Modern Irish States: A Standing Army', in *A Military History of Ireland*, 116–35, at 117.

102. *Song of Dermot*, ll. 2,864–979, and for Count Richard's part in the 'great war' of 1173–4 against Henry II, see Gillingham, *Richard I*, 42–51.

CHAPTER 6

1.   M. Bennett, 'The Crusaders' "Fighting March" Revisited', *War in History*, viii (2001), 1–18.

2.   For these armies see France, *Victory in the East*, 145–9 (Seljuk Turks), 200–6 (northern Syrian forces), 359–60 (Egyptians). See also *idem*, 'Technology and the Success of the First Crusade', in *War and Society in the Eastern Mediterranean, 7th–15th Centuries*, ed. Y. Lev (Leiden, 1997), 163–76.

3.   See, for example, W.E. Kaegi, Jnr, 'The Contribution of Archery to the Turkish Conquest of Anatolia', *Speculum*, xxxix (1964), 96–108; W.F. Paterson, 'The Archers of Islam', *Journal of the Economic and Social History of the Orient*, ix (1966), 69–89; J.D. Latham, 'The Archers of the Middle East. The Turco-Iranian Background', *Iran*, viii (1970), 97–103; D. Nicolle, *The Armies of Islam, 7–11th Centuries* (London, 1982), 16–24.

4.   For Turkish tactics, Smail, *Crusading Warfare*, 75–83.

5.   Ambroise, *Estoire de la Guerre Sainte*, ed. G. Paris (Paris, 1897); trans. M.J. Hubert and J. La Monte, *The Crusade of Richard Lion-Heart* (New York, 1941), ll. 5,647–62. All subsequent references to Ambroise cite this translation by line reference, which corresponds to Paris's edition.

6.   *Alexiad*, 479–80.

7.   Nicolle, *Arms and Armour*, I, 107; *idem*, *The Armies of Islam*, 14–16.

8.   J.D. Latham and W.F. Paterson, *Saracen Archery. An English Version and Exposition of a Mamluke Work on Archery (ca. 1368)* (London, 1970), xxiii–iv.

9.   *Gesta Francorum et aliorum Hierosolimitanum*, ed. and trans. R. Hill (London, 1962), 19.

10. Latham and Patterson, *Saracen Archery*, 106–10, and for arrow-guides, 145–51; P.E. Klopsteg, *Turkish Archery and the Composite Bow (Illinois, 1934)*, 15–32.

11. Ambroise, ll. 6, 282–91.

12. A.J. Boase, *Crusader Archaeology. The Material Culture of the Latin East* (London and New York, 1999), 118–19.

13. *De Expugnatione Terrae Sanctae per Saladinum Libellus*, in Ralph of Coggeshall, *Chronicon Anglicanum*, ed. J. Stevenson (Rolls Series, London, 1875), 242–3; trans. J. Brundage, *The Crusades: A Documentary Survey* (Milwaukee, 1962), 160.

14. *Gesta Francorum*, 4; Fulcher of Chartres, *Historia Hierosolymitana*, ed. H. Hagenmeyer (Heidelberg, 1913), 400. English translation by E.R. Ryan, *A History of the Expedition to Jerusalem,*

1095–1127, ed. H.S. Fink (Knoxville, 1969), 153.

15. William of Malmesbury, *Gesta Regum*, I, 466–7. John of Worcester, *sub anno* 1135, has a clearly apocryphal tale, told to him by the Abbot of St Valéry, of a Christian knight captured by Saracens in Apulia, who, refusing to renounce his faith under torture, 'was shot at by archers for his faith' (*John of Worcester*, III, 212–15). Cf. Orderic VI, 111–12, for similar accusations.

16. Howden, III, 180.

17. E. McEwen, 'Nomadic Archery. Some Observations on Composite Bow Design and Construction', in P. Denwood, ed., *Arts of the Eurasian Steppelands* (London, 1978), 188–202. For the Huns' bows and their deployment in war see J.O. Maenchen-Helfen, *The World of the Huns. Studies in their History and Culture* (Berkeley, 1973), 221–32.

18. E. McEwen and W. McLeod, 'The Ancient Egyptian Composite Bow: Some Notes on its Structure and Performance', *American Journal of Archaeology*, 1989.

19. See, *inter alia*, R. Payne-Gallwey, 'A Treatise on Turkish and other Oriental Bows', in *idem*, *The Crossbow* (London, 1903, repr. 1990), Appendix II, 1–23; Klopsteg, *Turkish Archery*; Latham and Patterson, *Saracen Archery*. A helpful summary of German and Turkish literature can be found in G. Grimley, *The Book of the Bow* (London, 1963).

20. D. Nicolle, *Saladin and the Saracens* (London, 1986), 6–7.

21. A Tartar bow shot by E. McEwen had a pull of 80lb (36.3kg) and could shoot a 34in (0.86cm) arrow over 300 yards (*JSAA*, xliv (2001), 4, and cf. vol. 27 (1984)). Bergman, McEwen and Miller, 'Experimental Archery', 665–6, note that the weapon used by Crimean Tartars in the Ottoman period had a greater length (and thus shot less fast) than most composite bows, but considerably outdistanced a self-bow of equal draw-weight using arrows of the same weight. The example tested had a pull of 60lb (27.2kg), and attained a velocity of 114mph (51m/s) with a 1¾oz (50g) arrow, having a cast of 98½yd (90m) further than the 80lb longbow.

22. Latham and Patterson, *Saracen Archery*, xxv, 30

23. Payne-Gallwey, *The Crossbow*, Appendix II, 3.

24. McEwen, Miller and Bergman, 'Early Bow Design', 53.

25. McEwen, Miller and Bergman, 'Early Bow Design', 54; Bergman, McEwen and Miller, 'Experimental Archery', 660–1.

26. For construction details see Klopsteg, *Turkish Archery*; and Grimley, *The Book of the Bow*, 46–50.

27. Clark, 'Neolithic Bows', 50–1.

28. McEwen, Miller and Bergman, 'Early Bow Design', 54, who note that the inherent power of the limbs of a composite bow enables them 'to be shortened significantly without loss of draw length or increased risk of breakage. . . . Reflex places the limbs under greater tension when the bow is strung, storing more power than self-bows can. Shorter limbs also mean a more efficient transfer of energy.'

29. Latham and Paterson, *Saracen Archery*, 80–3.

30. Odo of Deuil, *De Profectione Ludovici in Orientem*, ed. and trans. V.G. Berry (New York, 1948), 111.

31. Nicolle, *Saladin and the Saracens*, 9.

32. McEwen, Miller and Bergman, 'Early Bow Design', 54. The composite bow's construction allows it 'to be drawn much farther relative to the overall length of the weapon. The combination of extended draw length and short limbs enables the composite bow to shoot an arrow faster and farther than can a wooden self-bow of equal draw weight.' Cf. W. McLeod, 'The Range of the Ancient Bow', *Pheonix*, xix (1965), 1–14.

33. C. Cahen, 'Les changements techniques militaires dans le Proche Orient médiéval et leur importance historique', in V.J. Parry and M.E. Yapp, *War, Technology and Society in the Middle East* (London, 1975), 113–24, at 116–17.

34. Albert of Aix, *Historia Hierosolymitana, Recueil des Historiens des Croisades, Historiens Occidentaux*, 5 vols (Paris, 1844–95), IV, 265–713 at 331–2; France, *Victory in the East*, 148.

35. Ralph of Caen, *Gesta Tancredi*, RHC, Oc, III, 603–716.

36. *Alexiad*, 416. Anna Comnena further notes that Frankish armour 'consists of a tunic interwoven with iron rings linked one with another; the iron is good quality, capable of resisting an arrow and giving protection to the soldier's body', while their long shields were also capable of stopping an arrow 'whether it be Scythian or Persian or fired by the arms of a giant' (*ibid.*, 416).

37. Odo of Deuil, 119; Ambroise, ll. 11, 626–30.

38. David Nicolle, *Hattin, 1187* (London, 1993), 39, has noted that 'sources indicating the ineffectiveness of Islamic archery against Crusader armour are widely misunderstood, referring as they do to long-range harassment intended to injure unprotected horses rather than to kill men'. Nevertheless, it is striking how few casualties among knights on the Third Crusade are recorded as having been caused by arrows – in contrast to their horses which were frequently wounded or killed. At Jaffa, moreover, we do not know at what range the Turkish arrows which lodged in the king's armour were shot; certainly the battle itself involved a considerable degree of close combat between Franks and Muslim troops in which one might have expected horse-archers to have inflicted more significant casualties had they been able to penetrate the crusaders' armour.

39. See pp. 269–70.

40. Beha ad-Din (Ibn Shaddad), *The Life of Saladin*, trans. C.L. Conder (Palestine Pilgrims Text Society, xiii, London, 1897), 282.

41. Joinville, *The Life of Saint Louis*, trans. M.R.B. Shaw in *Chronicles of the Crusades. Joinville and Villehardouin* (Harmondsworth, 1963), 225.

42. Vale, *War and Chivalry*, 112.

43. France, *Victory in the East*, 280–2.

44. Smail, *Crusading Warfare*, 114–15, 164–5; C.J. Marshall, 'The Use of the Charge in Battles in the Latin East, 1192–1291', *Historical Research*, lxiii (1990), 221–6; idem, *Warfare in the Latin East, 1192–1291* (Cambridge, 1992) 158–67.

45. France, *Victory in the East*, 281–2; Ambroise, ll. 11,339–40; 11,411–30; 11,532–64. Ralph of Coggeshall believed the king had only six horses and a mule (Coggeshall, 46).

46. Bennett, 'The Crusaders' "Fighting March" Revisited', 2–10, provides a good analysis of the development of Byzantine defensive formations in theory and in practice.

47. Leo's *Taktica*, cited in Chaliand, *The Art of War*, 362, 363–4.

48. E. McGreer, *Sowing the Dragon's Teeth: Byzantine Warfare in the Tenth Century* (Washington, D.C., 1995), 136–40.

49. Fulcher, 180, trans. Ryan, 80, 84–5. Cf. France, *Victory in the East*, 148, 182.

50. Fulcher, 194–5, trans. Ryan, 85.

51. France, *Victory in the East*, 143ff.; idem, *Western Warfare in the Age of the Crusades*, 213.

52. For the battle, France, *Victory in the East*, 172–84.

53. Raymond d'Aguilers, *Historia Francorum qui Ceperunt Iherusalem*, RHC, Oc, III (Paris, 1886), 259; trans. J.H. and L.L. Hill (Philadelphia, 1968), 61; Fulcher, 84–5. On Frankish formations, Smail, *Crusading Warfare*, 173, 175, 179; and for detailed accounts of these battles, France, *Victory in the East*, 280–96, 360–5.

54. Fulcher, 126–7; *Gesta Francorum*, 95–6.

55. Fulcher, 452; trans. Ryan, 173.

56. *Alexiad*, 478–92; Bennett, 'The Crusaders' "Fighting March" Revisited', 17.

57. Smail, *Crusading Warfare*, 115–21; France, 'Technology and the Success of the First Crusade', 170.

58. *Gesta Francorum*, 15.

59. Fulcher, 168, trans. Ryan, 75.

60. Fulcher, 452.

61. Albert of Aix, 475, 602; France, *Victory in the East*, 36.

62. See pp. 71–2.

63. Walter the Chancellor, *Bella Antiochena*, ed. T.S. Ashbridge and S.B. Edgington, *Walter the Chancellor's The Antiochene Wars* (Aldershot, 1999), 152–5; Odo of Deuil, 125. Similarly, Turkish arrows caused heavy losses among the crusaders sheltering in Adalia, but the French archers forced the Turks to retire some distance (Odo of Deuil, 139–41).

64. Odo of Deuil, 25–6, 'pluvia sagittarum'.

65. Odo of Deuil, 117–19; Bennett, 'The Crusaders' "Fighting March" Revisited', 12–13.

66. B.Z. Kedar, 'The Battle of Hattin Revisited', in *The Horns of Hattin*, ed. B.Z. Kedar (London, 1992), 190–207; Nicolle, *Hattin*, 65–79.

67. *Continuation de Guillaume de Tyr de 1229 à 1261*, RHC, Oc, ii, 544. For a detailed discussion of this battle, Marshall, *Warfare in the Latin East*, 177–8.

68. Marshall, *Warfare in the Latin East*, 160.

69. Usamah ibn Munquidh, *Kitab al-I'tibar*, trans. P.K. Hitti, *Memoirs of an Arab-Syrian Gentleman or an Arab Knight in the Crusades* (Beirut, 1964), 86–7.

70. Devizes, 22.

71. Ambroise, ll. 1,476–544.

72. Ambroise, ll. 1,523–5.

73. *Gesta*, II, 164.

74. Devizes, 43. The name meant 'Kill-the-Greeks', an insulting reference to the inhabitants of Messina. For a good analysis of Richard's campaigns in the Holy Land see Gillingham, *Richard I*, 155–221.

75. A detailed account of the great siege of Acre, which lasted from August 1189 to July 1192, is given by R. Rogers, *Latin Siege Warfare in the Twelfth Century* (Oxford, 1992), 212–35.

76. Beha ad-Din, 260.

77. Ambroise, ll. 3,731–70. The story was one of a number of doubtless apocryphal tales in circulation concerning the siege of Acre, which was also known to the author of the *Itinerarium Peregrinorum et Gesta Regis Ricardi*, trans. H. Nicholson, *Chronicle of the Third Crusade* (Ashgate, 1997), 111–12.

78. *Gesta*, II, 186.

79. Ambroise, ll. 1,911–26. For turcopoles, see p. 109.

80. For Richard's tactics on his march from Acre to Jaffa see Verbruggen, *Art of Warfare*, 232–9; Gillingham, *Richard I*, 172–8. Helpful maps and diagrams of Richard's formation are given in J. Riley-Smith, ed. *The Atlas of the Crusades* (London, 1991), 64; M. Bennett, and N. Hooper, *Cambridge Illustrated Atlas: Warfare. The Middle Ages, 768–1487* (Cambridge, 1996). Bennett, 'The Crusaders' "Fighting March" Revisited', 14, makes the significant point that King Guy of Jerusalem, who was closely allied to Richard from 1191, had earlier in 1190 formed a similar defensive formation, guarding one flank by marching along the Nahr N'amien river.

81. *Itinerarium*, 237; Beha ad-Din, 283.

82. Beha ad-Din, 282–3.

83. Beha ad-Din, 282.

84. On the tactical context of Arsuf, see Smail, *Crusading Warfare*, 163–5.

85. Ambroise, ll. 6,253–6.

86. *Pipe Roll 2 Richard I*, 3, 53, 127, 131.

87. Beha ad-Din, 290–1.

88. Ambroise, ll. 10,404–8.

89. Ambroise, ll. 10,409–41.

90. Ambroise, ll. 10,807–11,289; Gillingham, *Richard I*, 211–14.

91. Ambroise, ll. 11,327–40, reckoned that Richard had some 50–60 knights and around 2,000 crossbowmen and other troops. Less plausibly, Coggeshall, 44 and n. 2, puts Richard's forces at only 80 knights and 400 infantry.

92. Ambroise, ll. 11,451–91.

93. Coggeshall, 45; trans. Delbrück, *History of the Art of War*, II, 411–12.

94. Ambroise, ll. 11,409–652; Coggeshall, 48–50.

95. Coggeshall, 49–50.

96. The essential work here is Marshall, *Warfare in the Latin East*, especially 151–2, and the tables of garrison and army composition at 115–17, and 148–50.

97. Marshall, *Warfare in the Latin East*, 174.

98. *CCR, 1254–56*, 221; C. Tyerman, *England and the Crusades, 1095–1588* (Chicago, 1988), 168.

99. *Liber recuperationis Terre Sancte*, ed. P.G. Golubovitch, in *Biblioteca Bio-Bibliografica della Terra Sancta*, II (Florence, 1913), 29–30. For Fidenzio, see N. Housley, *The Later Crusades, 1274–1580* (Oxford, 1992), 23–4.

100. *Liber recuperationis*, 29–30.

101. Vale, *War and Chivalry*, 112.

102. Cahen, 'Les changements techniques militaires', 117–18, and appendix, 123–4; K. Huuri, *Zur Geschichte des mittelalterliche Geschützwesens aus orientalischen Quellen* (Helsinki, 1941).

103. C. Cahen, 'Un traité d'armurie composé pour Saladin', *Bulletin d'Etudes Orientales*, xii (1947–8), 103–63, who gives a partial translation; A. Boudot-Lamotte, *Contribution à l'étude de l'archerie musulmanne* (Damascus, 1968), with a complete French translation; C. Hillenbrand, *The Crusades. Islamic Perspectives* (Edinburgh, 1999), 435–6, 456–8; Alm, *European Crossbows*, 18 n. 7, where the date of Saladin's death is wrongly given as 1190.

104. Ambroise, ll. 3,561–82; *Itinerarium*, 104–5. Both sources recount the same miracle story of how a Turk shot at a Frankish sergeant with his crossbow from the ramparts of the city. The bolt pierced the soldier's mail coif, his padded doublet of quilted linen (i.e. a gambeson) 'whose skilful cross-seaming makes it difficult for a weapon to pierce it', and then his hauberk, but was stopped by a small piece of parchment he wore around his neck bearing the name of God.

105. Latham and Paterson, *Saracen Archery*, 9.

106. Quoted by L. White, 'The Crusades and the Technological Thrust of the West', in V.J. Parry and M.E. Yapp, ed. *War, Technology and Society in the Middle East* (London, 1975), 239–56. For the Muslim adoption of the 'couched lance' see D. Nicolle, 'The Impact of the European Couched Lance on Muslim Military Tradition', *Journal of the Arms and Armour Society* (June 1980), 6–40.

107. Smail, *Crusading Warfare*, 111–12; Y. Harari, 'The Military Role of the Frankish Turcopoles: A Reassessment', *Mediterranean History Review*, xii (1997), 75–116; France, *Western Warfare*, 219–20 and n. 29.

108. Usamah, 79; *La Règle du Temple*, ed. H. De Curzon (Paris, 1886), nos 167–70; J. Upton-Ward, ed., *The Rule of the Templars* (Woodbridge, 1992), 45, 59–60, 61; Marshall, *Warfare in the Latin East*, 59.

109. Similarly, the Byzantine emperor Alexius had employed Turkish horse-archers as part of his forces sent against the Normans at Dyrrachium in 1081 (*Alexiad*, 146).

110. *La Continuation de Guillaume de Tyr (1184–1197)*, ed. M.R. Morgan (Paris, 1982).

111. F.M. Powicke, 'The Saracen Mercenaries of Richard I', *SHR*, viii (1910), 104–5; Stapleton, I, clix; Powicke, *Loss of Normandy*, 196 n. 117; *L'Estoire de Eracles Empereur et la Conqueste de la Terre d'Outremer* in *RHC, Oc*, II, 196.

112. *Pipe Roll 6 Richard I*, 176.

113. P. Pieri, 'I Saraceni di Lucera nella storia militare medievale', *Archivo Storico Pugliese*, vi (1953), 94–101. Cf. P. Herde, 'Taktiken mulimischer Heere vom ersten Kreuzug bis Ayn Djalut (1260) und ihre Einwirkung auf die Schlacht bei Tagliacozzo (1268)', in *Das Heilige Land im Mittelalter* (Wurzburg, 1981).

114. Oman, *Art of War*, I, 493–515.

115. See pp. 241–3.

116. *Beowulf*, l. 2,437.

117. R. Christlein, *Die Alamannen* (Stuttgart, 1978), 73; Manley, 'The Archer and the Army', 227.

118. For Avar bows, see I. Korvig and A. Kiss, *Cemeteries of the Avar Period in Hungary*, 2 vols (Budapest, 1975, 1977); Rausing, *The Bow*, 69; and cf. Bachrach, 'A Picture of Avar-Frankish Warfare', 10–21.

119. J.C. Coulston, 'Roman Archery Equipment', in *The Production and Distribution of Roman Military Equipment*, ed. M.C. Bishop (Oxford, 1985), 220–366.

120. Rausing, *The Bow*, 65–6; J.L. Davies, 'Roman Arrowheads from Dinorben and the *Sagitarii* of the Roman Army, *Britannia*, viii (1997), 357–70; G. Webster, *The Roman Imperial Army of the First and Second Centuries AD* (3rd edn, Oklahoma, 1988), 154–5, and

121. pl. xxi; D. Massey 'Roman Archery Tested', *Military Illustrated*, LXXIV (1994), 36–9.

121. Nicolle, *Arms and Armour*, I, 503–25; II, 915–29.

122. Such influence might still continue. The composite bows depicted in the Paris Psalter produced at Christchurch, Canterbury, in about 1180–1200 (BN, MS Lat 8846, f. 19r), for example, were heavily influenced by the Carolingian Utrecht Psalter (*The Utrecht Psalter*, 163).

123. B.G. Vigi, *Il Museo della Cattedrale di Ferra* (Florence, 2001), 34; Lewis, *The Art of Matthew Paris*, 273, 185.

124. *A Picture Book of Old Testament Stories of the Thirteenth Century*, ed. S.C. Cockerell (Roxburghe Club, London, 1924), ff. 2r, 23v, 32r, 34v, 42r.

125. *Life, Death and Art: The Medieval Stained Glass of Fairford Parish Church*, ed. S. Brown and L. Macdonald (Stroud, 1997), pls 26, 30.

126. While Bradbury, *The Medieval Archer*, 24, is right to point to classical influence in Carolingian depictions of the bow, his statement would seem untenable that 'there is no evidence of the West possessing the necessary skill for producing such bows'. Cf. B.S. Hall, *Weapons and Warfare in Renaissance Europe* (Baltimore, 1997), 18.

127. See pp. 120–6.

128. Fulcher (Bk I, c. 34), 342, trans. Ryan, 134. It was for the same reason that the Syrian Taybugha al-Ahrafi advised in 1368 that for crossbows used aboard ship, the bow arms or lathes should be made simply of yew and not composite materials (Latham and Paterson, *Saracen Archery*, 8).

129. Oman, *Art of War*, II, 349–53; D. Nicolle, *Nicopolis, 1396*, 48–64; cf. pp. 326–7.

CHAPTER 7

1. See Ch. 8, pp. 138–48.

2. S.D. Church, 'The 1210 Campaign in Ireland: Evidence for a Military Revolution?', *Anglo-Norman Studies*, xx (1997), 45–57 at 48–9 and 51 n. 17. Though their numbers are unknown, the wage bill of £2,382 14s 4d for crossbowmen and serjeants suggests a substantial force, with about 1,500 as a possible estimate. For Lincoln, F.M. Powicke, *King Henry III and the Lord Edward. The Community of the Realm in the Thirteenth Century* (Oxford, 1947), 13. Louis's army of invasion included 1,200 knights and numerous crossbowmen. Thus, for example, one small expeditionary unit that sailed ahead of the main force in 1216 under the French marshal Walter de Nemours contained over 100 knights, 40 horsed crossbowmen, 100 foot-crossbowmen and many serjeants (C. Petit Dutaillis, *Étude sur la vie et la règne de Louis VIII (1187–1226)* (Paris, 1894), 89–90).

3. Matthew Paris, IV, 211–13, where Paris puts the number of crossbowmen at 700 (*septigenti*), of whom 100 were from England, and other infantry at an improbably large 20,000. For the campaign, C. Bemont, 'La campagne de Poitou, 1242–1243.

Taillebourg et Saintes', *Annales du Midi*, v (1893), 289–314; R.C. Stacey, *Politics, Policy and Finance under Henry III, 1216–1245* (Oxford, 1987), 192–6.

4. Morris, *Welsh Wars*, 188–9; M. Prestwich, *Edward I* (London, 1988), 192–3. At its peak in early 1283 the Gascon contingent in Edward's Welsh campaign of 1282–3 was 40 knights, 120 mounted crossbowmen and 1,300 infantry (Prestwich, *Edward I*, 197).

5. *Cal. Docs. Scot.*, V, no. 492, v–x.

6. M.R. Powicke, *Military Obligation in Medieval England: A Study in Liberty and Duty* (Oxford, 1962), 122, 132. London once again supplied crossbowmen for Edward II's levy of 1312 (*ibid.*, 141).

7. *Parliamentary Writs and Writs of Military Summoms*, ed. F. Palgrave, 2 vols (London, 1827–34), I, 270 (15).

8. *Parl. Writs*, II, 433–4 (10–13).

9. E. Audoin, *Essai sur l'armée royale au temps de Philippe Auguste* (Paris, 1913), 111, 112; J.W. Baldwin, *The Government of Philip Augustus: Foundations of French Royal Power in the Middle Ages* (Berkeley, 1986), 168. For Cadoc, see Delisle in his preface to

inquests of St Louis, *RHF*, xxiv, part I, 130–3. Rigord, I, 162, however, notes that Philip also gathered horse-archers for his attack on the last remaining Angevin strongholds in 1205.

10. Marshall, *Warfare in the Latin East*, 171–4.

11. Oliver of Paderborn, *Historia Damiatina*, ed. H. Hoogeweg, *Bibliothek des Litterischen Vereins in Stuttgart*, ccii (1894), 259; Marshall, *Warfare in the Latin East*, 58, 172–3.

12. J.S.C. Riley-Smith, 'A Note on the Confraternities in the Latin Kingdom of Jerusalem', *Historical Research*, xxxxiv (1971), 301–8, at 307; W.C. Jordan, *Louis IX and the Challenge of Crusade: A Study in Rulership* (Princeton, 1979), 65.

13. Marshall, *Warfare in the Latin East*, 50 and n. 15, 76. In 1248 Louis's army has been estimated at around 15,000 men, including under 3,000 knights, 5,000 crossbowmen and 5,000–6,000 mounted serjeants, with the remainder being light infantry (Jordan, *Louis IX*, 65).

14. Marshall, *Warfare in the Latin East*, 77–83.

15. J.S.C. Riley-Smith, *The Knights of St John in Jerusalem and Cyprus, c. 1050–1310* (London, 1967), 325–6; *De Constructione Castri Saphet*, trans. H.N. Kennedy, *Crusader Castles* (Cambridge, 1994), 190–8 at 196.

16. *Annales Januenses*, *MGH, SS*, viii, ed. G.H. Pertz (Hanover, 1863), 226–48. The figure of 20,000 foot is greatly exaggerated.

17. F.W. Brooks, *The English Naval Forces, 1199–1272* (London, 1932), 60–3, which draws on his earlier 'Naval Armament in the Thirteenth Century', *The Mariner's Mirror*, xiv (1928), 115–31.

18. N.A.M. Rodger, *The Safeguard of the Sea: a naval history of Britain*, I (London, 1997), 162, and c.f. pp. 50–60, 61–72.

19. F.C. Lane, 'The Crossbow and the Nautical Revolution of the Middle Ages', in *Economy, Society and Government in Medieval Italy* (Kent, Ohio, 1969), 161–71. The number required per ship in 1255 was only modest. A two-decked ship of 100–150 tonnes was to have 3; large merchantmen of around 400 tonnes 8 to 10 crossbows, and smaller one-decked vessels were to have 2 crank-spanned crossbows (with 100 bolts each) and 6 stirrup-spanned (with 300 bolts each). The type of weapons included both hand-held crossbows, spanned by stirrup and hook (*de strevo* or *de strepa*), each with 150 bolts, and large crossbows with a windlass (*del torno vel de pesarola*), each with 50 bolts.

20. Powicke, *Loss of Normandy*, 225 n. 95.

21. C. de la Roncière, *Histoire de la marine française*, 6 vols (Paris, 1889–1932), I, 333–63; C. Jourdain, 'Mémoire sur les commencements de la marine militaire sous Philippe le Bel', *Mémoires de l'académie des inscriptions et belles lettres*, xxx (1881), 377–418; M.C. Prestwich, *War, Politics and Finance under Edward I* (London, 1972), 138; *idem*, *Edward I*, 383.

22. C.E. Dufourcq, *L'Espagne Catalane et le Mahgrib aux XIII et XIV siècles* (Paris, 1966), 50–2; Paterson, *The Crossbow*, 37.

23. Geoffrey le Baker, *Chronicon*, ed. E.M. Thompson (Oxford, 1889), 68; *The French Chronicle of London*, ed. G.J. Aungier (Camden Society, xxviii, 1844), 76; trans. C.J. Rogers, *The Wars of Edward III: Sources and Interpretations* (Woodbridge, 1999), 85, 'our archers and crossbowmen began to fire so thickly, like hail falling in winter, and our artillerymen shot so fiercely, that the French were unable to look out or to hold their heads up'.

24. See p. 209, and for the nature of naval warfare, Brooks, *The English Naval Forces*, 54–69, 196–226.

25. *Philippidos*, Bk VII, ll. 664, 263–4, 663; and *ibid.*, 186 n. 2, 187, 1 and 2, 202 n. 1, for details of several of these men and grants they received.

26. L. Landon, *Itinerary of King Richard I* (London, Pipe Roll Society, 1935), 36; Ambroise, ll. 324–5.

27. *Pipe Roll 30 Henry II*, 1183–4, xxix, 53.

28. Powicke, *Loss of Normandy*, 224–5; R.A. Brown, 'Royal Castle Building in England, 1154–1216', *EHR*, lxx (1955), 353–98, at 369–72.

29. *Rot. Scacc.*, II, 483–4.

30. Stacey, *Politics, Policy and Finance under Henry III*, 186 and n. 119.

31. Matthew Paris, II, 110–11.

32. Henry III, for example, raised 200 Gascon crossbowmen in 1232 and 500 in 1242 (*CCR, 1237–42*, 41, 392).

33. Hence we find men with names such as Lambert de Cassel, Gerard de la Barre, Peter de Limoges, Nicholas de Limes, William and Peter de Azay, Philippus Britoni, Andrew de Pamplona and Luce Hispaniens (*Rotuli Litterarum Clausarum in Turri Londinensi Asservati*, ed. T.D. Hardy, 2 vols (London, 1833, 44), 511–12 (1222); H.L. Blackmore, *Hunting Weapons* (London, 1971), 180.

34. Powicke, *Loss of Normandy*, 333; see p. 107.

35. Powicke, *Loss of Normandy*, 196 and n.

36. *Rot. Litt. Claus.*, 44.

37. *Rot. Scacc.*, II, 483–4; Powicke, *Loss of Normandy*, 225. Gascon crossbowmen in Edward's service during the campaigns in Aquitaine in 1294–7 received 1s a day, one-eighth of the wages of a knight, whereas English and Welsh infantry received the equivalent of one-twelfth of a knight's wages (Prestwich, *War, Politics and Finance*, 93).

38. Baldwin, *The Government of Philip Augustus*, 169. By contrast, a knight received 72d (*ibid.*, 169).

39. *Rot. de Lib.*, 6; cf. *Rot. Litt. Claus.*, I, 28, 250b.

40. For which see p. 101.

41. *RHF*, III, *Comptes Royaux, 1285–1314*, vol. II, 611–25; P. Wolff, 'Achat d'armes pour Philippe le Bel dans la région toulousaine', *Annales du Midi*, lxi (1948), 84–91; M. Vale, *The Angevin Legacy and the Hundred Years War, 1250–1340* (Oxford, 1990), 202.

42. Palgrave, *Documents*, I, 211; *Parl. Writs*, II, 433–4 (10–13).

43. *Ordonnances des roys de France de la troisième race recueillies par ordre chronologique*, ed. E. de Lauriere, 23 vols (Paris, 1723–1849), IV, 67ff.

44. Payne-Gallwey, *The Crossbow*; Harmuth, *Die Armbrust*; G.M. Wilson, *Crossbows* (London, 1976); Paterson, *Guide to the Crossbow*; Alm, *European Crossbows*, which contains an extensive bibliography.

45. See p. 62.

46. II Lateran Council (1139) c. 29, in *Conciliorum oecumenicorum decreta*, ed. G. Alberigo *et al.* (2nd edn, Basel, 1962), 179; '*Artam illam mortiferam et odibilem balistariorum et sagittariorum adversus*

Christianos et Catholicos exerci de caetero sub anathenate prohibemus.' On the canon *Artam illam* see J.A. Brundage, 'The Limits of War-Making Power; The Contribution of Medieval Canonists', in *Peace in a Nuclear Age: The Bishops' Pastoral Letter in Perspective*, ed. C.J. Reid, Jnr (Washington, DC, 1986), 69–85, at 77–8.

47. Galbert of Bruges, *The Murder of Charles the Good*, trans. J.B. Ross (New York, 1960), 83 and n. 11.

48. A.J. Hatto, 'Archery and Chivalry: A Noble Prejudice', *Modern Language Review*, xxxv (1940), 40–54 at 40–5; Gaier, 'Quand l'arbalète était une nouveauté', 168–9. Brundage, 'The Limits of War-Making Power', 78, makes the interesting connection between the reissue of the prohibition by the Third Lateran Council in 1179 and the defeat of Frederick Barbarossa at the hands of the infantry of the Lombard League, who made extensive use of the crossbow, at the battle of Legnano in 1176.

49. J.W. Baldwin, *Masters, Princes and Merchants: The Circle of Peter the Chanter*, 2 vols (Princeton, 1970), II, 204, 223–4.

50. J.A. Brundage, *Medieval Canon Law and the Crusader* (Madison, Milwaukee, and London, 1969), 28–9; *idem*, 'Holy War and the Medieval Lawyers', in *The Holy War*, ed. T.P. Murphy (Columbus, Ohio, 1976), 99–140, at 111–12; *Itinerarium peregrinorum*, ed. W. Stubbs (London, Rolls Series, 1864), 93.

51. Thus in 1239 Gregory IX had no objection to the promise of Raymond VII of Provence to serve the papacy in Italy with a force of 40 knights and 10 mounted crossbowmen (Contamine, *War in the Middle Ages*, 67); cf. D.P. Waley, 'Papal Armies in the Thirteenth Century', *EHR*, lxxii (1957), 1–30.

52. The thirteenth century saw an increasing trend to subvert the prohibition by the argument that its use was licit in a just war (Brundage, 'The Limits of War-Making Power', 79–82).

53. P. Fournier, 'La prohibition par le IIe Concile Latran d'armes jugées trop meurtrières (1139)', *Revue générale du droit international public*, xxiii (1916), 471–9. It is perhaps no coincidence that Fournier was writing during the First World War, when new types of deadly weapons such as gas were being unleashed for the first time.

54. *Philippidos*, Bk V, 440–620. For the circumstances of Richard's death see J. Gillingham, 'The Unromantic Death of Richard I', *Speculum*, liv (1979), 18–41, and reprinted in *idem*, *Richard Coeur de Lion. Kingship, Chivalry and War in the Twelfth Century* (London, 1994), 155–80; and cf. *idem*, *Richard I*, 321–34.

55. Audoin, *Essai sur l'armée royale*, 36 n. 1.

56. *The Letters of Innocent III (1198–1216) concerning England and Wales*, ed. C.R. Cheney and M.G. Cheney (Oxford, 1967), 6–7.

57. Baldwin, *Masters, Princes and Merchants*, II, 160 and n. 128; Brundage, 'The Limits of War-Making Power', 79–82, who notes 'Peter the Chanter and his circle had perhaps invented and certainly publicised a loophole in the ban on the dreaded weapons'.

58. J.C. Holt, *Magna Carta* (2nd edn, Cambridge, 1992), 464–5.

59. Accounts of the Treasurer of the Household reveal Edward III had 111 crossbowmen in his army in 1347 for the siege of Calais,

while Henry V employed crossbowmen at the siege of Harfleur and even had 38 crossbowmen at Agincourt (Bradbury, *The Medieval Archer*, 18–19).

60. Payne-Gallwey, *The Crossbow*, 32. Aesthetics, however, were a different matter: 'The longbow, glorious as its achievements were in the hands of our ancestors, was but a hewn stick of foreign yew of no intrinsic value. On the other hand, the crossbow gave the artist, the engraver, the inlayer and the mechanic every chance of exercising their talents to the utmost' (*ibid.*, vii).

61. C.H. Ashdown, *British and Foreign Arms and Armour* (London, 1909), 130.

62. Oman, *Art of War*, II, 58: 'The conclusion is inevitable that the weapon superseded by the arblast was merely the old shortbow which had been in constant use since Saxon times.' For the Assize of Arms, see pp. 82–3.

63. Ambroise, ll. 4,967–72, 4,927–40. At his landing at Jaffa in 1192 he waded ashore bearing a crossbow, laying low any Turk who crossed his path (*ibid.*, ll. 11,138–9).

64. Howden, III, 238–9; *Pipe Roll 6 Richard I*, 43, 68, 175–6, 212, 25. For details of the siege see T. Foulds, 'The Siege of Nottingham Castle in 1194', *Transactions of the Thoroton Society of Nottinghamshire*, xcv (1991), 20–8.

65. Bartlett, *The Making of Europe*, 63–4.

66. Ambroise, ll. 2,171–2, referring to the munitions on the great Saracen dromond heading for Acre destroyed by Richard in 1191.

67. *CCR, 1227–31*, 217, 312. On yew laths see Paterson, *The Crossbow*, 66–7.

68. The basic construction of such composite weapons was similar in principle to those of composite handbows, though there was much variation in detail. A crossbow of 1460, for instance, had its bow formed of a strip of whalebone between two lengths of yew, covered with tendon and glue, then finally encased in birch bark, with the bow tips protected by fittings of horn; Barron de Cosson, 'The Crossbow of Ulrich V, Count of Wurtemburg, 1460, with remarks on its Construction', *Archaeologia*, lii (1892), 445–65; H.L. Blackmore, *Hunting Weapons* (London, 1971), 180.

69. Wilson, *Crossbows*, 3.

70. E. Harmuth, 'Belt Spanners for Crossbows', in *Art, Arms and Armour. An International Anthology, I: 1979–80*, ed. R. Held (Chiasso, Switzerland, 1979), 100–7, at 101.

71. Blackmore, *Hunting Weapons*, 183, gives other variants of this term. An early example occurs in the list of armaments in Capetian castles in 1210; *Cartulaire Normande de Phillipe Auguste, Louis VIII, Saint-Louis et Phillipe-le-Hardi*, ed. L. Delisle (Caen, 1882, repr. Geneva 1978), nos 214 and 215, at 33–44.

72. Harmuth, 'Belt Spanners for Crossbows', 102.

73. Blackmore, *Hunting Weapons*, 178, and Paterson, *The Crossbow*, 35. The crossbow described had a simple bow of yew.

74. He also received 6,050 quarrels for the two-foot bows and 18,000 quarrels for the one-foot bows, all in nine coffers; *Cal. Docs. Scot.*, II, no. 1539.

75. Harmuth, 'Belt Spanners for Crossbows', 102.

76. H. Nickel, 'Bow and Arrow/Crossbow', *Dictionary of the Middle Ages*, ed. J.R. Strayer, 13 vols (New York, 1982–9), II, 353.

77. Payne-Gallwey judged from examples in his own collection that a siege crossbow, just capable of being hand-held but probably intended to be fired from a rest, weighed 18lb (8.2kg), while a large steel-bowed military crossbow of the type used at Agincourt weighed 15–16lb (6.8–7.3kg) without its windlass.

78. P.S. Ferguson, 'Notes on the Initial letter of a Charter of Edward II to the City of Carlisle', *Archaeological Journal*, xxxix (1882), 291–5; for the handle and screw mechanism, Paterson, *The Crossbow*, 44–5. For these weapons see J. Liebel, *Springalds and Great Crossbows* (Leeds, Royal Armouries, 1998).

79. J.F. Fino, 'Machines de jet médiévales', *Gladius*, x (1972), 26–7. Extant examples of bows for these large springalds are in the Musée de l'Armée, Paris, and a complete one is at the castle museum in Quedlinburg, Germany.

80. Q. Hughes, 'Medieval Firepower', *Fortress*, viii (1991), 31–43, at 34, 41. Springalds are also recorded at Conwy, and were probably standard equipment in major fortresses.

81. Marshall, *Warfare in the Latin East*, 174.

82. *Scalacronica*, 25–6.

83. *HGM*, III, 138.

84. Bolts in the Metropolitan Museum, New York, vary from 1.5 to 2.75oz for those with pyramidal heads, and 4 to 5oz for those with crown-shaped heads (S.V. Grancsay, 'Just How Good was Armor?', *True. The Man's Magazine*, April 1954, 45–7, 89–92, at 90). For velocities see below, n. 93.

85. Stone or pellet bows were also used for birding or sport. In London in 1280 John de Burton 'and some of his neighbours of Flete street were shooting with crossbows at a mark (*metam*) fixed in a target (*bersorio*), but as John shot, the ball (*pila*) glanced off a pear tree, accidentally striking William, son of Gillott le Cordwaner in the head, a wound from which he later died' (*Calendar of Inquisitions, Miscellaneous*, I, no. 2233).

86. Paterson, *The Crossbow*, 31.

87. Gervase of Canterbury, I, 246; *Gesta*, I, 49; Diceto, I, 373; Matthew Paris, II, 666; Guisborough, 275.

88. *The Song of the Cathar Wars*, trans. J. Shirley (Aldershot, 1996), 172.

89. Coggeshall, 206; *AM*, III, 87–8; Matthew Paris, III, 85.

90. Gaier, 'Quand l'arbalète était une nouveauté', 171 n. 22.

91. *The Miracles of Elizabeth of Thuringia*, ed. A. Huysken in *Quellenstudien zur der Geschichte der heiligen Elizabeth* (Marburg, 1908), 187. This reference was kindly supplied by Professor Robert Bartlett.

92. Thirteenth-century crossbows have been estimated to have had a range of 200–50 yards (180–230m), while the most powerful bows of the fifteenth and sixteenth centuries could have an effective range of 200m and an extreme range of 400m (Hughes, 'Medieval Firepower', 33; Gaier, 'Quand l'arbalète etait une nouveauté'), but evidence for these ranges is not given.

93. Thus the crossbow used by Bergman, McEwen and Miller, 'Experimental Archery', 663, Table, was only a modern commercial weapon, which though steel-bowed was spanned by hand and had a relatively small draw-weight of 90lb (40.8kg), while the bolts used were of aluminium weighing only ½oz (13g), and thus much lighter than medieval bolts. As the authors note, the crossbow was only included to establish upper limits of projectile velocity in a study devoted primarily to self- and composite bows (*ibid.*, 666). The same criticisms are true of the experiments of Grancsay, 'Just How Good was Armor'. Granscay obtained a velocity of 94.6mph (42.3m/s) from a cranequin-spanned crossbow with a draw-weight of 740lb (335.7kg), but using a bolt weighing only 1¼oz (35g). By contrast, he achieved a velocity of 91.2mph (40.75m/s) using a rawhide-backed longbow of osage orange, but having a draw-weight of only 68lb (30.9kg), and using an arrow weighing 2½oz (71g). As Paterson, *The Crossbow*, 31, notes, the bolt's weight could have been increased to up to 4oz (113g) with little loss in velocity but a much greater penetrative power.

94. An extant example of an '*arcubalista unius pedis*' from the City Museum at Cologne is discussed by E. Harmuth, 'Concerning the One-Foot Crossbow of the High Gothic', *JSAA*, XXVIII (1985), 9–12. The date of this weapon is uncertain, but is possibly *c.* 1400 or earlier, while the composite bow (which lacks a stirrup) may be earlier than the stock.

95. E. Harmuth, 'Zur Leistung der Mittelalterlichen Armbrust', *Waffen- und Kostümkunde*, xiii (1971), 128–36, gives an estimate as 143lb (65kg), while Paterson, *The Crossbow*, 40, suggests 150lb (68kg) as a minimum figure 'though a little more can be allowed for a fit and well trained archer'.

96. Brown, 'Observations on the Berkhampstead Bow', 12–17; Renn, 'A Bowstave from Berkhampstead Castle', 72–4. (British Museum, 1931.7.9.1).

97. See p. 227.

98. M. Le Roux de Lincy, 'Inventaires des biens maubles et immaubles de la comtesse Mahaut d'Artois, pillés par l'armée de son neveu, en l'armée 1333', *Bibliothèque de l'Ecole des Chartes* (1853), 53–79 at 60–8, item 54, '*une arbaleste d'acier dorée ou pris de Cs.*'; H. Bartlett Wells, 'A Problem in the Techniques of the Medieval European Swordsmith', *Journal of the Arms and Armour Society*, iv (1964), 229.

99. Payne-Gallwey, *The Crossbow*, 20–2. Paterson, *The Crossbow*, 31, reckoned the effective range for shooting on a flat trajectory was around 60–70 yards, though professional crossbowmen would undoubtedly have been trained to shoot at varying trajectories.

100. See pp. 329–30; cf. Vale, *War and Chivalry*, 113: 'what seems certain is that the improved steel crossbows of the fifteenth century had a more effective penetrating power, over a longer range, than did the longbow'.

101. Hall, *Weapons and Warfare*, 17–18.

102. Wylie, *Henry V*, III, 44–5.

103. As John Paston complained to his brother Sir John Paston in 1469: 'Also, Sir, we poor *sans deniers* [moneyless men] of Caistor have broken three of four steel-bows, wherefore we beseech you and [if] there be any maker of steel-bows in London which is very

cunning, that ye will send me word, and I shall send you the bows that be broken, which be your own great bow, and Robert Jackson's bow, and John Pampyng's bow; these three have cast so many calvys [slivers of metal] that they shall never cast quarrels till they be new made.'

104. Harmuth, 'Zur Leistung der mittelalterlischen Armbrust', 135; Paterson, *The Crossbow*, 31.

105. Paterson, *The Crossbow*, 45.

106. Harmuth, 'Belt Spanners for Crossbows', 103–7.

107. Paterson, *The Crossbow*, 50.

108. A windlass from the Royal Armouries showed a power advantage of 45:1, compared to that of around 5:1 for a goat's-foot lever, and 2:1 for a single cord and pulley device, but 145:1 for a cranequin (Paterson, *The Crossbow*, 49, 45, 41, 52).

109. Paterson, *The Crossbow*, 52; A.R. Williams, 'Metallographic Examination of 16th Century Armour', *Bulletin of the Historical Metallurgy Group*, vi (1972), 15–23 at 15.

110. Paterson, *The Crossbow*, 31; Grancsay, 'Just How Good was Armor?', 90.

111. Payne-Gallwey, *The Crossbow*, 14–15.

112. See pp. 30–1.

113. C. Ffoulkes, *The Armourer and his Craft. From the XIth to the XVIth Century* (London, 1912), 64–5, 180; see p. 275.

114. Vale, *War and Chivalry*, 113; see p. 275.

115. Bartlett, *The Making of Europe*, 65–70.

116. Rigord, I, 162, '*equites sagittarios*'.

117. *Annals of Dunstable*, in *Annales Monastici*, ed. Luard, III, 87; W. Rishanger, *Chronicon de Bellis*, ed. J. Orchard Halliwell, *The Chronicle of William de Rishanger of the Barons' Wars: The Miracles of Simon de Montfort* (London, 1840), 56; and see p. 138.

118. R. Avent, *Castles of the Princes of Gwynedd* (Cardiff, 1982), 13; A.D. Carr, 'Teulu and Penteulu' in *The Welsh King and his Court*, ed. T-M. Charles-Edwards, M.E. Owen and P. Russell (Cardiff, 2000), 70–1.

119. *Brut y Tywysogyon*, s.a 1212/3. Examples of stipendiaries include Ralph the crossbowman, who took service with Henry III in 1244 after being retained by Llewelyn 'formerly Prince of Wales' (*Calendar of the Liberate Rolls Preserved in the The National Archive*, 6 vols (London, 1916–64), *1240–1245*, 226; Carr, 'Teulu and Penteulu', 70–1). In 1296 one of Edward I's messengers, a Welshman named Llewyn, defected to the Scots during the siege of Stirling Castle, taking with him not only the royal dispatches but also his crossbow, which he offered to use against his former employers (*Chronicon de Lanercost, MCCI–MCCCXLVI*, ed. J. Stevenson (Edinburgh, 1839), 178–9).

120. Hughes, 'Medieval Firepower', 33.

121. Ascham, *Toxophilus*, 149.

122. See, for example, Gaier, 'Quand l'arbalète était une nouveauté', 170 n. 20, who cites many twelfth-century examples from France and the Low Countries.

123. N.J.G. Pounds, *The Medieval Castle in England and Wales: a Social and Political History* (Cambridge, 1990), 108–9.

124. Audoin, *Essai sur l'armée royale*, for Register A; Contamine, *War in the Middle Ages*, 72.

125. *CCR, 1256–9*, 232; *Cal. Lib. Rolls, 1240–5*, 122. In 1260 Thomas de Sancto Sepulchro is mentioned as an *attilator* (*CCR, 1259–61*, 245), his name ('of the Holy Sepulchre') implying he was from the Latin kingdom of Jerusalem, while the German origin of Henry Teutonicus again stresses that many of Henry's experts were drawn from far afield. See now D. Bachrach, 'Origins of the Crossbow Industry in England', *JMMH*, ii (2004), 73–88.

126. *CCR, 1227–31*, 193; *Cal. Lib. Rolls, 1240–5*, 258; *Cal. Lib. Rolls, 1245–51*, 258.

127. *Cal. Lib. Rolls, 1226–40*, 444. *Ibid.*, 5, records the buying of cork (*cortice*) used, like bark, as a protective covering for the composite bow arms, as well as thread (*filum*), sinew (*nervos*) and glue (*glu*). In 1358 yew, wax, resinous pitch, tallow, charcoal, glue, shredded ox sinew, ram's horn and varnish were sent to Robert l'Artilleur of Rouen to make the composite bows for crossbows (De Cosson, 'The Crossbow of Ulrich', 447–8; Blackmore, *Hunting Weapons*, 181).

128. *CCR, 1237–42*, 409.

129. *CCR, 1231–34*, 212, 181.

130. C.E. Hart, *The Royal Forest* (Oxford, 1966), 267–72.

131. Pounds, *The Castle in England and Wales*, 110, maps this distribution.

132. *Cal. Lib. Rolls, 1245–1251*, 119, 287; Pounds, *The Castle in England and Wales*, 108–9.

133. *CCR, 1254–6*, 260.

134. *Documents relatif au comté de Champagne et Brie (1172–1361)*, ed. A. Longon, 3 vols (Paris, 1901–14), II, 33; Contamine, *War in the Middle Ages*, 72.

135. *Rot. Litt. Claus.*, I, 143.

136. For the background to the siege and its progress see Carpenter, *The Minority of Henry III*, 360–7. A detailed account, drawn from the rolls, of the equipment deployed by Henry at the siege is provided by G.H. Fowler, 'Munitions in 1224', *Bedfordshire Historical Record Society*, v (1920), 117–32; and see now E. Amt, 'Besieging Bedford: Military Logistics in 1224', *JMMH*, i (2002), 101–24.

137. *Rot. Litt. Claus.*, I, 606.

138. *Rot. Litt. Claus.*, I, 606. Ten of these large *ballistae*, plus ten protective manlets (*targiae*), were sent from London on wagons (*ibid.*).

139. *Rot. Litt. Claus.*, I, 609.

140. *Rot. Litt. Claus.*, I, 607, 608.

141. *Rot. Litt. Claus.*, I, 613; Fowler, 'Munitions in 1224', 126.

142. *CCR, 1272–9*, 373; Prestwich, *Edward I*, 179.

143. *Accounts of the Constables of Bristol Castle*, 65. Of these 18,000 were for two-foot crossbows and 32,000 were for one-foot crossbows.

144. *Accounts of the Constables of Bristol Castle*, 65.

145. Vale, *The Angevin Legacy*, 209–10. In 1254 30,000 bolts had been shipped from England to Gascony, and in 1294–5 another 37,700 (J. Miquel, 'L'armement des châteaux dans la Gascogne

anglaise de 1250 à 1325', in M.-P. Baudry, ed. *Les fortifications dans les domaines Plantagenêt, XIIe–XIVe siècle: actes du colloque international tenu à Poitiers du 11 au 13 novembre 1994* (Poitiers, 2000), 89–99, at 93–4).

146.   *CCR, 1232*, 175.

147.   Prestwich, *War, Politics and Finance*, 106. *Cal. Docs. Scot.*, II, 412.

148.   On such defences see R. Higham, 'Timber Castles: A Reassessment', *Fortress*, i (1989), 50–60; R. Higham and P. Barker, *Timber Castles* (London, 1992).

149.   The subsequent provision of wooden hourds or 'bretesches' in the later Middle Ages shows explicit provision for bowmen. Thus in 1356 fear of the Free Companies led the town of Anse, near Lyon, to strengthen its fortifications by repairing the walls, supplying gates with armaments, and erecting six bretesches, each with two crossbows. Trees within a crossbow's shot of the walls were cut down so as to give the enemy no cover (P. Contamine, *Guerre, état et sociétè à la fin du Moyen Age: études sur les armées des rois de France, 1337–1494* (Paris, 1972), 6).

150.   A modern reconstruction of such hourding can be seen at Caerphilly Castle.

151.   *Richmond Castle* (HMSO, 1953); D. Renn, 'The Norman Military Works', in *Ludlow Castle, its History and Buildings*, ed. R. Shoesmith and A. Johnson (Logaston, 2000), 125–38, who notes that absence of such loops is a characteristic feature of early Norman work.

152.   D. Renn, 'Defending Framlingham Castle', *Proceedings of the Suffolk Institute of Archaeology*, xxxiii (1973), 58–67.

153.   Renn, 'Defending Framlingham Castle', 65, fig. 25.

154.   Renn, 'Defending Framlingham Castle', 62.

155.   J. Mesqui, 'Les tours à archères dans le domaine Plantagenêt français, 1160–1205', in *Les fortifications dans les domaines Plantagenêt*, 77–88.

156.   J. Mesqui, *Les Châteaux-Forts en France* (Paris, 2000), 24–7, under 'archère'; and cf. *idem*, *Châteaux et enceintes de la France médiévale: de la défense à la résidence*, 2 vols (Paris, 1991).

157.   D. Renn, 'The Avranches Traverse at Dover Castle', *Archaeologia Cantiana*, lxxxiv (1969), 79–92. A similar construction, the Bell Tower, was added to the defences of the Tower of London at the same date (*ibid.*, 89 and figs 2 and 3). Similar embrasures can be found at the great Plantagenet keep at Niort in Poitou, built either by Henry II or Richard I (M.-P. Baudry, 'Le château des Plantagenet à Niort', in *Les fortifications dans les domaines Plantagenêt*, 23–40, at 30–1 and pl. III.

158.   Among the earliest examples is the great Hospitaller castle of Belvoir, begun in the 1160s to command the Jordan valley.

159.   P.E. Curnow, 'Some Developments in Military Architecture c. 1200: Le Coudray-Salbart', *Anglo-Norman Studies*, ii (1980), 42–62, at 56–7; M.-P. Baudry, 'Le château du Coudray-Salbart', *Bulletin archéologique du comité des travaux historiques et scientifiques*, nouv. sér., xxiii–iv (1991), 137–212, especially 173–81 for a detailed study of provision for archery.

160.   G.T. Clark, *Medieval Military Architecture*, 2 vols (London, 1884), I, 315–35; D. Renn, *Caerphilly Castle* (Cadw, Cardiff, revised edn, 1997), 3, 9–14, 34.

161.   G. Port, *Rochester Castle* (English Heritage, 1987), 14.

162.   J.K. Knight, *The Three Castles: Grosmont Castle, Skenfrith Castle, White Castle* (Cadw, Cardiff, 2nd edn, revised, 2000), 39–46; P.N. Jones and D. Renn. 'The Military Effectiveness of Arrow Loops. Some Experiments at White Castle', *Château Gaillard*, ix–x (1982), 447–56; cf. Hughes, 'Medieval Firepower', 33.

163.   Jones and Renn, 'The Military Effectiveness of Arrow Loops', 449, who note that the 'yaw problems associated with the launch of longbow arrows could be overcome with practice'.

164.   Jones and Renn, 'The Military Effectiveness of Arrow Loops', 450–1, and fig. 8.

165.   The classic study remains A.J. Taylor, *The Welsh Castles of Edward I* (London, 1986).

166.   Hughes, 'Medieval Firepower', 36–7. For the castle and town defences see A.J. Taylor, *Conway Castle and Town Walls, Caernarvonshire* (Cadw, Cardiff, revised edn, 2003), and further bibliography there cited.

167.   Taylor, *Conwy Castle*, 39–59.

168.   A.J. Taylor, *Caernarvon Castle and Town Walls* (5th edn, Cardiff, 2001), 27, 37.

169.   A.J. Taylor, *Harlech Castle* (Cadw, Cardiff, 4th edn, 2002), 17; *idem, Beaumaris Castle* (Cadw, Cardiff, 4th edn, 1999).

170.   Hughes, 'Medieval Firepower', 39–42.

171.   In 1403, during the revolt of Owain Glyn Dŵr, only 271 men in total were garrisoning the great castles of Conwy, Caernarfon, Harlech and Criccieth (C.T. Allmand, *Henry V* (London, 1992), 24). At Beaumaris lack of an adequate garrison led to the blocking, either at the period of the Glyn Dŵr revolt or in the Civil War from 1642, of 79 of the 164 loops at ground level in the outer curtain (Taylor, *Beaumaris Castle*, 39).

172.   R.A. Brown, 'Framlingham Castle and Bigod, 1154–1216', *Suffolk Institute of Archaeology and Natural History*, xxv (1950), 127–48; *idem, Castles, Conquest and Charters: Collected Papers* (Woodbridge, 1989), 204.

173.   *Calendar of Ancient Correspondence concerning Wales*, ed. J. Goronwy Edwards (Cardiff, 1935), 82; Suppe, *Military Institutions*, 82. In 1224 the garrison of Montgomery, a key royal castle in the marches, was garrisoned by 2 mounted and 4 foot crossbowmen, 12 serjeants and an unspecified number of knights (*Rot. Litt. Claus.*, I, 582, 617, 642).

174.   Morris, *Welsh Wars*, 193–4. The usual garrison for Harlech was about 40, including around ten crossbowmen (Hughes, 'Medieval Firepower', 41).

175.   Prestwich, *Edward I*, 426.

176.   Prestwich, *War, Politics and Finance*, 74; A.E. Prince, 'The Indenture System under Edward III', in *Historical Essays in Honour of James Tait*, ed. J.G. Edwards, W.H. Galbraith, E.F. Jacob (1933), 286 n. 4.

177.   *Cal. Lib. Rolls, 1240–5*, 144. This number fluctuated considerably.

In 1263 there were only 30 crossbowmen in Dover, and 11 *balistarii pedites* in Gloucester (*CLR, 1261–4*, 240).

178.   Renn, 'The Avranches Traverse', 85–6.

179.   *Rolls of the Justices in Eyre: being the Rolls of Pleas and Assizes for Yorkshire in 3 Henry III, 1218–19*, ed. D. Stenton (London, 1937), no. 889, 325.

180.   R.R. Davies, *The Revolt of Owain Glyn Dŵr* (Oxford, 1995), 250–1.

181.   Coggeshall, 206.

182.   Matthew Paris, II, 626; Walter of Coventry, *Memoriale fratris Walteri de Conventria: the historical collections of Walter of Coventry*, ed. W. Stubbs, 2 vols (London, 1872–3), II, 227.

183.   *The Old French Continuation of William of Tyre*, trans. in P. Edbury, *The Conquest of Jerusalem and the Third Crusade: Sources in Translation* (Aldershot, 1996), 98; Ambroise, ll. 4,815–22; *Itinerarium*, 220–1.

184.   *HGM*, ll. 10,200–34; Foulds, 'The Siege of Nottingham Castle', 23–4. In 1224 similar large protective shields were ordered for Henry III's siege of Bedford, while pavais for bowmen were among the supplies ordered for the French garrison of Calais in 1293, along with crossbows, bolts, helmets, lances and other weapons (Vale, *The Angevin Legacy*, 201).

185.   See p. 286.

186.   When, for example, at the siege of Toron in 1179, Reyner de Marun shot a great Turkish emir through the heart, the Muslims struck camp and departed (William of Tyre, XXI, c.25).

187.   *Chroniques des comtes d'Anjou*, 253.

188.   *Hystoria Albigensis*, ed. P. Guebin and E. Lyon, 3 vols (Paris, 1926–39), I, 193; II, 441–5.

189.   *Flores Historiarum*, ed. H.R. Luard, 3 vols (Rolls Series, London, 1890), III, 318. If this account, larded with biblical analogies, is to be believed, he also had narrow misses from the bolt of a springald and from a stone from an engine which caused his horse to stumble and the king to fall.

190.   *Feudal Society in Medieval France: documents from the County of Champagne*, ed. and trans. T. Evergates (Philadelphia, 1993), 7.

191.   Payne-Gallwey, *The Crossbow*, 9 n. 1.

192.   E.S. Eames, *Catalogue of Medieval Lead-Glazed Earthenware Tiles in the Department of Medieval and Later Antiquities, British Museum*, 2 vols (London, 1980), II, pls 468 and 474.

193.   J.F. Verbruggen, *De Krijgskunst in West-Europe in de Middeleeuwen, IXe tot begin XIVe eeuw* (Brussels, 1954), 38; C. Gaier, *Art et organisation militaires dans la principauté de Liège et dans le comté de Looz au moyen âge* (Brussels, 1968), 111.

194.   Matthew Paris, III, 19. Similarly, crossbowmen formed the leading unit of the Liègeois army defeated by John at Othée in 1408,

while as late as 1482 a charter confirming the crossbowmen of Liège in their ancient privileges stated that one of their primary functions was to go ahead of the main formations of the army as it advanced, and to cover it in retreat (Gaier, *Art et organisation*, 110).

195.   F. Lot, *L'Art Militaire et les Armées au Moyen Âge en Europe et dans le Proche Orient*, 2 vols (Paris, 1946), I, 241. Though Desclot's figures are wildly exaggerated, there is nothing inherently implausible about the basic order of march he gives.

196.   Lot, *L'art militaire*, II, 304.

197.   See pp. 107–8.

198.   Contamine, *War in the Middle Ages*, 73. Clearly these men would guard the front ranks, but the proportions might imply that two crossbowmen might shelter behind each pavise.

199.   See p. 88; *Cartulaire Normande*, no. 215, 34. At Vaudreuil the former type of shield is designated as 'knights' shields (*scuta militum*) (*ibid.*). It is possible that the spearmen who protected Richard's Genoese and Pisan crossbowmen at Jaffa in 1192 had large shields. Certainly by the mid-fourteenth century French armies contained not only *paviseurs* but serjeants armed with lances and *targe* or pavise (Contamine, *Guerre, état et société*, 22).

200.   Vale, *Angevin Legacy*, 201.

201.   Gaier, 'Quand l'arbalète était une nouveauté', 173 n. 27; Contamine, *Guerre, état, sociètè*, 22; *Ordonnances des roys*, IV, 67.

202.   R. Davidsohn, *Storia di Firenze*, 5 vols (Florence, 1957–73), II, 458–65; Mallet, *Mercenaries and their Masters*, 21–3.

203.   Verbruggen, *The Art of Warfare*, 190–4; K. De Vries, *Infantry Warfare in the Early Fourteenth Century: discipline, tactics and technology* (Woodbridge, 1996), 17.

204.   Verbruggen, *The Art of Warfare*, 198.

205.   Wilson, *Crossbows*, 31.

206.   Some fourteenth-century German examples from the city of Erfurt now in the Metropolitan Museum weigh 48lb (21.8kg) and 50lb (22.7kg) respectively, which must have restricted their use to siege operations.

207.   A. Credland, 'The Crossbow in Europe: A Historical Introduction', in Paterson, *The Crossbow*, 20.

208.   L.M. Paterson, *The World of the Troubadours: Medieval Occitan Society, c.1100–c.1300* (Cambridge, 1993), 45–8, 51–3.

209.   Contamine, *War in the Middle Ages*, 73, quoting the Catalan observer Bernat Desclot: 'the men whom we call Almogavars live exclusively by their arms and dwell neither in towns nor villages but only in mountains and forests. They fight daily against the Saracens, penetrating a day or two's march into Saracen territory and collecting booty and bringing back with them numerous prisoners and many goods. They live off this booty . . .'

CHAPTER 8

1.   *Adam Bell, Clym of the Clough and William of Cloudesly*, in R.B. Dobson and J. Taylor, *Rymes of Robyn Hood: An Introduction to the English Outlaw* (London, 1976), 260.

2.   Matthew Paris, IV, 209–13; Bemont, 'La campagne de Poitou',

289–314; Stacey, *Politics, Policy and Finance under Henry III*, 192–6.

3.   *Chronica de Mailros*, 194, notes the baronial army contained knights and '*pedestribus innumeris, inter quos erant multi balistarii et fundibularii*'. For the battle of Lewes, see especially Carpenter, *The*

Battles of Lewes and Evesham, 19–36. Older but still valuable accounts include W.H. Blaauw, *The Barons' War, including the Battles of Lewes and Evesham* (2nd edn, London, 1871); *The Battle of Lewes, 1264*, ed. F.M. Powicke (Lewes, 1964); T. Beamish, *Battle Royal* (London, 1965).

4.   Carpenter, *The Battles of Lewes and Evesham*, 31–2; Guisborough, 194.

5.   Guisborough, 194, who notes that the Londoners had requested the privilege of being the first to attack.

6.   For the battle of Evesham, D.C. Cox, *The Battle of Evesham* (Evesham, 1965); *idem*, 'The Battle of Evesham in the Evesham Chronicle', *Historical Research*, lxii (1989), 337–45; and *idem, The Battle of Evesham: A New Account* (Evesham, 1988); Carpenter, *The Battles of Lewes and Evesham*, 37–66; O. De Laborderie, J.R. Maddicott and D.A. Carpenter, 'The Last Hours of Simon de Montfort: A New Account', *EHR*, cxv (2000), 378–412.

7.   De Laborderie, Maddicott and Carpenter, 'The Last Hours of Simon de Montfort', 408, 411. Unfortunately, the description of the fighting itself is largely lost through a lacuna in the manuscript.

8.   See p. 149.

9.   Carpenter, *The Battles of Lewes and Evesham*, 64; *Political Songs*, 125, '*tot à cheval, fust le mal, sauntz nulle pedaile*'.

10.   Thomas of Wykes, *Chronicon vulgo dictum Thomae Wykes*, ed. H.R. Luard, *Annales Monastici*, iv (London, 1867), 173; *Chronicon de Bello*, in C. Bemont, *Simon de Montfort* (Paris, 1884), 373–80 at 380; *Chronica Minor S. Benedicti de Hulmo*, ed. H. Ellis, *Chronica Johannis de Oxenedes* (London, 1859), 412–39, 208; Carpenter, *The Battles of Lewes and Evesham*, 61.

11.   Carpenter, *The Battles of Lewes and Evesham*, 63–6.

12.   Cavalry were also used in the royalist assaults on some of the Cinque Ports in 1266, for the commander, Roger Leyburn, claimed expenses of £200 for horses killed in the attack on Sandwich and a further £140 for horses killed at Winchelsea (A. Lewis, 'Roger of Leyburn and the Pacification of England, 1265–7', *EHR*, ccxiv (1939), at 201–2).

13.   *CCR, 1261–4*, 376–7; Wykes, 147.

14.   Rishanger, *Chronicon de Bellis*, 56.

15.   *De antiquis legibus liber: Cronica maiorum et vicecomitatum Londoniarum*, ed. T. Stapleton (Camden Society, London, 1846); trans. *EHD*, III, 178.

16.   Guisborough, 190; Powicke, *Henry III and the Lord Edward*, 784–7, Appendix F.

17.   G.R. Stephens, 'A Note on William of Cassingham', *Speculum*, xvi (1941), 216–23, assembles what is known of William's life and career; cf. Powicke, *Henry III and the Lord Edward*, 9–10. William (*c.* 1195–1257) was a minor royal official in charge of the pastures owned in the Weald by the king's manor of Milton. He was subsequently granted wardenship of the Seven Hundreds of the Weald, with the right to draw resources from there to support his men in their hostilities against Louis.

18.   Matthew Paris, II, 655. His figure of 1,000 archers, taken from Roger of Wendover, is probably an exaggeration, but documentary sources reveal that the Weald could yield significant numbers of bowmen; *Annales Monastici*, III, 46, 48; *Histoire des Ducs de Normandie et des rois d'Angleterre*, ed. F. Michel (Paris, 1840), 181; *HGM*, III, 210; *Rot. Litt. Pat, 1216–25*, 56. King John wrote a letter of thanks to the men of the Weald in September 1216 (*Foedera*, I, pt 1, 142).

19.   *Histoire des Ducs*, 181–3; *RHF*, xxiv, 744.

20.   Stephens, 'William of Cassingham', 222–3.

21.   *William Thorne's Chronicle of Saint Augustine's Abbey Canterbury*, trans. A.H. Davis (Oxford, 1934), 47–9; J.C. Holt, 'The Origins of the Constitutional Tradition in England', in *idem*, *Magna Carta and Medieval Government* (London, 1985), 10.

22.   *CCR, 1261–4*, 360, 383–4.

23.   Carpenter, *The Battles of Lewes and Evesham*, 16; Wykes, 147–8; *Chronicon de Bello*, 375–6.

24.   Powicke, *Henry III and the Lord Edward*, 520.

25.   Lewis, 'Roger of Leyburn', 194–7.

26.   Lewis, 'Roger of Leyburn', 199.

27.   Lewis, 'Roger of Leyburn', 200; Rishanger, *Chronica et Annales*, H.T. Riley (Rolls Series, 1865), 56.

28.   There is sometimes confusion over the identity of these bowmen, for the Exchequer clerks rendered the term '*Waldenses*' in Leyburn's original invoice as '*Wallenses*' or Welsh – a clear sign of the automatic association of the Welsh with archery. But the fact that these men were hired for only one or two days, together with earlier unequivocal references to archers from the Weald as '*Waldenses*', makes it almost certain these were local men and not Welsh troops (Lewis, 'Roger of Leyburn', 201–2; *CCR, 1261–4*, 360, '*de melioribus sagittaris Waldensibus*'). Despite his own caveats, however, Lewis, 'Roger of Leyburn', 201 and 205, continues to refer to these archers as Welsh.

29.   Lewis, 'Roger of Leyburn', 208.

30.   *CCR, 1264–8*, 191; Lewis, 'Roger of Leyburn', 204. Leyburn's tactics were highly effective, but expensive: in 1267 the Treasury owed him £3,100 (Powicke, *Henry III and the Lord Edward*, 521 and n. 1: *CPR, 1266–72*, 251).

31.   *CPR, 1266–72*, 133; *CCR, 1264–8*, 300. In December 1265 Edward had moved against the rebels in the Isle of Axholme, levying loyal troops from Nottingham and Derby, and finally received their surrender at Bickersditch in Sherwood Forest (Lewis, 'Roger of Leyburn', 199–200).

32.   *CPR, 1266–72*, 20; Lewis, 'Roger of Leyburn', 208–9.

33.   Morris, *Welsh Wars*, 33.

34.   Morris, *Welsh Wars*, 33; Lewis, 'Roger of Leyburn', 208–9.

35.   See pp. 153–7.

36.   Cf. Powicke, *Henry III and the Lord Edward*, 529–30.

37.   M. Keen, *The Outlaws of Medieval England* (revised edn, London, 2000), 235.

38.   For valuable surveys of the debate see, *inter alia*, J.G. Bellamy, *Robin Hood: An Historical Enquiry* (London, 1985); Holt, *Robin Hood*; Bradbury, *The Medieval Archer*, 58–70; Keen, *The Outlaws of Medieval England*, Appendix IV, 'Robin Hood in Recent Historical Writing (1977–86): A Postscript'; R.B. Dobson and J. Taylor, 'Robin Hood of Barnsdale: A Fellow Thou Hast Long Sought',

Northern History, xix (1983), 218–19; *idem*, 'General Review: Robin Hood', *Northern History*, xxvi (1990), 229–32.

39. A. Ayton, 'Military Service and the Development of the Robin Hood Legend in the Fourteenth Century', *Nottingham Medieval Studies*, xxxvi (1992), 126–47, and especially 136.
40. Walter Bower, *Scotichronicon*, ed. S. Taylor, D.E.R. Watt and B. Scott, 9 vols (Aberdeen, 1987–98), v, 354–5, where he also records the popularity of the legend in his own day: 'The foolish common folk eagerly celebrate the deeds of these men [Robin and his band] with gawping enthusiasm in comedies and tragedies, and take pleasure in hearing jesters and bards singing [of them] more than in other romances.' In mentioning Robin in 1266 Bower departs from Andrew of Wyntoun, whose earlier *Original Chronicle*, completed before 1420, relates Robin's activities under the years 1284–5 (*The Original Chronicle of Andrew of Wyntoun*, ed. F.J. Amours, 6 vols (Scottish Text Society, 1903–14), V, 136–7). For these northern traditions, see Holt, *Robin Hood*, 40–1; Dobson and Taylor, *Rymes of Robyn Hood*, 4–5, 315.
41. D. Crook, 'Some Further Evidence Concerning the Dating of the Origins of the Legend of Robin Hood', *EHR*, xcix (1984), 530–4; repr. S. Knight, ed., *Robin Hood: An Anthology* (Cambridge, 1999), 257–61; *The Three Earliest Subsidies for the County of Sussex, 1296, 1327, 1332*, ed. W. Hudson (Sussex Record Society, x, 1910), 33.
42. *Historia Majoris Britanniae*, ed. R. Freebairn (Edinburgh, 1740), 128; trans. A. Constable, *A History of Greater Britain* (Scottish Historical Society, 1892), 156–7.
43. Howden, III, 240.
44. L.V.D. Owen, 'Robin Hood in the Light of Research', in *The Times, Trade and Engineering*, xxxviii new series (February, 1936), at xxix; J.C. Holt, 'The Ballads of Robin Hood' in *Peasants, Knights and Heretics*, ed. R.H. Hilton (Cambridge, 1976), 236–57, at 253–4; *idem*, *Robin Hood*, 53–4.
45. D. Crook, 'The Sheriff of Nottingham and Robin Hood: The Genesis of the Legend?', in *Thirteenth Century England, II. Proceedings of the Newcastle upon Tyne Conference, 1987*, ed. P.R. Coss and S.D. Lloyd (Woodbridge, 1988), 59–68, at 66–8.
46. Crook, 'The Sheriff of Nottingham', 68.
47. *The Three Earliest Subsidies for the County of Sussex*, 33; Crook, 'Some Further Evidence', 530–4; repr. in Knight, *Robin Hood: An Anthology*, 257–61.
48. Prestwich, *Armies and Warfare*, 235.
49. Ayton, 'Military Service and the Development of the Robin Hood Legend', 126–33, 135.
50. B.A. Hanawalt, 'Ballads and Bandits: Fourteenth Century Outlaws and the Robin Hood Poems', in *Chaucer's England: Literature in Historical Context*, ed. B.A. Hanawalt (Minneapolis, 1992), and reprinted in Knight, *Robin Hood: An Anthology*, 263–284.
51. F. Pollock and F.W. Maitland, *The History of the English Law before the time of Edward I*, 2 vols (Cambridge, 1895), II, 557.
52. *Political Songs*, 232–6; Dobson and Taylor, *Rymes of Robin Hood*, 252–4.
53. *Early English Lyrics: Amorous, Divine, Moral and Trivial*, ed. E.K. Chambers and F. Sidgwick (London, 1966), 41.
54. *CCR, 1302–7*, 396–7.
55. Stubbs, *Select Charters*, 465, 468.
56. Holt, *Robin Hood*, 52.
57. Dobson and Taylor, *Rymes of Robyn Hood*, 19, 79, 142, 144. For Barnsdale, Holt, *Robin Hood*, 83–8.
58. W.C. Bolland, *A Manual of Year Book Studies* (Cambridge, 1925), 107; Dobson and Taylor, *Rymes of Robyn Hood*, 3.
59. *Anonimalle Chronicle, 1333–1381*, ed. V.H. Galbraith (Manchester, 1927), 41, '*et le prince respondit qils furent gentz Dangleterre foresters vivaunt par sauvagine en lour dedute, et ceo fusst lour custome checun jour destre issint arrays*'.
60. *Select Pleas of the Forest*, 97, 102.
61. *The Hunting Book of Gaston Phébus*, ed. M. Thomas, F. Avril and W. Schlag (London, 1998), ff. 113v, 114r, 115r; *The Parlement of the Thre Ages*, ed. M.Y. Offord (Early English Text Society, vol. 246, London, 1959), 1–2.
62. Phébus, *Livre de chasse*, 269–70; Edward, Duke of York, *Master of the Game*, ed. W.A. and F. Baillie-Grohman (London, 1904).
63. Dobson and Taylor, *Rymes of Robyn Hood*, 109, 141, 144.
64. Keen, *The Outlaws of Medieval Legend*, 76.
65. *Rotuli Parliamentorum*, 6 vols (Record Commission, 1767–77), V, 16; Dobson and Taylor, *Rymes of Robyn Hood*, 3–4.
66. Phébus, *Livre de chasse*, 269–70; Cummins, *The Hound and the Hawk*, 53.
67. Cummins, *The Hound and the Hawk*, 113, 169.
68. 'Greybeard' [*sic*], 'Some Thoughts on "Nestroque" – an Agincourt Battle Command?', *JSAA*, xliv (2001), 22–3, who also suggests that different patterns of horn blast could have been used to issue 'predetermined and appropriate' commands to units of the army. For the use of the *menée* in hunting dangerous game like the boar, wolf or hart, see Cummins, *The Hound and the Hawk*, 166, and cf. 164. The metaphor of the hunt was certainly in Shakespeare's mind when he has Henry V conclude his speech before Harfleur with the words 'I see you stand like greyhounds at the slips, straining upon the start. The game's afoot! Follow your spirit and upon this charge cry "God for Harry, England and St George!"' (*Henry V*, III.1, 31–4).
69. See M. Bennett, 'The Battle', in *Agincourt, 1415: Henry V, Sir Thomas Erpingham and the Triumph of the English Archers*, ed. A. Curry (Stroud, 2000), 21–36, at 31, for the splendid suggestion that the command may have represented 'Now Strike!' in a pronounced Norfolk dialect!
70. *Chronique d'Enguerran de Monstrelet*, ed. L. Douet d'Arcq, 6 vols (Paris, 1857–62), III, who renders Erpingham's command as 'nescieque'; *The Battle of Agincourt: Sources and Interpretations*, ed. A. Curry (Woodbridge, 2000), 158, 160.
71. *Chronique de Jean le Bel*, ed. E. Deprez, and J. Viard, 2 vols (Paris, 1904–5), I, 39–42; Cummins, *The Hound and the Hawk*, 57, 169.
72. B.A. Hanawalt, 'Fur-Collar Crime: The Pattern of Crime among the Fourteenth-Century English Nobility', *Journal of Social History*, viii (1975), 1–17; J. Birrell, 'Who Poached the King's Deer?', *Midland History*, vii (1982), 9–25.
73. *II Cnut*, 80–80.1, in *EHD*, I, no. 50, 430.

74. For royal forests see J.C. Cox, *The Royal Forests of England* (London, 1905) and C.R. Young, *The Royal Forests of England* (University of Pennsylvania, 1979). For the forest and its officers in the fourteenth century see N. Nelson, 'The Forests', in *The English Government at Work, 1327–1336*, I, 394–467.

75. A.L. Poole, *From Domesday Book to Magna Carta* (Oxford, 1951), 29–35.

76. Stubbs, *Select Charters*, 344–8; Holt, *Magna Carta*, 338–40, and 512–17 for the text of the 1225 reissue of the Charter of the Forest.

77. Stubbs, *Select Charters*, 186; *EHD*, II, no. 28, 451 (clause 2).

78. Since their visitations could be as many as three or more years apart, many of those apprehended under the forest law languished for considerable periods in gaol, and some even died there.

79. *Royal and other Historical Letters illustrative of the Reign of Henry III*, ed. W.W. Shirley, 2 vols (Rolls Series, London, 1862, 1866), I, 348; C.R. Young, 'The Forest Eyre in England during the Thirteenth Century', *American Journal of Legal History*, xviii (1974), 321–31, provides the background to these judicial proceedings.

80. *Select Pleas of the Forest*, 5. Others were in mercy for keeping or hiding greyhounds or other dogs.

81. *Select Pleas of the Forest*, 109.

82. *The Lanercost Cartulary*, ed. J.M. Todd (Surtees Society, cciii, 1997), 240. This reference was kindly supplied by Mr David Sherlock of English Heritage.

83. For the organisation of the forest see *Select Pleas of the Forest*, ix ff.

84. *Adam Bell, Clym of the Clough and William of Cloudesly*, in Dobson and Taylor, *Rymes*, 272.

85. Cox, *The Royal Forests*, 20. Under Edward IV some foresters of Sherwood received 4d a day, but as they could serve by deputy it would seem these were men of higher status.

86. *Master of Game*, 189; trans. Orme, *From Childhood to Chivalry*, 199.

87. *General Prologue*, ll. 101–17.

88. T. Jones, *Chaucer's Knight. The Portrait of a Medieval Mercenary* (London, 1980, repr. 1985), 212. For Hawkwood and the White Company see pp. 246–51.

89. Jones, *Chaucer's Knight*, 212.

90. Ayton, 'The Development of the Robin Hood Legend', 137 and n. 62.

91. A. Goodman, *John of Gaunt. The Exercise of Princely Power in Fourteenth-Century Europe* (London, 1992), 218.

92. *Rot. Parl.*, II, 332.

93. Ayton, 'The Development of the Robin Hood Legend', 139–40.

94. J. Birrell, 'Peasant Deer Poachers in the Medieval Forest', in *Progress and Problems in Medieval England. Essays in Honour of Edward Miller*, ed. J. Britnell and J. Hatcher (Cambridge, 1996), 66–88, at 71–5.

95. *Select Pleas of the Forest*, 79–81.

96. *Select Pleas of the Forest*, 77–8. The term used for the three unbarbed arrows, '*genderatas*', is rare and its precise meaning is unclear.

97. For example, *Select Pleas of the Forest*, 77–8; 87, 90, 95, 96 bis.

98. *Select Pleas of the Forest*, 38–40.

99. *Select Pleas of the Forest*, 37–8; B.A. Hanawalt, 'Men's Games, King's Deer: Poaching in Medieval England', *Journal of Medieval and Renaissance Studies*, viii (1988), 175–93, at 188–90; J. Birrell, 'Forest Law and the Peasantry in the Later Thirteenth Century', in *Thirteenth Century England II. Proceedings of the Newcastle upon Tyne Conference, 1987*, ed. P.R. Coss and S.D. Lloyd (Woodbridge, 1988), 149–63, at 156.

100. *Select Pleas of the Forest*, 110.

101. Birrell, 'Forest Law and the Peasantry', 155; *idem*, 'Who Poached the King's Deer?', 11–13, 17; Hanawalt, 'Men's Games, King's Deer', 185–7.

102. Birrell, 'Forest Law and the Peasantry', 161.

103. See, *inter alia*, R.H. Hilton, 'The Origins of Robin Hood', *Past and Present*, xiv (1958); J.C. Holt, 'The Audience and Ballads of Robin Hood', *Past and Present*, xviii (1960); M. Keen, 'Robin Hood – Peasant or Gentleman?', *Past and Present*, xix (1961); J.C. Holt, 'Robin Hood: Some Comments', *Past and Present*, xix (1961). All of these articles are reprinted in R.H. Hilton, ed., *Peasants, Knights and Heretics. Studies in Medieval English Social History* (Cambridge, 1976), 221–70.

104. *A Lytell Geste*, verses 385, 386; *Robin Hood and the Monk*, verse 122, in Dobson and Taylor, *Rymes of Robin Hood*, 107–9, 115–25; Hanawalt, 'Men's Games, King's Deer', 181, 193; *idem*, 'Ballads and Bandits', in Knight, ed., *Robin Hood*, 283.

105. Morris, *Welsh Wars*, 174; Prestwich, *Edward I*, 198.

106. *CPR, 1324–7*, 27.

107. *CCR, 1227–31*, 398.

108. Stubbs, *Select Charters*, 468; *EHD*, III, no. 59, 60.

109. *Rôles Gascons*, ed. F. Michel and C. Bémont, 3 vols (Paris, 1885–1906), III, cxxxviii–cxxxix; Prestwich, *Edward I*, 202; Vale, *Angevin Legacy*, 202.

110. *Rotuli Scotiae in Turri Londinensi et in Domo Capitulari Westmonasteriensi asservati*, ed. D. Macpherson *et al*, 2 vols (Record Commission, London, 1814, 1819), I, 255 n; but cf. *CCR 1333–7*, 158. Taking issue with Morris's assertion that much of the English army consisted of 'murderers and robbers and poachers', R. Nicholson, *Edward III and the Scots: The Formative Years of a Military Career, 1327–1335* (London, 1965), 130, points out, however, that 'it soon appeared that the list of pardons was swollen with the names of many a felon who had never left home'. An idea of their numbers is given by the fact that in 1334–5 pardoned criminals formed two companies, each of 100 men (*ibid.*, 130 n. 5).

111. *Political Songs*, 128.

112. *CPR, 1258–66*, 534, Lewis, 'Roger of Leyburn', 199–200. In December 1265, for example, Edward had moved in person against the rebels in the Isle of Axholme, levying loyal troops from Nottingham and Derby, and finally received their surrender at Bickersditch in Sherwood Forest.

CHAPTER 9

1. Morris, *Welsh Wars*, 95.

2. Prestwich, 'English Armies', 338.

3. See the discussion by Prestwich, *Edward I*, 227–32.

4. The essential work on Edwardian armies is Prestwich, *War, Politics and Finance under Edward I* (Towta, New Jersey, 1972). This chapter owes much to this and Professor Prestwich's other work on Edward I and on his military organisation.

5. *Rot. Litt. Claus*, I, 632; *Foedera*, I, 281.

6. *CCR, 1227–31*, 595, which also refers to those '*jurati ad ferrum*', or 'sworn to serve with iron armour', namely with mail coats, haubergeons and gambesons (*loricas et hauberiones et purpunctos*); Powicke, *Military Obligation*, 82–95, at 86–7, 90.

7. *Foedera*, I, 281; Stubbs, *Select Charters*, 362–5, with a translation in *EHD*, III, no. 33, 357–59.

8. *Statutes of the Realm*, I, 96–8; Stubbs, *Select Charters*, 463–9, provides the text and translation, while the statute is also translated in *EHD*, III, no. 59, 460–2.

9. Stubbs, *Select Charters*, 463.

10. C. Homans, *English Villagers of the Thirteenth Century* (Cambridge, Mass., 1942), 329.

11. As Edward II later instructed his local agents concerning the muster of 1322, they were 'to ordain and array all horsemen and footmen of that wapentake [Anyesty, Yorkshire] between the ages of sixteen and sixty in twenties, hundreds and constabularies, and to see that they were well armed according to the statute of Winchester' (*CCR, 1318–23*, 555).

12. Prestwich, *War, Politics and Finance*, 107; *idem, Armies and Warfare*, 171.

13. Prestwich, *Edward I*, 199–200, 195; R.A. Brown, H.M. Colvin and A.J. Taylor, ed., *The History of the King's Works*, I (London, 1963), 336, no. 1. In 1327 infantry from Queen Isabella's lands in Holderness sent on the Weardale campaign were equipped with 'short cloaks (courtpies) of one suit [i.e. colour]', as well as aketons, bascinets and gauntlets (*CPR, 1327–30*, 280).

14. Palgrave, *Documents*, I, 218–19.

15. Prestwich, *War, Politics and Finance*, 101.

16. Miller, *War in the North*, 9.

17. See pp. 41–2.

18. Morris, *Welsh Wars*, 34.

19. Prestwich, *Armies and Warfare*, 115–17.

20. Prestwich, *War, Politics and Finance*, 92.

21. Morris, *Welsh Wars*, 95–6; Prestwich, *Edward I*, 190.

22. Prestwich, *Edward I*, 221.

23. Prestwich, *War, Politics and Finance*, 93–5; *idem, Armies and Warfare*, 117.

24. Prestwich, *War, Politics and Finance*, 93.

25. Prestwich, *War, Politics and Finance*, 95.

26. Prestwich, *War, Politics and Finance*, 93.

27. Prestwich, *War, Politics and Finance*, 95.

28. Rishanger, 177; *The Chronicle of Bury St Edmunds, 1212–1301*, ed. A. Gransden (London, 1964), 143–4; Prestwich, *Edward I*, 393.

29. Guisborough, 325.

30. See, for example, R.K. Turvey, 'Defences of Twelfth-Century Deheubarth and the Castle Strategy of the Lord Rhys', *Archaeologia Cambrensis*, cxliv (1997 for 1995), 103–32; J.R. Kenyon, 'Fluctuating Frontiers: Normano-Welsh Castle Warfare, c. 1075–1240', *Château Gaillard*, xvii (1996), 119–26.

31. In 1259, for example, Llewelyn ap Gruffyd had invaded Dyfed with 240 mailed horses (*equos loricatos*) among his forces, and in 1262 he entered the lands of Roger Mortimer with a large number of infantry and 300 barded horse (*equitaturis armatis*) (*Annales Cambriae*, ed. J. Williams (London, 1860), 98; *Cal. Anc Corr. Wales*, 15).

32. Morris, *Welsh Wars*, 160–1; Prestwich, *Edward I*, 189. During September and October 1282 the Welsh castles of Ruthin, Dinas Bran and Denbigh all fell (Morris, *Welsh Wars*, 177–8). In January 1283 Dolwyddelan fell without a struggle, probably by prior negotiation (*King's Works*, I, 336, no. 1; Prestwich, *Edward I*, 195).

33. Morris, *Welsh Wars*, 192–3.

34. Prestwich, *Edward I*, 218–19.

35. S.E. Rees and C. Caple, *Dinefŵr Castle, Dryslwyn Castle* (Cadw, Cardiff, 1999), 15–17, and for the castle itself, 36–48.

36. Prestwich, *Edward I*, 180.

37. Morris, *Welsh Wars*, 110–38; Prestwich, *Edward I*, 179–81.

38. Morris, *Welsh Wars*, 165–6.

39. Guisborough, 219, who puts Tany's force at 7 bannerets and around 300 men-at-arms.

40. Rishanger, 101–2; *Flores*, III, 57; *Annales of Dunstable*, 292; *The Chronicle of Pierre de Langtoft*, ed. T. Wright, 2 vols (London, Rolls Series, 1886), II, 178–9; Prestwich, *Edward I*, 191–2; L. Beverley-Smith, 'The Death of Llewelyn ap Gruffydd: The Narrative Reconsidered', *Welsh History Review*, xi (1982), 200–13.

41. *Ann. Worcester*, 483, '*cum vellent fugere a facie arcus, impediebantur a mari fluctuante*'.

42. Guisborough, 251–2; *Book of Prests, 1294–5*, ed. E.B. Fryde (Oxford, 1962), xxxii–iii; Prestwich, *Edward I*, 221.

43. Prestwich, *Edward I*, 179. An interesting reflection on how important dense forest might be regarded as strategic protection is revealed by a charter of Edward, issued in 1259, in which he granted the men of Lyme in Cheshire the right to freely clear their woods, just as they had done before Earl Rannulf of Chester had placed the woods 'in defence' for the security of those parts. The earl was, it seems, seeking to protect the eastern flank of his palatinate, probably in the 1220s (G. Barraclough, *The Earldom and County Palatinate of Chester* (Oxford, 1953), 38–9).

44. Guisborough, 219; Rishanger, 57.

45. Langtoft, II, 180–1.

46. *Cal. Anc. Corr. Wales*, 131–2.

47. *King's Works*, I, 336, no. 1; Prestwich, *Edward I*, 195.

48. *Book of Prests*, xxxii–iv, xxxix–xli; M.C. Prestwich, 'A New Account of the Welsh Campaign of 1294–1295', *Welsh History Review*, vi (1973–4), 89–94 at 90.

49. See p. 140. Reginald de Grey had been Justiciar of Chester from 1281 and had played a key role in containing the ambitions of Dafydd before 1282. On the outbreak of war in 1282 Grey was appointed to a northern command at Chester, guarding Edward's left flank as the king moved along the coast from Flint to Rhuddlan, while in the campaigns of 1294 he led a division along the coastal route while the king marched on Conwy via Denbighshire (Prestwich, *Edward I*, 183, 189).

50. *Cal. Anc. Corr. Wales*, 108–9.

51. Guisborough, 220–1; *Chronicon Petroburgense*, ed. T. Stapleton (Camden Society, 1849), 57–8. For a discussion of the conflicting narratives, see Beverley-Smith, 'The Death of Llewelyn ap Gruffydd'; and Prestwich, *Edward I*, 193–4.

52. *Cal. Anc. Corr. Wales*, 83–4.

53. Guisborough, 220, who credits one Helias Walwayn with this plan.

54. Guisborough, 220–1, '*et ascendentibus nostris, sagittas et telas multa direxerunt*'.

55. Guisborough, 221,'*facta consertacione aliqua per sagittarios nostros qui inter equestres innixi erant, corruerant multi eo quod animose steterunt expectantes dominum suum*'.

56. *Nicholai Triveti Annales*, ed. T. Hog (London, 1845), 225; trans. Morris, *Welsh Wars*, 256.

57. Morris, *Welsh Wars*, 256–7.

58. J.G. Edwards, 'The Battle of Maes Moydog and the Welsh campaign of 1294–5', *EHR*, xxxix (1924), 1–12; and cf. *idem*, 'The Site of the Battle of "Meismeidoc", 1295 (Note)', *EHR*, xlvi (1931), 262–5.

59. Morris, *Welsh Wars*, 256; Prestwich, *War, Politics and Finance*, 108.

60. Guisborough, 221; *Liber recuperationis*, 29, '*et semper debent equites habere ballistarios vel sagittarios multos secum intermixtos*'. See pp. 107–8.

61. Prestwich, 'A New Account of the Welsh Campaign', 94. The translation is taken from Prestwich, *Edward I*, 223, but with the last sentence following that given in Prestwich, *War, Politics and Finance*, 108, and R.F. Walker, 'The Hagnaby Chronicle and the Battle of Maes Moydog', *Welsh History Review*, viii (1976–7), 125–38, at 129. This contains the important implication that the Welsh took the offensive: '*les Galeis attendirent si bien e alerent a nos genz tut de front, et furent les plus beaus Waleis et le plus hardix qe oncque nul homme veist*'.

62. *Littere Wallie*, ed. J.G. Edwards (Cardiff, 1940), 1–4.

63. M.C. Prestwich, 'Military Logistics: The Case of 1322', in *Armies, Chivalry and Warfare*, ed. M. Strickland, 276–88; F. Watson, *Under the Hammer: Edward I and Scotland, 1286–1306* (Edinburgh, 1998).

64. S. Cameron, 'Chivalry in Barbow's *Bruce*', in *Armies, Warfare and Chivalry*, ed. Strickland, 13–29, at 15–19.

65. Apart from Largs in 1263, the last major military venture had been Alexander II's Galloway expedition of 1235 (G.W.S. Barrow, *Robert Bruce and the Community of the Realm of Scotland* (Edinburgh, 1988), 72).

66. *Lanercost*, 176; trans. Maxwell, 139–40.

67. Guisborough, 194.

68. Langtoft, 248–9.

69. Barrow, *Robert Bruce*, 100–1.

70. Rishanger, 441–2; Barrow, *Robert Bruce*, 84–5, 113.

71. *Lanercost*, 176; trans. Maxwell, 139–40.

72. For a full account of the battle, see Barrow, *Robert the Bruce*, 86–8.

73. Verbruggen, *Art of War*, 122, 169–70; Rogers, 'The Military Revolutions of the Hundred Years War', 241–78, at 247–8.

74. D. Adams, 'Archery in the Highlands', *Military Illustrated*, cxi (August, 1997), 44. The author comments that these are 'simple bows, not longbows', but the nature of the carving makes such a distinction extremely problematic. See W.D.H. Sellar, 'Sueno's Stone and Its Interpreters', in *Moray: Province and People* (Edinburgh, 1993), 97–116.

75. See p. 75.

76. *Regesta Regum Scottorum, I. The Acts of Malcolm IV, King of Scots, 1153–1165*, ed. G.W.S. Barrow (Edinburgh, 1960), 55–6; *Regesta Regum Scottorum, II. The Acts of William I, King of Scots, 1165–1214*, ed. G.W.S. Barrow (Edinburgh, 1971), 55–7.

77. *Reg. Scott. I.*, 152, 284, where Malcolm grants 2 ploughgates in Edman to Geoffrey de Melville for the service of one archer with a horse in the army (1153–65); *Reg. Scott. II.*, 389, where in 1198 William grants Walter, son of Walter Scott, Allardyce (Mearns) in feu and heritage for the service of one archer with horse and haubergel; *ibid.*, II, 452, where in 1211 Ranulf the Falconer receives Kingower in Gowrie for personal service, or if he cannot serve, for the service of one archer in the army.

78. The note is made in the margin of a sheet of coats of arms in Paris's *Liber Additamentorum* (BM, MS Cotton Nero D I, f.170a; T. Tremlett, 'The Matthew Paris Shields', *Aspilogia*, II (1967), 3–86 at 5); '*Pedites vero erant expediti et armis decenter communiti scilicet securibus peracutis, lanceis et arcubus, et animosa valde parati pro domino constanter vivere vel mori, vincere vel vinci reputantes mortem martirum et salvationem*'.

79. Anderson, II, 628, 630.

80. *Rotuli Scaccarii Regum Scotorum*, ed. J. Stuart and G. Burnett, I, 1264–1359 (Edinburgh, 1878), 5, where a payment of 2½ marks was also recorded to 'one crossbowman for that year'. At Aberdeen one William *balistarius* received money 'to purchase staves (*baculos*) and other things which pertain to his office', suggesting he was a maker and repairer of crossbows and not simply a crossbowman. He may be the same William mentioned at Roxburgh, who, together with Imbart, received cow hides '*ad machinas*' (*ibid.*, 12, 30).

81. *Rot. Scacc. Scot.*, I, 28.

82. *The Roll of Arms of the Princes, Barons and Knights who attended King Edward I to the Siege of Caerlaverock*, ed. and trans. T. Wright (London, 1864), 32; *The Siege of Carlaverock*, ed. and trans. N.H. Nicolas (London, 1828), 79–81.

83. S. Cruden, *The Scottish Castle* (Edinburgh and London, 1960), 34. The four round towers at Rothesay were added to the existing twelfth-century shell keep, which had been breached by the Norse in the siege of 1230 (*ibid.*, 29–36).

84. C.J. Tabraham, *Kildrummy Castle* (Historic Scotland, Edinburgh, 1986), 18–26. It is possible that the twin-towered gatehouse was added by Edward I's masons between 1296 and 1306, when Robert Bruce's brother Neil held it unsuccessfully against the English (*ibid.*, 6, 8–11, 23–4).

85. At Dirleton, which fell to Edward I in 1298, the surviving thirteenth-century towers in the south-west angle are defended by a number of loops, some with splayed bases (D. Grove, *Dirleton Castle* (Historic Scotland, Edinbugh, 1995), 5, 20–1, 24–5; Cruden, *The Scottish Castle*, 80).

86. *Argyll Castles in the Care of Historic Scotland: Extracts from RCAHMS Inventories of Argyll, Vols I, II and VII* (Edinburgh, 1997), 35–48.

87. W.D. Simpson, 'Skipness Castle', *Transactions of the Glasgow Archaeological Society*, n.s. xv, pt 3 (1966), 106; *Argyll Castles*, 9–26.

88. *Political Songs*, 170.

89. Guisborough, 328.

90. Barrow, *Robert Bruce*, 120.

91. *Calendar of Documents relating to Scotland*, ed. J. Bain, 4 vols (London, 1881–8); vol. V ed. R.R. Sharpe (London, 1901), II, 1432; IV, 474.

92. Rishanger, 383.

93. For a full discussion, see A.A.M. Duncan, 'The Seal of William Wallace', in *The Wallace Book*, ed. E. Cowan (Edinburgh, 2005).

94. For a discussion of Wallace's background see A. Young and M.J. Stead, *In the Footsteps of William Wallace* (Stroud, 2002), 21–39. For the wider context of Wallace's seal see P.D.A. Harvey, 'Personal Seals in Thirteenth-Century England', in *Church and Chronicle in the Middle Ages: Essays Presented to John Taylor*, ed. I. Wood and G. Loud (Hambledon, 1991), 117–27.

95. *Harry's Wallace*, ed. M.P. McDairmid, 2 vols (Edinburgh, 1968), I, 64–5 (Bk IV, ll. 548–54).

96. *Ibid.*, ll. 570–8.

97. Hence, for example, the comment of W.M. Mackenzie, *The Battle of Bannockburn. A Study of Medieval Warfare* (Glasgow, 1913), 77–8, that in the opening stages of Bannockburn 'the English longbow showed its native superiority'.

98. Adams, 'Archery in the Highlands', 46.

99. See Ch. 18, pp. 343–53.

100. Prestwich, *War, Politics and Finance*, 68–9, 87, 94–5.

101. Prestwich, *Edward I*, 479–81.

102. G.W.S. Barrow, *The Anglo-Norman Era in Scottish History* (Oxford, 1980), 161, 165; A.A.M. Duncan, *Scotland: The Making of the Kingdom* (Edinburgh, 1975), 387; *Regesta Regum Scottorum, V. The Acts of Robert I, King of Scots, 1306–1329*, ed. A.A.M. Duncan (Edinburgh, 1988), 51–4. A thirteenth-century writ indicates that service was owed at 24 hours' notice for 40 days.

103. *Scotichronicon* (Book XI, c.28). The overtly classical names given by Bower to these officers – quaternion, decurion, chiliarch – are, however, most improbable.

104. Barrow, *Robert Bruce*, 143, estimates each schiltrom as containing about 1,000 men. For the term 'schiltrum' (also used by Barbour

105. Guisborough, 327; trans. J.E. Morris, *Bannockburn* (Cambridge, 1914), 44.

106. Langtoft, 313.

107. For discussion and further references see M.J. Strickland, 'Military Technology and Conquest; the Anomaly of Anglo-Saxon England', *Anglo-Norman Studies*, xix (1996), 353–82.

108. *Lanercost*, 191; trans. Maxwell, 166.

109. John Fordun, *Chronica gentis Scotorum*, ed. W.F. Skene, 2 vols (Edinburgh, 1871–2), I, 330, II, 323.

110. Guisborough, 327.

111. R. Marchionni, *Sienese Battles (I). Montaperti* (Siena, 1996); Oman, *Art of War*, I, 496–515, and cf. 15–26 for the predominance of cavalry at the battle of the Marchefeld in 1278 between the German Emperor Rudolf and Ottokar of Bohemia; France, *Western Warfare*, 176–7.

112. Guisborough, 328.

113. Guisborough, 328.

114. Guisborough, 328.

115. *Political Songs*, 176; and cf. Fordun, *Chronica*, I, 331.

116. Rishanger, 441–2; *Lanercost*, 194; trans. Maxwell, 170.

117. *Political Songs*, 223.

118. Prestwich, *War, Politics and Finance*, 31–2, 108–9, 171–5; *idem*, *Edward I*, 382–6, 398–400.

119. Vale, *Angevin Legacy*, 202; *Rôles Gascons*, III, cxlix–cl.

120. *Rôles Gascons*, III, clxvii–clxix.

121. Prestwich, *Edward I*, 381. For a detailed narrative of the war see *Rôles Gascons*, III, cxxiv–clxxxii; Prestwich, *Edward I*, 376–86, 398–9; and for analysis of strategy, logistics and finance see Vale, *Angevin Legacy*, 200–15.

122. Vale, *Angevin Legacy*, 202.

123. Guisborough, 260–4.

124. Guisborough, 261.

125. Guisborough, 262.

126. Rishanger, 166–7, agrees that Artois attacked the English as they left a wood 3 miles from Bellegarde, but says that the English were in two divisions only, and that once the fighting started the Earl of Lincoln withdrew with the second division, leaving St John hopelessly outnumbered.

127. Guisborough, 263; Rishanger, 166–7; Langtoft, II, 282–3.

128. Guisborough, 263.

129. N.B. Lewis, 'The English Force in Flanders, August–November, 1297', in *Studies in Medieval History Presented to F.M. Powicke*, ed. R.W. Hunt, W.A. Pantin and R.W. Southern (Oxford, 1948), 310–18, at 311–12, and 317–18 for a detailed table of individual contingents from Welsh areas.

130. Lodewyk van Velthem, *Spiegel Historiaal*, Bk IV, c.5, translated in D.L. Evans, 'Some Notes on the Principality of Wales in the Time of the Black Prince', *Transactions of the Honourable Society of Cymmrodorion* (1925–6), 25–110, at 46 n. 1.

131. Prestwich, *War, Politics and Finance*, 32.

132. Guisborough, 316.

CHAPTER 10

1. A.A.M. Duncan, 'The War of the Scots, 1306–23', *TRHS*, 6th ser., ii (1992), 125–51.

2. John Barbour, *The Bruce*, ed. A.A.M. Duncan (Edinburgh, 1997), 410, n. 109–19.

3. Barrow, *Robert Bruce*, 207; C. McNamee, *The Wars of the Bruces. Scotland, Ireland and England, 1306–1328* (Edinburgh, 1997), 61–2; *Bruce*, 410 nn. 109–19; 428 n. 466.

4. Barrow, *Robert Bruce*, 208; *Bruce*, 416 n. 244.

5. *Bruce*, 296–309 (VIII, ll. 123–354).

6. *Bruce*, 308 n. 355–65 and n. 372.

7. T. Miller, 'The Site of the New Park in relation to the Battle of Bannockburn', *SHR*, xii (1915), 60–75; *idem, The Site of the Battle of Bannockburn* (Historical Association Pamphlet, London, 1931). The evidence is well reviewed by Barrow, *Robert Bruce*, 209–17, with important further comments by Duncan, *Bruce*, 440–7.

8. The close proximity of the major abbey of Cambuskenneth may in part explain this.

9. *Bruce*, 420 (XI, ll. 303–8).

10. *Bruce*, 422 (XI, ll. 365–80).

11. The course of this great battle has been told many times, with specific studies including R. White, *A History of the Battle of Bannockburn* (Edinburgh, 1871); Mackenzie, *The Battle of Bannockburn*; Morris, *Bannockburn*; A. Nusbacher, *The Battle of Bannockburn, 1314* (Stroud, 2000); P. Armstrong, *Bannockburn 1314* (Botley, 2002). The best account, however, remains that of Barrow, *Robert Bruce*, 202–32, to which the following paragraphs are indebted.

12. Moray's position is disputed. He may have come out of the New Park to prevent Clifford's force from skirting past St Ninian's Kirk, but Duncan, *Bruce*, 440–4, has recently argued that Moray's division was much further south, and based in the Torwood. By this interpretation Moray came out not of the New Park but out of the Torwood, to prevent Clifford outflanking him and cutting him off from the main Scots force.

13. *Vita Edwardi Secundi*, ed. N. Denholm-Young (London, 1957), 51.

14. The *Vita Edwardi*, 51–2, notes that the veterans and more experienced knights, including the Earl of Gloucester, advised against fighting the next day, not least because the army was seriously in need of rest, but that 'this practical and honourable advice was rejected by the younger men as idle and cowardly'.

15. Langtoft, II, 178–9.

16. *Scalacronica*, 142.

17. *Vita Edwardi*, 52.

18. *Bruce*, 470–1 (XII, ll. 435–7).

19. *Bruce*, 470–3 (XII, ll. 477–93).

20. *Lanercost*, 225; trans. Maxwell, 207.

21. John de Trokelowe, *Chronica monasterii S. Albani*, ed. H.T. Riley (London, 1866), 84; *Bruce*, 471 note to l. 437. The annals (1307–22) ascribed to John de Trokelowe, a monk of St Albans, may in fact have been written by William Rishanger, another chronicler of that abbey (Gransden, *Historical Writing in England*, II, 5–60).

22. Bruce seemingly had two small units of cavalry, one under Sir James Douglas, attached to Edward Bruce's division, and the other, led by Sir Robert Keith, the Scots marshal, attached to the king's own division.

23. *Bruce*, 482 (XIII, ll. 50–75).

24. *Bruce*, 484 (XIII, ll. 76–81). He continues, 'They behaved boldly and well, for after the enemy's archers were scattered . . . who were more numerous than they were by a large number, so that they [the English] did not fear their firing, they [the Scots archers] grew so bold that they thought they would completely defeat their enemies' (*Bruce*, 484 (XIII ll. 82–8)).

25. Mackenzie, *The Battle of Bannockburn*, 79, n. 1.

26. The view of Duncan, *Bruce*, 482, note to 1, 41–9.

27. Le Baker, 8 (and 185 for Stowe's rendering).

28. Le Baker, 8 and 186 for Stowe's rendering: 'Almost three hundreth men of armes were slaine in that place, our archers killing manie of them, who, seeing the Scottes cruellie bent upon our horsemen fallen in the ditche, shotte theire arrows with a high compass, that they might fall betwixt the armour of their enemies and which was all in vayne; and when they shotte right foorth, they slewe few Scottes, by reason of their armed breasts, but manie of the Englishmen, by reason of their naked backs.'

29. Orpen, *Ireland under the Normans*, IV, 200–6; Prestwich, *Armies and Warfare*, 318. For the context of the battle of Faughart or Fochart (Louth), see McNamee, *The Wars of the Bruces*, 184–6.

30. *Lanercost*, 225; trans. Maxwell, 208.

31. *Scalacronica*, 142; trans. Maxwell, 56.

32. Barrow, *Robert Bruce*, 228–32.

33. *Vita Edwardi*, 55. The *Annales Londonienses*, ed. W. Stubbs, *Chronicles of the Reigns of Edward I and Edward II*, I (Rolls Series, London, 1882), 231, notes that few among the foot and squires were slain, but the toll of knights was heavy.

34. *Lanercost*, 228; trans. Maxwell, 210.

35. *Bruce*, 488, says that when Edward II had initially approached the Scottish positions, he took counsel as to whether to stop and encamp or to attack directly, but the van knew nothing of this and attacked the Park. Within Clifford's division, a dispute arose between Beaumont and Sir Thomas Gray as to whether to wait for Moray's division to come on or to attack it at once. Gloucester and Hereford engaged in a bitter dispute about who was to lead the van even as the Scots were surging towards them, while Gloucester's impetuous charge to his death may well have been precipitated by the king's accusation of cowardice when the earl had advised caution in attacking the Scots formations (*Vita Edwardi*, 52–3).

36. *Vita Edwardi*, 54–6.

37. Barrow, *Robert Bruce*, 208.

38. R. Nicholson, *Scotland: The Later Middle Ages* (Edinburgh, 1974), 109.

39. *Bruce*, 258–60 (VII, ll. 1–52, 53–74).

40. *Bruce*, 278–80 (VI, ll. 438–54), and for other versions of the tale of an attack on Bruce, *ibid.*, 214 n. 495. In another version of this story Bruce is approached by three men he knows to be traitors; he seizes his page's crossbow – here the missile weapon is that only befitting a servant – and shoots the leading man through the eye and into his brain, before dispatching the other two with his sword (*Bruce*, 216–22 (V, ll. 523–658)).

41. *Bruce*, 260 (VII, ll. 53–78).

42. Barrow, *Robert Bruce*, 248.

43. *Bruce*, 361–3 (X, ll. 40–74); Barrow, *Robert Bruce*, 254–7.

44. *Bruce*, 596–604 (XVI, ll. 335–493).

45. *Registrum Magni Sigilli Regum Scottorum*, ed. J.M. Thomson *et al.*, 11 vols (1882–1914), I, 448–50; Barrow, *Robert Bruce*, 280, 284.

46. *Lanercost*, 223; *Bruce* (X, ll. 473–90).

47. *Lanercost*, 230–1; trans. Maxwell, 215; *Bruce*, 656 (XVII, ll. 815–26).

48. *Scalacronica*, 144; trans. Maxwell, 58. For the Scots' siege, *Bruce*, 616–27 (XVII, ll. 1–200). When the town was taken by surprise, some of its garrison, including 24 men-at-arms, 13 hobelars, 29 crossbowmen and 19 foot-archers, managed to escape back to England (*ibid.*, 622 n. 126, and cf. 626 n. 200).

49. *Bruce*, 628 (XVII, ll. 217–39).

50. *Bruce*, 626 n. 200. The size of Edward's main army is discussed by Duncan, *Bruce*, 630 n. 283. Of over 24,000 infantry summoned, some 8,000 were at the siege in late August but this figure quickly fell by early September to around 5,500, while the cavalry may have numbered some 1,340.

51. *Bruce*, 626 n. 200.

52. *Bruce*, 634, 636 (XVII, ll. 347–60, 382–3).

53. *Bruce*, 656 (XVII, ll. 815–26).

54. *Isle of Bute, Abstracts of Charters and Documents*, no. 2. I am grateful to Dr Steven Boardman for this reference.

55. Adams, 'Archery in the Highlands', 44–6.

56. For a discussion of the nature of military service under King Robert, see *Reg. Scott. V*, 48–54.

57. *Acts of the Parliaments of Scotland*, ed. T. Thomson and C. Innes, 12 vols (Edinburgh, 1814–75), I, 113; *Reg. Scott. V*, 414.

58. *APS*, I, 113–14; *Reg. Scott. V*, 414 (no. 139, c. 27), and 54. For the comparable subsistence and non-monetary economy of much of Wales beyond the Marches, see Prestwich, *Edward I*, 171.

59. Barrow, *Robert Bruce*, 287–9; *Reg. Scott. V*, 48–54.

60. *Reg. Scott. V*, 294 (no. 5), 537 (no. 276); Barrow, *Robert Bruce*, 287.

61. Barrow, *Robert Bruce*, 287.

62. Nicholson, *Scotland. The Later Middle Ages*, 110, who notes that Bruce's surviving charters suggest he obtained the services of only some 40 knights and 40 archers by new tenures; *Reg. Scott. V*, 48, corrects this to 43 known archers.

63. *Reg. Scott. V*, 50.

64. *Reg. Scott. V*, 420–1 (no. 143). Cf. *ibid.*, 544 (no. 286), for a grant to John de Mondforde for a similar render of arrows; and 381 (no.

105), where a charter of 1316 grants William Turnbull land for a still more token render of 'one large arrow'.

65. W.S. Reid, 'Trade, Traders and Scottish Independence', *Speculum*, xxix (1954), 210–22; Nicholson, *Scotland. The Later Middle Ages*, 15, 107.

66. The most detailed recent study of Bruce's highly lucrative policy of levying protection money in northern England is provided by McNamee, *The Wars of the Bruces*; see also J.F. Willard, 'The Scotch Raids and the Fourteenth-Century Taxation of Northern England', *University of Colorado Studies*, v, no. 4 (1908), 240–2; J. Scammell, 'Robert I and the North of England', *EHR*, lxxiii (1958), 385–403.

67. Jean Le Bel, *Chronique de Jean le Bel*, ed. J. Viard and E. Déprez, 2 vols (Paris, 1904–5), I, 51–2; trans. Rogers, *War, Cruel and Sharp*, 14; and cf. *EHD*, IV, no. 11, 59–60, for the translation by Lord Berners.

68. Barrow, *Robert Bruce*, 239–40; *Bruce*, 642–4.

69. *Lanercost*, 242; trans. Maxwell, 231. For a detailed discussion of the Boroughbridge campaign see J.R. Maddicott, *Thomas of Lancaster, 1307–1322* (Oxford, 1970), 303–11.

70. *Lanercost*, 242; trans. Maxwell, 231.

71. Morris, *Bannockburn*, 94–6.

72. *Bruce*, 630–1, n. 283.

73. *Lanercost*, 242–3; trans. Maxwell, 232; *The Brut*, ed. F.W.D. Brie (Early English Text Society, original series, cxxxi, London, 1906), 218, notes that troops were also raised by the sheriff of York Sir Simon Ward.

74. Gransden, *Historical Writing in England*, 14 and n. 75.

75. *Lanercost*, 243; trans. Maxwell, 232.

76. *Brut*, 217. Lack of support for Lancaster is indicated by the fact that one of Harclay's commanders was William Latimer, formerly one of Lancaster's retainers (Maddicott, *Thomas of Lancaster*, 311).

77. Le Baker, 13–14; Gransden, *Historical Writing in England*, II, 39.

78. *Lanercost*, 243; trans. Maxwell, 233.

79. *Lanercost*, 243–4; trans. Maxwell, 233.

80. *Brut*, 219, 'thoo might men seen Archieres drawen ham in that on side and in that othere'.

81. A.E. Prince, 'The Importance of the Campaign of 1327', *EHR*, l (1935), 299–302, at 300.

82. *Rot. Scot.*, I, 208. Le Bel notes that the majority of the men-at-arms were mounted 'on small hackneys (*sur petites hagnenees*)' (I, 51–2).

83. Le Bel, I, 52; Rogers, *War, Cruel and Sharp*, 14.

84. Le Bel, I, 65.

85. *Bruce*, 717.

86. *Bruce*, 727–31; Le Bel, I, 70; Nicholson, *Edward III and the Scots*, 26–41; Rogers, *War, Cruel and Sharp*, 19–23.

87. Le Bel, I, 39–42; Rogers, *Wars of Edward III*, 4–5. Le Bel's figure may be exaggerated but the *Brut* records no fewer than 80 slain and buried under a stone in Fossgate (*Brut*, 250). For the enquiry after the incident, *Foedera*, II, ii, 707.

88. *Chronicon Henrici Knighton*, ed. J. Lumby, 2 vols (Rolls Series, London, 1889–95), I, 460.

89. Prince, 'The Importance of the Campaign of 1327', 299–302.
90. *Rot. Scot.*, I, 208, '*et quod omnes et singuli, tam magnates quam alii, si conflictum cum ipsius Scotis habere contigerit, si expedire viderint, pedes pugnent*'.
91. Le Bel, I, 50.
92. Cf. C.J. Rogers, 'The Offensive/Defensive in Medieval Strategy', in *From Crécy to Mohacs: Warfare in the Late Middle Ages (1346–1526), Acta of the XXnd Colloquium of the International*

Commission of Military History (Vienna, 1996), 158–71, at 158–61; Oman, *Art of War*, II, 246–51.
93. *Bruce*, 719 (XIX, l. 403); Prince, 'The Importance of the Campaign of 1327', 301. The earliest illustration of a cannon appears in Walter Milmete's *De Officiis Regum*, presented to the young Edward that same year. See T.F. Tout, 'Firearms in England in the Fourteenth Century', *EHR*, xxvi (1911), 666–702.
94. *Brut*, 281; Prince, 'The Importance of the Campaign of 1327', 301.

CHAPTER 11

1. Ascham, *Toxophilus*, 51.
2. Rogers, *War, Cruel and Sharp*, 28–9.
3. For detailed accounts of the campaign see Nicholson, *Edward III and the Scots*, 75–90; and Rogers, *War, Cruel and Sharp*, 27–47.
4. *Gesta Edwardi de Carnarvon auctore canonico Bridlingtoniensi cum continuatione ad* AD *1377*, ed. W. Stubbs, *Chronicles of the Reign of Edward I and Edward II*, II (Rolls Series, London, 1883), 102, 106. Rogers, *War, Cruel and Sharp*, 33 and n. 32, notes that Edward III supplied Beaumont with £500, enough to pay 1,000 archers 2*d* a day for two months. For the overall strength of the English force see *ibid.*, 34 n. 38.
5. Bridlington, 104; le Baker, 49; and for collected reference to the importance of the archers at Kinghorn, Rogers, 'The Efficacy of the English Longbow', 236 n. 11.
6. *Andrew of Wyntoun's Orygynale Cronykil of Scotland*, ed. D. Laing, 3 vols (Edinburgh, 1872–9), II, 386. It seems likely that Beaumont and Balliol had been counting on the timely defection of Mar, but were disappointed in this (Bridlington, 104–5; Rogers, *War, Cruel and Sharp*, 34–5 and notes 39 and 40). For a discussion of the strategic objectives of the English force see Rogers, *War, Cruel and Sharp*, 36–8.
7. *Brut*, 278; Robert of Avesbury, *De gestis mirabilibus regis Edwardi tertii*, ed. E.M. Thompson (Rolls Series, London, 1889), 297.
8. Bridlington, 106, '*dispositis itaque turmis sagittariis suis, ut collaterales cuneos hostium invaderunt*'. The translation of Bridlington is taken here from *EHD, 1327–1485*, ed. A.R. Myers (London, 1969), no.7, 54–6. Bradbury, *The Medieval Archer*, 88, is cautious about placing the archers on the wings, but comparison with Bridlington's fuller comments about Edward III's deployment at Halidon make a flanking position for the archers at Dupplin very probable.
9. *Thomae Walsingham, quodam monachi Sancti Albani Historia Anglicana*, ed. H.T. Riley, 2 vols (Rolls Series, 1863–4), I, 194.
10. *Brut*, 276, who notes these weapons were given by Balliol to 'the most strongest of his company'; Rogers, *Wars of Edward III*, 27; *Scalacronica*, 159; trans. Maxwell, 89.
11. Rogers, *War, Cruel and Sharp*, 42 and n. 92.
12. Avesbury, 296; Nicholson, *Edward III and the Scots*, 80.
13. *Lanercost*, 268; Bridlington, 106; *Brut*, 278, alone has the Scots in three divisions.
14. *Brut*, 278; and for this incident in other versions of the *Brut*,

15. *Lanercost*, 268; trans. Maxwell, 270; cf. Rogers, *War, Cruel and Sharp*, 44 n. 103, for the alternative reading of '*non poterant se juvare*' as 'not able to help themelves'.
16. *Lanercost*, trans. Maxwell, 271. *Lanercost* is here followed by Wyntoun, II, 388, who similarly mentions Stafford as playing the key role in steadying the English line.
17. Wyntoun, II, 388.
18. *Scalacronica*, 160; trans. Maxwell, 91; le Baker, 49.
19. Wyntoun, II, 388; trans. Rogers, *The Wars of Edward III*, 29.
20. Bridlington, 106; *EHD*, IV, 56.
21. *Scalacronica*, 160; trans. Maxwell, 91; Walsingham, I, 194.
22. Bridlington, 106.
23. Bridlington, 107; *Lanercost*, 268; trans. Maxwell, 271, 'a marvellous thing happened that day, such as was never heared of or seen in any previous battle, to wit, that the pile of dead was greater in height from the earth toward the sky than one whole spear length'.
24. Bridlington, 107; cf. *Scalacronica*, 91. Wyntoun, II, 388, reckoned that over a thousand had perished in the great pile 'where a drop of blood was never drawn'.
25. Rogers, *War, Cruel and Sharp*, 45 and n. 113 (unpublished *Brut*, Corpus Christi College, Oxford, MS 78, f.171v); *Anonimalle Brut*, 150; Knighton, I, 463; *Historea Aurea*, 560.
26. Bridlington, 106; Wyntoun, II, 386.
27. Wyntoun, II, 385: 'Bot swa suld nane do, that were wys: Wys men suld drede thare innymys; For lychtlynes and succwdry Drawys in defowle comownaly'.
28. Wyntoun, II, 386–7, 'for swa suld men lychtly Oouercum thame; for qwha to the flycht Hym settis, tynys hart and mycht'.
29. Wyntoun, II, 389:
    Hereby men may ensawmpill ta,
    That bettyre is ordynans in till fycht
    Sum tyme, than owthir streynth or mycht.
    As Caton sayis, off othire thyng
    Men may offtys mak mendyng,
    Quhen men trespast has; bot in fycht
    Quhen that men rewlyd ar noucht rycht,
    Men sall it noucht welle mend agayne,
    For in the neck folowys the payne.
30. *Foedera*, II, ii, 864.

31. Nicholson, *Edward III and the Scots*, 131–8; and Rogers, *War, Cruel and Sharp*, 48–76, for a valuable analysis of the strategic context of the battle.

32. According to Bridlington, 114, this force consisted of 500 men-at-arms 'along with archers and foot-soldiers'.

33. Bridlington, 114; *Lanercost*, 274.

34. Bridlington, 114: '*sagittarii alis singulis deputantur*'.

35. Bridlington, 114–15; *EHD*, IV, 58.

36. Bridlington, 115.

37. Le Baker, 51; see p. 181.

38. Rogers, *War, Cruel and Sharp*, 70.

39. While Bradbury, *The Medieval Archer*, 89, refers to the Bridlington chronicle, his account strangely does not take into account what either it or the *Brut* says concerning the wings of archers for each division, and in his diagram of the battle only two wings of archers are depicted, on the extreme flanks of Edward's army.

40. *Brut*, 285; and cf. *Cleopatra Brut*, f.182v, trans. Rogers, *Wars of Edward III*, 38, 'each division of the English army had two wings of good archers'.

41. Nicholson, *Edward III and the Scots*, 133.

42. The sources, which are in disagreement here, are discussed in *The Anonimalle Chronicle 1307–1334*, ed. W.R. Childs and J. Taylor, *Yorkshire Archaeological Society Record Series*, cxlvii (Leeds, 1991), 58–9. The *Brut*, 283–4, gives a detailed breakdown of the composition of each of the Scottish divisions.

43. Bridlington, 115; *Polychronicon Radulphi Higden*, ed. C. Babington and J.R. Lumby, 9 vols (Rolls Series, London, 1865–86), viii, 329, who notes that the Scots fought 'alle on fote and ungert'.

44. *Chronicon domini Walteri de Hemingburgh de Gestis Regum Angliae*, ed. H.C. Hamilton, 2 vols (London, 1848), I, 308–9, an account which gives the constituent elements of the Scottish force in remarkable detail. According to this, the first division contained 300 men-at-arms (*armati*) and 2,200 more lightly equipped levies (*de communitate leviter armati*); the second, 11 knights and 300 men-at-arms and 3,000 infantry; the third, 17 knights, 300 men-at-arms and 4,400 infantry; the fourth, 12 knights, 200 men-at-arms and 4,000 infantry. The *Brut*, 283–4, says they had four divisions, then goes on to list the constituents of five 'wards', dividing the first division into two.

45. *Anonimalle*, 167. The Bridlington chronicler has echoes of this when he has Douglas say to the Scots, 'Now another fortune had led them [the English] into our borders, as it were prisoners, behind them a fine town defended by warlike men, on the right hand a wide deep sea, on the left hand the hollow of the River Tweed which the rising tide fills to the margin of its banks' (Bridlington, 115, trans. *EHD*, IV, 58). Cf. Hemingburgh, 309.

46. Thomas Burton, *Chronica Monasterii de Melsa*, ed. E.A. Bond, 2 vols (Rolls Series, London, 1866–8), ii, 370.

47. Wyntoun, II, 399–401; trans. Rogers, *Wars of Edward III*, 38. The marsh is now drained, and the land turned to arable, though in 1333 Halidon Hill was wasteland; D. Smurfitt, *The Battlefield of Halidon Hill*, National Army Museum Report, 2–3, 10.

48. *Lanercost*, 274.

49. *Cleopatra Brut*, f.182v; trans. Rogers, *Wars of Edward III*, 38; Nicholson, *Edward III and the Scots*, 135, citing BM, MS Harl. 4690, f.82v, 'as thik as motes on the sonne beme'.

50. *Lanercost*, 274; trans. Maxwell, 279. Cf. Bridlington, 116, trans. *EHD*, IV, 58, 'but they could bear neither the storm of arrows nor the weapons of the knights, and soon they took to flight'; the two versions of the *Brut* in Higden, *Polychronicon*, 329, 'Englisshe men archers beet doun the Scottes', and the Scots were 'oppresseded by the archers of Ynglonde'.

51. Nicholson, *Edward III and the Scots*, 135 n. 3.

52. Bridlington, 116, trans. *EHD*, IV, 58.

53. *Cleopatra Brut*, f.182v; trans. Rogers, *Wars of Edward III*, 38.

54. *Lanercost*, 274; trans. Maxwell, 280.

55. *Cleopatra Brut*, f.182v; trans. Rogers, *Wars of Edward III*, 38.

56. *Lanercost*, 274; trans. Maxwell, 280, where the figure of 36,320 foot-soldiers slain may be safely regarded as an exaggeration! Bridlington, 116; trans. *EHD*, IV, 59, says 7 earls, 25 bannerets and 47 knights were killed.

57. *Melsa*, II, 370; Bridlington, 116; Hemingburgh, 309.

58. A. Grant, 'Disaster at Neville's Cross: the Scottish Point of View', in *The Battle of Neville's Cross, 1346*, ed. D. Rollason and M. Prestwich (Stamford, 1998), 15–35, at 17–18.

59. *Knighton's Chronicle, 1337–1396*, ed. and trans. G.H. Martin (Oxford, 1995), 68–9. Cf. *Anonimalle Chronicle*, 25–6.

60. *Rot. Scot.*, I, 668–73.

61. Knighton, 70–1; le Baker, 87. The payment was due on the day after the battle, which of course freed them from the need to pay up.

62. Knighton, 70–1, who again notes 'for they believed that there was none in that country able to resist them, because all were at the siege of Calais'.

63. The campaign and battle of Neville's Cross has received extensive treatment in secondary works, notably: R. White, 'The Battle of Neville's Cross', *Archaeologia Aeliana* (1856), 271–303; Oman, *Art of War*, II, 149–51; A.H. Burne, 'The Battle of Neville's Cross', *Durham University Journal*, x (1948–9) and *idem, More Battlefields in England* (London, 1952), 178–89; Nicholson, *Scotland. The Later Middle Ages*, 144–7; J. Sumption, *The Hundred Years War: Trial by Battle* (London, 1990), 550–4; De Vries, *Infantry Warfare*, 176–87; C.J. Rogers, 'The Scottish Invasion of 1346', *Northern History*, xxxiv (1998), 51–69, which analyses much of the existing literature and makes use of three unpublished chronicle accounts; *The Battle of Neville's Cross*, ed. Rollason and Prestwich, which in addition to interpretative essays contains a valuable selection of primary sources in translation; and M. Penman, *David II, 1329–71* (East Linton, 2004).

64. *Anonimalle Chronicle*, 26. For Rokeby see R. Frame, 'Thomas Rokeby, Sheriff of Yorkshire, Custodian of David II', in *The Battle of Neville's Cross*, ed. Rollason and Prestwich, 50–6. In 1327, during the Weardale campaign, it was Rokeby who had located the position of the Scots army, thereby earning a knighthood and lands of an annual value of £100, which Edward III had promised to the first person to bring him this intelligence (*ibid.*, 52).

65. M.C. Prestwich, 'The English at the Battle of Neville's Cross', in Rollason and Prestwich, ed., *The Battle of Neville's Cross*, 1–14 at 8–9.

66. *Anonimalle Chronicle*, 24–5; *Lanercost*, 348–9. For Douglas see M.H. Brown, 'The Development of Scottish Border Lordship, 1332–1358', *Historical Research*, lxx (1997), 1–22.

67. *Melsa*, III, 61.

68. After the battle Neville replaced the existing cross by a new, more lavish cross to commemorate the victory. This was itself destroyed in 1589, but descriptions of it survive. For the cross and suggested reconstructions see Butler, *The Battle of Neville's Cross*, 23; J.L. Drury, 'The Monument at Neville's Cross, C. Durham', and G.A.L. Johnson, 'The Neville's Cross Monument: a Physical and Geological Report', both in *The Battle of Neville's Cross*, ed. Rollason and Prestwich, 78–96, 97–111.

69. For the Scots army see Grant, 'Disaster at Neville's Cross', 21–2. An estimate of around 12,000 would accord with the most plausible chronicle estimate for the army in 1333.

70. Knighton, 68–9.

71. Wyntoun, II, 475.

72. For the topography of the area see R.A. Lomas, 'The Durham Landscape and the Battle of Neville's Cross', in *The Battle of Neville's Cross*, ed. Rollason and Prestwich, 66–77.

73. This is the site suggested by Burne, *More Battlefields of England*, 118, but see the important caveats of Prestwich, 'The English at the Battle of Neville's Cross', 9–10, as to locating the battle with such precision and on the dangers of Burne's (in)famous 'inherent military probability'. Prestwich notes, however, that 'the steep fall down to the Browney Valley on the west, and to Flass Vale on the east, surely helped to define the best place for establishing a defensive line'. One should also note here that other aspects of Burne's reconstruction of the battle are highly questionable. Despite his own caveat that 'amid the usual welter of contradictory sources there is little to be gathered for certain regarding the course of the battle' (*More Battlefields of England*, 121), he creates an English cavalry reserve, not mentioned by any source. He then takes the remarks of Thomas Sampson that the English archers and commons twice retreated and rallied as implying that this cavalry force launched several counter-charges against the Scots' left!

74. Details of the army's composition are given in the newsletter of Thomas Samson (Froissart, *Oeuvres de Froissart*, ed. K. de Lettenhove *et al.*, 25 vols (Brussels, 1867–77), V, 490–1). The van contained Percy, Neville, Maulay, Scrope, Musgrave, Sir Andrew FitzRalph; the centre the archbishop, the Earl of Angus, Lord Deyncourt, Sir Roger la Zouche, Sir Ralph Hastings, the Provost of Beverley; in the rearguard were Mowbray, Leybourn and the Sheriff of York.

75. Prestwich, 'The English at the Battle of Neville's Cross', 6–7; and Rogers, 'The Scottish Invasion of 1346', 59–60 and nn. 40–3, who argues for a higher figure approaching around 10,000. Samson's letter (Froissart, *Oeuvres*, V, 490–1), gives the English army's strength as 10,000 archers, 1,000 men-at-arms and 1,000 hobelars, together with 20,000 commons from the region north of the Trent and Humber.

76. E 101/25/10, translated in *The Battle of Neville's Cross*, Appendix (i), 163; le Baker, 87.

77. Woodhouse's account roll, in *The Battle of Neville's Cross*, 163.

78. *Anonimalle Chronicle*, 25; Rogers, 'The Scottish Invasion of 1346', 59 and n. 40.

79. Knighton, 72–3, a description 'reported by one who was there to see, and bore witness'. The *Historia Roffensis* stated that the archbishop summoned to the army 'all the brave men, religious, priests, clerks and laymen who were subject to his jurisdiction in his province' and that in the battle itself, 'the Archbishop and all the religious and the clerks fought hand to hand with the Scots' (C.J. Rogers, and M. Buck, 'Three New Accounts of the Neville's Cross Campaign', *Northern History*, xxxiv (1998), 78–9).

80. The make-up of the majority of contingents in 1346 is unknown, but for examples of the size and composition of some of the northern magnates' retinues in the 1330s see Prestwich, 'The English at the Battle of Neville's Cross', 5.

81. *Melsa*, III, 61 '*interque autem exercitus, Anglorum videlicet et Scottorum, gentes suas in tres acies dividebat, sagittariis a latere constitutis*'; trans. in *The Battle of Neville's Cross*, Appendix (e). The statement implies that the Scots did likewise, but we find no further reference to any Scottish archers in the sources.

82. Burne, *More Battlefields of England*, 118, 125. The context of the English archers is discussed by R. Hardy, 'The Military Archery at Neville's Cross, 1346', in *The Battle of Neville's Cross*, ed. Rollason and Prestwich, 122–31.

83. *Melsa*, III, 61, '*missilibus multipliciter confossus*'; trans. in *The Battle of Neville's Cross*, Appendix (e).

84. Wyntoun, II, 475; trans. *The Battle of Neville's Cross*, 160.

85. A helpful table breaking down the various accounts is given by Grant, 'The Disaster at Neville's Cross', 26–7.

86. Gray began his chronicle during his imprisonment in Edinburgh Castle, following his capture by the Scots at Norham in 1355. The annals from 1340–55 have been lost, but the antiquary John Leland made abstracts from them before their disappearance; Maxwell, *Scalacronica*, 112–20; Gransden, *Historical Writing in England*, II, 92–3.

87. Wyntoun, II, 475; trans. *The Battle of Neville's Cross*, 160:
      Than gud Schyre Jhone the Grame can say
      To the Kyng, 'Gettis me, but ma
      Ane hundyre on hors wyth me to ga,
      And all yhone archerys skayle sall I:
      Swa sall we fecht mare sykkerly.'

88. Wyntoun, II, 475; *Scotichronicon*, VII, 258–9, which has Graham request 'a hundred mounted lancers' (*equestres lanceatos*), but says that 'none dared to commit himself to such a risk'.

89. Grant, 'Disaster at Neville's Cross', 30.

90. Wyntoun, II, 475; trans. *The Battle of Neville's Cross*, 161.

91. Wyntoun, II, 475:

   > The Erle off Murrawe and his menyhe
   > at hey dykis assemblid thai,
   > And thak brak getly thaire aray;
   > Tharfor thai war swne dyscumfyte.

92. The letter is printed in Froissart, *Oeuvres*, V, 490–1: '*Deux fois se retrairent les archers e comunes de nostre partie, mais nos gents darmes se combatierent e se continuerent durement bien tantq les archers e communes reassemblerent.*' It is translated in full in *The Battle of Neville's Cross*, ed. Rollason and Prestwich, Appendix (b), 134–6, and in extract in Rogers, *Wars of Edward III*, 138.

93. Le Baker, 87–8: '*Resistit animose nacio Scotia nescia fuge, et, capitibus ferro tectis inclinatis, acies densa Anglicos invadens, cassidibus politis et umbonibus numero firmatis, sagittas Anglicorum in primordio belli frustravit; set armatorum acies prima ictubus letalibus hostes salutavit.*'

94. *Scotichronicon*, VII, 254–7; and cf. Wyntoun's similar remark that the host contained 'off armyt men bot twa thowsande' (II, 473).

95. See pp. 235, 238, 239.

96. F. Michel, *Les Écossais en France, les Français en Écosse*, 2 vols (London and Edinburgh, 1862), I, 72. In 1385 the Scots received armour for 1,200 men, sent from Paris (*ibid.*, I, 89).

97. Grant, 'Disaster at Neville's Cross', 29. The reason, however, for his doubt that the 3,000 archers from Yorkshire actually took part in the battle – and that the Scots thus faced far fewer longbowmen – is unclear, and sits uneasily with the chroniclers' remarks about the impact of the English archers in the later stages of the battle. Cf. Rogers, 'The Scottish Invasion of 1346', 59.

98. Knighton, 68–9: '*bene in armis arraiatorum ad modum et formam francorum*'.

99. See p. 397.

100. Grant, 'Disaster at Neville's Cross', 18, noting his upbringing 'in a militaristic atmposhere at Château Gaillard in Normandy'.

101. Giovanni Villani, *Cronica*, ed. R. Palmarocchi, *Cronisti del Trecento* (Milan, 1935), 403; le Baker, 86.

102. For a spirited attempt, see Rogers, 'The Scottish Invasion of 1346', 63–6. An object lesson in the difficulties of reconciling medieval battle accounts is demonstrated by a comparison between the accounts of the Scots chroniclers Wyntoun and Bower, who seem to have drawn their accounts of the battle independently from a lost Latin chronicle composed in the 1390s, though Bower adds further details (*Scotichronicon*, VII, xvii). Nevertheless, their versions of the battle differ radically. While Wyntoun has the Scots make two attacks, Bower gives the course of the battle an entirely different emphasis. For him, the Scots were overcome 'from the two whirlwind attacks so fiercely launched by the English', first against Moray's division, then against that of the king (*Scotichronicon*, VII, 258–60).

103. Wyntoun, II, 475:

   > Thai, that held hale, sped thame ful tyte
   > To the Kyng, that assemblid was
   > In till a full anoyus plas,

   > Than nane, but hurt, mycht lyfft his hand,
   > Qwhen thai thaire fayis mycht noucht wythstand.
   > To the Stwartis rowt than went thai,
   > That was asemblyd nere that way.

104. The *Historia Roffensis* similarly believed that 'three times they drew apart from one another for rest so as to fight again more strongly' (Rogers and Buck, 'Three New Accounts', 78–9).

105. Wyntoun, II, 476; trans. *The Battle of Neville's Cross*, ed. Rollason and Prestwich, 161.

106. Le Baker, 88.

107. Unless, as suggested by Grant, 'Disaster at Neville's Cross', 30, the 2,000 well-armed troops comprised the entirety of both Moray and the king's division, with each containing 1,000.

108. Le Baker, 88.

109. Rogers and Buck, 'Three New Accounts', 78–9, 70–81 at 72–3. The authors have labelled this chronicle, from BL Tiberius A VI, 'The "Packington" Account', Version A, as it may well be a French epitome of a lost vernacular chronicle by William Packington, a clerk in the Black Prince's household.

110. *Melsa*, II, 62.

111. This is stressed by English chroniclers, e.g. *Anonimalle Chronicle*, 27, '*saunz coupe de espeie ou de lance doner ou prerdue*'; le Baker, 88.

112. Wyntoun, II, 476; trans. *The Battle of Neville's Cross*, 161.

113. Grant, 'Disaster at Neville's Cross', 32.

114. Wyntoun, II, 475; Bower, *Scotichronicon*, VII, 260–1. Coupland was richly rewarded by Edward III by promotion to banneret and an annuity of £600, the modern equivalent of nearly £230,000. Despite this, he proved to be a grasping and unscrupulous figure in northern society, and was finally murdered in 1363. For his career see M.C. Dixon, 'John de Coupland – Hero to Villain', in *The Battle of Neville's Cross*, ed. Rollason and Prestwich, 36–49.

115. Knighton, 72–3.

116. Le Baker, 88; letter of Thomas Samson, in Froissart, *Oeuvres*, V, 490–1.

117. *Historical Papers and Letters from the Northern Registers*, ed. J. Raine (Rolls Series, London, 1873), 387–9.

118. Knighton, 70–1, gives a substantial list of those taken and slain; le Baker, 88.

119. Knighton, 70–1; *VCH*, Durham, II, 98.

120. Butler, *The Battle of Neville's Cross*, 22.

121. *The Pipewell Chronicle*, in Rogers and Buck, 'Three New Accounts', 80–1: 'the battle was so severe and of such long duration that the convent of Durham twice chanted the Seven Psalms and the Fifteen Psalms with the litany before anyone could tell who would gain the victory'. Prestwich, 'The English at the Battle of Neville's Cross', 1, rightly remarks that of all the great English victories of 1346–7, that of Neville's Cross 'is perhaps the least simple to account for in military terms'.

122. *Anonimalle Chronicle*, 27; Froissart, *Oeuvres*, V, 490–1.

123. The *Historia Roffensis* similarly believed that 'three times they drew apart from one another for rest so as to fight again more strongly' (Rogers and Buck, 'Three New Accounts', 78–9).

CHAPTER 12

1. A. Ayton, *Knights and Warhorses. Military Service and the English Aristocracy under Edward III* (Woodbridge, 1994), 10; Le Bel, I, 156: *'les plus noble et le plus frisques combastans qu'on sache'*; Rogers, *War, Cruel and Sharp*, 9, 402; *Anonimalle Chronicle*, 43.

2. For these crucial reforms see A. Ayton, 'English Armies in the Fourteenth Century', in *Arms, Armies and Fortifications in the Hundred Years War*, ed. A. Curry and M. Hughes (Woodbridge, 1994), 21–38; and *idem, Knights and Warhorses*, especially Ch. 1, 'The Military Revolution in Edwardian England', 9–25, two important discussions to which this chapter owes much.

3. Prince, 'The Indenture System under Edward III', 283–97; *idem*, 'The Army and Navy', 352–5; N.B. Lewis, 'The Organization of Indentured Retinues in Fourteenth-Century England', *TRHS*, 4th ser., xxvii (1944), 29–39; J.W. Sherbourne, 'Indentured Retinues and English Expeditions to France, 1369–1380', *EHR*, lxxix (1964), 718–46; M. Jones and S. Walker, 'Private Indentures for Life Service in Peace and War, 1278–1476', in *Camden Miscellany*, xxxii (5th ser., iii, 1994), 1–190, which provides texts and a valuable introduction; Prestwich, *Armies and Warfare*, 88–100; and Ayton, 'English Armies', 22–3.

4. Prestwich, *Armies and Warfare*, 88–91; Morris, *Welsh Wars*, 68–9, 278–9; N.B. Lewis, 'An Early Indenture of Military Service, 27 July, 1287', *BIHR*, xiii (1935), 85–9; for early indentures by nobles in Edward I's reign, Jones and Walker, 'Private Indentures', 35–46.

5. Prince, 'The Indenture System', 186; Prestwich, *War, Politics and Finance*, 73–6; *idem*, 'English Armies in the Early Stages of the Hundred Years War', *BIHR*, lvi (1983), 106–7.

6. N.B. Lewis, 'The Recruitment and Organization of a Contract Army, May to November 1337', *BIHR*, xxxvii (1964), 1–19. The majority of archers were raised as in earlier periods from the shires through commissioners of array.

7. Lewis, 'Recruitment and Organization', 93. For Ughtred, see A. Ayton, 'Sir Thomas Ughtred and the Edwardian Military Revolution', in *The Age of Edward III*, ed. J.S. Bothwell (York, 2001), 107–32.

8. Prince, 'The Indenture System', 288 n. 10.

9. Sherbourne, 'Indentured Retinues and English Expeditions to France', 742–3. As the fifteen indentures only supplied 178 men-at-arms and 181 archers of his quota agreed with the crown, Felton must have entered into several other subcontracts now lost. For comparative examples, see A. Goodman, 'The Military Subcontracts of Sir Hugh Hastings, 1380', *EHR*, xcv (1980), 114–20; and S.K. Walker, 'Profit and Loss in the Hundred Years War: the Subcontracts of Sir John Strother, 1374', *BIHR*, lviii (1985), 100–6.

10. Prince, 'The Indenture System', 288–97; Curry, *Agincourt*, 437–41.

11. Goodman, 'The Military Subcontracts of Sir Hugh Hastings', 118–19; Sherbourne, 'Indentured Retinues', 742–4.

12. P. Morgan, *War and Society in Medieval Cheshire, 1277–1403* (Manchester, 1987), 39–41.

13. Prestwich, 'English Armies', 102–13.

14. Prestwich, *Armies and Warfare*, 93; Ayton, *Knights and Warhorses*, 11.

15. Nicholson, *Edward III and the Scots*, 198–200.

16. Ayton, *Knights and Warhorses*, 13–14.

17. Morgan, *War and Society*, 42.

18. Sumption, *The Hundred Years War: Trial by Fire* (London, 1999), 154.

19. *CCR, 1360–64*, 534–5. The order was reissued as statute in 1369 (*Foedera*, III, ii, 79).

20. *Statutes of the Realm*, II, 57, 163; *Rot. Parl.*, III, 643.

21. Prestwich, 'English Armies', 107; Morgan, *War and Society*, 42; Ayton, 'English Armies', 21–38.

22. *The Register of John of Gaunt*, ed. S. Armitage-Smith, 2 vols (London, 1911), I, 290ff; Goodman, *John of Gaunt*, 218–19; Jones and Walker, 'Private Indentures', 35ff.

23. Only once more, in 1385 for Richard II's Scottish expedition, were writs of summons issued for a general feudal levy, though in practice Richard's army was a standard contract army; N.B. Lewis, 'The Last Medieval Summons of the English Feudal Levy, 13 June, 1385', *EHR*, lxxii (1958), 1–26.

24. A.E. Prince, 'The Strength of English Armies in the Reign of Edward III', *EHR*, xlvi (1931), 353–71, at 367–8.

25. Curry, *Agincourt*, 420, 421.

26. A. Curry, 'The First English Standing Army? Military Organization in Lancastrian Normandy, 1420–1450', in *Pedigree, Patronage and Power in Late Medieval England*, ed. C. Ross (Gloucester, 1979), 193–214; *idem*, 'English Armies in the Fifteenth Century', in *Arms, Armies and Fortifications in the Hundred Years War*, ed. Curry and Hughes, 39–68; and *idem*, 'The Organization of Field Armies in Lancastrian Normandy', in *Armies, Chivalry and Warfare in Medieval Britain and France. Proceedings of the 1995 Harlaxton Symposium*, ed. M.J. Strickland (Stamford, 1998), 207–33.

27. Curry, *Agincourt*, 437–40.

28. Curry, *Agincourt*, 410, 420–1.

29. Curry, *Agincourt*, 421.

30. Curry, *Agincourt*, 422, 436.

31. Curry, *Agincourt*, 422.

32. Prestwich, 'English Armies', 109.

33. A. Ayton, 'The English Army and the Normandy Campaign of 1346', *England and Normandy in the Middle Ages*, ed. D. Bates and A. Curry (London, 1994), 253–68; Rogers, *War, Cruel and Sharp*, 422.

34. Prince, 'The Strength of English Armies', 364; Prestwich, *Armies and Warfare*, 342.

35. Ayton, 'English Armies', 21.

36. Curry, *Agincourt*, 406.

37. Prestwich, *Armies and Warfare*, 336.

38. Prestwich, 'English Armies', 109. But see Ayton, *Knights and Warhorses*, Appendix B.

39. M.R. Powicke, 'Lancastrian Captains', in *Essays in Medieval History Presented to Bertie Wilkinson*, ed. T.A. Sandquist and M.R. Powicke (Toronto, 1969), 371–82, at 378–9. The size of English expeditionary armies between 1415 and 1450 is tabulated in Bennett and Hooper, *Cambridge Illustrated Atlas, Warfare. The Middle Ages, 768–1487*, 133.

40. See p. 23.

41. Hanawalt, 'Men's Games, King's Deer', 186–7.

42. Sumption, *Trial by Fire*, 157.

43. Hewitt, *Organization of War*, 39, for white and green uniforms; Prestwich, *Armies and Warfare*, 141. The granting of livery to retainers was a practice of long standing, but by Richard II's reign legislation had been passed limiting the wearing of livery to service within the household and in time of war, when troops under their lord were in the king's service (K.B. McFarlane, *The Nobility of Later Medieval England* (Oxford, 1973), 106–7). McFarlane, *ibid.*, 107 n. 3, called the fourteenth century 'the century of unbridled livery', but it is not clear to what extent a lord's colours or badges were issued below the rank of squire. For the later fifteenth century a detailed record of livery badges used in an expeditionary army to France is provided by F.P. Barnard, *Edward IV's Expedition of 1475: the Leaders and their Badges* (Oxford, 1925).

44. *The Black Book of the Admiralty*, ed. T. Twiss, 4 vols (Rolls Series, London, 1871), I, 456, c. 18. For a valuable discussion of these ordinances and for military discipline in armies of the later fourteenth century see M. Keen, 'Richard II's Ordinances of War of 1385', *Rulers and Ruled in Late Medieval England. Essays Presented to Gerald Harriss*, ed. R.E. Archer and S. Walker (London, 1995), 33–48.

45. Prestwich, *Armies and Warfare*, 141. As early as 1188 it was stipulated that during the Third Crusade the English were to wear white crosses, the Flemish green and the French red (*Gesta*, II, 30).

46. *Black Book of the Admiralty*, I, 464, c. 18.

47. Ayton, 'English Armies', 26–31.

48. M. McKisack, *The Fourteenth Century: 1307–1399* (Oxford, 1959), 23, 253 n. 3; *Victoria County History, Derbyshire*, 2 vols (London, 1907), I, 168; *Rot. Parl.*, II, 149, 160. Similarly, the Black Prince had more troops than requested for the Nájera campaign (Prince, 'The Indenture System', 290 and n. 4).

49. Curry, *Agincourt*, 421, 413.

50. See, for example, Morgan, *War and Society in Medieval Cheshire*, 112–13, who suggests that the development of licences to return to England were in response to the problems of desertion.

51. *Black Book of the Admiralty*, I, 453–4; 460, c. 4; 457, c. 22; 466, c. 23; 454; 460, c.5; Keen, 'Richard II's Ordinances of War', 38–9.

52. Keen, 'Richard II's Ordinances of War', 39.

53. Prince, 'The Strength of English Armies', 355 n. 1. In 1342 the army in Brittany contained a force of 376 Welsh archers and their

54. leaders: a captain, 3 constables, 20 vintenars, a chaplain, a physician (*ibid.*, 363).

54. Prince, 'The Strength of English Armies', 366, 368 and n. 6.

55. Curry, *Agincourt*, 422; cf. Allmand, *Henry V*, 208.

56. See pp. 353–5.

57. Prince, 'The Army and Navy', 341.

58. J.E. Morris, 'Mounted Infantry in Medieval Warfare', *TRHS*, 3rd series, viii (1914), 77–102, at 93; *idem, Bannockburn*, 100; cf. Oman, *Art of War*, II, 119.

59. Lydon, 'The Hobelar: An Irish Contribution to Medieval Warfare', 12–16.

60. Morgan, *War and Society in Medieval Cheshire*, 43; Prince, 'The Strength of English Armies', 354 n. 7.

61. J.E. Morris, 'Cumberland and Westmorland Levies in the Time of Edward I and Edward II', *Cumberland and Westmorland Archaeological and Antiquarian Society*, new ser., iii (1903), 307–27, at 313–24.

62. Prince, 'The Strength of English Armies', 355–6; Nicholson, *Edward III and the Scots*, 199–200.

63. The Lochindorb raid is described by a contemporary English newsletter, printed in H. Ellis, *Original Letters Illustrative of English History*, 4 vols (3rd ser., London, 1846), I, 33–9, and trans. in Rogers, *Wars of Edward III*, 48–50. For its military significance, Morgan, *War and Society*, 41.

64. Prestwich, 'English Armies in the Hundred Years War', 109 and n. 46.

65. Prince, 'The Army and the Navy', 334.

66. Prince, 'The Strength of English Armies', 366.

67. Ayton, *Knights and Warhorses*, 10.

68. Prestwich, *Armies and Warfare*, 342.

69. Morgan, *War and Society*, 41.

70. Froissart, *Chroniques de Jean Froissart*, ed. S. Luce, 15 vols (Paris, 1869–99), III, 67–71, 288–90; Murimuth, 190, by contrast, regarded the victory as being primarily won by the bowmen. The battle is discussed by A.H. Burne, *The Crécy War: a Military History of the Hundred Years War from 1337 to the Peace of Brétigny, 1360* (London, 1955), 105–12, with sketch maps; Sumption, *Trial by Battle*, 468–9, who offers a very different account; De Vries, *Infantry Warfare*, 188–9, who classifies it as an infantry ambush. Unfortunately, no details of the battle are given by K. Fowler, *The King's Lieutenant. Henry of Grosmont, First Duke of Lancaster, 1310–1361* (London, 1969), 60.

71. Le Baker, 152, trans. R. Barber, ed. *The Life and Campaigns of the Black Prince* (Woodbridge, 1986), 80; Froissart, ed. Luce, V, 37–8.

72. Prince, 'The Strength of English Armies', 354–5.

73. Prince, 'The Strength of English Armies', 355. Similarly, for the Lochindorb raid in 1336 Edward's force was probably composed of equal numbers of men-at-arms and a combination of hobelars or mounted archers, though in the campaigns of 1337–8 the preponderance of mounted archers to men at arms – 2,350 mounted archers to 1,060 men-at-arms – was more than double (*ibid.*, 358, 358–60).

74.   Prince, 'The Strength of English Armies', 363.

75.   Prince, 'The Strength of English Armies', 367–8, 369–70.

76.   J.W. Sherbourne, 'The English Navy: Shipping and Manpower', *Past and Present*, xxxvii (1967), 163–75.

77.   Prince, 'The Strength of English Armies', 361.

78.   Ayton, *Knights and Warhorses*, 10.

79.   Prince, 'The Strength of English Armies', 363.

80.   Sherbourne, 'Indentured Retinues', 720. The retinue of the Earl of Hereford, one of the captains who accompanied him, was 300 men-at-arms and 600 archers (*ibid.*).

81.   Sherbourne, 'Indentured Retinues', 719, 723. Similarly, retinues in the expeditionary force to Portugal in 1381 were of equal numbers of men-at-arms and mounted archers (Ayton, *Knights and Warhorses*, 15).

82.   Ayton, *Knights and Warhorses*, 15 and n. 27; Allmand, *Henry V*, 213.

83.   Curry, *Agincourt*, 420, 423.

84.   Powicke, 'Lancastrian Captains', 379–82.

85.   Morgan, *War and Society*, 39–40; Ayton, 'English Armies in the Fourteenth Century', 32–3.

86.   C. Dyer, *Standards of Living in the Later Middle Ages* (Cambridge, 1989), 15, 23.

87.   McKisack, *The Fourteenth Century*, 245–6.

88.   Ayton, 'The Development of the Robin Hood Legend', 136 and n. 57.

89.   *CPR, 1343–5*, 427–8; Ayton, 'The English Army and the Normandy Campaign', 254–5.

90.   Powicke, *Military Obligation in Medieval England*, 196–7.

91.   Dyer, *Standards of Living*, 30–2. Cf. C. Given-Wilson, *The English Nobility in the Late Middle Ages* (London, 1987), 69–83, who suggests that gentry families in the fourteenth century numbered between 9,00 and 10,000.

92.   Sir John Fortescue, *De Laudibus Legum Angliae*, ed. S.B. Chrimes (Cambridge, 1942), 69; Dyer, *Standards of Living*, 30–2.

93.   Prince, 'The Army and Navy', 341. In 1318 24 foot-archers had formed part of the *garde corps le roi*, who accompanied the king on his progresses and might also be used as messengers (*The English Government at Work*, I, 223–4).

94.   Morgan, *War and Society in Medieval Cheshire*, 109.

95.   *Register of Edward the Black Prince*, 204, 491.

96.   Tout, *Chapters*, III, 487–9; *ibid.*, IV, 10, 199; Keen, *England in the Later Middle Ages*, 288.

97.   Bradbury, *The Medieval Archer*, 171–6.

98.   Ayton, *Knights and Warhorses*, 16, and cf. 5, where he notes that over 75 per cent of men-at-arms in English armies were below knightly status, and nicely sums up their diversity: 'men awaiting inheritances, younger sons who were never likely to inherit, members of modestly endowed families "hovering perilously close to the level of the richer peasantry", and "professional" soldiers, men from the yeomanry or below, whose status had been enhanced by a career in arms'. Cf. Morgan, *War and Society in Medieval Cheshire*, 109: 'it is apparent that recognition as a man-at-arms depended solely upon possession of the necessary equipment, and not upon a particular station or role in local society'.

99.   Ayton, *Knights and Warhorses*, 16 n. 33; *idem*, 'Development of the Robin Hood Legend', 136–7.

100. A.J. Pollard, *John Talbot and the War in France, 1427–1453* (London, 1983), 90.

101. *Black Book of the Admiralty*, I, 455, c. 11. By the time of Henry V's ordinances of 1419 this distinction had been dropped, and anyone guilty was placed under arrest until a fine was paid and was in the king's mercy for his life (*ibid.*, 462–3, c. 12).

102. M.J. Bennett, *Community, Class and Careerism. Cheshire and Lancashire Society in the Age of Sir Gawain and the Green Knight* (Cambridge, 1983), 182–3.

103. *Scalacronica*, 131, 134.

104. *DNB*, xxv, 236; for Knollys, *DNB*, xxxi, 281–6; and Bennett, *Community, Class and Careerism*, 182.

105. Knighton, 160–1. The word *garcio* may here also have the meaning of 'groom'.

106. *CPR, 1416–1422*, 341. Later in the century 'yeoman' was regarded as synonymous with 'husbondman' (*CPR, 1467–77*), 515, while the term itself seems to have derived from 'yongman', meaning a young man or servant of a noble (K. Mertes, *The Noble English Household, 1250–1600* (Oxford, 1987), 29).

107. *The Sermons of Hugh Latimer*, 101.

108. Ayton, *Knights and Warhorses*, 2. See also *idem*, 'Edward III and the English Aristocracy at the Beginning of the Hundred Years War', in *Armies, Chivalry and Warfare*, 173–206.

109. Curry, *Agincourt*, 413–14. This was the rate for service in Normandy and northern France, whereas that for service in Guienne was at the higher rate of 9*d* and 18*d* respectively (*ibid.*).

110. *Chronique normande de Pierre Cochon*, ed. C. de Robillard de Beaurepaire (Société de l'Histoire de Normandie, 1870), 275–6; Curry, *Agincourt*, 114.

111. Monstrelet, III, 106; Curry, *Agincourt*, 160.

112. *Chronique de Jean le Fèvre, Seigneur de Saint Remy*, ed. F. Morand, 2 vols (Société de l'Histoire de France, 1876–81), I, 254; Curry, *Agincourt*, 160.

113. A. Curry, 'Les "gens vivans sur le païs" pendant l'occupation anglaise de la Normandie (1417–1450)', in *La Guerre, la violence et les gens au Moyen Age, I: Guerre et violence*, ed. P. Contamine and O. Guyotjeannin (Paris, 1996), 209–21.

114. Monstrelet, IV, 330; trans. *Contemporary Chronicles of the Hundred Years War*, ed. P.E. Thompson (London, 1966), 305.

115. Bennett, 'The Battle', 28.

116. *Black Book of the Admiralty*, I, 464–5, c.19

117. Sherbourne, 'Indentured Retinues', 719 n. 3.

118. While rightly noting that 'the Knight and his little retinue together make up a perfect "lance"', Jones, *Chaucer's Knight*, 212, goes on to support his interpretation of the Knight as a ruthless mercenary by stating that such a grouping was 'the distinctive fighting unit of Hawkwood's White Company'. Yet while Hawkwood's forces indeed contained such units, this was surely a reflection of the fact that 'lances' consisting of man-at-arms,

squire or valet and archer had long been commonplace in English armies, and formed a natural model for Hawkwood's retinues from the 1360s.

119. See pp. 254–7.

120. See pp. 329–31.

121. *Le Religieux de St Denis*, in *Histoire de Charles VI*, ed. M.L. Bellaguet (*Collection des documents inédits sur l'histoire de France*, 6 vols, Paris, 1839–52), V (1844), 562–3; Curry, *Agincourt*, 108.

122. Prince, 'The Strength of English Armies', 362; Prestwich, 'English Armies in the Early Stages of the Hundred Years War'. For Welsh levies under Edward III see Evans, 'Notes on the History of the Principality of Wales in the Time of the Black Prince', 25–110.

123. Prestwich, 'English Armies', 108.

124. See p. 219.

125. See p. 326.

126. Ayton, *Knights and Warhorses*, 12.

127. *Rot. Scot.*, I, 225; *CCR, 1333–1337*, 622, 624; Prince, 'The Army and Navy', 342 and 343 n. 12.

128. Prince, 'The Army and Navy', 342; Curry, *Agincourt*, 421, for the Gascon unit.

129. Hewitt, *Organization for War*, 72; Wylie, *England under Henry IV*, II, 7, 101, 269n and III, 107.

130. Megson, *Such Goodly Company*.

131. In the expedition of 1369, however, some archers were among the retinues from Brabant, Limburg and Juliers which had been hired to join John of Gaunt's advanced guard (Sherbourne, 'Indentured Retinues', 723).

132. Sumption, *Trial by Fire*, 225.

133. Prince, 'The Strength of English Armies', 366, 368 and n. 6, 369; Sherbourne, 'Indentured Retinues', 722.

134. Curry, *Agincourt*, 422 and 423, for the suggestion that many archers recorded as 'foot' may well have been mounted, at least for any campaign beyond the siege of Harfleur.

135. W.T. Waugh, 'The Administration of Normandy, 1420–22', in *Essays Presented to Thomas Frederick Tout*, ed. A.G. Little and F.M. Powicke (Manchester, 1925), 349–59, at 352; R.A. Newhall, *The English Conquest of Normandy, 1416–1424* (New Haven, Connecticut, 1924); *idem, Muster and Review. A Problem of English Military Administration, 1420–1440* (Cambridge, Mass., 1940); C.T. Allmand, *Lancastrian Normandy, 1415–1450. The History of a Medieval Occupation* (Oxford, 1983); A. Curry, 'The First English Standing Army', 193–214; *idem*, 'English Armies in the Fifteenth Century', 39–68. A major new study on the English army in Normandy is currently under preparation by Professor Curry.

136. C.J. Rogers, 'An Unknown News Bulletin from the Siege of Tournai', *War in History*, v (1998), 358–66; *Eulogium historiarum*, ed. F.S. Haydon, 3 vols (Rolls Series, London, 1858–63), III, 219–20; le Baker, 141–2.

137. Froissart, ed. Luce, III, 47–8. For Derby, see now C.J. Rogers, 'The Bergerac Campaign (1345) and the Generalship of Henry of Lancaster', *JMMH*, ii (2004), 89–111.

138. Froissart, ed. Luce, III, 50–1; trans. Froissart, *Chroniques*, ed. T. Johnes, 13 vols (London, 1808), II, 58.

139. Froissart, ed. Luce, III, 75–6; trans. Johnes, II, 76–7.

140. Froissart, ed. Luce, IV, 164; Sumption, *Trial by Fire*, 179.

141. K.A. Fowler, 'News from the Front: Letters and Despatches of the Fourteenth Century', *Guerre et société en France, en Angleterre et en Bourgogne, XIVe–Xve siècle*, ed. P. Contamine, C. Giry-Deloison and M.H. Keen (1991), 63–92, at 71.

142. Le Bel, I, 307–15, 319–20; Froissart, ed. Luce, II, 167–8; *The Chronicles of Froissart*, ed. G.C. Macaulay and trans. Lord Berners (London, 1895), 108.

143. Monstrelet, V, 42–3.

144. H. Nicholas, *History of the Battle of Agincourt and the Expedition of Henry the Fifth into France* (3rd edn, London, 1971), Appendix, 42–3. I am grateful to Professor Anne Curry for pointing out that these ordinances, sometimes ascribed to Talbot, are in fact those of Salisbury.

145. I. Friel, 'Winds of Change? Ships and the Hundred Years War', in *Arms, Armies and Fortifications in the Hundred Years War*, ed. Curry and Hughes, 183–93, 183–93, at 184–6; and *idem*, 'Oars, Sails and Guns: The English and War at Sea, *c.* 1200–*c.* 1500', *War at Sea in the Middle Ages and the Renaissance*, ed. J.B. Hattendorf and R.W. Unger (Woodbridge, 2003), 69–79, especially 71–2.

146. Bradbury, *The Medieval Archer*, 102–3; Sumption, *Trial by Fire*, 324–7; K. De Vries, 'God, Admirals, Archery and Flemings: Perceptions of Victory and Defeat at the Battle of Sluys, 1340', *American Neptune*, lv (1995), 223–42.

147. *Melsa*, III, 44.

148. Froissart, ed. Luce, IV, 88–97.

149. Prestwich, 'English Armies', 110.

150. Sherbourne, 'The English Navy: Shipping and Manpower', 172.

151. Wylie, *Henry V*, III, 45. During Henry V's crossing to Normandy in 1415 the fleet had been escorted by three large vessels and twelve smaller craft, carrying a force of 150 men-at-arms and 300 archers (*ibid.*, II, 6–7).

152. J.W. Sherbourne, 'The Battle of La Rochelle and the War at Sea, 1372–5', *BIHR*, xlii (1969), 17–29.

153. *Ibid.*, 19–20.

154. Wylie, *Henry V*, II, 346–65.

155. Wylie, *Henry V*, III, 48–9.

156. C.F. Richmond, 'The Keeping of the Seas during the Hundred Years War: 1422–1440', *History*, xlix (1964), 283–98, at 289; and cf. *idem*, 'English Naval Power in the Fifteenth Century', *History*, lii (1967), 1–15.

157. *Lanercost*, 295; Froissart, ed. Luce, I, 136–7.

158. Avesbury, 363, 368; Le Bel, II, 96–8; Froissart, ed. Luce, V, 12–13.

159. *Gesta Henrici Quinti*, ed. F. Taylor and J.S. Roskell (Oxford, 1975), 70–3; le Fèvre, I, 235; Waurin, II, 193–4.

160. Wylie, *Henry V*, III, 114–16; A.H. Burne, *The Agincourt War: A Military History of the Latter Part of the Hundred Years War from 1369–1453* (London, 1956), 128–9.

161. Edward Hall, *The Union of Two Noble and Illustre Families of Lancaster and York*, ed. H. Ellis (London, 1809), 188.

162. Froissart, ed. Luce, VI, 125 (trans. Berners, 149): '*quand li arcier furent devant, si s'eslargirent et commencencièrent à traire de grant manière; mès li Francois estoient si fort armé et si bien paveschié contre le tret, que onques il n'en furent grevé, se petit non, ne pour ce n'en laissièrent il point à combatre, mès entrèrent, et tout à piet, ens ès Navarois et Englès, et cil entre eulz de grant volenté*'.

163. Froissart, ed. Luce, VI, 162, '*li arcier traiirent de commencement; mès leurs très ne grevanoient as François, car il estoient trop bien armet et fort, et ossi bien paveschiet contre le tret*'.

164. Le Baker, 84, trans. Barber, 44.

165. *Life of the Black Prince by the Herald of Sir John Chandos*, ed. M.K. Pope and E.C. Lodge (Oxford, 1910), 100–1.

166. Le Fèvre, I, 250; Waurin, II, 185–222 at 207; Tito Livio, 20; Curry, *Agincourt*, 62; Thomas of Elmham, *Liber metricus*, ed. C.A. Cole, *Memorials of Henry the Fifth, King of England* (London, 1858), 121–2; Curry, *Agincourt*, 47. For the (dubious) tradition that it was the Duke of Alençon who struck this blow, Wylie, *Henry V*, II, 164–5.

167. See p. 192.

168. Ayton, *Knights and Warhorses*, 27–8. It is noteworthy that though Jean Le Bel and Jacques de Hemricourt noted that such lavish apparel was increasingly giving way to more workaday equipment by the 1350s, both men regarded it as a cause for complaint that this was so (see pp. 273–4).

169. Le Baker, 152, trans. Barber, 80. Froissart believed that the cavalry assault led by Sir James Audley and other Anglo-Gascon knights was directed against the initial mounted attack by the French marshals, but it is far more probable that it was directed towards John's final French division at the crux of the battle.

170. Le Baker, 82, trans. Barber, 42; 142–3, trans. Barber, 72: 'the prince and everyone with him at once dismounted, handing their chargers and horses to their squires, to be kept in reserve for pursuing the enemy'.

171. P.E. Russell, *The English Intervention in Spain and Portugal in the Time of Edward III and Richard II* (Oxford, 1995), 103.

172. Froissart, ed. Luce, III, 47–8.

173. Letter of Bartholomew Burghersh to Archbishop Stratford (29 July 1346), in Adam of Murimuth, *Continuatio Chronicarum*, ed. E.M. Thompson (Rolls Series, London, 1889), 203–4; *Chronique Normande*, 76. Letter of Michael Northburgh in Avesbury, 359; *The Acts of War of Edward III*, in Barber, 32–3.

174. Rogers, *War, Cruel and Sharp*, 9, and cf. 7 and n. 27 for earlier criticisms of his strategic, as opposed to tactical, abilities.

175. Sumption, *Trial by Fire*, 154.

176. For these themes see J. Vale, *Edward III and Chivalry: Chivalric Society and its Context, 1270–1350* (Woodbridge, 1983).

177. Le Baker, 106, trans. Barber, 47.

178. Le Baker, 140, trans. Barber, 70

179. Ayton, 'English Armies in the Fourteenth Century', 26.

180. M. Jones, 'Edward III's Captains in Brittany', *England in the Fourteenth Century*, ed. W.M. Ormrod (Woodbridge, 1986), 99–118.

181. Rogers, *War, Cruel and Sharp*, 234 n. 82; Ayton, 'Sir Thomas Ughtred', 107ff; and *idem*, 'The English Army and the Normandy Campaign of 1346', 252–3.

182. Rogers, *War, Cruel and Sharp*, 264 and n. 149.

183. Sumption, *Trial by Fire*, 154. A sense of the range of military experience possessed by some of Edward's leading commanders is given by the career of Thomas Beauchamp, Earl of Warwick. He served on all of Edward's early Scottish campaigns and became commander of the army in Scotland in 1337, before acting as marshal of the army on the 1346 campaign (*Complete Peerage*, XII, ii, 372–4). At Crécy Ughtred acted as his deputy marshal.

184. Lewis, 'Recruitment and Organization', 3 and n. 3.

185. For the Order see J. D'Arcy Boulton, *Knights of the Crown: the Monarchal Orders of Knighthood in Late Medieval Europe* (Woodbridge, 2000); and H.E.L. Collins, *The Order of the Garter, 1348–1461: Chivalry and Politics in Late Medieval England* (Oxford, 2000).

186. At Falkirk, for example, the English knights in the battle commanded by Antony Bek, the Bishop of Durham, 'were pushing on too fast so as to have the honour of attacking first'. He bade them wait till Edward I should come up with the third battle, but received a round retort from Ralph Basset of Drayton that he should go and celebrate mass and leave the business of war to the knights (Guisborough, 327–8).

187. *Scalacronica*, 168; trans. Maxwell, 105.

188. *Chronique Normande*, 171–2, believed that the Anglo-Navarese first mounted for this pursuit, but when they saw the French about turn, they dismounted to fight.

189. Sherbourne, 'Indentured Retinues and English Expeditions to France', 723–5; *Chronicon Angliae*, ed. E.M. Thompson, *Chronicles and Memorials of Great Britain and Ireland* (London, 1974), vol. lxiv, 66; M. Collis, *The Hurling Time* (London, 1958), 156–8.

190. Froissart, ed. Luce, VI, 156–7.

191. Elmham, *Liber Metricus*, 120; Curry, *Agincourt*, 46. As York was already in command of the vanguard by 23 October, the story is hardly likely (Tito Livio, 15, Curry, *Agincourt*, 58).

192. *The Chronicle of John Hardyng*, ed. H. Ellis (London, 1812), 384; Allmand, *Henry V*, 159. For Baugé, see p. 345.

193. Flavius Vegetius Renatus, *Epitoma Rei Militaris*, ed. R. Dyboski and Z.M. Arend, *Knyghthode and Bataile: a XVth century verse paraphrase of Flavius Vegetius Renatus' treatise "De Rei Militari"* (London, 1935), 58–9, and cf. the comments of A. Goodman, *Wars of the Roses* (London, 1981), 123–4.

194. Le Baker, 148, trans. Barber 77.

195. Froissart, ed. Luce, V, 33, trans. Thompson, *Contemporary Chronicles*, 110.

196. Froissart, ed. Luce, VII, 43.

197. Monstrelet, III, 105–6; le Fèvre, I, 253; Curry, *Agincourt*, 158, 160. I owe the suggestion about Ughtred's role to Dr Ayton.

198. The Pseudo Elmham, *Thomae de Elmham Vita et Gesta Henrici Quinti*, ed. T. Hearne (Oxford, 1727), 59; Curry, *Agincourt*, 68, 69.

199. *Gesta Henrici Quinti*, 82–3, nos 3 and 4.

200. Monstrelet, IV, 293, 300, trans. Thompson, *Contemporary Chronicles*, 294, 295.

201. For Talbot's career see Pollard, *John Talbot*, and *ibid.*, 8, for his possible participation at Shrewsbury.

202. Ayton, 'Sir Thomas Ughtred', 107–32. Cf. Rogers, *War, Cruel and Sharp*, 234 n. 82, who suggests that a number of the king's household bannerets and knights serving on the Crécy campaign, including Thomas Bradstone, Maurice Berkeley and William fitzWarin, had probably been at Halidon Hill.

203. *English Suits before the Parlement of Paris, 1420–1436*, ed. C.T. Allmand and C.A.J. Armstrong, Camden Society, 4th ser., xxvi (London, 1982), 104, and cf. C. Allmand, 'Changing Views of the Soldier in Late Medieval France', in *Guerre et société en France, en Angleterre et en Bourgogne, XIVe–Xve siècle*, ed. P. Contamine, C. Giry-Deloison and M.H. Keen (Lille, 1991), 171–88, at 177.

204. K.B. McFarlane, 'Bastard Feudalism', *BIHR*, xx (1945), 161–80 and repr. in *idem, England in the Fifteenth Century: Collected Essays* (London, 1981), 23–44.

205. *Chandos Herald*, 96; trans. Barber, 125. In 1359 Chandos's retinue had comprised 7 knights, 54 esquires and 36 horsed archers (Prince, 'The Indenture System', 283).

206. Le Bel, II, 106; Rogers, *The Wars of Edward III*, 134.

207. *Black Book of the Admiralty*, I, 455, c. 10; 462, c. 11; Keen, 'Richard II's Ordinances of War', 43–4.

208. Avesbury, 354, 369.

209. Froissart, ed. Luce, V, 17; trans. Thompson, *Contemporary Chronicles*, 101.

210. Le Baker, 149; trans. Barber, 77.

211. Le Baker, 150; trans. Barber, 78.

212. Le Baker, 120.

213. *Gesta Henrici Quinti*, 80–1.

214. Keen, 'Richard II's Ordinances of War', 35ff.

215. Keen, 'Richard II's Ordinances of War', 44–5.

216. *Black Book of the Admiralty*, I, 455, c. 14; 459, 460, 467 (clauses 2, 3, 26, 28, 33, 37).

217. Rogers, *War, Cruel and Sharp*, 238–44. C.R. Rogers, 'By Fire and Sword. *Bellum Hostile* and "Civilians" in the Hundred Years War', in *Civilians in the Path of War*, ed. M. Grimsley and C. Rogers (Lincoln, Nebraska, and London, 2002), 33–78 for a detailed analysis of such ravaging.

218. *Gesta Henrici Quinti*, 26–7 and n. 1, 68–9. Henry's disciplinary measures, together with ordinances of 1419 and 1421, are given in Nicholas, *Agincourt*, Appendix 8, 31–40, and discussed by Wylie, *Henry V*, II, 20–4.

219. Religieux, V, 537, 547; Curry, *Agincourt*, 105: 'they showed more regard than the French for the local inhabitants who had declared themselves in their favour' and 'they strictly observed the rules of military discipline and scrupulously obeyed the orders of the king'.

220. Rogers, *War, Cruel and Sharp*, 241, citing the *Historia Roffensis* (BL, Cotton Faustina B V, f.91). It is noteworthy that such testimony should come from an English source, rather than a more overtly hostile French one.

221. Froissart, ed. Luce, III, 187: '*pillars et ribaus, Gallois et Cornillois*'.

222. *Gesta Henrici Quinti*, 93; Monstrelet, III, 121; Tito Livio, 21, Curry, *Agincourt*, 63.

223. Le Bel, II, 78, 83.

224. Wylie, *Henry V*, III, 60–1.

225. Froissart, ed. Lettenhove, VII, 333.

226. *Brut*, I, 378; Curry, *Agincourt*, 92.

227. Monstrelet, III, 106; le Fèvre, I, 253; Curry, *Agincourt*, 158.

228. See pp. 347–8.

229. Tito Livio, 19–20, Curry, *Agincourt*, 62.

230. Religieux, V, 562; Curry, *Agincourt*, 107.

231. Le Fèvre, I, 246; Curry, *Agincourt*, 155.

232. *The St Albans Chronicle, 1406–1420*, ed. V.H. Galbraith (Oxford, 1937), 94; Curry, *Agincourt*, 51.

233. *St Albans Chronicle*, 95; Curry, *Agincourt*, 52.

234. F. Taylor, 'The Chronicle of John Strecche for the Reign of Henry V (1414–1422)', *Bulletin of the John Rylands Library*, xvi (1932), 156.

235. For a detailed account of the battle, Wylie, *Henry V*, II, 333; *Gesta Henrici Quinti*, 114–21; Taylor, 'Strecche', 156–7.

236. Wylie, *Henry V*, II, 333.

237. Burne, *Agincourt War*, 104.

CHAPTER 13

1. For Edward's strategic aims see C.J. Rogers, 'Edward III and the Dialectics of Strategy, 1327–1360', *TRHS*, 6th ser., iv (1994), 83–102, and *idem, War, Cruel and Sharp*, 127–30.

2. Rogers, 'The Military Revolutions of the Hundred Years War', 244.

3. For an excellent overview of English tactical deployment see M. Bennett, 'The Development of Battle Tactics in the Hundred Years War', in *Arms, Armies and Fortifications*, 1–20.

4. Rogers, *War, Cruel and Sharp*, 162; Sumption, *Trial by Battle*, 280–5.

5. Knighton, 18–19.

6. The numbers of Welsh had fluctuated from over 1,000 to only 80 (Prince, 'The Strength of English Armies', 361 and n. 2).

7. Le Bel, I, 162–4; Froissart, ed. Luce, I, 177–80.

8. Knighton, 20–1.

9. Sumption, *Trial by Battle*, 288.

10. For Cassel see De Vries, *Infantry Warfare*, 105–11.

11. Sumption, *Trial by Battle*, 291–360; Rogers, *War, Cruel and Sharp*, 213–16; K. De Vries, 'Contemporary Views of Edward III's failure at the Siege of Tournai, 1340', *Nottingham Medieval Studies*, xxxix (1995), 70–105.

12. For the political and strategic context, see Sumption, *Trial by*

Battle, 398–402. The tactical interest of the battle, overlooked by Oman in his *Art of War*, was first highlighted by T.F. Tout, 'The Tactics of Boroughbridge and Morlaix', in *idem*, *Collected Works*, 2 vols (Manchester, 1934), II, 221–5, 223–5, while the battle is also discussed by Burne, *Crécy War*, 71–8; and De Vries, *Infantry Warfare*, 137–44.

13. Knighton, 42–3. An uncorroborated estimate of Charles's force put it at some 3,000 horse, 1,500 Genoese and an unknown number of Breton troops (Murimuth, 127).

14. *Scalacronica*, 170; trans. Maxwell, 108; le Baker, 67; Knighton, 26–7; Sumption, *Trial by Battle*, 311–12.

15. Sumption, *Trial by Battle*, 398–402; Murimuth, 125, states that his force on arrival in Brittany was 500 men-at-arms and 1,000 archers, while Walter Mauny's earlier detachment comprised 60 men-at-arms and 200 archers.

16. There is thus no contemporary authority for Burne's statement that 'the dismounted men-at-arms occupied the centre of the line, the archers were stationed on the flanks', and he himself later admits that 'the archers are not specifically referred to in the accounts' (*Crécy War*, 72, 88), as Tout, 'The Tactics of Boroughbridge and Morlaix', 714, had already pointed out. Bradbury, *The Medieval Archer*, 103–4, here relies on Tout and Burne, while De Vries, *Infantry Warfare*, 143–4, believes that the archers were placed in the main English formation, 'using weapons other than their longbows', though he does not state on what this assertion is based. Sumption, *Trial by Battle*, 402, more cautiously omits mention of archers. While it may be inferred from subsequent English formations that the archers were on the flanks, sketch maps such as that of Bennett, 'The Development of Battle Tactics', 6, must remain speculative.

17. Knighton, 42–3: 'the French were at once overcome by the English and put to flight'. According to Knighton's source, the French formed three battles, the first under Geoffroi de Charny '*cum multis galettis*'. This word is obscure. Tout took it to mean Breton light infantry, while the new editor of Knighton translates it as cavalry, a more plausible interpretation, and closer to *galeati* – helmets or 'bascinets' (Tout, 'The Tactics of the Battles of Boroughbridge and Morlaix', 224; Knighton, 42–3).

18. De Vries, *Infantry Warfare*, 108.

19. Sumption, *Trial by Battle*, 341–3; Bennett, 'The Development of Battle Tactics', 10.

20. Knighton, 42–3.

21. Knighton, 42–3.

22. Knighton, 42–3. Burne's depiction of the subsequent action of the English in forming '"a hedgehog", a defensive line along the edge of the wood and facing in all directions' is pure speculation (*Crécy War*, 74).

23. Le Baker, 76–7.

24. Gransden, *Historical Writing in England*, II, 39.

25. Jean de Venette calls him 'an illustrious nobleman, valiant and gentle, courteous and handsome' (Jean de Venette, *Chronicon*, ed. J. Birdsall and R.A. Newhall, *The Chronicle of Jean de Venette* (New York, 1953), 126).

26. Hence, for example, Sumption, *Trial by Fire*, 238, notes that at Poitiers, 'the French decided, for the first time in a major engagement, to abandon the mass cavalry charge which had been the main feature of their battle tactics for more than two centuries'.

27. V.H. Galbraith, 'Extracts from the *Historia Aurea* and a French 'Brut' (1317–47)', *EHR*, xliii (1928), 203–17, at 213–14, believed this battle to date to 1347, placing it three weeks before Dagworth's major victory and capture of Charles of Blois at La Roche-Derrien. But using an expanded version of this text (Bodleian, MS 462, ff.31–2), Prince, 'The Strength of English Armies', 364–5, showed that this engagement actually took place in June 1346, and thus several months before Crécy. For the context of this battle, unnoticed by Tout in his 'Some Neglected Fights', see Sumption, *Trial by Battle*, 495–6.

28. The exact size of Dagworth's retinue is given by Prince, 'The Strength of English Armies', 364, as 14 knights, 65 esquires, 120 horse-archers and 40 *bidauts* or light Breton infantry, which tallies closely with the figures in the *Historia Aurea*'s report of 80 men-at-arms and 100 archers ('Extracts from the *Historia Aurea*', 213). On Dagworth, see M. Jones, 'Sir Thomas Dagworth et la guerre civile en Bretagne au XIVe siècle: quelques documents inédits', *Annales de Bretagne*, lxxxviii (1980), 621–39; *Complete Peerage*, IV, 27–9; and McFarlane, *The Nobility of Later Medieval England*, 163–4.

29. *Historia Aurea*, 213: '*Anglici vero in arto sic positi locum quemdam illis aptum eligentes equos omnes et carectas a tergo statuerunt*'. The numbers given for Charles's army are clearly far too large – 1,500 men-at-arms, 2,000 Genoese crossbowmen, 30,000 foot – but the army was certainly a large one (*ibid.*, 213).

30. *Historia Aurea*, 213: '*multi nobiles et milites cum suis armatis pedites dismissis equites contra Anglicos pugnare proponebant*'.

31. *Historia Aurea*, 213; this force was led by the Viscount of Rouen and the Lords of Rochefort, Rothren, Lohéac and de Quintin.

32. It is thus hard to concur with Sumption, *Trial by Fire*, 246, that by 1356 the defeat at Poitiers was in part 'because the French were not used to fighting on foot'. For the nature of such techniques as set out in the following century see S. Anglo, 'Le Jeu de la Hache. A Fifteenth-century Treatise on the Technique of Chivalric Axe Combat', *Archaeologia*, cix (1991), 112–28; and J. Waller, 'Combat Techniques', in *Blood Red Roses. The Archaeology of a Mass Grave from the battle of Towton, AD 1461*, ed. V. Fiorato, A. Boylston and C. Knüsel (Oxford, 2000), 148–54.

33. See the important observations of Rogers, 'The Offensive/Defensive in Medieval Strategy', 158–71.

34. Ffoulkes, *The Armourer and his Craft*, 63.

35. *Historia Aurea*, 213 n. 10, 214.

36. Prince, 'The Strength of English Armies', 365 n. 3.

37. Jones, 'Sir Thomas Dagworth', 621–39.

38. The French text of the letter, with a translation, is given in Avesbury, 388–9. For the context of the battle, Sumption, *Trial by Battle*, 572–5.

39. Avesbury, 389–90.

40. Such was Dagworth's own estimate in his dispatch to Edward III (Avesbury, 389–90), but Prince, 'The Strength of English Armies', 365, calculates Dagworth's actual force at the battle to have been 300 men-at-arms and 600 mounted archers.

41. Avesbury, 389–90.

42. Rogers, *War, Cruel and Sharp*, Appendix, 423–6.

43. The following paragraph is drawn from the very full reanalysis of Edward's strategy and movements in Rogers, *War, Cruel and Sharp*, 237–64.

44. Fowler, 'News From the Front', 78–9, with the text printed 83–4.

45. Fowler, 'News From the Front', 79.

46. Among the more extended treatments of the battle see H. Belloc, *Crécy* (London, 1912); J.F.C. Fuller, *The Decisive Battles of the Western World and their Influence upon History*, 3 vols (London, 1954–6); G. Wrottesley, *Crécy and Calais* (London, 1955); Burne, *Crécy War*, 169–203; R. Barber, *Edward, Prince of Wales and Aquitaine* (London, 1978), 60–72; H. de Wailly, *Crécy, 1346: Anatomy of a Battle* (Poole, 1987); Sumption, *Trial by Battle*, 525–32; De Vries, *Infantry Warfare*, 155–75; Rogers, *War, Cruel and Sharp*, 238–72; and D. Nicolle, *Crécy, 1346. The Triumph of the Longbow* (Osprey, 2000). This latter work is particularly valuable for its illustrations. An important new collection of studies devoted to the battle, *The Battle of Crécy*, ed. A. Ayton and Sir Philip Preston (Woodbridge), is currently in press and should do much to increase our understanding of the engagement and its topography.

47. Bradbury, *The Medieval Archer*, 95–108.

48. Le Bel, II, 105–6; Rogers, *The Wars of Edward III*, 133–4.

49. Cf. Barber, *Edward, Prince of Wales*, 64.

50. Le Baker, 84, trans. Barber, 44: '*Sagitarris eciam sua loca designarunt, ut, non coram armatis, set a lateribus regis exercitus quasi ale astarent, et sic non impedirent armatos neque inimicis occurent in fronte, set in latera sagittas fulminarent.*' For the placing of Northampton and Warwick, see *The Acts of War*, in Barber, *Life and Campaigns*, 29.

51. Le Bel, II, 105; Rogers, *The Wars of Edward III*, 133.

52. Le Baker, 83, trans. Barber, 44.

53. Sumption, *Trial by Battle*, 527. This version of Edward's deployment seems to be based on the *Chronographia regnum Francorum, 1270–1405*, ed. H. Moranville, 3 vols (Paris, 1891–7), II, 231–2, which says that Edward 'had his army shut in with carts and wagons' (*exercitum suum claudi fecit curribus suis et quadrigis*), and that the English archers shot at the Genoese strongly, '*et fecerunt clausurum de curribus et sepibus nemorum*'. The *Chronique Normande*, 80–1, notes more ambiguously that the bolts of the Genoese did the English little harm because they were '*bien targiez de leur charroy*'.

54. Bennett, 'The Development of Battle Tactics', 8.

55. The evidence is reviewed in detail by A.H. Burne, 'Cannon at Crécy', *Royal Artillery Journal*, lxxvii (1939), 335ff; *idem, Crécy War*, 192–202. Cf. Tout, *Chapters*, II, 237–9, 254, 258–62; and Hall, *Weapons and Warfare*, 45–6; Sumption, *Trial by Battle*, 527–8.

56. *Chroniques des quatre premiers Valois (1327–1393)*, ed. S. Luce (Paris, 1862), 14–17; *Chronique Normande*, 80–1.

57. For Jean Le Bel and other chroniclers' treatment of the battle, see N. Chareyron, *Jean Le Bel. Le Maître de Froissart, Grand Imagier de la guerre de Cent Ans* (Brussels, 1996), 105–19.

58. Le Bel, II, 101–2; trans. Rogers, *The Wars of Edward III*, 131–2.

59. Le Bel, II, 101–2; trans. Rogers, *The Wars of Edward III*, 132.

60. *Chronique et Annales de Gilles le Muisit, abbé de Saint-Martin de Tournai (1272–1352)*, ed. H. Lemaître (Paris, 1906), 161; *Chronique Normande*, 80–1.

61. *Chronographia*, 231.

62. Sumption, *Trial by Battle*, 531–2.

63. Sumption, *Trial by Battle*, 526.

64. Rogers, *War, Cruel, and Sharp*, 267. The *Chronicle of St Omer*, cited in *ibid.*, 268, says that Louis, Count of Blois, attempted to dismount his men-at-arms and lead them forward on foot. But he was unable to retreat and was killed.

65. *Chronicle of St Omer*, f.262, cited in Rogers, *War, Cruel and Sharp*, 267 n. 166.

66. Froissart, ed. Luce, III, 174; trans. in *Chroniques*, ed. G. Brereton (Harmondsworth, 1968), 87. Froissart's treatment of the battle initially followed that of Le Bel, but developed considerably during his various recensions (Froissart, ed. Luce, III, xl–lxiii, 168–93, 403–37); and for the final redaction of Book I (Rome, Reg. Lat. 869), Froissart, *Chroniques*, ed. G.T. Diller (Geneva, 1972), 717–41. For a discussion see Lettenhove, *Oeuvres de Froissart*, V, 27–75, and Barber, *Edward, Prince of Wales*, 245–8.

67. Froissart, ed. Luce, V, 42–3; trans. Brereton, 138.

68. *Chronique et Annales de Gilles le Muisit*, 161; *Chronographia regum Francorum*, II, 232; *Chronique Normande*, 80.

69. Froissart, ed. Luce, III, 175–6, 418.

70. Le Baker, 83, trans. Barber, 43.

71. Burne, *Crécy War*, 188–9; and cf. Guillaume de Nangis, II, 202, and Jean de Venette, trans. 43 and n. 63.

72. *Chronique Normande*, 80–1; Le Muisit, 161, give their number as 10,000. Sumption, *Trial by Battle*, suggests that Philip had possibly as many as 6,000 Genoese, the figure given by Villani.

73. Paterson, *The Crossbow*, 33.

74. Le Baker, 83, trans. Barber, 43.

75. Le Muisit, 162.

76. Froissart, ed. Luce, III, 176–7; trans. Brereton, 89; Le Muisit, 162.

77. Giovanni Villani, *Nouva Chronica*, ed. G. Porta, 3 vols (Parma, 1991), III, 452.

78. Le Bel, II, 102–3; Rogers, *The Wars of Edward III*, 132.

79. Le Muisit, 162; Lescot, 74; *Chronographia*, 232.

80. Froissart, ed. Luce, III, 177.

81. Le Baker, 83, trans. Barber, 44.

82. Le Baker, 84, trans. Barber, 44.

83. Froissart, ed. Luce, III, trans. Brereton, 89.

84. Le Bel, II, 103; Rogers, *The Wars of Edward III*, 132; '*ces flesches barbelèes [qui] faisoient merveilles*'.

85. *Chronographia*, II, 233.

86. Froissart, ed. Luce, III, 182–3; Barber, *Edward, Prince of Wales*, 246–8, who notes that the prince had already been knighted at St Vaast-la-Hogue at the outset of the campaign. King Edward seems to have been gratified in this wish; writing in the 1380s for one of the prince's subsequent companions in arms, Chandos Herald remarked that, 'I know for certain that that day the brave and noble prince had the vanguard, and we should remember it, because it was through him and his qualities that the field was won' (Chandos Herald, ll. 355–7; trans. Barber, 89).

87. Le Baker, 84, trans. Barber, 44. That others distinguished themselves in the fighting is suggested by the fact that Edward III created Alan de la Zouche and John de Lisle barons, and made fifty knights (*Eulogium historiarum*, III, 211; Knighton, 64–5).

88. Le Bel, 108; le Baker, 85, notes his body was accorded full honours by the English.

89. *Récits d'un bourgeois de Valenciennes*, ed. K. de Lettenhove (Louvain, 1877), 233. Both these knights were well rewarded after the battle (Barber, *Edward Prince of Wales*, 67 and n. 26).

90. *Récits*, 233; le Baker, 84, trans. Barber, 44–5.

91. Le Baker, 84, trans. Barber, 44.

92. Le Baker, 84, '*orrida Martis facies ostensa*', trans. Barber, 45.

93. *Eulogium historiarum*, III, 211. Sumption, *Trial by Fire*, 218, notes that the values of French mounts revealed by restor or compensation payments show that the average cost of a destrier for a banneret was 270 livres tournois (£54), that for a knight 103 livres tournois (£21) and for a squire 40 livres tournois (£8).

94. See p. 279.

95. Le Bel, II, 103; Rogers, *The Wars of Edward III*, 133.

96. *Chronique normande de Pierre Cochon*, 69; Barber, *Edward, Prince of Wales*, 68 and n. 28.

97. Letter of Edward III in Chandos Herald, 354; le Baker, 85, 261–2; Murimuth, 248; Northburgh, in Avesbury, 369.

98. Le Bel, II, 109; Rogers, *The Wars of Edward III*, 135.

99. C. Given-Wilson and F. Bériac, 'Edward III's Prisoners of War: the Battle of Poitiers and its Context', *EHR*, cxvi (2001), 802–33; F. Bériac-Laine and C. Given-Wilson, *Les prisonniers de la bataille de Poitiers* (Paris, 2002), especially 307–28.

100. Barber, *Edward, Prince of Wales*, 70–2.

101. Froissart, ed. Luce, III, 186.

102. Knighton, 42–3.

103. Le Bel, II, 104; Rogers, *The Wars of Edward III*, 133.

104. See p. 214.

105. For the siege of Calais see Burne, *Crécy War*, 204–23; Sumption, *Trial by Battle*, 536–40, 554–83.

106. Avesbury, 393; and for a discussion of the context of this challenge, Rogers, *War, Cruel and Sharp*, 279–82.

107. For the context, and the large number of archers, Sumption, *Trial by Fire*, 60–2.

108. Le Baker, 106–7, trans. Barber, 47–8. Cf. Avesbury, 408–10, who gives the number of men-at-arms at 30 against Geoffrey's 16; Le Muisit, 260–3; *Les Grandes Chroniques de France*, ed. J. Viard, 10 vols (Paris, 1920–53), IX, 321–2.

109. T.F. Tout, 'Some Neglected Fights between Crécy and Poitiers', *The Collected Works of Thomas Frederick Tout*, 3 vols (Manchester, 1932–4), II, 227–31, was the first to draw attention to the significance of Lunalonge (1349), Taillebourg (1351) and Mauron (1352).

110. The site of the battle is uncertain, and the *Chronique Normande* simply remarks of the Anglo-Gascon position that 'it was very advantageous' ('*de grant aventaige estoit*') ibid., 95.

111. *Chronique Normande*, 94–5.

112. *Chronique Normande*, 97–8.

113. Le Baker, 115–16; Le Muisit, 294–5; *Chronique Normande*, 101–2; Knighton, 110–11; *Récits*, 268–9; *Istore et croniqes de Flandres*, ed. K. de Lettenhove, 2 vols (Brussels, 1879–80), II, 75.

114. Bennett, 'The Development of Battle Tactics', 11.

115. Le Bel, II, 194–8; Froissart, ed. Luce, IV, 111–15; Froissart, ed. Lettenhove, V, notes on 513–14; de la Broderie, *Histoire de Bretagne*, III, 514–29; H.R. Bush, ed., 'La bataille de Trente Anglois et Trente Bretons', *Modern Philology*, ix (1911–12), 511–44, and x (1912–13), 82–136.

116. Le Bel, II, 196. For other such engagements, Sumption, *Trial by Fire*, 34.

117. Le Bel, II, 197. According to a verse account of the battle (Froissart, ed. Lettenhove, V, 513). The Combat of Thirty was recorded by Wyntoun, II, 488–94, who stresses the vital role of one horseman in attacking the English from the flank. Richard Lescot, *Chronique (1328–1344), suivie de la continuation de cette chronique (1344–1364)*, ed. J. Lemoine (Paris, 1896), 86.

118. For Bentley's meteoric career, see Jones, 'Edward III's Captains in Brittany', 100.

119. *Chronique Normande*, 105. However Sumption, *Trial by Fire*, 94, suggests this was possibly double the number of Bentley's actual force.

120. The best contemporary descriptions are given by the *Chronique Normande*, 105–6; le Baker, 120; and with additional details of the slain and prisoners, but not of the fight itself, in Bentley's dispatches, given by Avesbury, 416–17. For secondary accounts of Mauron, see A. de la Broderie, *Histoire de Bretagne*, III (1899), 530–2; Tout, 'Some Neglected Fights between Crécy and Poitiers', 230–1; Burne, *Crécy War*, 236–45; Sumption, *Trial by Fire*, 94–5.

121. *Chronique Normande*, 105; '*le long d'une haie, laquele ilz mistrent derriere leur dos, et mistsrent leurs archiers sur leurs costez, dont ilz avoient bien viii cens*'.

122. *Chronique Normande*, 105–6. For the French captured or slain, ibid., 106; Bentley's report in Avesbury, 190; le Baker, 120.

123. Le Baker, 120; Sumption, *Trial by Fire*, 95.

124. Le Baker, 120. His account of Mauron is given in translation in *EHD*, IV, 92, but contains no tactical details.

125. Rogers, *War, Cruel and Sharp*, 348–58.

126. Froissart, ed. Luce, V, 29, trans. Thompson, *Contemporary Chronicles*, 108. Knighton, 142–3, similarly remarks on the English army's want of supplies.

127. As Prestwich, *Armies and Warfare*, 310, notes 'it is hard to believe that if the English had wanted to avoid fighting, they could not have succeeded in doing so'.

128. The battle of Poitiers has been treated by a number of authorities, including R. Delechenal, *Histoire de Charles V*, 5 vols (Paris, 1909–31), I, 212–44; A.H. Burne, 'The Battle of Poitiers', *EHR*, liii (1938), 21–52, which has a valuable discussion of the primary sources, and on which *idem*, *Crécy War*, 275–321, is in part based; J.M. Touneur-Aumont, *La bataille de Poitiers* (Paris, 1940); V.H. Galbraith, 'The Battle of Poitiers', *EHR*, liv (1939), 473–5; Hewitt, *The Black Prince's Expedition*, 112–31; Barber, *Edward, Prince of Wales*, 136–48; Rogers, *War, Cruel and Sharp*, 373–84; and D. Green, *The Battle of Poitiers, 1356* (Stroud, 2002). Bériac-Laine and Given-Wilson, *Les prisonniers de la bataille de Poitiers* provides an excellent study not only of the process of ransom but also of the *mentalité* of warfare, and discusses the battle at 39–50.

129. Le Baker, 146–7, trans. Barber, 75–6.

130. We have here followed the topography suggested by Green, *Battle of Poitiers*, 58–60 and pls 2–5, and see 58 n. 7 for references to map sources.

131. Froissart, ed. Luce, V, 31, trans. Thompson, *Contemporary Chronicles*, 109.

132. Le Baker, 147, trans. Barber, 76. '*insistentes aggeri tuto supra fossam et ultra sepem*'. Froissart believed that the English dug several ditches in front of their positions, Froissart, trans. Thompson, *Contemporary Chronicles*, 102.

133. Froissart, ed. Luce, V, 31, trans. Thompson, *Contemporary Chronicles*, 109.

134. Letter of Bartholemew Burghersh, in Froissart, ed. Lettenhove, XVIII, 387. These figures are also given in a marginal note, together with a list of French slain and prisoners, in a Canterbury manuscript, which numbers the prince's army at 3,000 men-at-arms, 2,000 archers and 1,000 '*sudamtyz*', with John's army reckoned at 8,000 men-at-arms and 3,000 infantry (Gervase of Canterbury, *Opera Historica*, II, lii). This may draw directly on Burghersh's letter, but the prince had close connections to Christchurch, Canterbury, and was buried there. Prince, 'The Strength of English Armies', 366–7, suggests, by contrast, that his army may not have been far off the size of that accompanying him on his 1355 expedition, which has been estimated at a little over 1,000 men-at-arms, the same number of mounted archers, around 300–400 foot-archers in his personal retinue, and a small body of some 170 Welsh. Knighton, 148–9, estimated the prince's force at 1,800 men-at-arms and 1,400 archers.

135. Sumption, *Trial by Fire*, 235. The *Anonimalle Chronicle*, 38, believed King John's battle alone contained 8,000 'bascinets' and large numbers of crossbowmen, pavise bearers and other infantry.

136. Froissart, ed. Luce, V, 22: '*et fisent fosser et haiier leurs archiers autour d'yaux, pou estre plus fort*'.

137. Froissart, ed. Luce, V, 22; adaption of the translation in Thompson, *Contemporary Chronicles*, 104.

138. Froissart, ed. Luce, V, 19–20, trans. Thompson, *Contemporary Chronicles*, 103.

139. *Ordonnances des rois de France*, 67–70. The ordinance is translated in Allmand, *Society at War*, 45–8.

140. K. Fowler, *The Age of Plantagenet and Valois: the Struggle for Supremacy, 1328–1498* (London, 1967), 94, 99, 101.

141. Le Baker, 143, trans. Barber, 73.

142. The *Chronographia*, II, 262, implies that King Jean's battle dismounted only after seeing the discomfiture of the marshals' mounted attack.

143. *Chronique Normande*, 98, 291 n. 1; he narrowly escaped being captured again at Comborn in 1353, in a hand-to-hand battle with English men-at-arms; *ibid.*, 101–2, 291.

144. *Chronique Normande*, 106–7: '*et descendirent à pié l'une parti et l'autre*'.

145. Froissart, ed. Luce, V, 22; trans. Thompson, *Contemporary Chronicles*, 105.

146. Froissart, ed. Luce, V, 22; trans. Thompson, *Contemporary Chronicles*, 104–5.

147. Le Baker, 143, trans, Barber, 73, who speaks of 'five hundred horses clad in mail to protect them from arrows, whose commanders ordered them to attack the archers at the beginning of the battle, and ride them down under their horses' hooves; but this order was not carried out as events showed'.

148. Froissart, ed. Luce, V, 23, trans. Thompson, *Contemporary Chronicles*, 105.

149. Chandos Herald, 28: *Anonimalle Chronicle*, 38. This, and evidence for crossbowmen supporting King Jean's main division, must qualify Bennett's remark, 'The Development of Battle Tactics', 13, that at Poitiers 'once again French missilemen are notable by their absence'.

150. Sumption, *Trial by Fire*, 238–9, believes it was a genuine attempt to retreat.

151. *Anonimalle Chronicle*, 38.

152. Le Baker, 144, trans. Barber 74, believed that Clermont, who had earlier urged Jean to accept the prince's offer of a truce, wanted to be the first in the attack to save his reputation from any allegations of cowardice that such counsel might bring, while d'Audenham was supporting his claim by his slanders, 'which were made out of envy'.

153. Chandos Herald, 34, trans. Barber, 99.

154. Chandos Herald, 35, trans. Barber, 100; and cf. Knighton, 'the first division of the French clashed with the Earl of Warwick, but they were quickly brought low by the archers'.

155. *Chronographia*, II, 262; Froissart, ed. Lettenhove, V, 425/439, similarly notes how 'the battle of the marshals was almost completely broken up and discomfited by the archers' shooting' (*la bataille des mareschaus fu tantos toute déreoute et desconfite par le trait des archiers*).

156. *Anonimalle Chronicle*, 38. Chandos Herald's belief that Salisbury's men 'defeated the marshals and the armed cavalry before the [English] vanguard could wheel round and come back over the river which they had just crossed' must surely be mistaken,

as only one part of the marshals' force attacked Salisbury's division.

157. Le Baker, 148, trans. Barber, 76.

158. *Chronique Normande*, 115.

159. Chandos Herald, 36–7, trans. Barber, 100.

160. Green, *Battle of Poitiers*, 54.

161. Le Baker, 150; trans. Barber, 78.

162. *Chronique Normande*, 115, 'y ot pluseurs Englois qui tournerent pour fuir, mais François s'entasserent si pour le grant trait des archiers, qui sur leurs tests leur venoit, que grand foison ne povoient combatre et chairent les uns sur l'autre. Lors se prindrent François à desconfire'.

163. Le Baker, 151, trans. Barber, 79.

164. Knighton, 144–5.

165. For a plausible suggestion of his route in a wide arc behind Salisbury's right wing, Green, *The Battle of Poitiers*, map 5.

166. Le Baker, 152, trans. Barber, 80.

167. Le Baker, 152, trans. Barber, 80.

168. Knighton, 142–3, noted that 'Sir Geoffrey de Charny bore the scarlet standard, which is the token of Death'.

169. Le Baker, 152–3, trans. Barber, 80–1

170. For casualties and prisoners, see Given-Wilson and Beriac, 'Edward III's Prisoners of War', 802–33; and Bériac-Laine and Given-Wilson, *Les prisonniers de la bataille de Poitiers*.

171. Sumption, *Trial by Fire*, 246.

172. Chandos Herald, 42; trans. Barber, 102.

173. *Chroniques des règnes de Jean II et Charles V*, ed. R. Delachenal (Paris, 1910), 72: 'autres dient que la cause de la desconfiture fu pour ce que l'on ne povoit entrer es diz Angloiz; car ilz s'estoient mis en trop forte place, et leurs archeirs traaioient si dru que les gens du dit roy de France ne povoient demourer en leur trait'.

174. *Eulogium historiarum*, 225; Prestwich, *Armies and Warfare*, 325.

175. Froissart, ed. Luce, V, 77; Prestwich, *Armies and Warfare*, 322.

176. A very full account of the battle and events leading up to it is provided by Delachenal, *Histoire de Charles V*, III, 27–64; see also S. Luce, *Histoire de Bertrand du Guesclin et de son époque* (Paris, 1882), 389–412.

177. Froissart, ed. Luce, VI, 110, gives the most precise figures, though their veracity cannot be ascertained; for other chronicle estimates, Delachenal, *Histoire de Charles V*, 36 n. 4.

178. Froissart, ed. Luce, VI, 113–15.

179. The *Chronique Normande*, 171–2, believed that the Anglo-Navarese first mounted for this pursuit, but when they saw the French about turn, they dismounted to fight.

180. *The Chronicles of Froissart*, trans. Berners, 149; Froissart, ed. Luce, VI, 125: 'quand li arcier furent devant, si s'eslargirent et commencencièrent à traire de grant manière; mès li Francois estoient si fort armé et si bien paveschié contre le tret, que onques il n'en furent grevé, se petit non, ne pour ce n'en laissièrent il point à combatre, mès entrèrent, et tout à piet, ens ès Navarois et Englès, et cil entre eulz de grant volenté'.

181. *Chronique des quatre premiers Valois*, 146–7; Froissart has a more pictureque story of how a picked force of 30 knights cut their way through to where the Captal was fighting and took him

prisoner (ed. Luce, VI, 126–7). According to the *Chronique Normande*, 172, a group of English had attempted to outflank the French position, but Du Guesclin had in turn succeeded in attacking the main Anglo-Navarese force from the rear.

182. Delachenal, *Histoire de Charles V*, 56–9, where the relevant sources are cited in the notes.

183. F. Buttin, 'La lance et l'arrêt de cuirasse', *Archaeologia*, xcix (1965), 77–114; Vale, *War and Chivalry*, 114–15, 118.

184. Chaucer, *Knight's Tale*, l. 2602, the English rendering of the commonly found French expression 'jeter les lances en l'arrêt'.

185. For accounts of Auray see de la Broderie, *Histoire de Bretagne*, II, 582–95; D. Plaine, 'La journée d'Auray d'après quelques documents nouveaux', *Association bretonne*, xvii (1874), 83–102; Luce, *Du Guesclin en Normandie*; *The Chronicles of Froissart translated out of the French by Sir John Bourchier, Lord Berners (1523–25)*, ed. W.P. Ker, 4 vols (London, 1901–2), II, 130–43.

186. Froissart, ed. Luce, VI, 155–6. Froissart believed that Chandos adopted this formation to mirror that of the French, though this seems unlikely.

187. Froissart, ed. Luce, VI, 155–7

188. Froissart, ed. Luce, VI, 154.

189. Froissart, ed. Luce, VI, 162.

190. Froissart, ed. Luce, VI, 162.

191. Froissart, ed. Luce, VI, 162: 'li arcier traiirent de commencement; mès leurs très ne grevanoient as François, car il estoient trop bien armet et fort, et ossi bien paveschiet contre le tret'.

192. Froissart, ed. Luce, VI, 162–3.

193. See the valuable discussion by Rogers, 'The Offensive/Defensive in Medieval Strategy', 158–171.

194. Jean de Bueil, *Le Jouvencel*, ed. L. Lecestre, 2 vols (Paris, 1887–9), I, 153; trans. Contamine, *War in the Middle Ages*, 231.

195. Jean Cuvelier, *Chronique de Bertrand de Guesclin*, ed. E. Charrière, 2 vols (Paris, 1839), II, 5875–9.

196. Burne, *Crécy War*, 49, calls this mounted counter-attack 'a dazzling decision which stamps him for all time as a great commander'.

197. The essential study for this campaign and its wider context remains Russell, *English Intervention*, to which the following account of Nájera is indebted.

198. Barber, *Black Prince*, 194.

199. Russell, *English Intervention*, 79.

200. Chandos Herald, 77–87, trans. Barber, 117–21.

201. The chief sources for the battle are Chandos Herald and the eye-witness account of Lopez de Ayala. Froissart's account, which is often confused, draws heavily on Chandos Herald. The campaign was also the subject of a Latin poem by Walter of Peterborough, *Prince Edward's Expedition into Spain and the Battle of Nájera*, ed. T. Wright, *Political Poems and Songs*, 2 vols (Rolls Series, London, 1859–), I, 97–122, and a much briefer anonymous verse (*ibid.*, I, 94–6). While of some value for the campaign, however, neither adds to our knowledge of the battle itself. A dispatch by the prince announcing his victory lists some of the prisoners, but

gives little information on the fighting (A.E. Prince, 'A Letter of Edward the Black Prince describing the battle of Nájera in 1367', *EHR*, xli (1926), 415–18. For secondary accounts of the battle see Delachenal, *Histoire de Charles V*, 400–7; Oman, *Art of War*, II, 184–90; Russell, *English Intervention*, 83–107; and cf. Barber, *Edward, Prince of Wales*, 199–202.

202. Russell, *English Intervention*, 99–101, with topographical map on p. 100.

203. Pero López de Ayala, *Crónica del rey Don Pedro*, ed. E. Llaguno y Amirola, *Crónicas de los reyes de Castiilla*, I (Madrid, 1779), 556.

204. Chandos Herald, 92; trans. Barber, 123, believed Enrique to have 6,000 crossbowmen, a clear exaggeration.

205. Chandos Herald, 94; trans. Barber, 124, believed that Denia and Count Sancho also fought on foot, and that the cavalry comprised 4,100 armed horse.

206. Ayala, I, 442–3.

207. Russell, *English Intervention*, 96–7. Ayala estimated the prince's force at 10,000 men-at-arms and the same number of archers, which clearly is a gross exaggeration.

208. Ayala, I, 454–5; Chandos Herald, 99–100; trans. Barber, 126.

209. Froissart, ed. Luce, VII, 37.

210. Chandos Herald, 100–1; Froissart, ed. Luce, VII, 38.

211. Chandos Herald, 103, trans. Barber, 128.

212. Froissart, ed. Luce, VII, 37.

213. Froissart, ed. Luce, VII, 41.

214. Ayala, I, 455.

215. Samuel Daniel, *The Collection of the History of England*, in *The Complete Works in Verse and Prose of Samuel Daniel*, ed. A.B. Grosart, 5 vols (London, 1885–96), V, 290; McKisack, *The Fourteenth Century*, 145.

CHAPTER 14

1. McKisack, *The Fourteenth Century*, 145.

2. Burne, *The Agincourt War*, 19–20, while his account of this period runs to fewer than seven pages.

3. For a discussion of the Gascon leaders in 1356 and formation of contingents see Bériac-Lainé and Given-Wilson, *Les prisonniers de la bataille de Poitiers*, 295–304.

4. K. Fowler, *Medieval Mercenaries. Volume I: The Great Companies* (Oxford, 2001), 64–7.

5. For Amory, Fowler, *Medieval Mercenaries*, 69–71.

6. P. Tucoo-Chala, *Gaston Fébus et la vicomté de Béarn, 1342–1391* (Bordeaux, 1960), 87.

7. Froissart, *Oeuvres*, ed. Lettenhove, VII, 380.

8. Fowler, *Medieval Mercenaries*, 24ff.

9. Walsingham, *Historia Anglicana*, I, 295, speaks, *s.a.* 1361, of '*illa magna et famosa Comitiva de diversis nationibus adunata, cujus duces pro majori parte erant Anglici*'.

10. Walsingham, *Historia Anglicana*, I, 295–6; E.R. Chamberlain, 'The English Mercenary Companies in Italy', *History Today*, vi, no. 5 (May 1956), 334–43, at 337; Fowler, *Medieval Mercenaries*, 3 n. 9, 45 and n. 5.

11. Fowler, *Medieval Mercenaries*, 262, and cf. 277.

12. Froissart, ed. Luce, IX, 156.

13. For Brignais see Froissart, ed. Luce, VI, 65–9; Fowler, *Medieval Mercenaries*, 46–51.

14. On the Free Companies in Spain see K. Fowler, 'L'emploi des mercenaires par les pouvoirs ibériques et l'intervention militaire anglaise en Espagne (vers 1361 – vers 1379)', *Realidad e imagines del poder: España a fines de la edad media*, ed. A. Rucquoi (Valladolid, 1998), 23–55: and *idem*, 'Deux entrepreneurs militaires au XIVe siècle: Bertrand du Guesclin et Sir Hugh Calveley', *Le combatant au moyen âge*, 243–56.

15. K. Fowler, 'Sir John Hawkwood and the English Condottieri in Trecento Italy', *Renaissance Studies*, xii (1998), 131–48, at 132, 137. A detailed modern study is currently in preparation by Professor Fowler and will appear as the second volume of his *Medieval Mercenaries*. Until then, the most detailed accounts of Hawkwood's career remain J. Temple-Leader and G. Marcotti, *Sir John Hawkwood, Story of a Condottieri* (London and Florence, 1889), who discuss what little is known of Hawkwood's origins at 5–9; and G. Trease, *The Condottieri* (London, 1971). A briefer summary is provided by F. Gaupp, 'The Condottiere John Hawkwood', *History*, xxiii (1939), 305–21.

16. Fowler, 'Sir John Hawkwood', 132, 137.

17. Temple-Leader and Marcotti, *Sir John Hawkwood*, 45–58.

18. Matteo Villani, *Chronica, con la continuazione di Filippo Villani*, ed. G. Porta, 2 vols (Parma, 1995), II, 702; the translation is from Chamberlain, 'The English Mercenary Companies', 337.

19. For the organisation and conditions in the Companies see Ricotti, *Storia delle Compagne di Ventura in Italia*; G. Canestrini, 'Documenti per sevire alla Storia della Milizia Italiana', *Archivio Storico Italiano*, xv (1851); Temple-Leader and Marcotti, *Sir John Hawkwood*, 38–45.

20. Jones, *Chaucer's Knight*, 16–18, 214–15; see p. 146. For a contrary view, see M. Keen, 'Chaucer's Knight, the English Aristocracy and the Crusade', *English Court Culture in the Later Middle Ages*, ed. V.J. Scattergood and J.W. Sherborne (London, 1981), 45–61.

21. Nicolle, *Arms and Armour*, I, 499–500, II, 910–11 (no. 1378), who suggests these may represent Cumans, Hungarians and Balkans, though the weapons seem disproportionately long for a representation of composite bows.

22. D.P. Waley, 'The Army of the Florentine Republic from the Twelfth to the Fourteenth Century', *Florentine Studies. Politics and Society in Renaissance Florence*, ed. N. Rubinstein (Evanston, 1968), 70–108, at 73.

23. D.P. Waley, '*Condotte* and *Condottieri* in the Thirteenth Century', *Proceedings of the British Academy*, lxi (1975), 337–71, at 339, 344.

24. Mallet, *Mercenaries and their Masters*, 21–2, 35. Similarly, in 1354 the league of Florence, Siena and Perugia formed in defence against the Company of Fra Moriale agreed to field 1,000 mercenary crossbowmen and 2,000 cavalry (W. Caferro, *Mercenary Companies and the Decline of Siena* (Baltimore, 1998), 100).

25. Contamine, *War in the Middle Ages*, 161.

26. Caferro, *Mercenary Companies*, 57–8.

27. Waley, 'The Army of the Florentine Republic', 72, 74, 76–8.

28. Mallet, *Mercenaries and their Masters*, 33.

29. See pp. 109–12.

30. Pietro Azario, *Liber gestorum in Lombardia*, ed. F. Cognasso, in *Rerum Italicarum Scriptores*, ed. L.A. Muratori, XVI, pt 4, 128, trans. Jones, *Chaucer's Knight*, 212; 'pedestres tam magnos et acutos arcus, quod ipsos fingunt a testa inferiori in terra et, trahendo, magnas et longas sagitas emitunt'.

31. Matteo Villani, *Chronica*, II, 702, 'altri di loro erano arcieri, e loro archi erano di nasso, e lunghi, e con essi erano presti e ubidenti, e facieno buona pruova'.

32. Fowler, 'Sir John Hawkwood', 137.

33. Ricotti, *Storia delle Compagnie*, II, 315–16: Jones, *Chaucer's Knight*, 133 n. 22.

34. P. Partner, *The Lands of St Peter: The Papal State in the Middle Ages and the Early Renaissance* (London, 1972), 353; *Codex diplomaticus Dominii Temporalis Sanctae Sedis*, ed. A. Theiner, 2 vols (Rome, 1861–2), II, no. 399.

35. For these merchants and the export of Italian armour, see p. 273.

36. Temple-Leader and Marcotti, *Sir John Hawkwood*, 237.

37. Oman, *Art of War*, II, 294.

38. Fowler, 'Sir John Hawkwood ', 137.

39. According to Froissart, VI, 68, the men of the Companies had done likewise at Brignais in 1362.

40. Matteo Villani, *Chronica*, II, 702–3; Azario, *Liber gestorum in Lombardia*, 128.

41. Matteo Villani, *Chronica*, II, 702. The translation is an amended version of that given in Jones, *Chaucer's Knight*, 133.

42. Pietro Azario, *Liber gestorum in Lombardia*, 128: '*Nam mos ipsorum est cum necessario habeant in aperto debellare, descentes ab equis, sola dipliode armati, ut plurimum, vel placa una ferrea supra pectus et capite ut plurimum decoperto vel cum solo cupo barbute et lanceis grandibus*'. My translation here differs somewhat from that of Jones, *Chaucer's Knight*, 135.

43. Matteo Villani, *Chronica*, II, 701–2.

44. Fowler, 'Sir John Hawkwood', 133.

45. For accounts of the battle see Temple-Leader and Marcotti, *Sir John Hawkwood*, 195–202; Oman, *Art of War*, II, 297–300; Trease, *The Condottieri*, 113–26; Mallet, *Mercenaries and their Masters*, 54–5; D. Nicolle, *Italian Medieval Armies, 1300–1500* (London, 1983), 24–5. For the political context of the engagement, see B.G. Kohl, *Padua under the Carrara, 1318–1405* (Baltimore and London, 1998), 233–40.

46. Fowler, 'Sir John Hawkwood', 133–4.

47. *Chronica Carrarese*, in Muratori, XVII, 268–71.

48. *Chronica Carrarese*, 270–5.

49. Trease, *The Condottieri*, 126.

50. Oman, *Art of War*, II, 296.

51. Fowler, 'Sir John Hawkwood', 131.

52. D.M. Bueno de Mesquita, 'Some Condottieri of the Trecento and their Relations with Political Authority', *Proceedings of the British Academy*, xxxii (1946), 219–41, at 225ff; Contamine, *War in the Middle Ages*, 158–61.

53. Nicolle, *Medieval Italian Armies*, 10–11.

54. For examples of comparative numbers of infantry to cavalry, Contamine, *War in the Middle Ages*, 133.

55. Mallet, *Mercenaries and their Masters*, 156–7.

56. *The St Albans Chronicle. The Chronica maiora of Thomas Walsingham*, ed. J. Taylor, W.R. Childs and L. Watkiss (Oxford, 2003) I, 408–9 and n. 477.

57. Russell, *English Intervention*, 302–44.

58. Russell, *English Intervention*, 365–6.

59. C. Bessa, 'Le Portugal 1383–1385: crise, art militaire et consolidation de l'indépendance', in *From Crécy to Móhacs*, 28–50, at 28–31; Fernão Lopez, *Cronica de Don Fernando*, ed. de Salvador Dias Arnaut (Porto, 1979), 233–49; Bessa, 'Le Portugal 1383–1385', 33.

60. *Cronica del Rey Don Juan Primero*, in *Cronicas de los Reyes de Castilla*, II, 219; Russell, *English Intervention*, 365–6.

61. The Monk of Westminster, in Ralph Higden, *Polychronicon*, 66; Russell, *English Intervention*, 354–6.

62. Bessa, 'Le Portugal 1383–1385', 31–3.

63. Ayala, *Cronica del Rey Don Juan*, 231.

64. A. Do Paço, 'The Battle of Aljubarotta', *Antiquity*, xxxvii (1963), 264–9. The main frontal ditch was 2.5m wide and had two stages, the first .8m deep, with a deeper central section (another .74m at deepest, making the deepest bottom 1.54m). The excavators found around 830 pits, but part of the site was covered with olive trees and could not be dug; they estimated there were probably more than a thousand on this flank alone.

65. Russell, *English Intervention*, 396 n. 3, completely dismisses Froissart's view here, and is generally sceptical about the reliability of his account.

66. Froissart, ed. Luce, XII, 148.

67. Ayala, *Cronica del Rey Don Juan*, 231.

68. Ayala, *Cronica del Rey Don Juan*, 230–3; Russell, *English Intervention*, 368, 393.

69. Froissart, ed. Luce, XII, 157.

70. Ayala, *Cronica del Rey Don Juan*, 235–7, lists some of the most important among the slain.

71. Froissart, ed. Luce, XII, 162–3, 164–5.

72. For the course of the war see Delachenal, *Histoire de Charles V*, IV, 147ff; F. Autrand, *Charles V le Sage* (Paris, 1994), 568–605.

73. For this campaign and the defeat at Pontvallain, Fowler, *Medieval Mercenaries*, 283–97.

74. Froissart, ed. Luce, XIV, 7.

75. For 'l'armée de la reconquête', see Contamine, *Guerre, État et Société*; Autrand, *Charles V*, 602–5.

76. *Ordonnances des Rois de France*, V.

77. Fowler, *Age of Plantagenet and Valois*, 134.

78. *Ordonnances des Rois de France*, V, 651.

79. Delaunay, *Étude sur les anciennes compagnies d'archers, d'arbalètriers, et d'arquebusiers* (Paris, 1879), 4–9.

80. Delaunay, *Étude sur les anciennes compagnies d'archers*, 4–9.

81. *Ordonnances des Rois de France*, V, 32.

82. *Ordonnances des Rois de France*, V, 144–5, 636.

83. *Ordonnances des Rois de France*, V, 16, c.7

84. Fowler, *Medieval Mercenaries*, 224–5.

85. *Ordonnances des Rois de France*, V, 14–22.

86. *Ordonnances des Rois de France*, V, 172.

87. Delauney, *Étude sur les anciennes compagnies d'archers*, 62.

88. Jean Juvenal des Ursins, *Histoire de Charles VI*, 385.

89. Sumption, *Trial by Fire*, 332–3, who remarks 'rarely had political divisions been so completely closed by the common interest of caste'.

90. Sumption, *Trial by Fire*, 332.

91. For Charles VII's armies and the Francs-archers, see pp. 353–6.

92. A.J. Macdonald, *Border Bloodshed. Scotland and England at War, 1369–1403* (Edinburgh, 2000), 87 and n. 50.

93. Bradbury, *The Medieval Archer*, 169–70.

94. W. Rye, 'The Riot between the Monks and Citizens of Norwich in 1272', *Norfolk Antiquarian Miscellany*, ii (1883); E.C. Fernie, *An Architectural History of Norwich Cathedral* (Oxford, 1993), 163–81.

95. J.A.F. Thomson, *The Transformation of Medieval England, 1370–1529* (London, 1983), 32–9.

96. Froissart, ed. Luce X, 108; N. Brooks, 'The Organization and Achievement of the Peasants of Kent and Essex in 1381', *Studies in Medieval History Presented to R.H.C. Davis*, ed. H. Mayr-Harting and R.I. Moore (London, 1985), 247–70. Military experience among leaders was also a factor visible in the near-contemporary Florentine peasants' movement of the Ciompi in 1379 (G.A. Brucker, 'The Ciompi Revolution', in *Florentine Studies. Politics and Society in Renaissance Florence*, ed. N. Rubinstein (London, 1968), 314–56 at 328–9), 'Evidence does not permit us to conclude that the revolution was primarily the work of disgruntled army veterans . . . But the concentration in the city of several hundred ex-soldiers . . . is an important factor. It influenced the selection of the Ciompi leaders, and also conditioned the mentality of the rank and file. Soldiers accustomed to handling arms are less docile than labourers.'

97. *Anonimalle Chronicle*, 148; Froissart, ed. Luce, X, 121, 'they arranged themselves on the place in manner of battle, and their bows before them'; R.B. Dobson, ed. *The Peasants' Revolt of 1381* (London, 1970), 166, 196.

98. Walsingham, *Historia Anglicana*, I, 464–5; Dobson, *Peasants Revolt*, 178–9.

99. *Eulogium historiarum*, III, 353–4.

100. *Anonimalle Chronicle*, 149; Walsingham, *Historia Anglicana*, I, 466; Knighton, 220–1; Froissart, ed. Luce, X, 122–3. The continuator of the *Eulogium historiarum* alone believed that it was rather Knollys who restrained the king's desire for vengeance, and, noting that many were there under duress, is said to have told them, 'Fall to the ground, you wretches, cut your bowstrings and depart' (*Eulogium historiarum*, III, 353–4; Dobson, *Peasants Revolt*, 206–8).

101. J.L. Gillespie, 'Richard II's Cheshire Archers', *Transactions of the Historic Society of Lancashire and Cheshire*, cxxv (1974), 1–39; and idem, 'Richard II's Archers of the Crown', *Journal of British Studies*, xviii (1979), 14–29.

102. In 1303 a safe-conduct was issued to 24 of the king's archers to serve in Scotland, and the same number are recorded as the king's guard in the 1318 household ordinances of Edward II (*CPR, 1301–1307*, 109; T.F. Tout, *The Place of Edward II in English History* (2nd edn, Manchester, 1936), 272).

103. Gillespie, 'Richard II's Archers of the Crown', 15. Some of these men had been of long service, such as Richard Pupplington, recorded as having served Edward III and Richard II for over forty years.

104. McKisack, *England in the Fourteenth Century*, 447.

105. *Polychronicon*, 94; Gillespie, 'Richard II's Cheshire Archers', 5–6; idem, 'Richard II's Archers of the Crown', 17–18.

106. Gillespie, 'Richard II's Cheshire Archers', 12–13; idem, 'Richard II's Archers of the Crown', 20–1.

107. Thomas Walsingham, *Annales Ricardi Secundi et Henrici Quarti, Regum Angliae*, ed. H.T. Riley (London, 1866), 153–420 at 218–19.

108. *Mum and the Sothsegger*, ed. M Day and R. Steele (Early English Texts Society, 1936), II, 41–3.

109. Gillespie, 'Richard II's Cheshire Archers', 3.

110. *Anglo-Norman Letters and Petitions from All Souls MS. 182*, ed. M.D. Legge (Oxford, 1941), 100, no. 52.

111. For a detailed discussion of these campaigns, Macdonald, *Border Bloodshed*, 75–93; Gillespie, 'Richard II: King of Battles?', 141–6.

112. Macdonald, *Border Bloodshed*, 89; J.L. Gillespie, 'Richard II: King of Battles?' in *The Age of Richard II*, ed. J.L. Gillespie (Stroud, 1997), 148–55.

113. B. McNab, 'Obligations of the Church in English Society: Military Arrays of the Clergy, 1369–1418', *Order and Innovation in the Middle Ages: Essays in Honor of Joseph R. Strayer*, ed. W.C. Jordan, B. McNab and T. Ruiz (Princeton, 1976), 293–314.

114. *Foedera*, VI, 631.

115. McNab, 'Military Arrays', 306.

116. McNab, 'Military Arrays', 306–13.

117. McNab, 'Military Arrays', 304.

118. Lydon, 'Richard II's Expeditions to Ireland', 140–1. For background E. Curtis, *Richard II in Ireland, 1394–5* (Oxford, 1927).

119. Gillespie, 'Richard II's Archers of the Crown', 19.

120. Lydon, 'Richard II's Expeditions to Ireland', 134–6; Gillespie, 'Richard II: King of Battles?', 151–3. For warfare in later medieval Ireland, R. Frame, 'War and Peace in the Medieval Lordship of Ireland', *The English in Ireland*, ed. J. Lydon (Dublin, 1984), 118–41.

121. Lydon, 'Richard II's Expeditions to Ireland', 147–8; Gillespie, 'Richard II: King of Battles?', 156–9.

122. Knighton, 506–7, 'whom for his valour the Scots called Harry Hotspur, because when others were given to sleep he would keep watch for his enemies'.

123. *The Westminster Chronicle: 1381–1394*, ed. and trans. L.C. Hector and B.F. Harvey (Oxford, 1982), 346–7; Froissart, ed. Mirot (Luce), XV, 132.

124. The battle of Otterburn and its wider context has been the subject of an excellent collection of papers, *War and Border Societies in the Middle Ages*, ed. A. Goodman and A. Tuck (London and New York, 1992), and of those in *The Battle of Otterburn, 600th Anniversary 1388–1988* (Newcastle upon Tyne, for the Redesdale Society, 1988). For other accounts of the battle, A.H. Burne, *The Battlefields of England* (London, 1973), 190–202, and C. Tyson, 'The Battle of Otterburn. When and Where was it Fought', in *War and Border Societies*, ed. Goodman and Tuck, 65–93, who at n. 28 gives further bibliography for the battle.

125. A. Goodman, 'Introduction', in *War and Border Societies*, at 3, and A. Grant, 'The Otterburn War from the Scottish Point of View', in *ibid.*, 30–64.

126. *Westminster Chronicle*, 348–9.

127. Froissart, ed. Mirot (Luce), XV, 139; trans. Brereton, 341.

128. *Scotichronicon: EHD*, IV, 163–4.

129. Froissart, ed. Mirot (Luce), XV, 143.

130. *Westminster Chronicle*, 856; Knighton, 506–7.

131. Froissart, ed. Mirot (Luce), XV, 143; *Scotichronicon*, VIII, 46. Swinton, a Berwickshire lord who would distinguish himself again at Homildon Hill in 1402, was well acquainted with English military practice, for he had earlier served the duke of Lancaster with a retinue of 60 men (N. Macdougall, *An Antidote to the English: The Auld Alliance, 1295–1560* (East Linton, 2001), 55).

132. *Westminster Chronicle*, 348–9; Knighton, 506–7.

133. *Westminster Chronicle*, 348–9.

134. The figure, which is probably somewhat inflated, is given by the *Historia Vitae et Regni Ricardi Secundo*, ed. G.B. Stow (Philadelphia, 1977), 174.

135. Bower, VIII, 44–7.

136. Walsingham, *Historia Anglicana*, II, 251; trans. *EHD*, IV, no. 86, 191.

137. See p. 162.

138. Macdougall, *An Antidote to the English*, 55.

139. D. Adams, 'Some Unrecognized Depictions of the Saffron Shirt in Scotland', *Northern Studies*, xxx (1993), 64–5; *idem*, 'Archery in the Highlands', 44.

140. *Scotichronicon*, VIII, 46–7.

141. *Scotichronicon*, VIII, 46–7.

142. Walsingham, *Historia Anglicana*, II, 251–2; trans. *EHD*, IV, no. 86, 191.

143. Walsingham, *Historia Anglicana*, II, 252; trans. *EHD*, IV, no. 86, 191.

144. Macdougall, *An Antidote to the English*, 58.

145. *The Chronicle of London*, ed. N.H. Nicolas (London, 1827), 88. Oman, *Art of War*, II, 375, was among several historians who have concurred with this verdict, regarding Shrewsbury as 'the first pitched battle between Englishmen since the bowman had become the great power in war'. He nevertheless treated the battle in a cursory paragraph.

146. For the political background see J.M.W. Bean, 'Henry IV and the Percies', *History*, xliv (1959), 212–27; A. King, '"They have the Hertes of the People by North": Northumberland, the Percies and Henry IV', in *Henry IV: The Establishment of the Regime, 1399–1406*, ed. G. Dodd and D. Biggs (York, 2003), 139–60; and for the family itself, A. Rose, *Kings in the North. The House of Percy in British History* (London, 2002).

147. *English Chronicle of the Reigns of Richard II, Henry IV, Henry V, and Henry VI, written before the year 1471*, ed. J.S. Davies (Camden Society, London, 1856), 28; *Eulogium historiarum*, III, 396.

148. Among the priests listed as armed rebels were the parsons of Rosthorne, Hawardyn, Pulforde, Dodleston, Hanley and Davenham (W.G.D. Fletcher, 'Some Documents Relative to the Battle of Shrewsbury', *Transactions of the Shropshire Archaeological Society*, x (1898), 236).

149. For secondary accounts of the battle see J.H. Wylie, *History of England under Henry the Fourth*, 4 vols (London, 1884–98), I, 358–65; A.H. Burne, 'The Battle of Shrewsbury: A Military Reconstruction', *Transactions of the Shropshire Archaeological Society*, lii (1947–8); *idem*, *Battlefields*, 203–13; E.J. Priestley, *The Battle of Shrewsbury, 1403* (Shrewsbury, 1979); *English Heritage, 1995 Battlefield Report: Shrewsbury 1403*.

150. For Henry's military career see A. Tuck, 'Henry IV and Chivalry', in *Henry IV: The Establishment of the Regime*, 55–71.

151. Priestley, *The Battle of Shrewsbury*, 6, 10–11; Wyntoun, III, 92, says of Dunbar 'and the King be [by] his counsale had all the bettyr of that battale'.

152. R. Griffiths, 'Prince Henry and Wales, 1400–1408', in *Profit, Piety and Professions in Later Medieval England*, ed. M. Hicks (Gloucester, 1990), 51–61, especially 52–5.

153. Estimates are collected by Wylie, *Henry the Fourth*, I, 359. Waurin, II, 59, 61, believed Percy had collected 24,000 archers and 2,000 lances in Northumberland, and that the king's force at Shrewsbury numbered 26,000 archers and 3,000 men-at-arms, with 60,000 in total!

154. E.F. Jacob, *The Fifteenth Century* (Oxford, 1961), 51. Records reveal that on 17 July 1403 Henry had paid the wages of 4 barons, 20 knights, 476 esquires and 2,500 archers, a force that may have been initially raised for operations with Prince Henry against the Welsh (Wylie, *Henry the Fourth*, I, 359–60).

155. Priestley, *The Battle of Shrewsbury*, 20. Adam of Usk, *Chronicon, 1377–1404*, ed. E.M. Thompson (London, 1876), 170–1, says it was fought at a place called Berwick, where in 1409 Henry IV founded a chantry chapel (*ibid.*, 170 n. 2). An inquisition post mortem, 1416–17, states the battle was at 'Bolefild in the town of Harlescote' (Fletcher, 'Some Documents Relative to the Battle of Shrewsbury', 249). A northern continuation of Higden's

Polychronicon, printed in C.L. Kingsford, *English Historical Literature of the Fifteenth Century* (Oxford, 1913), noted that some 1,500 bodies out of the 3,000 or so slain were buried in one mass grave on the site where the chantry was subsequently founded. The endowment was begun in 1406, with subsequent grants, and, save for a later tower, the present church dates from 1409. I am grateful to the custodian for opening the church and sharing his local knowledge with me on a cold late December afternoon in 2002 (MJS).

156. Burne, *Battlefields*, 72, discusses Percy's position, but his account contains a good deal of unsupported speculation and must be treated with considerable caution. Recent excavations have added little to our knowledge of the battle.

157. *Annales Henrici Quarti*, 365; Walsingham, *Historia Anglicana*, II, 257.

158. Oman, *Art of War*, II, 375.

159. *Annales Henrici Quarti*, 366, '*et arcitenentes praecipuos collocatos*'; Waurin, II, 60–1 (trans. W.L. Hardy and E.L.C.P. Hardy, *A Collection of Chronicles and Ancient Histories*, 3 vols (London, 1864–91), II, 58), noted '*il fist son ordnonnance davant-garde, bataille et arriere-garde*'. Waurin, however, is not reliable on the detail of their composition; he believed that Henry was joined in the centre battle by the Dukes of York and Gloucester and the Earls of Rutland and Arundel, that the van (whose commander Stafford he fails to mention) contained the Earls of Exeter, Warwick and Somerset, the Lord Ros and many other lords, and that the rearguard was under the command not of Prince Henry (whom he also omits to mention) but the Duke of Surrey. Waurin also confuses the Earl of Westmorland, Thomas Percy, with the Earl of Northumberland, who was not present at the battle. Burne, *Battlefields*, 67, inexplicably has only two royalist units, placing Prince Henry on the left and the king's main battle on the right.

160. Waurin, II, 63; trans. *Chronicles*, 60.

161. *Annales Henrici Quarti*, 367, '*sagitarii Henrici [Hotspur], quibus meliores non poterant inveniri in Comitatu Cestriae, fortiter sagittare coeperunt; quorum iaculis multi de parte Regis illico corruerunt*'. The account in the *Annales* is of particular value, since it was in part based on the eyewitness account of a squire of the Duchess of Norfolk who was wounded in the battle and crawled beneath a bush to escape. Usk, 170–1, says the king began the battle, but by this he may have been thinking less in terms of the opening attack than his breaking off negotiations with Worcester, mentioned in other accounts as being with the words 'Advance banner'.

162. Walsingham, *Historia Anglicana*, II, 257, '*Nec minus regii sagitarii suum peregere negotium, sed imbrem asperrimum spiculorum in adversarios emisere*'.

163. *Annales Henrici Quarti*, 367; Walsingham, *Historia Anglicana*, II, 257. Waurin, II, 64, 61, records the rout of the royalist vanguard, but only after close hand-to-hand fighting in which the prowess of Douglas and his companions gained the advantage.

164. *English Chronicle*, 28; *Annales Henrici*, 367; the *Eulogium historiarum*, III, 397, agrees with the *English Chronicle* that this attack was made by Percy with only 30 men. For a garbled account of Shrewsbury, in which Henry IV finds and slays Thomas Percy (sic), protected by only a few men after the rebel force had seemingly routed the royal forces, see Jean de Bueil, *Le Jouvencel*, II, 61–2.

165. *Annales Henrici Quarti*, 367; Walsingham, *Historia Anglicana*, II, 258; Usk, 170–1, who noted that when victory was proclaimed at the end of the battle for King Henry, Douglas is supposed to have cried in amazement, 'Have I not already killed two Henrys . . . with my own hands?'

166. Waurin, II, 64; trans. *Chronicles*, 61.

167. *Annales Henrici Quarti*, 367; Trokelowe, 368; Walsingham, *Historia Anglicana*, II, 258; *English Chronicle*, 29; *Eulogium historiarum*, III, 397–8.

168. *Annales Henrici Quarti*, 368.

169. *English Chronicle*, 28.

170. *Annales Henrici Quarti*, 368.

171. Usk, 170–1.

172. H. Owen and J.B. Blakeway, *History of Shrewsbury*, 2 vols (London, 1825), I, 194, citing the charter of the College of Battlefield, 5 December 1446.

173. Waurin, *Chronicles*, II, 62.

174. *English Chronicle*, 28; Waurin, *Chronicles*, II, 61.

175. Fletcher, 'Some Documents Relative to the Battle of Shrewsbury', 239.

176. Fletcher, 'Some Documents Relative to the Battle of Shrewsbury', 241.

177. Fletcher, 'Some Documents Relative to the Battle of Shrewsbury', 239.

CHAPTER 15

1. J. Keegan, *The Face of Battle* (London, 1976), 93.

2. K. De Vries, 'Catapults are Not Atomic Bombs: Towards a Redefinition of "Effectiveness" in Premodern Military Technology', *War in History*, iv (1997), 454–70, especially 460–2; and cf. *idem*, *Medieval Military Technology* (Peterborough, Ontario, 1994), 38; and *idem*, *Infantry Warfare*, 5–6, 127–8.

3. Rogers, 'The Efficacy of the English Longbow', 233–42.

4. Walsingham, II, 312; Curry, *Agincourt*, 52.

5. Wykes, 148; *Political Songs*, 170.

6. P. Jones, 'The Target', in R. Hardy, *Longbow: a Social and Military History* (Sparkford, 1992), 232–6.

7. The principal research in this field has been undertaken by Dr Alan Williams, an archaeometallurgist now based at the Wallace Collection in London. His method has been either to

detach a small flake from inside an armour plate, such as inside the rim of a breastplate or where corrosion has already created a fracture, or to place the edge of a plate on an inverted microscope, having first set it in resin, the area being polished and etched to form a suitable surface. The Vickers Pyramid Hardness scale is measured in kg/mm² (T.P.D. Blackburn, D. Edge, A.R. Williams and C.B.T. Adams, 'Head Protection in England Before the First World War', *Neurosurgery*, xlvii (December, 2000), 1,261–86, at 1,264). For an extensive analysis, see A.R. Williams, *The Knight and the Blast Furnace* (Leiden, 2002), which appeared after the completion of this chapter.

8.   For current perspectives see *Fields of Conflict. Progress and Prospect in Battlefield Archaeology*, ed. P.W.M. Freeman and A. Pollard, BAR International Series (Oxford, 2001), 958.

9.   Ffoulkes, *The Armourer and his Craft*, 44–8; M. Burgess, 'The Mail-maker's Technique', *Antiquaries Journal*, xxxiii (1953), 48–55; C.S. Smith, 'Methods of Making Chain Mail in the 14th–18th Centuries: A Metallographic Note', *Technology and Culture*, I (1960), 60–7; C. Blair, *European Arms and Armour, c. 1100–1850* (London, 1962), 19–29.

10.   Strickland, *War and Chivalry*, 169–71; P. Sigal, 'Les coups et blessures reçus par le combattant à cheval en occident aux XIIe et XIIIe siècles', in *Le Combattant au Moyen Âge*, 171–83.

11.   William of Malmesbury, *Gesta Regum Anglorum*, I, 726–9; see p. 86.

12.   Ffoulkes, *The Armourer and his Craft*, 63, '*un auberjon d'acier de toute botte*'; ibid., 62, '*camisam ferream, ex circulis ferreis contextam, per quae nulla sagitta arcus poterat hominem vulneare*'.

13.   See p. 44.

14.   Graham-Campbell, *Viking Artefacts*, 68.

15.   Jessop, 'A New Artefact Typology for the Study of Medieval Arrowheads', 192–205, at 195, 198. Similar heads are found in eleventh-century Europe, for example the long bodkin heads (6.5–10.56cm) from Hontheim, Rheinland-Pfalz (Kluge-Pinsken, 'Bogen und Armbrust', 99).

16.   I. MacIvor, D. Gallagher et al., 'Excavations at Caerlaverock Castle, 1955–66', *Archaeological Journal*, clvi (1999), 213. The arrows were of Jessop type MP7 (broadheads), and M7 (bodkins).

17.   S.V. Grancsay, 'Just How Good was Armor?', 45.

18.   Ffoulkes, *The Armourer and his Craft*, 44–5.

19.   Ffoulkes, *The Armourer and his Craft*, 63.

20.   I. Origo, *The Merchant of Prato* (New York and London, 1957), 12; R. Brun, 'Notes sur le commerce des armes à Avignon au XIVème siècle', *Bibliothèque de L'École des Chartes*, cix (1951), at 217–25.

21.   Ffoulkes, *The Armourer and his Craft*, 45.

22.   Blair, *European Arms and Armour*, 24.

23.   See the literary references to aketons worn beneath hauberks collected by S.J. Herben, 'Arms and Armour in Chaucer', *Speculum*, xii (1937), 475–87, at 480ff.

24.   Wyntoun, II, 431–2; Rogers, *Wars of Edward III*, 58.

25.   F. Lachaud, 'Armour and Military Dress in Thirteenth and Early Fourteenth Century England', in Strickland, ed., *Armies, Chivalry and Warfare*, 344–69.

26.   Blair, *European Armour*, 34 ill. 12.

27.   For coat-armour see Blair, *European Armour*, 75–6; and for the examples of coat-armour made for Edward III see N.H. Nichols, 'Expenses of the Great Wardrobe of Edward III from 21 December 1345 to 31 January 1349', *Archaeologia*, xxxi (1846), 34–5.

28.   J.G. Mann, *The Funeral Achievements of Edward, The Black Prince* (London, 1951), 17–18; M. Scalini, R.H. Wackernagel and I. Eaves, *The Armoury of the Castle of Churburg* (Udine, 1996), 50, for an illustration of Blois's jupon (now in the Musée Historique des Tissus, Lyons).

29.   Ffoulkes, *The Armourer and his Craft*, Appendix A, 169, and cf. 85–7 for similar French legislation.

30.   Ffoulkes, *The Armourer and his Craft*, 86–7.

31.   Ffoulkes, *The Armourer and his Craft*, 93; *Manners and Household Expenses of England in the Thirteenth and Fifteenth Centuries*, ed. T.H. Turner (London, 1841), 239.

32.   Cuvelier, *Chronique*, II, 95; Ffoulkes, *The Armourer and his Craft*, 86.

33.   Blackburn et al., 'Head Protection', 1280.

34.   *Philippidos*, 83, III, ll. 490–8.

35.   *Philippidos*, XI, ll. 116–32; trans. Duby, *The Legend of Bouvines*, 200.

36.   Lewis, *The Art of Matthew Paris*, pls iii, xiii, and figs 67, 112, 149, 227, 234. Similarly, a mid-thirteenth-century illustration of a crusader knight depicts two crosses projecting up from the surcoat to act as additional shoulder defences, and these doubtless form part of a similar form of solid body armour.

37.   *La Règle du Temple*, c. 138.

38.   Blair, *European Armour*, 39–41, 53–9.

39.   C. Paoli, *Libro di Montaperti* (Florence, 1889), 373–4; Contamine, *War in the Middle Ages*, 67; Oman, *Art of War*, I, 499–503, 513.

40.   T. Richardson, 'The Introduction of Plate Armour in Medieval Europe', *Royal Armouries Yearbook*, ii (1997), 40–5, at 40.

41.   Howden, IV, 58, '*equos coopertos ferro*'.

42.   Blackburn et al., 'Head Protection', 1264–5.

43.   Blackburn et al., 'Head Protection', 1266–7.

44.   Ffoulkes, *The Armourer and his Craft*, 49–51, and Appendix D, 177.

45.   B. Thordemann, *Armour from the Battle of Wisby, 1361*, 2 vols (Stockholm, 1939), 210–29.

46.   Blackburn et al., 'Head Protection', 1263.

47.   A.R. Williams, 'Four Helmets of the Fourteenth Century Compared', *Journal of the Arms and Armour Society*, x (1981), 80–102, at 83. This body armour (Swiss National Museum, Zurich, Inv. No. LM 13367), is discussed by E.A. Gessler, 'Die spangenharnische von Knüssnach', *Zeitschrift fur historische Waffen- und Kostümkunde* (new ser.), I, pt 8 (1925).

48.   Le Bel, I, 154.

49.   *Cal. Docs. Scot.*, II, 364–6; H. Johnstone, *Edward of Caernarvon, 1284–1307* (Manchester, 1946), 86; F.M. Kelly, 'A Knight's

Armour in the Early XIV Century, being the Inventory of Raoul de Nesle', *Burlington Magazine* (March 1905), 457–69.

50. The chronology is discussed by Richardson, 'The Introduction of Plate Armour', 41–2.

51. Powicke, *Military Obligation*, 145; Jones, *Chaucer's Knight*, 132.

52. *The Chronicle of Robert Manning of Brunne*, ed. F.J. Furnivall, 2 vols (Rolls Series, London, 1887), I, 350. Chaucer's later description of the arming of Sir Thopas is very similar, referring to the pair of plates as a 'hauberk' of plates:

> And next to his shirt an aketon,
> And over that a habergeoun
> To prevent his heart being pierced;
> And over that a fine hauberk,
> Which was all made by Jewish craftsmen
> Very strong and of steel plates;
> And over that his coat-armour
> As white as a lily flower,
> In which he will fight.

(Jones, *Chaucer's Knight*, 131, modernised from Sir Thopas, ll. 860–8.) Though Herben, 'Arms and Armour in Chaucer', 479–81, rightly refutes the view that Chaucer's description of Thopas's armour is satirical and ludicrous, it may well be that by the 1380s the kind of equipment here described was considered quite outmoded by the full 'white harness' of plate. Cf. L. Irving, 'The Arming of Sir Thopas', *Modern Language Notes*, li (1956), 300–11.

53. *Chroniques de Tournay*, in Froissart, *Oeuvres*, ed. Lettenhove, XXV, 355–7; Rogers, *Wars of Edward III*, 95.

54. Powicke, *Military Obligation*, 145.

55. *The Battle of Neville's Cross*, ed. Rollason and Prestwich, 163.

56. G.W. Henger, 'The Metallography and Chemical Analysis of Iron-based Samples dating from Antiquity to Modern Times', *Bulletin of the Historical Metallurgy Group*, iv (1970), 49–52; A.R. Williams, 'Medieval Metalworking: Armour Plate and the Advance of Metallurgy', *The Chartered Mechanical Engineer* (September, 1978), 109–14.

57. Steel could also be produced by 'case hardening', whereby the iron blooms or even finished objects were packed around with charcoal and subject to prolonged heating, or by decarburising carbon-rich cast iron (A.R. Williams, 'Fifteenth-Century Armour from Churburg: a Metallurgical Study', *Armi Antiche*, xxxii (1986), 3–82, at 4).

58. Williams, 'The Knight and the Blast Furnace', 486.

59. Figures from the tomb of Azzone Visconti, *c.* 1339, in San Gottardo in Corte, Milan, show some form of solid breastplate worn under armorial surcoats, from which chains hang, to attach to sword, dagger, helm and possibly shield (L. Boccia, *Armi et Armature Lombarde* (Milan, 1980), 28, ill. 9).

60. Williams, 'Fifteenth-Century Armour from Churburg', 5.

61. P.N. Jones, 'The Metallography and Relative Effectiveness of Arrowheads and Armour during the Middle Ages', *Materials Characterization*, xxix (1992), 111–17 at 117; *idem*, 'The Target', in Hardy, *Longbow*, 233.

62. Williams, 'Fifteenth-Century Armour from Churburg', 5. Air-cooled steel produces a crystalline structure called pearlite (ferrite and iron carbide), while 'slack-quenching' may produce a mixture of pearlite, bainite and martensite.

63. This bascinet (Poldi-Pezzuoli Museum, Inv. No. 3599), is analysed in A.R. Williams, 'Milanese Armour and its Metallurgy', in *Military Studies in Medieval Europe. Papers of the 'Medieval Europe Brugge 1997' Conference*, ed. G. De Boe and F. Verhaeghe (Zellik, 1997), II, 61–70, at 62–3, 66–7; Williams, 'Four Helmets of the Fourteenth Century', 83–4. The breastplate (Munich, Bayerisches Museum W 195), which retains its original velvet covering, is illustrated in Boccia, *Armi e Armature Lombarde*, 47, ills 28, 29, and L. Boccia and E.T. Coelho, *L'Arte dell'Armatura in Italia* (Milan, 1967), ills 36, 37.

64. Le Baker, 87–8.

65. Le Baker, 148.

66. This is clearly shown in details from the altarpiece depicting the life of St Jacopo from Pistoia Cathedral, *c.* 1367–71, illustrated in A.V. Norman, *Arms and Armour* (London, 1964), pl. 17. Richardson, 'The Introduction of Plate Armour', 42, suggests that such developments may have been encouraged by the needs of the tournament, and it is noteworthy that '*vj poitrines a jouster*' are mentioned in the inventory of Count William of Hainault in 1358.

67. This armour (Churburg, 13) is illustrated in Boccia, *Armi e Armature Lombarde*, 34–5, ills 13, 14, and in Boccia and Coelho, *L'Arte dell'Armatura in Italia*, pls 1–6, where the side and inside details of the breastplate are shown. The armour was tested and found to have a structure of ferrite and pearlite, suggesting it was quenched, with an average microhardness of 180 VPH (Williams, 'Fifteenth-Century Armour from Churburg', 11, 15).

68. The Churburg armour bears the repeated inscription, '*Jesus autem per medium illorum ibat*' (Luke 4:30); cf. Vale, *War and Chivalry*, 110, for further examples.

69. The earlier dating to the 1360s is suggested by Scalini in Scalini, Wackernagel and Eaves, *The Armoury of the Castle of Churburg*, II, 44, but this redating from the more traditional range of the last decades of the century has been challenged (Richardson, 'The Introduction of Plate Armour', 41–2).

70. Norman, *Arms and Armour*, 27–33.

71. For example the breastplate now part of a composite armour of *c.* 1390–1400 (Churburg 16, 14, 47, 53), illustrated in Boccia and Coelho, *L'Arte dell'Armatura in Italia*, 129, ills 28–30.

72. Ricotti, *Storia della Compagnie di Ventura in Italia*, II, 342; Jones, *Chaucer's Knight*, 133 n. 22, which reproduces the 'Tariff of Fines for the City of Florence, 1368', in translation.

73. That the effigy is representative of the prince's actual armour is shown not only by the surviving funeral achievements of helmet, jupon, shield and gauntlets, but by the injunction in the prince's will that his tomb should carry 'our image in relieved work of latten gilt . . . all armed in steel for battle, with our arms quartered; and my visage with our helmet of the leopard put under the head of the image . . .' (J. Mann, 'The Funeral

Achievements of Edward, The Black Prince' in *Edward, The Black Prince*, Canterbury Papers, viii (Canterbury, 1963), 15).

74. Origo, *The Merchant of Prato*, 11.

75. Origo, *The Merchant of Prato*, 12.

76. F. Menant, 'La metallurgie Lombarde au moyen âge', in *Hommes et travail du metal dans les villes médiévales*, ed. P. Benoit (Paris, 1988), 127–61.

77. Origo, *The Merchant of Prato*, 12; Brun, 'Notes sur le commerce des armes à Avignon au XIVème siècle', 217–25.

78. Origo, *The Merchant of Prato*, 36, 355; *Calendar of Pleas and Memoranda Rolls of the City of London*, III, 128.

79. Available armour prices from Datini's time show the best bascinets, lined with silk and leather or sheepskin, cost between 4 and 5 florins, compared to the more simple and visorless cervellières at only 33 *solidi* each; Origo, *The Merchant of Prato*, 12.

80. G.G. Astill, 'An Early Inventory of a Leicestershire Knight', *Midland History*, ii (1974), 274–83.

81. Astill, 'An Early Inventory', 279, 281. The 'cothsak' (sackcloth) mentioned with a leather jerkin, together worth 6*s* 8*d*, suggests that the former may have been some form of coat-armour, akin to the 'gypon' (jupon) of Chaucer's Knight: 'Of fustian he wered a gypon, Al bismotered with his habergeon' (*The Prologue*, 75–6). The inventory also refers to 'spurs, saddle, *souto* (possibly a crupper), a horse's headpiece (*testario*) and stirrups' worth 10 marks.

82. Though Chaucer arms Sir Thopas with a 'pair of plates', his leg defences are still of *cuir bouilli* (Thopas, l. 2065, 'his jambeux were of quyrboilly').

83. Froissart, *Oeuvres*, ed. Lettenhove, XXI, 350–6; Rogers, 'The Efficacy of the English Longbow', 238 n. 22.

84. Origo, *The Merchant of Prato*, 13.

85. Metropolitan Museum, New York, Inv. No. 29. 153. 3. This armour formed part of a major hoard of armour discovered at the Venetian fortress on the island of Negroponte (modern Euboea), which was buried when the fortress was destroyed in 1470. It also contained several brigandine plates of varying sizes, including some pairs of plates for the breast which covered much of the upper torso (Inv. No. 29. 150. 92.101). One of these large brigandine plates bears the mark of the famous Milanese armourer Antonio Missaglia; Ffoulkes, *The Armourer and his Craft*, 50, pl. XI; *idem*. 'Italian Armour at Chalcis in the Ethnological Museum at Athens', *Archaeologia*, lxii (1910), 381–90.

86. Walsingham, I, 467; trans. Dobson, *The Peasants' Revolt of 1381*, 170.

87. Le Bel, 119–28; Rogers, *Wars of Edward III*, 56.

88. *Traité des Guerres d'Awans et de Waroux*, 41, with partial translation in Jones, *Chaucer's Knight*, 135.

89. Glasgow Museum and Art Gallery, 39–65e; Williams, 'Fifteenth-Century Armour from Churburg', 27–38; Sir James Mann, *European Arms and Armour*, 2 vols (Wallace Collection Catalogues, London 1962), I, 13 (Wallace Collection, A 21); Vale, *War and Chivalry*, 184–5, tabulates the weights of various fifteenth-century armours and their constituent pieces.

90. *Codice degli stipendiarii della repubblica di Firenze 1369*, in Ricotti, *Storia delle Compagnie*, II, 315–16; Jones, *Chaucer's Knight*, 133–4; see p. 249.

91. Oman, *Art of War*, II, 178.

92. Williams, 'Four Helmets of the Fourteenth Century Compared', 82–3.

93. Wallace Collection, A 69 (weight 2.82kg: skull = 2kg, visor = .82kg); Williams, 'Fifteenth-Century Armour from Churburg', 19; Blackburn *et al.*, 'Head Protection', 1271; Williams, 'The Knight and the Blast Furnace', 485, fig. 1.

94. Murimuth, 190, believed that at Auberoche 'through the English archers, more than 1,000 infantry, called bidauts, were slain and seventy men-at-arms'.

95. A fine example of a Milanese 'great bascinet', *c.* 1390, with skull and broad gorget hammered from a single piece of steel (Venice, Palazzo Ducale, Sale d'Armi del Consiglio dei Dieci, E.1), Boccia, *Armi e Armature Lombarde*, 40, ill. 19.

96. 'How a man shall be armed at ease when he shall fight on foot', in Viscount Dillon, 'On an MS Collection of Ordinances of Chivalry of the Fifteenth Century Belonging to Lord Hastings', *Archaeologia*, lvii (1900), 29–70, at 43.

97. For example, the figure of St George in an altarpiece of 1425 by Gentile de Fabriano (Uffizi, Florence), where the saint has a mail shirt worn under the cuirass and pauldrons but over the upper vambraces (Boccia and Coelo, *L'arte dell'armatura in Italia*, ill. 59).

98. Monstrelet, I, 365.

99. *Gesta Henrici Quinti*, 86–7.

100. Williams, 'The Knight and the Blast Furnace', 487; *idem*, 'Fifteenth-Century Armour from Churburg', 27–38.

101. Glasgow Museum and Art Gallery, 39–65e. The metallurgy of this armour is examined by Williams, 'Fifteenth-Century Armour from Churburg', 27–38, and 11 for tabulated data; and cf. Williams, 'The Blast Furnace and the Mass Production of Plate Armour', 102–3.

102. For other examples of this breastplate of two parts see Boccia, *Armi e Armature Lombarde*, 52, ill. 35 (Churburg 18 and 22), 67, ill. 50, 71, ill. 53. Some breastplates, however, were solid, such as the armour from the church of the Madonna del Grazie, Udine (*ibid.*, 84–5, ills 73–4).

103. 'Gregory', 216; *The Paston Letters, A.D. 1422–1509*, ed. J. Gairdner, 6 vols (London, 1904), V, 99.

104. Ffoulkes, *The Armourer and his Craft*, Appendix E, 180.

105. Williams, 'The Blast Furnace and the Mass Production of Plate Armour', 101.

106. Gaier, *L'Industrie et le commerce des armes*, 279–80.

107. J.G. Mann, 'Notes on the Evolution of Plate Armour in Germany in the 14th and 15th Centuries', *Archaeologia*, lxxxvii (1934), 69–97.

108. Williams, 'Fifteenth-Century Armour from Churburg', 27–38. The average hardness of 11 tested specimens of Augsburg armour was 338 VPH, and those from Innsbruck 373 VPH, though 6 out of 20 specimens were not of hardened steel (*idem*, 'The Blast

Furnace and the Mass Production of Plate Armour', 103). In the sixteenth century the steel from 18 out of 51 Augsburg and 39 out of 63 Innsbruck armours had been fully hardened and tempered.

109. Vale, *War and Chivalry*, 121.

110. Ffoulkes, 'Some Aspects of the Craft of the Armourer', 25, for some of the sallet's drawbacks.

111. Le Baker, 88; Le Fèvre, I, 254; Waurin, II, 212

112. Churburg, 19; illustrated in Boccia *et al.*, *Armi e Armature Lombarde*, 65, ill. 48, and Boccia and Coelho, *L'Arte dell'Armatura in Italia*, ills 84–9.

113. See p. 397.

114. Jones, 'The Metallography and Relative Effectiveness of Arrowheads', 117.

115. A.R. Williams, 'Some Firing with Simulated Fifteenth-Century Handguns', *Journal of the Arms and Armour Society*, viii (1974), 114–20.

116. T. Richardson, 'Ballistic Testing of Historical Weapons', *Royal Armouries Yearbook*, iii (1998), 50–2.

117. For the mechanics, construction and range of the arrow see P.L. Pratt, 'The Arrow', in Hardy, *Longbow*, 226–32.

118. *CPR, 1358–61*, 323; see p. 9.

119. Ffoulkes, *The Armourer and his Craft*, 64. An account for 1416 mentions '*fleches à arc empanné a cire et ferres de fers d'espreuve*' (*ibid.*).

120. P.N. Jones, 'A Short History of the Attack on Armour', *Metallurgist and Materials Technologist* (1984), 247; Jones, 'The Metallography and Relative Effectiveness of Arrowheads', 112.

121. Jones, 'The Metallography and Relative Effectiveness of Arrowheads', 112.

122. Jones, 'The Metallography and Relative Effectiveness of Arrowheads', 112. This head is Jessop type M7.

123. Grancsay, 'Just How Good was Armor?', 45–7, 89–92.

124. Grancsay, 'Just How Good was Armor?', 92.

125. Grancsay, 'Just How Good was Armor?', 89–90.

126. Grancsay, 'Just How Good was Armor?', 90. The depth of penetration is not given.

127. Grancsay, 'Just How Good was Armor?', 90.

128. Jones, 'A Short History of the Attack on Armour'; and *idem*, 'The Metallography and Relative Effectiveness of Arrowheads' for a more detailed analysis of these tests.

129. Jones, 'The Metallography and Relative Effectiveness of Arrowheads', 115 gives the varying thicknesses of pieces of fourteenth- and fifteenth-century armour in Table 1.

130. Jones, 'A Short History of the Attack on Armour', 248.

131. Williams, Letter, in *Metals and Materials*, 736; Jones, 'The Target', 233.

132. William's research, particularly on early Italian armour, must seriously qualify the statements by Jones that 'with few exceptions armour manufacture is ferritic with occasional use of carburisation giving hardness in the range of 120–220 VHN' (Jones, 'A Short History of the Attack on Armour', 248), and that 'with the exception of one helmet, all armour prior to 1450 AD is

soft iron' (*ibid.*, 'The Metallography and Relative Effectiveness of Arrowheads', 114).

133. Blackburn *et al.*, 'Head Protection', 1,280.

134. Jones, 'The Metallography and Relative Effectiveness of Arrowheads', 116, Table 2.

135. Jones, 'The Target', 234–6.

136. It is a pity that Jones did not conduct further tests against thicker plates, analogous to those of his earlier tests against wrought iron. The range for these later tests is not given.

137. Richardson, 'Ballistic Testing of Historical Weapons', 50–2.

138. Blackburn *et al.*, 'Head Protection', 1,279.

139. Blackburn *et al.*, 'Head Protection', 1,281.

140. Orderic, IV, 48–9; V, 224–5; and see p. 56.

141. Robert of Torigny, IV, 147.

142. Ailred, *Relatio de Standardo*, 196; *Lanercost*, 274.

143. *Lanercost*, 274.

144. The few extant examples (around 14) of the thirteenth and fourteenth centuries are listed and discussed in H. Schneider, *Zeitschrift fur Schweizerische Archäologie und Kunstgeschichte*, xiv (1953), part I, 29–31; J.G. Scott, 'Two 14th c Helms Found in Scotland', *Journal of the Arms and Armour Society*, iv (1962), 68–79.

145. *Chronique Normande*, 115.

146. Knighton, 62–3; Letter of Richard Wynkeley, in Barber, *Life and Campaigns*, 20; *Eulogium historiarum*, II, 211; Walsingham, 269; Murimuth, 216; letter of Northburgh in Avesbury, 369; *Chronique des Pays-Bays, de France, d'Angleterre et de Tournai*, in *Corpus Chronicorum Flandriae*, ed. J.J. de Smet, 4 vols (Brussels, 1837–65), III, 172.

147. Letter of Prior Fossor to the Bishop of Durham, *Historical Papers and Letters from the Northern Registers*, 388, '*cum sagitta in facie graviter vulneratus*'. According to Murimuth, 219, and Bower, *Scotichronicon*, VII, 260–1, the king was wounded by two arrows, with the 'Packington' Account, Version A (Rogers and Buck, 'Three New Accounts of the Neville's Cross Campaign', 75), stating that both were in the face.

148. Le Baker, 101–2.

149. For Prince Henry's wound, Trokelowe, 368; Walsingham, II, 258; *English Chronicle*, 29; *Eulogium historiarum*, III, 397–8. For arrow wounds at St Albans, p. 371.

150. For examples of leading figures killed or wounded in the face after having removed their bevors, Vale, *War and Chivalry*, 119.

151. Letter of Sir John Wingfield to Sir Richard Stafford, trans. Barber, *Life and Campaigns*, 55.

152. Jones, 'A Short History of the Attack on Armour', 247.

153. Jones, 'A Short History of the Attack on Armour', 247.

154. *Calendar of Inquisitions, Miscellaneous*, I, no. 2165.

155. *Calendar of Inquisitions, Miscellaneous*, I, no. 2214.

156. *CPR, 1367–1370*, 42.

157. *Calendar of Inquisitions, Miscellaneous*, I, no. 566.

158. *Calendar of Inquisitions, Miscellaneous*, I, no. 579.

159. See p. 147.

160. At Agincourt the Bishop of Thérouanne is said to have had five grave-pits dug, each containing some 1,200 men, and to have placed a large wooden cross over each mass grave. He also had the site enclosed by thick hedges to keep out animals who might disturb the graves. (*Chronique de Ruisseauville*, in G. Bacquet, *Azincourt* (Bellegarde, 1977), 95–6; *Mémoires de Pierre de Fenin*, ed. E. Dupont (Paris, 1837), 66–7; Curry, *Agincourt*, 127, 119). Jean Juvenal des Ursins, *Histoire de Charles VI*, 518–19; Curry, *Agincourt*, 131, believed some of the dead were also interred in local churches and cemeteries.

161. A. Pollard and N. Oliver, *Two Men in a Trench* (London, 2002), Ch. 1.

162. Le Fèvre, I, 260; Waurin, II, 218.

163. Wylie, *England under Henry IV*, II, 94.

164. Fiorato, Boylston and Knüsel, *Blood Red Roses: The Archaeology of a Mass Grave from the Battle of Towton*; and V. Fiorato, 'Towton, AD 1461. Excavation of a Mass War Grave', *Current Archaeology*, clxxi (vol. VX, no. 3, December 2000), 98–103; A. Boylston, S. Sutherland, T. Holst and J. Coughlan, 'Burials from the battle of Towton', *Royal Armouries Yearbook*, ii (1997), 36–9. For the evidence of the few other known burials, such as Sandbjerget, Denmark, see *Blood Red Roses*, 180–1.

165. Fiorato, 'Towton, AD 1461', 98–103. For the battle itself, see pp. 374–7.

166. S.A. Novak, 'Battle Related Trauma', in Fiorato *et al.*, *Blood Red Roses*, 98–9.

167. At Wisby, despite the excavation of nearly 2,000 skeletons, the bolt wounds discovered were almost entirely on skulls, with wounds only found elsewhere on one tibia and one ilium (Thordemann, *Wisby*, 187). Clearly, there must have been far more wounds to the body than these two examples, but they are no longer recoverable.

168. Thordmann, *Wisby*, 191; C.B. Courville, 'War Wounds of the Cranium in the Middle Ages: As Disclosed in the Skeletal Material from the Battle of Wisby', *Bulletin of the Los Angeles Neurological Society*, xxx (1965), 27–33.

169. Thordmann, *Wisby*, 184–7, and figs 178–81. It is possible that in some cases a bolt had passed right through the skull and emerged the other side (186–7).

170. Thordmann, *Wisby*, 189.

171. Thordmann, *Wisby*, 187–9. The other suggestion made here that the bolt wounds were received after being felled by the blows is less plausible, though if a rain of bolts was falling this was not impossible.

172. Thordmann, *Wisby*, 188.

173. Thordmann, *Wisby*, 191.

174. Thordmann, *Wisby*, 190–1.

175. C. Rawcliffe, *Medicine and Society in Later Medieval England* (Stroud, 1995), 3. Compare Le Bel, I, 58, who paints a vivid picture of the miseries of campaigning in northern England in the Weardale campaign of 1327, where the knights, operating without tents and baggage in a desperate but fruitless attempt to catch their Scottish opponents, suffered privations of food and shelter during incessant rain, and were reduced to eating bread soaked with their horses' sweat and drinking river water.

176. Fiorato, 'Towton, AD 1461', 98–103.

177. M. Herbert, 'L'armée Provencale en 1374', *Annales du Midi*, xci (1979), 5–27.

178. Nor did his injuries stop there; 'also at the bataille of Agingcourt, and after the takyng of the carrakes on the see, there with a gadde of yren his plates smyten in sondre, and sore hurt, maymed and wounded; by meane wherof he being sore febeled and debrused, now falle to great age and poverty, gretly endetted, and may not helpe himself' (*Original Letters Illustrative of English History*, second series, IV, 95–6; Rawcliffe, *Medicine and Society*, 4).

179. *The Paston Letters*, V, 99.

180. L.M. Patterson, 'Military Surgery', in C. Harper-Bill and R. Harvey, eds, *The Ideals and Practice of Medieval Knighthood*, vol. II (1986), 117–46, 134.

181. *Miracula S. Mariae de Rupe Amatoris*, II, c. 39, 228–30; II, c. 42, 232–4; I, c. 29, 91–2; Sigal, 'Les coups et blessures', 182–3.

182. *Franklin's Tale*, ll. 1,113–15.

183. Patterson, 'Military Surgery', 134, 135.

184. Patterson, 'Military Surgery', 135.

185. Morris, 'Mounted Infantry in Medieval Warfare', 101–2.

186. A.A.M. Duncan, 'Honi soit qui mal y pense: David II and Edward III, 1346–52', *SHR*, lxvii (1988), 113–41, at 115.

187. *Scotichronicon*, VII, 260–1, and 464, nn. 36–42; *Rot. Scacc. Scot*, II, cvii; Duncan, 'Honi soit qui mal y pense', 15.

188. J.T. Beck, *The Cutting Edge. The Early History of the Surgeons of London* (London, 1974), 55, and for Bradmore's career see Rawcliffe, *Medicine and Society*, 75–6; and *idem*, 'Master Surgeons at the Lancastrian Court', in *The Lancastrian Court*, ed. J. Stratford (Dorington, 2003), 192–210, especially 203–8 for military surgery. I am grateful to Professor Rawcliffe for her assistance concerning Bradmore.

189. (Translation by the author.) The text of Bradmore's account is edited and discussed by S.J. Lang, 'John Bradmore and his Book *Philomena*', *Social History of Medicine*, v (1992), 121–30, who demonstrates that Bradmore's Latin text (BL, MS Sloane 2272) served as a major source, rendered not verbatim but as a detailed précis, for a surgical text of 1446 in Middle English (BL, MS Harley, 1736). Many thanks are due to Dr Tig Lang for drawing my attention to H. Cole and T. Lang, 'The Treating of Prince Henry's Arrow Wound, 1403', *JSAA* (2003), 95–101, and for sending illustrations of Bradmore's 'extractor'.

190. C. Rawcliffe, 'The Profits of Practice: the Wealth and Status of Medical Men in Later Medieval England', *Social History of Medicine*, I (1988), 61–78 at 69, suggests that his subsequent appointment to the post of 'searcher' of the port of London was a reward for healing Prince Henry.

191. R.I. Burns, 'The Medieval Crossbow as a Surgical Instrument: An Illustrated Case History', *Bulletin of the New York Academy of Medicine*, xlviii, no. 8 (September 1972), 983–9; Paterson, *The Crossbow*, 111–12.

192. J. Coplin, 'L'arbalète en médecine', *Les Arbaletrieri Bruxellois*, iv (1996), 4.

193. *The Retrial of Joan of Arc: The Evidence at the Trial for her Rehabilitation*, ed. R. Pernoud and trans. J.M. Cohen (London, 1955), 106–7.

194. *The First Biography of Joan of Arc*, trans. D. Rankin and C. Quintal (Pittsburg, 1964), 83; M. Warner, *Joan of Arc. The Image of Female Heroism* (London, 1981), 109.

195. Smythe, *Certain Discourses Military*, 75. Nevertheless, some shafts might be poisoned. In 1267 a woman called Desiderata wrestled in sport with William de Stanesgate, who was carrying a crossbow and poisoned bolts, but she accidentally fell on one of the bolts in his belt and was fatally wounded (*Calendar of Inquisitions, Miscellaneous*, I, no. 2133).

196. Orderic, IV, 128; *Chronicon de Hida*, 299.

197. Orderic, VI, 76–7; *Gesta*, II.

198. *The Waltham Chronicle*, ed. and trans. L. Watkiss and M. Chibnall (Oxford, 1994), 80.

199. William le Breton, II, 135 (*Philippidos*, V, ll. 258–68).

200. Coggeshall, 94–5; Howden, IV, 83; K. Norgate, *England under the Angevin Kings*, 2 vols (London, 1887), 382–6; Gillingham, *Richard I*, 324 n. 10.

201. Howden, IV, 84.

CHAPTER 16

1. H.J. Hewitt, *Organisation of War under Edward III* (Manchester, 1966).

2. R.A. Newhall, *Muster and Review: A Problem of English Military Administration, 1420–1440* (Cambridge, Mass., 1940), and *The English Conquest of Normandy 1416–1424* (New Haven, 1924, rpr. New York, 1971).

3. Hardy, *Longbow*, 75–95.

4. A. Curry, 'Isolated or Integrated? The English Soldier in Lancastrian Normandy', in *Courts and Regions in Medieval Europe*, ed. S.R. Jones, R. Marks and A.J. Minnis (Woodbridge, 2000), 191–210.

5. BN, MS français 25777/1725.

6. Curry, 'Isolated or Integrated?', 198.

7. *Ibid.*, 199.

8. *Ibid.*, 204.

9. *Ibid.*, 204.

10. Le Baker, 116–18, trans. Stowe, 284–6; Hardy, *Longbow*, 97.

11. Traditional.

12. Gillespie, 'Cheshire Archers', 1–39.

13. Gillespie, 'Cheshire Archers', 32.

14. H. Hutchinson, *The Hollow Crown* (1961), 170.

15. Gillespie, *Records of the Ormerod and Holmes families*, and *Heralds' Visitations*.

16. Gillespie, 'Archers of the Crown', 14–29.

17. Prestwich, *Armies and Warfare*, 137.

18. See p. 30.

19. Prestwich, 'Armies and Warfare', 137.

20. Prestwich, 'Armies and Warfare', 145.

21. We can only quote the frequent use of legislation to enforce such practice, and the fact that 'the Butts' is almost as common a location name as 'the Church' or 'the school' in very many cities, towns and villages.

22. Burne, *Crécy War* and *Agincourt War*.

23. It is perhaps useful to remember that throughout the period of this study the Scots, quite apart from providing in their time the archer-guard for the Kings of France, were the allies of France in war, and the enemies and frequent invaders of England in both war and peace (see Ch. 18).

24. 'Possibly', because we shall examine other factors which alter the situation at Agincourt.

25. Sumption, *Trial by Battle*, 51., quoting PRO, C76/23 mm 22, 22d, 21, 20, 19 *Foedera*, iii, 87 and PRO, C81/314/17803.

26. PRO, C76/24; Le Bel, II, 344–8.

27. On a visit some years ago to Crécy with the late Viscount de Lisle VC, KG, I indicated where I thought the Black Prince would have been. De Lisle said, 'A little further forward, surely . . . about here. Back there his view to the left was blocked and there was some dead ground to the front; *here* he and his archers could see everything.'

28. Sumption, *Trial by Fire*, 240.

29. Chandos Herald, ed. R. Barber, 88–9.

30. Rogers, *War, Cruel and Sharp*.

31. J.M. Tourneur-Aumont, *Bataille de Poitiers* (Paris-Presses Universitaires de France, 1940), 18–24.

32. A great ally of the Plantagenets, a Gascon baron and a Knight of the Garter.

33. John of Reading, *Chronica 1346–57*, ed. Tait (Manchester University Press, 1914).

34. Rogers, *War, Cruel and Sharp*, 374–5.

35. Le Baker, 151.

36. A. Curry, *Battle of Agincourt: Sources and Interpretations* (Woodbridge, 2000).

37. *Chronique de Ruisseauville*, 138.

38. Jean Juvenal des Ursins, 518.

39. Le Fèvre, I, 242, 252.

40. Religieux V, 558.

41. Bradbury, *The Medieval Archer*, 126–7.

42. Nicolas, *The Battle of Agincourt*, 405.

43. See also Wylie, *Henry V*, 131 n. 8.

44. Curry, *Agincourt*, 22–6.

45. Even the meticulous Wylie does not follow, or even seem to notice, the clear allusion to changes of position given by the Chaplain. Tito Livio (q.v.) mentions it, and the move to Maisoncelles 'not near'; Curry, *Agincourt*, 59.

46.   Veronique de Chabot-Tramecourt, *Patrimonie d'un Gentilhomme en Artois, XVII & XVIII siècles* (Lignereuil, 1979).

47.   *Vita Henrici*, 62, Tito Livio, in Curry, *Agincourt*, 60.

48.   Wylie, *Henry V*, II, 149.

CHAPTER 17

1.   *Agincourt, or the Bowman's Glory*, 1665, in *Bishop Percy's Folio Manuscript. Ballads and Romances*, ed. J.W. Hales and F.J. Furnival, 4 vols (London, 1867–8), II, 595; and reprinted in Curry, *Agincourt*, 302–4.

2.   Curry, *Agincourt*, 1–9, 301–31.

3.   Curry, *Agincourt*, 370–401.

4.   The only available edition of the French text of Christine's *Livre des fais* is that contained in C.M. Laennec, 'Christine *antygrafe*: Authorship and Self in the Prose Works of Christine de Pizan, with an Edition of B.N. Ms. 603, "Le Livre des Fais d'Armes et de Chevalerie"', 2 vols (Doctoral Thesis, Yale University, 1988: U.M.I, Ann Arbor, 1991), the edition being in the second volume. I am indebted to my colleague Professor Angus Kennedy for this reference, and for his assistance on further bibliography relating to the *Livre des fais*. A modern English text of Caxton's 1489 translation from the French is provided by Christine de Pizan, *The Book of Deeds of Arms and of Chivalry*, trans. S. Willard and C.C. Willard (Pennsylvania State University, 1999). Subsequent references to the *Livre des fais* cite the Laennec edition followed by the translation of Willard and Willard.

5.   Laennec, 'Christine *antygrafe*', 1ff; *The Book of Deeds of Arms*, 3–6. For further discussion of the work's context see *The Writings of Christine de Pizan*, ed. C.C. Willard (New York, 1994), 254–9; C.C. Willard, 'Christine de Pizan's Treatise on the Art of Medieval Warfare', in *Essays in Honor of Louis Francis Solano*, ed. R.J. Cormier and U.T. Holmes (Chapel Hill, North Carolina, 1970), 179–91.

6.   M.-A. Bossy, 'Arms and the Bride: Christine de Pizan's Military Treatise as a Wedding Gift for Margaret of Anjou', in *Christine de Pizan and the Categories of Difference*, ed. M. Desmond (Minneapolis, 1998), 236–56, 1498 for Talbot and the Shrewsbury Book (British Library, Royal MS E VI); William Caxton, *The Book of the Fayttes of Armes and of Chyvalrye*, ed. A.T.P. Byles (Early English Texts Society, 1937), 291; Goodman, *The Wars of the Roses*, 166–7.

7.   B.S. Hall, '"So notable Ordynaunce": Christine de Pizan, Firearms and Siegecraft in a Time of Transition', in *Cultuurhistorisches Caleidoscoop aangeboden an Prof. Dr. Willy L. Braekman*, ed. C. De Baeker (Ghent, 1992), 219–33, and especially at 223, where it is argued that Christine's detailed knowledge of gunpowder weaponry strongly supports the idea that the Duke of Burgundy was her primary source of information on military affairs.

8.   *Livre des fais*, 87 (Bk I, Ch. 23); *The Book of Deeds of Arms*, 65.

9.   *The Très Riches Heures of Jean, Duke of Berry*, ed. J. Longnon, R. Cazelles and M. Meiss (New York, 1969), pl. 1.

10.   *Livre des fais*, 87; *The Book of Deeds of Arms*, 65–6.

11.   *Livre des fais*, 88; *The Book of Deeds of Arms*, 66.

12.   *Livre des fais*, 88–9; *The Book of Deeds of Arms*, 66. The B.N. Ms 603 text of the *Livre des fais* only mentions Roosebeke, but the text used by Caxton makes reference to Othée (here called Liège) as well (*Book of Fayttes of Armes and of Chyvalrye*, ed. Byles, 82).

13.   Froissart, ed. Luce, XI, 43, 51.

14.   Froissart, ed. Luce, XI, 54–7.

15.   R. Vaughan, *John the Fearless* (London, 1966), 60.

16.   B. Schnerb, 'La bataille rangée dans la tactique des armées bourguignonnes au début du 15e siècle: essai de synthèse', *Annales de Bourgogne*, lxxi (1989), 5–32; *Livre des fais*, 88–9; *The Book of Deeds of Arms*, 66.

17.   Vaughan, *John the Fearless*, 60–2.

18.   B. Schnerb, *L'État bourguignon, 1363–1477* (Paris, 1999), 267.

19.   Vaughan, *John the Fearless*, 140.

20.   Vaughan, *John the Fearless*, 92, 141–2.

21.   C. Brusten, *L'armée bourguignonne de 1465 à 1468* (Brussels, 1953), 108.

22.   British Library Cotton Caligula Dv ff.43–4, edited and discussed by C. Philpotts, 'The French Plan of Battle During the Agincourt Campaign', *EHR*, xxx (1984), 59–68. The plan is translated by Allmand, *Society at War*, 194–5, and M. Bennett, *Agincourt: Triumph Against the Odds* (London, 1991), 62–6, and a plan is also given in *idem*, 'The Development of Battle Tactics', 17.

23.   For a detailed narrative of Henry's march, Wylie, *Henry V*, II, 88–120.

24.   Jean Juvenal des Ursins, *Histoire de Charles VI*, II, 518; Curry, *Agincourt*, 130.

25.   Bennett, *Agincourt*, 44–59.

26.   For the importance of the offices of Constable and Marshal in the French armies see Fowler, *Age of Plantagenet and Valois*, 116–20.

27.   He went on to be French governor of Genoa, then of Languedoc and Guyenne. He died in English captivity in 1421. For his career see D. Lalande, *Jean II le Maingre, dit Boucicaut (1366–1421): étude d'une biographie héroïque* (Geneva, 1988); N. Housley, 'Le Maréchal Boucicaut à Nicopolis', in *Nicopolis, 1396–1996*, ed. J. Paviot and M. Chauney-Bouillot (Dijon, 1997), and also printed in *Annales de Bourgogne*, lxvii (1996), fasc. 3, at 85–99; and *idem*, 'One Man and his Wars; the Depiction of Warfare by Marshal Boucicaut's Biographer', *Journal of Medieval History*, xxix (2003), 27–40. For the beautiful book of hours he commissioned see M. Meiss, *French Painting in the Time of Jean de Berry. The Boucicaut Master* (London, 1968), which contains a valuable introduction.

28.   Philpotts, 'The French Plan of Battle', 64–6; Allmand, *Society at War*, 194–5.

29.   Vaughan, *John the Fearless*, 208.

30.   Monstrelet, III, 108; le Fèvre, I, 256; Waurin, II, 215.

31.   See pp. 339–41.

32.   Bennett, *Agincourt*, 53–4.

33.   *Gesta Henrici Quinti*, 78–9.

34. *Gesta Henrici Quinti*, 78–9; Elmham, *Liber Metricus*, 119; Monstrelet, III, 102; Curry, *Agincourt*, 45, 155.

35. Tito Livio, 19; Curry, *Agincourt*, 69.

36. *Mémoires*, I, 360–4; trans. R. Vaughan, *Charles the Bold. The Last Valois Duke of Burgundy* (London, 1973), 201. The Burgundians similarly crossed themselves and commended themselves to God.

37. *Brut*, 596.

38. Elmham, *Liber Metricus*, 123–4; Curry, *Agincourt*, 48, 77.

39. Le Fèvre, I, 245.

40. *Brut*, 387, 'but God and our archers made hem to stomble'.

41. Burne, *Agincourt War*, 93–4.

42. Curry, *Agincourt*, 11–13.

43. For Henry's abilities see G.L. Harriss, ed. *Henry V. The Practice of Kingship* (Oxford, 1985), and especially C.T. Allmand, 'Henry V the Soldier and the War with France', in *ibid.*, 117–35.

44. For these men see *Gesta Henrici Quinti*, 74, ns 2 and 3.

45. *Chronique normande de Pierre Cochon*, 273–4; Curry, *Agincourt*, 113.

46. *Gesta Henrici Quinti*, 80–1.

47. Guillaume Cousinot, *Chronique de la Pucelle*, ed. V. de Viriville, 8 vols (Paris, 1859), 155–7; Curry, *Agincourt*, 111.

48. *Gesta Henrici Quinti*, 74–5, and n. 4

49. Juvenal des Ursins, *Histoire de Charles*, 519, 520. Des Ursins twice mentions the deployments agreed by this council. In the first, he notes that the flanking cavalry attacks were to be led by Gaulvet, Lord of la Freté-Hubert, Clignet de Brabant and Louis de Bosredon (also rendered Boisbourdon in Curry, *Agincourt*, 130). Clignet de Brabant was in the French vanguard, but unlike Bosredon he is not mentioned by name in the 'Somme Plan'. Des Ursins's second account (520), given as if reporting the accounts of others, gives the French deployment as a vanguard under Bourbon, Boucicaut and Guichard Dauphin, a main battle led by the Dukes of Orléans, Alençon, Brittany and the Constable, d'Albret, and a rearguard led by Bar, Nevers and the Count of Charolais. Two wings were to be commanded by the Count of Richemont and Tanneguy de Chastel, while the cavalry attack against the English was to be led by the Admiral, Clignet de Brabant and the senechal of Hainault. Several of these commanders, however, including Tanneguy de Chastel, the Count of Charolais and the Duke of Brittany, were not present for the battle itself. For details of the French commanders, see Philpotts, 'The French Plan of Battle', 59–66.

50. *Gesta Henrici Quinti*, 68–71.

51. Bennett, 'Battle Tactics'. 15–16.

52. For Nicopolis see A.S. Atiya, *The Crusade of Nicopolis* (London, 1934); K.M. Setton, *The Papacy and the Levant (1204–1571), I, The Thirteenth and Fourteenth Centuries* (Philadelphia, 1976), 345–69; Vaughan, *Philip the Bold*, 59–78; J. Paviot and M. Chauney-Bouillot, ed. *Nicopolis, 1396–1996* (Dijon, 1997); and D. Nicolle, *Nicopolis, 1396. The Last Crusade* (Osprey, 1999), particularly valuable for its maps and illustrations.

53. *Le Livre des fais du bon messire Jehan le Maingre, dit Bouciquaut, mareschal de France et gouverneur de Jennes*, ed. D. Lalande (Paris and Geneva, 1985), 104–5, '*firent planter grant foison de pieux agus que ilz avoient fait apprester pour ce faire, et estoient ces pieulx plantez en biesant, les pointes tournees devers noz gens, si hault que ilz pouoient aler jusques au ventres des chevaulx*'; Setton, *The Papacy and the Levant*, I, 353.

54. *Le Livre des fais*, 105.

55. Religieux, II, 500–18; *Le Livre des fais*, 106–11. The extent to which the French knights dismounted is discussed by Atiya, *Nicopolis*, 88–90, who analyses the conflicting evidence of the sources.

56. Religieux, II, 504–18; *Le Livre des fais*, 111–12.

57. Bennett, 'Battle Tactics', 16.

58. For Beaufort's participation, Wylie, *England under Henry IV*, III, 261 and n. 14 (correcting his earlier assumption in *ibid.* I, 6, that Henry of Bolingbroke was himself present at the battle); J.J.N. Palmer, *England, France and Christendom, 1377–99* (London, 1972), 184–5, 204, and for the nature of the English contingent, 239–40 9 (which supersedes the discussion by Atiya, *Nicopolis*, 44–8, 80 and refutes the argument of C.L. Tipton, 'The English at Nicopolis', *Speculum*, xxxvii (1962), 528–40, that no English were actually present); and Goodman, *John of Gaunt*, 202–3. The presence of the men of Cheshire, who had been enlisted following a rebellion in that county in 1393, is suggested by Palmer, *England, France and Christendom*, 184–5. Sir Ralph Percy, Hotspur's younger brother, was also probably among those slain by the Turks (*ibid.*, 240).

59. *Gesta Henrici Quinti*, 74–5.

60. *Gesta Henrici Quinti*, 83.

61. For York and Camoys, see *Gesta Henrici Quinti*, 82–3, ns 3 and 4.

62. Keen, 'Richard II's Ordinances of War', 39; S. Armitage-Smith, *John of Gaunt* (London, 1904), Appendix II, 437–9.

63. Above, Ch. 16, pp. 306–9.

64. Curry, *Agincourt*, 24–5.

65. In his *Liber metricus*, Thomas Elmham noted that Henry placed 'the vanguard as wing on the right, with the rearguard as a wing to the left. Among them he intermingled troops of archers (*hic intermisit turmas simul architenentium*)'. But if, as is now generally agreed, Elmham did not write the *Gesta*, he was heavily influenced by it, and given the still uncertain relationship between the texts, it is probably unwise to regard Elmham as independent on the nature of Henry's formations (*Liber Metricus*, 120; Curry, *Agincourt*, 46).

66. Robert Blondell, *De Reductione Normanniae*, ed. J. Stevenson, *Narratives of the Expulsion of the English from Normandy, MCCCCXLIX–MCCCCL* (London, 1863), 173; and see p. 359.

67. Monstrelet, III, 105; Curry, *Agincourt*, 158.

68. Le Fèvre, I, 253; Waurin, II, 211–12; Curry, *Agincourt*, 159.

69. Bennett, 'The Impact of English Tactics', 55.

70. *Gesta Henrici Quinti*, 82–3.

71. For Sir Thomas see A. Curry, 'Sir Thomas Erpingham', in *Agincourt, 1415*, ed. Curry, 53–77, especially 71–3 for his role in the battle.

72. The Italian chronicler Tito Livio (who seems to have had his account direct from the king's brother, the Duke of Gloucester) believed that thorn bushes and hedges also acted as a defence to the English flanks (Tito Livio, 16; Curry, *Agincourt*, 59, 'and on the

two flanks hedges and thorn bushes which protected the royal army from ambush and assault by the enemy').

73. Tito Livio, 17; Curry, *Agincourt*, 60. Elmham, 62; Curry, *Agincourt*, 71, believed that 'all the French lines were strengthened with ranks of twenty or more' deep, against the four-deep ranks of the English.

74. Religieux, 562; Curry, *Agincourt*, 107.

75. *Livre des fais*; *The Book of Deeds of Arms*, 7.

76. *Book of Fayttes of Armes*, ed. Byles, 83.

77. *Knyghthode and Bataile*, 39–40.

78. Monstrelet, III, 103, 104, '*en la bataille furent ordonnez autant de chevaliers et d'escuiers et de gens de traict comme en l'avengarde*'; le Fèvre, I, 248; Curry, *Agincourt*, 156.

79. Monstrelet, III, 102; *Gesta Henrici Quinti*, 92–3.

80. *Ordonnonces des roys de France*, IV, 70; Allmand, *Society at War*, 47–8.

81. Contamine, *War in the Middle Ages*, 129, 168; see pp. 254–6.

82. Wylie, *Henry V*, 59.

83. Wylie, *England under Henry IV*, II, 95.

84. Delauney, *Étude sur les anciennes compagnies d'archers*, 4ff.

85. *Ordonnances des rois de France*, IX, 522–6.

86. *Ordonnances des rois de France*, IX, 605–6, 595–8, 658–61.

87. *Ordonnances des rois de France*, X, 61–2.

88. *Extraits analytiques des registres des consaulx de la ville de Tournai, 1431–76*, ed. A. de la Grange (Tournai, 1893), 135, '*anchiennes ordonnances sur leur serment, du temps du roy Dangobiert*'. I am grateful to Dr Graeme Small for this reference.

89. *Ordonnances des rois de France*, IX, 589–90.

90. Le Fèvre, 253; Curry, *Agincourt*, 159.

91. Religieux, 559; Curry, *Agincourt*, 106.

92. *Gesta Henrici Quinti*. 87.

93. *Chronique normande de Pierre Cochon*, 273–4; Curry, *Agincourt*, 113.

94. *Récits*, 219.

95. *Le Songe du Vieil Pélerin*, ed. G.W. Coopland, 2 vols (Cambridge, 1969), II, 382–3; trans. Allmand, *Society at War*, 50.

96. *Chronique des quatres premiers Valois*, 46; Froissart, ed. Lettenhove, V, 381–2; Sumption, *Trial by Fire*, 227. Cf. Delachenal, *Histoire de Charles V*, I, 186; Lescot, 101–2.

97. See pp. 227–8.

98. Religieux, 549; Curry, *Agincourt*, 102–3. *The Histoire de Charles VI* attributed to Jean Juvenal des Ursins seems to be drawing directly on this passage from the Religieux, when he notes that at Agincourt the men-at-arms looked down on the infantry raised from Paris and other towns, 'as they had done at the battles of Courtrai, at the taking of King John at Poitiers, and in Turkey' (*Histoire de Charles VI*, 518; Curry, *Agincourt*, 129).

99. *Chronique de Ruisseauville*, in Bacquet, *Azincourt*, 94–5; Curry, *Agincourt*, 126

100. *Histoire de Charles VI*, 518; Curry, *Agincourt*, 130.

101. Meiss, *French Painting*, 8–9. This disdain may, as Meiss suggests, account for the 'wholly immoderate parade' of his armorial bearings throughout the book of hours.

102. *Livre des fais*, 24.

103. *Livre des fais*, xxi–xxix.

104. *Livre des fais*, 392–401.

105. *Chronique de la Pucelle*, 155–6; Curry, *Agincourt*, 111.

106. Religieux, 559, 571; Curry, *Agincourt*, 106, 109.

107. Le Fèvre, I, 249: Waurin, II, 207; Curry, *Agincourt*, 157.

108. This was a problem encountered by James IV at Flodden, who was to perish in the front ranks of his pikemen.

109. Commynes, *Memoirs*, trans. Jones, 73.

110. Monstrelet, III, 107; le Fèvre, I, 255; Waurin, II, 213–14.

111. Walsingham, 94–5; Curry, *Agincourt*, 51.

112. Religieux, 559; Curry, *Agincourt*, 106.

113. *Gesta Henrici Quinti*, 82–3.

114. Monstrelet, III, 106; le Fèvre, I, 253–4; Waurin, II, 212; Curry, *Agincourt*, 160.

115. Le Fèvre, I, 250–1; Waurin, II, 208–9.

116. Monstrelet, III, 106; Curry, *Agincourt*, 160.

117. Le Fèvre, I, 251; Waurin, II, 208–9; Curry, *Agincourt*, 158.

118. Walsingham, 95–6; Curry, *Agincourt*, 52.

119. Le Fèvre, 225; Waurin, II, 213–14; Monstrelet, accuses Saveuse of breaking ranks to be first into the attack (III, 107).

120. *Gesta Henrici Quinti*, 86–7.

121. Monstrelet, III, 107–8; Curry, *Agincourt*, 161.

122. Le Fèvre, I, 254; Waurin, II, 213; Curry, *Agincourt*, 160–1; Cf. Jean Juvenal des Ursins, *Histoire de Charles VI*, 520; Curry, *Agincourt*, 133, 'in order to better withstand and reply to the English fire, they lowered their heads and inclined them towards the ground'.

123. Le Fèvre, I, 252; Waurin, II, 211; Curry, *Agincourt*, 159.

124. Elmham, *Liber Metricus*, 122; Curry, *Agincourt*, 47.

125. *L'Apparicion Maistre Jehan de Meun et le Somnium super Materia Scismatis*, ed. I. Arnold (Paris, 1926), ll. 517–20 (cited in Jones, *Chaucer's Knight*, 273 n. 11).

126. Religieux, 559; Curry, *Agincourt*, 106. 'The French', he added, 'were too restricted and weighed down in their movements . . . they were already exhausted by a long march and were suffering under the weight of their armour.'

127. *Chronique normande de Pierre Cochon*, 273–4; Curry, *Agincourt*, 113.

128. Le Fèvre, I, 252–3; Waurin, II, 211; Curry, *Agincourt*, 159.

129. La Marche, *Mémoires*, II, 319.

130. *Chronique anonyme du regne de Charles VI*, in *La Chronique d'Enguerran de Monstrelet*, ed. L. Douet-D'Arcq, VI, 228–30, at 229; Curry, *Agincourt*, 115, which also notes the ploughed ground and the exhaustion caused by the armour of the French.

131. *Gesta Henrici Quinti*, 90–1, 88–9.

132. *Gesta Henrici Quinti*, 90–1, 'our archers notched their sharp-pointed arrows and loosed them into the enemy's flanks, keeping up the fight without pause'.

133. Tito Livio, 19; Curry, *Agincourt*, 61.

134. On these methods of fighting see *Medieval Combat. A Fifteenth Century Manual of Sword Fighting and Close-Quarter Combat by Hans Talhoffer*, ed. and trans. M. Rector (London, 2000), 1476; J.

Waller, 'Combat Techniques', in Fiorato *et al.*, *Blood Red Roses*, 148–54.

135. *Gesta Henrici Quinti*, 90–1.

136. *Gesta Henrici Quinti*, 88–9.

137. Le Fèvre, I, 260; Waurin, II, 218.

138. Le Fèvre, I, 256; Waurin, II, 215; Curry, *Agincourt*, 162.

139. Le Fèvre, I, 256; Waurin, II, 214–15; Curry, *Agincourt*, 162.

140. Newhall, 'Discipline in an English Army', 143.

141. Monstrelet, III, 106.

142. Religieux, 563; Curry, *Agincourt*, 107.

143. Waurin, II, 214; Monstrelet, III, 106; Curry, *Agincourt*, 162.

144. Religieux, 563; Curry, *Agincourt*, 107.

145. J.R. Hale, 'On a Tudor Parade Ground: the Captain's Handbook of Henry Barrett, 1562', *The Society for Renaissance Studies*, Occasional Papers, no. 5, reprinted in J.R. Hale, *Renaissance War Studies* (London, 1983), 247–90, at 276–7.

146. Monstrelet, III, 106; *Chronique de Ruisseauville*, in Bacquet, *Azincourt*, 91–4; Curry, *Agincourt*, 125.

147. Monstrelet, III, 108; Curry, *Agincourt*, 162.

148. *Book of Fayttes of Armes*, ed. Byles, 83.

149. *Mémoires de Pierre de Fenin*, 63–4; Curry, *Agincourt*, 118.

150. Religieux, 571; Curry, *Agincourt*, 109.

151. Monstrelet, III, 108.

152. Monstrelet, III, 108–9.

153. *Gesta Henrici Quinti*, 90–1.

154. Philpotts, 'The French Plan', 63.

155. *Gesta Henrici Quinti*, 92–3.

156. Just prior to the battle of Nicopolis the allies had executed their Turkish prisoners captured earlier (Religieux, II, 500–1).

157. Le Fèvre, I, 258; Waurin, II, 216.

158. Le Bel, II, 106.

159. Monstrelet, IV, 160.

160. On the comparative proportions of the slain compared to Crécy and Poitiers, see Curry, *Agincourt*, 472–3.

161. *Gesta Henrici Quinti*, 92–3.

162. *Gesta Henrici Quinti*, 92–3, 94–7.

163. Monstrelet, IV, 110. Le Fèvre and Waurin put the number at 1,600.

164. *The Earliest English Translations of Vegetius's De Re Militari*, ed. G. Lester (Heidelberg, 1988), 47. Earlier, around 1325, Jean de Vignai had translated Vegetius into French, stating it was good to be informed on military wisdom, '*car en toutes batailles seulent plus donner victoire sens et usage d'armes qu force ne multitude de gens mal endoctrines*' (P. Meyer, 'Les anciens traducteurs français de Végèce, et en particulier Jean de Vignai', *Romania*, xxv (1896), 401–23).

165. M. Howard, *War in European History* (Oxford, 1976), 30–5.

CHAPTER 18

1. Vaughan, *John the Fearless*, 91–3. As Duke of Nevers John had also archers and crossbowmen with him on the Nicopolis campaign. The names of some of the bowmen in his own household, including Andre le Petit Archer, are listed in the Burgundian ordinance drawn up on 28 March 1396, which is edited and discussed by Atiya, *Nicopolis*, 144–8, 41–2. Based on the proportions of knights and esquires to bowmen in Nevers's own retinue, Atiya estimates the French force contained around 500 archers and 1,000 crossbowmen (*ibid.*, 42), but the allies were relying primarily on the Hungarian light cavalry for their missile arm to counter the Turks.

2. On this battle plan see J.F. Verbruggen, 'Un plan de bataille du duc de Bourgogne (14 Septembre 1417) et la tactique de l'Époque', *Revue internationale d'histoire militaire*, xx (1959), 443–51. The text is given in Georges Chastellain, *Oeuvres de Georges Chastellain*, ed. K. de Lettenhove, 8 vols (Brussels, 1863–6), I, 324–7, and translated by Vaughan, *John the Fearless*, 148–50.

3. Vaughan, *John the Fearless*, 150.

4. Vaughan, *John the Fearless*, 149–50.

5. Vaughan, *John the Fearless*, 149.

6. Vaughan, *John the Fearless*, 149.

7. Bennett, 'The Development of Battle Tactics', 17–18, with the plan of 1417 illustrated on 19.

8. Vaughan, *John the Fearless*, 150.

9. Bennett, 'The Development of Battle Tactics', 18, drawing

attention to the disciplinary clause omitted by Vaughan, *John the Fearless*, 148–50.

10. For relations between England and Burgundy between 1419 and 1435 see R. Vaughan, *Philip the Good. The Apogee of Burgundy* (London, 1970), 1–28.

11. Monstrelet, IV, 159.

12. For this battle, Monstrelet, IV, 59–63; Vaughan, *Philip the Good*, 12–14.

13. Monstrelet, IV, 160.

14. For Cravant, Burne, *Agincourt War*, 184–95; J.-M. Dousseau, *La Bataille de Cravant* (Auxerre, 1987), and see p. 346.

15. Monstrelet, IV, 384.

16. For the battle see B. Schnerb, *Bulgnéville (1431): L'État bourguignon prend pied en Lorraine* (Paris, 1993), 76–87, on which the account which follows is based.

17. Monstrelet, IV, 459.

18. Le Fèvre, II, 260.

19. Monstrelet, IV, 461.

20. Monstrelet, IV, 461.

21. Monstrelet, IV, 461, '*si furent mis les archiers ou front devant, et une partie sur les hèles, et fichèrent leurs penchons devant eulx*'.

22. Monstrelet, IV, 461–3.

23. Schnerb, *Bulgnéville*, 80–3.

24. *Les chroniques du roi Charles VII par Gilles le Bouvier dit le hérault Berry*, ed. H. Courteault, L. Célier and M.-H. Julien de Pommerol (Paris, 1979), 149.

25. Monstrelet, IV, 464

26. Schnerb, *Bulgnéville*, 86, 89–91, 80.

27. Vaughan, *Philip the Good*, 14.

28. B. Schnerb, *L'État bourguignon*, 267; *idem*, *Bulgnéville*, 64–7.

29. Contamine, *War in the Middle Ages*, 168–9.

30. Michel, *Les Écossais*, 59–77; Macdougall, *An Antidote to the English*, 55; for his role at Poitiers, see. p. 234.

31. Michel, *Les Écossais*, I, 109–11, 113; Macdougall, *An Antidote to the English*, 59.

32. Macdougall, *An Antidote to the English*, 62. For the Scots forces, B.G.H. Ditcham, 'The Employment of Foreign Mercenary Troops in the French Royal Armies, 1415–70' (PhD thesis, University of Edinburgh, 1979); and B. Chevalier, 'Les Écossais dans les armées de Charles VII jusqu'à la bataille de Verneuil', *Jeanne d'Arc: une époque, un Rayonnement* (Paris, 1982).

33. *Scotichronicon*, VIII, 112–13; G. Du Fresne de Beaucourt, *Histoire de Charles VII*, 6 vols (Paris, 1881–91), I, 428–30; Vale, *Charles VII*, 33.

34. Macdougall, *An Antidote to the English*, 60.

35. Contamine, *Guerre, état, et société*, 272 n. 181. It is not a little ironic in view of subsequent events that in 1413 Henry V had granted Scots safe conduct to import, via England, arms purchased in France (*Rot. Scot*, II, 207; Michel, *Les Écossais*, I, 113).

36. A number of French had been captured in the battle and subsequently ransomed (*Foedera*, VIII, 393).

37. *Registrum Honoris de Morton*, ed. T. Thomson and A. Macdonald, 2 vols (Bannatyne Club, 1853), II, no. 129; Nicholson, *Scotland. The Later Middle Ages*, 213.

38. Macdougall, *An Antidote to the English*, 72.

39. Adams, 'Archery in the Highlands', 44–6.

40. Michel, *Les Écossais*, I, 118 n. 1; Wylie, *Henry V*, III, 216; Burne, *Agincourt War*, 145–6.

41. *Scotichronicon*, VIII, 114–15.

42. *Scotichronicon*, VIII, 114–15. On these tensions see B.G.H. Ditcham, '"Mutton Guzzlers and Wine Bags". Foreign Soldiers and Native Reactions in Fifteenth Century France', *Power, Culture and Religion in France*, ed. C.T. Allmand (Woodbridge, 1989), 1–13.

43. For the fullest account of the battle, its context and the problematic nature of the sources, see Wylie, *Henry V*, III, 293–310; R. Planchenault, 'La bataille de Baugé (22 mars 1421)', *Mémoires de la société nationale d'agriculture, sciences et arts d'Angers*, 5e série, xxviii (1925), 5–30; *idem*, 'Les suites de la bataille de Baugé (1421)', *ibid.*, 6e série, v (1930), 90–107; Allmand, *Henry V*, 158–9.

44. *Brut*, II, 447–8.

45. *Chronicle of John Hardyng*, 384; Allmand, *Henry V*, 159.

46. *Vita et Gesta Henrici Quinti*, ed. T. Hearne (Oxford, 1727), 302.

47. The statement by Bower, *Scotichronicon*, VIII, 118–19, that both sides negotiated a truce in observance of Easter Sunday is unlikely, and is used to highlight the perfidy of the English surprise attack.

48. *Scotichronicon*, VIII, 118–21; *The Book of Pluscarden*, ed. F.J.H. Skene, 2 vols (Edinburgh, 1877–80), II, 265–8.

49. Religieux, 456, says that some fought on foot, some on horseback, while Hardyng, *Chronicle*, 335, says the English dismounted.

50. See the discussion of the sources on this point by Wylie, *Henry V*, III, 303 n. 4.

51. *Scotichronicon*, VIII, 120–1. Clarence's death is variously reported, but Bower, *Scotichronicon*, VIII, 120–1, claims he was wounded in the face by the lance of Sir John Swinton – son of the man who fought at Otterburn and Homildon – then felled by Buchan's mace. *The Book of Pluscarden*, II, 268, noted 'it was commonly held that his slayer was 'a Highland Scot named Alexander Macausland, a native of Lennox', serving in Buchan's household, and noted that this Alexander sold the precious coronet taken from Clarence's helmet to the Earl of Darnley for 1,000 nobles.

52. Wylie, *Henry V*, III, 309.

53. *Scotichronicon*, VIII, 120–1. The English chronicler Adam of Usk ends his account with this defeat 'which caused much grief in England', noting 'it is this slaughter which the Earl of Salisbury has been charged with his followers to avenge, and is fiercely avenging, with fire and sword, to keep the country [Normandy] safe' (*The Chronicle of Adam Usk*, ed. C. Given-Wilson (Oxford, 1997), 270–1).

54. Vale, *Charles VII*, 33.

55. *Scotichronicon*, VIII, 294–5 and note to l. 38, where the slain are stated to have included 'six captains, two lieutenants and 1,200 others' and a further 200 slain by brigands following their rout.

56. Burne, *Agincourt War*, 185–95, provides an attempted reconstruction of the battle.

57. Waurin, III, 67; trans. *Chronicles*, III, 45, 70; trans. *Chronicles*, 47, says he was on the English expedition following up the victory, but it is uncertain if he was present at the battle itself. He only slightly expands the version given by Monstrelet, IV, 161–2.

58. Waurin, III, 68–9; trans. *Chronicles*, 46.

59. As Bower, *Scotichronicon*, VIII, 294–5, remarks, he was ransomed for 30,000 crowns 'and the high value placed on him was a measure of the special trust he enjoyed from the King of France'.

60. Beaucourt, *Histoire de Charles VII*, II, 14; Vale, *Charles VII*, 33.

61. Macdougall, *An Antidote to the English*, 69.

62. Macdougall, *An Antidote to the English*, 71–2.

63. M.K. Jones, 'The Battle of Verneuil (17 August 1424): Towards a History of Courage', *War in History*, ix (2002), 375–411, at 377–82.

64. *Revue des Questions Historiques*, lxxxvi (1909), 570, for Aumâle's own description of the battle; J. Le Fizelier, 'La bataille de la Brossinière', *Revue Historique et Archéologique du Maine*, i (1876), 28–42; Jones, 'Verneuil', 379–80.

65. Jones, 'Verneuil', 391.

66. Historisches Museum der Stadt Wein, Inv. No. 127153; illustrated in Norman, *Arms and Armour* ill. 46. Its metallurgy is discussed by A.R. Williams, 'The Blast Furnace and the Mass

Production of Plate Armour', 104. The average hardness of the peytral was 252 VPH, that of the chanfron varied between 150 and 236 VPH, side plates between 200 and 252 VPH.

67. For an example of such horse armour in about 1415, see P. Porter, *Medieval Warfare in Manuscripts* (London, 2000), 28.

68. Jones, 'Verneuil', 380–1.

69. Newhall, *Muster and Review*, 315–17; Curry, 'English Armies in the Fifteenth Century', 63; Jones, 'Verneuil', 383–4, 387 and n. 45.

70. Waurin, III, 110.

71. Monstrelet, IV, 193; Pluscarden, 272.

72. Jones, 'Verneuil', 395.

73. Jones, 'Verneuil', 388–96.

74. Thomas Basin, *Histoire de Charles VII*, ed. C. Samaran, 2 vols (Paris, 1933–44), I, 94–6; trans. M. Harbinson, 'Verneuil – the Events of 17 August, 1424: an Examination of the Sources and the Account of Thomas Basin', *The Hobilar*, xxx (1998), 18–22, at 19.

75. Jones, 'Verneuil', 395–6, 390; Berry Herald, *Chroniques de Roi Charles*, ed H. Corteault and L. Cellier (Paris 1979), 117–19.

76. *Les Chroniques de Normandie*, ed. A. Hellot (Rouen, 1881), 73; Jones, 'Verneuil', 392.

77. Waurin, III, 115.

78. Waurin, III, 115.

79. Jones, 'Verneuil', 397.

80. The 'army of Scotland', however, had left for France before the treaty began on 1 May.

81. Michel, *Les Écossais*, I, 152–4.

82. Monstrelet, IV, 310–11; trans. Thompson, *Contemporary Chronicles*, 296.

83. Oman, *Art of War*, II, 361–70; Hall, *Weapons and Warfare*, 107–14.

84. Such tactics, for example, had been used in a minor engagement in the 1350s, when 30 men-at-arms under Sir Nicholas Dagworth, protected by a formation of wagons, had vanquished 66 French and taken prisoner the Scottish lord Norman Lesley (Michel, *Les Écossais*, I, 69; John Leland, *De Rebus Britannicis Collectanea*, 6 vols (London, 1774), II, 574).

85. Monstrelet, IV, 312–13; trans. Thompson, *Contemporary Chronicles*, 297.

86. Monstrelet, IV, 313–14.

87. Monstrelet, IV, 313; trans. Thompson, *Contemporary Chronicles*, 297.

88. Monstrelet, IV, 331–2.

89. Monstrelet, IV, 329; trans. Thompson, *Contemporary Chronicles*, 305.

90. Monstrelet, IV, 330–2.

91. A. Curry, *The Hundred Years War* (London, 1993), 112.

92. Michel, *Les Écossais*, I, 168–71.

93. Michel, *Les Écossais*, I, 101–2.

94. Contamine, *Guerre, état et société*, 294.

95. 'Le recouvrement de Normendie par Berry, herault du roi', in *Narratives of the Expulsion of the English from Normandy*, ed. J. Stevenson (Rolls Series, London, 1869), 315.

96. C. Sterling and C. Schaefer, *The Hours of Etienne Chevalier* (New York, 1971), pl. 2.

97. Contamine, *Guerre, état et société*, 296.

98. *APS*, II, 6 c. 19; W.C. Dickinson, 'The Acts of Parliament at Perth, 6 March 1429/30', *SHR*, xxix (1950), 1–12.

99. *APS*, II, 5, c.18, 6, c.19.

100. *Scotichronicon*, VIII, 258–9.

101. *APS*, II, 8, c.23.

102. *APS*, II, 8, c.23; 10–11, c.17; 18, cc. 11–14; *Scotichronicon*, VIII, 262–5; M. Brown, *James I* (Edinburgh, 1994), 115.

103. *APS*, II, 9, c. 2 (1425).

104. *APS*, II, 18, cc.11, 12, 14. The parliament of March 1430 reissued these clauses in expanded legislation dealing with defence of the Marches (I.E. O'Brien, 'The Scottish Parliament in the Fifteenth and Sixteenth Centuries' (PhD Thesis, University of Glasgow, 1980), 338–46.

105. *Highland Papers*, ed. J.R.N. MacPhail, 4 vols (Scottish History Society, 1914–34), I, 40–3; Nicholson, *Scotland. The Later Middle Ages*, 316.

106. *Scotichronicon*, VIII, 296–7.

107. *Scotichronicon*, VIII, 296–7.

108. Brown, *James I*, 164.

109. *Scotichronicon*, VIII, 258–9.

110. Edinburgh University Library, MS 195; Adams, 'Some Unrecognized Depictions of the Saffron Shirt', 64–5, who plausibly suggests that the scene probably represents the meeting of Aeneas with Evander, 'King of the Arcadians, a wild woodland tribe'.

111. *APS*, II, 45 c. 14; Nicholson, *Scotland. The Later Middle Ages*, 393–4.

112. *APS*, II, 48 c.6.

113. J. Fergusson, 'A Pair of Butts', *SHR*, xxxiv (1955), 19–25, at 19.

114. *Calendar of Entries in the Papal Registers Relating to Great Britain and Ireland: Papal Letters* (London, 1893), XI, 519, 590 and cf. 661; R. Schwoebel, *The Shadow of the Crescent: The Renaissance Image of the Turk (1453–1517)* (New York, 1969), 136.

115. *Scotichronicon*, VIII, 362, note to l. 9.

116. *APS*, II, 100 c.6.

117. *APS*, 122 c.2, 3, 1. Spearmen were to possess jacks that were to reach to the knee or, if they wore leg harness, the jack covered the upper parts of such leg armour, while it was now stipulated that no spears were to be shorter than 5 or 5½ ells.

118. *The Poems of William Dunbar*, ed. J. Small, 3 vols (Scottish Text Society, Edinburgh, 1893), II, 187, ll. 129–30.

119. For the circumstances leading to their formation see *Chronique de Mathieu d'Escouchy*, ed. G. Fresne de Beaucourt, 3 vols (Paris, 1863–4), I, 51–60; Allmand, *Society at War*, 51–5.

120. Jean Chartier, *Chronique française du roi de France Charles VII*, ed. Vallet de Viriville, II, 235; Oman, *Art of War*, II, 432–4; Fowler, *Plantagenet and Valois*, 137.

121. *Le recouvrement de Normendie*, 370–1.

122. For these reforms see Contamine, *Guerre, état et société*, 277–319.

123. Contamine, *War in the Middle Ages*, 129.

124.   M. Vale, *Charles VII* (Berkeley and Los Angeles, 1974), 150.

125.   Delauney, *Etude sur les anciennes compagnies d'archers*, 4–9.

126.   *Ordonnances des rois de France*, XIII, 240, 242–3.

127.   *Ordonnances des rois de France*, XIII, 456–7.

128.   *Ordonnances des rois de France*, XIII, 483–4.

129.   Contamine, *Guerre, état et société*, 304–8.

130.   See p. 255.

131.   P-H. Morice, *Mémoires pour servir de preuves à l'histoire . . . de Bretagne*, 3 vols (Paris, 1742–6), II, 1166–7.

132.   *Ordonnances des rois de France*, XIV, 1–3; trans. Allmand, *Society at War*, 55–6.

133.   Vale, *Charles VII*, 150.

134.   Contamine, *Guerre, état et société*, 305.

135.   Contamine, *War in the Middle Ages*, 133.

136.   *Ibid.*, 157.

137.   Hall, *Weapons and Warfare*, 115, 118–21.

138.   Berry Herald, 347.

139.   *Ibid.*, 306.

140.   Commynes, *Memoirs*, trans. Jones, 379–80.

141.   Oman, *Art of War*, II, 434.

142.   Contamine, *War in the Middle Ages*, 133, 170.

143.   Chartier, *Chronique*, II, 235.

144.   Hall, *Weapons and Warfare*, 118–21.

145.   Berry Herald, 373.

146.   Oman, *Art of War*, II, 226.

147.   Berry Herald, 373; cf. Chartier, *Chronique*, II, 235.

148.   The most detailed analysis of Formigny remains that of C. Joret, *Le Bataille de Formigny* (Paris, 1903), while also of value is J. Lair, *Essai historique et topographique sur la bataille de Formigny, 15 avril, 1450* (Paris, 1903), and E. Cosneau, *Le connétable de Richemont, Arthur de Bretagne: 1393–1458* (Paris, 1886). More readily accessible is the account by Burne, *Agincourt War*, 313–30, with a briefer summary by Oman, *Art of War*, II, 400–2, and Lot, *L'Art militaire*, II, 80–2.

149.   Curry, 'The First English Standing Army', 196.

150.   For the career of Talbot see H. Talbot, *The English Achilles. The Life and Campaigns of John Talbot, 1st Earl of Shrewsbury* (London, 1981).

151.   Holinshed, *Chronicles*, III, 193.

152.   For these campaigns see Burne, *Agincourt War*, 281–91.

153.   M.K. Jones, 'The Relief of Avranches (1439): An English Feat of Arms at the End of the Hundred Years War', *England in the Fifteenth Century*, ed. N. Rogers (Stamford, 1994), 42–55.

154.   Oman, *Art of War*, II, 399.

155.   *Le Jouvencel*, I, 153.

156.   *Le Jouvencel*, II, 63; trans. Rogers, 'The Offensive/Defensive in Medieval Strategy', 158.

157.   Burne, *Agincourt War*, 283–9.

158.   Burne, *Agincourt War*, 293–9.

159.   M.K. Jones, 'Richard III as a Soldier', in *Richard III. A Medieval Kingship*, ed. J. Gillingham (London, 1993), 93–112, at 93.

160.   Newhall, *Muster and Review*, 120; Curry, 'The First English Standing Army', 202.

161.   Curry, 'The First English Standing Army', 200–1; idem, 'Les gens vivans sur le païs', 209–21.

162.   Curry, 'The First English Standing Army', 207–8.

163.   *Letters and Papers Illustrative of the Wars of the English in France during the Reign of Henry VI, King of England*, ed. J. Stevenson, 2 vols (Rolls Series, London, 1861–4), II, pt 2, 579–81.

164.   Curry, 'The First English Standing Army', 200 and n. 44.

165.   Chartier, *Chronique de Charles VII*, 191–2; Berry Herald, 331.

166.   Blondel, *De Reductione Normanniae*, 173: '*Profecto acies Anglorum perpulchre construuntur. Triplices enim ordines, ut solidi civitatis muri, hostium invasionem detrudunt. Tres vero turmae sagitariorum, qualibet ex septigentis compositae, duae bellorum extrema et altera medium tenetes, veluti tres turres firmae, hostium aggresionem ne frangat proeliorum ordines in praesidio constructae arcent.*'

167.   Blondel, *De Reductione Normanniae*, 171.

168.   Berry Herald, 333–4; *Chronique de Mathieu D'Escouchy*, I, 282.

169.   Chartier, *Chronique de Charles VII*, 195.

170.   Blondel, *De Reductione Normanniae*, 172; *Chronique de Mathieu D'Escouchy*, I, 283.

171.   Blondel, *De Reductione Normanniae*, 173; Berry Herald, 336–7, who ascribes the French counter-attack to the leadership of the seneschal of Poitou; Thomas Basin, *Histoire des règnes de Charles VII et de Louis XI*, ed. J. Quicherat, 4 vols (Paris, 1855–9), I, 236–7.

172.   Blondel, *De Reductione Normanniae*, 173, and Guillaume Gruel, *Chronique d'Arthur de Richemont*, ed. A. Le Vavasseur (Paris, 1890), 206, certainly believed as much.

173.   J.H. Ramsay, *Lancaster and York. A Century of English History*, 2 vols (Oxford, 1892), 107; Oman, *Art of War*, II, 400–1; but cf. Burne's more judicious comments, *Agincourt War*, 319–23.

174.   Chartier, *Chronique*, 195; Blondel, *De Reductione Normanniae*, 175–6; Gruel, *Chronique d'Arthur de Richemont*, 206; Burne, *Agincourt War*, 327–8.

175.   *Le Jouvencel*, II, 64–5; 'les Angloys se mirent en bataille devant les Françoys et, quant ilz virent les Françoys en plus grant nombre qu'ilz ne cuidoient, ilz se adviserent d'aler prendre place avantageuse et en y allant se desroyerent et par ce furent desconfiz'.

176.   Chartier, *Chronique*, 196; *Chronique de Mathieu D'Escouchy*, I, 284.

177.   Berry Herald, 335–6, who believed 1,400 prisoners were taken; *Chronique de Mathieu D'Escouchy*, I, 285; Basin, *Histoire de Charles VII*, I, 238.

178.   Grafton, *Henry VI*, year xxvii (quoted in Oman, *Art of War*, II, 402)

179.   Gruel, *Chronique d'Arthur de Richemont*, 206–7.

180.   Vale, *War and Chivalry*, 141–2.

181.   The fullest narratives of the battle of Castillon are those of Chartier, *Chronique*, III, 1–9 and Basin, *Histoire de Charles VII*, II, 194–201, the latter being translated by Allmand, *Society at War*, 111–13. The engagement is discussed in detail by Burne, *Agincourt War*, 331–45.

182.   Vale, *War and Chivalry*, 141.

183.   Basin, *Histoire de Charles VII*, II, 194–5.

184. Talbot's burial and the description of a nineteenth-century examination of his skeleton are discussed by Talbot, *The English Achilles*, 172–8.

185. Monstrelet, trans. Thompson, *Contemporary Chronicles*, 343.

186. For a valuable overview of Burgundian military campaigns see R. Vaughan, *Valois Burgundy* (London, 1975), 123–61.

187. Much of what follows on Charles's armies is drawn from Richard Vaughan's seminal study *Charles the Bold* which still provides the most authoritative account in English of Charles's campaigns, as well as a whole chapter devoted to a study of his armies. Important studies in French include J. de la Chauvelays, *Diverses organizations des armées de Charles le Téméraire*, and idem, *Les armées de Charles le Téméraire dans les deux bourgognes* (Paris, 1879). Brusten, *L'armée bourguignonne*, and idem, 'L'armée bourguignonne de 1465–1477', *Revue internationale de l'histoire militaire*, xx (1959), 452–66, are useful but have relatively little to say concerning archers. N. Michael, *Armies of Medieval Burgundy, 1364–1477* (London, 1983), provides a valuable summary, with excellent illustrations.

188. Commynes, *Memoirs*, trans. Jones, 72.

189. La Marche, *Mémoires*, II, 235, 321; *Le Jouvencel*, II, 203. For Gavre, L. De Vos, 'La bataille de Gavere le 23 juillet 1453. La victoire de l'organization', in *From Crécy to Mohacs*, 145–57.

190. Commynes, *Memoirs*, trans. Jones, 72.

191. Commynes, *Memoirs*, trans. Jones, 70.

192. Commynes, *Memoirs*, trans. Jones, 70.

193. Commynes, *Memoirs*, trans. Jones, 73.

194. Commynes, *Memoirs*, 122.

195. Commynes, *Memoirs*, 122. Here they were placed among the forces left to press home the siege of Saint-Trond, while the Burgundian army attacked the men of Liège.

196. Vaughan, *Charles the Bold*, 211, 217.

197. *Calendar of State Papers Relating to English Affairs Existing in the Archives and Collections of Venice*, ed. R. Brown, *et al.*, 38 vols (London, 1864–1947), I, 133–4.

198. Vaughan, *Charles the Bold*, 216–17.

199. Jean de Haynin, *Mémoires, 1465–77*, ed. D.D. Brouwers, 2 vols (Liège, 1905–6), II, 182–4; Vaughan, *Charles the Bold*, 327–8.

200. *Correspondance de la mairie de Dijon*, ed. J. Garnier, 3 vols (Dijon, 1868–70), I, 143–8 at 147; Vaughan, *Charles the Bold*, 324.

201. *Calendar of State Papers Existing in the Archives and Collections of Milan*, ed. A.B. Hinds (London, 1912), 225; Vaughan, *Charles the Bold*, 383–4.

202. Vaughan, *Charles the Bold*, 392.

203. Vaughan, *Charles the Bold*, 211.

204. According to the Ordinance of 1468, *Mémoires pour servir a l'histoire de France et Bourgogne*, 2 vols (Paris 1729), II, 283–5.

205. The ordinances of 1472 and 1473 were both printed in *Lois militaires de Charles de Bourgogne, Schweizerische Geschichtsforscher*,

206. Commynes, *Memoirs*, trans. Jones, 73.

207. Vaughan, *Charles the Bold*, 210.

208. For these engravings, F.W.H. Hollstein, *Dutch and Flemish Etchings, Engravings and Woodcuts, c.a 1450–1700, vol. XII: Masters and Monogrammists of the Fifteenth Century* (Amsterdam, 1956), 218–19.

209. Waurin, V, 625–6; trans. Vaughan, *Charles the Bold*, 220.

210. Bennett, 'The Battle', 30; and for the 'Double Armed Man', Hardy, *Longbow*, 140, 142.

211. For the great siege of Neuss, see Vaughan, *Charles the Bold*, 319–45.

212. *Mémoires*, I, 360–4; trans. Vaughan, *Charles the Bold*, 198.

213. Vaughan, *Charles the Bold*, 201–2.

214. Vaughan, *Charles the Bold*, 204.

215. Vaughan, *Charles the Bold*, 202.

216. Strikingly, while Charles's own lengthy account does not specify the nature of the enemy infantry, the dispatch of the Milanese ambassador, Panigarola, does so and gives estimates of their numbers (Vaughan, *Charles the Bold*, 204).

217. Thus the force contract by Charles with the Count of Campobasso in 1472 contained 400 lances, each of 4 horsemen, 400 mounted crossbowmen and 300 infantry (Vaughan, *Charles the Bold*, 215).

218. Vaughan, *Charles the Bold*, 216.

219. For Grandson see J.F. Kirk, *Charles the Bold*, 3 vols (London, 1863–8), III, 270–319; Vaughan, *Charles the Bold*, 369–77; F. Chabloz, *La bataille de Grandson d'après vingt-sept auteurs* (Lausanne, 1897); W. Schaufelberger, *Der alte Schweizer und sein Krieg. Studien zur Kriegführung vornehmlich im 15 Jahrhundert* (Zurich, 1952); F. Deuchler, *Die Burgundebeute* (Bern, 1963); D. Reichel, ed. *Grandson, 1476. Essai d'approche pluridisciplinaire d'une action militaire du XVe siècle* (Lausanne, 1976).

220. Oman, *Art of War*, II, 265–7; Vaughan, *Charles the Bold*, 374–6; D. Miller and G.A. Embleton, *The Swiss at War, 1300–1500* (London, 1979), 20–5.

221. Vaughan, *Charles the Bold*, 384–6, with a table of army composition.

222. Vaughan, *Charles the Bold*, 389.

223. See pp. 395–6.

224. Dispatch of the Milanese ambassador, Panigarola, given in translation in P.M. Kendall, *Louis IX* (New York, 1971), 436–9; Vaughan, *Charles the Bold*, 390–2.

225. Kendall, *Louis XI*, 306.

226. For what follows, C. Pfister, *Histoire de Nancy*, 3 vols (Paris, 1902–9), I, 464–525; Oman, *Art of War*, II, 271; Vaughan, *Charles the Bold*, 419–32, with a full list of primary sources and secondary authorities at 427 n. 1.

227. Kirk, *History of Charles the Bold*, III, 495; P. Frédérix, *Mort de Charles le Téméraire, 5 Janvier 1477* (Paris, 1966), 215–16.

228. Vaughan, *Charles the Bold*, 397.

CHAPTER 19

1. Samuel Daniel, *The Civil Wars between the Two Houses of Lancaster and York*, extracted in *The Oxford Book of War Poetry*, ed. J. Stallworthy (Oxford, 1984), 42–3.

2. Cf. Oman, *Art of War*, II, 405–6.

3. For England as a peaceable kingdom, J. Gillingham, *The Wars of the Roses. Peace and Conflict in Fifteenth-Century England* (London, 1981), 15–31.

4. R.A. Griffiths, *The Reign of Henry VI* (Berkeley and Los Angeles, 1981), 610–22; I.M.W. Harvey, *Jack Cade's Rebellion of 1450* (Oxford, 1991); M. Bohna, 'Armed Force and Civic Legitimacy in Jack Cade's Revolt, 1450', *EHR*, cxviii (2003), 563–82.

5. *Bale's Chronicle* in *Six Town Chronicles*, ed. R. Flenley (Oxford, 1911), 128.

6. *Paston Letters*, II, 154.

7. Harvey, *Jack Cade's Rebellion*, 86–7; 'Gregory', 190.

8. Bohna, 'Armed Force and Civic Legitimacy', 563–4.

9. 'Gregory', 196.

10. M. Keen, *England in the Later Middle Ages: A Political History* (London, 1973), 441.

11. C.L. Kingsford, 'Extracts from the First Version of Hardyng's Chronicle', *EHR*, xxvii (1912), 740–53, at 749.

12. Gillingham, *Wars of the Roses*, 16–23.

13. Gillingham, *Wars of the Roses*, 19–20.

14. Goodman, *Wars of the Roses*, 20–2, 39–40.

15. For the battle see C.A.J. Armstrong, 'Politics and the Battle of St Albans, 1455', *BIHR*, xxxiii (1960), 1–72; Goodman, *Wars of the Roses*, 23–5, 169, who suggests that by contrast the outnumbered Lancastrian forces were short of archers.

16. Armstrong, 'Politics and the Battle of St Albans', 63–5.

17. 'Gregory', 198; *Dijon Relation*, in Armstrong, 'Politics and the Battle of St Albans', 64–5; *Registrum Abbatiae Johannis Whethamstede*, ed. T. Riley, 2 vols (Rolls Series, London, 1872–3), I, 168; *English Chronicle*, 72. The *Dijon Relation*, 64, believed that the king was wounded in the shoulder, and notes Buckingham was hit by three arrows. Among the fullest contemporary reports of the battle are the accounts printed in *The Paston Letters*, III, no. 283 and no. 284, the latter listing the chief nobles involved and giving estimates of the numbers of men-at-arms, as well as of casualties.

18. For the context of the battle, Griffiths, *Reign of Henry VI*, 820–1. Estimates of numbers and the principal casualties are given by 'Gregory', 204.

19. For example F.R. Wemlowe, *The Battle of Blore Heath* (1912); P.A. Haigh, *Military Campaigns of the Wars of the Roses* (Stroud, 1995), 17–19. For a more cautious analysis, Goodman, *Wars of the Roses*, 27–8.

20. Waurin, V, 319–21.

21. Goodman, *Wars of the Roses*, 29; Griffiths, *Reign of Henry VI*, 820–1. For a revisionist discussion of the extent of casualties among the Cheshiremen see J.L. Gillespie, 'Cheshiremen at Blore

22. 'Gregory', 205; Griffiths, *Reign of Henry VI*, 822.

23. Goodman, *Wars of the Roses*, 37–8.

24. *Whetehamstede*, I, 372; *Benet's Chronicle*, in *Six Town Chronicles*, 226; Waurin, V, 299; *Bale's Chronicle*, 151; R.I. Jack, 'A Quincentenary: the Battle of Northampton, July 10th, 1460', *Northamptonshire Past and Present*, iii (1960), 21–5 at 23–4; Goodman, *Wars of the Roses*, 37–9.

25. 'Gregory', 212–13.

26. *Whethamstede*, I, 390.

27. *Whethamstede*, I, 390–2; Goodman, *Wars of the Roses*, 46–8.

28. 'Gregory', 212; *Calendar of State Papers, Venice*, I, 99.

29. 'Gregory', 213; trans. *EHD*, IV, 287.

30. 'Gregory', 213–14; trans. *EHD*, IV, 288.

31. 'Gregory', 214; trans. *EHD*, IV, 288.

32. 'Gregory', 212–13.

33. *The Great Chronicle of London*, ed. A.H. Thomas and I.D. Thornley (London, 1938), 216.

34. Hall, *Weapons and Warfare*, 95–100.

35. Jones, 'Richard III as a Soldier', 100.

36. Goodman, *Wars of the Roses*, 145.

37. Goodman, *Wars of the Roses*, 165.

38. C. Ross, *Edward IV* (New Haven and London, 1997), 37, draws a contrast between Edward's emphasis on the attack and Warwick's tendency to adopt defensive positions, while Warwick's most recent biographer has noted that he 'was too cautious to be a successful field commander' (M. Hicks, *Warwick the Kingmaker* (Oxford, 1998), 308, and cf. 215–16). While a very able tactician, however, Edward himself has been criticised as being 'too lazy to be a really good soldier', distracted by his notorious sexual dalliances from prosecuting effective campaigns against the French and Scots (Jones, 'Richard III as a Soldier', 95).

39. C.L. Schofield, *The Life and Reign of Edward the Fourth*, 2 vols (London, 1923), I, 137–9 and 138 n. 2 for the date; Ross, *Edward IV*, 31; Goodman, *Wars of the Roses*, 49.

40. See pp. 388–9.

41. *English Chronicle*, 110; 'A Short English Chronicle', in *Three Fifteenth-Century Chronicles*, ed. J. Gairdner (London, Camden Society, 1880), 77. Edward thereafter adopted the badge of the sun as one of his emblems in commemoration of this miraculous appearance.

42. 'Gregory', 216; Hall, *Chronicle*, 253, who records that the arrow was headless, but deadly none the less.

43. Goodman, *Wars of the Roses*, 50–1. The fierce nature of the fighting was noted by Warwick's brother George Neville in his letter to Francesco Coppini (*Calendar of State Papers, Venice*, I, 99), and by Waurin, V, 337–8.

44. Hall, *Chronicle*, 253, put the Lancastrian forces at 60,000, and Edward's army at the remarkably precise number of 48,660 men, a figure he says was confirmed by 'they that knew it and paid their wages'. On the improbably large figures given by the sources see Schofield, *The Life and Reign of Edward IV*, I, 165–6; Ross, *Edward IV*, 36.

45. Among the many accounts of the battle see C. Ransome, 'The Battle of Towton', *EHR*, iv (1889), 460–6; Burne, *Battlefields of England*, 245–56; Haigh, *Military Campaigns*, 58–65; A.W. Boardman, *The Medieval Soldier: The Men Who Fought in the Wars of the Roses* (Stroud, 1998); J.R. Lander, *The Wars of the Roses* (Gloucester, 1990), 92.

46. Hall, *Chronicle*, 255–6; *Whethamstede*, I, 409, also mentions the volleys of the Lancastrians.

47. Hall, *Chronicle*, 256.

48. Ross, *Edward IV*, 35; 'Gregory', 217. During the Yorkist invasion of 1460 Fauconberg had likewise led an advance guard from London towards the king's base at Northampton (*Benet's Chronicle*, 226). For a discussion of military commands, see Goodman, *Wars of the Roses*, 122–7.

49. *Calendar of State Papers, Venice*, I, 100.

50. Waurin, V, 339–41.

51. 'Hearne's Fragment', in *Chronicles of the White Rose of York*, ed. J.A. Giles (1845), 9.

52. Waurin, V, 341, '*mais en fin, par la grant proesse principalment du comte de La Marche, Dieu luy donna la victoire*'.

53. *Calendar of State Papers, Venice*, I, 100.

54. *Calendar of State Papers, Venice*, I, 102.

55. Hall, *Chronicle*, 253, 254, 'this battayl was sore foughten, for hope of life was set on sideon every parte and takynge of prisoners was proclaymed as a great offence'.

56. Hall, *Chronicle*, 256; *Calendar of State Papers, Venice*, I, 100.

57. *Calendar of State Papers, Venice*, I, 100.

58. *Calendar of State Papers, Venice*, I, 100, 102, 103, and cf. 106, 108; *Paston Letters*, III, 268.

59. *Calendar of State Papers, Venice*, I, 100, 103, 105; 'Gregory', 216–18; *Paston Letters*, III, 267; Schofield, *The Life and Reign of Edward IV*, I, 163, 165–6.

60. Schofield, *The Life and Reign of Edward IV*, I, 166 and n. 2; *Blood Red Roses*, ed. Fiorato *et al.*, 162, 98.

61. *Histoire of the Arrival of King Edward IV, 1471*, ed. J. Bruce (London, 1838), reprinted in *Three Chronicles of the Reign of Edward IV*, ed. K. Dockray (Gloucester, 1988), 18, 'undre an hedge-syde'. For Barnet, see Ross, *Edward IV*, 167–8; P.W. Hammond, *The Battles of Barnet and Tewkesbury* (Gloucester, 1990), 71–8; Hicks, *Warwick the Kingmaker*, 308–10.

62. Hicks, *Warwick the Kingmaker*, 215.

63. P. Vergil, *Anglica Historia*, ed. H. Ellis, *Three Books of Polydore Vergil's English History* (London, 1844), 145.

64. *Arrival of King Edward IV*, 19.

65. *Arrival of King Edward IV*, 19.

66. J. Warkworth, *A Chronicle of the First Thirteen Years of the Reign of King Edward IV*, ed. J.O. Halliwell (London, 1839), 16. For a sceptical view of Warkworth's story, Gillingham, *Wars of the Roses*, 38–9.

67. *Arrival of King Edward IV*, 20.

68. For an analysis of the text see J.A.F. Thomson, '"The Arrival of Edward IV" – The Development of the Text', *Speculum*, xlvi (1971), 84–93.

69. *Arrival of King Edward IV*, 28–9. For a detailed analysis of the site and the course of the engagement see J.D. Blyth, 'The Battle of Tewksbury', *Transactions of the Bristol and Gloucestershire Archaeological Society*, lxxx (1961), 99–120.

70. Blyth, 'The Battle of Tewkesbury', 102–5.

71. *Arrival of King Edward IV*, 29.

72. *Arrival of King Edward IV*, 29.

73. Jones, 'Richard III as a Soldier', 96–7.

74. *Arrival of King Edward IV*, 29.

75. For army composition and methods of recruitment see Goodman, *Wars of the Roses*, 127–52, 200–9; Gillingham, *Wars of the Roses*, 32–5.

76. Goodman, *Wars of the Roses*, 143–4.

77. *Kingsford's Stonor Letters and Papers, 1290–1483*, ed. C. Carpenter (Cambridge, 1996), 352–3 (no. 258); Goodman, *Wars of the Roses*, 144–5.

78. J. Nicolson and R. Brown, *History and Antiquities of the Counties of Westmorland and Cumberland*, 2 vols (1777), I, 96, 97n, 98; W.H. Dunham, *Lord Hastings' Indentured Retinues, 1461–1483* (Connecticut, 1955), 64; Oman, *Art of War*, II, 408.

79. In 1461 John Paston noted that because the countryside was in turmoil in the aftermath of the battle of Wakefield, his father John wished to keep his own men with him, but 'he will send up Dawbeney, his spere and bowes with hym, as Stapilton and Calthorp or other men of worship of this cuntree agree to do' (*Paston Letters*, III, 266). The meaning of 'spears' in this context is ambiguous, but probably refers to men-at-arms rather than billmen.

80. A.F. Pollard, *The Reign of Henry VII*, 3 vols (London, 1913), I, 94, where the rates of pay are set out at 12*d* a day for every 'spear and his custrell', 9*d* for a demi-lance, and 8*d* a day for mounted archers and billmen.

81. *CPR, 1452–61*, 406–10; Goodman, *Wars of the Roses*, 143.

82. *CPR, 1452–61*, 406–10.

83. *Foedera*, XI, 624; Goodman, *Wars of the Roses*, 141.

84. *Paston Letters*, VI, 89–90 (no. 1006).

85. 'Hearne's Fragment', in *Thomae Sprotti Chronica*, ed. T. Hearne (Oxford, 1719), 286; *EHD*, IV, 289; Goodman, *Wars of the Roses*, 50–1.

86. Schofield, *Life and Reign of Edward IV*, I, 167.

87. Letter of Thomas de Portinari, June, 1475, *Calendar of State Papers, Milan*, I, 197–8. On ratios, Gillingham, *Wars of the Roses*, 36–7, and see p. 203.

88. Dunham, *Lord Hastings' Indentured Retinues*, 53.

89. Dunham, *Lord Hastings' Indentured Retinues*, 35, 40.

90. For the size and composition of the contingents, E.A. Barnard, *Edward IV's French Expedition of 1475, the Leaders and their Badges*

(Oxford, 1925); J.R. Lander, 'The Hundred Years War and Edward IV's 1475 Campaign in France', in *Tudor Men and Institutions: Studies in English Law and Government*, ed. A.J. Salvin (Baton Rouge, Louisiana, 1972), 70–100, reprinted in his *Crown and Nobility*; Ross, *Edward IV*, 221–2. For the archers promised in 1468 and actually raised in 1472, Schofield, *The Life and Reign of Edward IV*, I, 448–51, II, 33–4; M. Ballard, 'An Expedition of English Archers in 1467, and the Anglo-Burgundian Marriage Alliance', *Nottingham Medieval Studies*, xxxiv (1990), 152–74, at 155.

91.   *CPR, Edward IV and Henry VI, 1467–1477*, 496.

92.   Commynes, *Memoirs*, 261; Jacob, *The Fifteenth Century*, 578.

93.   *Foedera*, XI, 837–9.

94.   Ross, *Edward IV*, 220.

95.   Ross, *Edward IV*, 220.

96.   *CPR, Edward IV and Henry VI, 1467–77*, 524. Of these archers 100 were to serve at the king's expense, but the wages of the others were to be borne by 'the inhabitants of Ireland'.

97.   5 Edward IV, c.4, 1465. In Dublin, the centre of the Pale, the butts were at Hoggen Green (C. Haliday, *The Scandinavian Kingdom of Dublin* (2nd edn, Dublin, 1884, facsimile, ed. B. ó Ríordáin, Shannon, 1969), 166–8).

98.   Boardman, *Medieval Soldier*, 147.

99.   *The Cely Letters, 1472–1488*, ed. A. Hanham (Early English Text Society, Oxford, 1975), 26–7 (no. 28).

100. *Manners and Household Expenses of England*, 248; Orme, *From Childhood to Chivalry*, 200.

101. A. Campbell, *Highland Dress, Arms and Ornament* (Westminster, 1899), 145.

102. *The Book of Fayttes of Armes*, ed. Byles, 34.

103. 'The Tudors and the Origins of the Modern Irish States', *A Military History of Ireland*, 117.

104. *Henry IV, Part 2*, III, ii, ll. 42–51.

105. Dobson and Taylor, *Rymes*, 99.

106. *Kingsford's Stonor Letters and Papers*, 352–3.

107. Commynes, *Memoirs*, 72.

108. Dominic Mancini, *The Usurpation of Richard the Third*, ed. C.A.J. Armstrong (2nd edn, London, 1969), 98–9.

109. Commynes, *Memoirs*, 72.

110. Mancini, *The Usurpation of Richard the Third*, 99.

111. Goodman, *Wars of the Roses*, 143–4. The York civic records note that men from the city sent to Duke Richard in June 1483 were to be paid 12*d* a day, but on condition that 'every socher [soldier] shall pay fot hys aun jaket', *York Civic Records*, ed. A. Raine, 9 vols (Yorkshire Archaeological Society, Record Series, 1939–78), I, 74.

112. 'Gregory', 205.

113. *CPR, Edward IV and Henry VI, 1467–77*, 524. As brigandines were worn by all ranks, these armourers may have been only for the use of the king and his retinue.

114. G. Wilson, 'Pavises in England', *Royal Armouries Yearbook* (2001, 72–87).

115. *Arrival of King Edward IV*, 37.

116. Dunham, *Lord Hastings' Indentured Retinues*, 40, 41n.

117. Dunham, *Lord Hastings' Indentured Retinues*, 40.

118. 'Gregory', 212.

119. Dunham, *Lord Hastings' Indentured Retinues*, 40.

120. *Paston Letters*, VI, 85 (no. 1002).

121. S.B. Chrimes, *Henry VII* (London, 1977), 46 and n. 2; Gillingham, *Wars of the Roses*, 242. For detailed attempts to reconstruct the battle see P.M. Kendall, *Richard III* (1955), 354–69; D.T. Williams, *The Battle of Bosworth* (1973); Chrimes, *Henry VII*, 47–9; C. Ross, *Richard III* (London, 1981), 216–15; Goodman, *Wars of the Roses*, 91–5; M. Bennett, *The Battle of Bosworth* (Gloucester, 1985), 107–18, which has a valuable collection of the primary sources in translation; P.J. Foss, *The Field of Redemore: The Battle of Bosworth, 1485* (2nd edn, Newton Linford, 1998), and *idem*, 'The Battle of Bosworth: A Reassessment', *Midland History*, xiii (1988), 21–33; C. Gravett, *The Battle of Bosworth* (Osprey, 2000) and M.K. Jones, *Bosworth, 1485* (Stroud, 2002).

122. For the traditional site see J. Gairdner, 'The Battle of Bosworth', *Archaeologia*, lv (1896), 159–78, and Ross, *Richard III*, 218; for Dadlington, whose church was said to be 'standing upon a parcell of the grounde wher Bosworth feld otherwise called Dadlynton feld . . . was done', see C.F. Richmond, 'The Battle of Bosworth', *History Today*, xxxv (August 1985), 17–22. For Atherstone, and a discussion of how traditions of the battle site developed, Jones, *Bosworth*, 147–57.

123. *English History*, 222.

124. *English History*, 223, who numbers Stanley's as yet uncommitted force at around 3,000 men.

125. Richmond, 'The Battle of Bosworth', 22.

126. M. Hicks, *Richard III. The Man Behind the Myth* (London, 1991), 51–2; Jones, 'Richard III as a Soldier', 96.

127. Ross, *Richard III*, 220.

128. Jones, 'Richard III as a Soldier', 101, 103.

129. *English History*, 233.

130. *English History*, 233.

131. *Historiae Croylandensis Continuatio*, in *Rerum Anglicarum Scriptorum Veterum*, I, ed. W. Fulman (Oxford, 1684), 574–5; Bennett, *The Battle of Bosworth*, 158; *Chroniques de Jean Molinet (1474–1506)*, ed. G. Doutrepont and O. Jodogne, 3 vols (Brussels, 1935–7), I, 434–5.

132. Jones, *Bosworth*, 162–3, 193–5.

133. Contamine, *Guerre, état et société*, 308–10. It is possible that Anthony Woodville, Lord Rivers, had been present at Morat (Jones, 'Richard III as a Soldier', 105).

134. Molinet, *Chroniques*, I, 434; trans. Bennett, *The Battle of Bosworth*, 161.

135. *English History*, 223.

136. *Bishop Percy's Folio Manuscript*, III (237–8), 256–7.

137. *English History*, 223.

138. British Library, Royal MS 16 G IX, f.76v.

139. Goodman, *Wars of the Roses*, 92–3.

140. On the key role of Northumberland see Goodman, *Wars of the Roses*, 93 and n. 44, 96; Richmond, 'The Battle of Bosworth', 22; cf. Horrox, *Richard III. A Study in Service*, 319; 'The last charge of

Richard and his knights can be seen as the military equivalent of the king's political reliance on a small circle of trusted men in response to treachery.' For a different view, stressing the coherence of Richard's army, and his attempts to boost morale through pre-battle ritual, see Jones, *Bosworth*, 157–61, and for the charge itself, 164–5.

141. *English History*, 224.

142. Jones, *Bosworth*, 194–5. The suggestion, however, that these troops were withdrawn in the nick of time from the vanguard seems more problematic. Such a manoeuvre would have been difficult if not impossible if Oxford's van was heavily engaged with Richard's forces, but a sudden cavalry strike by Richard would surely not have allowed sufficient time for the recall and reformation of these forces. Might it not be simply that Tudor himself had retained a small number of these French pikemen in his own division, and that they succeeded in holding off the Yorkist charge until the fateful moment Richard was slain?

143. Jones, *Bosworth*, 194.

144. Richmond, 'The Battle of Bosworth', 20; *English History*, 224–5; Molinet, *Chroniques*, I, 435.

145. *English History*, 244.

146. Hicks, *Richard III*, 63–4, 67–8; Jones, 'Richard III as a Soldier', 100.

147. *English History*, 244.

148. It was claimed that Simnel, the son of an Oxford artisan, was the young Earl of Warwick, son of the Duke of Clarence and thus nephew to Edward IV and Richard III (Chrimes, *Henry VII*, 75–6).

149. *The Anglica Historia of Polydore Vergil, 1485–1537*, ed. D. Hay (Camden Society, 1950), 20–1.

150. *Anglica Historia*, ed. Hay, 22–3.

151. *Anglica Historia*, ed. Hay, 24–5.

152. Molinet, *Chroniques*, I, 564; Goodman, *Wars of the Roses*, 169–70.

153. *Anglica Historia*, ed. Hay, 24–5.

154. *Anglica Historia*, ed. Hay, 24–5.

155. Goodman, *Wars of the Roses*, 30ff, 56, 189.

156. Gillingham, *Wars of the Roses*, 15; 'The Wars of the Roses . . . were intermittent and limited. By Henry VII's reign English society was no more organised for war than it had been in Henry VI's.'

CHAPTER 20

1. Sir Thomas Elyot, *The Boke Named the Governour*, ed. H.H.S. Croft, 2 vols (London, 1883), I, 301–2.

2. C.G. Cruickshank, *Elizabeth's Army* (2nd edn, Oxford, 1966), 282.

3. Orme, *From Childhood to Chivalry*, 198–205.

4. *The Oxford Book of Scottish Verse*, ed. J. MacQueen and T. Scott (Oxford, 1966, repr. 1981), 120–30.

5. *Treasurer's Accounts*, II, 390, 488, 329; Fergusson, 'A Pair of Butts', 20.

6. Hall, *Chronicle*, 515; *The Chronicle of Calais in the Reigns of Henry VII and Henry VIII, to the year 1540*, ed. J.G. Nichols (Camden Society, no. xxxv, 1846), 13; *Calendar of State Papers, Venice*, IV (1527–33), 293.

7. Reisch, 'Archery in Renaissance Germany', 63–5.

8. *Calendar of State Papers, Venice*, IV (1527–33), 293.

9. Hall, *Union*, 513. For the context of such revels, D. Loades, *The Tudor Court* (London, 1986), 99.

10. Hall, *Chronicle*, 582; cf. *Letters and Papers, Foreign and Domestic*, II, pt 1, 120 (no. 410).

11. Loades, *The Tudor Court*, 99.

12. J. Stevens, *Music and Poetry in the Early Tudor Court* (New York, 1979), 249–50; Hanawalt, 'Men's Games, King's Deer', 191.

13. For the context of Henry's aggression, S. Gunn, 'The French Wars of Henry VIII', *The Origins of War in Early Modern Europe*, ed. J. Black (Edinburgh, 1987), 28–51.

14. Vergil, *Anglica Historia*, 161.

15. Ferguson, *Indian Summer of English Chivalry*, 23–4, 70; L.B. Smith, *Henry VIII. The Mask of Royalty* (Boston, 1971), 156; C.S.L. Davies, 'Henry VIII and Henry V: the War in France', *The End of the Middle Ages? England in the Fifteenth and Sixteenth Centuries*, ed. J.L. Watts (Stroud, 1998), 235–62.

16. J.J. Scarisbrick, *Henry VIII* (London, 1968), 23.

17. *Letters and Papers*, I, pt 2, no. 2391, 1058; Cruickshank, *Army Royal*, 1–2.

18. Ascham, *Toxophilus*, 5; L.V. Ryan, *Roger Ascham* (1963), 82.

19. *Mémoires du maréchal Florange dit le jeune adventureux*, ed. R. Goubaux and P.-A. Lemoisne (Paris, 1913), I, 272; J.G. Russell, *The Field of Cloth of Gold* (London, 1969), 132.

20. J. Fortescue, *A History of the British Army*, 7 vols (London, 1899–1912), I, 118, n. 1.

21. *Tudor Proclamations*, I, no. 121, 177–8.

22. 3 Henry VIII, c. 3, 1511. A further statute concerning archery was passed in 1514; 6 Henry VIII, c. 2, 1514 (*Statutes of the Realm*, III, 123).

23. *Statutes of the Realm*, III, 837–41.

24. Roger Ascham, *English Works*, ed. W.A. Wright (Cambridge, 1904), 97.

25. M. Campbell, *The English Yeoman under Elizabeth and the Early Stuarts* (Yale, 1942), 272; W. Druett, *Harrow through the Ages* (1935), 120–1.

26. Orme, *From Childhood to Chivalry*, 204.

27. J.G. Nichols, *Narratives of the Days of the Reformation* (London, Camden Society, lxxvii (1859)), 238–40; Orme, *From Childhood to Chivalry*, 41.

28. *The Sermons of Hugh Latimer*, I, 196–7.

29. *A Relation, or Rather a True Account of the Island of England*, ed. C.A. Sneyd (Camden Society, 1847), 31, 23. His further comments are less flattering: 'But I have it on the best information that when the war is raging most furiously, they will seek for good eating, and all their other comforts, without thinking what harm will befall them. They have an antipathy to foreigners, and imagine that they never come into their island, but to make themselves masters of it and usurp their goods . . .' (*ibid.*, 23–4).

30. *Calendar of State Papers, Venice, II (1509–1519)*, ed. R. Brown (London, 1867), 562 (no. 1287). For the comments of other Venetians see E.G. Salter, *Tudor England through Venetian Eyes* (London, 1930), 112–13.

31. Miller, *Henry VIII and the English Nobility*, 137; S.J. Gunn, *Charles Brandon, Duke of Suffolk, c. 1484–1545* (Oxford, 1988), 24–5.

32. Miller, *Henry VIII and the English Nobility*, 139.

33. Miller, *Henry VIII and the English Nobility*, 136–8.

34. Miller, *Henry VIII and the English Nobility*, 138–40.

35. Cruickshank, *Army Royal*, 78.

36. Cruickshank, *Army Royal*, 142

37. *Letters and Papers,* III, pt 2, no. 2995; Cruickshank, *Army Royal*, 78.

38. Cruickshank, *Army Royal*, 78.

39. *Tudor Royal Proclamations*, I, no. 73, 109.

40. Edward Hall, *The Triumphant Reigne of Kyng Henry the VIII*, ed. C. Whibley (London, 1904), 64.

41. Cruickshank, *Army Royal*, 188–9.

42. Hall, *Chronicle*, 526; *The Great Chronicle of London*, ed. A.A. Thomas and I.D. Thornley (London, 1938), 379; Gunn, *Charles Brandon*, 12.

43. Hall, *Kyng Henry the VIII*, 65, 62.

44. Oman, *Art of War in the Sixteenth Century*, 293–96.

45. Cruickshank, *Army Royal*, 105, 112.

46. As Queen Catherine told Henry, 'this battle hath been to your grace and all your realm the greatest honour that could be, and more than ye should win the Crown of France, thanken be God for it'; Cruickshank, *Army Royal*, 118.

47. This fateful battle has generated many accounts, most recently N. Barr, *Flodden* (Stroud, 2001). See also W. Mackay Mackenzie, *The Secret of Flodden; with 'The Rout of the Scots', a Translation of the Contemporary Italian Poem La Rotta de Scocesi* (Edinburgh, 1931), and G.F.T. Leather, *New Light on Flodden* (2nd edn, Berwick, 1938).

48. *Calendar of State Papers, Venice*, I, no. 316; James's artillery is discussed by Mackenzie, *Secret of Flodden*, 49–51, 59–60.

49. Oman, *Art of War in the Sixteenth Century*, 311.

50. G. Dickinson, 'Some Notes on the Scottish Army in the First Half of the Sixteenth Century', *SHR*, xxviii (1949), 133–45, at 136–7.

51. John Major, *A History of Greater Britain*, trans. A. Constable (Edinburgh, 1892), 49.

52. Oman, *Art of War in the Sixteenth Century*, 303–5.

53. Oman, *Art of War in the Sixteenth Century*, 302.

54. Barr, *Flodden*, 129, with pls 15–16 for illustrations of a modern copy.

55. Barr, *Flodden*, pl. 15.

56. 'Trewe Encounter', *Letters and Papers*, I, pt 2, no. 2246 (4), 1007. See *Proc. Antiq Scot.*, vii, I, 141. For the Scottish ordnance see Dickinson, 'Scottish Army', 138–9.

57. Oman, *Art of War in the Sixteenth Century*, 310.

58. Letter to the King of Denmark, cited in Mackenzie, *The Secret of Flodden*, 21.

59. Barr, *Flodden*, 90.

60. 'Trewe Encounter', *Letters and Papers*, I, pt 2, no. 2246 (4), 1007.

61. 'Trewe Encounter', *Letters and Papers*, I, pt 2, no. 2246 (4), 1007.

62. 'Articles of the bataill', in *Letters and Papers*, I, pt 2, no. 2246, 1005. For discussion of the 'Almayns manner', Mackenzie, *The Secret of Flodden*, 61–8.

63. 'The Rout of the Scots', in Mackenzie, *The Secret of Flodden*, 113, and cf. 71–2.

64. Robert Lindsay of Pitscottie, *Historie and Cronicles of Scotland*, 3 vols (Edinburgh, 1899), I, 270.

65. Hall, *Kyng Henry the VIII*, 109; Oman, *Art of War in the Sixteenth Century*, 314.

66. As suggested by Barr, *Flodden*, 100.

67. *The Trewe Encountre*, 151.

68. *Letters and Papers*, no. 4,461; Oman, *Art of War in the Sixteenth Century*, 314. The 'Trewe Encounter' notes 'few of them were slain with arrows: the bills did hew and beat them down' (*ibid.*, 314).

69. Mackenzie, *The Secret of Flodden*, 84.

70. Mackenzie, *The Secret of Flodden*, 91–3.

71. Mackenzie, *The Secret of Flodden*, 91, 89.

72. 'Trewe Encounter', *Letters and Papers*, I, pt 2, no. 2246, 1005.

73. Hall, *Kyng Henry the VIII*, 564.

74. See the illustrations of these arms in Barr, *Flodden*, 126.

75. Barr, *Flodden*, 129.

76. J.R. Hale, *Artists and Warfare in the Renaissance* (New Haven and London, 1990), 263.

77. Ascham, *Toxophilus*, 88.

78. Williams, 'The Blast Furnace and the Mass-Production of Plate Armour'; Blackburn *et al.*, 'Head Protection', 1,280.

79. P. Krenn, 'Was leisten die alten Handfeuerwaffen?', *Waffen- und Kostümkunde*, xxxii (1990), 35–52; Blackburn *et al.*, 'Head Protection', 1,280.

80. Blackburn *et al.*, 'Head Protection', 1,280 and table 3.

81. Grancsay, 'Just How Good was Armor?', 89–91.

82. Oman, *Art of War in the Sixteenth Century*, 286–7; Monluc, *Mémoires*, II, 310–20.

83. Barwick in *Bow versus Gun*, ed. E.C. Heath (Wakefield, 1973), 17v. For a good overview see T. Esper, 'The Replacement of the Longbow by Firearms in the English Army', *Technology and Culture*, vi (1965), 382–93.

84. *The Art of War in Spain: The Conquest of Granada, 1481–1492*, ed. A.D. McJoynt (London, 1995), 36–7; Phillips, *The Anglo-Scottish Wars*, 14–15.

85. Blaise de Monluc, *The Valois-Habsburg Wars and the French Wars of Religion*, ed. I. Roy (London, 1971), 41; Oman, *Art of War in the Sixteenth Century*, 43–4, 48.

86. Oman, *Art of War in the Sixteenth Century*, 45–8. Within each 'band' of 1,000 men there were to be 600 pikemen, 300 arquebusiers and 100 halberdiers. On the French army under Francis I, see A. Spont, 'Marignan et l'organisation militaire sous François Ier', *Revue des questions historiques*, n. s., xxii (1899), 59–77; Potter, *War and Government*, 155–99; R.J. Knecht, *Renaissance Warrior and Patron: The Reign of Francis I* (Cambridge, 1994), 69–70.

87. *Letters and Papers*, III, pt II, no. 3368.

88. *APS*, II, 345, cc. 20, 21 (1535); 372, cc. 11, 12 (1540).

89. 19 Henry VII, c. 4, *Statutes of the Realm*, II, 649–50, with the proviso that it was lawful for such weapons to be used to defend one's house; 14 and 15 Henry VIII, c. 7, 1523 (*Statutes of the Realm*, III, 215). The act was renewed in 1526, *Tudor Royal Proclamations*, no. 107, 151–2.

90. *Tudor Royal Proclamations*, I, no. 121, 177–81; renewed 1537, no. 171, 249–50.

91. Elyot, *The Governor*, 303.

92. For Henry VII's ordnance, Hooker, 'Organization and Supply', 26–30.

93. A.F. Pollard, *Henry VIII* (1905), 126–8.

94. Davies, 'Henry VIII and Henry V', 247–9.

95. Oman, *Art of War in the Sixteenth Century*, 286; Pollard, *The Reign of Henry VII*, I, 80.

96. *Letters and Papers*, III, pt 2, 3039; Phillips, *The Anglo-Scottish Wars*, 142; Miller, *Henry VIII and the English Nobility*, 145.

97. *Original Letters Illustrative of English History*, ed. H. Ellis, 1st ser. (London, 1824), I, 94; Phillips, *The Anglo-Scottish Wars*, 134–5. In 1533 a unit of Cheshire archers were sent to the Isle of Man to help defend it against Scottish raids (*ibid.*, 146).

98. *The Hamilton Papers*, I, 1523–1543, xvi; and for the battle, Phillips, *The Anglo-Scottish Wars*, 150–3.

99. D.L.W. Tough, *The Last Years of a Frontier* (Oxford, 1928), 89.

100. Phillips, *The Anglo-Scottish Wars*, 146.

101. Dickinson, 'Scottish Army', 142.

102. Dunbar, *History of Highland Dress*, 34.

103. Dunbar, *History of Highland Dress*, 40

104. Miller, *Henry VIII and the English Nobility*, 143. For the continued reputation of the longbow, however, see C. Gaier, 'L'invincibilité anglaise et le grand arc après la guerre de cent ans; un myth tenace', *Tijdschrift voor Geschiedenis*, xci (1978), 379–85.

105. Phillips, *Anglo-Scottish Warfare*, 42–87.

106. *The Inventory of King Henry VIII*, ed. D. Starkey (London, 1998), 102ff.

107. *Inventory of King Henry VIII*, 120.

108. *Inventory of King Henry VIII*, 120–1. At the Tower there were a further 3,060 bows of yew, and 13,050 sheaves of livery arrows (*ibid.*, 103).

109. *Acts of the Privy Council of England*, ed. J.R. Dasent *et al.* (NS, 46 vols, London, 1890–1964), II, 348, 350.

110. *Letters and Papers*, III, pt 2, no. 2995.

111. *Letters and Papers*, III, pt 3, nos 3495, 3494. Oman, *Art of War in the Sixteenth Century*, 324; Cruickshank, *Army Royal*, 78.

112. Cruickshank, *Army Royal*, 78; *Letters and Papers*, III, pt 3, no. 3495; *APS*, II, 345, cc. 20, 21 (1535); 372, cc. 11, 12 (1540).

113. H.A. Dillon, 'Arms and Armour at Westminster, the Tower and Greenwich, 1547', *Archaeologia*, li (1888), pt 1, 219–80, at 263–4.

114. Dunham, *Lord Hastings' Indentured Retainers*, 137.

115. Oman, *Art of War in the Sixteenth Century*, 332–3.

116. A. Mas Chao, 'Cerignola, Bicocca et Pavia: L'arme à feu individuelle comme facteur décisif au combat', *From Crécy to Mohacs*, 195–206.

117. Oman, *Art of War in the Sixteenth Century*, 166.

118. F. de La Noue, *Discours Politique et Militaires*, ed. F.E. Sutcliffe (Geneva, 1967), 363–7.

119. Cruickshank, *Army Royal*, 109–10. For the text, Add. MS. 23971, with other versions cited in *ibid.*, 106 n. 1; and W. St P. Bunbury, 'A Treatise on the Art of War by Thomas Audley', *Journal of the Society for Army Historical Research*, vi (1927), 65–78, 129–33.

120. J.R. Hale, 'On a Tudor Parade Ground: the Captain's Handbook of Henry Barrett, 1562', The Society for Renaissance Studies, Occasional Papers, no. 5, reprinted in J.R. Hale, *Renaissance War Studies* (London, 1983), 251–2 and pl. 1.

121. Hale, 'On a Tudor Parade Ground', 247–84, at 276–7.

122. Oman, *Art of War in the Sixteenth Century*, 379–80.

123. Cruickshank, *Elizabeth's Army*, 108.

124. Smythe, *Certain Discourses Military*, 88, 85–7; Bennett, 'The Battle', 29.

125. 'A Military Discourse whether it be better for England to give an invader present battle, or to temporize and defend the same', cited in Cruickshank, *Elizabeth's Army*, 107–8.

126. J. Hale, 'Men and Weapons: the Fighting Potential of Sixteenth-Century Venetian Galleys', in *idem*, *Renaissance War Studies* (London, 1985), 322.

127. Smythe, *Certain Discourses Military*, 81–2.

128. 33 Henry VIII, c. 9.

129. *Tudor Royal Proclamations*, I, no. 213, 313–14. An ordinance of 1544 set the maximum price for an almain rivet of the best sort, 'with all the furniture', at 9*s* 6*d*; *ibid.*, no. 235, 337.

130. 3 Henry VIII, c. 9.

131. 19 Henry VIII, c. 2, *Statutes of the Realm*, II, 649.

132. *The Lisle Letters*, III, no. 704, 385; V, no. 1256, 261 and no. 1285, 307.

133. 13 Elizabeth I, c. 14.

134. *Tudor Royal Proclamations*, I, nos 230, 330.

135. 3 Henry VII, c. 13, *Statutes of the Realm*, II, 521; *Tudor Proclamations*, I, no. 213, 313–14.

136. Cruickshank, *Elizabeth's Army*, 104.

137. 8 Elizabeth I, c. 10; Cruickshank, *Elizabeth's Army*, 104.

138. J. Goring, 'Social Change and Military Decline', 185–97.

139. Oman, *Art of War in the Sixteenth Century*, 383–4.

140. Oman, *Art of War in the Sixteenth Century*, 384.

141.   Goring, 'Social Change and Military Decline', 188–91.

142.   Tough, *The Last Years of a Frontier*, 89.

143.   Oman, *Art of War in the Sixteenth Century*, 380.

144.   *State Papers Domestic*, Addenda, 121–3, 136.

145.   Cruickshank, *Elizabeth's Army*, 109–12.

146.   *State Papers Domestic*, Addenda, 78–80.

147.   Cruickshank, *Elizabeth's Army*, 111.

148.   Oman, *Art of War in the Sixteenth Century*, 381.

149.   *Calendar of State Papers Relating to Scotland and Mary Queen of Scots, 1547–1603*, ed. W.K. Boyd, IV (Edinburgh, 1905), 448 (no. 501).

150.   *Calendar of Letters and Papers Relating to the Affairs of the Borders of England and Scotland*, ed. J. Bain, 2 vols (Edinburgh, 1894), I, 42–53 (nos 90–2).

151.   *CBP*, I, 36–7 (no. 89).

152.   *CBP*, I, 43–53 (no. 92), 37–42 (no. 90), 42–3 (no. 91); Tough, *The Last Years of a Frontier*, 89.

153.   *CBP*, I, 154 (no. 255).

154.   *CBP*, I, 98–9 (no. 159).

155.   *CBP*, I, 270, no. 539; Tough, *The Last Years of a Frontier*, 90.

156.   *CBP*, I, 395 (no. 744).

157.   *CBP*, I, 395 (no. 744), 453 (no. 828).

158.   Oman, *Art of War in the Sixteenth Century*, 381. Only Oxfordshire and Buckinghamshire revealed slightly higher numbers of archers to arquebusiers, a phenomenon Oman suggests might be explained by the continued prevalence of shooting, licitly or not, in these still heavily wooded areas.

159.   Smythe, *Certain Discourses Military*, 85–7.

160.   L. Boynton, *The Elizabethan Militia* (London and Toronto, 1967), 66.

161.   Boynton, *The Elizabethan Militia*, 66.

162.   Oman, *Art of War in the Sixteenth Century*, 383–4.

163.   Smythe, *Certain Discourses Military*, 81; Oman, *Art of War in the Sixteenth Century*, 384.

164.   *The Description of England*, ed. F.J. Furnival (New Shakespeare Society, vi 1877), 279.

165.   Samuel Daniel, *The Civil Wars between the Two Houses of Lancaster and York*, extracted in *The Oxford Book of War Poetry*, 43.

Bibliography

PRINTED SOURCES

Abbo, *Bella Parisiacae urbis*, ed. H. Waquet, *Abbon. Le Siège de Paris par les Normands* (Paris, 1942)

Abbonis Floriacensis passio Sancti Edmundi, ed. T. Arnold, *Memorials of St Edmund's Abbey*, 3 vols (Rolls Series, London, 1890–6)

Accounts of the Constables of Bristol Castle in the Thirteenth and Early Fourteenth Centuries, ed. M. Sharp (Bristol Record Society, xxxiv, Gloucester, 1982)

Acta Sanctorum Bollandiana, ed. J. Bollandus *et al.*, 64 vols (Antwerp, Brussels etc., 1643–)

Acts of the Parliaments of Scotland, ed. T. Thomson and C. Innes, 12 vols (Edinburgh, 1814–75)

Acts of the Privy Council of England, ed. J.R. Darent *et al.* (NS, 46 vols, London, 1890–1964)

Adam Murimuth, *Continuatio Chronicarum*, ed. E.M. Thompson (Rolls Series, London, 1889)

Adam of Usk, *Chronicon, 1377–1404*, ed. E.M. Thompson (London, 1876)

Adam of Usk, *Chronicon*, ed. C. Given-Wilson, *The Chronicle of Adam Usk* (Oxford, 1997)

Agincourt, or the Bowman's Glory, in *Bishop Percy's Folio Manuscript. Ballads and Romances*, ed. J.W. Hales and F.J. Furnival, II (London, 1868)

Ailred of Rievaulx, *Relatio venerabilis Aelredi abbatis Rievallensis, de Standardo*, ed. R. Howlett, *Chronicles of the Reigns of Stephen, Henry II and Richard I*, III (Rolls Series, London, 1886)

Aimé du Mont Cassin, *Storia di Normanni*, ed. V. de Bartholomeis (Rome, 1935)

Albert of Aix, *Historia Hierosolymitana, Recueil des Historiens des Croisades, Historiens Occidentaux*, 5 vols (Paris, 1844–95), IV, 265–713

Ambroise, *Estoire de la Guerre Sainte*, ed. G. Paris (Paris, 1897); trans. M.J. Hubert and J. La Monte, *The Crusade of Richard Lion-Heart* (New York, 1941)

Andrew of Wyntoun's Orygnale Cronykil of Scotland, ed. D. Laing, 3 vols (Edinburgh, 1872–9)

The Anglica Historia of Polydore Vergil, 1485–1537, ed. D. Hay (Camden Society, 1950)

Anglo-Norman Letters and Petitions from All Souls MS. 182, ed. M.D. Legge (Oxford, 1941)

Anglo-Saxon Chronicle, ed. D. Whitelock, *English Historical Documents, c. 500–1042*, I (2nd edn, London, 1979)

Anna Comnena, *Alexiad*, trans. E.R.A. Sewter, *The Alexiad of Anna Comnena* (London, 1969)

Annales Bertiniani, ed. F. Grat, J. Vielliard, S. Clémencet and L. Levillain, *Annales de Saint-Bertin* (Paris, 1964)

Annales Cambriae, ed. J. Williams (London, 1860)

Annales Januenses, MGH, SS, viii, ed. G.H. Pertz (Hanover, 1863), 226–48

Annales Londonienses, ed. W. Stubbs, *Chronicles of the Reigns of Edward I and Edward II*, I (Rolls Series, London, 1882)

Annales Prioratus de Dunstaplia, A.D. 1–1297, ed. H.R. Luard, *Annales Monastici*, iii (Rolls Series, London, 1866)

Annales Prioratus de Wignoria, A.D. 1–1377, ed. H.R. Luard, *Annales Monastici*, iv (Rolls Series, London, 1867)

Annals of the Four Masters, Annals of the Kingdom of Ireland by the Four Masters, from the earliest period to 1066, ed. J. O'Donovan, 7 vols (Dublin, 1851)

Annals of Loch Cé, ed. and trans. W.M. Hennessy, 2 vols (London, 1871)

The Anonimalle Chronicle 1307–1334, ed. W.R. Childs and J. Taylor, *Yorkshire Archaeological Society Record Series*, cxlvii (Leeds, 1991)

Anonimalle Chronicle 1333–1381, ed. V.H. Galbraith (Manchester, 1927)

The Anthony Roll of Henry VIII's Navy: Pepys Library 2991 and British Library Additional MS 22047 with Related Documents, ed. C.S. Knighton and D.M. Loades (Aldershot, 2000)

The antient calendars and inventories of the treasury of His Majesty's exchequer, together with documents illustrating the history of that repository, ed. F. Palgrave, 3 vols (London, 1836)

L'Apparicion Maistre Jehan de Meun et le Somnium super Materia Scismatis, ed. I. Arnold (Paris, 1926)

Argyll Castles in the Care of Historic Scotland: Extracts from RCAHMS Inventories of Argyll, Vols I, II and VII (Edinburgh, 1997)

Ascham, Roger, *English Works: Toxophilus, Report of the Affaires and State of Germany and The Schoolmaster*, ed. W.A. Wright (Cambridge, 1904)

Ascham, Roger, *Toxophilus*, ed. E. Arber (Westminster, 1902)

Azario, Pietro, *Liber gestorum in Lombardia*, ed. F. Cognasso, in *Rerum Italicarum Scriptores*, ed. L.A. Muratori, XVI, pt 4.

Bale's Chronicle in Six Town Chronicles, ed. R. Flenley (Oxford, 1911)

Barbour, John, *The Bruce*, ed. A.A.M. Duncan (Edinburgh, 1997)

Basin, Thomas, *Histoire de Charles VII*, ed. C. Samaran, 2 vols (Paris, 1933–44)

Basin, Thomas, *Histoire des règnes de Charles VII et de Louis XI*, ed. J. Quicherat, 4 vols (Paris, 1855–9)

The Battle of Hastings: Sources and Interpretations, ed. S. Morillo (Woodbridge, 1996)

The Battle of Maldon, ed. D. Scragg (Manchester, 1981)

Baudri of Bourgeuil, *Les oeuvres poétiques de Baudri de Bourgeuil (1046–1130)*, ed. P. Abrahams (Paris, 1926)

The Bayeux Tapestry, ed. F. Stenton (London, 1957)

The Beauchamp Pageant, ed. A Sinclair (Donington, 2004)

Beha ad-Din, *The Life of Saladin*, trans. C.L. Conder (Palestine Pilgrims Text Society, xiii, London, 1897)

Beowulf, ed. and trans. M. Swanton (Manchester, 1978)

Beroul, *The Romance of Tristan*, ed. N.J. Lacy (New York and London, 1989)

Berry Herald, *Chroniques de Roi Charles*, ed. H. Corteault and L. Cellier (Paris 1979)

Bishop Percy's Folio Manuscript. Ballads and Romances, ed. J.W. Hales and F.J. Furnival, 4 vols (London, 1867–8)

The Black Book of the Admiralty, ed. T. Twiss, 4 vols (Rolls Series, London, 1871)

Blamires, A. and Holian, G.C., *The Romance of the Rose Illuminated* (Cardiff, 2001)

Blondell, Robert, *De Reductione Normanniae*, ed. J. Stevenson, *Narratives of the Expulsion of the English from Normandy, MCCCCXLIX–MCCCCL* (London, 1863)

The Book of Pluscarden, ed. F.J.H. Skene, 2 vols (Edinburgh, 1877–80)

Book of Prests, 1294–5, ed. E.B. Fryde (Oxford, 1962)

Bower, Walter, *Scotichronicon*, ed. S. Taylor, D.E.R. Watt and B. Scott, 9 vols (Aberdeen, 1987–98)

Brundage, J., *The Crusades: A Documentary Survey* (Milwaukee, 1962)

The Brut, ed. F.W.D. Brie (Early English Text Society, original series, cxxxi, London, 1906)

Brut y Tywysogyon or The Chronicle of the Princes, Peniarth MS. 20, trans. T. Jones (Cardiff, 1952)

Burton, Thomas, *Chronica Monasterii de Melsa*, ed. E.A. Bond, 2 vols (Rolls Series, London, 1866–8)

Calendar of Ancient Correspondence concerning Wales, ed. J. Goronwy Edwards (Cardiff, 1935)

Calendar of Close Rolls (1892–)

Calendar of Documents relating to Scotland, ed. J. Bain, 4 vols (London, 1881–8); vol. v, ed. R.R. Sharpe (London, 1901)

Calendar of Entries in the Papal Registers Relating to Great Britain and Ireland: Papal Letters, XI (London, 1893)

Calendar of Inquisitions Miscellaneous (Chancery), 7 vols (London, 1916–37)

Calendar of Letter-Books Preserved Among the Archives of the Corporation of the City of London, 1275–1498, ed. R.R. Sharpe, 11 vols (London, 1899–1912)

Calendar of Patent Rolls (1891–)

Calendar of Pleas and Memoranda Rolls Preserved Among the Archives of the City of London, ed. A.H. Thomas, 6 vols (Cambridge, 1926–61)

Calendar of State Papers Existing in the Archives and Collections of Milan, ed. A.B. Hinds (London, 1912)

Calendar of State Papers Relating to English Affairs Existing in the Archives and Collections of Venice, ed. R. Brown, *et al.*, 38 vols (London, 1864–1947)

Calendar of State Papers Relating to Scotland and Mary Queen of Scots, 1547–1603, ed. W.K. Boyd (Edinburgh, 1905)

Capitularia Aquisgranense, ed. A. Boretius, *MGH Capit*, I, n. 77

The Carmen de Hastingae Proelio of Guy, Bishop of Amiens, ed. C. Morton and H. Muntz (Oxford, 1972)

The Carmen de Hastingae Proelio of Guy, Bishop of Amiens, ed. F. Barlow (Oxford, 1999)

Cartulaire Normande de Phillipe Auguste, Louis VIII, Saint-Louis et Phillipe-le-Hardi, ed. L. Delisle (Caen, 1882, repr. Geneva, 1978)

Caxton, William, *The Book of the Fayttes of Armes and of Chyvalrye*, ed. A.T.P. Byles (Early English Texts Society, 1937)

The Cely Letters, 1472–1488, ed. A. Hanham (Early English Text Society, Oxford, 1975)

Certain Discourses Military, ed. J.R. Hale (Ithaca, New York, 1964)

Chartier, Jean, *Chronique française du roi de France Charles VII*, ed. Vallet de Viriville (Paris, 1858)

Chastelain, Georges, *Oeuvres de Georges Chastellain*, ed. K. de Lettenhove, 8 vols (Brussels, 1863–6)

Cheshire Chamberlains' Accounts, ed. R. Stewart-Brown (Record Society, 1910)

Christine de Pizan, *The Book of Deeds of Arms and of Chivalry*, trans. S. Willard and C.C. Willard (Pennsylvania State University, 1999)

Chronica de Mailros, ed. J. Stevenson (Edinburgh, 1835)

Chronica Minor S. Benedicti de Hulmo, ed. H. Ellis, *Chronica Johannis de Oxenedes* (London, 1859), 412–39

Chronica Monasterii de Hida juxta Wintoniam, in *Liber monasterii de Hyda*, ed. E. Edwards (Rolls Series, London, 1866)

The Chronicle of Battle Abbey, ed. C. Bémont, *Simon de Montfort, comte de Leicester: sa vie (1208–1265), son rôle politique en France et en Angleterre* (Paris, 1884)

The Chronicle of Bury St Edmunds, 1212–1301, ed. A. Gransden (London, 1964)

The Chronicle of Calais in the Reigns of Henry VII and Henry VIII, to the year 1540, ed. J.G. Nichols (Camden Society, xxxv, 1846)

The Chronicle of John Hardyng, ed. H. Ellis (London, 1812)

The Chronicle of John of Worcester, ed. and trans. R.R. Darlington, P. McGurk and J. Bray, 3 vols (Oxford, 1995–)

The Chronicle of Lanercost, 1272–1346, trans. H. Maxwell (Glasgow, 1913)

The Chronicle of London, ed. N.H. Nicolas (London, 1827)

The Chronicle of Pierre de Langtoft, ed. T. Wright, 2 vols (Rolls Series, London, 1886)

The Chronicle of Robert Manning of Brunne, ed. F.J. Furnivall, 2 vols (Rolls Series, London, 1887)

The Chronicle of Robert of Torigny, ed. R. Howlett, *Chronicles of the Reigns of Stephen, Henry II and Richard I*, IV (Rolls Series, London, 1889)

The Chronicle of Walter of Guisborough, ed. H. Rothwell (Camden Society, London, 1957)

Chronicles of the White Rose of York, ed. J.A. Giles (1845)

Chronicon Angliae, ed. E.M. Thompson, *Chronicles and Memorials of Great Britain and Ireland* (London, 1974), vol. lxiv

Chronicon de Bello, in C. Bémont, *Simon de Montfort, comte de Leicester: sa vie (1208–1265), son rôle politique en France et en Angleterre* (Paris, 1884), 373–80

Chronicon de Lanercost, MCCI–MCCCXLVI, ed. J. Stevenson (Edinburgh, 1839)

Chronicon domni Walteri de Hemingburgh de Gestis Regum Angliae, ed. H.C. Hamilton, 2 vols (London, 1848)

Chronicon Henrici Knighton, ed. J. Lumby, 2 vols (Rolls Series, London, 1889–95)

Chronicon Petroburgense, ed. T. Stapleton (Camden Society, 1849)

Chronique anonyme du règne de Charles VI, in *La Chronique d'Enguerran de Monstrelet*, ed. L. Douet-D'Arcq (Société de l'Histoire de France, 6 vols, Paris, 1857–62)

La Chronique d'Enguerran de Monstrelet, ed. L. Douet-D'Arcq, 6 vols (Société de l'Histoire de France, 1857–62)

Chronique de Jean le Bel, ed. E. Deprez, and J. Viard, 2 vols (Paris, 1904–5)

Chronique de Jean le Fèvre, Seigneur de Saint Remy, ed. F. Morand, 2 vols (Société de l'Histoire de France, 1876–81)

Chronique de Mathieu d'Escouchy, ed. G. Fresne de Beaucourt, 3 vols (Paris, 1863–4)

Chronique de Ruisseauville, in G. Bacquet, *Azincourt* (Bellegarde, 1977)

Chronique des Pays-Bays, de France, d'Angleterre et de Tournai, in *Corpus Chronicorum Flandriae*, ed. J.J. de Smet, 4 vols (Brussels, 1837–65)

Chronique et Annales de Gilles le Muisit, abbé de Saint-Martin de Tournai (1272–1352), ed. H. Lemaître (Paris, 1906)

Chronique normande de Pierre Cochon, ed. C. de Robillard de Beaurepaire (Société de l'Histoire de Normandie, 1870)

Chronique Normande du XIVe siècle, ed. A. and E. Moliner (Paris, 1882)

Chroniques de Jean Molinet (1474–1506), ed. G. Doutrepont and O. Jodogne, 3 vols (Brussels, 1935–7)

Les Chronicques de Normandie, ed. A. Hellot (Rouen, 1881)

Chroniques des Comtes d'Anjou, ed. P. Marchegay and A. Salmon (Paris, 2nd edn, 1871)

Chroniques des quatre premiers Valois (1327–1393), ed. S. Luce (Paris, 1862)

Chroniques des règnes de Jean II et Charles V, ed. R. Delachenal (Paris, 1910)

Les chroniques du roi Charles VII par Gilles le Bouvier dit le hérault Berry, ed. H. Courteault, L. Célier et M.-H. Julien de Pommerol (Paris, 1979)

Chronographia regnum Francorum, 1270–1405, ed. H. Moranville, 3 vols (Paris, 1891–7)

Codex diplomaticus Dominii Temporalis Sanctae Sedis, ed. A. Theiner, 2 vols (Rome, 1861–2)

Cogadh Gaedhel re Gallaibh. The War of the Gaedhil with the Gaill, ed. and trans. J.H. Todd (Rolls Series, London, 1867)

Conciliorum oecumenicorum decreta, ed. G. Alberigo et al. (2nd edn, Basel, 1962)

The Conquest of Jerusalem and the Third Crusade: sources in translation, trans. P. Edbury (Aldershot, 1996)

Contemporary Chronicles of the Hundred Years War, ed. P.E. Thompson (London, 1966)

La Continuation de Guillaume de Tyr (1184–1197), ed. M.R. Morgan (Paris, 1982)

Continuation de Guillaume de Tyr de 1229 à 1621, RHC, Oc, ii

Correspondance de la mairie de Dijon, ed. J. Garnier, 3 vols (Dijon, 1868–70)

Creton, Jean, *Histoire du Roy d'Angleterre Richard*, in J.A.C. Buchon, *Collection des Chroniques nationales françaises*, xxiv (Paris, 1826); trans. J. Webb, *Archaeologia*, xx (1824), 13–239

Crónicas de los reyes de Castilla, ed. E. Llaguno y Amirola, 2 vols (Madrid, 1779)

Crook, D., 'Some Further Evidence Concerning the Dating of the Origins of the Legend of Robin Hood', *EHR*, 99 (1984), 530–4; reprinted in Knight, ed., *Robin Hood* (Cambridge, 1999), 257–61

The Crusade against Heretics in Bohemia, 1418–1437: Sources and Documents for the Hussite Crusades, ed. T.A. Fudge (Aldershot, 2002)

Curry, A., *The Battle of Agincourt: Sources and Interpretations* (Woodbridge, 2000)

Cuvelier, Jean, *Chronique de Bertrand de Guesclin*, ed. E. Charrière, 2 vols (Paris, 1839)

Daniel, Samuel, *The Collection of the History of England*, in *The Complete Works in Verse and Prose of Samuel Daniel*, ed. A.B. Grosart, 5 vols (London, 1885–96)

De antiquis legibus liber: Cronica maiorum et vicecomitatum Londoniarum, ed. T. Stapleton (Camden Society, London, 1846)

De constructione castri Saphet, trans. H.N. Kennedy, *Crusader Castles* (Cambridge, 1994)

De Procinctu romanae miliciae, ed. E. Dümmler, *Zeitschrift für Deutsches Alterum*, xv (1872), 413–81

The Description of England, ed. F.J. Furnivall (New Shakespeare Society, vi, 1877)

Dialogus de Scaccario and Constitutio Domus Regis, ed. C. Johnson (London, 1950)

Dobson, R.B., ed. *The Peasants' Revolt of 1381* (London, 1970)

Dobson, R.B., and Taylor, J., *Rymes of Robyn Hood: an Introduction to the English Outlaw* (London, 1976)

Documents illustrating the History of Civilization in Medieval England (1066–1500), trans. R. Trevor Davies (London and New York, 1926, repr. 1969)

Documents relatif au comté de Champagne et Brie (1172–1361), ed. A. Longon, 3 vols (Paris, 1901–14)

Dominic Mancini, *The Usurpation of Richard the Third*, ed. C.A.J. Armstrong (2nd edn, London, 1969)

Dugdale, W., *Monasticon Anglicanum*, 6 vols (London, 1817–30)

Eames, E.S., *Catalogue of Medieval Lead-Glazed Earthenware Tiles in the Department of Medieval and Later Antiquities, British Museum*, 2 vols (London, 1980)

The Earliest English Translations of Vegetius' De Re Militari, ed. G. Lester (Heidelberg, 1988)

The Earliest Norwegian Laws, ed. L.M. Larson (New York, 1935)

Early English Lyrics: Amorous, Divine, Moral and Trivial, ed. E.K. Chambers and F. Sidgwick (London, 1966)

Early Gothic Manuscripts, I. 1190–1250, ed. N.J. Morgan (Oxford, 1982)

Early Sources of Scottish History, AD 500–1286, trans. A.O. Anderson, 2 vols (Edinburgh, 1922, repr. Stamford, 1990)

Edward, Duke of York, *Master of the Game*, ed. W.A. and F. Baillie-Grohman (London, 1904)

Elyot, Thomas, *The Boke Named the Governour*, ed. H.H.S. Croft, 2 vols (London, 1883)

English Chronicle of the Reigns of Richard II, Henry IV, Henry V, and Henry VI, written before the year 1471, ed. J.S. Davies (Camden Society, London, 1856)

English Historical Documents, I, c. 500–1042, ed. D. Whitelock (2nd edn, London, 1979)

English Historical Documents II, 1042–1189, ed. D.C. Douglas and G.W. Greenway (2nd edn, London, 1981)

English Historical Documents, IV, 1327–1485, ed. A.R. Myers (London, 1969)

English Suits before the Parlement of Paris, 1420–1436, ed. C.T. Allmand and C.A.J. Armstrong, Camden Society, 4th ser., xxvi (London, 1982)

L'Estoire de Eracles Empereur et la Conqueste de la Terre d'Outremer in *RHC, Oc*, II

Eulogium historiarum, ed. F.S. Haydon, 3 vols (Rolls Series, London, 1858–63)

'Extracts From the Coram Rege Rolls and Pleas of the Crown, Staffordshire, of the Reign of Edward II, A.D. 1307 to A.D. 1327', ed. G. Wrottesley, in *Collections for a History of Staffordshire*, x (Staffordshire Record Society, 1889)

Extraits analytiques des reigstres des consaulx de la ville de Tournai, 1431–76, ed. A. de la Grange (Tournai, 1893)

Feudal Society in Medieval France: documents from the County of Champagne, ed. and trans. T. Evergates (Philadelphia, 1993)

The First Biography of Joan of Arc, trans. D. Rankin and C. Quintal (Pittsburg, 1964)

Flavius Vegetius Renatus, *Epitoma Rei Militaris*, ed. R. Dyboski and Z.M. Arend, *Knyghthode and Bataile: a XVth century verse paraphrase of Flavius Vegetius Renatus' treatise "De Rei Militari"* (London, 1935)

Flavius Vegetius Renatus, *Epitoma Rei Militaris*, ed. L.F. Stelten (New York, 1990)

Flores Historiarum, ed. H.R. Luard, 3 vols (Rolls Series, London, 1890)

Fordun, John, *Chronica gentis Scotorum*, ed. W.F. Skene, 2 vols (Edinburgh, 1871–2)

Fortescue, John, *De Laudibus Legum Angliae*, ed. S.B. Chrimes (Cambridge, 1942)

The French Chronicle of London, ed. G.J. Aungier, *Camden Society*, xxviii (1844)

Froissart, Jean, *The Chronicles of Froissart translated out of the French by Sir John Bourchier, Lord Berners (1523–25)*, ed. W.P. Ker, 4 vols (London, 1901–2)

Froissart, Jean, *Chroniques*, ed. and trans. G. Brereton (Harmondsworth, 1968)

Froissart, Jean, *Chroniques*, ed. G.T. Diller (Geneva, 1972)

Froissart, Jean, *Chroniques*, ed. T. Johnes, *Sir John Froissart's Chronicles of England, France, Spain and the adjoining countries, from the latter part of the Reign of Edward II to the Coronation of Henry IV*, 13 vols (London, 1808)

Froissart, Jean, *Chroniques*, ed. G.C. Macaulay and trans. Lord Berners, *The Chronicles of Froissart* (London, 1895)

Froissart, Jean, *Chroniques de Jean Froissart*, ed. S. Luce, 15 vols (Paris, 1869–99)

Froissart, Jean, *Oeuvres de Froissart*, ed. K. de Lettenhove *et al.*, 25 vols (Brussels, 1867–77)

Fulcher of Chartres, *Historia Hierosolymitana*, ed. H. Hagenmeyer (Heidelberg, 1913); English translation by E.R. Ryan, *A History of the Expedition to Jerusalem, 1095–1127*, ed. H.S. Fink (Knoxville, 1969)

Galbraith, V.H., 'Extracts from the *Historia Aurea* and a French 'Brut' (1317–47)', *EHR*, xliii (1928), 203–17

Gaston Phébus, *Livre de Chasse*, ed. G. Tilander (Karlshamm, 1971)

Geoffrey le Baker, *Chronicon*, ed. E.M. Thompson (Oxford, 1889)

Gervase of Canterbury, *Opera Historica*, ed. W. Stubbs, 2 vols (Rolls Series, London, 1879–80)

Gesta Edwardi de Carnarvon auctore canonico Bridlingtoniensi cum continuatione ad AD 1377, ed. W. Stubbs, *Chronicles of the Reign of Edward I and Edward II*, vol. II (Rolls Series, London, 1883)

Gesta Francorum et aliorum Hierosolimitanum, ed. and trans. R. Hill (London, 1962)

The Gesta Guillelmi of William of Poitiers, ed. R.H.C. Davies and M. Chibnall (Oxford, 1998)

Gesta Henrici Quinti, ed. F. Taylor and J.S. Roskell (Oxford, 1975)

The Gesta Normannorum Ducum of William of Jumièges, Orderic Vitalis, and Robert of Torigni, ed. E.M.C. van Houts (Oxford, 1992–5)

Gesta Stephani, ed. K.R. Potter (Oxford, 1976)

Giraldus Cambrensis, *Expugnatio Hibernica. The Conquest of Ireland*, ed. and trans. A.B. Scott and F.X. Martin (Dublin, 1978)

Giraldus Cambrensis, *Opera*, ed. J.S. Brewer, J.F. Dimock, and G.F. Warner, 8 vols (Rolls Series, London, 1861–91). *Itinerarium Kambriae*, in *Opera*, vi and an English translation by L. Thorpe, *The Journey Through Wales and the Description of Wales* (Harmondsworth, 1978)

Giraldus Cambrensis, *Speculum Duorum*, ed. Y. Lefèvre, R.B.C. Huygens and trans. by B. Dawson (Cardiff, 1974)

Giraldus Cambrensis, *Topographia Hibernica*, in *Opera*, ed. J.F. Dimock and G.F. Warner, v (Rolls Series, London, 1867); trans. by J.J. O'Meara, *The History and Topography of Ireland* (revised edn, Harmondsworth, 1982)

Les Grandes Chroniques de France, ed. J. Viard, 10 vols (Paris, 1920–53)

The Great Chronicle of London, ed. A.H. Thomas and I.D. Thornley (London, 1938)

The Great Rolls of the Pipe, 1–14 John, ed. D.M. Stenton (Pipe Roll Society, London, 1933–55)

The Great Rolls of the Pipe, 2–4 Henry II, ed. J. Hunter (London, 1844); *5–34 Henry II* (London, 1884–1925)

The Great Rolls of the Pipe for the First Year of the Reign of Richard I, ed. J. Hunter (London, 1844); the rest ed. D.M. Stenton (London, 1925–33)

Gregory of Tours, *History of the Franks*, trans. L. Thorpe (Harmondsworth, 1974)

Gregory of Tours, *Decem libri historiarum*, ed. B. Krusch and W. Levison, *Gregorii episcopi Turonensis libri historiarum X*, MGH SRM, I.i (Hanover, 1951)

Guillaume Cousinot, *Chronique de la Pucelle*, ed. V. de Viriville, 8 vols (Paris, 1859)

Guillaume Gruel, *Chronique d'Arthur de Richemont*, ed. A. Le Vavasseur (Paris, 1890)

Hall, Edward, *Chronicle*, ed. H. Ellis, *The Union of Two Noble and Illustre Families of Lancaster and York* (London, 1809)

Halliwell, J.O., ed., *The Chronicle of William de Rishanger of the Barons' Wars* (Camden Society, London, 1840)

The Hamilton Papers, ed. J. Bain, 2 vols (Edinburgh, 1890, 1892)

Hanawalt, B.A., 'Ballads and Bandits: Fourteenth Century Outlaws and the Robin Hood Poems', in *Chaucer's England: Literature in Historical Context*, ed. B.A. Hanawalt (Minneapolis, 1992), and reprinted in Knight, ed., *Robin Hood*, 263–84

The Harley Psalter, ed. W. Noel (Cambridge, 1996)

Harry's Wallace, ed. M.P. McDairmid, 2 vols (Edinburgh, 1968)

Henry of Huntingdon, *Historia Anglorum*, ed. D. Greenway (Oxford, 1996)

Highland Papers, ed. J.R.N. MacPhail, 4 vols (Scottish History Society, 1914–34)

Histoire de Guillaume le Maréchal, ed. P. Meyer, 3 vols (Paris, 1891–1907)

Histoire des Ducs de Normandie et des rois d'Angleterre, ed. F. Michel (Paris, 1840)

Histoire of the Arrival of King Edward IV, 1471, ed. J. Bruce (London, 1838)

Histoire Naturelle des Indes. The Drake Manuscript in the Pierpont Morgan Library with an introduction by V. Klinkenborg and translations by R.S. Kraemer (New York and London, 1996)

Historia Majoris Britanniae, ed. R. Freebairn (Edinburgh, 1740)

Historia Vitae et Regni Ricardi Secundo, ed. G.B. Stow (Philadelphia, 1977)

Historiae Croylandensis Continuatio, in *Rerum Anglicarum Scriptorum Veterum*, I, ed. W. Fulman (Oxford, 1684)

Historical Papers and Letters from the Northern Registers, ed. J. Raine (Rolls Series, London, 1873)

The Historie and Cronicles of Scotland, written and collected by Robert Lindsay of Pitscottie, ed. A.E.J.G. Mackay, 3 vols (Edinburgh, 1899–1911)

The History of Gruffyd ap Cynan, trans. A. Jones (Manchester, 1910)

Holinshed, R., *Chronicles*, ed. H. Ellis, *Chronicles of England, Scotland and Ireland*, 6 vols (London, 1808)

Hollstein, F.W.H., *Dutch and Flemish Etchings, Engravings and Woodcuts, c.a 1450–1700, vol. XII: Masters and Monogrammists of the Fifteenth Century* (Amsterdam, 1956)

Hudson, W., ed., *The Three Earliest Subsidies for the County of Sussex, 1296, 1327, 1332* (Sussex Record Society, x, 1910)

The Hunting Book of Gaston Phébus, ed. M. Thomas, F. Avril and W. Schlag (London, 1998)

The Inventory of King Henry VIII, ed. D. Starkey (London, 1998)

Istore et croniqes de Flandres, ed. K. de Lettenhove, 2 vols (Brussels, 1879–80)

Itinerarium Peregrinorum et Gesta Regis Ricardi, trans. H. Nicholson, *Chronicle of the Third Crusade* (Ashgate, 1997)

Jean de Bueil, *Le Jouvencel*, ed. L. Lecestre, 2 vols (Paris, 1887–9)

Jean de Haynin, *Mémoires, 1465–77*, ed. D.D. Brouwers, 2 vols (Liège, 1905–6)

Jean de Venette, *Chronicon*, ed. J. Birdsall and R.A. Newhall, *The Chronicle of Jean de Venette* (New York, 1953)

Jean de Waurin, *Recueil des croniques et anchiennes istories de la Grant Bretaigne, a present nomme Engleterre*, ed. W.L. Hardy and E.L.C.P. Hardy, 5 vols (Rolls Series, London, 1864–91); trans. W.L. Hardy and E.L.C.P. Hardy, *A Collection of Chronicles and Ancient Histories*, 3 vols (London, 1864–91)

Jean Juvenal des Ursins, *Histoire de Charles VI, Roy de France*, in Mm. Michaud and Poujoulat, eds, *Nouvelle Collection des Mémoires relatifs à l'Histoire de France depuis le XIIIe siècle jusqu'à fin du XVIIIe siècle*, II (Paris, 1857)

Jean Le Bel, *Chronique de Jean le Bel*, ed. J. Viard and E. Déprez, 2 vols (Paris, 1904–5)

John de Trokelowe, *Chronica monasterii S. Albani*, ed. H.T. Riley (London, 1866)

John of Hexham, *Chronica in Symeonis Monachi Opera Omnia*, ed. T. Arnold, II, 284–332

John of Reading, *Chronica, 1346–1367*, ed. J. Tait (Manchester, 1914)

John of Salisbury, *Policraticus*, ed. C.C. Webb, 2 vols (Oxford, 1909)

John of Salisbury, *The Statesman's Book of John of Salisbury*, trans. J. Dickinson (New York, 1927)

Joinville, *The Life of Saint Louis*, trans. M.R.B. Shaw, *Chronicles of the Crusades. Joinville and Villehardouin* (Harmondsworth, 1963)

Karoli ad Fulradum abbatum epistola, MGH Capit, I, ed. A. Boretius (Hanover, 1883); trans. P.E. Dutton, *Carolingian Civilization: A Reader* (Ontario, 1993), 73

King Harald's Saga, trans. M. Magnusson (Harmondsworth, 1966)

Kingsford, C.L., 'Extracts from the First Version of Hardyng's Chronicle', EHR, xxvii (1912), 740–53

Kingsford's Stonor Letters and Papers, 1290–1483, ed. C. Carpenter (Cambridge, 1996)

Knighton's Chronicle, 1337–1396, ed. and trans. G.H. Martin (Oxford, 1995)

Laws of the Salian and Ripuarian Franks, trans. T.J. Rivers (New York, 1986)

Leges Henrici Primi, ed. L.J. Downer (Oxford, 1972)

Leges Visigothorum, ed. K. Zeumer, MGH LNG, I (Hanover, 1902)

Leland, John, *De Rebus Britannicis Collectanea*, 6 vols (London, 1774)

Le Roux de Lincy, M., 'Inventaires des biens maubles et immaubles de la comtesse Mahaut d'Artois, pillés par l'armée de son neveu, en l'armée 1333', *Bibliothèque de l'Ecole des Chartes* (1853), 53–79

Lescot, Richard, *Chronique (1328–1344), suivie de la continuation de cette chronique (1344–1364)*, ed. J. Lemoine (Paris, 1896)

Letters and Papers, Foreign and Domestic, of the Reign of Henry VIII, 22 vols (London, 1862–1932)

Letters and Papers Illustrative of the Wars of the English in France during the Reign of Henry VI, King of England, ed. J. Stevenson, 2 vols (Rolls Series, London, 1861–4)

Letters from the Mary Rose, ed. C.S. Knighton and D.M. Loades (Stroud, 2002)

The Letters of Innocent III (1198–1216) concerning England and Wales, ed. C.R. Cheney and M.G. Cheney (Oxford, 1967)

The Letters of Lanfranc, Archbishop of Canterbury, ed. and trans. H. Clover and M. Gibson (Oxford, 1979)

Liber recuperationis Terre Sancte, ed. P.G. Golubovitch, in *Biblioteca Bio-Bibliografica della Terra Sancta*, II (Florence, 1913)

Life of the Black Prince by the Herald of Sir John Chandos, ed. M.K. Pope and E.C. Lodge (Oxford, 1910)

The Life and Campaigns of the Black Prince, ed. R. Barber (Woodbridge, 1986)

Life, Death and Art: The Medieval Stained Glass of Fairford Parish Church, ed. S. Brown and L. Macdonald (Stroud, 1997)

The Lisle Letters, ed. M. St Clare Byrne, 6 vols (Chicago and London, 1981)

Littere Wallie, ed. J.G. Edwards (Cardiff, 1940)

Le 'livre des fais' du bon messire Jehan le Maingre, dit Bouciquaut, mareschal de France et gouverneur de Jennes, ed. D. Lalande (Paris and Geneva, 1985)

Lopez, Fernao, *Cronica de Don Fernando*, ed. de Salvador Dias Arnaut (Porto, 1979)

Luard, H.R., ed., *Annales Monastici*, 5 vols (London, 1864–9)

Lydgate, John, *The Horse, the Sheep and the Goose*, ed. J.H.F. Jenkinson (Cambridge, 1906)

Macpherson, D. *et al.*, *Rotuli Scotiae in Turri Londinensi et in Domo Capitulari Westmonasteriensi asservati*, 2 vols (Record Commission, London, 1814, 1819)

Magni Rotuli Scaccarii Normanniae, ed. T. Stapleton, 2 vols (London, 1840–84)

Major, John, *Historia Majoris Britanniae*, ed. R. Freebairn (Edinburgh, 1740), translated by A. Constable, *A History of Greater Britain* (Scottish Historical Society, 1892)

Manners and Household Expenses of England in the Thirteenth and Fifteenth Centuries, ed. T.H. Turner (London, 1841)

Materials for the History of Thomas Becket, ed. J.C. Robertson, 7 vols (London, 1875–85)

Maurice's Strategikon: Handbook of Byzantine Military Strategy, trans. G.T. Dennis (Philadelphia, 2001)

Medieval Combat. A Fifteenth Century Manual of Swordfighting and Close-Quarter Combat by Hans Talhoffer, ed. and trans. M. Rector (London, 2000)

Medieval Europe, ed. J. Kirshner and K.F. Morrison (Chicago and London, 1986)

Mémoires de Pierre de Fenin, ed. E. Dupont (Paris, 1837)

Mémoires du maréchal Florange dit le jeune adventureux, ed. R. Goubaux and P.-A. Lemoisne, 2 vols (Paris, 1913–24)

Mémoires pour servir à l'histoire de France et Bourgogne, 2 vols (Paris 1729)

Memorials of St Edmund's Abbey, ed. T. Arnold, 3 vols (Roll Series, 1890–6)

Michel, F., ed., *Histoire des Ducs de Normandie et des rois d'Angleterre* (Paris, 1840)

Michel, F. and Bémont, C., eds, *Rôles Gascons*, 3 vols (Paris, 1885–1906)

The Miracles of Elizabeth of Thuringia, ed. A. Huysken in *Quellenstudien zur der Geschichte der heiligen Elizabeth* (Marburg, 1908)

Monasterii de Hida juxta Wintoniam, ed. E. Edwards, *Liber Monasterii de Hyda* (London, Rolls Series, 1866)

Monluc, Blaise de, *The Valois–Habsburg Wars and the French Wars of Religion*, ed. I. Roy (London, 1971)

Morgan, N.J., *Early Gothic Manuscripts, I. 1190–1250* (Oxford, 1982)

Mülinen, N.F. von, ed., *Lois militaires de Charles de Bourgogne, Schweizerische Geschichtsforscher*, II (1817), 425–68

Mum and the Sothsegger, ed. M Day and R. Steele (Early English Texts Society, 1936)

Narratives of the Days of Reformation, ed. J.G. Nichols (Camden Society, London, 1859)

Nicholai Triveti Annales, ed. T. Hog (London, 1845)

Njal's Saga, trans. M. Magnusson and H. Pálsson (Harmondsworth, 1960)

Odo of Deuil, *De Profectione Ludovici in Orientem*, ed. and trans. V.G. Berry (New York, 1948)

Offord, M.Y., ed., *The Parlement of the Thre Ages* (Early English Text Society, ccxlvi, London, 1959)

The Old French Continuation of William of Tyre, trans. in P. Edbury, *The Conquest of Jerusalem and the Third Crusade: Sources in Translation* (Aldershot, 1996)

Oliver of Paderborn, *Historia Damiatina*, ed. H. Hoogeweg, *Bibliothek des Litterischen Vereins in Stuttgart*, ccii (1894)

Ordonnances des roys de France de la troisième race recueillies par ordre chronologique, ed. E. de Lauriere, 23 vols (Paris, 1723–1849)

The Original Chronicle of Andrew of Wyntoun, ed. F.J. Amours, 6 vols (Scottish Text Society, 1903–14)

Original Letters Illustrative of English History, ed. H. Ellis, 3 series in 11 vols (London, 1824–46)

Orkneyinga Saga, trans. H. Pálsson and P. Edwards (Harmondsworth, 1981)

The Oxford Book of Scottish Verse, ed. J. MacQueen and T. Scott (Oxford, 1966, repr. 1981)

The Oxford Book of War Poetry, ed. J. Stallworthy (Oxford, 1984)

Oxford City Documents, 1268–1665, ed. T. Rogers (Oxford, 1981)

Paris, Matthew, *Chronica majora*, ed. H.R. Luard, *Matthaei Parisiensis, monachi sancti Albani, chronica majora*, 7 vols (London, Rolls Series, 1872–3)

The Parlement of the Thre Ages, ed. M.Y. Offord (Early English Text Society, vol. 246, London, 1959)

The Paston Letters, A.D. 1422–1509, ed. J. Gairdner, 6 vols (London, 1904)

Philippe de Commynes, *Mémoires*, trans. M. Jones, *Memoirs. The Reign of Louis XI, 1461–1493* (Harmondsworth, 1972)

A Picture Book of Old Testament Stories of the Thirteenth Century, ed. S.C. Cockerell (Roxburghe Club, London, 1924)

The Pipewell Chronicle, in C.J. Rogers and M. Buck, 'Three New Accounts of the Neville's Cross Campaign'

Political Poems and Songs, ed. T. Wright, 2 vols (Rolls Series, London, 1859–61)

The Political Songs of England: from the Reign of John to that of Edward II, ed. T. Wright (Edinburgh, 1839)

Polychronicon Radulphi Higden, ed. C. Babington and J.R. Lumby, 9 vols (Rolls Series, London, 1865–86)

The Pseudo Elmham, *Thomae de Elmham Vita et Gesta Henrici Quinti*, ed. T. Hearne (Oxford, 1727)

Ralph of Caen, *Gesta Tancredi*, RHC, Oc, III, 603–716

Ralph of Coggeshall, *Chronicon Anglicanum*, ed. J. Stevenson (Rolls Series, London, 1875)

Ralph of Diceto, *Opera Historica*, ed. W. Stubbs, 2 vols (Rolls Series, London, 1876)

Raymond d'Aguilers, *Historia Francorum qui Ceperunt Iherusalem, RHC, Oc, III* (Paris, 1886)

Récits d'un bourgeois de Valenciennes, ed. K. de Lettenhove (Louvain, 1877)

Le recouvrement de Normendie par Berry, herault du roi, in *Narratives of the Expulsion of the English from Normandy*, ed. J. Stevenson (Rolls Series, London, 1869)

Recueil des Actes des Ducs de Normandie, 911–1066, ed. M. Faroux (Caen, 1961)

Recueil des historiens des Gaules et de la France, ed. M.L. Delisle, 24 vols (new edn, Paris, 1869–1904)

Regesta Regum Scottorum, I. The Acts of Malcolm IV, King of Scots, 1153–1165, ed. G.W.S. Barrow (Edinburgh, 1960)

Regesta Regum Scottorum, II. The Acts of William I, King of Scots, 1165–1214, ed. G.W.S. Barrow (Edinburgh, 1971)

Regesta Regum Scottorum, V. The Acts of Robert I, King of Scots, 1306–1329, ed. A.A.M. Duncan (Edinburgh, 1988)

Reginonis abbatis Prumiensis chronicon cum continuatione Treverensi, ed. F. Kurze, *MGH SRG* (Hanover, 1890)

Register of Edward, the Black Prince, ed. M.C.B. Dawes, 4 vols (London, 1930–3)

The Register of John of Gaunt, ed. S. Armitage-Smith, 2 vols (London, 1911)

Registrum Abbatiae Johannis Whethamstede, ed. T. Riley, 2 vols (Rolls Series, London, 1872–3)

Registrum honoris de Morton, ed. T. Thomson and A. Macdonald, 2 vols (Bannatyne Club, 1853)

Registrum Magni Sigilli Regnum Scottorum, ed. J.M. Thomson *et al.*, 11 vols (Edinburgh, 1882–1914)

La Règle du Temple, ed. H. De Curzon (Paris, 1886)

A Relation, or Rather a True Account of the Island of England, ed. C.A. Sneyd (Camden Society, London, 1847)

Le Religieux de Saint-Denis, ed. M.L. Bellaguet, *Histoire des Charles VI*, 6 vols (Paris, 1839–52)

The Retrial of Joan of Arc: The Evidence at the Trial for her Rehabilitation, ed. R. Pernoud and trans. J.M. Cohen (London, 1955)

Richard of Devizes, *Chronicon*, ed. and trans. J.T. Appelby (London, 1963)

Richard of Hexham, *De gestis regis Stephani et de bello Standardii*, ed. R. Howlett, *Chronicles of the Reigns of Stephen, Henry II and Richard I, III* (Rolls Series, London, 1886)

Richer, *Histoire de la France*, ed. R. Latouche, 2 vols (Paris, 1930)

Rigord, *Gesta Philippi Augusti*, ed. H.-F. Delaborde, *Oeuvres de Rigord et de Guillaume le Breton, historiens de Philippe-Auguste*, 2 vols (Paris, 1882)

Rishanger, William, *Chronica monasterii S. Albani, Chronica et Annales, regnantibus Henrico tertio et Edwardo primo*, ed. H.T. Riley (London, 1865)

Rishanger, William, *Chronicon de Bellis*, ed. J. Orchard Halliwell, *The Chronicle of William de Rishanger of the Barons' Wars: The Miracles of Simon de Montfort* (London, 1840)

Robbins, R.H., *Historical Poems of the 14th and 15th c* (New York, 1959)

Robert of Avesbury, *De gestis mirabilibus regis Edwardi tertii*, ed. E.M. Thompson (Rolls Series, London, 1889)

Roger of Howden, *Chronica*, ed. W. Stubbs, 4 vols (Rolls Series, London, 1868–71)

Roger of Howden, *Gesta Henrici II et Ricardi I*, ed. W. Stubbs, 2 vols (Rolls Series, London, 1867)

Rôles Gascons, ed. F. Michel and C. Bémont 3 vols (Paris, 1885–1906)

The Roll of Arms of the Princes, Barons and Knights who attended King Edward I to the Siege of Caerlaverock, ed. and trans. T. Wright (London, 1864)

Rolls of the Justices in Eyre: being the rolls of Pleas and Assizes for Yorkshire in 3 Henry III, 1218–19, ed. D. Stenton (London, 1937)

The Romance of the Rose by Guillaume de Lorris and Jean de Meun, trans. C. Dahlberg (Princeton, 3rd edn, 1995)

Romanesque Manuscripts, 1066–1190, ed. C.M. Kaufman (London, 1975)

Rotuli de Dominabus et Pueris et Puellis de Donatione Regis in XII Comitatibus, 31 Henry II, 1185, ed. J.H. Round (London, 1913)

Rotuli de Liberate ac de Misis et Praestitis Regnanate Johanne, ed. T. Duffus Hardy (London, 1844)

Rotuli Hundredorum, ed. W. Illingworth and J. Caley, 2 vols (London, 1812–18)

Rotuli Parliamentorum, 6 vols (Record Commission, 1767–77)

Rotuli Scaccarii Regum Scotorum, ed. J. Stuart and G. Burnett, 23 vols (Edinburgh, 1878–1908)

Rotuli Scotiae in Turri Londinensi et in Domo Capitulari Westmonasteriensi asservati, ed. D. Macpherson *et al.*, 2 vols (Record Commission, London, 1814, 1819)

Royal and other Historical Letters illustrative of the Reign of Henry III, ed. W.W. Shirley, 2 vols (Rolls Series, London, 1862, 1866)

The Rule of the Templars, ed. J. Upton-Ward (Woodbridge, 1992)

Rymer, T., ed., *Foedera, Conventiones, Literae*, 20 vols (London, 1704–35)

The St Albans Chronicle, 1406–1420, ed. V.H. Galbraith (Oxford, 1937)

The St Albans Chronicle. The Chronica maiora of Thomas Walsingham, ed. J. Taylor, W.R. Childs and L. Watkiss (Oxford, 2003)

Saxo Grammaticus, *Danorum regum heroumque historia*, ed. E. Christiansen, 3 vols (Oxford, 1980–1)

Saxo Grammaticus, *The History of the Danes, Books I–IX*, ed. H. Ellis Davidson and trans. P. Fisher (Cambridge, 1979, 1980 in 2 vols, repr. as one volume, 1996)

Scalacronica, ed. J. Stevenson (Edinburgh, Maitland Club, 1836)

Scottish Annals from English Chroniclers, AD 500 to 1286, trans. A.O. Anderson (London, 1902)

Select Pleas of the Forest, ed. G.J. Turner (Selden Society, 1901)

The Sermons of Hugh Latimer, ed. G.E. Corrie (Parker Society, 1844)

The Siege of Carlaverock, ed. and trans. N.H. Nicolas (London, 1828)

Simeon of Durham, *Historia regum*, ed. T. Arnold, *Symeonis Monachi Opera Omnia*, 2 vols (London, 1882–5)

The Skalds: A Selection of their Poems, ed. and trans. L.M. Hollander (New York, 1947)

Snorri Sturluson, *Heimskringla*, trans. S. Laing, 2 vols (revised edn, London, 1964)

The Song of the Cathar Wars, trans. J. Shirley (Aldershot, 1996)

The Song of Dermot and the Earl, ed. and trans. G.H. Orpen (Oxford, 1892)

Le Songe du Vieil Pélerin, ed. G.W. Coopland, 2 vols (Cambridge, 1969)

Stapleton, T., *De antiquis legibus liber: Cronica maiorum et vicecomitatum Londoniarum* (Camden Society, London, 1846)

Statutes of the Realm, 11 vols (Record Commission, 1810–28)

Stephen of Rouen, *Draco Normannicus*, ed. R. Howlett, *Chronicles of the Reigns of Stephen, Henry II and Richard I*, II (Rolls Series, London, 1885)

Stubbs, W., *Select Charters and other illustrations of English Constitutional History from the Earliest Times to the Reign of Edward the First* (9th edn, revised by H.W.C. Davis, Oxford, 1913)

Der Stuttgarter Bilderpsalter, 2 vols (Stuttgart, 1965–8)

Das Stuttgarter Passionale, ed. A. Boecker (Augsburg, 1923)

Suger, *Vie de Louis VI le Gros*, ed. H. Waquet (Paris, 1929)

Thomae Sprotti Chronica, ed. T. Hearne (Oxford, 1719)

Thomas, M., Avril, F. and Schlag, W., eds, *The Hunting Book of Gaston Phébus* (London, 1998)

Thomas of Elmham, *Liber metricus*, ed. C.A. Cole, *Memorials of Henry the Fifth, King of England* (London, 1858)

Thomas of Wykes, *Chronicon vulgo dictum Thomae Wykes*, ed. H.R. Luard, *Annales Monastici*, iv (London, 1867)

Three Chronicles of the Reign of Edward IV, ed. K. Dockray (Gloucester, 1988)

Three Earliest Subsidies for the County of Sussex, 1296, 1327, 1332, ed. W. Hudson (Sussex Record Society, x, 1910)

Three Fifteenth-Century Chronicles, ed. J. Gairdner (Camden Society, London, 1880)

Three Lives of English Saints, ed. M. Winterbotton (Toronto, 1972)

Titi Livii Foro-Juliensis Vita Henrici Quinti, ed. T Hearne (Oxford, 1716); partial translation in A. Curry, ed., *The Battle of Agincourt: sources and interpretations* (Woodbridge, 2000), 53–63

Todd, J.M., ed., *The Lanercost Cartulary* (Surtees Society, cciii, Gateshead, 1997)

The Très Riches Heures of Jean, Duke of Berry, ed. J. Longnon, R. Cazelles and M. Meiss (New York, 1969)

Tudor Royal Proclamations, ed. P.L. Hughes and J.F. Larkin, 3 vols (New Haven and London, 1964–9)

Trewe Encountre of Batayle Lately Don Betwene Englande and Scotlande (London 1809)

The Utrecht Psalter in Medieval Art: Picturing the Psalms of David, ed. K. van der Horst, W. Noel and W. Wustefeld (London, 1996)

Usamah ibn Munquidh, *Kitab al-I'tibar*, trans. P.K. Hitti, *Memoirs of an Arab-Syrian Gentleman or an Arab Knight in the Crusades* (Beruit, 1964)

Vergil, P., *Anglica Historia*, ed. H. Ellis, *Three Books of Polydore Vergil's English History* (London, 1844)

Victoria County History, Derbyshire, 2 vols (London, 1907)

Villani, Giovanni, *Cronica*, ed. G. Porta, 3 vols (Parma, 1991)

Villani, Matteo, *Chronica, con la continuazione di Filippo Villani*, ed. G. Porta, 2 vols (Parma, 1995)

Vita Edwardi Secundi, ed. N. Denholm-Young (London, 1957)

Vita et Gesta Henrici Quinti, ed. T. Hearne (Oxford, 1727)

Vita Landiberti vertustissima, ed. B. Krusch, *MGH SRM*, VI (Hanover and Leipzig, 1913), 353–84

Vitalis, Orderic, *Historia Ecclesiastica*, ed. M.M. Chibnall, *The Ecclesiastical History of Orderic Vitalis*, 6 vols (Oxford, 1969–80)

Vollstandige Faksimile – Ausgabe im Originalformat der Handschrift MS Ashmole 1511 – Bestiarum (Graz, 1992)

Wace, *Roman de Brut*, ed. I. Arnold, 2 vols (Paris, 1938–40)

Wace, *Roman de Rou*, ed. A.J. Holden, 3 vols (Paris, 1970–3)

Walsingham, Thomas, *Annales Ricardi Secundi et Henrici Quarti, Regum Angliae*, ed. H.T. Riley (London, 1866), 153–420

Walsingham, Thomas, *Historia Anglicana*, ed. H.T. Riley, 2 vols (Rolls Series, London, 1863–4)

Walter of Coventry, *Memoriale fratris Walteri de Conventria: the historical collections of Walter of Coventry*, ed. W. Stubbs, 2 vols (London, 1872–3)

Walter of Peterborough, *Prince Edward's Expedition into Spain and the Battle of Nájera*, ed. T. Wright, Political Poems and Songs, 2 vols (Rolls Series, London, 1859–61), I

Walter the Chancellor, *Bella Antiochena*, ed. T.A. Ashbridge and S.B. Edgington, *Walter the Chancellor's The Antiochene Wars* (Aldershot, 1999)

The Waltham Chronicle, ed. and trans. L. Watkiss and M. Chibnall (Oxford, 1994)

The War of Saint Sardos, 1323–1325. Gascon Correspondence and Diplomatic Documents, ed. P. Chaplais (Camden 3rd ser., lxxxvii, 1954)

Warkworth, J., *A Chronicle of the First Thirteen Years of the Reign of King Edward IV*, ed. J.O. Halliwell (London, 1839)

The Wars of Edward III: Sources and Interpretations, ed. C.J. Rogers (Woodbridge, 1999)

The Westminster Chronicle: 1381–1394, ed. and trans. L.C. Hector and B.F. Harvey (Oxford, 1982)

William 'Gregory', *Chronicle*, ed. J. Gairdner, *The Historical Collections of a Citizen of London in the Fifteenth Century* (London, 1876)

William le Breton, *Philippidos*, ed. H.-F. Delaborde, *Oeuvres de Rigord et de Guillaume le Breton, historiens de Philippe-Auguste*, 2 vols (Paris, 1882), II, 1–385

William of Apulia, *Gesta Roberti Wiscardi*, ed. D.R. Williams, MGH SS, IX (Hanover, 1851), 239–98

William of Apulia, *La Geste de Robert Guiscard*, ed. M. Mathieu (Palermo, 1961)

William of Malmesbury, *Gesta regum anglorum*, ed. and trans. R.A.B. Mynors, R.M. Thompson and M. Winterbottom, 2 vols (Oxford, 1998–9)

William of Malmesbury, *Historia Novella*, ed. E. King and K.R. Potter (Oxford, 1998)

William of Newburgh, *Historia Rerum Anglicarum*, ed. R. Howlett, *Chronicles of the Reigns of Stephen, Henry II and Richard I*, I (London, 1884)

William of Poitiers, *Gesta Guillelmi*, ed. and trans. R.H.C. Davies and M. Chibnall, *The Gesta Guillelmi of William of Poitiers* (Oxford, 1998)

William Thorne's Chronicle of Saint Augustine's Abbey Canterbury, trans. A.H. Davis (Oxford, 1934)

Wilson, D.M., *The Bayeux Tapestry* (London and New York, 1985)

The Writings of Christine de Pizan, ed. C.C. Willard (New York, 1994)

Wrottesley, C., *Crécy and Calais from the Public Records* (London, 1898)

York Civic Records, ed. A. Raine, 9 vols (Yorkshire Archaeological Society, Record Series, 1939–78)

York Memorandum Book, ed. M. Sellers (Surtees Society, cxx, 1911)

SECONDARY LITERATURE

Abels, R., *Lordship and Military Obligation in Anglo-Saxon England* (Berkeley, 1988)

Abratowski, A., 'The Bow in Poland', *JSAA*, xliv (2001)

Adams, D., 'Archer in the Highlands', *Military Illustrated*, cxi (August, 1997)

——, *Making the Boughstave Longbow* (Lincoln, 1988)

——, 'Some Unrecognized Depictions of the Saffron Shirt in Scotland', *Northern Studies*, xxx (1993)

Alcock, L., 'Gwyr y Gogledd: An Archaeological Approach', *Archaeologica Cambrensis*, cxxxii (1984 for 1983), 1–18

Allmand, C.T., 'Changing Views of the Soldier in Late Medieval France', in P. Contamine, C. Giry-Deloison and M.H. Keen, eds, *Guerre et société en France, en Angleterre et en Bourgogne, XIVe–XVe siècle* (Lille, 1991), 171–88

——, *Henry V* (London, 1992)

——, 'Henry V the Soldier and the War with France', in Harriss, ed., *Henry V*, 117–35

——, *Lancastrian Normandy, 1415–1450. The History of a Medieval Occupation* (Oxford, 1983)

——, *Society at War: The Experience of England and France During the Hundred Years War* (Edinburgh, 1973)

Alm, J., *European Crossbows: A Survey*, trans. H. Bartlett Wells, ed. G.M. Wilson (London, 1993)

Anglo, S., 'Le Jeu de la Hache. A Fifteenth century Treatise on the Technique of Chivalric Axe Combat', *Archaeologia*, cix (1991), 112–28

Armitage-Smith, S., *John of Gaunt* (London, 1904)

Armstrong, C.A.J., 'Politics and the Battle of St Albans, 1455', *BIHR*, xxxiii (1960)

Armstrong, P., *Bannockburn 1314* (Botley, 2002)

Arnold, C.J., *The Anglo-Saxon Cemeteries of the Isle of Wight* (London, 1982)

Ashdown, C.H., *British and Foreign Arms and Armour* (London, 1909)

Astill, G.G., 'An Early Inventory of a Leicestershire Knight', *Midland History*, ii (1974), 274–83

Atiya, A.S., *The Crusade of Nicopolis* (London, 1934)

Audoin, E., *Essai sur l'armée royale au temps de Philippe Auguste* (Paris, 1913)

Autrand, F., *Charles V le Sage* (Paris, 1994)

Avent, R., *Castles of the Princes of Gwynedd* (Cardiff, 1982)

Ayton, A., 'Edward III and the English Aristocracy at the Beginning of the Hundred Years War', in M. Strickland, ed., *Armies, Chivalry and Warfare*, 173–206

——, 'English Armies in the Fourteenth Century', in A. Curry and M. Hughes, eds, *Arms, Armies and Fortifications in the Hundred Years War* (Woodbridge, 1994), 21–38

——, 'The English Army and the Normandy Campaign of 1346', in *England and Normandy in the Middle Ages*, ed. D. Bates and A. Curry (London, 1994), 253–68

——, *Knights and Warhorses. Military Service and the English Aristocracy under Edward III* (Woodbridge, 1994)

——, 'Military Service and the Development of the Robin Hood Legend in the Fourteenth Century', *Nottingham Medieval Studies*, xxxvi (1992), 126–47

——, 'Sir Thomas Ughtred and the Edwardian Military Revolution', in *The Age of Edward III*, ed. J.S. Bothwell (York, 2001), 107–32

Baatz, D., 'Die Römische Jagdarmbrust', *Archäeologisches Korrespondenzblatt*, xxi (1991), 283–99

Bachrach, B., *Armies and Politics in the Early Medieval West* (Aldershot, 1993)

——, *Early Carolingian Warfare. Prelude to Empire* (Philadelphia, 2001)

——, 'On the Origins of William the Conqueror's Horse Transports', *Technology and Culture*, xxvi (1985), 505–31

——, 'A Picture of Avar–Frankish Warfare from a Carolingian Psalter of the Early Ninth Century in the Light of the *Strategicon*', *Archivum Eurasiae Medii Aevi*, iv (1986), 5–27; repr. in Bachrach, *Armies and Politics*, 5–27

——, 'Procopius, Agathias and the Frankish Military', *Speculum*, xlv (1970), 435–41

Backhouse, J., ed. *The Golden Age of Anglo-Saxon Art, 966–1066* (London, 1984)

Bacquet, G., *Azincourt* (Bellegarde, 1977)

Baldwin, J.W., *The Government of Philip Augustus: Foundations of French Royal Power in the Middle Ages* (Berkeley, 1986)

——, *Masters, Princes and Merchants: The Circle of Peter the Chanter*, 2 vols (Princeton, 1970)

Ballard, M., 'An Expedition of English Archers in 1467, and the Anglo-Burgundian Marriage Alliance', *Nottingham Medieval Studies*, xxxiv (1990), 152–74

Barber, R., *Edward, Prince of Wales and Aquitaine* (London, 1978)

Barker, J., *The Tournament in England, 1100–1400* (Woodbridge, 1986)

Barnard, F.P., *Edward IV's Expedition of 1475: The Leaders and their Badges* (Oxford, 1925)

Barr, N., *Flodden* (Stroud, 2003)

Barraclough, G., *The Earldom and County Palatinate of Chester* (Oxford, 1953)

Barrow, G.W.S., *The Anglo-Norman Era in Scottish History* (Oxford, 1980)

——, *Robert Bruce and the Community of the Realm of Scotland* (Edinburgh, 1988)

Bartlett, R., *Gerald of Wales, 1146–1223* (Oxford, 1982)

——, *The Making of Europe: Conquest, Colonization and Cultural Change, 950–1350* (London, 1993)

Bartlett, T. and Jeffery, K., *A Military History of Ireland* (Cambridge, 1996)

Bartlett Wells, H., 'A Problem in the Techniques of the Medieval European Swordsmith', *Journal of the Arms and Armour Society*, iv (1964)

Baudry, M.-P., 'Le château des Plantagenêt à Niort', in *Les fortifications dans les domaines Plantagenêt*, 23–40

——, 'Le château du Coudray-Salbart', *Bulletin archéologique du comité des travaux historiques et scientifiques*, nouv. sér., xxiii–iv (1991), 137–212

——, ed. *Les fortifications dans le domains Plantagenêt, XIIe–XIVe siècle: actes du colloque international tenu à Poitiers du 11 au 13 novembre 1994* (Poitiers, 2000)

Bayet, J., 'Le symbolisme du cerf et du centaure à la Porte rouge de Notre-Dame de Paris', *Revue archéologique*, xliv (1954)

Beamish, T., *Battle Royal: A New Account of Simon de Montfort's Struggle against King Henry III* (London, 1965)

Bean, J.M.W., 'Henry IV and the Percies', *History*, xliv (1959), 212–27

Beck, J.T., *The Cutting Edge. The Early History of the Surgeons of London* (London, 1974)

Beeler, J., *Warfare in England, 1066–1189* (New York, 1966)

Bellamy, J.G., *Robin Hood: An Historical Enquiry* (London, 1985)

Belloc, H., *Crécy* (London, 1912)

Bémont, C., 'La campagne de Poitou, 1242–1243. Taillebourg et Saintes', *Annales de Midi*, v (1893), 289–314

——, *Simont de Montfort* (Paris, 1884)

Bennett, M., *Agincourt: Triumph Against the Odds* (London, 1991)

——, 'The Battle', in A. Curry, ed., *Agincourt, 1415: Henry V, Sir Thomas Erpingham and the Triumph of the English Archers* (Stroud, 2000), 21–36

——, *The Battle of Bosworth* (Gloucester, 1985)

——, 'The Crusaders' "Fighting March" Revisited', *War in History*, vii (2001), 1–18

——, 'The Development of Battle Tactics in the Hundred Years War', in A. Curry and M. Hughes, eds, *Arms, Armies and Fortifications in the Hundred Years War* (Woodbridge, 1994), 1–20

——, 'The Knight Unmasked', *Military History Quarterly*, vii (1995), 8–19

——, 'The Medieval Warhorse Reconsidered', in S. Church and R. Harvey. eds, *Medieval Knighthood, V. Papers from the Sixth Strawberry Hill Conference, 1994* (Woodbridge, 1995), 19–40

——, 'Poetry and History? The Roman de Rou as a Source for the Norman Conquest', *Anglo-Norman Studies*, v (1982), 21–39

——, 'Wace and Warfare', *Anglo-Norman Studies*, xi (1988), 37–58; repr. in Strickland, ed. *Anglo-Norman Warfare*, 230–50

—— and Hooper, N., *Cambridge Illustrated Atlas: Warfare. The Middle Ages, 769–1487* (Cambridge, 1996)

Bennett, M.J., *Community, Class and Careerism. Cheshire and Lancashire Society in the Age of the Sir Gawain and the Green Knight* (Cambridge, 1983)

Benson, L.D., *The Riverside Chaucer* (3rd edn, Boston, 1987)

Bergman, C.A., Miller, R. and McEwen, E., 'Experimental Archery: Projectile Velocities and Comparison of Bow Performances', *Antiquity*, lxii (1988)

Bériac-Laine, F. and Given-Wilson, C., *Les prisonniers de la bataille de Poitiers* (Paris, 2002)

Bernstein, D.J., *The Mystery of the Bayeux Tapestry* (London, 1986)

Bessa, C., 'Le Portugal 1383–1385: crise, art militaire et consolidation de l'indépendence', in *From Crécy to Móhacs: Warfare in the Later Middle Ages (1346–1526)*, International Commission of Military History (Vienna, 1997), 28–50

Beverley-Smith, L., 'The Death of Llewelyn ap Gruffydd: The Narrative Reconsidered', *Welsh History Review*, xi (1982), 200–13

Birrell, J., 'Forest Law and the Peasantry in the Later Thirteenth Century', in P.R. Coss and S.D. Lloyd, eds, *Thirteenth Century England II. Proceedings of the Newcastle upon Tyne Conference, 1987*, 149–63

——, 'Peasant Deer Poachers in the Medieval Forest', in J. Britnell and J. Hatcher, eds, *Progress and Problems in Medieval England. Essays in Honour of Edward Miller* (Cambridge, 1996), 66–88

——, 'Who Poached the King's Deer?', *Midland History*, vii (1982)

Bivar, A.D.H., 'Cavalry Equipment and Tactics on the Euphrates Frontier', *Dumbarton Oaks Papers*, xxvi (1972), 271–92

Blaauw, W.H., *The Barons' War, including the Battles of Lewes and Evesham* (2nd edn, London, 1871)

Blackburn, T.P.D., Edge, D., Williams, A.R. and Adams, C.B.T., 'Head Protection in England Before the First World War', *Neurosurgery*, xlvii (December, 2000), 1261–86

Blackmore, H.L., *Hunting Weapons* (London, 1971)

Blair, C., *European Arms and Armour, c. 1100–1850* (London, 1962)

Blyth, J.D., 'The Battle of Tewksbury', *Transactions of the Bristol and Gloucestershire Archaeological Society*, lxxx (1961), 99–120

Boardman, A.W., *The Medieval Soldier: The Men Who Fought in the Wars of the Roses* (Stroud, 1998)

Boase, A.J., *Crusader Archaeology. The Material Culture of the Latin East* (London and New York, 1999)

Boccia, L., *Armi et Armature Lombarde* (Milan, 1980)

—— and Coelho, E.T., *L'Arte dell'Armatura in Italia* (Milan, 1967)

Bohna, M., 'Armed Force and Civic Legitimacy in Jack Cade's Revolt, 1450', *EHR*, cxviii (2003), 563–82

Bolland, W.C., *A Manual of Year Book Studies* (Cambridge, 1925)

Bossy, M.-A., 'Arms and the Bride: Christine de Pizan's Military Treatise as a Wedding Gift for Margaret of Anjou', in M. Desmond, ed., *Christine de Pizan and the Categories of Difference* (Minneapolis, 1998), 236–56

Boudot-Lamotte, A., *Contribution à l'étude de l'archerie musulmanne* (Damascus, 1968)

Boylston, A., Sutherland, S., Holst, T. and Coughlan, J., 'Burials from the battle of Towton', *Royal Armouries Yearbook*, ii (1997), 36–9

Boynton, L., *The Elizabethan Militia* (London and Toronto, 1967)

Bradbury, J., *The Battle of Hastings* (Stroud, 1998)

——, 'Battles in England and Normandy, 1066–1154', *Anglo-Norman Studies*, vi (1984), 1–12; repr. in Strickland, ed. *Anglo-Norman Warfare*, 182–93

——, *The Medieval Archer* (Woodbridge, 1985)

——, *The Medieval Siege* (Woodbridge, 1992)

——, *Stephen and Matilda* (Stroud, 1996)

Bradford, E., *The Story of the Mary Rose* (Book Club Associates, 1982)

Brookes, F.W., *The Battle of Stamford Bridge* (East Yorkshire Local History series, vi, 1956)

——, *The English Naval Forces, 1199–1272* (London, 1932)

——, 'Naval Armament in the Thirteenth Century', *The Mariner's Mirror*, xiv (1928), 115–31

—— and Oakley, F., 'The Campaign and Battle of Lincoln, 1217', *Associated Architectural Societies' Reports and Papers*, xxxvi, pt 2 (1922), 295–312

Brooks, N., 'The Organisation and Achievements of the Peasants of Kent and Essex in 1381', in H. Mayr-Harting and R.I. Moore, eds, *Studies in Medieval History presented to R.H.C. Davis* (London, 1985), 247–70

Brown, G.B., *The Arts in Early England*, 6 vols (London, 1903–37)

Brown, M., *James I* (Edinburgh, 1994)

——, 'The Development of Scottish Border Lordship, 1332–1358', *Historical Research*, lxx (1997), 1–22

Brown, R.A., 'The Battle of Hastings', *Proceedings of the Battle Conference on Anglo-Norman Studies*, iii (1980), 1–21; repr. in Strickland, ed. *Anglo-Norman Warfare*, 161–81

——, *Castles, Conquest and Charters: collected papers* (Woodbridge, 1989)

——, 'Framlingham Castle and Bigod, 1154–1216', *Suffolk Institute of Archaeology and Natural History*, xxv (1950), 127–48

——, 'Royal Castle Building in England, 1154–1216', *EHR*, lxx (1955), 353–98

——, Colvin, H.M. and Taylor, A.J., eds, *The History of the King's Works*, I (London, 1963)

Brown, R.C., 'Observations on the Berkhamstead Bow', *JSAA*, x (1967), 12–17

Brucker, G.A., 'The Ciompi Revolution', in N. Rubinstein, ed., *Florentine Studies. Politics and Society in Renaissance Florence* (London, 1968), 314–56

Brun, R., 'Notes sur le commerce des armes à Avignon au XIVème siècle', *Bibliothèque de L'École des Chartes* (1951), 217–25

Brundage, J.A., 'Holy War and the Medieval Lawyers', in T.P. Murphy, ed., *The Holy War* (Columbus, Ohio, 1976), 99–140

——, 'The Limits of War-Making Power: The Contribution of Medieval Canonists', in C.J. Reid, Jnr, ed., *Peace in a Nuclear Age: The Bishops' Pastoral Letter in Perspective* (Washington, DC, 1986), 69–85

——, *Medieval Canon Law and the Crusader* (Madison, Milwaukee and London, 1969)

Brusten, C., *L'armée bourguignonne de 1465 à 1468* (Brussels, 1953)

——, 'L'armée bourguignonne de 1465 à 1477', *Revue internationale de l'histoire militaire*, xx (1959), 452–66

Bueno de Mesquita, D.M., 'Some Condottieri of the Trecento and their Relations with Political Authority', *Proceedings of the British Academy*, xxxii (1946), 219–41

Burgess, M., 'The Mail-maker's Technique', *Antiquaries Journal*, xxxiii (1953), 48–55

Burne, A.H., *The Agincourt War: A Military History of the Latter Part of the Hundred Years War from 1369–1453* (London, 1956)

——, 'The Battle of Neville's Cross', *Durham University Journal*, x (1948–9)

——, 'The Battle of Poitiers', *EHR*, liii (1938), 21–52

——, 'The Battle of Shrewsbury: A Military Reconstruction', *Transactions of the Shropshire Archaeological Society*, lii (1947–8)

——, *The Battlefields of England* (London, 1973)

——, 'Cannon at Crécy', *Royal Artillery Journal*, lxxvii (1939)

——, *The Crécy War: A Military History of the Hundred Years War from 1337 to the Peace of Brétigny, 1360* (London, 1955)

——, *More Battlefields of England* (London, 1952)

Burns, R.I., 'The Medieval Crossbow as a Surgical Instrument: An Illustrated Case History', *Bulletin of the New York Academy of Medicine*, xlviii, no. 8 (September 1972), 983–9

Bush, H.R., ed., 'La bataille de Trente Anglois et Trente Bretons', *Modern Philology*, ix (1911–12), 511–44, and x (1912–13), 82–136

Buttin, F., 'La lance et l'arrêt de cuirasse', *Archaeologia*, xcix (1965), 77–114

Caferro, W., *Mercenary Companies and the Decline of Siena* (Baltimore, 1998)

Cahen, C., 'Les changements techniques militaires dans le Proche Orient médiéval et leur importance historique', in Parry and Yapp, eds, *War, Technology and Society in the Middle East*, 112–24

——, 'Une traité d'armurie composé pour Saladin', *Bulletin d'Etudes Orientales*, xii (1947–8), 103–63

Camille, M., *A Mirror in Parchment. The Luttrell Psalter and the Making of Medieval England* (London, 1998)

Campbell, A., *Highland Dress, Arms and Ornament* (Westminster, 1899)

Campbell, D.B., 'Auxiliary Artillery Revisited', *Bonner Jahrbücher*, clxxxvi (1986), 117–32

Campbell, M., *The English Yeoman under Elizabeth and the Early Stuarts* (Yale, 1942)

Canestrini, G., 'Documenti per sevire alla Storia della Milizia Italiana', *Archivio Storico Italiano*, xv (1851)

Carpenter, D.A., *The Battles of Lewes and Evesham, 1264/5* (Keele, 1987)

——, *The Minority of Henry III* (London, 1990)

Carpenter, D.M., 'The Pilgrim from Catalonia/Aragon: Ramon de Perellós, 1397', in M. Haren and Y. de Pontfarcy, eds, *The Medieval Pilgrimage to St Patrick's Purgatory Lough Derg and the European Tradition* (Enniskillen, 1988), 99–119

Carr, A.D., 'Teulu and Penteulu' in T.-M. Charles-Edwards, M.E. Owen and P. Russell, eds, *The Welsh King and his Court* (Cardiff, 2000)

Cathcart King, D.J., 'Henry II and the Fight at Coleshill', *Welsh History Review*, ii (1964–5), 367–75

Chabloz, F., *La bataille de Grandson d'après vingt-sept auteurs* (Lausanne, 1897)

Chabot-Tramecourt, V. de, *Patrimonie d'un Gentilhomme en Artois* (XVIIIe siècle)

Chaliand, G., *The Art of War in World History: from Antiquity to the Nuclear Age* (Berkeley, 1994)

Chamberlain, E.R., 'The English Mercenary Companies in Italy', *History Today*, vi, no. 5 (May, 1956), 334–43

Chareyron, N., *Jean le Bel. Le Maître de Froissart, Grand Imagier de la guerre de Cent Ans* (Brussels, 1996)

Charles-Edwards, T.M., 'Irish Warfare before 1100', in Bartlett and Jeffery, eds, *A Military History of Ireland*, 26–51

Chauvelays, J. de la, *Les armées de Charles le Téméraire dans les deux bourgognes* (Paris, 1879)

——, *Diverses organizations des armées de Charles le Téméraire*

Chenevix-Trench, C., *History of Marksmanship* (London, 1972)

Chevalier, B., 'Les Écossais dans les armées des Charles VII jusqu'à la bataille de Verneuil', *Jeanne d'Arc: une époque, un rayonnement* (Paris, 1982)

Chevedden, P.E., 'Artillery in Late Antiquity: Prelude to the Middle Ages', in I.A. Corfis and M. Wolfe, eds, *The Medieval City under Siege* (Woodbridge, 1995), 131–73

Chibnall, M., 'Mercenaries and the Familia Regis under Henry I', *History*, lxii (1977), 15–23; repr. in Strickland, ed., *Anglo-Norman Warfare*, 84–92

Chrimes, S.B., *Henry VII* (London, 1977)

Christlein, R., *Die Alamannen* (Stuttgart, 1978)

Church, S.D., 'The 1210 Campaign in Ireland: Evidence for a Military Revolution', *Anglo-Norman Studies*, xx (1997), 45–57

Clark, G. and Godwin, H., 'Prehistoric Ancestors of the Weapons which brought England victory at Crécy, Poitiers and Agincourt: Neolithic Longbows of 4,500 years ago, found in the Somersetshire Peat', *Illustrated London News* (10 February 1962)

Clark, G.T., *Medieval Military Architecture*, 2 vols (London, 1884)

Clark, J.D.G., 'Neolithic Bows from Somerset, England, and the Prehistory of Archery in North-western Europe', *Proceedings of the Prehistoric Society*, xxix (1963), 50–98

Colardelle, R. and Colardelle, M., 'L'habitat médiéval immergé de Colletière à Charavines (Isère)', *Archaelogie Medievale*, x (1980), 167–219

Cole, H. and Lang, T., 'Treating Prince Henry's Arrow Wound, 1403', *JSAA* (2003), 95–101

Collins, H.E.L., *The Order of the Garter, 1348–1461: Chivalry and Politics in Late Medieval England* (Oxford, 2000)

Collis, M., *The Hurling Time* (London, 1958)

Constable, A., *A History of Greater Britain* (Scottish Historical Society, 1892)

Contamine, P., *Guerre, état et société à la fin du Moyen Age: études sur les armées des rois de France, 1337–1494* (Paris, 1972)

——, *War in the Middle Ages* (Oxford, 1984)

Conti, F., *Castelli d'Itali* (Touring Club Italiano, 1995)

Cooper, J., ed., *The Battle of Maldon. Fiction and Fact* (London, 1993)

Coplin, J., 'L'arbalète en médecine', *Les Arbaletrieri Bruxellois*, iv (1996)

Cosgrove, A., ed., *A New History of Ireland, II. Medieval Ireland, 1169–1534* (Oxford, 1987)

Cosneau, E., *Le connétable de Richemont, Arthur de Bretagne: 1393–1458* (Paris, 1886)

Cosson, B. de, 'The Crossbow of Ulrich V Count of Wurtemburg, 1460, with remarks on its Construction', *Archaeologia*, lii (1892), 445–65

Cottrill, F., 'A Medieval Description of a Bow and Arrow', *The Antiquaries Journal*, xxiii (1943), 54–5

Coulston, J.C., 'Roman Archery Equipment', in M.C. Bishop, ed., *The Production and Distribution of Roman Military Equipment* (Oxford, 1985)

Coulton, G.G., *Social Life in Britain* (Cambridge, repr. 1968)

Coupland, S., 'Carolingian Arms and Armour in the Ninth Century', *Viator*, xxi (1990), 29–50

Cowdrey, H.E.J., 'Bishop Ermenfrid of Sion and the Penitential Ordinance following the Battle of Hastings', *Journal of Ecclesiastical History*, xx (1969), 225–42

Cox, D.C., *The Battle of Evesham* (Evesham, 1965)

——, *The Battle of Evesham: A New Account* (Evesham, 1988)

——, 'The Battle of Evesham in the Evesham Chronicle', *Historical Research*, lxii (1989), 337–45

Cox, J.C., *The Royal Forests of England* (London, 1905)

Credland, A.G., 'The Crossbow in Europe: A Historical Introduction', in Paterson, ed., *The Crossbow*

——, 'Crossbow Remains, Part 1', *JSAA*, xxiii (1980)

Crook, D., 'Concerning the Dating of the Origins of Robin Hood', *EHR*, lxxxxviiii (1984), 530–4; repr. in Knight, ed., *Robin Hood*, 257–61

——, 'The Sheriff of Nottingham and Robin Hood: The Genesis of the Legend?', in P.R. Coss and S.D. Lloyd, eds, *Thirteenth Century England, II. Proceedings of the Newcastle upon Tyne Conference, 1987* (Woodbridge, 1988), 59–68

——, 'Some Further Evidence Concerning the Dating of the Origins of the Legend of Robin Hood', *EHR*, 99 (1984), 530–4; repr. S. Knight, ed., *Robin Hood: An Anthology* (Cambridge, 1999) 257–61

Crouch, D., *The Beaumont Twins. The Roots and Branches of Power in the Twelfth Century* (Cambridge, 1986)

——, *The Image of Aristocracy in Britain, 1000–1300* (London, 1992)

——, 'The March and the Welsh Kings', in King, ed., *The Anarchy of King Stephen's Reign*, 255–89

Cruden, S., *The Scottish Castle* (Edinburgh and London, 1960)

Cruickshank, C., *Army Royal. Henry VIII's Invasion of France, 1513* (Oxford, 1969)

——, *Elizabeth's Army* (2nd edn, Oxford, 1966)

Cummings, J.G., *The Hound and the Hawk. The Art of Medieval Hunting* (London, 1988)

Curnow, P.E., 'Some Developments in Military Architecture c. 1200: Le Coudray-Salbart', *Anglo-Norman Studies*, ii (1980), 42–62

Curry, A., 'English Armies in the Fifteenth Century', in A. Curry and M. Hughes, eds, *Arms, Armies and Fortifications in the Hundred Years War* (Woodbridge, 1994), 39–68

——, 'The First English Standing Army? Military Organization in Lancastrian Normandy, 1420–1450', in C. Ross, ed., *Pedigree, Patronage and Power in Late Medieval England* (Gloucester, 1979), 193–214

——, 'Isolated or Integrated? The English Soldier in Lancastrian Normandy', in *Courts and Regions in Medieval Europe*, ed. S.R. Jones, R. Marks and A.J. Minnis (Woodbridge, 2000), 191–210

——, 'Les "gens vivans sur le païs" pendant l'occupation anglaise de la Normandie (1417–1450)', in P. Contamine and O. Guyotjeannin, eds, *La Guerre, la violence et les gens au Moyen Age, I: Guerre et violence* (Paris, 1996), 209–21

——, *The Hundred Years War* (London, 1993)

——, 'The Organisation of Field Armies in Lancastrian Normandy', in M. Strickland, ed., *Armies, Warfare and Chivalry*, 207–33

——, 'Sir Thomas Erpingham', in *Agincourt, 1415*, ed. Curry, 53–77

Curtis, E., *Richard II in Ireland, 1394–5* (Oxford, 1927)

Dalton, P., *Conquest, Anarchy and Lordship. Yorkshire, 1066–1154* (Cambridge, 1994)

D'Arcy Boulton, J., *Knights of the Crown: the Monarchal Orders of Knighthood in Late Medieval Europe* (Woodbridge, 2000)

Davidsohn, R., *Storia di Firenze*, 5 vols (Florence, 1957–73)

Davies, C.S.L., 'Henry VIII and Henry V: The War in France', in J.L. Watts, ed., *The End of the Middle Ages? England in the Fifteenth and Sixteenth Centuries* (Stroud, 1998)

Davies, J.L., 'Roman Arrowheads from Dinorben and the *Sagitarii* of the Roman Army', *Britannia*, viii (1997), 357–70

Davies, R.R., *Conquest, Coexistence and Change: Wales, 1063–1415* (Oxford, 1987)

Davies, S., 'Native Welsh Military Institutions, c. 1033–1283' (Doctoral thesis, University of Wales College, Cardiff, 2000)

Davis, R.H.C., 'William of Poitiers and his History of William the Conqueror', in *The Writing of History in the Middle Ages*, ed. R.H.C. Davis and J.M. Wallace-Hadrill (Oxford, 1981), 71–100

Delachenal, R., *Histoire de Charles V*, 5 vols (Paris, 1909–31)

Delauney, L.-A., *Etude sur les anciennes compagnies d'archers, d'arbalétriers, et d'arquebusiers* (Paris, 1879)

Delbrück, H., *A History of the Art of War Within the Framework of Political History*, trans. W.J. Renfroe, Jnr, 4 vols (Westport, 1975)

Deuchler, F., *Die Burgundebeute* (Bern, 1963)

De Laborderie, O., Maddicott, J.R., and Carpenter, D.A., 'The Last Hours of Simon de Montfort: A New Account', *EHR*, cxv (2000), 378–412

De Vos, L., 'La bataille de Gavere le 23 juillet 1453. La victoire de l'organization', in *From Crécy to Móhacs: Warfare in the Later Middle Ages (1346–1526)*, International Commission of Military History (Vienna, 1997), 145–57

DeVries, K., 'Catapults are Not Atomic Bombs: Towards a Redefinition of "Effectiveness" in Premodern Military Technology', *War in History*, iv (1997), 454–70

——, 'Contemporary Views of Edward III's failure at the Siege of Tournai, 1340', *Nottingham Medieval Studies*, xxxix (1995), 70–105

——, 'God, Admirals, Archery and Flemings: Perceptions of Victory and Defeat at the Battle of Sluys, 1340', *American Neptune*, lv (1995), 223–42

——, 'Harold Godwineson in Wales: Military Legitimacy in Late Anglo-Saxon England', in R.P. Abels and B.S. Bachrach, eds, *The Normans and their Adversaries at War* (Woodbridge, 2001), 65–86

——, *Infantry Warfare in the Early Fourteenth-Century: discipline, tactics and technology* (Woodbridge, 1996)

——, *Medieval Military Technology* (Peterborough, Ontario, 1994)

——, *The Norwegian Invasion of England in 1066* (Woodbridge, 1999)

Dickens, B., 'The Late Addition to *ASC* 1066 C', *Proceedings of the Leeds Philosophical and Literary Society*, v (1940)

Dickinson, G., 'Some Notes on the Scottish Army in the First Half of the Sixteenth Century', *SHR*, xxviii (1949), 133–45

Dickinson, W.C., 'The Acts of Parliament at Perth, 6 March 1429/30', *SHR*, xxix (1950), 1–12

Dillon, H.A., 'Arms and Armour at Westminster, the Tower and Greenwich, 1547', *Archaeologia*, li (1888), pt 1, 219–80

——, 'On an MS Collection of Ordinances of Chivalry of the Fifteenth Century Belonging to Lord Hastings', *Archaeologia*, lvii (1900), 29–70

Ditcham, B.G.H., 'The Employment of Foreign Mercenary Troops in the French Royal Armies, 1415–70' (Ph.D thesis, University of Edinburgh, 1979)

——, '"Mutton Guzzlers and Wine Bags". Foreign Soldiers and Native Reactions in Fifteenth Century France', in C.T. Allmand, ed., *Power, Culture and Religion in France* (Woodbridge, 1989), 1–13

Dixon, M.C., 'John de Coupland – Hero to Villain', in Rollason and Prestwich, eds, *The Battle of Neville's Cross*, 36–49

Dobson, R.B. and Taylor, J., 'General Review: Robin Hood', *Northern History*, xxvi (1990), 229

—— and ——, 'Robin Hood of Barnesdale: A Fellow Thou Hast long Sought', *Northern History*, xix (1983)

Do Paço, A., 'The Battle of Aljubarotta', *Antiquity*, xxxvii (1963)

Dousseau, J.-M., *La Bataille de Cravant (1423)* (Auxerre, 1987)

Druett, W., *Harrow Through the Ages* (Uxbridge, 1935)

Drury, J.L., 'The Monument at Neville's Cross, C. Durham', in Rollason and Prestwich, eds, *The Battle of Neville's Cross*, 78–96

Duby, G., *The Legend of Bouvines*, trans. C. Tihanyi (Cambridge, 1990)

Dufourcq, C.E., *L'Espagne Catalane et le Mahgrib aux XIII et XIV siècles* (Paris, 1966)

Du Fresne de Beaucourt, G., *Histoire de Charles VII*, 6 vols (Paris, 1881–91)

Dunbar, J.T., *History of Highland Dress* (Edinburgh, 1962)

Duncan, A.A.M., 'Honi soit qui mal y pense: David II and Edward III, 1346–52', *SHR*, lxvii (1988), 113–41

——, *Scotland: The Making of the Kingdom* (Edinburgh, 1975)

——, 'The War of the Scots, 1306–23', *TRHS*, 6th ser., ii (1992), 125–51

Dunham, W.H., *Lord Hastings' Indentured Retinues, 1461–1483* (Connecticut, 1955)

Dyer, C., *Everyday Life in Medieval England* (London, 1994)

——, *Standards of Living in the Later Middle Ages* (Cambridge, 1989)

Eames, E.S., *Catalogue of Medieval Lead-Glazed Earthenware Tiles in the Department of Medieval and Later Antiquities, British Museum*, 2 vols (London, 1980)

Edwards, J.G., 'The Battle of Maes Moydog and the Welsh campaign of 1294–5', *EHR*, xxxix (1924), 1–12

——, 'Henry II and the Fight at Coleshill: Some Further Reflections', *Welsh History Review*, iii (1966–7), 251–63

——, 'The Site of the Battle of "Meismeidoc", 1295 (Note)', *EHR*, xlvi (1931), 262–5

Ellis, H., *A General Introduction to Domesday Book* (London, 1833)

Ellis, S.G., 'The Tudors and the Origins of the Modern Irish States: A Standing Army', in Bartlett and Jeffery, eds, *A Military History of Ireland*, 116–35

Embleton, G., *Medieval Military Costume* (2000)

Engelhardt, H.C.C., *Nydam Mosefund, 1859–63* (Copenhagen, 1865)

Englehardt, C., *Denmark in the Early Iron Age* (London, 1866)

——, *Vimose Fundet* (Copenhagen, 1929)

Epstein, S.A., *Genoa and the Genoese, 958–1528* (North Carolina, 1996)

Esper, T., 'The replacement of the Longbow by Firearms in the English Army', *Technology and Culture*, vi (1965), 382–93

Evans, D.L., 'Some Notes on the Principality of Wales in the Time of the Black Prince', *Transactions of the Honourable Society of Cymmrodorion* (1926)

Evison, V.I., 'Sugar Loaf Shield Bosses', *Antiquaries Journal*, xliii (1963), 38–96

Farmer, D.H., *The Oxford Dictionary of Saints* (2nd edn, 1987)

Farnham, G.F. and Skillington, S.H., 'The Skeffingtons of Skeffington', *Leicestershire Archaeological Society Transactions*, xvi (1929–31)

Farrell, R.T.A., 'The Archer and Associated Figures on the Ruthwell Cross – A Reconsideration', in R.T.A. Farrell, ed., *Bede and Anglo-Saxon England*, British Archaeological Reports (British Series), xlvi (1978), 96–117

Ferguson, A.B., *The Indian Summer of English Chivalry: Studies in the Decline and Transformation of Chivalric Idealism* (Durham, NC, 1960)

Ferguson, P.S., 'Notes on the Initial Letter of a Charter of Edward II to the City of Carlisle', *Archaeological Journal*, xxxix (1882)

Fergusson, J., 'A Pair of Butts', *SHR*, xxxiv (1955), 19–25

Fernie, E.C., *An Architectural History of Norwich Cathedral* (Oxford, 1993)

Ffoulkes, C., *The Armourer and his Craft. From the XIth to the XVIth Century* (London, 1912)

——, 'Italian Armour at Chalcis in the Ethnological Museum at Athens', *Archaeologia*, lxii (1910), 381–90

Fino, J.F., 'Machines de jet médiévales', *Gladius*, x (1972), 25–43

Fiorato, V., 'Towton, AD 1461. Excavation of a Mass War Grave', *Current Archaeology*, clxxi (vol. VX, no. iii, December 2000), 98–103

——, Boylston, A. and Knusel, C., *Blood Red Roses: The Archaeology of a Mass Grave from the Battle of Towton AD 1461* (Oxbow, 2000)

Flanagan, M.T., 'Irish and Anglo-Norman Warfare in Twelfth-Century Ireland', in T. Bartlett and K. Jeffery, eds, *A Military History of Ireland* (Cambridge, 1996), 52–75

——, *Irish Society, Anglo-Norman Settlers, Angevin Kingship: Interactions in Ireland in the Late Twelfth Century* (Oxford, 1989)

Fletcher, W.G.D., 'Some Documents Relative to the Battle of Shrewsbury', *Transactions of the Shropshire Archaeological Society*, x (1898)

Foote, P.G. and Wilson, D.M., *The Viking Achievement* (London, 1970)

Foss, P.J., 'The Battle of Bosworth: A Reassessment', *Midland History*, xiii (1988)

——, *The Field of Redemore: The Battle of Bosworth, 1485* (2nd edn, Newton Linford, 1998)

Foulds, T., 'The Siege of Nottingham Castle in 1194', *Transactions of the Thoroton Society of Nottinghamshire*, xcv (1991), 20–8

Fournier, P., 'La prohibition par le IIe Concile Latran d'armes jugées trop meurtrières (1139)', *Revue générale du droit international public*, xxiii (1916), 471–9

Fowler, G.H., 'Munitions in 1224', *Bedfordshire Historical Record Society*, v (1920), 117–32

Fowler, K., *The Age of Plantagenet and Valois: The Struggle for Supremacy, 1328–1498* (London, 1967)

——, 'Deux entrepreneurs militaires au XIVe siècle: Bertrand du Guesclin et Sir Hugh Calveley', *Le Combattant au Moyen Age* (Paris, 2nd edn, 1995), 243–56

——, 'L'emploi des mercenaires par les pouvoirs ibériques et l'intervention militaire anglaise en Espagne (vers 1361 – vers 1379)', in A. Rucquoi, ed., *Realidad e imagines del poder: España a fines de la edad media* (Valladolid, 1998), 23–55

——, *The King's Lieutenant. Henry of Grosmont, First Duke of Lancaster, 1310–1361* (London, 1969)

——, *Medieval Mercenaries. Volume I: The Great Companies* (Oxford, 2001)

——, 'News from the Front: Letters and Despatches of the Fourteenth Century', in P. Contamine, C. Giry-Deloison and M.H. Keen, eds, *Guerre et société en France, en Angleterre et en Bourgogne, XIVe–XVe siècle* (Lille, 1991), 63–92

——, 'Sir John Hawkwood and the English Condottieri in Trecento Italy', *Renaissance Studies*, xii (1998), 131–48

Frame, R., 'Thomas Rokerby, Sheriff of Yorkshire, Custodian of David II', in Rollason and Prestwich, eds, *The Battle of Neville's Cross*, 50–6

——, 'War and Peace in the Medieval Lordship of Ireland', *The English in Ireland*, ed. J. Lydon (Dublin, 1984), 118–41

France, J., 'Anna Comnena, the Alexiad and the First Crusade', *Reading Medieval Studies*, x (1983), 20–32

——, 'The Composition and Raising of the Armies of Charlemagne', *JMMH*, I (2002), 61–82

——, 'The Military History of the Carolingian Period', *Revue Belge d'Histoire Militaire*, xxvi (1985), 81–99

——, 'Technology and the Success of the First Crusade', in Y. Lev, ed., *War and Society in the Eastern Mediterranean, 7th–15th Centuries* (Leiden, 1997), 163–76

——, *Victory in the East. A Military History of the First Crusade* (Cambridge, 1994)

——, *Western Warfare in the Ages of the Crusades* (London, 1999)

Frank, R., 'Skaldic Poetry', in J.R. Strayer, ed., *Dictionary of the Middle Ages*, 13 vols (New York, 1982–9), xi, 316–23

Franklin, J.A., 'The Romanesque Cloister Sculpture at Norwich Cathedral Priory', in F.H. Thompson, ed., *Studies in Medieval Sculpture* (Society of Antiquaries of London Occasional Paper, new ser., III, 1983)

Frédérix, P., *Mort de Charles le Téméraire, 5 Janvier 1477* (Paris, 1966)

Freeman, E.A., *The Reign of William Rufus and the Accession of Henry the First*, 2 vols (Oxford, 1882)

Freeman, P.W.M. and Pollard, A., eds, *Fields of Conflict. Progress and Prospect in Battlefield Archaeology*, BAR International Series, 958 (Oxford, 2001)

Friel, I., 'Oars, Sails and Guns: The English and War at Sea, c. 1200–c. 1500', in *War at Sea in the Middle Ages and Renaissance*, ed. J.B. Hattendorf and R.W. Unger (Woodbridge, 2003), 69–79

——, 'Winds of Change? Ships and the Hundred Years War', in Curry and Hughes, eds, *Arms, Armies and Fortifications in the Hundred Years War*, 183–93

Fuller, J.F.C., *The Decisive Battles of the Western World and their Influence upon History*, 3 vols (London, 1954–6)

Gaier, C., *Art et organisation militaires dans la principauté de Liège et dans le comté de Looz au moyen âge* (Brussels, 1968)

——, *L'Industrie et le commerce des armes dans les anciennes principautés belge du XIIIme à la fin du XIVme siècle* (Paris, 1973)

——, 'L'Invincibilité anglaise et le grand arc après la guerre de cent ans: un mythe tenace', *Tijdschrift voor Geschiedenis*, xci (1978), 379–85

——, 'Quand l'arbalète était une nouveauté. Réflexions sur son role militaire du Xe au XIIIe siècle', in Burst, ed., *Armes et combats dans lunivers médiéval* (Brussels, 1995), 159–82

Gaillard, G., *Les débuts de la sculpture Romane Espagnole* (Paris, 1938)

Gairdner, J., 'The Battle of Bosworth', *Archaeologia*, lv (1896), 159–78

Galbraith, V.H., 'The Battle of Poitiers', *EHR*, liv (1939), 473–5

Ganshof, F.L., 'À propos de la cavalerie dans les armeés de Charlemagne', *Comptes-rendus de l'Académie des inscriptions et belles-lettres* (1952), 531–6

——, 'Charlemagne's Army', *Frankish Institutions under Charlemagne* (New York, 1970), 59–68

——, 'L'armée sous les carolingiennes', *Ordinamenti militari in occidente nell'alto medioevo*, Settimane, xv, 2 vols (Spoleto, 1968), I, 109–30

Gaupp, F., 'The Condottiere John Hawkwood', *History*, xxiii (1939), 305–21

Gendall, J., 'The Arundell Archive of Arrows and Arrowheads', *JSAA*, xliv (2001)

Gessler, E.A., 'Die spangenharnische von Knussnach', *Zeitschrift fur historische Waffen- und Kostümkunde* (new ser.), I, pt 8 (1925)

Gilbert, J.M., 'Crossbows on Pictish Stones', *Proceedings of the Society of Antiquaries of Scotland*, cvii (1975–6), 316–17

Gillespie, J.L., 'Cheshiremen at Blore Heath: A Swan Dive', in J. Rosenthal and C. Richmond, eds, *People, Politics and Community in the Later Middle Ages* (Gloucester, 1987), 77–89

——, 'Richard II's Archers of the Crown', *Journal of British Studies*, xviii (1979), 14–29

——, 'Richard II's Cheshire Archers', *Transactions of the Historic Society of Lancashire and Cheshire*, cxxv (1974), 1–39

——, 'Richard II: King of Battles?' in *The Age of Richard II*, ed. J.L. Gillespie (Stroud, 1997), 148–55

Gillingham, J., *Richard I* (New Haven and London, 1999)

——, 'Richard I and the Science of War in the Middle Ages', in J. Gillingham and J.C. Holt, eds, *War and Government in the Middle Ages* (Woodbridge, 1984), 78–91; repr. in Strickland, ed., *Anglo-Norman Warfare*, 194–207

——, *Richard Coeur de Lion. Kingship, Chivalry and War in the Twelfth Century* (London, 1994)

——, 'The Unromantic Death of Richard I', Speculum, liv (1979), 18–41; repr. in idem, *Richard Coeur de Lion. Kingship, Chivalry and War in the Twelfth Century* (London, 1994), 155–80

——, '"Up with Orthodoxy!" In Defence of Vegetian Warfare', *JMMH*, ii (2004), 149–58

——, 'War and Chivalry in the History of William the Marshall', *Thirteenth Century England. Proceedings of the Newcastle upon Tyne Conference* (Suffolk, 1987), 1–14; repr. in Strickland, ed., *Anglo-Norman Warfare*, 251–63

——, *The Wars of the Roses. Peace and Conflict in Fifteenth-Century England* (London, 1981)

——, 'William the Bastard at War', in C. Harper-Bill, C. Holdsworth and J. Nelson, eds, *Studies in Medieval History presented to R.A. Brown* (Woodbridge, 1989), 141–58; repr. in Strickland, ed., *Anglo-Norman Warfare*, 143–60

Given-Wilson, C., *The English Nobility in the Late Middle Ages* (London, 1987)

—— and Bériac, F., 'Edward III's Prisoners of War: The Battle of Poitiers and its Context', *EHR*, cxvi (2001), 802–33

Glover, R., 'English Warfare in 1066', *EHR*, lxvii (1952), 1–18

Goldberg, P.J.P., 'Masters and Men in Later Medieval England', in D.M. Hadley, ed., *Masculinity in Medieval Europe* (London and New York, 1999), 56–70

Goodman, A., *John of Gaunt. The Exercise of Princely Power in Fourteenth-Century Europe* (London, 1992)

——, 'The Military Subcontracts of Sir Hugh Hastings, 1380', *EHR*, xcv (1980), 114–20

——, *The Wars of the Roses* (London, 1981)

—— and Tuck, A., eds, *War and Border Societies in the Middle Ages* (London and New York, 1992)

Gordon, D., *Making and Meaning. The Wilton Diptych* (London, 1993)

Gordon, H. and Webb, A., 'The Hedgeley Moor Bow at Alnwick Castle', *JSAA*, xv (1972)

Goring, J., 'Social Change and military Decline in Mid-Tudor England', *History*, lx (1975), 185–97

Graham-Campbell, J., *Viking Artefacts. A Select Catalogue* (London, 1980)

—— and Batey, C.E., *Vikings in Scotland. An Archaeological Survey* (Edinburgh, 1998)

Grancsay, S.V., 'Just How Good was Armor?', *True. The Man's Magazine*, April 1954

Gransden, A., *Historical Writing in England*, 2 vols (London, 1974, 1982)

Grant, A., 'Disaster at Neville's Cross: The Scottish Point of View', in Rollason and Prestwich, eds, *The Battle of Neville's Cross, 1346* (Stamford, 1998), 15–35

——, 'The Otterburn War from the Scottish Point of View', in Goodman and Tuck, eds, *War and Border Societies*, 30–64

Gras, N.S.B., *The Early English Customs System. A Documentary Study of the Institutional Economic History of the Customs from the Thirteenth to the Sixteenth Century* (Harvard, 1918)

Gravett, C., *The Battle of Bosworth* (Osprey, 2000)

Green, D., *The Battle of Poitiers, 1356* (Stroud, 2002)

'Greybeard' [sic], 'Some Thoughts on "Nestroque" – an Agincourt Battle Command?', *JSAA*, xliv (2001), 22–3

Griffith, P., *The Viking Art of War* (London, 1995)

Griffiths, R., 'Prince Henry and Wales, 1400–1408', in M. Hicks, ed., *Profit, Piety and Professions in Later Medieval England* (Gloucester, 1990), 51–61

Griffiths, R.A., *The Reign of Henry VI* (Berkeley and Los Angeles, 1981)

Grimley, G., *The Book of the Bow* (London, 1963)

Grove, D., *Dirleton Castle* (Historic Scotland, Edinbugh, 1995)

Guillaume, H.L.G., *Histoire de l'organization militaire sous les ducs de Bourgogne* (Mémoires de l'Academie Royale de Belgique, xxii, Brussels 1848)

Gunn, S.J., *Charles Brandon, Duke of Suffolk, c. 1484–1545* (Oxford, 1988)

——, 'The French Wars of Henry VIII', in J. Black, ed., *The Origins of War in Early Modern Europe* (Edinburgh, 1987)

Haigh, P.A., *Military Campaigns of the Wars of the Roses* (Stroud, 1995)

Haldon, J., '"Solenarion"–The Byzantine Crossbow', *Historical Journal of the University of Birmingham*, xii (1970)

Hale, J.R., *Artists and Warfare in the Renaissance* (New Haven and London, 1990)

——, 'Men and Weapons: the Fighting Potential of Sixteenth-Century Venetian Galleys', in idem, *Renaissance War Studies*

——, 'On a Tudor Parade Ground: the Captain's Handbook of Henry Barrett, 1562', *The Society for Renaissance Studies, Occasional Papers*, V; repr. in idem, *Renaissance War Studies* (London, 1983), 247–90

Haliday, C., *The Scandinavian Kingdom of Dublin* (2nd edn, Dublin, 1884, facsimile, ed. B. ó Rííordáin, Shannon, 1969)

Hall, B.S., '"So notable Ordynaunce": Christine de Pizan, Firearms and Siegecraft in a Time of Transition', in C. De Baeker, ed., *Cultuurhistorisches Caleidoscoop aangeboden an Prof. Dr. Willy L. Braekman* (Ghent, 1992), 219–33

——, *Weapons and Warfare in Renaissance Europe* (Baltimore, 1997)

Hall, R.A., 'A Viking Age Grave at Donnybrook, Co. Dublin', *Medieval Archaeology*, xxii (1978), 64–83

——, *The Viking Dig: The Excavations at York* (London, 1984)

Hammond, P.W., *The Battles of Barnet and Tewkesbury* (Gloucester, 1990)

Hanawalt, B.A., 'Ballads and Bandits: fourteenth-century outlaws and the Robin Hood poems', in Knight, ed., *Robin Hood*, 263–84

Hanawalt, B.A., 'Fur Collar Crime: The pattern of Crime among the Fourteenth-Century English Nobility', *Journal of Social History*, viii (1975), 1–17

——, *Growing up in Medieval London. The Experience of Childhood in History* (Oxford, 1993)

——, 'Men's Games, King's Deer: Poaching in Medieval England', *Journal of Medieval and Renaissance Studies*, viii (1988), 175–93

Harari, Y., 'The Military Role of the Frankish Turcopoles: A Reassessment', *Mediterranean History Review*, xii (1997), 75–116

Harbinson, M., 'Verneuil – the Events of 17 August, 1424: an Examination of the Sources and the Account of Thomas Basin', *The Hobilar*, xxx (1998), 18–22

Hardy, R., *Longbow: a social and military history* (Sparkford, 1992)

——, 'The Military Archery at Neville's Cross, 1346', in Rollason and Prestwich, eds, *The Battle of Neville's Cross*, 122–31

——, 'The Longbow', in A. Curry and M. Hughes, eds, *Arms, Armies and Fortifications in the Hundred Years War* (Woodbridge, 1994), 161–81.

Harmuth, E., *Die Armbrust* (Graz, 1975)

——, *Die Armbrust. Ein Handbuch* (Gratz, 1986)

——, 'Die Armbrustbilder von Haimo von Auxerre', *Waffen- und Kostümkunde*, 3rd ser., xii (1970), 127–30

——, 'Belt Spanners for Crossbows', in R. Held, ed., *Art, Arms and Armour. An International Anthology, I: 1979–80* (Chiasso, Switzerland, 1979), 100–7

——, 'Concerning the One-Foot Crossbow of the High Gothic', *JSAA*, 28 (1985)

——, 'Zur Leistung der Mittelalterlischen Armbrust', *Waffen- und Kostümkunde*, xiii (1971), 128–36

Harriss, G.L., ed., *Henry V. The Practice of Kingship* (Oxford, 1985)

Hart, C., 'The Bayeux Tapestry and Schools of Illumination at Canterbury', *Anglo-Norman Studies*, xxii (1999), 117–68

Hart, C.E., *Royal Forest* (Oxford, 1966)

Harvey, I.M.W., *Jack Cade's Rebellion of 1450* (Oxford, 1991)

Harvey, P.D.A., *Mappa Mundi. The Hereford World Map* (Hereford and London, 1996)

——, 'Personal Seals in Thirteenth-Century England', in I. Wood and G. Loud, eds, *Church and Chronicle in the Middle Ages: Essays Presented to John Taylor* (Hambledon, 1991), 117–27

Hatto, A.J., 'Archery and Chivalry : A Noble Prejudice', *Modern Language Review*, xxxv (1940), 40–54

Hayes-McCoy, G.A., *Irish Battles* (London, 1969)

Heath, E.G., 'The English War Arrow', *JSAA*, iii (1960)

Hencken, H.O'N., 'Ballinderry Crannog No. 1', *Proceedings of the Royal Irish Academy*, xliii (1935–7)

Henger, G.W., 'The Metallography and Chemical Analysis of Iron-based Samples dating from Antiquity to Modern Times', *Bulletin of the Historical Metallurgy Group*, iv (1970), 49–52

Herben, S.J., 'Arms and Armour in Chaucer', *Speculum*, xii (1937), 475–87

Herbert, M., 'L'armée Provencale en 1374', *Annales du Midi*, xci (1979), 5–27

Herde, P., 'Taktiken mulimischer Heere vom ersten Kreuzug bis Ayn djalut (1260) und ihre Einwirkung auf die Schlacht bei Tagliacozzo (1268)', in *Das Heilige Land im Mittelalter* (Wurzburg, 1981)

Hewitt, H.J., *The Black Prince's Expedition of 1355–1357* (Manchester, 1958)

——, *The Organization of War under Edward III, 1338–1362* (Manchester, 1966)

Hewitt, J., *Ancient Armour and Weapons* (Oxford, 1855, repr. London, 1996)

Hicks, M., *Richard III. The Man Behind the Myth* (London, 1991)

——, *Warwick the Kingmaker* (Oxford, 1998)

Higham, R., 'Timber Castles: A Reassessment', *Fortress*, i (1989), 50–60

—— and Barker, P., *Timber Castles* (London, 1992)

Hillenbrand, C., *The Crusades. Islamic Perspectives* (Edinburgh, 1999)

Hillier, G., *The History and Antiquities of the Isle of Wight* (London, 1850)

Hilton, R.H., 'The Origins of Robin Hood', *Past and Present*, xiv (1958)

——, ed., *Peasants, Knights and Heretics: studies in medieval English social history* (Cambridge, 1976)

Hollister, C.W., *Anglo-Saxon Military Institutions on the Eve of the Norman Conquest* (Oxford, 1962)

——, *The Military Organization of Norman England* (Oxford, 1965)

——, *Norman Military Obligation* (Oxford, 1965)

Holt, J.C., 'The Audience and Ballads of Robin Hood', *Past and Present*, xviii (1960)

——, 'The Ballads of Robin Hood' in Hilton, ed., *Peasants, Knights and Heretics*, 236–57

——, *Magna Carta* (2nd edn, Cambridge, 1992)

——, 'The Origins of the Constitutional Tradition in England', in *idem*, *Magna Carta and Medieval Government* (London, 1985)

——, *Robin Hood* (London, 2nd edn, 1989)

——, 'Robin Hood: Some Comments', *Past and Present*, xix (1961)

Homans, C., *English Villagers of the Thirteenth Century* (Cambridge, Mass., 1942)

Hooper, N. and Bennett, M., eds, *Cambridge Illustrated Atlas of Warfare. The Middle Ages, 768–1487* (Cambridge, 1996)

Hosler, J.D., 'Henry II's Military Campaigns in Wales, 1157–1165', *JMMH*, ii (2004), 53–72

Housley, N., *The Later Crusades, 1274–1580* (Oxford, 1992)

——, 'Le Maréchal Boucicaut à Nicopolis', in J. Paviot and M. Chauney-Bouillot, eds, *Nicopolis, 1396–1996* (Dijon, 1997), and also printed in *Annales de Bourgogne*, lxvii (1996), fasc. 3, at 85–99

——, 'One Man and his Wars; the Depiction of Warfare by Marshal Boucicaut's Biographer', *Journal of Medieval History*, xxix (2003), 27–40

Hughes, Q., 'Medieval Firepower', *Fortress*, viii (1991), 31–43

Huuri, K., *Zur Geschichte des mittelalterliche Geschützwesens aus orientalischen Quellen* (Helsinki, 1941)

Irving, L., 'The Arming of Sir Thopas', *Modern Language Notes*, li (1956), 300–11

Jack, R.I., 'A Quincentenary: the Battle of Northampton, July 10th, 1460', *Northamptonshire Past and Present*, iii (1960)

Jacob, E.F., *The Fifteenth Century* (Oxford, 1961)

Jessop, O., 'A New Artefact Typology for the Study of Medieval Arrowheads', *Medieval Archaeology*, xl (1996), 192–205

Jóhannesson, J., *Islendiga Saga: A History of the Old Icelandic Commonwealth*, trans. H. Bessason (University of Manitoba, 1974)

Johnson, G.A.L., 'The Neville's Cross Monument: A Physical and Geological Report', in Rollason and Prestwich, eds, *The Battle of Neville's Cross*, 97–111

Johnson, J.H., 'The King's Wardrobe and Household', in J.F. Willard, ed., *The English Government at Work, 1327–1336* (Cambridge, Mass., 1940–50), 206–29

Johnstone, H., *Edward of Caernarvon, 1284–1307* (Manchester, 1946)

Jones, M.C.E., 'Edward III's captains in Brittany', in W.M. Ormrod, ed., *England in the Fourteenth Century* (Woodbridge, 1986), 99–118

——, 'Sir Thomas Dagworth et la guerre civile en Bretagne au XIVe siècle: quelques documents inédits', *Annales de Bretagne*, lxxxviii (1980), 621–39

—— and Walker, S., 'Private Indentures for Life Service in Peace and War, 1278–1476', in *Camden Miscellany*, xxxii (5th ser., iii, 1994), 1–190

Jones, M.K., 'The Battle of Verneuil (17 August 1424): Towards a History of Courage', *War in History*, ix (2002), 375–411

——, *Bosworth, 1485* (Stroud, 2002)

——, 'The Relief of Avranches (1439): An English Feat of Arms at the End of the Hundred Years War', in N. Rogers, ed., *England in the Fifteenth Century* (Stamford, 1994), 42–55

——, 'Richard III as a Soldier', in J. Gillingham, ed., *Richard III. A Medieval Kingship* (London, 1993), 93–112

Jones, P.N., 'A Short History of the Attack on Armour', *Metallurgist and Materials Technologist* (1984)

——, 'The Metallography and Relative Effectiveness of Arrowheads and Armour during the Middle Ages', *Materials Characterization*, xxix (1992), 111–17

——, 'The Target', in Hardy, *Longbow*, 232–6

—— and Renn, D., 'The Military Effectiveness of Arrow Loops. Some Experiments at White Castle', *Château Gaillard*, ix–x (1982), 447–56

Jones, T., *Chaucer's Knight. The Portrait of a Medieval Mercenary* (London, 1980, repr. 1985)

Jordan, W.C., *Louis IX and the Challenge of Crusade: A Study in Rulership* (Princeton, 1979)

Joret, C., *Le Bataille de Formigny* (Paris, 1903)

Jourdain, C., 'Mémoire sur les commencements de la marine militaire sous Philippe le Bel', *Mémoires de l'académie des inscriptions et belles lettres*, xxx (1881), 377–418

Keagi, Jnr, W.E., 'The Contribution of Archery to the Turkish Conquest of Anatolia', *Speculum*, xxxix (1964), 96–108

Kedar, B.Z., 'The Battle of Hattin Revisited', in *idem*, ed., *The Horns of Hattin* (London, 1992)

Keegan, J., *The Face of Battle* (London, 1976)

Keen, M., 'Chaucer's Knight, the English Aristocracy and the Crusade', in V.J. Scattergood and J.W. Sherborne, eds, *English Court Culture in the Later Middle Ages* (London, 1981), 45–61

——, *England in the Later Middle Ages: A Political History* (London, 1973)

——, *The Outlaws of Medieval England* (rev. edn, London, 2000)

——, 'Richard II's Ordinances of War of 1385', in R.E. Archer and S. Walker, eds, *Rulers and Ruled in Late Medieval England. Essays Presented to Gerald Harriss* (London, 1995), 33–48

——, 'Robin Hood – Peasant or Gentleman?', *Past and Present*, xix (1961)

Kelly, F.M., 'A Knight's Armour in the Early XIV Century, being the Inventory of Raoul de Nesle', *Burlington Magazine* (March 1905), 457–69

Kendall, P.M., *Louis IX* (New York, 1971)

——, *Richard III* (1955)

Kenyon, J.R., 'Fluctuating Frontiers: Normano-Welsh Castle Warfare, *c*. 1075–1240', *Château Gaillard*, xvii (1996), 119–26

King, A., '"They have the Hertes of the People by North": Northumberland, the Percies and Henry IV', in G. Dodd and D. Biggs, eds, *Henry IV: The Establishment of the Regime, 1399–1406* (York, 2003), 139–60

King, E., ed., *The Anarchy of Stephen's Reign* (Oxford, 1994)

Kingsford, C.L., 'A Historical Collection of the Fifteenth Century', *EHR*, xxix (1914), 505–15

Kirk, J.F., *Charles the Bold*, 3 vols (London, 1863–8)

Klopsteg, P.E., *Turkish Archery and the Composite Bow* (Illinois, 1934)

Kluge-Pinsken, A., 'Bogen und Armbrust', in *Das Reich der Salier 1024–1125. Katalog zur Ausstellung des Landes Rhein-Pfalz* (Sigmaringen, 1992)

Knecht, R.J., *Renaissance Warrior and Patron: The Reign of Francis I* (Cambridge, 1994)

Knight, J.K., *The Three Castles: Grosmont Castle, Skenfrith Castle, White Castle* (Cadw, Cardiff, 2nd edn, revised, 2000)

Knight, R., 'Werewolves, Monsters and Miracles: Representing Colonial Fantasies in Gerald of Wales's *Topographia Hibernica*', *Studies in Iconography*, xx (2001), 55–86

Knight, S., ed., *Robin Hood: An Anthology of Scholarship and Criticism* (Woodbridge, 1999)

Kohl, B.G., *Padua under the Carrara, 1318–1405* (Baltimore and London, 1998)

Kooi, B.W., *The Mechanics of the Bow and Arrow* (PhD thesis, Ryksuniveristet, Groningen, 1983)

—— and Bergman, C.A., 'An Approach to the Study of Ancient Archery using Mathematical Modelling', *Antiquity*, lxxi (1997), 124–34

Korvig, I. and Kiss, A., *Cemeteries of the Avar Period in Hungary*, 2 vols (Budapest, 1975, 1977)

Krenn, P., 'Was leisten die alten Handfeuerwaffen?', *Waffen- und Kostümkunde*, xxxii (1990), 35–52

Lachaud, F., 'Armour and Military Dress in Thirteenth and Early Fourteenth Century England', in Strickland, ed., *Armies, Chivalry and Warfare*, 344–69

Laennec, C.M., 'Christine *antygrafe*: Authorship and Self in the Prose Works of Christine de Pizan, with an Edition of BN Ms. 603, "Le Livre des Fais d'Armes et de Chevalerie"', 2 vols (Doctoral Thesis, Yale University, 1988: U.M.I, Ann Arbor, 1991)

Lair, J., *Essai historique et topographique sur la bataille de Formigny, 15 avril, 1450* (Paris, 1903)

Lalande, D., *Jean II le Maingre, dit Boucicaut (1366–1421): étude d'une biographie héroïque* (Geneva, 1988)

Lander, J.R., 'The Hundred Years War and Edward IV's 1475 Campaign in France', in A.J. Salvin, ed., *Tudor Men and Institutions: Studies in English Law and Government* (Baton Rouge, Louisiana, 1972), 70–100

——, *The Wars of the Roses* (Gloucester, 1990)

Landon, L., *Itinerary of King Richard I* (London, Pipe Roll Society, 1935)

Lane, F.C., 'The Crossbow and the Nautical Revolution of the Middle Ages', *Economy, Society and Government in Medieval Italy* (Kent, Ohio, 1969), 161–71

Lang, S.J., 'John Bradmore and his Book Philomena', *Social History of Medicine*, v (1992), 121–30

Lapidge, M., 'The Welsh-Latin Poetry of Sulien's Family', *Studia Celtica*, viii–ix (1973–4), 68–106

Lasko, P., *The Kingdom of the Franks. North-West Europe before Charlemagne* (London, 1971)

Latham, J.D., 'The Archers of the Middle East. The Turco-Iranian Background', *Iran*, viii (1970), 97–103

—— and Patterson, W.F., *Saracen Archery. An English Version and Exposition of a Mamluke Work on Archery (ca. 1368)* (London, 1970)

Latimer, P., 'Henry II's Campaign against the Welsh in 1165', *Welsh History Review*, xiv (1989), 523–52

Leadman, A.D.H., 'The Battle of the Standard', *Yorkshire Archaeological and Topographical Journal*, x (1889), 377–86

Leather, G.F.T., *New Light on Flodden* (2nd edn, Berwick, 1938)

Le Fizelier, J., 'La bataille de la Brossiniere', *Revue Historique et Archaeologique du Maine*, i (1876), 28–42

Le-Jan-Hennebicque, R., 'Satellites et bandes armées dans le monde franc (VIIe–Xe siècles)', *Le Combattant au Moyen Age* (Paris, 2nd edn, 1995)

Leroux, M., *La bataille de Tinchebray* (Tinchebray, 1972)

Lewis, A., 'Roger of Leyburn and the Pacification of England, 1265–7', *EHR*, ccxiv (1939)

Lewis, C.T. and Short, C., *A Latin Dictionary* (Oxford, 1879)

Lewis, N.B., 'An Early Indenture of Military Service, 27 July, 1287', *BIHR*, xiii (1935), 85–9

——, 'The English Force in Flanders, August-November, 1297', in R.W. Hunt, W.A. Pantin and R.W. Southern, eds, *Studies in Medieval History Presented to F.M. Powicke* (Oxford, 1948), 310–18

——, 'The Last Medieval Summons of the English Feudal Levy, 13 June, 1385', *EHR*, lxxii (1958), 1–26

——, 'The Organization of Indentured Retinues in Fourteenth Century England', *TRHS*, 4th ser., xxvii (1944), 29–39

——, 'The Recruitment and Organization of a Contract Army, May to November 1337', *BIHR*, xxxvii (1964), 1–19

Lewis, S., *The Art of Matthew Paris in the Chronica Majora* (Berkeley and Los Angeles, 1987)

Liebel, J., *Springalds and Great Crossbows* (Leeds, Royal Armouries, 1998)

Lloyd, J.E., *A History of Wales*, 2 vols (London, 1911)

Loades, D., *The Tudor Court* (London, 1986)

Lomas, R.A., 'The Durham Landscape and the Battle of Neville's Cross', in Rollason and Prestwich, eds, *The Battle of Neville's Cross*, 66–77

Loomis, G., 'The Growth of the Saint Edmund Legend', *Harvard Studies and Notes in Philology and Literature*, xiv (1932), 83–113

Lot, F., *L'Art Militaire et les Armées au Moyen Age en Europe et dans le Proche Orient*, 2 vols (Paris, 1946)

Luce, S., *Histoire de Bertrand du Guesclin et de son époque* (Paris, 1882)

Lydon, J.F., 'The Hobelar: An Irish Contribution to Medieval Warfare', *The Irish Sword*, ii (1954–6), 12–16

——, 'Richard II's expeditions to Ireland', *Journal of the Royal Society of Antiquaries of Ireland*, xciii (1963), 135–49

——, 'The Scottish Soldier in Medieval Ireland: the Bruce Invasion and the Galloglass', in G.R. Simpson, ed., *The Scottish Soldier Abroad, 1247–1967* (Edinburgh, 1992), 1–15

Macdonald, A.J., *Border Bloodshed. Scotland and England at War, 1369–1403* (Edinburgh, 2000)

Macdougall, N., *An Antidote to the English: The Auld Alliance, 1295–1560* (East Linton, 2001)

MacGregor, A., 'Two Antler Crossbow Nuts and Some Notes of the Early Development of the Crossbow', *Proceedings of the Society of Antiquaries of Scotland*, cvii (1975–6), 317–21

MacIvor, I., Gallagher, D. *et al.*, 'Excavations at Caerlaverock Castle, 1955–66', *Archaeological Journal*, clvi (1999)

Mackenzie, W.M., *The Battle of Bannockburn. A Study of Medieval Warfare* (Glasgow, 1913)

——, *The Secret of Flodden* (Edinburgh, 1931)

McClintock, H.F., *Old Irish and Highland Dress* (2nd edn, Dundalk, 1950)

McEwen, E., 'Nomadic Archery. Some Observations on Composite Bow Design and Construction', in P. Denwood, ed., *Arts of the Eurasian Steppelands* (London, 1978)

—— and McLeod, W., 'The Ancient Egyptian Composite Bow: Some Notes on its Structure and Performance', *American Journal of Archaeology*

——, Miller, R.L. and Bergman, C.A., 'Early Bow Design and Construction', *Scientific American* (June, 1991), 76–82

McFarlane, K.B., *The Nobility of Later Medieval England* (Oxford, 1973)

——, 'Bastard Feudalism', *BIHR*, xx (1945), 161–80 and repr. in *idem*, *England in the Fifteenth Century: Collected Essays* (London, 1981), 23–44

McGreer, E., *Sowing the Dragon's Teeth: Byzantine Warfare in the Tenth Century* (Washington, DC, 1995)

McGurk, J., *The Elizabethan Conquest of Ireland: the 1590s Crisis* (Manchester, 1997)

McJoynt, A.D., *The Art of War in Spain: The Conquest of Granada, 1481–1492* (London, 1995)

McKerral, A., 'West Highland Mercenaries in Ireland', *Scottish Historical Review*, xxx (1951), 1–14

McKisack, M., *The Fourteenth Century: 1307–1399* (Oxford, 1959)

McLeod, W., 'The Range of the Ancient Bow', *Pheonix*, xix (1965), 1–14

McNab, B., 'Obligations of the Church in English Society: Military Arrays of the Clergy, 1369–1418', in W.C. Jordan, B. McNab and T. Ruiz, eds, *Order and Innovation in the Middle Ages: Essays in Honor of Joseph R. Strayer* (Princeton, 1976), 293–314

McNamee, C., *The Wars of the Bruces. Scotland, Ireland and England, 1306–1328* (Edinburgh, 1997)

Maddicott, J.R., *Thomas of Lancaster, 1307–1322* (Oxford, 1970)

Maenchen-Helfen, J.O., *The World of the Huns. Studies in their History and Culture* (Berkeley, 1973)

Mahaffy, J.P., 'Two Early Tours in Ireland', *Hermathena*, xl (1914)

Mallet, M.E., *Mercenaries and Their Masters: Warfare in Renaissance Italy* (London, 1974)

Manchester, K. and Elmhurst, O.E.C., 'Forensic Aspects of Anglo-Saxon Injury', *Ossa* (1982 for 1980), 179–88

Manley, J., 'The Archer and the Army in the Late Saxon Period', *Anglo-Saxon Studies in Archaeology and History*, iv (1985), 223–35

Mann, J.G., *The Funeral Achievements of Edward, The Black Prince* (London, 1951)

——, *European Arms and Armour*, 2 vols (Wallace Collection Catalogues, London 1962)

——, 'The Funeral Achievements of Edward, The Black Prince', in *Edward, The Black Prince*, Canterbury Papers, viii (Canterbury, 1963)

——, 'Notes on the Evolution of Plate Armour in Germany in the 14th and 15th Centuries', *Archaeologia*, lxxxvii (1934), 69–97

Marchionni, R., *Sienese Battles (I). Montaperti* (Siena, 1996)

Marsden, E.W., *Greek and Roman Artillery* (Oxford, 1969)

Marshall, C.J., 'The Use of the Charge in Battles in the Latin East, 1192–1291', *Historical Research*, lxiii (1990), 221–6

——, *Warfare in the Latin East, 1192–1291* (Cambridge, 1992)

Mas Chao, A., 'Cerignola, Bicocca et Pavia: l'arme a feu individuelle conne facteur decisif au combat', in *From Crécy to Mohacs*, 195–206

Massey, D., 'Roman Military Archery tested', *Military Illustrated*, lxxiv (1994), 36–9

Megson, B., *Such Goodly Company: A glimpse of life of the Bowyers of London, 1300–1600* (London, 1993)

Meiss, M., *French Painting in the Time of Jean de Berry. The Boucicaut Master* (London, 1968)

Menant, F., 'La métallurgie Lombarde au moyen age', in P. Benoit, ed., *Hommes et travail du métal dans les villes médiévales* (Paris, 1988), 127–61

Mertes, K., *The Noble English Household, 1250–1600* (Oxford, 1987)

Mesqui, J., *Châteaux et enceintes de la France médiévale: de la défense à la résidence*, 2 vols (Paris, 1991)

——, *Les Châteaux-Forts en France* (Paris, 2000)

——, 'Les tours à archères dans le domaine Plantagenêt français, 1160–1205', in *Les fortifications dans les domaines Plantagenêt*, 77–88

Meyer, P., 'Les anciens traducteurs français de Végece, et en particulier Jean de Vignai', *Romania*, xxv (1896)

Michael, N., *Armies of Medieval Burgundy, 1364–1477* (London, 1983)

Michel, F., *Les Écossais en France, les Francais en Écosse*, 2 vols (London and Edinburgh, 1862)

Miller, D. and Embleton, G.A., *The Swiss at War, 1300–1500* (London, 1979)

Miller, E., *War in the North. The Anglo-Scottish Wars of the Middle Ages* (Hull, 1960)

Miller, H., *Henry VIII and the English Nobility* (Oxford, 1986)

Miller, T., *The Site of the Battle of Bannockburn* (Historical Association Pamphlet, London, 1931)

——, 'The Site of the New Park in relation to the Battle of Bannockburn', *SHR*, xii (1915), 60–75

Miquel, J., 'L'armement des châteaux dans la Gascogne anglaise de 1250 à 1325', in *Les fortifications dans les domaines Plantagenêt*, 89–99

Moore, J.S., 'Anglo-Norman Garrison', *Anglo-Norman Studies*, xxii (1999), 205–59

Morgan, P., *War and Society in Medieval Cheshire, 1277–1403* (Manchester, 1987)

Morillo, S., 'Battle Seeking: The Contexts and Limits of Vegetian Strategy', *JMMH*, I (2002), 21–41

——, 'Hastings: An Unusual Battle', *Haskins Society Journal*, ii (1990), 95–103

——, *Warfare under the Anglo-Norman Kings, 1066–1135* (Woodbridge, 1994)

Morris, J.E., *Bannockburn* (Cambridge, 1914)

——, 'Cumberland and Westmorland Levies in the Time of Edward I and Edward II', *Cumberland and Westmorland Archaeological and Antiquarian Society*, new ser., iii (1903), 307–27

——, 'Mounted Infantry in Medieval Warfare', *TRHS*, 3rd ser., viii (1914), 77–102

——, *The Welsh Wars of Edward I* (Oxford, 1901, repr. Stroud, 1996, with a foreword by M. Prestwich)

Morris, R.H., *Chester in the Plantagenet and Tudor Reigns* (Chester, 1893)

Müller-Wille, M., 'Das Bootkammergrab von Haithabu', in *Berichte über die Ausgrabungen in Haithabu*, ed. K. Schietzel (Neumünster, 1976)

Nelson, L.H., *The Normans in South Wales, 1070–1171* (Austin and London, 1966)

Nelson, N., 'The Forests', in J.F. Willard, ed., *The English Government at Work, 1327–1336*, I, 394–467

Newhall, R.A., *The English Conquest of Normandy, 1416–1424* (New Haven, Connecticut, 1924)

——, *Muster and Review. A Problem of English Military Administration, 1420–1440* (Cambridge, Mass., 1940)

Nicholas, H., *History of the Battle of Agincourt and the Expedition of Henry the Fifth into France* (3rd edn, London, 1971)

Nichols, N.H., 'Expenses of the Great Wardrobe of Edward III from 21 December 1345 to 31 January 1349', *Archaeologia*, xxxi (1846), 34–5

Nicholson, R., *Edward III and the Scots: The Formative Years of a Military Career, 1327–1335* (London, 1965)

——, *Scotland: The Later Middle Ages* (Edinburgh, 1974)

Nickel, H., 'Bow and Arrow/Crossbow', J.R. Strayer, ed., *Dictionary of the Middle Ages*, 13 vols (New York, 1982–9), II, 353

Nicolle, D., *The Armies of Islam, 7–11th Centuries* (London, 1982)

——, *Arms and Armour of the Crusading Era, 1050–1350*, 2 vols (New York, 1988)

——, *Crécy, 1346. The Triumph of the Longbow* (Osprey, 2000)

——, *Hattin, 1187* (London, 1993)

——, 'The Impact of the European Couched Lance on Muslim Military Tradition', *Journal of the Arms and Armour Society* (June, 1980), 6–40

——, *Italian Medieval Armies, 1300–1500* (London, 1983)

——, *Nicopolis, 1396. The Last Crusade* (Osprey, 1999)

——, *Saladin and the Saracens* (London, 1986)

Nicolson, J. and Brown, R., *History and Antiquities of the Counties of Westmorland and Cumberland*, 2 vols (1777)

Norgate, K., *England under the Angevin Kings*, 2 vols (London, 1887)

——, *The Minority of Henry III* (London, 1912)

Norman, A.V., *Arms and Armour* (London, 1964)

Novak, S.A., 'Battle Related Trauma', in V. Fiorato, A. Boylston and C. Knüsel, eds, *Blood Red Roses. The Archaeology of a Mass Grave from the Battle of Towton, AD 1461* (Oxford, 2000)

Nusbacher, A., *The Battle of Bannockburn, 1314* (Stroud, 2000)

O'Brien, I.E., 'The Scottish Parliament in the Fifteenth and Sixteenth Centuries' (PhD thesis, University of Glasgow, 1980)

O'Curry, E., *On the Manners and Customs of the Ancient Irish*, 3 vols (London, 1873)

Oman, C.W.C., *A History of the Art of War in the Middle Ages*, 2 vols (London, 1924, repr. 1991)

——, *A History of the Art of War in the Sixteenth Century* (London, 1937)

Origo, I., *The Merchant of Prato* (New York and London, 1957)

O'Riordan, B., 'Excavations at High Street and Winetavern Street, Dublin', *Medieval Archaeology*, xv (1971), 73–85

Orme, N., *From Childhood to Chivalry. The Education of English Kings and Aristocracy, 1066–1530* (London and New York, 1984)

——, *Medieval Children* (New Haven and London, 2001)

Orpen, G.H., *Ireland under the Normans, 1169–1333*, 4 vols (Oxford, 1911–20)

Ottaway, P. and Rogers, N., *Craft, Industry and Everyday Life: Finds from Medieval York* (York, 2002)

Owen, H. and Blakeway, J.B., *History of Shrewsbury*, 2 vols (London, 1825)

Owen, L.V.D., 'Robin Hood in the Light of Research', in *The Times, Trade and Engineering*, xxxviii (new ser., February 1936)

Oxley, J.E., *The Fletchers and Longbowstring-makers of London* (Court of the Worshipful Company, 1968)

Palmer, J.J.N., *England, France and Christendom, 1377–99* (London, 1972)

Paoli, C., *Libro di Montaperti* (Florence, 1889)

Parry, V.J. and Yapp, M.E., eds, *War, Technology and Society in the Middle East* (London, 1975)

Partner, P., *The Lands of St Peter: The Papal State in the Middle Ages and the Early Renaissance* (London, 1972)

Paterson, L.M., *The World of the Troubadours: Medieval Occitan Society, c.1100–c.1300* (Cambridge, 1993)

Paterson, W.F., 'The Archers of Islam', *Journal of the Economic and Social History of the Orient*, ix (1966), 69–89

——, *A Guide to the Crossbow* (Society of Archer Antiquaries, 1990)

Patterson, L.M., 'Military Surgery', in C. Harper-Bill and R. Harvey, eds, *The Ideals and Practice of Medieval Knighthood*, vol. II (1986), 117–46

Paulsen, P., *Alamanische Adelsgräber von Niederstotzingen (Kreis Heidenheim)* (Stuttgart, 1967)

Paviot, J. and Chauney-Bouillot, M., eds, *Nicopolis, 1396–1996* (Dijon, 1997)

Payne-Gallwey, R., *The Crossbow. Medieval and Modern, Military and Sporting, its Construction, History and Management, with a treatise on the Ballista and Catapults of the Ancients* (London, 1903, repr. 1990)

——, *Projectile Throwing Engines of the Ancients with a Treatise on the Turkish Bow* (London, 1907)

Penman, M., *David II, 1329–71* (East Linton, 2004)

Petit-Dutaillis, C., *Étude sur la vie et la règne de Louis VIII (1187–1226)* (Paris, 1894)

Pfister, C., *Histoire de Nancy*, 3 vols (Paris, 1902–9)

Phillips, G., *The Anglo-Scottish Wars, 1513–1550* (Woodbridge, 1999)

Philpotts, C., 'The French Plan of Battle During the Agincourt Campaign', *EHR*, 30 (1984), 59–68

Piere, P., 'I Saraceni di Lucera nella storia militare medievale', *Archivo Storico Pugliese*, vi (1953), 94–101

Plaine, D., 'La journée d'Auray d'après quelques documents nouveaux', *Association bretonne*, XVII (1874), 83–102

Planchenault, R., 'La bataille de Baugé (22 mars 1421)', *Mémoires de la société nationale d'agriculture, sciences et arts d'Angers*, 5e série, xxviii (1925), 5–30

——, 'Les suites de la bataille de Baugé (1421)', *Mémoires de la société nationale d'agriculture, sciences et arts d'Angers*, 6e série, v (1930), 90–107

Pollard, A.F., *Henry VIII* (London, 1905)

——, *The Reign of Henry VII*, 3 vols (London, 1913)

——, *John Talbot and the War in France, 1427–1453* (London, 1983)

Pollock, F. and Maitland, F.W., *The History of the English Law before the time of Edward I*, 2 vols (Cambridge, 1895)

Poole, A.L., *From Domesday Book to Magna Carta* (Oxford, 1951)

Port, G., *Rochester Castle* (English Heritage, 1987)

Porter, P., *Medieval Warfare in Manuscripts* (London, 2000)

Postan, M., 'The Economic and Political Relations of England and the Hanse from 1400 to 1475', in E. Power and M. Postan, eds, *Studies in English Trade in the Fifteenth Century* (London, 1933), 91–153

Pounds, N.J.G., *The Medieval Castle in England and Wales: a Social and Political History* (Cambridge, 1990)

Powicke, F.M., ed., *The Battle of Lewes, 1264: its place in English History* (Lewes, 1964)

——, *King Henry III and the Lord Edward. The Community of the Realm in the Thirteenth Century* (Oxford, 1947)

——, *The Loss of Normandy, 1189–1204* (2nd edn, Manchester, 1961)

——, 'The Saracen Mercenaries of Richard I', *SHR*, viii (1910)

Powicke, M.R., 'Lancastrian Captains', in T.A. Sandquist and M.R. Powicke, eds, *Essays in Medieval History Presented to Bertie Wilkinson* (Toronto, 1969), 371–82

——, *Military Obligation in Medieval England: A Study in Liberty and Duty* (Oxford, 1962)

Pratt, P.L., 'The Arrow', in Hardy, *Longbow*, 226–32

Prestwich, J.O., 'The Military Household of the Norman Kings', *EHR*, xcvi (1981), 1–37; repr. in Strickland, ed., *Anglo-Norman Warfare*, 93–127

Prestwich, M.C., *Armies and Warfare in the Middle Ages: the English Experience* (New Haven and London, 1996)

——, *Edward I* (London, 1988)

——, 'English Armies in the Early Stages of the Hundred Years War: a scheme in 1341', *BIHR*, lvi (1983), 102–13

——, 'The English at the Battle of Neville's Cross', in Rollason and Prestwich, eds, *The Battle of Neville's Cross*, 1–14

——, 'Military Logistics: The Case of 1322', in Strickland, ed., *Armies, Chivalry and Warfare*, 276–88

——, 'A New Account of the Welsh Campaign of 1294–1295', *Welsh History Review*, vi (1973–4), 89–94

——, *War, Politics and Finance under Edward I* (London, 1972)

Price, L., 'Armed Forces of the Irish Chiefs in the Early Sixteenth Century', *Journal of the Royal Society of Antiquaries of Ireland*, lxii (1932), 201–7

Priestley, E.J., *The Battle of Shrewsbury, 1403* (Shrewsbury, 1979)

Prince, A.E., 'The Army and Navy', in J.F. Willard, ed., *The English Government at Work*, I (Cambridge, Mass., 1940), 332–93

——, 'The Importance of the Campaign of 1327', *EHR*, l (1935), 299–302

——, 'The Indenture System under Edward III', in J.G. Edwards, W.H. Galbraith and E.F. Jacob, eds, *Historical Essays in Honour of James Tait* (Manchester, 1933), 283–97

——, 'A Letter of Edward the Black Prince describing the battle of Nájera in 1367', *EHR*, xli (1926), 415–18

——, 'The Strength of English Armies in the Reign of Edward III', *EHR*, xlvi (1931), 353–71

Ramsay, J.H., *Lancaster and York. A Century of English History*, 2 vols (Oxford, 1892)

Randall, R., 'An Eleventh-Century Ivory Pectoral Cross', *Journal of the Warburg and Courtauld Institutes*, xxv (1962), 159–71

Ransome, C., 'The Battle of Towton', *EHR*, iv (1889), 460–6

Rausing, G., *The Bow. Some Notes on its Origins and Development* (Lund, 1967)

Rawcliffe, C., *Medicine and Society in Later Medieval England* (Stroud, 1995)

——, 'The Profits of Practice: the Wealth and Status of Medical Men in Later Medieval England', *Social History of Medicine*, I (1988), 61–78

——, 'Master Surgeons at the Lancastrian Court', in *The Lancastrian Court*, ed J. Stratford (Donington, 2003), 192–210

Rees, S.E. and Caple, C., *Dinefwr Castle, Dryslwyn Castle* (Cadw, Cardiff, 1999)

Reichel, D., ed., *Grandson, 1476. Essai d'approche pluridisciplinaire d'une action militaire du XVe siècle* (Lausanne, 1976)

Reid, W.S., 'Trade, Traders and Scottish Independence', *Speculum*, xxix (1954), 210–22

Renn, D., 'The Avranches Traverse at Dover Castle', *Archaeologia Cantiana*, lxxxiv (1969), 79–92

——, 'A Bowstave from Berkhamstead Castle', *Hertfordshire Archaeology* (St Albans, 1971)

——, *Caerphilly Castle* (Cadw, Cardiff, rev. edn, 1997)

——, 'Defending Framlingham Castle', *Proceedings of the Suffolk Institute of Archaeology*, xxxiii (1973), 58–67

——, 'The Keep at Wareham Castle', *Medieval Archaeology*, iv (1960), 56–68

——, 'The Norman Military Works', in R. Shoesmith and A. Johnson, eds, *Ludlow Castle, its History and Buildings* (Logaston, 2000), 125–38

Reuter, T., 'Carolingian and Ottonian Warfare', in M. Keen, ed., *Medieval Warfare. A History* (Oxford, 1999), 13–35

Rey, R., *La Sculpture Romane Languedocienne* (Paris, 1936)

Richardson, T., 'Ballistic Testing of Historical Weapons', *Royal Armouries Yearbook*, iii (1998), 50–2

——, 'The Introduction of Plate Armour in Medieval Europe', *Royal Armouries Yearbook*, ii (1997), 40–5

Richmond, C.F., 'Royal Administration and the Keeping of the Seas, 1422–1485' (Oxford University D. Phil. Thesis, 1963)

——, 'The Battle of Bosworth', *History Today*, xxxv (August 1985), 17–22

——, 'English Naval Power in the Fifteenth Century', *History*, lii (1967), 1–15

——, 'The Keeping of the Seas During the Hundred Years War: 1422–1440', *History*, xlix (1964), 283–98

Ricotti, E., *Storia della Compagnie di Ventura in Italia*, 4 vols (Torino, 1847)

Ridyard, S.J., *The Royal Saints of Anglo-Saxon England. A Study of West Saxon and East Anglian Cults* (Cambridge, 1988)

Riesch, H., 'Archery in Renaissance Germany', *JSAA*, xxxviii (1995)

——, '"Quod nullus in hostem habeat baculum sed arcum": Pfeil und Bogen als Biespiel für technologische Innovationen der Karolingerzeit', *Technikgeschichte*, lxi (1994), 209–26

Riley-Smith, J.S.C., ed., *The Atlas of the Crusades* (London, 1991)

——, *The Knights of St John in Jerusalem and Cyprus, c.1050–1310* (London, 1967)

——, 'A Note of the Confraternities in the Latin Kingdom of Jerusalem', *Historical Research*, xxxxiv (1971), 301–8

Rodger, N.A.M., *The Safeguard of the Sea: a naval history of Britain*, I (London, 1997)

Roesdahl, E., *The Vikings* (London, 1991)

Rogers, C.J., 'By Fire and Sword. *Bellum Hostile* and "Civilians" in the Hundred Years War', in *Civilians in the Path of War*, ed. M. Grimsley and C.J. Rogers (Lincoln, Nebraska, and London, 2002), 33–78

——, 'Edward III and the Dialectics of Strategy, 1327–1360', *TRHS*, 6th ser., iv (1994), 83–102

——, 'The Bergerac Campaign (1345) and the Generalship of Henry of Lancaster', *JMMH*, ii (2004), 89–111

——, 'The Efficacy of the English Longbow: A Reply to Kelly De Vries', *War in History*, v (1998), 233–42

——, 'The Military Revolutions of the Hundred Years War', *The Journal of Military History*, lvii (1993), 241–78

——, 'The Offensive/Defensive in Medieval Strategy from Crécy to Mohacs: Warfare in the Late Middle Ages (1346–1526)', *Acta of the XXnd Colloquium of the International Commission of Military History* (Vienna, 1996), 158–71

——, 'The Scottish Invasion of 1346', *Northern History*, xxxiv (1998), 51–69

——, 'An Unknown News Bulletin from the Siege of Tournai', *War in History*, v (1988), 358–66

——, 'The Vegetian "Science of Warfare" in the Middle Ages', *JMMH*, I (2002), 1–19

——, *War, Cruel and Sharp: English Strategy under Edward III, 1327–1360* (Woodbridge, 2000)

—— and Buck, M., 'Three New Accounts of the Neville's Cross Campaign', *Northern History*, xxxiv (1998)

Rogers, R., 'Aspects of the Military History of the Anglo-Norman Invasion of Ireland, 1169–1225', *Irish Sword*, xvi (1986), 135–46

——, *Latin Siege Warfare in the Twelfth Century* (Oxford, 1992)

Rolands, I.W., 'King John and Wales', in S.D. Church, ed., *King John: New Interpretations* (Woodbridge, 1998)

Rollason, D. and Prestwich, M., eds, *The Battle of Neville's Cross* (Stamford, 1998) de la Roncière, C., *Histoire de la marine française*, 6 vols (Paris, 1889–1932)

Rose, A., *Kings in the North. The House of Percy in British History* (London, 2002)

Rose, W., 'Anna Comnena über die Bewaffnung der Kreuzfahrer', *Zeitschrift für Historische Waffen- und Kostümkunde*, ix (1921), 1–10

Ross, C., *Edward IV* (New Haven and London, 1997)

——, *Richard III* (London, 1981)

Round, J.H., *Geoffrey de Mandeville* (London, 1892)

Rule, M., *The Mary Rose*, foreword by HRH the Prince of Wales (Conway Maritime Press, 1982)

Russell, J.G., *The Field of Cloth of Gold* (London, 1969)

Russell, P.E., *The English Intervention in Spain and Portugal in the Time of Edward III and Richard II* (Oxford, 1995)

Ryan, L.V., *Roger Ascham* (Stanford, 1963)

Rye, W., 'The Riot between the Monks and Citizens of Norwich in 1272', *Norfolk Antiquarian Miscellany*, ii (1883)

Rynne, E., 'The Impact of the Vikings on Irish Weapons', in *Atti del VI Congresso Internazionale delle Scienze Preistoriche et Protostoriche, Roma, 1962* (Rome, 1966), 181–5

Salin, E., *La Civilisation mérovingienne: d'après les sépultures, les textes et le laboratoire*, 2 vols (Paris, 1959)

Salter, E.G., *Tudor England through Venetian Eyes* (London, 1930)

Sandler, L.F., *The Peterborough Psalter in Brussels and Other Fenland Manuscripts* (London, 1974)

Scalini, M., Wackernagel, R.H. and Eaves, I., *The Armoury of the Castle of Churburg* (Udine, 1996)

Scammell, J., 'Robert I and the North of England', *EHR*, lxxiii (1958), 385–403

Scarisbrick, J.J., *Henry VIII* (London, 1968)

Schaufelberger, W., *Der alte Schweizer und sein Krieg. Studien zur Kriegführung vornehmlich im 15, Jahrhundert* (Zurich, 1952)

Schneider, H., *Zeitschrift fur Schweizerische Archäologie und Kunstgeschichte*, xiv (1953), pt I, 29–31

Schnerb, B., 'La bataille rangée dans la tactique des armées bourguignonnes au début du 15e siècle: essai de synthèse', *Annales de Bourgogne*, lxxi (1989), 5–32

——, *Bulgnéville (1431): L'État bourguignon prend pied en Lorraine* (Paris, 1993)

——, *L'État bourguignon, 1363–1477* (Paris, 1999)

Schofield, C.L., *The Life and Reign of Edward the Fourth*, 2 vols (London, 1923)

Schwoebel, R., *The Shadow of the Crescent: The Renaissance Image of the Turk (1453–1517)* (New York, 1969)

Scott, J.G., 'Two 14th c Helms Found in Scotland', *Journal of the Arms and Armour Society*, iv (1962), 68–79

Scragg, D., ed., *The Battle of Maldon AD 991* (Manchester, 1991)

Sellar, W.D.H., 'Sueno's Stone and Its Interpreters', in *Moray: Province and People* (Edinburgh, 1993)

Setton, K.M., *The Papacy and the Levant (1204–1571), I, The Thirteenth and Fourteenth Centuries* (Philadelphia, 1976)

Sherbourne, J.W., 'The Battle of La Rochelle and the War at Sea, 1372–5', *BIHR*, xlii (1969), 17–29

——, 'The English Navy: Shipping and Manpower, 1369–1389', *Past and Present*, xxxvii (1967), 163–75

——, 'Indentured Retinues and English Expeditions to France, 1369–1380', *EHR*, lxxix (1964), 718–46

Shetelig, H. and Falk, H., *Scandinavian Archaeology* (Oxford, 1937)

Sigal, P., 'Les coups et blessures reçus par le combattant à cheval en occident aux XIIe et XIIIe siècles', in *Le Combattant au Moyen Age* (Histoire ancienne et Médiévale, 36, Paris, 2nd edn, 1995), 171–83

Simms, K., *From Kings to Warlords: The Changing Political Structure of Gaelic Ireland in the later Middle Ages* (Woodbridge, 1987)

——, 'Gaelic Warfare in the Middle Ages', in Bartlett and Jeffery, eds, *A Military History of Ireland*, 99–116

——, 'Warfare in the medieval Gaelic Lordships', *The Irish Sword*, xii (1975–6), 98–108

Simpson, W.D., *The Earldom of Mar* (Aberdeen, 1949)

——, 'Skipness Castle', *Transactions of the Glasgow Archaeological Society*, new ser. xv, pt 3 (1966)

Smail, R.C., *Crusading Warfare, 1097–1193* (Cambridge, 2nd edn, 1995)

Smith, C.S., 'Methods of Making Chain Mail in the 14th–18th Centuries: A Metallographic Note', *Technology and Culture*, I (1960), 60–7

Smith, L.B., *Henry VIII. The Mask of Royalty* (Boston, 1971)

Spont, A., 'Marignan et l'organisation militaire sous Francois Ier', *Revue des questions historiques*, xxii (1899), 59–77

Stacey, R.C., *Politics, Policy and Finance under Henry III, 1216–1245* (Oxford, 1987)

Steer, K.A. and Bannerman, J.W.M., *Late Medieval Monumental Sculpture in the West Highlands* (Edinburgh, 1977)

Stephens, G.R., 'A Note on William of Cassingham', *Speculum*, xvi (1941), 216–223

Sterling, C. and Schaefer, C., *The Hours of Etienne Chevalier* (NewYork, 1971)

Stevens, J., *Music and Poetry in the Early Tudor Court* (New York, 1979)

Stirland, A.J., *Raising the Dead: the Skeleton Crew of Henry VIII's Great Ship the Mary Rose* (Chichester, 2002)

Strickland, M.J., ed., *Anglo-Norman Warfare. Studies in late Anglo-Saxon and Anglo-Norman Military Organization and Warfare* (Woodbridge, 1992)

——, ed., *Armies, Chivalry and Warfare in Medieval Britain and France*, Proceedings of the 1995 Harlaxton Symposium (Stanford, 1998)

——, 'Military Technology and Conquest: The Anomaly of Anglo-Saxon England', *Anglo-Norman Studies*, xix (1996), 353–82

——, *War and Chivalry. The Conduct and Perception of War in England and Normandy, 1066–1217* (Cambridge, 1996)

Sumption, J., *The Hundred Years War: Trial by Battle* (London, 1990)

——, *The Hundred Years War: Trial by Fire* (London, 1999)

Suppe, F.C., *Military Institutions on the Welsh Marches: Shropshire, AD. 1066–1300* (Woodbridge, 1994)

Tabraham, C.J., *Kildrummy Castle* (Historic Scotland, Edinburgh, 1986)

Talbot, H., *The English Achilles. The Life and Campaigns of John Talbot, 1st Earl of Shrewsbury* (London, 1981)

Tasker, E.G., *Encyclopedia of Medieval Church Art* (London, 1993)

Taylor, A.J., *Beaumaris Castle* (Cadw, Cardiff, 4th edn, 1999)

——, *Caernarvon Castle and Town Walls* (5th edn, Cardiff, 2001)

——, *Conway Castle and Town Walls, Caernarvonshire* (Cadw, Cardiff, rev. edn, 2003)

——, *Harlech Castle* (Cadw, Cardiff, 4th edn, 2002)

——, *The Welsh Castles of Edward I* (London, 1986)

Taylor, F., 'The Chronicle of John Strecche for the Reign of Henry V (1414–1422)', *Bulletin of the John Rylands Library*, xvi (1932)

Temple-Leader, J. and Marcotti, G., *Sir John Hawkwood, Story of a Condottieri* (London and Florence, 1889)

Thomson, D. et al., *Raeburn: The Art of Sir Henry Raeburn, 1756–1823* (Edinburgh, 1997)

Thomson, J.A.F., '"The Arrival of Edward IV" – The Development of the Text', *Speculum*, xlvi (1971), 84–93

——, *The Transformation of Medieval England, 1370–1529* (London, 1983)

Thomson, R.M., 'Early Romanesque Book Illustration in England: the Dates of the Pierpont Morgan "Vitae Sancti Edmundi" and the Bury Bible', *Viator*, ii (1971), 211–15

Thordemann, B., *Armour from the Battle of Wisby, 1361*, 2 vols (Stockholm, 1939)

Thorsilen, E., *Ladbyskibet* (Copenhagen, 1957)

Thrupp, S.L., *The Merchant Class of Medieval London* (Michigan, 1962)

Tipton, C.L., 'The English at Nicopolis', *Speculum*, xxxvii (1962), 528–40

Tough, D.L.W., *The Last Years of a Frontier: a history of the Borders during the reign of Elizabeth I* (Oxford, 1928)

Touneur-Aumont, J.M., *La bataille de Poitiers* (Paris, 1940)

Tout, T.F., *Chapters in the Administrative History of Medieval England: The Wardrobe, the Chamber and the Small Seals*, 6 vols (Manchester, 1920–33)

——, *The Collected Works of Thomas Frederick Tout*, 3 vols (Manchester, 1932–4)

——, 'The Fair of Lincoln and the "Histoire de Guillaume le Maréchal"', *EHR*, xviii (1903), 240–65

——, 'Firearms in England in the Fourteenth Century', *EHR*, xxvi (1911), 666–702

——, *The Place of Edward II in English History* (2nd edn, Manchester, 1936)

——, 'Some Neglected Fights between Crécy and Poitiers', *Collected Works*, II, 227–31

——, 'The Tactics of Boroughbridge and Morlaix', *Collected Works*, II, 221–5

Trease, G., *The Condottieri* (London, 1971)

Tremlett, T., 'The Matthew Paris Shields', *Aspilogia*, II (1967), 3–86

Tristram, E.W., *English Medieval Wall Painting: the Thirteenth Century*, 2 vols (Oxford, 1950)

Tuck, A., 'Henry IV and Chivalry', in G. Dodd and D. Biggs, eds, *Henry IV: The Establishment of the Regime, 1399–1406* (Woodbridge, 2003), 55–71

Tucoo-Chala, P., *Gaston Fébus et la vicomté de Béarn, 1342–1391* (Bordeaux, 1960)

Turvey, R.K., 'Defences of twelfth-century Deheubarth and the Castle Strategy of the Lord Rhys', *Archaeologia Cambrensis*, cxliv (1997 for 1995), 103–32

Turville-Petre, E.O.G., *Scaldic Poetry* (Oxford, 1976)

Tyerman, C., *England and the Crusades, 1095–1588* (Chicago, 1988)

Tyson, C., 'The Battle of Otterburn. When and Where was it Fought', in Goodman and Tuck, eds, *War and Border Societies*, 65–93

Vale, J., *Edward III and Chivalry: Chivalric Society and its Context, 1270–1350* (Woodbridge, 1983)

Vale, M., *The Angevin Legacy and the Hundred Years War, 1250–1340* (Oxford, 1990)

——, *Charles VII* (Berkeley and Los Angeles, 1974)

——, *War and Chivalry. Warfare and Aristocratic Culture in England, France and Burgundy at the End of the Middle Ages* (Athens, Georgia, 1981)

Van Houts, E., 'The Ship List of William the Conqueror', *Anglo-Norman Studies*, x (1987), 159–83

Vaughan, R., *Charles the Bold. The Last Valois Duke of Burgundy* (London, 1973)

——, *John the Fearless* (London, 1966)

——, *Philip the Good. The Apogee of Burgundy* (London, 1970)

——, *Valois Burgundy* (London, 1975)

Veeck, W., *Die Alamannen im Würtemberg* (Berlin and Leipzig, 1931)

Verbruggen, J.F., 'L'armée et la stratégie de Charlemagne', *Karl der Grosse. Lebenswerk und Nachleben* (Dusseldorf, 1965), 420–36

——, *The Art of Warfare in Western Europe during the Middle Ages*, trans. S. Willard and S.C.M. Southern (Woodbridge, 2nd edn, 1997)

——, *De Krijgskunst in West-Europe in de Middeleeuwen, IXe tot begin XIVe eeuw* (Brussels, 1954)

——, 'Un plan de bataille du duc de Bourgogne (14 Septembre 1417) et la tactique de l'époque', *Revue internationale d'histoire militaire*, xx (1959), 443–51

Vigi, B.G., *Il Museo della Cattedrale di Ferra* (Florence, 2001)

Wailly, H. de, *Crécy, 1346: Anatomy of a Battle* (Poole, 1987)

Waley, D.P., 'The Army of the Florentine Republic from the Twelfth to the Fourteenth Century', in N. Rubinstein, ed., *Florentine Studies. Politics and Society in Renaissance Florence* (Evanston, 1968), 70–108

——, '*Condotte* and *Condottieri* in the Thirteenth Century', *Proceedings of the British Academy*, lxi (1975), 337–71

——, 'Papal Armies in the Thirteenth Century', *EHR*, lxxii (1957), 1–30

Walker, R.F., 'The Hagnaby Chronicle and the Battle of Maes Moydog', *Welsh Historical Review*, viii (1976–7), 125–38

Walker, S.K., 'Profit and Loss in the Hundred Years War: the Subcontracts of Sir John Strother, 1374', *BIHR*, 58 (1985), 100–6

Waller, J., 'Combat Techniques', in V. Fiorato, A. Boylston and C. Knüsel, eds, *Blood Red Roses. The Archaeology of a Mass Grave from the battle of Towton, AD 1461* (Oxford, 2000), 148–54

Ward Perkins, J.B., *London Museum Medieval Catalogue* (London, 1940)

Warner, M., *Joan of Arc. The Image of Female Heroism* (London, 1981)

Warren, W.L., *Henry II* (London, 1973, repr. 1983)

——, *King John* (2nd edn, London, 1978)

Watson, F., *Under the Hammer: Edward I and Scotland, 1286–1306* (Edinburgh, 1998)

Waugh, W.T., 'The Administration of Normandy, 1420–22', in A.G. Little and F.M. Powicke, eds, *Essays Presented to Thomas Frederick Tout* (Manchester, 1925), 349–59

Webster, G., *The Roman Imperial Army of the First and Second Centuries AD* (3rd edn, Oklahoma, 1988)

Webster, L.E., 'Stylistic Aspects of the Franks Casket', in R.T. Farrell, ed., *The Vikings* (London, 1982), 20–32

——, and Backhouse, J., eds, *The Making of England. Anglo-Saxon Art and Culture, AD 600–900* (London, 1991)

Wemlowe, F.R., *The Battle of Blore Heath* (1912)

Werner, J., 'Bewaffnung und Waffenbeigrabe in der Merowingerzeit', *Ordinamenti militari in occidente nell'alto medioevo, Settimane*, xv, 2 vols, I (Spoleto, 1968), 95–108

White, G.H., *Complete Peerage*, 12 vols (London, 1910–59)

White, L., 'The Crusades and the Technological Thrust of the West', in V. Parry and M. Yapp, eds, *War, Technology and Society in the Middle East* (London, 1975), 239–56

——, *Medieval Technology and Social Change* (Oxford, 1962)

White, R., 'The Battle of Neville's Cross', *Archaeologia Aeliana* (1856), 271–303

——, *A History of the Battle of Bannockburn* (Edinburgh, 1871)

Whitelock, D., 'Fact and Fiction in the Legend of St Edmund', *Proceedings of the Suffolk Institute for Archaeology*, xxxi (1967–9), 217–33

Wilbur, C.M., 'A History of the Crossbow', *The Smithsonian Report for 1936* (Washington, 1937), 427–38

Willard, C.C., 'Christine de Pizan's Treatise on the Art of Medieval Warfare', in R.J. Cormier and U.T. Holmes, eds, *Essays in Honor of Louis Francis Solano* (Chapel Hill, North Carolina, 1970), 179–91

Willard, J.F., ed., *The English Government at Work, 1327–1336*, 3 vols (Cambridge, Mass., 1940–50)

——, 'The Scotch Raids and the Fourteenth-Century Taxation of Northern England', *University of Colorado Studies*, v, no. 4 (1908), 240–2

Williams, A.R., 'The Blast Furnace and the Mass Production of Plate Armour', in G. Hollister-Short and F.A.J.L. James, eds, *History of Technology* (London, 1994)

——, 'Fifteenth-Century Armour from Churburg: a metallurgical study', *Armi Antiche*, xxxii (1986), 3–82

——, 'Four Helmets of the Fourteenth Century Compared', *Journal of the Arms and Armour Society*, x (1981), 80–102

——, *The Knight and the Blast Furnace* (Leiden, 2002)

——, 'Medieval Metalworking: Armour Plate and the Advance of Metallurgy', *The Chartered Mechanical Engineer* (September, 1978), 109–14

——, 'Metallographic Examination of 16th century Armour', *Bulletin of the Historical Metallurgy Group*, vi (1972), 15–23

——, 'Milanese Armour and its Metallurgy', in G. De Boe and F. Verhaeghe, eds, *Military Studies in Medieval Europe. Papers of the 'Medieval Europe Brugge 1997' Conference* (Zellik, 1997), II, 61–70

——, 'Some Firing with Simulated Fifteenth-Century Handguns', *Journal of the Arms and Armour Society*, viii (1974), 114–20

Williams, D.T., *The Battle of Bosworth* (1973)

Wilson, G.M., *Crossbows* (London, 1976)

Wolff, P., 'Achat d'armes pour Philippe le Bel dans la région toulousaine', *Annales du Midi*, lxi (1948), 84–91

Wright, C.E., *The Cultivation of Saga in Anglo-Saxon England* (Edinburgh and London, 1939)

Wylie, J.H., *History of England under Henry the Fourth*, 4 vols (London, 1884–98)

—— and Waugh, W.T., *The Reign of Henry V*, 3 vols (Cambridge, 1914–29)

Young, A. and Stead, M.J., *In the Footsteps of William Wallace* (Stroud, 2002)

Young, C.R., 'The Forest Eyre in England during the Thirteenth Century', *American Journal of Legal History*, xviii (1974), 321–31

——, *The Royal Forests of England* (University of Pennsylvania, 1979)

Index

Bold type indicates main or substantial sections. Continuous page references ignore intervening illustrations. Dukes, Earls and Counts are indexed under their title, e.g., Cornwall, John de Eltham, Earl of; knights and baronets under their surname, e.g. Beaumont, Sir Henry de; other medieval persons under their given name, e.g. Baldwin de Carron; from about fifteenth century modern usage is followed.